INTRODUCTION TO MODERN ECONOMIC GROWTH

INTRODUCTION TO MODERN ECONOMIC GROWTH

DARON ACEMOGLU

PRINCETON UNIVERSITY PRESS

Princeton and Oxford

Published by Princeton University Press, 41 William Street, Princeton,
New Jersey 08540

In the United Kingdom: Princeton University Press, 6 Oxford Street, Woodstock,
Oxfordshire OX20 1TW

Library of Congress Cataloging-in-Publication Data

Acemoglu, Daron.
Introduction to modern economic growth / Daron Acemoglu.
p.   cm.
Includes bibliographical references and index.
ISBN 978-0-691-13292-1 (hardcover : alk. paper)
1. Economic development.   2. Macroeconomics.   I. Title.
HD75.A24   2009
338.9—dc22   2008038853

British Library Cataloging-in-Publication Data is available

This book has been composed in Times Roman and Myriad using ZzTEX
by Princeton Editorial Associates, Inc., Scottsdale, Arizona.

Printed on acid-free paper.   ∞

press.princeton.edu

Printed in the United States of America

1 3 5 7 9 10 8 6 4 2

To Asu, for her unending love and support

Contents

Preface   xv

Part I: Introduction

Chapter 1   Economic Growth and Economic Development:
                          The Questions   3

1.1   Cross-Country Income Differences   3
1.2   Income and Welfare   7
1.3   Economic Growth and Income Differences   9
1.4   Origins of Today's Income Differences and World Economic Growth   11
1.5   Conditional Convergence   15
1.6   Correlates of Economic Growth   18
1.7   From Correlates to Fundamental Causes   19
1.8   The Agenda   21
1.9   References and Literature   23

Chapter 2   The Solow Growth Model   26

2.1   The Economic Environment of the Basic Solow Model   27
2.2   The Solow Model in Discrete Time   34
2.3   Transitional Dynamics in the Discrete-Time Solow Model   43
2.4   The Solow Model in Continuous Time   47
2.5   Transitional Dynamics in the Continuous-Time Solow Model   51
2.6   A First Look at Sustained Growth   55
2.7   Solow Model with Technological Progress   56
2.8   Comparative Dynamics   67
2.9   Taking Stock   68
2.10   References and Literature   69
2.11   Exercises   71

Chapter 3   The Solow Model and the Data   77

3.1   Growth Accounting   77
3.2   The Solow Model and Regression Analyses   80
3.3   The Solow Model with Human Capital   85

3.4   Solow Model and Cross-Country Income Differences: Regression Analyses   90
3.5   Calibrating Productivity Differences   96
3.6   Estimating Productivity Differences   100
3.7   Taking Stock   105
3.8   References and Literature   106
3.9   Exercises   107

Chapter 4   Fundamental Determinants of Differences in Economic Performance   109
4.1   Proximate versus Fundamental Causes   109
4.2   Economies of Scale, Population, Technology, and World Growth   112
4.3   The Four Fundamental Causes   114
4.4   The Effect of Institutions on Economic Growth   123
4.5   What Types of Institutions?   136
4.6   Disease and Development   137
4.7   Political Economy of Institutions: First Thoughts   140
4.8   Taking Stock   140
4.9   References and Literature   141
4.10 Exercises   143

Part II: Toward Neoclassical Growth

Chapter 5   Foundations of Neoclassical Growth   147
5.1   Preliminaries   147
5.2   The Representative Household   149
5.3   Infinite Planning Horizon   156
5.4   The Representative Firm   158
5.5   Problem Formulation   160
5.6   Welfare Theorems   161
5.7   Proof of the Second Welfare Theorem (Theorem 5.7) *   168
5.8   Sequential Trading   171
5.9   Optimal Growth   174
5.10 Taking Stock   176
5.11 References and Literature   176
5.12 Exercises   178

Chapter 6   Infinite-Horizon Optimization and Dynamic Programming   182
6.1   Discrete-Time Infinite-Horizon Optimization   182
6.2   Stationary Dynamic Programming   185
6.3   Stationary Dynamic Programming Theorems   187
6.4   The Contraction Mapping Theorem and Applications *   190
6.5   Proofs of the Main Dynamic Programming Theorems *   194
6.6   Applications of Stationary Dynamic Programming   201
6.7   Nonstationary Infinite-Horizon Optimization   211
6.8   Optimal Growth in Discrete Time   215
6.9   Competitive Equilibrium Growth   219

6.10 Computation 221
6.11 Taking Stock 221
6.12 References and Literature 222
6.13 Exercises 223

Chapter 7   An Introduction to the Theory of Optimal Control 227

7.1 Variational Arguments 228
7.2 The Maximum Principle: A First Look 235
7.3 Infinite-Horizon Optimal Control 240
7.4 More on Transversality Conditions 250
7.5 Discounted Infinite-Horizon Optimal Control 253
7.6 Existence of Solutions, Concavity, and Differentiability * 259
7.7 A First Look at Optimal Growth in Continuous Time 268
7.8 The q-Theory of Investment and Saddle-Path Stability 269
7.9 Taking Stock 274
7.10 References and Literature 275
7.11 Exercises 278

Part III: Neoclassical Growth

Chapter 8   The Neoclassical Growth Model 287

8.1 Preferences, Technology, and Demographics 287
8.2 Characterization of Equilibrium 293
8.3 Optimal Growth 298
8.4 Steady-State Equilibrium 300
8.5 Transitional Dynamics and Uniqueness of Equilibrium 302
8.6 Neoclassical Growth in Discrete Time 305
8.7 Technological Change and the Canonical Neoclassical Model 306
8.8 The Role of Policy 312
8.9 Comparative Dynamics 313
8.10 A Quantitative Evaluation 315
8.11 Extensions 317
8.12 Taking Stock 317
8.13 References and Literature 318
8.14 Exercises 319

Chapter 9   Growth with Overlapping Generations 327

9.1 Problems of Infinity 328
9.2 The Baseline Overlapping Generations Model 329
9.3 The Canonical Overlapping Generations Model 335
9.4 Overaccumulation and Pareto Optimality of Competitive Equilibrium
in the Overlapping Generations Model 336
9.5 Role of Social Security in Capital Accumulation 339
9.6 Overlapping Generations with Impure Altruism 342
9.7 Overlapping Generations with Perpetual Youth 345
9.8 Overlapping Generations in Continuous Time 348
9.9 Taking Stock 353

9.10   References and Literature   354
9.11   Exercises   355

Chapter 10   Human Capital and Economic Growth   359

10.1   A Simple Separation Theorem   359
10.2   Schooling Investments and Returns to Education   361
10.3   The Ben-Porath Model   363
10.4   Neoclassical Growth with Physical and Human Capital   367
10.5   Capital-Skill Complementarity in an Overlapping Generations Model   371
10.6   Physical and Human Capital with Imperfect Labor Markets   374
10.7   Human Capital Externalities   379
10.8   The Nelson-Phelps Model of Human Capital   380
10.9   Taking Stock   382
10.10 References and Literature   384
10.11 Exercises   384

Chapter 11   First-Generation Models of Endogenous Growth   387

11.1   The *AK* Model Revisited   388
11.2   The *AK* Model with Physical and Human Capital   393
11.3   The Two-Sector *AK* Model   395
11.4   Growth with Externalities   398
11.5   Taking Stock   402
11.6   References and Literature   404
11.7   Exercises   404

Part IV: Endogenous Technological Change

Chapter 12   Modeling Technological Change   411

12.1   Different Conceptions of Technology   411
12.2   Science and Profits   414
12.3   The Value of Innovation in Partial Equilibrium   416
12.4   The Dixit-Stiglitz Model and Aggregate Demand Externalities   422
12.5   Individual R&D Uncertainty and the Stock Market   428
12.6   Taking Stock   429
12.7   References and Literature   430
12.8   Exercises   431

Chapter 13   Expanding Variety Models   433

13.1   The Lab-Equipment Model of Growth with Input Varieties   433
13.2   Growth with Knowledge Spillovers   444
13.3   Growth without Scale Effects   446
13.4   Growth with Expanding Product Varieties   448
13.5   Taking Stock   452
13.6   References and Literature   453
13.7   Exercises   453

Chapter 14   Models of Schumpeterian Growth   458

14.1   A Baseline Model of Schumpeterian Growth   459
14.2   A One-Sector Schumpeterian Growth Model   468
14.3   Innovation by Incumbents and Entrants   472
14.4   Step-by-Step Innovations *   479
14.5   Taking Stock   489
14.6   References and Literature   490
14.7   Exercises   491

Chapter 15   Directed Technological Change   497

15.1   Importance of Biased Technological Change   498
15.2   Basics and Definitions   500
15.3   Baseline Model of Directed Technological Change   503
15.4   Directed Technological Change with Knowledge Spillovers 514
15.5   Directed Technological Change without Scale Effects   518
15.6   Endogenous Labor-Augmenting Technological Change   519
15.7   Generalizations and Other Applications   522
15.8   An Alternative Approach to Labor-Augmenting Technological Change* 523
15.9   Taking Stock   526
15.10 References and Literature   527
15.11 Exercises   529

Part V: Stochastic Growth

Chapter 16   Stochastic Dynamic Programming   537

16.1   Dynamic Programming with Expectations   537
16.2   Proofs of the Stochastic Dynamic Programming Theorems * 544
16.3   Stochastic Euler Equations   549
16.4   Generalization to Markov Processes *   552
16.5   Applications of Stochastic Dynamic Programming   554
16.6   Taking Stock   561
16.7   References and Literature   561
16.8   Exercises   562

Chapter 17   Stochastic Growth Models   566

17.1   The Brock-Mirman Model   567
17.2   Equilibrium Growth under Uncertainty   571
17.3   Application: Real Business Cycle Models   579
17.4   Growth with Incomplete Markets: The Bewley Model   583
17.5   The Overlapping Generations Model with Uncertainty   586
17.6   Risk, Diversification, and Growth   588
17.7   Taking Stock   603
17.8   References and Literature   604
17.9   Exercises   605

Part VI: Technology Diffusion, Trade, and Interdependences

Chapter 18   Diffusion of Technology   611
18.1 Productivity Differences and Technology   611
18.2 A Benchmark Model of Technology Diffusion   613
18.3 Technology Diffusion and Endogenous Growth   619
18.4 Appropriate and Inappropriate Technologies and Productivity Differences   623
18.5 Contracting Institutions and Technology Adoption   630
18.6 Taking Stock   642
18.7 References and Literature   643
18.8 Exercises   644

Chapter 19   Trade and Growth   648
19.1 Growth and Financial Capital Flows   648
19.2 Why Does Capital Not Flow from Rich to Poor Countries?   653
19.3 Economic Growth in a Heckscher-Ohlin World   655
19.4 Trade, Specialization, and the World Income Distribution   663
19.5 Trade, Technology Diffusion, and the Product Cycle   674
19.6 Trade and Endogenous Technological Change   678
19.7 Learning-by-Doing, Trade, and Growth   680
19.8 Taking Stock   684
19.9 References and Literature   685
19.10 Exercises   687

Part VII: Economic Development and Economic Growth

Chapter 20   Structural Change and Economic Growth   697
20.1 Nonbalanced Growth: The Demand Side   697
20.2 Nonbalanced Growth: The Supply Side   703
20.3 Agricultural Productivity and Industrialization   715
20.4 Taking Stock   719
20.5 References and Literature   720
20.6 Exercises   721

Chapter 21   Structural Transformations and Market Failures
in Development   725
21.1 Financial Development   726
21.2 Fertility, Mortality, and the Demographic Transition   729
21.3 Migration, Urbanization, and the Dual Economy   736
21.4 Distance to the Frontier and Changes in the Organization of Production   744
21.5 Multiple Equilibria from Aggregate Demand Externalities and the Big Push   752
21.6 Inequality, Credit Market Imperfections, and Human Capital   758
21.7 Toward a Unified Theory of Development and Growth?   764
21.8 Taking Stock   768
21.9 References and Literature   769
21.10 Exercises   771

Part VIII: The Political Economy of Growth

Chapter 22   Institutions, Political Economy, and Growth   781

22.1   The Impact of Institutions on Long-Run Development   781
22.2   Distributional Conflict and Economic Growth in a Simple Society   784
22.3   The Canonical Cobb-Douglas Model of Distributional Conflict   792
22.4   Distributional Conflict and Competition   793
22.5   Subgame Perfect versus Markov Perfect Equilibria   799
22.6   Inefficient Economic Institutions: A First Pass   802
22.7   Heterogeneous Preferences, Social Choice, and the Median Voter *   805
22.8   Distributional Conflict and Economic Growth: Heterogeneity and the Median Voter   814
22.9   The Provision of Public Goods: Weak versus Strong States   817
22.10   Taking Stock   822
22.11   References and Literature   823
22.12   Exercises   825

Chapter 23   Political Institutions and Economic Growth   831

23.1   Political Regimes and Economic Growth   832
23.2   Political Institutions and Growth-Enhancing Policies   834
23.3   Dynamic Trade-offs   837
23.4   Understanding Endogenous Political Change   850
23.5   Taking Stock   856
23.6   References and Literature   857
23.7   Exercises   858

Epilogue: Mechanics and Causes of Economic Growth   861

What Have We Learned?   861
A Possible Perspective on Growth and Stagnation over the Past 200 Years   864
Many Remaining Questions   872

Part IX: Mathematical Appendixes

Appendix A   Odds and Ends in Real Analysis and Applications to Optimization   877

A.1   Distances and Metric Spaces   878
A.2   Mappings, Functions, Sequences, Nets, and Continuity   880
A.3   A Minimal Amount of Topology: Continuity and Compactness *   885
A.4   The Product Topology *   889
A.5   Absolute Continuity and Equicontinuity *   891
A.6   Correspondences and Berge's Maximum Theorem   894
A.7   Convexity, Concavity, Quasi-Concavity, and Fixed Points   898
A.8   Differentiation, Taylor Series, and the Mean Value Theorem   900
A.9   Functions of Several Variables and the Inverse and Implicit Function Theorems   904
A.10   Separation Theorems *   907

A.11 Constrained Optimization   910
A.12 Exercises   915

Appendix B   Review of Ordinary Differential Equations   917

B.1   Eigenvalues and Eigenvectors   917
B.2   Some Basic Results on Integrals   918
B.3   Linear Differential Equations   920
B.4   Solutions to Linear First-Order Differential Equations   921
B.5   Systems of Linear Differential Equations   924
B.6   Local Analysis and Stability of Nonlinear Differential Equations   926
B.7   Separable and Exact Differential Equations   927
B.8   Existence and Uniqueness of Solutions   929
B.9   Continuity and Differentiability of Solutions   930
B.10 Difference Equations   930
B.11 Exercises   932

Appendix C   Brief Review of Dynamic Games   934

C.1   Basic Definitions   934
C.2   Some Basic Results   937
C.3   Application: Repeated Games with Perfect Observability   941
C.4   Exercises   942

Appendix D   List of Theorems   944

Chapter 2   944
Chapter 5   944
Chapter 6   944
Chapter 7   945
Chapter 10   945
Chapter 16   945
Chapter 22   946
Appendix A   946
Appendix B   947
Appendix C   947

References   949

Name Index   971

Subject Index   977

Preface

As long as a branch of science offers an abundance of problems, so long is it alive.

—David Hilbert, Paris, 1900

This book is intended to serve two purposes. First and foremost, this is a book about economic growth and long-run economic development. The process of economic growth and the sources of differences in economic performance across nations are some of the most interesting, important, and challenging areas in modern social science. The primary purpose of this book is to introduce graduate students to these major questions and to the theoretical tools necessary for studying them. The book therefore strives to provide students with a strong background in dynamic economic analysis, since only such a background will enable a serious study of economic growth and economic development. I also try to provide a clear discussion of the broad empirical patterns and historical processes underlying the current state of the world economy. This narrative is motivated by my belief that to understand why some countries grow and others fail to do so, economists have to move beyond the mechanics of models and pose questions about the fundamental causes of economic growth.

Second, in a somewhat different capacity, this book is also a graduate-level introduction to modern macroeconomics and dynamic economic analysis. It is sometimes commented that, unlike basic microeconomic theory, there is no core of current macroeconomic theory that is shared by all economists. This is not entirely true. While there is disagreement among macroeconomists about how to approach short-run macroeconomic phenomena and what the boundaries of macroeconomics should be, there is broad agreement about the workhorse models of dynamic macroeconomic analysis. These include the Solow growth model, the neoclassical growth model, the overlapping generations model, and models of technological change and technology adoption. Since these are all models of economic growth, a thorough treatment of modern economic growth can also provide (and perhaps should provide) an introduction to this core material of modern macroeconomics. Although there are several good graduate-level macroeconomic textbooks, they typically spend relatively little time on the basic core material and do not develop the links between modern macroeconomic analysis and economic dynamics on the one hand and general equilibrium theory on the other. In contrast, the current book does not cover any of the short-run topics in macroeconomics, but provides a thorough and rigorous introduction to what I view to be the core of macroeconomics.

The selection of topics is designed to strike a balance between the two purposes of the book. Chapters 1, 3, and 4 introduce many of the salient features of the process of economic growth and the sources of cross-country differences in economic performance. Even though these chapters cannot do justice to the large literature on economic growth empirics, they provide a sufficient background for students to appreciate the issues that are central to the study of economic growth and a platform for further study of this large literature.

Chapters 5–7 cover the conceptual and mathematical foundations of modern macroeconomic analysis. Chapter 5 provides the microfoundations for much of the rest of the book (and for much of modern macroeconomics), while Chapters 6 and 7 supply a quick but relatively rigorous introduction to dynamic optimization. Most books on macroeconomics or economic growth use either continuous time or discrete time exclusively. I believe that a serious study of both economic growth and modern macroeconomics requires the student (and the researcher) to be able to move between formulations using discrete and continuous time, choosing the more convenient or appropriate approach for the set of questions at hand. Therefore I have deviated from standard practice and included both continuous-time and discrete-time material throughout the book.

Chapters 2, 8, 9, and 10 introduce the basic workhorse models of modern macroeconomics and traditional economic growth, while Chapter 11 presents the first-generation models of sustained (endogenous) economic growth. Chapters 12–15 cover models of technological progress, which are an essential part of any modern economic growth course.

Chapter 16 generalizes the tools introduced in Chapter 6 to stochastic environments. Using these tools, Chapter 17 presents a number of models of stochastic growth—most notably the neoclassical growth model under uncertainty, which is the foundation of much of modern macroeconomics (though it is often left out of courses on economic growth). The canonical Real Business Cycle model is presented as an application. This chapter also covers another major workhorse model of modern macroeconomics, the incomplete markets model of Bewley. Finally, Chapter 17 also presents a number of other approaches to modeling the interaction between incomplete markets and economic growth and shows how models of stochastic growth can be useful in understanding how economies transition from stagnation or slow growth to an equilibrium with sustained growth.

Chapters 18–21 cover topics that are sometimes left out of economic growth textbooks. These include models of technology adoption, technology diffusion, the interaction between international trade and technology, the process of structural change, the demographic transition, the possibility of poverty traps, the effects of inequality on economic growth, and the interaction between financial and economic development. These topics are important for creating a bridge between the empirical patterns we observe in practice and the theory. Most traditional growth models consider a single economy in isolation, often after it has already embarked on a process of steady economic growth. A study of models that incorporate cross-country interdependences, structural change, and the possibility of takeoffs makes it possible to link core topics of development economics, such as structural change, poverty traps, or the demographic transition, to the theory of economic growth.

Finally, Chapters 22 and 23 consider another topic often omitted from macroeconomics and economic growth textbooks: political economy. Inclusion of this material is motivated by my belief that the study of economic growth would be seriously hampered if we failed to ask questions about the fundamental causes of differences among countries in their economic performances. These questions inexorably bring us to differences in economic policies and institutions across nations. Political economy enables us to develop models to understand why economic policies and institutions differ across countries and must therefore be an integral part of the study of economic growth.

A few words on the philosophy and organization of the book might also be useful for students and teachers. The underlying philosophy of the book is that all the results that are stated should be proved or at least explained in detail. This implies a somewhat different organization than found in other books. Most textbooks in economics do not provide proofs for many of the results that are stated or invoked, and mathematical tools that are essential for the analysis are often taken for granted or developed in appendixes. In contrast, I have strived to provide simple proofs of almost all results stated in this book. It turns out that once unnecessary generality is removed, most results can be stated and proved in a way that is easily accessible to graduate students. In fact, I believe that even somewhat long proofs are much easier to understand than general statements made without proof, which leave the reader wondering why these statements are true.

I hope that the style I have chosen not only makes the book self-contained but also gives students an opportunity to develop a thorough understanding of the material. In line with this philosophy, I present the basic mathematical tools necessary for the development of the main material in the body of the text. My own experience suggests that a linear progression, where the necessary mathematical tools are introduced when needed, makes it easier for students to follow and appreciate the material. Consequently, analysis of the stability of dynamical systems, dynamic programming in discrete time, and optimal control in continuous time are all introduced in the main body of the text. This should both help students appreciate the foundations of the theory of economic growth and provide them with an introduction to the main tools of dynamic economic analysis, which are increasingly used in every subdiscipline of economics. Throughout, when some material is technically more difficult and can be skipped without loss of continuity, it is marked with an asterisk (*). Material that is only tangentially related to the main results in the text or that should be familiar to most graduate students is left for the appendixes.

I have also included a large number of exercises. Students can gain a thorough understanding of the material only by working through the exercises. Exercises that are somewhat more difficult are also marked with an asterisk.

This book can be used in a number of different ways. First, it can be used in a one-quarter or one-semester course on economic growth. Such a course might start with Chapters 1–4, then depending on the nature of the course, use Chapters 5–7 either for a thorough study of the general equilibrium and dynamic optimization foundations of growth theory or only for reference. Chapters 8–11 cover traditional growth theory, and Chapters 12–15 provide the basics of endogenous growth theory. Depending on time and interest, any selection of Chapters 16–23 can be used for the last part of such a course.

Second, the book can be used for a one-quarter first-year graduate-level course in macroeconomics. In this case, Chapter 1 would be optional. Chapters 2, 5–7, 8–11, 16–17, and a selection from 12–15 would be the core of such a course. The same material could also be covered in a one-semester course, but in this case, it could be supplemented either with some of the later chapters or with material from one of the leading graduate-level macroeconomic textbooks on short-run macroeconomics, fiscal policy, asset pricing, or other topics in dynamic macroeconomics.

Third, the book can be used for an advanced (second-year) course in economic growth or economic development. An advanced course on growth or development could use Chapters 1–11 as background and then focus on selected chapters from among Chapters 12–23.

Finally, since the book is self-contained, I also hope that it can be used for self-study.

Acknowledgments

This book grew out of the first graduate-level introduction to macroeconomics course I taught at MIT. Parts of the book have also been taught as part of second-year graduate courses on macroeconomics and economic growth. I thank the students who attended these lectures and made comments that have improved the manuscript. I owe special thanks to Nathan

Hendren, Derek Li, Monica Martinez-Bravo, Plamen Nemov, Samuel Pienknagura, Anna Zabai, and especially to Georgy Egorov, Michael Peters, and Alp Simsek for outstanding research assistance.

Alp deserves more than a special mention. He has been involved with almost every aspect of the book for more than two years. Without Alp's help, the book would have taken me much longer to complete and would have contained many more errors. I am deeply indebted to him.

I also thank Pol Antras, Gabriel Carroll, Francesco Caselli, Melissa Dell, Jesus Fernandez-Villaverde, Kiminori Matsuyama, James Robinson, and Pierre Yared for very valuable suggestions on multiple chapters, and George-Marios Angeletos, Binyamin Berdugo, Truman Bewley, Olivier Blanchard, Leopoldo Fergusson, Peter Funk, Oded Galor, Hugo Hopenhayn, Simon Johnson, Chad Jones, Christos Koulovatianos, Omer Moav, Eduardo Morales, Ismail Saglam, Ekkehart Schlicht, Patricia Waeger, Luis Zermeno, and Jesse Zinn for useful suggestions and corrections on individual chapters.

Last but not least, I thank Lauren Fahey for editorial suggestions on multiple chapters and help with the references, Cyd Westmoreland for truly exceptional copyediting and editorial suggestions, and Seth Ditchik and his colleagues at Princeton University Press for support and help throughout the process.

PART I

INTRODUCTION

Economic Growth and Economic Development: The Questions

1.1 Cross-Country Income Differences

There are very large differences in income per capita and output per worker across countries today. Countries at the top of the world income distribution are more than 30 times as rich as those at the bottom. For example, in 2000, gross domestic product (GDP; or income) per capita in the United States was more than $34,000. In contrast, income per capita is much lower in many other countries: about $8,000 in Mexico, about $4,000 in China, just over $2,500 in India, only about $1,000 in Nigeria, and much, much lower in some other sub-Saharan African countries, such as Chad, Ethiopia, and Mali. These numbers are all in 2000 U.S. dollars and are adjusted for purchasing power parity (PPP) to allow for differences in relative prices of different goods across countries.[1] The cross-country income gap is considerably larger when there is no PPP adjustment. For example, without the PPP adjustment, GDP per capita in India and China relative to the United States in 2000 would be lower by a factor of four or so.

Figure 1.1 provides a first look at these differences. It plots estimates of the distribution of PPP-adjusted GDP per capita across the available set of countries in 1960, 1980, and 2000. A number of features are worth noting. First, the 1960 density shows that 15 years after the end of World War II, most countries had income per capita less than $1,500 (in 2000 U.S. dollars); the mode of the distribution is around $1,250. The rightward shift of the distributions for 1980 and 2000 shows the growth of average income per capita for the next 40 years. In 2000, the mode is slightly above $3,000, but now there is another concentration of countries between $20,000 and $30,000. The density estimate for the year 2000 shows the considerable inequality in income per capita today.

The spreading out of the distribution in Figure 1.1 is partly because of the increase in average incomes. It may therefore be more informative to look at the logarithm (log) of

1. All data are from the Penn World tables compiled by Heston, Summers, and Aten (2002). Details of data sources and more on PPP adjustment can be found in the References and Literature section at the end of this chapter.

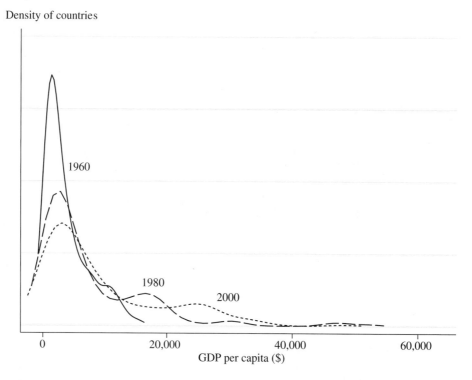

FIGURE 1.1 Estimates of the distribution of countries according to PPP-adjusted GDP per capita in 1960, 1980, and 2000.

income per capita. It is more natural to look at the log of variables, such as income per capita, that grow over time, especially when growth is approximately proportional, as suggested by Figure 1.8 below. This is for the simple reason that when $x(t)$ grows at a proportional rate, $\log x(t)$ grows linearly, and if $x_1(t)$ and $x_2(t)$ both grow by the same proportional amount, $\log x_1(t) - \log x_2(t)$ remains constant, while $x_1(t) - x_2(t)$ increases.

Figure 1.2 shows a similar pattern, but now the spreading is more limited, because the absolute gap between rich and poor countries has increased considerably between 1960 and 2000, while the proportional gap has increased much less. Nevertheless, it can be seen that the 2000 density for log GDP per capita is still more spread out than the 1960 density. In particular, both figures show that there has been a considerable increase in the density of relatively rich countries, while many countries still remain quite poor. This last pattern is sometimes referred to as the "stratification phenomenon," corresponding to the fact that some of the middle-income countries of the 1960s have joined the ranks of relatively high-income countries, while others have maintained their middle-income status or even experienced relative impoverishment.

Figures 1.1 and 1.2 demonstrate that there is somewhat greater inequality among nations today than in 1960. An equally relevant concept might be inequality among individuals in the world economy. Figures 1.1 and 1.2 are not directly informative on this, since they treat each country identically regardless of the size of its population. An alternative is presented in Figure 1.3, which shows the population-weighted distribution. In this case, countries such as China, India, the United States, and Russia receive greater weight because they have larger populations. The picture that emerges in this case is quite different. In fact, the 2000 distribution looks less spread out, with a thinner left tail than the 1960 distribution. This reflects the fact that

Density of countries

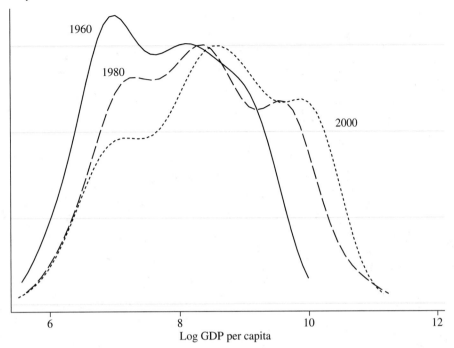

FIGURE 1.2   Estimates of the distribution of countries according to log GDP per capita (PPP adjusted) in 1960, 1980, and 2000.

Density of countries (weighted by population)

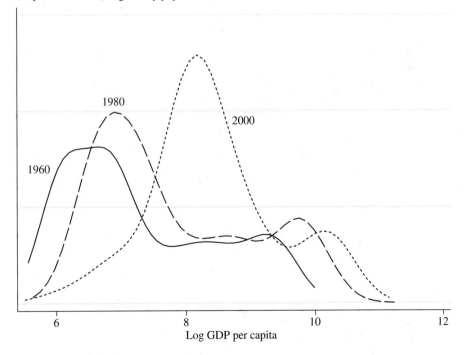

FIGURE 1.3   Estimates of the population-weighted distribution of countries according to log GDP per capita (PPP adjusted) in 1960, 1980, and 2000.

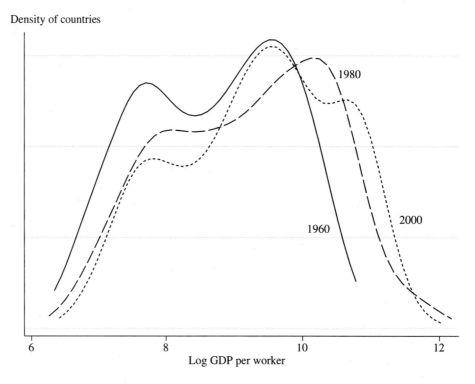

FIGURE 1.4   Estimates of the distribution of countries according to log GDP per worker (PPP adjusted) in 1960, 1980, and 2000.

in 1960 China and India were among the poorest nations in the world, whereas their relatively rapid growth in the 1990s puts them into the middle-poor category by 2000. Chinese and Indian growth has therefore created a powerful force for relative equalization of income per capita among the inhabitants of the globe.

Figures 1.1, 1.2, and 1.3 look at the distribution of GDP per capita. While this measure is relevant for the welfare of the population, much of growth theory focuses on the productive capacity of countries. Theory is therefore easier to map to data when we look at output (GDP) per worker. Moreover, key sources of difference in economic performance across countries are national policies and institutions. So for the purpose of understanding the sources of differences in income and growth across countries (as opposed to assessing welfare questions), the unweighted distribution is more relevant than the population-weighted distribution. Consequently, Figure 1.4 looks at the unweighted distribution of countries according to (PPP-adjusted) GDP per worker. "Workers" here refers to the total economically active population (according to the definition of the International Labour Organization). Figure 1.4 is very similar to Figure 1.2, and if anything, it shows a greater concentration of countries in the relatively rich tail by 2000, with the poor tail remaining more or less the same as in Figure 1.2.

Overall, Figures 1.1–1.4 document two important facts: first, there is great inequality in income per capita and income per worker across countries as shown by the highly dispersed distributions. Second, there is a slight but noticeable increase in inequality across nations (though not necessarily across individuals in the world economy).

1.2 Income and Welfare

Should we care about cross-country income differences? The answer is definitely yes. High income levels reflect high standards of living. Economic growth sometimes increases pollution or may raise individual aspirations, so that the same bundle of consumption may no longer satisfy an individual. But at the end of the day, when one compares an advanced, rich country with a less-developed one, there are striking differences in the quality of life, standards of living, and health.

Figures 1.5 and 1.6 give a glimpse of these differences and depict the relationship between income per capita in 2000 and consumption per capita and life expectancy at birth in the same year. Consumption data also come from the Penn World tables, while data on life expectancy at birth are available from the World Bank Development Indicators.

These figures document that income per capita differences are strongly associated with differences in consumption and in health as measured by life expectancy. Recall also that these numbers refer to PPP-adjusted quantities; thus differences in consumption do not (at least in principle) reflect the differences in costs for the same bundle of consumption goods in different countries. The PPP adjustment corrects for these differences and attempts to measure the variation in real consumption. Thus the richest countries are not only producing more than 30 times as much as the poorest countries, but are also consuming 30 times as much. Similarly, cross-country differences in health are quite remarkable; while life expectancy at birth is as

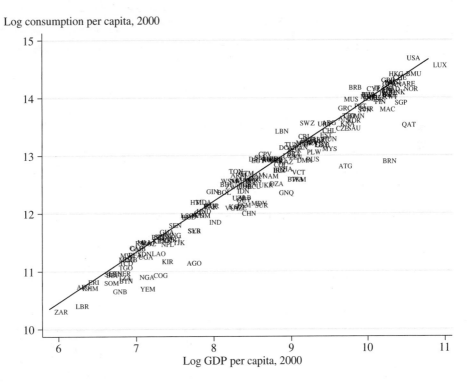

FIGURE 1.5 The association between income per capita and consumption per capita in 2000. For a definition of the abbreviations used in this and similar figures in the book, see http://unstats.un.org/unsd/methods/m49/m49alpha.htm.

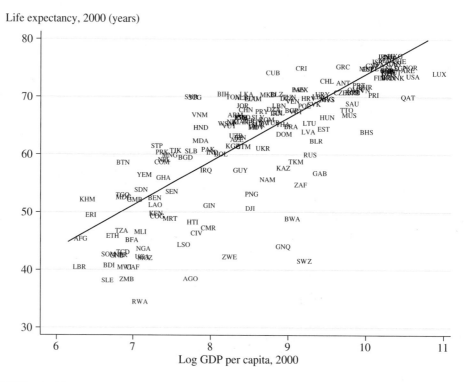

FIGURE 1.6 The association between income per capita and life expectancy at birth in 2000.

high as 80 in the richest countries, it is only between 40 and 50 in many sub-Saharan African nations. These gaps represent huge welfare differences.

Understanding why some countries are so rich while some others are so poor is one of the most important, perhaps *the* most important, challenges facing social science. It is important both because these income differences have major welfare consequences and because a study of these striking differences will shed light on how the economies of different nations function and how they sometimes fail to function.

The emphasis on income differences across countries implies neither that income per capita can be used as a "sufficient statistic" for the welfare of the average citizen nor that it is the only feature that we should care about. As discussed in detail later, the efficiency properties of the market economy (such as the celebrated First Welfare Theorem or Adam Smith's invisible hand) do not imply that there is no conflict among individuals or groups in society. Economic growth is generally good for welfare but it often creates winners and losers. Joseph Schumpeter's famous notion of creative destruction emphasizes precisely this aspect of economic growth; productive relationships, firms, and sometimes individual livelihoods will be destroyed by the process of economic growth, because growth is brought about by the introduction of new technologies and creation of new firms, replacing existing firms and technologies. This process creates a natural social tension, even in a growing society. Another source of social tension related to growth (and development) is that, as emphasized by Simon Kuznets and discussed in detail in Part VII, growth and development are often accompanied by sweeping structural transformations, which can also destroy certain established relationships and create yet other winners and losers in the process. One of the important questions of political economy, which is discussed in the last part of the book, concerns how institutions and policies can be arranged so that those who lose out from the process of economic growth can be compensated or prevented from blocking economic progress via other means.

A stark illustration of the fact that growth does not always mean an improvement in the living standards of all or even most citizens in a society comes from South Africa under apartheid. Available data (from gold mining wages) suggest that from the beginning of the twentieth century until the fall of the apartheid regime, GDP per capita grew considerably, but the real wages of black South Africans, who make up the majority of the population, likely fell during this period. This of course does not imply that economic growth in South Africa was not beneficial. South Africa is still one of the richest countries in sub-Saharan Africa. Nevertheless, this observation alerts us to other aspects of the economy and also underlines the potential conflicts inherent in the growth process. Similarly, most existing evidence suggests that during the early phases of the British industrial revolution, which started the process of modern economic growth, the living standards of the majority of the workers may have fallen or at best remained stagnant. This pattern of potential divergence between GDP per capita and the economic fortunes of large numbers of individuals and society is not only interesting in and of itself, but it may also inform us about why certain segments of the society may be in favor of policies and institutions that do not encourage growth.

1.3   Economic Growth and Income Differences

How can one country be more than 30 times richer than another? The answer lies in differences in growth rates. Take two countries, A and B, with the same initial level of income at some date. Imagine that country A has 0% growth per capita, so its income per capita remains constant, while country B grows at 2% per capita. In 200 years' time country B will be more than 52 times richer than country A. This calculation suggests that the United States might be considerably richer than Nigeria because it has grown steadily over an extended period of time, while Nigeria has not. We will see that there is a lot of truth to this simple calculation. In fact, even in the historically brief postwar era, there are tremendous differences in growth rates across countries. These differences are shown in Figure 1.7 for the postwar era, which plots the density of growth rates across countries in 1960, 1980, and 2000. The growth rate in 1960 refers to the (geometric) average of the growth rate between 1950 and 1969, the growth rate in 1980 refers to the average growth rate between 1970 and 1989, and 2000 refers to the average between 1990 and 2000 (in all cases subject to data availability). Figure 1.7 shows that in each time interval, there is considerable variability in growth rates; the cross-country distribution stretches from negative rates to average rates as high as 10% per year. It also shows that average growth in the world was more rapid in the 1950s and 1960s than in the subsequent decades.

Figure 1.8 provides another look at these patterns by plotting log GDP per capita for a number of countries between 1960 and 2000 (in this case, I plot GDP per capita instead of GDP per worker because of the availability of data and to make the figures more comparable to the historical figures below). At the top of the figure, U.S. and U.K. GDP per capita increase at a steady pace, with a slightly faster growth in the United States, so that the log (or proportional) gap between the two countries is larger in 2000 than it is in 1960. Spain starts much poorer than the United States and the United Kingdom in 1960 but grows very rapidly between 1960 and the mid-1970s, thus closing the gap between itself and the latter two countries. The three countries that show the most rapid growth in this figure are Singapore, South Korea, and Botswana. Singapore starts much poorer than the United Kingdom and Spain in 1960 but

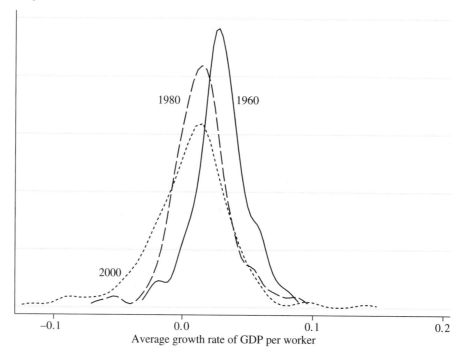

Density of countries

Average growth rate of GDP per worker

FIGURE 1.7 Estimates of the distribution of countries according to the growth rate of GDP per worker (PPP adjusted) in 1960, 1980, and 2000.

grows rapidly, and by the mid-1990s it has become richer than both. South Korea has a similar trajectory, though it starts out poorer than Singapore and grows slightly less rapidly, so that by the end of the sample it is still a little poorer than Spain. The other country that has grown very rapidly is the "African success story" Botswana, which was extremely poor at the beginning of the sample. Its rapid growth, especially after 1970, has taken Botswana to the ranks of the middle-income countries by 2000.

The two Latin American countries in this picture, Brazil and Guatemala, illustrate the often-discussed Latin American economic malaise of the postwar era. Brazil starts out richer than South Korea and Botswana and has a relatively rapid growth rate between 1960 and 1980. But it experiences stagnation from 1980 on, so that by the end of the sample South Korea and Botswana have become richer than Brazil. Guatemala's experience is similar but even more bleak. Contrary to Brazil, there is little growth in Guatemala between 1960 and 1980 and no growth between 1980 and 2000.

Finally, Nigeria and India start out at similar levels of income per capita as Botswana but experience little growth until the 1980s. Starting in 1980, the Indian economy experiences relatively rapid growth, though this has not been sufficient for its income per capita to catch up with the other nations in the figure. Finally, Nigeria, in a pattern that is unfortunately all too familiar in sub-Saharan Africa, experiences a contraction of its GDP per capita, so that in 2000 it is in fact poorer than it was in 1960.

The patterns shown in Figure 1.8 are what we would like to understand and explain. Why is the United States richer in 1960 than other nations and able to grow at a steady pace thereafter? How did Singapore, South Korea, and Botswana manage to grow at a relatively rapid pace for

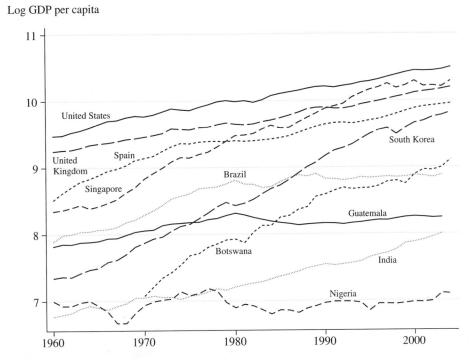

FIGURE 1.8 The evolution of income per capita in the United States, the United Kingdom, Spain, Singapore, Brazil, Guatemala, South Korea, Botswana, Nigeria, and India, 1960–2000.

40 years? Why did Spain grow relatively rapidly for about 20 years but then slow down? Why did Brazil and Guatemala stagnate during the 1980s? What is responsible for the disastrous growth performance of Nigeria?

1.4 Origins of Today's Income Differences and World Economic Growth

The growth rate differences shown in Figures 1.7 and 1.8 are interesting in their own right and could also be, in principle, responsible for the large differences in income per capita we observe today. But are they? The answer is largely no. Figure 1.8 shows that in 1960 there was already a very large gap between the United States on the one hand and India and Nigeria on the other.

This pattern can be seen more easily in Figure 1.9, which plots log GDP per worker in 2000 versus log GDP per capita in 1960 (in both cases relative to the U.S. value) superimposed over the 45° line. Most observations are around the 45° line, indicating that the relative ranking of countries has changed little between 1960 and 2000. Thus the origins of the very large income differences across nations are not to be found in the postwar era. There are striking growth differences during the postwar era, but the evidence presented so far suggests that world income distribution has been more or less stable, with a slight tendency toward becoming more unequal.

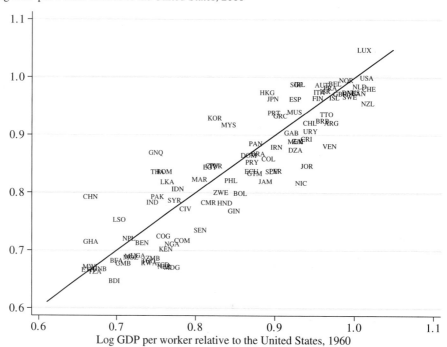

FIGURE 1.9 Log GDP per worker in 2000 versus log GDP per worker in 1960, together with the 45° line.

If not in the postwar era, when did this growth gap emerge? The answer is that much of the divergence took place during the nineteenth and early twentieth centuries. Figures 1.10–1.12 give a glimpse of these developments by using the data compiled by Angus Maddison for GDP per capita differences across nations going back to 1820 (or sometimes earlier). These data are less reliable than Summers-Heston's Penn World tables, since they do not come from standardized national accounts. Moreover, the sample is more limited and does not include observations for all countries going back to 1820. Finally, while these data include a correction for PPP, this is less complete than the price comparisons used to construct the price indices in the Penn World tables. Nevertheless, these are the best available estimates for differences in prosperity across a large number of nations beginning in the nineteenth century.

Figure 1.10 illustrates the divergence. It depicts the evolution of average income among five groups of countries: Africa, Asia, Latin America, Western Europe, and Western offshoots of Europe (Australia, Canada, New Zealand, the United States). It shows the relatively rapid growth of the Western offshoots and West European countries during the nineteenth century, while Asia and Africa remained stagnant and Latin America showed little growth. The relatively small (proportional) income gap in 1820 had become much larger by 1960.

Another major macroeconomic fact is visible in Figure 1.10: Western offshoots and West European nations experience a noticeable dip in GDP per capita around 1929 because of the famous Great Depression. Western offshoots, in particular the United States, only recovered fully from this large recession in the wake of World War II. How an economy can experience a sharp decline in output and how it recovers from such a shock are among the major questions of macroeconomics.

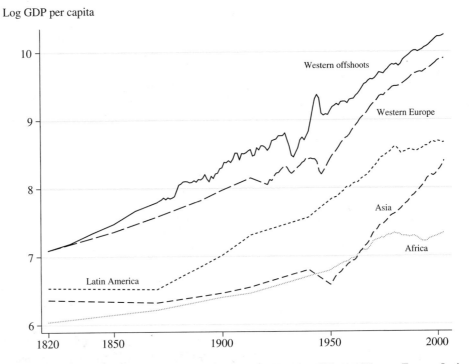

FIGURE 1.10 The evolution of average GDP per capita in Western offshoots, Western Europe, Latin America, Asia, and Africa, 1820–2000.

A variety of evidence suggests that differences in income per capita were even smaller before 1820. Maddison also has estimates for average income for the same groups of countries going back to 1000 A.D. or even earlier. Figure 1.10 can be extended back in time using these data; the results are shown in Figure 1.11. Although these numbers are based on scattered evidence and informed guesses, the general pattern is consistent with qualitative historical evidence and the fact that income per capita in any country cannot have been much less than $500 in terms of 2000 U.S. dollars, since individuals could not survive with real incomes much less than this level. Figure 1.11 shows that as we go further back in time, the gap among countries becomes much smaller. This further emphasizes that the big divergence among countries has taken place over the past 200 years or so. Another noteworthy feature that becomes apparent from this figure is the remarkable nature of world economic growth. Much evidence suggests that there was only limited economic growth before the eighteenth century and certainly before the fifteenth century. While certain civilizations, including ancient Greece, Rome, China, and Venice, managed to grow, their growth was either not sustained (thus ending with collapses and crises) or progressed only at a slow pace. No society before nineteenth-century Western Europe and the United States achieved steady growth at comparable rates.

Notice also that Maddison's estimates show a slow but steady increase in West European GDP per capita even earlier, starting in 1000. This assessment is not shared by all economic historians, many of whom estimate that there was little increase in income per capita before 1500 or even before 1800. For our purposes this disagreement is not central, however. What is important is that, using Walter Rostow's terminology, Figure 1.11 shows a pattern of *takeoff* into sustained growth; the economic growth experience of Western Europe and Western offshoots appears to have changed dramatically about 200 years or so ago. Economic historians also debate whether there was a discontinuous change in economic activity that deserves the

Log GDP per capita

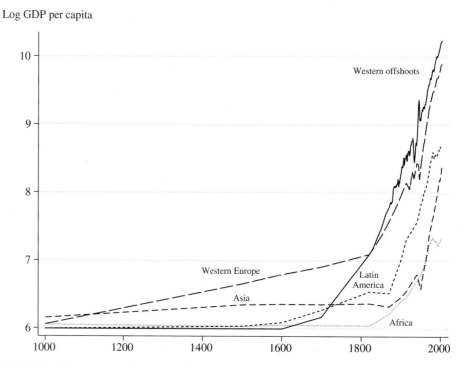

FIGURE 1.11 The evolution of average GDP per capita in Western offshoots, Western Europe, Latin America, Asia, and Africa, 1000–2000.

terms "takeoff" or "industrial revolution." This debate is again secondary to our purposes. Whether or not the change was discontinuous, it was present and transformed the functioning of many economies. As a result of this transformation, the stagnant or slowly growing economies of Europe embarked upon a path of sustained growth. The origins of today's riches and also of today's differences in prosperity are to be found in this pattern of takeoff during the nineteenth century. In the same time that Western Europe and its offshoots grew rapidly, much of the rest of the world did not experience a comparable takeoff (or did so much later). Therefore an understanding of modern economic growth and current cross-country income differences ultimately necessitates an inquiry into the causes of why the takeoff occurred, why it did so about 200 years ago, and why it took place only in some areas and not in others.

Figure 1.12 shows the evolution of income per capita for the United States, the United Kingdom, Spain, Brazil, China, India, and Ghana. This figure confirms the patterns shown in Figure 1.10 for averages, with the United States, the United Kingdom, and Spain growing much faster than India and Ghana throughout, and also much faster than Brazil and China except during the growth spurts experienced by these two countries.

Overall, on the basis of the available information we can conclude that the origins of the current cross-country differences in income per capita are in the nineteenth and early twentieth centuries (or perhaps even during the late eighteenth century). This cross-country divergence took place at the same time as a number of countries in the world "took off" and achieved sustained economic growth. Therefore understanding the origins of modern economic growth are not only interesting and important in their own right, but also holds the key to understanding the causes of cross-country differences in income per capita today.

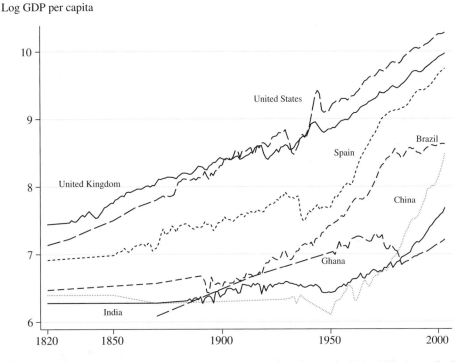

Log GDP per capita

FIGURE 1.12 The evolution of income per capita in the United States, the United Kindgom, Spain, Brazil, China, India, and Ghana, 1820–2000.

1.5 Conditional Convergence

I have so far documented the large differences in income per capita across nations, the slight divergence in economic fortunes over the postwar era, and the much larger divergence since the early 1800s. The analysis focused on the unconditional distribution of income per capita (or per worker). In particular, we looked at whether the income gap between two countries increases or decreases regardless of these countries' characteristics (e.g., institutions, policies, technology, or even investments). Barro and Sala-i-Martin (1991, 1992, 2004) argue that it is instead more informative to look at the conditional distribution. Here the question is whether the income gap between two countries that are similar in observable characteristics is becoming narrower or wider over time. In this case, the picture is one of conditional convergence: in the postwar period, the income gap between countries that share the same characteristics typically closes over time (though it does so quite slowly). This is important both for understanding the statistical properties of the world income distribution and also as an input into the types of theories that we would like to develop.

How do we capture conditional convergence? Consider a typical *Barro growth regression*:

$$g_{i,t,t-1} = \alpha \log y_{i,t-1} + \mathbf{X}_{i,t-1}^{T}\boldsymbol{\beta} + \varepsilon_{i,t}, \tag{1.1}$$

where $g_{i,t,t-1}$ is the annual growth rate between dates $t-1$ and t in country i, $y_{i,t-1}$ is output per worker (or income per capita) at date $t-1$, $\mathbf{X}$ is a vector of other variables included in the regression with coefficient vector $\boldsymbol{\beta}$ ($\mathbf{X}^{T}$ denotes the transpose of this vector), and $\varepsilon_{i,t}$

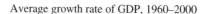

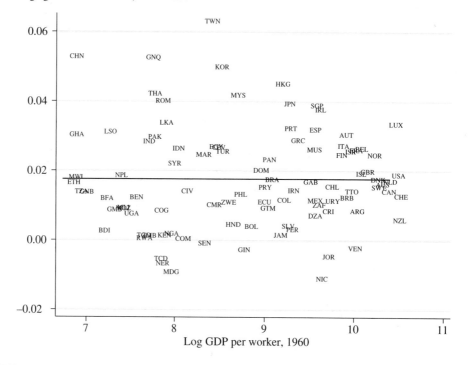

FIGURE 1.13 Annual growth rate of GDP per worker between 1960 and 2000 versus log GDP per worker in 1960 for the entire world.

is an error term capturing all other omitted factors. The variables in **X** are included because they are potential determinants of steady-state income and/or growth. First note that without covariates, (1.1) is quite similar to the relationship shown in Figure 1.9. In particular, since $g_{i,t,t-1} \approx \log y_{i,t} - \log y_{i,t-1}$, (1.1) can be written as

$$\log y_{i,t} \approx (1+\alpha) \log y_{i,t-1} + \varepsilon_{i,t}.$$

Figure 1.9 showed that the relationship between log GDP per worker in 2000 and log GDP per worker in 1960 can be approximated by the 45° line, so that in terms of this equation, α should be approximately equal to 0. This observation is confirmed by Figure 1.13, which depicts the relationship between the (geometric) average growth rate between 1960 and 2000 and log GDP per worker in 1960. This figure reiterates that there is no "unconditional" convergence for the entire world—no tendency for poorer nations to become relatively more prosperous—over the postwar period.

While there is no convergence for the entire world, when we look among the member nations of the Organisation for Economic Co-operation and Development (OECD),[2] we see a different pattern. Figure 1.14 shows that there is a strong negative relationship between log GDP per worker in 1960 and the annual growth rate between 1960 and 2000. What distinguishes this sample from the entire world sample is the relative homogeneity of the OECD countries, which

---

2. "OECD" here refers to the members that joined the OECD in the 1960s (this excludes Australia, New Zealand, Mexico, and Korea). The figure also excludes Germany because of lack of comparable data after reunification.

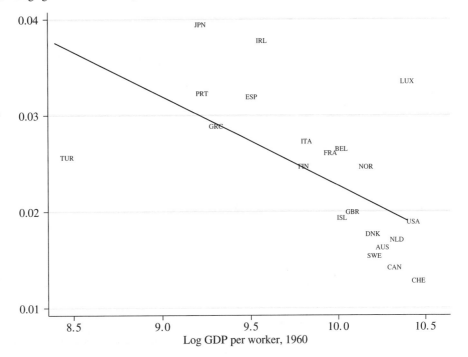

FIGURE 1.14 Annual growth rate of GDP per worker between 1960 and 2000 versus log GDP per worker in 1960 for core OECD countries.

have much more similar institutions, policies, and initial conditions than for the entire world. Thus there might be a type of conditional convergence when we control for certain country characteristics potentially affecting economic growth.

This is what the vector $\mathbf{X}$ captures in (1.1). In particular, when this vector includes such variables as years of schooling or life expectancy, using cross-sectional regressions Barro and Sala-i-Martin estimate α to be approximately -0.02, indicating that the income gap between countries that have the same human capital endowment has been narrowing over the postwar period on average at about 2 percent per year. When this equation is estimated using panel data and the vector $\mathbf{X}$ includes a full set of country fixed effects, the estimates of α become more negative, indicating faster convergence.

In summary, there is no evidence of (unconditional) convergence in the world income distribution over the postwar era (in fact, the evidence suggests some amount of divergence in incomes across nations). But there is some evidence for conditional convergence, meaning that the income gap between countries that are similar in observable characteristics appears to narrow over time. This last observation is relevant both for recognizing among which countries the economic divergence has occurred and for determining what types of models we should consider for understanding the process of economic growth and the differences in economic performance across nations. For example, we will see that many growth models, including the basic Solow and the neoclassical growth models, suggest that there should be transitional dynamics as economies below their steady-state (target) level of income per capita grow toward that level. Conditional convergence is consistent with this type of transitional dynamics.

1.6 Correlates of Economic Growth

The previous section emphasized the importance of certain country characteristics that might be related to the process of economic growth. What types of countries grow more rapidly? Ideally, this question should be answered at a causal level. In other words, we would like to know which specific characteristics of countries (including their policies and institutions) have a causal effect on growth. "Causal effect" refers to the answer to the following counterfactual thought experiment: if, all else being equal, a particular characteristic of the country were changed exogenously (i.e., not as part of equilibrium dynamics or in response to a change in other observable or unobservable variables), what would be the effect on equilibrium growth? Answering such causal questions is quite challenging, precisely because it is difficult to isolate changes in endogenous variables that are not driven by equilibrium dynamics or by omitted factors.

For this reason, let us start with the more modest question of what factors correlate with postwar economic growth. With an eye to the theories to come in the next two chapters, the two obvious candidates to look at are investments in physical and human capital (education).

Figure 1.15 shows a positive association between the average investment to GDP ratio and economic growth between 1960 and 2000. Figure 1.16 shows a positive correlation between average years of schooling and economic growth. These figures therefore suggest that the countries that have grown faster are typically those that have invested more in physical and human capital. It has to be stressed that these figures do not imply that physical or human capital investment are the causes of economic growth (even though we expect from basic economic theory that they should contribute to growth). So far these are simply correlations, and they

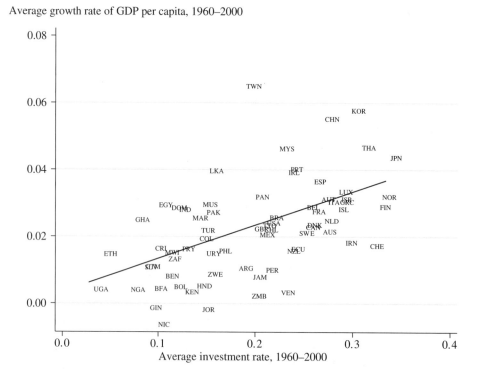

FIGURE 1.15 The relationship between average growth of GDP per capita and average growth of investments to GDP ratio, 1960–2000.

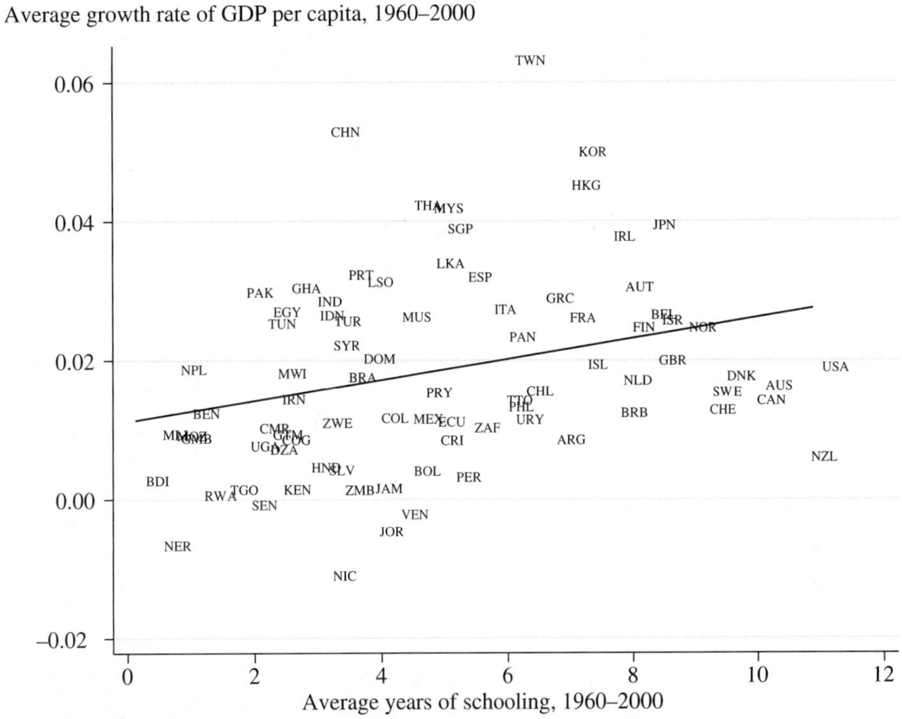

Average growth rate of GDP per capita, 1960–2000

FIGURE 1.16 The relationship between average growth of GDP per capita and average years of schooling, 1960–2000.

are likely driven, at least in part, by omitted factors affecting both investment and schooling on the one hand and economic growth on the other.

We investigate the role of physical and human capital in economic growth further in Chapter 3. One of the major points that emerges from the analysis in Chapter 3 is that focusing only on physical and human capital is not sufficient. Both to understand the process of sustained economic growth and to account for large cross-country differences in income, we also need to understand why societies differ in the efficiency with which they use their physical and human capital. Economists normally use the shorthand expression "technology" to capture factors other than physical and human capital that affect economic growth and performance. It is therefore important to remember that variations in technology across countries include not only differences in production techniques and in the quality of machines used in production but also disparities in productive efficiency (see in particular Chapter 21 on differences in productive efficiency resulting from the organization of markets and from market failures). A detailed study of technology (broadly construed) is necessary for understanding both the worldwide process of economic growth and cross-country differences. The role of technology in economic growth is investigated in Chapter 3 and later chapters.

1.7 From Correlates to Fundamental Causes

The correlates of economic growth, such as physical capital, human capital, and technology, is our first topic of study. But these are only proximate causes of economic growth and economic success (even if we convince ourselves that there is an element of causality in the correlations shown above). It would not be entirely satisfactory to explain the process of economic growth and cross-country differences with technology, physical capital, and human capital, since presumably there are reasons technology, physical capital, and human capital differ across countries. If these factors are so important in generating cross-country income differences and causing the takeoff into modern economic growth, why do certain societies fail to improve their technologies, invest more in physical capital, and accumulate more human capital?

Let us return to Figure 1.8 to illustrate this point further. This figure shows that South Korea and Singapore have grown rapidly over the past 50 years, while Nigeria has failed to do so. We can try to explain the successful performances of South Korea and Singapore by looking at the proximate causes of economic growth. We can conclude, as many have done, that rapid capital accumulation has been a major cause of these growth miracles and debate the relative roles of human capital and technology. We can simply blame the failure of Nigeria to grow on its inability to accumulate capital and to improve its technology. These perspectives are undoubtedly informative for understanding the mechanics of economic successes and failures of the postwar era. But at some level they do not provide answers to the central questions: How did South Korea and Singapore manage to grow, while Nigeria failed to take advantage of its growth opportunities? If physical capital accumulation is so important, why did Nigeria fail to invest more in physical capital? If education is so important, why are education levels in Nigeria still so low, and why is existing human capital not being used more effectively? The answer to these questions is related to the *fundamental causes* of economic growth—the factors potentially affecting why societies make different technology and accumulation choices.

At some level, fundamental causes are the factors that enable us to link the questions of economic growth to the concerns of the rest of the social sciences and ask questions about the roles of policies, institutions, culture, and exogenous environmental factors. At the risk of oversimplifying complex phenomena, we can think of the following list of potential fundamental causes: (1) luck (or multiple equilibria) that lead to divergent paths among societies with identical opportunities, preferences, and market structures; (2) geographic differences that affect the environment in which individuals live and influence the productivity of agriculture, the availability of natural resources, certain constraints on individual behavior, or even individual attitudes; (3) institutional differences that affect the laws and regulations under which individuals and firms function and shape the incentives they have for accumulation, investment, and trade; and (4) cultural differences that determine individuals' values, preferences, and beliefs. Chapter 4 presents a detailed discussion of the distinction between proximate and fundamental causes and what types of fundamental causes are more promising in explaining the process of economic growth and cross-country income differences.

For now, it is useful to briefly return to the contrast between South Korea and Singapore versus Nigeria and ask the questions (even if we are not in a position to fully answer them yet): Can we say that South Korea and Singapore owe their rapid growth to luck, while Nigeria was unlucky? Can we relate the rapid growth of South Korea and Singapore to geographic factors? Can we relate them to institutions and policies? Can we find a major role for culture? Most detailed accounts of postwar economics and politics in these countries emphasize the role of growth-promoting policies in South Korea and Singapore—including the relative security of property rights and investment incentives provided to firms. In contrast, Nigeria's postwar history is one of civil war, military coups, endemic corruption, and overall an environment that failed to provide incentives to businesses to invest and upgrade their technologies. It therefore seems necessary to look for fundamental causes of economic growth that make contact with these facts. Jumping ahead a little, it already appears implausible that luck can be the major explanation for the differences in postwar economic performance; there were already significant economic differences between South Korea, Singapore, and Nigeria at the beginning of the postwar era. It is also equally implausible to link the divergent fortunes of these countries to geographic factors. After all, their geographies did not change, but the growth spurts of South Korea and Singapore started in the postwar era. Moreover, even if Singapore benefited from being an island, without hindsight one might have concluded that Nigeria had the best environment for growth because of its rich oil reserves.[3] Cultural differences across countries are likely to be important in many respects, and the rapid growth of many Asian countries is often linked to certain "Asian values." Nevertheless, cultural explanations are also unlikely to adequately explain fundamental causes, since South Korean or Singaporean culture did not change much after the end of World War II, while their rapid growth is a distinctly postwar phenomenon. Moreover, while South Korea grew rapidly, North Korea, whose inhabitants share the same culture and Asian values, has endured one of the most disastrous economic performances of the past 50 years.

This admittedly quick (and partial) account suggests that to develop a better understanding of the fundamental causes of economic growth, we need to look at institutions and policies that affect the incentives to accumulate physical and human capital and improve technology. Institutions and policies were favorable to economic growth in South Korea and Singapore, but not in Nigeria. Understanding the fundamental causes of economic growth is largely about understanding the impact of these institutions and policies on economic incentives and why, for example, they have enhanced growth in South Korea and Singapore but not in Nigeria. The intimate link between fundamental causes and institutions highlighted by this discussion motivates Part VIII, which is devoted to the political economy of growth, that is, to the study of how institutions affect growth and why they differ across countries.

An important caveat should be noted at this point. Discussions of geography, institutions, and culture can sometimes be carried out without explicit reference to growth models or even to growth empirics. After all, this is what many social scientists do outside the field of economics. However, fundamental causes can only have a big impact on economic growth if they affect parameters and policies that have a first-order influence on physical and human capital and technology. Therefore an understanding of the mechanics of economic growth is essential for evaluating whether candidate fundamental causes of economic growth could indeed play the role that is sometimes ascribed to them. Growth empirics plays an equally important role in distinguishing among competing fundamental causes of cross-country income differences. It is only by formulating parsimonious models of economic growth and confronting them with data that we can gain a better understanding of both the proximate and the fundamental causes of economic growth.

1.8 The Agenda

The three major questions that have emerged from the brief discussion are:

1. Why are there such large differences in income per capita and worker productivity across countries?

2. Why do some countries grow rapidly while other countries stagnate?

3. What sustains economic growth over long periods of time, and why did sustained growth start 200 years or so ago?

---

3. One can turn this reasoning around and argue that Nigeria is poor because of a "natural resource curse," that is, precisely because it has abundant natural resources. But this argument is not entirely compelling, since there are other countries, such as Botswana, with abundant natural resources that have grown rapidly over the past 50 years. More important, the only plausible channel through which abundance of natural resources may lead to worse economic outcomes is related to institutional and political economy factors. Such factors take us to the realm of institutional fundamental causes.

For each question, a satisfactory answer requires a set of well-formulated models that illustrate the mechanics of economic growth and cross-country income differences together with an investigation of the fundamental causes of the different trajectories which these nations have embarked upon. In other words, we need a combination of theoretical models and empirical work.

The traditional growth models—in particular, the basic Solow and the neoclassical models—provide a good starting point, and the emphasis they place on investment and human capital seems consistent with the patterns shown in Figures 1.15 and 1.16. However, we will also see that technological differences across countries (either because of their differential access to technological opportunities or because of differences in the efficiency of production) are equally important. Traditional models treat technology and market structure as given or at best as evolving exogenously (rather like a black box). But if technology is so important, we ought to understand why and how it progresses and why it differs across countries. This motivates our detailed study of endogenous technological progress and technology adoption. Specifically, we will try to understand how differences in technology may arise, persist, and contribute to differences in income per capita. Models of technological change are also useful in thinking about the sources of sustained growth of the world economy over the past 200 years and the reasons behind the growth process that took off 200 years or so ago and has proceeded relatively steadily ever since.

Some of the other patterns encountered in this chapter will inform us about the types of models that have the greatest promise in explaining economic growth and cross-country differences in income. For example, we have seen that cross-country income differences can be accounted for only by understanding why some countries have grown rapidly over the past 200 years while others have not. Therefore we need models that can explain how some countries can go through periods of sustained growth while others stagnate.

Nevertheless, we have also seen that the postwar world income distribution is relatively stable (at most spreading out slightly from 1960 to 2000). This pattern has suggested to many economists that we should focus on models that generate large permanent cross-country differences in income per capita but not necessarily large permanent differences in growth rates (at least not in the recent decades). This argument is based on the following reasoning: with substantially different long-run growth rates (as in models of endogenous growth, where countries that invest at different rates grow at permanently different rates), we should expect significant divergence. We saw above that despite some widening between the top and the bottom, the cross-country distribution of income across the world is relatively stable over the postwar era.

Combining the postwar patterns with the origins of income differences over the past several centuries suggests that we should look for models that can simultaneously account for long periods of significant growth differences and for a distribution of world income that ultimately becomes stationary, though with large differences across countries. The latter is particularly challenging in view of the nature of the global economy today, which allows for the free flow of technologies and large flows of money and commodities across borders. We therefore need to understand how the poor countries fell behind and what prevents them today from adopting and imitating the technologies and the organizations (and importing the capital) of richer nations.

And as the discussion in the previous section suggests, all of these questions can be (and perhaps should be) answered at two distinct but related levels (and in two corresponding steps). The first step is to use theoretical models and data to understand the mechanics of economic growth. This step sheds light on the proximate causes of growth and explains differences in income per capita in terms of differences in physical capital, human capital, and technology, and these in turn will be related to other variables, such as preferences, technology, market structure, openness to international trade, and economic policies.

The second step is to look at the fundamental causes underlying these proximate factors and investigate why some societies are organized differently than others. Why do societies have different market structures? Why do some societies adopt policies that encourage economic growth while others put up barriers to technological change? These questions are central to a study of economic growth and can only be answered by developing systematic models of the political economy of development and looking at the historical process of economic growth to generate data that can shed light on these fundamental causes.

Our next task is to systematically develop a series of models to understand the mechanics of economic growth. I present a detailed exposition of the mathematical structure of a number of dynamic general equilibrium models that are useful for thinking about economic growth and related macroeconomic phenomena, and I emphasize the implications of these models for the sources of differences in economic performance across societies. Only by understanding these mechanics can we develop a useful framework for thinking about the causes of economic growth and income disparities.

1.9   References and Literature

The empirical material presented in this chapter is largely standard, and parts of it can be found in many books, though interpretations and emphases differ. Excellent introductions, with slightly different emphases, are provided in Jones's (1998, Chapter 1) and Weil's (2005, Chapter 1) undergraduate economic growth textbooks. Barro and Sala-i-Martin (2004) also present a brief discussion of the stylized facts of economic growth, though their focus is on postwar growth and conditional convergence rather than the very large cross-country income differences and the long-run perspective stressed here. Excellent and very readable accounts of the key questions of economic growth, with a similar perspective to the one here, are provided in Helpman (2005) and in Aghion and Howitt's new book (2008). Aghion and Howitt also provide a very useful introduction to many of the same topics discussed in this book.

Much of the data used in this chapter come from Summers-Heston's (Penn World) dataset (latest version, Summers, Heston, and Aten, 2006). These tables are the result of a careful study by Robert Summers and Alan Heston to construct internationally comparable price indices and estimates of income per capita and consumption. PPP adjustment is made possible by these data. Summers and Heston (1991) give a lucid discussion of the methodology for PPP adjustment and its use in the Penn World tables. PPP adjustment enables the construction of measures of income per capita that are comparable across countries. Without PPP adjustment, differences in income per capita across countries can be computed using the current exchange rate or some fundamental exchange rate. There are many problems with such exchange rate–based measures, however. The most important one is that they do not allow for the marked differences in relative prices and even overall price levels across countries. PPP adjustment brings us much closer to differences in real income and real consumption. GDP, consumption, and investment data from the Penn World tables are expressed in 1996 constant U.S. dollars. Information on workers (economically active population), consumption, and investment are also from this dataset. Life expectancy data are from the World Bank's World Development Indicators CD-ROM and refer to the average life expectancy of males and females at birth. This dataset also contains a range of other useful information. Schooling data are from Barro and Lee's (2001) dataset, which contains internationally comparable information on years of schooling. Throughout, cross-country figures use the World Bank labels to denote the identity of individual countries. A list of the labels can be found in http://unstats.un.org/unsd/methods/ m49/m49alpha.htm.

In all figures and regressions, growth rates are computed as geometric averages. In particular, the geometric average growth rate of output per capita y between date t and $t + T$ is

$$g_{t,t+T} \equiv \left(\frac{y_{t+T}}{y_t} \right)^{1/T} - 1.$$

The geometric average growth rate is more appropriate to use in the context of income per capita than is the arithmetic average, since the growth rate refers to proportional growth. It can be easily verified from this formula that if $y_{t+1} = (1 + g) \, y_t$ for all t, then $g_{t+T} = g$.

Historical data are from various works by Angus Maddison, in particular, Maddison (2001, 2003). While these data are not as reliable as the estimates from the Penn World tables, the general patterns they show are typically consistent with evidence from a variety of different sources. Nevertheless, there are points of contention. For example, in Figure 1.11 Maddison's estimates show a slow but relatively steady growth of income per capita in Western Europe starting in 1000. This growth pattern is disputed by some historians and economic historians. A relatively readable account, which strongly disagrees with this conclusion, is provided in Pomeranz (2000), who argues that income per capita in Western Europe and the Yangtze Valley in China were broadly comparable as late as 1800. This view also receives support from recent research by Allen (2004), which documents that the levels of agricultural productivity in 1800 were comparable in Western Europe and China. Acemoglu, Johnson, and Robinson (2002, 2005b) use urbanization rates as a proxy for income per capita and obtain results that are intermediate between those of Maddison and Pomeranz. The data in Acemoglu, Johnson, and Robinson (2002) also confirm that there were very limited income differences across countries as late as the 1500s and that the process of rapid economic growth started in the nineteenth century (or perhaps in the late eighteenth century). Recent research by Broadberry and Gupta (2006) also disputes Pomeranz's arguments and gives more support to a pattern in which there was already an income gap between Western Europe and China by the end of the eighteenth century.

The term "takeoff" used in Section 1.4 is introduced in Walter Rostow's famous book *The Stages of Economic Growth* (1960) and has a broader connotation than the term "industrial revolution," which economic historians typically use to refer to the process that started in Britain at the end of the eighteenth century (e.g., Ashton, 1969). Mokyr (1993) contains an excellent discussion of the debate on whether the beginning of industrial growth was due to a continuous or discontinuous change. Consistent with my emphasis here, Mokyr concludes that this is secondary to the more important fact that the modern process of growth *did* start around this time.

There is a large literature on the correlates of economic growth, starting with Barro (1991). This work is surveyed in Barro and Sala-i-Martin (2004) and Barro (1997). Much of this literature, however, interprets these correlations as causal effects, even when this interpretation is not warranted (see the discussions in Chapters 3 and 4).

Note that Figures 1.15 and 1.16 show the relationship between average investment and average schooling between 1960 and 2000 and economic growth over the same period. The relationship between the growth of investment and economic growth over this time is similar, but there is a much weaker relationship between growth of schooling and economic growth. This lack of association between growth of schooling and growth of output may be for a number of reasons. First, there is considerable measurement error in schooling estimates (see Krueger and Lindahl, 2001). Second, as shown in some of the models discussed later, the main role of human capital may be to facilitate technology adoption, and thus we may expect a stronger relationship between the level of schooling and economic growth than between the change in schooling and economic growth (see Chapter 10). Finally, the relationship between the level of schooling and economic growth may be partly spurious, in the sense that it may be capturing the influence of some other omitted factors also correlated with the level of schooling; if this is the case, these omitted factors may be removed when we look at changes. While we cannot reach a firm conclusion on these alternative explanations, the strong correlation between average schooling and economic growth documented in Figure 1.16 is interesting in itself.

The narrowing of differences in income per capita in the world economy when countries are weighted by population is explored in Sala-i-Martin (2005). Deaton (2005) contains a critique of Sala-i-Martin's approach. The point that incomes must have been relatively equal around 1800 or before, because there is a lower bound on real incomes necessary for the survival of an individual, was first made by Maddison (1991), and was later popularized by Pritchett (1997). Maddison's estimates of GDP per capita and Acemoglu, Johnson, and Robinson's (2002) estimates based on urbanization confirm this conclusion.

The estimates of the density of income per capita reported in this chapter are similar to those used by Quah (1993, 1997) and Jones (1997). These estimates use a nonparametric Gaussian kernel. The specific details of the kernel estimation do not change the general shape of the densities. Quah was also the first to emphasize the stratification in the world income distribution and the possible shift toward a bimodal distribution, which is visible in Figure 1.3. He dubbed this the "Twin Peaks" phenomenon (see also Durlauf and Quah, 1999). Barro (1991) and Barro and Sala-i-Martin (1992, 2004) emphasize the presence and importance of conditional convergence and argue against the relevance of the stratification pattern emphasized by Quah and others. The estimate of conditional convergence of about 2% per year is from Barro and Sala-i-Martin (1992). Caselli, Esquivel, and Lefort (1996) show that panel data regressions lead to considerably higher rates of conditional convergence.

Marris (1982) and Baumol (1986) were the first economists to conduct cross-country studies of convergence. However, the data at the time were of lower quality than the Summers-Heston data and also were available for only a selected sample of countries. Barro's (1991) and Barro and Sala-i-Martin's (1992) work using the Summers-Heston dataset has been instrumental in generating renewed interest in cross-country growth regressions.

The data on GDP growth and black real wages in South Africa are from Wilson (1972). Wages refer to real wages in gold mines. Feinstein (2005) provides an excellent economic history of South Africa. The implications of the British industrial revolution for real wages and living standards of workers are discussed in Mokyr (1993). Another example of rapid economic growth with falling real wages is provided by the experience of the Mexican economy in the early twentieth century (see Gomez-Galvarriato, 1998). There is also evidence that during this period, the average height of the population might have been declining, which is often associated with falling living standards (see López-Alonso and Porras Condey, 2004).

There is a major debate on the role of technology and capital accumulation in the growth experiences of East Asian nations, particularly South Korea and Singapore. See Young (1991, 1995) for the argument that increases in physical capital and labor inputs explain almost all of the rapid growth in these two countries. See Klenow and Rodriguez (1997) and Hsieh (2002) for the opposite point of view.

The difference between proximate and fundamental causes is discussed further in later chapters. This distinction is emphasized in a different context by Diamond (1997), though it is also implicitly present in North and Thomas's (1973) classic book. It is discussed in detail in the context of long-run economic development and economic growth in Acemoglu, Johnson, and Robinson (2005a). I revisit these issues in greater detail in Chapter 4.

2

The Solow Growth Model

The previous chapter introduced a number of basic facts and posed the main questions concerning the sources of economic growth over time and the causes of differences in economic performance across countries. These questions are central not only to growth theory but also to macroeconomics and the social sciences more generally. Our next task is to develop a simple framework that can help us think about the proximate causes and the mechanics of the process of economic growth and cross-country income differences. We will use this framework both to study potential sources of economic growth and also to perform simple comparative statics to gain an understanding of which country characteristics are conducive to higher levels of income per capita and more rapid economic growth.

Our starting point is the so-called Solow-Swan model named after Robert (Bob) Solow and Trevor Swan, or simply the Solow model, named after the more famous of the two economists. These economists published two pathbreaking articles in the same year, 1956 (Solow, 1956; Swan, 1956) introducing the Solow model. Bob Solow later developed many implications and applications of this model and was awarded the Nobel prize in economics for his contributions. This model has shaped the way we approach not only economic growth but also the entire field of macroeconomics. Consequently, a by-product of our analysis of this chapter is a detailed exposition of a workhorse model of macroeconomics.

The Solow model is remarkable in its simplicity. Looking at it today, one may fail to appreciate how much of an intellectual breakthrough it was. Before the advent of the Solow growth model, the most common approach to economic growth built on the model developed by Roy Harrod and Evsey Domar (Harrod, 1939; Domar, 1946). The Harrod-Domar model emphasized potential dysfunctional aspects of economic growth, for example, how economic growth could go hand-in-hand with increasing unemployment (see Exercise 2.23 on this model). The Solow model demonstrated why the Harrod-Domar model was not an attractive place to start. At the center of the Solow growth model, distinguishing it from the Harrod-Domar model, is the neoclassical aggregate production function. This function not only enables the Solow model to make contact with microeconomics, but as we will see in the next chapter, it also serves as a bridge between the model and the data.

An important feature of the Solow model, which is shared by many models presented in this book, is that it is a simple and abstract representation of a complex economy. At first, it may appear too simple or too abstract. After all, to do justice to the process of growth or macroeconomic equilibrium, we have to consider households and individuals with different tastes, abilities, incomes, and roles in society; various sectors; and multiple social interactions. The Solow model cuts through these complications by constructing a simple one-good economy, with little reference to individual decisions. Therefore, the Solow model should be thought of as a starting point and a springboard for richer models.

In this chapter, I present the basic Solow model. The closely related neoclassical growth model is presented in Chapter 8.

2.1 The Economic Environment of the Basic Solow Model

Economic growth and development are dynamic processes and thus necessitate dynamic models. Despite its simplicity, the Solow growth model is a dynamic general equilibrium model (though, importantly, many key features of dynamic general equilibrium models emphasized in Chapter 5, such as preferences and dynamic optimization, are missing in this model).

The Solow model can be formulated in either discrete or continuous time. I start with the discrete-time version, because it is conceptually simpler and more commonly used in macroeconomic applications. However, many growth models are formulated in continuous time, and I then provide a detailed exposition of the continuous-time version of the Solow model and show that it is often more convenient to work with.

2.1.1 Households and Production

Consider a closed economy, with a unique final good. The economy is in discrete time running to an infinite horizon, so that time is indexed by $t = 0, 1, 2, \ldots$. Time periods here may correspond to days, weeks, or years. For now, we do not need to specify the time scale.

The economy is inhabited by a large number of households. Throughout the book I use the terms *households, individuals,* and *agents* interchangeably. The Solow model makes relatively few assumptions about households, because their optimization problem is not explicitly modeled. This lack of optimization on the household side is the main difference between the Solow and the *neoclassical growth* models. The latter is the Solow model plus dynamic consumer (household) optimization. To fix ideas, you may want to assume that all households are identical, so that the economy trivially admits *a representative household*—meaning that the demand and labor supply side of the economy can be represented as if it resulted from the behavior of a single household. The representative household assumption is discussed in detail in Chapter 5.

What do we need to know about households in this economy? The answer is: not much. We have not yet endowed households with preferences (utility functions). Instead, for now, households are assumed to save a constant exogenous fraction $s \in (0, 1)$ of their disposable income—regardless of what else is happening in the economy. This assumption is the same as that used in basic Keynesian models and the Harrod-Domar model mentioned above. It is also at odds with reality. Individuals do not save a constant fraction of their incomes; if they did, then an announcement by the government that there will be a large tax increase next year should have no effect on their savings decisions, which seems both unreasonable and empirically incorrect. Nevertheless, the exogenous constant saving rate is a convenient starting point, and we will spend a lot of time in the rest of the book analyzing how consumers behave and make intertemporal choices.

The other key agents in the economy are firms. Firms, like consumers, are highly heterogeneous in practice. Even within a narrowly defined sector of an economy, no two firms are identical. But again for simplicity, let us start with an assumption similar to the representative household assumption, but now applied to firms: suppose that all firms in this economy have access to the same production function for the final good, or that the economy admits a *representative firm,* with a representative (or aggregate) production function. The conditions under which this representive firm assumption is reasonable are also discussed in Chapter 5. The aggregate production function for the unique final good is written as

$$Y(t) = F(K(t), L(t), A(t)), \tag{2.1}$$

where $Y(t)$ is the total amount of production of the final good at time t, $K(t)$ is the capital stock, $L(t)$ is total employment, and $A(t)$ is technology at time t. Employment can be measured in different ways. For example, we may want to think of $L(t)$ as corresponding to hours of employment or to number of employees. The capital stock $K(t)$ corresponds to the quantity of "machines" (or more specifically, equipment and structures) used in production, and it is typically measured in terms of the value of the machines. There are also multiple ways of thinking of capital (and equally many ways of specifying how capital comes into existence). Since the objective here is to start with a simple workable model, I make the rather sharp simplifying assumption that capital is the same as the final good of the economy. However, instead of being consumed, capital is used in the production process of more goods. To take a concrete example, think of the final good as "corn." Corn can be used both for consumption and as an input, as seed, for the production of more corn tomorrow. Capital then corresponds to the amount of corn used as seed for further production.

Technology, on the other hand, has no natural unit, and $A(t)$ is simply a *shifter* of the production function (2.1). For mathematical convenience, I often represent $A(t)$ in terms of a number, but it is useful to bear in mind that, at the end of the day, it is a representation of a more abstract concept. As noted in Chapter 1, we may often want to think of a broad notion of technology, incorporating the effects of the organization of production and of markets on the efficiency with which the factors of production are utilized. In the current model, $A(t)$ represents all these effects.

A major assumption of the Solow growth model (and of the neoclassical growth model we will study in Chapter 8) is that technology is *free:* it is publicly available as a nonexcludable, nonrival good. Recall that a good is *nonrival* if its consumption or use by others does not preclude an individual's consumption or use. It is *nonexcludable,* if it is impossible to prevent another person from using or consuming it. Technology is a good candidate for a nonexcludable, nonrival good; once the society has some knowledge useful for increasing the efficiency of production, this knowledge can be used by any firm without impinging on the use of it by others. Moreover, it is typically difficult to prevent firms from using this knowledge (at least once it is in the public domain and is not protected by patents). For example, once the society knows how to make wheels, everybody can use that knowledge to make wheels without diminishing the ability of others to do the same (thus making the knowledge to produce wheels nonrival). Moreover, unless somebody has a well-enforced patent on wheels, anybody can decide to produce wheels (thus making the knowhow to produce wheels nonexcludable). The implication of the assumptions that technology is nonrival and nonexcludable is that $A(t)$ is freely available to all potential firms in the economy and firms do not have to pay for making use of this technology. Departing from models in which technology is freely available is a major step toward understanding technological progress and will be our focus in Part IV.

As an aside, note that some authors use x_t or K_t when working with discrete time and reserve the notation $x(t)$ or $K(t)$ for continuous time. Since I go back and forth between continuous and discrete time, I use the latter notation throughout. When there is no risk of confusion, I drop the time arguments, but whenever there is the slightest risk of confusion, I err on the side of caution and include the time arguments.

Let us next impose the following standard assumptions on the aggregate production function.

Assumption 1 (Continuity, Differentiability, Positive and Diminishing Marginal Products, and Constant Returns to Scale) *The production function $F : \mathbb{R}_+^3 \to \mathbb{R}_+$ is twice differentiable in K and L, and satisfies*

$$F_K(K, L, A) \equiv \frac{\partial F(K, L, A)}{\partial K} > 0, \quad F_L(K, L, A) \equiv \frac{\partial F(K, L, A)}{\partial L} > 0,$$

$$F_{KK}(K, L, A) \equiv \frac{\partial^2 F(K, L, A)}{\partial K^2} < 0, \quad F_{LL}(K, L, A) \equiv \frac{\partial^2 F(K, L, A)}{\partial L^2} < 0.$$

Moreover, F exhibits constant returns to scale in K and L.

All of the components of Assumption 1 are important. First, the notation $F : \mathbb{R}_+^3 \to \mathbb{R}_+$ implies that the production function takes nonnegative arguments (i.e., $K, L \in \mathbb{R}_+$) and maps to nonnegative levels of output ($Y \in \mathbb{R}_+$). It is natural that the level of capital and the level of employment should be positive. Since A has no natural units, it could have been negative. But there is no loss of generality in restricting it to be positive. The second important aspect of Assumption 1 is that F is a continuous function in its arguments and is also differentiable. There are many interesting production functions that are not differentiable, and some interesting ones that are not even continuous. But working with differentiable functions makes it possible to use differential calculus, and the loss of some generality is a small price to pay for this convenience. Assumption 1 also specifies that marginal products are positive (so that the level of production increases with the amount of inputs); this restriction also rules out some potential production functions and can be relaxed without much complication (see Exercise 2.8). More importantly, Assumption 1 requires that the marginal products of both capital and labor are diminishing, that is, $F_{KK} < 0$ and $F_{LL} < 0$, so that more capital, holding everything else constant, increases output by less and less. And the same applies to labor. This property is sometimes also referred to as "diminishing returns" to capital and labor. The degree of diminishing returns to capital plays a very important role in many results of the basic growth model. In fact, the presence of diminishing returns to capital distinguishes the Solow growth model from its antecedent, the Harrod-Domar model (see Exercise 2.23).

The other important assumption is that of constant returns to scale. Recall that F exhibits *constant returns to scale* in K and L if it is *linearly homogeneous* (homogeneous of degree 1) in these two variables. More specifically:

Definition 2.1 *Let $K \in \mathbb{N}$. The function $g : \mathbb{R}^{K+2} \to \mathbb{R}$ is* homogeneous of degree m *in $x \in \mathbb{R}$ and $y \in \mathbb{R}$ if*

$$g(\lambda x, \lambda y, z) = \lambda^m g(x, y, z) \text{ for all } \lambda \in \mathbb{R}_+ \text{ and } z \in \mathbb{R}^K.$$

It can be easily verified that linear homogeneity implies that the production function F is concave, though not strictly so (see Exercise 2.2). Linearly homogeneous (constant returns to scale) production functions are particularly useful because of the following theorem.

Theorem 2.1 (Euler's Theorem) *Suppose that $g : \mathbb{R}^{K+2} \to \mathbb{R}$ is differentiable in $x \in \mathbb{R}$ and $y \in \mathbb{R}$, with partial derivatives denoted by g_x and g_y, and is homogeneous of degree m in x and y. Then*

$$mg(x, y, z) = g_x(x, y, z)x + g_y(x, y, z)y \text{ for all } x \in \mathbb{R}, y \in \mathbb{R}, \text{ and } z \in \mathbb{R}^K.$$

Moreover, $g_x(x, y, z)$ and $g_y(x, y, z)$ are themselves homogeneous of degree $m - 1$ in x and y.

Proof. We have that g is differentiable and

$$\lambda^m g(x, y, z) = g(\lambda x, \lambda y, z). \tag{2.2}$$

Differentiate both sides of (2.2) with respect to λ, which gives

$$m\lambda^{m-1} g(x, y, z) = g_x(\lambda x, \lambda y, z)x + g_y(\lambda x, \lambda y, z)y$$

for any λ. Setting $\lambda = 1$ yields the first result. To obtain the second result, differentiate both sides of (2.2) with respect to x:

$$\lambda g_x(\lambda x, \lambda y, z) = \lambda^m g_x(x, y, z).$$

Dividing both sides by λ establishes the desired result. ■

2.1.2 Endowments, Market Structure, and Market Clearing

The previous subsection has specified household behavior and the technology of production. The next step is to specify endowments, that is, the amounts of labor and capital that the economy starts with and who owns these endowments. We will then be in a position to investigate the allocation of resources in this economy. Resources (for a given set of households and production technology) can be allocated in many different ways, depending on the *institutional structure* of the society. Chapters 5–8 discuss how a social planner wishing to maximize a weighted average of the utilities of households might allocate resources, while Part VIII focuses on the allocation of resources favoring individuals who are politically powerful. The more familiar benchmark for the allocation of resources is to assume a specific set of market institutions, in particular, competitive markets. In competitive markets, households and firms act in a price-taking manner and pursue their own objectives, and prices clear markets. Competitive markets are a natural benchmark, and I start by assuming that all goods and factor markets are competitive. This is yet another assumption that is not totally innocuous. For example, both labor and capital markets have imperfections, with certain important implications for economic growth, and monopoly power in product markets plays a major role in Part IV. But these implications can be best appreciated by starting out with the competitive benchmark.

Before investigating trading in competitive markets, let us also specify the ownership of the endowments. Since competitive markets make sense only in the context of an economy with (at least partial) private ownership of assets and the means of production, it is natural to suppose that factors of production are owned by households. In particular, let us suppose that households own all labor, which they supply inelastically. Inelastic supply means that there is some endowment of labor in the economy, for example, equal to the population, $\bar{L}(t)$, and all of it will be supplied regardless of its (rental) price—as long as this price is nonnegative. The labor market clearing condition can then be expressed as:

$$L(t) = \bar{L}(t) \tag{2.3}$$

for all t, where $L(t)$ denotes the demand for labor (and also the level of employment). More generally, this equation should be written in complementary slackness form. In particular, let the rental price of labor or the wage rate at time t be $w(t)$, then the labor market clearing condition takes the form

$$L(t) \leq \bar{L}(t), w(t) \geq 0 \quad \text{and} \quad \left(L(t) - \bar{L}(t)\right) w(t) = 0. \tag{2.4}$$

The complementary slackness formulation ensures that labor market clearing does not happen at a negative wage—or that if labor demand happens to be low enough, employment could be below $\bar{L}(t)$ at zero wage. However, this will not be an issue in most of the models studied in this book, because Assumption 1 and competitive labor markets ensure that wages are strictly positive (see Exercise 2.1). In view of this result, I use the simpler condition (2.3) throughout and denote both labor supply and employment at time t by $L(t)$.

The households also own the capital stock of the economy and rent it to firms. Let us denote the rental price of capital at time t by $R(t)$. The capital market clearing condition is similar to (2.3) and requires the demand for capital by firms to be equal to the supply of capital by households:

$$K(t) = \bar{K}(t),$$

where $\bar{K}(t)$ is the supply of capital by households and $K(t)$ is the demand by firms. Capital market clearing is straightforward to ensure in the class of models analyzed in this book. In particular, it is sufficient that the amount of capital $K(t)$ used in production at time t (from firms' optimization behavior) be consistent with households' endowments and saving behavior.

Let us take households' initial holdings of capital, $K(0) \geq 0$, as given (as part of the description of the environment). For now how this initial capital stock is distributed among the households is not important, since households' optimization decisions are not modeled explicitly and the economy is simply assumed to save a fraction s of its income. When we turn to models with household optimization below, an important part of the description of the environment will be to specify the preferences and the budget constraints of households.

At this point, I could also introduce the price of the final good at time t, say $P(t)$. But there is no need, since there is a choice of a numeraire commodity in this economy, whose price will be normalized to 1. In particular, as discussed in greater detail in Chapter 5, Walras's Law implies that the price of one of the commodities, the numeraire, should be normalized to 1. In fact, throughout I do something stronger and normalize the price of the final good to 1 in all periods. Ordinarily, one cannot choose more than one numeraire—otherwise, one would be fixing the relative price between the numeraires. But as explained in Chapter 5, we can build on an insight by Kenneth Arrow (Arrow, 1964) that it is sufficient to price *securities* (assets) that transfer one unit of consumption from one date (or state of the world) to another. In the context of dynamic economies, this implies that we need to keep track of an *interest rate* across periods, denoted by $r(t)$, which determines intertemporal prices and enables us to normalize the price of the final good to 1 within each period. Naturally we also need to keep track of the wage rate $w(t)$, which determines the price of labor relative to the final good at any date t.

This discussion highlights a central fact: all of the models in this book should be thought of as general equilibrium economies, in which different commodities correspond to the same good at different dates. Recall from basic general equilibrium theory that the same good at different dates (or in different states or localities) is a different commodity. Therefore, in almost all of the models in this book, there will be an infinite number of commodities, since time runs to infinity. This raises a number of special issues, which are discussed in Chapter 5 and later.

Returning to the basic Solow model, the next assumption is that capital depreciates, meaning that machines that are used in production lose some of their value because of wear and tear. In terms of the corn example above, some of the corn that is used as seed is no longer available for consumption or for use as seed in the following period. Let us assume that this depreciation takes an exponential form, which is mathematically very tractable. Thus capital depreciates (exponentially) at the rate $\delta \in (0, 1)$, so that out of 1 unit of capital this period, only $1 - \delta$ is left for next period. Though depreciation here stands for the wear and tear of the machinery, it can also represent the replacement of old machines by new ones in more realistic models (see Chapter 14).

The loss of part of the capital stock affects the interest rate (rate of return on savings) faced by households. Given the assumption of exponential depreciation at the rate δ and the normalization of the price of the final good to 1, the interest rate faced by the households is $r(t) = R(t) - \delta$, where recall that $R(t)$ is the rental price of capital at time t. A unit of final good can be consumed now or used as capital and rented to firms. In the latter case, a household receives $R(t)$ units of good in the next period as the rental price for its savings, but loses δ units of its capital holdings, since δ fraction of capital depreciates over time. Thus the household has given up one unit of commodity dated $t-1$ and receives $1 + r(t) = R(t) + 1 - \delta$ units of commodity dated t, so that $r(t) = R(t) - \delta$. The relationship between $r(t)$ and $R(t)$ explains the similarity between the symbols for the interest rate and the rental rate of capital. The interest rate faced by households plays a central role in the dynamic optimization decisions of households below. In the Solow model, this interest rate does not directly affect the allocation of resources.

2.1.3 Firm Optimization and Equilibrium

We are now in a position to look at the optimization problem of firms and the competitive equilibrium of this economy. Throughout the book I assume that the objective of firms is to maximize profits. Given the assumption that there is an aggregate production function, it is sufficient to consider the problem of a representative firm. Throughout, unless otherwise stated, I also assume that capital markets are functioning, so firms can rent capital in spot markets. For a given technology level $A(t)$, and given factor prices $R(t)$ and $w(t)$, the profit maximization problem of the representative firm at time t can be represented by the following static problem:

$$\max_{K \geq 0, L \geq 0} F(K, L, A(t)) - R(t)K - w(t)L. \tag{2.5}$$

When there are irreversible investments or costs of adjustments, as discussed, for example, in Section 7.8, the maximization problem of firms becomes dynamic. But in the absence of these features, maximizing profits separately at each date t is equivalent to maximizing the net present discounted value of profits. This feature simplifies the analysis considerably.

A couple of additional features are worth noting:

1. The maximization problem is set up in terms of aggregate variables, which, given the representative firm, is without any loss of generality.

2. There is nothing multiplying the F term, since the price of the final good has been normalized to 1. Thus the first term in (2.5) is the revenues of the representative firm (or the revenues of all of the firms in the economy).

3. This way of writing the problem already imposes competitive factor markets, since the firm is taking as given the rental prices of labor and capital, $w(t)$ and $R(t)$ (which are in terms of the numeraire, the final good).

4. This problem is concave, since F is concave (see Exercise 2.2).

An important aspect is that, because F exhibits constant returns to scale (Assumption 1), the maximization problem (2.5) does not have a well-defined solution (see Exercise 2.3); either there does not exist any (K, L) that achieves the maximum value of this program (which is infinity), or $K = L = 0$, or multiple values of (K, L) will achieve the maximum value of this program (when this value happens to be 0). This problem is related to the fact that in a world with constant returns to scale, the size of each individual firm is not determinate (only aggregates are determined). The same problem arises here because (2.5) is written without imposing the condition that factor markets should clear. A competitive equilibrium requires that all firms (and thus the representative firm) maximize profits and factor markets clear. In particular, the demands for labor and capital must be equal to the supplies of these factors at all times (unless the prices of these factors are equal to zero, which is ruled out by Assumption 1). This observation implies that the representative firm should make zero profits, since otherwise it would wish to hire arbitrarily large amounts of capital and labor exceeding the supplies, which are fixed. It also implies that total demand for labor, L, must be equal to the available supply of labor, $L(t)$. Similarly, the total demand for capital, K, should equal the total supply, $K(t)$. If this were not the case and $L < L(t)$, then there would be an excess supply of labor and the wage would be equal to zero. But this is not consistent with firm maximization, since given Assumption 1, the representative firm would then wish to hire an arbitrarily large amount of labor, exceeding the supply. This argument, combined with the fact that F is differentiable (Assumption 1), implies that given the supplies of capital and labor at time t, $K(t)$ and $L(t)$, factor prices must satisfy the following familiar conditions equating factor prices to marginal products:[1]

$$w(t) = F_L(K(t), L(t), A(t)), \qquad (2.6)$$

and

$$R(t) = F_K(K(t), L(t), A(t)). \qquad (2.7)$$

Euler's Theorem (Theorem 2.1) then verifies that at the prices (2.6) and (2.7), firms (or the representative firm) make zero profits.

Proposition 2.1 *Suppose Assumption 1 holds. Then, in the equilibrium of the Solow growth model, firms make no profits, and in particular,*

$$Y(t) = w(t)L(t) + R(t)K(t).$$

Proof. This result follows immediately from Theorem 2.1 for the case of constant returns to scale ($m = 1$). ∎

Since firms make no profits in equilibrium, the ownership of firms does not need to be specified. All we need to know is that firms are profit-maximizing entities.

In addition to these standard assumptions on the production function, the following boundary conditions, the *Inada conditions*, are often imposed in the analysis of economic growth and macroeconomic equilibria.

Assumption 2 (Inada Conditions) *F satisfies the* Inada conditions

$$\lim_{K \to 0} F_K(K, L, A) = \infty \quad \text{and} \quad \lim_{K \to \infty} F_K(K, L, A) = 0 \text{ for all } L > 0 \text{ and all } A,$$

$$\lim_{L \to 0} F_L(K, L, A) = \infty \quad \text{and} \quad \lim_{L \to \infty} F_L(K, L, A) = 0 \text{ for all } K > 0 \text{ and all } A.$$

Moreover, $F(0, L, A) = 0$ for all L and A.

The role of these conditions—especially in ensuring the existence of *interior equilibria*—will become clear later in this chapter. They imply that the first units of capital and labor

---

1. An alternative way to derive (2.6) and (2.7) is to consider the cost minimization problem of the representative firm, which takes the form of minimizing $rK + wL$ with respect to K and L, subject to the constraint that $F(K, L, A) = Y$ for some level of output Y. This problem has a unique solution for any given level of Y. Then imposing market clearing, that is, $Y = F(K, L, A)$ with K and L corresponding to the supplies of capital and labor, yields (2.6) and (2.7).

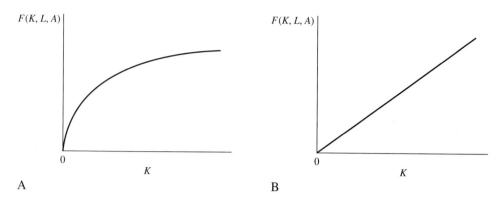

FIGURE 2.1 Production functions. (A) satisfies the Inada conditions in Assumption 2, while (B) does not.

are highly productive and that when capital or labor are sufficiently abundant, their marginal products are close to zero. The condition that $F(0, L, A) = 0$ for all L and A makes capital an essential input. This aspect of the assumption can be relaxed without any major implications for the results in this book. Figure 2.1 shows the production function $F(K, L, A)$ as a function of K, for given L and A, in two different cases; in panel A the Inada conditions are satisfied, while in panel B they are not.

I refer to Assumptions 1 and 2, which can be thought of as the neoclassical technology assumptions, throughout much of the book. For this reason, they are numbered independently from the equations, theorems, and proposition in this chapter.

2.2 The Solow Model in Discrete Time

I next present the dynamics of economic growth in the discrete-time Solow model.

2.2.1 Fundamental Law of Motion of the Solow Model

Recall that K depreciates exponentially at the rate δ, so that the law of motion of the capital stock is given by

$$K(t+1) = (1-\delta)\, K(t) + I(t), \tag{2.8}$$

where $I(t)$ is investment at time t.

From national income accounting for a closed economy, the total amount of final good in the economy must be either consumed or invested, thus

$$Y(t) = C(t) + I(t), \tag{2.9}$$

where $C(t)$ is consumption.[2] Using (2.1), (2.8), and (2.9), any feasible dynamic allocation in this economy must satisfy

$$K(t+1) \leq F(K(t),\, L(t),\, A(t)) + (1-\delta)K(t) - C(t)$$

---

2. In addition, we can introduce government spending $G(t)$ on the right-hand side of (2.9). Government spending does not play a major role in the Solow growth model, thus its introduction is relegated to Exercise 2.7.

for $t = 0, 1, \ldots$. The question is to determine the equilibrium dynamic allocation among the set of feasible dynamic allocations. Here the behavioral rule that households save a constant fraction of their income simplifies the structure of equilibrium considerably (this is a behavioral rule, since it is not derived from the maximization of a well-defined utility function). One implication of this assumption is that any welfare comparisons based on the Solow model have to be taken with a grain of salt, since we do not know what the preferences of the households are.

Since the economy is closed (and there is no government spending), aggregate investment is equal to savings:

$$S(t) = I(t) = Y(t) - C(t).$$

The assumption that households save a constant fraction $s \in (0, 1)$ of their income can be expressed as

$$S(t) = sY(t), \tag{2.10}$$

which, in turn, implies that they consume the remaining $1 - s$ fraction of their income, and thus

$$C(t) = (1 - s) Y(t). \tag{2.11}$$

In terms of capital market clearing, (2.10) implies that the supply of capital for time $t + 1$ resulting from households' behavior can be expressed as $K(t + 1) = (1 - \delta)K(t) + S(t) = (1 - \delta)K(t) + sY(t)$. Setting supply and demand equal to each other and using (2.1) and (2.8) yields *the fundamental law of motion* of the Solow growth model:

$$K(t + 1) = sF(K(t), L(t), A(t)) + (1 - \delta)K(t). \tag{2.12}$$

This is a nonlinear difference equation. The equilibrium of the Solow growth model is described by (2.12) together with laws of motion for $L(t)$ and $A(t)$.

2.2.2 Definition of Equilibrium

The Solow model is a mixture of an old-style Keynesian model and a modern dynamic macro-economic model. Households do not optimize when it comes to their savings or consumption decisions. Instead, their behavior is captured by (2.10) and (2.11). Nevertheless, firms still maximize profits, and factor markets clear. Thus it is useful to start defining equilibria in the way that is customary in modern dynamic macro models.

Definition 2.2 *In the basic Solow model for a given sequence of $\{L(t), A(t)\}_{t=0}^{\infty}$ and an initial capital stock $K(0)$, an equilibrium path is a sequence of capital stocks, output levels, consumption levels, wages, and rental rates $\{K(t), Y(t), C(t), w(t), R(t)\}_{t=0}^{\infty}$ such that $K(t)$ satisfies (2.12), $Y(t)$ is given by (2.1), $C(t)$ is given by (2.11), and $w(t)$ and $R(t)$ are given by (2.6) and (2.7), respectively.*

The most important point to note about Definition 2.2 is that an equilibrium is defined as an entire path of allocations and prices. An economic equilibrium does *not* refer to a static object; it specifies the entire path of behavior of the economy. Note also that Definition 2.2 incorporates the market clearing conditions, (2.6) and (2.7), into the definition of equilibrium. This practice is standard in macro and growth models. The alternative, which involves describing the equilibrium in more abstract terms, is discussed in Chapter 8 in the context of the neoclassical growth model (see, in particular, Definition 8.1).

2.2.3   Equilibrium without Population Growth and Technological Progress

It is useful to start with the following assumptions, which are relaxed later in this chapter:

1. There is no population growth; total population is constant at some level $L > 0$. Moreover, since households supply labor inelastically, this implies $L(t) = L$.
2. There is no technological progress, so that $A(t) = A$.

Let us define the capital-labor ratio of the economy as

$$k(t) \equiv \frac{K(t)}{L},$$ (2.13)

which is a key object for the analysis. Now using the assumption of constant returns to scale, output (income) per capita, $y(t) \equiv Y(t)/L$, can be expressed as

$$y(t) = F\left(\frac{K(t)}{L}, 1, A\right)$$

$$\equiv f(k(t)).$$ (2.14)

In other words, with constant returns to scale, output per capita is simply a function of the capital-labor ratio. Note that $f(k)$ here depends on A, so I could have written $f(k, A)$. I do not do this to simplify the notation and also because until Section 2.7, there will be no technological progress. Thus for now A is constant and can be normalized to $A = 1$.[3] The marginal product and the rental price of capital are then given by the derivative of F with respect to its first argument, which is $f'(k)$. The marginal product of labor and the wage rate are then obtained from Theorem 2.1, so that

$$R(t) = f'(k(t)) > 0 \quad \text{and}$$

$$w(t) = f(k(t)) - k(t)f'(k(t)) > 0.$$ (2.15)

The fact that both factor prices are positive follows from Assumption 1, which ensures that the first derivatives of F with respect to capital and labor are always positive.

Example 2.1 (The Cobb-Douglas Production Function)   *Let us consider the most common example of production function used in macroeconomics, the Cobb-Douglas production function. I hasten to add the caveat that even though the Cobb-Douglas form is convenient and widely used, it is also very special, and many interesting phenomena discussed later in this book are ruled out by this production function. The Cobb-Douglas production function can be written as*

$$Y(t) = F(K(t), L(t), A(t))$$

$$= AK(t)^\alpha L(t)^{1-\alpha}, 0 < \alpha < 1.$$ (2.16)

---

3. Later, when technological change is taken to be labor-augmenting, the term A can also be taken out, and the per capita production function can be written as $y = Af(k)$, with a slightly different definition of k as effective capital-labor ratio (see, e.g., (2.50) in Section 2.7).

It can easily be verified that this production function satisfies Assumptions 1 and 2, including the constant returns to scale feature imposed in Assumption 1. Dividing both sides by $L(t)$, the per capita production function in (2.14) becomes:

$$y(t) = Ak(t)^{\alpha},$$

where $y(t)$ again denotes output per worker and $k(t)$ is capital-labor ratio as defined in (2.13). The representation of factor prices as in (2.15) can also be verified. From the per capita production function representation, in particular (2.15), the rental price of capital can be expressed as

$$R(t) = \frac{\partial Ak(t)^{\alpha}}{\partial k(t)},$$

$$= \alpha Ak(t)^{-(1-\alpha)}.$$

Alternatively, in terms of the original production function (2.16), the rental price of capital in (2.7) is given by

$$R(t) = \alpha AK(t)^{\alpha-1}L(t)^{1-\alpha}$$

$$= \alpha Ak(t)^{-(1-\alpha)},$$

which is equal to the previous expression and thus verifies the form of the marginal product given in (2.15). Similarly, from (2.15),

$$w(t) = Ak(t)^{\alpha} - \alpha Ak(t)^{-(1-\alpha)} \times k(t)$$

$$= (1-\alpha)AK(t)^{\alpha}L(t)^{-\alpha},$$

which verifies the alternative expression for the wage rate in (2.6).

Returning to the analysis with the general production function, the per capita representation of the aggregate production function enables us to divide both sides of (2.12) by L to obtain the following simple difference equation for the evolution of the capital-labor ratio:

$$k(t+1) = sf(k(t)) + (1-\delta)k(t). \tag{2.17}$$

Since this difference equation is derived from (2.12), it also can be referred to as the *equilibrium difference equation* of the Solow model: it describes the equilibrium behavior of the key object of the model, the capital-labor ratio. The other equilibrium quantities can all be obtained from the capital-labor ratio $k(t)$.

At this point, let us also define a *steady-state equilibrium* for this model.

Definition 2.3 *A steady-state equilibrium without technological progress and population growth is an equilibrium path in which $k(t) = k^*$ for all t.*

In a steady-state equilibrium the capital-labor ratio remains constant. Since there is no population growth, this implies that the level of the capital stock will also remain constant. Mathematically, a steady-state equilibrium corresponds to a stationary point of the equilibrium difference equation (2.17). Most of the models in this book admit a steady-state equilibrium. This is also the case for this simple model.

The existence of a steady state can be seen by plotting the difference equation that governs the equilibrium behavior of this economy, (2.17), which is done in Figure 2.2. The thick curve

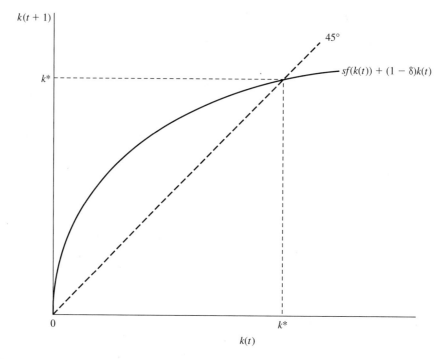

FIGURE 2.2 Determination of the steady-state capital-labor ratio in the Solow model without population growth and technological change.

represents the right-hand side of (2.17) and the dashed line corresponds to the 45° line. Their (positive) intersection gives the steady-state value of the capital-labor ratio k^*, which satisfies

$$\frac{f(k^*)}{k^*} = \frac{\delta}{s}. \tag{2.18}$$

Notice that in Figure 2.2 there is another intersection between (2.17) and the 45° line at $k = 0$. This second intersection occurs because, from Assumption 2, capital is an essential input, and thus $f(0) = 0$. Starting with $k(0) = 0$, there will then be no savings, and the economy will remain at $k = 0$. Nevertheless, I ignore this intersection throughout for a number of reasons. First, $k = 0$ is a steady-state equilibrium only when capital is an essential input and $f(0) = 0$. But as noted above, this assumption can be relaxed without any implications for the rest of the analysis, and when $f(0) > 0$, $k = 0$ is no longer a steady-state equilibrium. This is illustrated in Figure 2.3, which draws (2.17) for the case where $f(0) = \varepsilon$ for some $\varepsilon > 0$. Second, as we will see below, this intersection, even when it exists, is an unstable point; thus the economy would never travel toward this point starting with $K(0) > 0$ (or with $k(0) > 0$). Finally, and most importantly, this intersection holds no economic interest for us.[4]

An alternative visual representation shows the steady state as the intersection between a ray through the origin with slope δ (representing the function δk) and the function $sf(k)$. Figure 2.4, which illustrates this representation, is also useful for two other purposes. First, it depicts the levels of consumption and investment in a single figure. The vertical distance between the horizontal axis and the δk line at the steady-state equilibrium gives the amount of

---

4. Hakenes and Irmen (2006) show that even with $f(0) = 0$, the Inada conditions imply that in the continuous-time version of the Solow model $k = 0$ may not be the only equilibrium and the economy may move away from $k = 0$.

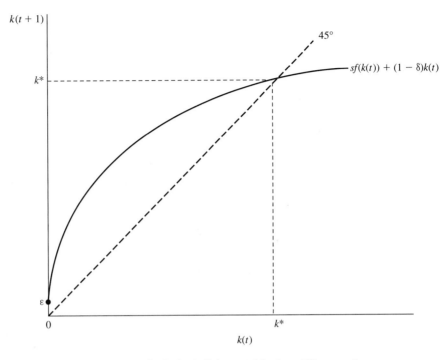

FIGURE 2.3 Unique steady state in the basic Solow model when $f(0) = \varepsilon > 0$.

investment per capita at the steady-state equilibrium (equal to δk^*), while the vertical distance between the function $f(k)$ and the δk line at k^* gives the level of consumption per capita. Clearly, the sum of these two terms make up $f(k^*)$. Second, Figure 2.4 also emphasizes that the steady-state equilibrium in the Solow model essentially sets investment, $sf(k)$, equal to the amount of capital that needs to be replenished, δk. This interpretation is particularly useful when population growth and technological change are incorporated.

This analysis therefore leads to the following proposition (with the convention that the intersection at $k = 0$ is being ignored even though $f(0) = 0$).

Proposition 2.2 *Consider the basic Solow growth model and suppose that Assumptions 1 and 2 hold. Then there exists a unique steady-state equilibrium where the capital-labor ratio $k^* \in (0, \infty)$ satisfies (2.18), per capita output is given by*

$$y^* = f(k^*), \tag{2.19}$$

and per capita consumption is given by

$$c^* = (1 - s) \, f(k^*). \tag{2.20}$$

Proof. The preceding argument establishes that any k^* that satisfies (2.18) is a steady state. To establish existence, note that from Assumption 2 (and from l'Hôpital's Rule, see Theorem A.21 in Appendix A), $\lim_{k \to 0} f(k)/k = \infty$ and $\lim_{k \to \infty} f(k)/k = 0$. Moreover, $f(k)/k$ is continuous from Assumption 1, so by the Intermediate Value Theorem (Theorem A.3) there exists k^* such that (2.18) is satisfied. To see uniqueness, differentiate $f(k)/k$ with respect to k, which gives

$$\frac{\partial(f(k)/k)}{\partial k} = \frac{f'(k)k - f(k)}{k^2} = -\frac{w}{k^2} < 0, \tag{2.21}$$

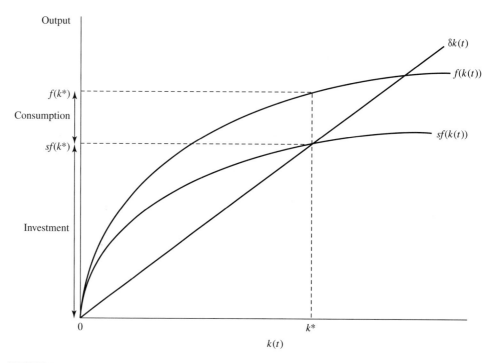

FIGURE 2.4 Investment and consumption in the steady-state equilibrium.

where the last equality in (2.21) uses (2.15). Since $f(k)/k$ is everywhere (strictly) decreasing, there can only exist a unique value k^* that satisfies (2.18). Equations (2.19) and (2.20) then follow by definition. ∎

Through a series of examples, Figure 2.5 shows why Assumptions 1 and 2 cannot be dispensed with for establishing the existence and uniqueness results in Proposition 2.2. In the first two panels, the failure of Assumption 2 leads to a situation in which there is no steady-state equilibrium with positive activity, while in the third panel, the failure of Assumption 1 leads to nonuniqueness of steady states.

So far the model is very parsimonious: it does not have many parameters and abstracts from many features of the real world. An understanding of how cross-country differences in certain parameters translate into differences in growth rates or output levels is essential for our focus. This connection will be made in the next proposition. But before doing so, let us generalize the production function in one simple way and assume that

$$f(k) = A\tilde{f}(k),$$

where $A > 0$, so that A is a shift parameter, with greater values corresponding to greater productivity of factors. This type of productivity is referred to as "Hicks-neutral" (see below). For now, it is simply a convenient way of parameterizing productivity differences across countries. Since $f(k)$ satisfies the regularity conditions imposed above, so does $\tilde{f}(k)$.

Proposition 2.3 *Suppose Assumptions 1 and 2 hold and $f(k) = A\tilde{f}(k)$. Denote the steady-state level of the capital-labor ratio by $k^*(A, s, \delta)$ and the steady-state level of output by*

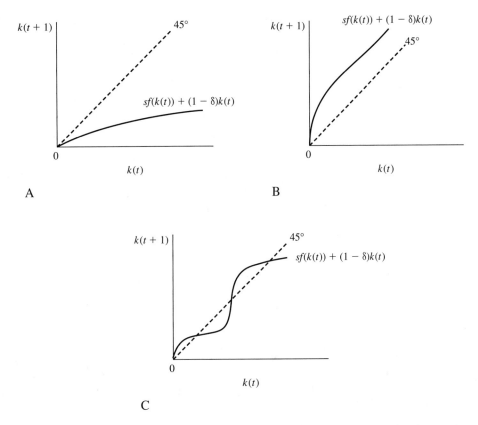

FIGURE 2.5 Examples of nonexistence and nonuniqueness of interior steady states when Assumptions 1 and 2 are not satisfied.

$y^*(A, s, \delta)$ *when the underlying parameters are A, s, and δ. Then*

$$\frac{\partial k^*(A, s, \delta)}{\partial A} > 0, \quad \frac{\partial k^*(A, s, \delta)}{\partial s} > 0, \quad \text{and} \quad \frac{\partial k^*(A, s, \delta)}{\partial \delta} < 0;$$

$$\frac{\partial y^*(A, s, \delta)}{\partial A} > 0, \quad \frac{\partial y^*(A, s, \delta)}{\partial s} > 0, \quad \text{and} \quad \frac{\partial y^*(A, s, \delta)}{\partial \delta} < 0.$$

Proof. The proof follows immediately by writing

$$\frac{\tilde{f}(k^*)}{k^*} = \frac{\delta}{As},$$

which holds for an open set of values of k^*, A, s, and δ. Now apply the Implicit Function Theorem (Theorem A.25) to obtain the results. For example,

$$\frac{\partial k^*}{\partial s} = \frac{\delta (k^*)^2}{s^2 w^*} > 0,$$

where $w^* = f(k^*) - k^* f'(k^*) > 0$. The other results follow similarly. ∎

Therefore countries with higher saving rates and better technologies will have higher capital-labor ratios and will be richer. Those with greater (technological) depreciation will tend to have lower capital-labor ratios and will be poorer. All of the results in Proposition 2.3 are intuitive, and they provide us with a first glimpse of the potential determinants of the capital-labor ratios and output levels across countries.

The same comparative statics with respect to A and δ also apply to c^*. However, it is straightforward to see that c^* is not monotone in the saving rate (e.g., think of the extreme case where $s = 1$). In fact, there exists a unique saving rate, s_{gold}, referred to as the "golden rule" saving rate, which maximizes the steady-state level of consumption. Since we are treating the saving rate as an exogenous parameter and have not specified the objective function of households yet, we cannot say whether the golden rule saving rate is better than some other saving rate. It is nevertheless interesting to characterize what this golden rule saving rate corresponds to. To do this, let us first write the steady-state relationship between c^* and s and suppress the other parameters:

$$c^*(s) = (1 - s) f(k^*(s))$$
$$= f(k^*(s)) - \delta k^*(s),$$

where the second equality exploits the fact that in steady state, $sf(k) = \delta k$. Now differentiating this second line with respect to s (again using the Implicit Function Theorem), we obtain

$$\frac{\partial c^*(s)}{\partial s} = [f'(k^*(s)) - \delta]\frac{\partial k^*}{\partial s}. \tag{2.22}$$

Let us define the golden rule saving rate s_{gold} to be such that $\partial c^*(s_{\text{gold}})/\partial s = 0$. The corresponding steady-state golden rule capital stock is defined as k^*_{gold}. These quantities and the relationship between consumption and the saving rate are plotted in Figure 2.6. The next proposition shows that s_{gold} and k^*_{gold} are uniquely defined.

Proposition 2.4 *In the basic Solow growth model, the highest level of steady-state consumption is reached for* s_{gold}, *with the corresponding steady-state capital level* k^*_{gold} *such that*

$$f'(k^*_{\text{gold}}) = \delta. \tag{2.23}$$

Proof. By definition $\partial c^*(s_{\text{gold}})/\partial s = 0$. From Proposition 2.3, $\partial k^*/\partial s > 0$; thus (2.22) can be equal to zero only when $f'(k^*(s_{\text{gold}})) = \delta$. Moreover, when $f'(k^*(s_{\text{gold}})) = \delta$, it can be verified that $\partial^2 c^*(s_{\text{gold}})/\partial s^2 < 0$, so $f'(k^*(s_{\text{gold}})) = \delta$ indeed corresponds to a local maximum. That $f'(k^*(s_{\text{gold}})) = \delta$ also yields the global maximum is a consequence of the following observations: for all $s \in [0, 1]$, we have $\partial k^*/\partial s > 0$, and moreover, when $s < s_{\text{gold}}$, $f'(k^*(s)) - \delta > 0$ by the concavity of f, so $\partial c^*(s)/\partial s > 0$ for all $s < s_{\text{gold}}$. By the converse argument, $\partial c^*(s)/\partial s < 0$ for all $s > s_{\text{gold}}$. Therefore only s_{gold} satisfies $f'(k^*(s)) = \delta$ and gives the unique global maximum of consumption per capita. ∎

In other words, there exists a unique saving rate, s_{gold}, and also a unique corresponding capital-labor ratio, k^*_{gold}, given by (2.23), that maximize the level of steady-state consumption. When the economy is below k^*_{gold}, a higher saving rate will increase consumption, whereas when the economy is above k^*_{gold}, steady-state consumption can be raised by saving less. In the latter case, lower savings translate into higher consumption, because the capital-labor ratio of the economy is too high; households are investing too much and not consuming enough. This is the essence of the phenomenon of *dynamic inefficiency,* discussed in greater detail in Chapter 9. For now, recall that there is no explicit utility function here, so statements about inefficiency

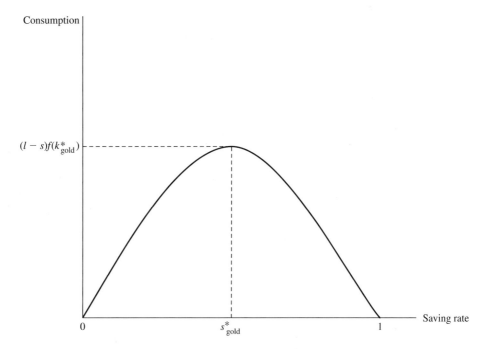

FIGURE 2.6 The golden rule level of saving rate, which maximizes steady-state consumption.

must be considered with caution. In fact, the reason this type of dynamic inefficiency does not generally apply when consumption-saving decisions are endogenized may already be apparent to many of you.

2.3 Transitional Dynamics in the Discrete-Time Solow Model

Proposition 2.2 establishes the existence of a unique steady-state equilibrium (with positive activity). Recall that an equilibrium path does not refer simply to the steady state but to the entire path of capital stock, output, consumption, and factor prices. This is an important point to bear in mind, especially since the term "equilibrium" is used differently in economics than in other disciplines. Typically, in engineering and the physical sciences, an equilibrium refers to a point of rest of a dynamical system, thus to what I have so far referred to as "the steady-state equilibrium." One may then be tempted to say that the system is in "disequilibrium" when it is away from the steady state. However, in economics, the non-steady-state behavior of an economy is also governed by market clearing and optimizing behavior of households and firms. Most economies spend much of their time in non-steady-state situations. Thus we are typically interested in the entire dynamic equilibrium path of the economy, not just in its steady state.

To determine what the equilibrium path of our simple economy looks like, we need to study the transitional dynamics of the equilibrium difference equation (2.17) starting from an arbitrary capital-labor ratio, $k(0) > 0$. Of special interest are the answers to the questions of whether the economy will tend to this steady state starting from an arbitrary capital-labor ratio and how it will behave along the transition path. Recall that the total amount of capital at the beginning of the economy, $K(0) > 0$, is taken as a state variable, while for now, the supply of labor L is fixed. Therefore at time $t = 0$, the economy starts with an arbitrary capital-labor ratio $k(0) = K(0)/L > 0$ as its initial value and then follows the law of motion given by the difference equation (2.17). Thus the question is whether (2.17) will take us to the unique steady state starting from an arbitrary initial capital-labor ratio.

Before answering this question, recall some definitions and key results from the theory of dynamical systems. Appendix B provides more details and a number of further results. Consider the nonlinear system of autonomous difference equations,

$$\mathbf{x}(t + 1) = \mathbf{G}(\mathbf{x}(t)), \tag{2.24}$$

where $\mathbf{x}(t) \in \mathbb{R}^n$ and $\mathbf{G} : \mathbb{R}^n \to \mathbb{R}^n$ (where $n \in \mathbb{R}$). Let $\mathbf{x}^*$ be a *fixed point* of the mapping $\mathbf{G}(\cdot)$, that is,

$$\mathbf{x}^* = \mathbf{G}(\mathbf{x}^*).$$

I refer to $\mathbf{x}^*$ as a "steady state" of the difference equation (2.24).[5] The relevant notion of stability is introduced in the next definition.

Definition 2.4 *A steady state $\mathbf{x}^*$ is* locally asymptotically stable *if there exists an open set $B(\mathbf{x}^*)$ containing $\mathbf{x}^*$ such that for any solution $\{\mathbf{x}(t)\}_{t=0}^{\infty}$ to (2.24) with $\mathbf{x}(0) \in B(\mathbf{x}^*)$, $\mathbf{x}(t) \to \mathbf{x}^*$. Moreover, $\mathbf{x}^*$ is* globally asymptotically stable *if for all $\mathbf{x}(0) \in \mathbb{R}^n$, for any solution $\{\mathbf{x}(t)\}_{t=0}^{\infty}$, $\mathbf{x}(t) \to \mathbf{x}^*$.*

The next theorem provides the main results on the stability properties of systems of linear difference equations. The following theorems are special cases of the results presented in Appendix B.

Theorem 2.2 (Stability for Systems of Linear Difference Equations) *Consider the following linear difference equation system:*

$$\mathbf{x}(t + 1) = \mathbf{A}\mathbf{x}(t) + \mathbf{b}, \tag{2.25}$$

with initial value $\mathbf{x}(0)$, where $\mathbf{x}(t) \in \mathbb{R}^n$ for all t, $\mathbf{A}$ is an $n \times n$ matrix, and $\mathbf{b}$ is a $n \times 1$ column vector. Let $\mathbf{x}^*$ be the steady state of the difference equation given by $\mathbf{A}\mathbf{x}^* + \mathbf{b} = \mathbf{x}^*$. Suppose that all of the eigenvalues of $\mathbf{A}$ are strictly inside the unit circle in the complex plane. Then the steady state of the difference equation (2.25), $\mathbf{x}^*$, is globally (asymptotically) stable, in the sense that starting from any $\mathbf{x}(0) \in \mathbb{R}^n$, the unique solution $\{\mathbf{x}(t)\}_{t=0}^{\infty}$ satisfies $\mathbf{x}(t) \to \mathbf{x}^*$.

Unfortunately, much less can be said about nonlinear systems, but the following is a standard local stability result.

Theorem 2.3 (Local Stability for Systems of Nonlinear Difference Equations) *Consider the following nonlinear autonomous system:*

$$\mathbf{x}(t + 1) = \mathbf{G}(\mathbf{x}(t)), \tag{2.26}$$

with initial value $\mathbf{x}(0)$, where $\mathbf{G} : \mathbb{R}^n \to \mathbb{R}^n$. Let $\mathbf{x}^*$ be a steady state of this system, that is, $\mathbf{G}(\mathbf{x}^*) = \mathbf{x}^*$, and suppose that $\mathbf{G}$ is differentiable at $\mathbf{x}^*$. Define

$$\mathbf{A} \equiv D\mathbf{G}(\mathbf{x}^*),$$

---

5. Various other terms are used to describe $\mathbf{x}^*$, for example, "equilibrium point" or "critical point." Since these other terms have different meanings in economics, I refer to $\mathbf{x}^*$ as a steady state throughout.

where $D\mathbf{G}$ *denotes the matrix of partial derivatives (Jacobian) of* $\mathbf{G}$. *Suppose that all of the eigenvalues of* $\mathbf{A}$ *are strictly inside the unit circle. Then the steady state of the difference equation (2.26),* $\mathbf{x}^*$, *is locally (asymptotically) stable, in the sense that there exists an open neighborhood of* $\mathbf{x}^*$, $\mathbf{B}(\mathbf{x}^*) \subset \mathbb{R}^n$, *such that starting from any* $\mathbf{x}(0) \in \mathbf{B}(\mathbf{x}^*)$, $\mathbf{x}(t) \to \mathbf{x}^*$.

An immediate corollary of Theorem 2.3 is the following useful result.

Corollary 2.1

1. *Let* $x(t)$, a, $b \in \mathbb{R}$. *If* $|a| < 1$, *then the unique steady state of the linear difference equation* $x(t+1) = ax(t) + b$ *is globally (asymptotically) stable, in the sense that* $x(t) \to x^* = b/(1-a)$.

2. *Let* $g : \mathbb{R} \to \mathbb{R}$ *be differentiable in the neighborhood of the steady state* x^*, *defined by* $g(x^*) = x^*$, *and suppose that* $|g'(x^*)| < 1$. *Then the steady state* x^* *of the nonlinear difference equation* $x(t+1) = g(x(t))$ *is locally (asymptotically) stable. Moreover, if* g *is continuously differentiable and satisfies* $|g'(x)| < 1$ *for all* $x \in \mathbb{R}$, *then* x^* *is globally (asymptotically) stable.*

Proof. The first part follows immediately from Theorem 2.2. The local stability of g in the second part follows from Theorem 2.3. Global stability follows since

$$|x(t+1) - x^*| = |g(x(t)) - g(x^*)|$$

$$= \left| \int_{x^*}^{x(t)} g'(x)dx \right|$$

$$< |x(t) - x^*|,$$

where the second line follows from the Fundamental Theorem of Calculus (Theorem B.2 in Appendix B), and the last inequality uses the hypothesis that $|g'(x)| < 1$ for all $x \in \mathbb{R}$. This implies that for any $x(0) < x^*$, $\{x(t)\}_{t=0}^{\infty}$ is an increasing sequence. Since $|g'(x)| < 1$, there cannot exist $x' \neq x^*$ such that $x' = g(x')$, and moreover $\{x(t)\}_{t=0}^{\infty}$ is bounded above by x^*. It therefore converges to x^*. The argument for the case where $x(0) > x^*$ is identical. ∎

We can now apply Corollary 2.1 to the equilibrium difference equation (2.17) of the Solow model to establish the local stability of the steady-state equilibrium. Global stability does not directly follow form Corollary 2.1 (since the equivalent of $|g'(x)| < 1$ for all x is not true), but a slightly different argument can be used to prove this property.

Proposition 2.5 *Suppose that Assumptions 1 and 2 hold. Then the steady-state equilibrium of the Solow growth model described by the difference equation (2.17) is globally asymptotically stable, and starting from any* $k(0) > 0$, $k(t)$ *monotonically converges to* k^*.

Proof. Let $g(k) \equiv sf(k) + (1-\delta)k$. First observe that $g'(k)$ exists and is always strictly positive, that is, $g'(k) > 0$ for all k. Next, from (2.17),

$$k(t+1) = g(k(t)), \tag{2.27}$$

with a unique steady state at k^*. From (2.18), the steady-state capital k^* satisfies $\delta k^* = sf(k^*)$, or

$$k^* = g(k^*). \tag{2.28}$$

Now recall that $f(\cdot)$ is concave and differentiable from Assumption 1 and satisfies $f(0) = 0$ from Assumption 2. For any strictly concave differentiable function, we have (recall Fact A.23 in Appendix A):

$$f(k) > f(0) + kf'(k) = kf'(k). \tag{2.29}$$

Since (2.29) implies that $\delta = sf(k^*)/k^* > sf'(k^*)$, we have $g'(k^*) = sf'(k^*) + 1 - \delta < 1$. Therefore

$$g'(k^*) \in (0, 1).$$

Corollary 2.1 then establishes local asymptotic stability.

To prove global stability, note that for all $k(t) \in (0, k^*)$,

$$k(t+1) - k^* = g(k(t)) - g(k^*)$$

$$= -\int_{k(t)}^{k^*} g'(k) dk,$$

$$< 0,$$

where the first line follows by subtracting (2.28) from (2.27), the second line again uses the Fundamental Theorem of Calculus (Theorem B.2), and the third line follows from the observation that $g'(k) > 0$ for all k. Next, (2.17) also implies

$$\frac{k(t+1) - k(t)}{k(t)} = s\frac{f(k(t))}{k(t)} - \delta$$

$$> s\frac{f(k^*)}{k^*} - \delta$$

$$= 0,$$

where the second line uses the fact that $f(k)/k$ is decreasing in k (from (2.29)) and the last line uses the definition of k^*. These two arguments together establish that for all $k(t) \in (0, k^*)$, $k(t+1) \in (k(t), k^*)$. Therefore $\{k(t)\}_{t=0}^{\infty}$ is monotonically increasing and is bounded above by k^*. Moreover, since k^* is the unique steady state (with $k > 0$), there exists no $k' \in (0, k^*)$ such that $k(t+1) = k(t) = k'$ for any t. Therefore $\{k(t)\}_{t=0}^{\infty}$ must monotonically converge to k^*. An identical argument implies that for all $k(t) > k^*$, $k(t+1) \in (k^*, k(t))$ and establishes monotonic convergence starting from $k(0) > k^*$. This completes the proof of global stability. ∎

This stability result can be seen diagrammatically in Figure 2.7. Starting from initial capital stock $k(0) > 0$, which is below the steady-state level k^*, the economy grows toward k^* and experiences *capital deepening*—meaning that the capital-labor ratio increases. Together with capital deepening comes growth of per capita income. If instead the economy were to start with $k'(0) > k^*$, it would reach the steady state by decumulating capital and contracting (i.e., by experiencing negative growth).

The following proposition is an immediate corollary of Proposition 2.5.

Proposition 2.6 *Suppose that Assumptions 1 and 2 hold, and $k(0) < k^*$. Then $\{w(t)\}_{t=0}^{\infty}$ is an increasing sequence, and $\{R(t)\}_{t=0}^{\infty}$ is a decreasing sequence. If $k(0) > k^*$, the opposite results apply.*

Proof. See Exercise 2.9. ∎

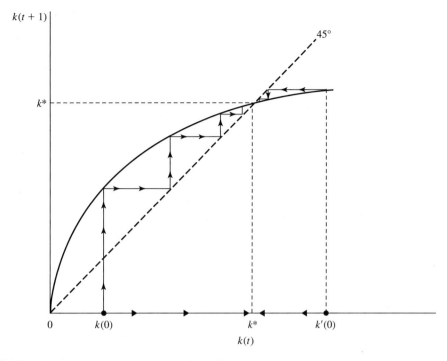

FIGURE 2.7 Transitional dynamics in the basic Solow model.

Recall that when the economy starts with too little capital relative to its labor supply, the capital-labor ratio will increase. Thus the marginal product of capital will fall due to diminishing returns to capital and the wage rate will increase. Conversely, if it starts with too much capital, it will decumulate capital, and in the process the wage rate will decline and the rate of return to capital will increase.

The analysis has established that the Solow growth model has a number of nice properties: unique steady state, global (asymptotic) stability, and finally, simple and intuitive comparative statics. Yet so far it has no growth. The steady state is the point at which there is no growth in the capital-labor ratio, no more capital deepening, and no growth in output per capita. Consequently, the basic Solow model (without technological progress) can only generate economic growth along the transition path to the steady state (starting with $k(0) < k^*$). However this growth is not sustained: it slows down over time and eventually comes to an end. Section 2.7 shows that the Solow model can incorporate economic growth by allowing exogenous technological change. Before doing this, it is useful to look at the relationship between the discrete- and continuous-time formulations.

2.4 The Solow Model in Continuous Time

2.4.1 From Difference to Differential Equations

Recall that the time periods $t = 0, 1, \ldots$ can refer to days, weeks, months, or years. In some sense, the time unit is not important. This arbitrariness suggests that perhaps it may be more convenient to look at dynamics by making the time unit as small as possible, that is, by going to continuous time. While much of modern macroeconomics (outside of growth theory) uses discrete-time models, many growth models are formulated in continuous time. The continuous-time setup has a number of advantages, since some pathological results of discrete-time models disappear when using continuous time (see Exercise 2.21). Moreover, continuous-time models have more flexibility in the analysis of dynamics and allow explicit-form solutions in a wider set of circumstances. These considerations motivate the detailed study of both the discrete- and continuous-time versions of the basic models in this book.

Let us start with a simple difference equation:

$$x(t+1) - x(t) = g(x(t)). \tag{2.30}$$

This equation states that between time t and $t+1$, the absolute growth in x is given by $g(x(t))$. Imagine that time is more finely divisible than that captured by our discrete indices, $t = 0, 1, \ldots$. In the limit, we can think of time as being as finely divisible as we would like, so that $t \in \mathbb{R}_+$. In that case, (2.30) gives us information about how the variable x changes between two discrete points in time, t and $t+1$. Between these time periods, we do not know how x evolves. However, if t and $t+1$ are not too far apart, the following approximation is reasonable:

$$x(t + \Delta t) - x(t) \simeq \Delta t \cdot g(x(t))$$

for any $\Delta t \in [0, 1]$. When $\Delta t = 0$, this equation is just an identity. When $\Delta t = 1$, it gives (2.30). In between it is a linear approximation. This approximation will be relatively accurate if the distance between t and $t+1$ is not very large, so that $g(x) \simeq g(x(t))$ for all $x \in [x(t), x(t+1)]$ (however, you should also convince yourself that this approximation could in fact be quite bad if the function g is highly nonlinear, in which case its behavior changes significantly between $x(t)$ and $x(t+1)$). Now divide both sides of this equation by Δt, and take limits to obtain

$$\lim_{\Delta t \to 0} \frac{x(t + \Delta t) - x(t)}{\Delta t} = \dot{x}(t) \simeq g(x(t)), \tag{2.31}$$

where, as throughout the book, I use the dot notation to denote time derivatives, $\dot{x}(t) \equiv dx(t)/dt$. Equation (2.31) is a differential equation representing the same dynamics as the difference equation (2.30) for the case in which the distance between t and $t+1$ is small.

2.4.2 The Fundamental Equation of the Solow Model in Continuous Time

We can now repeat all of the analysis so far using the continuous-time representation. Nothing has changed on the production side, so we continue to have (2.6) and (2.7) as the factor prices, but now these refer to instantaneous rental rates. For example, $w(t)$ is the flow of wages that workers receive at instant t. Savings are again given by

$$S(t) = sY(t),$$

while consumption is still given by (2.11).

Let us also introduce population growth into this model and assume that the labor force $L(t)$ grows proportionally, that is,

$$L(t) = \exp(nt)L(0). \tag{2.32}$$

The purpose of doing so is that in many of the classical analyses of economic growth, population growth plays an important role, so it is useful to see how it affects the equilibrium here. There is still no technological progress.

Recall that

$$k(t) \equiv \frac{K(t)}{L(t)},$$

which implies that

$$\frac{\dot{k}(t)}{k(t)} = \frac{\dot{K}(t)}{K(t)} - \frac{\dot{L}(t)}{L(t)},$$

$$= \frac{\dot{K}(t)}{K(t)} - n,$$

where I used the fact that, from (2.32), $\dot{L}(t)/L(t) = n$. From the limiting argument leading to equation (2.31) in the previous subsection, the law of motion of the capital stock is given by

$$\dot{K}(t) = sF(K(t), L(t), A(t)) - \delta K(t).$$

Using the definition of $k(t)$ as the capital-labor ratio and the constant returns to scale properties of the production function, the fundamental law of motion of the Solow model in continuous time is obtained as

$$\frac{\dot{k}(t)}{k(t)} = s\frac{f(k(t))}{k(t)} - (n + \delta), \tag{2.33}$$

where, following usual practice, I have transformed the left-hand side to the proportional change in the capital-labor ratio by dividing both sides by $k(t)$.[6]

Definition 2.5 *In the basic Solow model in continuous time with population growth at the rate n, no technological progress and an initial capital stock $K(0)$, an* equilibrium path *is given by paths (sequences) of capital stocks, labor, output levels, consumption levels, wages, and rental rates $[K(t), L(t), Y(t), C(t), w(t), R(t)]_{t=0}^{\infty}$ such that $L(t)$ satisfies (2.32), $k(t) \equiv K(t)/L(t)$ satisfies (2.33), $Y(t)$ is given by (2.1), $C(t)$ is given by (2.11), and $w(t)$ and $R(t)$ are given by (2.6) and (2.7), respectively.*

As before, a steady-state equilibrium involves $k(t)$ remaining constant at some level k^*.

It is easy to verify that the equilibrium differential equation (2.33) has a unique steady state at k^*, which is given by a slight modification of (2.18) to incorporate population growth:

$$\frac{f(k^*)}{k^*} = \frac{n + \delta}{s}. \tag{2.34}$$

In other words, going from discrete to continuous time has not changed any of the basic economic features of the model. Thus the steady state can again be plotted in a diagram similar to Figure 2.1 except that it now also incorporates population growth. This is done in Figure 2.8, which also highlights that the logic of the steady state is the same with population growth as it was without population growth. The amount of investment, $sf(k)$, is used to replenish the capital-labor ratio, but now there are two reasons for replenishments. The capital stock depreciates exponentially at the flow rate δ. In addition, the capital stock must also increase as

---

6. Throughout I adopt the notation $[x(t)]_{t=0}^{\infty}$ to denote the continuous-time path of variable $x(t)$. An alternative notation often used in the literature is $(x(t); t \geq 0)$. I prefer the former both because it is slightly more compact and also because it is more similar to the discrete-time notation for the time path of a variable, $\{x(t)\}_{t=0}^{\infty}$. When referring to $[x(t)]_{t=0}^{\infty}$, I use the terms "path," "sequence," and "function (of time t)" interchangeably.

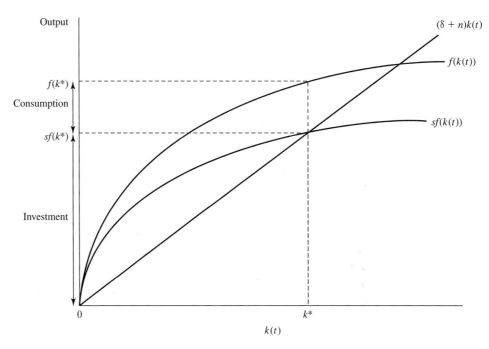

FIGURE 2.8 Investment and consumption in the steady-state equilibrium with population growth.

population grows to maintain the capital-labor ratio at a constant level. The amount of capital that needs to be replenished is therefore $(n + \delta)k$.

Proposition 2.7 *Consider the basic Solow growth model in continuous time and suppose that Assumptions 1 and 2 hold. Then there exists a unique steady-state equilibrium where the capital-labor ratio is equal to $k^* \in (0, \infty)$ and satisfies (2.34), per capita output is given by*

$$y^* = f(k^*),$$

and per capita consumption is given by

$$c^* = (1 - s) f(k^*).$$

Proof. See Exercise 2.5. ∎

Moreover, again defining $f(k) = A \tilde{f}(k)$, the following proposition holds.

Proposition 2.8 *Suppose Assumptions 1 and 2 hold and $f(k) = A \tilde{f}(k)$. Denote the steady-state equilibrium level of the capital-labor ratio by $k^*(A, s, \delta, n)$ and the steady-state level of output by $y^*(A, s, \delta, n)$ when the underlying parameters are given by A, s, δ, and n. Then we have*

$$\frac{\partial k^*(A,s,\delta,n)}{\partial A} > 0, \quad \frac{\partial k^*(A,s,\delta,n)}{\partial s} > 0, \quad \frac{\partial k^*(A,s,\delta,n)}{\partial \delta} < 0, \quad \text{and} \quad \frac{\partial k^*(A,s,\delta,n)}{\partial n} < 0;$$

$$\frac{\partial y^*(A,s,\delta,n)}{\partial A} > 0, \quad \frac{\partial y^*(A,s,\delta,n)}{\partial s} > 0, \quad \frac{\partial y^*(A,s,\delta,n)}{\partial \delta} < 0, \quad \text{and} \quad \frac{\partial y^*(A,s,\delta,n)}{\partial n} < 0.$$

Proof. See Exercise 2.6. ∎

The new result relative to the earlier comparative static proposition (Proposition 2.3) is that now a higher population growth rate, n, also reduces the capital-labor ratio and output per capita. The reason for this is simple: a higher population growth rate means there is more labor to use the existing amount of capital, which only accumulates slowly, and consequently the equilibrium capital-labor ratio ends up lower. This result implies that countries with higher population growth rates will have lower incomes per person (or per worker).

2.5 Transitional Dynamics in the Continuous-Time Solow Model

The analysis of transitional dynamics and stability with continuous time yields similar results to those in Section 2.3, but the analysis is slightly simpler. Let us first recall the basic results on the stability of systems of differential equations. Once again, further details are contained in Appendix B.

Theorem 2.4 (Stability of Linear Differential Equations) *Consider the following linear differential equation system:*

$$\dot{\mathbf{x}}(t) = \mathbf{A}\mathbf{x}(t) + \mathbf{b} \tag{2.35}$$

with initial value $\mathbf{x}(0)$, where $\mathbf{x}(t) \in \mathbb{R}^n$ for all t, $\mathbf{A}$ is an $n \times n$ matrix, and $\mathbf{b}$ is a $n \times 1$ column vector. Let $\mathbf{x}^*$ be the steady state of the system given by $\mathbf{A}\mathbf{x}^* + \mathbf{b} = 0$. Suppose that all eigenvalues of $\mathbf{A}$ have negative real parts. Then the steady state of the differential equation (2.35) $\mathbf{x}^*$ is globally asymptotically stable, in the sense that starting from any $\mathbf{x}(0) \in \mathbb{R}^n$, $\mathbf{x}(t) \to \mathbf{x}^*$.

Theorem 2.5 (Local Stability of Nonlinear Differential Equations) *Consider the following nonlinear autonomous differential equation:*

$$\dot{\mathbf{x}}(t) = \mathbf{G}(\mathbf{x}(t)) \tag{2.36}$$

with initial value $\mathbf{x}(0)$, where $\mathbf{G} : \mathbb{R}^n \to \mathbb{R}^n$. Let $\mathbf{x}^*$ be a steady state of this system, that is, $\mathbf{G}(\mathbf{x}^*) = 0$, and suppose that $\mathbf{G}$ is differentiable at $\mathbf{x}^*$. Define

$$\mathbf{A} \equiv D\mathbf{G}(\mathbf{x}^*),$$

and suppose that all eigenvalues of $\mathbf{A}$ have negative real parts. Then the steady state of the differential equation (2.36), $\mathbf{x}^*$, is locally asymptotically stable, in the sense that there exists an open neighborhood of $\mathbf{x}^*$, $\mathbf{B}(\mathbf{x}^*) \subset \mathbb{R}^n$, such that starting from any $\mathbf{x}(0) \in \mathbf{B}(\mathbf{x}^*)$, $\mathbf{x}(t) \to \mathbf{x}^*$.

Once again an immediate corollary is as follows.

Corollary 2.2

1. *Let $x(t) \in \mathbb{R}$. Then the steady state of the linear differential equation $\dot{x}(t) = ax(t)$ is globally asymptotically stable (in the sense that $x(t) \to 0$) if $a < 0$.*

2. *Let $g : \mathbb{R} \to \mathbb{R}$ be differentiable in the neighborhood of the steady state x^* defined by $g(x^*) = 0$ and suppose that $g'(x^*) < 0$. Then the steady state of the nonlinear differential equation $\dot{x}(t) = g(x(t))$, x^*, is locally asymptotically stable.*

3. *Let $g : \mathbb{R} \to \mathbb{R}$ be continuously differentiable. Suppose that $g(x^*) = 0$ and that $g(x) < 0$ for all $x > x^*$ and $g(x) > 0$ for all $x < x^*$. Then the steady state of the nonlinear differential equation $\dot{x}(t) = g(x(t))$, x^*, is globally asymptotically stable, that is, starting with any $x(0)$, $x(t) \to x^*$.*

Proof. See Exercise 2.10. ■

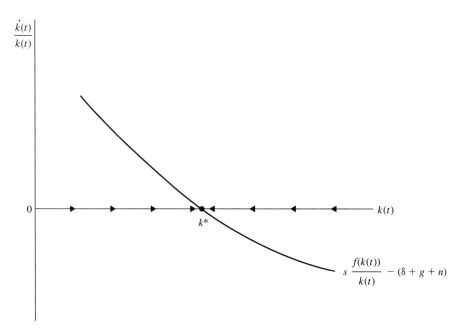

FIGURE 2.9 Dynamics of the capital-labor ratio in the basic Solow model.

Notice that the equivalent of part 3 of Corollary 2.2 is not true in discrete time. The implications of this observation are illustrated in Exercise 2.21.

In view of these results, Proposition 2.5 has a straightforward generalization of the results for discrete time.

Proposition 2.9 *Suppose that Assumptions 1 and 2 hold. Then the basic Solow growth model in continuous time with constant population growth and no technological change is globally asymptotically stable and, starting from any $k(0) > 0$, $k(t)$ monotonically converges to k^*.*

Proof. The proof of stability is now simpler and follows immediately from part 3 of Corollary 2.2 by noting that when $k < k^*$, we have $sf(k) - (n + \delta)k > 0$, and when $k > k^*$, we have $sf(k) - (n + \delta)k < 0$. ∎

Figure 2.9 shows the analysis of stability diagrammatically. The figure plots the right-hand side of (2.33) and makes it clear that when $k < k^*$, $\dot{k} > 0$, and when $k > k^*$, $\dot{k} < 0$, so that the capital-labor ratio monotonically converges to the steady-state value k^*.

Example 2.2 (Dynamics with the Cobb-Douglas Production Function) *Let us return to the Cobb-Douglas production function introduced in Example 2.1:*

$$F(K, L, A) = AK^\alpha L^{1-\alpha}, \quad \text{with } 0 < \alpha < 1.$$

As noted above, the Cobb-Douglas production function is special, mainly because it has an elasticity of substitution between capital and labor equal to 1. For a homothetic production function $F(K, L)$, the elasticity of substitution is defined by

$$\sigma \equiv -\left[\frac{\partial \log(F_K/F_L)}{\partial \log(K/L)} \right]^{-1}, \tag{2.37}$$

where F_K and F_L denote the marginal products of capital and labor. (F is homothetic when F_K/F_L is only a function of K/L). For the Cobb-Douglas production function $F_K/F_L = \alpha L/((1-\alpha)K)$, and thus $\sigma = 1$. This feature implies that when the production function is Cobb-Douglas and factor markets are competitive, equilibrium factor shares will be constant regardless of the capital-labor ratio. In particular, the share of capital in national income is

$$\alpha_K(t) = \frac{R(t)K(t)}{Y(t)}$$

$$= \frac{F_K(K(t), L(t))K(t)}{Y(t)}$$

$$= \frac{\alpha AK(t)^{\alpha-1}L(t)^{1-\alpha}K(t)}{AK(t)^{\alpha}L(t)^{1-\alpha}}$$

$$= \alpha.$$

Similarly, the share of labor is $\alpha_L(t) = 1 - \alpha$. Thus with an elasticity of substitution equal to 1, as capital increases, its marginal product decreases proportionally, leaving the capital share (the amount of capital times its marginal product) constant.

Recall that with the Cobb-Douglas technology, the per capita production function takes the form $f(k) = Ak^{\alpha}$, so the steady state is again given by (2.34) (with population growth at the rate n) as

$$A(k^*)^{\alpha-1} = \frac{n+\delta}{s},$$

or as

$$k^* = \left(\frac{sA}{n+\delta}\right)^{\frac{1}{1-\alpha}},$$

which is a simple expression for the steady-state capital-labor ratio. It follows that k^* is increasing in s and A and decreasing in n and δ (these results are naturally consistent with those in Proposition 2.8). In addition, k^* is increasing in α, because a higher α implies less diminishing returns to capital, thus a higher capital-labor ratio is necessary to reduce the average return to capital to a level consistent with the steady state as given in (2.34).

Transitional dynamics are also straightforward in this case. In particular,

$$\dot{k}(t) = sAk(t)^{\alpha} - (n+\delta)k(t)$$

with initial condition $k(0) > 0$. To solve this equation, let $x(t) \equiv k(t)^{1-\alpha}$, so the equilibrium law of motion of the capital-labor ratio can be written in terms of $x(t)$ as

$$\dot{x}(t) = (1-\alpha)sA - (1-\alpha)(n+\delta)x(t),$$

which is a linear differential equation with a general solution

$$x(t) = \frac{sA}{n+\delta} + \left[x(0) - \frac{sA}{n+\delta}\right]\exp(-(1-\alpha)(n+\delta)t)$$

(see Appendix B). Expressing this solution in terms of the capital-labor ratio yields

$$k(t) = \left\{\frac{sA}{n+\delta} + \left[k(0)^{1-\alpha} - \frac{sA}{n+\delta}\right]\exp\left(-(1-\alpha)(n+\delta)t\right)\right\}^{\frac{1}{1-\alpha}}.$$

This solution illustrates that starting from any $k(0)$, the equilibrium $k(t) \to k^* = (sA/(n+\delta))^{1/(1-\alpha)}$, and in fact, the rate of adjustment is related to $(1-\alpha)(n+\delta)$. More specifically, the gap between $k(0)$ and the steady-state value k^* narrows at the exponential rate $(1-\alpha)(n+\delta)$. This result is intuitive: a higher α implies less diminishing returns to capital, which slows down the rate at which the marginal and average products of capital decline as capital accumulates, and this reduces the rate of adjustment to the steady state. Similarly, a smaller δ means less depreciation and a smaller n means slower population growth, both of which slow down the adjustment of capital per worker and thus the rate of transitional dynamics.

Example 2.3 (The Constant Elasticity of Substitution Production Function)   *The Cobb-Douglas production function, which features an elasticity of substitution equal to 1, is a special case of the Constant Elasticity of Substitution (CES) production function, first introduced by Arrow et al. (1961). This production function imposes a constant elasticity, σ, not necessarily equal to 1. Consider a vector-valued index of technology $\mathbf{A}(t) = \left(A_H(t), A_K(t), A_L(t)\right)$. Then the CES production function can be written as*

$$Y(t) = F(K(t), L(t), \mathbf{A}(t))$$

$$\equiv A_H(t) \left[\gamma \left(A_K(t) K(t) \right)^{\frac{\sigma-1}{\sigma}} + (1-\gamma)(A_L(t)L(t))^{\frac{\sigma-1}{\sigma}} \right]^{\frac{\sigma}{\sigma-1}}, \qquad (2.38)$$

where $A_H(t) > 0$, $A_K(t) > 0$ and $A_L(t) > 0$ are three different types of technological change that are discussed further in Section 2.7; $\gamma \in (0, 1)$ is a distribution parameter, which determines how important labor and capital services are in determining the production of the final good; and $\sigma \in [0, \infty]$ is the elasticity of substitution. To verify that σ is the constant elasticity of substitution, let us use (2.37). The ratio of the marginal product of capital to the marginal productive labor, F_K/F_L, is then given by

$$\frac{F_K}{F_L} = \frac{\gamma A_K(t)^{\frac{\sigma-1}{\sigma}} K(t)^{-\frac{1}{\sigma}}}{(1-\gamma) A_L(t)^{\frac{\sigma-1}{\sigma}} L(t)^{-\frac{1}{\sigma}}},$$

so that the elasticity of substitution is indeed given by σ, that is,

$$\sigma = - \left[\frac{\partial \log(F_K/F_L)}{\partial \log(K/L)} \right]^{-1}.$$

The CES production function is particularly useful because it is more general and flexible than the Cobb-Douglas form while still being tractable. As $\sigma \to 1$, the CES production function (2.38) converges to the Cobb-Douglas function

$$Y(t) = A_H(t)(A_K(t))^{\gamma}(A_L(t))^{1-\gamma}(K(t))^{\gamma}(L(t))^{1-\gamma}.$$

As $\sigma \to \infty$, the CES production function becomes linear, that is,

$$Y(t) = \gamma A_H(t)A_K(t)K(t) + (1-\gamma) A_H(t)A_L(t)L(t).$$

Finally, as $\sigma \to 0$, the CES production function converges to the Leontief production function with no substitution between factors:

$$Y(t) = A_H(t) \min \left\{ \gamma A_K(t)K(t); (1-\gamma) A_L(t)L(t) \right\}.$$

The special feature of the Leontief production function is that if $\gamma A_K(t)K(t) \neq (1-\gamma)A_L(t)L(t)$, either capital or labor will be partially idle in the sense that a small reduction in capital or labor will have no effect on output or factor prices. Exercise 2.23 illustrates a number of the properties of the CES production function, while Exercise 2.16 provides an alternative derivation of this production function along the lines of the original article by Arrow et al. (1961). Notice also that the CES production function with $\sigma > 1$ violates Assumption 1 (see Exercise 2.24), so in the context of aggregate production functions with capital and labor, we may take $\sigma \leq 1$ as the benchmark.

2.6 A First Look at Sustained Growth

Can the Solow model generate sustained growth without technological progress? The answer is yes, but only if some of the assumptions imposed so far are relaxed. The Cobb-Douglas example (Example 2.2) already showed that when α is close to 1, the adjustment of the capital-labor ratio back to its steady-state level can be very slow. A very slow adjustment toward a steady state has the flavor of sustained growth rather than the economy (quickly) settling down to a steady state. In fact, the simplest model of sustained growth essentially takes $\alpha = 1$ in terms of the Cobb-Douglas production function. To construct such a model, let us relax Assumptions 1 and 2 (which do not allow $\alpha = 1$), and consider the so-called AK model, where

$$F(K(t), L(t), A(t)) = AK(t) \tag{2.39}$$

and $A > 0$ is a constant. The results here apply with more general constant returns to scale production functions that relax Assumption 2, for example, with

$$F(K(t), L(t), A(t)) = AK(t) + BL(t). \tag{2.40}$$

Nevertheless, it is simpler to illustrate the main insights with (2.39), leaving the analysis of the case when the production function is given by (2.40) to Exercise 2.22.

Let us continue to assume that population grows at a constant rate n as before (see (2.32)). Then combining (2.32) with the production function (2.39), the fundamental law of motion of the capital stock becomes

$$\frac{\dot{k}(t)}{k(t)} = sA - \delta - n.$$

This equation shows that when the parameters satisfy the inequality $sA - \delta - n > 0$, there will be sustained growth in the capital-labor ratio and thus in output per capita. This result is summarized in the next proposition.

Proposition 2.10 *Consider the Solow growth model with the production function (2.39) and suppose that $sA - \delta - n > 0$. Then in equilibrium there is sustained growth of output per capita at the rate $sA - \delta - n$. In particular, starting with a capital-labor ratio $k(0) > 0$, the economy has*

$$k(t) = \exp\left(\left(sA - \delta - n\right)t\right)k(0)$$

and

$$y(t) = \exp\left(\left(sA - \delta - n\right)t\right)Ak(0).$$

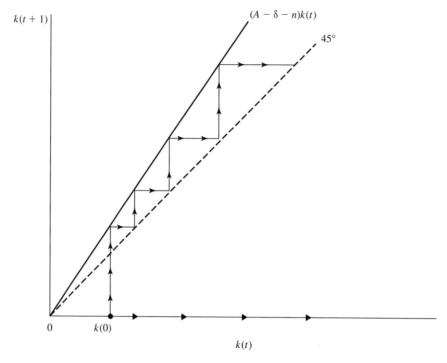

FIGURE 2.10 Sustained growth with the linear AK technology with $sA - \delta - n > 0$.

This proposition not only establishes the possibility of sustained growth but also shows that when the aggregate production function is given by (2.39), sustained growth is achieved without transitional dynamics. The economy always grows at a constant rate $sA - \delta - n$, regardless of the initial level of capital-labor ratio. Figure 2.10 shows this equilibrium diagrammatically.

Does the AK model provide an appealing approach to explaining sustained growth? While its simplicity is a plus, the model has a number of unattractive features. First, it is somewhat of a knife-edge case, which does not satisfy Assumptions 1 and 2; in particular, it requires the production function to be ultimately linear in the capital stock. Second and relatedly, this feature implies that as time goes by the share of national income accruing to capital will increase toward 1 (if it is not equal to 1 to start with). The next section shows that this tendency does not seem to be borne out by the data. Finally and most importantly, a variety of evidence suggests that technological progress is a major (perhaps the most significant) factor in understanding the process of economic growth. A model of sustained growth without technological progress fails to capture this essential aspect of economic growth. Motivated by these considerations, we next turn to the task of introducing technological progress into the baseline Solow growth model.

2.7 Solow Model with Technological Progress

2.7.1 Balanced Growth

The models analyzed so far did not feature technological progress. I now introduce changes in $A(t)$ to capture improvements in the technological knowhow of the economy. There is little doubt that today human societies know how to produce many more goods and can do so more efficiently than in the past. The productive knowledge of human society has

Labor and capital share in total value added

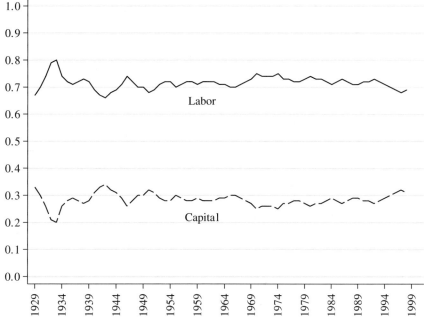

FIGURE 2.11 Capital and labor share in the U.S. GDP.

progressed tremendously over the past 200 years, and even more so over the past 1,000 or 10,000 years. This suggests that an attractive way of introducing economic growth in the framework developed so far is to allow technological progress in the form of changes in $A(t)$.

The key question is how to model the effects of changes in $A(t)$ on the aggregate production function. The standard approach is to impose discipline on the form of technological progress (and its impact on the aggregate production function) by requiring that the resulting allocations be consistent with balanced growth, as defined by the so-called Kaldor facts (Kaldor, 1963). Kaldor noted that while output per capita increases, the capital-output ratio, the interest rate, and the distribution of income between capital and labor remain roughly constant. Figure 2.11, for example, shows the evolution of the shares of capital and labor in the U.S. national income. Throughout the book, balanced growth refers to an allocation where output grows at a constant rate and capital-output ratio, the interest rate, and factor shares remain constant. (Clearly, three of these four features imply the fourth.)

Figure 2.11 shows that, despite fairly large fluctuations, there is no trend in factor shares. Moreover, a range of evidence suggests that there is no apparent trend in interest rates over long time horizons (see, e.g., Homer and Sylla, 1991). These facts and the relative constancy of capital-output ratios until the 1970s make many economists prefer models with balanced growth to those without. The share of capital in national income and the capital-output ratio are not exactly constant. For example, since the 1970s both the share of capital in national income and the capital-output ratio may have increased, depending on how one measures them. Nevertheless, constant factor shares and a constant capital-output ratio provide a good approximation to reality and a very useful starting point for our models.

Also for future reference, note that in Figure 2.11 the capital share in national income is about 1/3, while the labor share is about 2/3. This estimate ignores the share of land; land is not a major factor of production in modern economies (though this has not been true historically and is not true for the less-developed economies of today). Exercise 2.11 illustrates how incorporating land into this framework changes the analysis. Note also that this pattern of the factor distribution of income, combined with economists' desire to work with simple models, often makes them choose a Cobb-Douglas aggregate production function of the form $AK^{1/3}L^{2/3}$ as an approximation to reality (especially since it ensures that factor shares are constant by construction). However, Theorem 2.6 below shows that Cobb-Douglas technology is not necessary for balanced growth, and as noted in Example 2.2, the Cobb-Douglas form is both special and restrictive.

Another major advantage of models with balanced growth is that they are much easier to analyze than those with nonbalanced growth. Analysis is facilitated because with balanced growth, the equations describing the law of motion of the economy can be represented by difference or differential equations with well-defined steady states in transformed variables (thus, balanced growth will imply $\dot{k} = 0$, except that now the definition of k is different). This enables us to apply the tools used in the analysis of stationary models to study economies with sustained growth. It is nonetheless important to bear in mind that in reality, growth has many nonbalanced features. For example, the share of different sectors changes systematically over the growth process, with agriculture shrinking and manufacturing first increasing and then shrinking. Ultimately, we would like to develop models that combine certain balanced features with these types of structural transformations. I return to these issues in Part VII of the book.

2.7.2 Types of Neutral Technological Progress

What types of restrictions does balanced growth place on our models? It turns out that the answer to this question is "quite a few." The production function $F(K(t), L(t), A(t))$ is too general to achieve balanced growth, and only some very special types of production functions are consistent with balanced growth. To develop this point, consider an aggregate production function $\tilde{F}$ and let us define different types of neutral technological progress. A first possibility is

$$\tilde{F}(K(t), L(t), A(t)) = A(t)F(K(t), L(t))$$

for some constant returns to scale function F. This functional form implies that the technology term $A(t)$ is simply a multiplicative constant in front of another (quasi-) production function F. This type of technological progress is referred to as "Hicks-neutral" after the famous British economist John Hicks. Figure 2.12 illustrates this form of technological progress by plotting the isoquants of the function $\tilde{F}(K(t), L(t), A(t))$, which correspond to combinations of labor and capital for a given technology $A(t)$ such that the level of production is constant. Hicks-neutral technological progress, in the first panel, corresponds to a relabeling of the isoquants (without any change in their shape).

Another alternative is to have capital-augmenting or Solow-neutral technological progress in the form

$$\tilde{F}(K(t), L(t), A(t)) = F(A(t)K(t), L(t)),$$

which is also referred to as "capital-augmenting progress," because a higher $A(t)$ is equivalent to the economy having more capital. This type of technological progress corresponds to the isoquants shifting inward as if the capital axis were being shrunk (since a higher A now corresponds to a greater level of effective capital). This type of progress is shown in panel B of Figure 2.12 for a doubling of $A(t)$.

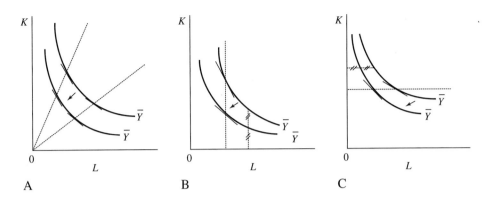

FIGURE 2.12 (A) Hicks-neutral, (B) Solow-neutral, and (C) Harrod-neutral shifts in isoquants.

Finally, we can have labor-augmenting or Harrod-neutral technological progress (panel C), named after Roy Harrod (whom we already encountered in the context of the Harrod-Domar model):

$$\tilde{F}(K(t), L(t), A(t)) = F[K(t), A(t)L(t)].$$

This functional form implies that an increase in technology $A(t)$ increases output as if the economy had more labor and thus corresponds to an inward shift of the isoquant as if the labor axis were being shrunk. The approximate form of the shifts in the isoquants are plotted in the third panel of Figure 2.12, again for a doubling of $A(t)$.

Of course in practice technological change can be a mixture of these, so we could have a vector-valued index of technology $\mathbf{A}(t) = \left(A_H(t), A_K(t), A_L(t)\right)$ and a production function that looks like

$$\tilde{F}(K(t), L(t), \mathbf{A}(t)) = A_H(t)F\left[A_K(t)K(t), A_L(t)L(t)\right], \tag{2.41}$$

which nests the CES production function introduced in Example 2.3. Nevertheless, even (2.41) is a restriction on the form of technological progress, since in general changes in technology, $A(t)$, could modify the entire production function.

Although all of these forms of technological progress look equally plausible ex ante, we will next see that balanced growth in the long run is only possible if all technological progress is labor-augmenting or Harrod-neutral. This result is very surprising and troubling, since there are no compelling reasons for why technological progress should take this form. I return to a discussion of why long-run technological change might be Harrod-neutral in Chapter 15.

2.7.3 Uzawa's Theorem

The discussion above suggests that the key elements of balanced growth are the constancy of factor shares and the constancy of the capital-output ratio, $K(t)/Y(t)$. The shares of capital and labor in national income are

$$\alpha_K(t) \equiv \frac{R(t)K(t)}{Y(t)} \quad \text{and} \quad \alpha_L(t) \equiv \frac{w(t)L(t)}{Y(t)}.$$

By Assumption 1 and Theorem 2.1, $\alpha_K(t) + \alpha_L(t) = 1$.

A version of the following theorem was first proved by the leading growth theorist, Hirofumi Uzawa (1961). The statement and the proof here build on the argument developed in the recent paper by Schlicht (2006). The theorem shows that constant growth of output, capital, and consumption combined with constant returns to scale implies that the aggregate production function must have a representation with Harrod-neutral (purely labor-augmenting) technological progress. For simplicity and without loss of any generality, I focus on continuous-time models.

Theorem 2.6 (Uzawa's Theorem I) *Consider a growth model with aggregate production function*

$$Y(t) = \tilde{F}(K(t), L(t), \tilde{A}(t)),$$

where $\tilde{F} : \mathbb{R}_+^2 \times \mathcal{A} \to \mathbb{R}_+$ and $\tilde{A}(t) \in \mathcal{A}$ represents technology at time t (where $\mathcal{A}$ is an arbitrary set, e.g., a subset of $\mathbb{R}^N$ for some natural number N). Suppose that $\tilde{F}$ exhibits constant returns to scale in K and L. The aggregate resource constraint is

$$\dot{K}(t) = Y(t) - C(t) - \delta K(t).$$

Suppose that there is a constant growth rate of population, $L(t) = \exp(nt)L(0)$, and that there exists $T < \infty$ such that for all $t \geq T$, $\dot{Y}(t)/Y(t) = g_Y > 0$, $\dot{K}(t)/K(t) = g_K > 0$, and $\dot{C}(t)/C(t) = g_C > 0$. Then

1. *$g_Y = g_K = g_C$; and*
2. *for any $t \geq T$, there exists a function $F : \mathbb{R}_+^2 \to \mathbb{R}_+$ homogeneous of degree 1 in its two arguments, such that the aggregate production function can be represented as*

$$Y(t) = F(K(t), A(t)L(t)),$$

where $A(t) \in \mathbb{R}_+$ and

$$\frac{\dot{A}(t)}{A(t)} = g = g_Y - n.$$

Proof. (Part 1) By hypothesis for $t \geq T$, we have $Y(t) = \exp(g_Y(t - T))Y(T)$, $K(t) = \exp(g_K(t - T))K(T)$, and $L(t) = \exp(n(t - T))L(T)$. Since $\dot{K}(t) = g_K K(t)$, the aggregate resource constraint at time t implies

$$(g_K + \delta)K(t) = Y(t) - C(t).$$

Dividing both sides of this equation by $\exp\left(g_K(t - T)\right)$, we obtain

$$(g_K + \delta)K(T) = \exp((g_Y - g_K)(t - T))Y(T) - \exp((g_C - g_K)(t - T))C(T)$$

for all $t \geq T$. Differentiating the previous equation with respect to time yields

$$(g_Y - g_K)\exp((g_Y - g_K)(t - T))Y(T) - (g_C - g_K)\exp((g_C - g_K)(t - T))C(T) = 0$$

for all $t \geq T$. This equation can hold for all t if any of the following four conditions is true: (i) $g_Y = g_K = g_C$, (ii) $g_Y = g_C$ and $Y(T) = C(T)$, (iii) if $g_Y = g_K$ and $C(T) = 0$, or (iv) $g_C = g_K$ and $Y(T) = 0$. The latter three possibilities contradict, respectively, that $g_K > 0$, that $g_C > 0$ (which implies $C(T) > 0$ and $K(T) > 0$, and hence $Y(T) > C(T)$), and that

$Y(T) > 0$. Therefore (i) must apply and $g_Y = g_K = g_C$, as claimed in the first part of the theorem.

(Part 2) For any $t \geq T$, the aggregate production function for time T can be written as

$$\exp\left(-g_Y\,(t - T)\right) Y(t) = \tilde{F}\left[\exp\left(-g_K\,(t - T)\right) K(t),\, \exp\left(-n(t - T)\right) L(t),\, \tilde{A}(T)\right].$$

Multiplying both sides by $\exp\left(g_Y(t - T)\right)$ and using the constant returns to scale property of $\tilde{F}$ yields

$$Y(t) = \tilde{F}\left[\exp\left((t - T)\left(g_Y - g_K\right)\right) K(t),\, \exp\left((t - T)(g_Y - n)\right) L(t),\, \tilde{A}(T)\right].$$

From part 1, $g_Y = g_K$ and thus for any $t \geq T$,

$$Y(t) = \tilde{F}\left[K(t),\, \exp\left((t - T)\left(g_Y - n\right)\right) L(t),\, \tilde{A}(T)\right]. \tag{2.42}$$

Since (2.42) is true for all $t \geq T$ and $\tilde{F}$ is homogeneous of degree 1 in K and L, there exists a function $F : \mathbb{R}_+^2 \to \mathbb{R}_+$ that is homogeneous of degree 1 such that

$$Y(t) = F(K(t),\, \exp((g_Y - n)t)L(t)).$$

Rewriting this as

$$Y(t) = F(K(t),\, A(t)L(t)),$$

with

$$\frac{\dot{A}(t)}{A(t)} = g_Y - n$$

establishes the second part of the theorem. ∎

A remarkable feature of this theorem is that it was stated and proved without any reference to equilibrium behavior. The theorem only exploits the fact that the production function exhibits constant returns to scale in K and L and that the allocation $[Y(t), K(t), C(t)]_{t=0}^\infty$ features output, capital, and consumption all growing at the same constant rate after time T. Notice, however, that the theorem holds under the hypothesis that $Y(t)$, $K(t)$, and $C(t)$ exhibit constant growth rates after some (finite) time T. A stronger result would require the same conclusions to hold as $t \to \infty$. Exercise 2.14 contains a generalization of Theorem 2.6 in this direction, but also shows why some additional conditions need to be imposed in this case.

Before providing an economic intuition for Theorem 2.6, let us state a simple corollary of this theorem, which will be useful both in the discussions below and for the intuition.

Corollary 2.3 *Under the assumptions of Theorem 2.6, for all $t \geq T$ technological progress can be represented as Harrod neutral (purely labor-augmenting).*

In light of Theorem 2.6 and this corollary, with a slight abuse of terminology, we can say that "technological change must be asymptotically Harrod neutral."

Let us now return to the intuition for Uzawa's Theorem. This theorem supposes that there is capital accumulation, that is, $g_K > 0$. Part 1 implies that this is possible only if output and capital grow at the same rate. Either this growth rate is equal to the rate of population growth, n, in which case there is no technological change (the proposition applies with $g_Y = 0$) or the economy exhibits growth of per capita income and the capital-labor ratio ($g_K = g_Y > 0$).

The latter case creates an asymmetry between capital and labor, in the sense that capital is accumulating faster than labor. Constancy of growth then requires technological change to make up for this asymmetry—that is, technology should take a labor-augmenting form.

This intuition does not provide a reason for why technology should take this labor-augmenting (Harrod-neutral) form, however. The theorem and its corollary simply state that if technology did not take this form, an (asymptotic) allocation with constant growth rates of output, capital and consumption (and thus balanced growth) would not be possible. At some level, this result is distressing, since it implies that balanced growth (in fact something weaker than balanced growth) is only possible under a very stringent assumption. Chapter 15 shows that when technology is endogenous the same intuition also implies that technology should be endogenously more labor-augmenting than capital-augmenting.

Notice also that Theorem 2.6 and its corollary do *not* state that technological change has to be labor-augmenting all the time. Instead, technological change ought to be labor-augmenting after time T (along the balanced growth path). This is the pattern that certain classes of endogenous technology models will generate (see again Chapter 15 for a discussion). More importantly, contrary to common claims in textbooks and the literature, Theorem 2.6 does *not* even state that capital-augmenting (Solow-neutral) technological change is impossible as $t \to \infty$. It states that such technological progress is not possible if there is balanced growth after some date T. Exercise 2.17 provides a simple example where asymptotic balanced growth (with the conditions in Theorem 2.6 being satisfied as $t \to \infty$) is possible in the presence of asymptotic capital-augmenting technological progress.

It should also be emphasized that Theorem 2.6 does not require that $Y(t) = F(K(t), A(t)L(t))$, but only that it has a representation of the form $Y(t) = F(K(t), A(t)L(t))$. For example, if the aggregate production function is Cobb-Douglas, that is,

$$Y(t) = (A_K(t)K(t))^\alpha (A_L(t)L(t))^{1-\alpha},$$

then both $A_K(t)$ and $A_L(t)$ could grow at constant rates while maintaining balanced growth. However, in this Cobb-Douglas example we can define $A(t) = A_K(t)^{\alpha/(1-\alpha)} A_L(t)$ and the production function can be represented as

$$Y(t) = K(t)^\alpha (A(t)L(t))^{1-\alpha},$$

so that technological change is represented as purely labor-augmenting, which is what Theorem 2.6 requires. Intuitively, the differences between labor-augmenting and capital-augmenting (and Hicks-neutral) forms of technological progress matter when the elasticity of substitution between capital and labor is not equal to 1. In the Cobb-Douglas case, as we have seen above, this elasticity of substitution is equal to 1; thus Harrod-neutral, Solow-neutral, and Hicks-neutral forms of technological progress are simple transforms of one another.

Theorem 2.6 does not specify how factor prices behave. As noted at the beginning of this section, the Kaldor facts also require constant factor shares. Since capital and output are growing at the same rate, the rental rate of capital must be constant. Does Theorem 2.6 (combined with competitive factor markets) imply constant factor shares? Unfortunately, the answer is not necessarily. This is related to an implicit limitation in Theorem 2.6. The theorem states that the original production function $\tilde{F}(K(t), L(t), \tilde{A}(t))$ has a representation of the form $F(K(t), A(t)L(t))$ along an asymptotic path with constant growth rates. This does not guarantee that the derivatives of $\tilde{F}$ and F with respect to K and L agree. Exercise 2.19 provides an example of production function $\tilde{F}$ that satisfies all of the conditions of Theorem 2.6 (and thus admits a representation of the form $F(K(t), A(t)L(t))$ as $t \to \infty$), but has derivatives that do not agree with those of F. In fact, the exercise shows that, with competitive markets, this $\tilde{F}$

leads to arbitrary behavior of factor prices as $t \to \infty$. The next theorem, however, shows that along a balanced growth path, where factor shares are also constant over time, the derivatives of $\tilde{F}$ and F must agree, and vice versa.

Theorem 2.7 (Uzawa's Theorem II) *Suppose that all hypotheses in Theorem 2.6 are satisfied, so that $\tilde{F} : \mathbb{R}_+^2 \times \mathcal{A} \to \mathbb{R}_+$ has a representation of the form $F(K(t), A(t)L(t))$ with $A(t) \in \mathbb{R}_+$ and $\dot{A}(t)/A(t) = g = g_Y - n$ (for $t \geq T$). In addition, suppose that factor markets are competitive and that for all $t \geq T$, the rental rate satisfies $R(t) = R^*$ (or equivalently, $\alpha_K(t) = \alpha_K^*$). Then, denoting the partial derivatives of $\tilde{F}$ and F with respect to their first two arguments by $\tilde{F}_K$, $\tilde{F}_L$, F_K, and F_L, we have*

$$\tilde{F}_K(K(t), L(t), \tilde{A}(t)) = F_K(K(t), A(t)L(t)) \text{ and}$$
$$\tilde{F}_L(K(t), L(t), \tilde{A}(t)) = A(t)F_L(K(t), A(t)L(t)). \tag{2.43}$$

Moreover, if (2.43) holds and factor markets are competitive, then $R(t) = R^*$ (and $\alpha_K(t) = \alpha_K^*$) for all $t \geq T$.

Proof. From Theorem 2.6, $g_Y = g_K = g_C = g + n$. Since $R(t) = R^*$ for all $t \geq T$, this also implies that the wage rate satisfies $w(t) = \big(Y(t) - R^*K(t)\big)/L(t) = \exp(g(t - T)) w^*$ (where $w^* = w(T)$). Therefore we have that for all $t \geq T$,

$$R^* = \tilde{F}_K(K(t), L(t), \tilde{A}(t))$$
$$\exp(g(t - T)) w^* = \tilde{F}_L(K(t), L(t), \tilde{A}(t)). \tag{2.44}$$

With the same argument as in the proof of Theorem 2.6, we can also write

$$R^* = \tilde{F}_K(\exp(-(g + n)(t - T)) K(t), \exp(-n(t - T)) L(t), \tilde{A}(T)),$$
$$w^* = \tilde{F}_L(\exp(-(g + n)(t - T)) K(t), \exp(-n(t - T)) L(t), \tilde{A}(T)).$$

Using the fact that $\tilde{F}_K$ and $\tilde{F}_L$ are homogeneous of degree 0 in K and L (see Theorem 2.1), the previous two equations can be rewritten as

$$R^* = \tilde{F}_K(K(t), \exp(g(t - T)) L(t), \tilde{A}(T)),$$
$$w^* = \tilde{F}_L(K(t), \exp(g(t - T)) L(t), \tilde{A}(T)).$$

Comparing these to (2.44), we can conclude that for all $t \geq T$,

$$\tilde{F}_K(K(t), \exp(g(t - T)) L(t), \tilde{A}(T)) = \tilde{F}_K(K(t), L(t), \tilde{A}(t)),$$
$$\exp(g(t - T)) \tilde{F}_L(K(t), \exp(g(t - T)) L(t), \tilde{A}(T)) = \tilde{F}_L(K(t), L(t), \tilde{A}(t)).$$

This implies that there exist functions homogeneous of degree 0, $\hat{F}_1, \hat{F}_2 : \mathbb{R}_+^2 \to \mathbb{R}_+$, such that

$$\hat{F}_1(K(t), A(t)L(t)) = \tilde{F}_K(K(t), L(t), \tilde{A}(t)),$$
$$A(t)\hat{F}_2(K(t), A(t)L(t)) = \tilde{F}_L(K(t), L(t), \tilde{A}(t)),$$

with $\dot{A}(t)/A(t) = g$. Define $\hat{F} : \mathbb{R}^2_+ \rightarrow \mathbb{R}_+$ as

$$\hat{F}(K, AL) \equiv \hat{F}_1(K, AL)K + \hat{F}_2(K, AL)AL. \tag{2.45}$$

From Theorem 2.1, $\hat{F}(K(t), A(t)L(t)) = \tilde{F}(K(t), L(t), \tilde{A}(t))$, and thus $\hat{F}$ is homogeneous of degree 1 in its two arguments and provides a representation of $\tilde{F}$ along the path $[K(t), L(t)]_{t=0}^\infty$. Since $\hat{F}$ is homogeneous of degree 1, (2.45) implies that its partial derivatives are given by $\hat{F}_1$ and $\hat{F}_2$ and thus agree with those of $\tilde{F}$, establishing (2.43).

To prove the second part of the theorem, simply note that with competitive factor markets, we have that for $t \geq T$,

$$\alpha_K(t) \equiv \frac{R(t)K(t)}{Y(t)}$$

$$= \frac{K(t)}{Y(t)} \frac{\partial \tilde{F}(K(t), L(t), \tilde{A}(t))}{\partial K(t)}$$

$$= \alpha^*_K,$$

where the second line uses the definition of the rental rate of capital in a competitive market, and the third line uses (2.43) together with the fact that F is homogeneous of degree 1. ∎

Theorem 2.7 implies that any allocation with constant growth rates for output, capital, and consumption must be a balanced growth path (where factor shares in national income are also constant). It also implies that balanced growth can only be generated by an aggregate production function that features Harrod-neutral technological change.

A further intuition for Theorem 2.6 comes from Theorem 2.7. Suppose the production function takes the special form $F(A_K(t)K(t), A_L(t)L(t))$. Theorem 2.7 implies that factor shares must be constant as $t \rightarrow \infty$. Thus, given constant returns to scale, balanced growth after some time T is possible only when total capital inputs, $A_K(t)K(t)$, and total labor inputs, $A_L(t)L(t)$, grow at the same rate; otherwise, the share of either capital or labor will not be constant. But if total labor and capital inputs grow at the same rate, then output $Y(t)$ must also grow at this rate (again because of constant returns to scale). The fact that the capital-output ratio is constant in steady state then implies that $K(t)$ must grow at the same rate as output and thus at the same rate as $A_L(t)L(t)$. Therefore, balanced growth is only possible if $A_K(t)$ is constant after date T.

2.7.4 The Solow Growth Model with Technological Progress: Continuous Time

I now present an analysis of the Solow growth model with technological progress in continuous time. The discrete-time case can be analyzed analogously, and I omit the details to avoid repetition. Theorem 2.6 implies that when the economy is experiencing balanced growth, the production function must have a representation of the form

$$Y(t) = F(K(t), A(t)L(t)),$$

with purely labor-augmenting technological progress. Most macroeconomic and growth analyses then assume that it takes this form throughout (for all t) and that there is technological progress at the rate $g > 0$, that is,

$$\frac{\dot{A}(t)}{A(t)} = g > 0. \tag{2.46}$$

Let us also start with this assumption. Suppose also that population grows at the rate n as in (2.32). Again using the constant saving rate, capital accumulates according to the differential equation

$$\dot{K}(t) = sF(K(t), A(t)L(t)) - \delta K(t). \tag{2.47}$$

The simplest way of analyzing this economy is to express everything in terms of a normalized variable. Since "effective" or efficiency units of labor are given by $A(t)L(t)$, and F exhibits constant returns to scale in its two arguments, I now define $k(t)$ as the *effective capital-labor* ratio (capital divided by efficiency units of labor) so that

$$k(t) \equiv \frac{K(t)}{A(t)L(t)}. \tag{2.48}$$

Although there is a slight danger that the use of the same symbol, $k(t)$, for capital-labor ratio earlier and effective capital-labor ratio now might cause some confusion, the important parallel between the roles of capital-labor ratio in the Solow model without technological progress and of the effective capital-labor ratio with labor-augmenting technological progress justifies this notation.

Differentiating this expression with respect to time, we obtain

$$\frac{\dot{k}(t)}{k(t)} = \frac{\dot{K}(t)}{K(t)} - g - n. \tag{2.49}$$

The quantity of output per unit of effective labor can be written as

$$\hat{y}(t) \equiv \frac{Y(t)}{A(t)L(t)}$$

$$= F\left(\frac{K(t)}{A(t)L(t)}, 1\right)$$

$$\equiv f(k(t)).$$

Income per capita is $y(t) \equiv Y(t)/L(t)$, so that

$$y(t) = A(t)\hat{y}(t) \tag{2.50}$$

$$= A(t)f(k(t)).$$

It should be clear that if $\hat{y}(t)$ is constant, income per capita, $y(t)$, will grow over time, since $A(t)$ is growing. This highlights that in this model, and more generally in models with technological progress, we should not look for a steady state where income per capita is constant, but for a *balanced growth path* (BGP), where income per capita grows at a constant rate, while transformed variables, such as $\hat{y}(t)$ or $k(t)$ in (2.49), remain constant. Since these transformed variables remain constant, BGPs can be thought of as steady states of a transformed model. Motivated by this observation, in models with technological change throughout I use the terms "steady state" and "BGP" interchangeably. We will see that consistent with the definition in Section 2.7.1, this BGP allocation will also feature constant capital-output ratio, interest rate, and factor shares in national income.

Next, substituting for $\dot{K}(t)$ from (2.47) into (2.49),

$$\frac{\dot{k}(t)}{k(t)} = \frac{sF(K(t), A(t)L(t))}{K(t)} - (\delta + g + n).$$

Using (2.48),

$$\frac{\dot{k}(t)}{k(t)} = \frac{sf(k(t))}{k(t)} - (\delta + g + n), \tag{2.51}$$

which is very similar to the law of motion of the capital-labor ratio in the model without technological progress (2.33). The only difference is the presence of g, which reflects the fact that now k is no longer the capital-labor ratio, but the *effective* capital-labor ratio. Thus for k to remain constant in the BGP, the capital-labor ratio needs to increase at the rate g.

An equilibrium in this model is defined similarly to before. A steady state or a BGP is, in turn, defined as an equilibrium in which the effective capital-labor ratio $k(t)$ is constant. Consequently the following proposition holds (proof omitted).

Proposition 2.11 *Consider the basic Solow growth model in continuous time with Harrod-neutral technological progress at the rate g and population growth at the rate n. Suppose that Assumptions 1 and 2 hold, and define the effective capital-labor ratio as in (2.48). Then there exists a unique BGP where the effective capital-labor ratio is equal to $k^* \in (0, \infty)$ given by*

$$\frac{f(k^*)}{k^*} = \frac{\delta + g + n}{s}. \tag{2.52}$$

Per capita output and consumption grow at the rate g.

Equation (2.52), which determines the BGP (steady-state) effective capital-labor ratio, emphasizes that now total savings, $sf(k)$, are used for replenishing the capital stock for three distinct reasons. The first is again depreciation at the rate δ. The second is population growth at the rate n (which reduces capital per worker). The third is Harrod-neutral technological progress, which reduces effective capital-labor ratio at the rate g when the capital-labor ratio is constant. Thus the replenishment of the effective capital-labor ratio requires total investment to be equal to $(\delta + g + n)k$, which is the intuitive explanation for (2.52).

The comparative static results are also similar to before, with the additional comparative static with respect to the initial level of the labor-augmenting technology, $A(0)$ (the level of technology at all points in time, $A(t)$, is completely determined by $A(0)$ given the assumption in (2.46)).

Proposition 2.12 *Suppose Assumptions 1 and 2 hold and let $A(0)$ be the initial level of technology. Denote the BGP level of effective capital-labor ratio by $k^*(A(0), s, \delta, n, g)$ and the level of output per capita by $y^*(A(0), s, \delta, n, g, t)$ (the latter is a function of time, since it is growing over time). Then*

$$\frac{\partial k^*(A(0), s, \delta, n, g)}{\partial A(0)} = 0, \quad \frac{\partial k^*(A(0), s, \delta, n, g)}{\partial s} > 0,$$

$$\frac{\partial k^*(A(0), s, \delta, n, g)}{\partial n} < 0, \quad \text{and} \quad \frac{\partial k^*(A(0), s, \delta, n, g)}{\partial \delta} < 0,$$

and also

$$\frac{\partial y^*(A(0), s, \delta, n, g, t)}{\partial A(0)} > 0, \quad \frac{\partial y^*(A(0), s, \delta, n, g, t)}{\partial s} > 0,$$

$$\frac{\partial y^*(A(0), s, \delta, n, g, t)}{\partial n} < 0, \quad \text{and} \quad \frac{\partial y^*(A(0), s, \delta, n, g, t)}{\partial \delta} < 0,$$

for each t.

Proof.   See Exercise 2.25.   ∎

Finally, the transitional dynamics of the economy with technological progress are similar to the dynamics without technological change.

Proposition 2.13   *Suppose that Assumptions 1 and 2 hold. Then the BGP of the Solow growth model with Harrod-neutral technological progress and population growth in continuous time is asymptotically stable; that is, starting from any $k(0) > 0$, the effective capital-labor ratio converges to the BGP value k^* ($k(t) \to k^*$).*

Proof.   See Exercise 2.26.   ∎

Therefore, with Harrod-neutral technological change, the dynamics of the equilibrium path and the comparative statics are very similar to those in the model without technological progress. The major difference is that now the model generates growth in output per capita, so it can be mapped to the data more successfully. However, the disadvantage is that growth is driven entirely exogenously. The growth rate of the economy is exactly the same as the exogenous growth rate of the technology stock. The model specifies neither where this technology stock comes from nor how fast it grows.

2.8   Comparative Dynamics

This section briefly undertakes some simple comparative dynamics exercises. Comparative dynamics are different from the comparative static results in Propositions 2.3, 2.8, or 2.12 in that the focus is now on the entire path of adjustment of the economy following a shock or a change in parameters. The basic Solow model is particularly well suited to such an analysis because of its simplicity. These exercises are also useful because the basic Solow model and its neoclassical cousin are often used for analysis of policy changes, medium-run shocks, and business cycle dynamics, so an understanding of how the basic model responds to various shocks is useful in a range of applications.

Recall that the law of motion of the effective capital-labor ratio in the continuous-time Solow model is given by (2.51), that is, $\dot{k}(t)/k(t) = sf(k(t))/k(t) - (\delta + g + n)$. The right-hand side of this equation is plotted in Figure 2.13. The intersection with the horizontal axis gives the unique BGP, with effective capital-labor ratio k^*. This figure is sufficient for the analysis of comparative dynamics. Consider, for example, a one-time, unanticipated, permanent increase in the saving rate from s to s'. This shifts the curve to the right as shown by the dashed line, with a new intersection with the horizontal axis at k^{**}. The dashed arrows under the horizontal axis show how the effective capital-labor ratio adjusts gradually to the new BGP effective capital-labor ratio, k^{**}. Immediately after the increase in the saving rate is realized, the capital stock and the effective capital-labor ratio remain unchanged (since they are state variables). After this point, k follows the dashed arrows and converges monotonically to k^{**}. The

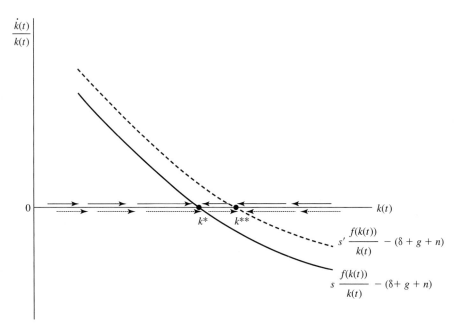

FIGURE 2.13 Dynamics following an increase in the saving rate from s to s'. The solid arrows show the dynamics for the initial steady state, while the dashed arrows show the dynamics for the new steady state.

comparative dynamics following a one-time, unanticipated, permanent decrease in δ or n are identical.

The same diagrammatic analysis can be used for studying the effect of an unanticipated but transitory change in parameters. For example, imagine that s changes in an unanticipated manner at $t = t'$, but this change will be reversed and the saving rate will return back to its original value at some known future date $t'' > t'$. In this case, starting at t', the economy follows the dashed arrows until t'. After t'', the original steady state of the differential equation applies and together with this, the solid arrows above the horizontal axis become effective. Thus from t'' onward, the economy gradually returns back to its original balanced growth equilibrium, k^*. We will see that similar comparative dynamics can be carried out in the neoclassical growth model as well, but the response of the economy to some of these changes will be more complex.

2.9 Taking Stock

What have we learned from the Solow model? At some level, a lot. We now have a simple and tractable framework that allows us to study capital accumulation and the implications of technological progress. As we will see in the next chapter, this framework is already quite useful in helping us think about the data.

However, at another level, we have learned relatively little. The questions that Chapter 1 posed are related to why some countries are rich while others are poor, why some countries grow while others stagnate, and why the world economy embarked upon the process of steady growth over the past few centuries. The Solow model shows us that if there is no technological progress, and as long as we are not in the AK world ruled out by Assumption 2, there will be no sustained growth. In this case, we can talk about cross-country output differences but not about growth of countries or of the world economy.

The Solow model generates per capita output growth only by introducing exogenous technological progress. But in this case, everything is driven by technological progress, and technological progress itself is exogenous, just a black box, outside the model and outside the influence of economic incentives. If technological progress is "where it's at," then we have to study and understand which factors generate technological progress, what makes some firms and societies invent better technologies, and what induces firms and societies to adopt and use these superior technologies.

Even on the question of capital accumulation, the Solow model is not entirely satisfactory. The rate of capital accumulation is determined by the saving rate, the depreciation rate, and the rate of population growth. All these rates are taken as exogenous.

In this light, the Solow growth model is most useful as a framework for laying out the general issues and questions. It emphasizes that to understand growth, we have to understand physical capital accumulation (and human capital accumulation, which is discussed in the next chapter) and perhaps most importantly, technological progress. All of these are black boxes in the Solow growth model. Therefore, much of the rest of the book will be about digging deeper, trying to uncover what lies in these black boxes. I start by introducing consumer optimization in Chapter 8, which enables a more systematic study of capital accumulation. Then I turn to models in which human capital accumulation and technological progress are endogenous. A model in which the rate of accumulation of factors of production and technology are endogenous gives us a framework for posing and answering questions related to the fundamental causes of economic growth.

Nevertheless, even in its bare-bones form, the Solow model is useful in helping us think about the world and bringing useful perspectives, especially related to the proximate causes of economic growth. This is the topic of the next chapter.

2.10 References and Literature

The model analyzed in this chapter was first developed in Solow (1956) and Swan (1956). Solow (1970) gives a nice and accessible treatment, with historical references. Barro and Sala-i-Martin's (2004, Chapter 1) textbook presents a more up-to-date treatment of the basic Solow model at the graduate level, while Jones (1998, Chapter 2) presents an excellent undergraduate treatment.

The treatment in the chapter made frequent references to basic consumer and general equilibrium theory. These are prerequisites for an adequate understanding of the theory of economic growth. Some of the important results from dynamic general equilibrium theory are discussed in Chapter 5. Mas-Colell, Whinston, and Green's (1995) graduate microeconomics textbook contains an excellent treatment of most of the necessary material, including producer theory and an accessible presentation of the basic notions of general equilibrium theory, including a discussion of Arrow securities and the definition of Arrow-Debreu commodities.

Properties of homogeneous functions and Euler's Theorem can be found, for example, in Simon and Blume (1994, Chapter 20). The reader should be familiar with the Implicit Function Theorem and properties of concave and convex functions, which are used throughout the book. A review is given in Appendix A.

Appendix B provides an overview of solutions to differential and difference equations and a discussion of stability. Theorems 2.2, 2.3, 2.4, and 2.5 follow from the results presented there. In addition, the reader may want to consult Boyce and DiPrima (1977), Luenberger (1979), or Simon and Blume (1994) for various results on difference and differential equations. Knowledge of solutions to simple differential equations and stability properties of difference and differential equations at the level of Appendix B is assumed in the text. In addition, the material in Luenberger (1979) is particularly useful, since it contains a unified treatment of difference and differential equations. Galor (2005) gives an introduction to difference equations and discrete-time dynamical systems for economists.

The golden rule saving rate was introduced by Edmund Phelps (1966). It is called the "golden rule" rate with reference to the biblical golden rule "do unto others as you would have them do unto you" applied in an intergenerational setting—that is, presuming that those living and consuming at each different date form a different generation. While the golden rule saving rate is of historical interest and is useful for discussions of dynamic efficiency, it has no intrinsic optimality property, since it is not derived from well-defined preferences. Optimal savings are discussed in greater detail in Chapter 8.

The balanced growth facts were first noted by Kaldor (1963). Figure 2.11 uses data from Piketty and Saez (2003). Homer and Sylla (1991) discuss the history of interest rates over many centuries and across different societies; they show that there is no notable upward or downward trend in interest rate. Nevertheless, not all aspects of the economic growth process are balanced, and the nonbalanced nature of growth is discussed in detail in Part VII of the book, which also contains references to changes in the sectoral composition of output in the course of the growth process.

A simpler version of Theorem 2.6 was first proved by Uzawa (1961). There are various different proofs in the literature, though many are not fully rigorous. The proof given here is adapted from Schlicht (2006), which is also discussed in Jones and Scrimgeour (2006). A similar proof also appears in Wan (1971). Barro and Sala-i-Martin (2004, Chapter 1) also suggest a proof. Nevertheless, their argument is incomplete, since it assumes that technological change must be a combination of Harrod- and Solow-neutral technological change, which is rather restrictive and is not necessary for the proof. The theorem and the proof provided here are therefore more general and complete. There are also a variety of misconceptions about the implications of Theorem 2.6. Many textbooks claim that this theorem rules out (asymptotic) capital-augmenting technological progress (unless the production function is Cobb-Douglas). Exercise 2.17 shows that this claim is not true and balanced growth is possible even with asymptotic capital-augmenting technological progress (with non–Cobb-Douglas production functions). Theorem 2.6 holds when balanced growth applies after some finite time T or under additional conditions, as discussed in Exercise 2.14. Moreover, it is also important to emphasize, as I did in the text, that Theorem 2.6 only provides a representation for a particular path of capital and labor. Consequently, this representation cannot always be used for equilibrium analysis (or for pricing capital and labor), as shown by Exercise 2.19. Theorem 2.7 was provided as a way of overcoming this difficulty. I am not aware of other results analogous to Theorem 2.7 in the literature.

As noted in the text, the CES production function was first introduced by Arrow et al. (1961). This production function plays an important role in many applied macroeconomic and economic growth models. The Inada conditions introduced in Assumption 2 are from Inada (1963).

Finally, the interested reader should look at the paper by Hakenes and Irmen (2006) for why Inada conditions can introduce an additional equilibrium path (other than the no-activity equilibrium) at $k = 0$ in continuous time even when $f(0) = 0$. Here it suffices to say that whether this steady state exists is a matter of the order in which limits are taken. In any case, as noted in the text, the steady state at $k = 0$ has no economic content and is ignored throughout the book.

2.11 Exercises

2.1 Show that competitive labor markets and Assumption 1 imply that the wage rate must be strictly positive and thus (2.4) implies (2.3).

2.2 Prove that Assumption 1 implies that $F(A, K, L)$ is concave in K and L but not strictly so.

2.3 Show that when F exhibits constant returns to scale and factor markets are competitive, the maximization problem in (2.5) either has no solution (the firm can make infinite profits), a unique solution $K = L = 0$, or a continuum of solutions (i.e., any (K, L) with $K/L = \kappa$ for some $\kappa > 0$ is a solution).

2.4 Consider the Solow growth model in continuous time with the following per capita production function:

$$f(k) = k^4 - 6k^3 + 11k^2 - 6k.$$

(a) Which parts of Assumptions 1 and 2 does the underlying production function $F(K, L)$ violate?

(b) Show that with this production function, there exist three steady-state equilibria.

(c) Prove that two of these steady-state equilibria are locally stable, while one of them is locally unstable. Can any of these steady-state equilibria be globally stable?

2.5 Prove Proposition 2.7.

2.6 Prove Proposition 2.8.

2.7 Let us introduce government spending in the basic Solow model. Consider the basic model without technological change and suppose that (2.9) takes the form

$$Y(t) = C(t) + I(t) + G(t),$$

with $G(t)$ denoting government spending at time t. Imagine that government spending is given by $G(t) = \sigma Y(t)$.

(a) Discuss how the relationship between income and consumption should be changed. Is it reasonable to assume that $C(t) = sY(t)$?

(b) Suppose that government spending partly comes out of private consumption, so that $C(t) = (s - \lambda\sigma)Y(t)$, where $\lambda \in [0, 1]$. What is the effect of higher government spending (in the form of higher σ) on the equilibrium of the Solow model?

(c) Now suppose that a fraction ϕ of $G(t)$ is invested in the capital stock, so that total investment at time t is given by

$$I(t) = (1 - s - (1 - \lambda)\sigma + \phi\sigma) Y(t).$$

Show that if ϕ is sufficiently high, the steady-state level of capital-labor ratio will increase as a result of higher government spending (corresponding to higher σ). Is this reasonable? How would you alternatively introduce public investments in this model?

2.8 Suppose that $F(K, L, A)$ is concave in K and L (though not necessarily strictly so) and satisfies Assumption 2. Prove Propositions 2.2 and 2.5. How do we need to modify Proposition 2.6?

2.9 Prove Proposition 2.6.

2.10 Prove Corollary 2.2.

2.11 Consider a modified version of the continuous-time Solow growth model where the aggregate production function is

$$F(K, L, Z) = L^\beta K^\alpha Z^{1-\alpha-\beta},$$

where Z is land, available in fixed inelastic supply. Assume that $\alpha + \beta < 1$, capital depreciates at the rate δ, and there is an exogenous saving rate of s.

(a) First suppose that there is no population growth. Find the steady-state capital-labor ratio in the steady-state output level. Prove that the steady state is unique and globally stable.

(b) Now suppose that there is population growth at the rate n, that is, $\dot{L}/L = n$. What happens to the capital-labor ratio and output level as $t \to \infty$? What happens to returns to land and the wage rate as $t \to \infty$?

(c) Would you expect the population growth rate n or the saving rate s to change over time in this economy? If so, how?

2.12 Consider the continuous-time Solow model without technological progress and with constant rate of population growth equal to n. Suppose that the production function satisfies Assumptions 1 and 2. Assume that capital is owned by capitalists and labor is supplied by a different set of agents, the workers. Following a suggestion by Kaldor (1957), suppose that capitalists save a fraction s_K of their income, while workers consume all of their income.

(a) Define and characterize the steady-state equilibrium of this economy and study its stability.

(b) What is the relationship between the steady-state capital-labor ratio k^* and the golden rule capital stock k^*_{gold} defined in Section 2.2.3?

2.13 Let us now make the opposite assumption of Exercise 2.12 and suppose that there is a constant saving rate $s \in (0, 1)$ out of labor income and no savings out of capital income. Suppose that the aggregate production function satisfies Assumptions 1 and 2. Show that in this case multiple steady-state equilibria are possible.

* 2.14 In this exercise, you are asked to generalize Theorem 2.6 to a situation in which, rather than

$$\dot{Y}(t)/Y(t) = g_Y > 0, \ \dot{K}(t)/K(t) = g_K > 0, \text{ and } \dot{C}(t)/C(t) = g_C > 0$$

for all $t \geq T$ with $T < \infty$, we have

$$\dot{Y}(t)/Y(t) \to g_Y > 0, \ \dot{K}(t)/K(t) \to g_K > 0, \text{ and} \dot{C}(t)/C(t) \to g_C > 0.$$

(a) Show, by constructing a counterexample, that Part 1 of Theorem 2.6 is no longer correct without further conditions. [Hint: consider $g_c < g_k = g_y$.] What conditions need to be imposed to ensure that these limiting growth rates are equal to one another?

(b) Now suppose that Part 1 of Theorem 2.6 has been established (in particular, $g_Y = g_K$). Show that the equivalent of the steps in the proof of the theorem imply that for any T and $t \geq T$, we have

$$\exp\left(-\int_T^t g_Y(s)ds\right) Y(t)$$

$$= \tilde{F}\left[\exp\left(-\int_T^t g_K(s)ds\right) K(t), \exp\left(-n(t-T)\right) L(t), \tilde{A}(T)\right],$$

where $g_Y(t) \equiv \dot{Y}(t)/Y(t)$, and $g_K(t)$ and $g_C(t)$ are defined similarly. Then show that

$$Y(t) = \tilde{F}\left[\exp\left(\int_T^t \left(g_Y(s) - g_K(s)\right) ds\right) K(t), \exp\left(\int_T^t \left(g_Y(s) - n\right) ds\right) L(t), \tilde{A}(T)\right]$$

Next observe that for any $\varepsilon_T > 0$, there exists $T < \infty$, such that $\left|g_Y(t) - g_Y\right| < \varepsilon_T/2$ and $\left|g_K(t) - g_Y\right| < \varepsilon_T/2$ (from the hypotheses that $\dot{Y}(t)/Y(t) \to g_Y > 0$ and $\dot{K}(t)/K(t) \to g_K > 0$). Consider a sequence (or net; see Appendix A) $\{\varepsilon_T\} \to 0$, which naturally corresponds to $T \to \infty$ in the above definition. Take $t = \xi T$ for some $\xi > 1$, and show that Part 2 of Theorem 2.6 holds if $\varepsilon_T T \to 0$ (as $T \to \infty$). Using this argument, show that if both $g_Y(t)$ and $g_K(t)$ converge to g_Y and g_K at a rate strictly faster than $1/t$, the asymptotic production function has a representation of the form $F(K(t), A(t)L(t))$, but that this conclusion does not hold if either $g_Y(t)$ or $g_K(t)$ converges at a slower rate. [Hint: here an asymptotic representation means that $\lim_{t \to \infty} \tilde{F}/F = 1$.]

2.15 Recall the definition of the elasticity of substitution σ in (2.37). Suppose labor markets are competitive and the wage rate is equal to w. Prove that if the aggregate production function $F(K, L, A)$ exhibits constant returns to scale in K and L, then

$$\varepsilon_{y,w} \equiv \frac{\partial y/\partial w}{y/w} = \sigma,$$

where, as usual, $y \equiv F(K, L, A)/L$.

* 2.16 In this exercise you are asked to derive the CES production function (2.38) following the method in the original article by Arrow et al. (1961). These authors noted that a good empirical approximation to the relationship between income per capita and the wage rate was provided by an equation of the form

$$y = \alpha w^\sigma,$$

where $y = f(k)$ is again output per capita and w is the wage rate. With competitive markets, recall that $w = f(k) - kf'(k)$. Thus the above equation can be written as

$$y = \alpha(y - ky')^\sigma,$$

where $y = y(k) \equiv f(k)$ and y' denotes $f'(k)$. This is a nonlinear first-order differential equation.

(a) Using separation of variables (see Appendix B), show that the solution to this equation satisfies

$$y(k) = \left(\alpha^{-1/\sigma} + c_0 k^{\frac{\sigma-1}{\sigma}}\right)^{\frac{\sigma}{\sigma-1}},$$

where c_0 is a constant of integration.

(b) Explain how you would put more structure on α and c_0 and derive the exact form of the CES production function in (2.38).

2.17 Consider the Solow growth model with constant saving rate s and depreciation rate of capital equal to δ. Assume that population is constant and the aggregate production function is given by the constant returns to scale production function

$$F(A_K(t)K(t), A_L(t)L(t)),$$

where $\dot{A}_L(t)/A_L(t) = g_L > 0$ and $\dot{A}_K(t)/A_K(t) = g_K > 0$.

(a) Suppose that F is Cobb-Douglas. Determine the BGP growth rate and the adjustment of the economy to the steady state.

(b) Suppose that F is not Cobb-Douglas (even asymptotically). Prove that there cannot exist $T < \infty$ such that the economy is on a BGP for all $t \geq T$. Explain why.

* 2.18 Consider the environment in Exercise 2.17. Suppose that F takes a CES form as in (2.38) with the elasticity of substitution between capital and labor $\sigma < 1$, $g_K > g_L$, and there is a constant saving rate s. Show that as $t \to \infty$, the economy converges to a BGP where the share of labor in national income is equal to 1 and capital, output, and consumption all grow at the rate g_L. In light of this result, discuss the claim in the literature that capital-augmenting technological change is inconsistent with balanced growth. Why is the claim in the literature incorrect? Relate your answer to Exercise 2.14.

* 2.19 In the context of Theorem 2.6, consider the production function

$$\tilde{F}(K(t), L(t), \tilde{A}(t)) = K(t)^{\tilde{A}(t)} L(t)^{1-\tilde{A}(t)},$$

where $\tilde{A}(t) : \mathbb{R}_+ \to (0, 1)$ is an arbitrary function of time, representing technology.

(a) Show that when $K(t) = \exp(nt)$ and $L(t) = \exp(nt)$ for $n \geq 0$, the conditions of Theorem 2.6 are satisfied and $\tilde{F}$ has a representation of the form $F(K(t), A(t)L(t))$. Determine a class of functions that provide such a representation.

(b) Show that the derivatives of $\tilde{F}$ and F are not equal.

(c) Suppose that factor markets are competitive. Show that while capital, output, and consumption grow at a constant rate, the capital share in national income behaves in an arbitrary fashion. [Hint: consider, for example, $\tilde{A}(t) = (2 + \sin(t))/4$.]

2.20 Consider the Solow model with noncompetitive labor markets. In particular, suppose that there is no population growth and no technological progress and output is given by $F(K, L)$. The saving rate is equal to s and the depreciation rate is given by δ.

(a) First suppose that there is a minimum wage $\bar{w}$, such that workers are not allowed to be paid less than $\bar{w}$. If labor demand at this wage falls short of L, employment is equal to the amount of labor demanded by firms, L^d (and the unemployed do not contribute to production and earn zero). Assume that $\bar{w} > f(k^*) - k^* f'(k^*)$, where k^* is the steady-state capital-labor ratio of the basic Solow model given by $f(k^*)/k^* = \delta/s$. Characterize the dynamic equilibrium path of this economy starting with some amount of physical capital $K(0) > 0$.

(b) Next consider a different form of labor market imperfection, whereby workers receive a fraction $\lambda > 0$ of output of their employer as their wage income. Characterize a dynamic equilibrium path in this case. [Hint: recall that the saving rate is still equal to s.]

2.21 Consider the discrete-time Solow growth model with constant population growth at the rate n, no technological change, and full depreciation (i.e., $\delta = 1$). Assume that the saving rate is a function of the capital-labor ratio and is thus given by $s(k)$.

(a) Suppose that $f(k) = Ak$ and $s(k) = s_0 k^{-1} - 1$. Show that if $A + \delta - n = 2$, then for any $k(0) \in (0, As_0/(1+n))$, the economy immediately settles into an asymptotic cycle and continuously fluctuates between $k(0)$ and $As_0/(1+n) - k(0)$. (Suppose that $k(0)$ and the parameters are given such that $s(k) \in (0, 1)$ for both $k = k(0)$ and $k = As_0/(1+n) - k(0)$.)

(b) Now consider the more general continuous production function $f(k)$ and saving function $s(k)$, such that there exist $k_1, k_2 \in \mathbb{R}_+$ with $k_1 \neq k_2$ and

$$k_2 = \frac{s(k_1)f(k_1) + (1-\delta)k_1}{1+n},$$

$$k_1 = \frac{s(k_2)f(k_2) + (1-\delta)k_2}{1+n}.$$

Show that when such (k_1, k_2) exist, there may also exist a stable steady state.

(c) Prove that such cycles are not possible in the continuous-time Solow growth model for any (possibly non-neoclassical) continuous production function $f(k)$ and continuous $s(k)$. [Hint: consider the equivalent of Figure 2.9.]

(d) What does the result in parts a–c imply for the approximations of discrete time by continuous time suggested in Section 2.4?

(e) In light of your answer to part d, what do you think of the cycles in parts a and b?

(f) Show that if $f(k)$ is nondecreasing in k and $s(k) = k$, cycles as in parts a and b are not possible in discrete time either.

2.22 Characterize the asymptotic equilibrium of the modified Solow/AK model mentioned in Section 2.6, with a constant saving rate s, depreciation rate δ, no population growth, and an aggregate production function of the form

$$F(K(t), L(t)) = A_K K(t) + A_L L(t).$$

2.23 Consider the basic Solow growth model with a constant saving rate s, constant population growth at the rate n, and no technological change, and suppose that the aggregate production function takes the CES form in (2.38).

(a) Suppose that $\sigma > 1$. Show that in this case equilibrium behavior can be similar to that in Exercise 2.22 with sustained growth in the long run. Interpret this result.

(b) Now suppose that $\sigma \to 0$, so that the production function becomes Leontief:

$$Y(t) = \min \left\{ \gamma A_K(t) K(t); (1 - \gamma) A_L(t) L(t) \right\}.$$

The model is then identical to the classical Harrod-Domar growth model developed by Roy Harrod and Evsey Domar (Harrod, 1939; Domar, 1946). Show that in this case there is typically no steady-state equilibrium with full employment and no idle capital. What happens to factor prices in these cases? Explain why this case is pathological, giving at least two reasons for why we may expect equilibria with idle capital or idle labor not to apply in practice.

2.24 Show that the CES production function (2.38) violates Assumption 2 unless $\sigma = 1$.

2.25 Prove Proposition 2.12.

2.26 Prove Proposition 2.13.

2.27 In this exercise, we work through an alternative conception of technology, which will be useful in the next chapter. Consider the basic Solow model in continuous time and suppose that $A(t) = A$, so that there is no technological progress of the usual kind. However, assume that the relationship between investment and capital accumulation is modified to

$$\dot{K}(t) = q(t)I(t) - \delta K(t),$$

where $[q(t)]_{t=0}^{\infty}$ is an exogenously given time-varying path (function). Intuitively, when $q(t)$ is high, the same investment expenditure translates into a greater increase in the capital stock.

Therefore we can think of $q(t)$ as the inverse of the relative price of machinery to output. When $q(t)$ is high, machinery is relatively cheaper. Gordon (1990) documented that the relative prices of durable machinery have been declining relative to output throughout the postwar era. This decline is quite plausible, especially given recent experience with the decline in the relative price of computer hardware and software. Thus we may want to suppose that $\dot{q}(t) > 0$. This exercise asks you to work through a model with this feature based on Greenwood, Hercowitz, and Krusell (1997).

(a) Suppose that $\dot{q}(t)/q(t) = \gamma_K > 0$. Show that for a general production function, $F(K, L)$, there exists no BGP.

(b) Now suppose that the production function is Cobb-Douglas, $F(K, L) = K^\alpha L^{1-\alpha}$, and characterize the unique BGP.

(c) Show that this steady-state equilibrium does not satisfy the Kaldor fact of constant K/Y. Is this discrepancy a problem? [Hint: how is K measured in practice? How is it measured in this model?]

3

The Solow Model and the Data

I n this chapter, we see how the Solow model or its simple extensions can be used to interpret both economic growth over time and cross-country output differences. The focus is on *proximate causes* of economic growth, that is, on such factors as investment or capital accumulation highlighted by the basic Solow model, as well as technology and human capital differences. What lies underneath these proximate causes is the topic of the next chapter.

There are multiple ways of using the basic Solow model to look at the data. I start with the growth accounting framework, which is most commonly applied for decomposing the sources of growth over time. After briefly discussing the theory of growth accounting and some of its uses, I discuss applications of the Solow model to cross-country output and growth differences. In this context, I also introduce the augmented Solow model with human capital and show how various different regression-based approaches can be motivated from this framework. Finally, I illustrate how the growth accounting framework can be modified to a development accounting framework to form another bridge between the Solow model and the data. A constant theme that emerges from many of these approaches concerns the importance of productivity differences over time and across countries. The chapter ends with a brief discussion of various other approaches to estimating cross-country productivity differences.

3.1 Growth Accounting

As discussed in the previous chapter, at the center of the Solow model is the aggregate production function, (2.1), which I rewrite here in its general form:

$$Y(t) = F(K(t), L(t), A(t)). \tag{3.1}$$

Another major contribution of Bob Solow to the study of economic growth was the observation that this production function, combined with competitive factor markets, also gives us a framework for accounting for the sources of economic growth. In particular, Solow (1957) developed what has become one of the most common tools in macroeconomics, the growth accounting framework.

For our purposes, it is sufficient to expose the simplest version of this framework. Consider a continuous-time economy, and suppose that the production function (3.1) satisfies

Assumptions 1 and 2 from Chapter 2. Differentiating with respect to time, dropping time dependence, and denoting the partial derivatives of F with respect to its arguments by F_A, F_K, and F_L, we obtain

$$\frac{\dot{Y}}{Y} = \frac{F_A A}{Y} \frac{\dot{A}}{A} + \frac{F_K K}{Y} \frac{\dot{K}}{K} + \frac{F_L L}{Y} \frac{\dot{L}}{L}. \tag{3.2}$$

Now denote the growth rates of output, capital stock, and labor by $g \equiv \dot{Y}/Y$, $g_K \equiv \dot{K}/K$ and $g_L \equiv \dot{L}/L$, respectively, and also define

$$x \equiv \frac{F_A A}{Y} \frac{\dot{A}}{A}$$

as the contribution of technology to growth. Defining $\varepsilon_k \equiv F_K K/Y$ and $\varepsilon_l \equiv F_L L/Y$ as the elasticities of output with respect to capital and labor, respectively (see also equation (3.9)), (3.2) implies

$$x = g - \varepsilon_k g_K - \varepsilon_l g_L.$$

This equation is no more than an identity. However, with competitive factor markets, it becomes useful for estimating the role of technological progress and economic growth. In particular, factor prices in competitive markets are given by $w = F_L$ and $R = F_K$ (equations (2.6) and (2.7) from the previous chapter), so that the elasticities ε_k and ε_l correspond to the factor shares $\alpha_K \equiv RK/Y$ and $\alpha_L \equiv wL/Y$. Putting all these together, we have

$$x = g - \alpha_K g_K - \alpha_L g_L. \tag{3.3}$$

Equation (3.3) is the fundamental growth accounting equation, which can be used to estimate the contribution of technological progress to economic growth using data on factor shares, output growth, labor force growth, and capital stock growth. The contribution from technological progress, x, is typically referred to as "total factor productivity" (TFP) or sometimes as "multi-factor productivity."

In particular, denoting an estimate by a hat "^", the estimate of TFP growth at time t is

$$\hat{x}(t) = g(t) - \alpha_K(t) g_K(t) - \alpha_L(t) g_L(t). \tag{3.4}$$

I put the hat only on x, but one may want to take into account that all terms on the right-hand side are also estimates obtained with a range of assumptions from national accounts and other data sources.

In continuous time, (3.4) is exact, because it is defined in terms of instantaneous changes (derivatives). In practice, we look at changes over discrete time intervals, for example, over a year (or sometimes with better data, over a quarter or a month). With discrete time intervals, there is a potential problem in using (3.4); over the time horizon in question, factor shares can change: should we use beginning-of-period or end-of-period values of α_K and α_L? It can be shown that the use of either beginning-of-period or end-of-period values might lead to biased estimates of the contribution of TFP to output growth, $\hat{x}$. Such a bias is particularly likely when the distance between the two time periods is large (see Exercise 3.1). The best way of avoiding such biases is to use data that are as high-frequency as possible.

For now, taking the available data as given, let us look at how one could use the growth accounting framework with data over discrete intervals. The most common way of dealing with the problems pointed out above is to use factor shares calculated as the average of the beginning-of-period and end-of-period values. Therefore in discrete time, for a change between times t and $t + 1$, the analogue of (3.4) becomes

$$\hat{x}_{t+1,t} = g_{t+1,t} - \bar{\alpha}_{K,t+1,t} g_{K,t+1,t} - \bar{\alpha}_{L,t+1,t} g_{L,t+1,t}, \tag{3.5}$$

where $g_{t,t+1}$ is the growth rate of output between t and $t + 1$, other growth rates are defined analogously, and

$$\bar{\alpha}_{K,t+1,t} \equiv \frac{\alpha_K(t) + \alpha_K(t + 1)}{2} \quad \text{and} \quad \bar{\alpha}_{L,t+1,t} \equiv \frac{\alpha_L(t) + \alpha_L(t + 1)}{2}$$

are average factor shares between t and $t + 1$. Equation (3.5) would be a fairly good approximation to (3.4) when the difference between t and $t + 1$ is small and the capital-labor ratio does not change much during this time interval.

Solow's (1957) article not only developed this growth accounting framework but also applied it to U.S. data for a preliminary assessment of the sources of growth during the early twentieth century. The question Bob Solow asked was: how much of the growth of the U.S. economy can be attributed to increased labor and capital inputs and how much of it is due to the residual, technological progress? Solow's conclusion was quite striking: a large part of the growth was due to technological progress. This has been a landmark finding, emphasizing the importance of technological progress as the driver of economic growth not only in theory but also in practice. It focused the attention of economists on sources of technology differences over time and across nations, industries, and firms.

From early days, however, it was recognized that calculating the contribution of technological progress to economic growth in this manner has a number of pitfalls. Moses Abramovitz (1957) famously dubbed the $\hat{x}$ term "the measure of our ignorance"—after all, it was the residual we could not explain and decided to call "technology." In its extreme form, this criticism is unfair, since $\hat{x}$ does correspond to technology according to (3.4); thus the growth accounting framework is an example of using theory to inform measurement. Yet at another level, the criticism has validity. If we underestimate the growth rates of labor and capital inputs, g_L and g_K, we will arrive at inflated estimates of $\hat{x}$. And in fact there are good reasons for suspecting that Solow's estimates and even the higher quality estimates that came later may be mismeasuring the growth of inputs. The most obvious reason for this error is that what matters is not labor hours, but effective labor hours, so it is important—though difficult—to make adjustments for changes in the human capital of workers. I discuss issues related to human capital in Section 3.3 and in greater detail in Chapter 10. Similarly, measurement of capital inputs is not straightforward. In the theoretical model, capital corresponds to the final good used as input to produce more goods. But in practice, capital comprises equipment (machinery) as well as structures (buildings). In measuring the amount of capital used in production one has to make assumptions about how relative prices of different types of equipment change over time. The typical approach, adopted for a long time in national accounts and also naturally in applications of the growth accounting framework, is to use capital expenditures. However, if the same machines are cheaper today than they were in the past (e.g., as has been the case for computers), then this methodology would underestimate g_K (recall Exercise 2.27 in the previous chapter). Therefore, when applying (3.4), underestimates of g_L and g_K will naturally inflate the estimates of the role of technology as a source of economic growth. Finally, changes in relative prices and the quality of products may also lead to the mismeasurement of the growth rate of output, g. If g is underestimated, then there will be a countervailing force toward underestimating $\hat{x}$.

There is still an active debate on how to adjust for the changes in the quality of labor and capital inputs to arrive at the best estimate of technology. Dale Jorgensen, for example, has shown that the residual technology estimates can be reduced very substantially (perhaps almost to zero) by making adjustments for changes in the quality of labor and capital (see, e.g., Jorgensen, Gollop, and Fraumeni, 1987; Jorgensen, 2005). These issues also become relevant when we attempt to decompose the sources of cross-country output differences. Before doing this, let us look at applications of the Solow model to data using regression analysis.

3.2 The Solow Model and Regression Analyses

Another popular approach of taking the Solow model to data is to use growth regressions, which involve estimating regression models with country growth rates on the left-hand side. These growth regressions have been used extensively following the work by Barro (1991). To see how these regressions are motivated and what their shortcomings are, let us return to the basic Solow model with constant population growth and labor-augmenting technological change in continuous time. Recall that, in this model, the equilibrium is described by the following equations:

$$y(t) = A(t) f(k(t)), \tag{3.6}$$

and

$$\frac{\dot{k}(t)}{k(t)} = \frac{sf(k(t))}{k(t)} - (\delta + g + n), \tag{3.7}$$

where $A(t)$ is the labor-augmenting (Harrod-neutral) technology term, $k(t) \equiv K(t)/(A(t)L(t))$ is the effective capital-labor ratio, and $f(\cdot)$ is the per capita production function. Equation (3.7) repeats (2.51) from the previous chapter. Differentiating (3.6) with respect to time and dividing both sides by $y(t)$ yields

$$\frac{\dot{y}(t)}{y(t)} = g + \varepsilon_k(k(t)) \frac{\dot{k}(t)}{k(t)}, \tag{3.8}$$

where

$$\varepsilon_k(k(t)) \equiv \frac{f'(k(t))k(t)}{f(k(t))} \in (0, 1) \tag{3.9}$$

is the elasticity of the $f(\cdot)$ function. The fact that it is between 0 and 1 follows from Assumption 1. For example, with the Cobb-Douglas technology from Example 2.1 in the previous chapter, $\varepsilon_k(k(t)) = \alpha$ (i.e., it is a constant independent of $k(t)$; see Example 3.1). However, generally, this elasticity is a function of $k(t)$.

Now let us consider a first-order Taylor expansion of (3.7) with respect to $\log k(t)$ around the steady-state value k^* (using Theorem A.22 in Appendix A and $\partial y / \partial \log x \equiv (\partial y / \partial x) \cdot x$). This expansion implies that for $k(t)$ in the neighborhood of k^*, we have

$$\frac{\dot{k}(t)}{k(t)} \approx \left(\frac{sf(k^*)}{k^*} - \delta - g - n \right) + \left(\frac{f'(k^*)k^*}{f(k^*)} - 1 \right) s \frac{f(k^*)}{k^*} (\log k(t) - \log k^*)$$

$$\approx \left(\varepsilon_k(k^*) - 1 \right) (\delta + g + n) (\log k(t) - \log k^*).$$

The use of the symbol $\approx$ here is to emphasize that this is an approximation ignoring second-order terms. In particular, the first line follows simply by differentiating $\dot{k}(t)/k(t)$ with respect to $\log k(t)$ and evaluating the derivatives at k^* (and ignoring second-order terms). The second line uses the fact that the first term in the first line is equal to zero by the definition of the steady-state value k^* (recall that from (2.52) in the previous chapter, $sf(k^*)/k^* = \delta + g + n$) and the definition of the elasticity of the f function, $\varepsilon_k(k(t))$. Now substituting this approximation into (3.8), we have

$$\frac{\dot{y}(t)}{y(t)} \approx g - \varepsilon_k(k^*)(1 - \varepsilon_k(k^*)) \, (\delta + g + n) \, (\log k(t) - \log k^*).$$

Let us define $y^*(t) \equiv A(t) f(k^*)$ as the steady-state level of output per capita, that is, the level of per capita output that would apply if the effective capital-labor ratio were at its steady-state value and technology were at its time t level. A first-order Taylor expansion of $\log y(t)$ with respect to $\log k(t)$ around $\log k^*(t)$ then gives

$$\log y(t) - \log y^*(t) \approx \varepsilon_k(k^*)(\log k(t) - \log k^*).$$

Combining this with the previous equation yields the following convergence equation:

$$\frac{\dot{y}(t)}{y(t)} \approx g - (1 - \varepsilon_k(k^*))(\delta + g + n)(\log y(t) - \log y^*(t)). \tag{3.10}$$

Equation (3.10) makes it clear that, in the Solow model, there are two sources of growth in output per capita: the first is g, the rate of technological progress, and the second is convergence. The latter is a consequence of the impact of the gap between the current level of output per capita and the steady-state level of output per capita on the rate of capital accumulation (recall that $0 < \varepsilon_k(k^*) < 1$). Intuitively, the further below its steady-state capital-labor ratio a country is, the faster it will grow. This pattern is already visible in Figure 2.7 in the previous chapter.

Another noteworthy feature is that the speed of convergence in (3.10), measured by the term $(1 - \varepsilon_k(k^*)) \, (\delta + g + n)$ multiplying the gap between $\log y(t)$ and $\log y^*(t)$, depends on $\delta + g + n$ and on the elasticity of the production function, $\varepsilon_k(k^*)$. Both of these terms capture intuitive effects. As discussed in the previous chapter, the term $\delta + g + n$ determines the rate at which the effective capital-labor ratio needs to be replenished. The higher this rate of replenishment the larger is the amount of investment in the economy (recall Figure 2.7 in the previous chapter) and the greater is the scope for faster adjustment. On the other hand, when $\varepsilon_k(k^*)$ is high, we are close to a linear—AK—production function, and as demonstrated in the previous chapter, in this case convergence should be slow. In the extreme case where $\varepsilon_k(k^*)$ is equal to 1, the economy takes the AK form, and there is no convergence.

Example 3.1 (Cobb-Douglas Production Function and Convergence)

Consider briefly the Cobb-Douglas production function from Example 2.1, where $Y(t) = A(t)K(t)^\alpha L(t)^{1-\alpha}$. This equation implies that $y(t) = A(t)k(t)^\alpha$. Consequently, as noted above, $\varepsilon_k(k(t)) = \alpha$. Therefore (3.10) becomes

$$\frac{\dot{y}(t)}{y(t)} \approx g - (1 - \alpha)(\delta + g + n)(\log y(t) - \log y^*(t)). \tag{3.11}$$

This equation also enables us to calibrate the speed of convergence—meaning to obtain a back-of-the-envelope estimate of the speed of convergence by using plausible values for the parameters. Let us focus on relatively developed economies. In that case, plausible values for these parameters might be $g \approx 0.02$ for approximately 2% per year output per capita *growth, $n \approx 0.01$ for approximately 1% population growth, and $\delta \approx 0.05$ for about 5% per year depreciation. Recall also from the previous chapter that the share of capital in national income is about 1/3, so with the Cobb-Douglas production function we should have $\alpha \approx 1/3$. Given these numbers, (3.11) suggests that the convergence coefficient in front of $\log y(t) - \log y^*(t)$ should be about 0.054 ($\approx 0.67 \times 0.08$). This value corresponds to a very rapid rate of convergence and would imply that the income gap between two similar countries that have the same technology, the same depreciation rate, and the same rate of population growth should narrow rather quickly. For example, it can be computed that with these numbers, the gap of income between two similar countries should be halved in little more than 10 years (see Exercise 3.4). This rapid convergence is clearly at odds with the patterns we saw in Chapter 1.*

Using a discrete-time approximation, (3.10) yields the regression equation

$$g_{i,t,t-1} = b^0 + b^1 \log y_{i,t-1} + \varepsilon_{i,t}, \tag{3.12}$$

where $g_{i,t,t-1}$ is the growth rate of country i between dates $t-1$ and t, $\log y_{i,t-1}$ is the initial (time $t-1$) log output per capita of this country, and $\varepsilon_{i,t}$ is a stochastic term capturing all omitted influences. Regressions of this form have been estimated by, among others, Baumol (1986), Barro (1991), and Barro and Sala-i-Martin (1992). If such an equation is estimated in the sample of core OECD countries, b^1 is indeed estimated to be negative; countries like Ireland, Greece, Spain, and Portugal that were relatively poor at the end of World War II have grown faster than the rest, as shown in Figure 1.14 in Chapter 1.

Yet Figure 1.13 in Chapter 1 shows that when we look at the whole world, there is no evidence for a negative b^1. Instead, this figure makes it clear that, if anything, b^1 would be positive. In other words, there is no evidence of worldwide convergence. However, as discussed in that chapter, this notion of unconditional convergence may be too demanding. It requires that there should be a tendency for the income gap between any two countries to decline, regardless of the technological opportunities, investment behavior, policies, and institutions of these countries. If they do differ with respect to these factors, the Solow model would *not* predict that they should converge in income level. In particular, in that case the term $y^*(t)$ in (3.10) would be country specific, and the model would predict that each country should converge to its own level of steady-state (BGP) income per capita. Thus in a world where countries differ according to their characteristics, a more appropriate regression equation may take the form

$$g_{i,t,t-1} = b_i^0 + b^1 \log y_{i,t-1} + \varepsilon_{i,t}, \tag{3.13}$$

where the key difference is that now the constant term, b_i^0, is country specific. (In principle, the slope term, measuring the speed of convergence, b^1, should also be country specific, but in empirical work, this term is generally taken to be constant, and I assume the same here to simplify the discussion.) One may then model b_i^0 as a function of country characteristics.

If the true equation is (3.13), in the sense that the Solow model applies but certain determinants of economic growth differ across countries, (3.12) may not be a good fit to the data. In that case, there is no guarantee that the estimates of b^1 resulting from this equation will be negative, even if there is convergence, as implied by the Solow model. In particular, it is natural to expect that $\text{Cov}(b_i^0, \log y_{i,t-1}) > 0$ (where Cov refers to the population covariance), since economies with certain growth-reducing characteristics are likely to have both low steady-state output levels and low initial levels. Therefore when data are generated by (3.13) and we use (3.12) for estimation, there will be an upward bias in the estimate of b^1, making it more difficult to detect negative b^1 values.

With this motivation, Barro (1991) and Barro and Sala-i-Martin (1992, 2004) favor the notion of conditional convergence, which means that the convergence effects emphasized by the Solow model should lead to negative estimates of b^1 once b_i^0 is allowed to vary across countries. To implement this idea of conditional convergence empirically, they estimate models where b_i^0 is assumed to be a function of, among other things, the male schooling rate, the female schooling rate, the fertility rate, the investment rate, the government-consumption ratio, the inflation rate, changes in terms of trades, openness, and such institutional variables as rule of law and democracy. The corresponding regression equation then takes the form

$$g_{i,t,t-1} = \mathbf{X}_{i,t}^T \boldsymbol{\beta} + b^1 \log y_{i,t-1} + \varepsilon_{i,t}, \tag{3.14}$$

where $\mathbf{X}_{i,t}$ is a (column) vector including the variables mentioned above (as well as a constant), with a vector of coefficients $\boldsymbol{\beta}$ (recall that $\mathbf{X}^T$ denotes the transpose of $\mathbf{X}$). In other words, this specification supposes that b_i^0 in (3.13) can be approximated by $\mathbf{X}_{i,t}^T \boldsymbol{\beta}$. Consistent with the emphasis on conditional convergence, regressions of (3.14) tend to show a negative estimate of b^1, but the magnitude of this estimate is much smaller than that suggested by the computations in Example 3.1.

Regressions similar to (3.14) have not only been used to support conditional convergence but also to estimate the determinants of economic growth. In particular, it may appear natural to presume that the estimates of the coefficient vector $\boldsymbol{\beta}$ will contain information about the causal effects of various variables on economic growth. For example, the fact that the schooling variables enter with positive coefficients in the estimates of regression (3.14) is interpreted as evidence that schooling causes growth. The simplicity of the regression equations of the form (3.14) and the fact that they create a bridge between theory and data have made them popular over the past two decades.

Nevertheless, regressions of this form are problematic for several reasons. These include:

1. Most, if not all, of the variables in $\mathbf{X}_{i,t}$, as well as $\log y_{i,t-1}$, are econometrically endogenous in the sense that they are jointly determined with the rate of economic growth between dates $t-1$ and t. For example, the same factors that make a country relatively poor in 1950, thus reducing $\log y_{i,t-1}$, should also affect its growth rate after 1950. Or the same factors that make a country invest little in physical and human capital could have a direct effect on its growth rate (through other channels, e.g., its technology or the efficiency with which the factors of production are being utilized). This tendency creates an obvious source of bias (and lack of econometric consistency) in the regression estimates of the coefficients. This bias makes it unlikely that the effects captured in the coefficient vector $\boldsymbol{\beta}$ correspond to causal effects of these characteristics on the growth potential of economies. One may argue that the convergence coefficient b^1 is of interest even if $\boldsymbol{\beta}$ does not have a causal interpretation. However, a basic result in econometrics is that if $\mathbf{X}_{i,t}$ is econometrically endogenous, so that the parameter vector $\boldsymbol{\beta}$ is estimated inconsistently, the estimate of the parameter b^1 will also be inconsistent unless $\mathbf{X}_{i,t}$ is independent from $\log y_{i,t-1}$.[1] This result makes the estimates of the convergence coefficient, b^1, difficult to interpret. In addition, transitory movements in income per capita (e.g., due to business cycles) or measurement error will also imply that the right-hand-side variables in (3.14) are econometrically endogenous and will typically create a downward bias in the estimates of b^1. Suppose, for example, that we only observe estimates of output per capita $\tilde{y}_{i,t} = y_{i,t} \exp\left(u_{i,t}\right)$, where $y_{i,t}$ is the true output per capita

---

1. An example of the potential endogeneity of these variables is given in Section 3.4.

and $u_{i,t}$ is a random and serially uncorrelated error term. When the variable $\log \tilde{y}_{i,t}$ is used in the regression, the error term $u_{i,t-1}$ appears both on the left- and right-hand sides of (3.14). In particular, note that

$$\log \tilde{y}_{i,t} - \log \tilde{y}_{i,t-1} = \log y_{i,t} - \log y_{i,t-1} + u_{i,t} - u_{i,t-1}.$$

Since the measured growth is

$$\tilde{g}_{i,t,t-1} \approx \log \tilde{y}_{i,t} - \log \tilde{y}_{i,t-1} = \log y_{i,t} - \log y_{i,t-1} + u_{i,t} - u_{i,t-1},$$

the measurement error $u_{i,t-1}$ will be part of both the error term $\varepsilon_{i,t}$ and the right-hand side variable $\log \tilde{y}_{i,t-1} = \log y_{i,t-1} + u_{i,t-1}$ in the regression equation

$$\tilde{g}_{i,t,t-1} = \mathbf{X}_{i,t}^T \boldsymbol{\beta} + b^1 \log \tilde{y}_{i,t-1} + \varepsilon_{i,t}.$$

This will naturally lead to a negative bias in the estimation of b^1. Therefore we can end up with a negative estimate of b^1, even when there is no conditional convergence.

2. The economic interpretation of regression equations like (3.14) is not always straightforward. Many of the regressions used in the literature include the investment rate as part of the vector $\mathbf{X}_{i,t}$ (and all of them include the schooling rate). However, in the Solow model, differences in investment rates (and in the extended Solow model, differences in schooling rates) are the primary channel by which the potential determinants included in the vector $\mathbf{X}_{i,t}$ (e.g., institutions, openness) will influence economic growth. Therefore, once we condition on the investment and schooling rates, the coefficients on the other variables in $\mathbf{X}_{i,t}$ no longer measure their (full) impact on economic growth. Consequently estimates of (3.14) with investment-like variables on the right-hand side are difficult to link to theory.

3. Finally, the motivating equation for the growth regression, (3.10), is derived for a closed Solow economy. When we look at cross-country income differences or growth experiences, the use of this equation imposes the assumption that each country is an island. In other words, the world is being interpreted as a collection of noninteracting closed economies. In practice, countries trade goods, exchange ideas, and borrow and lend in international financial markets. These interactions imply that the behavior of different countries will not be given by (3.10) but by a system of equations characterizing the entire world equilibrium. Interpreting cross-country growth experiences by (3.10) in a world with interacting economies can often lead to misleading results (see the discussion in Chapters 18 and 19).

This discussion does not imply that growth regressions are uninformative. At some basic level, these regressions (at least leaving aside the difficulties associated with the estimation of b^1) can be interpreted as providing information on salient correlations in the data. Knowing what these correlations are is an important input into the process of formulating empirically plausible theories.

In this context, a complementary, or perhaps a more natural, regression framework for investigating the (conditional) correlations in the data is

$$\log y_{i,t} = \alpha \log y_{i,t-1} + \mathbf{X}_{i,t}^T \boldsymbol{\beta} + \delta_i + \mu_t + \varepsilon_{i,t}, \tag{3.15}$$

where δ_i denotes a full set of country fixed effects and μ_t denotes a full set of year effects. This regression framework differs from the growth regressions in a number of respects. First, the regression equation is specified in levels rather than with the growth rate on the left-hand side. But this difference is mainly a rearrangement of (3.14)—since $g_{i,t,t-1} \approx \log y_{i,t} - \log y_{i,t-1}$. More importantly, by including the country fixed effects, this regression equation takes out fixed country characteristics that might be simultaneously affecting economic growth (or the level of income per capita) and the right-hand-side variables of interest. Therefore, panel data regressions as in (3.15) may be more informative about the statistical relationship between a range of factors and income per capita. However, it is important to emphasize that including country fixed effects is not a panacea against all omitted variable biases and econometric endogeneity problems. Simultaneity bias often results from time-varying influences, which cannot be removed by including fixed effects. Moreover, to the extent that some of the variables in the vector $\mathbf{X}_{i,t}$ are slowly varying themselves, the inclusion of country fixed effects will make it difficult to uncover the statistical relationship between these variables and income per capita and may increase potential biases due to measurement error in the right-hand-side variables.

In the remainder of this chapter, I discuss how the structure of the Solow model can be further exploited to look at the data. But first I present an augmented version of the Solow model incorporating human capital, which is useful in these empirical exercises.

3.3 The Solow Model with Human Capital

Human capital is a term we use to represent the stock of skills, education, competencies, and other productivity-enhancing characteristics embedded in labor. Put differently, human capital represents the efficiency units of labor embedded in raw labor hours.

The term "human capital" originates from the observation that individuals will invest in their skills, competencies, and earning capacities in the same way that firms invest in their physical capital—to increase their productivity. The seminal work by Ted Schultz, Jacob Mincer, and Gary Becker brought the notion of human capital to the forefront of economics. For now, all we need to know is that labor hours supplied by different individuals do not contain the same efficiency units; a highly trained carpenter can produce a chair in a few hours, while an amateur would spend many more hours to perform the same task. Economists capture this notion by thinking that the trained carpenter has greater human capital; that is, he has more efficiency units of labor embedded in the labor hours he supplies. The theory of human capital is vast and some of the important notions of this theory are discussed in Chapter 10. For now, our objective is more modest: to investigate how including human capital makes the Solow model a better fit to the data. The inclusion of human capital enables us to embed all three of the main proximate sources of income differences: physical capital, human capital, and technology.

For the purposes of this section, let us focus on continuous-time models and suppose that the aggregate production function of the economy is given by a variant of (2.1):

$$Y = F(K, H, AL), \tag{3.16}$$

where H denotes human capital. Notice that this production function is somewhat unusual, since it separates human capital H from labor L as potential factors of production. I start with this form, because it is commonly used in the growth literature. The more micro-founded models in Chapter 10 assume that human capital is embedded in workers. How human capital is measured in the data is discussed below. Let us also modify Assumptions 1 and 2 as follows.

Assumption 1' *The production function $F : \mathbb{R}^3_+ \to \mathbb{R}_+$ in (3.16) is twice differentiable in K, H, and L and satisfies*

$$\frac{\partial F(K,H,AL)}{\partial K} > 0, \quad \frac{\partial F(K,H,AL)}{\partial H} > 0, \quad \frac{\partial F(K,H,AL)}{\partial L} > 0;$$
$$\frac{\partial^2 F(K,H,AL)}{\partial K^2} < 0, \quad \frac{\partial^2 F(K,H,AL)}{\partial H^2} < 0, \quad \frac{\partial^2 F(K,H,AL)}{\partial L^2} < 0.$$

Moreover, F exhibits constant returns to scale in its three arguments.

Assumption 2' *F satisfies the Inada conditions:*

$$\lim_{K \to 0} \frac{\partial F(K, H, AL)}{\partial K} = \infty \quad \text{and} \quad \lim_{K \to \infty} \frac{\partial F(K, H, AL)}{\partial K} = 0 \quad \text{for all } H > 0 \text{ and } AL > 0,$$

$$\lim_{H \to 0} \frac{\partial F(K, H, AL)}{\partial H} = \infty \quad \text{and} \quad \lim_{H \to \infty} \frac{\partial F(K, H, AL)}{\partial H} = 0 \quad \text{for all } K > 0 \text{ and } AL > 0,$$

$$\lim_{L \to 0} \frac{\partial F(K, H, AL)}{\partial L} = \infty \quad \text{and} \quad \lim_{L \to \infty} \frac{\partial F(K, H, AL)}{\partial L} = 0 \quad \text{for all } K, H, A > 0.$$

In addition, let us assume that investments in human capital take a similar form to investments in physical capital: households save a fraction s_k of their income to invest in physical capital and a fraction s_h to invest in human capital. Human capital also depreciates in the same way as physical capital, and we denote the depreciation rates of physical and human capital by δ_k and δ_h, respectively.

There is again constant population growth and a constant rate of labor-augmenting technological progress, that is, $\dot{L}(t)/L(t) = n$ and $\dot{A}(t)/A(t) = g$. Defining effective human and physical capital ratios as

$$k(t) \equiv \frac{K(t)}{A(t)L(t)} \quad \text{and} \quad h(t) \equiv \frac{H(t)}{A(t)L(t)}$$

and using the constant returns to scale feature in Assumption 1', output per effective unit of labor can be written as

$$\hat{y}(t) \equiv \frac{Y(t)}{A(t)L(t)}$$

$$= F\left(\frac{K(t)}{A(t)L(t)}, \frac{H(t)}{A(t)L(t)}, 1\right)$$

$$\equiv f(k(t), h(t)).$$

Using the same steps as in Chapter 2, the laws of motion of $k(t)$ and $h(t)$ are

$$\dot{k}(t) = s_k f(k(t), h(t)) - (\delta_k + g + n)k(t),$$

$$\dot{h}(t) = s_h f(k(t), h(t)) - (\delta_h + g + n)h(t).$$

A steady-state equilibrium is now defined by effective human and physical capital ratios, (k^*, h^*), satisfying the following two equations:

$$s_k f(k^*, h^*) - (\delta_k + g + n)k^* = 0, \tag{3.17}$$

and

$$s_h f(k^*, h^*) - (\delta_h + g + n)h^* = 0. \tag{3.18}$$

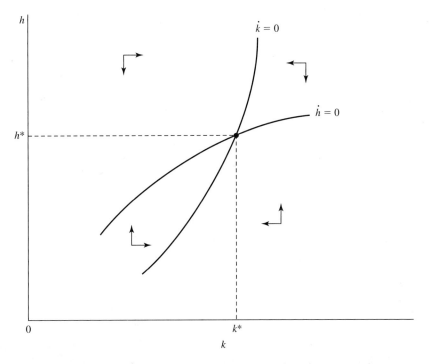

FIGURE 3.1 Dynamics of physical capital-labor and human capital-labor ratios in the Solow model with human capital.

As in the basic Solow model, the focus is on steady-state equilibria with $k^* > 0$ and $h^* > 0$ (if $f(0, 0) = 0$, then there exists a trivial steady state with $k = h = 0$, which I ignore for the same reasons as in the previous chapter).

Let us first prove that this steady-state equilibrium is unique. To see this heuristically, consider Figure 3.1, which is drawn in (k, h) space. The two curves represent (3.17) and (3.18) (corresponding to $\dot{k} = 0$ and $\dot{h} = 0$). Both curves are upward sloping, so that higher human capital is associated with higher physical capital in equilibrium. Moreover, the proof of the next proposition shows that (3.18) is always shallower in (k, h) space, so the two upward-sloping curves can only intersect once.

Proposition 3.1 *Suppose Assumptions 1′ and 2′ are satisfied. Then in the augmented Solow model with human capital there exists a unique steady-state equilibrium (k^*, h^*).*

Proof. First consider the slope of the curve (3.17), corresponding to the $\dot{k} = 0$ locus, in (k, h) space. Using the Implicit Function Theorem (Theorem A.25), we have

$$\frac{dh}{dk}\bigg|_{\dot{k}=0} = \frac{(\delta_k + g + n) - s_k f_k(k^*, h^*)}{s_k f_h(k^*, h^*)}, \tag{3.19}$$

where $f_k \equiv \partial f/\partial k$. Rewriting (3.17), we have $s_k f(k^*, h^*)/k^* - (\delta_k + g + n) = 0$. Now recall that since f is strictly concave in k in view of Assumption 1′ and $f(0, h^*) \geq 0$, we have

$$f(k^*, h^*) > f_k(k^*, h^*)k^* + f(0, h^*)$$

$$> f_k(k^*, h^*)k^*.$$

Therefore $(\delta_k + g + n) - s_k f_k(k^*, h^*) > 0$, and (3.19) is strictly positive.

Similarly, defining $f_h \equiv \partial f / \partial h$ and applying the Implicit Function Theorem to the $\dot{h} = 0$ locus (3.18) yields

$$\left. \frac{dh}{dk} \right|_{\dot{h}=0} = \frac{s_h f_k \left(k^*, h^* \right)}{\left(\delta_h + g + n \right) - s_h f_h \left(k^*, h^* \right)}. \tag{3.20}$$

With the same argument as that used for (3.19), this expression is also strictly positive.

Next we prove that (3.19) is steeper than (3.20) when (3.17) and (3.18) hold, so that there can be at most one intersection. First, observe that

$$\left. \frac{dh}{dk} \right|_{\dot{h}=0} < \left. \frac{dh}{dk} \right|_{\dot{k}=0}$$

$$\Updownarrow$$

$$\frac{s_h f_k \left(k^*, h^* \right)}{\left(\delta_h + g + n \right) - s_h f_h \left(k^*, h^* \right)} < \frac{\left(\delta_k + g + n \right) - s_k f_k \left(k^*, h^* \right)}{s_k f_h \left(k^*, h^* \right)}$$

$$\Updownarrow$$

$$s_k s_h f_k f_h < s_k s_h f_k f_h + \left(\delta_h + g + n \right) \left(\delta_k + g + n \right)$$
$$\qquad - \left(\delta_h + g + n \right) s_k f_k - \left(\delta_k + g + n \right) s_h f_h.$$

Now using (3.17) and (3.18) and substituting for $\left(\delta_k + g + n \right) = s_k f(k^*, h^*)/k^*$ and $\left(\delta_h + g + n \right) = s_h f(k^*, h^*)/h^*$, this is equivalent to

$$f(k^*, h^*) > f_k(k^*, h^*)k^* + f_h(k^*, h^*)h^*,$$

which is satisfied by the fact that $f(k^*, h^*)$ is a strictly concave function.

Finally, to establish existence, note that Assumption 2′ implies that

$$\lim_{h \to 0} f(k, h)/h = \infty, \quad \lim_{k \to 0} f(k, h)/k = \infty, \quad \lim_{h \to \infty} f(k, h)/h = 0,$$

$$\text{and } \lim_{k \to \infty} f(k, h)/k = 0,$$

so that the curves look as in Figure 3.1; that is, (3.17) is below (3.18) as $k \to 0$ and $h \to 0$, but it is above (3.18) as $k \to \infty$ and $h \to \infty$. This implies that the two curves must intersect at least once. ∎

This proposition shows that a unique steady state exists when the Solow model is augmented with human capital. The comparative statics are similar to those of the basic Solow model (see Exercise 3.7). Most importantly, both greater s_k and greater s_h will translate into higher normalized output per capita, $\hat{y}^*$.

Now turning to cross-country behavior, consider a set of countries experiencing the same rate of labor-augmenting technological progress, g. Then those with a greater propensity to invest in physical and human capital will be relatively richer. This is the type of prediction that can be investigated empirically to see whether the augmented Solow model (with similar technological possibilities across countries) provides a useful way of looking at cross-country income differences. Before doing this, the next proposition verifies that the unique steady state is globally stable.

Proposition 3.2 *Suppose Assumptions 1' and 2' are satisfied. Then the unique steady-state equilibrium of the augmented Solow model with human capital, (k^*, h^*), is globally stable in the sense that starting with any $k(0) > 0$ and $h(0) > 0$, we have $(k(t), h(t)) \to (k^*, h^*)$.*

Proof. See Exercise 3.6. ∎

Figure 3.1 gives the intuition for this result by showing that the law of motion of k and h depends on whether the economy is above or below the two curves representing the loci for $\dot{k} = 0$ and $\dot{h} = 0$, respectively, (3.17) and (3.18). To the right of the (3.17) curve, there is too much physical capital relative to human capital and consequently $\dot{k} < 0$. To its left, the converse holds, and $\dot{k} > 0$. Similarly, below the (3.18) curve, there is too little human capital relative to the amount of labor and physical capital and thus $\dot{h} > 0$. Above it, $\dot{h} < 0$. Given these arrows, the global stability of the dynamics follows.

Example 3.2 (Augmented Solow Model with Cobb-Douglas Production Functions) *Let us now work through a special case of the above model with a Cobb-Douglas production function. In particular, suppose that the aggregate production function is*

$$Y(t) = K(t)^{\alpha} H(t)^{\beta} (A(t)L(t))^{1-\alpha-\beta}, \tag{3.21}$$

where $0 < \alpha < 1$, $0 < \beta < 1$, and $\alpha + \beta < 1$. Output per effective unit of labor can then be written as $\hat{y}(t) = k^{\alpha}(t)h^{\beta}(t)$, with the same definition of $\hat{y}(t)$, $k(t)$, and $h(t)$ as above. Using the functional form in (3.21), (3.17) and (3.18) give the unique steady-state equilibrium as

$$k^* = \left(\left(\frac{s_k}{n + g + \delta_k} \right)^{1-\beta} \left(\frac{s_h}{n + g + \delta_h} \right)^{\beta} \right)^{\frac{1}{1-\alpha-\beta}}, \tag{3.22}$$

$$h^* = \left(\left(\frac{s_k}{n + g + \delta_k} \right)^{\alpha} \left(\frac{s_h}{n + g + \delta_h} \right)^{1-\alpha} \right)^{\frac{1}{1-\alpha-\beta}},$$

which shows that a higher saving rate in physical capital not only increases k^* but also h^*. The same applies for a higher saving rate in human capital. This reflects the fact that the higher saving rate in physical capital, by increasing k^*, raises overall output and thus the amount invested in schooling (since s_h is constant). Given (3.22), output per effective unit of labor in steady state is obtained as

$$\hat{y}^* = \left(\frac{s_k}{n + g + \delta_k} \right)^{\frac{\alpha}{1-\alpha-\beta}} \left(\frac{s_h}{n + g + \delta_h} \right)^{\frac{\beta}{1-\alpha-\beta}}. \tag{3.23}$$

Equation (3.23) shows that the relative contributions of the saving rates for physical and human capital on output per capita depend on the shares of physical and human capital—the larger is α, the more important is s_k and the larger is β, the more important is s_h.

3.4 Solow Model and Cross-Country Income Differences: Regression Analyses

3.4.1 A World of Augmented Solow Economies

An alternative to the growth regressions discussed in Section 3.2 is to exploit the steady-state implications of the Solow model. This line of attack was pioneered by an important paper by Mankiw, Romer, and Weil (1992; or MRW). These authors used the Cobb-Douglas model discussed in Example 3.2 and envisaged a world consisting of $j = 1, \ldots, J$ countries, each country isolated from the rest, thus following the laws of motion implied by the Solow model. Thus we are again using the assumption that each country is an island. Though unattractive for the reasons discussed above, much of the empirical growth literature starts from this assumption. It is therefore a useful starting place for our discussion of whether the standard Solow model provides a good account of the sources of cross-country differences in income (per capita).

Following Example 3.2, let us assume that country $j = 1, \ldots, J$ has the following aggregate production function:

$$Y_j(t) = K_j(t)^{\alpha} H_j(t)^{\beta} (A_j(t) L_j(t))^{1-\alpha-\beta}.$$

This production function nests the basic Solow model without human capital when $\beta = 0$. First, assume that countries differ in terms of their saving rates, $s_{k,j}$ and $s_{h,j}$; population growth rates, n_j; and technology growth rates, $\dot{A}_j(t)/A_j(t) = g_j$. As usual, define $k_j \equiv K_j/A_j L_j$ and $h_j \equiv H_j/A_j L_j$. Since our main interest here is cross-country income differences, rather than studying the dynamics of a particular country over time, let us focus on a world in which each country is in steady state (thus ignoring convergence dynamics, which was the focus in the previous section). To the extent that countries are not too far from their steady state, there will be little loss of insight from this assumption, though naturally this approach is not satisfactory for countries experiencing large growth spurts or collapses, as in some of the examples discussed in Chapter 1.

Given the steady-state assumption, the analogues of (3.22) apply here and imply that the steady-state physical and human capital to effective labor ratios of country j, (k_j^*, h_j^*), are given by (3.22), so that using (3.23), the steady-state income per capita of country j is obtained as

$$y_j^*(t) \equiv \frac{Y(t)}{L(t)} = A_j(t) \left(\frac{s_{k,j}}{n_j + g_j + \delta_k} \right)^{\frac{\alpha}{1-\alpha-\beta}} \left(\frac{s_{h,j}}{n_j + g_j + \delta_h} \right)^{\frac{\beta}{1-\alpha-\beta}}. \tag{3.24}$$

Here $y_j^*(t)$ stands for output per capita of country j along the BGP. An immediate implication of (3.24) is that if g_j values are not equal across countries, income per capita will diverge, since the term $A_j(t)$ will grow at different rates for different countries. As discussed in Chapter 1, there is some evidence for this type of divergent behavior, but the world (per capita) income distribution can also be approximated by a relatively stable distribution. This is an area of current research, and there is an active debate on whether the world economy in the postwar era should be modeled as having an expanding or a stable distribution of income per capita. The former would be consistent with a specification in which g_j differs across countries, while the latter would require all countries to have the same rate of technological progress, g (recall the discussion in Chapter 1). Mankiw, Romer, and Weil adopt the latter perspective and assume that technological know-how in all countries grows at some common rate g.

Common technology advances: $A_j(t) = \bar{A}_j \exp(gt)$.

Put differently, countries differ according to their technology *level*—in particular, according to their initial level of technology, $\bar{A}_j$—but they share the same common technology growth rate, g. Using this assumption together with (3.24) and taking logs, we obtain the following convenient log-linear equation for the BGP of income for country $j = 1, \ldots, J$:

$$\log y_j^*(t) = \log \bar{A}_j + gt + \frac{\alpha}{1 - \alpha - \beta} \log \left(\frac{s_{k,j}}{n_j + g + \delta_k} \right)$$

$$+ \frac{\beta}{1 - \alpha - \beta} \log \left(\frac{s_{h,j}}{n_j + g + \delta_h} \right). \tag{3.25}$$

Equation (3.25) is simple and attractive and can be estimated easily with cross-country data. Estimates for $s_{k,j}$, $s_{h,j}$, and n_j can be computed from the available data, and combined with values for the constants δ_k, δ_h, and g, they can be used to construct measures of the two key right-hand-side variables. Given these measures, (3.25) can be estimated by ordinary least squares (by regressing income per capita on these measures) to uncover the values of α and β.

MRW take $\delta_k = \delta_h = \delta$ and $\delta + g = 0.05$ as approximate depreciation rates for physical and human capital and as the growth rate for the world economy. These numbers are somewhat arbitrary, but their exact values are not important for the estimation. The literature typically approximates $s_{k,j}$ with average investment rates (investments/GDP). Investment rates, average population growth rates n_j, and log output per capita are from the Summers-Heston dataset discussed in Chapter 1. In addition, MRW use estimates of the fraction of the school-aged population that is enrolled in secondary school as a measure of the investment rate in human capital, $s_{h,j}$. I return to a discussion of this variable below.

These assumptions are still not sufficient for estimating (3.25) consistently, because the term $\log \bar{A}_j$ is unobserved (at least to the econometrician) and thus will be captured by the error term. Most reasonable models of economic growth would suggest that technological differences, $\log \bar{A}_j$, should be correlated with investment rates in physical and human capital. Thus an estimation of (3.25) would lead to the most standard form of omitted variable bias and inconsistent estimates. Consistency would only follow under a stronger assumption than the common technology advances assumption introduced above. Therefore, implicitly, MRW make another crucial assumption.

Orthogonal technology: $\bar{A}_j = \varepsilon_j A$, with ε_j orthogonal to all other variables.

Under the orthogonal technology assumption, $\log \bar{A}_j$, which is part of the error term, is orthogonal to the key right-hand-side variables, and (3.25) can be estimated consistently.

3.4.2 Mankiw, Romer, and Weil Estimation Results

MRW first estimate (3.25) without the human capital term (i.e., imposing $\beta = 0$) for the cross-sectional sample of non-oil-producing countries. In particular, their estimating equation in this case is

$$\log y_j^* = \text{constant} + \frac{\alpha}{1 - \alpha} \log(s_{k,j}) - \frac{\alpha}{1 - \alpha} \log(n_j + g + \delta_k) + \varepsilon_j.$$

This equation is obtained from (3.25) by setting $\beta = 0$ and specializing it to a single cross section. In addition, the terms $\log(s_{k,j})$ and $\log(n_j + g + \delta_k)$ are separated to test the restriction that their coefficients should be equal in absolute value and of opposite signs. Finally,

TABLE 3.1
Estimates of the basic Solow model

	MRW	Updated data	
	1985	1985	2000
$\log(s_k)$	1.42	1.01	1.22
	(.14)	(.11)	(.13)
$\log(n + g + \delta)$	−1.97	−1.12	−1.31
	(.56)	(.55)	(.36)
Adjusted R^2	.59	.49	.49
Implied α	.59	.50	.55
Number of observations	98	98	107

Note: Standard errors are in parentheses.

this equation also includes ε_j as an error term, capturing all omitted factors and influences on income per capita.

Their results from this estimation exercise are replicated in column 1 of Table 3.1 using the original MRW data (standard errors in parentheses). Their estimates suggest a coefficient of about 1.4 for $\alpha / (1 - \alpha)$, which implies a value of α about 2/3. Since α is also the share of capital in national income, it should be about 1/3 (recall Figure 2.11). Thus the regression estimates without human capital appear to lead to overestimates of α. Columns 2 and 3 report the same results with updated data. The fit of the model is slightly less good than was the case with the MRW data, but the general pattern is similar. The implied values of α are also a little smaller than the original estimates, but still substantially higher than the value of 1/3 one would expect on the basis of the underlying model.

The most natural reason for the high implied values of the parameter α in Table 3.1 is that ε_j is correlated with $\log(s_{k,j})$, either because the orthogonal technology assumption is not a good approximation to reality or because there are also human capital differences correlated with $\log(s_{k,j})$. MRW favor the second interpretation and estimate the augmented model:

$$\log y_j^* = \text{constant} + \frac{\alpha}{1 - \alpha - \beta} \log(s_{k,j}) - \frac{\alpha}{1 - \alpha - \beta} \log(n_j + g + \delta_k) \qquad (3.26)$$

$$+ \frac{\beta}{1 - \alpha - \beta} \log(s_{h,j}) - \frac{\beta}{1 - \alpha - \beta} \log(n_j + g + \delta_h) + \varepsilon_j.$$

The original MRW estimates are given in column 1 of Table 3.2. Now the estimation is more successful. Not only is the adjusted R^2 quite high (about 78%), the implied value for α is about 1/3. On the basis of this estimation result, MRW and others have interpreted the fit of the augmented Solow model to the data as a success: with common technology, human and physical capital investments appear to explain about three-quarters of the differences in cross-country income per capita, and the implied parameter values are reasonable. Columns 2 and 3 of the table show the results with updated data. The implied values of α are similar, though the adjusted R^2 is somewhat lower.

To the extent that these regression results are reliable, they give a big boost to the augmented Solow model. In particular, the estimate of adjusted R^2 suggests that a significant fraction of

TABLE 3.2
Estimates of the augmented Solow model

	MRW	Updated data	
	1985	1985	2000
$\log(s_k)$	.69	.65	.96
	(.13)	(.11)	(.13)
$\log(n + g + \delta)$	−1.73	−1.02	−1.06
	(.41)	(.45)	(.33)
$\log(s_h)$	.66	.47	.70
	(.07)	(.07)	(.13)
Adjusted R^2	.78	.65	.60
Implied α	.30	.31	.36
Implied β	.28	.22	.26
Number of observations	98	98	107

Note: Standard errors are in parentheses.

the differences in income per capita across countries can be explained by differences in their physical and human capital investment behavior. The immediate implication is that technology (TFP) differences have a somewhat limited role. If this conclusion were appropriate, it would imply that, as far as the proximate causes of prosperity are concerned, we could confine our attention to physical and human capital and also assume that countries have access to more or less the same world technology. The implications for the modeling of economic growth are of course quite major.

3.4.3 Challenges to the Regression Analyses of Growth Models

There are two major (and related) problems with the regression approach and the conclusion that the importance of technology differences is limited.

The first relates to the assumption that technology differences across countries are orthogonal to all other variables. While the constant technology advances assumption may be defended, the orthogonality assumption is too strong, almost untenable. When $\bar{A}_j$ varies across countries, it should also be correlated with measures of s_j^h and s_j^k: countries that are more productive also invest more in physical and human capital. This correlation is for two reasons. The first is a version of the *omitted variable bias* problem: technology differences are also outcomes of investment decisions. Thus societies with high levels of $\bar{A}_j$ are those that have invested more in technology for various reasons; it is then natural to expect the same reasons to induce greater investment in physical and human capital as well. Second, even if we ignore omitted variable bias, there is a *reverse causality* problem: complementarity between technology and physical or human capital implies that countries with high $\bar{A}_j$ find it more beneficial to increase their stock of human and physical capital. In terms of the regression (3.26), omitted variable bias and reverse causality problems imply that the key right-hand-side variables are correlated with the error term, ε_j. Consequently, ordinary least squares regressions of (3.26) lead to upwardly biased estimates of α and β. In addition, the estimate of R^2, which is a measure of how much of the cross-country variability in income per capita can be explained by physical and human capital, will also be biased upward.

The second problem with the regression analyses relates to the magnitudes of the estimates of α and β in (3.26). The regression framework above is attractive in part because we can gauge whether the estimate of α is plausible. We should do the same for the estimate of β. However, such an exercise reveals that the coefficient on the investment rate in human capital, s_j^h, appears too large relative to microeconometric evidence.

Recall first that MRW use the fraction of the working-age population enrolled in secondary school. This variable ranges from 0.4% to more than 12% in the sample of countries used for this regression. Their estimates therefore imply that, holding all other variables constant, a country with approximately 12% school enrollment should have income per capita of about 9 times that of a country with $s_j^h = 0.4$. More explicitly, the predicted log difference in incomes between these two countries is

$$\frac{\beta}{1 - \alpha - \beta}(\log 12 - \log (0.4)) = 0.70 \times (\log 12 - \log (0.4)) \approx 2.38.$$

Thus, holding all other factors constant, a country with school enrollment of more than 12% should be about $\exp(2.38) \approx 10.8$ times richer than a country with a level of schooling investment of about 0.4.

In practice, the difference in average years of schooling between any two countries in the MRW sample is less than 12. Chapter 10 shows that there are good economic reasons to expect additional years of schooling to increase earnings proportionally, for example, as in Mincer regressions of the form

$$\log w_i = \mathbf{X}_i^T \boldsymbol{\gamma} + \phi S_i + u_i, \tag{3.27}$$

where w_i denotes the wage earnings of individual i, $\mathbf{X}_i$ is a set of demographic controls, S_i is years of schooling, and u_i is an error term. The estimate of the coefficient ϕ is the rate of returns to education, measuring the proportional increase in earnings resulting from one more year of schooling. The microeconometrics literature suggests that (3.27) provides a good approximation to the data and estimates ϕ to be between 0.06 and 0.10, implying that a worker with one more year of schooling earns about 6–10% more than a comparable worker with one less year of schooling. If labor markets are competitive, or at the very least, if wages are, on average, proportional to productivity, (3.27) also implies that one more year of schooling increases worker productivity by about 6–10%.

Can we deduce from this information how much richer a country with 12 more years of average schooling should be? The answer is yes, but with two caveats. First, we need to assume that the micro-level relationship as captured by (3.27) applies identically to all countries. Let us, for now, ignore other potential determinants of wages and write the earnings of individual i as $w_i = \tilde{\phi}(S_i)$, where S_i denotes the individual's level of schooling. The first key assumption is that this $\tilde{\phi}$ function is identical across countries and can be approximated by an exponential function of the form $\tilde{\phi}(S_i) \approx \exp(\phi S_i)$ so that we obtain (3.27). Why this assumption may be reasonable is further discussed in Chapter 10.

Second, we need to assume that there are no *human capital externalities*—meaning that the human capital of a worker does not directly increase the productivity of other workers. There are reasons why human capital externalities may exist, and some economists believe that they are important. The evidence discussed in Chapter 10, however, suggests that human capital externalities—except those working through innovation—are unlikely to be large. Thus it is reasonable to start without them. The key result, which will enable us to go from the microeconometric wage regressions to cross-country differences is that with constant returns to scale, perfectly competitive markets, and no human capital externalities, differences in worker productivity directly translate into differences in income per capita. To see this, suppose that each firm f in country j has access to the production function

$$y_{fj} = K_f^\alpha (A_j H_f)^{1-\alpha},$$

where A_j is the productivity of all firms in the country, K_f is the capital stock, and H_f denotes the efficiency units of human capital employed by firm f (thus this production function takes the more usual form in which human capital is embedded in workers rather than the form in (3.16)). Here the Cobb-Douglas production function is chosen for simplicity and does not affect the argument. Suppose also that firms in this country face a cost of capital equal to R_j. With perfectly competitive factor markets, profit maximization implies that the cost of capital must equal its marginal product,

$$R_j = \alpha \left(\frac{K_f}{A_j H_f} \right)^{-(1-\alpha)}. \tag{3.28}$$

Therefore all firms ought to function at the same physical to human capital ratio, and consequently all workers, regardless of their level of schooling, ought to work at the same physical to human capital ratio. Another direct implication of competitive labor markets is that in country j, wages per unit of human capital are equal to

$$w_j = (1-\alpha)\, \alpha^{\alpha/(1-\alpha)} A_j R_j^{-\alpha/(1-\alpha)}.$$

Consequently a worker with human capital h_i receives a wage income of $w_j h_i$. Once again, this is a more general result: with aggregate constant returns to scale production technology, wage earnings are linear in the effective human capital of the worker, so that a worker with twice as much effective human capital as another should earn twice as much (see Exercise 3.9). Substituting for capital from (3.28), the total income in country j is

$$Y_j = (1-\alpha)\, \alpha^{\alpha/(1-\alpha)} R_j^{-\alpha/(1-\alpha)} A_j H_j,$$

where H_j is the total efficiency units of labor in country j. This equation implies that holding R_j and A_j constant, a doubling of human capital will translate into a doubling of total income. The MRW regression that controls for the investment rate can be thought of as holding R_j constant (see Exercise 3.10 on how R_j is constant when the capital-output ratio is constant). Thus doubling the human capital (i.e., doubling the efficiency units of labor) should have the same effect on the earnings of an individual as the effect of doubling the aggregate human capital has on total income.

This analysis implies that the estimated rates of return to schooling can be used to calculate differences in the stock of human capital across countries. So in the absence of human capital externalities, a country with 12 more years of average schooling should have a stock of human capital somewhere between $\exp(0.10 \times 12) \approx 3.3$ and $\exp(0.06 \times 12) \approx 2.05$ times the stock of human capital of a country with fewer years of schooling. So holding other factors constant, this country should be about 2–3 times as rich as a country with zero years of average schooling. This difference is much less than the almost 11-fold difference implied by the MRW analysis.

This discussion suggests that the estimate for β that is implied by the MRW regressions is too high relative to the microeconometric evidence, and thus is likely to be upwardly biased. The cause of this overestimation is, in turn, most likely related to the possible correlation between the error term ε_j and the key right-hand side regressors in (3.26). Consequently, regression analyses based on (3.26) appear unlikely to provide us with an accurate picture of the extent of cross-country productivity differences and of the proximate causes of income differences.

3.5 Calibrating Productivity Differences

What other approach can we use to gauge the importance of physical and human capital and technology differences? An alternative is to calibrate the total factor productivity (TFP) differences across countries rather than estimating them using a regression framework. These TFP estimates are then interpreted as a measure of the contribution of technology to cross-country income differences. The calibration approach was proposed and used by Klenow and Rodriguez (1997) and Hall and Jones (1999). Here I follow Hall and Jones's approach, which is slightly simpler. The advantage of the calibration approach is that the omitted variable bias underlying the estimates of MRW will be less important (since micro-level evidence is used to anchor the contribution of human capital to economic growth). The disadvantage is that certain assumptions on functional forms have to be taken much more seriously, and we must explicitly assume that there are no human capital externalities.

3.5.1 Basics

Suppose that each country j has access to the Cobb-Douglas aggregate production function

$$Y_j = K_j^\alpha (A_j H_j)^{1-\alpha}, \tag{3.29}$$

where H_j is the stock of human capital of country j, capturing the amount of efficiency units of labor available to this country, K_j is its stock of physical capital, and A_j is labor-augmenting technology. Since our focus is on cross-country comparisons, time arguments are omitted.

Suppose that each worker in country j has S_j years of schooling. Then, using the Mincer equation (3.27) from the previous section, ignoring the other covariates, and taking exponents, H_j can be estimated as $H_j = \exp(\phi S_j) L_j$, where L_j is employment in country j and ϕ is the rate on returns to schooling estimated from (3.27). This approach may not lead to accurate estimates of the stock of human capital of a country, however. First, it does not take into account differences in other "human capital" factors, such as training or experience (which are discussed in greater detail in Chapter 10). Second, countries may differ not only in the years of schooling of their labor forces, but in the quality of schooling and the amount of post-schooling human capital. Third, the rate of return to schooling may vary systematically across countries (e.g., it may be lower in countries with a greater abundance of human capital). It is possible to deal with each of these problems to some extent by constructing better estimates of the stocks of human capital.

Following Hall and Jones, let us make a partial correction for the last factor. Assume that the rate of return to schooling does not vary across countries but is potentially different for different years of schooling. For example, one year of primary schooling may be more valuable than one year of graduate school (e.g., because learning how to read might increase productivity more than a solid understanding of growth theory). In particular, let the rate of return to acquiring the Sth year of schooling be $\phi(S)$. The above equation would be the special case where $\phi(S) = \phi$

for all S. Given this assumption the estimate of the stock of human capital can be constructed as

$$H_j = \sum_S \exp\{\phi(S)S\}L_j(S),$$

where $L_j(S)$ now refers to the total employment of workers with S years of schooling in country j.

A series for $K_j(t)$ can be constructed from the Summers-Heston dataset using investment data and the *perpetual inventory* method. In particular, recall that, with exponential depreciation, the stock of physical capital evolves according to

$$K_j(t+1) = (1-\delta)\, K_j(t) + I_j(t),$$

where $I_j(t)$ is the level of investment in country j at time t. The perpetual inventory method involves using information on the depreciation rate, δ, and investments, $I_j(t)$, to estimate $K_j(t)$. Let us assume, following Hall and Jones, that $\delta = 0.06$. With a complete series for $I_j(t)$, this equation can be used to calculate the stock of physical capital at any point in time. However, the Summers-Heston dataset does not contain investment information before the 1960s. The equation can still be used by assuming that each country's investment was growing at the same rate before the sample to compute the initial capital stock. Using this assumption, Hall and Jones calculate the physical capital stock for each country in the year 1985. I do the same here for 1980 and 2000. Finally, with the same arguments as before, I choose a value of 1/3 for α.

Given series for H_j and K_j and a value for α, we can construct "predicted" incomes at a point in time using

$$\hat{Y}_j = K_j^{1/3}(A_{US}H_j)^{2/3}$$

for each country j, where A_{US} is the labor-augmenting technology level of the United States, computed so that this equation fits the United States perfectly: $Y_{US} = K_{US}^{1/3}\left(A_{US}H_{US}\right)^{2/3}$. Throughout, time indices are dropped. Once a series for $\hat{Y}_j$ has been constructed, it can be compared to the actual output series. The gap between the two series represents the contribution of technology. Alternatively, we could explicitly back out country-specific technology terms (relative to the United States) as

$$\frac{A_j}{A_{US}} = \left(\frac{Y_j}{Y_{US}}\right)^{3/2}\left(\frac{K_{US}}{K_j}\right)^{1/2}\left(\frac{H_{US}}{H_j}\right).$$

Figures 3.2 and 3.3 show the results of these exercises for 1980 and 2000. The following features are noteworthy:

1. Differences in physical and human capital still matter a great deal: the predicted and actual incomes are highly correlated. Thus the regression analysis was not entirely misleading in emphasizing the importance of physical and human capital.

2. However, in contrast to the regression analysis, this exercise shows that there are significant technology (productivity) differences. There are often large gaps between predicted and actual incomes, showing the importance of technology differences across countries. This gap can be seen most easily in Figure 3.2, where practically all observations are above the 45° line, which implies that the Solow model is overpredicting the income level of countries that are poorer than the United States.

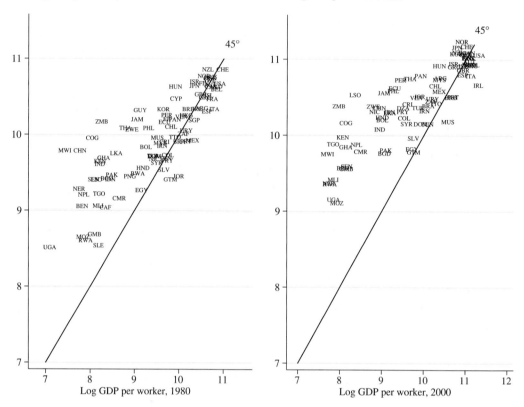

FIGURE 3.2 Predicted and actual log GDP per worker across countries, 1980 and 2000.

3. The same conclusion follows from Figure 3.3, which plots the estimates of the technology differences, A_j/A_{US}, against log GDP per capita. These differences are often substantial.

4. Also interesting is the pattern indicating that the empirical fit of the Solow growth model seems to deteriorate over time. In Figure 3.2, the observations are further above the 45° line in 2000 than in 1980, and in Figure 3.3, the relative technology differences become larger over time. Why the fit of the simple Solow growth model is better in 1980 than in 2000 is an interesting and largely unanswered question.

3.5.2 Challenges

In the same way as the regression analysis was based on a number of stringent assumptions (in particular, the assumption that technology differences across countries were orthogonal to other factors), the calibration approach also relies on certain important assumptions. The above exposition highlighted several of them. In addition to the standard assumption that factor markets are competitive, the calibration exercise had to assume no human capital externalities, impose a Cobb-Douglas production function, and make a range of approximations to measure cross-country differences in the stocks of physical and human capital.

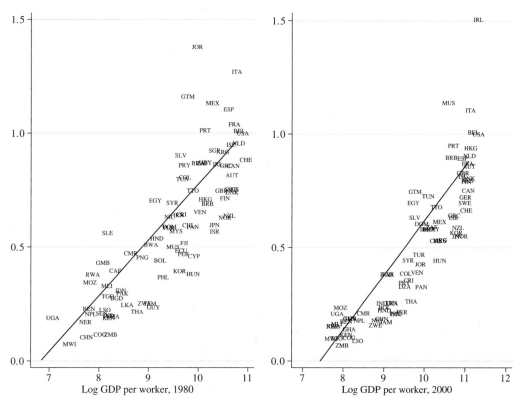

FIGURE 3.3 Calibrated technology levels relative to U.S. technology (from the Solow growth model with human capital) versus log GDP per worker, 1980 and 2000.

Let us focus on the assumptions about functional form. Could we relax the assumption that the production function is Cobb-Douglas? The answer is partly yes. The exercise here is similar to growth accounting, which does not need to make strong functional form assumptions (and this similarity to growth accounting is the reason this exercise is sometimes referred to as "development accounting" or "levels accounting"). In particular, recall (3.5), which showed how TFP estimates can be obtained from a general constant returns to scale production function (under competitive labor markets) by using average factor shares. Now instead imagine that the production function of all countries is given by $F(K_j, H_j, A_j)$ and that countries differ according to their physical and human capital as well as technology—but not according to F. Suppose also that we have data on K_j and H_j and on the share of capital in national income for each country. Then a natural adaptation of (3.5) can be used across countries rather than over time. In particular, let us rank countries in descending order according to their physical capital to human capital ratios, K_j/H_j (use Exercise 3.1 to see why this is the right way to rank countries rather than doing so randomly). Then we have

$$\hat{x}_{j,j+1} = g_{j,j+1} - \bar{\alpha}_{K,j,j+1} g_{K,j,j+1} - \bar{\alpha}_{L,j,j+1} g_{H,j,j+1}, \tag{3.30}$$

where $g_{j,j+1}$ is the proportional difference in output between countries j and $j+1$, $g_{K,j,j+1}$ is the proportional difference in capital stock between these countries, and $g_{H,j,j+1}$ is the proportional difference in human capital stocks. In addition, $\bar{\alpha}_{K,j,j+1}$ and $\bar{\alpha}_{Lj,j+1}$ are the average capital and labor shares between the two countries; $\hat{x}_{j,j+1}$ in (3.30) is then the estimate of the proportional TFP difference between the two countries.

Using this method and taking one of the countries (e.g., the United States) as the base, we can calculate relative technology differences across countries. This levels accounting exercise faces two major challenges, however. One is data related and the other is theoretical. First, data on capital and labor shares across countries are not available for most countries. This paucity of data makes the use of equation (3.30) far from straightforward. Consequently, almost all calibration or levels accounting exercises that estimate technology (productivity) differences use the Cobb-Douglas approach of the previous subsection (i.e., a constant value of α_K equal to 1/3).

Second, even if data on capital and labor shares were available, the differences in factor proportions (e.g., differences in K_j/H_j) across countries are large. An equation like (3.30) is a good approximation for small changes. As illustrated in Exercise 3.1, when factor proportion differences between observations are large, significant biases are possible.

To sum up, the approach of calibrating productivity differences across countries is a useful alternative to cross-country regression analysis but has to rely on a range of stringent assumptions on the form of the production function and can lead to biased estimates of technology differences. The biases come about both because these functional form assumptions may not be a good approximation to the data and because of mismeasurement of differences in the quality and quantity of physical and human capital across countries.

3.6   Estimating Productivity Differences

In the previous section, productivity (technology) differences are obtained as residuals from a calibration exercise, so we have to trust the functional form assumptions used in this strategy. But if we are willing to trust the functional forms, we can also estimate these differences econometrically rather than rely on calibration. The great advantage of econometrics relative to calibration is that not only do we obtain estimates of the objects of interest, but we also have standard errors, which show how much these estimates can be trusted. In this section, I briefly discuss two different approaches to estimating productivity differences.

3.6.1   A Naïve Approach

The first possibility is to take a production function of the form (3.29) as given and try to estimate it using cross-country data. In particular, taking logs:

$$\log Y_j = \alpha \log K_j + (1 - \alpha) \log H_j + \alpha \log A_j. \tag{3.31}$$

Given series for Y_j, K_j, and H_j, (3.31) can be estimated with ordinary least squares with the restriction that the coefficients on $\log K_j$ and $\log H_j$ sum to 1, and the residuals can be interpreted as estimates of technology differences. Unfortunately, this approach is not particularly attractive, since the potential correlation between $\log A_j$ and $\log K_j$ or $\log H_j$ implies that the estimates of α need not be unbiased even when constant returns to scale is imposed. Moreover, when constant returns is not imposed, the restriction that these coefficients sum to 1 will be rejected. Thus this regression approach runs into the same difficulties as the MRW approach discussed in Section 3.4.

Thus even if we are willing to presume that we know the functional form of the aggregate production function, it is difficult to directly estimate productivity differences. So how can we do better than this naïve approach? The answer involves making more use of economic theory. Estimating an equation of the form (3.31) does not make use of the fact that we are looking at the equilibrium of an economic system. A more sophisticated approach would use more of the restrictions imposed by equilibrium behavior (and would bring in additional relevant data). I next illustrate this approach using a specific attempt based on international trade theory. The reader who is not familiar with trade theory may want to skip this subsection.

3.6.2 Learning from International Trade*

Models of growth and international trade are studied in Chapter 19. Even without a detailed discussion of international trade theory, we can use data from international trade flows and some simple principles of international trade theory to obtain an alternate way of estimating productivity differences across countries.

Let us follow an important paper by Trefler (1993), which uses an augmented version of the standard Heckscher-Ohlin approach to international trade. The standard Heckscher-Ohlin approach assumes that countries differ according to their factor proportions (e.g., some countries have much more physical capital relative to their labor supply than others). In a closed economy, this disparity leads to differences in relative factor costs and in the relative prices of products using these factors in different intensities. International trade provides a way of taking advantage of these relative price differences. The most stylized form of the theory assumes no costs of shipping goods and no policy impediments to trade, so that international trade takes place costlessly between countries.

Trefler starts from the standard Heckscher-Ohlin model of international trade but allows for factor-specific productivity differences, so that capital in country j has productivity A_j^k; thus a stock of capital K_j in this country is equivalent to an effective supply of capital $A_j^k K_j$. Similarly for labor (human capital), country j has productivity A_j^h. In addition, Trefler assumes that all countries have the same homothetic preferences and there are sufficient differences in factor intensity across goods to ensure international trade between countries to arbitrage relative differences in factor cost (or in the jargon of international trade, countries are said to be in the "cone of diversification"). The latter assumption is important: when all countries have the same productivities both in physical and human capital, it leads to the celebrated *factor price equalization* result—all factor prices would be equal in all countries, because the world economy is sufficiently integrated. When there are productivity differences across countries, this assumption instead leads to *conditional factor price equalization*, meaning that factor prices are equalized once their different effective productivities are taken into consideration.

Under these assumptions, a standard equation in international trade links the net factor exports of each country to the abundance of that factor in the country relative to the world as a whole. The term "net factor exports" needs some explanation. It does not refer to actual trade in factors (e.g., migration of people, capital flows). Instead trading goods is a way of trading the factors that are embodied in that particular good. For example, a country that exports cars made with capital and imports corn made with labor is implicitly exporting capital and importing labor. More specifically, the net export of capital by country j, X_j^K, is calculated by considering the total exports of country j and computing how much capital is necessary to produce these exports and then subtracting the amount of capital necessary to produce its total imports. For our purposes, how factor contents are calculated is not important (it suffices to say that as with all things empirical, the devil is in the details and these calculations are far from straightforward and require a range of assumptions). Then the absence of trading frictions across countries and identical homothetic preferences imply that

$$X_j^K = A_j^k K_j - \gamma_j^C \sum_{i=1}^{J} A_i^k K_i \text{ and } X_j^H = A_j^h H_j - \gamma_j^C \sum_{i=1}^{J} A_i^h H_i, \tag{3.32}$$

where γ_j^C is the share of country j in world consumption (the value of this country's consumption divided by world consumption), and J is the total number of countries in the world. These equations simply restate the conclusion in the previous paragraph that a country will be a net exporter of capital if its effective supply of capital, $A_j^k K_j$, exceeds a fraction, here γ_j^C, of the world's effective supply of capital, $\sum_{i=1}^{J} A_i^k K_i$.

Consumption shares are easy to calculate. Then, given estimates for X_j^K and X_j^H, the above system of $2 \times J$ equations can be solved for the same number of unknowns, the A_i^k and A_i^h values for J countries. This solution gives estimates for factor-specific productivity differences across countries that are generated from an entirely different source of variation than those exploited before. In fact, this exercise provides us with a separate labor-augmenting (or human capital-augmenting) term and a capital-augmenting productivity term for each country.

How do we know that these numbers provide a good approximation to cross-country factor productivity differences? This problem is the same one we encountered in the previous section in judging whether the calibrated productivity (technology) differences were reliable. Fortunately, international trade theory gives us one more set of equations to check whether these numbers are reliable. As noted above, under the assumption that the world economy is sufficiently integrated, there is conditional factor price equalization. Thus for any two countries j and j', we have

$$\frac{R_j}{A_j^k} = \frac{R_{j'}}{A_{j'}^k} \quad \text{and} \quad \frac{w_j}{A_j^h} = \frac{w_{j'}}{A_{j'}^h}, \tag{3.33}$$

where R_j is the rental rate of capital in country j and w_j is the observed wage rate (which includes the compensation to human capital) in country j. The second equation in (3.33), for example, states that if workers in a particular country have, on average, half the efficiency units of those in the United States, their earnings should be roughly half those of American workers.

Using data on factor prices, we can therefore construct an alternative series for A_j^k and A_j^h. It turns out that the series for A_j^k and A_j^h implied by (3.32) and (3.33) are very similar, so there appears to be some validity to this approach. This validation gives us some confidence that there is relevant information in the numbers that Trefler obtains.

Figure 3.4 shows Trefler's original estimates. The numbers in this figure imply that there are very large differences in labor productivity and substantial, though much smaller, differences in capital productivity. For example, labor in Pakistan is 1/25th as productive as labor in the United States. In contrast, capital productivity differences are much more limited than labor productivity differences; capital in Pakistan is only half as productive as capital in the United States. This finding is not only intriguing in itself but is also quite consistent with models of directed technological change in Chapter 15 that may explain why technological change is labor-augmenting in the long run.

It is also informative to compare the productivity difference estimates from Trefler's approach to those from the previous section. Figures 3.5 and 3.6 undertake this comparison. The first plots the labor productivity difference estimates from the Trefler approach against the calibrated overall productivity differences from the Cobb-Douglas specification in the previous

Capital productivity

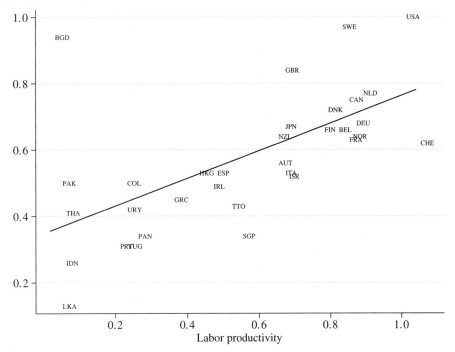

FIGURE 3.4   Comparison of labor-productivity and capital-productivity differences across countries.

Calibrated productivity differences, 1988

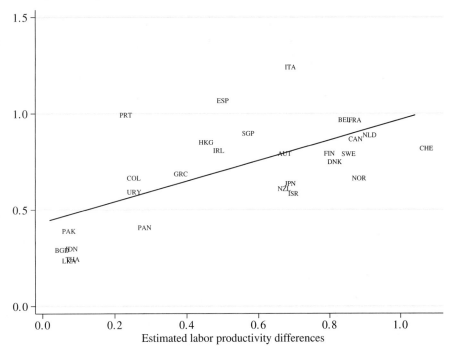
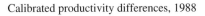

FIGURE 3.5   Comparison of the labor productivity estimates from the Trefler approach with the calibrated productivity differences from the Hall-Jones approach.

Calibrated productivity differences, 1988

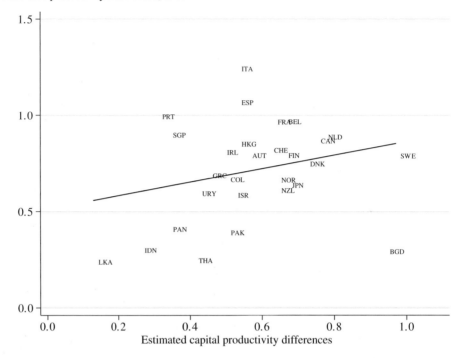

FIGURE 3.6 Comparison of the capital productivity estimates from the Trefler approach with the calibrated productivity differences from the Hall-Jones approach.

section. The similarity between the two series is remarkable, suggesting that both approaches are capturing some features of reality and that in fact there are significant productivity (technology) differences across countries. Interestingly, however, Figure 3.6 shows that the relationship between the calibrated productivity differences and the capital productivity differences is considerably weaker than for labor productivity.

Despite its apparent success, it is important to emphasize that Trefler's approach also relies on stringent assumptions. The four major assumptions are:

1. No international trading costs;
2. Identical production functions except for factor-augmenting technology differences;
3. Identical homothetic preferences; and
4. Sufficiently integrated world economy, leading to conditional factor price equalization.

All four of these assumptions are rejected in the data in one form or another. There are clearly international trading costs, including freight costs, tariff costs, and other trading restrictions. Productivity differences in practice are more complex than the simple factor-augmenting form assumed by Trefler. There is a very well-documented home bias in consumption, violating the assumption of identical homothetic preferences. Finally, most trade economists believe that conditional factor price equalization is not a good description of factor price differences across countries. In view of these concerns, the results from the Trefler exercise have to be interpreted with caution. Nevertheless, this approach is important both in showing how different sources of data and additional theory can be used to estimate cross-country technology differences and in providing a cross-validation for the calibration and estimation results discussed in Section 3.5.

3.7 Taking Stock

What have we learned? The major point of this chapter has not been the development of new theory. Instead it has been to see whether we could use the Solow model to obtain a more informed interpretation of cross-country differences and to use data to gauge the strengths and shortcomings of the Solow growth model.

At the end of this brief journey, the message is somewhat mixed. On the positive side, despite its simplicity, the Solow model has enough substance that we can take it to data in various different forms, including TFP accounting, regression analysis, and calibration. Moreover, each of these different methods gives us some idea about the sources of economic growth over time and of income differences across countries.

On the negative side, however, no single approach is entirely convincing. Each relies on a range of stringent auxiliary assumptions. Consequently, no firm conclusions can be drawn. The simplest applications of the Solow accounting framework suggest that technology is the main source of economic growth over time. However, this conclusion is disputed by those who point out that adjustments to the quality of physical and human capital substantially reduce or perhaps even totally eliminate residual TFP growth. The same debate recurs in the context of cross-country income differences; while some believe that accounting for differences in physical and human capital across countries leaves little need for technology differences, others show that, with reasonable models, most of the cross-country differences are due to technology.

While complete agreement is not possible, it is safe to say that the consensus in the literature today favors the interpretation that cross-country differences in income per capita cannot be understood solely on the basis of differences in physical and human capital; in other words, there are technology differences across countries, and these technology differences are likely to be at the heart of cross-country income and growth differences.

Hence an important potential lesson from this data detour is that technological progress is not only important in generating economic growth in the basic Solow model but also likely to be a major factor in cross-country differences in prosperity. A detailed study of technological progress and technology adoption decisions of households and firms is therefore necessary as part of the study of economic growth. This conclusion motivates the detailed analysis of technological progress and technology adoption later in the book. It is also useful to emphasize once again that differences in TFP are not necessarily due to technology in the narrow sense. If two countries have access to the same technology but make use of the available techniques in different ways with different degrees of efficiency, or if they are subject to different degrees of market or organizational failures, these differences will show up as TFP differences. One indication that TFP differences arising from market or organizational failures are important comes from episodes of severe crises. When countries have large drops in their income, due to civil wars, political instability, financial crises, or other reasons, these drops are almost always associated with corresponding declines in TFP (along with little change in capital stocks and much smaller changes in labor inputs). Naturally, these drops in TFP are not caused by technological regress but result from the breakdown of the market or increases in other sources of inefficiency. Therefore technology differences should always be construed rather broadly, and we should pay special attention to cross-country differences in the efficiency of production. By implication, to understand TFP differences across countries, we must study not only differences in the techniques that they use but also the way they organize markets and firms and how they provide incentives to different agents in the economy. This insight again shapes our agenda for the rest of the book, especially paving the way for investigating endogenous technological change in Part IV and differences in technology and productive efficiency across countries in Parts VI and VII.

There is one more sense in which what we have learned in this chapter is limited. What the Solow model makes us focus on—physical capital, human capital, and technology—are proximate causes of economic growth in cross-country differences. It is important to know which of these proximate causes are important and how they affect economic performance, both to have a better understanding of the mechanics of economic growth and also to know which classes of models to focus on. But at some level (and exaggerating somewhat) to say that a country is poor because it has insufficient physical capital, human capital, and inefficient technology is like saying that a person is poor because he or she does not have money. There are, in turn, other reasons some countries are more abundant in physical capital, human capital, and technology, in the same way as there are factors that cause one person to have more money than another. In Chapter 1, I referred to these as the *fundamental causes* of differences in prosperity, contrasting them with the proximate causes. A satisfactory understanding of economic growth and differences in prosperity across countries requires both an analysis of proximate causes and of fundamental causes of economic growth. The former is essential for the study of the mechanics of economic growth and to develop the appropriate formal models incorporating these insights. The latter is important for understanding why some societies make choices that lead them to low physical capital, low human capital, and inefficient technology and thus to relative poverty. This is the issue I turn to in the next chapter.

3.8 References and Literature

The growth accounting framework is introduced and applied in Solow (1957). Jorgensen, Gollop, and Fraumeni (1987) give a comprehensive development of this framework, emphasizing that competitive markets are necessary and essentially sufficient for this approach to work. They also highlight the measurement difficulties and emphasize that underestimates of improvements in the quality of physical and human capital lead to overestimates of the contribution of technology to economic growth. Jorgensen (2005) contains a more recent survey.

Regression analysis based on the Solow model has a long history. More recent contributions include Baumol (1986), Barro (1991), and Barro and Sala-i-Martin (1992). Barro (1991) has done more than anybody else to popularize growth regressions, which have become a very commonly used technique over the past two decades. See Durlauf (1996); Durlauf, Johnson and Temple (2005); and Quah (1993) for various critiques of growth regressions, especially focusing on issues of convergence. Wooldridge (2002) contains an excellent discussion of issues of omitted variable bias and the different approaches that can be used (see, e.g., Chapters 4, 5, and 8–11 in Wooldridge's book). You should read more about the economic limitations of growth regressions and the econometric problems facing such regressions before embarking upon your own empirical analyses.

The augmented Solow model with human capital is a generalization of the model presented in Mankiw, Romer, and Weil (1992). As noted in the text, treating human capital as a separate factor of production is somewhat unusual and difficult to micro-found. Different ways of introducing human capital in the basic growth model are discussed in Chapter 10.

Mankiw, Romer, and Weil (1992) also provide the first regression estimates of the Solow and the augmented Solow models. A detailed critique of Mankiw, Romer, and Weil is provided in Klenow and Rodriguez (1997). Hall and Jones (1999) and Klenow and Rodriguez (1997) provide the first calibrated estimates of productivity (technology) differences across countries. Caselli (2005) gives an excellent overview of this literature, with a detailed discussion of how one might correct for differences in the quality of physical and human capital across countries. He reaches the conclusion that such corrections will not change the basic conclusions of Klenow and Rodriguez and Hall and Jones that cross-country technology differences are important.

Subsection 3.6.2 draws on Trefler (1993). Trefler does not emphasize the productivity estimates implied by this approach, focusing more on the method as a way of testing the Heckscher-Ohlin model. Nevertheless these productivity estimates are an important input for growth economists. Trefler's approach has been criticized for various reasons, which are secondary for our focus here. The interested reader should look at Gabaix (2000) and Davis and Weinstein (2001).

3.9 Exercises

3.1 Suppose that output is given by the neoclassical production function $Y(t) = F(K(t), L(t), A(t))$ satisfying Assumptions 1 and 2, and that we observe output, capital, and labor at two dates t and $t + T$. Suppose that we estimate TFP growth between these two dates using the equation

$$\hat{x}(t, t + T) = g(t, t + T) - \alpha_K(t)g_K(t, t + T) - \alpha_L(t)g_L(t, t + T),$$

where $g(t, t + T)$ denotes output growth between dates t and $t + T$, and other growth terms are defined similarly, while $\alpha_K(t)$ and $\alpha_L(t)$ denote the factor shares at the beginning date. Let $x(t, t + T)$ be the true TFP growth between these two dates. Show that there exist functions F such that $\hat{x}(t, t + T)/x(t, t + T)$ can be arbitrarily large or small. Next show the same result when the TFP estimate is constructed using the end-date factor shares:

$$\hat{x}(t, t + T) = g(t, t + T) - \alpha_K(t + T)g_K(t, t + T) - \alpha_L(t + T)g_L(t, t + T).$$

Explain the importance of differences in factor proportions (capital-labor ratio) between the beginning and end dates in these results.

3.2 Consider the economy with labor market imperfections as in the second part of Exercise 2.20 from the previous chapter, where workers were paid a fraction $\lambda > 0$ of output. Show that in this economy the fundamental growth accounting equation leads to biased estimates of TFP.

3.3 For the Cobb-Douglas production function from Example 3.1, $Y(t) = A(t)K(t)^a L(t)^{1-\alpha}$, derive an exact analogue of (3.10) and show how the rate of convergence, that is, the coefficient in front of $\left(\log y(t) - \log y^*(t)\right)$, changes as a function of $\log y(t)$.

3.4 Consider once again the production function in Example 3.1. Suppose that two countries, 1 and 2, have exactly the same technology and the same parameters α, n, δ, and g, thus the same $y^*(t)$. Suppose that they start with $y_1(0) = 2y_2(0)$ at time $t = 0$. Using the parameter values in Example 3.1, calculate how long it would take for the income gap between the two countries to decline to 10%.

3.5 Consider a collection of Solow economies, each with different levels of δ, s, and n. Show that an equivalent of the conditional convergence regression equation (3.13) can be derived from an analogue of (3.10) in this case.

3.6 Prove Proposition 3.2.

3.7 In the augmented Solow model (see Propositions 3.1 and 3.2) determine the impact of increases in s_k, s_h, and n on h^* and k^*.

3.8 Consider a world economy consisting of countries represented by the augmented Solow growth model with the production functions given by (3.16). Derive the equivalent of the fundamental growth accounting equation in this case and explain how one might use available data to estimate TFP growth using this equation.

3.9   Consider the basic Solow model with no population growth and no technological progress and a production function of the form $F(K, H)$, where H denotes the efficiency units of labor (human capital) given by $H = \sum_{i \in N} h_i$, where N is the set of all individuals in the population, and h_i is the human capital of individual i. Assume that H is fixed. Suppose there are no human capital externalities and factor markets are competitive.

(a) Calculate the steady-state equilibrium of this economy.

(b) Prove that if 10% higher h at the individual level is associated with $a\%$ higher earnings, then a 10% increase in the country's stock of human capital H will lead to $a\%$ increase in steady-state output. Compare this result to the immediate impact of an unanticipated 10% increase in H (i.e., consider the impact of a 10% increase in H with the stock of capital unchanged).

3.10   Consider a constant returns to scale production function for country j, $Y_j = F(K_j, A_j H_j)$, where K_j is physical capital, H_j denotes the efficiency units of labor, and A_j is labor-augmenting technology. Prove that if $K_j / Y_j = K_{j'} / Y_{j'}$ in two different countries j and j', then the rental rates of capital in the two countries, R_j and $R_{j'}$ will also be equal.

3.11   Imagine you have a cross section of countries, $j = 1, \ldots, J$, and for each country, at a single point in time, you observe labor L_j, capital K_j, total output Y_j, and the share of capital in national income, α_j^K. Assume that all countries have access to a production technology of the form

$$F(K_j, L_j, A_j),$$

where A is technology. Assume that F exhibits constant returns to scale in K and L, and all markets are competitive.

(a) Explain how you would estimate relative differences in technology (productivity) across countries due to the term A without making any further assumptions. Write down the equations that are involved in estimating the contribution of A to cross-country income differences explicitly.

(b) Suppose that the exercise in part (a) leads to large differences in productivity due to the A term. How would you interpret this? Does it imply that countries have access to different production possibility sets?

(c) Now suppose that the true production function is $F(K, H, A)$, where H denotes efficiency units of labor. What other types of data would you need to estimate the contribution of technology (productivity) across countries to output differences?

(d) Show that if H is calculated as in Section 3.5, but there are significant quality-of-schooling differences and no differences in A, this strategy will lead to significant differences in the estimates of A.

4

Fundamental Determinants of Differences in Economic Performance

4.1 Proximate versus Fundamental Causes

"The factors we have listed (innovation, economies of scale, education, capital accumulation, etc.) are not causes of growth; *they are growth*." (North and Thomas, 1973, p. 2, italics in original)

The previous chapter illustrated how the Solow growth model can be used to understand cross-country income differences and the process of economic growth. In the context of the Solow growth model, the process of economic growth is driven by technological progress. Cross-country income differences, on the other hand, are due to a combination of technology differences and differences in physical capital per worker and in human capital per worker. While this approach provides us with a good starting point and delineates potential sources of economic growth and cross-country income differences, these sources are only proximate causes of economic growth and economic success. Let us focus on cross-country income differences, for example. As soon as we attempt to explain these differences with technology, physical capital, and human capital differences, an obvious question presents itself: if technology, physical capital, and human capital are so important in understanding differences in the wealth of nations and if they can account for 5-fold, 10-fold, 20-fold, or even 30-fold differences in income per capita across countries, then why is it that some societies do not improve their technologies, invest in physical capital, and accumulate human capital as much as others?

It appears therefore that any explanation that simply relies on technology, physical capital, and human capital differences across countries is, at some level, incomplete. There must be other, deeper reasons that we will refer to as "fundamental causes" of economic growth. It is these reasons that are preventing many countries from investing enough in technology, physical capital, and human capital.

An investigation of fundamental causes of economic growth is important for at least two reasons. First, any theory that focuses on the intervening variables (proximate causes) alone, without understanding the underlying driving forces, would be incomplete. Thus growth theory will not fulfill its full promise until it comes to grips with these fundamental causes. Second, if part of our study of economic growth is motivated by improving the growth performance of certain nations and the living standards of their citizens, understanding fundamental causes is central to this objective, since attempting to increase growth merely by focusing on proximate causes would be tantamount to dealing with symptoms of diseases without understanding what the diseases themselves are. While such attacks on symptoms can sometimes be useful, they are no substitute for a fuller understanding of the causes of the disease, which may allow a more satisfactory treatment. In the same way, we may hope that an understanding of the fundamental causes of economic growth could one day offer more satisfactory solutions to the major questions of social sciences concerning why some countries are poor and some are rich and how we can ensure that more nations grow faster.

What could these fundamental causes be? Can we make progress in understanding them? And, perhaps most relevant for this book, is growth theory useful in such an endeavor?

In this chapter, I develop some answers to these questions. Let us start with the last two questions. The argument in this book is that a good understanding of the mechanics of economic growth and thus the construction of detailed models of the growth process are essential for a successful investigation of the fundamental causes of economic growth. This understanding is crucial for at least two reasons; first, we can only pose useful questions about the fundamental causes of economic growth by understanding what the major proximate causes are and how they impact economic outcomes. Second, only models that provide a good approximation to reality and are successful in qualitatively and quantitatively matching the major features of the growth process can inform us about whether the potential fundamental causes that are proposed could indeed play a significant role in generating the huge differences observed in income per capita across countries. Our analysis of the mechanics of economic growth will often enable us to discard or refine certain proposed fundamental causes. As to the question of whether we can make progress, the vast economic growth literature is evidence that progress is being made and more progress is certainly achievable. In some sense, it is part of the objective of this book to convince you that the answer to this question is yes.

Returning to the first question, there are innumerable fundamental causes of economic growth that various economists, historians, and social scientists have proposed over the ages. Clearly, listing and cataloging them is neither informative nor useful. Instead, I classify the major candidate fundamental causes of economic growth into four categories of hypotheses. While such a classification undoubtedly fails to do justice to some of the nuances of the literature, it is satisfactory for our purposes of highlighting the main factors affecting cross-country income differences and economic growth. These are:

1. The luck hypothesis,
2. The geography hypothesis,
3. The culture hypothesis, and
4. The institutions hypothesis.

By "luck," I refer to the set of fundamental causes that explain divergent paths of economic performance among countries that are otherwise identical, either because some small uncertainty or heterogeneity between them has led to different choices with far-ranging consequences or because of different selection among multiple equilibria. Multiple equilibria correspond to different equilibrium configurations arising for the same underlying economic environment.

When models exhibit multiple equilibria, we are often unable to make specific predictions as to which of these equilibria will be selected by different countries, and it is possible for two otherwise identical countries to end up in different equilibria with quite distinct implications for economic growth and living standards. Luck and multiple equilibria can manifest themselves through any of the proximate causes discussed so far (and through some additional mechanisms discussed later in the book). For example, multiple equilibria can exist in technology adoption or in models that focus on investments in human and physical capital. Therefore explanations based on luck or multiple equilibria are often theoretically well grounded. Whether they are empirically plausible is another matter.

By "geography," I refer to all factors that are imposed on individuals as part of the physical, geographic, and ecological environment in which they live. Geography can affect economic growth through a variety of proximate causes. Geographic factors that can influence the growth process include soil quality, which can affect agricultural productivity; natural resources, which directly contribute to the wealth of a nation and may facilitate industrialization by providing certain key resources, such as coal and iron ore, during critical times; climate, which may affect productivity and attitudes directly; topography, which can affect the costs of transportation and communication; and disease environment, which can affect individual health, productivity and incentives to accumulate physical and human capital. For example, in terms of the aggregate production function of the Solow model, poor soil quality, lack of natural resources, or an inhospitable climate may correspond to a low level of A, that is, to a type of inefficient technology. Many philosophers and social scientists have suggested that climate also affects preferences in a fundamental way, so perhaps individuals living in certain climates have a preference for earlier rather than later consumption, thus reducing their saving rates of both physical and human capital. Finally, differences in the disease burden across areas may affect the productivity of individuals and their willingness to accumulate human capital. Thus geography-based explanations can easily be incorporated into both the simple Solow model and the more sophisticated models discussed later in the book.

By "culture," I refer to beliefs, values, and preferences that influence individual economic behavior. Differences in religious beliefs across societies are among the clearest examples of cultural differences that may affect economic behavior. Differences in preferences, for example, regarding how important wealth is relative to other status-generating activities and how patient individuals should be, might be as important as—or even more important than—luck, geography, and institutions in affecting economic performance. Broadly speaking, culture can affect economic outcomes through two major channels. First, it can influence the willingness of individuals to engage in different activities or to tradeoff consumption today versus consumption tomorrow. Via this channel, culture influences societies' occupational choices, market structure, saving rates, and individuals' willingness to accumulate physical and human capital. Second, culture may also affect the degree of cooperation and of trust in society, which are important foundations for productivity-enhancing activities.

By "institutions," I refer to rules, regulations, laws, and policies that affect economic incentives and thus the incentives to invest in technology, physical capital, and human capital. It is a truism of economic analysis that individuals only take actions that are rewarded. Institutions, which shape these rewards, must therefore be important in affecting all three of the proximate causes of economic growth. What distinguishes institutions from geography, luck, and culture is that they are social choices. Although laws and regulations are not directly chosen by individuals, and some institutional arrangements may be historically persistent, in the end the laws, policies, and regulations under which a society lives are the choices of the members of that society. If the members of the society collectively decide to change them, they can do so. This possibility implies that if institutions are a major fundamental cause of economic growth and cross-country differences in economic performance, they can potentially be reformed to achieve better outcomes. Such reforms may not be easy; they may encounter stiff opposition, and often we may not exactly know which reforms will work. But they are still within the realm of the possible, and further research might clarify how such reforms will affect economic incentives and how they can be implemented.

There is a clear connection between institutions and culture. Both affect individual behavior, and both are important determinants of incentives. Nevertheless, a crucial difference between the theories in these two categories justifies their separation. Institutions are directly under the control of the members of the society, in the sense that by changing the distribution of resources, constitutions, laws, and policies, individuals can collectively influence the institutions under which they live. In contrast, culture refers to a set of beliefs that have evolved over time and are outside the direct control of individuals.[1] Even though institutions might be hard to change in practice, culture is much harder to influence, and any advice to a society that it should change its culture is almost vacuous.

It is also important to emphasize that institutions themselves, even if they are a fundamental cause of differences in economic growth and income across countries, are endogenous. They are equilibrium choices made either by the society at large or by some powerful groups in society. One can then argue that luck, geography, or culture should be more important, because they may be "more exogenous" in the sense that they are *not* equilibrium choices in the same way as institutions are, and institutions vary across societies largely because of geographic, cultural, or random factors. While at some philosophical level this argument is correct, it is not a particularly useful observation. It neither obviates the need to understand the direct effects of luck, geography, culture, and institutions (and these direct effects have been the focus of much of the debate in this area) nor does it imply that understanding the specific role of institutions and economic development is secondary in any sense. After all, if we can understand what the effects of institutions are and which specific types of institutions matter, institutional reform can lead to major changes in economic behavior (even if part of the original variation in institutions was due to geography, luck, or culture).

In the rest of this chapter, I explain the reasoning motivating these different hypotheses and provide a brief overview of the empirical evidence pertaining to various fundamental causes of economic growth. The theoretical underpinnings and implications of the institutions view are further developed in Part VIII of the book. At this point, the reader should be warned that I am not an objective outside observer in this debate, but a strong proponent of the institutions hypothesis. Therefore, not surprisingly, this chapter concludes that the institutional differences are at the root of the important proximate causes that I have listed. Nevertheless, the same evidence can be interpreted in different ways, and the reader should feel free to draw his or her own conclusions.

Before delving into a discussion of the fundamental causes, one other topic deserves a brief discussion. This is where I start in the next section.

4.2 Economies of Scale, Population, Technology, and World Growth

As emphasized in Chapter 1, cross-country income differences result from the differential growth experiences of countries over the past two centuries. This makes it important for us to understand the process of economic growth. Equally remarkable is the fact that world economic growth is, by and large, a phenomenon of the past 200 years or so. Thus other major questions

---

1. A major and important exception to this lack of control is the effect of education on the beliefs and values of individuals.

concern why economic growth started so recently and why there was little economic growth before. The growth literature has provided a variety of interesting answers to these questions. Much of the literature focuses on the role of economies of scale and population. The argument goes as follows: in the presence of economies of scale (or increasing returns to scale), the population needs to have reached a certain critical level so that technological progress can gather speed. Alternatively, some natural (steady) progress of technology that may have been going on in the background needs to reach a critical threshold for the process of growth to begin. These scenarios are quite plausible. World population has indeed increased tremendously over the past million years, and the world's inhabitants today have access to a pool of knowledge and technology unimaginable to our ancestors. Could these long-run developments of the world economy also account for cross-country differences? Is the increase in world population a good explanation for the takeoff of the world economy?

Let us focus on population to give a preliminary answer to these questions. The simplest way of thinking of the relationship between population and technological change is the Simon-Kremer model (named after the demographer Julian Simon and the economist Michael Kremer). This model is implicitly one of the entire world economy, since there are no cross-country differences. Imagine that there is a small probability that each individual will discover a new idea that will contribute to the knowledge pool of the society. Crucially, these random discoveries are independent across individuals, so that a larger pool of individuals implies the discovery of more new ideas, increasing aggregate productivity. Let output be determined simply by technology (this condition can be generalized so that technology and capital determine output as in the Solow model, but this does not affect the point I make here):

$$Y(t) = L(t)^{\alpha} \, (A(t)Z)^{1-\alpha},$$

where $\alpha \in (0, 1)$, $Y(t)$ is world output, $A(t)$ is the world stock of technology, $L(t)$ is world population, and Z is some other fixed factor of production (e.g., land). I normalize $Z = 1$ without loss of any generality. Time is continuous, and ideas are discovered at the rate λ so that the knowledge pool of the society evolves according to the differential equation

$$\dot{A}(t) = \lambda L(t), \tag{4.1}$$

with $A(0) > 0$ taken as given. Population, in turn, is a function of output, for example because of the Malthusian channels discussed in Chapter 21. For instance, suppose that population increases linearly in output:

$$L(t) = \phi Y(t). \tag{4.2}$$

Combining these three equations, we obtain (see Exercise 4.1)

$$\dot{A}(t) = \lambda \phi^{\frac{1}{1-\alpha}} A(t). \tag{4.3}$$

The solution to this differential equation involves

$$A(t) = \exp\!\left(\lambda \phi^{1/(1-\alpha)} t\right) A(0). \tag{4.4}$$

Equation (4.4) shows how a model of economies of scale (increasing returns) in population can generate a steady increase in technology. It is also straightforward to verify that

$$Y(t) = \phi^{\frac{\alpha}{1-\alpha}} A(t),$$

so that aggregate income also grows at the constant level $\lambda \phi^{1/(1-\alpha)}$. Such a model would generate steady growth but no acceleration. Simon and Kremer, instead, assume that there are stronger externalities to population than in (4.1). They impose the following equation governing the accumulation of ideas:

$$\frac{\dot{A}(t)}{A(t)} = \lambda L(t).$$

This implies that the law of motion of technology is given by (see Exercise 4.2)

$$A(t) = \frac{1}{A(0)^{-1} - \lambda \phi^{1/(1-\alpha)} t}. \tag{4.5}$$

In contrast to (4.4), this equation implies an accelerating output level. Starting from a low level of $A(0)$ (or $L(0)$), this model would generate a long period of low output, followed by an acceleration or takeoff, reminiscent to the modern economic growth experience discussed in Chapter 1. Therefore a model with significant economies of scale is capable of generating the pattern of takeoff we see in the data.

While such a story, which has been proposed by many economists, may have some appeal for accounting for world growth, it is important to emphasize that it has little to say about cross-country income differences or why modern economic growth started in some countries (Western Europe) and not others (Asia, South America, Africa). In fact, if we take Western Europe and Asia as the relevant economic units, the European population has consistently been less than that of Asia over the past 2,000 years (see, e.g., Figure 21.1); thus it is unlikely that simple economies of scale in population are responsible for the economic takeoff in Western Europe while Asia stagnated.

This discussion therefore suggests that models based on economies of scale of one sort or another do not provide us with fundamental causes of cross-country income differences. At best, they are theories of growth of the world taken as a whole. Moreover, once we recognize that the modern economic growth process has been uneven, meaning that it took place in some parts of the world and not others, the appeal of such theories diminishes further. If economies of scale were responsible for modern economic growth, this phenomenon should also be able to explain when and where this process of economic growth started. Existing models based on economies of scale do not. In this sense, they are unlikely to provide the fundamental causes of modern economic growth. Then are these types of economies of scale and increasing returns to population unimportant? Certainly not. They may well be part of the proximate causes of the growth process (e.g., the part lying in the black box of technology). But this discussion suggests that these models need to be augmented by other fundamental causes to explain why, when, and where the takeoff occurred. This further motivates the investigation of the fundamental causes.

4.3 The Four Fundamental Causes

4.3.1 Luck and Multiple Equilibria

Chapter 21 presents a number of models in which multiple equilibria or multiple steady states can arise because of coordination failures in the product market or imperfections in credit markets. These models suggest that an economy, with given parameter values, can exhibit significantly different types of equilibrium behavior, some with higher levels of income or perhaps sustained growth, while other equilibria involve poverty and stagnation. To give a flavor of these models, consider the following simple game of investment played by a large number of agents in the society:

		Everybody else	
		High investment	Low investment
Individual	High investment	y^H, y^H	$y^L - \varepsilon, y^L$
	Low investment	$y^L, y^L - \varepsilon'$	y^L, y^L

Let us focus on symmetric equilibria. The first column indicates that all agents (except the individual in question) have chosen high investment, while the second corresponds to low investment by all agents. The first row, on the other hand, corresponds to high investment by the individual in question, and the second row is for low investment. In each cell, the first number refers to the income of the individual in question, while the second number is the payoff to each of the other agents in the economy. Suppose that $y^H > y^L$ and $\varepsilon, \varepsilon' > 0$. This payoff matrix then implies that high investment is more profitable when others are also undertaking high investment. For example, this may be because of technological complementarities or aggregate demand externalities (see Chapter 21).

It is then clear that there are two (pure-strategy) symmetric equilibria in this game. In one equilibrium, the individual expects all other agents to choose high investment, and he does so himself. Since the same calculus applies to each agent, each agent will also expect high investment by all others and will choose high investment himself. This establishes that high investment by all agents is an equilibrium. Similarly, when the individual expects all others to choose low investment, it is a best response for him to choose low investment, so that there also exists an equilibrium with low investment. Thus, this simple game exhibits two symmetric (pure-strategy) equilibria.

Two features are worth noting. First, depending on the extent of complementarities and other economic interactions, y^H can be quite large relative to y^L, so there may be significant income differences in the allocations implied by the two different equilibria. Thus if we believe that such a game is a good approximation to reality and different countries can end up in different equilibria, the economic interactions here could help explain large differences in income per capita. Second, the two equilibria in this game are also Pareto-ranked—all individuals are better off in the equilibrium in which everybody chooses high investment (see Chapter 5 on the Pareto criterion). Both of these features are shared by the Big Push models discussed in Chapter 21.

In addition to models of multiple equilibria, stochastic models, in which the realization of certain random variables determines when a particular economy transitions from low- to high-productivity technologies and starts the process of takeoff, might also be relevant in this context (see Section 17.6).

Both models of multiple equilibria and those in which stochastic variables determine the long-run growth properties of the economy are attractive as descriptions of certain aspects of the development process. They are also informative about the mechanics of economic development in an interesting class of models. But do they inform us about the fundamental causes of economic growth? Can we say that the United States is rich today while Nigeria is poor because the former has been lucky in its equilibrium selection while the latter has been unlucky? Can we pinpoint their divergent development paths to some small stochastic events 200, 300, or 400 years ago? The answer seems to be no.

U.S. economic growth is the cumulative result of a variety of processes, ranging from innovations and free entrepreneurial activity to significant investments in human capital and rapid capital accumulation. It is difficult to reduce these processes to a simple lucky break or the selection of the right equilibrium. Even 400 years ago, conditions were significantly different in the United States and in Nigeria, and this led to different opportunities, institutional paths, and incentives. It is the combination of the historical experiences of countries and different economic incentives that underlies their different processes of economic growth.

Equally important, models based on luck or multiple equilibria can explain why there might be a 20-year or perhaps a 50-year divergence between two otherwise identical economies. But how are we to explain a 500-year divergence? It certainly does not seem plausible to imagine that Nigeria, today, can suddenly switch equilibria and quickly achieve the level of income per capita in the United States.[2] Most models of multiple equilibria are unsatisfactory in another sense. As in the simple example discussed above, most models of multiple equilibria involve the presence of Pareto-ranked equilibria. This implies that one equilibrium gives higher utility or welfare to *all* agents than another. While such Pareto-ranked equilibria are a feature of parsimonious models, which do not specify many relevant dimensions of heterogeneity that are important in practice, it is not clear whether they are useful in thinking about why some countries are rich and others are poor. If indeed it were possible for Nigerians to change their behavior and for all individuals in the nation to become better off (say, by switching from low to high investment in terms of the game above), it is very difficult to believe that for 200 years they have not been able to coordinate on such a better action. Most readers are aware that Nigerian history is shaped by religious and ethnic conflict and by a civil war that ravaged the nation, and that the country is still adversely affected by the extreme corruption of politicians, bureaucrats, and soldiers who have enriched themselves at the expense of the population at large. That an easy Pareto-improving change exists against this historical and social background seems improbable, to say the least.

To be fair, not all models of multiple equilibria allow easy transitions from a Pareto-inferior equilibrium to a superior one. In the literature, a useful distinction can be made between models of multiple equilibria (in which different equilibria can be reached if individuals change their beliefs and behaviors simultaneously) versus models of multiple steady states with history dependence (in which once a particular path of equilibrium is embarked upon, it becomes much harder—perhaps impossible—to transition to the other steady-state equilibrium; see Chapter 21). Models with multiple steady states are more attractive for understanding persistent differences in economic performance across countries than models with multiple equilibria. Nevertheless, unless some other significant source of conflict of interest or distortions are incorporated, it seems unlikely that the difference between the United States and Nigeria can be explained by using models in which the two countries have identical parameters but have made different choices and stuck with them. The mechanics of how a particular steady-state equilibrium can be maintained would be the most important element of such a theory, and other fundamental causes of economic growth, including institutions, policies, or perhaps culture, must play a role in explaining this type of persistence. Put differently, in today's world of free information, technology, and capital flows, if Nigeria had the same parameters, the same opportunities, and the same institutions as the United States, there should exist some

---

2. Naturally, one can argue that reforms or major changes in the growth trajectory are always outcomes of a switch from one equilibrium to another. But such an explanation would not have much empirical content, unless it is based on a well-formulated model of equilibrium selection and can make predictions about when we might expect such switches.

arrangement such that these new technologies could be imported and everybody could be made better off.

Another challenge to models of multiple steady states concerns the ubiquity of growth miracles, such as South Korea and Singapore, which we discussed in Chapter 1. If cross-country income differences are due to multiple steady states, from which escape is totally or nearly impossible, then how can we explain countries that embark upon a very rapid growth process? The example of China may be even most telling here. While China stagnated under communism until Mao's death, the changes in economic institutions and policies that took place thereafter have led to very rapid economic growth. If China were in a low-growth steady state before Mao's death, then we need to explain how it escaped from this steady state after 1978 and why it did not do so before. Inevitably this line of reasoning brings us to the role of other fundamental causes, such as institutions, policies, and culture.

A different, and perhaps more promising, argument about the importance of luck can be made by emphasizing the role of leaders. Perhaps it was Mao who held back China, and his death and the identity, beliefs, and policies of his successors were at the root of its subsequent growth. Perhaps the identity of the leader of a country can thus be viewed as a stochastic event, shaping economic performance. This point of view probably has a lot of merit. Recent empirical work by Jones and Olken (2005) shows that leaders seem to influence the economic performance of nations. Thus luck could play a major role in cross-country income and growth differences by determining whether growth-enhancing or growth-retarding leaders are selected. Nevertheless, such an explanation is closer to the institutional approaches than the pure luck category. First, leaders often influence the economic performance of their societies by the policies they set and the institutions they develop. Second, the selection and behavior of leaders and the policies that they pursue are part of the institutional explanations. Third, Jones and Olken's research points to an important interaction between the effect of leaders and a society's institutions. Leaders seem to matter for economic growth only in countries where institutions are nondemocratic or weak (in the sense of not placing constraints on politicians or elites). In democracies and in societies where other institutions appear to place checks on the behavior of politicians and leaders, the identity of the leaders seems to play almost no role in economic performance.

Given these considerations, I tentatively conclude that models emphasizing luck and multiple equilibria are useful for our study of the mechanics of economic development, but they are unlikely to provide us with the fundamental causes of why world economic growth started 200 years ago and why some countries are rich while others are poor today.

4.3.2 Geography

While the approaches in the last subsection emphasize the importance of luck and multiple equilibria among otherwise identical societies, an alternative is to emphasize the deep hetero-geneity across societies. The geography hypothesis is, first and foremost, about the fact that not all areas of the world are created equal. "Nature," that is, the physical, ecological, and geographical environment of nations, plays a major role in their economic experiences. As pointed out above, geographic factors can play this role by determining both the preferences and the opportunity set of individual economic agents in different societies. There are at least three main versions of the geography hypothesis, each emphasizing a different mechanism for how geography affects prosperity.

The first and earliest version of the geography hypothesis goes back to Montesquieu ([1748], 1989). Montesquieu, who was a brilliant French philosopher and an avid supporter of republican forms of government, was also convinced that climate was among the main determinants of the fate of nations. He believed that climate, in particular heat, shaped human attitudes and effort, and through this channel, affected both economic and social outcomes. He wrote in his classic book *The Spirit of the Laws* (1989, p. 234):

> The heat of the climate can be so excessive that the body there will be absolutely without strength. So, prostration will pass even to the spirit; no curiosity, no noble enterprise, no generous sentiment; inclinations will all be passive there; laziness there will be happiness.
>
> People are . . . more vigorous in cold climates. The inhabitants of warm countries are like old men, timorous; the people in cold countries are like young men, brave.

Today some of the pronouncements in these passages appear somewhat naïve and perhaps bordering on "political incorrectness." They still have many proponents, however. Even though Montesquieu's eloquence makes him stand out among those who formulated this perspective, he was neither the first nor the last to emphasize such geographic fundamental causes of economic growth. Among economists a more revered figure is one of the founders of our discipline, Alfred Marshall. Almost a century and a half after Montesquieu, Marshall (1890, p. 195) wrote:

> [V]igor depends partly on race qualities: but these, so far as they can be explained at all, seem to be chiefly due to climate.

While the first version of the geography hypothesis appears naïve and raw to many of us, its second version, which emphasizes the impact of geography on the technologies available to a society, especially in agriculture, is more palatable and has many more supporters. This view is developed by an early Nobel Prize winner in economics, Gunnar Myrdal (1968, vol. 3, p. 2121), who wrote:

> [S]erious study of the problems of underdevelopment . . . should take into account the climate and its impacts on soil, vegetation, animals, humans and physical assets— in short, on living conditions in economic development.

More recently, Jared Diamond, in his widely popular *Guns, Germs and Steel*, espouses this view and argues that geographical differences between the Americas and Europe (or more appropriately, Eurasia) have determined the timing and nature of settled agriculture and, by means of this channel, shaped whether societies have been able to develop complex organizations and advanced civilian and military technologies (1997, e.g., p. 358). The economist Jeffrey Sachs (2001, p. 2) has been a recent and forceful proponent of the importance of geography in agricultural productivity, stating that

> By the start of the era of modern economic growth, if not much earlier, temperate-zone technologies were more productive than tropical-zone technologies.

There are also reasons for questioning this second, and more widely-held, view of geographic determinism. Most of the technological differences emphasized by these authors refer to agriculture. But as Chapter 1 emphasized, the origins of differential economic growth across countries goes back to the age of industrialization. Modern economic growth came with industry, and it is the countries that have failed to industrialize that are poor today. Low agricultural productivity, if anything, should create a comparative advantage in industry and encourage those countries with "unfavorable geography" to start investing in industry before others did. One might argue that reaching a certain level of agricultural productivity is a prerequisite for industrialization. While this suggestion is plausible (or at least possible), many of the societies that later failed to industrialize had already achieved a certain level of agricultural productivity and in fact were often ahead of those who later industrialized very rapidly (see Section 4.4). Thus a simple link between unfavorable agricultural conditions and the failure to take off seems to be absent.[3]

The third variant of the geography hypothesis, which has become particularly popular over the past decade, links poverty in many areas of the world to their disease burden, emphasizing that "the burden of infectious disease is . . . higher in the tropics than in the temperate zones" (Sachs, 2000, p. 32). Bloom and Sachs (1998) and Gallup and Sachs (2001, p. 91) claim that the prevalence of malaria alone reduces the annual growth rate of sub-Saharan African economies by as much as 2.6% a year. Such a magnitude implies that had malaria been eradicated in 1950, income per capita in sub-Saharan Africa would have been double what it is today. If we add to this the effect of other diseases, we would obtain even larger effects.

This third version of the geography hypothesis may be much more plausible than the first two, especially since the microeconomics literature shows that unhealthy individuals are less productive and perhaps less able to learn and thus accumulate human capital. I discuss both the general geography hypothesis and this specific version of it in greater detail in the next two sections. But an important caveat needs to be mentioned. The fact that the burden of disease is heavier in poor nations today is as much a consequence as a cause of poverty. European nations in the eighteenth and even nineteenth centuries were plagued by many diseases. It was the process of economic development that enabled them to eradicate these diseases and create healthier living environments. The fact that many poor countries have unhealthy environments is, at least in part, a consequence of their failure to develop economically.

4.3.3 Institutions

An alternative fundamental cause of differences in economic growth and income per capita is institutions. One problem with the institutions hypothesis is that it is somewhat difficult to define what "institutions" are. In daily usage, the word "institutions" refers to many different things, and the academic literature is sometimes not clear about its definition.

The economic historian Douglass North was awarded the Nobel Prize in economics largely because of his work emphasizing the importance of institutions in the historical development process. North (1990, p. 3) offers the following definition:

> Institutions are the rules of the game in a society or, more formally, are the humanly devised constraints that shape human interaction.

He goes on to emphasize the key implications of institutions:

> In consequence [institutions] structure incentives in human exchange, whether political, social, or economic.

This definition encapsulates the three important elements that make up institutions. First, they are humanly devised; that is, in contrast to geography, which is outside human control, institutions refer to man-made factors. Institutions are about the effect of societies' own choices on their own economic fates. Second, institutions place constraints on individual behavior. These constraints do not need to be unassailable: any law can be broken, any regulation can be ignored. Nevertheless policies, regulations, and laws that punish certain types of behavior

---

3. Ex post, one can in fact tell the opposite story: perhaps the poor nations of today had agriculturally superior land and this created a comparative advantage against industry. This is not an entirely convincing explanation either, since as discussed in Chapter 20, most less-developed economies today have lower agricultural as well as lower industrial productivity than the relatively advanced nations.

while rewarding others will naturally have an effect on behavior. And this brings us to the third important element in the definition. The constraints placed on individuals by institutions shape human interaction and affect incentives. In some deep sense, institutions, much more than the other candidate fundamental causes, are about the importance of incentives.

The reader may have already noted that the above definition makes the concept of institutions rather broad. In fact, this is precisely the sense in which I use the concept throughout this book; institutions refer to a broad cluster of arrangements that influence various economic interactions among individuals. These include economic, political, and social relations among households, individuals, and firms. The importance of political institutions, which determine the process of collective decision making in society, cannot be overstated and is the topic of analysis in Part VIII of this book.

A more natural starting point for the study of the fundamental causes of income differences across countries is in *economic institutions*, which comprise such things as the structure of property rights, the presence and (well or ill) functioning of markets, and the contractual opportunities available to individuals and firms. Economic institutions are important because they influence the structure of economic incentives in society. Without property rights, individuals do not have the incentive to invest in physical or human capital or adopt more efficient technologies. Economic institutions are also important because they ensure the allocation of resources to their most efficient uses and determine who obtains profits, revenues, and residual rights of control. When markets are missing or ignored (as was the case in many former socialist societies, for example), gains from trade go unexploited and resources are misallocated. Economic theory therefore suggests that societies with economic institutions that facilitate and encourage factor accumulation, innovation, and the efficient allocation of resources should prosper relative to societies that do not have such institutions.

The hypothesis that differences in economic institutions are a fundamental cause of different patterns of economic growth is intimately linked to the models I develop in this book. All economic models start with a specification of economic institutions, for example, the structure of markets, the set of feasible contracts and transactions, and allocations of endowments and ownership rights to individuals. Moreover, in all of these models, individuals respond to incentives. It is the economic institutions, determined broadly by the way in which individuals organize their societies, that shape these incentives. Some ways of organizing societies encourage people to innovate, take risks, save for the future, find better ways of doing things, learn and educate themselves, solve problems of collective action, and provide public goods. Others do not. Our theoretical models pinpoint what specific policy and institutional variables are important in retarding or encouraging economic growth.

Part VIII of the book develops theoretical approaches to the analysis of what constitutes "good economic institutions" that encourage physical and human capital accumulation and the development and adoption of better technologies (though good economic institutions do change with environment and time). It should already be intuitive to the reader that economic institutions that tax productivity-enhancing activities will not encourage economic growth. Economic institutions that ban innovation will not lead to technological improvements. Therefore enforcement of some basic property rights and some amount of free enterprise are indispensable. But other aspects of economic institutions matter as well. Human capital, for example, is important both for increasing productivity and for technology adoption. However, for a broad cross section of society to be able to accumulate human capital, some degree of equality of opportunity is necessary. Economic institutions that only protect the rights of a rich elite or the privileged will not achieve such equality of opportunity and will often create other distortions, potentially retarding economic growth. Chapter 14 emphasizes that the process of Schumpeterian creative destruction, in which new firms improve over and destroy incumbents, is an essential element of economic growth. Schumpeterian creative destruction requires a level playing field, so that incumbents are unable to block technological progress. Economic growth based on creative destruction therefore also requires economic institutions that guarantee some degree of equality of opportunity in the society.

Another question may have already occurred to the reader: why should any society have economic and political institutions that retard economic growth? Would it not be better for all parties to maximize the size of the national pie (level of GDP, consumption, or economic growth)? There are two possible answers to this question. The first takes us back to multiple equilibria. It may be that the members of the society cannot coordinate on the "right" (e.g., growth-enhancing) institutions. This answer is not satisfactory for the same reasons as other broad explanations based on multiple equilibria are unsatisfactory: if there exists an equilibrium institutional improvement that will make *all* members of a society richer and better off, it seems unlikely that the society will be unable to coordinate on this improvement for extended periods of time.

The second answer recognizes that there are inherent conflicts of interest within the society. There are no reforms, changes, or advances that would make everybody better off; as in the Schumpeterian creative destruction stories, each reform, change, or advance creates winners and losers. Part VIII shows that institutional explanations are intimately linked with conflicts of interest in society. Put simply, the distribution of resources cannot be separated from the aggregate economic performance of the economy—or perhaps in a more familiar form, efficiency and distribution cannot be decoupled. Institutions that fail to maximize the growth potential of an economy may nonetheless create benefits for some segments of the society, who then form a constituency in favor of these institutions. Thus to understand the sources of institutional variation we have to study the winners and losers of different institutional reforms and why, even when the institutional change in question may increase the size of the national pie, winners are unable to buy off or compensate losers, and why they are not powerful enough to overwhelm the potential losers. Such a study will not only help explain why some societies choose or end up with institutions that do not encourage economic growth, but it will also enable us to make predictions about institutional change. After all, the fact that institutions can and do change is a major difference between the institutions hypothesis and the geography and culture hypotheses. Questions about equilibrium institutions and endogenous institutional change are central for the institutions hypothesis but must be postponed until Part VIII. Here, note that the endogeneity of institutions has another important implication: the endogeneity of institutions makes empirical work on assessing the role of institutions more challenging, because it implies that the standard simultaneity biases in econometrics will be present when we look at the effect of institutions on economic outcomes.[4]

In this chapter I focus on the empirical evidence in favor of and against the various hypotheses. I argue that this evidence by and large suggests that institutional differences that societies choose and end up with are a primary determinant of their economic fortunes. The discussion below provides a summary of recent empirical work to bolster this case. Nevertheless, it is important to emphasize that luck, geography, and culture are also potentially important, and the four fundamental causes are complementary. The evidence suggests that institutions are the most important one among these four causes, but it does not deny the potential role of other factors, such as cultural influences.

4. Note also that although geography is "exogenous" in the sense that, with some notable exceptions (e.g., climate change, global warming) it is not much influenced by economic decisions, this does not make it econometrically exogenous. Geographic characteristics may still be (and in fact likely are) correlated with other factors that influence economic growth.

4.3.4 Culture

The final fundamental explanation for economic growth emphasizes the idea that different societies (or perhaps different races or ethnic groups) have distinct cultures because of different shared experiences or different religions. Culture is viewed by some social scientists as a key determinant of the values, preferences, and beliefs of individuals and societies and, the argument goes, these differences play a key role in shaping economic performance.

At some level, culture can be thought of as influencing equilibrium outcomes for a given set of institutions. Recall that in the presence of multiple equilibria, there is a central question of equilibrium selection. For example, in the simple game discussed in Section 4.3.1, culture may be one of the factors determining whether individuals coordinate on the high- or the low-investment equilibrium. "Good" cultures can be thought of as ways of coordinating on better (Pareto-superior) equilibria. Naturally, the arguments discussed above—that an entire society being stuck in an equilibrium in which all individuals are worse off than in an alternative equilibrium is implausible—would militate against the importance of this particular role of culture. Alternatively, different cultures generate different sets of beliefs about how people behave, and these distinctions can alter the set of equilibria for a given specification of institutions (e.g., some beliefs allow punishment strategies to be used whereas others do not).

The most famous link between culture and economic development is that proposed by Max Weber (1930, p. 11), who argued that the origins of industrialization in Western Europe could be traced to a cultural factor—the Protestant reformation and particularly the rise of Calvinism. Interestingly, Weber provided a clear summary of his views as a comment on Montesquieu's arguments:

> Montesquieu says of the English that they "had progressed the farthest of all peoples of the world in three important things: in piety, in commerce, and in freedom." Is it not possible that their commercial superiority and their adaptation to free political institutions are connected in some way with that record of piety which Montesquieu ascribes to them?

Weber argued that English piety, in particular, Protestantism, was an important driver of capitalist development. Protestantism led to a set of beliefs that emphasized hard work, thrift, and saving. It also interpreted economic success as consistent with, even as signaling, being chosen by God. Weber contrasted these characteristics of Protestantism with those of other religions, such as Catholicism, which, Weber argued, did not promote capitalism. More recently, similar ideas have been applied to emphasize different implications of other religions. Many historians and scholars have argued that the rise of capitalism, the process of economic growth, and industrialization are intimately linked to cultural and religious beliefs. Similar ideas have been proposed as explanations for why Latin American countries are relatively poor (because of their Iberian culture), while their North American neighbors are more prosperous (because of their Anglo-Saxon culture).

A related argument, originating in anthropology, argues that societies may become "dysfunctional" because their cultural values and their system of beliefs do not encourage cooperation. An original and insightful version of this argument is developed in Banfield's (1958) analysis of poverty in southern Italy. His ideas were later popularized by Putnam (1993), who suggested the notion of social capital, as a stand-in for cultural attitudes that lead to cooperation and other "good outcomes." Many versions of these ideas are presented in one form or another in the economics literature as well.

Two challenges confront theories of economic growth based on culture. The first is the difficulty of measuring culture. While there has been some progress in measuring certain cultural characteristics with self-reported beliefs and attitudes in social surveys, simply stating that the north of Italy is rich because it has good social capital, while the south is poor because it has poor social capital runs the risk of circularity. The second difficulty confronting cultural explanations is accounting for growth miracles, such as those of South Korea and Singapore. As mentioned above, if some Asian cultural values are responsible for the successful growth experiences of these countries, it becomes difficult to explain why these Asian values did not lead to growth before. Why do these values not spur economic growth in North Korea? If Asian values are important for Chinese growth today, why did they not lead to a better economic performance under Mao's dictatorship? Both of these challenges are, in principle, surmountable. One may be able to develop models of culture, with better mapping to data, and also with an associated theory of how culture may change rapidly under certain circumstances. While possible in principle, such theories have not been developed. Moreover, the evidence presented in the next section suggests that cultural effects are not the major force behind the large differences in economic growth experienced by many countries over the past few centuries. In this light, culture may be best viewed as a complement to institutional factors, for example, acting as one of the forces responsible for institutional persistence.

4.4 The Effect of Institutions on Economic Growth

I now argue that there is convincing empirical support for the hypothesis that differences in economic institutions, more than luck, geography, or culture, cause differences in incomes per capita. Let us start by looking at the simplest correlation between a measure of economic institutions and income per capita.

Figure 4.1 shows the cross-country correlation between the log of GDP per capita in 1995 and a broad measure of property rights, protection against expropriation risk, averaged over the period 1985 to 1995. The data on this measure of economic institutions come from Political Risk Services, a private company that assesses the expropriation risk that foreign investments face in different countries. These data are not perfect. They reflect the subjective assessments of some analysts about how secure property rights are. Nevertheless, they are useful for our purposes. First, they emphasize the security of property rights, which is an essential aspect of economic institutions, especially in regard to their effect on economic incentives. Second, these measures are purchased by businessmen contemplating investment in these countries, thus they reflect the market assessment of security of property rights.

Figure 4.1 shows that countries with more secure property rights—thus better economic institutions—have higher average incomes. One should not interpret the correlation in this figure as depicting a causal relationship—that is, as establishing that secure property rights cause prosperity. First, the correlation might reflect reverse causation; it may be that only countries that are sufficiently wealthy can afford to enforce property rights. Second and more importantly, there might be a problem of omitted variable bias. It could be something else, for example, geography or culture, that explains both why countries are poor and why they have insecure property rights. Thus if omitted factors determine institutions and incomes, we would spuriously infer the existence of a causal relationship between economic institutions and incomes when in fact no such relationship exists. This is the standard identification problem in econometrics resulting from simultaneity or omitted variable biases. Finally, security of property rights—or other proxy measures of economic institutions—are themselves equilibrium outcomes, presumably resulting from the underlying political institutions and political conflict. While this last point is important, a satisfactory discussion of institutional equilibria necessitates the modeling of political economy interactions and must wait until Part VIII.

To further illustrate these potential identification problems, suppose that climate or geography matter for economic performance. In fact, a simple scatterplot shows a positive association

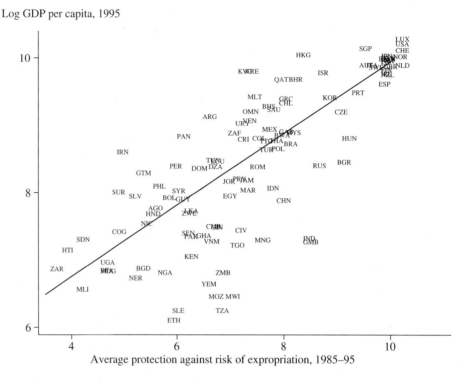

FIGURE 4.1 Relationship between economic institutions, as measured by average expropriation risk between 1985 and 1995, and GDP per capita.

between latitude (the absolute value of distance from the equator) and income per capita, which is consistent with the views of Montesquieu and other proponents of the geography hypothesis. Interestingly, Montesquieu not only claimed that warm climate makes people lazy and thus unproductive, but he also asserted that it made them unfit to be governed by democracy. Thus, according to Montesquieu, despotism is the "equilibrium" political system in warm climates. Therefore a potential explanation for the patterns in Figure 4.1 is that there is an omitted factor, geography, which explains both economic institutions and economic performance. Ignoring this potential third factor would lead to mistaken conclusions.

Even if Montesquieu's claim appears both unrealistic and condescending to our modern sensibilities, the general point should be taken seriously: the correlations depicted in Figure 4.1, and for that matter the correlations in Figure 4.2, do not necessarily reflect causal relationships. As noted in the context of the effect of religion or social capital on economic performance, these types of scatterplots, correlations, or their multidimensional version in ordinary least squares regressions, *cannot* establish causality. Doubt about the effect of omitted variables will almost always remain, even for careful regression analyses.

How can we overcome the challenge of establishing a causal relationship between (economic) institutions and economic outcomes? The answer to this question is to specify econometric approaches based on plausible identifying restrictions. This can be done by estimating structural econometric models or using more reduced-form approaches, based on instrumental variable strategies. We do not currently know enough about the evolution of economic institutions and their impact on economic outcomes to be able to specify and estimate fully structural econometric models. Thus as a first step, we can look at more reduced-form evidence that might still be informative about the causal relationship between institutions and economic growth.

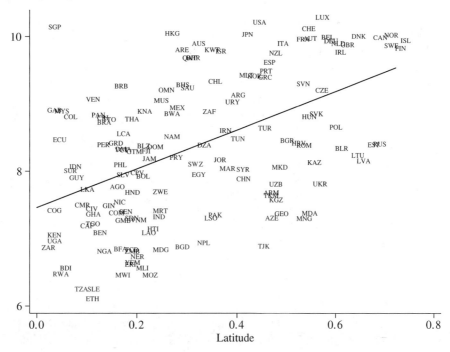

FIGURE 4.2 Relationship between latitude (distance of capital from the equator) and income per capita in 1995.

One way of doing so is to learn from history, in particular from the natural experiments—unusual historical events during which, while other fundamental causes of economic growth are held constant, institutions change because of potentially exogenous reasons. I now discuss lessons from two such natural experiments.

4.4.1 The Korean Experiment

Until the end of World War II, Korea was under Japanese occupation. Korean independence came shortly after the war. The major fear of the United States during this time was the takeover of the entire Korean peninsula either by the Soviet Union or by communist forces under the control of the former guerrilla fighter, Kim Il Sung. U.S. authorities therefore supported the influential nationalist leader Syngman Rhee, who was in favor of separation rather than a united communist Korea. Elections in the South were held in May 1948, amid a widespread boycott by Koreans opposed to separation. The newly elected representatives proceeded to draft a new constitution and established the Republic of Korea to the south of the 38th parallel. The North became the Democratic People's Republic of Korea, under the control of Kim Il Sung.

These two independent countries organized themselves in radically different ways and adopted completely different sets of (economic and political) institutions. The North followed the model of Soviet communism and the Chinese Revolution in abolishing private property in land and capital. Economic decisions were not mediated by the market but by the communist state. The South instead maintained a system of private property and capitalist economic institutions.

Before these institutional changes, North and South Korea shared the same history and cultural roots. In fact, Korea exhibited an unparalleled degree of ethnic, linguistic, cultural, geographic, and economic homogeneity. There are few geographic distinctions between the North and South, and both share the same disease environment. Moreover, before the separation the North and the South were at the same level of development. If anything, there was slightly more industrialization in the North. Maddison (2001) estimates that at the time of separation, North and South Korea had approximately the same income per capita.

We can therefore think of the splitting of the Koreas 60 years ago as a "natural experiment" that can be used to identify the causal influence of institutions on prosperity. Korea was split into two, with the two halves organized in radically different ways, while geography, culture, and many other potential determinants of economic prosperity were held constant. Thus any differences in economic performance can plausibly be attributed to differences in institutions.

In the 60 years following the split, the two Koreas have experienced dramatically diverging paths of economic development. By the late 1960s South Korea was transformed into one of the Asian "miracle" economies, experiencing one of the most rapid surges of economic prosperity in history. Meanwhile, North Korea stagnated. By 2000 the level of income per capita in South Korea was $16,100, while in North Korea it was only $1,000. There is only one plausible explanation for the radically different economic experiences of the two Koreas after 1950: their different institutions led to divergent economic outcomes. In this context, it is noteworthy that the two Koreas not only shared the same geography but also the same culture, so that neither geographic nor cultural differences could have much to do with the divergent paths of the two Koreas. Of course one can say that South Korea was lucky while the North was unlucky (even though this difference was not due to any kind of multiple equilibria but was a result of the imposition of different institutions). Nevertheless, the perspective of luck is unlikely to be particularly useful in this context, since what is remarkable is the persistence of the dysfunctional North Korean institutions. Despite convincing evidence that the North Korean system has been generating poverty and famine, the leaders of the Communist Party in North Korea have opted to use all the means available to them to maintain their regime.

However convincing on its own terms, the evidence from this natural experiment is not sufficient for the purposes of establishing the importance of economic institutions as the primary factor shaping cross-country differences in economic prosperity. First, this is only one case, and in controlled experiments in the natural sciences, a relatively large sample is essential. Second, here we have an example of an extreme case, the difference between a market-oriented economy and an extreme communist one. Few social scientists today would deny that a lengthy period of totalitarian centrally planned rule has significant economic costs. And yet many might argue that differences in economic institutions among capitalist economies or among democracies are not the major factor leading to differences in their economic trajectories. To establish the major role of economic institutions in the prosperity and poverty of nations we need to look at a larger-scale "natural experiment" in institutional divergence.

4.4.2   The Colonial Experiment: The Reversal of Fortune

The colonization of much of the world by Europeans provides such a large-scale natural experiment. Beginning in the early fifteenth century and especially after 1492, Europeans conquered many other nations. The colonization experience transformed the institutions in many diverse lands conquered or controlled by Europeans. Most importantly, Europeans imposed different sets of institutions in various parts of their global empire, as exemplified most sharply by the contrast of the institutional structure that developed in the northeastern United States, based on smallholder private property and democracy, versus the institutions in the

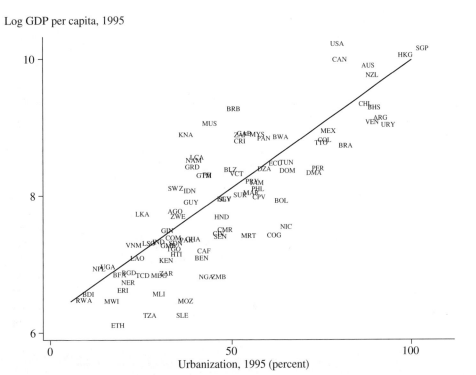

FIGURE 4.3 Urbanization and income, 1995.

Caribbean plantation economies, based on repression and slavery. As a result, while geography was held constant, Europeans initiated significant changes in the economic institutions of different societies.

The impact of European colonialism on economic institutions is perhaps most dramatically conveyed by a single fact—historical evidence shows that there has been a remarkable reversal of fortune in economic prosperity within former European colonies. Societies like the Mughals in India and the Aztecs and Incas in the Americas were among the richest civilizations in 1500; yet the nation-states that now exist in their boundaries are among the poorer nations of today. In contrast, countries occupying the territories of the less-developed civilizations of North America, New Zealand, and Australia are now much richer than those in the lands of the Mughals, Aztecs, and Incas.

The reversal of fortune is not confined to such comparisons. To document the reversal more broadly, we need a proxy for prosperity 500 years ago. Fortunately, urbanization rates and population density can serve the role of such proxies. Only societies with a certain level of productivity in agriculture and a relatively developed system of transport and commerce can sustain large urban centers and a dense population. Figure 4.3 shows the relationship between income per capita and urbanization (fraction of the population living in urban centers with more than 5,000 inhabitants) in 1995 and demonstrates that even today, long after industrialization, there is a significant relationship between urbanization and prosperity.

Naturally, high rates of urbanization do not mean that the majority of the population lived in prosperity. In fact, before the twentieth century urban areas were often centers of poverty and ill health. Nevertheless, urbanization is a good proxy for average prosperity and closely corresponds to the GDP per capita measures we are using to look at prosperity today. Another

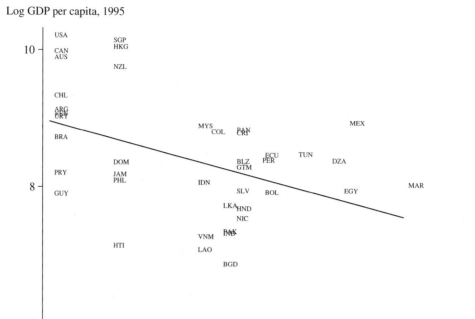

FIGURE 4.4 Reversal of fortune: urbanization in 1500 versus income per capita in 1995 among the former European colonies.

variable that is useful for measuring pre-industrial prosperity is the density of the population, which is closely related to urbanization.

Figures 4.4 and 4.5 show the relationship between income per capita today and urbanization rates and (log) population density in 1500 for the sample of (former) European colonies. I focus on 1500 since it is before European colonization had an effect on any of these societies. A strong negative relationship, indicating a reversal in the rankings in terms of economic prosperity between 1500 and today, is clear in both figures. In fact, the figures show that in 1500 the temperate areas were generally less prosperous than the tropical ones, but this pattern was also reversed by the twentieth century.

There is something extraordinary and unusual about this reversal. A wealth of evidence shows that after the initial spread of agriculture, there was remarkable persistence in urbanization and population density for all countries, including those that were subsequently colonized by Europeans. Extending the data on urbanization to earlier periods shows that both among former European colonies and noncolonies, urbanization rates and prosperity persisted for 500 years or longer. Though there are prominent examples of the decline and fall of empires, such as ancient Egypt, Athens, Rome, Carthage, and Venice, the overall pattern was one of persistence. Reversal was also not the general pattern in the world after 1500. When we look at Europe as a whole or at the entire world excluding the former European colonies, there is no evidence of a similar reversal between 1500 and 1995.

There is therefore no reason to think that the pattern in Figures 4.4 and 4.5 is some sort of natural reversion to the mean. Instead, the reversal of fortune among the former European colonies reflects something unusual, something related to the intervention that these countries experienced. The major intervention, of course, was related to the change in institutions. Not

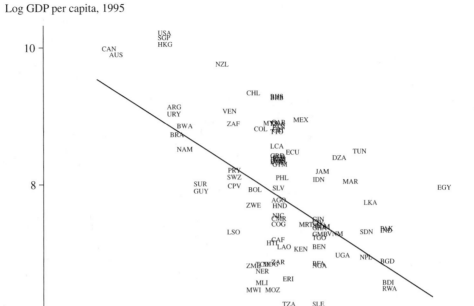

FIGURE 4.5 Reversal of fortune: population density in 1500 versus income per capita in 1995 among the former European colonies.

only did the Europeans impose a different order in almost all countries they conquered, there were also tremendous differences among the types of institutions they imposed in the different colonies.[5] These institutional differences among the former colonies are likely at the root of the reversal in economic fortunes. This conclusion is bolstered further when we look at the timing and the nature of the reversal. Acemoglu, Johnson, and Robinson (2002) show that the reversal took place largely in the nineteenth century and appears to be closely connected to industrialization.

These patterns are clearly inconsistent with the simplest and most common version of the geography hypothesis. In 1500, the countries in the tropics were relatively prosperous; today it is the reverse. Thus it is implausible to base a theory of relative prosperity on the intrinsic poverty of the tropics, climate, disease environments, or other fixed characteristics.

Nevertheless, following Diamond (1997), one could propose what Acemoglu, Johnson, and Robinson (2002) call a "sophisticated geography hypothesis," that geography matters but in a time-varying manner. For example, Europeans created latitude-specific technologies, such as heavy metal ploughs, that only worked in temperate latitudes and not with tropical soils. Thus when Europe conquered most of the world after 1492, they introduced specific technologies that functioned in some places (the United States, Argentina, Australia) but not

---

5. In some instances, including those in Central America and India, the colonial institutions were built on the precolonial institutions. In these cases, a major determinant of early institutions was whether Europeans maintained and further developed existing hierarchical institutions, such as those in the Aztec, Inca, or the Mughal empires, or whether they introduced or imposed political and economic institutions encouraging broad-based participation and investment.

others (Peru, Mexico, West Africa). However, the timing of the reversal, which was largely in the late eighteenth and nineteenth centuries, is inconsistent with the most plausible types of sophisticated geography hypotheses. Europeans did bring new technologies, but the timing of the reversal implies that the crucial technologies were industrial, not agricultural, and it is difficult to see why industrial technologies should not function in the tropics (and in fact, they have functioned quite successfully in tropical Singapore and Hong Kong).

Similar considerations weigh against the culture hypothesis. Although culture changes slowly, the colonial experiment was sufficiently radical to have caused major modifications in the cultures of many countries that fell under European rule. In addition, the destruction of many indigenous populations and immigration from Europe are likely to have created new cultures or at least modified existing ones in major ways. Nevertheless, the culture hypothesis does not provide a natural explanation for the reversal and has nothing to say about the timing of the reversal. Moreover, as discussed below, econometric models that control for the effect of institutions on income do not show a major effect of religion or culture on prosperity.

The importance of luck is also limited. The different institutions imposed by the Europeans were not random. They were instead very much related to the conditions they encountered in the colonies. In other words, the types of institutions that were imposed and developed in the former colonies were endogenous (equilibrium) outcomes that we need to study.

4.4.3 The Reversal and the Institutions Hypothesis

Is the reversal of fortune consistent with a dominant role for economic institutions in comparative development? The answer is yes. In fact, once we recognize the variation in economic institutions created by colonization, we see that the reversal of fortune is what the institutions hypothesis predicts.

The evidence in Acemoglu, Johnson, and Robinson (2002) shows a close connection between initial population density, urbanization, and the creation of good economic institutions. In particular, the evidence points out that, other things being equal, the higher the initial population density or the greater the initial urbanization, the worse were subsequent institutions, including both institutions right after independence and also institutions today. Figures 4.6 and 4.7 illustrate these relationships using the same measure of current economic institutions as in Figure 4.1, protection against expropriation risk today. They document that the relatively densely settled and highly urbanized colonies ended up with worse institutions, while sparsely settled and nonurbanized areas received an influx of European migrants and developed institutions protecting the property rights of a broad cross section of society. European colonialism therefore led to an institutional reversal, in the sense that the previously richer and more densely settled places ended up with "worse" institutions. The institutional reversal does not mean that institutions had been better in the previously more densely settled areas. It only implies a tendency for the relatively poorer and less densely settled areas to end up with more growth-enhancing institutions than previously rich and more densely settled areas had.

As discussed in footnote 5 above, it is possible that the Europeans did not actively introduce institutions discouraging economic progress in many of these places but inherited them from previous indigenous civilizations. The structure of the Mughal, Aztec, and Inca empires were already very hierarchical, with power concentrated in the hands of narrowly based ruling elites. These empires were structured to extract resources from the majority of the population for the benefit of a minority. Often Europeans simply took over these existing institutions. What is important in any case is that in densely settled and relatively developed places it was in the interests of the Europeans to have institutions facilitating the extraction of resources, without any respect for the property rights of the majority of the populace. In contrast, in the sparsely

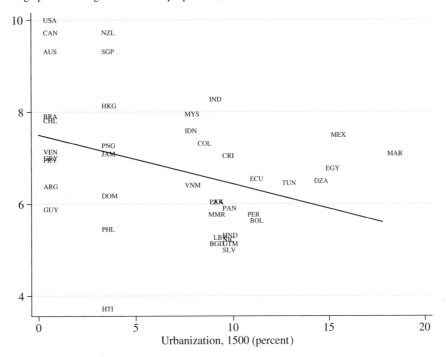

Average protection against risk of expropriation, 1985–95

FIGURE 4.6   The institutional reversal: urbanization in 1500 and economic institutions today among the former European colonies.

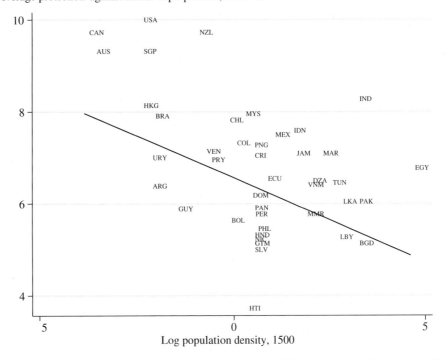

Average protection against risk of expropriation, 1985–95

FIGURE 4.7   The institutional reversal: population density in 1500 and economic institutions today among the former European colonies.

settled areas it was in their interests to develop institutions protecting property rights. These incentives led to an institutional reversal.

The institutional reversal, combined with the institutions hypothesis, predicts the reversal of fortune: relatively rich places ended up with relatively worse economic institutions. And if these institutions are important, we should see these countries become relatively poor over time.

Moreover, the institutions hypothesis is consistent with the timing of the reversal. Recall that the institutions hypothesis links incentives to invest in physical and human capital and in technology to economic institutions and argues that economic prosperity results from these investments. Therefore we expect economic institutions to play a more important role in shaping economic outcomes when there are major new investment opportunities—thus creating a greater need for new entrepreneurs and for the process of creative destruction. The opportunity to industrialize was the major investment opportunity of the nineteenth century. As documented in Chapter 1, countries that are rich today, among both the former European colonies and other countries, are those that industrialized successfully during this critical period. The timing of the reversal, in the late eighteenth and nineteenth centuries, is consistent with this perspective.

The explanation for the reversal that emerges from the discussion so far is one in which the economic institutions in various colonies were shaped by Europeans to serve their own (economic) interests. Moreover, because conditions and endowments differed among colonies, Europeans created disparate economic institutions, which, in many cases, still persist and continue to shape economic performance. Why did Europeans introduce better institutions in previously poor and unsettled areas than in previously rich and densely settled areas? Without going into details, a number of obvious ideas that have emerged from the research in this area can be mentioned.

Europeans were more likely to introduce or maintain economic institutions facilitating the extraction of resources in areas where they stood to benefit from this extraction. This typically meant areas controlled by a small group of Europeans as well as areas offering resources to be extracted. These resources included gold and silver; valuable agricultural commodities, such as sugar; but most importantly, what is perhaps the most valuable commodity of all, human labor. In places with a large indigenous population, Europeans could exploit the population in various ways, using taxes, tributes, or employment as forced labor in mines or plantations. This type of colonization was incompatible with institutions providing economic or civil rights to the majority of the population. Consequently, a more developed civilization and a denser population structure made it more profitable for the Europeans to introduce worse economic institutions.

In contrast, in places with little to extract, and in sparsely settled places where the Europeans themselves became the majority of the population, it was in their interests to introduce economic institutions protecting their own property rights.

4.4.4 Settlements, Mortality, and Development

The initial conditions of the colonies emphasized so far—indigenous population density and urbanization—are not the only factors that affected the Europeans' colonization strategy. In addition, the disease environments differed markedly among the colonies, with obvious consequences on the attractiveness of European settlement. As noted above, when Europeans settled, they established institutions that they themselves had to live under, so whether Europeans could settle had a major effect on the subsequent path of institutional development. In other words, the disease environment 200 or more years ago, especially the prevalence of malaria and yellow fever (which crucially affected European mortality), likely influenced the paths of institutional and economic development in the former European colonies. If, in addition, the disease environment of colonial times affects economic outcomes today only through its effect on institutions, then this historical disease environment can be used as an exogenous source of variation in current institutions. From an econometric point of view, this disease environment then corresponds to a valid instrument to estimate the causal effect of economic institutions on prosperity. Although mortality rates of potential European settlers could be correlated with indigenous mortality, which may affect income today, in practice local populations had developed much greater immunity to malaria and yellow fever. Acemoglu, Johnson, and Robinson (2001) present a variety of evidence suggesting that the major effect of European settler mortality is through institutions.

In particular, Acemoglu, Johnson, and Robinson's argument can be summarized as follows:

$$
\begin{array}{c} \text{(Potential) settler} \\ \text{mortality} \end{array} \Rightarrow \text{Settlements} \Rightarrow \begin{array}{c} \text{Early} \\ \text{institutions} \end{array} \Rightarrow \begin{array}{c} \text{Current} \\ \text{institutions} \end{array} \Rightarrow \begin{array}{c} \text{Current} \\ \text{performance} \end{array}
$$

That is, the European colonization strategy was influenced by the feasibility of settlements. Europeans were more likely to develop institutions providing property rights protection and basic political rights to the majority of the population in places where they themselves would settle (and become this majority), and they were unlikely to settle in lands where they faced very high mortality rates. Because the colonial state and institutions persisted to some degree, former European colonies that had disease environments more favorable to Europeans are also more likely to have better institutions today.

Based on this reasoning, Acemoglu, Johnson, and Robinson (2001) use the mortality rates expected by the first European settlers in the colonies as an instrument for current institutions in a sample of former European colonies. Their estimates of instrumental variables show a large and robust effect of institutions on economic growth and income per capita. Figures 4.8 and 4.9 provide an overview of the evidence. Figure 4.8 shows the cross-sectional relationship between income per capita and the measure of economic institutions depicted in Figure 4.1, protection against expropriation risk. It shows a strong relationship between the historical mortality risk faced by Europeans and the current extent to which property rights are enforced. A bivariate regression yields an R^2 of 0.26. It also shows that there were very large differences in European mortality. Countries such as Australia, New Zealand, and the United States were very healthy, and existing evidence suggests that life expectancy in Australia and New Zealand was in fact greater than in Britain. In contrast, Europeans faced extremely high mortality rates in Africa and parts of Central America and Southeast Asia. These differential mortality rates were largely due to tropical diseases, such as malaria and yellow fever, and at the time it was not understood how these diseases arose or how they could be prevented or cured.

Figures 4.8 and 4.9 already show that if the exclusion restriction—that the mortality rates of potential European settlers should have no effect on current economic outcomes other than through institutions—is valid, then there is a large impact of economic institutions on economic performance. This effect is documented in detail in Acemoglu, Johnson, and Robinson (2001), who present a range of robustness checks confirming this result. Their estimates suggest that most of the gap between rich and poor countries today is due to differences in economic institutions. For example, the evidence suggests that more than 75% of the income gap between relatively rich and relatively poor countries can be explained by differences in their economic institutions (as proxied by the security of property rights). Equally important, the evidence indicates that once the effect of institutions is estimated by this methodology, there appears to be no effect of geographic variables: latitude, whether a country is landlocked, and the current disease environment appear to have little effect on current economic outcomes. This evidence

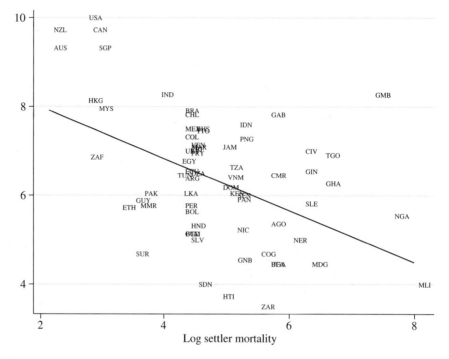

FIGURE 4.8 Relationship between mortality of potential European settlers and current economic institutions.

again suggests that institutional differences across countries are a major determinant of their economic fortunes, while geographic differences are much less important.

These results also provide an interpretation for why Figure 4.2 showed a significant correlation between latitude and income per capita. This correlation is accounted for by the association between latitude and the determinants of European colonization strategies. Europeans did not have immunity to tropical diseases during the colonial period, and thus settler colonies tended, other things being equal, to be established in temperate latitudes. Thus the historical creation of economic institutions was correlated with latitude. Without considering the role of economic institutions, one would find a spurious relationship between latitude and income per capita. However, once the influence of economic institutions is controlled for, this relationship disappears, and there appears to be no causal effect of geography on prosperity today.[6]

4.4.5 Culture, Colonial Identity, and Economic Development

One might think that culture played an important role in the colonial experience, since Europeans not only brought new institutions, but also their own cultures. European culture might have affected the economic development of former European colonies through three different channels. First, as already mentioned, the cultures of former European colonies are likely to have been affected by the identity of the colonizing powers. For example, the British may have

---

6. However, this conclusion does not imply that geography did not play an important role in the process of economic development before 1500.

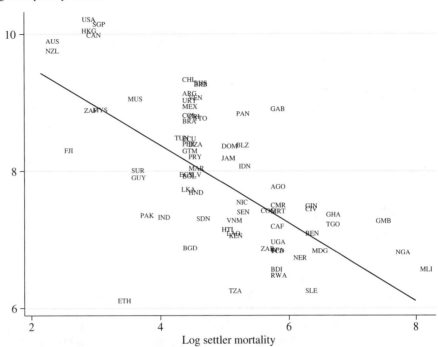

FIGURE 4.9 Relationship between mortality of potential European settlers and GDP per capita, 1995.

implanted a "superior" Anglo-Saxon culture into colonies such as Australia and the United States relative to the Iberian inheritance in Latin America. Second, European colonists may have brought a culture, work ethic, or set of beliefs that were conducive to prosperity in the lands that they conquered. Finally, Europeans also brought different religions with potentially different implications for prosperity.

Yet the econometric evidence in Acemoglu, Johnson, and Robinson (2001) is not consistent with any of these views. Similar to the evidence related to geographical variables, the econometric strategy discussed above suggests that, once the effect of economic institutions is taken into account, the identity of the colonial power, the contemporary fraction of Europeans in the population, and the proportions of the populations of various religions do not appear to have a direct effect on economic growth and income per capita.

These econometric results are supported by historical examples. Although no Spanish colony has been as successful economically as the United States, many former British colonies, such as those in Africa, India and Bangladesh, are poor today. It is also clear that the British in no way simply re-created British institutions in their colonies. For example, by 1619 the North American colony of Virginia had a representative assembly with universal male suffrage, something that did not arrive in Britain itself until 1919. Another telling example is that of Providence Island in the Caribbean. While the Puritan values are often credited with the arrival of democracy and equality of opportunity in the northeastern United States, the Puritan colony in Providence Island quickly became just like any other Caribbean slave colony despite its Puritanical inheritance.

Similarly, even though the seventeenth-century Dutch had perhaps the best domestic economic institutions in the world, their colonies in Southeast Asia ended up with institutions designed for the extraction of resources, providing little economic or civil rights to the indigenous population. These colonies consequently experienced slow growth relative to other countries.

Overall, the evidence does not appear to be consistent with a major role of geography, religion, or culture transmitted by the identity of the colonizer or the presence of Europeans. Instead, differences in economic institutions appear to be the robust causal factor underlying the differences in income per capita across countries. Institutions therefore appear to be the most important fundamental cause of income differences and long-run growth.

4.5 What Types of Institutions?

As already noted, the notion of institutions used in this chapter and in much of the literature is rather broad. It encompasses different types of social arrangements, laws, regulations, enforcement of property rights, and so on. One may, perhaps rightly, complain that we are learning relatively little by emphasizing the importance of such a broad cluster of institutions. It is therefore important to try to understand what types of institutions are most important for our purpose. Such a study will not only be useful in our empirical analysis of fundamental causes, but can provide us with a better sense of what types of models to develop to link fundamental causes to growth mechanics and to ultimate economic outcomes.

There is relatively little work on unbundling the broad cluster of institutions to understand what specific types of institutions might be important for economic outcomes. Much of this type of work remains to be done. Here it is useful to briefly mention some recent existing research attempting to distinguish the impact of contracting institutions from the influence of property rights institutions. One of the important roles of institutions is to facilitate contracting between lenders and borrowers or between different firms. Such contracting is only possible if laws, courts, and regulations uphold contracts in an appropriate way. Let us refer to institutional arrangements of this sort that support private contracts as "contracting institutions." The other cluster of institutions emphasized above relates to those constraining government and elite expropriation. Let us refer to these as "property rights institution" (because they potentially protect the property rights of a broad cross section of society). Although in many situations contracting and property rights institutions are intimately linked, they are nonetheless conceptually different. While contracting institutions regulate horizontal relationships in society between regular citizens, property rights institutions are about vertical relationships, that is, the protection of citizens against the power of elites, politicians, and privileged groups. These two sets of institutions are potentially distinct and can thus have distinct effects.

Acemoglu and Johnson (2005) investigate the relative roles of these two sets of institutions. Their strategy is again to make use of the natural experiments of colonial history. What helps this particular unbundling exercise is that in the sample of former European colonies, the legal system imposed by colonial powers appears to have a strong effect on contracting institutions but little influence on the available measures of property rights institutions. At the same time, both mortality rates for potential European settlers and population density in 1500 have a large effect on current property rights institutions and no impact on contracting institutions. Using these different sources of variation in the sample of former European colonies, it is possible to estimate the separate effects of contracting and property rights institutions.

The empirical evidence estimating the different sources of variation in colonial history finds that property rights institutions are more important for current economic outcomes than are contracting institutions. Countries with greater constraints on politicians and elites and more protection against expropriation by these powerful groups appear to have substantially higher long-run growth rates and higher levels of current income. They also have significantly greater investment levels and generate more credit for the private sector. In contrast, the role of contracting institutions is more limited. Once the effects of property rights institutions are controlled for, contracting institutions seem to have no impact on income per capita, the ratio of investment to GDP, and the ratio of private credit to GDP. Contracting institutions appear to have some effect on stock market development, however.

These results suggest that contracting institutions affect the form of financial intermediation but have less impact on economic growth and investment. It seems that economies can function in the face of weak contracting institutions without disastrous consequences, but not in the presence of a significant risk of expropriation from the government or other powerful groups. A possible interpretation is that private contracts or other reputation-based mechanisms can, at least in part, alleviate problems originating from weak contracting institutions. For example, when it is more difficult for lenders to collect on their loans, interest rates increase, banks that can monitor effectively play a more important role, or reputation-based credit relationships may emerge. In contrast, property rights institutions relate to the relationship between the state and its citizens. When there are no checks on the state, politicians, and elites, private citizens do not have the security of property rights necessary for investment.

Nevertheless, in interpreting the evidence in Acemoglu and Johnson (2005), one should also bear in mind that the sources of variation in income per capita and investment rates identifying the different effects of contracting and property rights institutions relate to the large differences discussed in Chapter 1. It is possible that contracting institutions have modest effects that are hard to detect when looking at countries with 30-fold differences in income per capita. Therefore, this evidence should be interpreted as suggesting that contracting institutions are less important in generating the large differences in economic development compared to property rights institutions, not necessarily as suggesting that contracting institutions do not matter for economic outcomes.

4.6 Disease and Development

The evidence presented in Section 4.4 already militates against a major role for geographic factors in economic development. One version of the geography hypothesis deserves further analysis, however. A variety of evidence suggests that unhealthy individuals are less productive and often less successful in acquiring human capital. Could the differences in the disease environments across countries have an important effect on economic development? Could the burden of disease be a major factor in explaining the very large income differences across countries? A recent paper by David Weil (2007), for example, argues that the framework used in the previous chapter, with physical capital, human capital, and technology, should be augmented by including health capital. In other words, the aggregate production function may take the form $F(K, H, Q, A)$, where H denotes efficiency units of labor (human capital as conventionally measured), while Q is health capital. Weil suggests a methodology for measuring the contribution of health capital to productivity from microestimates and argues that differences in health capital emerge as an important factor in accounting for cross-country differences in income levels.

The idea that the low productivity of less-developed nations is partly due to the unhealthy state of their workforces has obvious appeal. Existing econometric evidence shows that it has some empirical validity as well. But does it imply that geographic factors are an important fundamental cause of economic growth? Not necessarily. As already mentioned, the burden of disease is endogenous. Today's unhealthy nations are unhealthy precisely because they are poor and are unable to invest in health care, clean water, and other health-improving technologies. After all, much of Europe was unhealthy and suffering from short life expectancy only 200

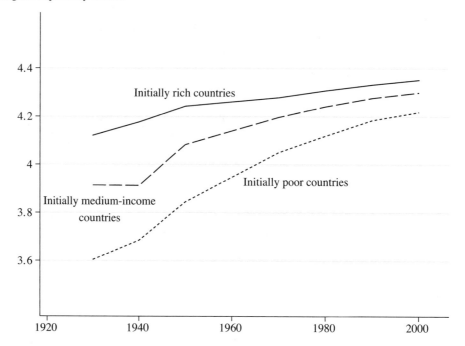

FIGURE 4.10   Evolution of life expectancy at birth among initially poor, initially middle-income, and initially rich countries, 1940–2000.

years ago. This changed *with* economic growth. In this sense, even if health capital is a useful concept and does contribute to accounting for cross-country income differences, it may itself be a proximate cause that is affected by other factors.

A recent paper by Acemoglu and Johnson (2007) directly investigates the impact of changes in disease burdens on economic development. They exploit the large improvements in life expectancy, particularly among the relatively poor countries, that took place starting in the 1940s. These health improvements were the direct consequence of significant international health interventions, more effective public health measures, and the introduction of new chemicals and drugs. More important for the purposes of understanding the effect of disease on economic growth, these health improvements were by and large exogenous from the viewpoint of individual nations. Moreover, their impact on specific countries also varied, depending on whether the country in question was affected by the specific diseases for which the cures and drugs had become internationally available. The impact of these health improvements was major, in fact so significant that it may deserve to be called the "international epidemiological transition," since it led to an unprecedented improvement in life expectancy in a large number of countries. Figure 4.10 shows this unprecedented convergence in life expectancy by plotting life expectancy in countries that were initially (circa 1940) poor, middle income, and rich. It illustrates that while in the 1930s life expectancy was low in many poor and middle-income countries, this transition brought their levels of life expectancy close to those prevailing in richer parts of the world. As a consequence of these developments, health conditions in many parts of the less-developed world today, though still in dire need of improvement, are significantly better than the corresponding health conditions were in the West at the same stage of development.

The international epidemiological transition allows a promising empirical strategy to isolate potentially exogenous changes in health conditions. The effects of the international epi-

Log GDP per capita

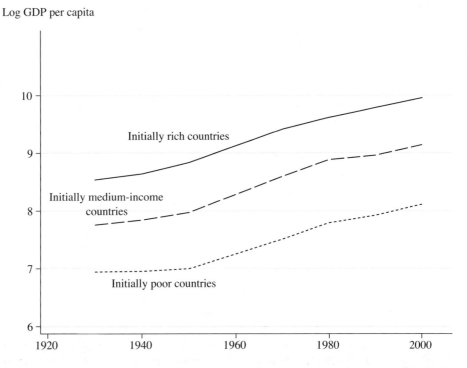

FIGURE 4.11 Evolution of GDP per capita among initially poor, initially middle-income, and initially rich countries, 1940–2000.

demiological transition on a country's life expectancy were related to the extent to which its population was initially (circa 1940) affected by various specific diseases, for example, tuberculosis, malaria, and pneumonia, and to the timing of the various health interventions. This reasoning suggests that potentially exogenous variation in the health conditions of the country can be measured by calculating a measure of predicted mortality, driven by the interaction of baseline cross-country disease prevalence with global intervention dates for specific diseases. Acemoglu and Johnson (2007) show that such measures of predicted mortality have a large and robust effect on changes in life expectancy starting in 1940 but have *no* effect on changes in life expectancy prior to this date (that is, before the key interventions). This observation suggests that the large increases in life expectancy experienced by many countries after 1940 were in fact related to the global health interventions.

Not surprisingly, Acemoglu and Johnson (2007) find that predicted mortality and the changes in life expectancy that it causes have a fairly large effect on population; a 1% increase in life expectancy is related to an approximately 1.3–1.8% increase in population. However, somewhat more surprisingly, they also find no evidence of a positive effect on GDP per capita. Figure 4.11 provides an aggregated version of this evidence. It shows no convergence in income per capita among initially poor, initially middle-income, and initially rich countries.

Why did the very significant increases in life expectancy and health not cause improvements in GDP per capita? The most natural answer to this question comes from neoclassical growth theory (presented in the previous two chapters and in Chapter 8). The first-order effect of increased life expectancy is to increase population, which initially reduces capital-labor and land-labor ratios, depressing income per capita. This initial decline is later compensated for by higher output as more people enter the labor force. However, there is no reason to expect a large significant increase in income per capita, especially when many of the affected countries are heavily vested in agriculture and experience a decline in land-labor ratios as a result of the rise in population. Consequently small beneficial effects of health on productivity may not be sufficient to offset or reverse the negative effects of population pressure on income per capita over periods as long as 50 years or more.

4.7 Political Economy of Institutions: First Thoughts

The evidence presented in this chapter suggests that institutions are a major—perhaps the most significant—fundamental cause of economic growth. We must therefore think about why institutions and policies differ across countries to understand why some countries are poor and others are rich. I also argue in the Epilogue that understanding institutional changes holds clues about why the process of world economic growth started 200 years or so ago.

However an explanation of differences in income across countries and over time in terms of institutional differences is also incomplete. If, as this chapter has documented, some institutions are conducive to rapid economic growth and others to stagnation, why would any society collectively choose institutions that condemn them to stagnation? The answer to this question relates to the nature of collective choices in societies. Institutions and policies, like other collective choices, are not taken for the good of the society at large, but are a result of political equilibria. To understand such political equilibria, we need to understand the conflicting interests of different individuals and groups in societies and analyze how they are mediated by different political institutions. Thus a proper understanding of how institutions affect economic outcomes and why institutions differ across countries (and why they sometimes change and pave the way for growth miracles) requires models of political economy, which explicitly study how the conflicting interests of different individuals are aggregated into collective choices. Models of political economy also specify why certain individuals and groups may be opposed to economic growth or prefer institutions that eschew growth opportunities.

The discussion in this chapter therefore justifies the inclusion of a study of political economy as part of any detailed investigation of economic growth. Much of the study of economic growth has to be about the structure of models, so that we understand the mechanics of economic growth and the proximate causes of income differences. But part of this broad study must also confront the fundamental causes of economic growth, which relate to policies, institutions, and other factors that lead to different investment, accumulation, and innovation decisions.

4.8 Taking Stock

This chapter has emphasized the differences between the proximate causes of economic growth, related to physical capital accumulation, human capital, and technology, and the fundamental causes, which influence the incentives to invest in these factors of production. I have argued that many of the questions motivating our study of economic growth must lead us to an investigation of the fundamental causes. But an understanding of fundamental causes is most useful when we can link them to the parameters of fully developed models of economic growth to see how they affect the mechanics of growth and what types of predictions they generate.

The institutions hypothesis, which seems to receive support from the evidence presented in this chapter, calls for a careful theoretical investigation. The institutions view makes sense only when there are groups in society that favor institutions that do not necessarily enhance the growth potential of the economy. Such groups do so because they do not directly or indirectly benefit from the process of economic growth. Thus it is important to develop a good understanding of the distributional implications of economic growth (e.g., how it affects relative prices and relative incomes, how it may destroy the rents of incumbents). This theoretical understanding of the implications of the growth process then needs to be combined with political economy models of collective decision making to investigate the circumstances under which groups opposed to economic growth can be powerful enough to maintain institutions that are inimical to growth.

In this chapter, my objective has been more limited (since many of the more interesting growth models are developed later in the book), and I have focused on the broad outlines of a number of alternative fundamental causes of economic growth and on a first look at the long-run empirical evidence relevant to these hypotheses. I argued that approaches emphasizing institutional differences (and differences in policies, laws, and regulations) across societies are most promising for understanding both the current growth experiences of countries and the historical process of economic growth. I also emphasized the importance of studying the political economy of institutions as a way of understanding why institutions differ across societies and lead to divergent economic paths.

4.9 References and Literature

The early part of this chapter builds on Acemoglu, Johnson, and Robinson (2005a), who discuss the distinction between proximate and fundamental causes and the various different approaches to the fundamental causes of economic growth. North and Thomas (1973) appear to be the first to implicitly criticize growth theory for focusing solely on proximate causes and ignoring the fundamental causes of economic growth. Diamond (1997) also draws a distinction between proximate and fundamental explanations.

The model presented in Section 4.2 draws on Simon (1977) and the more recent work by Michael Kremer (1993). Kremer (1993) argues for the importance of economies of scale and increasing returns to population based on the acceleration in the growth rate of world population. Another important argument relating population to technological change is proposed by Ester Boserup (1965) and is based on the idea that increases in population create scarcity, inducing societies to increase their productivity. Other models that build economies of scale to population and discuss the transition of the world economy from little or no growth to one of rapid economic growth include Galor and Weil (2000), Galor and Moav (2002), and Hansen and Prescott (2002). Some of these papers also try to reconcile the role of population in generating technological progress with the later demographic transition. Galor (2005) provides an excellent summary of this literature and an extensive discussion. McEvedy and Jones (1978) provide a concise history of world population and relatively reliable information going back to 10,000 B.C. Their data indicate that, as claimed in the text, the total population in Asia has been consistently greater than in Western Europe over this time period.

The geography hypothesis has many proponents. In addition to Montesquieu, Niccolò Machiavelli was an early proponent of the importance of climate and geographic characteristics. Marshall (1890) and Myrdal (1968) are among the economists who have most clearly articulated various versions of the geography hypothesis. It has more recently been popularized by Sachs (2001) and Bloom and Sachs (1998). Diamond (1997) offers a more sophisticated version of the geography hypothesis, in which the availability of different types of crops and animals, as well as the axes of communication within continents, influence the timing of settled agriculture and thus the possibility of developing complex societies. Diamond's thesis is therefore based on geographic differences but also relies on institutional factors as intervening variables.

Scholars emphasizing the importance of various types of institutions in economic development include John Locke, Adam Smith, John Stuart Mill, Arthur Lewis, Douglass North, and Robert Thomas. The recent economics literature includes many models highlighting the importance of property rights, for example, Skaperdas (1992), Tornell and Velasco (1992), Acemoglu (1995), Grossman and Kim (1995), Hirshleifer (2001), and Dixit (2004). Other models emphasize the importance of policies within a given institutional framework. Well-known examples of this approach include Saint-Paul and Verdier (1993), Alesina and Rodrik (1994), Persson and Tabellini (1994), Krusell and Ríos-Rull (1999), and Bourguignon and Verdier (2000). There is a much smaller literature on endogenous institutions and the effect of these institutions on economic outcomes. Surveys of this work can be found in Acemoglu (2007b) and Acemoglu and Robinson (2006a). The literature on the effect of economic institutions on economic growth is summarized and discussed in greater detail in Acemoglu, Johnson, and Robinson (2005a), which also provides an overview of the empirical literature on the topic. I return to many of these issues in Part VIII.

The importance of religion for economic development is most forcefully argued in Max Weber's work, for example Weber (1930, 1958). Many other scholars since then have picked up on this idea and have argued about the importance of religion. Prominent examples include the various papers in Harrison and Huntington (2000) and Landes (1998). Landes, for example, tries to explain the rise of the West based on cultural and religious variables. This evidence is criticized in Acemoglu, Johnson, and Robinson (2005a). Barro and McCleary (2003) provide evidence of a positive correlation between the prevalence of religious beliefs and economic growth. One has to be careful in interpreting this evidence as showing a causal effect of religion on economic growth, since religious beliefs are endogenous both to economic outcomes and to other fundamental causes of income differences.

The emphasis on the importance of cultural factors or social capital goes back to Banfield (1958) and has recently been popularized by Putnam (1993). The essence of these interpretations appears to be related to the role of culture or social capital in ensuring the selection of better equilibria. Similar ideas are also advanced in Greif (1994). Many scholars, including Véliz (1994); North, Summerhill, and Weingast (2000); and Wiarda (2001), emphasize the importance of cultural factors in explaining the economic backwardness of Latin American countries. Knack and Keefer (1997) and Durlauf and Fafchamps (2005) document positive correlations between measures of social capital and various economic outcomes. None of this work establishes a causal effect of social capital because of the potential endogeneity of social capital and culture. A number of recent papers attempt to overcome these difficulties, for example, Guiso, Sapienza, and Zingales (2004) and Tabellini (2007). The discussion of the Puritan colony in the Providence Island is based on Kupperman (1993).

The literature on the effect of economic institutions and policies on economic growth is vast. Most growth regressions include some controls for institutions or policies and find them to be significant (see, e.g., those reported in Barro and Sala-i-Martin, 2004). One of the first papers to examine the cross-country correlation between property rights measures and economic growth is Knack and Keefer (1995). This literature does not establish a causal effect of institutions on economic performance because of major simultaneity and endogeneity concerns. Mauro (1995) and Hall and Jones (1999) present the first instrumental-variable estimates on the effect of institutions (or corruption) on long-run economic development.

The evidence reported here, which exploits differences in colonial experience to create an instrumental variables strategy, is based on Acemoglu, Johnson, and Robinson (2001, 2002). The urbanization and population density data used here are from Acemoglu, Johnson, and Robinson (2002), who compiled these data based on work by McEvedy and Jones (1978);

Chandler (1987); Bairoch (1988); Bairoch, Batou, and Chèvre (1988); and Eggimann (1999). Further details and econometric results are presented in Acemoglu, Johnson, and Robinson (2002). The data on mortality rates of potential settlers are from Acemoglu, Johnson, and Robinson (2001), who compiled the data based on work by Gutierrez (1986) and Curtin (1989, 1998). That paper also provides a large number of robustness checks, documenting the influence of economic institutions on economic growth and showing that other factors, including religion and geography, have little effect on long-run economic development once the effect of institutions is controlled for.

The discussion of the role of leaders on growth draws on Jones and Olken (2005). The details of the Korean experiment and historical references are provided in Acemoglu (2003c) and Acemoglu, Johnson, and Robinson (2005a). The discussion of distinguishing the effects of different types of institutions draws on Acemoglu and Johnson (2005).

The discussion of the effect of disease on development is based on Weil (2007) and especially on Acemoglu and Johnson (2007), which used the econometric strategy described in the text. Figures 4.10 and 4.11 are from Acemoglu and Johnson (2007). In these figures, initially poor countries are those that are poorer than Spain in 1940 and include Bangladesh, Brazil, China, Ecuador, El Salvador, Honduras, India, Indonesia, Korea, Malaysia, Myanmar, Nicaragua, Pakistan, the Philippines, Sri Lanka, and Thailand. Initially rich countries are those that are richer than Argentina in 1940 and include Belgium, Netherlands, Sweden, Denmark, Canada, Germany, Australia, New Zealand, Switzerland, the United Kingdom, and the United States. Young (2005) investigates the effect of the HIV epidemic in South Africa and reaches a conclusion similar to that reported here, though his analysis relies on a calibration of the Solow growth model rather than on econometric estimation.

4.10 Exercises

4.1 Derive (4.3) and (4.4).

4.2 Derive equation (4.5). Explain how and why the behavior implied for technology by this equation differs from (4.4). Do you find the assumptions leading to (4.4) or to (4.5) more plausible?

4.3 (a) Show that the models leading to both (4.4) and (4.5) imply a constant income per capita over time.

   (b) Modify (4.2) to be

$$L(t) = \phi Y(t)^{\beta}$$

   for some $\beta \in (0, 1)$. Justify this equation and derive the law of motion for technology and income per capita under the two scenarios considered in Section 4.2. Are the implications of this model more reasonable than those considered in the text?

PART II

TOWARD NEOCLASSICAL GROWTH

This part of the book is a preparation for what is to come. In some sense, Part II can be viewed as the preliminaries for the rest of the book. The ultimate purpose is to enrich the basic Solow model by introducing well-defined household preferences and optimization, and in the process clarify the relationship between growth theory and general equilibrium theory. This will enable us to open the black box of savings and capital accumulation, turning these into forward-looking investment decisions. It will also permit us to make welfare statements about whether the rate of growth of an economy is too slow, too fast, or just right from a welfare-maximizing (Pareto optimality) viewpoint. The tools introduced in this part of the book are also essential for our study of technology as another forward-looking investment by firms, researchers, and individuals. However, much of this effort will have to wait for Parts III and IV of the book.

The three chapters in this part present the material necessary to appreciate subsequent chapters in the book. The next chapter makes more explicit the relationship between models of economic growth and general equilibrium theory. It also highlights some of the assumptions implicit in growth models. The two subsequent chapters develop the mathematical tools for dynamic optimization in discrete and continuous time. To avoid making these chapters purely about mathematics, I use a variety of economic models of some relevance to growth theory as examples and also present some results on equilibrium and optimal growth. Nevertheless, the material in the next three chapters is significantly more mathematical than anything else in the book (except the Appendixes at the end). The reader therefore may wish to first consult the Appendixes and/or skip some of the proofs presented in the next three chapters in a first reading.

5

Foundations of Neoclassical Growth

The Solow growth model is predicated on a constant saving rate. It would be more informative to specify the preference orderings of households (individuals), as in standard general equilibrium theory, and derive their decisions from these preferences. This specification would enable us both to have a better understanding of the factors that affect savings decisions and also to discuss the optimality of equilibria—in other words, to pose and answer questions related to whether the (competitive) equilibria of growth models can be improved. The notion of improvement here is based on the standard concept of Pareto optimality, which asks whether some households can be made better off without others being made worse off. Naturally, we can only talk of households being "better off" if we have some information about well-defined preference orderings.

5.1 Preliminaries

To prepare for this analysis, let us consider an economy consisting of a unit measure of infinitely-lived households. By a "unit measure of households" I mean an uncountable number of households with total measure normalized to 1; for example, the set of households $\mathcal{H}$ could be represented by the unit interval $[0, 1]$. This abstraction is adopted for simplicity, to emphasize that each household is infinitesimal and has no effect on aggregates. Nothing in this book hinges on this assumption. If the reader instead finds it more convenient to think of the set of households, $\mathcal{H}$, as a countable set, for example, $\mathcal{H} = \mathbb{N}$, this can be done without any loss of generality. The advantage of having a unit measure of households is that averages and aggregates are the same, enabling us to economize on notation. It would be even simpler to have $\mathcal{H}$ as a finite set of the form $\{1, 2, \ldots, M\}$. While this form would be sufficient in many contexts, overlapping generations models in Chapter 9 require the set of households to be infinite.

Households in this economy may be truly "infinitely lived," or alternatively they may consist of overlapping generations with full (or partial) altruism linking generations within the household. Throughout I equate households with individuals and thus ignore all possible sources of conflict or different preferences within the household. In other words, I assume that households have well-defined preference orderings.

As in basic general equilibrium theory, let us suppose that preference orderings can be represented by utility functions. In particular, suppose that there is a unique consumption good, and each household h has an *instantaneous utility function* given by

$$u^h(c^h(t)),$$

where $c^h(t)$ is the consumption of household h, and $u^h : \mathbb{R}_+ \to \mathbb{R}$ is increasing and concave. I take the domain of the utility function to be $\mathbb{R}_+$ rather than $\mathbb{R}$, so that negative levels of consumption are not allowed. Even though some well-known economic models allow negative consumption, this is not easy to interpret in general equilibrium or in growth theory. Thus this restriction is sensible in most models.

The instantaneous utility function captures the utility that an individual (or household) derives from consumption at time t. It is therefore not the same as a utility function specifying a complete preference ordering over all commodities—here all commodities corresponding to consumption levels at all dates. For this reason, the instantaneous utility function is sometimes also referred to as the "felicity function."

There are two major assumptions in writing an instantaneous utility function. First, it supposes that the household does not derive any utility from the consumption of other households, so consumption externalities are ruled out. Second, in writing the instantaneous utility function, I have already imposed the condition that overall utility is *time-separable and stationary;* that is, instantaneous utility at time t is independent of the consumption levels at past or future dates and is represented by the same utility function u^h at all dates. This second feature is important in enabling us to develop tractable models of dynamic optimization.

Finally, let us introduce a third assumption and suppose that households discount the future exponentially—or proportionally. In discrete time and ignoring uncertainty, this assumption implies that household preferences or utility (starting at time $t = 0$) can be represented as

$$U^h\big(c^h(1), c^h(2), \ldots, c^h(T)\big) \equiv \sum_{t=0}^{T} (\beta^h)^t u^h(c^h(t)), \tag{5.1}$$

where $\beta^h \in (0, 1)$ is the discount factor of household h, and the horizon T could be finite or equal to infinity (so that $T = \infty$ is allowed). Here U^h denotes the utility function of household h defined over the entire stream of consumption levels, while u^h is still the instantaneous utility function. The distinction between these two concepts is important to bear in mind. The functional form of the utility function U^h incorporates exponential discounting and time separability. It implies that the weight given to tomorrow's utility u^h is a fraction β^h of today's utility, and the weight given to the utility the day after tomorrow is a fraction $(\beta^h)^2$ of today's utility, and so on. Exponential discounting and time separability are convenient because they naturally ensure time-consistent behavior.

A solution $\{x(t)\}_{t=0}^{T}$ (possibly with $T = \infty$) to a dynamic optimization problem is *time-consistent* if the following is true: when $\{x(t)\}_{t=0}^{T}$ is a solution starting at time $t = 0$, $\{x(t)\}_{t=t'}^{T}$ is a solution to the continuation dynamic optimization problem starting from time $t = t' > 0$. If a problem is not time-consistent, it is *time-inconsistent*. Time-consistent problems are much more straightforward to work with and satisfy all the standard axioms of rational decision making. Although time-inconsistent preferences may be useful in the modeling of certain behaviors, such as problems of addiction or self-control, time-consistent preferences are ideal for the focus in this book, since they are tractable, relatively flexible, and provide a good approximation to reality in the context of aggregative models. It is also worth noting that many classes of preferences that do not feature exponential and time-separable discounting nonetheless lead to time-consistent behavior. Exercise 5.1 discusses issues of time-consistency further and shows how nonexponential discounting may lead to time-inconsistent behavior, while Exercise 5.2 introduces some common non-time-separable preferences that lead to time-consistent behavior.

There is a natural analogue to (5.1) in continuous time, again incorporating exponential discounting, which is introduced and discussed below and further in Chapter 7.

Equation (5.1) ignores uncertainty in the sense that it assumes the sequence of consumption levels for household h, $\{c^h(t)\}_{t=0}^T$, is known with certainty. If this sequence were uncertain, we would need to look at expected utility maximization. Most growth models do not necessitate an analysis of behavior under uncertainty, but a stochastic version of the neoclassical growth model is the workhorse of much of the rest of modern macroeconomics and will be presented in Chapter 17. For now, it suffices to say that in the presence of uncertainty, $u^h(\cdot)$ should be interpreted as a *Bernoulli utility function*, defined over risky acts, so that the preferences of household h at time $t = 0$ can be represented by the following *(von Neumann-Morgenstern) expected utility function U^h*:

$$U^h \equiv \mathbb{E}_0^h \sum_{t=0}^T (\beta^h)^t u^h(c^h(t)),$$

where $\mathbb{E}_0^h$ is the expectation operator with respect to the information set available to household h at time $t = 0$. In this expression, I did not explicitly write the argument of the expected utility function U^h, since this argument is now more involved; it no longer corresponds to a given sequence of consumption levels but to a probability distribution over consumption sequences. At this point, there is no need to introduce the notation for these distributions (see Chapter 16).

The formulation so far indexes the individual utility function $u^h(\cdot)$ and the discount factor β^h by "h" to emphasize that these preference parameters are potentially different across households. Households could also differ according to their income paths. For example, each household could have effective labor endowments of $\{e^h(t)\}_{t=0}^T$ and thus a sequence of labor income of $\{e^h(t)w(t)\}_{t=0}^T$, where $w(t)$ is the equilibrium wage rate per unit of effective labor.

Unfortunately, at this level of generality, this problem is not tractable. Even though we can establish the existence of equilibrium under some regularity conditions, it would be impossible to go beyond that. Proving the existence of equilibrium in this class of models is of some interest, but our focus is on developing workable models of economic growth that generate insights into the process of growth over time and cross-country income differences. I therefore follow the standard approach in macroeconomics and assume the existence of a representative household.

5.2 The Representative Household

An economy *admits a representative household* when the preference (demand) side of the economy can be represented as if there were a single household making the aggregate consumption and saving decisions (and also the labor supply decisions when these are endogenized) subject to an aggregate budget constraint. The major convenience of the representative household assumption is that rather than modeling the preference side of the economy as resulting from equilibrium interactions of many heterogeneous households, it allows us to model it as a solution to a single maximization problem. Note that this description is purely *positive*—it asks the question of whether the aggregate behavior can be represented as if it were generated by a single household. A stronger notion, the *normative* representative household, would also allow us to use the representative household's utility function for welfare comparisons and is introduced later in this section.

Let us start with the simplest case that leads to the existence of a representative household. For concreteness, suppose that all households are infinitely-lived and identical; that is, each household has the same discount factor β, the same sequence of effective labor endowments $\{e(t)\}_{t=0}^{\infty}$, and the same instantaneous utility function

$$u(c^h(t)),$$

where $u : \mathbb{R}_+ \to \mathbb{R}$ is increasing and concave, and $c^h(t)$ is the consumption of household h. Therefore there really is a representative household in this case. Consequently, again ignoring uncertainty, the demand side of the economy can be represented as the solution to the following maximization problem starting at time $t = 0$:

$$\max \sum_{t=0}^{\infty} \beta^t u(c(t)), \tag{5.2}$$

where $\beta \in (0, 1)$ is the common discount factor of all the households, and $c(t)$ is the consumption level of the representative household.

The economy described so far admits a representative household rather trivially; all households are identical. In this case, the representative household's preferences, (5.2), can be used not only for positive analysis (e.g., to determine the level of savings) but also for normative analysis, such as evaluating the optimality of equilibria.

The assumption that the economy is inhabited by a set of identical households is not very appealing. Instead, we would like to know when an economy with heterogeneity can be modeled as if aggregate consumption levels were generated by the optimization decision of a representative household. To illustrate the potential difficulties that the "as if" perspective might encounter, let us consider a simple exchange economy with a finite number of commodities and state an important theorem from general equilibrium theory. Recall that in an exchange economy, the equilibrium can be characterized in terms of excess demand functions for different commodities (or more generally, in terms of excess demand correspondences; see Appendix A). Let the equilibrium of the economy be represented by the aggregate excess demand function $\mathbf{x}(p)$ when the vector of prices is p. The demand side of an economy admits a representative household if $\mathbf{x}(p)$ can be obtained as a solution to the maximization problem of a single household. The next theorem shows that this is not possible in general.

Theorem 5.1 (Debreu-Mantel-Sonnenschein Theorem) *Let $\varepsilon > 0$ and $N \in \mathbb{N}$. Consider a set of prices $\mathbf{P}_\varepsilon = \{p \in \mathbb{R}_+^N : p_j/p_{j'} \geq \varepsilon$ for all j and $j'\}$ and any continuous function $\mathbf{x} : \mathbf{P}_\varepsilon \to \mathbb{R}_+^N$ that satisfies Walras's Law and is homogeneous of degree 0. Then there exists an exchange economy with N commodities and $H < \infty$ households, where the aggregate excess demand is given by $\mathbf{x}(p)$ over the set $\mathbf{P}_\varepsilon$.*

Proof. See Debreu (1974) or Mas-Colell, Whinston, and Green (1995, Proposition 17.E.3).
∎

Therefore the fact that excess demands result from aggregating the optimizing behavior of households places few restrictions on the form of these demands. In particular, recall from basic microeconomics that individual (excess) demands satisfy the weak axiom of revealed preference and have Slutsky matrices that are symmetric and negative semidefinite. These properties do not necessarily hold for the aggregate excess demand function $\mathbf{x}(p)$. Thus without imposing further structure, it is impossible to derive $\mathbf{x}(p)$ from the maximization behavior of a single household. Theorem 5.1 therefore raises a severe warning against the use of the representative household assumption.

Nevertheless, this result is an outcome of strong income effects, which can create unintuitive results even in basic consumer theory (recall, e.g., Giffen goods). Special but approximately realistic preference functions, as well as restrictions on the distribution of income across households, enable us to rule out arbitrary aggregate excess demand functions. To show that the representative household assumption is not as hopeless as Theorem 5.1 suggests, I now present a special but relevant case in which aggregation of individual preferences is possible and enables the modeling of the economy as if the demand side were generated by a representative household.

To prepare for this theorem, consider an economy with a finite number N of commodities and recall that an indirect utility function for household h, $v^h(p, w^h)$, specifies the household's (ordinal) utility as a function of the price vector $p = (p_1, \ldots, p_N)$ and the household's income w^h. Naturally, any indirect utility function $v^h(p, w^h)$ has to be homogeneous of degree 0 in p and w.

Theorem 5.2 (Gorman's Aggregation Theorem) *Consider an economy with $N < \infty$ commodities and a set $\mathcal{H}$ of households. Suppose that the preferences of each household $h \in \mathcal{H}$ can be represented by an indirect utility function of the form*

$$v^h(p, w^h) = a^h(p) + b(p)w^h \tag{5.3}$$

and that each household $h \in \mathcal{H}$ has a positive demand for each commodity. Then these preferences can be aggregated and represented by those of a representative household, with indirect utility

$$v(p, w) = a(p) + b(p)w,$$

where $a(p) \equiv \int_{h \in \mathcal{H}} a^h(p)dh$, and $w \equiv \int_{h \in \mathcal{H}} w^h dh$ is aggregate income.

Proof. See Exercise 5.3. ∎

This theorem implies that when preferences can be represented by the special linear indirect utility functions (5.3), aggregate behavior can indeed be represented as if it resulted from the maximization of a single household. This class of preferences are referred to as "Gorman preferences" after W. M. (Terence) Gorman, who was among the first economists studying issues of aggregation and proposed the special class of preferences used in Theorem 5.2. These preferences are convenient because they lead to linear Engel curves. Recall that *Engel curves* represent the relationship between expenditure on a particular commodity and income (for given prices). Gorman preferences imply that the Engel curve of each household (for each commodity) is linear and has the same slope as the Engel curve of the other households for the same commodity. In particular, assuming that $a^h(p)$ and $b(p)$ are differentiable, *Roy's Identity* implies that household h's demand for commodity j is given by

$$x_j^h(p, w^h) = -\frac{1}{b(p)}\frac{\partial a^h(p)}{\partial p_j} - \frac{1}{b(p)}\frac{\partial b(p)}{\partial p_j}w^h.$$

Therefore a linear relationship exists between demand and income (or between expenditure and income) for each household, and the slope of this relationship is independent of the household's identity. This property is in fact indispensable for the existence of a representative household and for Theorem 5.2, unless we wish to impose restrictions on the distribution of income. In particular, let us say that an economy admits a *strong representative household* if redistribution of income or endowments across households does not affect the demand side. The strong representative household applies when preferences take the Gorman form as shown by Theorem 5.2. Moreover, it is straightforward to see that, since without the Gorman form the Engel curves of some households have different slopes, there exists a specific scheme of income redistribution across households that would affect the aggregate demand for different goods. This reasoning establishes the following converse to Theorem 5.2: Gorman preferences (with the same $b(p)$ for all households) are necessary for the economy to admit a strong representative household.[1]

Notice that instead of the summation, Theorem 5.2 is stated with the integral over the set $\mathcal{H}$ to allow for the possibility that the set of households may be a continuum. The integral should be thought of as the Lebesgue integral, so that when $\mathcal{H}$ is a finite or countable set, $\int_{h \in \mathcal{H}} w^h dh$ is indeed equivalent to the summation $\sum_{h \in \mathcal{H}} w^h$.[2] Although Theorem 5.2 is stated for an economy with a finite number of commodities, this limitation is only for simplicity, and the results in this theorem hold in economies with an infinite number or a continuum of commodities.

Finally, note that Theorem 5.2 does not require that the indirect utility must take the form of (5.3). Instead, they must have a representation of the Gorman form. Recall that in the absence of uncertainty, monotone transformations of the utility or the indirect function have no effect on behavior, so all that is required in models without uncertainty is that there exist a monotone transformation of the indirect utility function that takes the form given in (5.3).

Many commonly used preferences in macroeconomics are special cases of Gorman preferences, as illustrated in the next example.

Example 5.1 (CES Preferences) *A very common class of preferences used in industrial organization and macroeconomics are the CES preferences, also referred to as "Dixit-Stiglitz preferences" after the two economists who first used these preferences. Suppose that each household $h \in \mathcal{H}$ has total income w^h and preferences defined over $j = 1, \ldots, N$ goods given by*

$$U^h\left(x_1^h, \ldots, x_N^h\right) = \left[\sum_{j=1}^{N}\left(x_j^h - \xi_j^h\right)^{\frac{\sigma-1}{\sigma}}\right]^{\frac{\sigma}{\sigma-1}}, \tag{5.4}$$

where $\sigma \in (0, \infty)$ and $\xi_j^h \in [-\bar{\xi}, \bar{\xi}]$ is a household-specific term, which parameterizes whether the particular good is a necessity for the household. For example, $\xi_j^h > 0$ may mean that household h needs to consume at least a certain amount of good j to survive. The utility function (5.4) is referred to as a CES function for the following reason: if we define the level

---

1. Naturally, we can obtain a broader class of preferences for which aggregate behavior can be represented as if it resulted from the maximization problem of a single representative household once attention is restricted to specific distributions of income (wealth) across households. The most extreme version of this restriction would be to impose the existence of a representative household by assuming that all households have identical utility functions and endowments.

2. Throughout the book I avoid the use of measure theory when I can, but I refer to the Lebesgue integral a number of times. It is a generalization of the standard Riemann integral. The few references to Lebesgue integrals simply signal that we should think of integration in a slightly more general context, so that the integrals could represent expectations or averages even with discrete random variables and discrete distributions (or mixtures of continuous and discrete distributions). References to some introductory treatments of measure theory and the Lebesgue integral are provided at the end of Chapter 16.

of consumption of each good as $\hat{x}_j^h = x_j^h - \xi_j^h$, then the elasticity of substitution between any two $\hat{x}_j^h$ and $\hat{x}_{j'}^h$ (with $j \neq j'$) is equal to σ.

Each consumer faces a vector of prices $p = (p_1, \ldots, p_N)$, and we assume that for all h,

$$\sum_{j=1}^{N} p_j \bar{\xi} < w^h,$$

so that each household $h \in \mathcal{H}$ can afford a bundle such that $\hat{x}_j^h \geq 0$ for all j. In Exercise 5.6 you are asked to derive the optimal consumption levels for each household and show that their indirect utility function is given by

$$v^h(p, w^h) = \frac{\left[-\sum_{j=1}^{N} p_j \xi_j^h + w^h \right]}{\left[\sum_{j=1}^{N} p_j^{1-\sigma} \right]^{\frac{1}{1-\sigma}}}, \tag{5.5}$$

which satisfies the Gorman form (and is also homogeneous of degree 0 in p and w). Therefore this economy admits a representative household with an indirect utility function given by

$$v(p, w) = \frac{\left[-\sum_{j=1}^{N} p_j \xi_j + w \right]}{\left[\sum_{j=1}^{N} p_j^{1-\sigma} \right]^{\frac{1}{1-\sigma}}},$$

where $w \equiv \int_{h \in \mathcal{H}} w^h dh$ is the aggregate income level in the economy, and $\xi_j \equiv \int_{h \in \mathcal{H}} \xi_j^h dh$. It can be verified that the utility function leading to this indirect utility function is

$$U(x_1, \ldots, x_N) = \left[\sum_{j=1}^{N} (x_j - \xi_j)^{\frac{\sigma-1}{\sigma}} \right]^{\frac{\sigma}{\sigma-1}}. \tag{5.6}$$

We will see in Chapter 8 that preferences closely related to the CES preferences presented here play a special role not only in aggregation, but also in ensuring balanced growth.

Most—but importantly, not all—macro models assume more than the existence of a representative household. First, many models implicitly assume the existence of a strong representative household, thus abstracting from the distribution of income and wealth among households and its implications for aggregate behavior. Second, most approaches also impose the existence of a *normative representative household:* not only does there exist a representative household whose maximization problem generates the relevant aggregate demands but also the utility function of this household can be used for welfare analysis.[3] More specifically, recall that an allocation is *Pareto optimal* (Pareto efficient) if no household can be made strictly better off without some other household being made worse off (see Definition 5.2 below). Equivalently, a Pareto optimal allocation is a solution to the maximization of a weighted average of the utilities of the households in the economy subject to the resource and technology constraints (and typically, different weights give different Pareto optimal allocations).

---

3. To emphasize the pitfalls of imposing this restriction without ensuring that the economy admits a normative representative household, I can do no better than directly quote Deaton and Muellbauer (1980, p. 163): "It is extremely dangerous to deduce microeconomic behavior on the basis of macroeconomic observations, particularly if such deductions are then used to make judgments about economic welfare."

When the economy admits a normative representative household, then we can model the demand side in a simple manner and use this modeling to make statements about whether a particular allocation is Pareto optimal and how it can be improved. The existence of a normative representative household is significantly stronger than the existence of a (positive) representative household. Nevertheless, the Gorman preferences in Theorem 5.2 not only imply the existence of a strong representative household (and thus aggregation of individual demands regardless of the exact distribution of income), but they also generally imply the existence of a normative representative household. The next theorem states a simple form of this result.

Theorem 5.3 (Existence of a Normative Representative Household) *Consider an economy with a finite number $N < \infty$ of commodities, a set $\mathcal{H}$ of households, and a convex aggregate production possibilities set Y. Suppose that the preferences of each household $h \in \mathcal{H}$ can be represented by Gorman form $v^h(p, w^h) = a^h(p) + b(p)w^h$, where $p = (p_1, \ldots, p_N)$ is the price vector, and that each household $h \in \mathcal{H}$ has a positive demand for each commodity.*

1. *Then any feasible allocation that maximizes the utility of the representative household, $v(p, w) = \sum_{h \in \mathcal{H}} a^h(p) + b(p)w$, with $w \equiv \sum_{h \in \mathcal{H}} w^h$, is Pareto optimal.*

2. *Moreover, if $a^h(p) = a^h$ for all p and all $h \in \mathcal{H}$, then any Pareto optimal allocation maximizes the utility of the representative household.*

Proof. Let Y represent the aggregate production possibilities set inclusive of endowments, and let $Y_j(p)$ denote the set of profit-maximizing levels of net supply of commodity j when the price vector is p. Since Y is convex, the planner can equivalently choose p and an element in $Y_j(p)$ for each j rather than directly choosing $y \in Y$ (see Theorems 5.4 and 5.7 below). Then a Pareto optimal allocation can be represented as

$$\max_{\{y_j\}_{j=1}^N, p, \{w^h\}_{h \in \mathcal{H}}} \sum_{h \in \mathcal{H}} \alpha^h v^h(p, w^h) = \max_{\{y_j\}_{j=1}^N, p, \{w^h\}_{h \in \mathcal{H}}} \sum_{h \in \mathcal{H}} \alpha^h \left(a^h(p) + b(p)w^h\right) \quad (5.7)$$

subject to

$$-\frac{1}{b(p)} \left(\sum_{h \in \mathcal{H}} \frac{\partial a^h(p)}{\partial p_j} + \frac{\partial b(p)}{\partial p_j} w \right) = y_j \in Y_j(p) \text{ for } j = 1, \ldots, N,$$

$$\sum_{h \in \mathcal{H}} w^h = w \equiv \sum_{j=1}^N p_j y_j,$$

$$\sum_{j=1}^N p_j \omega_j = w,$$

$$p_j \geq 0 \quad \text{for all } j,$$

where $\{\alpha^h\}_{h \in \mathcal{H}}$ are nonnegative Pareto weights with $\sum_{h \in \mathcal{H}} \alpha^h = 1$. The first set of constraints uses Roy's Identity to express the total demand for good j and set it equal to the supply of good j, which is given by some y_j in $Y_j(p)$. The second equation defines total income as the value of net supplies. The third equation makes sure that total income in the economy is equal to the value of the endowments. The fourth set of constraints requires that all prices be nonnegative.

Now compare the maximization problem (5.7) to the following problem:

$$\max_{\{y_j\}_{j=1}^N, p, \{w^h\}_{h \in \mathcal{H}}} \sum_{h \in \mathcal{H}} a^h(p) + b(p)w \quad (5.8)$$

subject to the same set of constraints. The only difference between the two problems is that in the latter, each household has been assigned the same weight. Let $\mathbf{w} \in \mathbb{R}^{|\mathcal{H}|}$ (note that here, w is a number, whereas $\mathbf{w} = (w^1, \ldots, w^{|\mathcal{H}|})$ is a vector).

Let $(p^*, \mathbf{w}^*)$ be a solution to (5.8) with $w^h = w^* / |\mathcal{H}|$ for all $h \in \mathcal{H}$ so that all households have the same income (together with an associated vector of net supplies $\{y_j\}_{j=1}^N$). By definition it is feasible and also a solution to (5.7) with $\alpha^h = \alpha$, and therefore it is Pareto optimal, which establishes the first part of the theorem.

To establish the second part, suppose that $a^h(p) = a^h$ for all p and all $h \in \mathcal{H}$. To obtain a contradiction, suppose that some feasible $(p_\alpha^{**}, \mathbf{w}_\alpha^{**})$, with associated net supplies $\{y_j\}_{j=1}^N$ is a solution to (5.7) for some weights $\{\alpha^h\}_{h \in \mathcal{H}}$, and suppose that it is not a solution to (5.8). Let

$$\alpha^M = \max_{h \in \mathcal{H}} \alpha^h$$

and

$$\mathcal{H}^M = \left\{ h \in \mathcal{H} \mid \alpha^h = \alpha^M \right\}$$

be the set of households given the maximum Pareto weight. Let $(p^*, \mathbf{w}^*)$ be a solution to (5.8) such that

$$w^{h*} = 0 \quad \text{for all } h \notin \mathcal{H}^M, \tag{5.9}$$

and $w^* = \sum_{h \in \mathcal{H}^M} w^{h*}$. Note that such a solution exists, since the objective function and the constraint set in the second problem depend only on the vector $(w^1, \ldots, w^{|\mathcal{H}|})$ through $w = \sum_{h \in \mathcal{H}} w^h$.

Since by definition $(p_\alpha^{**}, \mathbf{w}_\alpha^{**})$ is in the constraint set of (5.8) and is not a solution,

$$\sum_{h \in \mathcal{H}} a^h + b(p^*)w^* > \sum_{h \in \mathcal{H}} a^h + b(p_\alpha^{**})w_\alpha^{**}$$

$$b(p^*)w^* > b(p_\alpha^{**})w_\alpha^{**}. \tag{5.10}$$

The hypothesis that $(p_\alpha^{**}, \mathbf{w}_\alpha^{**})$ is a solution to (5.7) implies that

$$\sum_{h \in \mathcal{H}} \alpha^h a^h + \sum_{h \in \mathcal{H}} \alpha^h b(p_\alpha^{**})w_\alpha^{h**} \geq \sum_{h \in \mathcal{H}} \alpha^h a^h + \sum_{h \in \mathcal{H}} \alpha^h b(p^*)w^{h*}$$

$$\sum_{h \in \mathcal{H}} \alpha^h b(p_\alpha^{**})w_\alpha^{h**} \geq \sum_{h \in \mathcal{H}} \alpha^h b(p^*)w^{h*}, \tag{5.11}$$

where w^{h*} and w_α^{h**} denote the hth components of the vectors $\mathbf{w}^*$ and $\mathbf{w}_\alpha^{**}$.

Note also that any solution $(p^{**}, \mathbf{w}^{**})$ to (5.7) satisfies $w^{h**} = 0$ for any $h \notin \mathcal{H}^M$. In view of this and the choice of $(p^*, \mathbf{w}^*)$ in (5.9), equation (5.11) implies

$$\alpha^M b(p_\alpha^{**}) \sum_{h \in \mathcal{H}} w_\alpha^{h**} \geq \alpha^M b(p^*) \sum_{h \in \mathcal{H}} w^{h*}$$

$$b(p_\alpha^{**})w_\alpha^{**} \geq b(p^*)w^*,$$

which contradicts (5.10) and establishes that, under the stated assumptions, any Pareto optimal allocation maximizes the utility of the representative household. ∎

5.3 Infinite Planning Horizon

Another important aspect of the standard preferences used in growth theory and macroeconomics concerns the planning horizon of individuals. Although some growth models are formulated with finitely-lived households (see, e.g., Chapter 9), most growth and macro models assume that households have an infinite planning horizon as in (5.2) or (5.16) below. A natural question is whether this is a good approximation to reality. After all, most individuals we know are not infinitely lived.

There are two reasonable microfoundations for this assumption. The first comes from the "Poisson death model" or the *perpetual youth model*, which is discussed in greater detail in Chapter 9. The general idea is that, while individuals are finitely lived, they are not aware of when they will die. Even somebody who is 100 years old cannot consume all his assets, since there is a fair chance that he will live for another 5 or 10 years. At the simplest level, we can consider a discrete-time model and assume that each individual faces a constant probability of death equal to $\nu > 0$. This is a strong simplifying assumption, since the likelihood of survival to the next age in reality is not a constant, but a function of the age of the individual (a feature best captured by actuarial life tables, which are of great importance to the insurance industry). Nevertheless it is a good starting point, since it is relatively tractable and also implies that individuals have an expected lifespan of $1/\nu < \infty$ periods, which can be used to get a sense of what the value of ν should be.

Suppose also that each individual has a standard instantaneous utility function $u : \mathbb{R}_+ \to \mathbb{R}$, and a true or pure discount factor $\hat{\beta}$, meaning that $\hat{\beta}$ is the discount factor that the individual would apply between consumption today and tomorrow if he or she were sure to live between the two dates. Moreover, let us normalize $u(0) = 0$ to be the utility after death. Now consider an individual who plans to have a consumption sequence $\{c(t)\}_{t=0}^{\infty}$ (conditional on living). Clearly, after the individual dies, future consumption plans do not matter. Standard arguments imply that this individual would have expected utility at time $t = 0$ given by

$$U_0(c(0), c(1), \ldots) = u(c(0)) + \hat{\beta}(1 - \nu)u(c(1)) + \hat{\beta}\nu u(0)$$

$$+ \hat{\beta}^2(1 - \nu)^2 u(c(2)) + \hat{\beta}^2(1 - \nu)\nu u(0) + \ldots$$

$$= \sum_{t=0}^{\infty} (\hat{\beta}(1 - \nu))^t u(c(t))$$

$$\equiv \sum_{t=0}^{\infty} \beta^t u(c(t)), \tag{5.12}$$

where the second line collects terms and uses $u(0) = 0$, and the final line defines $\beta \equiv \hat{\beta}(1 - \nu)$ as the effective discount factor of the individual. With this formulation, the model with finite lives and random deaths leads to an individual maximization problem identical to that in the model with infinitely-lived households (though the reasonable values of β in this case would differ; see also Exercise 5.7 for a similar derivation in continuous time). While until now agents faced no uncertainty, the possibility of death implies that there is a nontrivial (in fact quite important!) uncertainty in individuals' lives. As a result, instead of the standard ordinal utility theory, we have to use the expected utility theory as developed by von Neumann and Morgenstern. In particular, (5.12) is already the expected utility of the individual, since probabilities have been substituted in and there is no need to include explicit expectations.[4]

A second justification for the infinite planning horizon comes from intergenerational altruism or the "bequest" motive. At the simplest level, imagine an individual who lives for one period and has a single offspring (who will also live for a single period and will beget a single offspring, and so on). Suppose that this individual not only derives utility from his consumption but also from the bequest he leaves to his offspring. For example, we could posit

$$U(c(t), b(t)) = u(c(t)) + U^b(b(t)),$$

where $c(t)$ is his consumption and $b(t)$ denotes the bequest left to his offspring. Suppose also that the individual has total income $y(t)$, so that his budget constraint is

$$c(t) + b(t) \leq y(t).$$

The function $U^b(\cdot)$ contains information about how much the individual values the bequest left to his offspring. In general, there may be various reasons why individuals leave bequests (including accidental bequests that will be left by an individual facing random death probability, as in the example discussed in the previous paragraph). Nevertheless, a natural benchmark might be one in which the individual is purely altruistic, so that he cares about the utility of his offspring (with some discount factor).[5] Let the discount factor between generations be β. Also assume that the offspring will have an income of w without the bequest. Then the utility of the individual can be written as

$$u(c(t)) + \beta V(b(t) + w),$$

where $V(\cdot)$ can now be interpreted as the continuation value, equal to the utility that the offspring will obtain from receiving a bequest of $b(t)$ (together with his own income of w). Naturally, the value of the individual at time t can in turn be written as

$$V(y(t)) = \max_{c(t)+b(t)\leq y(t)} \{u(c(t)) + \beta V(b(t) + w)\},$$

which defines the current value of the individual starting with income $y(t)$ and takes into account what the continuation value will be. The next chapter shows that this equation is the canonical form of a dynamic programming representation of an infinite-horizon maximization problem. In particular, under some mild technical assumptions, this dynamic programming representation is equivalent to maximizing

$$\sum_{s=0}^{\infty} \beta^s u(c_{t+s})$$

at time t. Intuitively, even though an individual lives for one period, he cares about the utility of his offspring, and realizes that in turn his offspring cares about the utility of his own offspring, and so on. Thus each individual internalizes the utility of all future members of the "dynasty."

---

4. Throughout, except in the stochastic growth analysis in Chapters 16 and 17, I directly specify the expected utility function of households rather than explicitly introducing expectations.

5. The alternative to purely altruistic preferences are those in which a parent receives utility from specific types of bequests or from a subcomponent of the utility of his offspring. Models with such impure altruism are sometimes quite convenient and are discussed in Chapters 9 and 21.

This argument establishes that fully altruistic behavior within a dynasty (so-called dynastic preferences) also leads to a situation in which decision makers act as if they have an infinite planning horizon.

5.4 The Representative Firm

The previous section discussed how an economy admits a representative household only under special circumstances. The other assumption commonly used in growth models, and already introduced in Chapter 2, is the representative firm assumption. In particular, recall from Chapter 2 that the entire production side of the economy was represented by an aggregate production possibilities set, which can be thought of as the production possibilities set or the production function of a representative firm. One may think that this representation also requires quite stringent assumptions on the production structure of the economy. This is not the case, however. While not all economies admit a representative household, the standard assumptions adopted in general equilibrium theory or dynamic general equilibrium analysis (in particular, the assumptions of no production externalities and competitive markets) are sufficient to ensure that the formulation with a representative firm is without loss of generality.

This result is stated in the next theorem. To prepare for this result, let us introduce the following notation: for two vectors of the same dimension, p and y, $p \cdot y$ denotes their *inner product* (i.e., if $p = (p_1, \ldots, p_N)$ and $y = (y_1, \ldots, y_N)$, then $p \cdot y = \sum_{j=1}^{N} p_j y_j$). In addition, let $\mathcal{F}$ be the set of firms in the economy and

$$Y \equiv \left\{ \sum_{f \in \mathcal{F}} y^f : y^f \in Y^f \text{ for each } f \in \mathcal{F} \right\}. \tag{5.13}$$

denote the *aggregate production possibilities set* of the economy.

Theorem 5.4 (Representative Firm Theorem) *Consider a competitive production economy with $N \in \mathbb{N} \cup \{+\infty\}$ commodities and a countable set $\mathcal{F}$ of firms, each with a production possibilities set $Y^f \subset \mathbb{R}^N$. Let $p \in \mathbb{R}_+^N$ be the price vector in this economy and denote the set of profit-maximizing net supplies of firm $f \in \mathcal{F}$ by $\hat{Y}^f(p) \subset Y^f$ (so that for any $\hat{y}^f \in \hat{Y}^f(p)$, we have $p \cdot \hat{y}^f \geq p \cdot y^f$ for all $y^f \in Y^f$). Then there exists a representative firm with production possibilities set $Y \subset \mathbb{R}^N$ and a set of profit-maximizing net supplies $\hat{Y}(p)$ such that for any $p \in \mathbb{R}_+^N$, $\hat{y} \in \hat{Y}(p)$ if and only if $\hat{y} = \sum_{f \in \mathcal{F}} \hat{y}^f$ for some $\hat{y}^f \in \hat{Y}^f(p)$ for each $f \in \mathcal{F}$.*

Proof. Let Y be the aggregate production possibilities set defined in (5.13). To prove the "if" part of the theorem, fix $p \in \mathbb{R}_+^N$ and construct $\hat{y} = \sum_{f \in \mathcal{F}} \hat{y}^f$ for some $\hat{y}^f \in \hat{Y}^f(p)$ for each $f \in \mathcal{F}$. Suppose, to obtain a contradiction, that $\hat{y} \notin \hat{Y}(p)$, so that there exists y' such that $p \cdot y' > p \cdot \hat{y}$. By definition of the set Y, this implies that there exists $\{y^f\}_{f \in \mathcal{F}}$ with $y^f \in Y^f$ such that

$$p \cdot \left(\sum_{f \in \mathcal{F}} y^f \right) > p \cdot \left(\sum_{f \in \mathcal{F}} \hat{y}^f \right)$$

$$\sum_{f \in \mathcal{F}} p \cdot y^f > \sum_{f \in \mathcal{F}} p \cdot \hat{y}^f,$$

so that there exists at least one $f' \in \mathcal{F}$ such that

$$p \cdot y^{f'} > p \cdot \hat{y}^{f'},$$

which contradicts the hypothesis that $\hat{y}^f \in \hat{Y}^f(p)$ for each $f \in \mathcal{F}$ and completes this part of the proof.

To prove the "only if" part of the theorem, let $\hat{y} \in \hat{Y}(p)$ be a profit-maximizing choice for the representative firm. Then, since $\hat{Y}(p) \subset Y$, we have

$$\hat{y} = \sum_{f \in \mathcal{F}} y^f$$

for some $y^f \in Y^f$ for each $f \in \mathcal{F}$. Let $\hat{y}^f \in \hat{Y}^f(p)$. Then

$$\sum_{f \in \mathcal{F}} p \cdot y^f \le \sum_{f \in \mathcal{F}} p \cdot \hat{y}^f,$$

which implies that

$$p \cdot \hat{y} \le p \cdot \sum_{f \in \mathcal{F}} \hat{y}^f. \tag{5.14}$$

Since by hypothesis, $\sum_{f \in \mathcal{F}} \hat{y}^f \in Y$ and $\hat{y} \in \hat{Y}(p)$, we have

$$p \cdot \hat{y} \ge p \cdot \sum_{f \in \mathcal{F}} \hat{y}^f.$$

Therefore inequality (5.14) must hold with equality, which implies $y^f \in \hat{Y}^f(p)$ for each $f \in \mathcal{F}$. This completes the proof of the theorem. ∎

Theorem 5.4 implies that when there are no externalities and all factors are priced competitively, focusing on the aggregate production possibilities set of the economy—or equivalently on the representative firm—is without any loss of generality (naturally, assuming that the representative firm acts taking prices as given). Why is there such a difference between the representative household and representative firm assumptions? The answer is related to income effects. The reason why the representative household assumption is restrictive is that changes in prices create income effects, which affect different households differently. A representative household exists only when these income effects can be ignored, which is what the Gorman preferences guarantee. Since there are no income effects in producer theory, the representative firm assumption can be made without loss of generality.

Naturally, the fact that the production side of an economy can be modeled via a representative firm does not mean that heterogeneity among firms is uninteresting or unimportant. On the contrary, productivity differences across firms and firms' attempts to increase their productivity relative to others are central phenomena in this study of economic growth. Theorem 5.4 simply says that, when there is price-taking behavior, the production side of the economy can be equivalently represented by a single representative firm or an aggregate production possibilities set. I return to the issue of firm heterogeneity in the context of monopolistic competition in Part IV.

5.5 Problem Formulation

Let us now consider a discrete-time infinite-horizon economy and suppose that the economy admits a representative household. In particular, once again ignoring uncertainty, the utility of the representative household (starting at time $t = 0$) is given by

$$\sum_{t=0}^{\infty} \beta^t u(c(t)), \qquad (5.15)$$

where $\beta \in (0, 1)$ is again the discount factor.

In continuous time, the utility function (5.15) of the representative household becomes

$$\int_0^{\infty} \exp(-\rho t) u(c(t)) dt, \qquad (5.16)$$

where $\rho > 0$ is now the discount rate of the household.

Where does the exponential form of the discounting in (5.16) come from? Discounting in the discrete-time case was already referred to as "exponential," so the link should be apparent. More explicitly, let us calculate the value of \$1 after time T. Divide the interval $[0, T]$ into $T/\Delta t$ equally sized subintervals. Let the interest rate in each subinterval be equal to $r\Delta t$. It is important that the quantity r is multiplied by Δt, otherwise as we vary Δt, we would be changing the interest rate per unit of time. Using the standard compound interest rate formula, the value of \$1 in T periods at this interest rate is given by

$$v(T \mid \Delta t) = (1 + r\Delta t)^{T/\Delta t}.$$

Next, let us approach the continuous time limit by letting $\Delta t \to 0$ to obtain

$$v(T) = \lim_{\Delta t \to 0} v(T \mid \Delta t) = \lim_{\Delta t \to 0} (1 + r\Delta t)^{T/\Delta t} = \lim_{\Delta t \to 0} \left[\exp\left(\log (1 + r\Delta t)^{T/\Delta t} \right) \right],$$

where the last equality uses the fact that $\exp(\log x) = x$ for any $x > 0$. Thus

$$v(T) = \exp\left[\lim_{\Delta t \to 0} \log(1 + r\Delta t)^{T/\Delta t} \right]$$

$$= \exp\left[\lim_{\Delta t \to 0} \frac{T}{\Delta t} \log(1 + r\Delta t) \right].$$

The last term in square brackets has a limit of the form $0/0$ (or of the form $\infty \times 0$). To evaluate this limit, write it as

$$\lim_{\Delta t \to 0} \frac{\log(1 + r\Delta t)}{\Delta t/T} = \lim_{\Delta t \to 0} \frac{r/(1 + r\Delta t)}{1/T} = rT,$$

where the first equality follows from l'Hôpital's Rule (Theorem A.21 in Appendix A). Therefore

$$v(T) = \exp(rT).$$

Conversely, \$1 in T periods from now is worth $\exp(-rT)$ today. The same reasoning applies to discounting utility, so the utility of consuming $c(t)$ in period t evaluated at time $t = 0$ is $\exp(-\rho t) u(c(t))$, where ρ denotes the (subjective) discount rate. Equivalently, one could also go from exponential discounting in continuous time to discrete-time discounting. In particular, given a discount rate $\rho > 0$, the discount factor that applies during a time interval of length Δt is $\beta_{\Delta t} = \exp(-\rho \Delta t)$.

5.6 Welfare Theorems

We are ultimately interested in equilibrium growth. But there is a close connection between Pareto optima and competitive equilibria. These connections could not be exploited in the preceding chapters, because household (individual) preferences were not specified. I now introduce the First and Second Welfare Theorems and develop the relevant connections between the theory of economic growth and dynamic general equilibrium models.

Let us start with models that have a finite number of households, so that in terms of the notation in Sections 5.1 and 5.2 the set $\mathcal{H}$ is finite. Throughout I allow an infinite number of commodities, since growth models almost always feature an infinite number of time periods and thus an infinite number of commodities. The results stated in this section have analogues for economies with a continuum of commodities (corresponding to dynamic economies in continuous time), but for the sake of brevity and to reduce technical details, I focus on economies with a countable number of commodities.

Let the commodities be indexed by $j \in \mathbb{N}$, $x^h \equiv \{x_j^h\}_{j=0}^{\infty}$ be the consumption bundle of household h, and $\omega^h \equiv \{\omega_j^h\}_{j=0}^{\infty}$ be its endowment bundle. In addition, let us assume that feasible x^h values must belong to some *consumption set* $X^h \subset \mathbb{R}_+^{\infty}$. The most relevant interpretation for us is that there is an infinite number of dates, say indexed by t, and at each date $t = 0, 1, \ldots$, each household consumes a finite-dimensional vector of products, so that $\tilde{x}_t^h = \{\tilde{x}_{1,t}^h, \ldots, \tilde{x}_{N,t}^h\} \in \tilde{X}_t^h \subset \mathbb{R}_+^N$ for some $N \in \mathbb{N}$, and $x^h = \{\tilde{x}_t^h\}_{t=0}^{\infty}$. The consumption sets are introduced to ensure that households do not have negative consumption levels and are thus subsets of $\mathbb{R}_+^{\infty}$ (this restriction can be relaxed by allowing some components of the vector, e.g., those corresponding to different types of labor supply, to be negative; this extension is straightforward, and I do not do it here to conserve notation).

Let $\mathbf{X} \equiv \prod_{h \in \mathcal{H}} X^h$ be the Cartesian product of these consumption sets, which can be thought of as the aggregate consumption set of the economy. I also use the notation $\mathbf{x} \equiv \{x^h\}_{h \in \mathcal{H}}$ and $\boldsymbol{\omega} \equiv \{\omega^h\}_{h \in \mathcal{H}}$ to describe the entire set of consumption allocations and endowments in the economy. Feasibility of a consumption allocation requires that $\mathbf{x} \in \mathbf{X}$.

Each household in $\mathcal{H}$ has a well-defined preference ordering over consumption bundles. Suppose again that for each household $h \in \mathcal{H}$, preferences can be represented by a real-valued utility function $U^h : X^h \to \mathbb{R}$. The domain of this function is $X^h \subset \mathbb{R}_+^{\infty}$. I also assume that U^h is nondecreasing in each of its arguments for each $h \in \mathcal{H}$. Let $\mathbf{U} \equiv \{U^h\}_{h \in \mathcal{H}}$ be the set of utility functions.

Let us next describe the production side. Suppose that there is a finite number of firms represented by the set $\mathcal{F}$ and that each firm $f \in \mathcal{F}$ is characterized by a production set Y^f, which specifies levels of output firm f can produce from specified levels of inputs. In other words, $y^f \equiv \{y_j^f\}_{j=0}^{\infty}$ is a feasible production plan for firm f if $y^f \in Y^f$. For example, if there were only two commodities, labor and a final good, Y^f would include pairs $(-l, z)$ such that with labor input l (hence the negative sign), the firm can produce at most z. As is usual in general equilibrium theory, let us take each Y^f to be a cone, so that if $y^f \in Y^f$, then $\lambda y^f \in Y^f$ for any $\lambda \in \mathbb{R}_+$. This implies two important features: first, $\underline{0} \in Y^f$ for each $f \in \mathcal{F}$ (where $\underline{0}$ denotes the infinite sequence whose elements consist of 0); and second, each Y^f exhibits constant returns to scale. If there are diminishing returns to scale because of the presence of some scarce factors, such as entrepreneurial talent, this is added as an additional factor of production, and Y^f is still interpreted as a cone. Let $\mathbf{Y} \equiv \prod_{f \in \mathcal{F}} Y^f$ represent the aggregate production set in this economy, and let $\mathbf{y} \equiv \{y^f\}_{f \in \mathcal{F}}$ be such that $y^f \in Y^f$ for all f, or equivalently, $\mathbf{y} \in \mathbf{Y}$.[6]

The final object that needs to be described is the ownership structure of firms. In particular, if firms make profits, these profits should be distributed to some agents in the economy. We capture this distribution by assuming that there exists a sequence of profit shares represented by $\boldsymbol{\theta} \equiv \{\theta_f^h\}_{f \in \mathcal{F}, h \in \mathcal{H}}$ such that $\theta_f^h \geq 0$ for all f and h, and $\sum_{h \in \mathcal{H}} \theta_f^h = 1$ for all $f \in \mathcal{F}$. The number θ_f^h is the share of profits of firm f that will accrue to household h.

An economy $\mathcal{E}$ is described by preferences, endowments, production sets, consumption sets, and allocation of shares, that is, $\mathcal{E} \equiv (\mathcal{H}, \mathcal{F}, \mathbf{U}, \boldsymbol{\omega}, \mathbf{Y}, \mathbf{X}, \boldsymbol{\theta})$. An allocation in this economy is $(\mathbf{x}, \mathbf{y})$ such that $\mathbf{x}$ and $\mathbf{y}$ are feasible: $\mathbf{x} \in \mathbf{X}$, $\mathbf{y} \in \mathbf{Y}$, and

$$\sum_{h \in \mathcal{H}} x_j^h \leq \sum_{h \in \mathcal{H}} \omega_j^h + \sum_{f \in \mathcal{F}} y_j^f$$

for all $j \in \mathbb{N}$. The last requirement implies that the total consumption of each commodity cannot be more than the sum of its total endowment and net production. Once an economy $\mathcal{E}$ is specified, we can discuss how resources are (or should be) allocated in it. For example, we can think of *dictatorial allocations*, which would be chosen by a single individual (according to his or her preferences). Alternatively, we can think of the choices of a social planner wishing to maximize the weighted sum of the utilities of the households in the economy (which, as noted above, are closely connected to Pareto optimal allocations). Our main interest, however, is with *competitive equilibria,* which correspond to allocations resulting from a specific set of institutions combined with household maximizing behavior. These institutions are those of competitive markets, where, because of the existence of a large number of participants, households and firms take prices as given, and these prices are determined to clear markets. The additional, implicit, assumption is that of *complete markets*, which means that there exists a separate market for each commodity. In particular, this assumption implicitly rules out externalities, since externalities result from the nonmarket impact of one agent's actions on the utility or productivity of another agent. Though clearly an abstraction from reality, competitive equilibria are a good approximation to behavior in a range of circumstances, motivating the practice of using such equilibria as the benchmark in much of economic analysis.

The key component of a competitive equilibrium is the price system. A *price system* is a sequence $p \equiv \{p_j\}_{j=0}^{\infty}$ such that $p_j \geq 0$ for all j, with one of the commodities chosen as the numeraire and its price normalized to 1. Recall that $p \cdot z$ is again the inner product of sequences p and z (where, e.g., $z = x^h$ or y^f), so that $p \cdot z \equiv \sum_{j=0}^{\infty} p_j z_j$.[7] Then a competitive equilibrium—where externalities are absent, all commodities are traded competitively, all firms maximize profits, all households maximize their utility given their budget sets, and all markets clear—can be defined as follows.

Definition 5.1   *A competitive equilibrium for economy* $\mathcal{E} \equiv (\mathcal{H}, \mathcal{F}, \mathbf{U}, \boldsymbol{\omega}, \mathbf{Y}, \mathbf{X}, \boldsymbol{\theta})$ *is given by an allocation* $(\mathbf{x}^* = \{x^{h*}\}_{h \in \mathcal{H}}, \mathbf{y}^* = \{y^{f*}\}_{f \in \mathcal{F}})$ *and a price system* p^* *such that*

---

6. In some dynamic models, it is also useful to explicitly insist that the aggregate production possibilities set $\mathbf{Y}$ should allow for the transformation of date t goods into date $t + 1$ capital. However, this stipulation is not typically necessary in the models studied in this book.

7. You may note that such an inner product may not always exist in infinite-dimensional spaces. This issue will be explicitly dealt with in the proofs of Theorems 5.6 and 5.7 below.

1. *The allocation* $(\mathbf{x}^*, \mathbf{y}^*)$ *is feasible, that is,* $x^{h*} \in X^h$ *for all* $h \in \mathcal{H}$, $y^{f*} \in Y^f$ *for all* $f \in \mathcal{F}$, *and*

$$\sum_{h \in \mathcal{H}} x_j^{h*} \leq \sum_{h \in \mathcal{H}} \omega_j^h + \sum_{f \in \mathcal{F}} y_j^{f*} \quad \text{for all } j \in \mathbb{N}.$$

2. *For every firm* $f \in \mathcal{F}$, y^{f*} *maximizes profits:*

$$p^* \cdot y^{f*} \geq p^* \cdot y^f \quad \text{for all } y^f \in Y^f.$$

3. *For every household* $h \in \mathcal{H}$, x^{h*} *maximizes utility:*

$$U^h(x^{h*}) \geq U^h(x^h) \quad \text{for all } x \text{ such that } x^h \in X^h \text{ and } p^* \cdot x^h \leq p^* \cdot \left(\omega^h + \sum_{f \in \mathcal{F}} \theta_f^h y^f \right).$$

A major focus of general equilibrium theory is to establish the existence of a competitive equilibrium under reasonable assumptions. When there is a finite number of commodities and standard convexity assumptions are made on preferences and production sets, this is straightforward (in particular, the proof of existence involves simple applications of Theorems A.16, A.17, and A.18 in Appendix A). When an infinite number of commodities exists, as in infinite-horizon growth models, proving the existence of a competitive equilibrium is somewhat more difficult and requires more sophisticated arguments. Here I present the First and Second Welfare Theorems, which concern the efficiency properties of competitive equilibria, when they exist, and the decentralization of efficient (Pareto optimal) allocations as competitive equilibria. These results are more important than existence theorems for the focus in this book, both because in most growth models we will be able to characterize competitive equilibrium explicitly and also because the Second Welfare Theorem indirectly establishes the existence of a competitive equilibrium. Let us first recall the standard definition of Pareto optimality.

Definition 5.2 *A feasible allocation* $(\mathbf{x}, \mathbf{y})$ *for economy* $\mathcal{E} \equiv (\mathcal{H}, \mathcal{F}, \mathbf{U}, \boldsymbol{\omega}, \mathbf{Y}, \mathbf{X}, \boldsymbol{\theta})$ *is Pareto optimal if there exists no other feasible allocation* $(\hat{\mathbf{x}}, \hat{\mathbf{y}})$ *such that* $\hat{x}^h \in X^h$ *for all* $h \in \mathcal{H}$, $\hat{y}^f \in Y^f$ *for all* $f \in \mathcal{F}$,

$$\sum_{h \in \mathcal{H}} \hat{x}_j^h \leq \sum_{h \in \mathcal{H}} \omega_j^h + \sum_{f \in \mathcal{F}} \hat{y}_j^f \quad \text{for all } j \in \mathbb{N},$$

and

$$U^h\left(\hat{x}^h\right) \geq U^h\left(x^h\right) \quad \text{for all } h \in \mathcal{H}$$

with at least one strict inequality in the preceding relationship.

Our next result is the celebrated First Welfare Theorem for competitive economies. Before presenting this result, we need the following definition.

Definition 5.3 *Household* $h \in \mathcal{H}$ *is* locally nonsatiated *if, at each* $x^h \in X^h$, $U^h(x^h)$ *is strictly increasing in at least one of its arguments and* $U^h(x^h) < \infty$.

The latter requirement in this definition is already implied by the fact that $U^h : X^h \to \mathbb{R}$, but it is included for additional emphasis, since it is important for the proof and also because if in fact $U^h(x^h) = \infty$, we could not meaningfully talk of $U^h(x^h)$ being strictly increasing. Also note that local nonsatiation at a price vector p implies that $p \cdot x^h < \infty$ (see Exercise 5.5).

Theorem 5.5 (First Welfare Theorem I)　*Suppose that* $(\mathbf{x}^*, \mathbf{y}^*, p^*)$ *is a competitive equilibrium of economy* $\mathcal{E} \equiv (\mathcal{H}, \mathcal{F}, \mathbf{U}, \boldsymbol{\omega}, \mathbf{Y}, \mathbf{X}, \boldsymbol{\theta})$ *with* $\mathcal{H}$ *finite. Assume that all households are locally nonsatiated. Then* $(\mathbf{x}^*, \mathbf{y}^*)$ *is Pareto optimal.*

Proof.　Suppose that $(\mathbf{x}^*, \mathbf{y}^*, p^*)$ is a competitive equilibrium. To obtain a contradiction, suppose that there exists a feasible $(\hat{\mathbf{x}}, \hat{\mathbf{y}})$ such that $U^h(\hat{x}^h) \geq U^h(x^{h*})$ for all $h \in \mathcal{H}$ and $U^h(\hat{x}^h) > U^h(x^{h*})$ for all $h \in \mathcal{H}'$, where $\mathcal{H}'$ is a nonempty subset of $\mathcal{H}$.

Since $(\mathbf{x}^*, \mathbf{y}^*, p^*)$ is a competitive equilibrium, it must be the case that for all $h \in \mathcal{H}$,

$$p^* \cdot \hat{x}^h \geq p^* \cdot x^{h*} \tag{5.17}$$

$$= p^* \cdot \left(\omega^h + \sum_{f \in \mathcal{F}} \theta_f^h y^{f*} \right)$$

and for all $h \in \mathcal{H}'$,

$$p^* \cdot \hat{x}^h > p^* \cdot \left(\omega^h + \sum_{f \in \mathcal{F}} \theta_f^h y^{f*} \right). \tag{5.18}$$

Inequality (5.18) follows immediately because x^{h*} is the utility-maximizing choice for household h; thus if $\hat{x}^h$ is strictly preferred, then it cannot be in the budget set. Inequality (5.17) follows with a similar reasoning. Suppose that it did not hold. Then, by the hypothesis of local nonsatiation, U^h must be strictly increasing in at least one of its arguments, let us say the j'th component of x. Then construct $\hat{x}^h(\varepsilon)$ such that $\hat{x}_j^h(\varepsilon) = \hat{x}_j^h$ and $\hat{x}_{j'}^h(\varepsilon) = \hat{x}_{j'}^h + \varepsilon$ for $\varepsilon > 0$. For ε sufficiently small, $\hat{x}^h(\varepsilon)$ is in household h's budget set and yields strictly greater utility than the original consumption bundle $\hat{x}^h$, contradicting the hypothesis that household h is maximizing utility. Also note that local nonsatiation implies that $U^h(x^h) < \infty$, and thus the right-hand sides of (5.17) and (5.18) are finite (and in particular, $p^* \cdot x^{h*} < \infty$ for all $h \in \mathcal{H}$).

Now summing (5.17) over $\mathcal{H} \backslash \mathcal{H}'$ and (5.18) over $\mathcal{H}'$ and combining the two, we have

$$p^* \cdot \sum_{h \in \mathcal{H}} \hat{x}^h > p^* \cdot \sum_{h \in \mathcal{H}} \left(\omega^h + \sum_{f \in \mathcal{F}} \theta_f^h y^{f*} \right) \tag{5.19}$$

$$= p^* \cdot \left(\sum_{h \in \mathcal{H}} \omega^h + \sum_{f \in \mathcal{F}} y^{f*} \right),$$

where the second line uses the fact that the sums are finite, so that the order of summation can be exchanged, and that by the definition of the shares $\sum_{h \in \mathcal{H}} \theta_f^h = 1$ for all $f \in \mathcal{F}$. Finally, since $\mathbf{y}^*$ is profit maximizing at prices p^*, we have

$$p^* \cdot \sum_{f \in \mathcal{F}} y^{f*} \geq p^* \cdot \sum_{f \in \mathcal{F}} y^f \quad \text{for any } \left\{ y^f \right\}_{f \in \mathcal{F}} \text{ with } y^f \in Y^f \text{ for all } f \in \mathcal{F}. \tag{5.20}$$

However, by feasibility of $\hat{x}^h$ (Condition 1 of Definition 5.1),

$$\sum_{h \in \mathcal{H}} \hat{x}_j^h \leq \sum_{h \in \mathcal{H}} \omega_j^h + \sum_{f \in \mathcal{F}} \hat{y}_j^f \quad \text{for all } j,$$

and therefore, by taking the inner products of both sides with p^*, and exploiting (5.20) and the fact that $p^* \geq \underline{0}$, we conclude

$$p^* \cdot \sum_{h \in \mathcal{H}} \hat{x}_j^h \leq p^* \cdot \left(\sum_{h \in \mathcal{H}} \omega_j^h + \sum_{f \in \mathcal{F}} \hat{y}_j^f \right)$$

$$\leq p^* \cdot \left(\sum_{h \in \mathcal{H}} \omega_j^h + \sum_{f \in \mathcal{F}} y_j^{f*} \right),$$

which contradicts (5.19), establishing that any competitive equilibrium allocation $(\mathbf{x}^*, \mathbf{y}^*)$ is Pareto optimal. ∎

The proof of the First Welfare Theorem is both intuitive and simple. The proof is based on two simple ideas. First, if another allocation Pareto dominates the competitive equilibrium prices, then it must be nonaffordable in the competitive equilibrium for at least one household. Second, profit maximization implies that any competitive equilibrium already maximizes the set of affordable allocations. The proof is also simple, since it only uses the summation of the values of commodities at a given price vector. In particular, it makes no convexity assumption. However, the proof also highlights the importance of the feature that the relevant sums exist and are finite. Otherwise, the last step would lead to the conclusion that "$\infty < \infty$," which may or may not be a contradiction. The fact that these sums exist, in turn, follows from two assumptions: finiteness of the number of individuals and nonsatiation. However, as noted before, working with economies that have only a finite number of households (even if there is an infinite number of commodities) is not always sufficient for our purposes. For this reason, the next theorem provides a version of the First Welfare Theorem with an infinite number of households. For simplicity, here I take $\mathcal{H}$ to be a countably infinite set (e.g., $\mathcal{H} = \mathbb{N}$). The next theorem generalizes the First Welfare Theorem to this case. It makes use of an additional assumption to take care of infinite sums.

Theorem 5.6 (First Welfare Theorem II) *Suppose that* $(\mathbf{x}^*, \mathbf{y}^*, p^*)$ *is a competitive equilibrium of the economy* $\mathcal{E} \equiv (\mathcal{H}, \mathcal{F}, \mathbf{U}, \boldsymbol{\omega}, \mathbf{Y}, \mathbf{X}, \boldsymbol{\theta})$ *with* $\mathcal{H}$ *countably infinite. Assume that all households are locally nonsatiated and*

$$p^* \cdot \omega^* \equiv \sum_{h \in \mathcal{H}} \sum_{j=0}^{\infty} p_j^* \omega_j^h < \infty.$$

Then $(\mathbf{x}^*, \mathbf{y}^*, p^*)$ *is Pareto optimal.*

Proof. The proof is the same as that of Theorem 5.5 with a major difference. Local nonsatiation does not guarantee that the summations are finite in (5.19), since the summations are over an infinite number of households. In particular, (5.17) and (5.18) from the proof of Theorem 5.5 still apply, and we have $p^* \cdot x^{h*} < \infty$ for each $h \in \mathcal{H}$. Moreover, by profit maximization, $p^* \cdot \sum_{f \in \mathcal{F}} y^{f*} < \infty$. Now summing (5.17) over $\mathcal{H} \backslash \mathcal{H}'$ and (5.18) over $\mathcal{H}'$ yields (5.19), provided that

$$p^* \cdot \omega^* \equiv \sum_{h \in \mathcal{H}} \sum_{j=0}^{\infty} p_j^* \omega_j^h < \infty.$$

Then the remaining relations in the proof of Theorem 5.5 apply and yield a contradiction, establishing the desired result. ∎

Theorem 5.6 is particularly useful in the analysis of overlapping generations models in Chapter 9. The assumption that $\sum_{h \in \mathcal{H}} \sum_{j=0}^{\infty} p_j^* \omega_j^h < \infty$ is not very restrictive; for example, in dynamic models, discounting ensures that this condition is generally satisfied. The reader may also note that when we apply Theorem 5.5 to a infinite-horizon economy with infinitely-lived agents, this condition is satisfied automatically (since, otherwise, local nonsatiation would be violated). However there also exist reasonable and important economic models, such as the overlapping generations models, that can lead to equilibria where $\sum_{h \in \mathcal{H}} \sum_{j=0}^{\infty} p_j^* \omega_j^h = \infty$.

Let us next turn to the Second Welfare Theorem, which is the converse of the First Welfare Theorem. It answers the question of whether a Pareto optimal allocation can be decentralized as a competitive equilibrium. The Second Welfare Theorem requires a number of additional assumptions on preferences and technology, such as the convexity of consumption and production sets and of preferences. When the set of commodities is infinite, this theorem also requires several technical assumptions (the equivalents of which are trivially satisfied when the number of commodities is finite). Convexity assumptions are necessary because the Second Welfare Theorem implicitly contains an argument for the existence of equilibrium, which runs into problems in the presence of nonconvexities. Before stating this theorem, recall that the consumption set of each household $h \in \mathcal{H}$ is $X^h \subset \mathbb{R}_+^\infty$, so a typical element of X^h is $x^h = (x_0^h, x_1^h, x_2^h, \ldots)$, where x_t^h can be interpreted as the (finite-dimensional) vector of consumption of individual h at time t, that is, $x_t^h = (x_{1,t}^h, x_{2,t}^h, \ldots, x_{N,t}^h)$. Similarly, a typical element of the production set of firm $f \in \mathcal{F}$, Y^f, is of the form $y^f = (y_0^f, y_1^f, y_2^f, \ldots)$.

Let us also define $x^h[T] = (x_0^h, x_1^h, x_2^h, \ldots, x_T^h, 0, 0, \ldots)$ and $y^f[T] = (y_0^f, y_1^f, y_2^f, \ldots, y_T^f, 0, 0, \ldots)$. In other words, these are truncated sequences that involve zero consumption or zero production after some date T. It can be verified that $\lim_{T \to \infty} x^h[T] = x^h$ and $\lim_{T \to \infty} y^f[T] = y^f$ in the product topology (see Section A.4 in Appendix A). Finally, since in this case each x^h (or y^f) is an N-dimensional vector, with a slight abuse of notation, I use $p \cdot x^h$ for an appropriately defined inner product, for example,

$$p \cdot x^h = \sum_{t=0}^{\infty} \sum_{j=1}^{N} p_{j,t} x_{j,t}^h.$$

Theorem 5.7 (Second Welfare Theorem) *Consider a Pareto optimal allocation $(\mathbf{x}^*, \mathbf{y}^*)$ in an economy with endowment vector ω, production sets $\{Y^f\}_{f \in \mathcal{F}}$, consumption sets $\{X^h\}_{h \in \mathcal{H}}$, and utility functions $\{U^h(\cdot)\}_{h \in \mathcal{H}}$. Suppose that all production and consumption sets are convex, all production sets are cones, and all utility functions are continuous and quasi-concave and satisfy local nonsatiation. Moreover, suppose also that (i) there exists $\chi < \infty$ such that $\sum_{h \in \mathcal{H}} x_{j,t}^h < \chi$ for all j and t; (ii) $\underline{0} \in X^h$ for each h; (iii) for any h and $x^h, \bar{x}^h \in X^h$ such that $U^h(x^h) > U^h(\bar{x}^h)$, there exists $\bar{T}$ (possibly as a function of h, x^h, and $\bar{x}^h$) such that $U^h(x^h[T]) > U^h(\bar{x}^h)$ for all $T \geq \bar{T}$; and (iv) for any f and $y^f \in Y^f$, there exists $\tilde{T}$ such that $y^f[T] \in Y^f$ for all $T \geq \tilde{T}$. Then there exist a price vector p^* and endowment and share allocations (ω^*, θ^*) such that in economy $\mathcal{E} \equiv (\mathcal{H}, \mathcal{F}, \mathbf{U}, \omega^*, \mathbf{Y}, \mathbf{X}, \theta^*)$:*

1. *the endowment allocation ω^* satisfies $\omega = \sum_{h \in \mathcal{H}} \omega^{h*}$;*
2. *for all $f \in \mathcal{F}$,*

$$p^* \cdot y^{f*} \geq p^* \cdot y^f \quad \text{for any } y^f \in Y^f; \quad \text{and}$$

3. *for all $h \in \mathcal{H}$,*

$$\text{if } U^h(x^h) > U^h(x^{h*}) \quad \text{for some } x^h \in X^h \text{ then } p^* \cdot x^h \geq p^* \cdot w^{h*},$$

where

$$w^{h*} \equiv \omega^{h*} + \sum_{f \in \mathcal{F}} \theta_f^{h*} y^{f*}.$$

Moreover, if $p^* \cdot w^{h*} > 0$ for each $h \in \mathcal{H}$, then economy $\mathcal{E}$ has a competitive equilibrium $(\mathbf{x}^*, \mathbf{y}^*, p^*)$.

The proof of this theorem involves the application of the Geometric Hahn-Banach Theorem (Theorem A.27). It is somewhat long and involved. For this reason, its proof is provided in the next (starred) section. Here notice that if, instead of an infinite-dimensional economy, we were dealing with an economy with a finite commodity space, say with N commodities, then parts ii–iv of the hypothesis in the theorem, would be satisfied automatically by taking $\bar{T} = \tilde{T} = N$. In fact, this condition is not imposed in the statement of the Second Welfare Theorem in economies with a finite number of commodities. Its role in dynamic economies is that changes in allocations that are very far in the future should not have a large effect on utility. This condition is naturally satisfied in infinite-horizon economies with discounted utility and separable production structure. Intuitively, if a sequence of consumption levels x^h is strictly preferred to the sequence $\bar{x}^h$, then setting the elements of x^h and $\bar{x}^h$ to 0 in the very far (and thus heavily discounted) future should not change this conclusion (since discounting implies that x^h could not be strictly preferred to $\bar{x}^h$ because of higher consumption under x^h in the arbitrarily far future). Similarly, if some production vector y^f is feasible, the separable production structure implies that $y^f[T]$, which involves zero production after some date T, must also be feasible. Exercise 5.13 demonstrates these claims more formally. One difficulty in applying this theorem is that U^h may not be defined when the vector x^h involves zeros (e.g., when instantaneous utility of consumption is given by $\log c$). Exercise 5.14 shows that the theorem can be generalized to the case in which there exists a sufficiently small positive scalar $\varepsilon > 0$ and a sequence $\underline{\varepsilon}$ with each element equal to ε such that X^h (for all $h \in \mathcal{H}$) is restricted to $x^h \geq \underline{\varepsilon}$.

The conditions for the Second Welfare Theorem are more difficult to satisfy than those for the First Welfare Theorem because of the convexity requirements. In many ways, it is also the more important of the two theorems. While the First Welfare Theorem is celebrated as a formalization of Adam Smith's invisible hand, the Second Welfare Theorem establishes the stronger result that any Pareto optimal allocation can be decentralized as a competitive equilibrium. An immediate corollary of this property is an existence result; since the Pareto optimal allocation can be decentralized as a competitive equilibrium, a competitive equilibrium must exist (at least for the endowments leading to Pareto optimal allocations).

The Second Welfare Theorem motivates many macroeconomists to look for the set of Pareto optimal allocations instead of explicitly characterizing competitive equilibria. This approach is especially useful in dynamic models, in which competitive equilibria can sometimes be quite difficult to characterize or even to specify, while the characterization of Pareto optimal allocations is typically more straightforward.

The real power of the Second Welfare Theorem in dynamic macro models comes when it is combined with a normative representative household. Recall that Theorem 5.3 shows an equivalence between Pareto optimal allocations and optimal allocations for the representative household. In certain models, including many—but not all—growth models studied in this book, the combination of a normative representative household and the Second Welfare Theorem enables us to characterize *the optimal growth path* that maximizes the utility of the representative household and assert that this path corresponds to a competitive equilibrium.

5.7 Proof of the Second Welfare Theorem (Theorem 5.7) *

In this section, I provide a proof of the Second Welfare Theorem. The most important part of the theorem is proved using the Geometric Hahn-Banach Theorem (Theorem A.27).

Proof of Theorem 5.7. First, I establish that there exist a price vector p^* and an endowment and share allocation (ω^*, θ^*) that satisfy conditions 1–3 of Theorem 5.7. This proof has two parts.

(Part 1) This part follows from the Geometric Hahn-Banach Theorem (Theorem A.27). Define the "more preferred" sets for each $h \in \mathcal{H}$ as

$$P^h = \left\{ x^h \in X^h : U^h(x^h) > U^h(x^{h*}) \right\}.$$

Clearly, each P^h is convex. Let $P = \sum_{h \in \mathcal{H}} P^h$ and $Y' = \sum_{f \in \mathcal{F}} Y^f + \{\omega\}$, where recall that $\omega = \sum_{h \in \mathcal{H}} \omega^{h*}$, so that Y' is the sum of the production sets shifted by the endowment vector. Both P and Y' are convex (since each P^h and each Y^f is convex). Let the sequences of production plans for each firm be elements of the vector space ℓ_∞^N, which includes infinite sequences of vectors of the form $y^f = (y_0^f, y_1^f, \ldots)$, with each $y_j^f \in \mathbb{R}_+^N$. Since each production set is a cone, $Y' = \sum_{f \in \mathcal{F}} Y^f + \{\omega\}$ has an interior point (the argument is identical to that of Exercise A.31 in Appendix A). Moreover, let $x^* = \sum_{h \in \mathcal{H}} x^{h*}$ (and similarly $x = \sum_{h \in \mathcal{H}} x^h$). By feasibility and local nonsatiation, $x^* = \sum_{f \in \mathcal{F}} y^{f*} + \omega$. Then $x^* \in Y'$ and also $x^* \in \overline{P}$ (where recall that $\overline{P}$ is the closure of P).

Next observe that $P \cap Y' = \emptyset$. Otherwise, there would exist $\tilde{y} \in Y'$, which is also in P. The existence of such a $\tilde{y}$ would imply that, if distributed appropriately across the households, $\tilde{y}$ would make all households equally well off and at least one of them would be strictly better off (e.g., by the definition of the set P, there would exist $\{\tilde{x}^h\}_{h \in \mathcal{H}}$ such that $\sum_{h \in \mathcal{H}} \tilde{x}^h = \tilde{y}$, $\tilde{x}^h \in X^h$, and $U^h(\tilde{x}^h) \geq U^h(x^{h*})$ for all $h \in \mathcal{H}$ with at least one strict inequality). This would contradict the hypothesis that $(\mathbf{x}^*, \mathbf{y}^*)$ is a Pareto optimum.

Since Y' has an interior point, P and Y' are convex, and $P \cap Y' = \emptyset$, Theorem A.27 implies that there exists a nonzero continuous linear functional ϕ such that

$$\phi(y) \leq \phi(x^*) \leq \phi(x) \quad \text{for all } y \in Y' \quad \text{and all } x \in P. \tag{5.21}$$

(Part 2) I next show that the linear functional ϕ can be interpreted as a price vector, in particular, that it has an inner product representation. Consider the functional

$$\bar{\phi}(x) = \lim_{T \to \infty} \phi(x[T]), \tag{5.22}$$

where recall that for $x^h = (x_0^h, x_1^h, x_2^h, \ldots)$, $x^h[T] = (x_0^h, x_1^h, x_2^h, \ldots, x_T^h, 0, 0, \ldots)$. The main step of this part of the theorem involves showing that $\bar{\phi}$ is a well-defined continuous linear functional, also separating Y' and P as in (5.21). In what follows, let $\|x\|$ be the sup norm of x (short for $\|\cdot\|_\infty$) and let $\|\phi\|$ be the norm of the linear operator ϕ (see Appendix A).

First, let us define $\underline{x}_t^h \equiv (0, 0, \ldots, x_t^h, 0, \ldots,)$. That is, $\underline{x}_t^h$ is the same as the sequence x^h with zeros everywhere except its tth element. Next, note that by the linearity of ϕ,

$$\phi(x[T]) = \sum_{t=0}^{T} \phi(\underline{x}_t).$$

Clearly, if $\lim_{T\to\infty}\sum_{t=0}^{T}\left|\phi(\underline{x}_t)\right|$ exists and is well defined, then $\sum_{t=0}^{T}\phi(\underline{x}_t)$ would be absolutely convergent and thus $\lim_{T\to\infty}\phi(x[T])$ would exist (see Fact A.7). To show this, let us also define $\underline{z}^{\phi}\equiv(\underline{z}_0^{\phi},\underline{z}_1^{\phi},\ldots)$, where

$$\underline{z}_t^{\phi}\equiv\begin{cases}\underline{x}_t & \text{if } \phi(\underline{x}_t)\geq 0,\\ -\underline{x}_t & \text{if } \phi(\underline{x}_t)<0.\end{cases}$$

Then by definition,

$$\sum_{t=0}^{T}\left|\phi(\underline{x}_t)\right|=\phi(\underline{z}^{\phi}[T])$$

$$\leq\|\phi\|\left\|\underline{z}^{\phi}[T]\right\|$$

$$=\|\phi\|\,\|x[T]\|$$

$$\leq\|\phi\|\,\|x\|,$$

where the first line uses the definition of $\underline{z}^{\phi}$, the second line uses the fact that ϕ is a linear functional, the third line exploits the fact that the norm $\|\cdot\|$ does not depend on whether the elements are negative or positive, and the final line uses $\|x\|\geq\|x[T]\|$. This string of relationships implies that the sequence $\{\sum_{t=0}^{T}|\phi(\underline{x}_t)|\}_{T=1}^{\infty}$, which naturally dominates the sequence $\{\phi(x[T])\}_{T=1}^{\infty}$, is bounded (by $\|\phi\|\,\|x\|<\|\phi\|\,\chi<\infty$, since $\|x\|<\chi$ by hypothesis). This establishes that $\{\phi(x[T])\}_{T=1}^{\infty}$ converges and thus $\bar{\phi}(x)$ in (5.22) is well defined. The last inequality above also implies that $\bar{\phi}(x)\leq\|\phi\|\,\|x\|$, so $\bar{\phi}$ is a bounded, and thus continuous, linear functional (see Theorem A.26).

Next, for $t\in\mathbb{N}$, define $\bar{\phi}_t:X_t\to\mathbb{R}$ as $\bar{\phi}_t:x_t\mapsto\phi(\underline{x}_t)$ (where recall that $x=(x_0,x_1,\ldots,x_t,\ldots)$, $\underline{x}_t=(0,0,\ldots,x_t,0,\ldots)$, and $X_t\subset\mathbb{R}_+^N$, with $x_t\in X_t$). Clearly, $\bar{\phi}_t$ is a linear functional (since ϕ is linear) and moreover, since the domain of $\bar{\phi}_t$ is a subset of a Euclidean space, it has an inner product representation, and in particular, there exists $p_t^*\in\mathbb{R}^N$ such that

$$\bar{\phi}_t(x_t)=p_t^*\cdot x_t\quad\text{for all } x_t\in\mathbb{R}^N.$$

This representation also implies that

$$\bar{\phi}(x)=\lim_{T\to\infty}\phi(x[T])=\lim_{T\to\infty}\sum_{t=0}^{T}\bar{\phi}_t(x_t)=\lim_{T\to\infty}\sum_{t=0}^{T}p_t^*\cdot x_t,$$

so that $\bar{\phi}$ is a continuous linear functional with an inner product representation.

To complete this part of the proof, we need to show that $\bar{\phi}(x)=\sum_{j=0}^{\infty}\bar{\phi}(x_j)$ can be used instead of ϕ as the continuous linear functional in (5.21). We will first establish the following four steps:

(a) $\phi(x^*)\leq\bar{\phi}(x)$ for all $x\in P$,

(b) $\phi(x^*)\geq\bar{\phi}(y')$ for all $y'\in Y'$,

(c) $\bar{\phi}(x^*)\leq\phi(x^*)$,

(d) $\phi(x^*)\leq\bar{\phi}(x^*)$.

The desired result follows by combining these four steps. To prove each of these steps, we will make use of the hypotheses that $\underline{0} \in X^h$ for each $h \in \mathcal{H}$, and moreover that (i) for any $h \in \mathcal{H}$ and $x^h, \bar{x}^h \in X^h$ with $U^h(x^h) > U^h(\bar{x}^h)$, there exists $\bar{T}^h$ such that $U^h(x^h[T]) > U^h(\bar{x}^h)$ for all $T \geq \bar{T}^h$, and (ii) for any $f \in \mathcal{F}$ and $y^f \in Y^f$, there exists $\tilde{T}$ such that $y^f[T] \in Y^f$ for all $T \geq \tilde{T}$.

In particular, take $x \in P$ and recall that $x = \sum_{h \in \mathcal{H}} x^h$, with $x^h \in P^h$. Let $T^h(T) \equiv \max\{\bar{T}^h, \tilde{T}, T\}$, and drop the dependence on T to simplify notation. Since each x^h has the property that $U^h(x^h) > U^h(x^{h*})$ for each $h \in \mathcal{H}$, we have that $U^h(x^h[T^h]) > U^h(x^{h*})$ for each $h \in \mathcal{H}$. Moreover, since $\sum_{h \in \mathcal{H}} x^h[T^h]$ is in P, we also have

$$\phi(x^*) \leq \phi\left(\sum_{h \in \mathcal{H}} x^h[T^h]\right),$$

(where again recall that $x^* = \sum_{h \in \mathcal{H}} x^{h*}$). Since ϕ is linear, we also have

$$\phi\left(\sum_{h \in \mathcal{H}} x^h[T^h]\right) = \sum_{h \in \mathcal{H}} \phi(x^h[T^h]).$$

By definition $\lim_{T \to \infty} \phi(x^h[T^h]) = \bar{\phi}(x^h)$ (where recall that $T^h = T^h(T)$). Since each $\bar{\phi}(x^h)$ is well defined and ϕ is linear, this implies that as $T \to \infty$, $\phi\left(\sum_{h \in \mathcal{H}} x^h[T^h]\right) \to \bar{\phi}(x)$ and establishes step (a).

Next, take $y' \in Y'$. By hypothesis, $y'[T] \in Y'$ for T sufficiently large. Then

$$\phi(x^*) \geq \phi(y'[T]) = \bar{\phi}(y'[T]) \text{ for } T \text{ sufficiently large.}$$

Taking the limit as $T \to \infty$ establishes step (b).

Now, take $y' \in \text{Int } Y'$ and construct the sequence $\{y'_n\}$ with $y'_n = (1 - 1/n)x^* + y'/n$. Clearly, $y'_n \in Y'$ for each n and again by hypothesis, $y'_n[T] \in Y'$ for T sufficiently large. Thus with the same argument as in the previous paragraph, $\phi(x^*) \geq \bar{\phi}(y'_n[T])$ for each n (and for T sufficiently large). Taking the limit as $T \to \infty$ and then $n \to \infty$, we obtain step (c).

Finally, let $x^*_n = (1 + 1/n)x^*$. By local nonsatiation $x^*_n \in P$ for each n. This implies that $x^*_n[T] \in P$ for T sufficiently large and therefore

$$\phi(x^*_n[T]) = \bar{\phi}(x^*_n[T]) \geq \phi(x^*)$$

for each n and for T sufficiently large. Taking the limit as $T \to \infty$ and then $n \to \infty$, we obtain step (d).

Combining steps (a)–(d) establishes that $\bar{\phi}(x)$ can be used as the continuous linear functional separating P and Y'. As shown above, $\bar{\phi}(x)$ has an inner product representation of the form $\bar{\phi}(x) = \sum_{t=0}^{\infty} \phi_t(x_t) = p^* \cdot x$. Moreover, since each U^h is nondecreasing in its arguments, we have that $p^* \geq \underline{0}$. Thus, p^* can be interpreted as a price vector (functional).

Parts 1 and 2 have therefore established that there exists a price vector p^* such that conditions 1–3 in the theorem hold. Then, condition 1 of Definition 5.1 is satisfied by feasibility. Condition 2 in the theorem is sufficient to establish that all firms maximize profits at the price vector p^* (condition 2 of Definition 5.1). To show that all households maximize utility at the price vector p^* (condition 3 of Definition 5.1), use the hypothesis that $p^* \cdot w^{h*} > 0$ for each $h \in \mathcal{H}$. We know from condition 3 of the theorem that if $x^h \in X^h$ involves $U^h(x^h) > U^h(x^{h*})$, then $p^* \cdot x^h \geq p^* \cdot w^{h*}$. It is then straightforward to show that there cannot exist such an x^h that is strictly preferred to x^{h*} and satisfies $p^* \cdot x^h \leq p^* \cdot w^{h*}$. In particular, let

$\underline{\varepsilon} = (0, 0, \ldots, , \varepsilon, 0, \ldots)$, with ε corresponding to some $x^h_{j,t} > 0$ (such a strictly positive $x^h_{j,t}$ exists, since $p^* \cdot x^h \geq p^* \cdot w^{h*} > 0$). Then for $\varepsilon > 0$ and small enough,

$$x^h - \underline{\varepsilon} \in X^h, \quad U^h\left(x^h - \underline{\varepsilon}\right) > U^h\left(x^{h*}\right), \quad \text{and} \quad p^* \cdot \left(x^h - \underline{\varepsilon}\right) < p^* \cdot w^{h*},$$

thus violating condition 3 of the theorem. This establishes that for all $x^h \in X^h$ with $p^* \cdot x^h \leq p^* \cdot w^{h*}$, we have $U^h(x^h) \leq U^h(x^{h*})$, and thus condition 3 of Definition 5.1 holds and all households maximize utility at the price vector p^*. Thus $(\mathbf{x}^*, \mathbf{y}^*, p^*)$ is a competitive equilibrium. ∎

5.8 Sequential Trading

A final issue that is useful to discuss at this point relates to *sequential trading*. Standard general equilibrium models, in particular, the *Arrow-Debreu equilibrium* notion, assume that all commodities are traded at a given point in time—and once and for all. In the context of a dynamic model, where some of the different commodities correspond to the same product at different times, this assumption implies that trading takes place at the initial date, and there are no further trades in the future. This is not a good approximation to reality, and as we have already seen in the context of the Solow growth model in Chapter 2, growth models typically assume that firms hire capital and labor at each t, and households make their consumption decisions for time t at time t. Does the presence of this type of sequential trading make any difference to the insights of general equilibrium analysis? If so, then the applicability of the lessons from general equilibrium theory to dynamic macroeconomic models would be limited. Fortunately, in the presence of complete markets, sequential trading gives the same result as trading at a single point in time.

More explicitly, in the Arrow-Debreu equilibrium of a dynamic general equilibrium model at time $t = 0$, households agree on all future trades (including trades of goods that are not yet produced). Sequential trading, on the other hand, corresponds to separate markets opening at each t and households trading labor, capital, and consumption goods in each such market at each period. Clearly, both for mathematical convenience and descriptive realism, we would like to think of macroeconomic models as involving sequential trading, with separate markets at each date.

The key result concerning the comparison of models with trading at a single point in time and those with sequential trading is due to Kenneth Arrow (1964). Arrow's focus was on trading across states of nature. However, his results also imply that with complete markets trading at a single point in time and sequential trading are equivalent. The easiest way of seeing this equivalence is to consider the Arrow securities already discussed in Chapter 2. (Basic) Arrow securities provide an economical means of transferring resources across different dates and different states of nature. Instead of completing all trades at a single point in time, say at time $t = 0$, households can trade Arrow securities and then use these securities to purchase goods at different dates or after different states of nature have been revealed. While Arrow securities are most useful when there is uncertainty as well as a temporal dimension, for our purposes it is sufficient to focus on the transfer of resources across different dates.

The reason sequential trading with Arrow securities achieves the same result as trading at a single point in time is simple: by the definition of a competitive equilibrium, households correctly anticipate all prices that they will be facing at different dates (and in different states of nature) and purchase sufficient Arrow securities to cover the expenses that they will incur once the time to trade comes. In other words, instead of buying claims at time $t = 0$ for $x^h_{j,t'}$

units of commodity $j = 1, \ldots, N$ at date $t' > 0$ at prices $(p_{1,t'}, \ldots, p_{N,t'})$, it is sufficient for household h to have an income of $\sum_{j=1}^{N} p_{j,t'} x_{j,t'}^h$ and know that it can purchase as many units of each commodity as it wishes at time t' at the price vector $(p_{1,t'}, \ldots, p_{N,t'})$.

This result can be stated in a slightly more formal manner. Let us consider a dynamic exchange economy running across periods $t = 0, 1, \ldots, T$, possibly with $T = \infty$ (with the convention that when $T = \infty$, all summations are assumed to take finite values). Nothing here depends on the assumption that we are focusing on an exchange economy, but suppressing production simplifies notation. Imagine that there are N goods at each date, denoted by $(x_{1,t}, \ldots, x_{N,t})$, and let the consumption of good j by household h at time t be denoted by $x_{j,t}^h$. Suppose that these goods are perishable, so that they are indeed consumed at time t. Denote the set of households by $\mathcal{H}$ and suppose that each household $h \in \mathcal{H}$ has a vector of endowments $(\omega_{1,t}^h, \ldots, \omega_{N,t}^h)$ at time t and preferences given by the time-separable function of the form

$$\sum_{t=0}^{T} (\beta^h)^t u^h (x_{1,t}^h, \ldots, x_{N,t}^h),$$

for some $\beta^h \in (0, 1)$. These preferences imply that there are no externalities and preferences are time-consistent. I also assume that all markets are open and competitive.

Let an Arrow-Debreu equilibrium be given by $(\mathbf{p}^*, \mathbf{x}^*)$, where $\mathbf{x}^*$ is the complete list of consumption vectors of each household $h \in \mathcal{H}$, that is,

$$\mathbf{x}^* = (x_{1,0}, \ldots x_{N,0}, \ldots, x_{1,T}, \ldots x_{N,T}),$$

with $x_{j,t} = \{x_{j,t}^h\}_{h \in \mathcal{H}}$ for each j and t, and $\mathbf{p}^*$ is the vector of complete prices

$$\mathbf{p}^* = (p_{1,0}^*, \ldots, p_{N,0}^*, \ldots, p_{1,T}^*, \ldots, p_{N,T}^*),$$

with one of the prices, say $p_{1,0}^*$, chosen as the numeraire, so that $p_{1,0}^* = 1$. In the Arrow-Debreu equilibrium, each household $h \in \mathcal{H}$ purchases and sells claims on each of the commodities only at $t = 0$ and thus simply chooses an allocation that satisfies the budget constraint

$$\sum_{t=0}^{T} \sum_{j=1}^{N} p_{j,t}^* x_{j,t}^h \leq \sum_{t=0}^{T} \sum_{j=1}^{N} p_{j,t}^* \omega_{j,t}^h.$$

Market clearing then requires

$$\sum_{h \in \mathcal{H}} x_{j,t}^h \leq \sum_{h \in \mathcal{H}} \omega_{j,t}^h$$

for each $j = 1, \ldots, N$ and $t = 0, 1, \ldots, T$.

In the equilibrium with sequential trading, markets for goods dated t open at time t. In addition, there are T bonds—Arrow securities—that are in zero net supply and can be traded among the households at time $t = 0$.[8] The bond indexed by t pays 1 unit of one of the goods, say good $j = 1$ at time t. Let the prices of bonds be denoted by $(q_1, \ldots, q_T)$, again expressed in units of good $j = 1$ (at time $t = 0$). Thus a household can purchase a unit of bond t at time

---

8. Note that the Arrow securities do not correspond to technologies for transforming goods dated t into goods dated $t' > t$. Instead they are simply units of account specifying what the income levels of different households are at different dates.

0 by paying q_t units of good 1, and in return, it will receive 1 unit of good 1 at time t (or conversely can sell short 1 unit of such a bond) The purchase of bond t by household h is denoted by $b_t^h \in \mathbb{R}$, and since each bond is in zero net supply, market clearing requires that

$$\sum_{h \in \mathcal{H}} b_t^h = 0 \quad \text{for each } t = 0, 1, \ldots, T.$$

Notice that this specification assumes that there are only T bonds (Arrow securities). More generally, we could have introduced additional bonds, for example, bonds traded at time $t > 0$ for delivery of good 1 at time $t' > t$. This restriction to only T bonds is without loss of any generality (see Exercise 5.10).

Sequential trading corresponds to each individual using their endowment plus (or minus) the proceeds from the corresponding bonds at each date t. Since there is a market for goods at each t, it turns out to be convenient (and possible) to choose a separate numeraire for each date t. Let us again suppose that this numeraire is good 1, so that $p_{1,t}^{**} = 1$ for all t. Therefore the budget constraint of household $h \in \mathcal{H}$ at time t, given the equilibrium price vector for goods and bonds, $(\mathbf{p}^{**}, \mathbf{q}^{**})$, can be written as

$$\sum_{j=1}^{N} p_{j,t}^{**} x_{j,t}^h \leq \sum_{j=1}^{N} p_{j,t}^{**} \omega_{j,t}^h + b_t^h \tag{5.23}$$

for $t = 0, 1, \ldots, T$, together with $\sum_{t=0}^{T} q_t^{**} b_t^h \leq 0$ and the normalization $q_0^{**} = 1$. Let an equilibrium of the sequential trading economy be denoted by $(\mathbf{p}^{**}, \mathbf{q}^{**}, \mathbf{x}^{**}, \mathbf{b}^{**})$, where once again $\mathbf{p}^{**}$ and $\mathbf{x}^{**}$ denote the entire lists of prices and quantities of consumption by each household, and $\mathbf{q}^{**}$ and $\mathbf{b}^{**}$ denote the vectors of bond prices and bond purchases by each household. Given this specification, the following theorem can be established.

Theorem 5.8 (Sequential Trading) *For the above-described economy, if $(\mathbf{p}^*, \mathbf{x}^*)$ is an Arrow-Debreu equilibrium, then there exists a sequential trading equilibrium $(\mathbf{p}^{**}, \mathbf{q}^{**}, \mathbf{x}^{**}, \mathbf{b}^{**})$, such that $\mathbf{x}^* = \mathbf{x}^{**}$, $p_{j,t}^{**} = p_{j,t}^*/p_{1,t}^*$ for all j and t, and $q_t^{**} = p_{1,t}^*$ for all $t > 0$. Conversely, if $(\mathbf{p}^{**}, \mathbf{q}^{**}, \mathbf{x}^{**}, \mathbf{b}^{**})$ is a sequential trading equilibrium, then there exists an Arrow-Debreu equilibrium $(\mathbf{p}^*, \mathbf{x}^*)$ with $\mathbf{x}^* = \mathbf{x}^{**}$, $p_{j,t}^* = p_{j,t}^{**} p_{1,t}^*$ for all j and t, and $p_{1,t}^* = q_t^{**}$ for all $t > 0$.*

Proof. See Exercise 5.9. ∎

This theorem implies that all the results concerning Arrow-Debreu equilibria apply to economies with sequential trading. In most of the models studied in this book the focus is on economies with sequential trading and (except in the context of models with explicit financial markets and with possible credit market imperfections) we assume that there exist Arrow securities to transfer resources across dates. These securities might be riskless bonds in zero net supply, or in models without uncertainty, this role is typically played by the capital stock. We also follow the approach leading to Theorem 5.8 and normalize the price of one good at each date to 1. Thus in economies with a single consumption good, like the Solow or the neoclassical growth models, the price of the consumption good in each date is normalized to 1, and the interest rates directly give the intertemporal relative prices. This is the justification for focusing on interest rates as the key relative prices in macroeconomic (economic growth) models. It should also be emphasized that the presence of Arrow securities to transfer resources across dates also implies that capital (financial) markets are perfect, and in particular, that there are no credit constraints. When such constraints exist, we need to be much more explicit about whether and how each household can transfer resources across different dates (see, e.g., Chapter 21).

One final point implicit in the argument leading to Theorem 5.8 should be highlighted. The equivalence of the Arrow-Debreu equilibria and sequential trading equilibria is predicated on the requirement that the budget constraints facing households are the same under both formulations. Though this stipulation seems obvious, it is not always trivial to ensure that households face exactly the same budget constraints in sequential trading equilibria as in the Arrow-Debreu equilibria. This issue is discussed further at the beginning of Chapter 8, when we introduce the neoclassical growth model.

5.9 Optimal Growth

Motivated by the discussion at the end of Section 5.6, let us start with an economy characterized by an aggregate production function, and a normative representative household (recall Theorem 5.3). The *optimal growth problem* in this context refers to characterizing the allocation of resources that maximizes the utility of the representative household. For example, if the economy consists of a number of identical households, then this problem corresponds to the Pareto optimal allocation giving the same (Pareto) weight to all households (recall Definition 5.2).[9] Therefore the optimal growth problem in discrete time with no uncertainty, no population growth, and no technological progress can be written as follows:

$$\max_{\{c(t),k(t)\}_{t=0}^{\infty}} \sum_{t=0}^{\infty} \beta^t u(c(t)), \tag{5.24}$$

subject to

$$k(t+1) = f(k(t)) + (1-\delta)k(t) - c(t), \tag{5.25}$$

with $k(t) \geq 0$ and given $k(0) > 0$. Here $u : \mathbb{R}_+ \to \mathbb{R}$ is the instantaneous utility function of the representative household. The objective function represents the discounted sum of instantaneous utilities. The constraint (5.25) is also straightforward to understand: total output per capita produced with capital-labor ratio $k(t)$, $f(k(t))$, together with a fraction $1 - \delta$ of the capital that is undepreciated make up the total resources of the economy at date t. Out of these resources, $c(t)$ is spent as consumption per capita and the rest becomes next period's capital-labor ratio, $k(t+1)$.

The optimal growth problem requires that the social planner chooses an entire sequence of consumption levels and capital stocks, subject only to the resource constraint (5.25). There are no additional equilibrium constraints. The initial level of capital stock $k(0) > 0$ has been specified as one boundary condition. But in contrast to the basic Solow model, the solution to this problem involves two, not one, dynamic (difference or differential) equations and thus necessitates two boundary conditions. The additional boundary condition does take the form of an initial condition but comes from the optimality of a dynamic plan in the form of a transversality condition. The relevant transversality conditions for this class of problems will be discussed in the next two chapters.

---

9. One can also imagine allocations in which ex ante identical households receive different weights and utility levels. Throughout, whenever the economy admits a normative representative household, I follow the standard practice of focusing on optima with equal Pareto weights.

This maximization problem can be solved in a number of ways, for example, by setting up an infinite-dimensional Lagrangian. But the most convenient and common way of approaching it is by using dynamic programming, which we will study in the next chapter.

An important question for us is whether the solution to the optimal growth problem can be decentralized as a competitive equilibrium; that is, whether the Second Welfare Theorem (Theorem 5.7) can be applied to this environment. The answer to this question is yes. In fact, one of the main motivations for developing Theorem 5.7 in this chapter has been its use in discounted growth problems, such as the baseline neoclassical growth model presented in this section. The details of how this theorem can be applied to the optimal growth problem are developed in Exercises 5.12–5.14.

It is also useful to note that even if we wished to bypass the Second Welfare Theorem and directly solve for competitive equilibria, we would have to solve a problem similar to the maximization of (5.24) subject to (5.25). In particular, to characterize the equilibrium, we would need to start with the maximizing behavior of households. Since the economy admits a representative household, we need only look at the maximization problem of this household. Assuming that the representative household has 1 unit of labor supplied inelastically and denoting its assets at time t by $a(t)$, this problem can be written as

$$\max_{\{c(t),a(t)\}_{t=0}^{\infty}} \sum_{t=0}^{\infty} \beta^t u(c(t))$$

subject to some given $a(0) > 0$ and

$$a(t+1) = (1+r(t))a(t) - c(t) + w(t), \tag{5.26}$$

where $r(t)$ is the net rate of return on assets (so that $1 + r(t)$ is the gross rate of return) and $w(t)$ is the equilibrium wage rate (and thus the wage earnings of the representative household). Market clearing then requires that $a(t) = k(t)$. The constraint (5.26) is the flow budget constraint, meaning that it links tomorrow's assets to today's. Here we need an additional condition to ensure that the flow budget constraint eventually converges (so that $a(t)$ should not go to negative infinity). This can be ensured by imposing a lifetime budget constraint. Since a flow budget constraint in the form of (5.26) is both more intuitive and often more convenient to work with, we will not work with the lifetime budget constraint but instead augment the flow budget constraint with a limiting condition, which is introduced and discussed in the next three chapters.

The formulation of the optimal growth problem in continuous time is very similar and takes the form

$$\max_{[c(t),k(t)]_{t=0}^{\infty}} \int_0^{\infty} \exp(-\rho t)u(c(t))dt \tag{5.27}$$

subject to

$$\dot{k}(t) = f(k(t)) - c(t) - \delta k(t), \tag{5.28}$$

with $k(t) \geq 0$ and given $k(0) > 0$. The objective function (5.27) is the direct continuous-time analogue of (5.24), and (5.28) gives the resource constraint of the economy, similar to (5.25) in discrete time. Once again this problem lacks one boundary condition, which is supplied by the transversality condition. The most convenient way of characterizing the solution to this problem is by optimal control theory, which is developed in Chapter 7.

5.10 Taking Stock

This chapter introduced the preliminaries necessary for an in-depth study of equilibrium and optimal growth theory. At some level it can be thought of as an "odds-and-ends" chapter, introducing the reader to the notions of representative household, dynamic optimization, welfare theorems, and optimal growth. However, the material here is more than odds and ends, since a good understanding of the general equilibrium foundations of economic growth and the welfare theorems is necessary for what is to come in Part III and later.

The most important messages from this chapter are as follows. First, the set of models in this book are examples of more general dynamic general equilibrium models. It is therefore important to understand which features of the growth models are general (in the sense that they do not depend on the specific simplifying assumptions) and which results depend on the further simplifying assumptions. In this respect, the First and the Second Welfare Theorems are essential. They show that, provided that all product and factor markets are competitive and that there are no externalities in production or consumption (and under some relatively mild technical assumptions), dynamic competitive equilibria are Pareto optimal and any Pareto optimal allocation can be decentralized as a dynamic competitive equilibrium. These results are especially relevant in Part III, where the focus is on competitive economies. Importantly, these results do not directly apply in our analysis of technological change, where product markets are monopolistic, or in our study of economic development, where various market imperfections play an important role.

Second, the most general class of dynamic general equilibrium models are not tractable enough for us to derive sharp results about the process of economic growth. For this reason, we often adopt a range of simplifying assumptions. The most important of these is the representative household assumption, which enables us to model the demand side of the economy as if it were generated by the optimizing behavior of a single household. We saw how this assumption is generally not satisfied but also how a certain class of preferences (the Gorman preferences) enable us to model economies as if they admitted a representative household, even with arbitrary distributions of wealth and income.

In addition, this chapter introduced the first formulation of the optimal growth problems in discrete and in continuous time. These are used as examples in the next two chapters.

5.11 References and Literature

This chapter covered a great deal of ground and often many details were omitted for brevity. Many readers will be familiar with some of the material in this chapter. Deaton and Muellbauer (1980), Hildenbrand and Kirman (1988), and Mas-Colell, Whinston, and Green (1995) provide excellent discussions of the issues related to aggregation and the representative household assumption. Some of the original contributions on this topic are contained in Gorman (1953, 1959, 1976, 1980) and Pollak (1971). These and many other relevant results on separability and aggregation appear in the works of W. M. (Terence) Gorman. Deaton and Muellbauer (1980) provide an excellent discussion of Gorman's work and the implications of Gorman preferences. Caselli and Ventura (2000) use Gorman preferences in the context of a model of capital accumulation with heterogeneous agents. Mas-Colell, Whinston, and Green also discuss the concepts of positive and normative representative households. The concept of normative representative household in Theorem 5.3 is motivated by the use of the representative household assumption in dynamic macroeconomic models (which focus on the maximization of the utility of a representative household to characterize all Pareto optimal allocations and competitive equilibria). This concept is stronger than the one in Mas-Colell, Whinston, and Green, who define a normative representative household for a given social welfare function.

The Debreu-Mantel-Sonnenschein Theorem (Theorem 5.1) was originally proved by Sonnenschein (1972) and then extended by Debreu (1974) and Mantel (1976). Both Mas-Colell, Whinston, and Green (1995) and Hildenbrand and Kirman (1988) present this theorem and sketch its proof. Both Deaton and Muellbauer (1980) and Hildenbrand and Kirman (1988) also show how such aggregation is possible under weaker assumptions on utility functions together with certain restrictions on the distribution of income (or endowments).

Some basic concepts from microeconomic theory were assumed in this chapter, and the reader can find a thorough exposition of these in Mas-Colell, Whinston, and Green (1995). These include Roy's Identity, used following Theorem 5.2 and then again in Theorem 5.3, and Walras's Law, the concept of a numeraire, and expected utility theory of von Neumann and Morgenstern, used throughout the analysis. The reader is also referred to Chapter 16 of Mas-Colell, Whinston, and Green and to Bewley (2007) for clear expositions of the different representation of Pareto optima (including the result that every Pareto optimal allocation is a solution to the maximization of the weighted average of utilities of households in the economy).

The Representative Firm Theorem (Theorem 5.4) presented here is quite straightforward, but I am not aware of any discussion of this theorem in the literature (or at least in the macroeconomics literature). It is important to distinguish the subject matter of this theorem from the Cambridge controversy in early growth theory, which revolved around the issue of whether different types of capital goods could be aggregated into a single capital index (see, e.g., Wan, 1971). The Representative Firm Theorem says nothing about this issue.

The best reference for the analysis of the existence of competitive equilibria and the welfare theorems with a finite number of households and a finite number of commodities is still Debreu's (1959) *Theory of Value*. This short book introduces all mathematical tools necessary for general equilibrium theory and gives a very clean exposition. Equally lucid and more modern are the treatments of the same topics in Mas-Colell, Whinston, and Green (1995) and Bewley (2007). The reader may also wish to consult Mas-Colell, Whinston, and Green (their Chapter 16) for a proof of the Second Welfare Theorem with a finite number of commodities (Theorem 5.7 in this chapter is more general, because it covers the case of an infinite number of commodities). Both of these books also have an excellent discussion of the necessary restrictions on preferences to allow preferences to be represented by utility functions. Mas-Colell, Whinston, and Green (their Chapter 19) also gives a very clear discussion of the role of Arrow securities and the relationship between trading at a single point in time and sequential trading. The classic reference on Arrow securities is Arrow (1964).

Neither Debreu (1959) nor Mas-Colell, Whinston, and Green (1995) discuss infinite-dimensional economies. The seminal reference for infinite-dimensional welfare theorems is Debreu (1954). Bewley (2007) contains a number of useful results on infinite-dimensional economies. Stokey, Lucas, and Prescott (1989, their Chapter 15) present existence and welfare theorems for economies with a finite number of households and countably infinite number of commodities. The mathematical prerequisites for their treatment are greater than what has been assumed here, but their treatment is both thorough and straightforward, once the reader makes the investment in the necessary mathematical techniques. The most accessible references for the Hahn-Banach Theorem, which is necessary for a proof of Theorem 5.7 in infinite-dimensional spaces, are Luenberger (1969), Kolmogorov and Fomin (1970), and Kreyszig (1978). Luenberger (1969) is also an excellent source for all the mathematical techniques used in Stokey, Lucas, and Prescott (1989) and also contains much material useful for appreciating continuous-time optimization.

On the distinction between the coefficient of relative risk aversion and the intertemporal elasticity of substitution discussed in Exercise 5.2, see Kreps (1988), Epstein and Zin (1989), and Becker and Boyd (1997).

5.12 Exercises

5.1 Recall that a solution $\{x(t)\}_{t=0}^{T}$ to a dynamic optimization problem is time-consistent if the following is true: if $\{x(t)\}_{t=0}^{T}$ is a solution starting at time $t = 0$, then $\{x(t)\}_{t=t'}^{T}$ is a solution to the continuation dynamic optimization problem starting from time $t = t' > 0$.

(a) Consider the following optimization problem

$$\max_{\{x(t)\}_{t=0}^{T}} \sum_{t=0}^{T} \beta^t u(x(t))$$

subject to

$$x(t) \in [0, \bar{x}], \quad \text{and}$$

$$G(x(0), \dots, x(T)) \leq 0.$$

Although you do not need to, you may assume that G is continuous and convex, and u is continuous and concave. Prove that any solution $\{x^*(t)\}_{t=0}^{T}$ to this problem is time-consistent.

(b) Consider the optimization problem

$$\max_{\{x(t)\}_{t=0}^{T}} u(x(0)) + \delta \sum_{t=1}^{T} \beta^t u(x(t))$$

subject to

$$x(t) \in [0, \bar{x}],$$

$$G(x(0), \dots, x(T)) \leq 0.$$

Suppose that the objective function at time $t = 1$ becomes $u(x(1)) + \delta \sum_{t=2}^{T} \beta^{t-1} u(x(t))$. Interpret this objective function (sometimes referred to as "hyperbolic discounting").

(c) Let $\{x^*(t)\}_{t=0}^{T}$ be a solution to the maximization problem in part b. Assume that the individual chooses $x^*(0)$ at $t = 0$ and then is allowed to reoptimize at $t = 1$, that is, she can now solve the problem

$$\max_{\{x(t)\}_{t=1}^{T}} u(x(1)) + \delta \sum_{t=2}^{T} \beta^{t-1} u(x(t))$$

subject to

$$x(t) \in [0, \bar{x}], \quad \text{and}$$

$$G(x^*(0), \dots, x(T)) \leq 0.$$

Prove that the solution from $t = 1$ onward, $\{x^{**}(t)\}_{t=1}^{T}$, is not necessarily the same as $\{x^*(t)\}_{t=1}^{T}$.

(d) Explain which standard axioms of preferences in basic general equilibrium theory are violated by the preferences in parts b and c of this exercise.

5.2 This exercise asks you to work through an example that illustrates the difference between the coefficient of relative risk aversion and the intertemporal elasticity of substitution. Consider a household with the following non-time-separable preferences over consumption levels at two dates:

$$V(c_1, c_2) = \mathbb{E}\left[\left(\frac{c_1^{1-\theta} - 1}{1-\theta}\right)^{\frac{\alpha-1}{\alpha}} + \beta\left(\frac{c_2^{1-\theta} - 1}{1-\theta}\right)^{\frac{\alpha-1}{\alpha}}\right]^{\frac{\alpha}{\alpha-1}},$$

where $\mathbb{E}$ is the expectations operator. The budget constraint of the household is

$$c_1 + \frac{1}{1+r}c_2 \leq W,$$

where r is the interest rate and W is its total wealth, which may be stochastic.

(a) First suppose that W is nonstochastic and equal to $W_0 > 0$. Characterize the utility maximizing choice of c_1 and c_2.

(b) Now suppose that W is distributed over the support $[\underline{W}, \overline{W}]$ with some distribution function $G(W)$, where $0 < \underline{W} < \overline{W} < \infty$. Characterize the utility maximizing choice of c_1 (made before the realization of W). Define the coefficient of relative risk aversion and the intertemporal elasticity of substitution in this case. Explain why these two measures are not necessarily the same.

5.3 Prove Theorem 5.2.

* 5.4 Generalize Theorem 5.3 to an economy with a continuum of commodities.

5.5 Show that if a household chooses a consumption bundle x^h at price vector p and is locally non-satiated, then $p \cdot x^h < \infty$.

5.6 (a) Derive the utility-maximizing demands for households in Example 5.1 and show that the resulting indirect utility function for each household is given by (5.5).

(b) Show that maximization of (5.6) leads to the indirect utility function corresponding to the representative household.

(c) Now suppose that $U^h(x_1^h, \ldots, x_N^h) = \sum_{j=1}^{N}(x_j^h - \xi_j^h)^{\frac{\sigma-1}{\sigma}}$. Repeat the same computations as in parts a and b and verify that the resulting indirect utility function is homogeneous of degree 0 in p and y but does not satisfy the Gorman form. Show, however, that a monotone transformation of the indirect utility function satisfies the Gorman form. Is this sufficient to ensure that the economy admits a representative household?

5.7 Construct a continuous-time version of the model with finite lives and random deaths (recall (5.12) in the text). In particular suppose that an individual faces a constant (Poisson) flow rate of death equal to $\nu > 0$ and has a true discount factor equal to ρ. Show that this individual behaves as if she were infinitely lived with an effective discount factor of $\rho + \nu$.

5.8 (a) Will dynastic preferences, such as those discussed in Section 5.2, lead to infinite-horizon maximization if the instantaneous utility functions of future generations are different ($u_t(\cdot)$ potentially different for each generation t)?

(b) How would the results be different if an individual cares about the continuation utility of his offspring with discount factor β, but also cares about the continuation utility of the offspring of his offspring with a smaller discount factor δ?

5.9 Prove Theorem 5.8.

5.10 Consider the sequential trading model discussed in Section 5.8 and suppose now that households can trade bonds at time t that deliver one unit of good t at time t'. Denote the price of such bonds by $q_{t,t'}$.

(a) Rewrite the budget constraint of household h at time t, (5.23), including these bonds.

(b) Prove an equivalent of Theorem 5.8 in this environment with the extended set of bonds.

5.11 Consider a two-period economy consisting of two types of households. N_A households have the utility function

$$u(c_1^h) + \beta_A u(c_2^h),$$

where c_1^h and c_2^h denote the consumption of household h in the two periods. The remaining N_B households have the utility function

$$u(c_1^h) + \beta_B u(c_2^h),$$

with $\beta_B < \beta_A$. The two groups have, respectively, incomes w_A and w_B at date 1 and can save this income to the second date at some exogenously given gross interest rate $R > 0$. Show that for general $u(\cdot)$, this economy does not admit a strong representative household, that is, a representative household without restricting the distribution of incomes. [Hint: show that different distributions of income will lead to different demands.]

5.12 Consider an economy consisting of H households each with a utility function at time $t = 0$ given by

$$\sum_{t=0}^{\infty} \beta^t u(c^h(t)),$$

with $\beta \in (0, 1)$, where $c^h(t)$ denotes the consumption of household h at time t. Suppose that $u(0) = 0$. The economy starts with an endowment of $y > 0$ units of the final good and has access to no production technology. This endowment can be saved without depreciating or gaining interest rate between periods.

(a) What are the Arrow-Debreu commodities in this economy?

(b) Characterize the set of Pareto optimal allocations of this economy.

(c) Prove that the Second Welfare Theorem (Theorem 5.7) can be applied to this economy.

(d) Consider an allocation of y units to the households, $\{y^h\}_{h=1}^{H}$, such that $\sum_{h=1}^{H} y^h = y$. Given this allocation, find the unique competitive equilibrium price vector and the corresponding consumption allocations.

(e) Are all competitive equilibria Pareto optimal?

(f) Derive a redistribution scheme for decentralizing the entire set of Pareto optimal allocations.

5.13 (a) Suppose that utility of household h given by

$$U(x^h(0), x^h(1), \ldots) = \sum_{t=0}^{\infty} \beta^t v^h(x^h(t))$$

where $x^h(t) \in X \subset \mathbb{R}_+^N$, $v^h : X \to \mathbb{R}$ is continuous, X is compact, and $\beta < 1$. Show that the hypothesis that for any x^h, $\bar{x}^h \in X^h$ with $U^h(x^h) > U^h(\bar{x}^h)$, there exists $\bar{T}$ (as a function of x^h and $\bar{x}^h$) such that $U^h(x^h[T]) > U^h(\bar{x}^h)$ for all $T \geq \bar{T}$ in Theorem 5.7 (hypothesis iii) is satisfied.

(b) Suppose that the production structure is given by a neoclassical production function, where the production vector at time t is only a function of inputs at time t and capital stock chosen at time $t - 1$, that higher capital stock contributes to greater production, and there is free disposal. Show that the second hypothesis in Theorem 5.7, which states that for each $y^f \in Y^f$, there exists $\tilde{T}$ such that $y^f[T] \in Y^f$ for all $T \geq \tilde{T}$, is satisfied.

* 5.14 (a) Show that Theorem 5.7 does not cover the one-good neoclassical growth model with instantaneous preferences given by $u(c) = (c^{1-\theta} - 1)/(1 - \theta)$ with $\theta \geq 1$.

(b) For $\varepsilon > 0$, construct the sequence $\underline{\varepsilon}$ with each element equal to ε. Reformulate and prove a version of Theorem 5.7 such that that X^h (for all $h \in \mathcal{H}$) is restricted to have elements $x^h \geq \underline{\varepsilon}$ for $\varepsilon > 0$ sufficiently small. [Hint: redefine $x^h[T]$ to have ε rather than 0 after the Tth element and reformulate the hypothesis of the theorem accordingly.]

(c) Show that this modified version of Theorem 5.7 covers the economy in part a of this exercise.

Infinite-Horizon Optimization and Dynamic Programming

This chapter provides a brief introduction to infinite-horizon optimization in discrete time under certainty. The main purpose of the chapter is to introduce the reader to infinite-horizon optimization techniques and dynamic programming. These techniques are used in the rest of the book. Since dynamic programming has become an important tool in many areas of economics and especially in macroeconomics, a great deal of the emphasis is placed on dynamic programming methods.

The material in this chapter is presented in four parts. The first part (Sections 6.1–6.3) introduces the problem and provides a number of results necessary for applications of stationary dynamic programming techniques in infinite-dimensional optimization problems. Since understanding how these results are derived is often useful in various applications, the second part, in particular Sections 6.4 and 6.5, provides additional tools necessary for a more detailed analysis of dynamic programming and the proofs of the main theorems. The material in these two sections is not necessary for the rest of the book, and those readers who wish to acquire only a working knowledge of dynamic programming techniques can skip them. The third part then provides several results for nonstationary optimization problems (Section 6.7). Finally, the fourth part of the chapter (Sections 6.6, 6.8, and 6.9) provides a more detailed discussion of how dynamic programming techniques can be used in applications and also presents a number of results on optimal growth using these tools.

Throughout this chapter, the focus is on discounted maximization problems under certainty, similar to the maximization problems introduced in the previous chapter. Dynamic optimization problems under uncertainty are discussed in Chapter 16.

6.1 Discrete-Time Infinite-Horizon Optimization

The canonical discrete-time infinite-horizon optimization program can be written as

$$\sup_{\{x(t),y(t)\}_{t=0}^{\infty}} \sum_{t=0}^{\infty} \beta^t \tilde{U}(t, x(t), y(t))$$

subject to

$$y(t) \in \tilde{G}(t, x(t)) \quad \text{for all } t \geq 0,$$

$$x(t + 1) = \tilde{f}(t, x(t), y(t)) \quad \text{for all } t \geq 0,$$

$$x(0) \text{ given.}$$

Here $\beta \in [0, 1)$ is the discount factor, $t = 0, 1, \ldots$ denotes time, and $x(t) \in X \subset \mathbb{R}^{K_x}$ and $y(t) \in Y \subset \mathbb{R}^{K_y}$ for some $K_x, K_y \geq 1$. We can think of $x(t)$ as the *state variables* (state vector) of the problem, while $y(t)$ denotes the *control variables* (control vector) at time t. The real-valued function

$$\tilde{U} : \mathbb{Z}_+ \times X \times Y \to \mathbb{R}$$

is the instantaneous *payoff function* of this problem ($\mathbb{Z}_+$ denotes the nonnegative integers), while $\sum_{t=0}^{\infty} \beta^t \tilde{U}(t, x(t), y(t))$ is the overall *objective function*. The problem formulation has already imposed the condition that the objective function is a discounted sum of instantaneous payoffs. $\tilde{G}(t, x)$ is a set-valued mapping or a correspondence (see Appendix A), also written as

$$\tilde{G} : \mathbb{Z}_+ \times X \rightrightarrows Y.$$

Thus the first constraint specifies what values of the control vector $y(t)$ are allowed, given the value $x(t)$ at time t. In addition, $\tilde{f} : \mathbb{Z}_+ \times X \times Y \to X$ specifies the evolution of the state vector as a function of last period's state and control vectors. While this formulation is useful in highlighting the distinction between state and control variables, it is often more convenient to work with a transformation to eliminate $y(t)$ and write the optimization problem as

Problem 6.1

$$V^*(0, x(0)) = \sup_{\{x(t)\}_{t=0}^{\infty}} \sum_{t=0}^{\infty} \beta^t U(t, x(t), x(t + 1))$$

subject to

$$x(t + 1) \in G(t, x(t)) \quad \text{for all } t \geq 0,$$

$$x(0) \text{ given.}$$

Here $x(t) \in X \subset \mathbb{R}^K$ ($K = K_x$ in terms of the notation above), and now $x(t)$ corresponds to the state vector, while $x(t + 1)$ plays the role of the control vector at time t. In addition, $U : \mathbb{Z}_+ \times X \times X \to \mathbb{R}$ is the instantaneous payoff function with arguments $x(t)$ and $x(t + 1)$, as well as time t (instead of having arguments $x(t)$ and $y(t)$), and $G : \mathbb{Z}_+ \times X \rightrightarrows X$ specifies the constraint correspondence. Finally, I have also defined the *value function* $V^* : \mathbb{Z}_+ \times X \to \mathbb{R}$, which specifies the supremum (highest possible value) that the objective function can reach or approach (starting with some $x(t)$ at time t).

In the problem formulation, I used "sup," to denote the supremum of the problem (rather than "max" for the maximum), since there is no guarantee that the maximal value is attained by any feasible plan. However, in all cases studied in this book the maximal value is attained, so the reader may wish to substitute "max" for "sup." When the maximal value is attained by some sequence $\{x^*(t + 1)\}_{t=0}^{\infty} \in X^{\infty}$, I refer to this sequence as a solution or as an *optimal* *plan.*[1] Here X^∞ is the countable infinite product of the set X, so that an element of X^∞ is a sequence with each member in X (also note that $X^\infty \subset \ell^\infty$, where ℓ^∞ is the vector space of infinite sequences that are bounded with the sup norm $\|\cdot\|_\infty$, which I denote throughout by the simpler notation $\|\cdot\|$; see Appendix A). Of particular importance in this chapter is the function $V^*(t, x)$, which can be thought of as the value function, meaning the value of pursuing the optimal strategy starting with initial state x at time t. Our objective is to characterize the optimal plan $\{x^*(t+1)\}_{t=0}^\infty$ and the value function $V^*(0, x(0))$.

A more general formulation would involve an undiscounted objective function, written as

$$\sup_{\{x(t)\}_{t=0}^\infty} U(x(0), x(1), \ldots).$$

This added generality is not particularly useful for most problems in economic growth, and the discounted time-separable objective function ensures time consistency of the optimal plan, as discussed in the previous chapter (recall, in particular, Exercise 5.1).

Problem 6.1 is somewhat abstract. However, it has the advantage of being tractable and general enough to nest many interesting economic applications. The following example shows how the canonical optimal growth problem can be put into this form.

Example 6.1 *Recall the optimal growth problem (5.24) and (5.25) introduced in Section 5.9:*

$$\max_{\{k(t),c(t)\}_{t=0}^\infty} \sum_{t=0}^\infty \beta^t u(c(t)),$$

subject to

$$k(t+1) = f(k(t)) + (1-\delta)k(t) - c(t),$$

with $k(t) \geq 0$ and given $k(0) > 0$, and $u : \mathbb{R}_+ \to \mathbb{R}$. This problem maps into the general formulation here with one-dimensional state and control variables. In particular, let $x(t) = k(t)$ and $x(t+1) = k(t+1)$. Then use the constraint to write

$$c(t) = f(k(t)) - k(t+1) + (1-\delta)k(t)$$

and substitute this into the objective function to obtain

$$\max_{\{k(t)\}_{t=0}^\infty} \sum_{t=0}^\infty \beta^t u(f(k(t)) - k(t+1) + (1-\delta)k(t)),$$

subject to $k(t) \geq 0$. Now it can be verified that this problem is a special case of Problem 6.1 with $U(t, k(t), k(t+1)) = u(f(k(t)) - k(t+1) + (1-\delta)k(t))$ and with the constraint correspondence $G(t, k(t))$ given by $k(t+1) \in [0, f(k(t)) + (1-\delta)k(t)]$ (since $c(t) \geq 0$).

A notable feature emphasized by Example 6.1 is that once the optimal growth problem is formulated in the language of Problem 6.1, U and G do not explicitly depend on time. This feature is fairly common. Many interesting problems in economics can be formulated in such a stationary form. A stationary problem involves an objective function that is a discounted sum

---

1. I also sometimes use the term "solution" to denote the function V^* defined in Problems 6.1 or 6.2 (or V in Problem 6.3), but the context will make it clear whether the term "solution" refers to the optimal plan or the functions V^* or V.

and U and G functions that do not explicitly depend on time. In the next section, I start with the study of stationary dynamic optimization problems, returning to the more general case of Problem 6.1 in Section 6.7.

6.2 Stationary Dynamic Programming

Let us consider the stationary form of Problem 6.1.

Problem 6.2

$$V^*(x(0)) = \sup_{\{x(t)\}_{t=0}^\infty} \sum_{t=0}^\infty \beta^t U(x(t), x(t+1))$$

subject to

$$x(t+1) \in G(x(t)) \quad \text{for all } t \geq 0,$$

$$x(0) \text{ given.}$$

Here again $\beta \in [0, 1)$, and now the constraint correspondence and the instantaneous payoff functions take the form $G : X \rightrightarrows X$ and $U : X \times X \to \mathbb{R}$ respectively. Since this problem is stationary, I also write the value function without the time argument as $V^*(x(0))$.

Problem 6.2, like Problem 6.1, corresponds to the *sequence problem;* it involves choosing an infinite sequence $\{x(t)\}_{t=0}^\infty \in X^\infty$. Sequence problems sometimes have nice features, but their solutions are often difficult to characterize both analytically and numerically.

The basic idea of dynamic programming is to turn the sequence problem into a *functional equation;* that is, to transform the problem into one of finding a function rather than a sequence. The relevant functional equation can be written as follows.

Problem 6.3

$$V(x) = \sup_{y \in G(x)} \{U(x, y) + \beta V(y)\}, \quad \text{for all } x \in X. \tag{6.1}$$

Here $V : X \to \mathbb{R}$. Throughout, I use the notation V to refer to the function defined in Problem 6.3 and V^* for the function defined in Problem 6.2.

Intuitively, in Problem 6.3 instead of explicitly choosing the sequence $\{x(t)\}_{t=0}^\infty$, in (6.1), we choose a *policy*, which determines what the control vector $x(t+1)$ should be for a given value of the state vector $x(t)$. Since the instantaneous payoff function $U(\cdot, \cdot)$ does not depend on time, there is no reason for this policy to be time-dependent either, and I denote the control vector by y and the state vector by x. Then the problem is equivalent to choosing $y \in G(x) \subset X$ for a given value of $x \in X$. Mathematically, this corresponds to maximizing $V(x)$ for any $x \in X$. The only subtlety in (6.1) is the presence of $V(\cdot)$ on the right-hand side, which is explained below. This is the reason (6.1) is also called the "recursive formulation"—the function $V(x)$ appears both on the left- and right-hand sides of (6.1) and is thus defined recursively. The functional equation in Problem 6.3 is also called the "Bellman equation," after Richard Bellman, who was the first to introduce the dynamic programming formulation.

At first sight, the recursive formulation might not appear as a great advance over the sequence formulation. After all, functions might be trickier to work with than sequences. Nevertheless, it turns out that the functional equation of dynamic programming is easy to manipulate in many instances. In applied mathematics and engineering it is favored because it is computationally convenient. In economics the major advantage of the recursive formulation is that it often gives better economic insights, similar to the logic of comparing today to tomorrow. In particular, $U(x, y)$ is the return for today and $\beta V(y)$ is the continuation return from the next date onward, equivalent to the return for tomorrow. Consequently in many applications we can use our intuitions from two-period maximization problems. Finally, in some special but important cases, the solution to Problem 6.3 is simpler to characterize analytically than the corresponding solution to the sequence problem (Problem 6.2).

In fact, the form of Problem 6.3 suggests itself naturally from the formulation in Problem 6.2. Suppose Problem 6.2 has a maximum starting at $x(0)$ attained by the optimal sequence $\{x^*(t)\}_{t=0}^{\infty}$ with $x^*(0) = x(0)$. Then under some relatively weak technical conditions, we have that

$$V^*(x(0)) = \sum_{t=0}^{\infty} \beta^t U(x^*(t), x^*(t+1))$$

$$= U(x(0), x^*(1)) + \beta \sum_{s=0}^{\infty} \beta^s U(x^*(s+1), x^*(s+2))$$

$$= U(x(0), x^*(1)) + \beta V^*(x^*(1)).$$

This equation encapsulates the basic idea of dynamic programming, the *Principle of Optimality*, which is stated more formally in Theorem 6.2. It states that an optimal plan can be broken into two parts: what is optimal today, and the optimal continuation path. Dynamic programming exploits this principle.

A particularly notable advantage of the stationary dynamic programming formulation is that the solution can be represented by a time invariant *policy function* (or policy mapping)

$$\pi : X \rightarrow X,$$

determining which value of $x(t+1)$ to choose for a given value of the state variable $x(t)$. In general, there are two complications. First, a control reaching the optimal value may not exist, which was the reason I originally used the "sup" notation. Second, the solution to Problem 6.3 may involve not a policy function, but a *policy correspondence*, $\Pi : X \rightrightarrows X$, because there may be more than one maximizer for a given state variable. Let us ignore these complications for now and present a heuristic exposition. These issues are dealt with in greater detail in Sections 6.3 and 6.5.

Once the value function V is determined, the policy function is straightforward to characterize. In particular, by definition it must be the case that if the optimal policy is given by a policy function $\pi(x)$, then

$$V(x) = U(x, \pi(x)) + \beta V(\pi(x)) \quad \text{for all } x \in X,$$

which is one way of determining the policy function. This equation simply follows from the fact that $\pi(x)$ is the optimal policy, so when $y = \pi(x)$, the right-hand side of (6.1) reaches the maximal value $V(x)$.

The usefulness of the recursive formulation in Problem 6.3 comes from the fact that there are powerful tools that not only establish the existence of a solution but also some of its properties. These tools are also utilized directly in a variety of problems in economic growth, macroeconomics, and other areas of economic dynamics.

In the next section, I present results on the relationship between the solution to the sequence problem (Problem 6.2) and the recursive formulation (Problem 6.3). I also establish a number of results on concavity, monotonicity, and differentiability of the value function $V(\cdot)$ (and of the value function $V^*(\cdot)$ in Problem 6.2).

6.3 Stationary Dynamic Programming Theorems

Let us start with a number of assumptions on Problem 6.2. I number these assumptions separately to distinguish them from the assumptions on technology and preferences used throughout the book. Consider first a sequence $\{x^*(t)\}_{t=0}^{\infty} \in X^{\infty}$, which attains the supremum in Problem 6.2. Our main purpose is to ensure that this sequence satisfies the recursive equation of dynamic programming, written here by substituting in for the sequence $\{x^*(t)\}_{t=0}^{\infty}$ (instead of the "max" operator) as

$$V(x^*(t)) = U(x^*(t), x^*(t+1)) + \beta V(x^*(t+1)) \quad \text{for all } t = 0, 1, \ldots, \tag{6.2}$$

and that any solution to (6.2) is also a solution to Problem 6.2, in the sense that it will attain its supremum. In other words, we are interested in establishing equivalence results between the solutions to Problems 6.2 and 6.3.

To prepare for these results, let us define the set of feasible sequences or *plans,* starting with an initial value $x(t)$ as

$$\Phi(x(t)) = \{\{x(s)\}_{s=t}^{\infty} : x(s+1) \in G(x(s)) \quad \text{for } s = t, t+1, \ldots\}.$$

Intuitively, $\Phi(x(t))$ is the set of feasible choices of vectors starting from $x(t)$. Let us denote a typical element of the set $\Phi(x(0))$ by $\mathbf{x} = (x(0), x(1), \ldots) \in \Phi(x(0))$. Our first assumption is as follows.

Assumption 6.1 $G(x)$ *is nonempty for all* $x \in X$*; and for all* $x(0) \in X$ *and* $\mathbf{x} \in \Phi(x(0))$*,* $\lim_{n \to \infty} \sum_{t=0}^{n} \beta^t U(x(t), x(t+1))$ *exists and is finite.*

This assumption is stronger than what is necessary to establish the results that follow. In particular, for much of the theory of dynamic programming, it is sufficient that the limit in Assumption 6.1 exists. However, in economic applications, we are not interested in optimization problems in which households or firms achieve infinite value for two obvious reasons. First, when some agents can achieve infinite value, the mathematical problems are typically not well defined.[2] Second, the essence of economics, trade-offs in the face of scarcity, would be absent in these cases.

Assumption 6.2 X *is a compact subset of* $\mathbb{R}^K$*,* G *is nonempty-valued, compact-valued, and continuous. Moreover,* $U : \mathbf{X}_G \to \mathbb{R}$ *is continuous, where* $\mathbf{X}_G = \{(x, y) \in X \times X : y \in G(x)\}$*.*

This assumption is also natural. We need to impose the condition that $G(x)$ is compact-valued, since optimization problems with choices from noncompact sets are not well behaved (see Appendix A). In addition, the assumption that U is continuous leads to little loss of generality for most economic applications. In all the models in this book, U is continuous. The most restrictive assumption here is that the state variable lies in a compact set—that is, X is

---

2. Mathematical analysis of certain infinite-horizon optimization problems in which households or firms can achieve infinite value can be carried out using notions such as the "overtaking criterion" or "weak optimality" (see, e.g., Puterman, 1994). None of the models in this book require these more general optimality concepts.

compact. Most results in this chapter can be generalized to the case in which X is not compact, though this requires additional notation and somewhat more difficult analysis. The case in which X is not compact is important in the analysis of economic growth, since most interesting models of growth involve the state variable (e.g., capital stock) growing steadily. Nevertheless, in many cases, with a convenient normalization, the mathematical problem can be turned into one in which the state variable lies in a compact set. One class of important problems that cannot be treated without allowing for a noncompact X are those with endogenous growth. However, since the methods developed in the next chapter do not require this type of compactness assumption and since I often use continuous-time methods to study endogenous growth models, I simplify the discussion here by assuming that X is compact.

Note also that since X is compact and $G(x)$ is continuous and compact-valued, $\mathbf{X}_G$ is also compact. Since a continuous function on a compact domain is also bounded (Corollary A.1 in Appendix A), Assumption 6.2 also implies that U is bounded, which is important for some of the results below.

Many (but not all) economic problems impose additional structure on preferences and technology, for example, in the form of concavity or monotonicity of the instantaneous payoff function U and convexity of the constraints. These properties enable us to establish additional structural results. I now introduce these assumptions formally.

Assumption 6.3 *U is concave. That is, for any $\alpha \in (0, 1)$ and any (x, y), $(x', y') \in \mathbf{X}_G$, we have*

$$U\big(\alpha x + (1 - \alpha)x', \, \alpha y + (1 - \alpha)y'\big) \geq \alpha U(x, y) + (1 - \alpha)U(x', y').$$

Moreover, if $x \neq x'$,

$$U\big(\alpha x + (1 - \alpha)x', \, \alpha y + (1 - \alpha)y'\big) > \alpha U(x, y) + (1 - \alpha)U(x', y').$$

In addition, G is convex. That is, for any $\alpha \in [0, 1]$, and $x, x', y, y' \in X$ such that $y \in G(x)$ and $y' \in G(x')$, we have

$$\alpha y + (1 - \alpha)y' \in G\big(\alpha x + (1 - \alpha)x'\big).$$

This assumption imposes conditions similar to those used in many economic applications: the constraint set is assumed to be convex and the (instantaneous) payoff function is concave. It also imposes a condition similar to, though weaker than, strict concavity.

The next assumption puts more structure on the payoff function; in particular it ensures that the payoff function is increasing in the state variables (its first K arguments), and that larger values of the state variables are also attractive from the viewpoint of relaxing the constraints (i.e., a greater x means more choice).

Assumption 6.4 *For each $y \in X$, $U(\cdot, y)$ is strictly increasing in each of its first K arguments, and G is monotone in the sense that $x \leq x'$ implies $G(x) \subset G(x')$.*

The final assumption is that of differentiability and is also common in most economic models. This assumption enables us to work with first-order necessary conditions.

Assumption 6.5 *U is continuously differentiable on the interior of its domain $\mathbf{X}_G$.*

Given these assumptions, the following sequence of results can be established. The proofs for these results are provided in Section 6.5.

Theorem 6.1 (Equivalence of Values) *Suppose Assumption 6.1 holds. Then for any $x \in X$, any solution $V^*(x)$ to Problem 6.2 is also a solution to Problem 6.3. Moreover, any* *solution $V(x)$ to Problem 6.3 is also a solution to Problem 6.2, so that $V^*(x) = V(x)$ for all $x \in X$.*

Therefore under Assumption 6.1 both the sequence problem and the recursive formulation achieve the same value. The next theorem establishes the more important result that solutions to Problems 6.2 and 6.3 coincide.

Theorem 6.2 (Principle of Optimality) *Suppose Assumption 6.1 holds. Let $\mathbf{x}^* \in \Phi(x(0))$ be a feasible plan that attains $V^*(x(0))$ in Problem 6.2. Then*

$$V^*(x^*(t)) = U(x^*(t), x^*(t+1)) + \beta V^*(x^*(t+1)) \tag{6.3}$$

for $t = 0, 1, \ldots$, with $x^*(0) = x(0)$.

Moreover, if any $\mathbf{x}^* \in \Phi(x(0))$ satisfies (6.3), then it attains the optimal value in Problem 6.2.

This theorem is the major conceptual result in the theory of dynamic programming. It states that the returns from an optimal plan (sequence) $\mathbf{x}^* \in \Phi(x(0))$ can be broken into two parts: the current return, $U(x^*(t), x^*(t+1))$, and the continuation return, $\beta V^*(x^*(t+1))$, where the continuation return is given by the discounted value of a problem starting from the state vector from tomorrow onward, $x^*(t+1)$. In view of the fact that V^* in Problem 6.2 and V in Problem 6.3 are identical (see Theorem 6.1), (6.3) also implies (6.2).

The second part of Theorem 6.2 is equally important. It states that if any feasible plan $\mathbf{x}^*$ starting with $x(0)$—that is, $\mathbf{x}^* \in \Phi(x(0))$—satisfies (6.3), then $\mathbf{x}^*$ attains $V^*(x(0))$. Therefore this theorem states that we can go from the solution of the recursive problem to the solution of the original problem and vice versa. Consequently, as long as Assumption 6.1 is satisfied, there is no risk of excluding solutions when the problem is formulated recursively.

The next results summarize certain important features of the value function V in Problem 6.3. These results are useful for characterizing the qualitative features of optimal plans in dynamic optimization problems without explicitly finding the solutions.

Theorem 6.3 (Existence of Solutions) *Suppose that Assumptions 6.1 and 6.2 hold. Then there exists a unique continuous and bounded function $V : X \to \mathbb{R}$ that satisfies (6.1). Moreover, for any $x(0) \in X$, an optimal plan $\mathbf{x}^* \in \Phi(x(0))$ exists.*

This theorem establishes two major results. The first is the uniqueness of the value function (and hence of the Bellman equation) in dynamic programming problems. The second is the existence of an optimal plan. Combined with Theorem 6.1, this theorem further implies that an optimal policy function (correspondence) achieving the supremum V^* in Problem 6.2 exists and also that like V, V^* is continuous and bounded. The optimal plan in Problem 6.2 (or 6.3) may not be unique, however, even though the value function is unique. This may be the case when two alternative feasible sequences achieve the same maximal value. As in static optimization problems, nonuniqueness of solutions is a consequence of the lack of strict concavity of the objective function. When the conditions are strengthened by including Assumption 6.3, uniqueness of the optimal plan is guaranteed. I first show that this assumption implies that the value function V is strictly concave.

Theorem 6.4 (Concavity of the Value Function) *Suppose that Assumptions 6.1, 6.2, and 6.3 hold. Then the unique $V : X \to \mathbb{R}$ that satisfies (6.1) is strictly concave.*

In addition, it is straightforward to verify that if Assumption 6.3 is relaxed so that U is concave (without the additional requirement for $x \neq x'$ in the assumption), then a weaker version of Theorem 6.4 applies and implies that V is concave. Combining the previous two theorems yields the following corollary.

Corollary 6.1 *Suppose that Assumptions 6.1, 6.2, and 6.3 hold. Then there exists a unique optimal plan* $\mathbf{x}^* \in \Phi(x(0))$ *for any* $x(0) \in X$. *Moreover, the optimal plan can be expressed as* $x^*(t+1) = \pi(x^*(t))$, *where* $\pi : X \to X$ *is a continuous policy function.*

The important result in this corollary is that the "policy function" π is indeed a function, not a correspondence. This result is a consequence of the fact that x^* is uniquely determined. The result also implies that the policy mapping π is continuous in the state vector. Moreover, if there exists a vector of parameters $\mathbf{z}$ continuously affecting either the constraint correspondence Φ or the instantaneous payoff function U, then the same argument establishes that π is also continuous in this vector of parameters. This feature enables qualitative analysis of dynamic macroeconomic models under a variety of circumstances.

Our next result shows that under Assumption 6.4, the value function V is also strictly increasing.

Theorem 6.5 (Monotonicity of the Value Function) *Suppose that Assumptions 6.1, 6.2, and 6.4 hold and let* $V : X \to \mathbb{R}$ *be the unique solution to (6.1). Then* V *is strictly increasing in all of its arguments.*

Our purpose in developing the recursive formulation is to use it for characterizing the solution to dynamic optimization problems. As with static optimization problems, this is often made easier by using differential calculus. The difficulty in using differential calculus with (6.1) is that the right-hand side of this expression includes the value function V, which is endogenously determined. We can only use differential calculus if we know from more primitive arguments that this value function is indeed differentiable. The next theorem ensures that this is the case and also provides an expression for the gradient of the value function by exploiting a version of the familiar Envelope Theorem (Theorem A.31 in Appendix A). Recall that $\text{Int}X$ denotes the interior of the set X, $D_x f$ denotes the gradient of the function f with respect to the vector x, and Df denotes the gradient of the function f with respect to all of its arguments (see Appendix A).

Theorem 6.6 (Differentiability of the Value Function) *Suppose that Assumptions 6.1, 6.2, 6.3, and 6.5 hold. Let* $\pi(\cdot)$ *be the policy function defined in Corollary 6.1 and assume that* $x \in \text{Int } X$ *and* $\pi(x) \in \text{Int } G(x)$. *Then* $V(\cdot)$ *is differentiable at* x, *with gradient given by*

$$DV(x) = D_x U(x, \pi(x)). \tag{6.4}$$

These results allow us to use dynamic programming techniques in a wide variety of dynamic problems. Before doing so, I discuss how these results are proved. The next section introduces a number of mathematical tools from basic functional analysis necessary for proving some of these theorems, and Section 6.5 provides the proofs of all results stated in this section.

6.4 The Contraction Mapping Theorem and Applications *

In this section, I present several mathematical results that are necessary for making progress with the dynamic programming formulation. In this sense, the current section is a digression from the main story line. Therefore, this section and the next can be skipped without interfering with the study of the rest of the book. Nevertheless, the material in this and the next sections is useful for a good understanding of the foundations of dynamic programming and should enable the reader to achieve a better grasp of these methods. The reader may also wish to consult Appendix A before reading this section.

Recall from Appendix A that (S, d) is a metric space if S is a space and d is a metric defined over this space with the usual properties (in particular, the triangle inequality; recall Definition A.1). The metric is referred to as "d," since it loosely corresponds to the distance between two elements of S. A metric space is more general than a finite-dimensional Euclidean space, such as a subset of $\mathbb{R}^K$. But as with the Euclidean space, we are most interested in defining mappings from the metric space into itself. These mappings are referred to as "operators" to distinguish them from real-valued functions and are often denoted by the letter T (thus $T : S \to S$), and the standard notation often involves writing Tz for the image of a point $z \in S$ under T (rather than the more familiar $T(z)$). Instead, the notation $T(Z)$ stands for the image of a subset Z of S under T, that is, $T(Z) = \{x \in S : \exists z \in Z \text{ with } Tz = x\}$. I use this standard notation here.

Definition 6.1 *Let (S, d) be a metric space and $T : S \to S$ be an operator mapping S into itself. If for some $\beta \in (0, 1)$,*

$$d(Tz_1, Tz_2) \leq \beta d(z_1, z_2) \quad \text{for all } z_1, z_2 \in S,$$

then T is a contraction mapping *(with modulus β).*

In other words, a contraction mapping brings elements of the space S uniformly closer to one another.

Example 6.2 *Let us take a simple interval of the real line as our space, $S = [a, b]$, with the usual metric of this space: $d(z_1, z_2) = |z_1 - z_2|$. Then $T : S \to S$ is a contraction if for some $\beta \in (0, 1)$,*

$$\frac{|Tz_1 - Tz_2|}{|z_1 - z_2|} \leq \beta < 1, \quad \text{all } z_1, z_2 \in S, \quad \text{with } z_1 \neq z_2.$$

Definition 6.2 *A* fixed point *of T is any element of S satisfying $Tz = z$.*

Recall also that a metric space (S, d) is complete if every Cauchy sequence (i.e., a sequence whose elements are getting closer) in S converges to an element in S (see Sections A.1 and A.2 in Appendix A). Despite its simplicity, the following theorem is one of the most powerful results in functional analysis.

Theorem 6.7 (Contraction Mapping Theorem) *Let (S, d) be a complete metric space and suppose that $T : S \to S$ is a contraction. Then T has a unique fixed point, $\hat{z}$; that is, there exists a unique $\hat{z} \in S$ such that*

$$T\hat{z} = \hat{z}.$$

Proof. (Existence) Note that $T^n z = T(T^{n-1}z)$ for any $n = 1, 2, \ldots$ (with $T^0 z = z$). Choose $z_0 \in S$, and construct a sequence $\{z_n\}_{n=1}^{\infty}$ with each element in S such that $z_{n+1} = Tz_n$ so that

$$z_n = T^n z_0.$$

Since T is a contraction, we have

$$d(z_2, z_1) = d(Tz_1, Tz_0) \leq \beta d(z_1, z_0).$$

Repeating this argument yields

$$d(z_{n+1}, z_n) \leq \beta^n d(z_1, z_0), \quad n = 1, 2, \ldots. \tag{6.5}$$

Hence, for any $m > n$,

$$d(z_m, z_n) \leq d(z_m, z_{m-1}) + \cdots + d(z_{n+2}, z_{n+1}) + d(z_{n+1}, z_n) \tag{6.6}$$

$$\leq \left(\beta^{m-1} + \cdots + \beta^{n+1} + \beta^n \right) d(z_1, z_0)$$

$$\leq \frac{\beta^n}{1 - \beta} d(z_1, z_0),$$

where the first inequality uses the triangle inequality (see Appendix A). The second inequality uses (6.5). The last inequality uses

$$1/(1 - \beta) = 1 + \beta + \beta^2 + \cdots > 1 + \beta + \cdots + \beta^{m-n-1}.$$

The string of inequalities in (6.6) implies that for n and m sufficiently large, z_m and z_n will approach each other, so that $\{z_n\}_{n=1}^\infty$ is a Cauchy sequence. Since S is complete, every Cauchy sequence in S has an limit point in S and therefore $z_n \to \hat{z} \in S$.

The next step is to show that $\hat{z}$ is a fixed point. Note that for any $z_0 \in S$ and any $n \in \mathbb{N}$, we have

$$d(T\hat{z}, \hat{z}) \leq d(T\hat{z}, T^n z_0) + d(T^n z_0, \hat{z})$$

$$\leq \beta d(\hat{z}, T^{n-1} z_0) + d(T^n z_0, \hat{z}),$$

where the first relationship again uses the triangle inequality, and the second inequality utilizes the fact that T is a contraction. Since $z_n \to \hat{z}$, both of the terms on the right tend to zero as $n \to \infty$, which implies that $d(T\hat{z}, \hat{z}) = 0$, and therefore $T\hat{z} = \hat{z}$, establishing that $\hat{z}$ is a fixed point.

(Uniqueness) Suppose, to obtain a contradiction, that there exist $\hat{z}, z \in S$, such that $Tz = z$ and $T\hat{z} = \hat{z}$ with $\hat{z} \neq z$. This implies

$$0 < d(\hat{z}, z) = d(T\hat{z}, Tz) \leq \beta d(\hat{z}, z),$$

which delivers a contradiction in view of the fact that $\beta < 1$ and establishes uniqueness. ∎

The Contraction Mapping Theorem can be used to prove many well-known results. The next example and Exercise 6.4 show how it can be used to prove existence and uniqueness of solutions to differential equations. Exercise 6.5 shows how it can be used to prove the Implicit Function Theorem (Theorem A.25 in Appendix A).

Example 6.3 *Consider the following one-dimensional differential equation:*

$$\dot{x}(t) = f(x(t)), \tag{6.7}$$

with a boundary condition $x(0) = c \in \mathbb{R}$. Suppose that $f : [0, \bar{x}] \to \mathbb{R}$ is Lipschitz continuous in the sense that it is continuous and also for some $M < \infty$, it satisfies the following boundedness condition: $\left| f(x'') - f(x') \right| \leq M \left| x'' - x' \right|$ for all $x', x'' \in [0, \bar{x}]$. The Contraction Mapping Theorem (Theorem 6.7) can be used to prove the existence of a continuous function $x^*(t)$ that is the unique solution to this differential equation on any compact interval, in particular on $[0, s]$ for some $s \in [0, \bar{x}]$. To prove this assertion, consider the space of continuous functions on $[0, s]$, $\mathbf{C}[0, s]$, and define the operator T such that for any $g \in \mathbf{C}[0, s]$,

$$Tg(z) = c + \int_0^z f(g(x)) dx \quad \text{for all } z \in [0, s].$$

Notice that T is a mapping from the space of continuous functions on $[0, s]$ into itself, that is, $T : \mathbf{C}[0, s] \to \mathbf{C}[0, s]$. Moreover, it can be verified T is a contraction for some s. This follows because for any $z \in [0, s]$, we have

$$\left| \int_0^z f\left(g(x)\right) dx - \int_0^z f\left(\tilde{g}(x)\right) dx \right| \le \int_0^z M \left| g(x) - \tilde{g}(x) \right| dx \tag{6.8}$$

by the Lipschitz continuity of $f(\cdot)$. Equation (6.8) implies that

$$\left\| Tg(z) - T\tilde{g}(z) \right\| \le M \times s \times \left\| g - \tilde{g} \right\|,$$

where recall that $\|\cdot\|$ denotes the sup norm, now defined over the space of functions. Choosing $s < 1/M$ establishes that for s sufficiently small, T is indeed a contraction. Then from Theorem 6.7, there exists a unique fixed point of T over $\mathbf{C}[0, s]$. This fixed point is the unique solution to the differential equation, and it is also continuous. Exercise 6.4 asks you to verify some of these steps and shows how the result can be extended so that it applies to $\mathbf{C}[0, \bar{x}]$.

The main use of the Contraction Mapping Theorem for us is that it establishes the existence of a unique value function V in Problem 6.3, greatly facilitating the analysis of dynamic programming problems. Before doing this, let us consider another useful result. Recall that if (S, d) is a complete metric space and S' is a closed subset of S, then (S', d) is also a complete metric space.

Theorem 6.8 (Applications of Contraction Mappings) *Let (S, d) be a complete metric space and $T : S \to S$ be a contraction mapping with $T\hat{z} = \hat{z}$.*

1. If S' is a closed subset of S, and $T(S') \subset S'$, then $\hat{z} \in S'$.

2. Moreover, if $T(S') \subset S'' \subset S'$, then $\hat{z} \in S''$.

Proof. Take $z_0 \in S'$, and construct the sequence $\{T^n z_0\}_{n=1}^{\infty}$. Each element of this sequence is in S', since $T(S') \subset S'$. Theorem 6.7 implies that $T^n z_0 \to \hat{z}$. Since S' is closed, $\hat{z} \in S'$, proving Part 1.

We know that $\hat{z} \in S'$. Then $T(S') \subset S'' \subset S'$ implies that $\hat{z} = T\hat{z} \in T(S') \subset S''$, establishing Part 2. ∎

The second part of this theorem is very important to prove results, such as strict concavity or strict monotonicity of a function. This is because the set (space) of strictly concave functions or the set of the strictly increasing functions is not closed (and complete). Therefore the Contraction Mapping Theorem cannot be directly applied to these spaces of functions. The second part of this theorem enables us to circumvent this problem.

The previous two theorems show that the contraction mapping property is both simple and powerful. Nevertheless, beyond some simple cases, such as in Example 6.2, it is difficult to check whether an operator is indeed a contraction. This problem may seem particularly difficult in the case of spaces whose elements correspond to functions, which are those that are relevant in the context of dynamic programming. The next theorem provides us with straightforward sufficient conditions for an operator to be a contraction. For this theorem, let us use the following notation: for a real-valued function $f(\cdot)$ and some constant $c \in \mathbb{R}$, we define $(f + c)(x) \equiv f(x) + c$. Then the following theorem holds.

Theorem 6.9 (Blackwell's Sufficient Conditions for a Contraction) *Let $X \subseteq \mathbb{R}^K$, and $\mathbf{B}(X)$ be the space of bounded functions $f : X \to \mathbb{R}$ defined on X equipped with the sup norm*

$\|\cdot\|$. *Suppose that* $\mathbf{B}'(X) \subset \mathbf{B}(X)$, *and let* $T : \mathbf{B}'(X) \to \mathbf{B}'(X)$ *be an operator satisfying the following two conditions:*

1. *Monotonicity: For any* $f, g \in \mathbf{B}'(X)$, $f(x) \leq g(x)$ *for all* $x \in X$ *implies* $(Tf)(x) \leq (Tg)(x)$ *for all* $x \in X$; *and*

2. *Discounting: There exists* $\beta \in (0, 1)$ *such that*

$$[T(f + c)](x) \leq (Tf)(x) + \beta c \quad \text{for all } f \in B(X), c \geq 0, \text{ and } x \in X.$$

Then T *is a contraction with modulus* β *on* $\mathbf{B}'(X)$.

Proof. By the definition of the sup norm, $\|f - g\| = \max_{x \in X} |f(x) - g(x)|$. Then for any $f, g \in \mathbf{B}'(X) \subset \mathbf{B}(X)$,

$$f(x) \leq g(x) + \|f - g\| \qquad \text{for any } x \in X,$$

$$(Tf)(x) \leq T[g + \|f - g\|](x) \qquad \text{for any } x \in X,$$

$$(Tf)(x) \leq (Tg)(x) + \beta \|f - g\| \quad \text{for any } x \in X, \tag{6.9}$$

where the second line applies the operator T on both sides and uses monotonicity, and the third line uses discounting (together with the fact that $\|f - g\|$ is simply a number). By the converse argument,

$$g(x) \leq f(x) + \|g - f\| \qquad \text{for any } x \in X,$$

$$(Tg)(x) \leq T[f + \|g - f\|](x) \qquad \text{for any } x \in X,$$

$$(Tg)(x) \leq (Tf)(x) + \beta \|g - f\| \quad \text{for any } x \in X. \tag{6.10}$$

Combining the inequalities (6.9) and (6.10) yields

$$\|Tf - Tg\| \leq \beta \|f - g\| ,$$

proving that T is a contraction on $\mathbf{B}'(X)$. ∎

We will see that Blackwell's sufficient conditions are straightforward to check in many economic applications, including the models of optimal or equilibrium growth.

6.5 Proofs of the Main Dynamic Programming Theorems *

I now provide proofs of Theorems 6.1–6.6. The first step is a straightforward lemma, which is useful in these proofs. For a feasible infinite sequence $\mathbf{x} = (x(0), x(1), \ldots) \in \Phi(x(0))$ starting at $x(0)$, let

$$\bar{\mathbf{U}}(\mathbf{x}) \equiv \sum_{t=0}^{\infty} \beta^t U(x(t), x(t + 1))$$

be the value of choosing this potentially nonoptimal infinite feasible sequence. In view of Assumption 6.1, $\bar{\mathbf{U}}(\mathbf{x})$ exists and is finite. The next lemma shows that $\bar{\mathbf{U}}(\mathbf{x})$ can be separated into two parts, the current return and the continuation return.

Lemma 6.1 *Suppose that Assumption 6.1 holds. Then for any* $x(0) \in X$ *and any* $\mathbf{x} \in \Phi(x(0))$,

$$\bar{\mathbf{U}}(\mathbf{x}) = U(x(0), x(1)) + \beta \bar{\mathbf{U}}(\mathbf{x}'),$$

where $\mathbf{x}' = (x(1), x(2), \ldots)$.

Proof. Since under Assumption 6.1 $\bar{\mathbf{U}}(\mathbf{x})$ exists and is finite, it can be written as

$$\bar{\mathbf{U}}(\mathbf{x}) = \sum_{t=0}^{\infty} \beta^t U(x(t), x(t+1))$$

$$= U(x(0), x(1)) + \beta \sum_{s=0}^{\infty} \beta^s U(x(s+1), x(s+2))$$

$$= U(x(0), x(1)) + \beta \bar{\mathbf{U}}(\mathbf{x}'),$$

as defined in the lemma. ∎

Before providing a proof of Theorem 6.1, it is useful to be more explicit about what it means for V and V^* to be solutions to Problems 6.2 and 6.3. Let us start with Problem 6.2. Using the notation introduced in this section, for any $x(0) \in X$,

$$V^*(x(0)) = \sup_{\mathbf{x} \in \Phi(x(0))} \bar{\mathbf{U}}(\mathbf{x}). \tag{6.11}$$

In view of Assumption 6.1, which ensures that all values are bounded, (6.11) implies

$$V^*(x(0)) \geq \bar{\mathbf{U}}(\mathbf{x}) \text{ for all } \mathbf{x} \in \Phi(x(0)), \tag{6.12}$$

since no other feasible sequence of choices can give higher value than the supremum, $V^*(x(0))$. However, if some function $\tilde{V}(\cdot)$ satisfies condition (6.12), so will $\tilde{V}(\cdot) + \alpha$ for $\alpha > 0$. Therefore this condition is not sufficient. In addition, we also require that for any $\varepsilon > 0$, there exists $\mathbf{x}' \in \Phi(x(0))$ such that

$$V^*(x(0)) \leq \bar{\mathbf{U}}(\mathbf{x}') + \varepsilon. \tag{6.13}$$

The conditions for $V(\cdot)$ to be a solution to Problem 6.3 are similar. For any $x(0) \in X$,

$$V(x(0)) \geq U(x(0), y) + \beta V(y'), \tag{6.14}$$

for all $y \in G(x(0))$. Moreover, for any $\varepsilon > 0$, there exists $y' \in G(x(0))$ such that

$$V(x(0)) \leq U(x(0), y') + \beta V(y') + \varepsilon. \tag{6.15}$$

Proof of Theorem 6.1. If $\beta = 0$, Problems 6.2 and 6.3 are identical, thus the result follows immediately. Suppose that $\beta > 0$ and take arbitrary $x(0) \in X$ and $x(1) \in G(x(0))$. By (6.13) for any $\varepsilon > 0$, there exists $\mathbf{x}'_\varepsilon \in \Phi(x(1))$ such that $\bar{\mathbf{U}}(\mathbf{x}'_\varepsilon) \geq V^*(x(1)) - \varepsilon$. Moreover, by (6.12), for any $\mathbf{x} = (x(0), x(1), \ldots) \in \Phi(x(0))$, and thus in particular for $\mathbf{x}_\varepsilon = (x(0), \mathbf{x}'_\varepsilon)$, $\bar{\mathbf{U}}(\mathbf{x}_\varepsilon) \leq V^*(x(0))$. Lemma 6.1 then implies

$$V^*(x(0)) \geq U(x(0), x(1)) + \beta \bar{\mathbf{U}}(\mathbf{x}'_\varepsilon)$$

$$\geq U(x(0), x(1)) + \beta V^*(x(1)) - \beta \varepsilon.$$

Since $\varepsilon > 0$ is arbitrary, this inequality implies

$$V^*(x(0)) \geq U(x(0), x(1)) + \beta V^*(x(1)),$$

and thus $V^*(\cdot)$ satisfies (6.14).

Next, take an arbitrary $\varepsilon > 0$. By (6.13), there exists a feasible infinite sequence $\mathbf{x}'_\varepsilon = (x(0), x'_\varepsilon(1), x'_\varepsilon(2), \ldots) \in \Phi(x(0))$ such that

$$\bar{U}(\mathbf{x}'_\varepsilon) \geq V^*(x(0)) - \varepsilon.$$

Now since $\mathbf{x}''_\varepsilon = \left(x'_\varepsilon(1), x'_\varepsilon(2), \ldots\right) \in \Phi\left(x'_\varepsilon(1)\right)$ and $V^*\left(x'_\varepsilon(1)\right)$ is the supremum in Problem 6.2 starting with $x'_\varepsilon(1)$, Lemma 6.1 implies

$$V^*(x(0)) - \varepsilon \leq U\left(x(0), x'_\varepsilon(1)\right) + \beta\bar{U}\left(\mathbf{x}''_\varepsilon\right)$$

$$\leq U\left(x(0), x'_\varepsilon(1)\right) + \beta V^*\left(x'_\varepsilon(1)\right).$$

The last inequality implies that $V^*(\cdot)$ satisfies (6.15) since $x'_\varepsilon(1) \in G(x(0))$ for any $\varepsilon > 0$. This proves that any solution to Problem 6.2 satisfies (6.14) and (6.15), and is thus a solution to Problem 6.3.

To establish the converse, note that (6.14) implies that for any $x(1) \in G(x(0))$,

$$V(x(0)) \geq U(x(0), x(1)) + \beta V(x(1)).$$

Now substituting recursively for $V(x(1))$, $V(x(2))$, and so on, and defining $\mathbf{x} = (x(0), x(1), \ldots)$, we have

$$V(x(0)) \geq \sum_{t=0}^{n} U(x(t), x(t+1)) + \beta^{n+1} V(x(n+1)).$$

Moreover,

$$\lim_{n \to \infty} \sum_{t=0}^{n} \beta^t U(x(t), x(t+1)) = \bar{U}(\mathbf{x})$$

and

$$\lim_{n \to \infty} \beta^{n+1} V(x(n+1)) = \lim_{n \to \infty} \left[\beta^{n+1} \lim_{m \to \infty} \sum_{t=n}^{m} \beta^t U(x(t), x(t+1))\right] = 0$$

(since Assumption 6.1 ensures that $\lim_{m \to \infty} \sum_{t=n}^{m} \beta^t U(x(t), x(t+1))$ is finite). Therefore

$$V(x(0)) \geq \bar{U}(\mathbf{x})$$

for any $\mathbf{x} \in \Phi(x(0))$. Thus $V(\cdot)$ satisfies (6.12).

Next let $\varepsilon > 0$ be a positive number. From (6.15), for any $\varepsilon' = \varepsilon(1 - \beta) > 0$ there exists $x_\varepsilon(1) \in G(x(0))$ such that

$$V(x(0)) \leq U\left(x(0), x_\varepsilon(1)\right) + \beta V\left(x_\varepsilon(1)\right) + \varepsilon'.$$

Next, choose $x_\varepsilon(t) \in G(x(t-1))$, with $x_\varepsilon(0) = x(0)$. Define $\mathbf{x}_\varepsilon \equiv \left(x(0), x_\varepsilon(1), x_\varepsilon(2), \ldots\right)$. Again substituting recursively for $V\left(x_\varepsilon(1)\right)$, $V\left(x_\varepsilon(2)\right), \ldots,$ yields

$$V(x(0)) \leq \sum_{t=0}^{n} U\left(x_\varepsilon(t), x_\varepsilon(t+1)\right) + \beta^{n+1} V(x(n+1)) + \varepsilon' + \varepsilon'\beta + \cdots + \varepsilon'\beta^n$$

$$\leq \bar{U}\left(\mathbf{x}_\varepsilon\right) + \varepsilon,$$

where the last step follows using the definition of ε (in particular, $\varepsilon = \varepsilon' \sum_{t=0}^{\infty} \beta^t$) and because $\lim_{n \to \infty} \sum_{t=0}^{n} U(x_\varepsilon(t), x_\varepsilon(t+1)) = \bar{U}(\mathbf{x}_\varepsilon)$. This inequality establishes that $V(\cdot)$ also satisfies (6.13) and completes the proof. ∎

In economic problems, we are often interested not in the maximal value of the program but in the optimal plans that achieve this maximal value. Recall that the question of whether the optimal paths resulting from Problems 6.2 and 6.3 are equivalent was addressed by Theorem 6.2. I now provide a proof of this theorem.

Proof of Theorem 6.2. By hypothesis $\mathbf{x}^* \equiv (x(0), x^*(1), x^*(2), \ldots)$ is a solution to Problem 6.2, that is, it attains the supremum, $V^*(x(0))$, starting from $x(0)$. Let us define $\mathbf{x}_t^* \equiv (x^*(t), x^*(t+1), \ldots)$.

The first step is to show that for any $t \geq 0$, $\mathbf{x}_t^*$ attains the supremum starting from $x^*(t)$, so that

$$\bar{U}(\mathbf{x}_t^*) = V^*(x^*(t)). \tag{6.16}$$

The proof is by induction. The base step of induction (for $t = 0$) is straightforward, since by definition, $\mathbf{x}_0^* = \mathbf{x}^*$ attains $V^*(x(0))$.

Next suppose that the statement is true for t (that is, (6.16) is true for t), and we establish that it is also true for $t + 1$. Equation (6.16) implies that

$$V^*(x^*(t)) = \bar{U}(\mathbf{x}_t^*) \tag{6.17}$$

$$= U(x^*(t), x^*(t+1)) + \beta \bar{U}(\mathbf{x}_{t+1}^*).$$

Let $\mathbf{x}_{t+1} = (x^*(t+1), x(t+2), \ldots) \in \Phi(x^*(t+1))$ be any feasible plan starting with $x^*(t+1)$. By definition, $\mathbf{x}_t = (x^*(t), \mathbf{x}_{t+1}) \in \Phi(x^*(t))$. Since $V^*(x^*(t))$ is the supremum starting with $x^*(t)$,

$$V^*(x^*(t)) \geq \bar{U}(\mathbf{x}_t)$$

$$= U(x^*(t), x^*(t+1)) + \beta \bar{U}(\mathbf{x}_{t+1}).$$

Combining this inequality with (6.17) yields

$$\bar{U}(\mathbf{x}_{t+1}^*) \geq \bar{U}(\mathbf{x}_{t+1})$$

for all $\mathbf{x}_{t+1} \in \Phi(x^*(t+1))$. Thus $\mathbf{x}_{t+1}^*$ attains the supremum starting from $x^*(t+1)$ and the induction step is complete, proving that (6.16) holds for all $t \geq 0$.

Equation (6.16) then implies that

$$V^*(x^*(t)) = \bar{U}(\mathbf{x}_t^*)$$

$$= U(x^*(t), x^*(t+1)) + \beta \bar{U}(\mathbf{x}_{t+1}^*)$$

$$= U(x^*(t), x^*(t+1)) + \beta V^*(x^*(t+1)),$$

establishing (6.3) and thus completing the proof of the first part of the theorem.

Now suppose that (6.3) holds for $\mathbf{x}^* \in \Phi(x(0))$. Then substituting repeatedly for $\mathbf{x}^*$ yields

$$V^*(x(0)) = \sum_{t=0}^{n} \beta^t U(x^*(t), x^*(t+1)) + \beta^{n+1} V^*(x(n+1)).$$

In view of the fact that $V^*(\cdot)$ is bounded (see Assumption 6.1), we have

$$\bar{\mathbf{U}}(\mathbf{x}^*) = \lim_{n \to \infty} \sum_{t=0}^{n} \beta^t U(x^*(t), x^*(t+1))$$

$$= V^*(x(0)).$$

Thus $\mathbf{x}^*$ attains the optimal value in Problem 6.2, completing the proof of the second part of Theorem 6.2. ∎

These two theorems establish that under Assumption 6.1, we can freely interchange Problems 6.2 and 6.3. Our next task is to prove that a policy achieving the optimal path exists for both problems. I provide two alternative proofs to show how this conclusion can be reached by looking at either Problem 6.2 or Problem 6.3 and then exploiting their equivalence. The first proof is more abstract and works directly on the sequence problem (Problem 6.2). This method of proof is particularly useful for nonstationary problems.

Proof of Theorem 6.3. (Version 1) Consider Problem 6.2. The objective function in Problem 6.2 is continuous in the product topology in view of Assumptions 6.1 and 6.2 (see Theorem A.12 in Appendix A). Moreover, the constraint set $\Phi(x(0))$ is a closed subset of X^∞ (the infinite product of X). Since X is compact (Assumption 6.2), Tychonoff's Theorem (Theorem A.13) implies that X^∞ is compact in the product topology. A closed subset of a compact set is compact (Lemma A.2 in Appendix A), which implies that $\Phi(x(0))$ is compact. From Weierstrass' Theorem (Theorem A.9) applied to Problem 6.2, there exists $\mathbf{x} \in \Phi(x(0))$ attaining $V^*(x(0))$. Moreover, the constraint set is a continuous correspondence (again in the product topology), so Berge's Maximum Theorem (Theorem A.16) implies that $V^*(x(0))$ is continuous. Since $x(0) \in X$ and X is compact, this implies that $V^*(x(0))$ is bounded (Corollary A.1 in Appendix A). ∎

Proof of Theorem 6.3. (Version 2) Let $\mathbf{C}(X)$ be the set of continuous functions defined on X, endowed with the sup norm, $\|f\| = \sup_{x \in X} |f(x)|$. In view of Assumption 6.2, the relevant set X is compact, and therefore all functions in $\mathbf{C}(X)$ are bounded, since they are continuous (Corollary A.1 in Appendix A). For $V \in \mathbf{C}(X)$, define the operator T as

$$TV(x) = \max_{y \in G(x)} \{U(x, y) + \beta V(y)\}. \tag{6.18}$$

A fixed point of this operator, $V = TV$, will be a solution to Problem 6.3. We first prove that such a fixed point (solution) exists. The maximization problem on the right-hand side of (6.18) is one of maximizing a continuous function over a compact set, and by Weierstrass's Theorem (Theorem A.9) it has a solution. Consequently, T is well defined. Moreover, because $G(x)$ is a nonempty-valued continuous correspondence by Assumption 6.1, and $U(x, y)$ and $V(y)$ are continuous by hypothesis, Berge's Maximum Theorem (Theorem A.16) implies that

$$\max_{y \in G(x)} \{U(x, y) + \beta V(y)\}$$

is continuous in x. Thus $TV(x) \in \mathbf{C}(X)$, and T maps $\mathbf{C}(X)$ into itself.

It is also straightforward to verify that T satisfies Blackwell's sufficient conditions for a contraction in Theorem 6.9 (see Exercise 6.6). Therefore, applying Theorem 6.7, a unique fixed point $V \in \mathbf{C}(X)$ to (6.18) exists and is also the unique solution to Problem 6.3.

Now consider the maximization in Problem 6.3. Since U and V are continuous and $G(x)$ is compact-valued, another application of Weierstrass's Theorem implies that there exists

$y \in G(x)$ that achieves the maximum. This defines the set of maximizers $\Pi(x)$ for Problem 6.3:

$$\Pi(x) = \arg \max_{y \in G(x)} \{U(x, y) + \beta V(y)\}. \tag{6.19}$$

Let $\mathbf{x}^* = (x(0), x^*(1), \ldots)$, with $x^*(t+1) \in \Pi(x^*(t))$ for all $t \geq 0$. Then from Theorems 6.1 and 6.2, $\mathbf{x}^*$ is also an optimal plan for Problem 6.2. ∎

An additional result that follows from the second version of the proof (which can also be derived from version 1, but would require more work) concerns the properties of the set of maximizers $\Pi(x)$ (or equivalently the correspondence $\Pi : X \rightrightarrows X$) defined in (6.19). An immediate application of the Berge's Maximum Theorem (Theorem A.16) implies that Π is a upper hemicontinuous and compact-valued correspondence. This observation is used in the proof of Corollary 6.1. Before turning to this corollary, I provide a proof of Theorem 6.4. This proof also shows how the Contraction Mapping Theorem (Theorem 6.8) is often used in the study of dynamic optimization problems.

Proof of Theorem 6.4. Recall that $\mathbf{C}(X)$ is the set of continuous (and bounded) functions over the compact set X. Let $\mathbf{C}'(X) \subset \mathbf{C}(X)$ be the set of bounded, continuous, (weakly) concave functions on X, and let $\mathbf{C}''(X) \subset \mathbf{C}'(X)$ be the set of strictly concave functions. Clearly, $\mathbf{C}'(X)$ is a closed subset of the complete metric space $\mathbf{C}(X)$, but $\mathbf{C}''(X)$ is not a closed subset. Let T be as defined in (6.18). Since T is a contraction, it has a unique fixed point in $\mathbf{C}(X)$. By Theorem 6.8, proving that $T[\mathbf{C}'(X)] \subset \mathbf{C}''(X) \subset \mathbf{C}'(X)$ would be sufficient to establish that this unique fixed point is in $\mathbf{C}''(X)$ and hence the value function is strictly concave. Let $V \in \mathbf{C}'(X)$, and for $x' \neq x''$ and $\alpha \in (0, 1)$, let

$$x_\alpha \equiv \alpha x' + (1 - \alpha) x''.$$

Let $y' \in G(x')$ and $y'' \in G(x'')$ be solutions to Problem 6.3 with state vectors x' and x'', respectively. Then

$$\begin{aligned} TV(x') &= U(x', y') + \beta V(y'), \\ TV(x'') &= U(x'', y'') + \beta V(y''). \end{aligned} \tag{6.20}$$

In view of Assumption 6.3 (that G is convex), $y_\alpha \equiv \alpha y' + (1 - \alpha) y'' \in G(x_\alpha)$, so that

$$\begin{aligned} TV(x_\alpha) &\geq U(x_\alpha, y_\alpha) + \beta V(y_\alpha) \\ &> \alpha \big[U(x', y') + \beta V(y')\big] + (1 - \alpha)[U(x'', y'') + \beta V(y'')] \\ &= \alpha TV(x') + (1 - \alpha) TV(x''), \end{aligned}$$

where the first line follows from the fact that $y_\alpha \in G(x_\alpha)$ is not necessarily the maximizer starting with state x_α. The second line uses Assumption 6.3 (strict concavity of U and the concavity of V), and the third line is simply the definition introduced in (6.20). This argument implies that for any $V \in \mathbf{C}'(X)$, TV is strictly concave, and thus $T[\mathbf{C}'(X)] \subset \mathbf{C}''(X)$. Then Theorem 6.8 implies that the unique fixed point V^* is in $\mathbf{C}''(X)$, and hence it is strictly concave. ∎

Proof of Corollary 6.1. Assumption 6.3 implies that $U(x, y)$ is concave in y, and under this assumption, Theorem 6.4 established that $V(y)$ is strictly concave in y. The sum of a concave function and a strictly concave function is strictly concave, and thus the right-hand side of Problem 6.3 is strictly concave in y. Therefore, combined with the fact that $G(x)$ is convex for each $x \in X$ (again Assumption 6.3), there exists a unique maximizer $y \in G(x)$ for each

$x \in X$. Then the policy correspondence $\Pi(x)$ is single-valued and is thus a function and can be expressed as $\pi(x)$. Since $\Pi(x)$ is upper hemicontinuous as observed above, so is $\pi(x)$. Since a single-valued upper hemicontinuous correspondence is a continuous function, the corollary follows. ∎

Proof of Theorem 6.5. The proof again follows from Theorem 6.8. Let $\mathbf{C}'(X) \subset \mathbf{C}(X)$ be the set of bounded, continuous, nondecreasing functions on X, and let $\mathbf{C}''(X) \subset \mathbf{C}'(X)$ be the set of strictly increasing functions. Since $\mathbf{C}'(X)$ is a closed subset of the complete metric space $\mathbf{C}(X)$, Theorem 6.8 implies that if $T[\mathbf{C}'(X)] \subset \mathbf{C}''(X)$, then the fixed point to (6.18) is in $\mathbf{C}''(X)$, and therefore it is a strictly increasing function. To see that this is the case, consider any $V \in \mathbf{C}'(X)$, that is, any nondecreasing function. In view of Assumption 6.4, $\max_{y \in G(x)}\{U(x, y) + \beta V(y)\}$ is strictly increasing. This fact establishes that $TV \in \mathbf{C}''(X)$ and completes the proof. ∎

For Theorem 6.6, I also provide two proofs. The first one is simpler and only establishes that $V(x)$ has a well-defined vector of partial derivatives (the Jacobian), $DV(x)$. The second proof appeals to a powerful result from convex analysis and establishes that $V(x)$ is differentiable (see Section A.9 in Appendix A for examples of functions that may possess well-defined Jacobians but may not be differentiable). Moreover, the second proof is more widely known and used in the literature. For the first proof, recall that $\varepsilon \downarrow 0$ implies that ε is a positive decreasing sequence approaching 0 and $\varepsilon \uparrow 0$ that ε is a negative increasing sequence approaching 0.

Proof of Theorem 6.6. (Version 1) From Corollary 6.1, $\Pi(x)$ is single-valued and is thus a function that can be represented by $\pi(x)$. By hypothesis $\pi(x) = x' \in \text{Int } G(x)$. Now consider the initial value $x + \tilde{\varepsilon}_K$, where $\tilde{\varepsilon}_K$ is a K-dimensional vector with the first element equal to the number $\varepsilon > 0$, which is taken to be small, and the remaining elements equal to 0. By definition,

$$V^*(x) = V(x)$$

$$= \bar{\mathbf{U}}(\mathbf{x}^*),$$

where $\mathbf{x}^* = (x, x', \ldots) \in \Phi(x^*(0))$ is the optimal plan Now consider the alternative plan $\mathbf{x}_\varepsilon = (x + \tilde{\varepsilon}_K, x', \ldots)$ starting with initial value $x + \tilde{\varepsilon}_K$. For ε sufficiently small, this plan is feasible, that is, $\mathbf{x}_\varepsilon \in \Phi(x + \tilde{\varepsilon}_K)$. To see this, observe that $x' \in \text{Int } G(x)$ and from Assumption 6.2 G is continuous and thus $x' \in \text{Int } G(x + \tilde{\varepsilon}_K)$. Using Lemma 6.1 and the fact that $V^*(x) = V(x)$ for all x, the value of this plan can be written as

$$V(x + \tilde{\varepsilon}_K) \geq U(x + \tilde{\varepsilon}_K, x') + \beta V(x').$$

Therefore

$$V(x + \tilde{\varepsilon}_K) - V(x) \geq U(x + \tilde{\varepsilon}_K, x') - U(x, x').$$

Since by Assumption 6.5 U is differentiable, we have

$$V_1^+(x) \equiv \lim_{\varepsilon \downarrow 0} \frac{V(x + \tilde{\varepsilon}_K) - V(x)}{\varepsilon} \geq U_1(x, x'), \qquad (6.21)$$

where U_1 denotes the partial derivative of the U function with respect to the first element of the x vector. Next, consider the initial value $x - \tilde{\varepsilon}_K$. Again since $x' \in \text{Int } G(x)$ and G is continuous, $(x - \tilde{\varepsilon}_K, x', \ldots) \in \Phi(x - \tilde{\varepsilon}_K)$. The same argument then establishes that

$$V(x - \tilde{\varepsilon}_K) - V(x) \geq U(x - \tilde{\varepsilon}_K, x') - U(x, x'),$$

and then dividing by $-\varepsilon$, yields

$$V_1^-(x) \equiv \lim_{\varepsilon \uparrow 0} \frac{V(x + \tilde{\varepsilon}_K) - V(x)}{\varepsilon} \leq U_1(x, x'). \tag{6.22}$$

The same argument clearly applies to any partial derivative, so that

$$V_k^-(x) \leq U_k(x, x') \leq V_k^+(x)$$

for each $k = 1, 2, \ldots, K$. Since from Theorem 6.4, V is concave, $V_k^-(x) \geq V_k^+(x)$ for each k. This establishes that $V_k^+(x) = V_k^-(x) = U_k(x, x')$, and thus $DV(x) = D_x U(x, \pi(x))$, completing the proof. ■

Proof of Theorem 6.6. (Version 2) From Corollary 6.1, $\Pi(x)$ is single-valued and is thus a function that can be represented by $\pi(x)$. By hypothesis, $\pi(x) \in \text{Int } G(x)$, and from Assumption 6.2 G is continuous. Therefore there exists a neighborhood $\mathcal{N}(x)$ of x such that $\pi(x) \in \text{Int } G(x)$ for all $x \in \mathcal{N}(x)$. Define $W(\cdot)$ on $\mathcal{N}(x)$ by

$$W(x') = U(x', \pi(x)) + \beta V(\pi(x)) \quad \text{for all } x' \in \mathcal{N}(x).$$

In view of Assumptions 6.3 and 6.5, the fact that $V(\pi(x))$ is a number (independent of x') and that U is concave and differentiable implies that $W(\cdot)$ is concave and differentiable. Moreover, since $\pi(x) \in G(x')$ for all $x' \in \mathcal{N}(x)$, it follows that

$$W(x') \leq \max_{y \in G(x')} \{U(x', y) + \beta V(y)\} = V(x') \quad \text{for all } x' \in \mathcal{N}(x), \tag{6.23}$$

with equality at $x' = x$.

Since $V(\cdot)$ is concave, $-V(\cdot)$ is convex, and by a standard result in convex analysis, it possesses subgradients. Moreover, any subgradient $-p$ of $-V$ at x must satisfy

$$p \cdot (x' - x) \geq V(x') - V(x) \geq W(x') - W(x) \quad \text{for all } x' \in \mathcal{N}(x),$$

where the first inequality uses the definition of a subgradient and the second uses the fact that $W(x') \leq V(x')$, with equality at x, as established in (6.23). Thus every subgradient p of $-V$ is also a subgradient of $-W$. Since W is differentiable at x, its subgradient p must be unique, and another standard result in convex analysis implies that any convex function with a unique subgradient at an interior point x is differentiable at x. This reasoning establishes that $-V(\cdot)$, and thus $V(\cdot)$, is differentiable, as desired. The expression for the gradient (6.4) then follows from the Envelope Theorem (Theorem A.31). ■

6.6 Applications of Stationary Dynamic Programming

In this section, I return to the fundamentals of stationary dynamic programming and show how they can be applied to a range of problems. The main result in this section is Theorem 6.10, which shows how dynamic first-order conditions, the Euler equations, together with the transversality condition are sufficient to characterize solutions to dynamic optimization problems. This theorem is arguably more useful in practice than the main dynamic programming theorems presented above.

6.6.1 Basic Equations

Consider the functional equation corresponding to Problem 6.3:

$$V(x) = \max_{y \in G(x)} \{U(x, y) + \beta V(y)\} \quad \text{for all } x \in X. \tag{6.24}$$

Let us assume throughout that Assumptions 6.1–6.5 hold. Then from Theorem 6.4, the maximization problem in (6.24) is strictly concave, and from Theorem 6.6, the maximand is also differentiable. Therefore for any interior solution $y \in \text{Int } G(x)$, the first-order conditions are necessary and sufficient for an optimum (taking $V(\cdot)$ as given). In particular, (optimal) solutions can be characterized by the following convenient *Euler equations:*

$$D_y U(x, y^*) + \beta D V(y^*) = 0, \tag{6.25}$$

where I use an asterisk to denote optimal values, and once again D denotes gradients. (Recall that, in the general case, x is a vector, not a real number, and thus $D_x U$ is a vector of partial derivatives. I denote the vector of partial derivatives of the value function V evaluated at y by $DV(y)$.) Throughout the rest of the chapter, I adopt the convention that $D_y U$ (or $D_y U(x(t), x(t+1))$) denotes the gradient vector of U with respect to its last K arguments, whereas $D_x U$ is the gradient with respect to the first K arguments.

The set of first-order conditions in (6.25) would be sufficient to solve for the optimal policy, y^*, if we knew the form of the $V(\cdot)$ function. Since this function is determined recursively as part of the optimization problem, there is a little more work to do before we obtain the set of equations that can be solved for the optimal policy.

Fortunately, we can use the equivalent of the Envelope Theorem (Theorem A.31) for dynamic programming and differentiate (6.24) with respect to the state vector x to obtain:

$$DV(x) = D_x U(x, y^*). \tag{6.26}$$

The reason equation (6.26) is the equivalent of the Envelope Theorem is that the term $[D_y U(x, y^*) + \beta D V(y^*)]dy/dx$ (i.e., the effect of a change in y times the induced change in y in response to the change in x) is absent from the expression. Naturally this is because $D_y U(x, y^*) + \beta D V(y^*) = 0$ from (6.25).

Now using the notation $y^* = \pi(x)$ to denote the optimal policy function (which is single-valued in view of Assumption 6.3 and Corollary 6.1) and the fact that $DV(y) = D_x V(\pi(x), \pi(\pi(x)))$, we can combine these two equations to write a more convenient form of the Euler equations expressed simply in terms of the payoff functions:

$$D_y U(x, \pi(x)) + \beta D_x U(\pi(x), \pi(\pi(x))) = 0, \tag{6.27}$$

where $D_x U$ represents the gradient vector of U with respect to its first K arguments, and $D_y U$ represents its gradient with respect to the second set of K arguments. Notice that (6.27) is a functional equation in the unknown function $\pi(\cdot)$ and characterizes the optimal policy function.

These equations become even simpler and more transparent in the case where both x and y are real numbers. In this case (6.25) becomes

$$\frac{\partial U(x, y^*)}{\partial y} + \beta V'(y^*) = 0, \tag{6.28}$$

where V' the notes the derivative of the V function with respect to its single argument.

This equation is intuitive; it requires the sum of the marginal gain today from increasing y and the discounted marginal gain from increasing y on the value of all future returns to be equal to zero. For instance, as in Example 6.1, we can think of U as decreasing in y and increasing in x; (6.28) would then require the current cost of increasing y to be compensated by higher values tomorrow. In the context of economic growth, this condition corresponds to the current cost of reducing consumption to be compensated by higher consumption tomorrow. As with (6.25), the value of higher consumption in (6.28) is expressed in terms of the derivative of the value function, $V'(y^*)$, which is one of the unknowns. Let us now use the one-dimensional version of (6.26) to find an expression for this derivative:

$$V'(x) = \frac{\partial U(x, y^*)}{\partial x}. \tag{6.29}$$

Combining (6.28) and (6.29) yields the following simple condition:

$$\frac{\partial U(x, \pi(x))}{\partial y} + \beta \frac{\partial U(\pi(x), \pi(\pi(x)))}{\partial x} = 0,$$

where, in line with the notation for gradients, $\partial U/\partial x$ denotes the derivative of U with respect to its first argument and $\partial U/\partial y$ with respect to the second argument.

Alternatively, explicitly including the time arguments, the Euler equation can be written as

$$\frac{\partial U(x(t), x^*(t + 1))}{\partial y} + \beta \frac{\partial U(x^*(t + 1), x^*(t + 2))}{\partial x} = 0. \tag{6.30}$$

However, Euler equation (6.30) is not sufficient for optimality. In addition we need the transversality condition. The transversality condition is essential in infinite-dimensional problems, because it ensures that there are no beneficial simultaneous changes in an infinite number of choice variables. In contrast, in finite-dimensional problems, there is no need for such a condition, since the first-order conditions are sufficient to rule out possible gains when we change many or all of the control variables at the same time. The role that the transversality condition plays in infinite-dimensional optimization problems will become more apparent after Theorem 6.10 is established and after the discussion in Section 6.6.2.

In the general case, the transversality condition takes the form

$$\lim_{t \to \infty} \beta^t D_x U(x^*(t), x^*(t + 1)) \cdot x^*(t) = 0, \tag{6.31}$$

where "·" denotes the inner product operator. In the one-dimensional case, we have the simpler transversality condition:

$$\lim_{t \to \infty} \beta^t \frac{\partial U(x^*(t), x^*(t + 1))}{\partial x} \cdot x^*(t) = 0. \tag{6.32}$$

This condition requires that the product of the marginal return from the state variable x times the value of this state variable does not increase asymptotically at a rate faster than or equal to $1/\beta$.

The next theorem shows that the transversality condition and the Euler equations in (6.27) are necessary and sufficient to characterize a solution to Problem 6.2 and therefore to Problem 6.3.

Theorem 6.10 (Euler Equations and the Transversality Condition) *Let $X \subset \mathbb{R}_+^K$, and suppose that Assumptions 6.1–6.5 hold. Then a sequence $\{x^*(t)\}_{t=0}^{\infty}$ such that $x^*(t + 1) \in$ Int $G(x^*(t))$, $t = 0, 1, \ldots$, is optimal for Problem 6.2 given $x(0)$ if and only if it satisfies (6.27) and (6.31).*

Proof.   (Sufficiency) Consider an arbitrary $x(0)$, and let $\mathbf{x}^* \equiv (x(0), x^*(1), \ldots) \in \Phi(x(0))$ be a feasible (nonnegative) sequence satisfying (6.27) and (6.31). I first show that $\mathbf{x}^*$ yields higher value than any other $\mathbf{x} \equiv (x(0), x(1), \ldots) \in \Phi(x(0))$. For any $\mathbf{x} \in \Phi(x(0))$, define

$$\Delta_{\mathbf{x}} \equiv \lim_{T \to \infty} \inf \sum_{t=0}^{T} \beta^t [U(x^*(t), x^*(t+1)) - U(x(t), x(t+1))]$$

as the lim inf of the difference of the values of the objective function evaluated at the feasible sequences $\mathbf{x}^*$ and $\mathbf{x}$ as the time horizon goes to infinity. Here lim inf is used instead of lim, since there is no guarantee that for an arbitrary $\mathbf{x} \in \Phi(x(0))$, the limit exists.

From Assumptions 6.2 and 6.5, U is continuous, concave, and differentiable. Since U is concave, Theorem A.23 and the multivariate equivalent of Corollary A.4 in Appendix A imply that

$$\Delta_{\mathbf{x}} \geq \lim_{T \to \infty} \inf \sum_{t=0}^{T} \beta^t [D_x U(x^*(t), x^*(t+1)) \cdot (x^*(t) - x(t))$$

$$+ D_y U(x^*(t), x^*(t+1)) \cdot (x^*(t+1) - x(t+1))]$$

for any $\mathbf{x} \in \Phi(x(0))$. Since $x^*(0) = x(0)$, $D_x U(x^*(0), x^*(1)) \cdot (x^*(0) - x(0)) = 0$. Using Fact A.5(5), we can rearrange terms in this expression to obtain

$$\Delta_{\mathbf{x}} \geq \lim_{T \to \infty} \inf \sum_{t=0}^{T} \beta^t \left[D_y U(x^*(t), x^*(t+1)) + \beta D_x U(x^*(t+1), x^*(t+2)) \right]$$

$$\cdot (x^*(t+1) - x(t+1))$$

$$- \lim_{T \to \infty} \sup \beta^T D_x U(x^*(T+1), x^*(T+2)) \cdot x^*(T+1)$$

$$+ \lim_{T \to \infty} \inf \beta^T D_x U(x^*(T+1), x^*(T+2)) \cdot x(T+1).$$

Since $\mathbf{x}^*$ satisfies (6.27), the terms in the first line are all equal to zero. Moreover, since it satisfies (6.31), the second line is also equal to zero. Finally, from Assumption 6.4, U is increasing in x, that is, $D_x U \geq 0$, and moreover, $x \geq 0$ by hypothesis, so the last term is nonnegative, establishing that $\Delta_{\mathbf{x}} \geq 0$ for any $\mathbf{x} \in \Phi(x(0))$. Consequently, $\mathbf{x}^*$ yields higher value than any feasible $\mathbf{x} \in \Phi(x(0))$ and is therefore optimal.

(Necessity) Now define

$$\Delta'_{\mathbf{x}} \equiv \lim_{T \to \infty} \sup \sum_{t=0}^{T} \beta^t [U(x^*(t), x^*(t+1)) - U(x(t), x(t+1))].$$

Suppose that $\{x^*(t+1)\}_{t=0}^{\infty}$, with $x^*(t+1) \in \text{Int } G(x^*(t))$ for all t constitutes an optimal plan, which implies that $\Delta'_{\mathbf{x}}$ is nonnegative for any $\mathbf{x} \in \Phi(x(0))$. Consider $\mathbf{x} \in \Phi(x(0))$ such that $x(t) = x^*(t) - \varepsilon z(t)$, where $z(t) \in \mathbb{R}^K$ for each t, and ε is a real number. For ε sufficiently small, such an $\mathbf{x}$ in $\Phi(x(0))$ can be found by virtue of the fact that $x^*(t+1) \in \text{Int } G(x^*(t))$ for all t. Then by Theorem A.23 and Fact A.5(5), we have

$$\Delta'_{\mathbf{x}} \leq \lim_{T \to \infty} \sup \sum_{t=0}^{T} \beta^t [D_x U(x^*(t), x^*(t+1)) \cdot \varepsilon z(t)$$

$$+ D_y U(x^*(t), x^*(t+1)) \cdot \varepsilon z(t+1)]$$

$$+ \lim_{T \to \infty} \sup \sum_{t=0}^{T} \beta^t o(\varepsilon, t),$$

where $o(\varepsilon, t)$ is the residual in the Taylor expansion for the term corresponding to time t and satisfies $\lim_{\varepsilon \to 0} o(\varepsilon, t)/\varepsilon = 0$ for each t. Now if (6.27) is violated at some t', take $y(t) = 0$ for all $t \neq t'$, and choose ε and $z(t')$ such that $D_x U(x^*(t'), x^*(t'+1)) \cdot z(t') < 0$ and $\varepsilon \to 0$. This choice guarantees that $\Delta'_{\mathbf{x}} < 0$, yielding a contradiction to the hypothesis that (6.27) is not satisfied.

Next, suppose that (6.27) is satisfied but (6.31) is violated. Choosing $x(t) = (1 - \varepsilon)x^*(t)$ and repeating the same steps as above, we have

$$\Delta'_{\mathbf{x}} \leq -\varepsilon \lim_{T \to \infty} \inf \beta^T D_x U(x^*(T), x^*(T+1)) \cdot x^*(T+1) \tag{6.33}$$

$$+ \lim_{T \to \infty} \sup \sum_{t=0}^{T} \beta^t o(\varepsilon, t),$$

where the remaining terms have been canceled by using (6.27). Let us next prove that

$$\lim_{\varepsilon \to 0} \lim_{T \to \infty} \sup \sum_{t=0}^{T} \beta^t \frac{o(\varepsilon, t)}{\varepsilon} = 0. \tag{6.34}$$

Since $\lim_{\varepsilon \to 0} o(\varepsilon, t)/\varepsilon = 0$ for each t, there exists $M < \infty$ such that for ε sufficiently small, $|o(\varepsilon, t)/\varepsilon| < M$ for each t. For any $\delta > 0$, choose $\bar{T}$ such that $M\beta^{T+1}/(1 - \beta) \leq \delta/2$ for all $T > \bar{T}$. Then

$$\lim_{T \to \infty} \sup \sum_{t=0}^{T} \beta^t \left| \frac{o(\varepsilon, t)}{\varepsilon} \right| \leq \sum_{t=0}^{\bar{T}} \beta^t \left| \frac{o(\varepsilon, t)}{\varepsilon} \right| + \frac{\delta}{2} \tag{6.35}$$

for ε sufficiently small. Moreover, since $\sum_{t=0}^{\bar{T}} \beta^t |o(\varepsilon, t)/\varepsilon|$ is a finite sum, there exists $\bar{\varepsilon}$ such that for $\varepsilon \leq \bar{\varepsilon}$, $\sum_{t=0}^{\bar{T}} \beta^t |o(\varepsilon, t)/\varepsilon| \leq \delta/2$. This implies that the left-hand side of (6.35) is less than δ. Since δ is arbitrary, (6.34) follows. Next, note that if (6.31) is violated, the first term in (6.33) can be made strictly negative (by choosing ε negative or positive). Combined with (6.34), this implies that $\Delta'_{\mathbf{x}} < 0$, contradicting the hypothesis that (6.31) does not hold and completing the proof. ∎

Theorem 6.10 shows that the simple form of the transversality condition (6.31) is both necessary and sufficient for an interior optimal plan as long as the Euler equations (6.27) are also satisfied. The Euler equations are also necessary for an interior solution. Theorem 6.10 is therefore often all we need to characterize solutions to (discrete-time) dynamic optimization problems.

I now illustrate how the tools that have been developed so far can be used in the context of the problem of optimal growth, which is further discussed in Section 6.8.

Example 6.4 *Consider the following optimal growth problem, with log preferences, Cobb-Douglas technology, and full depreciation of capital stock:*

$$\max_{\{k(t),c(t)\}_{t=0}^{\infty}} \sum_{t=0}^{\infty} \beta^t \log c(t)$$

subject to

$$k(t+1) = k(t)^{\alpha} - c(t),$$

$$k(0) > 0,$$

where, as usual, $\beta \in (0, 1)$, k denotes the capital-labor ratio (capital stock), and the resource constraint follows from the production function $K^{\alpha}L^{1-\alpha}$, written in per capita terms.

This problem is one of the canonical examples that admit an explicit-form characterization. To derive this characterization, let us follow Example 6.1 and set up the maximization problem in recursive form as

$$V(x) = \max_{y \geq 0}\{\log(x^{\alpha} - y) + \beta V(y)\},$$

with x corresponding to today's capital stock and y to tomorrow's capital stock. Our main objective is to find the policy function $y = \pi(x)$, which determines tomorrow's capital stock as a function of today's capital stock. Once this is done, we can easily determine the level of consumption as a function of today's capital stock from the resource constraint.

It can be verified that this problem satisfies Assumptions 6.1–6.5. In particular, using the same argument as in Section 6.8 below, x and y again can be restricted to be in a compact set. Consequently, Theorems 6.1–6.6 apply. In particular, since $V(\cdot)$ is differentiable, the Euler equation for the one-dimensional case (6.28) implies

$$\frac{1}{x^{\alpha} - y} = \beta V'(y).$$

The Envelope Condition (6.29) gives

$$V'(x) = \frac{\alpha x^{\alpha-1}}{x^{\alpha} - y}.$$

Thus using the notation $y = \pi(x)$ and combining these two equations, we obtain

$$\frac{1}{x^{\alpha} - \pi(x)} = \beta \frac{\alpha \pi(x)^{\alpha-1}}{\pi(x)^{\alpha} - \pi(\pi(x))} \quad \text{for all } x,$$

which is a functional equation in a single function, $\pi(x)$. There are no straightforward ways of solving functional equations, but in most cases guess-and-verify methods are most fruitful. For example in this case, let us conjecture that

$$\pi(x) = ax^{\alpha}. \tag{6.36}$$

Substituting (6.36) in the previous expression, we have

$$\frac{1}{x^{\alpha} - ax^{\alpha}} = \beta \frac{\alpha a^{\alpha-1} x^{\alpha(\alpha-1)}}{a^{\alpha} x^{\alpha^2} - a^{1+\alpha} x^{\alpha^2}}$$

$$= \frac{\beta}{a} \frac{\alpha}{x^{\alpha} - ax^{\alpha}},$$

which implies that $a = \beta\alpha$ satisfies this equation. The policy function $\pi(x) = \beta\alpha x^{\alpha}$ also implies that the law of motion of the capital stock is

$$k(t+1) = \beta\alpha k(t)^{\alpha}, \tag{6.37}$$

and the optimal consumption level is

$$c(t) = (1 - \beta a)k(t)^{\alpha}.$$

It can then be verified that the capital-labor ratio $k(t)$ converges to a steady state k^{*}, which is sufficient to ensure the transversality condition (6.32). Corollary 6.1 and Theorem 6.10 then imply that $\pi(x) = \beta\alpha x^{\alpha}$ must be the unique policy function for this problem. Exercise 6.7 continues with some of the details of this example and also shows that the optimal growth path involves a sequence of capital-labor ratios converging to a unique steady state.

Finally, let us have a brief look at the intertemporal utility maximization problem of a consumer facing a certain income sequence.

Example 6.5 *Consider the problem of an infinitely-lived consumer with instantaneous utility function defined over consumption, $u(c)$, where $u : \mathbb{R}_{+} \to \mathbb{R}$ is strictly increasing, continuously differentiable, and strictly concave. The consumer discounts the future exponentially with the constant discount factor $\beta \in (0, 1)$. He also faces a certain (nonnegative) labor income stream of $\{w(t)\}_{t=0}^{\infty}$ and starts life with a given amount of assets $a(0) \in \mathbb{R}$. He receives a constant net rate of interest $r > 0$ on his asset holdings (so that the gross rate of return is $1 + r$). To start with, let us suppose that wages are constant, that is, $w(t) = w \in \mathbb{R}_{+}$. Then the utility maximization problem of the consumer can be written as*

$$\max_{\{c(t),a(t)\}_{t=0}^{\infty}} \sum_{t=0}^{\infty} \beta^{t} u(c(t)),$$

subject to the flow budget constraint

$$a(t+1) = (1+r)a(t) + w - c(t),$$

with initial assets, $a(0)$, given. This maximization problem, without further constraints, is not well defined and in fact does not capture the utility maximization problem of the consumer. In particular, Exercise 6.11 shows that this problem allows the consumer to build up debt without limit (so that $\lim_{t \to \infty} a(t) = -\infty$). This scenario is sometimes referred to as a "Ponzi game" and involves the consumer continuously borrowing and rolling over debt. If allowed, the consumer will clearly prefer consumption paths that allow this, since they enable him to increase his consumption at all dates. However, from an economic point of view this solution is nonsensical and would not be feasible in a market economy, because the financial market (lenders) transacting with the consumer would incur very large losses. This result emerges because we have not imposed the appropriate budget constraint on the consumer. As discussed in greater detail in Chapter 8, the flow budget constraint is not sufficient to capture the lifetime budget constraint of the consumer (as evidenced by the fact that the consumer can have consumption paths with $\lim_{t \to \infty} a(t) = -\infty$). An additional constraint needs to be imposed so that the consumer cannot run such Ponzi games.

There are three solutions to this problem. The first, which is discussed in greater detail in Chapter 8, is to impose a no-Ponzi condition that rules out such schemes. The second is to assume that the consumer cannot borrow, so $a(t+1) \geq 0$ for all t. While this constraint prevents the problem, it is somewhat too draconian. For example, we may wish to allow the *consumer to borrow temporarily, as many financial markets do, but not allow him to have an asset position reaching negative infinity. The third solution is to impose the natural debt limit. This restriction essentially involves computing the maximum debt that the consumer can repay and then requiring that his debt level should never exceed this level. It is clear that, since consumption is nonnegative, the consumer can never repay more than his total wage income. Given a constant wage rate w and a constant interest rate r, the net present discounted value of the consumer's wage income is w/r. This is a finite number, since w ∈ ℝ₊ and r > 0. Therefore, if his asset holdings, a(t + 1), ever fall below −w/r, the consumer will never be able to repay. It is therefore natural to expect the financial markets, even if they have the power to confiscate all of the income of the consumer, never to lend so much that the consumer reaches an asset position a(t + 1) < −w/r for any t. In this light, the natural debt limit requires*

$$a(t + 1) \geq \underline{a} \equiv -\frac{w}{r} \quad \text{for all } t.$$

The next challenge is that, even with the natural debt limit, the assets of the consumer, a, which correspond to the state variable of this maximization problem, do not necessarily belong to a compact set. Consequently, the theorems developed so far cannot be directly applied to this problem. One way of proceeding is to strengthen these theorems, so that they cover situations in which the feasible set (X in terms of the above notation) is potentially unbounded. While such a strengthening is possible, it requires additional mathematical details. An alternative approach is to make use of the economic structure of the model. In particular, the following method works in general (but not always; see Exercise 6.12). Let us choose some $\bar{a}$ and restrict a to lie in the interval $[\underline{a}, \bar{a}]$. Solve the problem and then verify that a is in the interior of this set. In this example, again using the fact that the net present discounted value of the future labor income of the consumer is w/r, an obvious choice is $\bar{a} \equiv a(0) + w/r < \infty$ (since $a(0) \in \mathbb{R}$ and w/r < ∞). Exercise 6.12 shows the conditions under which a(t) always lies in the interior of the interval $[\underline{a}, \bar{a}]$. This strategy of finding an upper bound for the state variable and thus ensuring that it lies in a compact set is often used in applications.

Finally, before characterizing the solution to this problem, note that the budget constraint could have been written as a(t + 1) = (1 + r)(a(t) + w − c(t)). The difference between these two alternative budget constraints involves the timing of interest payments. The one I use above presumes that a(t) is asset holdings at the beginning of time t and earns interest this period, whereas the alternative supposes that the consumer starts the period with assets a(t), then receives his labor income w at time t, and then consumes c(t). Whatever is left is saved for the next date and earns the gross interest rate (1 + r). The choice between these two formulations has no bearing on the results.

With these assumptions, the recursive formulation of the consumer's maximization problem can be written in a straightforward manner. The state variable is a(t), and consumption c(t) can be expressed as

$$c(t) = (1 + r)a(t) + w − a(t + 1).$$

With standard arguments and denoting the current value of the state variable by a and its future value by a', the recursive form of this dynamic optimization problem can be written as

$$V(a) = \max_{a' \in [\underline{a}, \bar{a}]} \{u((1 + r)a + w − a') + \beta V(a')\}.$$

Clearly u(·) is strictly increasing in a, continuously differentiable in a and a' and is strictly concave in a. Moreover, since u(·) is continuously differentiable in $a \in (\underline{a}, \bar{a})$ and the individ-

ual's wealth is finite, $V(a(0))$ is also finite. Thus all of the results from our analysis above, in particular Theorems 6.1–6.6, apply and imply that $V(a)$ is differentiable and that a continuous solution $a' = \pi(a)$ exists. Moreover, we can use the Euler equation (6.25), or its more specific form (6.28) for one-dimensional problems, to characterize the optimal consumption plan. In particular, we have

$$u'((1+r)a + w - a') = u'(c) = \beta V'(a'). \tag{6.38}$$

This important equation is often referred to as the "consumption Euler" equation. It states that the marginal utility of current consumption must be equal to the marginal increase in the continuation value multiplied by the product of the discount factor, β. It captures the economic intuition of the dynamic programming approach, which reduces the complex infinite-dimensional optimization problem to one of comparing today to tomorrow. As usual, the only difficulty here is that tomorrow itself involves a complicated maximization problem and hence tomorrow's value function and its derivative are endogenous. But here the Envelope Condition (6.29) again comes to our rescue and yields

$$V'(a') = (1+r)u'(c'),$$

where c' refers to next period's consumption. Using this relationship, the consumption Euler equation (6.38) becomes

$$u'(c) = \beta(1+r)u'(c'). \tag{6.39}$$

This form of the consumption Euler equation is more familiar and requires the marginal utility of consumption today to be equal to the marginal utility of consumption tomorrow multiplied by the product of the discount factor and the gross rate of return. Since we have assumed that β and $(1+r)$ are constant, the relationship between today's and tomorrow's consumption never changes. In particular, since $u(\cdot)$ is assumed to be continuously differentiable and strictly concave, $u'(\cdot)$ always exists and is strictly decreasing. Therefore the intertemporal consumption maximization problem implies the following simple rule:

$$\text{if } r = \beta^{-1} - 1, \quad c = c' \text{ and consumption is constant over time,}$$

$$\text{if } r > \beta^{-1} - 1, \quad c < c' \text{ and consumption increases over time,} \tag{6.40}$$

$$\text{if } r < \beta^{-1} - 1, \quad c > c' \text{ and consumption decreases over time.}$$

The remarkable feature is that these statements have been made without any reference to the initial level of asset holdings $a(0)$ and the wage rate w. It turns out that these only determine the initial level of consumption. The slope of the optimal consumption path is independent of the wealth of the individual. Exercise 6.13 asks you to determine the level of initial consumption using the transversality condition and the intertemporal budget constraint, while Exercise 6.12 asks you to verify that when $r \leq \beta - 1$, $a(t+1) \in (\underline{a}, \bar{a})$ for all t (so that the artificial bounds on asset holdings that I imposed have no bearing on the results).

Example 6.5 is somewhat restrictive, because wages are assumed to be constant over time. What happens if instead there is a time-varying sequence of wages $\{w(t)\}_{t=0}^{\infty}$ or a time-varying sequence of interest rates $\{r(t)\}_{t=0}^{\infty}$? Unfortunately, with a time-varying sequence of wages or interest rates, the problem becomes nonstationary, and the theorems developed for Problems 6.2 and 6.3 no longer apply. Nevertheless, many equilibrium problems will have this time-varying feature, because individuals face time-varying market prices. This motivates my discussion of nonstationary problems in Section 6.7.

6.6.2 Dynamic Programming versus the Sequence Problem

Before turning to nonstationary problems, let us compare the dynamic programming formulation to the sequence problem and motivate the transversality condition using the sequence problem. Let us also suppose that x is one dimensional and that there is a finite horizon T. Then the problem becomes

$$\max_{\{x(t)\}_{t=0}^{T}} \sum_{t=0}^{T} \beta^t U(x(t), x(t+1)),$$

subject to $x(t+1) \geq 0$, with $x(0)$ as given. Moreover, let $U(x(T), x(T+1))$ be the last period's utility, with $x(T+1)$ as the state variable left after the last period (this utility could be thought of as the "salvage value").

In this case, we have a finite-dimensional optimization problem, and we can simply look at first-order conditions. Moreover, let us again assume that the solution lies in the interior of the constraint set, that is, $x^*(t) > 0$, so that first-order conditions do not need to be expressed as complementary-slackness conditions. In particular, in this case they take the following simple form, equivalent to the Euler equation (6.30):

$$\frac{\partial U(x^*(t), x^*(t+1))}{\partial y} + \beta \frac{\partial U(x^*(t+1), x^*(t+2))}{\partial x} = 0$$

for any $0 \leq t \leq T - 1$, which are identical to the Euler equations for the infinite-horizon case (recall that $\partial U/\partial x$ denotes the derivative of U with respect to its first argument and $\partial U/\partial y$ with respect to the second argument). In addition, for $x(T+1)$, the following boundary condition is also necessary:

$$x^*(T+1) \geq 0, \text{ and } \beta^T \frac{\partial U(x^*(T), x^*(T+1))}{\partial y} x^*(T+1) = 0. \tag{6.41}$$

Intuitively, this boundary condition requires that $x^*(T+1)$ should be positive only if an interior value of it maximizes the salvage value at the end. To provide more intuition for this expression, let us return to the formulation of the optimal growth problem in Example 6.1.

Example 6.6 *Recall that in terms of the optimal growth problem,*

$$U(x(t), x(t+1)) = u(f(x(t)) + (1-\delta)x(t) - x(t+1)),$$

with $x(t) = k(t)$ and $x(t+1) = k(t+1)$. Suppose that, in contrast to the infinite-horizon models, the world comes to an end at date T. Then at the last date T,

$$\frac{\partial U(x^*(T), x^*(T+1))}{\partial y} = -u'(c^*(T+1)) < 0.$$

From (6.41) and the fact that U is increasing in its first argument (Assumption 6.4), an optimal path must have $k^*(T+1) = x^*(T+1) = 0$. Intuitively, there should be no capital left at the end of the world. If any resources were left after the end of the world, utility could be improved by consuming them either at the last date or at some earlier date.

The transversality condition can be derived heuristically as an extension of condition (6.41) to the case $T = \infty$. Taking this limit yields

$$\lim_{T \to \infty} \beta^T \frac{\partial U(x^*(T), x^*(T+1))}{\partial y} x^*(T+1) = 0.$$

Moreover, the Euler equation implies

$$\frac{\partial U(x^*(T), x^*(T+1))}{\partial y} + \beta \frac{\partial U(x^*(T+1), x^*(T+2))}{\partial x} = 0.$$

Substituting this relationship into the previous equation gives

$$-\lim_{T\to\infty} \beta^{T+1} \frac{\partial U(x^*(T+1), x^*(T+2))}{\partial x} x^*(T+1) = 0.$$

Canceling the negative sign and changing the timing for convenience, we obtain

$$\lim_{T\to\infty} \beta^T \frac{\partial U(x^*(T), x^*(T+1))}{\partial x} x^*(T) = 0,$$

which is exactly the transversality condition (6.32). This derivation also highlights that the transversality condition can equivalently be written as

$$\lim_{T\to\infty} \beta^T \frac{\partial U(x^*(T), x^*(T+1))}{\partial y} x^*(T+1) = 0.$$

Thus there is no unique representation of the transversality condition but instead various different equivalent forms. They all correspond to a "boundary condition at infinity" that rules out variations that change an infinite number of control variables at the same time.

6.7 Nonstationary Infinite-Horizon Optimization

6.7.1 Main Results

Let us now return to Problem 6.1. Nonstationarity makes analysis more difficult than in Problems 6.2 and 6.3. Nevertheless, many important economic problems, for example, utility maximization by a household in a dynamic competitive equilibrium, correspond to such a nonstationary problem. One way of making progress is to introduce additional assumptions on U and G to obtain the equivalents of Theorems 6.1–6.6 (see, e.g., Exercise 6.14). A simpler line of attack is to establish the existence of solutions and the equivalent of Theorem 6.10, which shows the necessity and sufficiency of Euler equations and the transversality conditions, which is the approach I use in this section. In particular, let us again define the set of feasible sequences or *plans* starting with an initial value $x(t)$ at time t as:

$$\Phi(t, x(t)) = \{\{x(s)\}_{s=t}^{\infty} : x(s+1) \in G(t, x(s)) \quad \text{for } s = t, t+1, \ldots\}.$$

Also denote an element of this set by $\mathbf{x}[t] = (x(t), x(t+1), \ldots) \in \Phi(t, x(t))$. The key assumptions are as follows.

Assumption 6.1N *$G(t, x)$ is nonempty for all $x \in X$ and $t \in \mathbb{Z}_+$, and $U(t, x, y)$ is uniformly bounded (from above); that is, there exists $M < \infty$ such that $U(t, x, y) \leq M$ for all $t \in \mathbb{Z}_+$, $x \in X$, and $y \in G(t, x)$.*

Assumption 6.2N *X is a compact subset of $\mathbb{R}^K$, G is nonempty-valued, compact-valued, and continuous. Moreover, $U : \mathbf{X}_G \to \mathbb{R}$ is continuous in x and y, where $\mathbf{X}_G = \{(t, x, y) \in X \times X : y \in G(t, x)\}$.*

Assumption 6.3N *U is concave. That is, for any $\alpha \in (0, 1)$ and any (t, x, y), $(t, x', y') \in \mathbf{X}_G$, we have*

$$U(t, \alpha x + (1 - \alpha)x', \alpha y + (1 - \alpha)y') \geq \alpha U(t, x, y) + (1 - \alpha)U(t, x', y').$$

Moreover, if $x \neq x'$,

$$U\big(t, \alpha x + (1 - \alpha)x', \alpha y + (1 - \alpha)y'\big) > \alpha U(t, x, y) + (1 - \alpha)U(t, x', y').$$

In addition, G is convex. That is, for any $\alpha \in [0, 1]$, and $x, x', y, y' \in X$ such that $y \in G(t, x)$ and $y' \in G(t, x')$, we have

$$\alpha y + (1 - \alpha)y' \in G\big(t, \alpha x + (1 - \alpha)x'\big).$$

Assumption 6.4N *For each $t \in \mathbb{Z}_+$ and $y \in X$, $U(t, x, y)$ is strictly increasing in each component of x, and G is monotone in x in the sense that $x \leq x'$ implies $G(t, x) \subset G(t, x')$ for any $t \in \mathbb{Z}_+$.*

Assumption 6.5N *U is continuously differentiable in x and y on Int $\mathbf{X}_G$ (where Int $\mathbf{X}_G$ refers to the interior of the set $\mathbf{X}_G$ with respect to x and y).*

The two key results are the following. The proofs of both theorems are given in Section 6.7.2.

Theorem 6.11 (Existence of Solutions) *Suppose that Assumptions 6.1N and 6.2N hold. Then there exists a unique function $V^* : \mathbb{Z}_+ \times X \to \mathbb{R}$ that is a solution to Problem 6.1. V^* is continuous in x and bounded. Moreover, for any $x(0) \in X$, an optimal plan $\mathbf{x}^*[0] \in \Phi(0, x(0))$ exists.*

Theorem 6.12 (Euler Equations and the Transversality Condition) *Let $X \subset \mathbb{R}_+^K$, and suppose that Assumptions 6.1N–6.5N hold. Then a sequence $\{x^*(t + 1)\}_{t=0}^\infty$, with $x^*(t + 1) \in$ Int $G(t, x^*(t))$, $t = 0, 1, \ldots,$ is optimal for Problem 6.1 given $x(0)$ if and only if it satisfies the Euler equation*

$$D_y U(t, x^*(t), x^*(t + 1)) + \beta D_x U(t + 1, x^*(t + 1), x^*(t + 2)) = 0, \tag{6.42}$$

and the transversality condition

$$\lim_{t \to \infty} \beta^t D_x U(t, x^*(t), x^*(t + 1)) \cdot x^*(t) = 0. \tag{6.43}$$

In (6.42), as in stationary problems, $D_y U$ denotes the vector of partial derivatives of U with respect to the control vector (its last K arguments), whereas $D_x U$ denotes the vector of partial derivatives with respect to the state vector. In (6.43), "$\cdot$" again denotes the inner product of the two vectors.

These two theorems provide us with the necessary tools to tackle nonstationary discrete-time infinite-horizon optimization problems. In particular, Theorem 6.11 ensures that the solution exists, and Theorem 6.12 shows that, as in the stationary case, we can simply use the Euler equations and the transversality condition to characterize this solution (as long as it is interior).

6.7.2 Proofs of Theorems 6.11 and 6.12*

Proof of Theorem 6.11. Since U is uniformly bounded (Assumption 6.1N) and continuous (Assumption 6.2N), Theorem A.12 in Appendix A implies that the objective function in Problem 6.1 is continuous in $\mathbf{x}[0]$ in the product topology. Moreover, the constraint set $\Phi(0, x(0))$

is a closed subset of X^∞ (the infinite product of X). Since X is compact (Assumption 6.2N), Tychonoff's Theorem (Theorem A.13) implies that X^∞ is compact in the product topology. A closed subset of a compact set is compact (Lemma A.2 in Appendix A), which implies that $\Phi(0, x(0))$ is compact. From Weierstrass's Theorem (Theorem A.9) applied to Problem 6.1, there exists $\mathbf{x}^*[0] \in \Phi(0, x(0))$ attaining $V^*(0, x(0))$. Moreover, the constraint set is a continuous correspondence (again in the product topology), so Berge's Maximum Theorem (Theorem A.16) implies that $V^*(0, x(0))$ is continuous in $x(0)$. Since $x(0) \in X$ and X is compact, this implies that $V^*(0, x(0))$ is bounded (Corollary A.1 in Appendix A). ∎

Proof of Theorem 6.12. The proof is similar to that of Theorem 6.10.

(Sufficiency) Consider an arbitrary $x(0)$ and let $\mathbf{x}^*[0] \equiv (x(0), x^*(1), \ldots) \in \Phi(0, x(0))$ be a feasible (nonnegative) sequence satisfying (6.42) and (6.43). For any feasible sequence $\mathbf{x}[0] \equiv (x(0), x(1), \ldots) \in \Phi(0, x(0))$, define

$$\Delta_{\mathbf{x}} \equiv \lim_{T \to \infty} \inf \sum_{t=0}^{T} \beta^t [U(t, x^*(t), x^*(t+1)) - U(t, x(t), x(t+1))]$$

as the difference of the objective function between the feasible sequences $\mathbf{x}^*$ and $\mathbf{x}$.

From Assumptions 6.2N and 6.5N, U is continuous, concave, and differentiable. By the definition of a concave function, we have

$$\Delta_{\mathbf{x}} \geq \lim_{T \to \infty} \inf \sum_{t=0}^{T} \beta^t [D_x U(t, x^*(t), x^*(t+1)) \cdot (x^*(t) - x(t))$$
$$+ D_y U(t, x^*(t), x^*(t+1)) \cdot (x^*(t+1) - x(t+1))]$$

for any $\mathbf{x}[0] \in \Phi(0, x(0))$. Using the fact that $x^*(0) = x(0)$ and rearranging terms yields

$$\Delta_{\mathbf{x}} \geq \lim_{T \to \infty} \inf \sum_{t=0}^{T} \beta^t \left[D_y U(t, x^*(t), x^*(t+1)) + \beta D_x U(t+1, x^*(t+1), x^*(t+2)) \right]$$
$$\cdot (x^*(t+1) - x(t+1))$$
$$- \lim_{T \to \infty} \sup \beta^T D_x U(T+1, x^*(T+1), x^*(T+2)) \cdot x^*(T+1)$$
$$+ \lim_{T \to \infty} \inf \beta^T D_x U(T+1, x^*(T+1), x^*(T+2)) \cdot x(T+1).$$

Since $\mathbf{x}^*[0]$ satisfies (6.42), the terms in first line are all equal to zero. Moreover, since it satisfies (6.43), the second line is also equal to zero. Finally, from Assumption 6.4N, U is increasing in x, that is, $D_x U \geq 0$, and moreover $x \geq 0$ by hypothesis, so the last term is nonnegative, establishing that $\Delta_{\mathbf{x}} \geq 0$ for any $\mathbf{x}[0] \in \Phi(0, x(0))$. Consequently, $\mathbf{x}^*[0]$ yields higher value than any feasible $\mathbf{x}[0] \in \Phi(0, x(0))$ and is therefore optimal.

(Necessity) Now define

$$\Delta'_{\mathbf{x}} \equiv \lim_{T \to \infty} \sup \sum_{t=0}^{T} \beta^t [U(t, x^*(t), x^*(t+1)) - U(t, x(t), x(t+1))]$$

Suppose that $\{x^*(t+1)\}_{t=0}^{\infty}$, with $x^*(t+1) \in \text{Int } G(t, x^*(t))$ for all t constitutes an optimal plan. Then $\Delta'_{\mathbf{x}}$ is nonnegative for any $\mathbf{x}[0] \in \Phi(0, x(0))$. Consider $\mathbf{x}[0] \in \Phi(x(0))$ such that $x(t) = x^*(t) - \varepsilon z(t)$, where $z(t) \in \mathbb{R}^K$, and ε is a real number. For ε sufficiently small, such an $\mathbf{x}[0]$ in $\Phi(0, x(0))$ can be found by virtue of the fact that $x^*(t+1) \in \text{Int } G(t, x^*(t))$ for all t. Then as in the proof of Theorem 6.10, we have

$$\Delta'_{\mathbf{x}} \leq \lim_{T \to \infty} \inf \sum_{t=0}^{T} \beta^t [D_x U(t, x^*(t), x^*(t+1)) \cdot \varepsilon z(t)$$

$$+ D_x U(t, x^*(t), x^*(t+1)) \cdot \varepsilon z(t+1)]$$

$$+ \lim_{T \to \infty} \sup \sum_{t=0}^{T} \beta^t o(\varepsilon, t),$$

with $\lim_{\varepsilon \to 0} o(\varepsilon, t)/\varepsilon = 0$. If (6.42) is violated at some t', take $z(t) = 0$ for all $t \neq t'$, ε and $z(t')$ such that $D_x U(t, x^*(t'), x^*(t'+1)) \cdot z(t') < 0$, and $\varepsilon \to 0$. Then $\Delta'_{\mathbf{x}} < 0$, yielding a contradiction to the hypothesis that (6.42) is not satisfied.

Next, suppose that (6.42) is satisfied but (6.43) is violated. Choosing $x(t) = (1 - \varepsilon)x^*(t)$ and repeating the same steps as in the proof of Theorem 6.10, we have

$$\Delta'_{\mathbf{x}} \leq -\varepsilon \lim_{T \to \infty} \inf \beta^T D_x U(T, x^*(T), x^*(T+1)) \cdot x^*(T+1).$$

If (6.43) is violated, by choosing ε negative or positive this inequality would imply $\Delta'_{\mathbf{x}} < 0$, contradicting the hypothesis that (6.43) does not hold. ∎

6.7.3 Application

As an application of nonstationary infinite-horizon optimization, let us consider the consumption problem in a market environment in which wages and interest rates are potentially changing over time.

Example 6.5 (continued). *The consumer is again infinitely lived, with instantaneous utility function defined over consumption $u(c)$, where $u : \mathbb{R}_+ \to \mathbb{R}$ is strictly increasing, continuously differentiable, and strictly concave. The discount factor is $\beta \in (0, 1)$. Now both the sequence of labor income, $\{w(t)\}_{t=0}^{\infty}$, and interest rates, $\{r(t)\}_{t=0}^{\infty}$, are potentially time varying, though there is still no uncertainty. The consumer starts life with a given amount of assets $a(0)$. His utility maximization problem can then be written as*

$$\max_{\{c(t), a(t)\}_{t=0}^{\infty}} \sum_{t=0}^{\infty} \beta^t u(c(t)),$$

subject to the flow budget constraint

$$a(t+1) = (1 + r(t))a(t) + w(t) - c(t),$$

with $a(0)$ given. As in the case with constant wage and interest rates, we need to introduce an additional constraint to complement the flow budget constraint. Let us again impose the natural debt limit. Exercise 6.13 shows that the natural debt limit at time t takes the form

$$a(t) \geq -\sum_{s=0}^{\infty} \left\{ \left(\prod_{j=0}^{s} \frac{1}{1 + r(t+j)} \right) w(t+s) \right\}. \tag{6.44}$$

Moreover, let us assume that the right-hand side of (6.44) is bounded above by some $\bar{W} < \infty$ for all t. Then a natural hypothesis is that $a(t)$ should always lie in some set of the form $[-\bar{W}, a(0) + \bar{W}]$ (see Exercise 6.13). Repeating the same arguments as in part 1 of Example 6.5, the consumer maximization problem can be written as

$$\max_{\{a(t)\}_{t=0}^{\infty}} \sum_{t=0}^{\infty} \beta^t u((1+r(t))a(t) + w(t) - a(t+1))$$

for given $a(0)$. The Euler equation in this case is

$$u'(c(t)) = \beta(1 + r(t+1))u'(c(t+1)) \tag{6.45}$$

for all t. Thus instead of (6.40), we have the following more general consumption rule:

if $r(t+1) = \beta^{-1} - 1$, $c(t) = c(t+1)$ and consumption is constant between t and $t+1$,

if $r(t+1) > \beta^{-1} - 1$, $c(t) = c(t+1)$ and consumption increases between t and $t+1$,

if $r(t+1) < \beta^{-1} - 1$, $c(t) = c(t+1)$ and consumption decreases between t and $t+1$.

In some ways, this result is even more remarkable than (6.40), since the slope of the optimal consumption path is not only independent of $a(0)$, but it is also independent of current income and in fact of the entire sequence of income levels $\{w(t)\}_{t=0}^{\infty}$.

6.8 Optimal Growth in Discrete Time

Let us now return to the optimal growth problem, introduced in Section 5.9, and use the main results from stationary dynamic programming to obtain a characterization of the optimal growth path of a neoclassical economy. Example 6.4 already showed how this can be done in the special case with logarithmic utility, a Cobb-Douglas production function, and full depreciation. In this section, the results are more general and are stated for the canonical optimal growth model introduced in Chapter 5.

Recall the optimal growth problem for a one-sector economy admitting a representative household with instantaneous utility function u and discount factor $\beta \in (0, 1)$. This problem can be written as

$$\max_{\{k(t),c(t)\}_{t=0}^{\infty}} \sum_{t=0}^{\infty} \beta^t u(c(t)), \tag{6.46}$$

subject to

$$k(t+1) = f(k(t)) + (1 - \delta)k(t) - c(t) \text{ and } k(t) \geq 0, \tag{6.47}$$

with the initial capital stock given by $k(0) > 0$. The standard assumptions on the production function, Assumptions 1 and 2 (from Chapter 2), are still in effect. In addition, let us impose the following assumption.

Assumption 3′ $u : [\varepsilon, \infty) \to \mathbb{R}$ *is continuously differentiable and strictly concave for some $\varepsilon > 0$ sufficiently small.*

This is considerably stronger than necessary. In fact, concavity or even continuity is enough for most results. But this assumption helps us avoid inessential technical details. It is referred to as "Assumption 3′" to distinguish it from the very closely related Assumption 3 that is introduced and used in Chapter 8 and thereafter.

The first step is to write the optimal growth problem as a (stationary) dynamic programming problem. This can be done along the lines of Examples 6.1 and 6.4. In particular, let the choice variable be next date's capital stock, denoted by s. Then the resource constraint (6.47) implies that current consumption is given by $c = f(k) + (1 - \delta)k - s$, and thus the optimal growth problem can be written in the following recursive form:

$$V(k) = \max_{s \in G(k)} \{u(f(k) + (1 - \delta)k - s) + \beta V(s)\}, \tag{6.48}$$

where $G(k)$ is the constraint correspondence, given by the interval $[0, f(k) + (1 - \delta)k]$. This constraint requires that consumption and the capital stock be nonnegative.

It can be verified that under Assumptions 1, 2, and 3′, the optimal growth problem satisfies Assumptions 6.1–6.5 of the dynamic programming problems. The only nonobvious feature is that the level of consumption and capital stock belong to a compact set. To verify that this is the case, note that the economy can never settle into a level of capital-labor ratio greater than $\bar{k}$, defined by

$$\delta \bar{k} = f(\bar{k}),$$

since this value is the capital-labor ratio that would sustain itself when consumption is set equal to 0. If the economy starts with $k(0) < \bar{k}$, it can never exceed $\bar{k}$. If it starts with $k(0) > \bar{k}$, it can never exceed $k(0)$. Therefore without loss of generality we can restrict consumption and capital stock to lie in the compact set $[0, \vec{k}]$, where

$$\vec{k} \equiv f\left(\max\left\{k(0), \bar{k}\right\}\right) + (1 - \delta) \max\left\{k(0), \bar{k}\right\}.$$

Consequently, Theorems 6.1–6.6 can be directly applied to this problem.

Proposition 6.1   *Given Assumptions 1, 2, and 3′, the optimal growth model as specified in (6.46) and (6.47) has a solution characterized by the unique value function $V(k)$ and consumption function $c(k)$. The capital stock in the next period is given by $s(k) = f(k) + (1 - \delta)k - c(k)$. Moreover, $V(k)$ is strictly increasing and strictly concave, and $s(k)$ is nondecreasing in k.*

Proof.   That the value function (6.48) is a solution to (6.46) and (6.47) follows from Theorems 6.1 and 6.2. That $V(k)$ exists follows from Theorem 6.3, and the fact that it is increasing and strictly concave, with the policy correspondence being a policy function, follows from Theorem 6.4 and Corollary 6.1.

Thus we only have to show that $s(k)$ is nondecreasing. This can be proved by contradiction using a "revealed preference" argument. Suppose, to arrive at a contradiction, that $s(k)$ is decreasing, that is, there exists k and $k' > k$ such that $s(k) > s(k')$. Since $k' > k$, $s(k)$ is feasible when the capital stock is k'. Moreover, since by hypothesis, $s(k) > s(k')$, $s(k')$ is feasible at capital stock k. By optimality and feasibility, we have

$$V(k) = u(f(k) + (1 - \delta)k - s(k)) + \beta V(s(k))$$

$$\geq u(f(k) + (1 - \delta)k - s(k')) + \beta V(s(k')),$$

$$V(k') = u(f(k') + (1 - \delta)k' - s(k')) + \beta V(s(k'))$$

$$\geq u(f(k') + (1 - \delta)k' - s(k)) + \beta V(s(k)).$$

Combining and rearranging these relations yields

$$u(f(k) + (1-\delta)k - s(k)) - u(f(k) + (1-\delta)k - s(k')) \geq \beta[V(s(k')) - V(s(k))]$$
$$\geq u(f(k') + (1-\delta)k' - s(k))$$
$$- u(f(k') + (1-\delta)k' - s(k')).$$

Denoting $z \equiv f(k) + (1-\delta)k$ and $x \equiv s(k)$ and similarly for z' and x', we have

$$u(z-x') - u(z-x) \leq u(z'-x') - u(z'-x). \tag{6.49}$$

But clearly,

$$(z-x') - (z-x) = (z'-x') - (z'-x),$$

which—combined with the fact that $z' > z$ (since $k' > k$) and $x > x'$ by hypothesis, and that u is strictly concave and increasing—implies

$$u(z-x') - u(z-x) > u(z'-x') - u(z'-x),$$

contradicting (6.49). This establishes that $s(k)$ must be nondecreasing everywhere. ∎

In addition, Assumption 2 implies that savings and consumption levels have to be interior. Thus an application of Theorem 6.6 establishes the following proposition.

Proposition 6.2 *Given Assumptions 1, 2, and 3′, the value function $V(k)$ defined above is differentiable.*

Let us next exploit Theorem 6.10, and study the Euler equation and the transversality condition of this dynamic optimization problem. The Euler equation from (6.48) takes the simple form

$$u'(c) = \beta V'(s),$$

where s denotes the next date's capital stock. Applying the Envelope Condition gives

$$V'(k) = [f'(k) + (1-\delta)] u'(c).$$

Consequently, we obtain the familiar condition

$$u'(c(t)) = \beta[f'(k(t+1)) + (1-\delta)] u'(c(t+1)). \tag{6.50}$$

The transversality condition also follows in a straightforward fashion from the more general transversality condition (6.32). In particular, since the instantaneous payoff function, U, now corresponds to $u(f(k) + (1-\delta)k - s)$ as a function of the current state variable k and tomorrow's state variable s, the transversality condition takes the form

$$\lim_{t \to \infty} [\beta^t (f'(k(t)) + (1-\delta))u'(c(t))k(t)] = 0. \tag{6.51}$$

As before, a steady state (of the optimal growth problem) is an allocation in which the capital-labor ratio and consumption do not depend on time, so again denoting this allocation by an asterisk, the steady-state capital-labor ratio must satisfy

$$\beta[f'(k^*) + (1-\delta)] = 1. \tag{6.52}$$

Equation (6.52) is a remarkable result; it shows that the steady-state capital-labor ratio does not depend on household preferences except via the discount factor. In particular, technology, the depreciation rate, and the discount factor fully characterize the steady-state capital-labor ratio.

In addition, since $f(\cdot)$ is strictly concave, k^* is uniquely defined. Finally, since $c(t) = c^*$ and $k(t) = k^*$ in the steady state, $\beta[f'(k^*) + (1 - \delta)] = 1$, and $\beta < 1$, the transversality condition (6.51) is automatically satisfied. This analysis leads to the following important proposition.

Proposition 6.3 *In the neoclassical optimal growth model specified in (6.46) and (6.47) with Assumptions 1, 2, and 3′, there exists a unique steady-state capital-labor ratio k^* given by (6.52), and starting from any initial $k(0) > 0$, the economy monotonically converges to this unique steady state; that is, if $k(0) < k^*$, then $k(t) \uparrow k^*$ and if $k(0) > k^*$, then $k(t) \downarrow k^*$.*

Proof.   Uniqueness and existence were established above. To establish monotone convergence, we start with arbitrary initial capital stock $k(0)$ and observe that $k(t + 1) = s(k(t))$ for all $t \geq 0$, where $s(\cdot)$ was defined and shown to be nondecreasing in Proposition 6.1. It must be the case that either $k(1) = s(k(0)) \geq k(0)$ or $k(1) = s(k(0)) < k(0)$.

Consider the first case. Since $s(\cdot)$ is nondecreasing and $k(2) = s(k(1))$, we must have $k(2) \geq k(1)$. By induction, $k(t) = s(k(t - 1)) \geq k(t - 1) = s(k(t - 2))$. Moreover, by definition $k(t) \in [0, \vec{k}]$. Therefore in this case $\{k(t)\}_{t=0}^{\infty}$ is a nondecreasing sequence in a compact set starting with $k(0) > 0$. Thus it necessarily converges to some limit $k(\infty) > 0$, which by definition satisfies $k(\infty) = s(k(\infty))$. Since k^* is the unique steady state (corresponding to positive capital-labor ratio), this implies that $k(\infty) = k^*$, and thus $k(t) \to k^*$. Moreover, since $\{k(t)\}_{t=0}^{\infty}$ is nondecreasing, it must be the case that $k(t) \uparrow k^*$. This argument thus completes the proof for the case $k(0) \leq k^*$.

Next consider the case in which $k(1) = s(k(0)) < k(0)$. The same argument as above applied in reverse now establishes that $\{k(t)\}_{t=0}^{\infty}$ is a nonincreasing sequence in the compact set $[0, \vec{k}]$, and thus it converges to a unique limit point $k(\infty)$. In this case, there are two candidate values for $k(\infty)$, $k(\infty) = 0$ or $k(\infty) = k^*$. The former is not possible, since as Exercise 6.19 shows, Assumption 2 implies that $s(\varepsilon) > \varepsilon$ for ε sufficiently small. Thus $k(\infty) = k^*$. Since $\{k(t)\}_{t=0}^{\infty}$ is nonincreasing, in this case we must have $k(0) > k^*$ and thus $\{k(t)\}_{t=0}^{\infty} \downarrow k^*$, completing the proof.   ∎

Consequently, in the optimal growth model there exists a unique steady state, and the economy monotonically converges to this unique steady state, for example, by accumulating more and more capital (if it starts with a capital-labor ratio that is too low).

In addition, consumption also monotonically increases (or decreases) along the path of adjustments to the unique-steady state, as stated in the following proposition.

Proposition 6.4 *We have that $c(k)$ defined in Proposition 6.1 is nondecreasing. Moreover, if $k(0) < k^*$, then the equilibrium consumption sequence satisfies $c(t) \uparrow c^*$, and if $k(0) > k^*$, then $c(t) \downarrow c^*$, where c^* is given by*

$$c^* = f(k^*) - \delta k^*.$$

Proof.   See Exercise 6.17.   ∎

This discussion illustrates that the optimal growth model is very tractable and shares many features with the Solow growth model, for example, a unique steady state and global monotonic convergence. There is no immediate counterpart of a saving rate, since the amount of savings

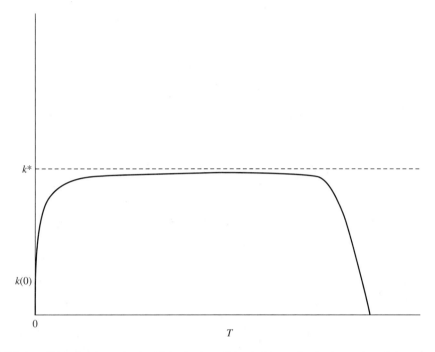

FIGURE 6.1 Turnpike dynamics in a finite-horizon (T periods) neoclassical growth model starting with initial capital-labor ratio $k(0)$.

depends on the utility function and changes over time, though the discount factor is closely related to the saving rate.

The convergence behavior of the optimal growth model is both important and remarkable in its simplicity. Such convergence results, which were first studied in the context of finite-horizon economies, are sometimes referred to as "Turnpike Theorems." To understand the meaning of this term, suppose that the economy ends at some date $T > 0$. What do optimal growth and capital accumulation look like in this economy? The early literature on optimal growth showed that as $T \to \infty$, the optimal capital-labor ratio sequence $\{k(t)\}_{t=0}^{T}$ would become arbitrarily close to k^* as defined by (6.52), but then in the last few periods it would sharply decline to zero to satisfy the transversality condition (recall the discussion of the finite-horizon transversality condition in Section 6.6). The path of the capital-labor ratio thus resembles a turnpike approaching a highway, as shown in Figure 6.1 (see Exercise 6.18).

6.9   Competitive Equilibrium Growth

Our main interest in this book is not optimal growth but equilibrium growth. A detailed analysis of competitive equilibrium growth is presented in Chapter 8. For now a brief discussion of how the competitive equilibrium can be obtained from the optimal growth problem is sufficient. The Second Welfare Theorem (Theorem 5.7 of the previous chapter) implies that the optimal growth path characterized in Section 6.8 also corresponds to an equilibrium growth path (in the sense that it can be decentralized as a competitive equilibrium). In fact, since we have focused on an economy admitting a representative household, the most straightforward competitive allocation would be a symmetric one, where all households, each with the instantaneous utility function $u(c)$, make the same decisions and receive the same allocations. I now discuss this symmetric (or "representative household") competitive equilibrium briefly.

Rather than appealing to the Second Welfare Theorem, a direct argument can be used to show the equivalence of optimal and competitive growth problems. Suppose that each household starts with an endowment of capital stock $K(0)$, meaning that the initial endowments are also symmetric (recall that there is a mass 1 of households, and the total initial endowment of capital of the economy is $K(0)$). The other side of the economy is populated by a large number of competitive firms, which are modeled using the aggregate production function. The definition of a competitive equilibrium in this economy is standard.

Definition 6.3 *A competitive equilibrium consists of paths of consumption, capital stock, wage rates, and rental rates of capital, $\{C(t), K(t), w(t), R(t)\}_{t=0}^{\infty}$, such that the representative household maximizes its utility given initial capital stock K_0 and prices $\{w(t), R(t)\}_{t=0}^{\infty}$, and the path of prices $\{w(t), R(t)\}_{t=0}^{\infty}$ is such that given the path of capital stock and labor $\{K(t), L(t)\}_{t=0}^{\infty}$, all markets clear.*

Households rent their capital to firms. As in the basic Solow model, they receive the competitive rental price of

$$R(t) = f'(k(t)),$$

and thus face a gross rate of return equal to

$$1 + r(t+1) = f'(k(t)) + (1 - \delta) \tag{6.53}$$

for renting 1 unit of capital at time t in terms of date $t+1$ goods. Notice that the gross rate of return on assets is defined as $1 + r$ (which enables me to use r for the net interest rate both in the discrete-time and the continuous-time models). In addition to capital income, households in this economy receive wage income for supplying their labor at the market wage of $w(t) = f(k(t)) - k(t) f'(k(t))$.

Now consider the maximization problem of the representative household:

$$\max_{\{c(t),a(t)\}_{t=0}^{\infty}} \sum_{t=0}^{\infty} \beta^t u(c(t)),$$

subject to the flow budget constraint

$$a(t+1) = (1 + r(t))a(t) - c(t) + w(t), \tag{6.54}$$

with $a(0) > 0$, where $a(t)$ denotes asset holdings at time t and as before, $w(t)$ is the wage income of the household (since labor supply is normalized to 1). The timing underlying the flow budget constraint (6.54) is that the household rents its capital or asset holdings, $a(t)$, to firms at the beginning of time period t to be used as capital during that period. Once again, we impose the natural debt limit, which takes the form (6.44), and market clearing again implies $a(t) = k(t)$.

With an argument identical to that in Example 6.5, the Euler equation for the consumer maximization problem yields

$$u'(c(t)) = \beta(1 + r(t+1))u'(c(t+1)). \tag{6.55}$$

Imposing steady state implies that $c(t) = c(t+1)$. Therefore, in steady state, we have

$$\beta(1 + r(t+1)) = 1.$$

Next, market clearing immediately implies that $1 + r(t + 1)$ is given by (6.53), so the capital-labor ratio of the competitive equilibrium is given by

$$\beta[f'(k(t + 1)) + (1 - \delta)] = 1.$$

The steady state then satisfies

$$\beta[f'(k^*) + (1 - \delta)] = 1.$$

This equation is identical to (6.52), which characterizes the solution to the optimal growth problem. A similar argument establishes that the entire competitive equilibrium path is identical to the optimal growth path. Specifically, substituting for $1 + r(t + 1)$ from (6.53) into (6.55) yields

$$u'(c(t)) = \beta[f'(k(t + 1)) + (1 - \delta)]u'(c(t + 1)), \tag{6.56}$$

which is identical to (6.50). This condition also implies that given the same initial condition, the trajectory of capital-labor ratio in the competitive equilibrium is identical to the behavior of the capital-labor ratio in the optimal growth path (see Exercise 6.21). This behavior is, of course, exactly what should be expected given the Second (and First) Welfare Theorems.

6.10 Computation

All the results presented here have been about existence of solutions and characterization of the form of the value functions, solutions, and the properties of the policy functions or optimal plans. Dynamic programming techniques are also widely used in explicit (numerical) computations (Exercise 6.3 below provides one useful starting point in this respect). In particular, the recursive formulation of dynamic programming problems also presents an effective computational approach. This formulation is particularly useful, since as suggested by the discussion in Example 6.4, only certain special dynamic optimization problems yield closed-form solutions. Therefore economists, like engineers, must often use computational tools to obtain qualitative and quantitative insights about solutions to optimization and equilibrium problems. The dynamic programming formulation is often the starting point of these computational approaches.

Space restrictions preclude me from providing a discussion of various computational tools and how dynamic programming methods are used in numerical analysis. This omission should not be interpreted as downplaying the importance of computation in the study of economic growth or the usefulness of dynamic programming approaches in computation. The reader is encouraged to consult Judd (1998) for an excellent and thorough discussion of computational issues in economics and the role of dynamic programming. Ljungqvist and Sargent (2005) also provide a brief introduction to the application of computational methods in macroeconomics.

6.11 Taking Stock

This chapter has been concerned with basic dynamic programming techniques for discrete-time infinite-dimensional problems. These techniques are not only essential for the study of economic growth but are also widely used in many diverse areas of macroeconomics and economic dynamics more generally. A good understanding of these techniques is essential for an appreciation of the mechanics of economic growth. In particular, they shed light on how different models of economic growth work, how they can be improved, and how they can be taken to the data. For this reason, this chapter is part of the main body of the text rather than being relegated to the appendixes at the end.

This chapter also presented a number of applications of dynamic programming, including a preliminary analysis of the one-sector optimal growth problem. The reader will have already noted the parallels between this model and the basic Solow model discussed in Chapter 2. These parallels are developed further in Chapter 8. I also briefly discussed the decentralization of the optimal growth path and the problem of utility maximization in a dynamic competitive equilibrium.

It is important to emphasize that the treatment in this chapter has assumed away a number of difficult technical issues. First, the focus has been on discounted problems, which are simpler than undiscounted problems. In economics, very few situations involve undiscounted objective functions ($\beta = 1$ rather than $\beta \in [0, 1)$). More important, throughout I have assumed that payoffs are bounded and the state vector x belongs to a compact subset of the Euclidean space X. These restrictions rule out many interesting problems, such as endogenous growth, where the state vector grows over time. Almost all of the results presented here have equivalents for these cases, but these require somewhat more advanced treatments.

6.12 References and Literature

At some level the main idea of dynamic programming, the Principle of Optimality, is straightforward. Nevertheless, it is also a powerful concept, as will be best appreciated once a number of its implications are derived. The basic ideas of dynamic programming, including the Principle of Optimality, were introduced by Richard Bellman in his famous monograph (Bellman, 1957). Most of the basic results about finite- and infinite-dimensional dynamic programming problems are contained in this monograph. Many of these ideas are also contained in Shapley's (1953) study of stochastic games. Shapley analyzed the characterization of equilibrium points of zero-sum stochastic games. His formulation of these games anticipated what later became known as Markov decision problems, which are closely related to dynamic programming problems. Moreover, Shapley used ideas similar to the Principle of Optimality and the Contraction Mapping Theorem to show the existence of a unique solution to these dynamic zero-sum games. A more detailed treatment of Markov decision problems can be found in Puterman (1994), who also discusses the relationship between Shapley's (1953) work, the general theory of Markov decision problems, and dynamic programming.

To the best of my knowledge, Karlin (1955) was the first to provide a simple formal proof of the Principle of Optimality, which is similar to the one presented here. Denardo (1967) developed the use of the contraction mappings in the theory of dynamic programming. Puterman (1994) contain a more detailed analysis of discounted stochastic dynamic programming problems. Blackwell (1965) introduced the Blackwell's sufficient conditions for a contraction mapping and applied them in the context of stochastic discounted dynamic programming problems. The result on the differentiability of the value function was first proved in Benveniste and Scheinkman (1979). The second version of the proof of Theorem 6.6 follows their approach closely. The first version of the proof extends the earlier proof by Mirman and Zilcha (1975), which was only for the neoclassical growth model.

The most complete treatment of discounted stationary dynamic programming problems is in Stokey, Lucas, and Prescott (1989). My treatment here is heavily influenced by theirs and borrows much from their insights. Relative to their treatment, some of the proofs have been simplified, and I have limited the analysis to the case with compact sets and bounded payoff functions. The reader can find generalizations of Theorems 6.1–6.6 to certain problems with unbounded returns and choice sets in Stokey, Lucas, and Prescott (1989, Chapter 4). In contrast to Stokey, Lucas, and Prescott, I also discuss and provide necessary and sufficient conditions for nonstationary infinite-horizon optimization problems.

The issue of the necessity and sufficiency of the transversality condition discussed in Theorem 6.10 is discussed briefly in Stokey, Lucas, and Prescott (1989) and in greater detail in Ekeland and Scheinkman (1986) and Kamihigashi (2001). Kamihigashi provides weaker and more general versions of the transversality condition, though the version provided here is sufficient for most economic applications. A much simpler but insightful exposition of dynamic programming is in Sundaram (1996), which also has a proof of Proposition 6.1 similar to the one given here.

Some useful references on the Contraction Mapping Theorem and its applications include Denardo (1967), Kolmogorov and Fomin (1970), Kreyszig (1978), and the eminently readable Bryant (1985), which contains applications of the Contraction Mapping Theorem to prove the existence and uniqueness of solutions to differential equations and the Implicit Function Theorem. The reader may also wish to consult Aczel (1966) for various methods of characterizing the solutions to functional equations.

6.13   Exercises

6.1   Consider the formulation of the discrete-time optimal growth model as in Example 6.1. Show that with this formulation and Assumptions 1 and 2 from Chapter 2, the discrete-time optimal growth model satisfies Assumptions 6.1–6.5.

* 6.2   Prove that if, for some $n \in \mathbb{N}$, T^n is a contraction over a complete metric space (S, d), then T has a unique fixed point in S.

* 6.3   Suppose that T is a contraction over the metric space (S, d) with modulus $\beta \in (0, 1)$. Prove that for any $z, z' \in S$ and $n \in \mathbb{N}$,

$$d(T^n z, z') \le \beta^n d(z, z').$$

Discuss how this result can be useful in numerical computations.

* 6.4   (a) Prove the claims made in Example 6.3, and show that the differential equation (6.7) has a unique continuous solution.

(b) Recall (6.8) from Example 6.3. Apply the same argument to Tg and $T\tilde{g}$, and prove that

$$\left\| T^2 g - T^2 \tilde{g} \right\| \le M^2 \times \frac{s^2}{2} \times \left\| g - \tilde{g} \right\|.$$

(c) Applying this argument recursively, prove that for any $n \in \mathbb{N}$, we have

$$\left\| T^n g - T^n \tilde{g} \right\| \le M^n \times \frac{s^n}{n!} \times \left\| g - \tilde{g} \right\|.$$

(d) Using the inequality in part c, the fact that for any $B < \infty$, $B^n/n! \to 0$ as $n \to 0$, and the result in Exercise 6.2, prove that the differential equation (6.7) has a unique continuous solution on the compact interval $[0, s]$ for any $s \in \mathbb{R}_+$.

* 6.5   Recall the Implicit Function Theorem (Theorem A.25 in Appendix A). Here is a slightly simplified version of it: consider the function $\phi(y, x)$ such that $\phi : \mathbb{R} \times [a, b] \to \mathbb{R}$ is continuously

differentiable with bounded first derivatives. In particular, there exists $0 < m < M < \infty$ such that

$$m \leq \frac{\partial \phi(y, x)}{\partial y} \leq M$$

for all x and y. Then the Implicit Function Theorem states that there exists a continuously differentiable function $y : [a, b] \to \mathbb{R}$ such that

$$\phi(y(x), x) = 0 \text{ for all } x \in [a, b].$$

Provide a proof for this theorem using the Contraction Mapping Theorem (Theorem 6.7) along the following lines:

(a) Let $\mathbf{C}^1([a, b])$ be the space of continuously differentiable functions defined on $[a, b]$. Then for every $y \in \mathbf{C}^1([a, b])$, construct the operator

$$Ty = y(x) - \frac{\phi(y(x), x)}{M} \text{ for } x \in [a, b].$$

Show that $T : \mathbf{C}^1([a, b]) \to \mathbf{C}^1([a, b])$ and is a contraction.

(b) Applying Theorem 6.7, derive the Implicit Function Theorem.

* 6.6 Prove that T defined in (6.18) is a contraction.

6.7 Let us return to Example 6.4.

(a) Prove that the law of motion of capital stock given by (6.37) monotonically converges to a unique steady-state value of k^* starting with any $k_0 > 0$. What happens to the level of consumption along the transition path?

(b) Now suppose that instead of (6.37), you hypothesize that

$$\pi(x) = ax^\alpha + bx + c.$$

Verify that the same steps lead to the conclusion that $b = c = 0$ and $a = \beta a$.

(c) Now let us characterize the explicit solution by guessing and verifying the form of the value function. In particular, make the following guess: $V(x) = A \log x$, and using this form together with the first-order conditions, derive the explicit-form solution.

6.8 Consider the following discrete-time optimal growth model with full depreciation:

$$\max_{\{k(t), c(t)\}_{t=0}^{\infty}} \sum_{t=0}^{\infty} \beta^t \left(c(t) - \frac{a}{2} c(t)^2 \right),$$

subject to

$$k(t + 1) = Ak(t) - c(t)$$

and $k(0) = k_0$. Assume that $k(t) \in [0, \bar{k}]$ and $a < \bar{k}^{-1}$, so that the utility function is always increasing in consumption.

(a) Formulate this maximization problem as a dynamic programming problem.

(b) Argue without solving this problem that there exists a unique value function $V(k)$ and a unique policy rule $c = \pi(k)$ determining the level of consumption as a function of the level of capital stock.

(c) Solve explicitly for $V(k)$ and $\pi(k)$. [Hint: guess the form of the value function $V(k)$, and use this together with the Bellman and Euler equations. Verify that this guess satisfies these equations, and argue that this solution must be unique.]

6.9 Consider Problem 6.2 or 6.3 with $x \in X \subset \mathbb{R}$, and suppose that Assumptions 6.1–6.3 and 6.5 hold, and that $\partial^2 U(x, y)/\partial x \partial y \geq 0$. Show that the optimal policy function $y = \pi(x)$ is nondecreasing.

6.10 Show that in Theorem 6.10, a sequence $\{x'(t)\}_{t=0}^{\infty}$ that satisfies the Euler equations but not the transversality condition could yield a suboptimal plan.

6.11 Consider the consumer utility maximization problem in Example 6.5, without the borrowing limits (i.e., with only the flow budget constraint). Show that for any path of consumption $\{c(t)\}_{t=0}^{\infty}$ that satisfies the flow budget constraint starting with an initial asset level $a(0)$, so does the path of consumption $\{c'(t)\}_{t=0}^{\infty}$, where $c'(t) = c(t) + \gamma$ for $\gamma > 0$. Using this result, show that the consumer can reach infinite utility by choosing a consumption path that leads to $\lim_{t \to \infty} a(t) = -\infty$. Explain why such paths cannot be feasible in market economies.

6.12 Consider Example 6.5, with $w(t) = w$ and $r(t) = r$ for all t.

 (a) Show that when $r \leq \beta^{-1} - 1$, $a(t) \in [\underline{a}, \bar{a}]$ for all t, where $\bar{a} \equiv a(0) + w/r$ and $\underline{a} = -w/r$.

 (b) Show that when $r > \beta^{-1} - 1$, there does not exist $\bar{a} < \infty$ such that $a(t) \in [\underline{a}, \bar{a}]$ for all t.

6.13 Consider the continuation of Example 6.5.

 (a) Show that the natural debt limit at time t takes the form (6.44).

 (b) Suppose that

$$\bar{W} = \max_{t=0,1,\ldots} \left\{ \sum_{s=0}^{\infty} \left(\prod_{j=0}^{s} \frac{1}{1+r(t+j)} \right) w(t+s) \right\}$$

 and that $\bar{W} < \infty$. Provide conditions such that $a(t) \in [-\bar{W}, a(0) + \bar{W}]$ for all t.

 (c) Using the transversality condition together with $a(0)$, $\{w(t)\}_{t=0}^{\infty}$ and $\{r(t)\}_{t=0}^{\infty}$, find an expression implicitly determining the initial level of consumption, $c(0)$. What happens to this level of consumption when $a(0)$ increases?

 (d) Suppose that $r(t) = r$ for all t. Consider a change in the earnings profile to a new sequence $\{\tilde{w}(t)\}_{t=0}^{\infty}$ such that for some $T < \infty$, $w(t) < \tilde{w}(t)$ for all $t < T$, $w(t) \geq \tilde{w}(t)$ for all $t \geq T$, and

$$\sum_{t=0}^{\infty} (1+r)^{-t} w(t) = \sum_{t=0}^{\infty} (1+r)^{-t} \tilde{w}(t).$$

 What is the effect of this change on the initial consumption level and the consumption path? Provide a detailed economic intuition for this result.

* 6.14 Consider the nonstationary infinite-horizon optimization problem introduced in Section 6.7. Provide conditions on G and U such that the operator defined by

$$TV(t, x) = \max_{y \in G(t,x)} \{U(t, x, y) + \beta V(t + 1, y)\}$$

for $V \in \mathbf{C}(\mathbb{Z}_+ \times X)$ is a contraction. Using these conditions, state and sketch the proofs of the appropriate equivalents of Theorems 6.2–6.6.

6.15 Consider the following discrete-time optimal growth model

$$\max_{\{k(t),c(t)\}_{t=0}^{\infty}} \sum_{t=0}^{\infty} u(c(t)),$$

subject to $k(t + 1) = k(t) - c(t)$, $k(0) \in (0, \infty)$. Assume that $u(\cdot)$ is a strictly increasing, strictly concave, and bounded function. Prove that there exists no solution to this problem. Explain why.

6.16 Consider the following discrete-time optimal growth model with full depreciation:

$$\max_{\{k(t),c(t)\}_{t=0}^{\infty}} \sum_{t=0}^{\infty} \beta^t u(c(t)),$$

subject to

$$k(t+1) = f(k(t)) - c(t)$$

and

$$k(0) = k_0 > 0.$$

Assume that $u(\cdot)$ is strictly concave and increasing for $c \geq 0$, and $f(\cdot)$ is concave and increasing.

(a) Formulate this maximization problem as a dynamic programming problem.

(b) Prove that there exists a unique value function $V(k)$ and a unique policy rule $c = \pi(k)$, and that $V(k)$ is continuous and strictly concave and $\pi(k)$ is continuous and increasing.

(c) When will $V(k)$ be differentiable?

(d) Assuming that $V(k)$ and all other functions are differentiable, characterize the Euler equation that determines the optimal path of consumption and capital accumulation.

(e) Is this Euler equation enough to determine the path of k and c? If not, what other condition do we need to impose? Write down this condition and explain intuitively why it makes sense.

6.17 Prove that, as claimed in Proposition 6.4, in the basic discrete-time optimal growth model, the optimal consumption plan $c(k)$ is nondecreasing, and when the economy starts with $k_0 < k^*$, the unique equilibrium involves $c(t) \uparrow c^*$.

* 6.18 Consider the finite-horizon optimal growth model described at the end of Section 6.8. Let the optimal capital-labor ratio sequence of the economy with horizon T be denoted by $\{k^T(t)\}_{t=0}^{T}$ with $k^T(0) > 0$. Show that for every $\varepsilon > 0$, there exists $T < \infty$ and $t' < T$ such that $|k^T(t') - k^*| < \varepsilon$. Show that $k^T(T) = 0$. Then assuming that $k^T(0)$ is sufficiently small, show that the optimal capital-labor ratio sequence looks as in Figure 6.1.

6.19 Prove that as claimed in the proof of Proposition 6.3, Assumption 2 implies that $s(\varepsilon) > \varepsilon$ for ε sufficiently small. Provide an intuition for this result.

* 6.20 Provide a proof of Proposition 6.1 without the differentiability assumption on the utility function $u(\cdot)$ (which was imposed in Assumption 3').

6.21 Prove that the optimal growth path starting with capital-labor ratio $k(0)$, which satisfies (6.50), is identical to the competitive equilibrium starting with the same capital-labor ratio and satisfying the same condition (or equivalently, (6.56)).

An Introduction
to the Theory
of Optimal Control

The previous chapter introduced the basic tools of dynamic optimization in discrete time. I now present a number of basic results in dynamic optimization in continuous time—particularly the so-called optimal control approach. Both dynamic optimization in discrete time and in continuous time are useful tools for macroeconomics and other areas of dynamic economic analysis. One approach is not superior to the other; instead, certain problems become simpler in discrete time while others are naturally formulated in continuous time.

Continuous-time optimization introduces several new mathematical issues, largely because even with a finite horizon, the maximization is with respect to an infinite-dimensional object (in fact an entire function: $y : [t_0, t_1] \to \mathbb{R}$). A brief review of some basic ideas from the calculus of variations and from the theory of optimal control is thus required. The main tools and ideas that are necessary for this book are straightforward and are presented here in the simplest way. A reader who simply wishes to apply these tools may decide to skim most of this chapter, focusing on the main theorems, especially Theorems 7.13 and 7.14, and their application to the canonical continuous-time optimal growth problem in Section 7.7.

In the rest of this chapter, I first review the finite-horizon continuous-time maximization problem and provide the simplest treatment of this problem (which is more similar to the calculus of variations than to optimal control). I then present the more powerful theorems from the theory of optimal control as developed by Pontryagin and coauthors.

The canonical continuous-time optimization problem can be written as

$$\max_{\mathbf{x}(t), \mathbf{y}(t)} W(\mathbf{x}(t), \mathbf{y}(t)) \equiv \int_0^{t_1} f(t, \mathbf{x}(t), \mathbf{y}(t)) dt \qquad (7.1)$$

subject to

$$\dot{\mathbf{x}}(t) = G(t, \mathbf{x}(t), \mathbf{y}(t))$$

and

$$\mathbf{x}(t) \in \mathcal{X}(t), \mathbf{y}(t) \in \mathcal{Y}(t) \quad \text{for all } t, \text{ and } \mathbf{x}(0) = \mathbf{x}_0,$$

where for each t, $\mathbf{x}(t)$ and $\mathbf{y}(t)$ are finite-dimensional vectors for each t (i.e., $\mathcal{X}(t) \subset \mathbb{R}^{K_x}$ and $\mathcal{Y}(t) \subset \mathbb{R}^{K_y}$, where K_x, $K_y \in \mathbb{N}$). In addition, we have $f : \mathbb{R} \times \mathbb{R}^{K_x} \times \mathbb{R}^{K_y} \to \mathbb{R}$ and $G : \mathbb{R} \times \mathbb{R}^{K_x} \times \mathbb{R}^{K_y} \to \mathbb{R}^{K_x}$. Here the vector $\mathbf{x}$ denotes the state variables. The behavior of this vector is governed by a system of differential equations, given the behavior of the vector of control variables $\mathbf{y}$ (or expressed differently, given the control function $\mathbf{y}(t)$). The end of the planning horizon t_1 can be equal to infinity. The function $W(\mathbf{x}(t), \mathbf{y}(t))$ denotes the value of the objective function when controls are given by $\mathbf{y}(t)$ and the resulting behavior of the state variables is summarized by $\mathbf{x}(t)$.[1] I also refer to f as the (instantaneous) payoff function and to G as the constraint function (though note that here G is vector valued). This problem formulation is general enough to incorporate discounting and time-varying constraints, since both the payoff function f and the constraint function G depend directly on time. I start with the finite-horizon case and then treat the infinite-horizon maximization problem, focusing particularly on the case where discounting is exponential.

7.1 Variational Arguments

Consider the following special case of (7.1), where the horizon is finite and both the state and control variables are one dimensional. This problem can be written as

$$\max_{x(t), y(t), x_1} W(x(t), y(t)) \equiv \int_0^{t_1} f(t, x(t), y(t))dt \tag{7.2}$$

subject to

$$\dot{x}(t) = g(t, x(t), y(t)) \tag{7.3}$$

and

$$x(t) \in \mathcal{X}, \ y(t) \in \mathcal{Y} \quad \text{for all } t, x(0) = x_0 \text{ and } x(t_1) = x_1. \tag{7.4}$$

Here the state variable $x(t) \in \mathcal{X} \subset \mathbb{R}$ is one dimensional, and its behavior is governed by the differential equation (7.3). The control variable $y(t)$ must belong to the set $\mathcal{Y} \subset \mathbb{R}$ (the sets $\mathcal{X}(t)$ and $\mathcal{Y}(t)$ in the more general problem (7.1) are now taken to be independent of time for simplicity). Consequently, $f : \mathbb{R} \times \mathbb{R} \times \mathbb{R} \to \mathbb{R}$ and $g : \mathbb{R} \times \mathbb{R} \times \mathbb{R} \to \mathbb{R}$. We assume throughout that $\mathcal{X}$ and $\mathcal{Y}$ are nonempty and convex.

A pair of functions $(x(t), y(t))$ that satisfies (7.3) and (7.4) are referred to as an admissible pair.[2] Throughout, as in the previous chapter, suppose that the value of the objective function is finite, that is, $W(x(t), y(t)) < \infty$ for any admissible pair $(x(t), y(t))$.

---

1. Notice that $W(\mathbf{x}(t), \mathbf{y}(t))$ in (7.1) is *not* the maximized value, but is simply defined as the value of the objective $\int_0^{t_1} f(t, \mathbf{x}(t), \mathbf{y}(t))dt$ associated with the state and control functions $\mathbf{x}(t)$ and $\mathbf{y}(t)$.

2. More precisely, an admissible pair is $(x(t), y(t))$ such that $x(t)$ is absolutely continuous, $y(t)$ is (Lebesgue) measurable, and $(x(t), y(t))$ satisfies (7.3) almost everywhere. Absolute continuity is defined in Appendix A and is a stronger form of continuity. In particular, a function defined by $F(x) = \int_0^x f(s)ds$ for $x \in [0, X]$ is absolutely continuous on $[0, X]$ if $f(s)$ is piecewise continuous on $[0, X]$ (or less stringently, if $f(s)$ is integrable). Fact A.17 in Appendix A shows that differentiability implies absolute continuity (though absolute continuity is weaker than differentiability). Except in Section 7.6, $x(t)$ is taken to be differentiable, and thus explicit reference to absolute continuity is suppressed. The requirement that $y(t)$ is measurable is not very restrictive either. Nevertheless, since I do not introduce concepts from measure theory explicitly, I will not provide a formal definition for measurability.

Let us first suppose that $t_1 < \infty$, so that we have a finite-horizon optimization problem. Notice that there is also a terminal value constraint $x(t_1) = x_1$, but x_1 is included as an additional choice variable. Thus the terminal value of the state variable x is free. In the context of finite-horizon economic problems, the formulation in which x_1 is not a choice variable may be simpler (see Example 7.1), but it is more natural to start with the case where the terminal value x_1 is free.

In addition, to simplify the exposition, throughout I assume that f and g are continuously differentiable functions of x, y, and t, and I simply state this as "f and g are continuously differentiable."

The challenge in characterizing the (optimal) solution to this problem lies in two features:

1. We are choosing a function $y : [0, t_1] \to \mathcal{Y}$ rather than a vector or a finite-dimensional object.

2. The constraint takes the form of a differential equation rather than a set of inequalities or equalities.

These features make it difficult for us to know what type of optimal policy to look for. For example, y may be a highly discontinuous function. It may also hit the boundary of the feasible set—thus corresponding to a corner solution. Fortunately, in most economic problems there is enough structure to make solutions continuous functions. Moreover, in most macroeconomic and growth applications the Inada conditions (e.g., Assumption 2 from Chapter 2) ensure that solutions to the relevant dynamic optimization problems lie in the interior of the feasible set. These features considerably simplify the characterization of the solution. In fact, when y is a continuous function of time and lies in the interior of the feasible set, it can be characterized by using variational arguments similar to those developed by Euler, Lagrange, and others in the context of the theory of calculus of variations. Since these tools are not only simpler but also more intuitive than the optimal control approach, I start with these variational arguments.

The *variational approach* simplifies the above maximization problem by first assuming that there exists a continuous solution (function) $\hat{y}$ that lies everywhere in the interior of the set $\mathcal{Y}$ (with corresponding state variable $\hat{x}$ everywhere in the interior of $\mathcal{X}$). It then characterizes the properties of this solution (see Exercise 7.3).[3]

More formally let us assume that $(\hat{x}(t), \hat{y}(t))$ is an admissible pair such that $\hat{y}(\cdot)$ is continuous on $[0, t_1]$, $\hat{x}(t) \in \text{Int } \mathcal{X}$ and $\hat{y}(t) \in \text{Int } \mathcal{Y}$ for all t (or more simply, $(\hat{x}(t), \hat{y}(t)) \in \text{Int } \mathcal{X} \times \mathcal{Y}$) and that we have

$$W(\hat{x}(t), \hat{y}(t)) \geq W(x(t), y(t))$$

for any other admissible pair $(x(t), y(t))$.

The important and stringent assumption here is that $(\hat{x}(t), \hat{y}(t))$ is a solution that never hits the boundary and does not involve discontinuities. Even though this feature is true of optimal controls in most economic applications, in purely mathematical terms it is a strong assumption. Recall, for example, that the previous chapter did not make such an assumption and instead started with a result on the existence of solutions and then proceeded to characterizing the properties of this solution (e.g., continuity and differentiability of the value function). However the problem of continuous-time optimization is sufficiently difficult that proving existence of solutions is not a trivial matter. I return to this issue below, but for now I follow the standard practice and assume that an interior continuous solution $(\hat{x}(t), \hat{y}(t)) \in \text{Int } \mathcal{X} \times \mathcal{Y}$ exists. Note

---

3. In addition, the calculus of variations approach compares this candidate solution to other continuous paths. In the optimal control approach, used in Theorem 7.9 below, the candidate path is compared to any other admissible path (in the sense of footnote 2).

also that since the behavior of the state variable x is given by the differential equation (7.3), when $y(t)$ is continuous, $\dot{x}(t)$ will also be continuous, so that $x(t)$ is in fact continuously differentiable.

I now exploit these features to derive necessary conditions for an interior continuous solution. Take an arbitrary fixed continuous function $\eta(t)$ and let $\varepsilon \in \mathbb{R}$ be a real number. Then a *variation* of the function $\hat{y}(t)$ is defined by

$$y(t, \varepsilon) \equiv \hat{y}(t) + \varepsilon \eta(t).$$

Given $\eta(t)$, $y(t, \varepsilon)$ is obtained by varying ε, hence the terminology. Naturally, some of these variations may be infeasible, that is, $y(t, \varepsilon) \notin \mathcal{Y}$ for some t. However, since $\hat{y}(t) \in \text{Int } \mathcal{Y}$ and a continuous function over a compact set $[0, t_1]$ is bounded and uniformly continuous (recall Theorem A.10 in Appendix A), for any fixed $\eta(\cdot)$ function we can always find $\varepsilon'_\eta > 0$ such that

$$y(t, \varepsilon) = \hat{y}(t) + \varepsilon \eta(t) \in \text{Int } \mathcal{Y}$$

for all $t \in [0, t_1]$ and for all $\varepsilon \in \left[-\varepsilon'_\eta, \varepsilon'_\eta\right]$, so that $y(t, \varepsilon)$ constitutes a *feasible variation*. Consequently, variational arguments can be used for sufficiently small values of ε. The fact that we have to look at small values of ε is not a drawback for deriving necessary conditions for optimality. In analogy with standard calculus, necessary conditions require that there should be no small change in controls that increases the value of the objective function.

Let us also define $x(t, \varepsilon)$ as the path of the state variable corresponding to the path of control variable $y(t, \varepsilon)$, that is,

$$\dot{x}(t, \varepsilon) = g(t, x(t, \varepsilon), y(t, \varepsilon)) \quad \text{for all } t \in [0, t_1], \text{ with } x(0, \varepsilon) = x_0. \tag{7.5}$$

Since $x(t) \in \text{Int } \mathcal{X}$ for all t, for ε sufficiently small, in particular, for $\varepsilon \in [-\varepsilon_\eta, \varepsilon_\eta] \subset \left[-\varepsilon'_\eta, \varepsilon'_\eta\right]$ for some $\varepsilon_\eta \leq \varepsilon'_\eta$, we also have that $x(\varepsilon, t) \in \mathcal{X}$ (because solutions to differential equations are continuous; in particular, recall Theorem B.13 in Appendix B). In view of this, for $\varepsilon \in [-\varepsilon_\eta, \varepsilon_\eta]$, $(x(t, \varepsilon), y(t, \varepsilon))$ is an admissible pair. Define

$$\mathcal{W}(\varepsilon) \equiv W(x(t, \varepsilon), y(t, \varepsilon)) \tag{7.6}$$

$$= \int_0^{t_1} f(t, x(t, \varepsilon), y(t, \varepsilon)) dt.$$

Since $\hat{y}(t)$ is optimal and for $\varepsilon \in [-\varepsilon_\eta, \varepsilon_\eta]$, $y(t, \varepsilon)$ and $x(t, \varepsilon)$ are feasible, we have

$$\mathcal{W}(\varepsilon) \leq \mathcal{W}(0) \quad \text{for all } \varepsilon \in [-\varepsilon_\eta, \varepsilon_\eta].$$

Next, rewrite (7.5), so that

$$g(t, x(t, \varepsilon), y(t, \varepsilon)) - \dot{x}(t, \varepsilon) = 0$$

for all $t \in [0, t_1]$. Thus for any function $\lambda : [0, t_1] \to \mathbb{R}$, we have

$$\int_0^{t_1} \lambda(t)[g(t, x(t, \varepsilon), y(t, \varepsilon)) - \dot{x}(t, \varepsilon)] dt = 0, \tag{7.7}$$

since the term in square brackets is identically equal to zero. In what follows, suppose that the function $\lambda(\cdot)$ is continuously differentiable. This function, when chosen suitably, is the *costate* variable, with an interpretation similar to the Lagrange multipliers in standard (constrained) optimization problems. As with Lagrange multipliers, only $\lambda(\cdot)$ that is chosen appropriately will play the role of the costate variable.

Adding (7.7) to (7.6) yields

$$\mathcal{W}(\varepsilon) = \int_0^{t_1} \{f(t, x(t, \varepsilon), y(t, \varepsilon)) + \lambda(t)[g(t, x(t, \varepsilon), y(t, \varepsilon)) - \dot{x}(t, \varepsilon)]\}dt. \quad (7.8)$$

To evaluate (7.8), let us first consider the integral $\int_0^{t_1} \lambda(t)\dot{x}(t, \varepsilon)dt$. Integrating this expression by parts (see Theorem B.3), we obtain

$$\int_0^{t_1} \lambda(t)\dot{x}(t, \varepsilon)dt = \lambda(t_1)x(t_1, \varepsilon) - \lambda(0)x_0 - \int_0^{t_1} \dot{\lambda}(t)x(t, \varepsilon)dt.$$

Substituting this expression back into (7.8) yields

$$\mathcal{W}(\varepsilon) = \int_0^{t_1} [f(t, x(t, \varepsilon), y(t, \varepsilon)) + \lambda(t)g(t, x(t, \varepsilon), y(t, \varepsilon)) + \dot{\lambda}(t)x(t, \varepsilon)]dt$$
$$- \lambda(t_1)x(t_1, \varepsilon) + \lambda(0)x_0. \quad (7.9)$$

Recall that f and g are continuously differentiable, and $y(t, \varepsilon)$ is continuously differentiable in ε by construction, which also implies that $x(t, \varepsilon)$ is continuously differentiable in ε. Denote the partial derivatives of x and y with respect to ε by x_ε and y_ε, respectively, and the partial derivatives of f and g by f_t, f_x, f_y, and so on. Differentiating (7.9) with respect to ε (making use of Leibniz's Rule [Theorem B.4]) gives

$$\mathcal{W}'(\varepsilon) \equiv \int_0^{t_1} [f_x(t, x(t, \varepsilon), y(t, \varepsilon)) + \lambda(t)g_x(t, x(t, \varepsilon), y(t, \varepsilon)) + \dot{\lambda}(t)]x_\varepsilon(t, \varepsilon)dt$$

$$+ \int_0^{t_1} [f_y(t, x(t, \varepsilon), y(t, \varepsilon)) + \lambda(t)g_y(t, x(t, \varepsilon), y(t, \varepsilon))]\eta(t)dt$$

$$- \lambda(t_1)x_\varepsilon(t_1, \varepsilon).$$

Let us next evaluate this derivative at $\varepsilon = 0$ to obtain

$$\mathcal{W}'(0) \equiv \int_0^{t_1} [f_x(t, \hat{x}(t), \hat{y}(t)) + \lambda(t)g_x(t, \hat{x}(t), \hat{y}(t)) + \dot{\lambda}(t)]x_\varepsilon(t, 0)dt$$

$$+ \int_0^{t_1} [f_y(t, \hat{x}(t), \hat{y}(t)) + \lambda(t)g_y(t, \hat{x}(t), \hat{y}(t))]\eta(t)dt$$

$$- \lambda(t_1)x_\varepsilon(t_1, 0),$$

where, as above, $\hat{x}(t) = x(t, \varepsilon = 0)$ denotes the path of the state variable corresponding to the optimal plan $\hat{y}(t)$. As with standard finite-dimensional optimization, if there exists some function $\eta(t)$ for which $\mathcal{W}'(0) \neq 0$, then $W(x(t), y(t))$ can be increased and thus the pair $(\hat{x}(t), \hat{y}(t))$ could not be a solution. Consequently, optimality requires that

$$\mathcal{W}'(0) = 0 \quad \text{for all } \eta(t). \quad (7.10)$$

Recall that the expression for $\mathcal{W}'(0)$ applies for any continuously differentiable $\lambda(t)$ function. Let us consider the function $\lambda(t)$ that is a solution to the differential equation

$$\dot{\lambda}(t) = -[f_x(t, \hat{x}(t), \hat{y}(t)) + \lambda(t)g_x(t, \hat{x}(t), \hat{y}(t))], \qquad (7.11)$$

with boundary condition $\lambda(t_1) = 0$. Since f_x and g_x are continuous functions (by the assumption that f and g are continuously differentiable), they are bounded for $t \in [0, t_1]$. Theorem B.8 then implies that this differential equation has a solution (given $(\hat{x}(t), \hat{y}(t))$). Since $\eta(t)$ is arbitrary, $\lambda(t)$ and $(\hat{x}(t), \hat{y}(t))$ need to be such that

$$f_y(t, \hat{x}(t), \hat{y}(t)) + \lambda(t)g_y(t, \hat{x}(t), \hat{y}(t)) = 0 \quad \text{for all } t \in [0, t_1]. \qquad (7.12)$$

Therefore

$$\int_0^{t_1} [f_y(t, \hat{x}(t), \hat{y}(t)) + \lambda(t)g_y(t, \hat{x}(t), \hat{y}(t))]\eta(t)dt = 0 \quad \text{for all } \eta(t).$$

Conversely, if (7.12) were not satisfied, there would exist some variation $\eta(t)$ that would make the previous integral either positive or negative and thus the necessary condition (7.10) could not be satisfied. This argument establishes the necessary conditions for $(\hat{x}(t), \hat{y}(t))$ to be an interior continuous solution to the problem of maximizing (7.2) subject to (7.3) and (7.4). These necessary conditions are that there should exist a continuously differentiable function $\lambda(\cdot)$ that satisfies (7.11), (7.12), and $\lambda(t_1) = 0$. Exercise 7.1 outlines a different argument to reach the same conclusion.

The condition that $\lambda(t_1) = 0$ is the *transversality condition* of continuous-time optimization problems. It is naturally related to the transversality condition we encountered in the previous chapter. Intuitively, this condition captures the fact that after the planning horizon, there is no value to having more (or less) x. This derivation establishes the following theorem (see also Section 7.3).

Theorem 7.1 (Necessary Conditions) *Consider the problem of maximizing (7.2) subject to (7.3) and (7.4), with f and g continuously differentiable. Suppose that this problem has an interior continuous solution $(\hat{x}(t), \hat{y}(t)) \in \text{Int } \mathcal{X} \times \mathcal{Y}$. Then there exists a continuously differentiable costate function $\lambda(\cdot)$ defined on $t \in [0, t_1]$ such that (7.3), (7.11), and (7.12) hold, and moreover $\lambda(t_1) = 0$.*

Note that the conditions in this theorem are necessary for an interior continuous solution. Solutions that are not interior need not satisfy (7.3), (7.11), and (7.12). Our strategy is to use these necessary conditions to locate a candidate optimal path and then use sufficiency conditions, developed below, to verify that they indeed correspond to (optimal) solutions.

Let us next consider a slightly different version of Theorem 7.1, in which the terminal value of the state variable, x_1, is fixed, so that the maximization problem is

$$\max_{x(t),y(t)} W(x(t), y(t)) \equiv \int_0^{t_1} f(t, x(t), y(t))dt \qquad (7.13)$$

subject to (7.3) and (7.4). The only difference is that there is no longer a choice over the terminal value of the state variable, x_1. In this case, we have the following theorem.

Theorem 7.2 (Necessary Conditions II) *Consider the problem of maximizing (7.13) subject to (7.3) and (7.4), with f and g continuously differentiable. Suppose that this problem has an interior continuous solution $(\hat{x}(t), \hat{y}(t)) \in \text{Int } \mathcal{X} \times \mathcal{Y}$. Then there exists a continuously* *differentiable costate function $\lambda(\cdot)$ defined over $t \in [0, t_1]$ such that (7.3), (7.11), and (7.12) hold.*

Proof. The proof is similar to the argument used in Exercise 7.1 for establishing Theorem 7.1, the main change being that now $x(t_1, \varepsilon)$ must equal x_1 for feasibility, so $x_\varepsilon(t_1, 0) = 0$ and $\lambda(t_1)$ is unrestricted. Exercise 7.5 asks you to complete the details. ∎

The new feature in this theorem is that the transversality condition $\lambda(t_1) = 0$ is no longer present, but instead the terminal value of the state variable x is specified as part of the constraints.[4] Let us start with an application of the necessary conditions in Theorem 7.2 to a simple economic problem. More interesting economic examples are provided later in the chapter and in the exercises.

Example 7.1 *Consider the utility-maximizing problem of a consumer living between two dates, 0 and 1. The individual has an instantaneous utility function $u(c)$ and discounts the future exponentially at the rate $\rho > 0$. Suppose that $u : [0, 1] \to \mathbb{R}$ is a strictly increasing, continuously differentiable, and strictly concave function. The individual starts with a level of assets equal to $a(0) > 0$, earns an interest rate equal to r on her asset holdings and also has a constant flow of labor earnings equal to w. Let us also suppose that she can never have a negative asset position, so that $a(t) \geq 0$ for all t. Therefore the utility-maximization problem can be written as*

$$\max_{[c(t), a(t)]_{t=0}^{1}} \int_0^1 \exp(-\rho t) u(c(t)) dt$$

subject to

$$\dot{a}(t) = ra(t) + w - c(t)$$

and $a(t) \geq 0$, with the initial value of $a(0) > 0$. In this problem, consumption is the control variable, while the asset holdings of the individual are the state variable.

To be able to apply Theorem 7.2, we need a terminal condition for $a(t)$, that is, some value a_1 such that $a(1) = a_1$. The economics of the problem makes it clear that the individual would like to have zero assets at the end of her planning horizon (since she could consume all of these at date $t = 1$ or slightly before, and $u(\cdot)$ is strictly increasing). Therefore, we must have $a(1) = 0$.

With this observation, Theorem 7.2 provides the following necessary conditions for an interior continuous solution: there exists a continuously differentiable costate variable $\lambda(t)$ such that the optimal path of consumption and asset holdings, $(\hat{c}(t), \hat{a}(t))$, satisfies a consumption Euler equation similar to (6.38) in Example 6.5 in the previous chapter:

$$\exp(-\rho t) u'(\hat{c}(t)) = \lambda(t). \tag{7.14}$$

In particular, we will see below that the term $\lambda(t)$ on the right-hand side is related to the derivative of the value function as in (6.38) in Example 6.5.

The next necessary condition determines the behavior of $\lambda(t)$ as

$$\dot{\lambda}(t) = -r\lambda(t). \tag{7.15}$$

---

4. It is also worth noting that the hypothesis that there exists an interior solution is more restrictive in this case than in Theorem 7.1. This is because the set of admissible control and state variables, Ω, may be empty or may have an empty interior, making an interior solution impossible. See Exercise 7.23 for an example and Section 7.6 for a formal definition of the set Ω.

Now using this condition and differentiating (7.14) yields a differential equation in consumption. This differential equation, derived in the next chapter in a somewhat more general context, is the key consumption Euler equation in continuous time. Leaving the derivation of this equation to the next chapter, we can simply integrate (7.15) to obtain

$$\lambda(t) = \lambda(0) \exp(-rt).$$

Combining this equation with the first-order condition for consumption yields a straightforward expression for the optimal consumption level at time t:

$$\hat{c}(t) = u'^{-1}[r\lambda(0) \exp((\rho - r)t)],$$

where $u'^{-1}[\cdot]$ is the inverse function of the marginal utility u'. This inverse exists and is strictly decreasing in view of the fact that u is strictly concave. This equation therefore implies that when $\rho = r$, so that the discount factor and the rate of return on assets are equal, the individual will have a constant consumption profile. When $\rho > r$, the argument of u'^{-1} is increasing over time, so consumption must be declining. Thus when the individual discounts the future more heavily than the rate of return, she wishes to have a front-loaded consumption profile. In contrast, when $\rho < r$, the opposite reasoning applies, and she chooses a back-loaded consumption profile. These are naturally identical to the conclusions reached in the discrete-time intertemporal consumer optimization problem in Example 6.5, in particular, (6.40).

The only variable left to determine to completely characterize the consumption profile is the initial value of the costate variable (and thus the initial value of consumption). This comes from the observation that the individual will run down all her assets by the end of her planning horizon, that is, $a(1) = 0$. Using the consumption rule, we have

$$\dot{a}(t) = ra(t) + w - u'^{-1}[r\lambda(0) \exp((\rho - r)t)].$$

The initial value of the costate variable, $\lambda(0)$, then has to be chosen such that $a(1) = 0$. You are asked to complete the details of this step in Exercise 7.6.

Example 7.1 applied the results of Theorem 7.2. It may at first appear that Theorem 7.1 is more convenient to use than Theorem 7.2, since it enables us to directly formulate the problem as one of dynamic optimization rather than first having to guess the terminal value of the state variable, $a(1)$ (as we did in Example 7.1). However, as the continuation of the previous example illustrates, this is not necessarily the case.

Example 7.1 (continued) *Let us try to apply Theorem 7.1 to the economic environment in Example 7.1. The first-order necessary conditions still give*

$$\lambda(t) = \lambda(0) \exp(-rt).$$

However, since $\lambda(1) = 0$, this equation holds only if $\lambda(t) = 0$ for all $t \in [0, 1]$. But the necessary conditions still imply the Euler equation,

$$\exp(-\rho t)u'(\hat{c}(t)) = \lambda(t),$$

which cannot be satisfied since $u' > 0$. Thus when the terminal value of the assets, $a(1)$, is a choice variable, there exists no solution (at least no solution with an interior continuous control). How is this possible?

The answer is that Theorem 7.1 cannot be applied to this problem, because there is an additional constraint that $a(t) \geq 0$. We would need to consider a version of Theorem 7.1 with inequality constraints. The necessary conditions with inequality constraints are somewhat *more difficult to work with. Using a little bit of economic reasoning to observe that the terminal value of the assets must be equal to zero and then applying Theorem 7.2 simplifies the analysis considerably.*

This discussion highlights that it may also be useful to have a version of Theorem 7.2 in which the terminal condition is specified as an inequality—as $x(t_1) \geq x_1$ rather than as $x(t_1) = x_1$. This alternative is presented next.

Theorem 7.3 (Necessary Conditions III) *Consider the problem of maximizing (7.2) subject to (7.3) and to $(x(t), y(t)) \in X \times Y$ for all t, $x(0) = x_0$, and $x(t_1) \geq x_1$, with f and g continuously differentiable. Suppose that this problem has an interior continuous solution $(\hat{x}(t), \hat{y}(t)) \in \text{Int } X \times Y$. Then there exists a continuously differentiable costate function $\lambda(\cdot)$ defined over $t \in [0, t_1]$ such that (7.3), (7.11) and (7.12) hold, and moreover $\lambda(t_1)(x(t_1) - x_1) = 0$.*

Proof. See Exercise 7.9. ∎

7.2 The Maximum Principle: A First Look

7.2.1 The Hamiltonian and the Maximum Principle

By analogy with the Lagrangian, a more economical way of expressing Theorem 7.2 is to construct the *Hamiltonian:*

$$H(t, x(t), y(t), \lambda(t)) \equiv f(t, x(t), y(t)) + \lambda(t)g(t, x(t), y(t)). \tag{7.16}$$

I often write $H(t, x, y, \lambda)$ for the Hamiltonian to simplify notation.[5] Since f and g are continuously differentiable, so is H. Denote the partial derivatives of the Hamiltonian with respect to $x(t)$, $y(t)$, and $\lambda(t)$, by H_x, H_y, and H_λ, respectively. Theorem 7.2 then immediately leads to the following result.

Theorem 7.4 (Simplified Maximum Principle) *Consider the problem of maximizing (7.2) subject to (7.3) and (7.4), with f and g continuously differentiable. Suppose that this problem has an interior continuous solution $(\hat{x}(t), \hat{y}(t)) \in \text{Int } X \times Y$. Then there exists a continuously differentiable function $\lambda(t)$ such that the optimal control $\hat{y}(t)$ and the corresponding path of the state variable $\hat{x}(t)$ satisfy the following necessary conditions:*

$$H_y(t, \hat{x}(t), \hat{y}(t), \lambda(t)) = 0 \text{ for all } t \in [0, t_1], \tag{7.17}$$

$$\dot{\lambda}(t) = -H_x(t, \hat{x}(t), \hat{y}(t), \lambda(t)) \quad \text{for all } t \in [0, t_1], \tag{7.18}$$

and

$$\dot{x}(t) = H_\lambda(t, \hat{x}(t), \hat{y}(t), \lambda(t)) \quad \text{for all } t \in [0, t_1], \tag{7.19}$$

---

5. More generally, the Hamiltonian should be written as

$$H(t, x, y, \lambda) \equiv \lambda_0 f(t, x(t), y(t)) + \lambda(t)g(t, x(t), y(t))$$

for some $\lambda_0 \geq 0$. In some pathological cases λ_0 may be equal to 0. However, in all economic applications this will not be the case, and we will have $\lambda_0 > 0$. When $\lambda_0 > 0$, it can be normalized to 1 without loss of any generality. Thus the definition of the Hamiltonian in (7.16) is appropriate for economic applications.

with $x(0) = x_0$ and $\lambda(t_1) = 0$, where the Hamiltonian $H(t, x, y, \lambda)$ is defined in (7.16). Moreover, the Hamiltonian $H(t, x, y, \lambda)$ also satisfies the Maximum Principle *that*

$$H(t, \hat{x}(t), \hat{y}(t), \lambda(t)) \geq H(t, \hat{x}(t), y, \lambda(t)) \quad \text{for all } y \in \mathcal{Y},$$

for all $t \in [0, t_1]$.

For notational simplicity, in (7.19), I wrote $\dot{x}(t)$ instead of $\hat{x}(t)(= d\hat{x}(t)/dt)$. The latter notation is rather cumbersome, and I refrain from using it as long as the context makes it clear that $\dot{x}(t)$ stands for this expression.[6]

Theorem 7.4 is a simplified version of the celebrated *Maximum Principle* of Pontryagin. A more general version of the Maximum Principle is given below. For now, a couple of features are worth noting:

1. As in the usual constrained maximization problems, a solution is characterized jointly with a set of "multipliers," here the *costate* variable $\lambda(t)$, and the optimal path of the control and state variables, $\hat{y}(t)$ and $\hat{x}(t)$.

2. Again as with the Lagrange multipliers in the usual constrained maximization problems, the costate variable $\lambda(t)$ is informative about the value of relaxing the constraint (at time t). In particular, $\lambda(t)$ is the value of an infinitesimal increase in $x(t)$ at time t (see Section 7.3.4).

3. With this interpretation, it makes sense that $\lambda(t_1) = 0$ is part of the necessary conditions. After the planning horizon, there is no value to having more (or less) x. This is therefore the finite-horizon equivalent of the transversality condition in the previous chapter.

As emphasized above, Theorem 7.4 gives necessary conditions for an interior continuous solution. However we do not know whether such a solution exists. Moreover these necessary conditions may characterize a stationary point rather than a maximum or simply a local rather than a global maximum. Therefore a sufficiency result is even more important in this context than in finite-dimensional optimization problems. Sufficiency is again guaranteed by imposing concavity. The following theorem, first proved by Mangasarian, shows that concavity of the Hamiltonian ensures that conditions (7.17)–(7.19) are not only necessary but also sufficient for a maximum.

Theorem 7.5 (Mangasarian's Sufficiency Conditions) *Consider the problem of maximizing (7.2) subject to (7.3) and (7.4), with f and g continuously differentiable. Define $H(t, x, y, \lambda)$ as in (7.16), and suppose that an interior continuous pair $(\hat{x}(t), \hat{y}(t)) \in \text{Int } \mathcal{X} \times \mathcal{Y}$ exists and satisfies (7.17)–(7.19). Suppose also that $\mathcal{X} \times \mathcal{Y}$ is a convex set and given the resulting costate variable $\lambda(t)$, $H(t, x, y, \lambda)$ is jointly concave in $(x, y) \in \mathcal{X} \times \mathcal{Y}$ for all $t \in [0, t_1]$. Then the pair $(\hat{x}(t), \hat{y}(t))$ achieves the global maximum of (7.2). Moreover, if $H(t, x, y, \lambda)$ is strictly concave in (x, y) for all $t \in [0, t_1]$, then the pair $(\hat{x}(t), \hat{y}(t))$ is the unique solution to (7.2).*

---

6. Conditions (7.18) and (7.19) also clarify why H is referred to as a "Hamiltonian." Given vectors $\mathbf{x}$ and $\mathbf{z}$, a *Hamiltonian dynamical system* is a dynamical system (set of differential equations) with a representation of the form $\dot{\mathbf{x}} = D_{\mathbf{z}} H(\mathbf{x}, \mathbf{z})$ and $\dot{\mathbf{z}} = -D_{\mathbf{x}} H(\mathbf{x}, \mathbf{z})$ for some function H. The Hamiltonian function H then plays the role of potential energy and is constant along the solution trajectories of this dynamical system (see, e.g., Perko, 2001). If H in Theorem 7.4 were independent of time, it would indeed be such a function, and the resulting dynamical system would be a Hamiltonian system. This is generally not the case when there is dependence on t, that is, discounting.

The proof of Theorem 7.5 follows from that of the next result.[7] Theorem 7.6, which was first derived by Arrow, weakens the condition that $H(t, x, y, \lambda)$ is jointly concave in (x, y). Before stating this result, let us define the *maximized Hamiltonian* as

$$M(t, x(t), \lambda(t)) \equiv \max_{y \in \mathcal{Y}} H(t, x(t), y, \lambda(t)), \tag{7.20}$$

with $H(t, x(t), y(t), \lambda(t))$ itself defined as in (7.16). Clearly, a necessary condition for an interior maximum in (7.20) is (7.17). Therefore, if an interior pair of state and control variables $(\hat{x}(t), \hat{y}(t))$ satisfies (7.17)–(7.19), then $M(t, \hat{x}(t), \lambda(t)) \equiv H(t, \hat{x}(t), \hat{y}(t), \lambda(t))$.

Theorem 7.6 (Arrow's Sufficiency Conditions) *Consider the problem of maximizing (7.2) subject to (7.3) and (7.4), with f and g continuously differentiable. Define $H(t, x, y, \lambda)$ as in (7.16), and suppose that an interior continuous pair $(\hat{x}(t), \hat{y}(t)) \in$ Int $\mathcal{X} \times \mathcal{Y}$ exists and satisfies (7.17)–(7.19). Given the resulting costate variable $\lambda(t)$, define the maximized Hamiltonian $M(t, x, \lambda)$ as in (7.20). If $\mathcal{X}$ is a convex set and $M(t, x, \lambda)$ is concave in $x \in \mathcal{X}$ for all $t \in [0, t_1]$, then $(\hat{x}(t), \hat{y}(t))$ achieves the global maximum of (7.2). Moreover, if $M(t, x, \lambda)$ is strictly concave in x for all $t \in [0, t_1]$, then the pair $(\hat{x}(t), \hat{y}(t))$ is the unique solution to (7.2).*

Proof. Consider an admissible pair $(\hat{x}(t), \hat{y}(t))$ satisfying the necessary conditions (7.17)–(7.19) as well as (7.3) and (7.4). Consider also an arbitrary pair $(x(t), y(t))$ that satisfies (7.3) and (7.4), and define $M(t, x, \lambda)$ as in (7.20). Since f and g are differentiable, $H(t, x(t), y(t), \lambda(t))$ and $M(t, x(t), \lambda(t))$ are also differentiable in x at time t. Denote the derivative of M with respect to x by M_x. Since M is concave, we have (recall, e.g., Corollary A.4)

$$M(t, x(t), \lambda(t)) \leq M(t, \hat{x}(t), \lambda(t)) + M_x(t, \hat{x}(t), \lambda(t))(x(t) - \hat{x}(t)) \quad \text{for all } t \in [0, t_1].$$

Integrating both sides over $[0, t_1]$ yields

$$\int_0^{t_1} M(t, x(t), \lambda(t))dt \leq \int_0^{t_1} M(t, \hat{x}(t), \lambda(t))dt + \int_0^{t_1} M_x(t, \hat{x}(t), \lambda(t))(x(t) - \hat{x}(t))dt. \tag{7.21}$$

Moreover,

$$M_x(t, \hat{x}(t), \lambda(t)) = H_x(t, \hat{x}(t), \hat{y}(t), \lambda(t)) \tag{7.22}$$

$$= -\dot{\lambda}(t),$$

where the first line follows from an Envelope Theorem–type reasoning (since $H_y = 0$ from (7.17)), while the second line follows from (7.18). Next, exploiting the definitions of $W(x(t), (t))$ and the maximized Hamiltonian in (7.2) and (7.20) yields

$$\int_0^{t_1} M(t, x(t), \lambda(t))dt \geq W(x(t), y(t)) + \int_0^{t_1} \lambda(t)g(t, x(t), y(t))dt,$$

---

7. The statement that $(\hat{x}(t), \hat{y}(t))$ is unique in the last part of the theorem requires some comment. When the problem is formulated in its most general form, $\hat{y}(t)$ needs to be Lebesgue measurable, and thus $(\hat{x}(t), \hat{y}(t))$ will be unique with the qualification "almost everywhere," though $\hat{x}(t)$ would continue to be uniquely defined. When $\hat{y}(t)$ is required to be continuous or piecewise continuous, there is no need for this qualification. I ignore this qualification throughout.

and

$$\int_0^{t_1} M(t, \hat{x}(t), \lambda(t))dt = W(\hat{x}(t), \hat{y}(t)) + \int_0^{t_1} \lambda(t)g(t, \hat{x}(t), \hat{y}(t))dt.$$

Combining these relations with (7.21) and (7.22) then yields

$$W(x(t), y(t)) \leq W(\hat{x}(t), \hat{y}(t)) \tag{7.23}$$

$$+ \int_0^{t_1} \lambda(t)[g(t, \hat{x}(t), \hat{y}(t)) - g(t, x(t), y(t))]dt$$

$$- \int_0^{t_1} \dot{\lambda}(t)(x(t) - \hat{x}(t))dt.$$

Integrating the last term by parts (Theorem B.3) and using the fact that by feasibility $x(0) = \hat{x}(0) = x_0$ and by the transversality condition $\lambda(t_1) = 0$ yields

$$\int_0^{t_1} \dot{\lambda}(t)(x(t) - \hat{x}(t))dt = - \int_0^{t_1} \lambda(t)(\dot{x}(t) - \dot{\hat{x}}(t))dt.$$

Substituting this expression into (7.23) gives

$$W(x(t), y(t)) \leq W(\hat{x}(t), \hat{y}(t)) \tag{7.24}$$

$$+ \int_0^{t_1} \lambda(t)[g(t, \hat{x}(t), \hat{y}(t)) - g(t, x(t), y(t))]dt$$

$$+ \int_0^{t_1} \lambda(t)(\dot{x}(t) - \dot{\hat{x}}(t))dt.$$

By definition of the admissible pairs $(x(t), y(t))$ and $(\hat{x}(t), \hat{y}(t))$, $\dot{\hat{x}}(t) = g(t, \hat{x}(t), \hat{y}(t))$ and $\dot{x}(t) = g(t, x(t), y(t))$. Thus (7.24) implies that $W(x(t), y(t)) \leq W(\hat{x}(t), \hat{y}(t))$ for any admissible pair $(x(t), y(t))$, establishing the first part of the theorem.

If M is strictly concave in x, then the inequality in (7.21) is strict. Therefore the same argument establishes $W(x(t), y(t)) < W(\hat{x}(t), \hat{y}(t))$, and no other admissible $(x(t), y(t))$ could achieve the same value, establishing the second part. ∎

Given Theorem 7.6, the proof of Theorem 7.5 follows as a direct corollary, since if a function $H(t, x, y, \lambda)$ is jointly [strictly] concave in (x, y), then $M(t, x, \lambda) \equiv \max_y H(t, x, y, \lambda)$ is [strictly] concave in x (see Exercise 7.7). Nevertheless in some applications it may be easier to verify that $H(t, x, y, \lambda)$ is jointly concave in (x, y) rather than looking at the maximized Hamiltonian. Moreover in some problems $M(t, x, \lambda)$ may be concave in x, while $H(t, x, y, \lambda)$ is concave in (x, y) and strictly concave in y, and this information may be useful in establishing uniqueness (see Exercise 8.11). However, to economize on space, I focus on sufficiency theorems along the lines of Theorem 7.6.

Sufficiency results as in Theorems 7.5 and 7.6 play an important role in the applications of optimal control. They ensure that an admissible pair $(\hat{x}(t), \hat{y}(t))$ that satisfies the necessary conditions specified in Theorem 7.4 is indeed a solution. This is important, since without the sufficiency results, Theorem 7.4 does not tell us that there exists an interior continuous solution; thus an admissible pair that satisfies the conditions of Theorem 7.4 may not be optimal or the (optimal) solution may not satisfy these "necessary conditions" (because it is not interior or continuous). Sufficiency results circumvent these problems by establishing that a candidate admissible pair (satisfying the necessary conditions for an interior continuous solution) corresponds to a global maximum or a unique global maximum.

One difficulty in verifying that the conditions in Theorems 7.5 and 7.6 are satisfied is that neither the concavity nor the convexity of $g(\cdot)$ guarantees the concavity of the Hamiltonian unless we know something about the sign of the costate variable $\lambda(t)$. Nevertheless, in many economically interesting situations, we can ascertain that the costate variable $\lambda(t)$ is everywhere nonnegative. For example, $f_y(t, \hat{x}(t), \hat{y}(t), \lambda(t)) \geq 0$ and $g_y(t, \hat{x}(t), \hat{y}(t), \lambda(t)) \leq 0$ are sufficient to ensure that $\lambda(t) \geq 0$. Once we know that $\lambda(t)$ is nonnegative, checking the sufficiency conditions is straightforward, especially when f and g are concave functions.

7.2.2 Generalizations

The above theorems can be generalized to the case in which the state variable and the controls are vectors and also to the case in which there are other constraints. The constrained case requires constraint qualification conditions as in the standard finite-dimensional optimization case (see, e.g., Theorems A.29 and A.30). These conditions are slightly more complicated to write down. Since I make no use of the constrained maximization problems (except in Exercise 10.7 in Chapter 10), I only discuss constrained problems in Exercise 7.10.

The vector-valued theorems are direct generalizations of the ones presented above and are useful in growth models with multiple capital goods. In particular, let

$$\max_{\mathbf{x}(t), \mathbf{y}(t), \mathbf{x}_1} W(\mathbf{x}(t), \mathbf{y}(t)) \equiv \int_0^{t_1} f(t, \mathbf{x}(t), \mathbf{y}(t)) dt \qquad (7.25)$$

subject to

$$\dot{\mathbf{x}}(t) = G(t, \mathbf{x}(t), \mathbf{y}(t)), \qquad (7.26)$$

and

$$\mathbf{x}(t) \in \mathcal{X} \text{ and } \mathbf{y}(t) \in \mathcal{Y} \quad \text{for all } t, \mathbf{x}(0) = \mathbf{x}_0 \text{ and } \mathbf{x}(t_1) = \mathbf{x}_1, \qquad (7.27)$$

where $\mathcal{X} \subset \mathbb{R}^{K_x}$ and $\mathcal{Y} \subset \mathbb{R}^{K_y}$ (with $K_x, K_y \in \mathbb{N}$).

Theorem 7.7 (Maximum Principle for Multivariate Problems) *Suppose that the problem of maximizing (7.25) subject to (7.26) and (7.27), with f and G continuously differentiable, has an interior continuous solution $(\hat{\mathbf{x}}(t), \hat{\mathbf{y}}(t)) \in \text{Int } \mathcal{X} \times \mathcal{Y}$. Let $H(t, \mathbf{x}, \mathbf{y}, \lambda)$ be given by*

$$H(t, \mathbf{x}, \mathbf{y}, \lambda) \equiv f(t, \mathbf{x}(t), \mathbf{y}(t)) + \lambda(t) \cdot G(t, \mathbf{x}(t), \mathbf{y}(t)), \qquad (7.28)$$

where $\lambda(t) \in \mathbb{R}^{K_x}$ (and $\lambda \cdot G$ denotes the inner product of the vectors λ and G). Then the optimal control $\hat{\mathbf{y}}(t)$ and the corresponding path of the state variable $\mathbf{x}(t)$ satisfy the following necessary conditions:

$$D_{\mathbf{y}} H(t, \hat{\mathbf{x}}(t), \hat{\mathbf{y}}(t), \lambda(t)) = 0 \quad \text{for all } t \in [0, t_1], \qquad (7.29)$$

$$\dot{\lambda}(t) = -D_{\mathbf{x}} H(t, \hat{\mathbf{x}}(t), \hat{\mathbf{y}}(t), \lambda(t)) \quad \text{for all } t \in [0, t_1], \qquad (7.30)$$

and

$$\dot{\mathbf{x}}(t) = D_\lambda H(t, \hat{\mathbf{x}}(t), \hat{\mathbf{y}}(t), \lambda(t)) \quad \text{for all } t \in [0, t_1], \mathbf{x}(0) = \mathbf{x}_0, \text{ and } \lambda(t_1) = 0. \quad (7.31)$$

Proof. See Exercise 7.11. ∎

Note also that various conditions in this theorem, or equivalently in the one-dimensional Theorem 7.4, can be relaxed further. For example, the requirement that $(\hat{\mathbf{x}}(t), \hat{\mathbf{y}}(t)) \in \text{Int } \mathcal{X} \times \mathcal{Y}$ is not necessary, and when either the state or the control variables take boundary values, there may be jumps in the control variables and the Hamiltonian may not be differentiable everywhere (see below). These possibilities can be incorporated by allowing $\hat{\mathbf{y}}(t)$ to be only piecewise continuous. Since in most economic applications both state and control variables are interior and the corresponding Hamiltonian is differentiable everywhere, the form of Theorem 7.7 stated here is sufficient for most problems of interest.

The sufficiency conditions provided above also have straightforward generalizations, which are presented next.

Theorem 7.8 (Sufficiency Conditions For Multivariate Problems) *Consider the problem of maximizing (7.25) subject to (7.26) and (7.27), with f and G continuously differentiable. Define $H(t, \mathbf{x}, \mathbf{y}, \lambda)$ as in (7.28), and suppose that an interior continuous pair $(\hat{\mathbf{x}}(t), \hat{\mathbf{y}}(t)) \in$ Int $\mathcal{X} \times \mathcal{Y}$ satisfies (7.29)–(7.31). If $\mathcal{X}$ is convex and $M(t, \mathbf{x}, \lambda) \equiv \max_{\mathbf{y}(t) \in \mathcal{Y}} H(t, \mathbf{x}, \mathbf{y}, \lambda)$ is concave in $\mathbf{x} \in \mathcal{X}$ for all $t \in [0, t_1]$, then the pair $(\hat{\mathbf{x}}(t), \hat{\mathbf{y}}(t))$ achieves the global maximum of (7.25). Moreover, if $M(t, \mathbf{x}, \lambda)$ is strictly concave in $\mathbf{x}$, then the pair $(\hat{\mathbf{x}}(t), \hat{\mathbf{y}}(t))$ is the unique solution to (7.25).*

Proof. See Exercise 7.12. ■

7.2.3 Limitations

The limitations of the results presented so far are obvious. First, the existence of a continuous and interior solution to the optimal control problem has been assumed. Second, and equally important, the analysis has focused on the finite-horizon case, whereas the study of growth models requires us to solve infinite-horizon problems. To deal with both of these issues, we need to look at the more modern theory of optimal control. This is done in the next section.

7.3 Infinite-Horizon Optimal Control

The results presented so far are most useful in developing an intuition for how dynamic optimization in continuous time works. While some problems in economics require finite-horizon optimal control, most economic problems—including almost all growth models—are more naturally formulated as infinite-horizon problems. This is obvious in the context of economic growth, but is also the case in repeated games, political economy, or industrial organization, where even though individuals may have finite expected lives, the end date of the game or of their lives may be uncertain. For this reason, the canonical model of optimization in economic problems is the infinite-horizon one. In this section, I provide necessary and sufficient conditions for optimality in infinite-horizon optimal control problems. Since these are the results that are most often used in economic applications, I simplify the exposition and state these results for the case in which both the state and the control variables are one dimensional. The more general, multivariate case is discussed in Section 7.6, when I return to the issue of existence of solutions and to the properties of the value functions.

7.3.1 The Basic Problem: Necessary and Sufficient Conditions

Let us focus on infinite-horizon control with a single control and a single state variable. For reasons that will be explained below, it is useful to generalize the terminal value constraint on the state variable. For this purpose, throughout this chapter, let $b : \mathbb{R}_+ \to \mathbb{R}_+$, such that $\lim_{t \to \infty} b(t)$ exists and satisfies $\lim_{t \to \infty} b(t) < \infty$. Then the terminal value condition on the state variable is specified as $\lim_{t \to \infty} b(t)x(t) \geq x_1$ for some $x_1 \in \mathbb{R}$. The special case where $b(t) = 1$ (for all t) gives us the terminal value constraint as $\lim_{t \to \infty} x(t) \geq x_1$ and is sufficient in many applications. But for the analysis of competitive equilibrium in continuous time, we need a terminal value constraint of the form $\lim_{t \to \infty} b(t)x(t) \geq x_1$. Using the same notation as above, the infinite-horizon optimal control problem is

$$\max_{x(t), y(t)} W(x(t), y(t)) \equiv \int_0^\infty f(t, x(t), y(t))dt \tag{7.32}$$

subject to

$$\dot{x}(t) = g(t, x(t), y(t)), \tag{7.33}$$

and

$$x(t) \in \mathfrak{X}, \text{ and } y(t) \in \mathfrak{Y} \quad \text{for all } t, x(0) = x_0 \text{ and } \lim_{t \to \infty} b(t)x(t) \geq x_1, \tag{7.34}$$

with again $f : \mathbb{R} \times \mathbb{R} \times \mathbb{R} \to \mathbb{R}$ and $g : \mathbb{R} \times \mathbb{R} \times \mathbb{R} \to \mathbb{R}$.

The main difference is that now time runs to infinity. Note also that this problem allows for an implicit choice over the endpoint x_1, since there is no terminal date. The last part of (7.34) imposes a lower bound on this endpoint. Notice that $\mathfrak{X}$ and $\mathfrak{Y}$ need not be bounded sets, so that the results developed here can be applied to endogenous growth models.

An admissible pair $(x(t), y(t))$ is defined in the same way as above, except that $y(t)$ can now be a piecewise continuous function (recall also footnote 2). Since $x(t)$ is given by a continuous differential equation, when $y(t)$ is continuous, $x(t)$ will be differentiable. When $y(t)$ is piecewise continuous, $x(t)$ will be continuous and differentiable almost everywhere.

There are additional technical difficulties when dealing with the infinite-horizon case, which are similar to those in the discrete-time analysis. Primary among those is the fact that the value of the functional in (7.32) may not be finite. These issues are dealt with in Section 7.6.

Before stating the more general version of the Maximum Principle relevant for infinite-horizon problems, recall that the Hamiltonian is defined by (7.16), with the only difference being that the horizon is now infinite. In addition, let us define the value function, which is the analogue of the value function in discrete-time dynamic programming introduced in the previous chapter:

$$V(t_0, x(t_0)) = \sup_{(x(t), y(t)) \in \mathfrak{X} \times \mathfrak{Y}} \int_{t_0}^\infty f(t, x(t), y(t))dt \tag{7.35}$$

$$\text{subject to } \dot{x}(t) = g(t, x(t), y(t)) \text{ and } \lim_{t \to \infty} b(t)x(t) \geq x_1.$$

In words, $V(t_0, x(t_0))$ gives the optimal value of the dynamic maximization problem starting at time t_0 with state variable $x(t_0)$. Clearly,

$$V(t_0, x(t_0)) \geq \int_{t_0}^\infty f(t, x(t), y(t))dt \quad \text{for any admissible pair } (x(t), y(t)). \tag{7.36}$$

Our focus throughout is on problems where there exist admissible pairs $(\hat{x}(t), \hat{y}(t))$ that reach $V(t_0, x(t_0)) < \infty$ (see Theorem 7.15 below for sufficient conditions). When $(\hat{x}(t), \hat{y}(t))$ is such a pair, then

$$V(t_0, x(t_0)) = \int_{t_0}^\infty f(t, \hat{x}(t), \hat{y}(t))dt. \tag{7.37}$$

Our first result is a weaker version of the Principle of Optimality, which we encountered in the context of discrete-time dynamic programming in the previous chapter.

Lemma 7.1 (Principle of Optimality) *Suppose that the pair $(\hat{x}(t), \hat{y}(t))$ is a solution to (7.32) subject to (7.33) and (7.34), that is, it reaches the maximum value $V(t_0, x(t_0))$. Then*

$$V(t_0, x(t_0)) = \int_{t_0}^{t_1} f(t, \hat{x}(t), \hat{y}(t))dt + V(t_1, \hat{x}(t_1)) \tag{7.38}$$

for all $t_1 \geq t_0$.

Proof. We have

$$V(t_0, x(t_0)) = \int_{t_0}^{\infty} f(t, \hat{x}(t), \hat{y}(t))dt$$

$$= \int_{t_0}^{t_1} f(t, \hat{x}(t), \hat{y}(t))dt + \int_{t_1}^{\infty} f(t, \hat{x}(t), \hat{y}(t))dt.$$

The proof is completed if $V(t_1, \hat{x}(t_1)) = \int_{t_1}^{\infty} f(t, \hat{x}(t), \hat{y}(t))dt$. By definition $V(t_1, \hat{x}(t_1)) \geq \int_{t_1}^{\infty} f(t, x(t), y(t))dt$ for all admissible $(x(t), y(t))$. Thus this equality can only fail if

$$V(t_1, \hat{x}(t_1)) > \int_{t_1}^{\infty} f(t, \hat{x}(t), \hat{y}(t))dt.$$

To obtain a contradiction, suppose that this inequality is true. Then there must exist an admissible pair $(\tilde{x}(t), \tilde{y}(t))$ from t_1 onward with $\tilde{x}(t_1) = \hat{x}(t_1)$ such that

$$\int_{t_1}^{\infty} f(t, \tilde{x}(t), \tilde{y}(t))dt > \int_{t_1}^{\infty} f(t, \hat{x}(t), \hat{y}(t))dt.$$

Then construct the pair $(\vec{x}(t), \vec{y}(t))$ such that $(\vec{x}(t), \vec{y}(t)) = (\hat{x}(t), \hat{y}(t))$ for all $t \in [t_0, t_1]$ and $(\vec{x}(t), \vec{y}(t)) = (\tilde{x}(t), \tilde{y}(t))$ for all $t \geq t_1$. Since $(\tilde{x}(t), \tilde{y}(t))$ is admissible from t_1 onward with $\tilde{x}(t_1) = \hat{x}(t_1)$, $(\vec{x}(t), \vec{y}(t))$ is admissible, and moreover

$$\int_{t_0}^{\infty} f(t, \vec{x}(t), \vec{y}(t))dt = \int_{t_0}^{t_1} f(t, \vec{x}(t), \vec{y}(t))dt + \int_{t_1}^{\infty} f(t, \vec{x}(t), \vec{y}(t))dt$$

$$= \int_{t_0}^{t_1} f(t, \hat{x}(t), \hat{y}(t))dt + \int_{t_1}^{\infty} f(t, \tilde{x}(t), \tilde{y}(t))dt$$

$$> \int_{t_0}^{t_1} f(t, \hat{x}(t), \hat{y}(t))dt + \int_{t_1}^{\infty} f(t, \hat{x}(t), \hat{y}(t))dt$$

$$= \int_{t_0}^{\infty} f(t, \hat{x}(t), \hat{y}(t))dt$$

$$= V(t_0, x(t_0)),$$

which contradicts (7.36), establishing that $V(t_1, \hat{x}(t_1)) = \int_{t_1}^{\infty} f(t, \hat{x}(t), \hat{y}(t))dt$ and thus (7.38). ∎

Two features in this version of the Principle of Optimality are noteworthy. First, in contrast to the similar equation (6.3) in the previous chapter, it may appear that there is no discounting in (7.38). This is not the case, since the discounting is embedded in the instantaneous payoff function f and is thus implicit in $V(t_1, \hat{x}(t_1))$. Second, Lemma 7.1 may appear to contradict the discussion of time consistency in Chapter 5, since this lemma is stated without additional assumptions that ensure time consistency. The important point here is that in the time-consistency discussion, the decision maker considered updating his or her continuation plan from t_1 onward at date t_1. In contrast, Lemma 7.1 considers the optimality of the plan after t_1 at time t_0. The issue of time consistency, that is, whether the individual would like to change his or her plan at date t_1, is discussed further in Exercise 7.22.

I next state the main result on necessary conditions for infinite-horizon optimal control problems. In this theorem, I also slightly relax the assumption that the optimal control $\hat{y}(t)$ is continuous.

Theorem 7.9 (Infinite-Horizon Maximum Principle) *Suppose that the problem of maximizing (7.32) subject to (7.33) and (7.34), with f and g continuously differentiable, has a piecewise continuous interior solution $(\hat{x}(t), \hat{y}(t)) \in \text{Int } \mathcal{X} \times \mathcal{Y}$. Let $H(t, x, y, \lambda)$ be as defined in (7.16). Then given $(\hat{x}(t), \hat{y}(t))$, the Hamiltonian $H(t, x, y, \lambda)$ satisfies the Maximum Principle*

$$H(t, \hat{x}(t), \hat{y}(t), \lambda(t)) \geq H(t, \hat{x}(t), y(t), \lambda(t))$$

for all $y(t) \in \mathcal{Y}$ and for all $t \in \mathbb{R}$. Moreover, for all $t \in \mathbb{R}_+$ for which $\hat{y}(t)$ is continuous, the following necessary conditions are satisfied:

$$H_y(t, \hat{x}(t), \hat{y}(t), \lambda(t)) = 0, \tag{7.39}$$

$$\dot{\lambda}(t) = -H_x(t, \hat{x}(t), \hat{y}(t), \lambda(t)), \tag{7.40}$$

and

$$\dot{x}(t) = H_\lambda(t, \hat{x}(t), \hat{y}(t), \lambda(t)), \quad \text{with } x(0) = x_0 \text{ and } \lim_{t \to \infty} b(t)x(t) \geq x_1. \tag{7.41}$$

The proof of this theorem is relatively long and is provided later in this section. For now, notice that when a solution of the specified form exists, it satisfies the Maximum Principle. Thus in some ways Theorem 7.9 can be viewed as stronger than the theorems presented in the previous chapter, especially since it does not impose compactness-type conditions. Nevertheless, this theorem only applies when the maximization problem has a piecewise continuous solution $\hat{y}(t)$. In addition, Theorem 7.9 states that if the optimal control, $\hat{y}(t)$, is a continuous function of time, conditions (7.39)–(7.41) are satisfied everywhere. Since $\hat{y}(t)$ is a piecewise continuous function, the optimal control may include discontinuities, but these will be relatively rare—in particular, it will be continuous "most of the time." The added generality of allowing discontinuities is somewhat superfluous in most economic applications, because economic problems often have enough structure to ensure that $\hat{y}(t)$ is indeed a continuous function of t. Consequently, in most economic problems (and in all models studied in this book) it is sufficient to focus on the necessary conditions (7.39)–(7.41).

The necessary conditions in Theorem 7.9 can also be expressed in the form of the so-called *Hamilton-Jacobi-Bellman* (HJB) equation, which is analogous to the dynamic programming formulation in the previous chapter.

Theorem 7.10 (Hamilton-Jacobi-Bellman Equation) *Let $V(t, x)$ be as defined in (7.35), and suppose that the hypotheses in Theorem 7.9 hold. Then when $V(t, x)$ is differentiable in (t, x), the optimal pair $(\hat{x}(t), \hat{y}(t))$ satisfies the HJB equation:*

$$f(t, \hat{x}(t), \hat{y}(t)) + \frac{\partial V(t, \hat{x}(t))}{\partial t} + \frac{\partial V(t, \hat{x}(t))}{\partial x} g(t, \hat{x}(t), \hat{y}(t)) = 0 \tag{7.42}$$

for all $t \in \mathbb{R}$.

Proof.   From Lemma 7.1, for the optimal pair $(\hat{x}(t), \hat{y}(t))$, we have

$$V(t_0, x_0) = \int_{t_0}^{t} f(s, \hat{x}(s), \hat{y}(s))ds + V(t, \hat{x}(t))$$

for all t. Differentiating this equation with respect to t and using the differentiability of V and Leibniz's Rule (Theorem B.4) yields

$$f(t, \hat{x}(t), \hat{y}(t)) + \frac{\partial V(t, \hat{x}(t))}{\partial t} + \frac{\partial V(t, \hat{x}(t))}{\partial x} \dot{x}(t) = 0 \quad \text{for all } t \geq t_0.$$

Setting $\dot{x}(t) = g(t, \hat{x}(t), \hat{y}(t))$ gives (7.42).   ∎

The HJB equation is useful for providing an intuition for the Maximum Principle. More importantly, it is used directly in many economic models, including the endogenous technology models studied in Part IV.

A few important features of the HJB equation are worth noting. First, given the continuous differentiability of f and g, the assumption that $V(t, x)$ is differentiable is not very restrictive, though it is not always satisfied. From (7.35), when $\hat{y}(t)$ is continuous and $g(t, x, y)$ is differentiable in t, $V(t, x)$ will also be differentiable in t. Moreover, an Envelope Theorem–type argument also implies that when $\hat{y}(t)$ is continuous, $V(t, x)$ should also be differentiable in x (the differentiability of $V(t, x)$ in x can also be established directly; see Theorem 7.17 below). Second, (7.42) is a partial differential equation, since it features the derivative of V with respect to both time and the state variable x. Third, this partial differential equation also has a similarity to the Euler equation derived in the context of discrete-time dynamic programming. In particular, recall that the simplest Euler equation, (6.28) in the previous chapter, required the current gain from increasing the control variable to be equal to the discounted loss of value. The HJB equation has a similar interpretation, with the first term corresponding to the current gain and the last term to the potential discounted loss of value. The second term results from the fact that the maximized value can also change over time.

7.3.2   Heuristic Derivation of the Stationary HJB Equation

Given its prominent role in dynamic economic analysis, it is useful to provide an alternative heuristic derivation of the HJB equation. For this purpose, let us focus on the simpler stationary version of the HJB equation. This stationary version applies to exponentially discounted maximization problems with time-autonomous constraints (see, e.g., Section 7.7). Briefly, in these problems $f(t, x(t), y(t)) = \exp(-\rho t)f(x(t), y(t))$, and the law of motion of the state variable is given by an autonomous differential equation, that is, $g(t, x(t), y(t)) = g(x(t), y(t))$. In this case, one can easily verify that if an admissible pair $(\hat{x}(t), \hat{y}(t))_{t \geq 0}$ is optimal starting at $t = 0$ with initial condition $x(0) = x_0$, then it is also optimal starting at $s > 0$, starting with the same initial condition; that is, $(\hat{x}(t), \hat{y}(t))_{t \geq s}$ is optimal for the problem with initial condition $x(s) = x_0$ (see Exercise 7.16). In view of this, let us define $v(x) \equiv V(0, x)$. Since $(\hat{x}(t), \hat{y}(t))$ is an optimal plan regardless of the starting date, we have

$$V(t, x(t)) = \exp(-\rho t)v(x(t)) \quad \text{for all } t. \tag{7.43}$$

Then by definition,

$$\frac{\partial V(t, x(t))}{\partial t} = -\rho \exp(-\rho t)v(x(t)).$$

Moreover, let

$$\dot{v}(x(t)) \equiv dV(t, x(t))/dt = (\partial V(t, x(t))/\partial x)\dot{x}(t)$$

be the change in the function v over time (which only results from the change in the state variable $x(t)$, since V does not directly depend on t). Substituting these expressions into (7.42) and noting that $\dot{x}(t) = g(\hat{x}(t), \hat{y}(t))$, we obtain the stationary form of the Hamilton-Jacobi-Bellman equation:

$$\rho v(\hat{x}(t)) = f(\hat{x}(t), \hat{y}(t)) + \dot{v}(\hat{x}(t)). \tag{7.44}$$

This stationary HJB equation is widely used in dynamic economic analysis and can be interpreted as a "no-arbitrage asset value equation" (see Section 7.3.4). The following heuristic argument not only shows how this equation is derived, but also provides a further intuition.

Heuristic Derivation of the Stationary HJB equation (7.44): Consider the discounted infinite-horizon problem described above and suppose that the admissible pair $(\hat{x}(t), \hat{y}(t))$ is optimal starting at $t = 0$ with initial condition $x(0)$. Recall that the value function starting at $x(0)$ is defined as

$$v(x(0)) \equiv \int_0^\infty \exp(-\rho t)f(\hat{x}(t), \hat{y}(t))dt,$$

with $\hat{x}(0) = x(0)$. Now for a time interval $\Delta t > 0$, we have

$$v(x(0)) = \int_0^{\Delta t} \exp(-\rho t)f(\hat{x}(t), \hat{y}(t))dt + \int_{\Delta t}^\infty \exp(-\rho t)f(\hat{x}(t), \hat{y}(t))dt,$$

$$= f((\hat{x}(0), \hat{y}(0)))\Delta t + o(\Delta t) + \int_{\Delta t}^\infty \exp(-\rho t)f(\hat{x}(t), \hat{y}(t))dt,$$

where the second line approximates $\int_0^{\Delta t} \exp(-\rho t)f(\hat{x}(t), \hat{y}(t))dt$ with $f(\hat{x}(0), \hat{y}(0))\Delta t$, and $o(\Delta t)$ is the residual from this approximation (which results from ignoring both the fact that there is discounting between 0 and Δt and that $(\hat{x}(t), \hat{y}(t))$ is not necessarily equal to $(\hat{x}(0), \hat{y}(0))$ for all $t \in [0, \Delta t]$). The $o(\Delta t)$ term is second order in the sense that $\lim_{\Delta t \to 0} o(\Delta t)/\Delta t = 0$. Therefore, as $\Delta t \to 0$, this term vanishes faster than the rate at which Δt approaches 0. Next, using (7.43),

$$v(x(0)) = f(\hat{x}(0), \hat{y}(0))\Delta t + o(\Delta t) + \exp(-\rho\Delta t)v(\hat{x}(\Delta t)).$$

Subtracting $v(\hat{x}(\Delta t))$ from both sides and dividing both sides by Δt yields

$$\frac{v(\hat{x}(0)) - v(\hat{x}(\Delta t))}{\Delta t} = f(\hat{x}(0), \hat{y}(0)) + \frac{o(\Delta t)}{\Delta t} + \frac{\exp(-\rho\Delta t) - 1}{\Delta t}v(\hat{x}(\Delta t)). \tag{7.45}$$

Next take the limit as $\Delta t \to 0$. Under the assumption that $v(x)$ is differentiable at $x(0)$, the left-hand side becomes $-\dot{v}(\hat{x}(0))$. The first term on the right-hand side does not depend on Δt, so it remains unaltered. The second term vanishes by definition. The limit of the third term can be written as

$$\lim_{\Delta t \to 0} \frac{\exp(-\rho \Delta t) - 1}{\Delta t} \times \lim_{\Delta t \to 0} v(\hat{x}(\Delta t)) = -\rho v(\hat{x}(0)).$$

This follows because $\exp(-\rho \times 0) = 1$ and thus as $\Delta t \to 0$, the expression $(\exp(-\rho \Delta t) - 1)/\Delta t = (\exp(-\rho \Delta t) - \exp(-\rho \times 0))/\Delta t$ is simply the derivative of $\exp(-\rho t)$ at $t = 0$. Substituting these terms into (7.45) gives

$$-\dot{v}(\hat{x}(0)) = f(\hat{x}(0), \hat{y}(0)) - \rho v(\hat{x}(0)).$$

Rearranging, this equation is identical to (7.44).

7.3.3 Transversality Condition and Sufficiency

Since there is no terminal value constraint of the form $x(t_1) = x_1$ in Theorem 7.9, we may expect that there should be a transversality condition similar to the condition that $\lambda(t_1) = 0$ in Theorem 7.1. For example, we may be tempted to impose a transversality condition of the form $\lim_{t \to \infty} \lambda(t) = 0$, which is a generalization of the condition that $\lambda(t_1) = 0$ in Theorem 7.1 to an infinite horizon. But this is not in general the case. An alternative transversality condition is

$$\lim_{t \to \infty} H(t, \hat{x}(t), \hat{y}(t), \lambda(t)) = 0, \tag{7.46}$$

but (7.46) is not always easy to check. Stronger transversality conditions apply when we put more structure on the problem (see Section 7.4). Before presenting these results, it is useful to state the following generalization of the sufficiency theorem to the infinite-horizon case.

Theorem 7.11 (Sufficiency Conditions for Infinite-Horizon Optimal Control) *Consider the problem of maximizing (7.32) subject to (7.33) and (7.34), with f and g continuously differentiable. Define $H(t, x, y, \lambda)$ as in (7.16), and suppose that an admissible pair $(\hat{x}(t), \hat{y}(t))$ satisfies (7.39)–(7.41). Given the resulting costate variable $\lambda(t)$, define $M(t, x, \lambda) \equiv \max_{y(t) \in \mathcal{Y}(t)} H(t, x, y, \lambda)$ as in (7.20). If $\mathcal{X}$ is a convex set, $M(t, x, \lambda)$ is concave in $x \in \mathcal{X}$ for all t and $\lim_{t \to \infty} \lambda(t)(\hat{x}(t) - \tilde{x}(t)) \leq 0$ for all $\tilde{x}(t)$ implied by an admissible control path $\tilde{y}(t)$, then the pair $(\hat{x}(t), \hat{y}(t))$ achieves the global maximum of (7.32). Moreover, if $M(t, x, \lambda)$ is strictly concave in x, then $(\hat{x}(t), \hat{y}(t))$ is the unique solution to (7.32).*

Proof. See Exercise 7.13. ∎

This sufficiency result involves the difficult-to-check condition $\lim_{t \to \infty} \lambda(t)(x(t) - \tilde{x}(t)) \leq 0$ for all $\tilde{x}(t)$ (i.e., for all $\tilde{x}(t)$ implied by an admissible control path $\tilde{y}(t)$). When we impose the appropriate transversality condition, sufficiency becomes much more straightforward to verify.

7.3.4 Economic Intuition

The Maximum Principle is not only a powerful mathematical tool, but from an economic point of view, it is the right tool, because it captures the essential economic intuition of dynamic economic problems. In this section, I provide two different and complementary economic intuitions for the Maximum Principle. One of them is based on the original form as stated in

Theorem 7.4 or Theorem 7.9, while the other is based on the dynamic programming (HJB) version provided in Theorem 7.10.

To obtain the first intuition, consider the problem of maximizing

$$\int_0^{t_1} H(t, \hat{x}(t), y(t), \lambda(t))dt = \int_0^{t_1} [f(t, \hat{x}(t), y(t)) + \lambda(t)g(t, \hat{x}(t), y(t))]dt \quad (7.47)$$

with respect to the entire function $y(t)$ for given $\lambda(t)$ and $\hat{x}(t)$, where t_1 can be finite or equal to $+\infty$. The condition $H_y(t, \hat{x}(t), y(t), \lambda(t)) = 0$ would then be a necessary condition for this alternative maximization problem. Therefore the Maximum Principle (implicitly) involves the maximization of the sum of the original maximand $\int_0^{t_1} f(t, \hat{x}(t), y(t))dt$ plus an additional term $\int_0^{t_1} \lambda(t)g(t, \hat{x}(t), y(t))dt$. Understanding the reason for this provides much of the intuition for the Maximum Principle.

First recall that $V(t, \hat{x}(t))$ is defined in (7.38) as the value of starting at time t with state variable $\hat{x}(t)$ and pursuing the optimal policy from then on. Thus an Envelope Theorem–type argument implies that

$$\lambda(t) = \frac{\partial V(t, \hat{x}(t))}{\partial x}.$$

That is, $\lambda(t)$ measures the impact of a small increase in x on the optimal value of the program (see (7.55) in the next section). Consequently, similar to the Lagrange multipliers in the theory of constrained optimization, $\lambda(t)$ is the (shadow) value of relaxing the constraint (7.33) by increasing the value of $x(t)$ at time t.[8] Moreover, recall that $\dot{x}(t) = g(t, \hat{x}(t), y(t))$, so that the second term in the Hamiltonian is equal to $\int_0^{t_1} \lambda(t)\dot{x}(t)dt$. This term is the shadow value of $x(t)$ at time t and the increase in the stock of $x(t)$ at this point. Moreover, recall that $x(t)$ is the state variable; thus we can think of it as a "stock" variable in contrast to the control $y(t)$, which corresponds to a "flow" variable.

Therefore, maximizing (7.47) is equivalent to maximizing instantaneous returns as given by the function $f(t, \hat{x}(t), y(t))$, plus the value of stock of $x(t)$, as given by $\lambda(t)$, times the increase in the stock, $\dot{x}(t)$. Thus the essence of the Maximum Principle is to maximize the flow return plus the value of the current stock of the state variable. This stock-flow type maximization has a clear economic logic.

Let us next turn to the interpretation of the costate equation,

$$\dot{\lambda}(t) = -H_x(t, \hat{x}(t), \hat{y}(t), \lambda(t))$$

$$= -f_x(t, \hat{x}(t), \hat{y}(t)) - \lambda(t)g_x(t, \hat{x}(t), \hat{y}(t)).$$

This equation is also intuitive. Since $\lambda(t)$ is the value of the stock of the state variable $x(t)$, $\dot{\lambda}(t)$ is the appreciation in this stock variable. A small increase in x changes the current flow return plus the value of the stock by the amount H_x, but it also affects the value of the stock by the amount $\dot{\lambda}(t)$. The Maximum Principle states that this gain should be equal to the depreciation in the value of the stock, $-\dot{\lambda}(t)$, since otherwise it would be possible to change $x(t)$ and increase the value of (7.47).

The second and complementary intuition for the Maximum Principle comes from the HJB equation (7.42) in Theorem 7.10. In particular, let us consider the exponentially discounted

8. Here I am using the language of "relaxing the constraint," implicitly presuming that a high value of $x(t)$ contributes to increasing the value of the objective function. This usage simplifies terminology, but it is not necessary for any of the arguments, since $\lambda(t)$ can be negative.

problem discussed above (and in greater detail in Section 7.5). Recall that in this case, the stationary form of the HJB equation is

$$\rho v(\hat{x}(t)) = f(\hat{x}(t), \hat{y}(t)) + \dot{v}(\hat{x}(t)), \tag{7.48}$$

where v depends only on the state variable x and not directly on time. This widely used equation (or in fact the HJB equation (7.42) more generally) can be interpreted as a no-arbitrage asset value equation. Intuitively, we can think of v as the value of an asset traded in the stock market and ρ as the required rate of return for (a large number of) investors. When will investors be happy to hold this asset? Loosely speaking, they will do so when the asset pays out at least the required rate of return. In contrast, if the asset pays out more than the required rate of return, there will be excess demand for it from the investors until its value adjusts so that its rate of return becomes equal to the required rate of return. Therefore we can think of the return on this asset in equilibrium as being equal to the required rate of return ρ. The return on the assets come from two sources. The first is dividends, that is, current returns paid out to investors. In the current context, this corresponds to the flow payoff $f(\hat{x}(t), \hat{y}(t))$. If this dividend were constant and equal to d and there were no other returns, then the no-arbitrage condition would imply $v = d/\rho$ or $\rho v = d$. The second source of returns from holding an asset comes from capital gains or losses (appreciation or depreciation of the asset). In the current context, this is equal to $\dot{v}$. Therefore, instead of $\rho v = d$, the no-arbitrage condition becomes

$$\rho v(x) = d + \dot{v}(x).$$

Thus at an intuitive level, the Maximum Principle (for stationary problems) amounts to requiring that the maximized value of the dynamic maximization program, $v(x)$, and its rate of change, $\dot{v}(x)$, should be consistent with this no-arbitrage condition.

7.3.5 Proof of Theorem 7.9*

In this section, I provide a sketch of the proof of Theorem 7.9. A fully rigorous proof of Theorem 7.9 is quite long and involved. It can be found in a number of sources mentioned in Section 7.10. The version provided here contains all the basic ideas but is stated under the assumption that $V(t, x)$ is twice differentiable in t and x. The assumption that $V(t, x)$ is differentiable in t and x is not particularly restrictive, and Theorem 7.17 provides sufficient conditions for this to be the case. Nevertheless, the additional assumption that it is twice differentiable is somewhat more stringent.

The main idea of the proof is due to Pontryagin and coauthors. Instead of smooth variations from the optimal pair $(\hat{x}(t), \hat{y}(t))$, the method of proof considers needle-like variations, that is, piecewise continuous paths for the control variable that can deviate from the optimal control path by an arbitrary amount for a small interval of time.

Sketch of Proof of Theorem 7.9. Suppose that the admissible pair $(\hat{x}(t), \hat{y}(t))$, with $\hat{y}(t) \in \text{Int } \mathcal{Y}$ and $\hat{x}(t) \in \text{Int } \mathcal{X}$, is a solution and attains the maximal value $V(0, x_0)$. Take an arbitrary $t_0 \in \mathbb{R}_+$. Construct the following perturbation: $y_\delta(t) = \hat{y}(t)$ for all $t \in [0, t_0)$ and for $\delta \in \mathbb{R}$ and some sufficiently small Δt, $y_\delta(t) = \delta$ for $t \in [t_0, t_0 + \Delta t]$ for all $t \in [t_0, t_0 + \Delta t]$. Moreover, let $y_\delta(t)$ for $t \geq t_0 + \Delta t$ be the optimal control for $V(t_0 + \Delta t, x_\delta(t_0 + \Delta t))$, where $x_\delta(t)$ is the value of the state variable resulting from the perturbed control y_δ, with $x_\delta(t_0 + \Delta t)$ being the value at time $t_0 + \Delta t$. Note that by construction, $x_\delta(t_0) = \hat{x}(t_0)$ (since $y_\delta(t) = \hat{y}(t)$ for all $t \in [0, t_0]$).

Since the pair $(\hat{x}(t), \hat{y}(t))$ is optimal, it follows that

$$V(t_0, \hat{x}(t_0)) = \int_{t_0}^{\infty} f(t, \hat{x}(t), \hat{y}(t))dt$$

$$\geq \int_{t_0}^{\infty} f(t, x_\delta(t), y_\delta(t))dt$$

$$= \int_{t_0}^{t_0+\Delta t} f(t, x_\delta(t), y_\delta(t))dt + V(t_0 + \Delta t, x_\delta(t_0 + \Delta t)),$$

where the last equality uses the fact that the admissible pair $(x_\delta(t), y_\delta(t))$ is optimal starting with state variable $x_\delta(t_0 + \Delta t)$ at time $t_0 + \Delta t$. Rearranging terms and dividing by Δt yields

$$\frac{V(t_0 + \Delta t, x_\delta(t_0 + \Delta t)) - V(t_0, \hat{x}(t_0))}{\Delta t} \leq -\frac{\int_{t_0}^{t_0+\Delta t} f(t, x_\delta(t), y_\delta(t))dt}{\Delta t} \qquad (7.49)$$

for all $\Delta t > 0$. Now take limits as $\Delta t \to 0$, and note that $x_\delta(t_0) = \hat{x}(t_0)$ and that

$$\lim_{\Delta t \to 0} \frac{\int_{t_0}^{t_0+\Delta t} f(t, x_\delta(t), y_\delta(t))dt}{\Delta t} = f(t_0, x_\delta(t_0), y_\delta(t_0)). \qquad (7.50)$$

Moreover, let $\mathcal{T} \subset \mathbb{R}_+$ be the set of points where the optimal control $\hat{y}(t)$ is a continuous function of time. Note that $\mathcal{T}$ is a dense subset of $\mathbb{R}_+$, since $\hat{y}(t)$ is a piecewise continuous function. Let us now take V to be a differentiable function of time at all $t \in \mathcal{T}$, so that

$$\lim_{\Delta t \to 0} \frac{V(t_0 + \Delta t, x_\delta(t_0 + \Delta t)) - V(t_0, \hat{x}(t_0))}{\Delta t}$$

$$= \frac{\partial V(t_0, x_\delta(t_0))}{\partial t} + \frac{\partial V(t_0, x_\delta(t_0))}{\partial x} \dot{x}_\delta(t_0) \qquad (7.51)$$

$$= \frac{\partial V(t_0, x_\delta(t_0))}{\partial t} + \frac{\partial V(t_0, x_\delta(t_0))}{\partial x} g(t_0, x_\delta(t_0), y_\delta(t_0)),$$

where the second line uses the fact that $\dot{x}_\delta(t) = g(t, x_\delta(t), y_\delta(t))$ from (7.33) given the control y_δ. Combining (7.49)–(7.51), we have

$$f(t_0, x_\delta(t_0), y_\delta(t_0)) + \frac{\partial V(t_0, x_\delta(t_0))}{\partial t} + \frac{\partial V(t_0, x_\delta(t_0))}{\partial x} g(t_0, x_\delta(t_0), y_\delta(t_0)) \leq 0 \quad (7.52)$$

for all $t_0 \in \mathcal{T}$ (which correspond to points of continuity of $\hat{y}(t)$) and for all admissible perturbation pairs $(x_\delta(t), y_\delta(t))$. Moreover, using Lemma 7.1 (or the same argument as in the proof of Theorem 7.10), we have that for all $t_0 \in \mathcal{T}$,

$$f(t_0, \hat{x}(t_0), \hat{y}(t_0)) + \frac{\partial V(t_0, \hat{x}(t_0))}{\partial t} + \frac{\partial V(t_0, \hat{x}(t_0))}{\partial x} g(t_0, \hat{x}(t_0), \hat{y}(t_0)) = 0. \quad (7.53)$$

Combining (7.52) with (7.53) and using the fact that $x_\delta(t_0) = \hat{x}(t_0)$, we have

$$f(t_0, \hat{x}(t_0), \hat{y}(t_0)) + \frac{\partial V(t_0, \hat{x}(t_0))}{\partial x} g(t_0, \hat{x}(t_0), \hat{y}(t_0)) \geq$$

$$f(t_0, x_\delta(t_0), y_\delta(t_0)) + \frac{\partial V(t_0, \hat{x}(t_0))}{\partial x} g(t_0, x_\delta(t_0), y_\delta(t_0)) \qquad (7.54)$$

for all $t_0 \in \mathcal{T}$ and for all admissible perturbation pairs $(x_\delta(t), y_\delta(t))$. Now defining

$$\lambda(t_0) \equiv \frac{\partial V(t_0, \hat{x}(t_0))}{\partial x}, \tag{7.55}$$

inequality (7.54) can be written as

$$f(t_0, \hat{x}(t_0), \hat{y}(t_0)) + \lambda(t_0)g(t_0, \hat{x}(t_0), \hat{y}(t_0)) \geq f(t_0, x_\delta(t_0), y_\delta(t_0)) + \lambda(t_0)g(t_0, x_\delta(t_0), y_\delta(t_0))$$

or equivalently as

$$H(t_0, \hat{x}(t_0), \hat{y}(t_0)) \geq H(t_0, \hat{x}(t_0), y_\delta(t_0)) \quad \text{for all admissible } y_\delta(t_0).$$

Since t_0 was arbitrary, we have

$$H(t, \hat{x}(t), \hat{y}(t)) \geq \max_y H(t, \hat{x}(t), y) \quad \text{for all } t,$$

establishing the Maximum Principle.

The necessary condition (7.39) directly follows from the Maximum Principle together with the fact that H is differentiable in x and y (because f and g are differentiable in x and y). Condition (7.41) holds because $(\hat{x}(t), \hat{y}(t))$ is admissible. Finally, (7.40) follows from differentiating (7.53) with respect to x at all points of continuity of $\hat{y}(t)$, which gives

$$\frac{\partial f(t, \hat{x}(t), \hat{y}(t))}{\partial x} + \frac{\partial^2 V(t, \hat{x}(t))}{\partial t \partial x}$$

$$+ \frac{\partial^2 V(t, \hat{x}(t))}{\partial x^2} g(t, \hat{x}(t), \hat{y}(t)) + \frac{\partial V(t, \hat{x}(t))}{\partial x} \frac{\partial g(t, \hat{x}(t), \hat{y}(t))}{\partial x} = 0$$

for all $t \in \mathcal{T}$. Using the definition of the Hamiltonian, this expression implies (7.40) and completes the proof. ∎

7.4 More on Transversality Conditions

Let us next turn to a more detailed discussion of the boundary conditions at infinity in infinite-horizon maximization problems. As in discrete-time optimization problems, these limiting boundary conditions are referred to as "transversality conditions." As mentioned in Section 7.3.3, a natural conjecture might be that, as in the finite-horizon case, the transversality condition should be similar to that in Theorem 7.1, with t_1 replaced with the limit of $t \to \infty$, that is, $\lim_{t \to \infty} \lambda(t) = 0$. The following example, which is very close to the original model studied by Frank Ramsey in 1928, illustrates that this conjecture is not true. In particular, without further assumptions, the valid transversality condition is given by the weaker condition (7.46).

Example 7.2 *Consider the following problem without discounting:*

$$\max \int_0^\infty [\log(c(t)) - \log c^*]dt$$

subject to

$$\dot{k}(t) = k(t)^\alpha - c(t) - \delta k(t),$$

$$k(0) = 1,$$

and

$$\lim_{t \to \infty} k(t) \geq 0,$$

where $c^* \equiv (k^*)^\alpha - \delta k^*$ and $k^* \equiv (\alpha/\delta)^{1/(1-\alpha)}$. In other words, c^* is the maximum level of consumption that can be achieved in the steady state of this model, and k^* is the corresponding steady-state level of capital. This way of writing the objective function makes sure that the integral converges and takes a finite value (since, for any $\varepsilon > 0$, $c(t)$ cannot exceed $c^* + \varepsilon$ forever).

The Hamiltonian is straightforward to construct; it does not explicitly depend on time and takes the form

$$H(k, c, \lambda) = \log c(t) - \log c^* + \lambda(t)[k(t)^\alpha - c(t) - \delta k(t)]$$

and implies the following necessary conditions:

$$H_c(k, c, \lambda) = \frac{1}{c(t)} - \lambda(t) = 0,$$

and

$$H_k(k, c, \lambda) = \lambda(t)[\alpha k(t)^{\alpha-1} - \delta] = -\dot{\lambda}(t).$$

It can be verified that any optimal path must feature $c(t) \to c^*$ as $t \to \infty$. This condition, however, implies that

$$\lim_{t \to \infty} \lambda(t) = \frac{1}{c^*} > 0, \quad \text{and} \quad \lim_{t \to \infty} k(t) = k^*.$$

Now recall from Theorem 7.3 that the finite-horizon transversality condition in this case would have been $\lambda(t_1)k(t_1) = 0$, whereas here $\lim_{t \to \infty} \lambda(t)k(t) = k^*/c^* > 0$. Therefore the equivalent of the finite-horizon transversality condition does not hold. It can be verified, however, that along the optimal path the following condition holds instead:

$$\lim_{t \to \infty} H(k(t), c(t), \lambda(t)) = 0.$$

The next theorem shows that this equation is indeed one version of the transversality condition for infinite-horizon optimization problems.

Theorem 7.12 (Transversality Condition for Infinite-Horizon Problems) *Suppose that the problem of maximizing (7.32) subject to (7.33) and (7.34), with f and g continuously differentiable, has a piecewise continuous optimal control $\hat{y}(t) \in \text{Int } \mathcal{Y}(t)$ with a corresponding path of state variable $\hat{x}(t) \in \text{Int } \mathcal{X}(t)$. Let $V(t, x(t))$ be the value function defined in (7.35). Suppose that $V(t, \hat{x}(t))$ is differentiable in x and t for t sufficiently large and that $\lim_{t \to \infty} \partial V(t, \hat{x}(t))/\partial t = 0$. Let $H(t, x, y, \lambda)$ be given by (7.16). Then the pair $(\hat{x}(t), \hat{y}(t))$ satisfies the necessary conditions (7.39)–(7.41) and the transversality condition*

$$\lim_{t \to \infty} H(t, \hat{x}(t), \hat{y}(t), \lambda(t)) = 0. \tag{7.56}$$

Proof. For t sufficiently large, $V(t, x)$ is differentiable in t and x, thus $\partial V(t, \hat{x}(t))/\partial x = \lambda(t)$ (see (7.55)). Then the HJB equation (7.42) holds and implies

$$\frac{\partial V(t, \hat{x}(t))}{\partial t} + f(t, \hat{x}(t), \hat{y}(t)) + \lambda(t)g(t, \hat{x}(t), \hat{y}(t)) = 0 \text{ for } t \text{ large,}$$

$$\frac{\partial V(t, \hat{x}(t))}{\partial t} + H(t, \hat{x}(t), \hat{y}(t), \lambda(t)) = 0 \text{ for } t \text{ large.} \tag{7.57}$$

Now take the limit as $t \to \infty$. Since $\lim_{t\to\infty} \partial V(t, \hat{x}(t))/\partial t = 0$ by hypothesis, (7.57) then implies (7.56). ∎

As discussed in the previous chapter, the condition that $\lim_{t\to\infty} V(t, \hat{x}(t))$ is finite is natural, since economic problems in which agents reach infinite value are not relevant (and moreover, if this limit were equal to infinity, there would typically be no pair $(x(t), y(t))$ reaching this value). The hypothesis here, $\lim_{t\to\infty} \partial V(t, \hat{x}(t))/\partial t = 0$, is only slightly stronger than assuming that $\lim_{t\to\infty} V(t, \hat{x}(t))$ exists and is finite. It is again satisfied in almost all economic problems and is satisfied in all models studied in this book. However, the transversality condition (7.56) is not particularly convenient. In the next section, I present a stronger and more useful version of this transversality condition that applies in the context of discounted infinite-horizon problems.

Example 7.3 *One of the important examples of infinite-horizon dynamic optimization problems is that of the optimal time path of consuming a nonrenewable resource. In particular, imagine the problem of an infinitely-lived individual who has access to a nonrenewable or exhaustible resource of size 1. The instantaneous utility of consuming a flow of resources y is $u(y)$, where $u : [0, 1] \to \mathbb{R}$ is a strictly increasing, continuously differentiable, and strictly concave function. The individual discounts the future exponentially with discount rate $\rho > 0$, so that her objective function at time $t = 0$ is to maximize*

$$\int_0^\infty \exp(-\rho t)u(y(t))dt.$$

The constraint is that the remaining size of the resource at time t, $x(t)$, evolves according to

$$\dot{x}(t) = -y(t),$$

which captures the fact that the resource is not renewable and becomes depleted as more of it is consumed. Naturally, we also need that $x(t) \geq 0$. The Hamiltonian takes the form

$$H(x(t), y(t), \lambda(t)) = \exp(-\rho t)u(y(t)) - \lambda(t)y(t).$$

Theorem 7.9 implies the following necessary conditions that an interior continuously differentiable solution $(\hat{x}(t), \hat{y}(t))$ to this problem must satisfy. There should exist a continuously differentiable function $\lambda(t)$ such that

$$u'(\hat{y}(t)) = \exp(\rho t)\lambda(t) \tag{7.58}$$

and

$$\dot{\lambda}(t) = 0. \tag{7.59}$$

The second condition follows since neither the constraint nor the payoff function depends on $x(t)$. Now anticipating the results in the next section, let us define $\mu(t) \equiv \exp(\rho t)\lambda(t)$.

Equation (7.58) then implies that $\mu(t)$ is the marginal value *of the exhaustible resource at time t. Differentiating the definition of $\mu(t)$ and using (7.59), we obtain the famous* Hotelling Rule *for the exploitation of exhaustible resources:*

$$\frac{\dot{\mu}(t)}{\mu(t)} = \rho.$$

This rule states that the optimal exploitation of an exhaustible resource involves its shadow value increasing at the same rate as the discount rate. We can also obtain a more explicit characterization of the time path of consumption $y(t)$ from (7.58):

$$\hat{y}(t) = u'^{-1}[\exp(\rho t)\lambda(0)],$$

where $u'^{-1}[\cdot]$ is the inverse function of u', which exists and is strictly decreasing by virtue of the fact that u is strictly concave (and naturally $\lambda(0) = \mu(0)$). This equation immediately implies that the amount of the resource consumed is monotonically decreasing over time. This is economically intuitive: due to discounting, there is preference for early consumption, but the entire resource is not consumed immediately, because there is also a preference for a smooth consumption path (since $u(\cdot)$ is strictly concave).

Combining the previous equation with the resource constraint gives

$$\dot{x}(t) = -u'^{-1}[\exp(\rho t)\lambda(0)].$$

Integrating this equation and using the terminal value constraint that $x(0) = 1$, we obtain

$$\hat{x}(t) = 1 - \int_0^t u'^{-1}[\exp(\rho s)\lambda(0)]ds.$$

Since along any optimal path, $\lim_{t\to\infty} \hat{x}(t) = 0$, we also have

$$\int_0^\infty u'^{-1}[\exp(\rho s)\lambda(0)]ds = 1.$$

Therefore the initial value of the costate variable $\lambda(0)$ must be chosen to satisfy this equation. You are asked to verify that the transversality condition (7.56) is satisfied in this case in Exercise 7.20.

7.5 Discounted Infinite-Horizon Optimal Control

Our main interest is in growth models in which the utility is discounted exponentially. Consequently, economically interesting problems often take the following more specific form:

$$\max_{x(t),y(t)} W(x(t), y(t)) \equiv \int_0^\infty \exp(-\rho t) f(x(t), y(t))dt, \quad \text{with } \rho > 0, \quad (7.60)$$

subject to

$$\dot{x}(t) = g(t, x(t), y(t)), \quad (7.61)$$

and

$$x(t) \in \text{Int } \mathcal{X}(t) \text{ and } y(t) \in \text{Int } \mathcal{Y}(t) \text{ for all } t, x(0) = x_0, \text{ and } \lim_{t\to\infty} b(t)x(t) \geq x_1, \quad (7.62)$$

where recall again that $b : \mathbb{R}_+ \to \mathbb{R}_+$, and $\lim_{t\to\infty} b(t) < \infty$. Throughout, the assumption that there is *discounting*, that is, $\rho > 0$, is implicit.

The special feature of this problem is that the payoff function f depends on time only through exponential discounting. The Hamiltonian in this case is

$$H(t, x(t), y(t), \lambda(t)) = \exp(-\rho t) f(x(t), y(t)) + \lambda(t) g(t, x(t), y(t))$$

$$= \exp(-\rho t) \left[f(x(t), y(t)) + \mu(t) g(t, x(t), y(t)) \right],$$

where the second line uses the definition

$$\mu(t) \equiv \exp(\rho t) \lambda(t). \tag{7.63}$$

In fact, in this case, rather than working with the standard Hamiltonian, we can work with *the current-value Hamiltonian*, defined as

$$\hat{H}(t, x(t), y(t), \mu(t)) \equiv f(x(t), y(t)) + \mu(t) g(t, x(t), y(t)). \tag{7.64}$$

When $g(t, x(t), y(t))$ is also an autonomous differential equation of the form $g(x(t), y(t))$, I simplify the notation by writing $\hat{H}(x(t), y(t), \mu(t))$ instead of $\hat{H}(t, x(t), y(t), \mu(t))$.

The next result establishes the necessity of a stronger transversality condition under some additional assumptions. These assumptions can be relaxed, though the result is simpler to understand and prove under these assumptions, and they are typically met in economic applications. Throughout, f and g are continuously differentiable for all admissible $(x(t), y(t))$ (with derivatives denoted f_x, f_y, g_x, and g_y).

Assumption 7.1 *In the maximization of (7.60) subject to (7.61) and (7.62),*

1. *f is weakly monotone in x and y, and g is weakly monotone in (t, x, y) (e.g., f could be nondecreasing in x and nonincreasing in y, and so on);*
2. *there exists $m > 0$ such that $\left| g_y(t, x(t), y(t)) \right| \geq m$ for all t and for all admissible pairs $(x(t), y(t))$; and*
3. *there exists $M < \infty$ such that $\left| f_y(x, y) \right| \leq M$ for all x and y.*

Theorem 7.13 (Maximum Principle for Discounted Infinite-Horizon Problems)
Suppose that the problem of maximizing (7.60) subject to (7.61) and (7.62), with f and g continuously differentiable, has an interior piecewise continuous optimal control $\hat{y}(t) \in$ Int $\mathcal{Y}(t)$ with corresponding state variable $\hat{x}(t) \in$ Int $\mathcal{X}(t)$. Let $V(t, x(t))$ be the value function defined in (7.35). Suppose that $V(t, \hat{x}(t))$ is differentiable in x and t for t sufficiently large, that $V(t, \hat{x}(t))$ exists and is finite for all t, and that $\lim_{t\to\infty} \partial V(t, \hat{x}(t))/\partial t = 0$. Let $\hat{H}(t, x, y, \mu)$ be the current-value Hamiltonian given by (7.64). Then except at points of discontinuity of $\hat{y}(t)$, the optimal control pair $(\hat{x}(t), \hat{y}(t))$ satisfies the following necessary conditions:

$$\hat{H}_y(t, \hat{x}(t), \hat{y}(t), \mu(t)) = 0 \quad \text{for all } t \in \mathbb{R}_+, \tag{7.65}$$

$$\rho\mu(t) - \dot{\mu}(t) = \hat{H}_x(t, \hat{x}(t), \hat{y}(t), \mu(t)) \quad \text{for all } t \in \mathbb{R}_+, \tag{7.66}$$

and

$$\dot{x}(t) = \hat{H}_\mu(t, \hat{x}(t), \hat{y}(t), \mu(t)) \quad \text{for all } t \in \mathbb{R}_+, \ x(0) = x_0, \ \text{and} \ \lim_{t\to\infty} b(t) x(t) \geq x_1, \tag{7.67}$$

and the transversality condition

$$\lim_{t \to \infty} [\exp(-\rho t) \hat{H}(t, \hat{x}(t), \hat{y}(t), \mu(t))] = 0. \tag{7.68}$$

Moreover, suppose that Assumption 7.1 holds and that either $\lim_{t \to \infty} \hat{x}(t) = x^* \in \mathbb{R}$ *or* $\lim_{t \to \infty} \dot{\hat{x}}(t)/\hat{x}(t) = \chi \in \mathbb{R}$. *Then the transversality condition can be strengthened to*

$$\lim_{t \to \infty} \left[\exp(-\rho t) \mu(t) \hat{x}(t) \right] = 0. \tag{7.69}$$

Proof. The necessary conditions (7.65)–(7.67) and the transversality condition (7.68) follow by using the definition of the current-value Hamiltonian and from Theorem 7.12. They are left as an exercise (see Exercise 7.14).

I only give the proof for the stronger transversality condition (7.69). The weaker transversality condition (7.68) can be written as

$$\lim_{t \to \infty} \left[\exp(-\rho t) f(\hat{x}(t), \hat{y}(t)) + \exp(-\rho t) \mu(t) g(t, \hat{x}(t), \hat{y}(t)) \right] = 0. \tag{7.70}$$

Recall from (7.37) that

$$V(t, \hat{x}(t)) = \int_t^\infty \exp(-\rho s) f(\hat{x}(s), \hat{y}(s)) ds.$$

Since $\lim_{t \to \infty} V(t, \hat{x}(t))$ exists and is finite, the first term in (7.70) must be equal to zero. Therefore

$$\lim_{t \to \infty} \left[\exp(-\rho t) \mu(t) g(t, \hat{x}(t), \hat{y}(t)) \right] = \lim_{t \to \infty} \left[\exp(-\rho t) \mu(t) \dot{x}(t) \right] = 0. \tag{7.71}$$

In the rest of the proof, let lim stand for $\lim_{t \to \infty}$.

I next present a result that is used in the rest of the proof. Recall the definition of a net from Definition A.7. In view of this definition, the function $[\mu(t)]_{t=0}^\infty$ can be viewed as a net and denoted by $\{\mu(t)\}_{t \in \mathbb{R}_+}$ or simply by $\{\mu(t)\}$. Then $\{\mu(t)\}_{t \in \mathcal{T}}$ for $\mathcal{T} \subset \mathbb{R}_+$ is a subnet of $\{\mu(t)\}$.

Claim 7.1 *The function (net)* $[\mu(t)]_{t=0}^\infty$ *defined by (7.71) is bounded in the sense that there exists* $B < \infty$ *such that* $|\mu(t)| < B$ *for all* t.

Proof. Suppose, to obtain a contradiction, that $\{\mu(t)\}$ is not bounded. Then there exists a subnet $\{\mu(t)\}_{t \in \mathcal{T}}$ limiting to $+\infty$ or $-\infty$ (for $\mathcal{T} \subset \mathbb{R}_+$). Since $g_y \geq m > 0$ or $g_y \leq -m < 0$ (see Assumption 7.1 parts 1 and 2), $\lim_{t \in \mathcal{T}} \mu(t) g_y(t, \hat{x}(t), \hat{y}(t)) = \pm\infty$. But in this case, (7.65) implies $\lim_{t \in \mathcal{T}} f_y(\hat{x}(t), \hat{y}(t)) = \mp\infty$, which contradicts Assumption 7.1 part 3. This establishes that $\{\mu(t)\}$ is bounded. ∎

Now let us consider three cases, which together make up the proof of the result.

First, suppose that $\lim \hat{x}(t) = \hat{x}^* \in \mathbb{R}$. Taking limits in (7.65) yields

$$\lim \left[f_y(\hat{x}(t), \hat{y}(t)) + \mu(t) g_y(t, \hat{x}(t), \hat{y}(t)) \right] = 0. \tag{7.72}$$

Since $\lim \hat{x}(t) = \hat{x}^*$ (and thus $\lim |\hat{x}(t)| = |\hat{x}^*|$), $\lim \exp(-\rho t) = 0$, and $|\mu(t)| < B$, we have

$$\lim \left[\exp(-\rho t) \mu(t) |\hat{x}(t)| \right] \leq B \lim \left[\exp(-\rho t) |\hat{x}(t)| \right] = B |\hat{x}^*| \lim \exp(-\rho t) = 0.$$

But in addition we have

$$\lim \left[\exp(-\rho t) \mu(t) |\hat{x}(t)| \right] \geq -B \lim \left[\exp(-\rho t) |\hat{x}(t)| \right] = -B |\hat{x}^*| \lim \exp(-\rho t) = 0.$$

Therefore

$$\lim \left[\exp(-\rho t)\mu(t) \left| \hat{x}(t) \right| \right] = \lim \left[\exp(-\rho t)\mu(t)\hat{x}(t) \right] = 0,$$

establishing (7.69).

Second, suppose that $\lim_{t\to\infty} \dot{\hat{x}}(t)/\hat{x}(t) = \chi \neq 0$. Then for each $\varepsilon \in (0, \chi)$, there exists $T < \infty$ such that for all $t \geq T$,

$$\left| \dot{\hat{x}}(t) \right| \geq \left| \chi - \varepsilon \right| \left| \hat{x}(t) \right|.$$

Multiplying both sides by $\left| \exp(-\rho t)\mu(t) \right|$ and taking limits, we have

$$\lim \left| \exp(-\rho t)\mu(t) \right| \left| \dot{\hat{x}}(t) \right| \geq \lim \left| \exp(-\rho t)\mu(t) \right| \left| \chi - \varepsilon \right| \left| \hat{x}(t) \right| \geq 0. \qquad (7.73)$$

Since $\lim \left| \exp(-\rho t)\mu(t) \right| \left| \dot{\hat{x}}(t) \right| = 0$ from (7.71) (see Fact A.5(4)) and $\left| \chi - \varepsilon \right| > 0$, both inequalities in (7.73) must hold as equalities and therefore $\lim \left[\exp(-\rho t)\mu(t)\hat{x}(t) \right] = 0$.

Third, consider the remaining case, where $\lim \hat{x}(t)$ does not exist (may be equal to infinity) and $\lim_{t\to\infty} \dot{\hat{x}}(t)/\hat{x}(t) = 0$. Then for any $\gamma > 0$ there exists $T < \infty$, such that $\left| \dot{\hat{x}}(t)/\hat{x}(t) \right| < \gamma$ for all $t \geq T < \infty$. Since $\rho > 0$, this implies that $\lim \left| \exp(-\rho t) \right| \left| \hat{x}(t) \right| = 0$. Claim 7.1 again implies that

$$0 = -B \lim \left[\exp(-\rho t)\mu(t) \left| \hat{x}(t) \right| \right] \leq \lim \left[\exp(-\rho t)\mu(t) \left| \hat{x}(t) \right| \right]$$

$$\leq B \lim \left[\exp(-\rho t) \left| \hat{x}(t) \right| \right] = 0,$$

and thus $\lim \left[\exp(-\rho t)\mu(t)\hat{x}(t) \right] = 0$, completing the proof. ∎

The proof of Theorem 7.13 clarifies the importance of discounting. For example, neither the key equation, (7.72), nor the argument in the second case in the proof apply without discounting. Exercise 7.17 discusses how a similar result can be established without discounting under stronger assumptions. Exercise 7.18 shows why Assumption 7.1 part 3 is necessary.

Notice that compared to the transversality condition in the finite-horizon case (e.g., Theorem 7.1), there is the additional term $\exp(-\rho t)$ in (7.69). This is because the transversality condition applies to the original costate variable $\lambda(t)$ (i.e., $\lim_{t\to\infty}[\lambda(t)x(t)] = 0$), and as shown above, the current-value costate variable $\mu(t)$ is given by $\mu(t) = \exp(\rho t)\lambda(t)$. Note also that the stronger transversality condition takes the form

$$\lim_{t\to\infty} \left[\exp(-\rho t)\mu(t)\hat{x}(t) \right] = 0,$$

not simply $\lim_{t\to\infty} \left[\exp(-\rho t)\mu(t) \right] = 0$. Exercise 7.19 illustrates why.

It is important to emphasize that Theorem 7.13 only provides necessary conditions for interior continuous solutions (with $\lim_{t\to\infty} \hat{x}(t) = x^*$ or $\lim_{t\to\infty} \dot{\hat{x}}(t)/\hat{x}(t) = \chi$). In this light, (7.69) should be interpreted as a necessary transversality condition for such a solution. But then (7.69) is neither sufficient nor necessary for a general solution (the solution may not be interior or continuous). However the next theorem shows that under the appropriate concavity conditions, (7.69) is also a sufficient transversality condition. It further shows that for such concave problems, Assumption 7.1 or the limiting conditions in Theorem 7.13 are no longer required. Therefore the next theorem is the most important result of this chapter and is used repeatedly in applications.

Theorem 7.14 (Sufficiency Conditions for Discounted Infinite-Horizon Problems)

Consider the problem of maximizing (7.60) subject to (7.61) and (7.62), with f and g continuously differentiable. Define $\hat{H}(t, x, y, \mu)$ as the current-value Hamiltonian as in (7.64), and suppose that some $\hat{y}(t)$ and the corresponding path of state variable $\hat{x}(t)$ satisfy (7.65)–(7.68). Given the resulting current-value costate variable $\mu(t)$, define $M(t, x, \mu) \equiv \max_{y(t) \in \mathcal{Y}(t)} \hat{H}(t, x, y, \mu)$. Suppose that $V(t, \hat{x}(t))$ exists and is finite for all t (where $V(t, x(t))$ is defined in (7.38)), that for any admissible pair $(x(t), y(t))$, $\lim_{t \to \infty}[\exp(-\rho t)\mu(t)x(t)] \geq 0$, and that $\mathcal{X}(t)$ is convex and $M(t, x, \mu)$ is concave in $x \in \mathcal{X}(t)$ for all t. Then the pair $(\hat{x}(t), \hat{y}(t))$ achieves the global maximum of (7.60). Moreover, if $M(t, x, \mu)$ is strictly concave in x, $(\hat{x}(t), \hat{y}(t))$ is the unique solution to (7.60).

Proof. Consider $(\hat{x}(t), \hat{y}(t))$ satisfying (7.65)–(7.68) and an arbitrary admissible pair $(x(t), y(t))$. By the same argument as in the proof of Theorem 7.6, we have

$$M(t, x(t), \mu(t)) \leq M(t, \hat{x}(t), \mu(t)) + M_x(t, \hat{x}(t), \mu(t))(x(t) - \hat{x}(t))$$

for all $t \geq 0$. Multiplying by $\exp(-\rho t)$ and integrating both sides over $[0, \infty)$ yields

$$\int_0^\infty \exp(-\rho t)M(t, x(t), \mu(t))dt \leq \int_0^\infty \exp(-\rho t)M(t, \hat{x}(t), \mu(t))dt$$
$$+ \int_0^\infty \exp(-\rho t)M_x(t, \hat{x}(t), \mu(t))(x(t) - \hat{x}(t))dt.$$

Moreover,

$$M_x(t, \hat{x}(t), \mu(t)) = \hat{H}_x(t, \hat{x}(t), \hat{y}(t), \mu(t)) = -\dot{\mu}(t).$$

Next, exploiting the definition of the maximized Hamiltonian yields

$$\int_0^\infty \exp(-\rho t)M(t, x(t), \mu(t))dt \geq W(x(t), y(t)) + \int_0^\infty \lambda(t)g(t, x(t), y(t))dt,$$

and

$$\int_0^\infty \exp(-\rho t)M(t, \hat{x}(t), \mu(t))dt = W(\hat{x}(t), \hat{y}(t)) + \int_0^\infty \lambda(t)g(t, \hat{x}(t), \hat{y}(t))dt,$$

where recall that $\lambda(t) \equiv \exp(-\rho t)\mu(t)$. Combining these equations, we have

$$W(x(t), y(t)) \leq W(\hat{x}(t), \hat{y}(t)) \tag{7.74}$$
$$+ \int_0^\infty \lambda(t)[g(t, \hat{x}(t), \hat{y}(t)) - g(t, x(t), y(t))]dt$$
$$- \int_0^\infty \dot{\lambda}(t)(x(t) - \hat{x}(t))dt.$$

Integrating the last term in (7.74) by parts and recalling that $x(0) = \hat{x}(0) = x_0$, we obtain

$$\int_0^\infty \dot{\lambda}(t)(x(t) - \hat{x}(t))dt = \lim_{t \to \infty}\left[\lambda(t)(x(t) - \hat{x}(t))\right] - \int_0^\infty \lambda(t)(\dot{x}(t) - \dot{\hat{x}}(t))dt.$$

In addition, from (7.68), we have

$$\lim_{t \to \infty} \left[\exp(-\rho t)\mu(t)\hat{x}(t)\right] = \lim_{t \to \infty} \left[\lambda(t)\hat{x}(t)\right] = 0.$$

Moreover, by hypothesis, $\lim_{t \to \infty} \lambda(t)x(t) \geq 0$, and thus

$$\int_0^\infty \dot{\lambda}(t)(x(t) - \hat{x}(t))dt \geq -\int_0^\infty \lambda(t)(\dot{x}(t) - \dot{\hat{x}}(t))dt.$$

Combining this expression with (7.74) yields

$$W(x(t), y(t)) \leq W(\hat{x}(t), \hat{y}(t)) \tag{7.75}$$

$$+ \int_0^\infty \lambda(t)[g(t, \hat{x}(t), \hat{y}(t)) - g(t, x(t), y(t))]dt$$

$$+ \int_0^\infty \lambda(t)\left[\dot{x}(t) - \dot{\hat{x}}(t)\right]dt.$$

By definition of the admissible pairs $(x(t), y(t))$ and $(\hat{x}(t), \hat{y}(t))$, $\dot{\hat{x}}(t) = g(t, \hat{x}(t), \hat{y}(t))$ and $\dot{x}(t) = g(t, x(t), y(t))$. Thus (7.75) implies that $W(x(t), y(t)) \leq W(\hat{x}(t), \hat{y}(t))$ for any admissible pair $(x(t), y(t))$, establishing the first part of the theorem.

If M is strictly concave in x, then the inequality in (7.75) is strict, and therefore the same argument establishes $W(x(t), y(t)) < W(\hat{x}(t), \hat{y}(t))$, and no other $(\hat{x}(t), \hat{y}(t))$ could achieve the same value, establishing the second part. ∎

Theorem 7.14 is very useful and powerful. It states that, for a concave problem, an admissible pair $(\hat{x}(t), \hat{y}(t))$ satisfying (7.65)–(7.67) as well as the transversality condition (7.68) necessarily dominates any other admissible pair $(x(t), y(t))$ for which $\lim_{t \to \infty}[\exp(-\rho t)\mu(t)x(t)] \geq 0$ (where $\mu(t)$ is the costate variable associated with the candidate solution $(\hat{x}(t), \hat{y}(t))$). For this sufficiency result, we do not need to check Assumption 7.1. Given this result, the following strategy will be used in most problems:

1. Use the conditions in Theorem 7.13 to locate *a candidate interior solution* $(\hat{x}(t), \hat{y}(t))$ satisfying (7.65)–(7.68).

2. Then verify the concavity conditions of Theorem 7.14 and simply check that $\lim_{t \to \infty}[\exp(-\rho t)\mu(t)x(t)] \geq 0$ for other admissible pairs (with $\mu(t)$ associated with the candidate solution $(\hat{x}(t), \hat{y}(t))$). If these conditions are satisfied, we will have characterized a global maximum.

An important feature of this theorem and the strategy outlined here is that they can be directly applied to unbounded problems (e.g., to endogenous growth models). Therefore, as long as the conditions of Theorem 7.14 are satisfied, there is no need to make boundedness assumptions on $\mathcal{X}$ or $\mathcal{Y}$ to characterize solutions to household utility maximization or optimal growth problems. Recall, however, that throughout it is assumed that $V(t, \hat{x}(t))$ exists and is finite (for all t). When there exist admissible pairs $(x(t), y(t))$ that reach infinite value, then the problem is not economically interesting, and the transversality condition ceases to be meaningful (and is neither necessary nor sufficient for a solution).

Theorem 7.14 provides sufficient conditions for an optimal control to concave problems. It does not require the optimal control, $\hat{y}(t)$, to be continuous (recall that Theorem 7.13 assumed piecewise continuity of $\hat{y}(t)$). However, it is straightforward to establish that when the optimal control problem is strictly concave, $\hat{y}(t)$ must be continuous. This result is stated and proved in the next corollary.

Corollary 7.1 *Suppose that the hypotheses in Theorem 7.14 are satisfied, $M(t, x, \mu)$ is strictly concave in x for all t, and $\mathcal{Y}$ is compact. Then $\hat{y}(t)$ is a continuous function of t on $\mathbb{R}_+$.*

Proof. Given the strict concavity of $M(t, x, \mu)$, Theorem 7.14 established the uniqueness of $(\hat{x}(t), \hat{y}(t))$. Now take some $\hat{t} \in \mathbb{R}_+$ and any sequence $\{t_n\}$ in $\mathbb{R}_+$ converging to $\hat{t}$. Since $\mathcal{Y}$ is compact, the corresponding sequence $\{\hat{y}(t_n)\}$ converges to some $\hat{y}^*$ (Theorem A.7). We have that $\hat{x}(t)$ and $\mu(t)$, given by the differential equations in (7.66) and (7.67), are continuous, and thus $\{\hat{x}(t_n)\}$ and $\{\mu(t_n)\}$ converge to $\hat{x}(\hat{t})$ and $\mu(\hat{t})$. Moreover, by the Maximum Principle $\hat{H}(t_n, \hat{x}(t_n), \hat{y}(t_n), \mu(t_n)) \geq \hat{H}(t_n, \hat{x}(t_n), y, \mu(t_n))$ for all $y \in \mathcal{Y}$. Using the fact that $\hat{H}$ is also continuous and taking limits, we obtain

$$\hat{H}(\hat{t}, \hat{x}(\hat{t}), \hat{y}^*, \mu(\hat{t})) \geq \hat{H}(\hat{t}, \hat{x}(\hat{t}), y, \mu(\hat{t})) \quad \text{for all } y \in \mathcal{Y}.$$

Since $(\hat{x}(t), \hat{y}(t))$ is unique, this implies that $\hat{y}(\hat{t}) = \hat{y}^*$, and therefore, $\hat{y}(t)$ is continuous at $\hat{t}$. Since this is true for any $\hat{t} \in \mathbb{R}_+$, $\hat{y}(t)$ is continuous on $\mathbb{R}_+$. ∎

Although Corollary 7.1 is useful, it should be noted that it does not provide primitive conditions for the existence of a continuous optimal control. It is stated and proved under the hypothesis that there exists a pair $(\hat{x}(t), \hat{y}(t))$ satisfying (7.65)–(7.68). Conditions on objective and constraint functions that guarantee the existence of a solution are presented in the next section.

7.6 Existence of Solutions, Concavity, and Differentiability *

The theorems presented so far characterize the properties of a solution to a continuous-time maximization problem. The natural question of when a solution exists has not been posed or answered. This omission might appear curious, since in both finite-dimensional and discrete-time infinite-horizon optimization problems studied in the previous chapter the analysis starts with existence theorems. There is a good reason for this omission, however. In continuous-time optimization problems, establishing the existence of solutions is considerably more difficult than the characterization of solutions. I now present the general theorem on existence of solutions to continuous-time optimization problems and two additional results providing conditions under which the value function $V(t, x)$, defined in (7.35) and Lemma 7.1, is concave and differentiable.

The reader may have already wondered how valid the approach of using the necessary conditions provided so far, which did not verify the existence of a solution, would be in practice. This concern is important, and ordinarily such an approach would open the door for potential mistakes. One line of defense, however, is provided by the sufficiency theorems, for example, Theorems 7.11 or 7.14 for infinite-horizon problems. If, given a continuous-time optimization problem, we find an admissible pair $(\hat{x}(t), \hat{y}(t))$ that satisfies the necessary conditions (e.g., those in Theorem 7.9) and we can then verify that the optimization problem satisfies the conditions in either of Theorems 7.11 or 7.14, then we must have characterized a solution and can dispense with an existence theorem. Therefore the sufficiency results contained in these theorems enable us to bypass the step of checking for the existence of a solution (or it amounts to proof by construction). Nevertheless, this approach is only valid when the problem possesses sufficient concavity to satisfy the conditions of Theorems 7.11 or 7.14. For problems that do not fall into this category, the justification for using the necessary conditions is much weaker. For this reason, and to provide a more complete treatment of continuous-time optimization problems, in this section I present an existence theorem for optimal control problems. Unfortunately, however, existence theorems for this class of problems are both somewhat complicated to state and difficult to prove. In particular, they require measure-theoretic ideas and more advanced tools (some of them stated in Section A.5). Here I provide a proof of one of the most useful and powerful theorems, giving only a sketch of some of the measure-theoretic details.

For the purposes of this existence theorem, I consider the most general problem studied so far, which is

$$\max_{\mathbf{x}(t),\mathbf{y}(t)} W(\mathbf{x}(t), \mathbf{y}(t)) \equiv \int_0^\infty f(t, \mathbf{x}(t), \mathbf{y}(t))dt \tag{7.76}$$

subject to

$$\dot{\mathbf{x}}(t) = G(t, \mathbf{x}(t), \mathbf{y}(t)), \tag{7.77}$$

and

$$\mathbf{x}(t) \in \mathcal{X}(t) \text{ and } \mathbf{y}(t) \in \mathcal{Y}(t) \text{ for all } t, \mathbf{x}(0) = \mathbf{x}_0, \text{ and } \lim_{t\to\infty} \mathbf{x}(t) \geq \mathbf{x}_1, \tag{7.78}$$

where $\mathcal{X}(t) \subset \mathbb{R}^{K_x}$ and $\mathcal{Y}(t) \subset \mathbb{R}^{K_y}$ with $K_x, K_y \in \mathbb{N}$, $f : \mathbb{R} \times \mathbb{R}^{K_x} \times \mathbb{R}^{K_y} \to \mathbb{R}$, and $G : \mathbb{R} \times \mathbb{R}^{K_x} \times \mathbb{R}^{K_y} \to \mathbb{R}^{K_x}$. As usual f and G are continuously differentiable in all of their arguments.

Clearly, finite-horizon problems are special cases of this more general problem, obtained by setting $f(t, \mathbf{x}, \mathbf{y}) \equiv 0$ for all $t \geq t_1$ for some $t_1 > 0$. Also the terminal value constraint is taken to be of the specific form $\lim_{t\to\infty} \mathbf{x}(t) \geq \mathbf{x}_1$ for concreteness. Different forms of the terminal value constraints, which may involve some of the state variables being entirely free and others having to satisfy equality constraints, can be handled using exactly the same strategy of proof as in Theorem 7.15 below.

To state the result on existence of solutions, let us define

$$M \equiv \left\{ (t, \mathbf{x}, \mathbf{y}) : \mathbf{x} \in \mathcal{X}(t), \mathbf{y} \in \mathcal{Y}(t) \text{ and } t \in \mathbb{R}_+ \right\},$$

and

$$M' \equiv \left\{ (t, \mathbf{x}) : \mathbf{x}(t) \in \mathcal{X}(t) \text{ and } t \in \mathbb{R}_+ \right\}.$$

Recall also $(\mathbf{x}(t), \mathbf{y}(t))$ is an admissible pair if $\mathbf{x}(t) \in \mathcal{X}(t)$ is absolutely continuous and $\mathbf{y}(t) \in \mathcal{Y}(t)$ is (Lebesgue) measurable for all t, $\mathbf{x}(t)$ and $\mathbf{y}(t)$ satisfy (7.77), and $\mathbf{x}(t)$ satisfies the initial and terminal value constraints $\mathbf{x}(0) = \mathbf{x}_0$ and $\lim_{t\to\infty} \mathbf{x}(t) \geq \mathbf{x}_1$ (recall footnote 2 and see Definition A.26). For a given initial condition $\mathbf{x}(0) = \mathbf{x}_0$, I denote the set of admissible pairs by

$$\Omega(0, \mathbf{x}_0) \equiv \left\{ \left[\mathbf{x}(t), \mathbf{y}(t) \right]_{t=0}^\infty : (\mathbf{x}(t), \mathbf{y}(t)) \text{ admissible} \right\}$$

and a generic element of $\Omega(0, \mathbf{x}_0)$ by $(\mathbf{x}(t), \mathbf{y}(t))$. The set $\Omega(0, \mathbf{x}_0)$ can be more explicitly written as

$$\Omega(0, \mathbf{x}_0) \equiv \left\{ \left[\mathbf{x}(t), \mathbf{y}(t) \right]_{t=0}^{\infty} : \mathbf{y}(t) \in \mathcal{Y}(t), \right.$$

$$\mathbf{x}(t) = \int_0^t G(s, \mathbf{x}(s), \mathbf{y}(s))ds + \mathbf{x}_0 \in \mathcal{X}(t) \quad \text{for all } t \in \mathbb{R}_+, \text{ and } \lim_{t \to \infty} \mathbf{x}(t) \geq \mathbf{x}_1 \right\}.$$

Theorem 7.15 (Existence of Solutions) *Consider the maximization of (7.76) subject to (7.77) and (7.78). Suppose that the following conditions hold:*

1. *The correspondences $\mathcal{X}(t) : \mathbb{R}_+ \rightrightarrows \mathbb{R}^{K_x}$ and $\mathcal{Y}(t) : \mathbb{R}_+ \rightrightarrows \mathbb{R}^{K_y}$ are nonempty-valued, compact-valued, closed-valued, and upper hemicontinuous correspondences.*

2. *The functions f and G are continuous on M.*

3. *The sets $\Omega(0, \mathbf{x}_0)$ and*

$$Q(t, \mathbf{x}) \equiv \left\{ (p, \mathbf{z}) \in \mathbb{R} \times \mathbb{R}^{K_x} : p \leq f(t, \mathbf{x}, \mathbf{y}) \text{ and } \mathbf{z} = G(t, \mathbf{x}, \mathbf{y}) \text{ for some } \mathbf{y} \in \mathcal{Y}(t) \right\}$$

   are nonempty for $\mathbf{x}_0 \in \mathcal{X}(t)$ and for all $(t, \mathbf{x}) \in M'$. Moreover the correspondence $Q(t, \mathbf{x})$ is closed-valued, convex-valued, and upper hemicontinuous for $(t, \mathbf{x}) \in M'$.

4. *For any interval $[t_1, t_1 + \delta]$ and any real number $\varepsilon > 0$, there exists a continuous function $\Phi_{t_1 \delta \varepsilon}(t)$ such that for any $T \in [0, \infty]$, $\int_0^T \Phi_{t_1 \delta \varepsilon}(t)dt$ exists and is less than or equal to $\Phi < \infty$, and*

$$\varepsilon f(t, \mathbf{x}, \mathbf{y}) \leq \Phi_{t_1 \delta \varepsilon}(t) - \|G(t, \mathbf{x}, \mathbf{y})\|$$

   for all $t \in [t_1, t_1 + \delta]$ and for all $(t, \mathbf{x}, \mathbf{y}) \in M$.

5. *There exists a positive function $\phi(t)$ (i.e., $\phi(t) \geq 0$ for all t) such that $\int_0^\infty \phi(t)dt$ exists and is less than or equal to $\phi < \infty$, and*

$$f(t, \mathbf{x}, \mathbf{y}) \leq \phi(t)$$

   for all $(t, \mathbf{x}, \mathbf{y}) \in M$.

   Under hypotheses 1–5, there exists an admissible pair $(\hat{\mathbf{x}}(t), \hat{\mathbf{y}}(t)) \in \Omega(0, \mathbf{x}_0)$ that is a solution to the maximization problem (7.76) subject to (7.77) and (7.78). That is, $W(\hat{\mathbf{x}}(t), \hat{\mathbf{y}}(t)) = \bar{W} \geq W(\mathbf{x}'(t), \mathbf{y}'(t))$ for any $(\mathbf{x}'(t), \mathbf{y}'(t)) \in \Omega(0, \mathbf{x}_0)$.

Proof. From hypothesis 5,

$$\int_0^\infty f(t, \mathbf{x}(t), \mathbf{y}(t))dt \leq \int_0^\infty \phi(t)dt \leq \phi < \infty$$

for all $(t, \mathbf{x}(t), \mathbf{y}(t)) \in M$. Since $\Omega(0, \mathbf{x}_0)$ is nonempty,

$$\bar{W} = \sup_{(\mathbf{x}(t), \mathbf{y}(t)) \in \Omega(0, \mathbf{x}_0)} \int_0^\infty f(t, \mathbf{x}(t), \mathbf{y}(t))dt \leq \phi < \infty.$$

For a sequence of admissible pairs $\{(\mathbf{x}^n(t), \mathbf{y}^n(t))\}_{n=1}^{\infty}$, define

$$w^n(t) \equiv \int_0^t f(s, \mathbf{x}^n(s), \mathbf{y}^n(s))\,ds,$$

$$w_+(t) \equiv \int_0^t \phi(s)\,ds \ \in [0, \phi],$$

$$w_-^n(t) \equiv -\int_0^t [\phi(s) - f(s, \mathbf{x}^n(s), \mathbf{y}^n(s))]\,ds,$$

where the inequality that $0 \leq w_+(t) \leq \phi$ follows from hypothesis 5. Moreover, again from hypothesis 5, $\phi(t) - f(t, \mathbf{x}^n(t), \mathbf{y}^n(t)) \geq 0$, so $w_-^n(t)$ is negative and nonincreasing in t. Also, evidently,

$$w_-^n(t) + w_+(t) = w^n(t).$$

Since $w_-^n(t)$ is nonincreasing, it converges on the extended real line, so that

$$\lim_{t \to \infty} w_-^n(t) = -W_-^n,$$

where W_-^n is bounded above (by $\bar{W} < +\infty$, since $\phi(t) - f(t, \mathbf{x}^n(t), \mathbf{y}^n(t)) \geq 0$ and $\int_0^t \phi(t)\,dt \leq \phi < \infty$) and is also nonpositive, since $w_-^n(t) \leq 0$ for all t. Then we can write

$$\lim_{t \to \infty} w_-^n(t) = \lim_{t \to \infty}\left[w_-^n(t) + w_+(t) - w_+(t)\right]$$

$$= \lim_{t \to \infty}\left[w^n(t) - w_+(t)\right]$$

$$= -W_-^n$$

The last equality ensures that $\lim_{t \to \infty} w^n(t)$ converges (on the extended real line) to W^n, which is less than $\phi - W_-^n < \infty$. Therefore, by the definition of the supremum, the sequence $\{(\mathbf{x}^n(t), \mathbf{y}^n(t))\}_{n=1}^{\infty}$ in Ω can be chosen such that

$$\bar{W} - \frac{K}{n} \leq \bar{W}^n \leq \bar{W}$$

for some real number $K > 0$. Consequently, $\lim_{n \to \infty} \bar{W}^n$ must exist and must be equal to $\bar{W}$.

To complete the proof, we must show that $\{(\mathbf{x}^n(t), \mathbf{y}^n(t))\}_{n=1}^{\infty}$ converges to an admissible pair. This step has four parts. We must show: (1) $\mathbf{x}^n(t) \to \hat{\mathbf{x}}(t)$ such that $\hat{\mathbf{x}}(t) \in X(t)$; (2) $\hat{\mathbf{x}}(t)$ is absolutely continuous; (3) when it exists, $\dot{\mathbf{x}}(t)$ satisfies (7.77); and (4) $\mathbf{y}^n(t) \to \hat{\mathbf{y}}(t) \in Y(t)$, where $\hat{\mathbf{y}}(t)$ is (Lebesgue) measurable.

Since $Y(t)$ and $X(t)$ are closed-valued (hypothesis 1), M is closed. This also implies that M' is closed. Since any interval $[t_1, t_1 + \delta]$ is closed and compact and $X(t)$ is compact for each t, $M_{t_1\delta} \equiv M' \cap ([t_1, t_1 + \delta] \times \mathbb{R}^{K_x})$ is compact (Lemma A.2), and thus any sequence of (vector) functions $\mathbf{x}^n(t) \in M_{t_1\delta}$ is uniformly bounded. We next show that the sequence of continuous functions $\{\mathbf{x}^n(t)\}_{n=1}^{\infty}$ in $M_{t_1\delta}$ is equicontinuous (Definition A.30). Let $\varepsilon > 0$. Since $\int_0^T \Phi_{t_1\delta\varepsilon}(t)\,dt$ exists for any T and $\Phi_{t_1\delta\varepsilon}(t)$ is continuous (hypothesis 4), there exists $\chi > 0$ such that

$$\int_{t_1}^{t_1+\delta} \Phi_{t_1\delta\varepsilon}(t)\,dt < \frac{\chi}{2}.$$

Using hypothesis 4 again and setting

$$\varepsilon \equiv \frac{\chi}{2(\Phi - \bar{W})} > 0$$

for each $n = 1, 2, \ldots$, we have that

$$\int_{t_1}^{t_1+\delta} \left\| \dot{\mathbf{x}}^n(t) \right\| dt = \int_{t_1}^{t_1+\delta} \left\| G(t, \mathbf{x}^n(t), \mathbf{y}^n(t)) \right\| dt$$

$$\leq \int_{t_1}^{t_1+\delta} \left[\Phi_{t_1\delta\varepsilon}(t) - \varepsilon f(t, \mathbf{x}^n(t), \mathbf{y}^n(t)) \right] dt$$

$$\leq \int_{t_1}^{t_1+\delta} \Phi_{t_1\delta\varepsilon}(t) d + \varepsilon \int_0^{\infty} [\phi(t) - f(t, \mathbf{x}^n(t), \mathbf{y}^n(t))] dt$$

$$\leq \frac{\chi}{2} + \varepsilon(\Phi - \bar{W})$$

$$\leq \chi.$$

Since this relation is true for each $n = 1, 2, \ldots$, and each interval $[t_1, t_1 + \delta]$, the vector functions $\mathbf{x}^n(t)$ are equicontinuous on each $[t_1, t_1 + \delta]$. Now the corollary to the Arzela-Ascoli Theorem (Corollary A.2) implies that there exists a subsequence $\{\mathbf{x}^{n_k}(t)\}$ of $\{\mathbf{x}^n(t)\}$ such that $\mathbf{x}^{n_k}(t) \to \hat{\mathbf{x}}(t)$ and that $\hat{\mathbf{x}}(t)$ is absolutely continuous on $[t_1, t_1 + \delta]$. Since $[0, \infty)$ is a countable union of intervals of the form $[t_1, t_1 + \delta]$, repeated application of the preceding argument countably many times implies that there exists a subsequence $\{\mathbf{x}^{n_{k'}}(t)\}$ of $\{\mathbf{x}^n(t)\}$ such that $\mathbf{x}^{n_{k'}}(t) \to \hat{\mathbf{x}}(t)$ on $[0, \infty)$. Definition A.26 then implies that $\hat{\mathbf{x}}(t)$ is absolutely continuous on $[0, \infty)$, completing the proof of parts 1 and 2 above.

For part 3, we need to show that when $\dot{\mathbf{x}}(t)$ exists, there is $a(t)$ such that $(a(t), \dot{\mathbf{x}}(t)) \in Q(t, \hat{\mathbf{x}}(t))$ for all t. For an arbitrary real number $\varepsilon > 0$, consider $Q_\varepsilon(t, \mathbf{x})$ be the ε neighborhood of the set $Q(t, \hat{\mathbf{x}})$, that is,

$$Q_\varepsilon(t, \hat{\mathbf{x}}) = \left\{ (p, \mathbf{z}) : d((p, \mathbf{z}), Q(t, \hat{\mathbf{x}})) < \varepsilon \right\},$$

where d is the Euclidean metric. Since $Q(t, \hat{\mathbf{x}})$ is convex-valued (hypothesis 3), so is $Q_\varepsilon(t, \hat{\mathbf{x}})$. By definition of admissibility, for the sequence $\{(\mathbf{x}^n(t), \mathbf{y}^n(t))\}_{n=1}^{\infty}$ considered above, $(p^n(t), \dot{\mathbf{x}}^n(t)) \in Q(t, \mathbf{x}^n(t))$ for all t (where $p^n(t) = f(t, \mathbf{x}^n(t), \mathbf{y}^n(t))$). And since $Q(t, \mathbf{x}^n(t)) \subset Q_\varepsilon(t, \mathbf{x}^n(t))$ for each t, $(p^n(t), \dot{\mathbf{x}}^n(t)) \in Q_\varepsilon(t, \mathbf{x}^n(t))$. Moreover, since $\varepsilon > 0$, there exists $h > 0$ such that

$$(p^n(t + \eta), \dot{\mathbf{x}}^n(t + \eta)) \in Q_\varepsilon(t, \mathbf{x}^n(t))$$

for all $\eta \leq h$ and for each $n = 1, 2, \ldots$. Integrating (7.77) between t and $t + h$ for an admissible pair $(\mathbf{x}^n(t), \mathbf{y}^n(t))$, we obtain

$$\mathbf{x}^n(t + h) = \int_t^{t+h} G(s, \mathbf{x}^n(s), \mathbf{y}^n(s)) ds + \mathbf{x}^n(t),$$

and therefore

$$\frac{\mathbf{x}^n(t + h) - \mathbf{x}^n(t)}{h} = \frac{\int_t^{t+h} \dot{\mathbf{x}}^n(s) ds}{h}$$

for each $n = 1, 2, \ldots$. Since $Q_\varepsilon(t, \mathbf{x}^n(t))$ is convex-valued and $\dot{\mathbf{x}}^n(s) \in Q_\varepsilon(t, \mathbf{x}^n(t))$ for all $s \in [t, t + h]$,

$$\left(\int_t^{t+h} \dot{\mathbf{x}}^n(s)ds \right) / h \in \overline{Q_\varepsilon(t, \mathbf{x}^n(t))}$$

(recall that $\overline{Q_\varepsilon(t, \mathbf{x}^n(t))}$ is the closure of $Q_\varepsilon(t, \mathbf{x}^n(t))$). By hypothesis 3, $Q_\varepsilon(t, \mathbf{x}^n(t))$ is closed-valued, convex-valued, and upper hemicontinuous and thus $\overline{Q_\varepsilon(t, \mathbf{x}^n(t))}$ is also closed-valued, convex-valued, and upper hemicontinuous. In view of this, taking the limit $n \to \infty$ yields

$$\frac{\hat{\mathbf{x}}(t + h) - \hat{\mathbf{x}}(t)}{h} \in \overline{Q_\varepsilon(t, \mathbf{x}(t))}.$$

Now taking the limit as $h \to 0$ and using the hypothesis that $\dot{\mathbf{x}}(t)$ exists, we have

$$\dot{\mathbf{x}}(t) \in \overline{Q_\varepsilon(t, \hat{\mathbf{x}}(t))}.$$

Since $\varepsilon > 0$ and t were arbitrary, we conclude that

$$\dot{\mathbf{x}}(t) \in \overline{Q(t, \hat{\mathbf{x}}(t))} = Q(t, \hat{\mathbf{x}}(t))$$

for all t, completing the proof of part 3.

For part 4, note that for each $n = 1, 2, \ldots$, $(\mathbf{x}^n(t), \mathbf{y}^n(t))$ is admissible, and thus $\mathbf{y}^n(t)$ must be measurable in t. Moreover, since $\mathcal{Y}(t)$ is compact, by Helly's Selection Theorem (e.g., Kolmogorov and Fomin, 1970, Theorem 5, p. 372), there exists a subsequence of $\{\mathbf{y}^n(t)\}$, denoted by $\{\mathbf{y}^{n_k}(t)\}$, such that $\mathbf{y}^{n_k}(t) \to \hat{\mathbf{y}}(t)$. Since $\hat{\mathbf{x}}(t)$ is absolutely continuous, it is differentiable almost everywhere (Fact A.17). Therefore $\dot{\mathbf{x}}(t)$ exists almost everywhere and is thus measurable. Moreover $\hat{\mathbf{x}}(t)$ is absolutely continuous and thus measurable. Next let $D = \left\{ (t, \hat{\mathbf{y}}(t)) \in \mathbb{R}_+ \times \mathcal{Y}(t) : \dot{\mathbf{x}}(t) = G(t, \hat{\mathbf{x}}(t), \hat{\mathbf{y}}(t)) \right\}$. Since $\mathbb{R}_+$ is a countable union of compact intervals and $\mathcal{Y}(t)$ is closed, D can be expressed as a countable union of compact sets. Since G is continuous in all of its arguments on D (hypothesis 2) and $\dot{\mathbf{x}}(t) = G(t, \hat{\mathbf{x}}(t), \hat{\mathbf{y}}(t))$ is measurable for all $t \in \mathbb{R}_+$, $\hat{\mathbf{y}}(t)$ is also measurable for all $t \in \mathbb{R}_+$. ∎

Theorem 7.15 establishes the existence of solutions to continuous-time maximization problems under relatively mild assumptions (at least from an economic point of view). Hypotheses 1 and 2 are the usual compactness and continuity assumptions, necessary in finite-dimensional and discrete-time optimization problems as well (recall, e.g., Theorem A.9). Hypotheses 4 and 5 are somewhat stronger versions of the boundedness assumptions that are also necessary in finite-dimensional and discrete-time optimization problems (these are sometimes referred to as "growth conditions" since they restrict the rate at which the payoff function can grow). Hypothesis 3 is rather unusual. Such a convexity assumption is not necessary in finite-dimensional and discrete-time optimization problems. However, in continuous-time problems this assumption cannot be dispensed with (see Exercise 7.24).

While Theorem 7.15 establishes the existence of solutions, providing sufficient conditions for the solution (the control $\mathbf{y}(t)$) to be continuous turns out to be much harder. Without knowing that the solution is continuous, the necessary conditions in Theorems 7.9 and/or 7.13 may appear incomplete. Although there is some truth to this, recall that both Theorems 7.9 and 7.13 provided necessary conditions only for all t except those at which $\mathbf{y}(t)$ is discontinuous. Moreover, Corollary 7.1 provided conditions for continuity (for concave problems). However, instead of using these conditions to prove the existence of continuous solutions, the indirect approach outlined above turns out to be more useful. In particular, in most economic problems the following approach works: (1) characterize a candidate solution that satisfies the necessary conditions in Theorem 7.9 or in Theorem 7.13 (provided that such a solution exists) and (2) verify the sufficiency conditions in one of Theorems 7.11 or 7.14. This approach, when it works, guarantees both the existence of a solution and continuity of the control (and smoothness of the state variable). Since all the problems in this book satisfy these conditions, this approach is the one I adopt henceforth.

Let us next discuss how the conditions of Theorem 7.15 can be verified in the context of the optimal growth example, which is discussed in greater detail in the next section.

Example 7.4 *Consider the problem*

$$\max_{[k(t),c(t)]_{t=0}^{\infty}} \int_0^\infty \exp(-\rho t)u(c(t))dt$$

subject to

$$\dot{k}(t) = f(k(t)) - \delta k(t) - c(t),$$

$k(t) \geq 0$ for all t, and $k(0) > 0$. Recall that $u : \mathbb{R}_+ \to \mathbb{R}$ is strictly increasing, continuously differentiable, and strictly concave, while $f(\cdot)$ satisfies our basic assumptions (Assumptions 1 and 2 from Chapter 2; this also implies that $c(t) \geq 0$ for all t). Let us now check that hypotheses 1–5 of Theorem 7.15 are satisfied. First, note that in view of the Inada conditions in Assumption 2, there exists $\bar{k} > 0$ such that $f(\bar{k}) = \delta\bar{k}$, so that for any $k > \bar{k}$, $\dot{k}$ would necessarily be strictly negative (even if $c = 0$). Thus we can restrict attention to $k(t) \in [0, \vec{k}]$, where $\vec{k} \equiv \max\{\bar{k}, k(0)\}$. Thus $k(t) \in \mathcal{X}(t) \equiv [0, \vec{k}]$ with $\mathcal{X}(t)$ compact and thus closed-valued, and also continuous in t. Similarly, $c(t) \in [0, f(\vec{k})]$; thus $c(t) \in \mathcal{Y}(t) \equiv [0, f(\vec{k})]$, so that $\mathcal{Y}(t)$ is compact-valued and continuous in t. Therefore hypothesis 1 is verified. Both u and f are continuous, so that hypothesis 2 is verified as well. The correspondence $Q(t, \mathbf{x})$ takes the form

$$Q(t, k) = \left\{(p, z) \in \mathbb{R} \times \mathbb{R}: p \leq \exp(-\rho t)u(c), z = f(k) - \delta k - c \text{ and } c \in [0, f(\vec{k})]\right\},$$

which is clearly closed- and convex-valued and continuous, and both $Q(t, \mathbf{x})$ and $\Omega(\mathbf{x}_0)$ are nonempty-valued; thus hypothesis 3 is also satisfied.

In view of the fact that $c(t) \in [0, f(\vec{k})]$, we have

$$\exp(-\rho t)u(t) \leq \exp(-\rho t) \max\{0, u(f(\vec{k}))\},$$

so that hypothesis 5 is satisfied as well. Finally, let

$$\Phi(t) \equiv \exp(-\rho t)\left[u(\vec{k}) + \max\{\vec{k}, [f(\vec{k}) - \delta\vec{k}]\}\right].$$

Then, using once more the fact that $c(t) \in [0, f(\vec{k})]$ and $k(t) \in [0, \vec{k}]$, we have that for any interval $[t_1, t_1 + \delta]$ and any $\varepsilon > 0$,

$$\varepsilon u(c) + |f(k) - \delta k - c| \leq \Phi(t)$$

for any $t \in [t_1, t_1 + \delta]$ and

$$\int_0^\infty \exp(-\rho t)\Phi(t) \leq \frac{u(\vec{k}) + \max\{\vec{k}, [f(\vec{k}) - \delta\vec{k}]\}}{\rho} < \infty,$$

thus verifying hypothesis 4. Theorem 7.15 therefore guarantees the existence of solutions in this problem. In the next section we will see that Theorem 7.14 in fact ensures the existence of a continuous solution to this problem.

I next briefly present conditions under which the value function $V(t, x)$ is concave and differentiable. Recall the definition of $V(t, x)$ in (7.35), which was done for the case of a one-dimensional state variable. Let us consider the more general problem of maximizing (7.76) subject to (7.77) and (7.78). Presuming that the solution exists, the value function is defined as

$$V(t_0, \mathbf{x}_0) = \max_{[\mathbf{x}(t), \mathbf{y}(t)]_{t=t_0}^\infty \in \Omega(t_0, \mathbf{x}_0)} \int_{t_0}^\infty f(t, \mathbf{x}(t), \mathbf{y}(t))dt.$$

Notice that all of the constraints are already incorporated into the set $\Omega(t_0, \mathbf{x}_0)$.

The next theorem provides sufficient conditions for the value function $V(t, \mathbf{x})$ to be concave in $\mathbf{x}$. The theorem is simple, though in many problems ensuring the condition that the constraint set $\Omega(t, \mathbf{x})$ is convex may be difficult. In particular, $\Omega(t_0, \mathbf{x})$ is convex when $[\mathbf{x}(t), \mathbf{y}(t)]_{t=t_0}^\infty \in \Omega(t_0, \mathbf{x})$ and $[\mathbf{x}'(t), \mathbf{y}'(t)]_{t=t_0}^\infty \in \Omega(t_0, \mathbf{x}')$ imply that $[\mathbf{x}_\alpha(t), \mathbf{y}_\alpha(t)]_{t=t_0}^\infty \in \Omega(t_0, \mathbf{x}_\alpha)$ for any $\alpha \in [0, 1]$, where

$$\mathbf{x}_\alpha(t) \equiv \alpha\mathbf{x}(t) + (1 - \alpha)\mathbf{x}'(t),$$

$$\mathbf{y}_\alpha(t) \equiv \alpha\mathbf{y}(t) + (1 - \alpha)\mathbf{y}'(t),$$

and

$$\mathbf{x}_\alpha \equiv \alpha\mathbf{x} + (1 - \alpha)\mathbf{x}'.$$

For example, linear systems of differential equations of the form $\dot{\mathbf{x}}(t) = A(t) + B(t)\mathbf{x}(t) + C(t)\mathbf{y}(t)$ satisfy this convexity condition.

Theorem 7.16 (Concavity of the Value Function)   *Consider the problem of maximizing (7.76) subject to (7.77) and (7.78), and suppose that the hypotheses of Theorem 7.15 are satisfied, so that a solution to this maximization problem exists. Let the value function starting with initial value $\mathbf{x}_0$ at time t_0 be $V(t_0, \mathbf{x}_0)$. Suppose also that $f(t, \mathbf{x}(t), \mathbf{y}(t))$ is jointly concave in $\mathbf{x}(t)$ and $\mathbf{y}(t)$ for all $t \in [t_0, \infty)$ and $\Omega(t_0, \mathbf{x})$ is convex for all $\mathbf{x} \in X(t_0)$. Then $V(t_0, \mathbf{x})$ is concave in $\mathbf{x}$.*

Proof.   Suppose $[\mathbf{x}(t), \mathbf{y}(t)]_{t=t_0}^\infty \in \Omega(t_0, \mathbf{x})$ and $[\mathbf{x}'(t), \mathbf{y}'(t)]_{t=t_0}^\infty \in \Omega(t_0, \mathbf{x}')$ are solutions. Then

$$V(t_0, \mathbf{x}) = \int_{t_0}^\infty f(t, \mathbf{x}(t), \mathbf{y}(t))dt, \text{ and } V(t_0, \mathbf{x}') = \int_{t_0}^\infty f(t, \mathbf{x}'(t), \mathbf{y}'(t))dt. \quad (7.79)$$

Now consider $V(t_0, \mathbf{x}_\alpha)$ with $\mathbf{x}_\alpha$ defined as above. By the hypothesis that $\Omega(t_0, \mathbf{x})$ is convex, $[\mathbf{x}_\alpha(t), \mathbf{y}_\alpha(t)]_{t=t_0}^\infty \in \Omega(t_0, \mathbf{x}_\alpha)$ with $\mathbf{x}_\alpha(t)$ and $\mathbf{y}_\alpha(t)$ defined as above. Therefore

$$V(t_0, \mathbf{x}_\alpha) \geq \int_{t_0}^\infty f(t, \mathbf{x}_\alpha(t), \mathbf{y}_\alpha(t))dt$$

$$= \int_{t_0}^\infty f(t, \alpha\mathbf{x}(t) + (1 - \alpha)\mathbf{x}'(t), \alpha\mathbf{y}(t) + (1 - \alpha)\mathbf{y}'(t))dt$$

$$\geq \alpha \int_{t_0}^\infty f(t, \mathbf{x}(t), \mathbf{y}(t))dt + (1 - \alpha) \int_{t_0}^\infty f(t, \mathbf{x}'(t), \mathbf{y}'(t))dt$$

$$= \alpha V(t_0, \mathbf{x}) + (1 - \alpha)V(t_0, \mathbf{x}'),$$

where the first line uses the fact that $[\mathbf{x}_\alpha(t), \mathbf{y}_\alpha(t)]_{t=t_0}^\infty$ is feasible, and thus $V(t_0, \mathbf{x}_\alpha)$ must be at least as large as the returns from $[\mathbf{x}_\alpha(t), \mathbf{y}_\alpha(t)]_{t=t_0}^\infty$. The second line writes out $\mathbf{x}_\alpha(t)$ and $\mathbf{y}_\alpha(t)$ explicitly, the third line uses the joint concavity of f, and the fourth line uses (7.79). This establishes the concavity of $V(t_0, \mathbf{x})$. ∎

Theorem 7.17 (Differentiability of the Value Function) *Consider the problem of maximizing (7.76) subject to (7.77) and (7.78), and suppose that the hypotheses of Theorems 7.15 and 7.16 are satisfied so that a solution exists and $V(t_0, \mathbf{x})$ is concave. Suppose also that f and G are differentiable in $(\mathbf{x}, \mathbf{y})$ for all t and that the optimal pair $(\hat{\mathbf{x}}(t), \hat{\mathbf{y}}(t))$ is such that there exists $\Delta t > 0$, with $\hat{\mathbf{x}}(t) \in \text{Int } \mathcal{X}(t)$ and $\hat{\mathbf{y}}(t) \in \text{Int } \mathcal{Y}(t)$ for $t \in [t_0, t_0 + \Delta t]$. Then $V(t_0, \mathbf{x})$ is differentiable in $\mathbf{x}$ at $\hat{\mathbf{x}}(t_0)$.*

Proof. Use the equivalent of Lemma 7.1 for multivariate problems to write

$$V(t_0, \hat{\mathbf{x}}(t_0)) = \int_{t_0}^{t_0+\Delta t} f(t, \hat{\mathbf{x}}(t), \hat{\mathbf{y}}(t))dt + V(t_0 + \Delta t, \hat{\mathbf{x}}(t_0 + \Delta t)).$$

Since $\hat{\mathbf{x}}(t) \in \text{Int } \mathcal{X}(t)$ and $\hat{\mathbf{y}}(t) \in text Int \; \mathcal{Y}(t)$ for $t \in [t_0, t_0 + \Delta t]$, for $\varepsilon > 0$ and sufficiently small, there exists a neighborhood $\mathcal{N}_\varepsilon(\hat{\mathbf{x}}(t_0))$ of $\hat{\mathbf{x}}(t_0)$ such that for all $\mathbf{x} \in \mathcal{N}_\varepsilon(\hat{\mathbf{x}}(t_0))$, there exists $[\mathbf{x}'(t), \mathbf{y}'(t)]_{t=t_0}^\infty \in \Omega(t_0, \mathbf{x})$ with $\mathbf{x}'(t + \Delta t) = \hat{\mathbf{x}}(t + \Delta t)$ and $[\mathbf{x}'(t), \mathbf{y}'(t)]_{t=t_0+\Delta t}^\infty = [\hat{\mathbf{x}}(t), \hat{\mathbf{y}}(t)]_{t=t_0}^\infty$. Let the value from this potentially suboptimal admissible pair be

$$\bar{V}(t_0, \mathbf{x}) = \int_{t_0}^{t_0+\Delta t} f(t, \mathbf{x}'(t), \mathbf{y}'(t))dt + V(t_0, \hat{\mathbf{x}}(t_0 + \Delta t)).$$

By definition, $\bar{V}(t_0, \mathbf{x}))$ exists and satisfies $\bar{V}(t_0, \mathbf{x}) \leq V(t_0, \mathbf{x})$ for all $\mathbf{x} \in \mathcal{N}_\varepsilon(\hat{\mathbf{x}}(t_0))$. Moreover $\bar{V}(t_0, \mathbf{x})$ is differentiable in $\mathbf{x}$ by the fact that f is differentiable and $[\mathbf{x}'(t), \mathbf{y}'(t)]_{t=t_0}^{t_0+\Delta t}$ is a differentiable trajectory by Theorem B.13. Moreover, by Theorem 7.16, $V(t_0, \mathbf{x})$ is concave, and appealing to the same result from convex analysis as in the proof of Theorem 6.6 in the previous chapter, the convex function $-V(t_0, \mathbf{x})$ is subdifferentiable and has a nonempty, closed, and convex set of subgradients, such that for any subgradient $\mathbf{p}$ and for all $\mathbf{x} \in \mathcal{N}_\varepsilon(\hat{\mathbf{x}}(t_0))$,

$$\mathbf{p}\cdot(\mathbf{x} - \hat{\mathbf{x}}(t_0)) \geq V(t_0, \mathbf{x}) - V(t_0, \hat{\mathbf{x}}(t_0)).$$

Moreover, since $\bar{V}(t_0, \mathbf{x}) \leq V(t_0, \mathbf{x})$ and $\bar{V}(t_0, \hat{\mathbf{x}}(t_0)) = V(t_0, \hat{\mathbf{x}}(t_0))$, we have

$$\mathbf{p}\cdot(\mathbf{x} - \hat{\mathbf{x}}(t_0)) \geq V(t_0, \mathbf{x}) - V(t_0, \hat{\mathbf{x}}(t_0)) \geq \bar{V}(t_0, \mathbf{x}) - \bar{V}(t_0, \hat{\mathbf{x}}(t_0))$$

for all $\mathbf{x} \in \mathcal{N}_\varepsilon(\hat{\mathbf{x}}(t_0))$. Since $\bar{V}(t_0, \mathbf{x})$ is differentiable for all $\mathbf{x} \in \mathcal{N}_\varepsilon(\hat{\mathbf{x}}(t_0))$, $\mathbf{p}$ must be uniquely defined, which implies that $V(t_0, \mathbf{x})$ is also differentiable at $\hat{\mathbf{x}}(t_0)$. ∎

7.7 A First Look at Optimal Growth in Continuous Time

In this section, I briefly show how the main results developed so far, Theorems 7.13 and 7.14, can be applied to the problem of optimal growth. Recall that the optimal growth problem involves the maximization of the utility of the representative household. I do not provide a full treatment of this model here, since it is the topic of the next chapter. My objective is to illustrate how Theorems 7.13 and 7.14 can be applied in economic growth problems by using this canonical problem. I show that checking the conditions for Theorem 7.13 requires some work, while verifying the conditions for Theorem 7.14 is much more straightforward.

Consider the neoclassical economy without population growth and without technological progress. In this case, the optimal growth problem in continuous time can be written as

$$\max_{[k(t),c(t)]_{t=0}^{\infty}} \int_0^{\infty} \exp(-\rho t)u(c(t))dt$$

subject to

$$\dot{k}(t) = f(k(t)) - \delta k(t) - c(t),$$

$k(t) \geq 0$ for all t, and $k(0) > 0$. Let us suppose that the utility function $u(c)$ is defined as $u : \mathbb{R}_+ \setminus \{0\} \to \mathbb{R}$ or as $u : \mathbb{R}_+ \to \mathbb{R}$ and is strictly increasing, continuously differentiable and strictly concave (e.g., when $u(c) = \log c$, the domain is $\mathbb{R}_+ \setminus \{0\}$). Suppose also that $f(\cdot)$ satisfies Assumptions 1 and 2 from Chapter 2 and that $\lim_{c \to 0} u'(c) = \infty$.

Let us first set up the current-value Hamiltonian, which, in this case, does not directly depend on time and can be written as

$$\hat{H}(k, c, \mu) = u(c(t)) + \mu(t)[f(k(t)) - \delta k(t) - c(t)], \qquad (7.80)$$

with state variable k, control variable c, and current-value costate variable μ.

From Theorem 7.13, let us look for a path of capital stock and consumption per capita that satisfies the necessary conditions

$$\hat{H}_c(k, c, \mu) = u'(c(t)) - \mu(t) = 0 \qquad (7.81)$$

and

$$\hat{H}_k(k, c, \mu) = \mu(t)[f'(k(t)) - \delta] = \rho\mu(t) - \dot{\mu}(t). \qquad (7.82)$$

In addition, we would like to use the stronger transversality condition (7.69), which here takes the form

$$\lim_{t \to \infty} \left[\exp(-\rho t)\mu(t)k(t) \right] = 0. \qquad (7.83)$$

If we wish to show that this transversality condition is necessary (for an interior solution), we need to verify that Assumption 7.1 is satisfied. First, the instantaneous utility function $u(c)$ is increasing in c and is independent of k, so it is weakly monotone. The constraint function $f(k) - \delta k - c$ is decreasing in c but may be nonmonotone in k. However, without any loss of generality, attention can be restricted to $k(t) \in [0, \bar{k}]$, where $\bar{k}$ is defined such that $f'(\bar{k}) = \delta$. Since increasing the capital stock above this level would reduce output and thus consumption both today and in the future, optimal control never involves $k(t) \notin [0, \bar{k}]$ for any $t > 0$. When $k(t) \in [0, \bar{k}]$, the constraint function is also weakly monotone in k. This ensures that part 1 of Assumption 7.1 is satisfied. Part 2 of Assumption 7.1 is immediate, since the derivative of $f(k) - \delta k - c$ with respect to c is equal to -1 and is thus uniformly bounded away from 0. Part 3 of Assumption 7.1 is not necessarily satisfied, however (e.g., with $u(c) = \log c$, $\lim_{c \to 0} u'(c) = \infty$). Nevertheless we could modify the problem by taking the utility function as $u : [\varepsilon, +\infty) \to \mathbb{R}$ for some $\varepsilon > 0$ sufficiently small. In this case, Assumption 7.1 part 3 would also be satisfied. We can then verify that any solution to this modified problem that involves $c(t) > \varepsilon$ for all t is also a solution to the original problem where the domain of the utility function is $\mathbb{R}_+ \backslash \{0\}$ (see Exercise 7.25). Moreover, it can also be shown that for any optimal growth problem as formulated here, there exists $\varepsilon > 0$ such that $c(t) > \varepsilon$ for all t (see again Exercise 7.25). Thus there is no loss of generality in choosing the domain of the utility function as $[\varepsilon, +\infty)$. This establishes that the necessary conditions in Theorem 7.13, including the strong version of the transversality condition, (7.69), can be used in the optimal growth problem. These conditions in this problem take the form of (7.81)–(7.83).

However a more direct line of attack would be to use Theorem 7.14. Recall that this theorem does not require Assumption 7.1. Therefore there is no need to look for a modified problem with the restriction that $c(t) \in [\varepsilon, +\infty)$. We simply look for a candidate path that satisfies conditions (7.81) and (7.82) as well as the transversality condition (7.83). First, we can observe that (7.81) implies $\mu(t) > 0$ along this candidate path (since $u' > 0$ everywhere). Consequently the current-value Hamiltonian given in (7.80) consists of the sum of two strictly concave functions and is itself strictly concave (and since $\hat{H}(k, c, \mu)$ is strictly concave, so is $M(k, \mu) \equiv \max_c \hat{H}(k, c, \mu)$). Second, since $\mu(t) > 0$ and $k(t) > 0$ (by feasibility), any alternative path must satisfy $\lim_{t \to \infty} \left[\exp(-\rho t) \mu(t) k(t) \right] \geq 0$. Therefore the conditions in Theorem 7.14 are satisfied. We can thus conclude that the candidate solution that satisfies (7.81)–(7.83) is a global maximum. Notice that in applying Theorem 7.14, we are using the equivalent of (7.69)—namely, (7.83)—as a sufficient transversality condition under concavity (and thus we do not need to check Assumption 7.1).

Since an analysis of optimal growth in the neoclassical model is more relevant in the context of the next chapter, I do not provide further details here.

7.8 The q-Theory of Investment and Saddle-Path Stability

As another application of the methods developed in this chapter, I now consider the canonical model of investment under adjustment costs, also known as the "q-theory of investment." This problem is not only useful as an application of optimal control techniques, but it is one of the basic models of standard macroeconomic theory. Moreover I use this model to illustrate the notion of *saddle-path stability*, which plays a central role in the analysis of optimal and equilibrium growth.

The economic problem is that of a price-taking firm trying to maximize the present discounted value of its profits. The only twist relative to the problems studied so far is that this firm is subject to adjustment costs when it changes its capital stock. In particular, let the capital stock of the firm be $K(t) \geq 0$, and suppose that the firm has access to a production function $f(K)$ that satisfies Assumptions 1 and 2 of Chapter 2. For simplicity, let us normalize the price of the output of the firm to 1 in terms of the final good at all dates. The firm is subject to adjustment costs captured by the function $\phi(I)$, which is strictly increasing, continuously differentiable, and strictly convex, and satisfies $\phi(0) = \phi'(0) = 0$. Thus in addition to the cost of purchasing investment goods (which, given the normalization of price, is equal to I for an amount of investment I), the firm incurs a cost of adjusting its production structure given by the convex function $\phi(I)$. In some models, the adjustment cost is taken to be a function of investment relative to capital—$\phi(I/K)$ instead of $\phi(I)$—but this modification makes no difference for our main focus. I also assume that installed capital depreciates at an exponential rate δ and that the firm maximizes its net present discounted earnings with a discount rate equal to the interest rate r, which is assumed to be constant.

The firm's problem can be written as

$$\max_{[K(t),I(t)]_{t=0}^{\infty}} \int_0^{\infty} \exp(-rt)[f(K(t)) - I(t) - \phi(I(t))]dt$$

subject to

$$\dot{K}(t) = I(t) - \delta K(t) \tag{7.84}$$

and $K(t) \geq 0$, with $K(0) > 0$ given. Notice that $\phi(I)$ does not contribute to capital accumulation; it is simply a cost. Moreover, since ϕ is strictly convex, it implies that the firm prefers not to make "large" adjustments. Therefore ϕ acts as a force for a smoother time path of investment.

To characterize the optimal investment plan of the firm, let us use the same strategy as in the previous section. In particular, write the current-value Hamiltonian as

$$\hat{H}(K, I, q) \equiv [f(K(t)) - I(t) - \phi(I(t))] + q(t)[I(t) - \delta K(t)],$$

where I used $q(t)$ instead of the familiar $\mu(t)$ for the costate variable, for reasons that will soon be apparent.

The necessary conditions for an interior solution to this problem, including the transversality condition, can be written as

$$\hat{H}_I(K, I, q) = -1 - \phi'(I(t)) + q(t) = 0,$$

$$\hat{H}_K(K, I, q) = f'(K(t)) - \delta q(t) = rq(t) - \dot{q}(t), \tag{7.85}$$

$$\lim_{t \to \infty} \exp(-rt)q(t)K(t) = 0.$$

The first necessary condition implies that

$$q(t) = 1 + \phi'(I(t)) \quad \text{for all } t. \tag{7.86}$$

Let us next check sufficiency. Since $q(t) > 0$ for all t, $\hat{H}$ is strictly concave. Moreover, since $K(t) \geq 0$ by feasibility, we also have $\lim_{t \to \infty} \exp(-rt)q(t)K(t) \geq 0$ for any feasible investment and capital stock paths. Consequently Theorem 7.14 applies and shows that a solution to (7.85) characterizes the unique profit-maximizing investment and capital stock paths. Once again, it turns out that using Theorem 7.14 is both straightforward and powerful. In particular, the transversality condition corresponding to (7.69) is being used as a sufficient condition, and there is no need to check Assumption 7.1.

Next, differentiating (7.86) with respect to time yields

$$\dot{q}(t) = \phi''(I(t))\dot{I}(t). \tag{7.87}$$

Substituting (7.87) this into the second necessary condition in (7.85), we obtain the following law of motion for investment:

$$\dot{I}(t) = \frac{1}{\phi''(I(t))}[(r + \delta)(1 + \phi'(I(t))) - f'(K(t))]. \tag{7.88}$$

Several interesting economic features emerge from this equation. First, as $\phi''(I)$ tends to zero, it can be verified that $\dot{I}(t)$ diverges, meaning that investment jumps to a particular value. In other words, it can be shown that this value is such that the capital stock immediately reaches its steady-state value (see Exercise 7.28). This result is intuitive. As $\phi''(I)$ tends to zero, $\phi(I)$ becomes linear. In this case, adjustment costs simply increase the cost of investment linearly and do not create any need for smoothing. In contrast, when $\phi''(I(t)) > 0$, there is a motive for smoothing, $\dot{I}(t)$ takes a finite value, and investment adjusts slowly. Therefore, as claimed above, adjustment costs lead to a smoother path of investment.

The behavior of investment and capital stock can now be analyzed using the differential equations (7.84) and (7.88). First, it can be verified easily that there exists a unique steady-state solution with $K > 0$. This solution involves a level of capital stock K^* for the firm and investment just sufficient to replenish the depreciated capital, $I^* = \delta K^*$. This steady-state level of capital satisfies the first-order condition (corresponding to the right-hand side of (7.88) being equal to zero):

$$f'(K^*) = (r + \delta)(1 + \phi'(\delta K^*)).$$

This first-order condition differs from the standard "modified golden rule" condition, which requires the marginal product of capital to be equal to the interest rate plus the depreciation rate, because an additional cost of having a higher capital stock is that there must be more investment to replenish depreciated capital. This is captured by the term $\phi'(\delta K^*)$. Since ϕ is strictly convex and f is strictly concave and satisfies the Inada conditions (from Assumption 2), there exists a unique value of K^* that satisfies this condition.

The analysis of dynamics in this case requires somewhat different ideas than those used in the basic Solow growth model (compare Theorems 2.4 and 2.5). In particular, instead of global stability in the K-I space, the correct concept is one of saddle-path stability. The reason for this is that instead of an initial value constraint, $I(0)$ is pinned down by a boundary condition at infinity, that is, to satisfy the transversality condition,

$$\lim_{t \to \infty} [\exp(-rt)q(t)K(t)] = 0.$$

Thus in the context of the current theory, with one state and one control variable, we should have a one-dimensional manifold (a curve) along which capital-investment pairs tend toward the steady state. This manifold is also referred to as the *stable arm*. The initial value of investment, $I(0)$, will then be determined so that the economy starts along this curve. In fact, if any capital-investment pair (rather than only pairs along this curve) were to lead to the steady state, we would not know how to determine $I(0)$; in other words, there would be an indeterminacy of equilibria. Mathematically, rather than requiring all eigenvalues of the linearized system to be negative, what we require now is saddle-path stability, which involves the number of (strictly) negative eigenvalues to be the same as the number of state variables.

This notion of saddle-path stability is central in most growth models. Let us now make these ideas more precise by considering the following generalizations of Theorems 2.4 and 2.5 (see Appendix B).

Theorem 7.18 (Saddle-Path Stability in Linear Systems) *Consider the following linear differential equation system:*

$$\dot{\mathbf{x}}(t) = \mathbf{A}\mathbf{x}(t) + \mathbf{b}, \qquad (7.89)$$

with initial value $\mathbf{x}(0)$*, where* $\mathbf{x}(t) \in \mathbb{R}^n$ *for all* t *and* $\mathbf{A}$ *is an* $n \times n$ *matrix. Let* $\mathbf{x}^*$ *be the steady state of the system, given by* $\mathbf{A}\mathbf{x}^* + \mathbf{b} = 0$*. Suppose that* $m \leq n$ *of the eigenvalues of* $\mathbf{A}$ *have* *negative real parts. Then there exists an m-dimensional subspace M of $\mathbb{R}^n$ such that starting from any $\mathbf{x}(0) \in M$, the differential equation (7.89) has a unique solution with $\mathbf{x}(t) \to \mathbf{x}^*$.*

Theorem 7.19 (Saddle-Path Stability in Nonlinear Systems)   *Consider the following nonlinear autonomous differential equation:*

$$\dot{\mathbf{x}}(t) = \mathbf{G}(\mathbf{x}(t)), \tag{7.90}$$

where $\mathbf{G} : \mathbb{R}^n \to \mathbb{R}^n$, and suppose that $\mathbf{G}$ is continuously differentiable, with initial value $\mathbf{x}(0)$. Let $\mathbf{x}^*$ be a steady state of this system, given by $\mathbf{G}(\mathbf{x}^*) = 0$. Define

$$\mathbf{A} = D\mathbf{G}(\mathbf{x}^*),$$

where $D\mathbf{G}(\mathbf{x}^*)$ is the Jacobian of $\mathbf{G}$ at $\mathbf{x}$. Suppose that $m \leq n$ of the eigenvalues of $\mathbf{A}$ have strictly negative real parts and the rest have strictly positive real parts. Then there exists an open neighborhood of $\mathbf{x}^*$, $\mathbf{B}(\mathbf{x}^*) \subset \mathbb{R}^n$, and an m-dimensional manifold $M \subset \mathbf{B}(\mathbf{x}^*)$ such that starting from any $\mathbf{x}(0) \in M$, the differential equation (7.90) has a unique solution with $\mathbf{x}(t) \to \mathbf{x}^*$.

Put differently, these two theorems state that when only a subset of the eigenvalues have negative real parts, a lower-dimensional subset of the original space leads to stable solutions. Fortunately, in this context this is exactly what we require, since $I(0)$ should adjust to place us on exactly such a lower-dimensional subspace (manifold) of the original space.

Armed with these theorems, we can now investigate the transitional dynamics in the q-theory of investment. To see that the equilibrium tends to this steady-state level of capital stock, let us plot (7.84) and (7.88) in the K-I space (Figure 7.1). The curve corresponding to $\dot{K} = 0$, (7.84), is upward sloping, since a greater level of capital stock requires more investment to replenish the depreciated capital. Above this curve, there is more investment than necessary for replenishment, so that $\dot{K} > 0$. Below this curve, $\dot{K} < 0$. On the other hand, the curve corresponding to $\dot{I} = 0$, (7.88), can be nonmonotonic. Nevertheless it is straightforward to verify that in the neighborhood of the steady state it is downward sloping (see Exercise 7.28). To the right of this curve, $f'(K)$ is lower, and thus $\dot{I} > 0$. To its left, $\dot{I} < 0$. The resulting phase diagram and the one-dimensional stable curve (manifold), often referred to as the stable arm, are shown in Figure 7.1.

Next we see that starting with an arbitrary level of capital stock, $K(0) > 0$, the unique solution involves an initial level of investment $I(0) > 0$, followed by convergence to the steady-state investment level of δK^* along the stable arm. In particular, it can easily be shown that when $K(0) < K^*$, $I(0) > I^*$, and it monotonically decreases toward I^* (see Exercise 7.28). This conlcusion is intuitive. Adjustment costs discourage large values of investment; thus the firm cannot adjust its capital stock to its steady-state level immediately. However, because of diminishing returns, the benefit of increasing the capital stock is greater when the level of capital stock is low. Therefore initially the firm is willing to incur greater adjustment costs to increase its capital stock and $I(0)$ is high. As capital accumulates and $K(t) > K(0)$, the benefit of boosting the capital stock declines, and the firm also reduces investment toward the steady-state investment level.

There are two ways of seeing why the solution corresponding to the stable arm in Figure 7.1—the one starting with $(K(0), I(0))$ and converging to (K^*, I^*)—is the unique solution. The first way, which is more rigorous and straightforward, is to use Theorem 7.14. As noted above, the conditions of this theorem hold in this problem. Thus we know that a path of capital and investment that satisfies the necessary conditions (i.e., a path starting with $(K(0), I(0))$ and converging to (K^*, I^*)) is the unique optimal path. By implication, other paths, for example, those that start in $I'(0)$ or $I''(0)$ in Figure 7.1, cannot be optimal.

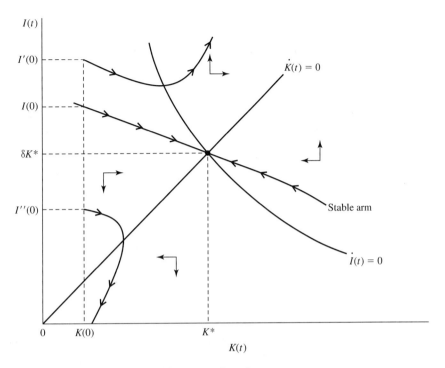

FIGURE 7.1 Dynamics of capital and investment in q-theory.

The second argument is common in the literature, though it is somewhat less complete and rigorous than the application of Theorem 7.14. It involves showing that initial investment levels other than $I(0)$ would violate either the transversality condition or the first-order necessary conditions. Consider, for example, $I'(0) > I(0)$ as the initial level of investment. The phase diagram Figure 7.1 makes it clear that starting from such a level of investment, the necessary conditions imply that $I(t)$ and $K(t)$ tend to infinity. It can be verified that in this case $q(t)K(t)$ would tend to infinity at a rate faster than r, violating the transversality condition $\lim_{t \to \infty} \exp(-rt)q(t)K(t) = 0$. To see this more explicitly, note that along a trajectory starting at $I'(0)$, $\dot{K}(t)/K(t) > 0$, and thus

$$\frac{d(q(t)K(t))/dt}{q(t)K(t)} \geq \frac{\dot{q}(t)}{q(t)} = \frac{\dot{I}(t)\phi''(I(t))}{1 + \phi'(I(t))} = r + \delta - f'(K(t))/(1 + \phi'(I(t))),$$

where the second relation uses (7.86) and (7.87), while the third substitutes from (7.88). As $K(t) \to \infty$, $f'(K(t)) \to 0$, implying that

$$\lim_{t \to \infty} \exp(-rt)q(t)K(t) \geq \lim_{t \to \infty} \exp(-rt) \exp((r + \delta)t) = \lim_{t \to \infty} \exp(\delta t) > 0,$$

violating the transversality condition.

In contrast, if we start with $I''(0) < I(0)$ as the initial level, $I(t)$ would tend to zero in finite time (as shown by the fact that the trajectories hit the horizontal axis) and $K(t)$ would also tend to zero (though not reaching it in finite time). After the time when $I(t) = 0$, we also have $q(t) = 1$ and thus $\dot{q}(t) = 0$ (from (7.86)). Moreover, by the Inada conditions, as $K(t) \to 0$, $f'(K(t)) \to \infty$. Consequently after $I(t)$ reaches 0, the necessary condition $\dot{q}(t) = (r + \delta)q(t) - f'(K(t))$ would be violated, which rules out paths starting with $I''(0) < I(0)$. The reason this argument is not entirely correct is that it is exploiting the necessary conditions for an interior continuous solution. However when $I(0) = 0$, we are no longer in the interior of the feasibility set for the control variable (here $\mathbb{R}_+$). Despite this potential problem, this argument is often used in many different contexts (including in the analysis of the neoclassical growth model). Nevertheless the same result can be established more rigorously, and the conclusion from this argument is valid (see Exercise 7.29 in this chapter and Exercise in 8.14 in the next chapter for the neoclassical growth model)

Let us next turn to the q-theory aspects. James Tobin argued that the value of an extra unit of capital to the firm divided by its replacement cost is a measure of the value of investment to the firm. In particular, when this ratio is high, the firm would like to invest more. In steady state, the firm settles where this ratio is 1 or close to 1. In our formulation, the costate variable $q(t)$ measures Tobin's q. To see this, let us denote the current (maximized) value of the firm when it starts with a capital stock of $K(t)$ by $V(K(t))$. The same arguments as above imply that

$$V'(K(t)) = q(t), \tag{7.91}$$

so that $q(t)$ measures exactly by how much a 1-dollar increase in capital raises the value of the firm.

In steady state, $\dot{q}(t) = 0$, so that $q^* = f'(K^*)/(r + \delta)$, which is approximately equal to 1 when $\phi'(\delta K^*)$ is small. Nevertheless, away from the steady state, $q(t)$ can differ significantly from this amount. When it is greater, this signals that there is need for further investments. Therefore in this model, Tobin's q, or alternatively the costate variable $q(t)$, signals when investment demand is high.

The q-theory of investment is one of the workhorse models of macroeconomics and finance, since proxies for Tobin's q can be constructed using stock market prices and book values of firms. When stock market prices are greater than book values, this corresponds to periods in which the firm in question has a high Tobin's q—meaning that the value of installed capital is greater than its replacement cost, which appears on the books. Nevertheless, whether this approach is satisfactory in practice is intensely debated, in part because Tobin's q does not contain all the relevant information when there are irreversibilities or fixed costs of investment, and also perhaps more importantly, what is relevant in theory (and in practice) is the marginal q, which corresponds to the marginal increase in value (as suggested by (7.91)). However, in the data most measures compute average q. The discrepancy between these two concepts can be large.

7.9 Taking Stock

This chapter has reviewed the basic tools of dynamic optimization in continuous time. By its nature, the chapter has been technical. The material covered here may have been less familiar to many readers than the discrete-time optimization methods presented in Chapter 6. Part of the difficulty arises from the fact that optimization in continuous time is with respect to functions, even when the horizon is finite (rather than with respect to vectors or infinite sequences as in the discrete-time case). This introduces a range of complications and some technical difficulties, which are not of great interest in the context of economic applications. As a result, this chapter has provided an overview of the main results, with an emphasis on those that are most useful in economic applications, together with some of the proofs. These proofs are included to provide readers with a sense of where the results come from and to develop a better intuition for the results.

It is useful to recap the main approach developed in this chapter. Most of the problems in economic growth and macroeconomics require the use of discounted infinite-horizon optimal control methods. Theorem 7.13 provides necessary conditions for an interior continuous solution to such problems. Theorem 7.14 provides sufficient conditions, related to the concavity of the maximized Hamiltonian, for such a solution to be a global or unique global maximum (these conditions require the existence of a candidate solution, since they use information on the costate variable of this solution). More importantly, the conditions in Theorem 7.14 are more straightforward to verify than those in Theorem 7.13 (in particular, than Assumption 7.1). Therefore the following strategy is used in the rest of this book:

1. Start with the necessary conditions in Theorem 7.13 to construct a *candidate solution*, which can be done even when Assumption 7.1 is not satisfied.

2. Once a candidate path has been located, verify that the concavity conditions in Theorem 7.14 are satisfied. If they are, then we have located a path that is optimal. If, in addition, the maximized Hamiltonian is strictly concave, then this solution is unique.

It is also worth noting that while the basic ideas of optimal control may be a little less familiar than those of discrete-time dynamic programming, these methods are used in much of growth theory and in other areas of macroeconomics. Moreover, while some problems naturally lend themselves to analysis in discrete time, other problems become easier in continuous time. Some argue that this is indeed the case for growth theory. Regardless of whether one agrees with this assessment, it is important to have a good command of both discrete-time and continuous-time models in macroeconomics, since it should be the context and economic questions that dictate which type of model is used, not the force of habit. This consideration motivated my choice of giving roughly equal weight to the two sets of techniques.

There is another reason for studying optimal control. The most powerful theorem in optimal control, Pontryagin's Maximum Principle, is as much an economic result as a mathematical one. As discussed in this chapter, the Maximum Principle has a very natural interpretation both in terms of maximizing flow returns plus the value of the stock and in terms of an asset value equation for the value of the maximization problem. These economic intuitions are not only useful in illustrating the essence of this mathematical technique, but they also provide a useful perspective on a large set of questions that involve the use of dynamic optimization techniques in macroeconomics, labor economics, finance, and other fields.

This chapter also concludes our exposition of the foundations of growth theory, which comprised general equilibrium foundations of aggregative models as well as an introduction to the mathematical tools necessary for dynamic economic analysis. I next turn to economically more substantive issues.

7.10 References and Literature

The main material covered in this chapter is the topic of many excellent applied mathematics textbooks. The purpose here has been to provide a review of the results that are most relevant for economists, together with simplified versions of the most important proofs. The first part of the chapter is closer to the theory of the calculus of variations, because it makes use of variational arguments combined with continuity properties. Nevertheless, most economists do not need to study the calculus of variations in detail, both because it has been superseded by optimal control theory and because most of the natural applications of the calculus of variations are in physics and the other natural sciences. The interested reader can look at Gelfand and

Fomin (2000). Chiang (1992) provides a readable and simple introduction to the calculus of variations with economic examples.

The theory of optimal control was originally developed by Pontryagin et al. (1962). For this reason, the main necessary condition is also referred to as the Pontryagin's (Maximum) Principle. The type of problem considered here (and in economics more generally) is referred to as the "Lagrange problem" in optimal control theory. The Maximum Principle is generally stated either for the somewhat simpler so-called Meyer problem or the more general Bolza problem, though all of these problems are essentially equivalent, and when the problem is formulated in vector form, one can easily go back and forth between these different problems by simple transformations. A more modern approach, which underlies the necessary conditions used in infinite-horizon problems, is developed in Rockefeller (1971).

There are several books with varying levels of difficulty dealing with optimal control. Many of these books are not easy to read but are also not entirely rigorous in their proofs. An excellent source that provides an advanced and complete treatment is Fleming and Rishel (1975). The first part of this book provides a complete (but rather different) proof of Pontryagin's Maximum Principle and various applications. This book also provides a number of theorems on existence and continuity of optimal controls, though for more specialized problems than those covered in Theorem 7.15 (or necessary for economic applications). The proof of existence of solutions in Section 7.6 combines certain ideas from Baum's (1976) proof, which in turn extends Cesari's (1966) classic proof of existence of solutions to infinite-horizon problems, with part of the proof in Fleming and Rishel (1975, Chapter 3). In particular, the last part of Theorem 7.15, which established the measurability of control $\hat{\mathbf{y}}(t)$, can be shown in greater detail using a similar line of argument to that in Fleming and Rishel (which involves the use of Lusin's Theorem). In the economics literature, existence theorems are provided in Magill (1981) and Romer (1986b), but under somewhat more restrictive conditions and using a different method of proof.

A deeper understanding of sufficient conditions for existence of solutions and the structure of necessary conditions can be gained from the excellent (but abstract and difficult) book by Luenberger (1969). The results in this book are general enough to cover both discrete-time and continuous-time dynamic optimization. Luenberger also gives a very good sense of why maximization in function spaces is different from finite-dimensional maximization and when such infinite-dimensional maximization problems may fail to have solutions.

The main theorems in the infinite-horizon case (Theorems 7.9, 7.13, 7.11, and 7.14) have been presented with the terminal value constraint $\lim_{t \to \infty} b(t)x(t) \geq x_1$. This is important, since the constraint on household assets in the competitive equilibrium of the neoclassical growth model (the no-Ponzi condition) takes this form. The standard results with terminal value constraints of the form $\lim_{t \to \infty} x(t) \geq x_1$ cannot be applied directly. Many authors seem to use the following reasoning: ignore the terminal value constraint; apply the Maximum Principle, and then if necessary, use the terminal value constraint at the end. While this procedure typically gives the "right" answer, it is not mathematically correct. The Maximum Principle cannot be applied in economic problems without a terminal value constraint, since in that case a solution typically fails to exist (see, e.g., Exercise 8.2 in the next chapter). Therefore the application of the Maximum Principle to these problems is vacuous. A slight strengthening of the terminal value constraints of the Maximum Principle circumvents this problem.

Note also that in contrast to the standard practice in economic growth and macroeconomics, the emphasis here has been mostly on the sufficiency results for concave problems, in particular, on Theorem 7.14. This approach has been taken because the standard form of the Maximum Principle only gives necessary conditions for interior continuous solutions. But it is not easy to verify that such a solution exists. Since most problems in economics are concave, Theorem 7.14

or other sufficiency results (e.g., Theorems 7.5, 7.6, 7.8, or 7.11) are easy to apply and enable us to verify that a candidate solution that satisfies the Maximum Principle is indeed a solution and achieves the global optimum. It should also be noted that all of the sufficiency results here have been stated and proved assuming that the control function $y(t)$ (or $\mathbf{y}(t)$) is continuous. The logic of the proof is very similar when these functions are piecewise continuous, and a formal proof along these lines is provided in Seierstad and Sydsaeter (1977).

Books that develop the theory of optimal control with economic applications may be more accessible for economists. The best reference is Seierstad and Sydsaeter (1987). This book is not as rigorous as Fleming and Rishel (1975) and in fact does not contain detailed proofs. Nevertheless it does provide a number of useful results and is more interesting to read for economists. It also shows how the results can be applied to economic problems. Other references in economics are Kamien and Schwartz (1981) and Leonard and Van Long (1992). Another classic book is Arrow and Kurz (1970), which covers the same material and also presents rich economic insights on growth theory and related problems. This book also states Arrow's Sufficiency Theorem, which first appeared in Arrow (1968). This theorem strengthens Mangasarian's Sufficiency Theorem, stated in Theorem 7.5, which appears in Mangasarian (1966).

Two recent books on applications of optimal control in economics, Weitzman (2003) and Caputo (2005), are somewhat more accessible. My treatment of the sufficiency results here is similar to Caputo (2005). Weitzman (2003) provides a lively discussion of the applications of the Maximum Principle, especially in the context of environmental economics and the depletion of natural resources.

There is some confusion in the literature over the role of the transversality condition. The example provided in Section 7.4 shows that the stronger transversality condition, which is very useful in many applications, does not always hold. Halkin (1974) was the first to provide an example to show this failure. The weaker form of the transversality condition (7.56) was derived in Michel (1982). His results are similar to those of Theorem 7.12, though Theorem 7.12 is stated under stronger assumptions. Michel instead considers stationary problems, assumes that the payoff function is nonnegative, and imposes an additional technical assumption that is not easy to verify. Michel (1982) also provides another set of sufficient conditions for the stronger transversality condition (7.69). More general (weaker) transversality conditions appropriate for economic models are presented in Benveniste and Scheinkman (1982) and Araujo and Scheinkman (1983). Theorem 7.14 is stated under somewhat different, and easy to check, assumptions.

The original economic interpretation of the Maximum Principle appeared in Dorfman (1969). The interpretation here builds on the discussion by Dorfman, but also extends it based on the no-arbitrage interpretation of asset values in the HJB equation. This interpretation of HJB is well known in many areas of macroeconomics and labor economicsis. Weitzman (2003) also provides an economic interpretation for the Maximum Principle related to the HJB equation.

The classic reference for exploitation of a nonrenewable resource is Hotelling (1931). Weitzman (2003) provides a detailed treatment and a very insightful discussion. Dasgupta and Heal (1979) and Conrad (1999) are also useful references for applications of similar ideas to sustainability and environmental economics. Classic references on investment with costs of adjustment and the q-theory of investment include Tobin (1969) and Hayashi (1982). Detailed treatments of the q-theory of investment can be found in any graduate-level macroeconomics textbook, for example, Blanchard and Fischer (1989) or Romer (2006), as well as in Dixit and Pindyck's (1994) book on investment under uncertainty and Caballero's (1999) survey. Caballero (1999) also includes a critique of the q-theory.

7.11 Exercises

7.1 Consider the problem of maximizing (7.2) subject to (7.3) and (7.4), as in Section 7.1. Suppose that $\lambda(t)$ is defined by (7.12). Suppose also that given the pair $(\hat{x}(t), \hat{y}(t))$, there exists a time interval (t', t'') with $t' < t''$ such that

$$\dot{\lambda}(t) \neq -\left[f_x(t, \hat{x}(t), \hat{y}(t)) + \lambda(t)g_x(t, \hat{x}(t), \hat{y}(t))\right] \text{ for all } t \in (t', t'').$$

Prove that the pair $(\hat{x}(t), \hat{y}(t))$ could not be an interior continuous solution containing the optimal value of (7.2). Using this argument establish that (7.12), (7.11), and $\lambda(t_1) = 0$ are necessary conditions for an interior solution $(\hat{x}(t), \hat{y}(t))$. [Hint: you may wish to assume that $g_y \neq 0$ to simplify the derivation.]

* 7.2 Let $(\hat{x}(t), \hat{y}(t))$ be a solution to (7.2). Prove that the maximized Hamiltonian defined in (7.20) and evaluated at $\hat{x}(t)$, $M(t, \hat{x}(t), \lambda(t))$, is differentiable in x and satisfies $\dot{\lambda}(t) = -M_x(t, \hat{x}(t), \lambda(t))$ for all $t \in [0, t_1]$. [Hint: recall that the solution is assumed to be continuous.]

7.3 The key equation of the calculus of variations is the Euler-Lagrange equation, which characterizes the solution to the following problem (under regularity conditions similar to those of Theorem 7.2):

$$\max_{x(t)} \int_0^{t_1} F(t, x(t), \dot{x}(t))dx$$

subject to $x(t) = 0$. Suppose that F is differentiable in all of its arguments and an interior continuously differentiable solution exists. The so-called Euler-Lagrange equation, which provides the necessary conditions for a solution, is

$$\frac{\partial F(t, x(t), \dot{x}(t))}{\partial x(t)} - \frac{\partial^2 F(t, x(t), \dot{x}(t))}{\partial \dot{x}(t)\partial t} = 0.$$

Derive this equation from Theorem 7.2. [Hint: define $y(t) \equiv \dot{x}(t)$.]

7.4 This exercise asks you to use the Euler-Lagrange equation derived in Exercise 7.3 to solve the canonical problem that motivated Euler and Lagrange, that of finding the shortest distance between two points in a plane. In particular, consider a two-dimensional plane and two points on this plane with coordinates (z_0, u_0) and (z_1, u_1). We would like to find the curve that has the shortest length that connects these two points. Such a curve can be represented by a function $x : \mathbb{R} \to \mathbb{R}$ such that $u = x(z)$, together with initial and terminal conditions $u_0 = x(z_0)$ and $u_1 = x(z_1)$. It is also natural to require that this curve $u = x(z)$ be smooth, which corresponds to requiring that the solution be continuously differentiable so that $x'(z)$ exists.

To solve this problem, observe that the (arc) length along the curve x can be represented as

$$A[x(z)] \equiv \int_{z_1}^{z_2} \sqrt{1 + [x'(z)]^2}dz.$$

The problem is to minimize this object by choosing $x(z)$.

Without loss of any generality let us take $(z_0, u_0) = (0, 0)$ and let $t = z$ to transform the problem into a more familiar form, which becomes that of maximizing

$$-\int_0^{t_1} \sqrt{1 + [x'(t)]^2}dt.$$

Prove that the solution to this problem requires that

$$\frac{d\left[x'(t)(1 + (x'(t))^2)\right]}{dt} = 0.$$

Show that this is possible only if $x''(t) = 0$, so that the shortest path between two points is a straight line.

7.5 Prove Theorem 7.2, paying particular attention to constructing feasible variations that ensure $x(t_1, \varepsilon) = x_1$ for all ε in some neighborhood of 0. What happens if there are no such feasible variations?

7.6 (a) Provide an expression for the initial level of consumption $c(0)$ as a function of $a(0)$, w, r, and β in Example 7.1.

(b) What is the effect of an increase in $a(0)$ on the initial level of consumption $c(0)$? What is the effect on the consumption path?

(c) How would the consumption path change if instead of a constant level of labor earnings, w, the individual faced a time-varying labor income profile given by $[w(t)]_{t=0}^{1}$? Explain in detail the reasoning for the answer.

7.7 Prove that if a function $\phi(x, y)$ is jointly [strictly] concave in (x, y), then $\Phi = \max_y \phi(x, y)$ is [strictly] concave in x.

* 7.8 Prove a version of Theorem 7.6 corresponding to Theorem 7.2. [Hint: instead of $\lambda(t_1) = 0$, the proof should exploit the fact that $x(1) = \hat{x}(1) = x_1$.]

7.9 Prove Theorem 7.3. [Hint: show that if the solution involves $x(t_1) > x_1$, then $\lambda(t_1)$ must be equal to 0, but not necessarily so when $x(t_1) = x_1$.]

7.10 Consider the problem of maximizing (7.2) subject to (7.3) and (7.4), and the additional constraint that $y(t) \geq 0$ for all t (instead of $y(t) \in \text{Int } \mathcal{Y}(t)$). Assume as usual that f and g are continuously differentiable. Show that the necessary conditions for optimality are: $x(0) = x_0$,

$$H_y(t, \hat{x}(t), \hat{y}(t), \lambda(t)) \leq 0 \quad \text{for all } t \in [0, t_1],$$

$$\dot{\lambda}(t) = -H_x(t, \hat{x}(t), \hat{y}(t), \lambda(t)) \quad \text{for all } t \in [0, t_1],$$

$$\dot{x}(t) = H_\lambda(t, \hat{x}(t), \hat{y}(t), \lambda(t)) \quad \text{for all } t \in [0, t_1],$$

and $\lambda(t_1) = 0$, with the Hamiltonian $H(t, x, y, \lambda)$ given by (7.16). Moreover the Hamiltonian $H(t, x, y, \lambda)$ also satisfies the Maximum Principle that for all $t \in [0, t_1]$,

$$H(t, \hat{x}(t), \hat{y}(t), \lambda(t)) \geq H(t, \hat{x}(t), y, \lambda(t)) \quad \text{for all } y \text{ such that } y(t) \geq 0 \quad \text{for all } t.$$

* 7.11 Prove Theorem 7.7.

7.12 Prove Theorem 7.8.

7.13 Prove Theorem 7.11. [Hint: apply the proof of Theorem 7.6, except that when the expression with $\dot{\lambda}$ is integrated by parts, there is an additional term, which you should show increases the right-hand side of the inequality corresponding to (7.24).]

7.14 Prove that in the discounted infinite-horizon optimal control problem considered in Theorem 7.13, conditions (7.65)–(7.67) are necessary. [Hint: use Theorem 7.9.]

7.15 Consider a finite-horizon continuous-time maximization problem in which the objective function is

$$W(x(t), y(t)) = \int_0^{t_1} f(t, x(t), y(t))dt,$$

with $x(0) = x_0$ and $t_1 < \infty$, and the constraint equation is

$$\dot{x}(t) = g(t, x(t), y(t)).$$

Imagine that t_1 is also a choice variable.

(a) Show that $W(x(t), y(t))$ can be written as

$$W(x(t), y(t)) = \int_0^{t_1} [H(t, x(t), y(t)) + \dot{\lambda}(t)x(t)]dt - \lambda(t_1)x(t_1) + \lambda(0)x_0,$$

where $H(t, x, y) \equiv f(t, x(t), y(t)) + \lambda(t)g(t, x(t), y(t))$ is the Hamiltonian, and $\lambda(t)$ is the costate variable.

(b) Now suppose that the pair $(\hat{x}(t), \hat{y}(t))$ together with terminal date $\hat{t}_1$ constitutes a solution for this problem. Consider the following class of variations:

$$y(t, \varepsilon) = \hat{y}(t) + \varepsilon\eta(t) \text{ for } t \in [0, \hat{t}_1],$$

and

$$y(t, \varepsilon) = \hat{y}(\hat{t}_1) + \varepsilon\eta(t) \text{ for } t \in [\hat{t}_1, \hat{t}_1 + \varepsilon\Delta t], \, t_1 = \hat{t}_1 + \varepsilon\Delta t.$$

Denote the corresponding path of the state variable by $x(t, \varepsilon)$. Evaluate $W(x(t, \varepsilon), y(t, \varepsilon))$ at this variation. Explain why this variation is feasible for ε sufficiently small.

(c) Show that for a feasible variation,

$$\frac{dW(x(t, \varepsilon), y(t, \varepsilon))}{d\varepsilon}\bigg|_{\varepsilon=0} = \int_0^{\hat{t}_1} [H_x(t, \hat{x}(t), \hat{y}(t)) + \dot{\lambda}(t)]\frac{\partial x(t, \varepsilon)}{\partial\varepsilon}dt$$

$$+ \int_0^{\hat{t}_1} H_y(t, \hat{x}(t), \hat{y}(t))\eta(t)dt$$

$$+ H(\hat{t}_1, \hat{x}(\hat{t}_1), \hat{y}(\hat{t}_1))\Delta t - \lambda(\hat{t}_1)\frac{\partial x(\hat{t}_1, \varepsilon)}{\partial\varepsilon} + \lambda(\hat{t}_1)\dot{x}(\hat{t}_1)\Delta t.$$

(d) Explain why the expression in part c has to be equal to zero.

(e) What happens if you take limit $\hat{t}_1 \to \infty$ in part c?

7.16 Consider the discounted infinite-horizon problem, with $f(t, x(t), y(t)) = \exp(-\rho t)f(x(t), y(t))$ and $g(t, x(t), y(t)) = g(x(t), y(t))$. Prove that if an admissible pair $(\hat{x}(t), \hat{y}(t))_{t\geq 0}$ is optimal starting at $t = 0$, with initial condition $x(0) = x_0$, then $(\hat{x}(t), \hat{y}(t))_{t\geq s}$ is also admissible and optimal for the problem starting at $t = s$, with initial condition $x(s) = x_0$.

* 7.17 Consider the general infinite-horizon optimal control problem, where the payoff function is $f(t, x, y)$. Generalize the transversality condition (7.69) in Theorem 7.13 to this case by strengthening Assumption 7.1 so that there exists $M < \infty$ such that $|f_y(t, x, y)| \leq M\exp(-\kappa t)$ for some $\kappa > 0$.

7.18 Consider a modified version of the Hotelling resource extraction problem

$$\max \int_0^\infty \exp(-\rho t)\log y(t)dt$$

subject to

$$\dot{x}(t) = -y(t),$$

$$x(0) = x_0 > 0, \text{ and } \lim_{t\to\infty} x(t) \geq x_1 \in (0, x_0),$$

with $\rho > 0$ and $y \in (0, +\infty)$.

(a) Show that this problem does not satisfy Assumption 7.1.

(b) Set up the current-value Hamiltonian $\hat{H}(x, y, \mu)$ with costate variable $\mu(t)$ and show that the Maximum Principle implies that

$$\mu(t) = \mu(0) \exp(\rho t),$$

and

$$y(t) = \mu(0)^{-1} \exp(-\rho t)$$

for some $\mu(0) > 0$.

(c) Show that the weaker transversality condition (7.68) is satisfied.
[Hint: $\lim_{t \to \infty}[\exp(-\rho t)\hat{H}(x, y, \mu)] = \lim_{t \to \infty}[\exp(-\rho t)(-\log \mu(0) - \rho t - 1)] = 0$.]

(d) Show that the stronger transversality condition (7.69) is not satisfied.
[Hint: $\lim_{t \to \infty}[\exp(-\rho t)\mu(t)x(t)] = \mu(0)x_1 > 0$.]

(e) Explain why the stronger transversality condition does not hold here and how it should be modified. [Hint: try $\lim_{t \to \infty}[\exp(-\rho t)\mu(t)(x(t) - x_1)] = 0$.]

* 7.19 Consider the following discounted infinite-horizon maximization problem:

$$\max \int_0^\infty \exp(-\rho t)[2y(t)^{1/2} + \log(x(t))]\, dt,$$

subject to $x(0) = \rho^{-1}$ and

$$\dot{x}(t) = -\rho x(t)y(t).$$

(a) Show that this problem satisfies all the assumptions of Theorem 7.14.

(b) Set up the current-value Hamiltonian, and derive the necessary conditions with the costate variable $\mu(t)$.

(c) Show that the following is a solution: $y(t) = 1$, $x(t) = \exp(-\rho t)/\rho$, and $\mu(t) = \exp(\rho t)$ for all t.

(d) Show that the solution in part c violates the "naïve transversality condition" that $\lim_{t \to \infty} \exp(-\rho t)\mu(t) = 0$. What is the appropriate transversality condition in this case?

7.20 Consider the problem of consuming a nonrenewable resource in Example 7.3. Show that the solution outlined in that example satisfies the transversality condition (7.56).

7.21 This exercise generalizes Example 7.2. Consider the following optimal growth model without discounting:

$$\max \int_0^\infty [u(c(t)) - u(c^*)]\, dt$$

subject to

$$\dot{k}(t) = f(k(t)) - c(t) - \delta k(t),$$

with initial condition $k(0) > 0$, and c^* defined as the golden rule consumption level

$$c^* = f(k^*) - \delta k^*,$$

where k^* is the golden rule capital-labor ratio given by $f'(k^*) = \delta$.

(a) Set up the Hamiltonian for this problem with costate variable $\lambda(t)$.

(b) Characterize the solution to this optimal growth problem.

(c) Show that the transversality condition $\lim_{t \to \infty} \lambda(t)k(t) = 0$ is not satisfied at the solution. Explain why.

7.22   Consider the infinite-horizon optimal control problem given by the maximization of (7.32) subject to (7.33) and (7.34). Suppose that the problem has a quasi-stationary structure, so that

$$f(t, x, y) \equiv \beta(t)f(x, y),$$

and

$$g(t, x, y) \equiv g(x, y),$$

where $\beta(t)$ is the discount factor that applies to returns that are an interval of time t away from the present.

(a) Set up the Hamiltonian, and characterize the necessary conditions for this problem.

(b) Prove that the solution to this problem is time consistent (meaning that the solution chosen at some date s cannot be improved upon at some future date s' by changing the continuation plans after this date) if and only if $\beta(t) = \exp(-\rho t)$ for some $\rho \geq 0$.

(c) Interpret the result in part b and explain how the conclusion is different from that of Lemma 7.1.

7.23   Consider the following maximization problem:

$$\max_{x(t), y(t)} \int_0^1 f(x(t), y(t))dt$$

subject to

$$\dot{x}(t) = y(t)^2,$$

$x(0) = 0$, and $x(1) = 0$, where $y(t) \in \mathbb{R}$ and f is an arbitrary continuously differentiable function. Show that the unique solution to this maximization problem does not satisfy the necessary conditions in Theorem 7.2. Explain why, and relate your answer to Exercise 7.5.

* 7.24   Consider the following infinite-horizon utility maximization problem

$$\max \int_0^\infty \exp(-\rho t)u(c(t))dt,$$

subject to initial capital $k(0)$ and law of motion of capital given by

$$\dot{k}(t) = \begin{cases} f(k(t)) - \delta k(t) - c(t) & \text{if } f(k(t)) - c(t) \geq \underline{k} \\ 0 & \text{if } f(k(t)) - c(t) < \underline{k}, \end{cases}$$

where $\underline{k} > \delta k^*$ for $k^* = f^{-1}(\rho + \delta)$ is a minimum investment size requirement. Suppose that $k(0) = k^*$. Show that there does not exist a solution to this optimal control problem. Explain why and relate your answer to Theorem 7.15. [Hint: Show that $k(t) = k^*$ for all t, which would have been the optimal policy without the minimum investment size requirement, is not feasible. Then show that the value function that would obtain for $k(t) = k^*$ can be approximated arbitrarily closely by a policy that alternates between $f(k(t)) - c(t) = 0$ for an interval of length $\Delta_1 > 0$ and $f(k(t)) - c(t) = \underline{k}$ for an interval of length $\Delta_2 > 0$ so as to keep $k(t)$ close to k^* on average. Then argue that any admissible pair $(k(t), c(t))$ can always be improved by a policy of this kind.]

7.25   (a) Consider the optimal growth problem in Section 7.7. Show that if $u(c) = \log c$, part 3 of Assumption 7.1 is violated.

(b) Suppose next that $u : \mathbb{R}_+ \setminus \{0\} \to \mathbb{R}$ is continuous, strictly increasing, and concave, and that u is continuously differentiable on $[\varepsilon, +\infty)$ for some $\varepsilon > 0$ sufficiently small. Show that if the modified problem in which $c(t)$ is restricted to be in $[\varepsilon, +\infty)$ has an optimal control, where

$c(t) > \varepsilon$ for all t, then this optimal control also constitutes a solution to the original problem, where $u : \mathbb{R}_+ \setminus \{0\} \to \mathbb{R}$. [Hint: use Theorem 7.14.]

(c) Show that for any optimal growth problem as described in Section 7.7, there exists $\varepsilon > 0$ such that the optimal control involves $c(t) > \varepsilon$ for all t.

7.26 Consider the following continuous-time discounted infinite-horizon problem:

$$\max \int_0^\infty \exp(-\rho t) u(c(t)) dt$$

subject to $x(0) > 0$ and

$$\dot{x}(t) = g(x(t)) - c(t).$$

Suppose that $u(\cdot)$ is strictly increasing and strictly concave, with $\lim_{c \to \infty} u'(c) = 0$ and $\lim_{c \to 0} u'(c) = \infty$, and $g(\cdot)$ is increasing and strictly concave, with $\lim_{x \to \infty} g'(x) = 0$ and $\lim_{x \to 0} g'(x) = \infty$.

(a) Set up the current-value Hamiltonian and derive the Euler equations for an optimal path.

(b) Show that the standard transversality condition and the Euler equations are necessary and sufficient for a solution.

(c) Characterize the optimal path of solutions and their limiting behavior.

7.27 Consider the q-theory model of Section 7.8.

(a) Verify that when $k \in [\varepsilon, \bar{k}]$, Assumption 7.1 is satisfied.

(b) Consider the modified problem with $k \in [\varepsilon, \bar{k}]$. Show that if there exists a solution to this modified problem with $k(t) > \varepsilon$ for all t, then it is also a solution to the original problem, where $k \in \mathbb{R}_+$. [Hint: use the same line of argument as in Exercise 7.25.]

(c) Show that there always exists $\varepsilon > 0$ sufficiently small such that the solution to the modified problem involves $k(t) > \varepsilon$ for all t.

7.28 (a) In the q-theory of investment discussed in Section 7.8, prove that when $\phi''(I) = 0$ (for all I), investment jumps so that the capital stock reaches its steady-state value K^* immediately.

(b) Prove that as shown in Figure 7.1, the curve for (7.88) is downward sloping in the neighborhood of the steady state.

(c) As an alternative to the diagrammatic analysis of Figure 7.1, linearize (7.84) and (7.88), and show that in the neighborhood of the steady state this system has one positive and one negative eigenvalue. Explain why this result implies that optimal investment plans tend toward the stationary solution (steady state).

(d) Prove that when $K(0) < K^*$, $I(0) > I^*$ and $I(t) \downarrow I^*$.

(e) Derive the equations for the q-theory of investment when the adjustment cost takes the form $\phi(I/K)$. How does this form affect the steady-state marginal product of capital?

(f) What will the optimal path look like when investment is irreversible, in the sense that there is an additional constraint, $I \geq 0$?

7.29 Consider a candidate optimal path that reaches $I = 0$ at some finite time t'. Construct the following deviation: for $\Delta > 0$ small and $T > t'$ large, set $I(t) = \Delta$ for all $t \geq T$. Using this deviation, show that this candidate path cannot be optimal. [Hint: let the capital stock in the candidate optimal path be $K(t)$, so that the change in profits from this deviation is approximately equal to

$$\Delta \Pi = \Delta \times \int_T^\infty \exp(-rt)[f'(K(t)) - 1] dt,$$

and show that for T sufficiently large, $f'(K(t)) > 1$ for all $t \geq T$ and thus $\Delta \Pi > 0$.]

PART III

NEOCLASSICAL GROWTH

This part of the book covers the basic workhorse models of economic growth. I start with the infinite-horizon neoclassical growth model, which has already been discussed in the previous three chapters. A closely related model is the baseline overlapping generations model of Samuelson and Diamond, which is the topic of Chapter 9. Despite the similarities between the two models, they have quite different normative and positive implications, and each model may be appropriate for different sets of issues. It is therefore important to discuss both in detail.

This part of the book also presents an introduction to models that endogenize human capital investments. Human capital plays an increasingly important role in the analysis of economic growth and in macroeconomics. These models allow us to study the interactions between human capital and growth and to link macroeconomic approaches to growth to microdata on schooling and returns to education.

Finally, Chapter 11 introduces the simplest models of sustained economic growth. These are contained in this part of the book rather than the next, because they are models of sustained growth without technological change. Despite their simplicity, these models lead to a number of important economic insights and provide a good introduction to the issues discussed in the Part IV of the book.

8

The Neoclassical Growth Model

We are now ready to start our analysis of the standard neoclassical growth model (also known as the Ramsey or Cass-Koopmans model). This model differs from the Solow model in only one crucial respect: it explicitly models the consumer side and endogenizes savings. In other words, it introduces household optimization. Beyond its use as a basic growth model, this model has become a workhorse for many areas of macroeconomics, including the analysis of fiscal policy, taxation, business cycles, and even monetary policy.

Since both the basic equilibrium and optimal growth models in discrete time have already been presented as applications of dynamic programming in Chapter 6, much of this chapter focuses on the continuous-time neoclassical growth model. Section 8.6 provides the characterization of the competitive equilibrium in discrete time.

8.1 Preferences, Technology, and Demographics

8.1.1 Basic Environment

Consider an infinite-horizon economy in continuous time and suppose that the economy admits a *normative* representative household (as defined in Theorem 5.3) with instantaneous utility function

$$u(c(t)). \tag{8.1}$$

The following standard assumption on this utility function is maintained throughout the book unless stated otherwise.

Assumption 3 (Neoclassical Preferences) *The instantaneous utility function $u(c)$ is defined on $\mathbb{R}_+$ or $\mathbb{R}_+\backslash\{0\}$. It is strictly increasing, concave, and twice differentiable, with derivatives $u'(c) > 0$ and $u''(c) < 0$ for all c in the interior of its domain.*

More explicitly, the reader may wish to suppose that the economy consists of a set of identical households (with measure normalized to 1). Each household has an instantaneous

287

utility function given by (8.1). Population within each household grows at the rate n, starting with $L(0) = 1$, so that total population in the economy is

$$L(t) = \exp(nt). \tag{8.2}$$

All members of the household supply their one unit of labor inelastically.

Our baseline assumption is that the household is fully altruistic toward all of its future members and always makes the allocations of consumption (among household members) cooperatively. Then the utility (objective) function of each household at time $t = 0$ can be written as

$$\int_0^\infty \exp(-(\rho - n)t)u(c(t))dt, \tag{8.3}$$

where $c(t)$ is consumption per capita at time t; ρ is the subjective discount rate; and the effective discount rate is $\rho - n$, because the household derives utility from the consumption per capita of its additional members in the future as well. More specifically, the form of the objective function (8.3) can be derived as follows. First, given the strict concavity of $u(\cdot)$ and the assumption that within-household allocation decisions are cooperative, each household member has an equal consumption (Exercise 8.1). Thus each member consumes $c(t) \equiv C(t)/L(t)$ at date t, where $C(t)$ is total consumption and $L(t)$ is the size of the representative household (equal to total population, since the measure of households is normalized to 1). This implies that the household receives a utility of $u(c(t))$ per household member at time t, or a total utility of $L(t)u(c(t)) = \exp(nt)u(c(t))$. Since utility at time t is discounted back to time 0 with a discount rate of $\exp(-\rho t)$, we obtain the expression in (8.3).

Let us also assume the following.

Assumption 4′ (Discounting) $\rho > n$.

This condition ensures that there is *discounting* of future utility streams. Otherwise, (8.3) would typically have infinite value, which would not correspond to an interesting economic model of household choice (e.g., the local nonsatiation assumption of Section 5.6 would be violated, and standard techniques would no longer be sufficient to characterize optimal plans). Assumption 4′ ensures that in the model without growth, discounted utility is finite. When the discussion is extended to sustained growth, this condition will be strengthened to Assumption 4 (see Section 8.7).

Let us start with an economy without any technological progress. Factor and product markets are competitive, and the production possibilities set of the economy is represented by the aggregate production function

$$Y(t) = F(K(t), L(t)),$$

which is a simplified version of the production function (2.1) used in the Solow growth model in Chapter 2. In particular, there is now no technology term (labor-augmenting technological change is introduced below). As in the Solow model, Assumptions 1 and 2 (see Chapter 2) are imposed throughout. The constant returns to scale feature enables us to work with the per capita production function $f(\cdot)$ such that output per capita is given by

$$y(t) \equiv \frac{Y(t)}{L(t)}$$

$$= F\left(\frac{K(t)}{L(t)}, 1\right)$$

$$\equiv f(k(t)),$$

where, as before,

$$k(t) \equiv \frac{K(t)}{L(t)}. \tag{8.4}$$

Competitive factor markets then imply that the rental rate of capital and the wage rate at time t are given by, respectively,

$$R(t) = F_K(K(t), L(t)) = f'(k(t)), \tag{8.5}$$

and

$$w(t) = F_L(K(t), L(t)) = f(k(t)) - k(t)f'(k(t)). \tag{8.6}$$

The demand side is somewhat more complicated, since each household solves a continuous-time optimization problem in deciding how to use their assets and allocate consumption over time. To prepare for this, let us denote the asset holdings of the representative household at time t by $\mathcal{A}(t)$. Then the law of motion for the total assets of the household is

$$\dot{\mathcal{A}}(t) = r(t)\mathcal{A}(t) + w(t)L(t) - c(t)L(t), \tag{8.7}$$

where $c(t)$ is consumption per capita of the household, $r(t)$ is the risk-free market rate of return on assets, and $w(t)L(t)$ is the flow of labor income earnings of the household. Defining per capita assets as

$$a(t) \equiv \frac{\mathcal{A}(t)}{L(t)},$$

dividing (8.7) by $L(t)$, substituting for the definition of $a(t)$, and using the fact that $L(t)$ grows at the rate n (see (8.2)), the law of motion of per capita assets is obtained as

$$\dot{a}(t) = (r(t) - n)a(t) + w(t) - c(t). \tag{8.8}$$

In practice, household assets can consist of (claims to) capital stock $K(t)$, which the households rent to firms, and government bonds $B(t)$. In models with uncertainty, households would have a portfolio choice between the capital stock of the corporate sector and riskless bonds (typically assumed to be supplied by the government). Bonds play an important role in models with incomplete markets, allowing households to smooth idiosyncratic shocks. Since these bonds are in zero net supply, in the aggregate $B(t) = 0$, and thus market clearing implies that assets per capita must be equal to the capital stock per capita. That is,

$$a(t) = k(t). \tag{8.9}$$

Because there is no uncertainty here, I ignore government bonds (until Chapter 17).[1] Since household assets are the same as the capital stock and capital depreciates at the rate δ, the market rate of return on assets is

$$r(t) = R(t) - \delta. \tag{8.10}$$

---

1. In particular, if bonds were present, by a no-arbitrage argument, they would have exactly the same rate of return as capital and thus would be redundant.

8.1.2 The Natural Debt Limit and the No-Ponzi Game Condition

Equation (8.8) is a flow constraint and is not sufficient for our modeling of dynamic competitive equilibria for two reasons. First, as already discussed in detail in Example 6.5 in Chapter 6, this flow constraint is not sufficient as a proper budget constraint on household behavior. One can impose a lower bound on assets, such as $a(t) \geq 0$ for all t to turn (8.8) into a proper infinite-horizon budget constraint, but this condition would be too restrictive (see Exercise 8.30). And if we do not ensure that there is a proper budget constraint on household behavior, the analysis of household maximization leads to nonsensical results. In particular, Exercise 8.2 shows that any solution to the maximization of (8.3) with respect to (8.8)—without an additional condition—involves $a(t)$ becoming arbitrarily negative for all t; that is, the representative household would hold an arbitrarily negative asset position. But then the market clearing condition (8.9) would imply that $k(t) = a(t)$ becomes arbitrarily negative, which violates the feasibility constraint that $k(t)$ has to be nonnegative. Clearly the flow budget constraint (8.8) is not sufficient to capture the full set of constraints on household behavior.

Second, as already discussed in Chapter 5, it is important to ensure that the sequential trading formulation adopted in dynamic (competitive) macro models corresponds to the appropriate Arrow-Debreu equilibrium (where, recall, all trades take place at the initial date). This requires that households face the same budget constraint in the sequential trading and in the Arrow-Debreu equilibrium formulations. For example, if we were to impose $a(t) \geq 0$ for all t, we would obtain a well-defined solution to the household maximization problem, but we would have broken the equivalence between the sequential trading formulation used in dynamic macro models and the underlying Arrow-Debreu equilibrium (see Exercise 8.30).

There are two ways to proceed. The first is to impose the no-Ponzi condition, which turns out to be both the more flexible and also the theoretically more rigorous approach. The second involves imposing a natural debt limit (as in Example 6.5). Since this second approach is used quite widely, I start with a brief discussion of the natural debt limit, emphasizing when it can be used and when it ceases to be useful.

Recall that the natural debt limit requires that $a(t)$ should never become so negative that the household cannot repay its debts even if it henceforth chooses zero consumption. Using (8.8) and assuming that the household does not consume from time t onward, the natural debt limit for time t is found to be

$$a(t) \geq - \int_t^{\infty} w(s) \exp\left(- \int_t^s (r(z) - n)dz \right) ds. \tag{8.11}$$

Equation (8.11) is the direct analogue of the discrete-time natural debt limit (6.44) in Chapter 6. In particular, the right-hand side is the negative of the net present discounted value of labor income for the household. Exercise 8.3 asks you to work through a more detailed derivation of this condition. Any path of consumption and assets for the household that violates (8.11) is not feasible (unless we allow for bankruptcy). Thus the problem of the representative household can be expressed as the maximization of (8.3) subject to (8.8) and (8.11). In fact, one could simply impose the limiting version of this constraint,

$$\lim_{t \to \infty} a(t) \geq \hat{a} \equiv - \lim_{t \to \infty} \left[\int_t^{\infty} w(s) \exp\left(- \int_t^s (r(z) - n)dz \right) ds \right]. \tag{8.12}$$

This is because, if the natural debt limit is violated for some $t' < \infty$, then (8.12) cannot be satisfied either (see Exercise 8.4). There is therefore no loss of generality in imposing (8.12) instead of (8.11).

There are two problems with the natural debt limit. First, it does not create the most direct link between dynamic macro models with sequential trading and the corresponding Arrow-Debreu economy. Second, it is not useful when we look at economies with sustained growth (because in that case $\hat{a} = -\infty$; see Exercise 8.8). For this reason, we next turn to the no-Ponzi condition, which overcomes both of these problems.

To start with, let us write the lifetime budget constraint of a household as

$$
\int_0^T c(t)L(t) \exp\left(\int_t^T r(s)\,ds\right) dt + \mathcal{A}(T)
$$

$$
= \int_0^T w(t)L(t) \exp\left(\int_t^T r(s)\,ds\right) dt + \mathcal{A}(0) \exp\left(\int_0^T r(s)\,ds\right)
$$

(8.13)

for some arbitrary $T > 0$, with $\mathcal{A}(T)$ denoting the household's asset position at time T. This constraint states that the household's asset position at time T is given by its total income plus initial assets minus expenditures, all carried forward to date T units. Differentiating this expression with respect to T and dividing by $L(t)$ gives (8.8) (see Exercise 8.5).

Now imagine that (8.13) applies to a finite-horizon economy ending at date T. At this point, the household cannot have negative asset holdings; thus (8.13) must hold with $\mathcal{A}(T) \geq 0$. However, inspection of the flow budget constraint (8.8) makes it clear that this constraint does not guarantee $\mathcal{A}(T) \geq 0$. Therefore in the finite horizon we also need to impose $\mathcal{A}(T) \geq 0$ as an additional *terminal value constraint*. In fact, it can be verified easily that $\mathcal{A}(T) \geq 0$ is exactly the condition that ensures that the household's lifetime budget constraint in this finite-horizon economy holds (as an inequality). Thus this constraint is the right one for ensuring the equivalence of the sequential trading and the Arrow-Debreu formulations.

In the infinite-horizon case, we need a similar constraint. The appropriate restriction is the no-Ponzi condition (or the no-Ponzi game condition). It takes the form

$$
\lim_{t \to \infty} \left[a(t) \exp\left(-\int_0^t (r(s) - n)\,ds\right) \right] \geq 0.
$$

(8.14)

This condition is stated as an inequality to ensure that the representative household does not asymptotically tend to a negative wealth. Intuitively, without (8.14), there is no proper lifetime budget constraint on the representative household (and by implication on any of the households in the economy), and they all increase their consumption by borrowing to such a level that feasibility is violated. Such an allocation could clearly not be an equilibrium. In the finite-horizon economy, the constraint $\mathcal{A}(T) \geq 0$ rules out this behavior. In the infinite-horizon economy, this role is played by (8.14). The reader may also wish to think of these constraints as resulting from the relationship between the representative household and the financial markets. Financial markets must impose a proper lifetime budget constraint on households, otherwise they would lose money.

At a more fundamental level, the no-Ponzi condition (8.14), as the infinite-horizon analogue of terminal value constraint $\mathcal{A}(T) \geq 0$, ensures the equivalence between the sequential trading formulation of dynamic competitive equilibria and the Arrow-Debreu formulation. To see this more clearly, multiply both sides of (8.13) by $\exp\left(-\int_0^T r(s)\,ds\right)$ to obtain

$$\int_0^T c(t)L(t) \exp\left(-\int_0^t r(s)\,ds\right) dt + \exp\left(-\int_0^T r(s)\,ds\right)\mathcal{A}(T)$$

$$= \int_0^T w(t)L(t)\exp\left(-\int_0^t r(s)\,ds\right) dt + \mathcal{A}(0).$$

Then divide everything by $L(0)$, and note that $L(t)$ grows at the rate n, to obtain

$$\int_0^T c(t)\exp\left(-\int_0^t (r(s)-n)\,ds\right) dt + \exp\left(-\int_0^T (r(s)-n)\,ds\right) a(T)$$

$$= \int_0^T w(t)\exp\left(-\int_0^t (r(s)-n)\,ds\right) dt + a(0).$$

Now take the limit as $T \to \infty$ and use the no-Ponzi condition (8.14) to obtain

$$\int_0^\infty c(t)\exp\left(-\int_0^t (r(s)-n)\,ds\right) dt \leq a(0) + \int_0^\infty w(t)\exp\left(-\int_0^t (r(s)-n)\,ds\right) dt, \tag{8.15}$$

which requires the discounted sum of expenditures to be no greater than initial income plus the discounted sum of labor income. This argument establishes the equivalence between the lifetime budget constraint (or the single time $t = 0$ budget constraint) in the Arrow-Debreu formulation and the flow constraints combined with the terminal value constraint in the form of the no-Ponzi condition (8.14) in the sequential trading formulation.

The name "no-Ponzi condition" for (8.14) comes from the chain-letter or pyramid schemes, which are sometimes called Ponzi games, in which an individual can continuously borrow from a competitive financial market (or more often, from unsuspecting souls that become part of the chain-letter scheme) and pay his or her previous debts using current borrowings. The consequence of this scheme would be that the asset holding of the individual would tend to $-\infty$ over time, violating feasibility at the economy level.

To complete this discussion, let us momentarily return to the finite-horizon problem. In this case, financial markets would impose $\mathcal{A}(T) \geq 0$. But the household itself would never choose $\mathcal{A}(T) > 0$ (because of local nonsatiation, as defined in Section 5.6), so the budget constraint could be simplified and written with $\mathcal{A}(T) = 0$, which essentially means that the lifetime budget constraint of the household holds as equality. In the same way, when the lifetime budget constraint in the infinite-horizon economy holds as equality, the no-Ponzi condition can be written in a stronger form as:

$$\lim_{t \to \infty}\left[a(t)\exp\left(-\int_0^t (r(s)-n)\,ds\right)\right] = 0. \tag{8.16}$$

We will see below that household optimization (in particular, the transversality condition of the households) combined with (8.14) will imply (8.16).

8.2 Characterization of Equilibrium

8.2.1 Definition of Equilibrium

Let us now define an equilibrium in this dynamic economy. I provide two definitions, each emphasizing different aspects of the nature of the equilibrium. In what follows, I typically make use of the second definition, though the first one is particularly useful in clarifying what a competitive equilibrium corresponds to conceptually.

As background for the first definition, recall that we have described the environment in terms of demographics, preferences, and technology. Given this description, we can ask the question of how resources should be allocated in this environment. One way of doing this is by vesting all power to allocate resources in a single body, for example, a social planner (or in less fortunate situations, a dictator). The optimal growth problem, already introduced in the previous two chapters and discussed further in Section 8.3, focuses on the allocation of resources by a social planner wishing to maximize the utility of the representative household. The competitive equilibrium, instead, imposes a different set of *institutions*—competitive markets for factors and goods, and private ownership of capital and labor. It then allows households to make their own choices given market prices. The first definition states this explicitly.

Definition 8.1   *A* competitive equilibrium *of the neoclassical growth model consists of paths of consumption, capital stock, wage rates, and rental rates of capital, $[C(t), K(t), w(t), R(t)]_{t=0}^{\infty}$, such that the representative household maximizes its utility given initial asset holdings (capital stock) $K(0) > 0$ and taking the time path of prices $[w(t), R(t)]_{t=0}^{\infty}$ as given; firms maximize profits taking the time path of factor prices $[w(t), R(t)]_{t=0}^{\infty}$ as given; and factor prices $[w(t), R(t)]_{t=0}^{\infty}$ are such that all markets clear.*

This definition states that households and firms act in a price-taking manner and that competitive markets clear. While Definition 8.1 emphasizes the important conceptual aspects of a competitive equilibrium, it is often more mathematically convenient to define an equilibrium by incorporating some of the equilibrium relationships. This is done in the next definition, which imposes the equations that the factor prices $[w(t), R(t)]_{t=0}^{\infty}$ must satisfy. In addition, this definition expresses the key objects in terms of per capita terms, which also facilitates further characterization.

Definition 8.2   *A* competitive equilibrium *of the neoclassical growth model consists of paths of per capita consumption, capital-labor ratio, wage rates, and rental rates of capital, $[c(t), k(t), w(t), R(t)]_{t=0}^{\infty}$, such that factor prices $[w(t), R(t)]_{t=0}^{\infty}$ are given by (8.5) and (8.6), and the representative household maximizes (8.3) subject to (8.8) and (8.14) given initial per capita asset holdings (capital-labor ratio) $k(0) > 0$ and factor prices $[w(t), R(t)]_{t=0}^{\infty}$ (with the rate of return on assets $r(t)$ given by (8.10)).*

Since this definition of equilibrium already incorporates some of the equilibrium behavior, one might have a preference for Definition 8.1 on theoretical grounds. Nevertheless definitions of equilibria similar to Definition 8.2 are often more convenient to work with and are more widely used, because they explicitly state the equations corresponding to the equilibrium and thus facilitate the characterization of allocations that solve the specified maximization problem subject to the relevant constraints. In the remainder of the book, I follow the standard practice of using definitions of equilibria similar to Definition 8.2, though the reader should bear in mind that it is derived from the more primitive Definition 8.1 by incorporating some of the equilibrium conditions.

Finally, recall also that an equilibrium corresponds to the entire time path of real quantities and the associated prices. We may sometimes focus on the steady-state equilibrium, but an equilibrium always refers to the entire path.

8.2.2 Household Maximization

Let us start with the problem of the representative household. From the definition of equilibrium we know that this is to maximize (8.3) subject to (8.8) and (8.14). This is a special case of the discounted infinite-horizon control problems discussed in Theorem 7.13 in the previous chapter. Our strategy is once again to apply Theorem 7.13 to obtain a candidate solution and then to verify that it is a solution by using Theorem 7.14.[2] Let us first set up the current-value Hamiltonian:

$$\hat{H}(t, a, c, \mu) = u(c(t)) + \mu(t) [w(t) + (r(t) - n) a(t) - c(t)],$$

with state variable a, control variable c, and current-value costate variable μ. This problem is closely related to that of optimal growth discussed in Section 7.7 in the previous chapter, but with two main differences: first, the rate of return on assets is time varying; second, the terminal value constraint is represented by the no-Ponzi condition (8.14), which is different from the transversality condition in Section 7.7 (which was $\lim_{t \to \infty} k(t) \geq 0$).

Now applying Theorem 7.13, the conditions for a candidate interior solution are

$$\hat{H}_c(t, a, c, \mu) = u'(c(t)) - \mu(t) = 0, \tag{8.17}$$

$$\hat{H}_a(t, a, c, \mu) = \mu(t)(r(t) - n) = -\dot{\mu}(t) + (\rho - n)\mu(t), \tag{8.18}$$

and the transition equation (8.8). The transversality condition (the equivalent of (7.69) in the previous chapter) is

$$\lim_{t \to \infty} \left[\exp\left(-(\rho - n) t\right) \mu(t)a(t) \right] = 0. \tag{8.19}$$

The transversality condition is written in terms of the current-value costate variable, which is more convenient given the rest of the necessary conditions.

Next, it is straightforward to verify that (8.17), (8.18), and (8.19) indeed characterize a solution. The current-value Hamiltonian $\hat{H}(t, a, c, \mu)$ is the sum of a concave function of c and a linear function of (a, c). Therefore it is concave in (a, c). To be able to apply Theorem 7.14, it only remains to show that for any feasible $(a(t), c(t))$, $\lim_{t \to \infty} \left[\exp\left(-(\rho - n) t\right) \mu(t)a(t) \right] \geq 0$. Substituting for $\mu(t)$ from (8.24) below, this again requires that

$$\lim_{t \to \infty} \left[a(t) \exp\left(-\int_0^t (r(s) - n)ds \right) \right] \geq 0.$$

But, this inequality is identical to the no-Ponzi condition (8.14). Thus no feasible $(a(t), c(t))$ can violate this condition. Theorem 7.14 therefore implies that any solution to (8.17)–(8.19) is a solution to the household maximization problem. Moreover, Exercise 8.11 shows that this solution is unique.

---

2. An argument similar to that in Section 7.7 can be used to show that the conditions in Theorem 7.13 are also necessary (see, e.g., Exercise 8.7). Nevertheless, the approach of using Theorem 7.13 to generate a candidate solution and then verifying optimality with Theorem 7.14 is both more direct and simpler.

Let us now use these equations to derive a more explicit characterization. First, rearrange the second condition (8.18) to obtain:

$$\frac{\dot{\mu}(t)}{\mu(t)} = -(r(t) - \rho), \tag{8.20}$$

which states that the multiplier changes depending on whether the rate of return on assets is currently greater than or less than the discount rate of the household.[3]

Next, the first necessary condition (8.17) implies that

$$u'(c(t)) = \mu(t). \tag{8.21}$$

Since u' is continuously differentiable, when (8.18) holds, $c(t)$ is also differentiable in time, and thus we can differentiate the previous expression with respect to time and divide by $\mu(t)$ to obtain

$$\frac{u''(c(t))c(t)}{u'(c(t))} \frac{\dot{c}(t)}{c(t)} = \frac{\dot{\mu}(t)}{\mu(t)}.$$

Substituting this expression into (8.20) yields the continuous-time consumption Euler equation

$$\frac{\dot{c}(t)}{c(t)} = \frac{1}{\varepsilon_u(c(t))} (r(t) - \rho), \tag{8.22}$$

where

$$\varepsilon_u(c(t)) \equiv -\frac{u''(c(t))c(t)}{u'(c(t))} \tag{8.23}$$

is the elasticity of the marginal utility $u'(c(t))$. Equation (8.22) is closely related to the consumption Euler equation (6.39) derived in the context of the discrete-time problem, as well as to the consumption Euler equation in continuous time with constant interest rates in Example 7.1 in the previous chapter. As in (6.39), it states that consumption grows over time when the discount rate is less than the rate of return on assets. Equation (8.22) also specifies the speed at which consumption grows in response to a gap between this rate of return and the discount rate. This speed is related to the elasticity of marginal utility of consumption, $\varepsilon_u(c(t))$. The interpretation of $\varepsilon_u(c(t))$ and of this equation is discussed further below.

Next, integrating equation (8.20) yields

$$\mu(t) = \mu(0) \exp\left(-\int_0^t (r(s) - \rho) \, ds\right)$$
$$= u'(c(0)) \exp\left(-\int_0^t (r(s) - \rho) \, ds\right), \tag{8.24}$$

where the first line uses the form of the solutions to linear nonhomogeneous differential equations (see Section B.4 in Appendix B), and the second line uses (8.17) evaluated at time

3. This condition also implies that $\mu(t)$ is continuously differentiable only when $r(t)$ is a continuous function of time. Once we impose market clearing together with the time path of $k(t)$ consistent with household maximizing behavior, $r(t)$ will indeed be a continuous function of time.

$t = 0$. Substituting (8.24) into the transversality condition (8.19) yields

$$\lim_{t \to \infty} \left[\exp\left(-(\rho - n) \, t \right) a(t) u' \left(c(0) \right) \exp\left(-\int_0^t \left(r(s) - \rho \right) ds \right) \right] = 0$$

$$\lim_{t \to \infty} \left[a(t) \exp\left(-\int_0^t \left(r(s) - n \right) ds \right) \right] = 0. \quad (8.25)$$

The second line follows by dividing the first by noting that $u'\left(c(0)\right) > 0$ and combining $\exp\left(-(\rho - n)\, t \right)$ with $\exp\left(-\int_0^t \left(r(s) - \rho \right) ds \right)$.

An immediate implication of (8.25) is that household maximization, together with the transversality condition (8.19), implies that the no-Ponzi condition (8.14) must hold as equality (i.e., (8.16) must apply). This result is not surprising; it states that the lifetime budget constraint of the individual should hold as equality. In the context of the Arrow-Debreu equilibrium, this is an implication of the local nonsatiation assumption—the household should never leave any money unspent. The derivation also emphasizes that it is the transversality condition that implies that the no-Ponzi condition (8.14)—which, from the lifetime budget constraint, is formulated as an inequality—should hold as equality. It is therefore the transversality condition that makes sure that the household uses its resources to maximize its utility even in the very far future and thus implies the infinite-horizon analogue of the condition that the household should not end its planning horizon with unspent resources.

This derivation and the corresponding discussion show the intimate connection between the transversality condition (8.19) and the stronger (equality) version of the no-Ponzi condition (8.16). However, it is important to emphasize that these two conditions are *not* the same thing (even though some such claims are made in the literature and in textbooks); (8.19) is an optimality condition, whereas (8.16) is a (lifetime) budget constraint holding as equality.

Since $a(t) = k(t)$, the transversality condition of the representative household can alternatively be written as

$$\lim_{t \to \infty} \left[k(t) \exp\left(-\int_0^t \left(r(s) - n \right) ds \right) \right] = 0. \quad (8.26)$$

Equation (8.26) emphasizes that the transversality condition requires the discounted market value of the capital stock in the very far future to be equal to zero. This "market value" version of the transversality condition is both intuitive and often more convenient to work with than (8.19). In particular, suppose that there exists a limiting interest rate r^* such that $r(t) \to r^*$. Then the transversality condition is satisfied only when $r^* > n$ (provided that $k(t)$ does not limit to zero). This conclusion is intuitive, since if it were the case that $r^* < n$, households would have infinite wealth (recall (8.15)). Thus $r^* > n$ is a natural condition to expect. We will see in the next chapter that this condition is closely connected to the issue of dynamic efficiency discussed in that chapter.

As noted above, Theorem 7.14 and the preceding analysis implies that the pair $(\hat{a}(t), \hat{c}(t))$ that satisfies (8.22) and (8.25) is the unique solution to the household maximization problem. Therefore any pair $(\hat{k}(t), \hat{c}(t))$ that satisfies (8.22) and (8.26) corresponds to a competitive equilibrium. A full competitive equilibrium is then given by the pair $(\hat{k}(t), \hat{c}(t))$ combined with market clearing prices. Recall that equilibrium prices are given by (8.5) and (8.6). From (8.10), this implies that the interest rate $r(t)$ is given by

$$r(t) = f'(k(t)) - \delta. \quad (8.27)$$

Substituting (8.27) into the household's maximization problem, we obtain

$$\frac{\dot{c}(t)}{c(t)} = \frac{1}{\varepsilon_u(c(t))} \left(f'(k(t)) - \delta - \rho \right) \tag{8.28}$$

as the equilibrium version of the consumption growth equation (8.22). Substituting (8.28) into (8.26), the transversality condition becomes

$$\lim_{t \to \infty} \left[k(t) \exp\left(- \int_0^t \left(f'(k(s)) - \delta - n \right) ds \right) \right] = 0. \tag{8.29}$$

Conditions (8.28) and (8.29) are expressed only in terms of the path of the capital-labor ratio and fully characterize a competitive equilibrium. Moreover we will see shortly that these equilibrium conditions are identical to the Euler equation and the transversality condition that characterize the optimal growth path (see Exercise 8.11).

8.2.3 Consumption Behavior

Let us now return to the dynamics of the representative household's consumption. First, recall that the Euler equation (8.22) relates the slope of the consumption profile of the representative household to $\varepsilon_u(c(t))$, which was defined as the elasticity of the marginal utility function, $u'(c)$. Notice, however, that $\varepsilon_u(c(t))$ is not only the elasticity of marginal utility, but even more importantly, it is also the inverse of the *intertemporal elasticity of substitution*, which plays a crucial role in macro models. The intertemporal elasticity of substitution regulates the willingness of households to substitute consumption (or labor or any other attribute that yields utility) over time. The elasticity of marginal utility of consumption between the dates t and $s > t$ is defined as

$$\sigma_u(t, s) = - \frac{d \log(c(s)/c(t))}{d \log(u'(c(s))/u'(c(t)))}.$$

As $s \downarrow t$,

$$\sigma_u(t, s) \to \sigma_u(t) = - \frac{u'(c(t))}{u''(c(t))c(t)} = \frac{1}{\varepsilon_u(c(t))}. \tag{8.30}$$

This result is not surprising, since the concavity of the utility function $u(\cdot)$—or equivalently, the elasticity of marginal utility—determines how willing households are to substitute consumption over time.

It is also possible to derive some further results on the consumption behavior of households. Notice that the term $\exp(- \int_0^t r(s)\, ds)$ is a present-value factor that converts a unit of income at time t to a unit of income at time 0. In the special case where $r(s) = r$, this factor would be equal to $\exp(-rt)$. But more generally, we can define an average interest rate between dates 0 and t as

$$\bar{r}(t) = \frac{1}{t} \int_0^t r(s)\, ds. \tag{8.31}$$

In that case, the conversion factor between dates 0 and t is $\exp(-\bar{r}(t)t)$, and the transversality condition can be written as

$$\lim_{t \to \infty} \left[\exp\left(- (\bar{r}(t) - n)\, t \right) a(t) \right] = 0. \tag{8.32}$$

Now integrating (8.22), we obtain (recall again Section B.4 in Appendix B):

$$c(t) = c(0) \exp\left(\int_0^t \frac{r(s) - \rho}{\varepsilon_u(c(s))} \, ds\right)$$

as the consumption function. Therefore, given the initial consumption level $c(0)$, the path of consumption is determined. In the special case where $\varepsilon_u(c(s))$ is constant (e.g., $\varepsilon_u(c(s)) = \theta$) this equation simplifies to

$$c(t) = c(0) \exp\left(\left(\frac{\bar{r}(t) - \rho}{\theta}\right) t\right),$$

The lifetime budget constraint can also be written as

$$\int_0^\infty c(t) \exp(-(\bar{r}(t) - n)t) \, dt = a(0) + \int_0^\infty w(t) \exp(-(\bar{r}(t) - n)t) \, dt.$$

Substituting for $c(t)$ into this lifetime budget constraint in this isoelastic case, we obtain

$$c(0) = \left[\int_0^\infty \exp\left(-\left(\frac{(1-\theta)\bar{r}(t)}{\theta} - \frac{\rho}{\theta} + n\right)t\right)dt\right]$$
$$\times \left[a(0) + \int_0^\infty w(t) \exp(-(\bar{r}(t) - n)t)\right] \qquad (8.33)$$

as the initial value of consumption. Once the initial consumption level is determined, the Euler equation (8.22) gives the entire path of utility-maximizing consumption of the household. The determination of the initial level of consumption is discussed further in Section 8.5.

8.2.4 Using the Natural Debt Limit

Let us now return to the alternative approach of using the natural debt limit (8.12) instead of the no-Ponzi condition (8.14). In principle, $\hat{a}$ in (8.12) could be equal to minus infinity. However, the same steps as in Exercise 8.2 show that this value of $\hat{a}$ would violate the feasibility constraint that $k(t)$ has to be nonnegative. Thus a well-defined equilibrium must involve $\hat{a} > -\infty$. We will see below that factor prices satisfy $\lim_{t\to\infty} r(t) > n$ and $\lim_{t\to\infty} w(t) = w \geq 0$, and this is sufficient for $\hat{a} > -\infty$ (see Exercise 8.9). When $\hat{a} > -\infty$, the maximization of (8.3) subject to (8.8) and (8.11) again satisfies the conditions of Theorems 7.13 and 7.14. Therefore the alternative approach of modeling the household's problem as maximizing (8.3) subject to (8.8) and (8.11) leads to the same characterization as the one using the no-Ponzi condition (see Exercise 8.10). It can then be verified that in equilibrium $\lim_{t\to\infty} r(t) > n$ and $\lim_{t\to\infty} w(t) = w \geq 0$, so that $\hat{a} > -\infty$, and the approach is indeed valid. However, as Exercise 8.8 shows, this approach does not work when there is sustained growth, as in Section 8.7.

8.3 Optimal Growth

Before further characterizing the competitive equilibrium, let us turn to the optimal growth problem. Recall that, since we have assumed the existence of a normative representative household, the optimal growth problem is equivalent to characterizing the capital-labor ratio and consumption path that maximizes the utility of this representative household. This problem can be written as

$$\max_{[k(t),c(t)]_{t=0}^{\infty}} \int_0^{\infty} \exp(-(\rho-n)t)u(c(t))\, dt$$

subject to

$$\dot{k}(t) = f(k(t)) - (n+\delta)k(t) - c(t),$$

and $k(0) > 0$.[4] As noted in Chapter 5, versions of the First and Second Welfare Theorems for economies with a continuum of commodities would imply that the solution to this problem should be the same as the equilibrium growth problem of the previous section. However in the present context there is no need to appeal to these theorems, since it is straightforward to characterize both allocations and show their equivalence.

To do this, let us once again set up the current-value Hamiltonian, which in this case takes the form

$$\hat{H}(k, c, \mu) = u(c(t)) + \mu(t)[f(k(t)) - (n+\delta)k(t) - c(t)],$$

with state variable k, control variable c, and current-value costate variable μ (the argument t is omitted since this is a stationary problem). With the same argument as in Section 7.7 in the previous chapter, it can be shown that Theorems 7.13 and 7.14 can be applied to this problem and characterize the unique optimal growth path. Consequently the necessary and sufficient conditions for this optimal path are

$$\hat{H}_c\,(k, c, \mu)\; = 0 = u'\,(c(t)) - \mu(t), \tag{8.34}$$

$$\hat{H}_k\,(k, c, \mu)\; = -\dot{\mu}(t) + (\rho - n)\,\mu(t) = \mu(t)\left(f'(k(t)) - \delta - n\right),$$

$$\lim_{t\to\infty}\left[\exp\left(-(\rho-n)\,t\right)\mu(t)k(t)\right] = 0.$$

Repeating the same steps as before, we can combine the first two optimality conditions in (8.34) and obtain (8.28) for the path of consumption of the representative household. In addition, once again integrating the second first-order condition, we have

$$\mu(t) = \mu(0)\exp\left(-\int_0^t \left(f'(k(s)) - \delta - \rho\right) ds\right).$$

Combining this equation with the first condition in (8.34) evaluated at $t = 0$ implies that $\mu(0) = u'\,(c(0)) > 0$. Substituting this expression into the transversality condition (the third condition in (8.34)), simplifying, and canceling out $\mu(0) > 0$, we obtain (8.29).

These steps establish that the competitive equilibrium is a Pareto optimum and that the optimal growth path can be decentralized as a competitive equilibrium. This result is stated in the next proposition.

---

4. In the case where the infinite-horizon problem represents dynastic utilities as discussed in Chapter 5, this specification presumes that the social planner gives the same weights to different generations as the current dynastic decision maker. Naturally, there also exist Pareto optimal allocations with unequal distribution of consumption across households or generations, though these are less natural and less interesting in the context of economies with a normative representative household.

Proposition 8.1 *In the neoclassical growth model described in Section 8.1, with Assumptions 1, 2, 3, and 4′, the equilibrium is Pareto optimal and coincides with the optimal growth path maximizing the utility of the representative household.*

8.4 Steady-State Equilibrium

As in Chapter 2, a steady-state equilibrium is defined as an equilibrium path in which the capital-labor ratio, consumption, and output are constant. The steady-state equilibrium (and, also, by the equivalence between the two problems, the stationary solution to the optimal growth problem) is straightforward to characterize. Steady state requires that consumption per capita is constant, thus

$$\dot{c}(t) = 0.$$

From (8.28), this expression implies that regardless of the exact utility function (as long as $f(k^*) > 0$), we must have a capital-labor ratio k^* that satisfies

$$f'(k^*) = \rho + \delta, \tag{8.35}$$

which is the equivalent of the steady-state relationship in the discrete-time optimal growth model.[5] Equation (8.35) pins down the steady-state capital-labor ratio as a function only of the production function, the discount rate, and the depreciation rate. The steady-state condition (8.35) corresponds to the modified golden rule, rather than to the golden rule in the Solow model (see Exercise 8.12). The modified golden rule involves a level of the capital stock that does not maximize steady-state consumption, because earlier consumption is preferred to later consumption. This preference is because of discounting, which means that the objective is not to maximize steady-state consumption, but instead involves giving a higher weight to earlier consumption.

Note also at this point that Assumption 4′ ($\rho > n$) and (8.35) together imply that the steady-state interest rate is

$$r^* = f'(k^*) - \delta > n \tag{8.36}$$

and thus satisfies the natural requirement that $r^* > n$. Since in steady state the wage rate is $w^* = f(k^*) - k^* f'(k^*) < \infty$, it can also be verified that households have finite wealth at all points in time.

Given k^*, the steady-state consumption level is also straightforward to determine as

$$c^* = f(k^*) - (n + \delta)k^*, \tag{8.37}$$

which is similar to the consumption level in the basic Solow model. Moreover, given Assumption 4′, a steady state where the capital-labor ratio and thus output are constant necessarily satisfies the transversality condition. This analysis therefore establishes the following result.

Proposition 8.2 *In the neoclassical growth model described in Section 8.1, with Assumptions 1, 2, 3, and 4′, the steady-state equilibrium capital-labor ratio k^* is uniquely determined*

---

5. In addition, there again exists another, economically uninteresting steady state at $k = 0$. As in Chapter 2, I ignore this steady state throughout. Moreover, as in Chapter 2, starting with any $k(0) > 0$ the economy will always tend to the steady-state capital-labor ratio k^* given by (8.35).

by (8.35) and is independent of the instantaneous utility function. The steady-state consumption per capita c^* is given by (8.37).

As with the basic Solow growth model, there are also several straightforward comparative static results that show how the steady-state values of capital-labor ratio and consumption per capita change with the underlying parameters. For this reason, let us again parameterize the production function as

$$f(k) = A\tilde{f}(k),$$

where $A > 0$, so that A is again a shift parameter, with greater values corresponding to greater productivity of factors. Since $f(k)$ satisfies the regularity conditions imposed above, so does $\tilde{f}(k)$.

Proposition 8.3 *Consider the neoclassical growth model described in Section 8.1, with Assumptions 1, 2, 3, and 4′, and suppose that $f(k) = A\tilde{f}(k)$. Denote the steady-state level of the capital-labor ratio by $k^*(A, \rho, n, \delta)$ and the steady-state level of consumption per capita by $c^*(A, \rho, n, \delta)$ when the underlying parameters are A, ρ, n and δ. Then*

$$\frac{\partial k^*(A, \rho, n, \delta)}{\partial A} > 0, \ \frac{\partial k^*(A, \rho, n, \delta)}{\partial \rho} < 0, \ \frac{\partial k^*(A, \rho, n, \delta)}{\partial n} = 0, \text{ and } \frac{\partial k^*(A, \rho, n, \delta)}{\partial \delta} < 0;$$

$$\frac{\partial c^*(A, \rho, n, \delta)}{\partial A} > 0, \ \frac{\partial c^*(A, \rho, n, \delta)}{\partial \rho} < 0, \ \frac{\partial c^*(A, \rho, n, \delta)}{\partial n} < 0, \text{ and } \frac{\partial c^*(A, \rho, n, \delta)}{\partial \delta} < 0.$$

Proof. See Exercise 8.17. ∎

The new results here relative to the basic Solow model concern the comparative statics with respect the discount rate ρ. In particular, instead of the saving rate, it is now the discount rate that affects the rate of capital accumulation. There is a close link between the discount rate in the neoclassical growth model and the saving rate in the Solow model. Loosely speaking, a lower discount rate implies greater patience and thus greater savings. In the model without technological progress, the steady-state saving rate can be computed as

$$s^* = \frac{(n + \delta)k^*}{f(k^*)}, \tag{8.38}$$

where k^* is the steady-state capital-labor ratio given in (8.35). Exercise 8.19 investigates the relationship between the discount rate, the saving rate, and the steady-state per capita consumption level.

A further interesting result is that the rate of population growth has no impact on the steady-state capital-labor ratio, which contrasts with the basic Solow model. Exercise 8.16 shows that this result depends on the way in which intertemporal discounting takes place. Another important result, which is more general, is that k^* and thus c^* do not depend on the instantaneous utility function $u(\cdot)$. The form of the utility function only affects the transitional dynamics but has no impact on steady states. This is because the steady state is determined by the modified golden rule. This result is not true in the presence of technological change and sustained growth.

8.5 Transitional Dynamics and Uniqueness of Equilibrium

Recall that transitional dynamics in the basic Solow model are given by a single differential equation with an initial condition. This is no longer the case, since the equilibrium is determined by two differential equations, repeated here for convenience:

$$\dot{k}(t) = f(k(t)) - (n + \delta)k(t) - c(t), \tag{8.39}$$

and

$$\frac{\dot{c}(t)}{c(t)} = \frac{1}{\varepsilon_u(c(t))} \left(f'(k(t)) - \delta - \rho \right). \tag{8.40}$$

Moreover, we have an initial condition $k(0) > 0$ and also a boundary condition at infinity, which takes the form

$$\lim_{t \to \infty} \left[k(t) \exp \left(- \int_0^t \left(f'(k(s)) - \delta - n \right) ds \right) \right] = 0. \tag{8.41}$$

As already discussed in the context of the q-theory of investment in the previous chapter (see Section 7.8), this combination of boundary conditions consisting of an initial condition and a transversality condition is quite typical for economic problems involving the behavior of both state and control variables. The appropriate notion of stability is again that of saddle-path stability introduced in Theorems 7.18 and 7.19 (instead of the stability results in Theorems 2.4 and 2.5). In particular, the consumption level (or equivalently the costate variable μ) is the control variable, and its initial value $c(0)$ (or equivalently $\mu(0)$) is free. It has to adjust to satisfy the transversality condition (the boundary condition at infinity). Since $c(0)$ or $\mu(0)$ can jump to any value, we again need the existence of a unique one-dimensional manifold (curve) tending to the steady state. As in the q-theory of investment, if there were multiple paths tending to the steady state, the equilibrium would not be unique (there would be multiple values of $c(0)$ consistent with equilibrium).

Fortunately the economic forces ensure (saddle-path) stability and the existence of a unique competitive equilibrium path. In particular, in the neoclassical growth model there exists a unique equilibrium, represented by a one-dimensional manifold (curve) of k-c combinations—the stable arm—converging to the steady state. This stable arm is shown in Figure 8.1. The vertical line is the locus of points where $\dot{c} = 0$. The $\dot{c} = 0$ locus is just a vertical line because, in view of the consumption Euler equation (8.40), only the unique level of k^* given by (8.35) can keep per capita consumption constant. The inverse U-shaped curve is the locus of points where $\dot{k} = 0$ in (8.39). The intersection of these two loci defines the steady state (k^*, c^*). The shape of the $\dot{k} = 0$ locus can be understood by analogy to Figure 2.6 in Chapter 2. Recall that steady-state consumption per capita is maximized at the golden rule capital-labor ratio k_{gold}, and levels of capital stock higher than this reduce steady-state consumption. The $\dot{c} = 0$ locus intersects the $\dot{k} = 0$ locus at the modified golden rule k^*, which is always to the left of k_{gold} (see Exercise 8.12). Once these two loci are drawn, the rest of the diagram can be completed by looking at the direction of motion according to the differential equations (8.39) and (8.40). Given these directions of movements, it is clear that there exists a unique stable arm tending to the steady state. This observation implies that starting with an initial capital-labor ratio $k(0) > 0$, there exists a unique $c(0)$ on the stable arm. If the representative household starts with a per capita consumption level of $c(0)$ at date $t = 0$ and then follows the consumption path given by the Euler equation (8.40), consumption per capita and the capital-labor ratio converge to the unique steady state (k^*, c^*).

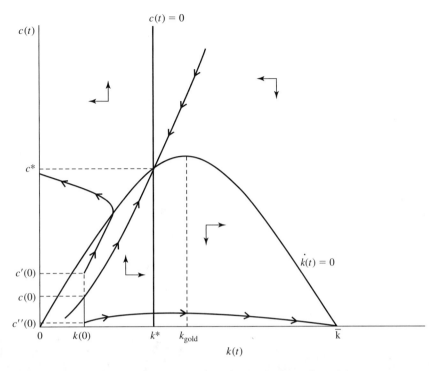

FIGURE 8.1 Transitional dynamics in the baseline neoclassical growth model.

Is the path starting with $(k(0), c(0))$ and converging to (k^*, c^*) the unique equilibrium? The answer is yes, and there are two complementary ways of seeing this. The first exploits the fact that we have already established the equivalence between competitive equilibria and Pareto optimal allocations (directly in Section 8.3 or by appealing to the Second Welfare Theorem [Theorem 5.7]). Given this equivalence, we can apply the sufficiency results in Theorem 7.14 to the optimal growth problem and conclude that the path starting with $(k(0), c(0))$ and converging to (k^*, c^*), which satisfies (8.39), (8.40), and (8.41), gives the unique optimal growth path. Therefore it is also the unique competitive equilibrium. This argument establishes the next proposition.

Proposition 8.4 *In the neoclassical growth model described in Section 8.1, with Assumptions 1, 2, 3, and 4′, there exists a unique equilibrium path starting from any $k(0) > 0$ and converging monotonically to the unique steady-state (k^*, c^*) with k^* given by (8.35). Moreover, if $k(0) < k^*$, then $k(t) \uparrow k^*$ and $c(t) \uparrow c^*$, whereas if $k(0) > k^*$, then $k(t) \downarrow k^*$ and $c(t) \downarrow c^*$. This equilibrium path is also identical to the unique optimal growth path.*

The second strategy for establishing the uniqueness of the equilibrium path is more popular in the literature and involves ruling out all paths other than the stable arm in Figure 8.1. As already discussed, given paths of interest and wage rates, $[r(t), w(t)]_{t=0}^{\infty}$, the representative household's utility-maximization problem has a unique solution (see Exercise 8.11). When these prices are given by (8.5), (8.6), and (8.10), this unique solution starts with $(k(0), c(0))$ and defines precisely the path of capital-labor ratio that leads to these equilibrium prices. To see that this equilibrium is unique, let us return to Figure 8.1. This figure makes it clear that all points away from the stable arm (different from $(k(0), c(0))$) diverge, and eventually reach zero consumption or zero capital stock. If the initial level of consumption were below the stable arm (e.g., at $c''(0)$), then consumption would reach zero in finite time, and thus capital would accumulate continuously until the maximum level of capital $\bar{k} > k_{gold}$ (reached with zero consumption). It can be verified that $f'\left(\bar{k}\right) < \delta + n$ (see Exercise 8.13), which implies that

$$\lim_{t \to \infty} \left[k(t) \exp\left(-\int_0^t \left(f'\left(k(s)\right) - \delta - n \right) ds \right) \right]$$
$$= \bar{k} \lim_{t \to \infty} \left[\exp\left(-\int_0^t \left(f'\left(\bar{k}\right) - \delta - n \right) ds \right) \right] > 0,$$

violating the transversality condition (8.29) or (8.41). Since in this case it can be shown that the transversality condition is not just sufficient but also necessary (by applying Theorem 7.13; see Exercise 8.7), paths starting below the stable arm cannot be part of an equilibrium. Next suppose that initial consumption starts above this stable arm, say at $c'(0)$. In this case, the capital stock would reach zero in finite time, while household consumption implied by (8.40) would remain positive (see again Exercise 8.13).[6] But this behavior violates feasibility and establishes that initial values of consumption above this stable arm cannot be part of the equilibrium (or the optimal growth solution). This line of argument then also leads to the conclusion that the transitional dynamics in the neoclassical growth model involves the initial consumption per capita jumping to $c(0)$ on the stable arm, and then (k, c) monotonically travels along this arm toward the steady state.

A complement to the second strategy is provided by the analysis of local stability. This method involves linearizing the two differential equations (8.39) and (8.40). A first-order Taylor expansion around the steady state $\left(k^*, c^*\right)$ (recall Theorem A.23 in Appendix A) gives

$$\dot{k} \simeq \text{constant} + (f'(k^*) - n - \delta)(k - k^*) - c,$$

and

$$\dot{c} \simeq \text{constant} + \frac{c^* f''(k^*)}{\varepsilon_u(c^*)} (k - k^*),$$

where, to simplify notation, I suppressed time dependence and used the approximately equal sign "$\simeq$" instead of explicitly including second-order terms. From (8.35), $f'(k^*) - \delta = \rho$, so the eigenvalues of this two-equation system are given by the values of ξ that solve the following quadratic form:

$$\det \begin{pmatrix} \rho - n - \xi & -1 \\ \frac{c^* f''(k^*)}{\varepsilon_u(c^*)} & 0 - \xi \end{pmatrix} = 0.$$

It is straightforward to verify that, since $c^* f''(k^*)/\varepsilon_u(c^*) < 0$, there are two real eigenvalues, one negative and one positive. Thus there exists a one-dimensional curve—the stable arm—converging to the steady state (see Exercise 8.15). Therefore, not surprisingly, the local analysis leads to the same conclusion as the global analysis of stability. However the local analysis can only establish local (saddle-path) stability, whereas the above analysis establishes global stability and the uniqueness of the competitive equilibrium.

---

6. One needs to take care of the same technical problem here as that pointed out in the context of the q-theory of investment in Section 7.8; when k reaches zero, the necessary conditions no longer apply. Nevertheless Exercise 8.14 proves from first principles that a jump in consumption down to zero can never be optimal for the representative household, establishing that paths that reach $k = 0$ in finite time can indeed be ruled out.

8.6 Neoclassical Growth in Discrete Time

It is useful to briefly discuss the baseline neoclassical growth model in discrete time to highlight its close connection to the continuous-time analysis. Discrete-time equilibrium growth models are discussed in greater detail in Chapter 17, when I introduce uncertainty.

For now let us suppose that there is no population growth, so that $c(t)$ denotes per capita consumption, the representative household inelastically supplies one unit of labor, and as usual, $\beta \in (0, 1)$ is the discount factor. The representative household then maximizes

$$\sum_{t=0}^{\infty} \beta^t u(c(t))$$

subject to the budget constraint

$$a(t + 1) = (1 + r(t))a(t) + w(t) - c(t),$$

where $a(t)$ is the asset holdings of the household at time t; $w(t)$ is the equilibrium wage rate, which is also equal to the labor income of the representative household, which supplies one unit of labor to the market; and $r(t)$ is the rate of return on asset holdings at time t. As in the continuous-time model, this flow budget constraint needs to be augmented with a no-Ponzi condition. Using similar reasoning to that leading to (8.14) in Section 8.1, this condition takes the form

$$\lim_{t \to \infty} \left[a(t) \prod_{s=1}^{t-1} \frac{1}{1 + r(s)} \right] \geq 0 \tag{8.42}$$

and ensures that the present discounted value of the representative household's asymptotic debt is nonnegative (see Exercise 8.25). Moreover the same argument as in Section 8.1 establishes that (8.42) is exactly the condition necessary to ensure the equivalence between the Arrow-Debreu and the sequential trading formulations of the competitive equilibrium.

Furthermore the representative household's transversality condition then implies that $a(t)$ cannot limit to a negative value; therefore the stronger form of the no-Ponzi condition, which must hold in equilibrium, is

$$\lim_{t \to \infty} \left[a(t) \prod_{s=1}^{t-1} \frac{1}{1 + r(s)} \right] = 0. \tag{8.43}$$

The production side of the economy is identical to that in the continuous-time model. Specifically the rental rate of capital $R(t)$ and the wage rate $w(t)$ are given by (8.5) and (8.6), respectively. Moreover, given depreciation at the rate $\delta > 0$, the rate of return on assets, $r(t)$, is again given by (8.27). A straightforward application of the results in Chapter 6 implies that the representative household will choose a consumption path that satisfies the Euler equation

$$u'(c(t)) = \beta(1 + r(t + 1))u'(c(t + 1)). \tag{8.44}$$

The reader will recall from the analysis of optimal growth in discrete time in Section 6.8 in Chapter 6 that (8.44) is identical to the Euler equation for the optimal growth problem (6.45) (since from (8.27), $r(t) = f'(k(t)) - \delta$). To establish the equivalence of the competitive equilibrium and the optimal growth paths, we need only to show that the no-Ponzi condition

(8.43) implies the transversality condition in the optimal growth problem (6.51) and vice versa. To see this, let us rewrite (6.51) here:

$$\lim_{t\to\infty} \left[\beta^t \left(f'(k(t)) + (1-\delta) \right) u'(c(t))k(t) \right] = 0.$$

Recursively substituting from (8.44) for $t, t-1$, and so on, and using (8.27), this equation is equivalent to

$$\lim_{t\to\infty} \left[\beta^{t-1} u'(c(t-1))k(t) \right] = 0,$$

$$\lim_{t\to\infty} \left[\beta^{t-2} \frac{1}{1+r(t-1)} u'(c(t-2))k(t) \right] = 0,$$

$$\lim_{t\to\infty} \left[\beta^{t-3} \frac{1}{(1+r(t-1))(1+r(t-2))} u'(c(t-3))k(t) \right] = 0,$$

$$\vdots$$

$$\lim_{t\to\infty} \left[k(t) \prod_{s=0}^{t-1} \frac{1}{1+r(s)} \right] = 0,$$

where the last line cancels out $u'(c(0))$, which is strictly positive by assumption. Since from market clearing $a(t) = k(t)$, this condition is the same as (8.43) and thus establishes that the competitive equilibrium and optimal growth paths coincide. This result is not surprising, since the neoclassical growth model satisfies the conditions of the First and Second Welfare Theorems (Theorems 5.6 and 5.7). Nevertheless, the explicit derivation here shows how the equivalence manifests itself in the context of this workhorse model of growth theory and macroeconomics.

Given the equivalence between the equilibrium and optimal growth paths, Proposition 6.3 from Section 6.8 characterizes the dynamics of the equilibrium allocation. In particular, this proposition implies that starting with any initial level of capital stock $k(0) > 0$, the competitive equilibrium path of the neoclassical growth model monotonically converges to the unique steady-state allocation. This result therefore highlights the parallel between the general insights from the discrete-time and continuous-time models.

8.7 Technological Change and the Canonical Neoclassical Model

As in the basic Solow model, the neoclassical growth model does not account for long-run growth without exogenous technological change. Therefore the more interesting version of the neoclassical model is the one that incorporates technological change, which I present here. The production function in this case takes the form

$$Y(t) = F(K(t), A(t)L(t)), \tag{8.45}$$

where

$$A(t) = \exp(gt) A(0).$$

Notice that the production function (8.45) imposes purely labor-augmenting (Harrod-neutral) technological change. This is because Theorem 2.6 in Chapter 2 still applies and implies that balanced growth is possible only with technological change that is labor-augmenting after some time T. As in that chapter, I simplify the analysis by assuming that technological change is labor-augmenting throughout.

Assumptions 1, 2, and 3 on the production and utility functions are still in effect. Assumption $4'$ will be strengthened further to ensure finite discounted utility in the presence of sustained economic growth.

The constant returns to scale feature again enables us to work with normalized variables. Let us define

$$\hat{y}(t) \equiv \frac{Y(t)}{A(t)L(t)}$$

$$= F\left(\frac{K(t)}{A(t)L(t)}, 1\right)$$

$$\equiv f(k(t)),$$

where

$$k(t) \equiv \frac{K(t)}{A(t)L(t)} \tag{8.46}$$

is the effective capital-labor ratio, incorporating labor-augmenting technology in the denominator. Naturally (8.46) is similar to the way that the effective capital-labor ratio was defined in the basic Solow growth model.

In addition to the assumptions on technology, we also need to impose a further assumption on preferences to ensure balanced growth. As in the basic Solow model, balanced growth is defined as a pattern of growth consistent with the Kaldor facts of constant rate of output growth, and constant capital-output ratio and capital share in national income. These two observations together also imply that the rental rate of return on capital, $R(t)$, has to be constant, which, from (8.10), implies that $r(t)$ has to be constant. Let us again refer to an equilibrium path that satisfies these conditions as a balanced growth path (BGP). Balanced growth also requires that consumption and output grow at a constant rate. The Euler equation implies that

$$\frac{\dot{c}(t)}{c(t)} = \frac{1}{\varepsilon_u(c(t))}(r(t) - \rho).$$

If $r(t) \to r^*$, then $\dot{c}(t)/c(t) \to g_c$ is possible only if $\varepsilon_u(c(t)) \to \varepsilon_u$, that is, if the elasticity of marginal utility of consumption is asymptotically constant. Therefore balanced growth is only consistent with utility functions that have asymptotically constant elasticity of marginal utility of consumption. Since this result is important, I state it as a proposition.

Proposition 8.5 *Balanced growth in the neoclassical model requires that asymptotically all technological change is purely labor-augmenting and the elasticity of intertemporal substitution, $\varepsilon_u(c(t))$, tends to a constant ε_u.*

The next example shows the family of utility functions with constant intertemporal elasticity of substitution, which are also those functions with a constant coefficient of relative risk aversion. This example also demonstrates that utility functions with constant intertemporal elasticity of substitution are the same as the Gorman preferences in this economy, so that the assumption that $\varepsilon_u(c(t)) \to \varepsilon_u$ is not much more restrictive than assuming the presence of a (strong) representative household (recall Chapter 5).

Example 8.1 (CRRA Utility) *Recall that the Arrow-Pratt coefficient of relative risk aversion for a twice differentiable concave utility function $u(c)$ is*

$$\mathcal{R} = -\frac{u''(c)c}{u'(c)}.$$

The constant relative risk aversion (CRRA) utility function satisfies the property that $\mathcal{R}$ is constant. Setting $\mathcal{R}$ to a constant, say $\theta > 0$, and integrating both sides gives the family of CRRA utility functions as

$$u(c) = \begin{cases} \frac{c^{1-\theta}-1}{1-\theta} & \text{if } \theta \neq 1 \text{ and } \theta \geq 0, \\ \log c & \text{if } \theta = 1, \end{cases}$$

with the coefficient of relative risk aversion given by θ (see Exercise B.9 in Appendix B for a formal derivation). In writing this expression, I separated the case where $\theta = 1$, since $\left(c^{1-\theta} - 1\right) / (1 - \theta)$ is undefined at $\theta = 1$. However it can easily be shown that $\log c$ is indeed the right limit when $\theta \to 1$.

With time-separable utility functions, the inverse of the elasticity of intertemporal substitution (defined in (8.30)) and the coefficient of relative risk aversion are identical. Therefore the family of CRRA utility functions also consists of those functions with constant elasticity of intertemporal substitution (see Exercise 5.2).

To link this utility function to the Gorman preferences discussed in Chapter 5, let us consider a slightly different problem in which an individual has preferences defined over the consumption of N commodities $\{c_1, \ldots, c_N\}$ given by

$$U(\{c_1, \ldots, c_N\}) = \begin{cases} \sum_{j=1}^{N} \frac{c_j^{1-\theta}}{1-\theta} & \text{if } \theta \neq 1 \text{ and } \theta \geq 0, \\ \sum_{j=1}^{N} \log c_j & \text{if } \theta = 1. \end{cases} \tag{8.47}$$

Suppose also that this individual faces a price vector $\mathbf{p} = (p_1, \ldots, p_N)$ and has income y, so that her budget constraint can be expressed as

$$\sum_{j=1}^{N} p_j c_j \leq y. \tag{8.48}$$

Maximizing (8.47) subject to the budget constraint (8.48) leads to the following indirect utility function:

$$v(p, y) = \frac{y^{1-\theta}}{(1-\theta) \left[\sum_{j=1}^{N} p_j^{\frac{\theta-1}{\theta}} \right]^{-\frac{1}{\theta}}}$$

(see Exercise 5.6). Although this indirect utility function does not satisfy the Gorman form in Theorem 5.2, a monotone transformation thereof does (simply raise it to the power $1/(1-\theta)$). Thus CRRA utility functions are within the Gorman class, and if all households have CRRA utility functions, then we can aggregate their preferences and represent them as if they belonged to a single individual.

Now consider a dynamic version of these preferences (defined over an infinite horizon):

$$U\left(c(0), c\left(1\right), \ldots\right) = \begin{cases} \sum_{t=0}^{\infty} \beta^t \frac{c(t)^{1-\theta}-1}{1-\theta} & \text{if } \theta \neq 1 \text{ and } \theta \geq 0, \\ \sum_{t=0}^{\infty} \beta^t \log c(t) & \text{if } \theta = 1. \end{cases}$$

The important feature of these preferences in growth theory is not that the coefficient of relative risk aversion is constant but that the intertemporal elasticity of substitution is constant (because most growth models do not feature uncertainty). The intertemporal elasticity of substitution regulates how willing individuals are to substitute consumption over time, thus determining their savings and consumption behavior. In view of this observation, it may be more appropriate to refer to CRRA preferences as "constant intertemporal elasticity of substitution" preferences. Nevertheless, I follow the standard convention in the literature and use the term "CRRA."

Finally, note that a more general family of utility functions within the Gorman class, with

$$\sum_{t=0}^{\infty} \beta^t \left[(c(t) - \gamma(t))^{1-\theta} - 1 \right] / (1-\theta) \text{ or } U = \sum_{t=0}^{\infty} \beta^t \log \left(c(t) - \gamma(t) \right)$$

is also consistent with balanced growth as long as $\lim_{t \to \infty} \gamma(t) = \bar{\gamma} < \infty$. These preferences are further discussed in Exercise 8.31.

Given the restriction that balanced growth is only possible with preferences featuring a constant elasticity of intertemporal substitution, let us start with the CRRA instantaneous utility function

$$u(c(t)) = \begin{cases} \frac{c(t)^{1-\theta}-1}{1-\theta} & \text{if } \theta \neq 1 \text{ and } \theta \geq 0, \\ \log c(t) & \text{if } \theta = 1, \end{cases}$$

where the elasticity of marginal utility of consumption, ε_u, is given by the constant θ. When $\theta = 0$, this function represents linear preferences, whereas when $\theta = 1$, it corresponds to log preferences. As $\theta \to \infty$, households become infinitely risk-averse and infinitely unwilling to substitute consumption over time.

More specifically, let us consider an economy with a (normative) representative household with CRRA preferences,

$$\int_0^{\infty} \exp\left(-(\rho - n)t\right) \frac{c(t)^{1-\theta} - 1}{1 - \theta} dt, \tag{8.49}$$

where $c(t) \equiv C(t)/L(t)$ is per capita consumption. I refer to this model, with labor-augmenting technological change and CRRA preference as given by (8.49) as the *canonical model*, since it is the model used in almost all applications of the neoclassical growth model. In this model, the representative household's problem is given by the maximization of (8.49) subject to (8.8) and (8.14). Once again using the necessary conditions from Theorem 7.13, the Euler equation of the representative household is obtained as

$$\frac{\dot{c}(t)}{c(t)} = \frac{1}{\theta} \left(r(t) - \rho \right). \tag{8.50}$$

Let us first characterize the steady-state equilibrium in this model with technological progress. Since with technological progress there is growth in per capita income, per capita consumption $c(t)$ also grows. In analogy with $k(t)$, let us define

$$\tilde{c}(t) \equiv \frac{C(t)}{A(t)L(t)}$$

$$\equiv \frac{c(t)}{A(t)}.$$

This normalized consumption level remains constant along the BGP. Naturally,

$$\frac{d\tilde{c}(t)/dt}{\tilde{c}(t)} = \frac{\dot{c}(t)}{c(t)} - g$$

$$= \frac{1}{\theta}\left(r(t) - \rho - \theta g\right).$$

Moreover the accumulation of capital stock is given by

$$\dot{k}(t) = f(k(t)) - \tilde{c}(t) - (n + g + \delta)\, k(t), \tag{8.51}$$

where recall that $k(t) \equiv K(t)/A(t)L(t)$ as in (8.46).

The transversality condition in turn can be expressed as

$$\lim_{t \to \infty} \left[k(t) \exp\left(-\int_0^t [f'(k(s)) - g - \delta - n]ds \right) \right] = 0. \tag{8.52}$$

In addition, the equilibrium interest rate $r(t)$ is still given by (8.27). Moreover, since in steady state (BGP) $\tilde{c}(t)$ must remain constant, $r(t) = \rho + \theta g$, which implies that

$$f'(k^*) = \rho + \delta + \theta g. \tag{8.53}$$

This equation uniquely determines the steady-state value of the effective capital-labor ratio k^*. The level of normalized consumption in steady state is then given by

$$\tilde{c}^* = f(k^*) - (n + g + \delta)\, k^*, \tag{8.54}$$

while per capita consumption grows at the rate g.

The only additional complication in this case is that because of sustained growth, the transversality condition becomes more demanding. In particular, substituting (8.53) into (8.52), the transversality condition requires that

$$\lim_{t \to \infty} \left[k(t) \exp\left(-\int_0^t [\rho - (1-\theta)\, g - n]ds \right) \right] = 0,$$

which can hold only if the integral in the exponent goes to minus infinity, that is, only if $\rho - (1-\theta)\, g - n > 0$. Thus to ensure a well-defined solution to the household maximization problem and a well-defined competitive equilibrium, we need to modify Assumption 4′ as follows.

Assumption 4 (Discounting with Technological Progress) $\rho - n > (1 - \theta)g.$

This assumption strengthens Assumption 4′ when $\theta < 1$. The steady-state interest rate in this economy is $r^* = \rho + \theta g$, and the growth rate of output is $g + n$. Therefore, in the same way as Assumption 4′ ensured $r^* > n$, Assumption 4 guarantees $r^* > g + n$. Assumption 4 emerges as a necessary condition in a variety of models both for household utility to be finite and for the transversality condition to hold. Imposing a condition to ensure that the transversality condition holds may appear strange, since the (necessary) transversality condition should be satisfied by an optimal solution—without the need to impose additional conditions. However, similar to Assumption 4′, the main role of Assumption 4 is not to satisfy the transversality condition but to ensure that households do not achieve infinite utility (which would again make the economic problem uninteresting and violate the local nonsatiation assumption from Chapter 5). Exercise 8.20 shows the link between Assumption 4 and the finiteness of the utility of the representative household. Recall that the transversality condition ceases to be meaningful when households achieve infinite utility. In fact, when this assumption is violated, the transversality condition also fails to hold. In what follows, checking that the transversality condition is satisfied turns out to be equivalent to (but somewhat simpler than) verifying that household utility is finite.

At this point, we can use a similar reasoning to that in Section 8.2 and establish that, given Assumption 4, the sufficiency conditions in Theorem 7.14 are satisfied. Thus the solution to the household maximization problem derived above indeed corresponds to a global maximum (see Exercise 8.21). The following is therefore an immediate generalization of Proposition 8.2.

Proposition 8.6 *Consider the neoclassical growth model with labor-augmenting technological progress at the rate g and preferences given by (8.49). Suppose that Assumptions 1, 2, 3, and 4 hold. Then there exists a unique BGP, where the effective capital-labor ratio k^* is given by (8.53), and output per capita and consumption per capita grow at the rate g.*

The steady-state (BGP) capital-labor ratio is no longer independent of the instantaneous utility function of the representative household, since now the steady-state capital-labor ratio k^*, given by (8.53), depends on the elasticity of marginal utility (or the inverse of the intertemporal elasticity of substitution) θ. This is because there is now growth in output per capita and thus in consumption per capita. Since households face an upward-sloping consumption profile, their willingness to substitute consumption today for consumption tomorrow determines how much they accumulate and thus the equilibrium effective capital-labor ratio.

Perhaps the most important implication of Proposition 8.6 is that, while the steady-state effective capital-labor ratio k^* is determined endogenously, the steady-state growth rate of the economy is given exogenously and is equal to the rate of labor-augmenting technological progress, g. Therefore the neoclassical growth model, like the basic Solow growth model, endogenizes the capital-labor ratio but not the growth rate of the economy. The advantage of the neoclassical growth model is that the capital-labor ratio and the equilibrium level of (normalized) output and consumption are determined by the preferences of the individuals rather than by an exogenously fixed saving rate. This model also enables us to compare equilibrium and optimal growth (and in this case conclude that the competitive equilibrium is Pareto optimal and that any Pareto optimum can be decentralized). But the determination of the rate of growth of the economy is still outside the scope of analysis.

An analysis similar to that for Proposition 8.6 leads to a generalization of Proposition 8.4.

Proposition 8.7 *Consider the neoclassical growth model with labor-augmenting technological progress at the rate g and preferences given by (8.49). Suppose that Assumptions 1, 2, 3, and 4 hold. Then there exists a unique equilibrium path, where $(k(t), \tilde{c}(t))$ converges monotonically to the unique steady-state $\left(k^*, \tilde{c}^*\right)$ with k^* given by (8.53) and $\tilde{c}^*$ given by (8.54).*

Proof. See Exercise 8.22. ∎

It is also useful to briefly look at an example with Cobb-Douglas technology.

Example 8.2 *Consider the model with CRRA utility and labor-augmenting technological progress at the rate g. Dropping time dependence to simplify notation, the production function is $F(K, AL) = K^\alpha (AL)^{1-\alpha}$, and thus*

$$f(k) = k^\alpha,$$

so that $r = \alpha k^{\alpha-1} - \delta$. The Euler equation written in terms of normalized consumption then becomes

$$\frac{d\tilde{c}/dt}{\tilde{c}} = \frac{1}{\theta}(\alpha k^{\alpha-1} - \delta - \rho - \theta g),$$

and the accumulation equation can be written as

$$\frac{\dot{k}}{k} = k^{\alpha-1} - \delta - g - n - \frac{\tilde{c}}{k}.$$

Now define $z \equiv \tilde{c}/k$ and $x \equiv k^{\alpha-1}$, which implies that $\dot{x}/x = (\alpha - 1)\dot{k}/k$. Therefore we have

$$\frac{\dot{x}}{x} = -(1-\alpha)(x - \delta - g - n - z), \tag{8.55}$$

and also

$$\frac{\dot{z}}{z} = \frac{d\tilde{c}/dt}{\tilde{c}} - \frac{\dot{k}}{k},$$

which implies that

$$\frac{\dot{z}}{z} = \frac{1}{\theta}(\alpha x - \delta - \rho - \theta g) - x + \delta + g + n + z$$

$$= \frac{1}{\theta}((\alpha - \theta)x - (1 - \theta)\delta + \theta n) - \frac{\rho}{\theta} + z. \tag{8.56}$$

The two differential equations (8.55) and (8.56) together with the initial condition $x(0)$ and the transversality condition completely determine the dynamics of the system. In Exercise 8.24, you are asked to complete this example for the special case in which $\theta \leq 1$ (log preferences).

8.8 The Role of Policy

In the model developed in Section 8.7, the rate of growth of per capita consumption and output per worker (per capita) are determined exogenously by the growth rate of labor-augmenting technological progress. The level of income, on the other hand, depends on the intertemporal elasticity of substitution $1/\theta$, the discount rate ρ, the depreciation rate δ, the population growth rate n, and naturally the form of the production function $f(\cdot)$.

Returning to the proximate causes of cross-country differences in income per capita and growth, this model gives us a way of understanding those differences in terms of preference and technology parameters. As discussed in Chapter 4, we also wish to link the proximate causes of economic growth to potential fundamental causes. The intertemporal elasticity of substitution and the discount rate can be viewed as potential determinants of economic growth related to cultural or geographic factors. However, an explanation for cross-country and over-time differences in economic growth based on differences or changes in preferences is unlikely to be satisfactory. A more appealing approach may be to link the incentives to accumulate physical capital (and later to accumulate human capital and technology) to the institutional environment of an economy, as done in Part VIII. For now, it is useful to focus on a particularly simple way in which institutional differences might affect investment decisions. Let us extend the above framework in a simple way and introduce linear tax policy. Suppose that returns on capital net of depreciation are taxed at the rate τ and the proceeds are redistributed lumpsum back to households. In that case, the capital accumulation equation is still given by (8.51), but the net interest rate faced by households changes to

$$r(t) = (1 - \tau)(f'(k(t)) - \delta),$$

because of the taxation of capital returns. The growth rate of normalized consumption is then obtained from the Euler equation (8.50) as

$$\frac{d\tilde{c}(t)/dt}{\tilde{c}(t)} = \frac{1}{\theta}(r(t) - \rho - \theta g)$$

$$= \frac{1}{\theta}((1 - \tau)(f'(k(t)) - \delta) - \rho - \theta g).$$

An identical argument to that above immediately implies that the steady-state capital to effective labor ratio is given by

$$f'(k^*) = \delta + \frac{\rho + \theta g}{1 - \tau}. \tag{8.57}$$

Equation (8.57) shows the effects of taxing steady-state capital on effective labor ratio and output per capita. A higher tax rate τ increases the right-hand side of (8.57), and since from Assumption 1, $f'(\cdot)$ is decreasing, it reduces k^*. Therefore higher taxes on capital have the effect of depressing capital accumulation and reducing income per capita. Thus (8.57) shows one channel through which policy (and thus institutional) differences might affect economic performance. Similar results apply if, instead of being imposed on the returns to capital, taxes were imposed on the amount of investment (see Section 8.10).

8.9 Comparative Dynamics

Comparative dynamics are a little different in the neoclassical growth model than those in the basic Solow model. Recall that while comparative statics refer to changes in steady state in response to changes in parameters, comparative dynamics look at how the entire equilibrium path of variables changes in response to a change in policy or parameters. Since the purpose here is to give a sense of how these results differ, I briefly consider the model with capital taxation discussed in the previous section and consider the effects of a change in the tax rate τ. Suppose that there is population growth at the rate n and labor-augmenting technological progress at the rate g and that capital is taxed at the rate τ. Suppose also that the economy is initially in a steady state represented by $(k^*, \tilde{c}^*)$. Now imagine that the capital tax rate declines from τ to $\tau' < \tau$. How does the equilibrium path change?

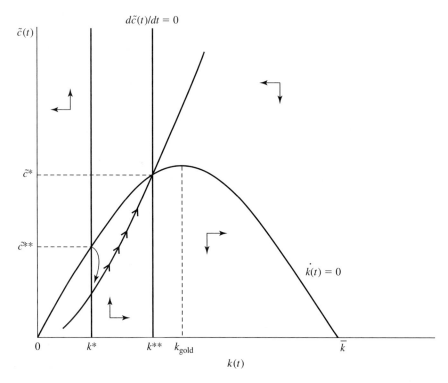

FIGURE 8.2 Dynamic response of capital and consumption to a decline in the tax rate from τ to $\tau' < \tau$.

We know from the analysis so far that at the new tax rate $\tau' > 0$, there exists a unique steady-state equilibrium that is saddle-path stable. Let this steady state be denoted by $\left(k^{**}, \tilde{c}^{**}\right)$. Therefore the economy will ultimately tend to this new steady-state equilibrium. Moreover, since $\tau' < \tau$, we know that the new steady-state effective capital-labor ratio has to be greater than k^*, that is, $k^{**} > k^*$ (while the equilibrium growth rate remains unchanged). Figure 8.2 shows diagrammatically the comparative dynamics. This figure is drawn under the assumption that the change in the tax rate is unanticipated and occurs at some date T. At this point, the curve corresponding to $(d\tilde{c}(t)/dt)/\tilde{c}(t) = 0$ shifts to the right and the laws of motion represented by the phase diagram change (in the figure, the arrows represent the dynamics of the economy after the change). It can be seen that following this decline in the tax rate, the previous steady-state level of consumption $\tilde{c}^*$ is above the stable arm of the new dynamical system. Therefore consumption must drop immediately to reach the new stable arm, so that capital can accumulate toward its new steady-state level. This drop is shown in the figure with the arc representing the jump in consumption immediately following the decline in the tax rate. Following this initial reaction, consumption slowly increases along the stable arm to a higher level of (normalized) consumption. Therefore a decline in the tax rate leads to a temporary decline in consumption but is followed by a rapid increase in consumption (along the stable arm). The overall level of normalized consumption will necessarily increase, since the intersection between the curve for $(d\tilde{c}(t)/dt)/\tilde{c}(t) = 0$ and the inverse U-shaped curve for $\dot{k}/k = 0$ is necessarily to the left side of k_{gold}.

Comparative dynamics in response to changes in other parameters, including the rate of labor-augmenting technological progress g, the rate of population growth n, the discount rate ρ, and other aspects of the utility function, can also be analyzed similarly. Exercise 8.28 asks you to work through the comparative dynamics in response to a change in the rate of labor-augmenting technological progress, g, and in response to an anticipated future change in τ.

8.10 A Quantitative Evaluation

Let us next investigate the quantitative implications of the neoclassical growth model for cross-country income differences resulting from differences in policies. Consider a world consisting of J closed neoclassical economies (with all the caveats of ignoring technological, trade, and financial linkages across countries discussed in Chapter 3; see also Chapter 19). Suppose that each country j admits a representative household with identical preferences given by

$$\int_0^\infty \exp(-\rho t)\frac{C_j(t)^{1-\theta} - 1}{1 - \theta}\,dt. \tag{8.58}$$

Let us assume that there is no population growth, so that C_j is both total and per capita consumption. Equation (8.58) stipulates that all countries have the same discount rate ρ (see Exercise 8.32). All countries also have access to the same production technology given by the Cobb-Douglas production function

$$Y_j(t) = K_j(t)^\alpha (A H_j(t))^{1-\alpha}, \tag{8.59}$$

with H_j representing the exogenously given stock of effective labor (human capital). The accumulation equation is

$$\dot{K}_j(t) = I_j(t) - \delta K_j(t). \tag{8.60}$$

The only difference across countries is in the budget constraint for the representative household, which takes the form

$$(1 + \tau_j)I_j(t) + C_j(t) \leq Y_j(t), \tag{8.61}$$

where τ_j is the (constant) tax on investment. This tax varies across countries, for example because of policies or differences in institutions. Notice, however, that I have not so far offered a reason why some countries may tax investment at a higher rate than others; this topic is discussed in Part VIII. For now, let us note that $1 + \tau_j$ can also be interpreted as the price of investment goods (relative to consumption goods) in country j: 1 unit of consumption goods can only be transformed into $1/(1 + \tau_j)$ units of investment goods.

The right-hand side of the budget constraint (8.61) is still $Y_j(t)$, which implicitly assumes that $\tau_j I_j(t)$ is wasted, rather than being redistributed back to the representative household. This assumption is without any major consequence, since, as noted in Theorem 5.2, CRRA preferences as in (8.58) have the nice feature that they can be exactly aggregated across individuals, so we do not have to worry about the distribution of income in the economy.

The competitive equilibrium can be characterized as the solution to the maximization of (8.58) subject to (8.60) and (8.61). With the same steps as above, the Euler equation of the representative household is

$$\frac{\dot{C}_j(t)}{C_j(t)} = \frac{1}{\theta}\left(\frac{\alpha}{(1+\tau_j)}\left(\frac{AH_j(t)}{K_j(t)}\right)^{1-\alpha} - \delta - \rho\right).$$

Consider the steady state. Because A is constant, the steady state requires that $\dot{C}_j(t)/C_j(t) = 0$ for all j. This requirement immediately implies that

$$K_j(t) = \left(\frac{\alpha}{(1+\tau_j)(\rho+\delta)}\right)^{\frac{1}{1-\alpha}} AH_j(t). \qquad (8.62)$$

So countries with higher taxes on investment have a lower capital stock in steady state. Equivalently, they also have lower capital per worker or a lower capital-output ratio (using (8.59), the capital output ratio is simply $K/Y = (K/AH)^{1-\alpha}$). Most importantly, they will also be relatively poor. Substituting (8.62) into (8.59), comparing two countries with different taxes (but the same human capital), and denoting the steady-state income level of a country with a tax rate equal to τ by $Y(\tau)$, we obtain the relative steady-state income differences as

$$\frac{Y(\tau)}{Y(\tau')} = \left(\frac{1+\tau'}{1+\tau}\right)^{\frac{\alpha}{1-\alpha}}. \qquad (8.63)$$

This equation therefore summarizes the intuitive notion that countries that tax investment, either directly or indirectly, at a higher rate will be poorer. More interestingly, this equation can be used for a quantitative evaluation of how large the effects of such policy differences might be. The advantage of using the neoclassical growth model for quantitative evaluation relative to the Solow growth model is that the extent to which different types of distortions (here captured by the tax rates on investment) affect income and capital accumulation is determined endogenously. In contrast, in the Solow growth model, what matters, besides technology, is the saving rate, so to evaluate the effect of policy on cross-country income differences, we would need to link taxes or distortions to savings. Such linkages might be done by using other sources of evidence to estimate the effect of these distortions on savings (though in general this is not an easy task).

How large are the effects of tax distortions captured by (8.63)? Put differently, can the neoclassical growth model account for quantitatively large cross-country income differences? Equation (8.63) shows that the answer depends on differences in τ across countries and the value of the parameter α. Recall that a plausible value for α is 1/3, since this is the share of capital income in national product which, with Cobb-Douglas production function, is equal to α, so this parameter can be easily mapped to data. Where can we obtain estimates of differences in the value of τ across countries? There is no obvious answer to this question. A popular approach in the literature is to exploit the fact that, in the closed-economy neoclassical model with investment-tax distortions, the price of investment goods relative to consumption goods is $1+\tau$. Data from the Penn World tables suggest that there is a large amount of variation in this relative price. For example, in some countries the relative price of investment goods is almost eight times as high as in others. Motivated by this observation, let us consider an eightfold difference in the value of τ. Combining this spread with $\alpha = 1/3$, (8.63) implies that the income gap between two such countries should be approximately threefold, that is,

$$\frac{Y(\tau)}{Y(\tau')} \approx 8^{1/2} \approx 3.$$

Therefore differences in capital-output ratios or capital-labor ratios caused by taxes or tax-like distortions, even by very large differences in taxes or distortions, are unlikely to account for the large differences in income per capita that we observe in practice. This result is not surprising and parallels our discussion of the Mankiw-Romer-Weil approach in Chapter 3. In particular, recall that the discussion in Chapter 3 showed that differences in income per capita across countries are unlikely to be accounted for solely by differences in capital per worker. To explain such large differences in income per capita across countries, we need sizable differences in the efficiency with which these factors are being used in different countries. Such efficiency differences are not present in this model. Therefore the simplest neoclassical model does not generate sufficient differences in capital-labor ratios to explain cross-country income differences.

Nevertheless, many economists have tried (and still try) to use versions of the neoclassical model to go further. The motivation is simple. If instead of using $\alpha = 1/3$, we take $\alpha = 2/3$, the ratio of incomes in the two countries would be

$$\frac{Y(\tau)}{Y(\tau')} \approx 8^2 \approx 64.$$

Thus if the responsiveness of capital or other factors to policy distortions were higher than that implied by the neoclassical growth model with $\alpha = 1/3$ (e.g., corresponding to the case where $\alpha = 2/3$), then the predicted differences across countries can be made much larger. How could we have a model in which $\alpha = 2/3$? Such a model must have additional accumulated factors while still keeping the share of capital income in national product at roughly $1/3$. One possibility might be to include human capital (see Chapter 10). However, the discussion in Chapter 3 showed that human capital differences appear to be insufficient to explain a large portion of the income per capita differences across countries. Another possibility is to introduce other types of capital or perhaps technology that responds to distortions in the same way as capital. While these are all logically possible, a systematic analysis of these issues requires models of endogenous technology, which is our focus in the next part of the book.

8.11 Extensions

There are many empirically and theoretically relevant extensions of the neoclassical growth model. I do not present them here for the sake of brevity. The most important ones are presented as exercises instead. In particular, Exercise 8.33 endogenizes the labor supply decisions of households by introducing leisure in the utility function. The model presented in this exercise is particularly important, since it corresponds to the version of the neoclassical growth model most often employed in short-run and medium-run macroeconomic analyses. This exercise also shows that further restrictions on the form of the utility function need to be imposed to preserve balanced growth in this case. Exercise 8.34 further studies models that incorporate government expenditures and taxation. Exercise 8.36 looks at the behavior of the basic neoclassical growth model with a free capital account, representing borrowing and lending opportunities for the economy at some exogenously given international interest rate r^*. Exercise 8.37 combines the costs of adjustments in investment as in the q-theory with the basic neoclassical model. Finally, Exercise 8.38 looks at a version of the neoclassical model with multiple sectors.

8.12 Taking Stock

This chapter presented arguably the most important model in macroeconomics; the one-sector neoclassical growth model. Recall that our study of the basic models of economic growth started in Chapter 2 with the Solow growth model. We saw that while this model gives a number of important insights, it treats much of the mechanics of economic growth as a black box. Growth can only be generated by technological progress (unless we are in the special

AK model without diminishing returns to capital), but technological progress is outside the model. The next important element in determining cross-country differences in income is the saving rate, but in the Solow growth model the saving rate was also taken as exogenous. The major contribution of the current chapter has been to open the black box of savings and capital accumulation by specifying the preferences of households. Consequently we can link saving rates to preferences, technology, and prices in the economy. Moreover, as Exercise 8.39 shows, the implications of policy on equilibrium quantities are different in the neoclassical model than in the Solow growth model with exogenously specified saving rates. Another major advantage of the neoclassical growth model is that because preferences are explicitly specified, equilibrium and optimal growth can be compared.

Perhaps the most important contribution of this model is that it paves the way for further analysis of capital accumulation, human capital investments, and endogenous technological progress, which is our topic in the next few chapters (starting with the analysis of human capital in Chapter 10). Therefore this chapter is the first, and perhaps conceptually the most important, step toward a systematic study of economic growth. It provides us with the mathematical and conceptual tools necessary for modeling capital accumulation, human capital accumulation, and technological change endogenously.

Did our study of the neoclassical growth model generate new insights about the sources of cross-country income differences and economic growth relative to the Solow growth model? The answer here is largely no. While the current model is an important milestone in the study of the mechanics of economic growth, as with the Solow growth model, the focus is on the proximate causes of these differences—we are still looking at differences in saving rates, investments in human capital, and technology, perhaps as determined by preferences and other dimensions of technology (e.g., the rate of labor-augmenting technological change). It is therefore important to bear in mind that this model by itself does not enable us to answer questions about the fundamental causes of economic growth. What it does, however, is to clarify the nature of the economic decisions so that we are in a better position to ask such questions.

8.13   References and Literature

The neoclassical growth model goes back to Frank Ramsey's (1928) classic article and for that reason is often referred to as the "Ramsey model." Ramsey's model was very similar to the standard neoclassical growth model, except that it did not feature discounting. Another early optimal growth model was presented by John von Neumann (1945), focusing on the limiting behavior of the dynamics in a linear model. The current version of the neoclassical growth model is most closely related to the analysis of optimal growth by David Cass (1965) and Tjalling Koopmans (1965). An excellent discussion of optimal growth is provided in Arrow and Kurz's (1970) volume.

All growth and macroeconomic textbooks cover the neoclassical growth model. Ljungqvist and Sargent (2005, Chapter 14) provides an introductory treatment of the neoclassical growth model in discrete time. Barro and Sala-i-Martin (2004, Chapter 2) provides a detailed treatment focusing on continuous-time models. Blanchard and Fischer (1989, Chapter 2) and Romer (2006, Chapter 2) also present the continuous-time version of the neoclassical growth model. These books use the necessary conditions implied by the Maximum Principle, including the strong version of the transversality condition, and characterize utility-maximizing consumption behavior. The typical approach is to first ignore the no-Ponzi condition and then rule out paths that violate this condition. As also pointed out in the previous chapter, more care is necessary in characterizing utility-maximizing behavior. First, when the no-Ponzi condition is ignored, households can reach unbounded levels of consumption, and the Maximum Principle is no longer valid. Second, even setting this problem aside, the Maximum Principle provides necessary conditions for interior solutions, whereas to establish uniqueness of equilibria (or optimal allocations), we need to rule out paths that are not everywhere interior. Instead of focusing on necessary conditions, the treatment in this chapter used Theorem 7.13 to generate the candidate solution and then verified the sufficiency conditions in Theorem 7.14. This approach is both simpler and more rigorous than the typical approach. I also sketched how such noninterior paths can be ruled out (from first principles) without using the Maximum Principle.

A quantitative evaluation of the effects of policy differences is provided in Chari, Kehoe, and McGrattan (1997). These authors follow Jones (1995) in emphasizing differences in the relative prices of investment goods (compared to consumption goods) in the Penn World tables and interpret these as due to taxes and other distortions. This interpretation is not without problems. In particular, in the presence of international trade, these relative price differences will reflect other technological factors or possible factor proportion differences (see Chapter 19; see also Acemoglu and Ventura, 2002; Hsieh and Klenow, 2006). Parente and Prescott (1994) perform similar quantitative exercises using an extended version of the neoclassical growth model (where the "stock of technology," which is costly to adopt from the world frontier, is interpreted as an additional capital good). Other authors have introduced yet other accumulable factors to increase the elasticity of output to distortions (i.e., to increase the α parameter in Section 8.10).

Ricardian equivalence discussed in Exercise 8.35 was first proposed by Barro (1974). It is further discussed in Chapter 9. The preferences used in Exercise 8.31 are referred to as "Stone-Geary preferences" after Geary (1950) and Stone (1954). They are a special case of the Gorman preferences discussed in Theorems 5.2 and 5.3.

8.14 Exercises

8.1 Consider the consumption allocation decision of an infinitely-lived household with (a continuum of) $L(t)$ members at time t, with $L(0) = 1$. Suppose that the household has total consumption $C(t)$ to allocate at time t. The household has utilitarian preferences with instantaneous utility function $u(c)$ and discounts the future at the rate $\rho > 0$.

(a) Show that the problem of the household can be written as

$$\max \int_0^\infty \exp(-\rho t)\left[\int_0^{L(t)} u\left(c_i(t)\right) di\right] dt$$

subject to

$$\int_0^{L(t)} c_i(t) di \le C(t),$$

and subject to the budget constraint

$$\dot{A}(t) = r(t)A(t) + W(t) - C(t),$$

where i denotes a generic member of the household, $A(t)$ is the total asset holdings of the household, $r(t)$ is the rate of return on assets, and $W(t)$ is total labor income.

(b) Show that as long as $u(\cdot)$ is strictly concave, this problem becomes

$$\max \int_0^\infty \exp\left(-(\rho - n)\,t\right) u(c(t))\, dt$$

subject to

$$\dot{a}(t) = (r(t) - n)\, a(t) + w(t) - c(t),$$

where $w(t) \equiv W(t)/L(t)$ and $a(t) \equiv A(t)/L(t)$. Provide an intuition for this transformed problem.

8.2 Consider the maximization of (8.3) subject to (8.8) without any other constraints.

(a) Show that for any candidate consumption plan $[c(t)]_{t=0}^\infty$, there exists another consumption plan $[c'(t)]_{t=0}^\infty$ that satisfies the flow budget constraint (8.8), involves $c'(t) > c(t)$, and yields strictly higher utility.

(b) Using the argument in part a, show that the household will choose asset levels $a(t)$ becoming arbitrarily negative for all t. [Hint: this problem does not have a sequence of consumption and asset levels that reach the maximum value of the objective function; so here you should simply show that $a(t)$ arbitrarily negative for all t approaches the maximum value of the objective function (which may be, but does not need to be, $+\infty$).]

(c) Explain why an allocation with these features would violate feasibility.

8.3 Start with the law of motion of the total assets of the households, given by (8.7). Using this equation, show that if the household starts with $A(t) = 0$ at time t and chooses zero consumption thereafter, then it asymptotically generates asset holdings of

$$\bar{W}(t) \equiv \int_t^\infty w(s)L(s) \exp\left(-\int_t^s r(z)\,dz\right) ds.$$

Explain why the natural debt limit requires that $A(t) \geq -\bar{W}(t)$. Using the definition of $A(t)$ and the fact that $L(t)$ grows at the rate n, derive (8.11). Relate this natural debt limit to its discrete-time analogue (6.44) in Chapter 6.

8.4 Show that the relaxed natural debt limit (8.12) implies that the original debt limit (8.11) holds for all t.

8.5 Derive (8.8) from (8.13).

8.6 Derive (8.16) from (8.14) and (8.19). [Hint: use (8.18) to substitute for $\mu(t)$ in (8.19).]

8.7 Verify that Theorem 7.13 can be applied to the household maximization problem in Section 8.2.2. In particular, following the same steps as in Section 7.7, show that Assumption 7.1 is satisfied when $c(t) \in [\varepsilon, +\infty)$ and when $r(t) > n$ for all t. Then show that the restriction to $c \in [\varepsilon, +\infty)$ has no effect on the results and that any equilibrium must involve $r(t) > n$ for all t.

8.8 (a) Show that the natural debt limit (8.12) with $\hat{a} > -\infty$ implies the no-Ponzi condition (8.14), but (8.14) does not imply (8.12) with $\hat{a} > -\infty$. [Hint: consider an economy where $w(t) = \exp(gt)\, w(0)$ and $r(t) = r$ for all t.]

(b) Show that in the neoclassical growth model with technological progress studied in Section 8.7, it is not possible to apply Theorems 7.13 or 7.14 using the natural debt limit.

8.9 Show that $\lim_{t\to\infty} r(t) > n$ and $\lim_{t\to\infty} w(t) = w \geq 0$ are sufficient to guarantee that $\hat{a} > -\infty$ in the natural debt limit (8.12).

8.10 (a) Show that imposing the natural debt limit with $\hat{a} > -\infty$ leads to the same household behavior as in the maximization problem with the no-Ponzi condition. [Hint: consider the maximization of (8.3) subject to (8.8) and (8.11) with $\hat{a} > -\infty$, and show that this problem satisfies the conditions of Theorems 7.13 and 7.14. Then derive the necessary conditions and compare them to those in Section 8.2.]

(b) Verify that in equilibrium $\hat{a} > -\infty$.

8.11 Use an argument similar to that of the proof of Mangasarian's sufficiency result (Theorem 7.5) to show that because the representative household's Hamiltonian in the neoclassical growth model, $H(t, a, c, \mu)$, is concave in (a, c) and strictly concave in c, the path of consumption and assets given by (8.17)–(8.19) is the unique solution to the household's maximization problem.

8.12 In the dynamics of the basic neoclassical growth model, depicted in Figure 8.1, prove that the $\dot{c} = 0$ locus always intersects the $\dot{k} = 0$ locus to the left of k_{gold}. Based on this analysis, explain why the modified golden rule capital-labor ratio k^* given by (8.35) differs from k_{gold}.

8.13 (a) In the analysis of transitional dynamics, show that if initial consumption $c(0)$ started above the stable arm, the capital stock would reach zero at some finite time. Explain why this would violate feasibility. [Hint: be specific on what you assume about the necessary conditions when $c = 0$.]

(b) Show that if the initial level of consumption starts below the stable arm, then the capital-labor ratio converges to $\bar{k}$, where $f'(\bar{k}) < \delta + n$. [Hint: use the facts that $\bar{k} > k_{\text{gold}}$ and that $f'(k_{\text{gold}}) = \delta + n$.]

8.14 Consider a candidate equilibrium path in Figure 8.1 where the capital stock (capital-labor ratio $k(t)$) reaches zero at some finite time $T < \infty$.

(a) Show that in the candidate equilibrium path, $c(t) = 0$ for all $t \geq T$, and as $t \to T$, $r(t) \to \infty$.

(b) Show that this candidate path cannot be an equilibrium by considering the following deviation for a household: reduce consumption by a small amount $\Delta > 0$ at $t' < T$ and save until T. [Hint: the utility cost is approximately $\exp(-(\rho - n)t')u'(c(t'))\Delta < \infty$, whereas with the proceeds the household can increase consumption by $\exp(\int_{t'}^{T} r(t)dt)\Delta$ at T, with utility gain approximately equal to $\exp(-(\rho - n)T + \int_{t'}^{T} r(t)dt)u'(0)\Delta$, where $u'(0) > u'(c(t'))$ and $\exp(-(\rho - n)T + \int_{t'}^{T} r(t)dt)u'(0) > \exp(-(\rho - n)t')$ for t' sufficiently close to T (from the fact that $\lim_{t \to T} r(t) \to \infty$).]

8.15 Consider the baseline neoclassical model with no technological progress.

(a) Show that in the neighborhood of the steady state k^*, the law of motion of $k(t) \equiv K(t)/L(t)$ can be represented as

$$k(t) \simeq k^* + \eta_1 \exp(\xi_1 t) + \eta_2 \exp(\xi_2 t),$$

where ξ_1 and ξ_2 are the eigenvalues of the linearized system.

(b) Compute these eigenvalues and show that one of them, say ξ_2, is positive.

(c) What does the result of part b imply about the value of η_2?

(d) How is the value of η_1 determined? [Hint: for this part, assume that the equation in part 1 holds exactly.]

(e) What determines the speed of adjustment of $k(t)$ toward its steady-state value k^*?

8.16 Consider a variant of the neoclassical model (with constant population growth at the rate n) in which preferences are given by

$$\max \int_0^\infty \exp(-\rho t)u(c(t))dt,$$

and there is population growth at the constant rate n. How does this modification affect the equilibrium? How should the transversality condition be modified? What is the relationship between the rate of population growth n and the steady-state capital-labor ratio k^*?

8.17 Prove Proposition 8.3.

8.18 Explain why the steady-state capital-labor ratio k^* does not depend on the form of the instantaneous utility function without technological progress but does depend on the intertemporal elasticity of substitution when there is positive technological progress.

8.19 (a) Show that the steady-state saving rate s^* defined in (8.38) is decreasing in ρ, so that lower discount rates lead to higher steady-state savings.

(b) Show that in contrast to the Solow model, the saving rate s^* can never be so high that a decline in savings (or an increase in ρ) can raise the steady-state level of consumption per capita.

8.20 Consider the BGP of the neoclassical model with technological progress studied in Section 8.7 (where consumption grows at the rate g). Show that household utility is finite if and only if Assumption 4 is satisfied.

8.21 Consider the neoclassical model with technological progress studied in Section 8.7. Show that when Assumption 4 is satisfied, the household maximization problem, that of maximizing (8.49) subject to (8.8) and (8.14), satisfies the sufficiency conditions in Theorem 7.14. What happens if Assumption 4 is not satisfied?

8.22 Prove that, as stated in Proposition 8.7, in the neoclassical model with labor-augmenting technological change and the standard assumptions, starting with $k(0) > 0$, there exists a unique equilibrium path where normalized consumption and the capital-labor ratio monotonically converge to the BGP.

8.23 Consider a neoclassical economy with a representative household with preferences at time $t = 0$ given by

$$\int_0^\infty \exp(-\rho t) \frac{c(t)^{1-\theta} - 1}{1 - \theta} \, dt.$$

There is no population growth and labor is supplied inelastically. Assume that the aggregate production function is given by $Y(t) = F(A(t)K(t), L(t))$, where F satisfies the standard assumptions (constant returns to scale, differentiability, and the Inada conditions).

(a) Define a competitive equilibrium for this economy.

(b) Suppose that $A(t) = A(0)$ for all t, and characterize the steady-state equilibrium. Explain why the steady-state capital-labor ratio is independent of θ.

(c) Now assume that $A(t) = \exp(gt)A(0)$, and show that a BGP (with constant capital share in national income, and constant and equal rates of growth of output, capital, and consumption) exists only if F takes the Cobb-Douglas form, $Y(t) = (A(t)K(t))^\alpha L(t)^{1-\alpha}$.

(d) Characterize the BGP in the Cobb-Douglas case. Derive the common growth rate of output, capital, and consumption.

8.24 Derive closed-form equations for the solution to the differential equations of transitional dynamics presented in Example 8.2 with log preferences.

8.25 Derive (8.42) from the $(T-1)$-period lifetime budget constraint of the representative household. In particular, write this budget constraint as

$$\sum_{t=0}^{T-1} \left(\prod_{s=0}^{t-1} \frac{1}{1+r(s)} \right) c(t) + \left(\prod_{s=0}^{t-1} \frac{1}{1+r(s)} \right) a(T)$$

$$\leq \sum_{t=0}^{T-1} \left(\prod_{s=0}^{t-1} \frac{1}{1+r(s)} \right) w(t) + a(0).$$

Explain the budget constraint. By taking the limit as $T \to \infty$, show that this constraint implies the infinite-horizon lifetime budget constraint only if (8.42) is satisfied.

8.26   Consider the discrete-time version of the neoclassical growth model. Suppose that the economy admits a representative household with log preferences ($\theta = 1$ in terms of (8.49)) and the production function is Cobb-Douglas. Assume also that $\delta = 1$, so that there is full depreciation. Characterize the steady-state equilibrium, and derive a difference equation that explicitly characterizes the behavior of capital stock away from the steady state.

8.27   In the discrete-time version of the neoclassical growth model in Exercise 8.26, suppose that there is labor-augmenting technological progress at the rate g:

$$A(t+1) = (1+g) A(t).$$

For simplicity, suppose that there is no population growth.

(a) Prove that balanced growth requires preferences to take the CRRA form

$$U(c(0), c(1), \ldots) \equiv \begin{cases} \sum_{t=0}^{\infty} \beta^t \frac{c(t)^{1-\theta}-1}{1-\theta} & \text{if } \theta \neq 1 \text{ and } \theta \geq 0 \\ \sum_{t=0}^{\infty} \beta^t \log c(t) & \text{if } \theta = 1. \end{cases}$$

(b) Assuming the form of preferences given in part a, prove that there exists a unique steady-state equilibrium in which effective capital-labor ratio remains constant.

(c) Prove that this steady-state equilibrium of part b is globally stable and that convergence to this steady state starting from a non-steady-state level of effective capital-labor ratio is monotonic.

8.28   (a) Analyze the comparative dynamics of the basic model in response to an unanticipated increase to $g' > g$ in the rate of labor-augmenting technological progress. Does consumption increase or decrease with this change?

(b) Analyze the comparative dynamics in response to the announcement at time T that at some future date $T' > T$ the tax rate will decline to $\tau' < \tau$. Does consumption increase or decrease at time T?

8.29   Consider the basic neoclassical growth model with technological change and CRRA preferences (8.49). Explain why $\theta > 1$ ensures that the transversality condition is always satisfied.

8.30   Consider the basic neoclassical growth model with CRRA preferences but with consumer heterogeneity in initial asset holdings (you may assume no technological change if you wish). In particular, there is a set $\mathcal{H}$ of households, and household $h \in \mathcal{H}$ starts with initial assets $a_h(0)$. Households are otherwise identical.

(a) Characterize the competitive equilibrium of this economy and show that the behavior of per capita variables is identical to that in a representative household economy, with the representative household starting with assets $a(0) = |\mathcal{H}|^{-1} \int_{\mathcal{H}} a_h(0)dh$, where $|\mathcal{H}|$ is the measure (number) of households in this economy. Interpret this result and relate it to Theorem 5.2.

(b) Show that if, instead of the natural debt limit or the no-Ponzi condition, we impose $a_h(t) \geq 0$ for all $h \in \mathcal{H}$ and for all t, then a different equilibrium allocation may result. In light of this finding, discuss whether (and when) it is appropriate to use a no-borrowing constraint instead of the no-Ponzi condition.

8.31   Consider a variant of the neoclassical economy with the so-called Stone-Geary preferences given by

$$\int_0^{\infty} \exp(-\rho t) \frac{(c(t)-\gamma)^{1-\theta}-1}{1-\theta} dt,$$

where $\gamma > 0$. There is no population growth. Assume that the production function is given by $Y(t) = F(K(t), A(t)L(t))$, which satisfies all the standard assumptions, and $A(t) = \exp(gt) A(0)$.

(a) Interpret the utility function.

(b) Define the competitive equilibrium for this economy.

(c) Characterize the equilibrium of this economy. Does a BGP with positive growth in consumption exist? Why or why not?

(d) Derive a parameter restriction ensuring that the standard transversality condition is satisfied.

(e) Characterize the transitional dynamics of the economy.

(f) Show that if preferences are given by

$$\sum_{t=0}^{\infty} \beta^t [(c(t) - \gamma(t))^{1-\theta} - 1]/(1 - \theta),$$

with $\lim_{t \to \infty} \gamma(t) = \bar{\gamma} < \infty$, a BGP equilibrium again exists and is identical to the BGP characterized in parts a–e of this exercise.

8.32 Consider a world consisting of a collection of closed neoclassical economies. Each country j has access to the same neoclassical production technology and admits a representative household with preferences $(1 - \theta)^{-1} \int_0^\infty \exp(-\rho_j t)(c_j^{1-\theta} - 1)dt$. Characterize the cross-country differences in income per capita in this world economy. What is the effect of a 10% difference in discount factor (e.g., a difference between a discount rate of 0.02 versus 0.022) on steady-state per capita income differences? [Hint: use the fact that the capital share of income is about 1/3.]

8.33 Consider a neoclassical growth model augmented with labor supply decisions. In particular, total population is normalized to 1, and all households have utility function given by $\int_0^\infty \exp(-\rho t) u(c(t), 1 - l(t))$, where $l(t) \in (0, 1)$ is labor supply. In a symmetric equilibrium, employment $L(t)$ is equal to $l(t)$. Assume that the production function is $Y(t) = F(K(t), A(t)L(t))$, and $A(t) = \exp(gt) A(0)$.

(a) Define a competitive equilibrium.

(b) Set up the current-value Hamiltonian that each household solves, taking wages and interest rates as given, and determine the necessary and sufficient conditions for the allocation of consumption over time and leisure-labor trade-off.

(c) Set up the current-value Hamiltonian for a planner maximizing the utility of the representative household, and derive the necessary and sufficient conditions for a solution.

(d) Show that the two problems are equivalent given competitive markets.

(e) Show that along a BGP, the utility function needs to have a representation of the form

$$u(c(t), 1 - l(t)) = \begin{cases} \frac{Ac(t)^{1-\theta}}{1-\theta} h(1 - l(t)) & \text{for } \theta \neq 1, \\ A \log c(t) + Bh(1 - l(t)) & \text{for } \theta = 1, \end{cases}$$

for some $h(\cdot)$ with $h'(\cdot) > 0$. [Hint: to simplify you may assume that the intertemporal elasticity of substitution for consumption, $\varepsilon_u \equiv -u_{cc}c/u_c$, is only a function of c.] Provide an intuition for this functional form in terms of income and substitution effects.

8.34 Consider the standard neoclassical growth model with a representative household with preferences

$$\int_0^\infty \exp(-\rho t)\left(\frac{c(t)^{1-\theta} - 1}{1 - \theta} + G(t)\right) dt,$$

where $G(t)$ is a public good financed by government spending. Assume that the production function is given by $Y(t) = F(K(t), L(t))$, which satisfies all the standard assumptions, and the budget set of the representative household is $C(t) + I(t) \leq Y(t)$, where $I(t)$ is private investment.

Assume that $G(t)$ is financed by taxes on investment. In particular, the capital accumulation equation is

$$\dot{K}(t) = (1 - \tau(t))\, I(t) - \delta K(t),$$

and the fraction $\tau(t)$ of the private investment $I(t)$ is used to finance the public good, that is, $G(t) = \tau(t)I(t)$. Take the path of tax rates $[\tau(t)]_{t=0}^{\infty}$ as given.

(a) Define a competitive equilibrium.

(b) Set up the individual maximization problem, and characterize consumption and investment behavior.

(c) Assuming that $\lim_{t \to \infty} \tau(t) = \tau$, characterize the steady state.

(d) What value of τ maximizes the steady-state utility of the representative household? Is this value also the tax rate that would maximize the initial utility level when the economy starts away from the steady state? Why or why not?

8.35 Consider the neoclassical growth model with a government that needs to finance a flow expenditure of $G > 0$. Suppose that government spending does not affect utility and that the government can finance this expenditure by using lump-sum taxes (that is, some amount $\mathcal{T}(t)$ imposed on each household at time t regardless of the household's income level and capital holdings) and debt, so that the government budget constraint takes the form

$$\dot{b}(t) = r(t)b(t) + g - \mathcal{T}(t),$$

where $b(t)$ denotes its debt level. The no-Ponzi condition for the government is

$$\lim_{t \to \infty} \left[b(t) \exp\left(- \int_0^t (r(s) - n)\, ds \right) \right] = 0.$$

Prove the following *Ricardian equivalence* result: any path of lump-sum taxes $[\mathcal{T}(t)]_{t=0}^{\infty}$ that satisfies the government's budget constraint (together with the no-Ponzi condition) leads to the same equilibrium path of capital-labor ratio and consumption. Interpret this result.

8.36 Consider the baseline neoclassical growth model with no population growth, no technological change, and preferences given by the standard CRRA utility function (8.49). Assume, however, that the representative household can borrow and lend at the exogenously given international interest rate r^*. Characterize the steady-state equilibrium and transitional dynamics in this economy. Show that if the economy starts with less capital than its steady-state level, it will immediately jump to the steady state by borrowing internationally. How will the economy repay this debt?

8.37 Modify the neoclassical economy (without technological change) by introducing costs of adjustment in investment as in the q-theory of investment studied in Section 7.8. Characterize the steady-state equilibrium and the transitional dynamics. How do the implications of this model differ from those of the baseline neoclassical model?

* 8.38 Consider a version of the neoclassical model that admits a representative household with preferences given by (8.49), no population growth, and no technological progress. The main difference from the standard model is that there are multiple capital goods. In particular, suppose that the production function of the economy is given by

$$Y(t) = F\left(K_1(t), \ldots, K_M(t), L(t) \right),$$

where K_m denotes the mth type of capital, and L is labor. F is homogeneous of degree 1 in all of its variables. Capital in each sector accumulates in the standard fashion,

$$\dot{K}_m(t) = I_m(t) - \delta_m K_m(t),$$

for $m = 1, \ldots, M$. The resource constraint of the economy at time t is

$$C(t) + \sum_{m=1}^{M} I_m(t) \leq Y(t).$$

(a) Write budget constraint of the representative household in this economy. Show that this can be done in two alternative and equivalent ways; first, with M separate assets, and second with only a single asset that is a claim to all of the capital in the economy.

(b) Define equilibrium and BGP allocations.

(c) Characterize the BGP by specifying the profit-maximizing decision of firms in each sector and the dynamic optimization problem of consumers.

(d) Write down the optimal growth problem in the form of a multidimensional current-value Hamiltonian, and show that the optimum growth problem coincides with the equilibrium growth problem. Interpret this result.

(e) Define and discuss the appropriate notion of saddle-path stability for transitional dynamics. Show that the equilibrium is always saddle-path stable and the equilibrium dynamics can be reduced to those in the one-sector neoclassical growth model.

(f) How are the transitional dynamics different when investment is irreversible in each sector (i.e., $I_m(t) \geq 0$ for all t and each $m = 1, \ldots, M$)?

8.39 Contrast the effects of taxing capital income at the rate τ in the Solow growth model and the neoclassical growth model. Show that capital income taxes have no effect in the former, while they depress the effective capital-labor ratio in the latter. Explain why there is such a difference.

9

Growth with Overlapping Generations

A key feature of the neoclassical growth model of the previous chapter is that it admits a (normative) representative household. This model provides us with a tractable framework for the analysis of capital accumulation. Moreover, it enables us to appeal to the First and Second Welfare Theorems to establish the equivalence between equilibrium and optimum growth problems. In many situations, however, the assumption of a representative household is not appropriate. One important set of circumstances that may require departure from this assumption is in the analysis of an economy in which new households arrive (or are born) over time. The arrival of new households in the economy is not only a realistic feature, but it also introduces a range of new economic interactions. In particular, decisions made by older generations will affect the prices faced by younger generations. These economic interactions have no counterpart in the neoclassical growth model. They are most succinctly captured in the *overlapping generations (OLG) models* introduced and studied by Paul Samuelson and later by Peter Diamond.

These models are useful for a number of reasons. First, they capture the potential interaction of different generations of individuals in the marketplace. Second, they provide a tractable alternative to the infinite-horizon representative agent models. Third, some of their key implications are different from those of the neoclassical growth model. Fourth, the dynamics of capital accumulation and consumption in some special cases of these models are quite similar to the basic Solow model rather than to the neoclassical model. Finally, they generate new insights about the role of national debt and social security in the economy.

I start with an illustration of why the First Welfare Theorem cannot be applied in OLG models. I then discuss the baseline OLG model and a number of applications of this framework. Finally, I present the OLG model in continuous time. The latter model, originally developed by Menahem Yaari and Olivier Blanchard and also referred to as the *perpetual youth* model, is a tractable alternative to the basic OLG model. This model is also used in the context of human capital investments in the next chapter.

9.1   Problems of Infinity

This section illustrates why the First Welfare Theorem does not apply to OLG models using an abstract general equilibrium economy introduced by Karl Shell. This model is interesting in part because it is closely related to the baseline OLG model of Samuelson and Diamond, which is presented in the next section.

Consider the following static economy with a countably infinite number of households, each denoted by $i \in \mathbb{N}$, and a countably infinite number of commodities, denoted by $j \in \mathbb{N}$. Assume that all households behave competitively (alternatively, we can assume that there are M households of each type, where M is a large number). Household i has preferences given by

$$u_i = c_i^i + c_{i+1}^i,$$

where $c_j^i \geq 0$ denotes the consumption of the jth type of commodity by household i. These preferences imply that household i enjoys the consumption of the commodity with the same index as its own and the next indexed commodity (e.g., the household indexed by 3 only derives utility from the consumption of goods indexed by 3 and 4).

The endowment vector ω of the economy is as follows: each household has one unit endowment of the commodity with the same index as its own. Let us choose the price of the first commodity as the numeraire, so that $p_0 = 1$. A competitive equilibrium in this economy is defined in the usual manner (e.g., Definition 5.1 in Chapter 5). The following proposition characterizes a competitive equilibrium (see Exercise 9.1 for the uniqueness of equilibrium).

Proposition 9.1   *In the above-described economy, the price vector* $\bar{\mathbf{p}}$ *such that* $\bar{p}_j = 1$ *for all* $j \in \mathbb{N}$ *is a competitive equilibrium price vector and induces an equilibrium with no trade, denoted by* $\bar{\mathbf{x}}$.

Proof.   At $\bar{\mathbf{p}}$, each household has income equal to 1. Therefore the budget constraint of household i can be written as

$$c_i^i + c_{i+1}^i \leq 1.$$

Thus consuming its own endowment is optimal for each household, establishing that the price vector $\bar{\mathbf{p}}$ and no trade, $\bar{\mathbf{x}}$, constitute a competitive equilibrium.   ■

However the competitive equilibrium in Proposition 9.1 is not Pareto optimal. To see this, consider the following alternative allocation: $\tilde{\mathbf{x}}_{i'}$ for $i' \in \mathbb{N}$. In this allocation, each household $i < i'$ consumes one unit of good $j = i$. Household i' consumes one unit of good $j = i'$ and one unit of good $j = i' + 1$. Finally, each household $i > i'$ consumes one unit of good $i + 1$. In other words, household i' consumes its own endowment and that of household $i' + 1$, while all other households, indexed $i > i'$, consume the endowment of the neighboring household, $i + 1$ (while the consumption bundles of all households $i < i'$ are the same as in $\bar{\mathbf{x}}$). In this allocation, all households with $i \neq i'$ are as well off as in the competitive equilibrium $(\bar{\mathbf{p}}, \bar{\mathbf{x}})$, and household i' is strictly better off. This argument establishes the following proposition.

Proposition 9.2   *In the above-described economy, the competitive equilibrium at* $(\bar{\mathbf{p}}, \bar{\mathbf{x}})$ *is not Pareto optimal.*

In fact, it is also straightforward to construct alternative allocations that make more than a single agent strictly better off relative to the equilibrium allocation $\bar{\mathbf{x}}$ (see Exercise 9.1). So why does the First Welfare Theorem not apply in this economy? Recall that the first version of this theorem (Theorem 5.5) is for an economy with a finite number of households, whereas there are an infinite number of households and commodities here. The extended version of the First Welfare Theorem (Theorem 5.6) covers this case, but only under the assumption that $\sum_{i \in \mathcal{H}} \sum_{j=0}^{\infty} p_j^* \omega_j^i < \infty$, where ω_j^i is the endowment of household h of commodity j and p_j^* is the price of this commodity in the competitive equilibrium in question. It can be verified that this assumption is not satisfied in the current example, since $\sum_{i \in \mathcal{H}} \omega_j^i = 1$ for all $j \in \mathbb{N}$, and the competitive equilibrium in question features $p_j^* = 1$ for all $j \in \mathbb{N}$, so that $\sum_{i \in \mathcal{H}} \sum_{j=0}^{\infty} p_j^* \omega_j^i = \infty$. As discussed in Chapter 5, when the total value of endowments at equilibrium prices is equal to infinity, there might exist feasible allocations for the economy as a whole that Pareto dominate the competitive equilibrium. The economy discussed here gives a simple example of this phenomenon.

If the failure of the First Welfare Theorem were a specific feature of this abstract (perhaps artificial) economy, it would not be of great interest to us. However, the next section shows that this abstract economy shares many crucial features with the baseline OLG model, and Section 9.4 shows that the Pareto suboptimality of the competitive equilibrium in this economy is closely connected to potential inefficiencies in the OLG model.

Even though Theorem 5.6 cannot be applied in this economy, it is possible to decentralize the Pareto optimal allocations. The following proposition shows how the Pareto optimal allocation $\tilde{\mathbf{x}}_{i'}$ described above can be decentralized as a competitive equilibrium.

Proposition 9.3 *In the above-described economy, there exists a reallocation of the endowment vector $\boldsymbol{\omega}$ to $\tilde{\boldsymbol{\omega}}_{i'}$, and an associated competitive equilibrium $(\bar{\mathbf{p}}, \tilde{\mathbf{x}}_{i'})$ that is Pareto optimal where $\tilde{\mathbf{x}}_{i'}$ is as described above, and $\bar{\mathbf{p}}$ is such that $\bar{p}_j = 1$ for all $j \in \mathbb{N}$.*

Proof. Consider the following reallocation of the endowment vector $\boldsymbol{\omega}$. The endowment of household $i > i'$ is given to household $i - 1$. Consequently, at the new endowment vector $\tilde{\boldsymbol{\omega}}_{i'}$, households $i < i'$ have one unit of good $j = i$, household i' has one unit of good i' and one unit of good $j = i' + 1$, while all households $i > i'$ have one unit of good $i + 1$. At the price vector $\bar{\mathbf{p}}$, household i' has a budget set

$$c_{i'}^{i'} + c_{i'+1}^{i'} \leq 2,$$

and thus it is utility maximizing for this household to choose $c_{i'}^{i'} = c_{i'+1}^{i'} = 1$. All other households have budget sets given by

$$c_i^i + c_{i+1}^i \leq 1;$$

thus it is feasible and optimal for each household $i < i'$ to consume one unit of good c_i and for each household $i > i'$ to consume one unit of good c_{i+1}. Thus $(\bar{\mathbf{p}}, \tilde{\mathbf{x}}_{i'})$ is a competitive equilibrium given the endowment vector $\tilde{\boldsymbol{\omega}}_{i'}$. ∎

9.2 The Baseline Overlapping Generations Model

I now discuss the baseline two-period OLG economy.

9.2.1 Demographics, Preferences, and Technology

In this economy, time is discrete and runs to infinity. Each individual lives for two periods. For example, all individuals born at time t live for dates t and $t + 1$. For now let us assume a general (separable) utility function for individuals born at date t of the form

$$U_t(c_1(t), c_2(t+1)) = u(c_1(t)) + \beta u(c_2(t+1)), \tag{9.1}$$

where $u : \mathbb{R}_+ \to \mathbb{R}$ satisfies the conditions in Assumption 3 (from Chapter 8), $c_1(t)$ denotes the consumption of an individual born at time t when young (at date t), and $c_2(t+1)$ is this individual's consumption when old (at date $t+1$). Also $\beta \in (0, 1)$ is the discount factor. There is no need to distinguish among different individuals of the same generation, and I do not do so to economize on notation.

Factor markets are competitive. Individuals can only work in the first period of their lives, and they supply one unit of labor inelastically, earning the equilibrium wage rate $w(t)$. Suppose also that there is exponential population growth, and in particular, the size of generation t (born at time t) is

$$L(t) = (1+n)^t L(0). \tag{9.2}$$

The production side of the economy is the same as before, characterized by a set of competitive firms, and it is represented by a standard constant returns to scale aggregate production function, satisfying Assumptions 1 and 2 (from Chapter 2):

$$Y(t) = F(K(t), L(t)),$$

which uses the fact that employment at time t is equal to the size of the group at this date, $L(t)$. To simplify the analysis let us assume that $\delta = 1$, so that capital fully depreciates after use (see Exercise 9.4). Thus, again defining $k \equiv K/L$, the (gross) rate of return to saving, which equals the rental rate of capital, is given by

$$1 + r(t) = R(t) = f'(k(t)), \tag{9.3}$$

where $f(k) \equiv F(k, 1)$ is the standard per capita production function. As usual, the wage rate is

$$w(t) = f(k(t)) - k(t)f'(k(t)). \tag{9.4}$$

9.2.2 Consumption Decisions

Let us start with the individual consumption decisions. Savings by an individual of generation t, $s(t)$, are determined as a solution to the following maximization problem:

$$\max_{c_1(t), c_2(t+1), s(t)} u(c_1(t)) + \beta u(c_2(t+1)),$$

subject to

$$c_1(t) + s(t) \le w(t),$$

and

$$c_2(t+1) \le R(t+1)s(t),$$

where I am using the convention that young individuals rent their savings as capital to final good producers at the end of time t and receive the return at time $t+1$ (after production is carried out).[1] The gross rate of return they receive on their savings is $R(t + 1) = 1 + r(t + 1)$. The second constraint incorporates the notion that individuals only spend money on their own end-of-life consumption (since there is no altruism or bequest motive). There is no need to introduce the additional constraint that $s(t) \geq 0$, since negative savings would violate the second-period budget constraint (given that $c_2(t + 1) \geq 0$).

Since the utility function $u(\cdot)$ is strictly increasing (Assumption 3), both constraints hold as equalities. Therefore the first-order condition for a maximum can be written in the familiar form of the consumption Euler equation (recall Chapter 6, e.g., (6.45)):

$$u'(c_1(t)) = \beta R(t + 1) u'(c_2(t + 1)). \tag{9.5}$$

Moreover, since the problem of each individual is strictly concave, this Euler equation is sufficient to characterize an optimal consumption path given market prices. Combining this equation with the budget constraint, we obtain the following implicit function that determines savings per person as

$$s(t) = s(w(t), R(t + 1)), \tag{9.6}$$

where $s : \mathbb{R}_+^2 \to \mathbb{R}$ is strictly increasing in its first argument and may be increasing or decreasing in its second argument (see Exercise 9.5). Total savings in the economy is equal to

$$S(t) = s(t)L(t),$$

where $L(t)$ denotes the size of generation t, who are saving for time $t + 1$. Since capital depreciates fully after use and all new savings are invested in the only productive asset of the economy—capital—the law of motion of the capital stock is given by

$$K(t + 1) = L(t)s(w(t), R(t + 1)). \tag{9.7}$$

9.2.3 Equilibrium

A competitive equilibrium in the OLG economy can be defined as follows.

Definition 9.1 *A competitive equilibrium* can be represented by sequences of aggregate capital stocks, household consumption, and factor prices, $\{K(t), c_1(t), c_2(t), R(t), w(t)\}_{t=0}^{\infty}$, such that the factor price sequence $\{R(t), w(t)\}_{t=0}^{\infty}$ is given by (9.3) and (9.4), individual consumption decisions $\{c_1(t), c_2(t)\}_{t=0}^{\infty}$ are given by (9.5) and (9.6), and the aggregate capital stock $\{K(t)\}_{t=0}^{\infty}$ evolves according to (9.7).

A steady-state equilibrium is defined in the usual fashion as an equilibrium in which the capital-labor ratio $k \equiv K/L$ is constant.

---

1. Here we could have used a number of different conventions, all with identical results. For example, it could be assumed that the young keep their savings from time t until the beginning of time $t + 1$, and at that point, they rent this as capital to final good producers. Or alternatively, one could introduce another set of (competitive) firms transforming savings in terms of date t commodities to date $t + 1$ commodities. In this case, the young would use these firms to transfer resources from t to $t + 1$. The convention used in the text is the simplest.

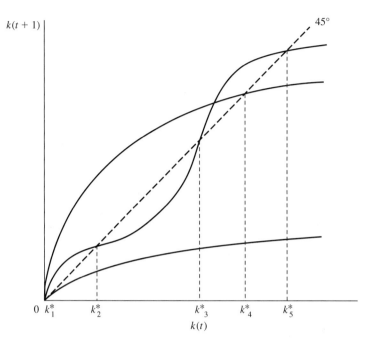

FIGURE 9.1 Various types of steady-state equilibria in the baseline overlapping generations model.

To characterize the equilibrium, divide (9.7) by labor supply at time $t + 1$, $L(t + 1) = (1 + n)L(t)$, to obtain the capital-labor ratio as

$$k(t + 1) = \frac{s(w(t), R(t + 1))}{1 + n}.$$

Now substituting for $R(t + 1)$ and $w(t)$ from (9.3) and (9.4), we obtain

$$k(t + 1) = \frac{s(f(k(t)) - k(t)f'(k(t)), f'(k(t + 1)))}{1 + n} \tag{9.8}$$

as the fundamental law of motion of the OLG economy. A steady state is given by a solution to this equation such that $k(t + 1) = k(t) = k^*$, that is,

$$k^* = \frac{s(f(k^*) - k^*f'(k^*), f'(k^*))}{1 + n}. \tag{9.9}$$

Since the savings function $s(\cdot, \cdot)$ can take any form, the difference equation (9.8) can lead to quite complicated dynamics, and multiple steady states are possible. Figure 9.1 illustrates some of the potential forms linking today's capital-labor ratio to tomorrow's that are consistent with (9.8). The figure illustrates that the OLG model can lead to a unique stable equilibrium, to multiple equilibria, or to an equilibrium with zero capital stock. In other words, without putting more structure on utility and production functions, the model makes few predictions.

9.2.4 Restrictions on Utility and Production Functions

In this section I characterize the steady-state equilibrium and transitional dynamics when further assumptions are imposed on the utility and production functions. In particular, let us suppose that the utility functions take the familiar CRRA form:

$$U_t\left(c_1(t), c_2(t+1)\right) = \frac{c_1(t)^{1-\theta} - 1}{1-\theta} + \beta\left(\frac{c_2(t+1)^{1-\theta} - 1}{1-\theta}\right), \tag{9.10}$$

where $\theta > 0$ and $\beta \in (0, 1)$. Furthermore, assume that technology is Cobb-Douglas, so that

$$f(k) = k^\alpha.$$

The rest of the environment is as described above. The CRRA utility simplifies the first-order condition for consumer optimization and implies

$$\frac{c_2(t+1)}{c_1(t)} = (\beta R(t+1))^{1/\theta}.$$

Once again this expression is the discrete-time consumption Euler equation from Chapter 6, now for the CRRA utility function. This Euler equation can be alternatively expressed in terms of savings as

$$s(t)^{-\theta}\beta R(t+1)^{1-\theta} = (w(t) - s(t))^{-\theta}, \tag{9.11}$$

which gives the following equation for the saving rate:

$$s(t) = \frac{w(t)}{\psi(t+1)}, \tag{9.12}$$

where

$$\psi(t+1) \equiv [1 + \beta^{-1/\theta} R(t+1)^{-(1-\theta)/\theta}] > 1,$$

which ensures that savings are always less than earnings. The impact of factor prices on savings is summarized by the following derivatives:

$$s_w \equiv \frac{\partial s(t)}{\partial w(t)} = \frac{1}{\psi(t+1)} \in (0, 1),$$

and

$$s_R \equiv \frac{\partial s(t)}{\partial R(t+1)} = \left(\frac{1-\theta}{\theta}\right)(\beta R(t+1))^{-1/\theta}\frac{s(t)}{\psi(t+1)}.$$

Since $\psi(t+1) > 1$, we also have that $0 < s_w < 1$. Moreover, in this case $s_R < 0$ if $\theta > 1$, $s_R > 0$ if $\theta < 1$, and $s_R = 0$ if $\theta = 1$. The relationship between the rate of return on savings and the level of savings reflects the counteracting influences of income and substitution effects. For example, when $\theta > 1$, the income effect dominates the substitution effect, so even though R increases (and thus consumption when young becomes more expensive relative to consumption when old), individuals wish to increase their consumption in both periods of their lives, and thus they reduce their savings. In contrast, when $\theta < 1$, the substitution effect dominates, and individuals reduce their consumption when young and thus increase their savings. The case of $\theta = 1$ (log preferences) is of special importance and is often used in applications. This special case with log preferences and Cobb-Douglas production function is sufficiently common and useful that it may deserve to be called the *canonical overlapping generations model* and is analyzed separately in the next section.

In the current somewhat more general context, (9.8) implies

$$k(t+1) = \frac{s(t)}{(1+n)} \tag{9.13}$$

$$= \frac{w(t)}{(1+n)\psi(t+1)},$$

or more explicitly,

$$k(t+1) = \frac{f(k(t)) - k(t)f'(k(t))}{(1+n)[1 + \beta^{-1/\theta}f'(k(t+1))^{-(1-\theta)/\theta}]}. \tag{9.14}$$

The steady state then involves a solution to the following implicit equation:

$$k^* = \frac{f(k^*) - k^*f'(k^*)}{(1+n)[1 + \beta^{-1/\theta}f'(k^*)^{-(1-\theta)/\theta}]}.$$

Now using the Cobb-Douglas formula, the steady state is obtained as the solution to

$$(1+n)\left[1 + \beta^{-1/\theta}\left(\alpha(k^*)^{\alpha-1}\right)^{(\theta-1)/\theta}\right] = (1-\alpha)(k^*)^{\alpha-1}. \tag{9.15}$$

For simplicity, define $R^* \equiv \alpha(k^*)^{\alpha-1}$ as the marginal product of capital in steady state. Equation (9.15) can then be rewritten as

$$(1+n)\left[1 + \beta^{-1/\theta}\left(R^*\right)^{(\theta-1)/\theta}\right] = (1-\alpha)\,R^*/\alpha. \tag{9.16}$$

The steady-state value of R^*, and thus of k^*, can now be determined from (9.16), which always has a unique solution. Let us next investigate the stability of this steady state. Substitute for the Cobb-Douglas production function in (9.14) to obtain

$$k(t+1) = \frac{(1-\alpha)\,k(t)^{\alpha}}{(1+n)[1 + \beta^{-1/\theta}\left(\alpha k(t+1)^{\alpha-1}\right)^{-(1-\theta)/\theta}]}. \tag{9.17}$$

Using (9.17), the following proposition can be proved.[2]

Proposition 9.4 *In the overlapping generations model with two-period lived households, Cobb-Douglas technology, and CRRA preferences, there exists a unique steady-state equilibrium with the capital-labor ratio k^* given by (9.15), and for any $\theta > 0$, this steady-state equilibrium is globally stable for all $k(0) > 0$.*

Proof. See Exercise 9.6. ∎

In this particular (well-behaved) case, the equilibrium dynamics are very similar to those of the basic Solow model and are shown in Figure 9.2. The figure shows that convergence to the unique steady-state capital-labor ratio k^* is monotonic. In particular, starting with an initial capital-labor ratio $k(0) < k^*$, the OLG economy steadily accumulates more capital and converges to k^*. Starting with $k'(0) > k^*$, the equilibrium involves progressively lower levels of capital-labor ratio, ultimately converging to k^*.

---

2. In this proposition and throughout the rest of this chapter, I again ignore the trivial steady state with $k = 0$.

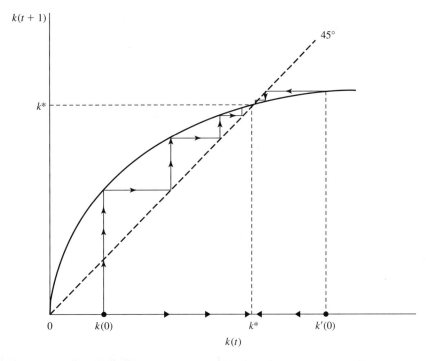

FIGURE 9.2 Equilibrium dynamics in the canonical overlapping generations model.

9.3 The Canonical Overlapping Generations Model

Even the model with CRRA utility and a Cobb-Douglas production function is relatively involved. For this reason, many of the applications of the OLG model use an even more specific utility function, log preferences (or equivalently $\theta = 1$ in terms of the CRRA preferences of the last section). Log preferences are particularly useful in this context, since, as noted above, they ensure that income and substitution effects exactly cancel out, so that changes in the interest rate (and therefore changes in the capital-labor ratio of the economy) have no effect on the saving rate. This independence makes the structure of equilibrium in the canonical OLG model essentially identical to that of the basic Solow model in Chapter 2.

Suppose that the utility of a (typical) individual of generation t is given by

$$U_t(c_1(t), c_2(t + 1)) = \log c_1(t) + \beta \log c_2(t + 1), \tag{9.18}$$

where as before $\beta \in (0, 1)$ (even though $\beta \geq 1$ could be allowed here without any change in the analysis). The aggregate production technology is again Cobb-Douglas, that is, $f(k) = k^{\alpha}$. The consumption Euler equation now becomes even simpler:

$$\frac{c_2(t + 1)}{c_1(t)} = \beta R(t + 1),$$

and it implies that savings should satisfy

$$s(t) = \frac{\beta}{1 + \beta} w(t), \tag{9.19}$$

which corresponds to a constant saving rate, equal to $\beta / (1 + \beta)$, out of labor income for each individual. This constant saving rate makes the model very similar to the baseline Solow growth model of Chapter 2.

Combining (9.19) with the capital accumulation equation (9.8), we have

$$
\begin{aligned}
k(t + 1) &= \frac{s(t)}{(1 + n)} \\
&= \frac{\beta w(t)}{(1 + n)(1 + \beta)} \\
&= \frac{\beta (1 - \alpha) k(t)^{\alpha}}{(1 + n)(1 + \beta)},
\end{aligned}
$$

where the second line uses (9.19) and the last line uses the fact that, given competitive factor markets, the wage rate is $w(t) = (1 - \alpha) k(t)^{\alpha}$.

It is straightforward to verify that there exists a unique steady state with the capital-labor ratio given by

$$
k^* = \left[\frac{\beta(1 - \alpha)}{(1 + n)(1 + \beta)} \right]^{\frac{1}{1-\alpha}}. \tag{9.20}
$$

Moreover, starting with any $k(0) > 0$, equilibrium dynamics are identical to those of the basic Solow model and monotonically converge to k^*. This behavior is illustrated in Figure 9.2 and stated in the next proposition.

Proposition 9.5 *In the canonical OLG model with log preferences and Cobb-Douglas technology, there exists a unique steady state, with capital-labor ratio k^* given by (9.20). Starting with any $k(0) \in (0, k^*)$, equilibrium dynamics are such that $k(t) \uparrow k^*$, and starting with any $k'(0) > k^*$, equilibrium dynamics involve $k(t) \downarrow k^*$.*

This canonical OLG model can be extended in a straightforward way by introducing technological progress. This extension is discussed in Exercise 9.7. Exercise 9.8 asks you to analyze the same economy without Cobb-Douglas technology.

9.4 Overaccumulation and Pareto Optimality of Competitive Equilibrium in the Overlapping Generations Model

Let us now return to the general problem and compare the competitive equilibrium of the OLG economy to the choice of a social planner wishing to maximize a weighted average of all generations' utilities. In particular, suppose that the social planner maximizes

$$
\sum_{t=0}^{\infty} \xi_t U_t(c_1(t), c_2(t + 1)),
$$

where recall that U_t is given by (9.1), and ξ_t is the weight that the social planner places on generation t's utility (with the assumption that $\sum_{t=0}^{\infty} \xi_t < \infty$ so that the planner's problem is well behaved). Substituting from (9.1), this expression implies that the planner maximizes

$$\sum_{t=0}^{\infty} \xi_t (u(c_1(t)) + \beta u(c_2(t + 1))),$$

subject to the resource constraint

$$F(K(t), L(t)) = K(t + 1) + L(t)c_1(t) + L(t - 1) c_2(t).$$

Dividing by $L(t)$ and using (9.2), the resource constraint can be written in per capita terms as

$$f(k(t)) = (1 + n)k(t + 1) + c_1(t) + \frac{c_2(t)}{1 + n}.$$

The social planner's maximization problem then implies the following first-order necessary condition:

$$u'(c_1(t)) = \beta f'(k(t + 1))u'(c_2(t + 1)).$$

Since $R(t + 1) = f'(k(t + 1))$, this equation is identical to (9.5). This result is not surprising: the social planner prefers to allocate consumption of a given individual in exactly the same way as the individual himself would do—there are no "market failures" in the allocation of consumption over time for an individual at given market prices.

However the social planner's allocation of resources across generations differs from that in the competitive equilibrium, since the social planner is giving different weights to different generations. More interesting than contrasting the social planner's allocation for a given set of weights to the equilibrium is the question of whether the competitive equilibrium is Pareto optimal. The parallel between the OLG model and the economy in Section 9.1 suggests that it may not be.

In fact the competitive equilibrium is not in general Pareto optimal. Suppose that the steady-state level of capital-labor ratio, k^*, given by (9.9) is greater than the golden rule capital-labor ratio k_{gold}. Recall from Chapter 2 that k_{gold} maximizes the steady-state level of consumption. In contrast to the neoclassical growth model of the previous chapter, there is no natural reason for the equilibrium (or steady-state) capital-labor ratio to be less than the golden rule level, k_{gold}, in the OLG model. When $k^* > k_{gold}$, reducing savings can increase consumption for every generation. In particular, in the steady state of the OLG economy, we have

$$f(k^*) - (1 + n)k^* = c_1^* + (1 + n)^{-1}c_2^*$$

$$\equiv c^*,$$

where the first line follows by national income accounting, and the second defines c^* as the total steady-state consumption. Therefore

$$\frac{\partial c^*}{\partial k^*} = f'(k^*) - (1 + n),$$

and the golden rule capital-labor ratio k_{gold} is defined by

$$f'(k_{gold}) = 1 + n.$$

Now if $k^* > k_{\text{gold}}$, then $\partial c^*/\partial k^* < 0$, so reducing savings can increase (total) consumption for everybody. If this is the case, the economy is said to be *dynamically inefficient*—it over-accumulates capital. Another way of expressing dynamic inefficiency is that

$$r^* < n,$$

that is, the steady-state (net) interest rate $r^* = R^* - 1$ is less than the rate of population growth. Recall that in the infinite-horizon Ramsey economy (see Chapter 8), the transversality condition (which follows from individual optimization) ensures that the steady-state interest rate satisfies $r^* > g + n$. Therefore dynamic inefficiency could never arise in this Ramsey economy. Dynamic inefficiency arises because of the specific form of household heterogeneity inherent in the OLG model, which removes the neoclassical transversality condition.

In the OLG economy, suppose we start from a steady state at time T with $k^* > k_{\text{gold}}$. Consider the following variation in which the capital stock for the next period is reduced by a small amount. In particular, change next period's capital-labor ratio by $-\Delta k$, where $\Delta k \in \left(0, k^* - k_{\text{gold}}\right)$, and from then on, keep the capital-labor ratio at $k^* - \Delta k$ (which is clearly feasible). Then the following changes occur in consumption levels:

$$\Delta c(T) = (1 + n)\Delta k > 0,$$

and

$$\Delta c(t) = -\left(f'(k^* - \Delta k) - (1 + n)\right)\Delta k \quad \text{for all } t > T.$$

The first expression reflects the direct increase in consumption due to the decrease in savings. In addition, since $k^* > k_{\text{gold}}$, for small enough Δk, $f'(k^* - \Delta k) - (1 + n) < 0$, and thus $\Delta c(t) > 0$ for all $t \geq T$, which explains the second expression. The increase in consumption for each generation can be allocated equally during the two periods of their lives, thus necessarily increasing the utility of all generations. This variation clearly creates a Pareto improvement in which all generations are better off and establishes the following result.

Proposition 9.6 *In the baseline OLG economy, the competitive equilibrium is not necessarily Pareto optimal. More specifically, when $r^* < n$, the economy is dynamically inefficient. In this case, it is possible to reduce the capital stock starting from the competitive steady state and increase the consumption level of all generations.*

As the above derivation makes clear, Pareto inefficiency of the competitive equilibrium is intimately connected to *dynamic inefficiency*. Dynamic inefficiency, the rate of interest being less than the rate of population growth, is not a theoretical curiosity. Exercise 9.9 shows that dynamic inefficiency can arise under reasonable circumstances (though this does not mean that issues of dynamic inefficiency are particularly important when thinking about growth or income differences across countries or over time).

Why is the equilibrium of the OLG economy potentially inefficient? This question is more challenging than it at first appears. In particular, in this economy all markets are competitive, and there are no externalities. Thus the usual sources of market failures are absent. It was once believed that the source of the potential inefficiency was the "incompleteness of markets," resulting from the fact that individuals from generation t cannot directly trade with individuals from generation $t + s$ for $s \geq 2$. When markets are incomplete, there is no guarantee that competitive equilibria are Pareto optimal, which might explain the potential inefficiency of OLG equilibrium. In particular, with incomplete markets, *pecuniary externalities*, which are the price-related effects of the trading decisions of others on the utility of a household, may have first-order welfare consequences and may cause (Pareto) inefficiencies. However this reasoning is incorrect. The simplest way of seeing its fallacy involves returning to the economy discussed in Section 9.1, which featured a similar inefficiency to that in the baseline OLG model. But in that economy all individuals could trade all commodities.

Though wrong this reasoning correctly emphasizes the importance of pecuniary externalities. Individuals from generation t face wages determined by the capital stock decisions of those from generation $t - 1$. Similarly, an individual from generation $t - 1$ receives a rate of return on her savings determined by the savings decisions of others of generation $t - 1$. Consequently, the savings decisions of each generation create pecuniary externalities on both workers and capital holders at the next date. These pecuniary externalities are related to the source of inefficiency in the OLG model, but not because the markets are incomplete. Pecuniary externalities are always present, but in competitive economies they are typically second-order, and thus do not matter for welfare. In a sense the fact that pecuniary externalities do not lead to Pareto suboptimal allocations could be viewed as the essence of the First Welfare Theorem (Theorems 5.5 and 5.6). However, the First Welfare Theorem does not apply to the economy in Section 9.1 and need not apply to the OLG economy. This point is further developed in Exercise 9.11, which shows that when the economy is dynamically inefficient, the condition that $\sum_{h \in \mathcal{H}} \sum_{j=0}^{\infty} p_j^* \omega_j^h < \infty$ in Theorem 5.6 is not satisfied, while this condition is satisfied when $r^* > n$. Intuitively, pecuniary externalities need not cancel out when there is an infinite stream of newborn agents joining the economy. These agents are affected by the pecuniary externalities created by previous generations, and it is possible to rearrange accumulation decisions and consumption plans in such a way that these pecuniary externalities can be exploited (in a manner similar to the way that consumption plans were rearranged to create a Pareto improvement over the competitive equilibrium in the economy of Section 9.1).

A complementary intuition for dynamic inefficiency, which is particularly useful in the next section, is as follows. Dynamic inefficiency arises from overaccumulation, which, in turn, results from the need of the current young generation to save for old age. However, the more they save, the lower is the rate of return to capital, and this may encourage them to save even more. Once again the effect of the savings by the current generation on the future rate of return to capital is a pecuniary externality. Had the First Welfare Theorem applied, these pecuniary externalities would not have led to Pareto suboptimal allocations. But this reasoning need not apply when there are infinite numbers of commodities and households. This second intuition also suggests that if alternative ways of providing consumption to individuals in old age were available, the overaccumulation problem might be solved or at least ameliorated. This topic is discussed in the next section.

9.5 Role of Social Security in Capital Accumulation

I now briefly discuss how social security can be introduced as a way of dealing with overaccumulation in the OLG model. Let us first consider a fully funded system, in which the young make contributions to the social security system, and their contributions are paid back to them in their old age. The alternative is an unfunded or *pay-as-you-go* social security system, in which transfers from the young go directly to the current old. We will see that, as is typically presumed, pay-as-you-go (unfunded) social security discourages aggregate savings. However, when there is dynamic inefficiency, discouraging savings may lead to a Pareto improvement.

9.5.1 Fully Funded Social Security

In a fully funded social security system, the government at date t raises some amount $d(t)$ from the young, for example, by compulsory contributions to their social security accounts.

These funds are invested in the only productive asset of the economy, the capital stock, and the workers receive the returns, given by $R(t + 1)d(t)$, when they are old. Thus the individual maximization problem under a fully funded social security system becomes

$$\max_{c_1(t),c_2(t+1),s(t)} u(c_1(t)) + \beta u(c_2(t + 1))$$

subject to

$$c_1(t) + s(t) + d(t) \le w(t),$$

and

$$c_2(t + 1) \le R(t + 1)\,(s(t) + d(t))$$

for a given choice of $d(t)$ by the government. Notice that now the total amount invested in capital accumulation is $s(t) + d(t) = (1 + n)k(t + 1)$.

It is also no longer the case that individuals always choose $s(t) > 0$, since they have the income from social security. Therefore this economy can be analyzed under two alternative assumptions: with the constraint that $s(t) \ge 0$ and without it.

It is clear that as long as $s(t)$ is free, the competitive equilibrium applies regardless of the sequence of feasible social security payments $\{d(t)\}_{t=0}^{\infty}$. When $s(t) \ge 0$ is imposed as a constraint, then the competitive equilibrium applies if, given the sequence $\{d(t)\}_{t=0}^{\infty}$, the privately optimal saving sequence $\{s(t)\}_{t=0}^{\infty}$ is such that $s(t) > 0$ for all t.

Proposition 9.7 *Consider a fully funded social security system in the above-described environment whereby the government collects $d(t)$ from young individuals at date t.*

1. *Suppose that $s(t) \ge 0$ for all t. If, given the feasible sequence $\{d(t)\}_{t=0}^{\infty}$ of social security payments, the utility-maximizing sequence of savings $\{s(t)\}_{t=0}^{\infty}$ is such that $s(t) > 0$ for all t, then the set of competitive equilibria without social security is the same as the set of competitive equilibria with social security.*

2. *Without the constraint $s(t) \ge 0$, given any feasible sequence $\{d(t)\}_{t=0}^{\infty}$ of social security payments, the set of competitive equilibria with social security is identical to the set of competitive equilibria without social security.*

Proof. See Exercise 9.13. ∎

This result is intuitive: the amount $d(t)$ taken out by the government is fully offset by a decrease in $s(t)$ as long as individuals are accumulating enough savings (or always when there are no constraints to force positive savings privately). Exercise 9.14 shows that even when there is the restriction that $s(t) \ge 0$, a fully funded social security program cannot lead to a Pareto improvement.

9.5.2 Unfunded Social Security

The situation is different with unfunded social security. Now the government collects $d(t)$ from the young at time t and distributes it to the current old with per capita transfer $b(t) = (1 + n)\,d(t)$ (which takes into account that there are more young than old because of population growth). Therefore the individual maximization problem becomes

$$\max_{c_1(t),c_2(t+1),s(t)} u(c_1(t)) + \beta u(c_2(t + 1))$$

subject to

$$c_1(t) + s(t) + d(t) \leq w(t),$$

and

$$c_2(t+1) \leq R(t+1)s(t) + (1+n)\,d(t+1),$$

for a given feasible sequence of social security payment levels $\{d(t)\}_{t=0}^{\infty}$.

In this environment the rate of return on social security payments is n rather than $r(t+1) = R(t+1) - 1$, because unfunded social security is a pure transfer system. Only $s(t)$—rather than $s(t) + d(t)$ as in the funded scheme—goes into capital accumulation. This observation is the basis of the claim that unfunded social security systems discourage aggregate savings. Consequently unfunded social security reduces capital accumulation. Discouraging capital accumulation can have negative consequences for growth and welfare. In fact, the empirical evidence in Chapters 1–4 suggest that there are many societies in which the level of capital accumulation is suboptimally low. In contrast, in the present model reducing aggregate savings and capital accumulation may be lead to a Pareto improvement when the economy exhibits dynamic inefficiency (and overaccumaltion).

More specifically, suppose that individuals of generation t can choose how much to contribute to unfunded social security (i.e., $d(t)$ is a choice variable). Whatever they contribute is given to the current old generation as consumption, and they receive $1 + n$ dollars for every dollar invested when they become old themselves. In this case, there would be no investment in physical capital until $r(t+1) \geq n$. Thus the unfunded social security system would increase the interest rate enough so that the economy is no longer in the dynamic inefficiency region. This analysis establishes the following proposition.

Proposition 9.8 *Consider the above-described OLG economy and suppose that the decentralized competitive equilibrium is dynamically inefficient. Then there exists a feasible sequence of unfunded social security payments $\{d(t)\}_{t=0}^{\infty}$ that leads to a competitive equilibrium starting from any date t that Pareto dominates the competitive equilibrium without social security.*

Proof. See Exercise 9.16. ∎

Unfunded social security reduces overaccumulation and improves the allocation of resources. The similarity between the way in which unfunded social security achieves a Pareto improvement in the OLG model and the way in which the Pareto optimal allocation was decentralized in the example economy of Section 9.1 is evident. In essence, unfunded social security transfers resources from future generations to the initial old generation, and when designed appropriately, it can do so without hurting future generations. Once again, this result depends on dynamic inefficiency; when there is no dynamic inefficiency, any transfer of resources (and any unfunded social security program) makes some future generation worse off. You are asked to prove this result in Exercise 9.17.

Another interesting aspect of unfunded social security is also worth noting. With this type of social security system the government is essentially running a Ponzi game or pyramid scheme. Each generation sacrifices an amount d when young and receives $(1 + n)\,d$ from the current young when they are old. This pattern is typical of a pyramid scheme. In the previous chapter, such schemes were ruled out, so why are they possible (and in fact desirable) here? The answer is related to the fact that in the neoclassical growth model, there exists a representative household whose utility maximization decision ensures that the economy is never in the dynamic inefficiency region. In particular, the transversality condition—or equivalently the finiteness of the utility—of the representative household rules out equilibria where $r^* < n$ (recall (8.36)). This is no longer the case in the OLG economy, and unfunded social security is one way of running a Pareto improving pyramid scheme in an economy with dynamic inefficiency. Interestingly, it is not the only such scheme possible. When $r^* < n$, the equilibrium allows for a range of "bubbles" that can play the same role as unfunded social security. We say that there is a *bubble* when an asset trades at a value greater than its intrinsic value. A bubble on any asset could play the same role as unfunded social security, because it can create a way of transferring resources across dates. The maximum rate of return on any bubble is n, which is also the maximum rate of return on unfunded social security. When there is dynamic inefficiency and $r^* < n$, a bubble provides a better way of transferring resources across dates than investing in physical capital. A simple example of a bubble that can play this role is fiat money, which has no intrinsic value. But all agents might expect fiat money to appreciate over time, so that the purchasing power of fiat money increases by some factor ($\leq 1 + n$) at each period. In this case, giving a limited amount of fiat money to some generation would also play the same role as unfunded social security. Equivalently, however, the same role can be played by other assets (generating similar bubbles). Finally, it is interesting to note that if the OLG economy has a family structure, so that future generations are linked to previous generations as members of a particular family or dynasty, within-family transfers (e.g., supported by social norms or repeated game punishment strategies; see Appendix C) could play the same role. In this case, we would see within-family transfers, which could improve the allocation of resources, and these transfers could be supported even though there is no altruism across family members.

9.6 Overlapping Generations with Impure Altruism

Section 5.3 in Chapter 5 demonstrated that altruism within families (e.g., of parents toward their offspring) can lead to a structure of preferences identical to those of the representative household in the neoclassical growth model. In contrast, this chapter has so far ignored altruistic preferences to emphasize the effect of finite lives and the economic implications of the arrival of new agents in the economy. As briefly noted in Section 5.3, the exact form of altruism within a family determines whether the representative household assumption is a good approximation to the preference side of the economy. In particular, a potentially empirically relevant form of altruism is one in which parents care about certain dimensions of the consumption vector of their offspring instead of their total utility. This type of preference is often referred to as "impure altruism" to distinguish it from the pure altruism discussed in Section 5.3. One particular type of impure altruism, commonly referred to as "warm glow preferences," plays an important role in many growth models because of its tractability. Warm glow preferences assume that parents derive utility from (the warm glow of) their bequest, rather than from their offspring's utility or consumption. These preferences constitute another convenient alternative to the neoclassical growth and the baseline OLG models. This alternative has some clear parallels to the canonical OLG model of the last section, since it also leads to equilibrium dynamics similar to those of the Solow growth model. Given the importance of this class of preferences in many applied growth models, it is useful to review them briefly. These preferences are also used in the next chapter and in Chapter 21.

Suppose that the production side of the economy is given by the standard neoclassical production function, satisfying Assumptions 1 and 2 from Chapter 2. Let us write this in per capita form as $f(k)$.

The economy is populated by a continuum of individuals with measure normalized to 1. Each individual lives for two periods, childhood and adulthood. In the second period of his life, each individual begets an offspring, works, and then his life comes to an end. For simplicity, let us assume that there is no consumption in childhood (or that it is incorporated in the parent's consumption). There are no new households, so population is constant at 1. Each individual supplies 1 unit of labor inelastically during his adulthood.

Let us assume that preferences of individual (i, t), who reaches adulthood at time t, are

$$\log(c_i(t)) + \beta \log(b_i(t)), \tag{9.21}$$

where $c_i(t)$ denotes the consumption of this individual, and $b_i(t)$ is the bequest to his offspring. Log preferences are assumed to simplify the analysis (see Exercise 9.20). The offspring starts the following period with the bequest, rents it out as capital to firms, supplies labor, begets his own offspring, and makes consumption and bequest decisions. I also assume that capital fully depreciates after use.

This formulation implies that the maximization problem of a typical individual can be written as

$$\max_{c_i(t), b_i(t)} \log(c_i(t)) + \beta \log(b_i(t)) \tag{9.22}$$

subject to

$$c_i(t) + b_i(t) \leq y_i(t) \equiv w(t) + R(t)b_i(t-1), \tag{9.23}$$

where $y_i(t)$ denotes the income of this individual,

$$w(t) = f(k(t)) - k(t)f'(k(t)) \tag{9.24}$$

is the equilibrium wage rate,

$$R(t) = f'(k(t)) \tag{9.25}$$

is the rate of return on capital, and $b_i(t-1)$ is the bequest received by this individual from his parent.

The total capital-labor ratio at time $t+1$ is given by aggregating the bequests of all adults at time t:

$$k(t+1) = \int_0^1 b_i(t)di, \tag{9.26}$$

which exploits the fact that the total measure of workers is 1, so that the capital stock and capital-labor ratio are identical.

An equilibrium in this economy is a somewhat more complicated object than before, because we may want to keep track of the consumption and bequest levels of all individuals. Let us denote the distribution of consumption and bequests across households at time t by $[c_i(t)]_{i \in [0,1]}$ and $[b_i(t)]_{i \in [0,1]}$, respectively, and assume that the economy starts with the distribution of wealth (bequests) at time t given by $[b_i(0)]_{i \in [0,1]}$, which satisfies $\int_0^1 b_i(0)di > 0$.

Definition 9.2 *A competitive equilibrium in this OLG economy with warm glow preferences is a sequence of consumption and bequest levels for each household,*

$$\left\{ [c_i(t)]_{i \in [0,1]}, [b_i(t)]_{i \in [0,1]} \right\}_{t=0}^{\infty},$$

that solves (9.22) subject to (9.23); a sequence of capital-labor ratios $\{k(t)\}_{t=0}^{\infty}$ given by (9.26) with some initial distribution of bequests $[b_i(0)]_{i \in [0,1]}$; and a sequences of factor prices $\{w(t), R(t)\}_{t=0}^{\infty}$ that satisfies (9.24) and (9.25).

The solution of (9.22) subject to (9.23) is straightforward because of the log preferences and gives

$$b_i(t) = \frac{\beta}{1+\beta} y_i(t)$$

$$= \frac{\beta}{1+\beta} [w(t) + R(t)b_i(t-1)] \tag{9.27}$$

for all i and t. This equation shows that individual bequest levels follow nontrivial dynamics. Since $b_i(t)$ determines the asset holdings of individual i of generation t, it can alternatively be interpreted as his wealth level. Consequently, this economy features a distribution of wealth that evolves endogenously over time. This evolution depends on factor prices. To obtain the equilibrium factor prices, let us aggregate bequests to obtain the capital-labor ratio of the economy via equation (9.26). Integrating (9.27) across all individuals yields

$$k(t+1) = \int_0^1 b_i(t)di$$

$$= \frac{\beta}{1+\beta} \int_0^1 [w(t) + R(t)b_i(t-1)]\, di \tag{9.28}$$

$$= \frac{\beta}{1+\beta} f(k(t)).$$

The last equality follows from the fact that $\int_0^1 b_i(t-1)\, di = k(t)$ and because by Euler's Theorem [Theorem 2.1], $w(t) + R(t)k(t) = f(k(t))$.

Consequently, aggregate equilibrium dynamics in this economy are straightforward and again closely resemble those in the baseline Solow growth model. Moreover, it is worth noting that these aggregate dynamics do not depend on the distribution of bequests or income across households (we will see in Chapter 21 that this is no longer true when there are other imperfections).

Solving for the steady-state equilibrium capital-labor ratio from (9.28) gives

$$k^* = \frac{\beta}{1+\beta} f(k^*), \tag{9.29}$$

which is uniquely defined and strictly positive in view of Assumptions 1 and 2. Moreover equilibrium dynamics are again given by Figure 9.2 and involve monotone convergence to this unique steady state.

A complete characterization of the equilibrium can now be obtained by looking at the dynamics of bequests. Different types of bequest dynamics are possible along the transition path. More can be said regarding the limiting distribution of wealth and bequests. In particular, we know that $k(t) \rightarrow k^*$, so the ultimate bequest dynamics are given by steady-state factor prices. Let these be denoted by $w^* = f(k^*) - k^* f'(k^*)$ and $R^* = f'(k^*)$. Then once the economy is at the steady-state capital-labor ratio k^*, individual bequest dynamics are given by

$$b_i(t) = \frac{\beta}{1+\beta} [w^* + R^* b_i(t-1)].$$

When $R^* < (1+\beta)/\beta$, starting from any level, $b_i(t)$ converges to a unique bequest (wealth) level given by

$$b^* = \frac{\beta w^*}{1 + \beta(1 - R^*)}. \tag{9.30}$$

Moreover it can be verified that the steady-state equilibrium must involve $R^* < (1+\beta)/\beta$. This follows from the fact that in steady state

$$R^* = f'(k^*) < \frac{f(k^*)}{k^*} = \frac{1+\beta}{\beta},$$

where the strict inequality exploits the strict concavity of $f(\cdot)$, and the last equality uses the definition of the steady-state capital-labor ratio k^* from (9.29). The following proposition summarizes this analysis.

Proposition 9.9 *Consider the OLG economy with warm glow preferences described above. In this economy, there exists a unique competitive equilibrium. In this equilibrium the aggregate capital-labor ratio is given by (9.28) and monotonically converges to the unique steady-state capital-labor ratio k^* given by (9.29). The distribution of bequests and wealth ultimately converges to full equality, with each individual having a bequest (wealth) level of b^* given by (9.30) with $w^* = f(k^*) - k^* f'(k^*)$ and $R^* = f'(k^*)$.*

9.7 Overlapping Generations with Perpetual Youth

A key feature of the baseline OLG model is that individuals have finite lives and know exactly when their lives will come to an end. An alternative way of modeling finite lives is along the lines of the "Poisson death model" or the *perpetual youth model* introduced in Section 5.3 of Chapter 5. Let us start with the discrete-time version of that model. Recall that in that model each individual is potentially infinitely lived, but faces a probability $\nu \in (0, 1)$ that her life will come to an end at any date (and all realizations are independent). Recall from (5.12) that the expected utility of an individual with a pure discount factor β is given by

$$\sum_{t=0}^{\infty} (\beta(1 - \nu))^t u(c(t)),$$

where $u(\cdot)$ is a standard instantaneous utility function satisfying Assumption 3, with the additional normalization that $u(0) = 0$. Since the probability of death is ν and is independent across periods, the expected lifetime of an individual in this model can be written as (see Exercise 9.18):

$$\text{Expected life} = \nu + 2(1 - \nu)\nu + 3(1 - \nu)^2 \nu + \cdots = \frac{1}{\nu} < \infty. \tag{9.31}$$

This equation captures the fact that with probability ν the individual will have a total life of length 1, with probability $(1 - \nu)\nu$, she will have a life of length 2, and so on. This model is referred to as the "perpetual youth model," since even though each individual has a finite expected life, all individuals who have survived up to a certain date have exactly the same expectation of further life. Therefore individuals who survive in this economy are "perpetually young;" their age has no effect on their future longevity and has no predictive power on how many more years they will live.

Individual i's flow budget constraint can be written as

$$a_i(t+1) = (1+r(t))a_i(t) - c_i(t) + w(t) + z_i(t), \qquad (9.32)$$

which is similar to the standard flow budget constraint, for example, (6.54) in Chapter 6. Recall that the gross rate of return on savings is $1 + r(t)$. The only difference from the standard budget constraint is the additional term, $z_i(t)$, which reflects transfers to the individual. The reason these transfers are introduced is as follows: since individuals face an uncertain time of death, there may be accidental bequests. In particular, individuals typically come to the end of their lives while their asset positions are positive. When this happens, one possibility is that the accidental bequests might be collected by the government and redistributed equally across all households in the economy. In this case, $z_i(t)$ would represent these receipts for individual i. However, this modeling assumption would require that we impose a constraint of the form $a_i(t) \geq 0$ to prevent individuals from accumulating debts by the time their lives come to an end.

An alternative, which avoids this additional constraint and makes the model more tractable, has been proposed and studied by Menahem Yaari and Olivier Blanchard. This alternative involves introducing life insurance or annuity markets, where competitive life insurance firms make payments to individuals (as a function of their asset levels) in return for receiving their positive assets when they die. The term $z(t)$ captures these annuity payments. In particular, imagine the following type of life insurance contract: a company would make a payment equal to $z(a(t))$ to an individual as a function of her asset holdings during every period in which she is alive.[3] When the individual dies, all her assets go to the insurance company. The fact that the payment level $z(a(t))$ depends only on the asset holdings of the individual and not on her age is a consequence of the perpetual youth assumption—the conditional expectation of further life is independent of when the individual was born (in fact, it is independent of everything else in the model). The profits of a particular insurance company contracting with an individual with asset holding equal to $a(t)$, at time t are

$$\pi(a, t) = -(1 - v)z(a) + va.$$

With free entry, insurance companies should make zero expected profits (in terms of net present discounted value), which requires that $\pi(a(t), t) = 0$ for all t and a; thus we have

$$z(a(t)) = \frac{v}{1 - v}a(t). \qquad (9.33)$$

The other important element of the model is the evolution of demographics. Since each agent faces a probability of death equal to v at every date, there is a natural force toward decreasing population. We assume, however, that there are also new agents who are born at every date. In contrast to the basic neoclassical growth model, suppose that these new agents are not born into a dynasty; instead they become separate households themselves. We assume that when the population at time t is $L(t)$, there are $nL(t)$ new households born. Consequently the evolution of the total population is given by

$$L(t+1) = (1 + n - v)L(t), \qquad (9.34)$$

---

3. The reader might note that this contract is the opposite of the most common type of life insurance contract where individuals make payments for their families to receive payments after their deaths. These types of insurance contracts are not useful in the current model, since individuals do not have offspring or are not altruistic toward them.

with the initial value $L(0) = 1$, and with $n > v$, so that there is positive population growth. Throughout this section, we ignore technological progress.

Perpetual youth, together with exponential population growth, leads to a simple pattern of demographics in this economy. In particular, it is easy to verify that at some point in time $t > 0$, there will be $n(1 + n - v)^{t-1}$ 1-year-olds, $n(1 + n - v)^{t-2}(1 - v)$ 2-year-olds, $n(1 + n - v)^{t-3}(1 - v)^2$ 3-year-olds, and so on (see Exercise 9.23).

The production side of the economy is standard and is represented by an aggregate production function $F(K(t), L(t))$ satisfying Assumptions 1 and 2. Suppose that capital depreciates at the rate δ. Factor markets are competitive, and factor prices are determined in the usual fashion. The rental return of capital at time t is again given by $R(t) = f'(k(t))$, so that the net return on savings is $r(t + 1) = f'(k(t)) - \delta$, and the wage rate is $w(t) = f(k(t)) - k(t)f'(k(t))$.

An allocation in this economy is similar to one in the neoclassical growth model and involves time paths for the aggregate capital stock, wage rates, and rental rates of capital, $\{K(t), w(t), R(t)\}_{t=0}^{\infty}$. However it is no longer sufficient to specify aggregate consumption, since the level of consumption is not the same for all individuals. Instead, individuals born at different times will have accumulated different amounts of assets and will consume different amounts. Let us denote the consumption at date t of a household born at date $\tau \leq t$ by $c(t \mid \tau)$. An allocation must now specify the entire sequence $\{c(t \mid \tau)\}_{t=0, \tau \leq t}^{\infty}$. Using this notation and the life insurance contracts introduced by (9.33), the flow budget constraint of an individual of generation τ can be written as:

$$a(t + 1 \mid \tau) = \left(1 + r(t) + \frac{v}{1 - v}\right) a(t \mid \tau) - c(t \mid \tau) + w(t). \tag{9.35}$$

A competitive equilibrium is again defined in the usual manner.

Definition 9.3 *A competitive equilibrium* consists of paths of capital stock, wage rates, and rental rates of capital, $\{K(t), w(t), R(t)\}_{t=0}^{\infty}$, and paths of consumption for each generation, $\{c(t \mid \tau)\}_{t=0, \tau \leq t}^{\infty}$, such that each individual maximizes utility, and the time path of factor prices, $\{w(t), R(t)\}_{t=0}^{\infty}$, is such that given the time path of capital stock and labor, $\{K(t), L(t)\}_{t=0}^{\infty}$, all markets clear.*

In addition to the competitive factor prices, the key equation is the consumption Euler equation for an individual of generation τ at time t. Taking into account that the gross rate of return on savings is $1 + r(t) + v/(1 - v)$ and that the effective discount factor of the individual is $\beta(1 - v)$, this Euler equation can be written as

$$u'(c(t \mid \tau)) = \beta[(1 + r(t + 1))(1 - v) + v]u'(c(t + 1 \mid \tau)). \tag{9.36}$$

Equation (9.36) looks similar to be standard consumption Euler equation, for example (6.45) in Chapter 6. It differs from (6.45) only because it applies separately to each generation τ and includes the term v (the probability of death facing each individual). Note, however, that when both r and v are small we have

$$(1 + r)(1 - v) + v \approx 1 + r,$$

and the terms involving v disappear. In fact, the reason these terms are present is because of the discrete-time nature of the current model. In the next section I present the continuous-time version of the perpetual youth model, where the approximation in the previous equation is exact. Moreover the continuous-time model allows us to obtain closed-form solutions for aggregate consumption and capital stock dynamics. Thus this model gives one example of a situation in which continuous-time methods turn out to be more appropriate than discrete-time methods (whereas the baseline OLG model required discrete time).

9.8 Overlapping Generations in Continuous Time

9.8.1 Demographics, Technology, and Preferences

Consider a continuous-time version of the perpetual youth model. Suppose that each individual faces a Poisson death rate of $\nu \in (0, \infty)$. Suppose also that individuals have logarithmic preferences and a pure discount rate of $\rho > 0$. As demonstrated in Exercise 5.7 in Chapter 5, individual i then maximizes the objective function

$$\int_0^\infty \exp(-(\rho + \nu)t) \log c_i(t) \, dt. \tag{9.37}$$

Demographics in this economy are similar to those in the discrete-time perpetual youth model of the previous section. In particular, the expected further life of an individual is independent of when he was born and is equal to $1/\nu < \infty$. This is both the life expectancy at birth and the expected further life of an individual who has survived up to a certain point. Let the population at time t be $L(t)$. Then the Poisson death rate implies that a total flow of $\nu L(t)$ individuals dies at time t. Once again, new households arrive at the exponential rate $n > \nu$, so that aggregate population dynamics are given by

$$\dot{L}(t) = (n - \nu) L(t). \tag{9.38}$$

We assume that $n - \nu < \rho$. The measure ("number") of individuals of the cohort born at time $\tau < t$ who are alive at time t is

$$L(t \mid \tau) = n \exp(-\nu(t - \tau) + (n - \nu)\tau). \tag{9.39}$$

In this equation and throughout the section, suppose that at $t = 0$, the economy starts with a population of $L(0) = 1$ who are all newborn at that point. (Equation (9.39) is derived in Exercise 9.25.)

As in the previous section, it is sufficient to specify the consumption behavior and the budget constraints for each cohort. In particular, the flow budget constraint for cohort τ at time t is

$$\dot{a}(t \mid \tau) = r(t)a(t \mid \tau) - c(t \mid \tau) + w(t) + z(a(t \mid \tau) \mid t, \tau),$$

where again $z(a(t \mid \tau) \mid t, \tau)$ is the transfer or annuity payment at time t to an individual born at time τ holding assets $a(t \mid \tau)$. Let us follow Yaari and Blanchard and again assume complete annuity markets with free entry. The instantaneous profits of a life insurance company providing such annuities at time t for an individual born at time τ with assets $a(t \mid \tau)$ is

$$\pi(a(t \mid \tau) \mid t, \tau) = \nu a(t \mid \tau) - z(a(t \mid \tau) \mid t, \tau),$$

since the individual will die and leave his assets to the life insurance company at the flow rate ν. The zero-profits condition now implies that

$$z(a(t \mid \tau) \mid t, \tau) = \nu a(t \mid \tau).$$

Substituting this equation into the flow budget constraint above, we obtain the more useful expression

$$\dot{a}(t \mid \tau) = (r(t) + \nu)a(t \mid \tau) - c(t \mid \tau) + w(t). \tag{9.40}$$

Let us assume that the production side is given by the per capita aggregate production function $f(k)$ satisfying Assumptions 1 and 2, where k is the aggregate capital-labor ratio. Capital is assumed to depreciate at the rate δ. Factor prices are given by the usual expressions

$$R(t) = f'(k(t)) \text{ and } w(t) = f(k(t)) - k(t)f'(k(t)), \tag{9.41}$$

and as usual $r(t) = R(t) - \delta$. The law of motion of the capital-labor ratio is given by

$$\dot{k}(t) = f(k(t)) - (n - \nu + \delta)k(t) - c(t), \tag{9.42}$$

where $c(t)$ is average consumption per capita, given by

$$c(t) = \frac{\int_{-\infty}^{t} c(t \mid \tau)L(t \mid \tau)d\tau}{\int_{-\infty}^{t} L(t \mid \tau)d\tau}$$

$$= \frac{\int_{-\infty}^{t} c(t \mid \tau)L(t \mid \tau)d\tau}{L(t)},$$

recalling that $L(t \mid \tau)$ is the size of the cohort born at τ at time t, and the lower limit of the integral is set to $-\infty$ to include all cohorts, even those born in the distant past.

9.8.2 Equilibrium

A competitive equilibrium is again defined in a straightforward manner.

Definition 9.4 *A competitive equilibrium* consists of paths of capital stock, wage rates, and rental rates of capital, $[K(t), w(t), R(t)]_{t=0}^{\infty}$, and paths of consumption for each generation, $[c(t \mid \tau)]_{t=0, \tau \leq t}^{\infty}$, such that each individual maximizes (9.37) subject to (9.40), the time path of prices, $[w(t), R(t)]_{t=0}^{\infty}$, is given by (9.41), and the capital-labor ratio evolves according to (9.42).

Let us start with consumer optimization. The maximization of (9.37) subject to (9.40) gives the usual Euler equation

$$\frac{\dot{c}(t \mid \tau)}{c(t \mid \tau)} = r(t) - \rho, \tag{9.43}$$

where $\dot{c}(t \mid \tau) \equiv \partial c(t \mid \tau)/\partial t$. Notice that, in contrast to the discrete-time version of this equation, (9.36), the probability (flow rate) of death, ν, does not feature here, since it exactly cancels out (the rate of return on assets is $r(t) + \nu$ and the effective discount factor is $\rho + \nu$, so that their difference is equal to $r(t) - \rho$).

The transversality condition for an individual of cohort τ can be written as

$$\lim_{t \to \infty} \exp(-(\bar{r}(t, \tau) + \nu))a(t \mid \tau) = 0, \tag{9.44}$$

where

$$\bar{r}(t, \tau) \equiv \frac{1}{t - \tau} \int_{\tau}^{t} r(s)ds$$

is the average interest rate between dates τ and t, as in (8.31) in Chapter 8, and the transversality condition here is the analogue of (8.32). The transversality condition (9.44) requires the net present discounted value of the assets in the very far future of an individual born at the time τ discounted back to this time to be equal to 0.

Combining (9.43) with (9.40) and (9.44) gives the following consumption "function" for an individual of cohort τ (see Exercise 9.26):

$$c(t \mid \tau) = (\rho + v)[a(t \mid \tau) + \omega(t)]. \tag{9.45}$$

This linear form of the consumption function is a particularly attractive feature of logarithmic preferences. The term in square brackets is the asset and human wealth of the individual, with the second term defined as

$$\omega(t) = \int_t^\infty \exp(-(\bar{r}(s, t) + v))w(s)ds.$$

This term represents the net present discounted value of future wage earnings of an individual discounted to time t. It is independent of τ, since the future expected earnings of all individuals are the same regardless of when they are born. The additional discounting with v in this term arises because individuals die at this rate and thus lose future earnings from then on.

Equation (9.45) implies that each individual consumes a fraction of this wealth equal to his effective discount rate $\rho + v$. Now integrating (9.45) across cohorts and using the fact that the size of the cohort τ at time t is $\exp(-v(t - \tau) + (n - v)\tau)$, (average) per capita consumption at time t is then obtained as

$$c(t) = (\rho + v)(a(t) + \omega(t)), \tag{9.46}$$

where $a(t)$ is average assets per capita. Since the only productive asset in this economy is capital, we also have that $a(t) = k(t)$. Finally, differentiating (9.46) yields

$$\dot{c}(t) = (\rho + v)(\dot{a}(t) + \dot{\omega}(t)). \tag{9.47}$$

The law of motion of assets per capita can be written as

$$\dot{a}(t) = (r(t) - (n - v))a(t) + w(t) - c(t).$$

This equation is intuitive. Aggregate wealth $a(t)L(t)$ increases because of the returns to capital at the rate $r(t)$ and because of the wage income $w(t)L(t)$. The total consumption $c(t)L(t)$ needs to be subtracted from the aggregate wealth. Finally, $L(t)$ grows at the rate $n - v$, which reduces the rate of growth of assets per capita. Human wealth per capita, on the other hand, satisfies

$$(r(t) + v)\omega(t) = \dot{\omega}(t) + w(t).$$

The intuition for this equation comes from the HJB equations discussed in Chapter 7. We can think of $\omega(t)$ as the value of an asset with a claim to the future earnings of a typical individual. The required rate of return on this is $r(t) + v$, which takes into account that the individual loses his future earnings stream at the rate v when he dies. The return on this asset is equal to its capital gains $\dot{\omega}(t)$ and dividends $w(t)$. Substituting for $\dot{a}(t)$ and $\dot{\omega}(t)$ from these two equations into (9.47), we have

$$
\begin{aligned}
\dot{c}(t) &= (\rho + v)[(r(t) - (n - v))a(t) + w(t) - c(t) + (r(t) + v)\omega(t) - w(t)] \\
&= (\rho + v)[(r(t) + v)(a(t) + \omega(t)) - na(t) - c(t)] \\
&= (\rho + v)\left[\frac{(r(t) + v)}{\rho + v} c(t) - na(t) - c(t) \right] \\
&= (r(t) - \rho)c(t) - (\rho + v)na(t),
\end{aligned}
$$

where the third line uses (9.46). Dividing both sides by $c(t)$, using the fact that $a(t) = k(t)$, and substituting $r(t) = f'(k(t)) - \delta$ yields

$$
\frac{\dot{c}(t)}{c(t)} = f'(k(t)) - \delta - \rho - (\rho + v)n\frac{k(t)}{c(t)}. \tag{9.48}
$$

Equation (9.48) is similar to the standard Euler equation (under logarithmic preferences) except for the last term. This last term reflects the fact that consumption growth per capita is slowed down by the arrival at each instant of new individuals, who have less wealth than the average individual. Their below-average wealth implies lower consumption and reduces the average consumption growth in the economy. This intuitively explains why the last term depends on n (the rate of arrival of new individuals) and on k/c (the size of average asset holdings relative to consumption).

The equilibrium path of the economy is completely characterized by the two differential equations (9.42) and (9.48)—together with an initial condition for $k(0) > 0$ and the transversality condition (9.44) applied to average assets and thus to the capital-labor ratio $k(t)$. A steady-state equilibrium is obtained when both $\dot{k}(t)/k(t)$ and $\dot{c}(t)/c(t)$ are equal to zero, and thus it satisfies the following two equations:

$$
\frac{c^*}{k^*} = \frac{(\rho + v)n}{f'(k^*) - \delta - \rho}, \tag{9.49}
$$

and

$$
\frac{f(k^*)}{k^*} - (n - v + \delta) - \frac{(\rho + v)n}{f'(k^*) - \delta - \rho} = 0. \tag{9.50}
$$

The second equation pins down the unique (positive) steady-state capital-labor ratio k^* (since both $f(k)/k$ and $f'(k)$ are decreasing). Given k^*, the first equation then determines the unique level of average consumption per capita c^*. It can also be verified that at k^*,

$$
f'(k^*) > \rho + \delta,
$$

so that the capital-labor ratio is lower than the level consistent with the modified golden rule k_{mgr}, given by $f'(k_{\text{mgr}}) = \rho + \delta$. Recall that the optimal steady-state capital-labor ratio of the neoclassical growth model satisfied the modified golden rule. In comparison, in this economy there is always underaccumulation. This behavior contrasts with the baseline OLG model, which potentially led to dynamic inefficiency and overaccumulation.

Let us next turn to equilibrium dynamics. Figure 9.3 plots (9.42) and (9.48). The arrows indicate how average consumption per capita and the capital-labor ratio change in different

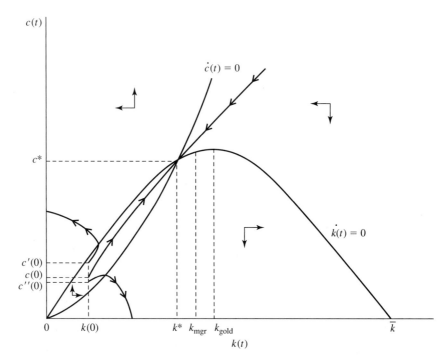

FIGURE 9.3 Steady-state and transitional dynamics in the overlapping generations model in continuous time.

regions. Both (9.42) and (9.48) are upward sloping and start at the origin. It is also straight-forward to verify that while (9.42) is concave in k-c space, (9.48) is convex. Thus they have a unique intersection (other than at $k = c = 0$). We also know from the preceding discussion that this unique intersection is at a capital-labor ratio less than that satisfying the modified golden rule, which is marked as k_{mgr} in the figure. Naturally k_{mgr} itself is less than k_{gold}. The phase diagram also makes it clear that there exists a unique stable arm that is upward sloping in k-c space. The shape of the stable arm is the same as that in the basic neoclassical growth model. If the initial level of consumption is above this stable arm, feasibility is violated, while if it is below, the economy tends toward zero consumption and violates the transversality condition given in (9.44). Consequently the steady-state equilibrium is globally saddle-path stable: consumption starts along the stable arm, and consumption and the capital-labor ratio mono-tonically converge to the steady state. Exercise 9.28 asks you to verify local saddle-path stability by linearizing (9.42) and (9.48) around the steady state.

The following proposition summarizes this analysis.

Proposition 9.10 *In the continuous-time perpetual youth model, there exists a unique steady state (k^*, c^*) given by (9.49) and (9.50). The steady-state capital-labor ratio k^* is less than the level of capital-labor ratio that satisfies the modified golden rule, k_{mgr}. Starting with any $k(0) > 0$, equilibrium dynamics monotonically converge to this unique steady state.*

Perhaps the most interesting feature of this equilibrium is that, despite finite lives and OLG, there is no overaccumulation. The reason for this is that individuals have a constant stream of labor income throughout their lives and thus do not need to save excessively to ensure smooth consumption. Is it possible to obtain overaccumulation in the continuous-time perpetual youth model? The answer is yes and is demonstrated by Blanchard (1985). He assumes that each individual starts life with one unit of effective labor, and then her effective labor units decline at some positive exponential rate $\zeta > 0$ throughout her life, so that the labor earnings of an individual of generation τ at time t is $\exp(-\zeta(t - \tau))w(t)$, where $w(t)$ is the market wage per unit of effective labor at time t. Consequently the individual consumption function changes from (9.45) to

$$c(t \mid \tau) = (\rho + vright)left[a(t \mid \tau) + \omega(t \mid \tau)],$$

where now $\omega(t \mid \tau)$ is the human wealth of an individual of generation τ at time t, given by

$$\omega(t \mid \tau) = \int_t^\infty \exp(-(\bar{r}(t, s) + v)) \exp(-\zeta(s - \tau))w(s)\,ds, \tag{9.51}$$

and $\exp(-\zeta(s - \tau))$ is the correction factor that accounts for the decline in effective labor units (see Exercise 9.30). Repeating the same steps as before with this new expression for human wealth, we obtain

$$\frac{\dot{c}(t)}{c(t)} = f'(k(t)) - \delta - \rho + \zeta - (\rho + v)(n + \zeta)\frac{k(t)}{c(t)}, \tag{9.52}$$

while the behavior of the capital-labor ratio is still given by (9.42). It can now be shown that for ζ sufficiently large, the steady-state capital-labor ratio k^* can exceed both the modified golden rule level k_{mgr} and the golden rule level, k_{gold} (see Exercise 9.30). This discussion therefore illustrates that overaccumulation emerges when there are both overlapping generations and a strong motive for saving for the future. Interestingly, it can be shown that what is important is not finite lives per se but instead the overlapping generations structure. In particular, Exercise 9.32 shows that when $n = 0$, overaccumulation is not possible, so that finite lives is not sufficient for overaccumulation. However, $k^* > k_{\text{gold}}$ is possible when $n > 0$, $\zeta > 0$, and $v = 0$, so that the OLG model with infinite lives can also generate overaccumulation.

9.9 Taking Stock

This chapter has continued our investigation of the mechanics of capital accumulation in dynamic equilibrium models. The main departure from the baseline neoclassical growth model of the previous chapter has been the relaxation of the representative household assumption. The simplest way of accomplishing this is to introduce two-period lived OLG (without pure altruism). In the baseline OLG model of Samuelson and Diamond, each individual lives for two periods, but can only supply labor during the first period of his life. I have also discussed alternative models without representative households, in particular, OLG with impure altruism and models of perpetual youth. In models of OLG with impure altruism, individuals transfer resources to their offspring, but they do not care directly about the utility of their offspring. Instead, they derive utility from the act of giving or from some subcomponent of the consumption vector of their descendent(s). In models of perpetual youth, the economy features expected finite lives and overlapping generations, but each individual still has an infinite planning horizon, because the time of death is uncertain.

These models may fail to satisfy the conditions of the First Welfare Theorem. As a result, there is no guarantee that the resulting equilibrium path is Pareto optimal. In fact, the extensive study of the baseline OLG models was partly motivated by the possibility of Pareto suboptimal allocations in such models. We have seen that these equilibria may be dynamically inefficient and feature overaccumulation—a steady-state capital-labor ratio greater than the golden rule capital-labor ratio. We have also seen how an unfunded social security system can reduce aggregate savings and thus ameliorate the overaccumulation problem. The important role that unfunded social security (or national debt) plays in the OLG model has made this model a workhorse for analysis of transfer programs and fiscal policies.

Our analysis of perpetual youth models, especially Yaari and Blanchard's continuous-time perpetual youth model, further clarified the roles of the path of labor income, finite horizons, and arrival of new individuals in generating overaccumulation. In particular, this model shows that the declining path of labor income is important for the overaccumulation result (the Samuelson-Diamond two-period model is an extreme case, since there is no labor income in the second period of the life of the individual). But perhaps the more important insight generated by these models is that what matters is not the finite horizons per se but the arrival of new individuals.

While overaccumulation and dynamic inefficiency have dominated much of the discussion of OLG models in the literature, one should not overemphasize the importance of dynamic inefficiency. As discussed in Chapter 1, the major question of economic growth is why so many countries have so little capital for their workers and why the process of economic growth and capital accumulation started only in the past 200 years. It is highly doubtful that overaccumulation is a major problem for most countries in the world.

The models presented in this chapter are useful for another reason, however. They significantly enrich our arsenal in the study of the mechanics of economic growth and capital accumulation. All three of the models presented in this chapter, the baseline OLG model, the OLG model with impure altruism, and the perpetual youth model, are tractable and useful vehicles for the study of economic growth in a variety of circumstances. For example, the first two lead to equilibrium dynamics similar to those of the baseline Solow growth model but without explicitly imposing an exogenously constant saving rate. The latter model, on the other hand, allows an analysis of equilibrium dynamics similar to that of the basic neoclassical growth model but also incorporates finite lives and overlapping generations, which are essential in many problems, for example, in the context of human capital investments studied in the next chapter.

In summary, this chapter has provided us with new modeling tools and different perspectives for the analyses of capital accumulation, aggregate saving, and economic growth. Although these perspectives do not directly offer fresh answers to the questions of why countries grow and why some countries are much poorer than others, they will be useful in developing such answers in subsequent chapters.

9.10 References and Literature

The baseline OLG model with two-period lived agents is due to Samuelson (1958) and Diamond (1965). A related model appears in French in the work of Maurice Allais. Blanchard and Fischer (1989, Chapter 3) provide an excellent textbook treatment of the baseline OLG model. Some textbooks use this setup as the main workhorse macroeconomic model, for example, McCandless and Wallace (1991), Azariadis (1993), and De La Croix and Michel (2002). See Galor and Ryder (1989) on the multiplicity of steady-state equilibria in the OLG model and Galor (1996) for a discussion of the similarities between the Solow growth model and the OLG model (recall also Exercise 2.13 in Chapter 2).

The economy studied in Section 9.1 is due to Shell (1971). The source of inefficiency in the OLG model is much discussed in the literature. Shell's (1971) example economy in Section 9.1

provides the clearest intuitive explanation for why the First Welfare Theorem does not apply. A lucid discussion is contained in Bewley (2007).

The issues of dynamic inefficiency in OLG models are discussed in Samuelson (1958) and Diamond (1965). A more complete treatment, without restricting attention to steady states, is provided in Cass (1972) (in the text, I simplified the discussion of dynamic inefficiency by focusing on steady states). The role of unfunded social security when there is dynamic inefficiency is discussed in Samuelson (1975), while the role of national debt in the same context is studied in Diamond (1965). Samuelson (1958) also notes how fiat money can play this role, and this point is further developed in Wallace (1980) and Weil (1987). See Blanchard (1979), Tirole (1985), and Gilles and LeRoy (1992) for some of the early important work on bubbles in OLG models; Tirole (1982) on the importance of infinite horizon for the possibility of bubbles; and Ventura (2002) for the relationship between asset bubbles and capital flows.

The model of OLG with impure altruism is due to Andreoni (1989). This model has been used extensively in the economic growth and economic development literatures, especially for the analysis of equilibrium dynamics in the presence of imperfect capital markets. Well-known examples include the models by Banerjee and Newman (1991, 1993), Galor and Zeira (1993), Aghion and Bolton (1997), and Piketty (1997), which are studied in Chapter 21. I am not aware of an analysis of the dynamics of wealth inequality with perfect markets in this economy along the lines of the model presented in Section 9.6, even though the analysis is quite straightforward. A similar analysis of wealth inequality dynamics is included in Stiglitz's (1969) model, but he assumes that each household can only use its savings in its own diminishing return technology (thus creating a strong force toward convergence of incomes).

The continuous-time perpetual youth model is due to Yaari (1965) and Blanchard (1985). The discrete-time version of this model was presented to facilitate the transition to the continuous-time version. My treatment of the continuous-time version closely followed Blanchard (1985). The importance of the path of labor income is emphasized and analyzed in Blanchard (1985). The importance of new arrivals in the market is emphasized and explained in Weil (1989). Models with OLG and finite lives are used extensively in the analysis of Ricardian Equivalence, introduced in Exercise 8.35. Blanchard (1985) includes extensive discussions of this issue.

9.11 Exercises

9.1 (a) Prove that the allocation characterized in Proposition 9.1 is the unique competitive equilibrium allocation.

(b) Show that, in addition to the allocations $\tilde{\mathbf{x}}_{i'}$ discussed in Proposition 9.3, it is possible to construct an allocation $\tilde{\mathbf{x}}_{i_1 i_2}$ for $i_1, i_2 \in \mathbb{N}$ that makes all individuals with index $i \in [i_1, i_2]$ strictly better off and all other individuals as well off as in allocation $\bar{\mathbf{x}}$.

9.2 Show that the allocation $\tilde{\mathbf{x}}_{i'}$ in Proposition 9.3 can also be decentralized as a competitive equilibrium with the price vector $\tilde{\mathbf{p}}$ such that $\tilde{p}_j = 1$ for all $j \leq i'$ and $\tilde{p}_j = \rho^{(j-i'-1)}$ for $j > i'$ with $\rho \in (0, 1)$.

9.3 Consider the following variant of the economy in Section 9.1. The utility of the individual indexed $i = j$ is

$$u(c(j)) + \beta u(c(j + 1)),$$

where $\beta \in (0, 1)$, and each individual has one unit of the good with the same index as his own.

(a) Define a competitive equilibrium for this economy.

(b) Characterize the set of competitive equilibria in this economy.

(c) Characterize the set of Pareto optima in this economy.

(d) Can all Pareto optima be decentralized without changing endowments? Can they be decentralized by redistributing endowments?

9.4 Show that in the model of Section 9.2 the dynamics of capital stock are identical to those derived in the text even when $\delta < 1$. [Hint: you have to specify what happens to undepreciated capital.]

9.5 In the baseline OLG model, verify that savings $s(w, R)$, given by (9.6), are increasing, w. Provide conditions on the utility function $u(\cdot)$ such that they are also increasing in their second argument (the gross rate of return R).

9.6 Prove Proposition 9.4

9.7 Consider the canonical OLG model with log preferences,

$$\log(c_1(t)) + \beta \log(c_2(t+1)),$$

for each individual. Suppose that there is population growth at the rate n. Individuals work only when they are young and supply one unit of labor inelastically. Production technology is given by

$$Y(t) = A(t)K(t)^\alpha L(t)^{1-\alpha},$$

where $A(t+1) = (1+g)A(t)$, with $A(0) > 0$ and $g > 0$.

(a) Define a competitive equilibrium and the steady-state equilibrium.

(b) Characterize the steady-state equilibrium, and show that it is globally stable.

(c) What is the effect of an increase in g on the equilibrium?

(d) What is the effect of an increase in β on the equilibrium? Provide an intuition for this result.

9.8 Consider the canonical model with log preferences, $\log(c_1(t)) + \beta \log(c_2(t))$, and the general neoclassical technology $F(K, L)$ satisfying Assumptions 1 and 2 (see Chapter 2). Show that multiple steady-state equilibria are possible in this economy.

9.9 Consider the canonical OLG model with log preferences and a Cobb-Douglas production function (as in Exercise 9.8).

(a) Define a competitive equilibrium.

(b) Characterize the competitive equilibrium, and derive explicit conditions under which the steady-state equilibrium is dynamically inefficient.

(c) Using plausible numbers discuss whether dynamic inefficiency can arise in "realistic" economies.

(d) Show that when there is dynamic inefficiency, it is possible to construct an unfunded social security system that creates a Pareto improvement relative to the competitive allocation.

9.10 Consider again the canonical OLG model with log preferences and a Cobb-Douglas production function, but assume that individuals now work in both periods of their lives.

(a) Define a competitive equilibrium and the steady-state equilibrium.

(b) Characterize the steady-state equilibrium and the transitional dynamics in this economy.

(c) Can this economy generate overaccumulation?

9.11 This exercise draws the parallels between Pareto inefficiency in the OLG model and the failure of the First Welfare Theorem (Theorem 5.6) with an infinite number of households.

(a) Show that when there is dynamic inefficiency, that is, $r^* < n$, the condition that $\sum_{h \in \mathcal{H}} \sum_{j=0}^{\infty} p_j^* \omega_j^h < \infty$ in Theorem 5.6 is violated. [Hint: note that in this case the endowments consist of labor at different dates, and the prices of the endowments are given by

$w(t)/R(t)$, thus by $w^*/\left(1+r^*\right)$ in steady state; conclude from this observation that in steady state the equivalent of $\sum_{h\in\mathcal{H}}\sum_{j=0}^{\infty}p_j^*\omega_j^h$ in this economy is $w^*\sum_{t=0}^{\infty}((1+n)/(1+r^*))^t]$.

(b) Show that when $r^* > n$, the condition that $\sum_{h\in\mathcal{H}}\sum_{j=0}^{\infty}p_j^*\omega_j^h < \infty$ in Theorem 5.6 is satisfied. Then use this theorem to establish that the OLG equilibrium is Pareto efficient.

* 9.12   Show that Theorem 5.6 is not informative about whether an OLG steady-state equilibrium with $r^* = n$ is Pareto optimal. In particular, show that this equilibrium is Pareto optimal when $u\,(\cdot)$ and $f\,(\cdot)$ are strictly concave. Can you construct an example in which it can be Pareto suboptimal?

9.13   Prove Proposition 9.7.

9.14   Consider the OLG model with fully funded social security in Section 9.5. Prove that even when the restriction $s(t) \geq 0$ for all t is imposed, no fully funded social security program can lead to a Pareto improvement.

9.15   Consider an OLG economy with the dynamically inefficient steady-state equilibrium. Show that the government can improve the allocation of resources by introducing national debt. [Hint: suppose that the government borrows from the current young and redistributes to the current old, paying back the current young the following period with another round of borrowing]. Contrast this result with the Ricardian Equivalence result in Exercise 8.35 in Chapter 8.

9.16   Prove Proposition 9.8.

9.17   Consider the baseline OLG model and suppose that the equilibrium is dynamically efficient, that is, $r^* > n$. Show that any unfunded social security system increases the welfare of the current old generation and reduces the welfare of some future generation.

9.18   Derive (9.31).

9.19   Consider the OLG model with warm glow preferences in Section 9.6, and suppose that preferences are given by $c(t)^\eta b(t)^{1-\eta}$, with $\eta \in (0, 1)$, instead of (9.21). The production side is the same as in Section 9.6. Characterize the dynamic equilibrium of this economy.

9.20   Consider the OLG model with warm glow preferences in Section 9.6, and suppose that preferences are given by $u_1(c_i(t)) + u_2(b_i(t))$, where u_1 and u_2 are strictly increasing and concave functions. The production side is the same as in the text. Characterize a dynamic equilibrium of this economy. Provide sufficient conditions on $u_1\,(\cdot)$ and $u_2\,(\cdot)$ such that (1) aggregate dynamics are globally stable, and (2) all individuals asymptotically tend to the same wealth level.

9.21   Characterize the aggregate equilibrium dynamics and the dynamics of wealth distribution in the OLG model with warm glow preferences as in Section 9.6 when the per capita production function is given by the Cobb-Douglas form $f\,(k) = Ak^\alpha$. Show that away from the steady state, there can be periods during which wealth inequality increases. Explain why.

9.22   Show that the steady-state capital labor ratio in the OLG model with impure altruism (of Section 9.6) can lead to overaccumulation, that is, to $k^* > k_{\text{gold}}$.

9.23   Prove that given the perpetual youth assumption and population dynamics in (9.34), at time $t > 0$, there will be $n\,(1+n-\nu)^{t-s}\,(1-\nu)^{s-1}$ s-year-olds for any $s \in \{1, 2, \ldots, t-1\}$.

* 9.24   Consider the discrete-time perpetual youth model discussed in Section 9.7 and assume that preferences are logarithmic. Characterize the steady-state equilibrium and the equilibrium dynamics of the capital-labor ratio.

9.25   Consider the continuous-time perpetual youth model of Section 9.8.

(a) Show that given $L\,(0) = 1$, the initial size of a cohort born at time $\tau \geq 0$ is $\exp\left((n-\nu)\,\tau\right)$.

(b) Show that the probability that an individual born at time τ is alive at time $t \geq \tau$ is $\exp(-\nu(t-\tau))$.

(c) Derive (9.39).

(d) Show that (9.39) does not apply at any finite time if the economy starts at $t = 0$ with an arbitrary age distribution.

9.26 Derive (9.45). [Hint: first integrate the flow budget constraint of the individual (9.40) using the transversality condition (9.44), and then use (9.43).]

9.27 Generalize the analysis of the continuous-time perpetual youth model of Section 9.8 to an economy with labor-augmenting technological progress at the rate g. Prove that the steady-state equilibrium is unique and globally (saddle-path) stable. What is the impact of a higher rate of technological progress?

9.28 Linearize the differential equations (9.42) and (9.48) around the steady state (k^*, c^*), and show that the linearized system has one negative and one positive eigenvalue.

9.29 Determine the effects of n and ν on the steady-state equilibrium (k^*, c^*) in the continuous-time perpetual youth model of Section 9.8.

9.30 (a) Derive equations (9.51) and (9.52).

(b) Show that for ζ sufficiently large, the steady-state equilibrium capital-labor ratio k^* can exceed k_{gold}, so that there is overaccumulation. Provide an intuition for this result.

9.31 Consider the continuous-time perpetual youth model with a constant flow of government spending G. Suppose that this spending does not affect consumer utility and that lump-sum taxes $[\mathcal{T}(t)]_{t=0}^{\infty}$ are allowed. Specify the government budget constraint as in Exercise 8.35 in Chapter 8. Prove that contrary to the Ricardian Equivalence result in Exercise 8.35, the sequence of taxes affects the equilibrium path of capital-labor ratio and consumption. Interpret this result, and explain the difference between the OLG model and the neoclassical growth model.

* 9.32 Consider the continuous-time perpetual youth model with labor income declining at the rate $\zeta > 0$. Show that there exists $\zeta > 0$ sufficiently high such that if $n > 0$ and $\nu = 0$, $k^* > k_{\text{gold}}$.

9.33 Consider an economy with aggregate production function

$$Y(t) = AK(t)^{1-\alpha}L(t)^{\alpha}.$$

All markets are competitive, the labor supply is normalized to 1, capital fully depreciates after use, and the government imposes a linear tax on capital income at the rate τ and uses the proceeds for government consumption. Consider two alternative demographic structures:

1. Agents are infinitely lived, with preferences

$$\sum_{t=0}^{\infty} \beta^t \log c(t).$$

2. Agents work in the first period and consume the capital income from their savings in the second period (an OLG model). The preferences of a generation born at time t are

$$\log c_1(t) + \beta \log c_2(t+1).$$

Characterize the equilibria in these two economies, and show that in the first economy, taxation reduces output, while in the second, it does not. Interpret this result. In light of this result discuss the applicability of models that try to explain income differences across countries with differences in the rates of capital income taxation.

10

Human Capital and Economic Growth

his chapter investigates the role of human capital in economic growth and in cross-country income differences. Our main purpose is to understand which factors affect human capital investments and how these influence the process of economic growth and economic development. Human capital refers to all the attributes of workers that potentially increase their productivity in all or some productive tasks. The term was coined because many of these attributes are accumulated by workers through investments. Human capital theory, developed primarily by Becker (1965) and Mincer (1974), is about the role of human capital in the production process and about the incentives to invest in skills, including pre–labor market investments (in the form of schooling) and on-the-job investments (in the form of training). It would not be an exaggeration to say that this theory is the basis of much of labor economics and plays an equally important role in macroeconomics. The literature on education and other types of human capital investments is vast, so only parts of this literature that are relevant to the main focus of this book are covered here. Other important connections between human capital and economic growth, especially those related to its effect on technological progress and its role in economic takeoff, are discussed later in the book.

10.1 A Simple Separation Theorem

Let us start with the partial equilibrium schooling decisions and establish a simple result, sometimes referred to as a "separation theorem" for human capital investments. I set up the basic model in continuous time for simplicity.

Consider the schooling decision of a single individual facing exogenously given prices for human capital. Throughout I assume that there are perfect capital markets. The separation theorem shows that, with perfect capital markets, schooling decisions maximize the net present discounted value of the individual and can thus be "separated from" consumption decisions (I return to human capital investments with imperfect capital markets in Chapter 21). In particular, consider an individual with an instantaneous utility function $u(c)$ that satisfies Assumption 3 (from Chapter 8). Suppose that the individual has a planning horizon of T (where $T = \infty$ is allowed), discounts the future at the rate $\rho > 0$, and faces a constant flow rate of death equal to

$v \geq 0$ (as in the perpetual youth model studied in the previous chapter). The objective function of this individual at time $t = 0$ is

$$\max \int_0^T \exp(-(\rho + v)t)u(c(t))\, dt. \tag{10.1}$$

Now suppose that this individual is born with some human capital $h(0) \geq 0$. Suppose that her human capital evolves over time according to the differential equation

$$\dot{h}(t) = G(t, h(t), s(t)), \tag{10.2}$$

where $s(t) \in [0, 1]$ is the fraction of time that the individual spends for human capital investments (i.e., schooling), and $G : \mathbb{R}_+^2 \times [0, 1] \to \mathbb{R}_+$ determines how human capital evolves as a function of time, the individual's stock of human capital, and schooling decisions. In addition, we may impose a further restriction on schooling decisions, for example,

$$s(t) \in \mathcal{S}(t), \tag{10.3}$$

where $\mathcal{S}(t) \subset [0, 1]$ and captures the fact that all schooling may have to be full-time (i.e., $s(t) \in \{0, 1\}$), or that there may exist other restrictions on schooling decisions.

The individual is assumed to face an exogenous path of wage per unit of human capital given by $[w(t)]_{t=0}^T$, so that her labor earnings at time t are

$$W(t) = w(t)[1 - s(t)][h(t) + \omega(t)],$$

where $1 - s(t)$ is the fraction of time spent supplying labor to the market, and $\omega(t)$ is raw (non–human capital) labor that the individual may be supplying to the market at time t. The path of non–human capital labor that the individual can supply to the market, $[\omega(t)]_{t=0}^T$, is exogenous. This formulation assumes that the only margin of choice is between market work and schooling (i.e., there is no leisure).

Finally, let us assume that the individual faces a constant (flow) interest rate equal to r on her savings (potentially including annuity payments, as discussed in the previous chapter). Using the equation for labor earnings, the lifetime budget constraint of the individual can be written as

$$\int_0^T \exp(-rt)c(t)dt \leq \int_0^T \exp(-rt)w(t)[1 - s(t)][h(t) + \omega(t)]\, dt. \tag{10.4}$$

Theorem 10.1 (Separation Theorem) *Suppose that the instantaneous utility function $u(\cdot)$ is strictly increasing. Then $[\hat{c}(t), \hat{s}(t), \hat{h}(t)]_{t=0}^T$ is a solution to the maximization of (10.1) subject to (10.2), (10.3), and (10.4) if and only if $[\hat{s}(t), \hat{h}(t)]_{t=0}^T$ maximizes*

$$\int_0^T \exp(-rt)w(t)[1 - s(t)][h(t) + \omega(t)]\, dt, \tag{10.5}$$

subject to (10.2) and (10.3), and $[\hat{c}(t)]_{t=0}^T$ maximizes (10.1) subject to (10.4) and given $[\hat{s}(t), \hat{h}(t)]_{t=0}^T$. That is, human capital accumulation and supply decisions can be separated from consumption decisions.

Proof. To prove the "only if" part, suppose that $[\hat{s}(t), \hat{h}(t)]_{t=0}^T$ does not maximize (10.5), but there exists $\hat{c}(t)$ such that $[\hat{c}(t), \hat{s}(t), \hat{h}(t)]_{t=0}^T$ is a solution to (10.1). Let the value of

(10.5) generated by $[\hat{s}(t), \hat{h}(t)]_{t=0}^{T}$ be denoted by $\hat{Y}$. Since $[\hat{s}(t), \hat{h}(t)]_{t=0}^{T}$ does not maximize (10.5), there exists $[\tilde{s}(t), \tilde{h}(t)]_{t=0}^{T}$ reaching a value of (10.5) $\tilde{Y} > \hat{Y}$. By the hypothesis that $[\hat{c}(t), \hat{s}(t), \hat{h}(t)]_{t=0}^{T}$ is a solution to (10.1), the budget constraint (10.4) implies

$$\int_{0}^{T} \exp(-rt)\hat{c}(t)dt \leq \hat{Y}.$$

Let $\varepsilon > 0$ and consider $[c(t), s(t), h(t)]_{t=0}^{T}$ such that $c(t) = \hat{c}(t) + \varepsilon$, $s(t) = \tilde{s}(t)$, and $h(t) = \tilde{h}(t)$ for all t. We have that

$$\int_{0}^{T} \exp(-rt)c(t)dt = \int_{0}^{T} \exp(-rt)\hat{c}(t)dt + \frac{[1 - \exp(-rT)]}{r}\varepsilon.$$

$$\leq \hat{Y} + \frac{[1 - \exp(-rT)]}{r}\varepsilon.$$

Since $\tilde{Y} > \hat{Y}$, for ε sufficiently small, $\int_{0}^{T} \exp(-rt)c(t)\,dt \leq \tilde{Y}$, and thus $[c(t), s(t), h(t)]_{t=0}^{T}$ is feasible. Since $u(\cdot)$ is strictly increasing, $[c(t), s(t), h(t)]_{t=0}^{T}$ is strictly preferred to $[\hat{c}(t), \hat{s}(t), \hat{h}(t)]_{t=0}^{T}$, leading to a contradiction and proving the "only if" part.

The proof of the "if" part is similar. Suppose that $[\hat{s}(t), \hat{h}(t)]_{t=0}^{T}$ maximizes (10.5). Let the maximum value be denoted by $\hat{Y}$. Consider the maximization of (10.1) subject to the constraint that $\int_{0}^{T} \exp(-rt)c(t)dt \leq \hat{Y}$. Let $[\hat{c}(t)]_{t=0}^{T}$ be a solution. Thus if $[\tilde{c}'(t)]_{t=0}^{T}$ is strictly preferred to $[\hat{c}(t)]_{t=0}^{T}$, then $\int_{0}^{T} \exp(-rt)\tilde{c}'(t)dt > \hat{Y}$. Then $[\hat{c}(t), \hat{s}(t), \hat{h}(t)]_{t=0}^{T}$ must be a solution to the original problem, because any other $[s(t), h(t)]_{t=0}^{T}$ leads to a value of (10.5) equal to $Y \leq \hat{Y}$, and if $[\tilde{c}'(t)]_{t=0}^{T}$ is strictly preferred to $[\hat{c}(t)]_{t=0}^{T}$, then $\int_{0}^{T} \exp(-rt)c'(t)dt > \hat{Y} \geq Y$ for any Y associated with any feasible $[s(t), h(t)]_{t=0}^{T}$. ∎

The intuition for this theorem is straightforward: in the presence of perfect capital markets, the best human capital accumulation decisions are those that maximize the lifetime budget set of the individual. Exercise 10.2 shows that this theorem does not hold when there are imperfect capital markets and also does not generalize to the case where leisure is also an argument of the utility function.

10.2 Schooling Investments and Returns to Education

Let us next turn to the simplest model of schooling decisions in partial equilibrium, which illustrate the main trade-offs in human capital investments. The model presented here is a version of Mincer's (1974) seminal contribution. This model also enables a simple mapping from the theory of human capital investments to the large empirical literature on returns to schooling.

Let us first assume that $T = \infty$, which simplifies the expressions. The flow rate of death, v, is positive, so that individuals have finite expected lives. Suppose that (10.2) is such that the individual has to spend an interval S with $s(t) = 1$—that is, in full-time schooling—and $s(t) = 0$ thereafter. At the end of the schooling interval, the individual has a schooling level of

$$h(S) = \eta(S),$$

where $\eta(\cdot)$ is a continuous, increasing, differentiable, and concave function. For $t \in [S, \infty)$, human capital accumulates over time (as the individual works) according to the differential equation

$$\dot{h}(t) = g_h h(t), \tag{10.6}$$

for some $g_h \geq 0$. Suppose also that wages grow exponentially,

$$\dot{w}(t) = g_w w(t), \tag{10.7}$$

with initial value $w(0) > 0$. Suppose that

$$g_w + g_h < r + v,$$

so that the net present discounted value of the individual is finite. Now using Theorem 10.1, the optimal schooling decision must be a solution to the following maximization problem:

$$\max_S \int_S^\infty \exp(-(r + v)t) w(t) h(t) dt. \tag{10.8}$$

Using (10.6) and (10.7), this equation is equivalent to (see Exercise 10.3):

$$\max_S \frac{\eta(S) w(0) \exp(-(r + v - g_w)S)}{r + v - g_h - g_w}. \tag{10.9}$$

Since $\eta(S)$ is concave, the objective function in (10.9) is strictly concave. Therefore the unique solution to this problem is characterized by the first-order condition

$$\frac{\eta'(S^*)}{\eta(S^*)} = r + v - g_w. \tag{10.10}$$

Equation (10.10) shows that higher interest rates and higher values of v (corresponding to shorter planning horizons) reduce human capital investments, while higher values of g_w increase the value of human capital and thus encourage further investments.

Integrating both sides of this equation with respect to S (or taking the antiderivative), we obtain

$$\log \eta(S^*) = \text{constant} + (r + v - g_w)S^*. \tag{10.11}$$

Next, the wage earnings of the worker of age $\tau \geq S^*$ in the labor market at time t are

$$W(S^*, t) = \exp(g_w t) \exp(g_h(t - S^*)) \eta(S^*).$$

Taking logs and using (10.11) implies that

$$\log W(S^*, t) = \text{constant} + (r + v - g_w)S^* + g_w t + g_h(t - S^*),$$

where $t - S^*$ can be thought of as worker experience (time after schooling). If we make a cross-sectional comparison across workers, the time trend term $g_w t$ is also included in the constant, so that we obtain the canonical Mincer equation, where, in the cross section, log wage earnings are proportional to schooling and experience. Written differently, we have the following cross-sectional equation:

$$\log W_j = \text{constant} + \gamma_s S_j + \gamma_e \text{ experience}, \tag{10.12}$$

where j refers to individual j. However, there is so far no source of heterogeneity that can generate different levels of schooling across individuals. Nevertheless (10.12) is important, since it is the typical empirical model for the relationship between wages and schooling estimated in labor economics.

The economic insight provided by this equation is quite important. It suggests that the functional form of the Mincerian wage equation is not a mere coincidence, but has economic content: the opportunity cost of one more year of schooling is foregone earnings. So the benefit has to be commensurate with these foregone earnings, and thus should lead to a proportional increase in earnings in the future. In particular, this proportional increase should be at the rate $(r + v - g_w)$.

As already discussed in Chapter 3, empirical work using equations of the form (10.12) leads to estimates for the returns to schooling coefficient, γ_s, in the range of 0.06–0.10. Equation (10.12) suggests that these returns to schooling are not unreasonable. For example, we can think of the annual interest rate r as approximately 0.10, v as corresponding to 0.02 (which gives an expected life of 50 years), and g_w corresponding to the rate of wage growth holding the human capital level of the individual constant (which should be approximately 0.02). Thus we should expect an estimate of γ about 0.10, which is consistent with the upper range of the empirical estimates.

10.3 The Ben-Porath Model

The baseline Ben-Porath model enriches the model studied in the previous section by allowing human capital investments and nontrivial labor supply decisions throughout the lifetime of the individual. In particular, we now let $s(t) \in [0, 1]$ for all $t \geq 0$. Together with the Mincer equation (10.12) (and the model underlying this equation presented in the previous section), the Ben-Porath model is the basis of much of labor economics. Here it is sufficient to consider a simple version of this model in which the human capital accumulation equation (10.2) takes the form

$$\dot{h}(t) = \phi(s(t)h(t)) - \delta_h h(t), \tag{10.13}$$

where $\delta_h > 0$ captures the depreciation of human capital, which comes about, for example, because new machines and techniques are introduced that erode the existing human capital of the worker. The individual starts with an initial value of human capital $h(0) > 0$. The function $\phi : \mathbb{R}_+ \to \mathbb{R}_+$ is strictly increasing, twice differentiable, and strictly concave. Furthermore, let us simplify the analysis by assuming that this function satisfies the Inada-type conditions

$$\lim_{x \to 0} \phi'(x) = \infty, \quad \text{and} \quad \lim_{x \to h(0)} \phi'(x) = 0.$$

The latter condition removes the need to impose additional constraints to ensure $s(t) \in (0, 1)$ (see Exercise 10.6).

Let us also suppose that there is no non–human capital component of labor, so that $\omega(t) = 0$ for all t, $T = \infty$, and there is a flow rate of death $v > 0$. Finally let us assume that the wage per unit of human capital is constant at w and the interest rate is constant and equal to r. We can also normalize $w = 1$ without loss of generality.

Again using Theorem 10.1, human capital investments can be determined as a solution to the following problem:

$$\max \int_0^\infty \exp(-(r + v)t)(1 - s(t))h(t)\, dt,$$

subject to (10.13).

Let us next set up the current-value Hamiltonian, which in this case takes the form

$$\mathcal{H}(h, s, \mu) = (1 - s(t))h(t) + \mu(t)(\phi(s(t)h(t)) - \delta_h h(t)),$$

where $\mathcal{H}$ is used to denote the Hamiltonian to avoid confusion with human capital. The necessary and sufficient conditions for this problem are (see Exercise 10.5):

$$\mathcal{H}_s(h, s, \mu) = -h(t) + \mu(t)h(t)\phi'(s(t)h(t)) = 0,$$

$$\mathcal{H}_h(h, s, \mu) = (1 - s(t)) + \mu(t)(s(t)\phi'(s(t)h(t)) - \delta_h)$$

$$= (r + v)\mu(t) - \dot{\mu}(t), \tag{10.14}$$

and

$$\lim_{t \to \infty} \exp(-(r + v)t)\mu(t)h(t) = 0.$$

To solve for the optimal path of human capital investments, let us adopt the following transformation of variables:

$$x(t) \equiv s(t)h(t).$$

Instead of $s(t)$ (or $\mu(t)$) and $h(t)$, we can look at the dynamics of the optimal path in $x(t)$ and $h(t)$. The first condition in (10.14) implies that

$$1 = \mu(t)\phi'(x(t)), \tag{10.15}$$

while the second necessary condition can be expressed as

$$\frac{\dot{\mu}(t)}{\mu(t)} = r + v + \delta_h - s(t)\phi'(x(t)) - \frac{1 - s(t)}{\mu(t)}.$$

Substituting for $\mu(t)$ from (10.15) and simplifying yields

$$\frac{\dot{\mu}(t)}{\mu(t)} = r + v + \delta_h - \phi'(x(t)). \tag{10.16}$$

The steady-state (stationary) solution of this optimal control problem involves $\dot{\mu}(t) = 0$ and $\dot{h}(t) = 0$, and thus implies that

$$x^* = \phi'^{-1}(r + v + \delta_h), \tag{10.17}$$

where $\phi'^{-1}(\cdot)$ is the inverse function of $\phi'(\cdot)$ (which exists and is strictly decreasing, since $\phi(\cdot)$ is strictly concave). Equation (10.17) shows that $x^* \equiv s^*h^*$ will be higher when the interest rate is low, when the life expectancy of the individual is high, and when the rate of depreciation of human capital is low.

To determine s^* and h^* separately, we set $\dot{h}(t) = 0$ in the human capital accumulation equation (10.13), which gives

$$h^* = \frac{\phi(x^*)}{\delta_h}$$

$$= \frac{\phi(\phi'^{-1}(r + v + \delta_h))}{\delta_h}. \tag{10.18}$$

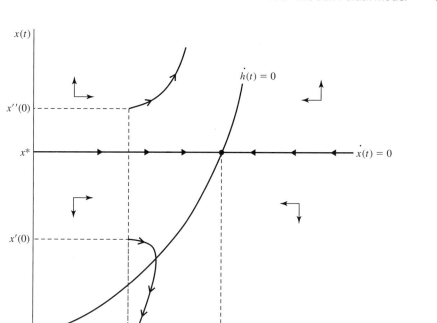

FIGURE 10.1 Equilibrium dynamics in the simplified Ben-Porath model.

Since $\phi'^{-1}(\cdot)$ is strictly decreasing and $\phi(\cdot)$ is strictly increasing, (10.18) implies that the steady-state solution for the human capital stock is uniquely determined and is decreasing in r, ν, and δ_h.

More interesting than the stationary (steady-state) solution to the optimization problem is the time path of human capital investments in this model. Differentiate (10.15) with respect to time to obtain

$$\frac{\dot{\mu}(t)}{\mu(t)} = \varepsilon_{\phi'}(x)\frac{\dot{x}(t)}{x(t)},$$

where

$$\varepsilon_{\phi'}(x) = -\frac{x\phi''(x)}{\phi'(x)} > 0$$

is the elasticity of the function $\phi'(\cdot)$ and is positive, since $\phi'(\cdot)$ is strictly decreasing (thus $\phi''(\cdot) < 0$). Combining this equation with (10.16) gives

$$\frac{\dot{x}(t)}{x(t)} = \frac{1}{\varepsilon_{\phi'}(x(t))}(r + \nu + \delta_h - \phi'(x(t))). \tag{10.19}$$

Figure 10.1 plots (10.13) and (10.19) in h-x space. The upward-sloping curve corresponds to the locus for $\dot{h}(t) = 0$, while (10.19) can only be zero at x^*; thus the locus for $\dot{x}(t) = 0$ corresponds to the horizontal line in the figure. The arrows of motion are also plotted in this phase diagram and make it clear that the steady-state solution (h^*, x^*) is globally saddle-path stable, with the stable arm coinciding with the horizontal line for $\dot{x}(t) = 0$. Starting with

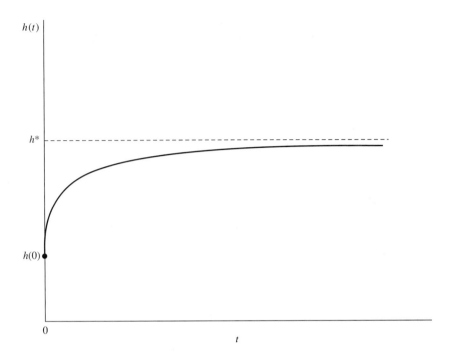

FIGURE 10.2   Time path of human capital investments in the simplified Ben-Porath model.

$h(0) \in (0, h^*)$, $s(0)$ jumps to the level necessary to ensure $s(0)h(0) = x^*$. From then on, $h(t)$ increases and $s(t)$ decreases so as to keep $s(t)h(t) = x^*$. Therefore the pattern of human capital investments implied by the Ben-Porath model is one of high investment at the beginning of an individual's life followed by lower investments later on.

In our simplified version of the Ben-Porath model this process takes place smoothly. In the original Ben-Porath model, which involves the use of other inputs in the production of human capital and finite horizons, the constraint $s(t) \leq 1$ typically binds early in the life of the individual, and the interval during which $s(t) = 1$ can be interpreted as full-time schooling. After full-time schooling, the individual starts working ($s(t) < 1$). But even on the job, the individual continues to accumulate human capital ($s(t) > 0$), which can be interpreted as spending time in training programs or allocating some time on the job to learning rather than to production. Moreover, because the horizon is finite, if the Inada conditions were relaxed, the individual could prefer to stop investing in human capital at some point. As a result, the time path of human capital generated by the standard Ben-Porath model may be hump-shaped, with a possibly declining portion at the end (see Exercise 10.7). Instead, the path of human capital (and the earning potential of the individual) in the current model is always increasing as shown in Figure 10.2.

The importance of the Ben-Porath model is twofold. First, it emphasizes that schooling is not the only way in which individuals can invest in human capital, and there is a continuity between schooling and other investments in human capital. Second, it suggests that in societies where schooling investments are high we may also expect higher levels of on-the-job investments in human capital. Thus there may be systematic mismeasurement of the amount or quality of human capital across societies.

10.4 Neoclassical Growth with Physical and Human Capital

Our next task is to incorporate human capital investments into the baseline neoclassical growth model. This exercise is useful both to investigate the interactions between physical and human capital and also to generate a better sense of the impact of differential human capital investments on economic growth. Physical-human capital interactions could potentially be important, since a variety of evidence suggests that physical capital and human capital (capital and skills) are complementary, meaning that greater capital increases the productivity of workers with high human capital more than that of low-skill workers. Such interactions may play an important role in economic growth, for example, by inducing a "virtuous cycle" of investments in physical and human capital. These types of virtuous cycles are discussed in greater detail in Chapter 21. It is instructive to see to what extent these types of complementarities manifest themselves in the neoclassical growth model. The potential for complementarities also raises the issue of imbalances. If physical and human capital are complementary, the society will achieve the highest productivity when there is a balance between these two different types of capital. However, whether the decentralized equilibrium ensures such a balance is a question that needs to be investigated.

Consider the following continuous-time economy admitting a representative household with preferences:

$$\int_0^\infty \exp(-\rho t)u(c(t))dt, \tag{10.20}$$

where the instantaneous utility function $u(\cdot)$ satisfies Assumption 3 (from Chapter 8) and $\rho > 0$. I ignore technological progress and population growth to simplify the discussion. Labor is again supplied inelastically.

Let us follow the specification in Chapter 3 and assume that the aggregate production possibilities frontier of the economy is represented by the aggregate production function

$$Y(t) = F(K(t), H(t), L(t)),$$

where $K(t)$ is the stock of physical capital, $L(t)$ is total employment, and $H(t)$ represents human capital. Since there is no population growth and labor is supplied inelastically, $L(t) = L$ for all t. This production function is assumed to satisfy Assumptions 1' and 2' in Chapter 3 (recall that these assumptions generalize Assumptions 1 and 2 to this aggregate production function with three inputs). As already discussed in that chapter, a production function in which "raw" labor and human capital are separate factors of production may be less natural than one in which human capital increases the effective units of labor of workers (as in the analysis of the previous two sections). Nevertheless, this production function allows a simple analysis of neoclassical growth with physical and human capital. As usual, it is more convenient to express all objects in per capita units; thus I write

$$y(t) \equiv \frac{Y(t)}{L} = f(k(t), h(t)),$$

where

$$k(t) \equiv \frac{K(t)}{L} \text{ and } h(t) \equiv \frac{H(t)}{L}$$

are the per capita levels of physical and human capital, respectively. In view of Assumptions 1' and 2', $f(k, h)$ is strictly increasing, differentiable, and jointly strictly concave in both of its arguments. Let us denote its derivatives by f_k, f_h, f_{kh}, and so on. Throughout, I assume that physical and human capital are complementary, that is, $f_{kh}(k, h) > 0$ for all $k, h > 0$.

Physical and human capital per capita evolve according to the following two differential equations:

$$\dot{k}(t) = i_k(t) - \delta_k k(t), \tag{10.21}$$

and

$$\dot{h}(t) = i_h(t) - \delta_h h(t), \tag{10.22}$$

where $i_k(t)$ and $i_h(t)$ are the investment levels in physical and human capital, respectively, while δ_k and δ_h are the depreciation rates of these two capital stocks. The resource constraint for the economy, expressed in per capita terms, is

$$c(t) + i_k(t) + i_h(t) \le f(k(t), h(t)) \quad \text{for all } t. \tag{10.23}$$

Since the environment described here is similar to the standard neoclassical growth model, equilibrium and optimal growth coincide. For this reason, I focus on the optimal growth problem (the competitive equilibrium is discussed in Exercise 10.12). The optimal growth problem involves the maximization of (10.20) subject to (10.21), (10.22), and (10.23). The solution to this maximization problem can again be characterized by setting up the current-value Hamiltonian (and using Theorems 7.13 and 7.14). To simplify the analysis, observe first that since $u(c)$ is strictly increasing, (10.23) will always hold as equality. Then substitute for $c(t)$ using this constraint, and write the current-value Hamiltonian as

$$\mathcal{H}(k(t), h(t), i_k(t), i_h(t), \mu_k(t), \mu_h(t)) = u(f(k(t), h(t)) - i_h(t) - i_k(t)) \tag{10.24}$$

$$+ \mu_h(t)(i_h(t) - \delta_h h(t)) + \mu_k(t)(i_k(t) - \delta_k k(t)),$$

where now there are two control variables, $i_k(t)$, and $i_h(t)$, and two state variables, $k(t)$ and $h(t)$, as well as two costate variables, $\mu_k(t)$ and $\mu_h(t)$, corresponding to the two constraints, (10.21) and (10.22). The candidate solution (from Theorem 7.13) satisfies

$$\mathcal{H}_{i_k}(k(t), h(t), i_k(t), i_h(t), \mu_k(t), \mu_h(t)) = -u'(c(t)) + \mu_k(t) = 0,$$

$$\mathcal{H}_{i_h}(k(t), h(t), i_k(t), i_h(t), \mu_k(t), \mu_h(t)) = -u'(c(t)) + \mu_h(t) = 0,$$

$$\mathcal{H}_k(k(t), h(t), i_k(t), i_h(t), \mu_k(t), \mu_h(t)) = f_k(k(t), h(t))u'(c(t)) - \mu_k(t)\delta_k$$

$$= \rho\mu_k(t) - \dot{\mu}_k(t),$$

$$\mathcal{H}_h(k(t), h(t), i_k(t), i_h(t), \mu_k(t), \mu_h(t)) = f_h(k(t), h(t))u'(c(t)) - \mu_h(t)\delta_h$$

$$= \rho\mu_h(t) - \dot{\mu}_h(t),$$

$$\lim_{t \to \infty} \exp(-\rho t)\mu_k(t)k(t) = 0,$$

$$\lim_{t \to \infty} \exp(-\rho t)\mu_h(t)h(t) = 0.$$

The last two are the two transversality conditions, since there are two state variables (and two costate variables). It can next be verified that $\mathcal{H}(k(t), h(t), i_k(t), i_h(t), \mu_k(t), \mu_h(t))$ is concave given the costate variables $\mu_k(t)$ and $\mu_h(t)$, so that Theorem 7.14 can be applied to conclude that these conditions indeed generate an optimal path (see Exercise 10.8).

The first two conditions immediately imply that

$$\mu_k(t) = \mu_h(t) = \mu(t).$$

Combining this equation with the next two conditions gives

$$f_k(k(t), h(t)) - f_h(k(t), h(t)) = \delta_k - \delta_h, \qquad (10.25)$$

which (together with $f_{kh} > 0$) implies that there is a one-to-one relationship between physical and human capital of the form

$$h = \xi(k),$$

where $\xi(\cdot)$ is uniquely defined, strictly increasing, and differentiable (with its derivative denoted by $\xi'(\cdot)$; see Exercise 10.9).

This observation makes it clear that the model can be reduced to the baseline neoclassical growth model and has the same dynamics as the neoclassical growth model, thus establishing the following proposition.

Proposition 10.1 *In the neoclassical growth model with physical and human capital investments described above, the optimal path of physical capital and consumption are given as in the one-sector neoclassical growth model and satisfy the following two differential equations:*

$$\frac{\dot{c}(t)}{c(t)} = \frac{1}{\varepsilon_u(c(t))}[f_k(k(t), \xi(k(t))) - \delta_k - \rho],$$

and

$$\dot{k}(t) = \frac{1}{1 + \xi'(k)}[f(k(t), \xi(k(t))) - \delta_h\xi(k(t)) - \delta_k k(t) - c(t)],$$

where

$$\varepsilon_u(c(t)) = -u''(c(t))c(t)/u'(c(t)),$$

together with the transversality condition

$$\lim_{t \to \infty} \left[k(t) \exp(- \int_0^t f_k(k(s), \xi(k(s)))ds) \right] = 0,$$

while the level of human capital at time t is given by $h(t) = \xi(k(t))$.

Proof. See Exercise 10.10. ■

At first, the implication of (10.25) that human and physical capital are always in balance is somewhat surprising. Initially, one may have conjectured that an economy that starts with a high stock of physical capital relative to human capital will have a relatively high physical-human capital ratio for an extended period of time. However, Proposition 10.1 and, in particular, (10.25) show that this is not the case, becasue there is no nonnegativity constraint on the investment levels. If the economy starts with a high level of physical capital and a low level of human capital, at the first instant it experiences a high level of $i_h(0)$, compensated with a very negative $i_k(0)$, so that at the next instant the physical-human capital ratio has been brought back to balance. After this adjustment, the dynamics of the economy are identical to those of the baseline neoclassical growth model. Therefore issues of imbalance do not arise in this version of the neoclassical growth model. This result is an artifact of the lack of nonnegativity constraints on physical and human capital investments. The situation is somewhat different when there are such nonnegativity, or irreversibility, constraints, that is, if $i_k(t) \geq 0$ and $i_h(t) \geq 0$ for all t. In this case, initial imbalances persist for a while. In particular, it can be shown that starting with a ratio of physical-human capital stock $(k(0)/h(0))$ that does not satisfy (10.25), the optimal path involves investment only in one of the two stocks until balance is reached (see Exercise 10.14). Therefore, with irreversibility constraints, some amount of imbalance can arise, but the economy quickly moves to correct this imbalance.

Another potential application of the neoclassical growth model with physical and human capital is in the analysis of the impact of policy distortions. Recall the discussion in Section 8.10 in Chapter 8, and suppose that the resource constraint of the economy is modified to be

$$c(t) + (1 + \tau)(i_k(t) + i_h(t)) \leq f(k(t), h(t)),$$

where $\tau \geq 0$ is a tax affecting both types of investments. Using an analysis parallel to that in Section 8.10, we can characterize the steady-state income ratio of two countries with different policies represented by τ and τ'. In particular, suppose that the aggregate production function takes the Cobb-Douglas form

$$Y = F(K, H, L) = K^\alpha H^\beta L^{1-\alpha-\beta}.$$

In this case, the ratio of income in the two economies with taxes/distortions of τ and τ' is given by (see Exercise 10.11):

$$\frac{Y(\tau)}{Y(\tau')} = \left(\frac{1 + \tau'}{1 + \tau}\right)^{\frac{\alpha+\beta}{1-\alpha-\beta}}. \tag{10.26}$$

If we again take α to be approximately 1/3, then the ability of this modified model to account for income differences using tax distortions increases because of the responsiveness of human capital accumulation to these distortions. For example, with $\alpha = \beta = 1/3$ and eightfold distortion differences, we would have

$$\frac{Y(\tau)}{Y(\tau')} \approx 8^2 = 64,$$

which is a huge difference in economic performance across countries.

Therefore, incorporating human capital into the neoclassical growth model provides one potential way of generating large differences in income per capita. Nevertheless, this result has to be interpreted with caution. First, the large impact of distortions on income per capita here is driven by a very elastic response of human capital accumulation. It is not clear whether human capital investments indeed respond so much to tax distortions. For instance, if these distortions correspond to differences in corporate taxes or corruption, we would expect them to affect corporate rather than individual human capital decisions. Of course this logic does not deny that in societies where policies discourage capital accumulation, there may also be barriers to schooling and other types of human capital investments. Nevertheless the impact of these barriers on physical and human capital investments may be quite different. Second, and more important, the large implied elasticity of output to distortions when both physical and human capital are endogenous has an obvious similarity to the Mankiw-Romer-Weil approach to explaining cross-country differences in terms of physical and human capital stocks. As discussed in Chapter 3, while this possibility is logical, existing evidence does not support the notion that human capital differences across countries can have such a large impact on income differences. This conclusion equally casts doubt on the importance of the large contribution of human capital differences induced by policy differences in the current model. Nevertheless, the conclusions in Chapter 3 were subject to two caveats that could potentially increase the role of human capital: large human capital externalities and significant differences in the quality of schooling across countries. These issues are discussed in Sections 10.6 and 10.7.

10.5 Capital-Skill Complementarity in an Overlapping Generations Model

The analysis in the previous section suggests that the neoclassical growth model with physical and human capital does not generate significant imbalances between these two different types of capital (unless we impose irreversibilities, in which case it can do so along the transition path). I next investigate the possibility of capital-skill imbalances in a simple OLG model with impure altruism, similar to the models introduced in Section 9.6 of the previous chapter. We will see that this class of models also generates only limited capital-skill imbalances. Nevertheless it provides a simple framework in which labor market frictions can be introduced, and capital-skill imbalances become much more important in the presence of such frictions. We also use the model in this section to go back to the more natural production function, which features capital and effective units of labor (with human capital augmenting the effective units of labor), as opposed to the production function used in the previous section with human capital as a separate factor of production.

The economy is in discrete time and consists of a continuum 1 of dynasties. Each individual lives for two periods, childhood and adulthood. Individual i of generation t works during adulthood at time t and earns labor income equal to $w(t)h_i(t)$, where $w(t)$ is the wage rate per unit of human capital and $h_i(t)$ is the individual's human capital. The individual also earns capital income equal to $R(t)b_i(t-1)$, where $R(t)$ is the gross rate of return on capital and $b_i(t-1)$ is his asset holdings, inherited as a bequest from his parent. The human capital of the individual is determined at the beginning of his adulthood by an effort decision. Labor is supplied to the market after this effort decision. At the end of adulthood, after labor and capital incomes are received, the individual decides on his level of consumption and on the level of bequest to his offspring.

Preferences of individual i (or of dynasty i) of generation t are given by

$$\eta^{-\eta}(1-\eta)^{-(1-\eta)}c_i(t)^{\eta}b_i(t)^{1-\eta} - \gamma(e_i(t)),$$

where $\eta \in (0, 1)$; $c_i(t)$ is own consumption; $b_i(t)$ is the bequest to the offspring; $e_i(t)$ is effort expended for human capital acquisition; and $\gamma(\cdot)$ is a strictly increasing, differentiable, and strictly convex cost of effort function. The term $\eta^{-\eta}(1-\eta)^{-(1-\eta)}$ is included as a normalizing factor to simplify the algebra.

The human capital of individual i is given by

$$h_i(t) = ae_i(t), \tag{10.27}$$

where a corresponds to "ability" and increases the effectiveness of effort in generating human capital for the individual. Substituting for $e_i(t)$ in the above expression, the preferences of individual i of generation t can be written as

$$\eta^{-\eta}(1-\eta)^{-(1-\eta)}c_i(t)^{\eta}b_i(t)^{1-\eta} - \gamma\left(\frac{h_i(t)}{a}\right). \tag{10.28}$$

The budget constraint of the individual is

$$c_i(t) + b_i(t) \leq m_i(t) = w(t)h_i(t) + R(t)b_i(t-1),$$ (10.29)

which defines $m_i(t)$ as the current income of individual i at time t, consisting of labor earnings, $w(t)h_i(t)$, and asset income, $R(t)b_i(t-1)$ (I use m rather than y, since y will have a different meaning below).

The production side of the economy is given by an aggregate production function

$$Y(t) = F(K(t), H(t))$$

that satisfies Assumptions 1 and 2 from Chapter 2, where $H(t)$ is "effective units of labor," or alternatively the total stock of human capital, given by

$$H(t) = \int_0^1 h_i(t)di,$$

while $K(t)$, the stock of physical capital, is given by

$$K(t) = \int_0^1 b_i(t-1)di.$$

Note also that this specification ensures that capital and skill (K and H) are complements: a production function with two factors and constant returns to scale necessarily implies that the two factors must be complements (see Exercise 10.15), that is,

$$\frac{\partial^2 F(K, H)}{\partial K \partial H} \geq 0.$$ (10.30)

Furthermore, let us again simplify the notation by assuming capital depreciates fully after use, that is, $\delta = 1$ (see Exercise 10.16).

Since the amount of human capital per worker is an endogenous variable in this economy, it is more useful to define a normalized production function expressing output per unit of human capital rather than the usual per capita production function. In particular, let $\kappa \equiv K/H$ be the capital–human capital ratio (or the effective capital-labor ratio), and let

$$y(t) \equiv \frac{Y(t)}{H(t)}$$

$$= F\left(\frac{K(t)}{H(t)}, 1\right)$$

$$= f(\kappa(t)),$$

where the second line uses the linear homogeneity of $F(\cdot, \cdot)$, while the last line uses the definition of κ. Here I use κ instead of the more usual k to preserve the notation k for capital per worker in the next section. From the definition of κ, we can write

$$\kappa(t) \equiv \frac{K(t)}{H(t)} = \frac{\int_0^1 b_i(t-1)di}{\int_0^1 h_i(t)di}.$$ (10.31)

Factor prices are then given by the usual competitive pricing formulas:

$$R(t) = f'(\kappa(t)), \quad \text{and} \quad w(t) = f(\kappa(t)) - \kappa(t)f'(\kappa(t)),$$ (10.32)

with the only noteworthy feature being that $w(t)$ now denotes wage per unit of human capital.

An equilibrium in this economy is a path of human capital, consumption and bequest levels for each individual, $\{[h_i(t)]_{i\in[0,1]}, [c_i(t)]_{i\in[0,1]}, [b_i(t)]_{i\in[0,1]}\}_{t=0}^{\infty}$, that solve (10.28) subject to (10.29) a sequence of effective capital-labor ratios, $\{\kappa(t)\}_{t=0}^{\infty}$, given by (10.31) with some initial distribution of bequests $[b_i(0)]_{i\in[0,1]}$, and sequences of factor prices, $\{w(t), R(t)\}_{t=0}^{\infty}$, that satisfy (10.32).

The characterization of an equilibrium is simplified by the fact that the solution to the maximization problem of (10.28) subject to (10.29) involves

$$c_i(t) = \eta m_i(t), \quad \text{and} \quad b_i(t) = (1-\eta)m_i(t), \tag{10.33}$$

and substituting these into (10.28), we obtain the indirect utility function (see Exercise 10.17)

$$m_i(t) - \gamma\left(\frac{h_i(t)}{a}\right), \tag{10.34}$$

which the individual maximizes by choosing $h_i(t)$ and recognizing that $m_i(t) = w(t)h_i(t) + R(t)b_i(t-1)$. The first-order condition of this maximization gives the human capital investment of individual i at time t as

$$aw(t) = \gamma'\left(\frac{h_i(t)}{a}\right). \tag{10.35}$$

Equivalently, inverting this relationship, defining $\gamma'^{-1}(\cdot)$ as the inverse function of $\gamma'(\cdot)$ (which is strictly increasing), and using (10.32), we obtain

$$h_i(t) = h(t) \equiv a\gamma'^{-1}\left[a(f(\kappa(t)) - \kappa(t)f'(\kappa(t)))\right]. \tag{10.36}$$

An important implication of this equation is that the human capital investment of each individual is identical and only depends on the effective capital-labor ratio in the economy. This result is a consequence of the specific utility function in (10.28), which ensures that there are no income effects in human capital decisions, so that all agents choose the same income-maximizing level of human capital (as in Theorem 10.1).

Next, note that since bequest decisions are linear, as shown in (10.33), we have

$$K(t+1) = \int_0^1 b_i(t)di$$

$$= (1-\eta)\int_0^1 m_i(t)di$$

$$= (1-\eta)f(\kappa(t))h(t),$$

where the last line uses the fact that, since all individuals choose the same human capital level given by (10.36), $H(t) = h(t)$, and thus $Y(t) = f(\kappa(t))h(t)$.

Now combining this equation with (10.31) gives

$$\kappa(t+1) = \frac{(1-\eta)f(\kappa(t))h(t)}{h(t+1)}.$$

Using (10.36), this expression becomes

$$\kappa(t+1)\gamma'^{-1}[a(f(\kappa(t+1)) - \kappa(t+1)f'(\kappa(t+1)))]$$
$$= (1-\eta)f(\kappa(t))\gamma'^{-1}[a(f(\kappa(t)) - \kappa(t)f'(\kappa(t)))]. \quad (10.37)$$

A steady state, as usual, involves a constant effective capital-labor ratio: $\kappa(t) = \kappa^*$ for all t. Substituting this into (10.37) yields

$$\kappa^* = (1-\eta)f(\kappa^*), \quad (10.38)$$

which defines the unique positive steady-state effective capital-labor ratio κ^* (since $f(\cdot)$ is strictly concave).

Proposition 10.2 *In the OLG economy with physical and human capital described above, there exists a unique steady state with positive activity, and the effective capital-labor ratio κ^* is given by (10.38).*

This steady-state equilibrium is also typically stable, but some additional conditions need to be imposed on $f(\cdot)$ and $\gamma(\cdot)$ to ensure stability (see Exercise 10.18).

An interesting implication of this equilibrium is that the capital-skill (k-h) complementarity in the production function $F(\cdot, \cdot)$ implies that a certain target level of physical to human capital ratio, κ^*, has to be reached in equilibrium. In other words, physical capital will not be too abundant relative to human capital, and neither will human capital be excessive relative to physical capital. Consequently, this model also limits equilibrium imbalances between physical and human capital. A possible and arguably attractive way of introducing such imbalances is to depart from perfectly competitive labor markets. This is also useful for illustrating how the role of human capital can be quite different in models with imperfect labor markets.

10.6 Physical and Human Capital with Imperfect Labor Markets

In this section, I analyze the implications of labor market frictions that lead to factor prices that differ from the ones used so far (in particular, prices that deviate from the competitive pricing formula (10.32)). The literature on labor market imperfections is vast, and my purpose here is not to provide an overview. For this reason, I adopt the simplest representation. In particular, imagine that the economy is identical to that described in the previous section, except that there is a continuum of firms with measure normalized 1 as well as a continuum of individuals, also with measure 1, at any point in time, and each firm can only hire one worker. Let us first suppress time dependence to simplify notation. Then the production function of each firm can be written as

$$y_j = F(k_j, h_i),$$

where y_j refers to the output of firm j, k_j is its capital stock (equivalently capital per worker, since the firm is hiring only one worker), and h_i is the human capital of worker i employed by the firm. This production function again satisfies Assumptions 1 and 2. The main departure from the models analyzed so far is in the structure for the labor market, which is summarized next.

1. Firms choose their physical capital level irreversibly (incurring the cost Rk_j, where R is the market rate of return on capital), and simultaneously workers choose their human capital level irreversibly.

2. After workers complete their human capital investments, they are randomly matched with firms. Random matching here implies that each worker has the same probability of matching with each firm, and in particular, workers with high human capital are not more likely to be matched with firms having high physical capital.

3. After matching, each worker-firm pair bargains over the division of output between themselves. Let us assume that they simply divide the output according to some pre-specified rule, and the worker receives total earnings of

$$W_j(k_j, h_i) = \lambda F(k_j, h_i),$$

for some $\lambda \in (0, 1)$.

This specification is admittedly very simple and reduced form. Nevertheless, it is sufficient to emphasize the main economic issues. A more detailed game-theoretic justification for a closely related environment is provided in Acemoglu (1996).

Let us also introduce heterogeneity in the cost of human capital acquisition by modifying (10.27) to be

$$h_i = a_i e_i,$$

where a_i differs across dynasties (individuals). A high value of a_i naturally corresponds to an individual who can more effectively accumulate human capital.

An equilibrium is defined similarly to that in Section 10.5 except that factor prices are no longer determined by (10.32). Let us start with the physical capital choices of firms. At the time each firm chooses its physical capital, it is unsure about the human capital of the worker it will employ. Given the random matching assumption, the expected return of firm j can be written as

$$(1 - \lambda) \int_0^1 F(k_j, h_i) di - Rk_j. \tag{10.39}$$

This expression takes into account that the firm will receive a fraction $1 - \lambda$ of the output produced jointly by itself and the worker that it is matched with. The integration of $F(k_j, h_i)$ over the human capital choices of all workers takes care of the fact that the firm does not know which worker it will be matched with. The last term is the cost of making an irreversible capital investment at the market price R. This investment is made before the firm knows which worker it will be matched with. Given the strict concavity of $F(\cdot, \cdot)$ in k (from Assumption 1), the objective function in (10.39) is also strictly concave in k_j. Therefore each firm chooses the same level of physical capital $\hat{k}$ such that

$$(1 - \lambda) \int_0^1 \frac{\partial F(\hat{k}, h_i)}{\partial k} di = R.$$

Now given this (expected) capital investment by firms, and using (10.34) from the previous section, each worker's objective function can be written as

$$\lambda F(\hat{k}, h_i) + Rb_i - \gamma\left(\frac{h_i}{a_i}\right),$$

which substitutes for the income m_i of the worker in terms of his wage earnings and capital income and introduces the heterogeneity in human capital decisions. This equation implies the following choice of human capital investment by a worker i:

$$\lambda a_i \frac{\partial F(\hat{k}, h_i)}{\partial h_i(t)} = \gamma'\left(\frac{h_i}{a_i}\right).$$

This equation yields a unique equilibrium human capital investment $\hat{h}_i(\hat{k})$ for each i. This human capital investment directly depends on the capital choice $\hat{k}$ of firms (since this choice affects the marginal product of human capital) and also depends implicitly on a_i. Moreover, given (10.30) and the facts that $\gamma(\cdot)$ is convex and F is concave in k, $\hat{h}_i(\hat{k})$ is strictly increasing in $\hat{k}$. Substituting $\hat{h}_i(\hat{k})$ into the first-order condition of firms, we obtain

$$(1 - \lambda) \int_0^1 \frac{\partial F(\hat{k}, \hat{h}_i(\hat{k}))}{\partial k} di = R.$$

Finally, to satisfy market clearing in the capital market, the rate of return to capital at time t, $R(t)$, has to equate the demand for capital to the supply of capital. As in the model of the previous section, supply comes from bequests from the previous period, so that the market clearing condition takes the form $\hat{k}(t) = \int_0^1 b_i(t-1)di$. This equation implies that in the closed-economy version of the current model, capital per firm is fixed by bequest decisions from the previous period. The main economic forces I wish to emphasize here are seen more clearly when physical capital is not predetermined. For this reason, let us imagine that the economy in question is small and open, so that $R(t) = R^*$ is pinned down by international financial markets (the closed-economy version is further discussed in Exercise 10.19).

Under this assumption, the equilibrium level of capital per firm is determined by

$$(1 - \lambda) \int_0^1 \frac{\partial F(\hat{k}, \hat{h}_i(\hat{k}))}{\partial k} di = R^*. \tag{10.40}$$

Proposition 10.3 *In the open-economy version of the model described above, there exists a unique positive level of capital per worker $\hat{k}$ given by (10.40) such that the equilibrium capital per worker is always equal to $\hat{k}$. Given $\hat{k}$, the human capital investment of worker i is uniquely determined by $\hat{h}_i(\hat{k})$ such that*

$$\lambda a_i \frac{\partial F(\hat{k}, \hat{h}_i(\hat{k}))}{\partial h} = \gamma'\left(\frac{\hat{h}_i(\hat{k})}{a_i}\right). \tag{10.41}$$

Here $\hat{h}_i(\hat{k})$ is increasing in $\hat{k}$, and a decline in R^* increases $\hat{k}$ and $\hat{h}_i$ for all $i \in [0, 1]$.

In addition to this equilibrium, there also exists a no-activity equilibrium where $\hat{k} = 0$ and $\hat{h}_i = 0$ for all $i \in [0, 1]$.

Proof. Note that since $F(k, h)$ exhibits constant returns to scale and γ is strictly convex, $\partial \hat{h}_i(\hat{k})/\partial k < 1$ for each i. Suppose instead that $\partial \hat{h}_i(\hat{k})/\partial k = 1$ at some $\hat{k}'$. Then when $\hat{k}$ is increased starting from $\hat{k}'$, the left-hand side of (10.41) would remain constant (because F is homogeneous of degree 1). However, since $\hat{h}_i(\hat{k})$ is strictly increasing and γ is strictly convex, the right-hand side would increase, yielding a contradiction. Therefore, $\int_0^1 (\partial F(\hat{k}, \hat{h}_i(\hat{k}))/\partial k)di$ is strictly decreasing in $\hat{k}$ for a given distribution of $[a_i]_{i \in [0,1]}$. Thus the equilibrium value of $\hat{k}$ is uniquely determined. Given this $\hat{k}$, (10.41) determines $\hat{h}_i(\hat{k})$ uniquely for each i. Applying the Implicit Function Theorem (Theorem A.25) to (10.41) implies that $\hat{h}_i(\hat{k})$ is increasing in $\hat{k}$. Finally, (10.40) implies that a lower R^* increases $\hat{k}$, and from the previous observation, $\hat{h}_i$ for all $i \in [0, 1]$ increases as well.

The existence of the no-activity equilibrium follows, since when all firms choose $\hat{k} = 0$, output is equal to zero, and it is a best response for workers to choose $\hat{h}_i = 0$, and when $\hat{h}_i = 0$ for all $i \in [0, 1]$, $\hat{k} = 0$ is a best response for all firms. ∎

Observe that there is underinvestment both in human capital and physical capital (for the positive activity equilibrium; clearly, there is an even more severe underinvestment in the no-activity equilibrium). Consider a social planner wishing to maximize output. Suppose that the social planner is restricted by the same random matching technology, so that she cannot allocate workers to firms as she wishes. A similar analysis to the above implies that the social planner would also like each firm to choose an identical level of capital per firm, say $\bar{k}$. However, this level of capital per firm will be different than in the competitive equilibrium, and she will also choose a different relationship between human capital and physical capital investments. In particular, given $\bar{k}$, she would make human capital investments so that

$$a_i \frac{\partial F(\bar{k}, \bar{h}_i(\bar{k}))}{\partial h} = \gamma'\left(\frac{\bar{h}_i(\bar{k})}{a_i}\right),$$

which is similar to (10.41) except that λ is absent from the left-hand side. This omission is because each worker takes into account only his share of output, λ, when undertaking human capital investments, while the social planner considers the entire output. Consequently, as long as $\lambda < 1$,

$$\bar{h}_i(k) > \hat{h}_i(k) \quad \text{for all } k > 0.$$

Similarly the social planner would also choose a higher level of capital investment for each firm, in particular, one that satisfies the equation

$$\int_0^1 \frac{\partial F(\bar{k}, \bar{h}_i(\bar{k}))}{\partial k} di = R^*,$$

which differs from (10.40) both because now the term $1 - \lambda$ is not present on the left-hand side and also because the planner takes into account the differential human capital investment behavior of workers given by $\bar{h}_i(\bar{k})$. This discussion establishes the following result.

Proposition 10.4 *In the equilibrium described in Proposition 10.3, there is underinvestment both in physical and human capital.*

More interesting than the underinvestment result is the imbalance in the physical-human capital ratio of the economy, which did not feature in the previous two environments we discussed. The following proposition summarizes this imbalance result in a sharp way.

Proposition 10.5 *Consider the positive activity equilibrium described in Proposition 10.3. Output is equal to 0 if either $\lambda = 0$ or $\lambda = 1$. Moreover, there exists $\lambda^* \in (0, 1)$ that maximizes output.*

Proof. See Exercise 10.20. ∎

Intuitively, different levels of λ create different types of imbalances between physical and human capital. A high level of λ implies that workers have a strong bargaining position, and this encourages their investment in human capital. But symmetrically, it discourages the physical capital investments of firms, since they only receive a small fraction of the output. Therefore a high level of λ (as long as $\lambda < 1$) creates an imbalance with an excessive amount of human capital relative to physical capital. This imbalance effect becomes more extreme as $\lambda \to 1$. In this limit, workers' investment behavior converges to the first-order condition of the social planner (that is, $\hat{h}_i(k) \to \bar{h}_i(k)$ for all $k > 0$). However at the same time, the physical capital investment of each firm, $\hat{k}$, converges to 0, so that $\bar{h}_i(k) \to 0$, and production collapses. The same happens, in reverse, when λ is too low. Now there is an excess of physical capital relative to human capital. An intermediate value of λ^* achieves a balance, though the equilibrium continues to be inefficient, as shown in Proposition 10.5.

Physical-human capital imbalances can also increase the role of human capital in cross-country income differences. In the current model, the proportional impact of a change in human capital on aggregate output (or on labor productivity) is greater than the return to human capital, since the latter is determined not by the marginal product of human capital but by the bargaining parameter λ. The deviation from competitive factor prices therefore decouples the contribution of human capital to productivity from market prices.

At the root of the inefficiencies and of the imbalance effect in this model are *pecuniary externalities*. Recall that pecuniary externalities refer to external effects that work through prices (not through direct technological spillovers). By investing more, workers (and symmetrically firms) increase the return to capital (symmetrically wages), and there is underinvestment because they do not take these external effects into consideration. As discussed in the previous chapter, pecuniary external effects are also present in competitive markets (since, e.g., supply affects price), but these are typically second order, because prices are such that they are equal to both the marginal benefit of buyers (marginal product of firms in the case of factors of production) and the marginal cost of suppliers. The presence of labor market frictions causes a departure from this type of marginal pricing and is the reason why pecuniary externalities are not second order here.

Perhaps even more interesting is the fact that pecuniary externalities in this model take the form of *human capital externalities*. Thus greater investments in human capital by a group of workers increase other workers' wages. Notice that in competitive markets (without externalities), if a group of workers increases its human capital investments, this typically depresses the physical-human capital ratio in the economy, reducing wages per unit of human capital and thus the earnings of other workers.[1] Interestingly, the opposite may happen in the presence of labor market imperfections. To illustrate this point, let us suppose that there are two types of workers, a fraction of workers χ with ability a_1 and $1 - \chi$ with ability $a_2 < a_1$. Using this specific structure, the first-order condition of firms (10.40) can be written as

$$(1 - \lambda) \left[\chi \frac{\partial F(\hat{k}, \hat{h}_1(\hat{k}))}{\partial k} + (1 - \chi) \frac{\partial F(\hat{k}, \hat{h}_2(\hat{k}))}{\partial k} \right] = R^*, \qquad (10.42)$$

while the first-order conditions for human capital investments for the two types of workers take the form

$$\lambda a_i \frac{\partial F(\hat{k}, \hat{h}_i(\hat{k}))}{\partial h} = \gamma' \left(\frac{\hat{h}_i(\hat{k})}{a_i} \right) \quad \text{for } i = 1, 2. \qquad (10.43)$$

Clearly, $\hat{h}_1(k) > \hat{h}_2(k)$, since $a_1 > a_2$. Now imagine an increase in χ, which corresponds to an increase in the fraction of high-ability workers in the population. Holding $\hat{h}_1(\hat{k})$ and $\hat{h}_2(\hat{k})$ constant, (10.42) implies that $\hat{k}$ should increase, since the left-hand side has increased (because $\hat{h}_1(\hat{k}) > \hat{h}_2(\hat{k})$ and $\partial^2 F(k, h)/\partial k \partial h > 0$). Therefore capital-skill complementarity combined with the pecuniary externalities implies that an improvement in the pool of workers leads to greater investments by firms.

---

1. For example, in the economy studied in the previous section, an increase in the human capital of a group of workers would reduce the wages of other workers. If, on the other hand, the rate to return to capital were held constant, then this increase would have no effect on the wages of other workers.

Intuitively, each firm expects the average worker that it will be matched with to have higher human capital, and since physical and human capital are complements, it is more profitable for each firm to increase its physical capital investment. Greater investments by firms, in turn, raise $F(\hat{k}, h)$ for each h, in particular for $\hat{h}_2(\hat{k})$. Since the earnings of type 2 workers is equal to $\lambda F(\hat{k}, \hat{h}_2(\hat{k}))$, their earnings also increase as a result of the response of firms to the change in the composition of the workforce. These interactions correspond to human capital externalities, because greater human capital investments by one group of workers increase the earnings of the remaining workers. In fact, human capital externalities, in this economy, are even stronger, because the increase in $\hat{k}$ also raises $\partial F(\hat{k}, \hat{h}_2(\hat{k}))/\partial h$ and thus encourages further investments by type 2 workers. This discussion is summarized in the following result.

Proposition 10.6 *The positive activity equilibrium described in Proposition 10.3 exhibits human capital externalities in the sense that an increase in the human capital investments of a group of workers raises the earnings of the remaining workers.*

10.7 Human Capital Externalities

The previous section illustrated how a natural form of human capital externalities can emerge in the presence of capital-skill complementarities combined with labor market imperfections. This channel is not the only one through which human capital externalities may arise. Many economists believe that the human capital stock of the workforce creates a direct nonpecuniary (technological) spillover on the productivity of each worker. In *The Economy of Cities*, Jane Jacobs (1970), for example, argues for the importance of human capital externalities and suggests that the concentration of economic activity in cities is partly a result of these externalities and also acts as an engine of economic growth because it facilitates the exchange of ideas among workers and entrepreneurs. In the growth literature, a number of well-known papers, including those by Robert Lucas (1988) and Azariadis and Drazen (1990), suggest that such technological externalities are important and play a major role in the process of economic growth. Human capital externalities are interesting in their own right. For example, when such external effects are present, the competitive price system is likely to be inefficient. Human capital externalities are also important for our understanding of the sources of income differences across countries. The discussion of the contribution of physical and human capital to cross-country income differences in Chapter 3 showed that differences in human capital are unlikely to account for a large fraction of cross-country income differences unless external effects are important.

At this point, it is therefore useful to briefly review the empirical evidence on the extent of human capital externalities. Early work in the area—in particular, the paper by James Rauch (1993)—tried to measure the extent of human capital externalities by estimating quasi-Mincerian wage regressions, with the major difference that average human capital of workers in the local labor market is also included on the right-hand side. More specifically, Rauch estimated models of the following form:

$$\log W_{j,m} = \mathbf{X}_{j,m}^T \boldsymbol{\beta} + \gamma_p S_{j,m} + \gamma_e S_m,$$

where $\mathbf{X}_{j,m}$ is a vector of controls, $S_{j,m}$ is the years of schooling of individual j working in labor market m, and S_m is the average years of schooling of workers in labor market m. Without this last term, this equation would be similar to the standard Mincerian wage regressions discussed in Section 10.2, and we would expect an estimate of the *private return* to schooling γ_p between 6 and 10%. When the average years of schooling S_m is also included in the regression, its coefficient γ_e measures the *external return* to schooling in the same units. For example, if γ_e is estimated to be of the same magnitude as γ_p, we would conclude that external returns to schooling are as important as private returns (which would correspond to very large externalities).

Rauch estimated significant external returns, with the magnitude of the external returns often exceeding that of the private returns. External returns of this magnitude would imply that human capital differences could play a much more important role as a proximate source of cross-country differences in income per capita than implied by the computations in Chapter 3. However, Rauch's regressions exploited differences in average schooling levels across cities, which could reflect many other factors that also directly affect wages. For example, wages are much higher in New York City than Ames, Iowa, but this difference is not only the result of the higher average education of New Yorkers. A more convincing estimate of external returns necessitates a source of exogenous variation in average schooling.

Acemoglu and Angrist (2000) exploited differences in average schooling levels across states and cohorts resulting from changes in compulsory schooling and child labor laws. These laws appear to have had a large effect on schooling, especially at the high school margin. Exploiting changes in average schooling in state labor markets driven by these law changes, Acemoglu and Angrist estimate external returns to schooling that are typically about 1–2% and are statistically insignificant (compared to private returns of about 10%). These results suggest that there are relatively small human capital externalities in local labor markets. This result is confirmed by Duflo (2004) using Indonesian data and by Ciccone and Peri (2006) on U.S. data.[2] Overall the evidence appears to suggest that local human capital externalities are not very large, and calibration exercises such as those in Chapter 3 that ignore these externalities are unlikely to lead to significant downward bias in the contribution of human capital to cross-country income differences.

The qualification "local" in the above discussion has to be emphasized. These estimates focus on local externalities originally emphasized by Jacobs. Nevertheless, if a few very talented scientists and engineers, or other very skilled workers, generate ideas that are then used in other parts of the country or even in the world economy, there may exist significant global human capital externalities. Such global external effects would not be captured by the currently available empirical strategies. Whether such global human capital externalities are important is an interesting area for future research.

10.8 The Nelson-Phelps Model of Human Capital

The discussion in this chapter so far has focused on the productivity-enhancing role of human capital, emphasized by Becker and Mincer's seminal analyses. This is arguably the most important role of human capital. An alternative perspective on human capital is provided by Richard Nelson and Edmund Phelps in their short and influential paper (Nelson and Phelps, 1966) and also by Ted Schultz (1964, 1975). According to this perspective, the major role of human capital is not to increase productivity in existing tasks but to enable workers to cope with change, disruptions, and especially new technologies. The Nelson-Phelps view of human

---

2. Moretti (2004) also estimates human capital externalities, and he finds larger effects. This may be because he focuses on college graduation, but it also partly reflects the fact that the source of variation that he exploits, changes in age composition and the presence of land-grant colleges, may have other effects on average earnings in an area.

capital has played an important role in a variety of different literatures and features in a number of growth models. Here I provide a simple presentation of the main ideas along the lines of their original model and a discussion of how this new dimension of human capital may enrich our view of its role in economic growth and development. This model also acts as a stepping stone toward our study of technology adoption in Part VI.

Consider the following continuous-time model to illustrate the basic ideas. Suppose that output in the economy is given by

$$Y(t) = A(t)L, \tag{10.44}$$

where L is the constant labor force, supplying its labor inelastically, and $A(t)$ is the technology level of the economy. There is no capital (and thus no capital accumulation decision) and also no labor supply margin. The only variable that changes over time is technology $A(t)$.

Suppose that the world technological frontier is given by $A_F(t)$. This frontier might correspond to technology in some other country or perhaps to the technological knowhow of scientists that has not yet been applied to production processes. Suppose that $A_F(t)$ evolves exogenously according to the differential equation

$$\frac{\dot{A}_F(t)}{A_F(t)} = g_F,$$

with initial condition $A_F(0) > 0$.

Let the human capital of the workforce be denoted by h. Notice that this human capital does not feature in the production function (10.44). This case is an extreme one in which human capital does not play any productivity-enhancing role. Instead the only role of human capital in the current model is to facilitate the implementation and use of frontier technology in the production process. In particular, the evolution of the technology level of the country in question, $A(t)$, is governed by the differential equation

$$\dot{A}(t) = gA(t) + \phi(h)A_F(t),$$

with initial condition $A(0) \in (0, A_F(0))$. The parameter g is strictly less than g_F and measures the growth rate of technology $A(t)$, resulting from learning-by-doing or other sources of productivity growth. But first term is only one source of improvement in technology. The other one comes from the second term and can be interpreted as improvements in technology because of implementation and adoption of frontier technologies. The extent of the second source of improvement is determined by the average human capital of the workforce, h. The second source captures the above-mentioned role of human capital in the context of adoption and adaptation of technology. In particular, suppose that $\phi(\cdot)$ is nondecreasing and satisfies

$$\phi(0) = 0 \quad \text{and} \quad \phi(h) = g_F - g > 0 \quad \text{for all } h \geq \bar{h},$$

where $\bar{h} > 0$. This specification implies that the human capital of the workforce regulates the ability of the economy to cope with new developments embedded in the frontier technologies; if the workforce has no human capital, there is no adoption or implementation of frontier technologies, and $A(t)$ grows at the rate g. If, in contrast, $h \geq \bar{h}$, there is rapid adoption of frontier technologies.

Since $A_F(t) = \exp(g_F t)A_F(0)$, the differential equation for $A(t)$ can be written as

$$\dot{A}(t) = gA(t) + \phi(h)A_F(0)\exp(g_F t).$$

The solution to this differential equation is (recall again Section B.4 in Appendix B):

$$A(t) = \left[\left(A(0) - \frac{\phi(h)A_F(0)}{g_F - g} \right) \exp(gt) + \frac{\phi(h)A_F(0)}{g_F - g} \exp(g_F t) \right],$$

which shows that the growth rate of $A(t)$ is faster when $\phi(h)$ is higher. Moreover, it can be verified that

$$A(t) \rightarrow \frac{\phi(h)}{g_F - g} A_F(t) \quad (\text{as } t \rightarrow \infty),$$

so that the ratio of the technology of the country to the frontier technology is also determined by human capital.

The role of human capital emphasized by Nelson and Phelps is undoubtedly important in several situations. For example, a range of empirical evidence shows that more educated farmers are more likely to adopt new technologies and seeds (e.g., Foster and Rosenzweig, 1995). Nelson and Phelps's conception of human capital has also been emphasized in the growth literature in connection with the empirical evidence already discussed in Chapter 1, which shows that there is a stronger correlation between economic growth and levels of human capital than between economic growth and changes in human capital. Some authors—most notably, Benhabib and Spiegel (1994)—suggest that this result may be because the most important role of human capital is not to increase the productive capacity with existing tasks but to facilitate technology adoption. One might then conjecture that if the role of human capital emphasized by Nelson and Phelps is important in practice, human capital might play a more important role in economic growth and development than the discussion so far has suggested. While this hypothesis is interesting, it is not entirely convincing. If the role of human capital in facilitating technology adoption is taking place within the firm's boundaries, then this will be reflected in the marginal product and earnings of more skilled workers. Workers that contribute to faster and more effective technology adoption would be compensated in line with the increase in the net present value of the firm. Then the returns to schooling and human capital used in the calculations in Chapter 3 should have already taken into account the contribution of human capital to aggregate output (thus to economic growth) working through technology adoption. If, on the other hand, human capital facilitates technology adoption not at the level of the firm but at the level of the labor market, it would be a form of local human capital externalities and should appear in the estimates of local external effects of human capital. Thus unless this particular role of human capital is external and these external effects work at a global level, the calibration exercises in Chapter 3, which use labor market returns to human capital, should not seriously underestimate the contribution of human capital to cross-country differences in income per capita.

10.9 Taking Stock

This chapter has presented several models of human capital investments that emphasize how human capital investments (including schooling and on-the-job training) respond to future rewards and how they evolve over time.

Four sets of related but distinct issues arise in connection with the role of human capital in economic growth. First, if some part of the earnings of labor we observe are rewards to accumulated human capital, then the effect of policies (and perhaps technology) on income per capita could be larger than estimated, because these would affect not only physical capital accumulation but also human capital accumulation. The neoclassical economy with physical and human capital studied in Section 10.4 models and quantifies this effect. It also provides a tractable framework in which physical and human capital investments can be studied. Nevertheless any effect of human capital differences resulting from differences in distortions or policies across countries should have shown up in the measurements in Chapter 3. The findings there suggest that human capital differences, though important, can only explain a small fraction of cross-country income differences (unless there is a significant mismeasurement of the impact of human capital on productivity).

The second important issue connected to the role of human capital relates to the measurement of the contribution of education and skills to productivity. A possible source of mismeasurement of these effects is the presence of human capital externalities. There are many compelling reasons why significant pecuniary or technological human capital externalities may exist. Section 10.6 illustrated how capital-skill complementarities in imperfect labor markets can lead to pecuniary externalities. Nevertheless, existing evidence suggests that the extent of human capital externalities is rather limited—with the important caveat that there might be global externalities that remain unmeasured. Specific channels through which global externalities may arise are R&D and technological progress, which are the topics of the next part of the book. An alternative source of mismeasurement of the contribution of human capital is differences in human capital quality. There are significant differences in school and teacher quality even within a narrow geographical area, so we may expect much larger differences across countries. In addition, most available empirical approaches measure human capital differences across countries by using differences in formal schooling. But the Ben-Porath model, analyzed in Section 10.3, suggests that human capital continues to be accumulated even after individuals complete their formal schooling. When human capital is highly rewarded, we expect both higher levels of formal schooling and greater levels of on-the-job investment. Consequently, the Ben-Porath model suggests that there might be higher quality of human capital (or greater amounts of unmeasured human capital) in economies where the level of formal schooling is high. If this is the case, the empirical measurements reported in Chapter 3 may understate the contribution of human capital to productivity. The exploration of this issue is an interesting area for future research.

The third set of novel issues raised by the modeling of human capital is the possibility of an imbalance between physical and human capital. Empirical evidence suggests that physical and human capital are complementary. Thus productivity will be high when the correct balance is achieved between physical and human capital. Could equilibrium incentives lead to an imbalance, whereby too much or too little physical capital is accumulated relative to human capital? We saw that such imbalances are unlikely or rather short lived in models with competitive labor markets. However the analysis in Section 10.6 shows that they become a distinct possibility when factor prices do not necessarily reflect marginal products, as in labor markets with frictions. The presence of such imbalances might increase the impact of human capital on aggregate productivity.

The final issue relates to the role of human capital in technological change and technology adoption. Section 10.8 presented the Nelson-Phelps view of human capital, which emphasizes the role of skills in facilitating the adoption and implementation of new technologies. While this perspective is likely to be important in a range of situations, it seems that, in the absence of significant external effects, this particular role of human capital should also not lead to a major mismeasurement of the contribution of human capital to aggregate productivity, especially in the types of exercises reported in Chapter 3.

This chapter contributes to our quest toward understanding the sources of economic growth and cross-country income differences and offers a useful framework for understanding both physical and human capital accumulation decisions. Our next task is to develop models for the other major proximate source of economic growth and income differences: technology.

10.10   References and Literature

The concept of human capital is due to Gary Becker (1965), Ted Schultz (1965), and Jacob Mincer (1974). The standard models of human capital, used extensively in labor and other areas of economics, have been developed by Becker (1965), Yoram Ben-Porath (1967), and Mincer (1974). These models have been the basis of the first three sections of this chapter. Recently there has been a renewed interest in the Ben-Porath model among macroeconomists. Recent contributions include Heckman, Lochner, and Taber (1998); Guvenen and Kuruscu (2006); and Manuelli and Seshadri (2006). These models make parametric assumptions (Cobb-Douglas functional forms) and try to gauge the quantitative implications of the Ben-Porath model for cross-country income differences and for the evolution of wage inequality. Caselli (2005), on the other hand, argues that quality differences are unlikely to increase the contribution of human capital to aggregate productivity.

There is a large literature on returns to schooling. As noted in the text and in Chapter 3, this literature typically finds that one more year of schooling increases earnings by about 6–10% (see, e.g., the survey in Card, 1999).

There is also a large literature on capital-skill complementarity. The idea was first put forward and empirically supported in Griliches (1969). Katz and Autor (2000) summarize more recent evidence on capital-skill complementarities.

Technological human capital externalities are emphasized in Jacobs (1970), Lucas (1988), and Azariadis and Drazen (1990), while pecuniary human capital externalities were first discussed by Marshall (1890), who argued that increasing the geographic concentration of specialized inputs increases productivity, since the matching between factor inputs and industries is improved. Models of pecuniary human capital externalities are constructed in Acemoglu (1996, 1997a). The model with capital-skill complementarity and labor market imperfections is based on Acemoglu (1996). In that paper, I provided a more detailed and microfounded model leading to similar results to those presented in Section 10.6 and derived the results on pecuniary externalities and human capital externalities discussed here.

The empirical literature on human capital externalities includes Rauch (1993), Acemoglu and Angrist (2000), Duflo (2004), Moretti (2004), and Ciccone and Peri (2006).

The role of human capital in adapting to change and implementing new technologies was first suggested by Schultz (1975) in the context of agricultural technologies (he emphasized the role of ability rather than human capital and stressed the importance of "disequilibrium" situations). Nelson and Phelps (1966) formulated the same ideas and presented a simple model, similar to that presented in Section 10.8. Foster and Rosenzweig (1995) provide evidence consistent with this role of human capital. Benhabib and Spiegel (1994) and Aghion and Howitt (1998) also include extensive discussions of the Nelson-Phelps view of human capital. Recent macroeconomic models that feature this role of human capital include Galor and Tsiddon (1997); Greenwood and Yorukoglu (1997); Caselli (1999); Galor and Moav (2000); and Aghion, Howitt, and Violante (2004).

10.11   Exercises

10.1   Formulate, state, and prove the Separation Theorem (Theorem 10.1) in an economy in discrete time.

10.2   (a) Consider the environment discussed in Section 10.1. Write the flow budget constraint of the individual as

$$\dot{a}(t) = ra(t) - c(t) + W(t),$$

and suppose that there are credit market imperfections so that $a(t) \geq 0$. Construct an example in which Theorem 10.1 does not apply. Can you generalize this example to the case in which the individual can save at the rate r but can only borrow at the rate $r' > r$?

(b) Now modify the environment in part a so that the instantaneous utility function of the individual is

$$u(c(t), 1 - l(t)),$$

where $l(t)$ denotes total hours of work, and labor supply at the market is equal to $l(t) - s(t)$, so that the individual has a nontrivial leisure choice. Construct an example in which Theorem 10.1 does not apply.

10.3 Derive (10.9) from (10.8).

10.4 Consider the model presented in Section 10.2 and suppose that the effective discount rate r varies across individuals (e.g., because of credit market imperfections). Show that individuals facing a higher r would choose lower levels of schooling. What happens if you estimate the wage regression similar to (10.12) in a world in which the source of disparity in schooling is differences in discount rates across individuals?

10.5 Verify that Theorems 7.13 and 7.14 from Chapter 7 can be applied to the Ben-Porath and lead to (10.14) as necessary and sufficient conditions for an optimal path of human capital investments. [Hint: use a similar argument to that in Section 7.7 in Chapter 7.]

10.6 Consider the following variant of the Ben-Porath model, in which the human capital accumulation equation is given by

$$\dot{h}(t) = s(t)\phi(h(t)) - \delta_h h(t),$$

where ϕ is strictly increasing, differentiable, and strictly concave, with $s(t) \in [0, 1]$. Assume that individuals are potentially infinitely lived and face a Poisson death rate of $\nu > 0$. Show that the optimal path of human capital investments involves $s(t) = 1$ for some interval $[0, T]$ and then $s(t) = s^*$ for $t \geq T$.

10.7 Modify the Ben-Porath model studied in Section 10.3 as follows. Assume that the horizon is finite, and suppose that $\phi'(0) < \infty$. Also, suppose that

$$\phi'(h(0)) > \delta_h/(1 - \exp(-\delta_h T)),$$

where recall that δ_h is the rate of depreciation of human capital.

(a) Provide the necessary conditions for an interior solution. Highlight how these necessary conditions should be modified to allow for corner solutions where $s(t)$ might take the value of 0 or 1.

(b) Show that under these conditions the optimal path of human capital accumulation involves an interval $[0, t')$ of full-time schooling with $s(t) = 1$ for all $t \in [0, t')$, where $t' > 0$, followed by another interval of on-the-job investment $s(t) \in (0, 1)$, and finally an interval of no human capital investment, that is, $s(t) = 0$ for all $t \in (t'', T]$, where $t'' < T$. [Hint: Suppose that the first part of the claim is not true, and show that in this case the necessary conditions must hold as equality. Combining the two necessary conditions, derive a first-order linear nonautonomous differential equation for the costate variable $\lambda(t)$, and solve this differential equation with the boundary condition $\lambda(T) = 0$. Then show that given the implied value for $\lambda(0)$ and the inequality above, the necessary conditions at $t = 0$ cannot be satisfied. Next use the assumption that $\phi' < \infty$ together with the fact that the costate variable $\lambda(t)$ is continuous and must satisfy $\lambda(T) = 0$ to prove that $s(t)$ must be equal to zero for some interval $[T - \xi, T]$. Finally, using these intermediate steps, conclude that $s(t)$ must take intermediate values before this final interval.]

(c) How do the earnings of the individual evolve over the life cycle?

(d) How would you test the implications of this model?

10.8 Prove that the current-value Hamiltonian in (10.24) is jointly concave in $(k(t), h(t), i_k(t), i_h(t))$.

10.9 Prove that (10.25) implies the existence of a relationship between physical and human capital of the form $h = \xi(k)$, where $\xi(\cdot)$ is uniquely defined, strictly increasing, and differentiable.

10.10 (a) Prove Proposition 10.1.

(b) Show that the differential equation for consumption growth alternatively could have been written as

$$\frac{\dot{c}(t)}{c(t)} = \frac{1}{\varepsilon_u(c(t))}[f_h(k(t), \xi(k(t))) - \delta_h - \rho].$$

10.11 Derive (10.26).

10.12 Consider the neoclassical growth model with physical and human capital discussed in Section 10.4.

(a) Specify the consumer maximization problem in this economy.

(b) Define a competitive equilibrium (specifying firm optimization and market clearing conditions).

(c) Characterize the competitive equilibrium, and show that it coincides with the solution to the optimal growth problem.

10.13 Introduce labor-augmenting technological progress at the rate g into the neoclassical growth model with physical and human capital discussed in Section 10.4.

(a) Define a competitive equilibrium.

(b) Determine transformed variables that remain constant in a steady-state allocation.

(c) Characterize the steady-state equilibrium and the transitional dynamics.

(d) Why does faster technological progress lead to more rapid accumulation of human capital?

* 10.14 Characterize the optimal growth path of the economy in Section 10.4 subject to the additional constraints that $i_k(t) \geq 0$ and $i_h(t) \geq 0$.

10.15 Prove that as long as $Y(t) = F(K(t), H(t))$ satisfies Assumptions 1 and 2 (see Chapter 2), the inequality in (10.30) holds.

10.16 Show that the equilibrium dynamics in Section 10.5 remain unchanged if $\delta < 1$.

10.17 Derive (10.33) and (10.34).

10.18 Provide conditions on $f(\cdot)$ and $\gamma(\cdot)$ such that the unique steady-state equilibrium in the model of Section 10.5 is locally stable.

10.19 Analyze the economy in Section 10.6 under the closed-economy assumption. Show that an increase in a_1 for group 1 workers now creates a dynamic externality, in the sense that current output increases, which leads to greater physical and human capital investments in the next period.

10.20 Prove Proposition 10.5.

11

First-Generation Models of Endogenous Growth

The models presented so far focus on physical and human capital accumulation and generate growth because of exogenous technological progress. While such models are useful in thinking about sources of income differences among countries that have (free) access to the same set of technologies, they do not generate sustained long-run growth (of the country or of the world economy) and have relatively little to say about sources of technology differences. A systematic analysis of both cross-country income differences and the process of world economic growth requires models in which technology choices and technological progress are endogenized. This topic is discussed in Part IV. While models in which technology evolves as a result of firms' and workers' decisions are most attractive in this regard, sustained economic growth is possible in the neoclassical model as well. I end this part of the book by investigating sustained endogenous economic growth in neoclassical or quasi-neoclassical models.

We have already encountered the *AK* model in Chapter 2. This model relaxed one of the key assumptions on the aggregate production function of the economy (Assumptions 1 and 2 from Chapter 2) and prevented diminishing returns to capital. Consequently, continuous capital accumulation could act as the engine of sustained economic growth. This chapter starts with a "neoclassical" version of the *AK* model, which not only shows the possibility of endogenous growth in the neoclassical growth model, but also provides us with a tractable model that has applications in diverse areas. This model is not without shortcomings, however. The most important one is that capital is the only (or essentially the only) factor of production, and asymptotically, the share of national income accruing to capital tends to 1. I then present two different two-sector endogenous growth models, which behave very similarly to the baseline *AK* model but avoid this counterfactual prediction. The first of these models incorporates physical and human capital accumulation and is thus a close cousin of the neoclassical growth model with physical and human capital studied in Section 10.4. The second, which builds on the work by Rebelo (1991), is a substantially richer model and is also interesting since it allows investment and consumption goods sectors to have different capital intensities.

I conclude this chapter with a presentation of Paul Romer's (1986a) article that started the endogenous growth literature and rejuvenated the interest in economic growth among economists. While Romer's objective was to model technological change, he achieved this by introducing technological spillovers—similar to those we encountered in Chapter 10.

Consequently, while the competitive equilibrium of Romer's model is not Pareto optimal and the engine of economic growth can be interpreted as a form of knowledge accumulation, in many ways the model is still neoclassical in nature. In particular, we will see that in reduced form it is very similar to the baseline AK model (except for its welfare implications).

11.1 The *AK* Model Revisited

Let us start with the simplest neoclassical model of sustained growth, which we already encountered in the context of the Solow growth model, in particular, Proposition 2.10 in Section 2.6. This is the so-called AK model, in which the production technology is linear in capital. The analysis below shows that what matters is not the linearity of the production technology but the linearity of the accumulation technology. But for now it makes sense to start with the simpler case of the AK economy.

11.1.1 Demographics, Preferences, and Technology

Our focus in this chapter and in Part IV of the book is on economic growth, and as a first pass we focus on balanced economic growth, defined as a growth path consistent with the Kaldor facts (recall Chapter 2). As demonstrated in Chapter 8, balanced growth forces us to adopt CRRA preferences as in the canonical neoclassical growth model (to ensure a constant intertemporal elasticity of substitution).

Let us assume that the economy admits an infinitely-lived representative household, with household size growing at the exponential rate n. The preferences of the representative household at time $t = 0$ are given by

$$\int_0^\infty \exp(-(\rho - n)t)\frac{c(t)^{1-\theta} - 1}{1 - \theta}dt. \tag{11.1}$$

Labor is supplied inelastically. The flow budget constraint of the household can be written as

$$\dot{a}(t) = (r(t) - n)a(t) + w(t) - c(t), \tag{11.2}$$

where $a(t)$ denotes assets per capita at time t, $r(t)$ is the interest rate, $w(t)$ is the wage rate per capita, and n is the growth rate of population. As usual, let us impose the no-Ponzi game constraint,

$$\lim_{t\to\infty} \left[a(t) \exp\left(-\int_0^t (r(s) - n)ds\right)\right] \geq 0. \tag{11.3}$$

The Euler equation for the representative household is the same as before and implies the following rate of consumption growth per capita:

$$\frac{\dot{c}(t)}{c(t)} = \frac{1}{\theta}(r(t) - \rho). \tag{11.4}$$

The transversality condition of the households then implies that

$$\lim_{t\to\infty} \left[a(t) \exp\left(-\int_0^t (r(s) - n)ds\right)\right] = 0. \tag{11.5}$$

As before, this maximization is concave, and thus any solution to these conditions is in fact an optimal plan for the representative household.

The final good sector is similar to before, except that Assumptions 1 and 2 are not satisfied. More specifically, suppose that the aggregate production function is given by

$$Y(t) = AK(t),$$

with $A > 0$. Notice that this production function does not depend on labor, and thus wage earnings $w(t)$ in (11.2) are equal to zero. This is one of the unattractive features of the baseline *AK* model, but it is relaxed below (it is also relaxed in Exercises 11.3 and 11.4). Dividing both sides of this equation by $L(t)$ and as usual defining $k(t) \equiv K(t)/L(t)$ as the capital-labor ratio, we obtain per capita output as

$$y(t) \equiv \frac{Y(t)}{L(t)}$$

$$= Ak(t). \tag{11.6}$$

Equation (11.6) has a number of notable differences from the production functions that satisfy Assumptions 1 and 2. First, output is only a function of capital, and there are no diminishing returns (i.e., it is no longer the case that $f''(\cdot) < 0$). This feature is included only for simplicity, and introducing diminishing returns to capital does not affect the main results of this section (see Exercise 11.4). The more important assumption is that the Inada conditions embedded in Assumption 2 are no longer satisfied. In particular,

$$\lim_{k \to \infty} f'(k) = A > 0.$$

This feature is essential for sustained growth.

The conditions for profit-maximization are similar to those given before and require that the marginal product of capital is equal to the rental price of capital: $R(t) = r(t) + \delta$. Since the marginal product of capital is constant and equal to A from (11.6), we have that for all t, $R(t) = A$ and

$$r(t) = r = A - \delta. \tag{11.7}$$

Since the marginal product of labor is zero, labor earnings are also equal to zero.

11.1.2 Equilibrium

A *competitive equilibrium* in this economy consists of paths of per capita consumption, capital-labor ratio, wage rates, and rental rates of capital, $[c(t), k(t), w(t), R(t)]_{t=0}^{\infty}$, such that the representative household maximizes (11.1) subject to (11.2) and (11.3) given initial capital-labor ratio $k(0)$ and factor prices $[w(t), r(t)]_{t=0}^{\infty}$ such that $w(t) = 0$ for all t, and $r(t)$ is given by (11.7).

To characterize the equilibrium, note again that $a(t) = k(t)$. Using the facts that $r = A - \delta$ and $w = 0$, (11.2), (11.4), and (11.5) imply that

$$\dot{k}(t) = (A - \delta - n)k(t) - c(t), \tag{11.8}$$

$$\frac{\dot{c}(t)}{c(t)} = \frac{1}{\theta}(A - \delta - \rho), \tag{11.9}$$

and

$$\lim_{t \to \infty} \left[k(t) \exp(-(A - \delta - n)t) \right] = 0. \tag{11.10}$$

Since the right-hand side of (11.9) is constant, there must be a constant rate of consumption growth (and growth is positive as long as $A - \delta - \rho > 0$). The rate of growth of consumption is therefore independent of the level of capital stock per person, $k(t)$. This independence also implies that there are no transitional dynamics in this model. Starting from any $k(0) > 0$, consumption per capita (and as we will see, the capital-labor ratio) immediately starts growing at a constant rate. To establish this point more formally, let us integrate (11.9) starting from some initial level of consumption $c(0)$, which, as usual, will be determined from the lifetime budget constraint. This gives

$$c(t) = c(0) \exp\left(\frac{1}{\theta}(A - \delta - \rho)t\right). \tag{11.11}$$

Since there is growth in this economy, we have to ensure that household utility is bounded away from infinity, which is again equivalent to ensuring that the transversality condition is satisfied. We also want to ensure positive growth. Let us therefore impose

$$A > \rho + \delta > (1 - \theta)(A - \delta) + \theta n + \delta. \tag{11.12}$$

The first part of this condition ensures that there will be positive output and consumption growth, while the second part is the analogue of the condition that $\rho + \theta g > g + n$ in the neoclassical growth model with technological progress.

11.1.3 Equilibrium Characterization

Let us first show that there are no transitional dynamics in this economy. In particular, not only the growth rate of consumption but also the growth rates of capital and output are constant at all points in time and are equal to the growth rate of consumption given in (11.9). Substituting for $c(t)$ from (11.11) into (11.8), we obtain

$$\dot{k}(t) = (A - \delta - n)k(t) - c(0) \exp\left(\frac{1}{\theta}(A - \delta - \rho)t\right), \tag{11.13}$$

which is a first-order nonautonomous linear differential equation in $k(t)$. The solution is (recall again Section B.4):

$$k(t) = \kappa \exp((A - \delta - n)t)$$
$$+ [(A - \delta)(\theta - 1)\theta^{-1} + \rho\theta^{-1} - n]^{-1}[c(0) \exp(\theta^{-1}(A - \delta - \rho)t)], \tag{11.14}$$

where κ is a constant to be determined. Assumption (11.12) ensures that

$$(A - \delta)(\theta - 1)\theta^{-1} + \rho\theta^{-1} - n > 0.$$

From (11.14), it may look like capital (capital-labor ratio) is not growing at a constant rate, since it is the sum of two components growing at different rates. This is where the transversality condition becomes useful. Let us substitute from (11.14) into the transversality condition (11.10), which yields

$$\lim_{t \to \infty}\left[\kappa + [(A - \delta)(\theta - 1)\theta^{-1} + \rho\theta^{-1} - n]^{-1}\right.$$
$$\left. \times c(0) \exp(-((A - \delta)(\theta - 1)\theta^{-1} + \rho\theta^{-1} - n)t)\right] = 0.$$

Since $(A - \delta)(\theta - 1)\theta^{-1} + \rho\theta^{-1} - n > 0$, the second term in this expression converges to zero as $t \to \infty$. But the first term is a constant. Thus the transversality condition can only be satisfied if $\kappa = 0$. Therefore (11.14) implies that

$$k(t) = [(A - \delta)(\theta - 1)\theta^{-1} + \rho\theta^{-1} - n]^{-1}[c(0)\exp(\theta^{-1}(A - \delta - \rho)t)] \qquad (11.15)$$

$$= k(0)\exp(\theta^{-1}(A - \delta - \rho)t),$$

where the second line immediately follows from the fact that capital is equal to $k(0)$ at $t = 0$. Therefore capital and output grow at the same rate as consumption.

Equation (11.15) pins down the initial level of consumption per capita as

$$c(0) = [(A - \delta)(\theta - 1)\theta^{-1} + \rho\theta^{-1} - n]k(0). \qquad (11.16)$$

Note that in this simple *AK* model, growth is not only sustained but is also endogenous in the sense of being affected by underlying parameters. For example, consider an increase in the discount rate, ρ. Recall that in the Ramsey model, such a change only influenced the level of income per capita—it could have no effect on the growth rate, which was determined by the exogenous labor-augmenting rate of technological progress. Here it is straightforward to verify that an increase in ρ reduces the growth rate; households become less patient, and the rate of capital accumulation declines. Since capital accumulation is the engine of growth, the equilibrium rate of growth will decline. Similarly, changes in A and θ affect the levels and growth rates of consumption, capital, and output.

Finally, let us calculate the (equilibrium) saving rate. It is defined as total investment (which is equal to increase in capital plus replacement investment) divided by output. Thus we have

$$s = \frac{\dot{K}(t) + \delta K(t)}{Y(t)}$$

$$= \frac{\dot{k}(t)/k(t) + n + \delta}{A}$$

$$= \frac{A - \rho + \theta n + (\theta - 1)\delta}{\theta A}, \qquad (11.17)$$

where the last equality exploits the fact that $\dot{k}(t)/k(t) = (A - \delta - \rho)/\theta$. This equation implies that the saving rate, which was taken as constant and exogenous in the basic Solow model, is again constant over time, but now depends on preferences and technology.

Proposition 11.1 *Consider the AK economy with a representative household with preferences given by (11.1) and the production technology given by (11.6). Suppose that condition (11.12) holds. Then there exists a unique equilibrium path in which consumption, capital, and output per capita all grow at the same rate $g^* \equiv (A - \delta - \rho)/\theta > 0$ starting from any initial positive capital stock per capita $k(0) > 0$, and the saving rate is given by (11.17).*

One important implication of the *AK* model is that since all markets are competitive, there is a representative household, and there are no externalities, the competitive equilibrium will be Pareto optimal. This can be proved either using the First Welfare Theorem (Theorem 5.6) or by directly constructing the optimal growth solution.

Proposition 11.2 *Consider the AK economy with a representative household with prefer-ences given by (11.1) and the production technology given by (11.6). Suppose that condition (11.12) holds. Then the unique competitive equilibrium is Pareto optimal.*

Proof. See Exercise 11.2. ■

11.1.4 The Role of Policy

It is straightforward to incorporate policy differences into this framework and investigate their implications for the equilibrium growth rate. Suppose that there is a tax rate equal to τ on capital income as in Chapter 8. The budget constraint of the representative household then becomes

$$\dot{a}(t) = ((1 - \tau)r(t) - n)a(t) + w(t) - c(t). \tag{11.18}$$

Repeating the analysis above immediately implies that this tax adversely affects the growth rate of the economy, which becomes (see Exercise 11.5):

$$g = \frac{(1 - \tau)(A - \delta) - \rho}{\theta}. \tag{11.19}$$

Moreover it can be calculated that the saving rate is

$$s = \frac{(1 - \tau)A - \rho + \theta n - (1 - \tau - \theta)\delta}{\theta A}, \tag{11.20}$$

which is a decreasing function of τ provided that $A - \delta > 0$. Therefore in this model the equilibrium saving rate responds endogenously to policy. In addition, since the saving rate is constant, differences in policies lead to permanent differences in the rate of capital accumu-lation. This observation has an important implication. While in the baseline neoclassical growth model, even reasonably large differences in distortions (e.g., eightfold differences in τ) could only have limited effects on differences in income per capita, here even small differences in τ can have very large effects. In particular, consider two economies with the same technology and preferences but with different (constant) tax rates on capital income, τ and $\tau' > \tau$. Then for any $\tau' > \tau$,

$$\lim_{t \to \infty} \frac{Y(\tau', t)}{Y(\tau, t)} = 0,$$

where $Y(\tau, t)$ denotes aggregate output in the economy with tax τ at time t. Therefore even small policy differences can have very large effects in the long run. So why does the literature focus on the inability of the standard neoclassical growth model to generate large differences rather than the possibility that the *AK* model can generate arbitrarily large differences? The reason is twofold: first, as noted above, the *AK* model—with no diminishing returns and the share of capital in national income asymptoting to 1—is not viewed as a good approximation to reality. Second, and related to the discussion in Chapter 1, most economists believe that the relative stability of the world income distribution in the postwar era makes it more attractive to focus on models in which there is a stationary world income distribution rather than on models in which small policy differences can lead to permanent growth differences. Whether this last belief is justified is, in part, an empirical question.

11.2 The *AK* Model with Physical and Human Capital

As pointed out in the previous section, a major shortcoming of the baseline *AK* model is that the share of capital in national income is equal to 1 (or limits to 1 as in the variants of the *AK* model studied in Exercises 11.3 and 11.4). One way of enriching the *AK* model and avoiding these problems is to include both physical and human capital. I now briefly discuss this extension. Suppose that the economy admits a representative household with preferences given by (11.1). The production side of the economy is similar to Section 10.4, except that human capital now more plausibly increases the efficiency units of labor (rather than being a separate factor of production). In particular, the aggregate production function takes the form

$$Y(t) = F(K(t), H(t)), \tag{11.21}$$

where $H(t)$ denotes efficiency units of labor (or human capital), which accumulate in the same way as physical capital. The production function $F(\cdot, \cdot)$ now satisfies Assumptions 1 and 2. Suppose, to simplify the analysis, that there is no population growth, and thus $n = 0$.

The budget constraint of the representative household is given by

$$\dot{a}(t) = r(t)a(t) + w(t)h(t) - c(t) - i_h(t), \tag{11.22}$$

where $h(t)$ denotes the effective units of labor (human capital) of the representative household, $w(t)$ is wage rate per unit of human capital, and $i_h(t)$ is investment in human capital. As in Section 10.4, human capital evolves according to the differential equation

$$\dot{h}(t) = i_h(t) - \delta_h h(t), \tag{11.23}$$

where δ_h is the depreciation rate of human capital. The evolution of the capital stock is again given from the observation that $k(t) = a(t)$, and the depreciation rate of physical capital is denoted by δ_k. In this model, the representative household maximizes its utility by choosing the paths of consumption, human capital investments, and asset holdings. Competitive factor markets imply that

$$R(t) = f'(k(t)) \quad \text{and} \quad w(t) = f(k(t)) - k(t)f'(k(t)), \tag{11.24}$$

where, the effective capital-labor ratio is now given by dividing the capital stock by the stock of human capital in the economy:

$$k(t) \equiv \frac{K(t)}{H(t)}.$$

A *competitive equilibrium* of this economy consists of paths of per capita consumption, capital-labor ratio, wage rates, and rental rates of capital, $[c(t), k(t), w(t), R(t)]_{t=0}^{\infty}$, such that the representative household maximizes (11.1) subject to (11.3), (11.22), and (11.23) given the initial effective capital-labor ratio $k(0)$ and factor prices $[w(t), R(t)]_{t=0}^{\infty}$ that satisfy (11.24).

To characterize the competitive equilibrium, let us set up the current-value Hamiltonian for the representative household with costate variables μ_a and μ_h:

$$\mathcal{H}(a, h, c, i_h, \mu_a, \mu_k) = \frac{c(t)^{1-\theta} - 1}{1 - \theta} + \mu_a(t) \left[r(t)a(t) + w(t)h(t) - c(t) - i_h(t) \right]$$

$$+ \mu_h(t) \left[i_h(t) - \delta_h h(t) \right].$$

Once again, using Theorem 7.13 we can generate the following candidate solution to this maximization problem (see Exercise 11.8):

$$\mu_a(t) = \mu_h(t) = \mu(t) \quad \text{for all } t,$$

$$w(t) - \delta_h = r(t) \quad \text{for all } t, \qquad (11.25)$$

$$\frac{\dot{c}(t)}{c(t)} = \frac{1}{\theta}(r(t) - \rho) \quad \text{for all } t.$$

Intuitively, there are no constraints on human and physical capital investments; thus the shadow values of these two different types of investments have to be equal at all points in time as stated in the first condition in (11.25). This in turn yields the second condition in (11.25), equating the rates of return on human and physical capital. The third condition is the standard Euler equation. It can be verified that the current-value Hamiltonian is concave and satisfies the sufficiency conditions in Theorem 7.14. Therefore a solution to the conditions in (11.25) necessarily solves the representative household's maximization problem. Moreover, with the same argument as in Exercise 8.11, this solution is unique.

Combining (11.25) with (11.24) yields

$$f'(k(t)) - \delta_k = f(k(t)) - k(t)f'(k(t)) - \delta_h \quad \text{for all } t.$$

Since the left-hand side is decreasing in $k(t)$, while the right-hand side is increasing, the effective capital-labor ratio must satisfy

$$k(t) = k^* \quad \text{for all } t.$$

Proposition 11.3 *Consider the AK economy with physical and human capital, with preferences given by (11.1), and the production technology given by (11.21). Let k^* be given by*

$$f'(k^*) - \delta_k = f(k^*) - k^* f'(k^*) - \delta_h. \qquad (11.26)$$

Suppose that $f'(k^*) > \rho + \delta_k > (1 - \theta)(f'(k^*) - \delta) + \delta_k$. Then in this economy there exists a unique equilibrium path in which consumption, human capital, physical capital, and output all grow at the same rate $g^* \equiv (f'(k^*) - \delta_k - \rho)/\theta > 0$ starting from any initial conditions, where k^* is given by (11.26). The share of capital in national income is constant and less than 1 at all times.

Proof. See Exercise 11.9. ∎

The advantage of the economy studied here compared to the baseline *AK* model is that it generates a stable factor distribution of income, with a significant fraction of national income accruing to labor (as rewards to human capital). Consequently the current model cannot be criticized on the basis of generating counterfactual results on the capital share of GDP. A similar analysis to that in the previous section also shows that the current model generates long-run differences in growth rates from small policy differences. Therefore it can account for arbitrarily large differences in income per capita across countries. Nevertheless it does so partly by generating large human capital differences across countries. As such, the empirical mechanism through which these large cross-country income differences are generated may again not fit with the empirical patterns discussed in Chapter 3. Moreover, given substantial differences in policies across economies in the postwar period, like the baseline *AK* economy, the current model suggests significant changes in the world income distribution, whereas the evidence in Chapter 1 points to a relatively stable postwar world income distribution.

11.3   The Two-Sector *AK* Model

The models studied in the previous two sections are attractive in many respects: they generate sustained growth, and the equilibrium growth rate responds to policy, underlying preferences, and technology. Moreover, these are very close cousins of the neoclassical model. In fact, as argued there, the endogenous growth equilibrium is Pareto optimal.

One unattractive feature of the baseline *AK* model of Section 11.1 is that all national income accrues to capital. Essentially it is a one-sector model with only capital as the factor of production. This limitation makes it difficult to apply this model to real-world situations. The model in the previous section avoids this problem, but at some level it does so by creating another factor of production that accumulates linearly, so that the equilibrium structure is again equivalent to the one-sector *AK* economy. Therefore in some deep sense the economies of both sections are one-sector models. Another important shortcoming in addition to this one-sector property is that these models do not delineate the key feature driving sustained growth. What is important for sustained growth is not that the production technology is *AK* but instead the related feature that the *accumulation technology* is linear. In this section, I discuss a richer two-sector model of neoclassical endogenous growth based on Rebelo (1991). This model generates constant factor shares in national income without introducing human capital accumulation. It also illustrates the role of differences in the capital intensity of the production functions of consumption and investment goods.

The preference and demographics are the same as in Section 11.1; in particular, (11.1)–(11.5) apply as before (but with a slightly different interpretation for the interest rate in (11.4) as discussed below). Moreover, to simplify the analysis, suppose that there is no population growth, that is, $n = 0$, and that the total amount of labor in the economy, L, is supplied inelastically.

The main difference is in the production technology. Rather than a single good used for consumption and investment, let us now envisage an economy with two sectors. The first sector produces consumption goods with the following technology:

$$C(t) = BK_C(t)^\alpha L_C(t)^{1-\alpha}, \tag{11.27}$$

where the subscript "*C*" denotes that these are capital and labor used in the consumption sector, which has a Cobb-Douglas technology. In fact, the Cobb-Douglas assumption here is quite important in ensuring that the share of capital in national income is constant (see Exercise 11.12). The capital accumulation equation is given by

$$\dot{K}(t) = I(t) - \delta K(t),$$

where $I(t)$ denotes investment. Investment goods are produced in the second sector, which has a different technology from (11.27):

$$I(t) = AK_I(t). \tag{11.28}$$

The distinctive feature of the technology for the investment goods sector, (11.28), is that it is linear in the capital stock and does not feature labor. This assumption is an extreme version of one often made in two-sector models, that the investment good sector is more capital intensive than the consumption good sector. In the data there seems to be some support for this assumption, though the capital intensities of many sectors have been changing over time as the nature of consumption and investment goods has changed.

Market clearing implies that for all t, we have

$$K_C(t) + K_I(t) \le K(t)$$

for capital, and

$$L_C(t) \le L$$

for labor (since labor is only used in the consumption sector).

An equilibrium in this economy is defined similarly to that in the neoclassical economy but also features an allocation decision of capital between the two sectors. Moreover, since the two sectors are producing two different goods—consumption and investment goods—there is a relative price between the two sectors that adjusts endogenously.

Since both market clearing conditions will hold as equalities (the marginal product of both factors is always positive), we can simplify notation by letting $\kappa(t)$ denote the share of capital used in the investment sector, so that

$$K_C(t) = (1 - \kappa(t))K(t), \quad \text{and} \quad K_I(t) = \kappa(t)K(t).$$

From profit maximization, the rate of return to capital has to be the same when it is employed in the two sectors. Let the price of the investment good be denoted by $p_I(t)$ and that of the consumption good by $p_C(t)$. Then (11.27) and (11.28) imply

$$p_I(t)A = p_C(t)\alpha B \left(\frac{L}{(1 - \kappa(t))K(t)} \right)^{1-\alpha}. \tag{11.29}$$

Define a balanced growth path (BGP) as an equilibrium path in which $\kappa(t)$ is constant and equal to some $\kappa^* \in [0, 1]$. Moreover let us choose the consumption good as the numeraire, so that $p_C(t) = 1$ for all t. Then differentiating (11.29) implies that in the BGP,

$$\frac{\dot{p}_I(t)}{p_I(t)} = -(1 - \alpha)g_K, \tag{11.30}$$

where g_K is the BGP growth rate of capital.

As noted above, the Euler equation (11.4) still holds, but the relevant interest rate has to be for *consumption-denominated loans,* denoted by $r_C(t)$. This is the interest rate that measures how many units of consumption good an individual will receive tomorrow by giving up one unit of consumption today. Since the relative prices of consumption goods and investment goods are changing over time, the proper calculation goes as follows. By giving up one unit of consumption, the individual will buy $1/p_I(t)$ units of capital goods. These goods have an instantaneous return of $r_I(t)$. In addition the individual receives the one unit of capital, which has now experienced a change in its price of $\dot{p}_I(t)/p_I(t)$. Finally, she has to buy consumption goods, whose prices change by $\dot{p}_C(t)/p_C(t)$. Therefore the general formula of the rate of return denominated in consumption goods in terms of the rate of return denominated in investment goods is

$$r_C(t) = \frac{r_I(t)}{p_I(t)} + \frac{\dot{p}_I(t)}{p_I(t)} - \frac{\dot{p}_C(t)}{p_C(t)}. \tag{11.31}$$

Given the choice of numeraire, $\dot{p}_C(t)/p_C(t) = 0$. Moreover, $\dot{p}_I(t)/p_I(t)$ is given by (11.30). Finally,

$$\frac{r_I(t)}{p_I(t)} = A - \delta$$

given the linear technology in (11.28). Therefore we have

$$r_C(t) = A - \delta + \frac{\dot{p}_I(t)}{p_I(t)}.$$

and from (11.30), the BGP consumption-denominated rate of return is

$$r_C = A - \delta - (1 - \alpha)g_K.$$

From (11.4), this rate of return implies a consumption growth rate of

$$g_C = \frac{\dot{C}(t)}{C(t)} = \frac{1}{\theta}(A - \delta - (1 - \alpha)g_K - \rho). \tag{11.32}$$

Now differentiate (11.27) and use the fact that labor is always constant to obtain

$$\frac{\dot{C}(t)}{C(t)} = \alpha \frac{\dot{K}_C(t)}{K_C(t)},$$

which, from the constancy of $\kappa(t)$ in BGP, implies the following BGP relationship:

$$g_C = \alpha g_K.$$

Substituting this equation into (11.32), we obtain

$$g_K^* = \frac{A - \delta - \rho}{1 - \alpha(1 - \theta)}, \tag{11.33}$$

and

$$g_C^* = \alpha \frac{A - \delta - \rho}{1 - \alpha(1 - \theta)}. \tag{11.34}$$

What about wages? Because labor is being used in the consumption good sector, wages are positive. Since labor markets are competitive, the wage rate at time t is given by

$$w(t) = (1 - \alpha)p_C(t)B\left(\frac{(1 - \kappa(t))K(t)}{L}\right)^\alpha.$$

Therefore in the BGP we have

$$\frac{\dot{w}(t)}{w(t)} = \frac{\dot{p}_C(t)}{p_C(t)} + \alpha\frac{\dot{K}(t)}{K(t)}$$

$$= \alpha g_K^*,$$

which implies that wages also grow at the same rate as consumption.

Moreover, with the same arguments as in Section 11.2, it can be shown that there are no transitional dynamics in this economy. This analysis establishes the following proposition.

Proposition 11.4 *In the above-described two-sector neoclassical economy, there exists a unique equilibrium where, for any $K(0) > 0$, consumption and labor income grow at the constant rate given by (11.34), while the capital stock grows at the constant rate given by (11.33).*

Policy analysis in this model is similar to that in the basic *AK* model: taxes on investment income or other policies that discourage investment will depress growth.

One important implication of this model that differs from the neoclassical growth model is that there is continuous *capital deepening*. Capital grows at a faster rate than consumption and output. Whether this feature is realistic is debatable. The Kaldor facts, discussed in Chapter 2, include constant capital-output ratio as one of the requirements of balanced growth. The "balanced growth" here does not have this feature. For much of the twentieth century, the capital-output ratio appears to have been constant, but it has been increasing steadily over the past 30 years. Part of the reason is relative price adjustments. New capital goods are of higher quality, which needs to be incorporated in calculating the capital-output ratio. These calculations have only been performed in the recent past, which may explain why capital-output ratio has been constant in the earlier part of the twentieth century but not recently. Thus it is not clear whether a constant or an increasing capital-output ratio is a better approximation to reality.

11.4   Growth with Externalities

The model that started much of endogenous growth theory and revived economists' interest in economic growth was presented in Paul Romer's (1986a) paper. Romer's objective was to model the process of knowledge accumulation. He realized that this would be difficult in the context of a competitive economy. His initial solution (later updated and improved in his and others' work during the 1990s) was to consider knowledge accumulation to be a *by-product* of capital accumulation. In other words, Romer introduced technological spillovers, similar to the human capital externalities discussed in Chapter 10. While arguably crude, this approach captures an important dimension of knowledge, namely, that knowledge is a largely *nonrival* good—once a particular technology has been discovered, many firms can make use of this technology without preventing others from using the same knowledge. Nonrivalry does not imply knowledge is also nonexcludable (which would make it a pure public good). A firm that discovers a new technology may use patents or trade secrecy to prevent others from using it, for example, to gain a competitive advantage. These issues are discussed in Part IV of the book. For now it suffices to note that some of the important characteristics of knowledge and its role in the production process can be captured in a reduced-form way by introducing technological spillovers. I next discuss a version of the model in Romer's (1986a) paper that introduces such technological spillovers as the engine of economic growth. While the type of technological spillovers used in this model are unlikely to be the engine of sustained growth in practice, the model is a good starting point for our analysis of endogenous technological progress, since its similarity to the baseline *AK* economy makes it a tractable model of knowledge accumulation.

11.4.1 Preferences and Technology

Consider an economy without any population growth (we will see why this condition is important). For reasons that will become clear, instead of working with the aggregate production function, let us assume that the production side of the economy consists of a set [0, 1] of firms. The production function of each firm $i \in [0, 1]$ is

$$Y_i(t) = F(K_i(t), A(t)L_i(t)), \tag{11.35}$$

where $K_i(t)$ and $L_i(t)$ are capital and labor rented by a firm i. Notice that the labor-augmenting technology, $A(t)$, is not indexed by i, since it is common to all firms. Suppose that the production function F satisfies Assumptions 1 and 2. Let us normalize the measure of final good producers to 1, so that

$$\int_0^1 K_i(t)di = K(t),$$

and

$$\int_0^1 L_i(t)di = L$$

for all t, where L is the constant level of labor (supplied inelastically). Firms are competitive in all markets, which implies that they all have the same capital–effective labor ratio, and moreover factor prices are given by their marginal products:

$$w(t) = \frac{\partial F(K(t), A(t)L)}{\partial L},$$

and

$$R(t) = \frac{\partial F(K(t), A(t)L)}{\partial K(t)}.$$

The key assumption of Romer (1986a) is that although firms take $A(t)$ as given, this stock of technology (knowledge) advances endogenously for the economy as a whole. In particular, Romer assumes that this takes place because of spillovers across firms and attributes these spillovers to physical capital. Robert Lucas (1988) develops a similar model in which the structure is identical, but spillovers work through human capital (i.e., Romer has physical capital externalities, but Lucas has human capital externalities).

The idea of externalities is not uncommon to economists, but both Romer and Lucas make an extreme assumption of sufficiently strong externalities that $A(t)$ can grow continuously at the economy level. In particular, Romer assumes that

$$A(t) = BK(t), \tag{11.36}$$

so that the knowledge stock of the economy is proportional to its capital stock. This assumption can be motivated by "learning-by-doing," whereby greater investments in certain sectors increase the experience (of firms, workers, and managers) in the production process, making the production process itself more productive. Alternatively the knowledge stock of the economy could be a function of the cumulative output that the economy has produced up to now, thus giving it more of a flavor of "learning-by-doing." Notice also that (11.35) and (11.36) imply that the aggregate production function of this economy exhibits increasing returns to scale. As discussed in detail in Part IV, this property is a very common feature of models of endogenous growth. This feature also highlights that in this class of models we can no longer appeal to the Representative Firm Theorem (Theorem 5.4). Thus I specified the production function and equilibrium behavior of each firm in the economy. More generally, Theorem 5.4 applies when there are no externalities and all firms are price-taking, whereas almost all models of endogenous technology—starting with the Romer model in this section—involve either technological externalities or monopolistic competition.

Substituting for (11.36) into (11.35) and using the fact that all firms are functioning at the same capital–effective labor ratio and that F is homogeneous of degree 1, the production function of each firm can be written as

$$Y(t) = F(K(t), BK(t)L).$$

Since the measure of firms is equal to 1, this equation also gives aggregate output. Using the fact that $F(\cdot, \cdot)$ is homogeneous of degree 1, we can write

$$\frac{Y(t)}{K(t)} = F(1, BL)$$

$$\equiv \tilde{f}(L).$$

Output per capita is therefore

$$y(t) \equiv \frac{Y(t)}{L}$$

$$= \frac{Y(t)}{K(t)} \frac{K(t)}{L}$$

$$= k(t)\tilde{f}(L),$$

where again $k(t) \equiv K(t)/L$ is the capital-labor ratio in the economy.

Marginal products and factor prices can then be expressed in terms of the normalized production function, now $\tilde{f}(L)$:

$$w(t) = K(t)\tilde{f}'(L), \tag{11.37}$$

and the rental rate of capital is constant at

$$R(t) = R = \tilde{f}(L) - L\tilde{f}'(L). \tag{11.38}$$

11.4.2 Equilibrium

A *competitive equilibrium* is defined similarly to that in the neoclassical growth model as a path of consumption and capital stock for the economy, $[C(t), K(t)]_{t=0}^{\infty}$, that maximizes the utility of the representative household and wage and rental rates, $[w(t), R(t)]_{t=0}^{\infty}$, that clear markets. The important feature is that because the knowledge spillovers in (11.36) are external to each firm, equilibrium factor prices are given by (11.37) and (11.38)—that is, they do not price the role of the capital stock in increasing future productivity.

Since the market rate of return is $r(t) = R(t) - \delta$, it is also constant. The usual consumption Euler equation (11.4) then implies that consumption must grow at the constant rate given by

$$g_C^* = \frac{1}{\theta}(\tilde{f}(L) - L\tilde{f}'(L) - \delta - \rho). \tag{11.39}$$

It is also clear that capital grows at the same rate as consumption, so the rate of capital, output, and consumption growth are all given by (11.39) (see Exercise 11.15).

Let us assume that

$$\tilde{f}(L) - L\tilde{f}'(L) - \delta - \rho > 0, \tag{11.40}$$

so that there is positive growth, but the growth is not fast enough to violate the transversality condition (finiteness of utility):

$$(1 - \theta)(\tilde{f}(L) - L\tilde{f}'(L) - \delta) < \rho. \tag{11.41}$$

Proposition 11.5 *Consider the Romer model with physical capital externalities. Suppose that conditions (11.40) and (11.41) are satisfied. Then there exists a unique equilibrium path where starting with any level of capital stock $K(0) > 0$, capital, output, and consumption grow at the constant rate (11.39).*

Proof. Much of this proposition is proved in the preceding discussion. You are asked to verify the transversality conditions and show that there are no transitional dynamics in Exercise 11.16. ∎

This model therefore provides us with the first example of endogenous technological change. The technology of the economy, $A(t)$ as given in (11.36), evolves endogenously as a result of the investment decisions of firms. Consequently the growth rate of the economy is endogenous, even though none of the firms purposefully invest in research or acquiring new technologies.

Population must be constant in this model because of a *scale effect*. Since $\tilde{f}(L) - L\tilde{f}'(L)$ is always increasing in L (by Assumption 1), a higher population (labor force) L leads to a higher growth rate. The scale effect refers to this relationship between population and the equilibrium rate of economic growth. If population were growing, then the economy would not admit a steady state (BGP), and the growth rate of the economy would increase over time (with output reaching infinity in finite time, thus violating the finiteness of household utility and the transversality condition). The implications of positive population growth are discussed further in Exercise 11.18. Scale effects and how they can be removed are discussed in detail in Chapter 13.

11.4.3 Pareto Optimal Allocations

Given the presence of externalities, it is not surprising that the decentralized equilibrium characterized in Proposition 11.5 is not Pareto optimal. To characterize the allocation that maximizes the utility of the representative household, let us again set up the current-value Hamiltonian and look for a candidate path that satisfies the conditions in Theorem 7.13 (see Exercise 11.17). The per capita accumulation equation for this economy can be written as

$$\dot{k}(t) = \tilde{f}(L)k(t) - c(t) - \delta k(t).$$

The current-value Hamiltonian is

$$\hat{H}(k, c, \mu) = \frac{c(t)^{1-\theta} - 1}{1 - \theta} + \mu(t)[\tilde{f}(L)k(t) - c(t) - \delta k(t)],$$

and the necessary conditions for a candidate solution are

$$\hat{H}_c(k, c, \mu) = c(t)^{-\theta} - \mu(t) = 0,$$

$$\hat{H}_k(k, c, \mu) = \mu(t)[\tilde{f}(L) - \delta] = -\dot{\mu}(t) + \rho\mu(t),$$

$$\lim_{t \to \infty} \left[\exp(-\rho t)\mu(t)k(t)\right] = 0.$$

Using standard arguments (recall Section 7.7 in Chapter 7), it is straightforward to verify that the current-value Hamiltonian satisfies the conditions in Theorem 7.14, so that these conditions are sufficient for a unique Pareto optimum (see Exercise 11.17).

Combining these equations immediately yields that the social planner's allocation also features a constant growth rate of consumption (and output) given by

$$g_C^S = \frac{1}{\theta}(\tilde{f}(L) - \delta - \rho).$$

This rate is always greater than g_C^* as given by (11.39), since $\tilde{f}(L) > \tilde{f}(L) - L\tilde{f}'(L)$. Essentially the social planner takes into account that by accumulating more capital, she is improving productivity in the future. Since this effect is external to the firms, the decentralized economy fails to internalize this spillover. This result is summarized in the next proposition.

Proposition 11.6 *In the above-described Romer model with physical capital externalities, the decentralized equilibrium is Pareto suboptimal and grows at a slower rate than the allocation that would maximize the utility of the representative household.*

Exercise 11.19 asks you to characterize various different types of policies that can close the gap between the equilibrium and Pareto optimal allocations.

11.5 Taking Stock

This chapter ends our investigation of (closed-economy) neoclassical growth models. It also opens the way for the analysis of endogenous technological progress in the next part of the book. The models presented in this chapter are, in many ways, more tractable and easier than those in earlier chapters. This tractability is a feature of the linearity of the models (most clearly visible in the *AK* model). Such linearity removes transitional dynamics and leads to a more tractable mathematical structure. Linearity, of course, is essential for sustained economic growth. If strong concavity sets in (especially concavity consistent with the Inada conditions as in Assumption 2), sustained (endogenous) growth will not be possible. Therefore (asymptotic) linearity is an essential ingredient of any model that leads to sustained growth. The baseline *AK* model and its cousins make this linear structure quite explicit. While this type of linearity is not as apparent (and is often derived rather than assumed), it is also a feature of the endogenous technology models studied in the next part of the book. Nevertheless we will also see that linearity in the endogenous technology models often results from more interesting economic interactions than those in the models of this chapter.

There is another sense in which the material in this chapter does not do justice to issues of sustained growth. As discussed in Chapter 3, modern economic growth appears to be intimately connected to technological progress. Except for the Romer model of Section 11.4, the models studied in this chapter do not feature technological progress. This omission does not imply that they are necessarily inconsistent with the data. As already noted in Chapter 3, there is a lively debate about whether the observed total factor productivity growth is partly a result of the mismeasurement of inputs. If so, it could be that much of what we measure as technological progress is in fact capital deepening, which is the essence of economic growth in the AK model and its variants. Consequently the debate about the measurement of total factor productivity has important implications for what types of models we should use for thinking about world economic growth and cross-country income differences. In the final analysis, however, it seems unlikely that some form of technological progress has not played an important role in the process of economic growth over the past 200 years.

The discussion in this chapter has also revealed another important tension. Chapters 3 and 8 demonstrated that the neoclassical growth model (or the simpler Solow growth model) has difficulty in generating the very large income differences across countries that we observe in the data. Even if we choose quite large differences in cross-country distortions (e.g., eightfold differences in effective tax rates), the implied steady-state differences in income per capita are relatively modest. As noted before, this observation has generated a large literature that seeks reasonable extensions of the neoclassical growth model in order to derive more elastic responses to policy distortions and so provide a better mapping of these models to differences across countries. The models presented in this chapter, like those that we will encounter in the next part of the book, suffer from the opposite problem. They imply that even small differences in policies, technological opportunities, or other characteristics of societies lead to permanent differences in long-run growth rates. Consequently these models can explain very large differences in living standards from small policy, institutional, or technological differences. But this ability is both a blessing and a curse. The by-product of generating large cross-country differences from small policy or technological differences is that these models also predict an ever-expanding world income distribution—countries with different characteristics should grow at permanently different rates. The relative stability of the world income distribution in the postwar era pointed out in Chapter 1 is then a challenge to the baseline endogenous growth models.

Although one can debate whether endogenous growth models, with each country growing at a potentially different long-run rate, are a better approximation to postwar data than models in which there is a stable world income distribution, at some level this debate is not particularly interesting. First, there is more to understanding the nature of the growth process and the role of technological progress than simply looking at the postwar data. As illustrated in Chapter 1, the era of divergence is not the past 60 years, but the nineteenth century. Therefore we should not just focus on postwar data but also confront our growth models with historical data. These data are both richer and more informative about the era when the divergence across countries began. Second, as discussed in Chapters 18 and 19, most economies do not generate their own technology by R&D but largely import or adopt these technologies from more advanced nations (or from the world technology frontier). They also engage in substantial trade with other countries. Once technological, financial, and trade interdependences across countries are modeled, the sharp distinction between models of exogenous and endogenous growth disappears. This point again reiterates the potential pitfalls in modeling "each country as an island," especially when we wish to map these models to data. Having noted the importance of understanding interdependences across nations, in Part IV I follow the established literature and develop the models of endogenous technological progress without international interdependences, only returning to these themes in Chapters 18 and 19.

11.6 References and Literature

The *AK* model discussed in Section 11.1 is a special case of Rebelo's (1991) model (discussed in greater detail in Section 11.3). It is also a special case of von Neumann's (1945) seminal contribution to growth economics (this 1945 paper is the translation of the original, 1937, German article). Solow's (1970) book also discussed the *AK* model (naturally with exogenous savings), but dismissed it as uninteresting. A more complete treatment of sustained neoclassical economic growth is provided in Jones and Manuelli (1990), who show that even convex models (with production functions that satisfy Assumption 1 but, naturally, not Assumption 2) are consistent with sustained long-run growth. Exercise 11.4 is a version of the convex neoclassical endogenous growth model of Jones and Manuelli.

Barro and Sala-i-Martin (2004) discuss a variety of two-sector endogenous growth models with physical and human capital, similar to the model presented in Section 11.2, though the model presented here is much simpler than those analyzed in the literature.

Romer (1986a) is a pioneering paper of the endogenous growth literature, and the model presented in Section 11.4 is based on this paper. The importance of Romer's paper stems not only from the model itself but also from two other features. The first is its emphasis on potential noncompetitive elements to generate long-run economic growth (in this case knowledge spillovers). The second is its emphasis on the nonrival nature of knowledge and ideas. These issues are discussed in greater detail in Part IV.

Another paper that has played a major role in the new growth literature is Lucas (1988), which constructs an endogenous growth model similar to that of Romer (1986a), but with human capital accumulation and human capital externalities. Lucas's model also builds on the important work by Uzawa (1964). Lucas's paper has played two major roles in the literature. First, it emphasized the empirical importance of sustained economic growth and thus was instrumental in generating interest in the newly emerging endogenous growth models. Second, it emphasized the importance of human capital and especially of human capital externalities. Since the role of human capital was discussed extensively in Chapter 10, which also showed that the evidence for human capital externalities is rather limited, I focused on the Romer rather than the Lucas model in this chapter. It turns out that the Lucas model also generates transitional dynamics, which are slightly more difficult to characterize than the standard neoclassical transitional dynamics. A version of the Lucas model is discussed in Exercise 11.21.

11.7 Exercises

11.1 Derive (11.14).

11.2 Prove Proposition 11.2.

11.3 Consider the following continuous-time neoclassical growth model:

$$\int_0^\infty \exp(-(\rho - n)t)\frac{c(t)^{1-\theta} - 1}{1 - \theta}dt,$$

with aggregate production function

$$Y(t) = AK(t) + BL(t),$$

where A, $B > 0$.

(a) Define a competitive equilibrium for this economy.

(b) Set up the current-value Hamiltonian for the representative household. Characterize the solution. Combine this solution with equilibrium factor prices, and derive the equilibrium path. Show that the equilibrium path displays nontrivial transitional dynamics.

(c) Determine the evolution of the labor share of national income over time.

(d) Analyze the impact of an unanticipated increase in B on the equilibrium path.

(e) Prove that the equilibrium is Pareto optimal.

11.4   Consider the following continuous-time neoclassical growth model:

$$\int_0^\infty \exp(-(\rho - n)t) \frac{c(t)^{1-\theta} - 1}{1 - \theta} dt,$$

with production function

$$Y(t) = A\left[L(t)^{\frac{\sigma-1}{\sigma}} + K(t)^{\frac{\sigma-1}{\sigma}}\right]^{\frac{\sigma}{\sigma-1}}.$$

(a) Define and characterize a competitive equilibrium for this economy.

(b) Prove that the equilibrium is Pareto optimal.

(c) Show that if $\sigma \leq 1$, sustained growth is not possible.

(d) Show that if A and σ are sufficiently large, this model generates asymptotically sustained growth because of capital accumulation. Interpret this result.

(e) Characterize the transitional dynamics of the equilibrium path.

(f) What is happening to the share of capital in national income? Is this behavior plausible? How would you modify the model to ensure that the share of capital in national income remains constant?

(g) Now assume that returns from capital are taxed at the rate τ. Determine the asymptotic growth rate of consumption and output.

11.5   Derive (11.19) and (11.20).

11.6   Consider the neoclassical growth model with Cobb-Douglas technology $y(t) = Ak(t)^\alpha$ (expressed in per capita terms) and log preferences. Characterize the equilibrium path of this economy, and show that as $\alpha \to 1$, the equilibrium path approaches that of the baseline AK economy. Interpret this result.

11.7   Consider the baseline AK model of Section 11.1 and suppose that two otherwise-identical countries have different taxes on the rate of return on capital. Consider the following calibration of the model: $A = 0.15$, $\delta = 0.05$, $\rho = 0.02$, and $\theta = 3$. Suppose that the first country has a capital income tax rate of $\tau = 0.2$, while the second country has a tax rate of $\tau' = 0.4$. Suppose that the two countries start with the same level of income in 1900 and experience no change in technology or policies for the next 100 years. What will be the relative income gap between the two countries in 2000? Discuss this result and explain why you do (or do not) find the implications plausible.

11.8   (a) Verify that Theorems 7.13 and 7.14 from Chapter 7 can be applied to the two-sector model in Section 11.2. [Hint: use a similar argument to that in Section 7.7.]

(b) Prove that the consumer optimization problem in Section 11.2 leads to the conditions enumerated in (11.25).

11.9   Prove Proposition 11.3.

11.10   Prove that the competitive equilibrium of the economy in Section 11.2, characterized in Proposition 11.3, is Pareto optimal and coincides with the solution to the optimal growth problem.

11.11   Show that the rate of population growth has no effect on the equilibrium growth rate of the economies studied in Sections 11.1 and 11.2. Explain why. Do you find this prediction to be plausible?

11.12 Show that in the model of Section 11.3, if the Cobb-Douglas assumption is relaxed, there does not exist a BGP with a constant share of capital income in GDP.

11.13 Consider the effect of an increase in α on the competitive equilibrium of the model in Section 11.3. Why does it increase the rate of capital accumulation in the economy?

11.14 Consider a variant of the model studied in Section 11.3 in which the technology in the consumption good sector is still given by (11.27), while the technology in the investment good sector is modified to

$$I(t) = A(K_I(t))^\beta (L_I(t))^{1-\beta},$$

where $\beta \in (\alpha, 1)$. The labor market clearing condition now requires $L_C(t) + L_I(t) \le L(t)$. The rest of the environment is unchanged.

(a) Define a competitive equilibrium.

(b) Characterize the steady-state equilibrium, and show that it does not involve sustained growth.

(c) Explain why the long-run growth implications of this model differ from those of Section 11.3.

(d) Analyze the steady-state income differences between two economies taxing capital at the rates τ and τ'. What are the roles of the parameters α and β in determining these relative differences? Why do the implied magnitudes differ from those in the one-sector neoclassical growth model?

11.15 In the Romer model presented in Section 11.4, let g_C^* be the growth rate of consumption and g^* the growth rate of aggregate output. Show that $g_C^* > g^*$ is not feasible, while $g_C^* < g^*$ would violate the transversality condition.

11.16 Consider the Romer model presented in Section 11.4. Prove that the allocation in Proposition 11.5 satisfies the transversality condition. Prove also that there are no transitional dynamics in this equilibrium.

11.17 In the Romer model presented in Section 11.4, verify that Theorems 7.13 and 7.14 can be applied both to the representative household's problem and to the social planner's problem.

11.18 Consider the Romer model presented in Section 11.4, and suppose that population grows at the rate $n > 0$. Characterize the labor market clearing conditions. Formulate the dynamic optimization problem of a representative household, and show that any interior solution to this problem violates the transversality condition. Interpret this result.

11.19 Consider the Romer model presented in Section 11.4. Provide two different types of tax/subsidy policies that would make the equilibrium allocation identical to the Pareto optimal allocation.

11.20 Consider the following infinite-horizon economy in discrete time that admits a representative household with preferences at time $t = 0$ as

$$\sum_{t=0}^{\infty} \beta^t \frac{C(t)^{1-\theta} - 1}{1 - \theta},$$

where $C(t)$ is consumption, and $\beta \in (0, 1)$. Total population is equal to L, there is no population growth, and labor is supplied inelastically. The production side of the economy consists of a continuum 1 of firms, each with production function $Y_i(t) = F(K_i(t), A(t)L_i(t))$, where $L_i(t)$ is employment of firm i at time t, $K_i(t)$ is capital used by firm i at time t, and $A(t)$ is a common technology term. Market clearing implies that $\int_0^1 K_i(t)di = K(t)$, where $K(t)$ is the total capital stock at time t, and $\int_0^1 L_i(t)di = L(t)$. Assume that capital fully depreciates, so that the resource constraint of the economy is

$$K(t+1) = \int_0^1 Y_i(t)di - C(t).$$

Assume also that labor-augmenting productivity at time t, $A(t)$, is given by $A(t) = K(t)$.

(a) Define a competitive equilibrium (where all agents are price takers).

(b) Show that there exists a unique BGP competitive equilibrium, where the economy grows (or shrinks) at a constant rate every period. Provide a condition on F, β, and θ such that this growth rate is positive, but the transversality condition is still satisfied.

(c) Explain why any equilibrium must be along the BGP characterized in part c at all points.

* 11.21 Consider the following endogenous growth model due to Uzawa and Lucas. The economy admits a representative household, and preferences are given by

$$\int_0^\infty \exp(-\rho t) \frac{C(t)^{1-\theta} - 1}{1 - \theta} dt,$$

where $C(t)$ is consumption of the final good, which is produced as

$$Y(t) = AK(t)^\alpha H_P^{1-\alpha}(t),$$

where $K(t)$ is capital, $H(t)$ is human capital, and $H_P(t)$ denotes human capital used in production. The accumulation equations are

$$\dot{K}(t) = I(t) - \delta K(t),$$

and

$$\dot{H}(t) = BH_E(t) - \delta H(t),$$

where $H_E(t)$ is human capital devoted to education (further human capital accumulation), and for simplicity the depreciation of human capital is assumed to be at the same rate δ as physical capital. The resource constraints of the economy are $I(t) + C(t) \le Y(t)$, and $H_E(t) + H_P(t) \le H(t)$.

(a) Interpret the second resource constraint.

(b) Denote the fraction of human capital allocated to production by $h(t)$ (so that $h(t) \equiv H_P(t)/H(t)$) and calculate the growth rate of final output as a function of $h(t)$ and the growth rates of accumulable factors.

(c) Assume that $h(t)$ is constant, and characterize the BGP of the economy (with constant interest rate and constant rate of growth for capital and output). Show that in this BGP, $r^* \equiv B - \delta$, and the growth rate of consumption, capital, human capital, and output are given by $g^* \equiv (B - \delta - \rho)/\theta$. Show also that there exists a unique value of $k^* \equiv K/H$ consistent with BGP.

(d) Determine the parameter restrictions to make sure that the transversality condition is satisfied.

(e) Analyze the transitional dynamics of the economy starting with K/H different from k^*. [Hint: look at the dynamics in three variables, $k \equiv K/H$, $\chi \equiv C/K$, and h, and consider the cases $\alpha < \theta$ and $\alpha \ge \theta$ separately.]

PART IV

ENDOGENOUS TECHNOLOGICAL CHANGE

This part of the book focuses on models of endogenous technological change. Chapter 12 discusses various approaches to technological change and provides a brief overview of some workhorse models from the literature on industrial organization. Chapters 13 and 14 present the baseline endogenous technological progress models developed by Romer, Grossman and Helpman, and Aghion and Howitt. Chapter 15 considers a richer class of models in which the direction of technological change—for example, which factors technological change will augment or complement—is also endogenous.

The models presented in this part of the book are useful for two related purposes. First, by making technological progress respond to incentives, market structure, and policies, they allow us to develop a more satisfactory framework for the study of cross-country and over-time differences in economic performance. Second, they provide a tractable approach to modeling sustained growth, in which technological progress acts as the engine of long-run growth.

12

Modeling Technological Change

We have so far investigated models of economic growth of the exogenous and endogenous varieties. But economic growth has not resulted from technological change. It has been exogenous, sustained by (linear) capital accumulation, or taken place as a by-product of knowledge spillovers. Since our purpose is to understand the process of economic growth, models in which growth results from technological progress and technological change itself—as a consequence of purposeful investments by firms and individuals—are much more attractive. These models not only endogenize technological progress, but they also relate the process of technological change to market structure and to policies concerning antitrust, competition, and intellectual property rights. They also enable us to discuss issues of directed technological change. In this chapter, I begin with a brief discussion of different conceptions of technological change and provide some foundations for the models that come later.

12.1 Different Conceptions of Technology

12.1.1 Types of Technological Change

The literature on technological change often distinguishes among different types of innovations. A first common distinction is between *process* and *product* innovations. The latter refers to the introduction of a new product (e.g., the introduction of the first DVD player). The former is concerned with innovations that reduce the costs of production of existing products (e.g., the introduction of new machines to produce existing goods). Models of process and product innovations are often mathematically similar. Nevertheless the distinction between the two types of innovations is still useful in mapping these theories to data.

Process innovations that introduce higher quality versions of existing products or generate a lower cost technology to produce an existing product might be more important in practice than innovations reducing costs in production processes. The introduction of a better DVD player and the innovation to manufacture an existing DVD player at a lower cost would be examples of such process innovations. These innovations typically lead to the replacement of older vintages of the same good or machine and to potential competition between existing producers and the innovator.

In this context, one might additionally wish to distinguish between the introduction of a higher quality DVD player and the production of a cheaper DVD player, because heterogeneous consumers may have differential willingness to pay for quality than for quantity. Issues of differential willingness to pay for quality are important in the theory of industrial organization and for constructing accurate quality-adjusted price indices. However most growth models represent the consumer side by a representative household and implicitly assume perfect substitution between quality and quantity. These features create a close connection between process innovations that increase the quality of existing products and those that reduce the costs of production. The following example illustrates why, in the context of typical growth models, quality improvements and cost reductions are essentially equivalent.

Example 12.1   *Consider an economy admitting a representative household with preferences $U(qc(q), y \mid q)$, where y stands for a generic good (perhaps representing all other goods), and c is a particular consumption good available in different qualities. Here $c(q)$ denotes the amount consumed of the "vintage" of quality q. The utility function is also conditioned on q. This specification, with q multiplying $c(q)$, implies that quality and quantity are perfect substitutes, so that higher quality products increase the effective units of consumption. This assumption is typical in growth models, though it is clearly restrictive: the consumption (use) of five 1-GHz computers would not give the same services as the use of a single 5-GHz computer.*

Let the budget constraint of the representative household be

$$p(q)c(q) + y \leq m,$$

where $p(q)$ is the price of the good of quality (vintage) q, the price of the generic good is normalized to 1, and m denotes the resources available to the consumer. The problem of the household can then be equivalently written as

$$\max_{x(q), y} \; U(x(q), y \mid q)$$

subject to

$$\frac{p(q)}{q} x(q) + y \leq m,$$

where $x(q) \equiv qc(q)$ corresponds to the effective units of consumption of good c. It is straightforward to see from this problem formulation that proportional increases in quality q and declines in the price $p(q)$ have the same effects on the effective units of consumption and on welfare. This observation justifies the claim above that in many models, process innovations reducing costs of production and quality improvements have identical effects.

Another important distinction in the technological change literature is between macro and micro innovations (see Mokyr, 1990). The first refers to radical innovations, including the introduction of general-purpose technologies, such as electricity or the computer, which potentially change the organization of production in many different product lines. In contrast, micro innovations refer to the more common innovations that introduce newer models of existing products, improve the quality of a certain product line, or simply reduce costs. Most of the innovations modeled below can be viewed as micro innovations, though most endogenous technology models do not make an explicit distinction between micro and macro innovations. Empirically it appears that micro innovations are responsible for most productivity growth, though they often build upon some macro or general-purpose innovation, such as the invention of electricity or the microchip (see the evidence and discussion in Abernathy, 1978, and Freeman, 1982).

12.1.2 A Production Function for Technology

A potentially confusing issue in the study of technological progress is how to conceptualize the menu of technologies available to firms or individuals. Since our purpose is to develop models of endogenous technology, firms and/or individuals must have a choice among different types of technologies, and greater effort, research spending, and investment should lead to the invention of better technologies. These requirements imply that there must exist a *meta production function* (a production function over production functions) that determines how new technologies are generated as a function of inputs. In what follows I refer to this meta production function as the "innovation possibilities frontier" (or as the "R&D production function").

While a meta production function may appear natural to some, there are various economists and social scientists who do not find this approach compelling. Their argument against the production function approach to technology is that, by its nature, innovation includes the discovery of the unknown: how could we put the unknown in the context of a production function where inputs go in and outputs come out in a deterministic fashion?

Although this question has some descriptive merit (in the sense that describing the discovery of new technologies with a production function obscures some important details of the innovation process), the concern is largely irrelevant. There is no reason to assume that the meta production function for technology is deterministic. Both the success of a research project and the quality of the research output conditional on success can be uncertain, corresponding to a meta production function with stochastic output. Therefore the production function approach to technology is not particularly restrictive, as long as uncertain outcomes are allowed, and we are willing to assume that individuals can make calculations about the effect of their actions on the probability of success and quality of the research project. Naturally, some observers may argue that such calculations are not possible. But without such calculations we would have little hope of modeling the process of technological change (or technology adoption). Since our objective is to model purposeful innovations, assuming that individuals and firms can make such calculations is natural, and this assumption is equivalent to assuming the existence of a meta production function for technologies.

12.1.3 Nonrivalry of Ideas

Another important aspect of technology is emphasized in Paul Romer's work. As already discussed in the previous chapter, Romer's (1986a) first model of endogenous growth introduced increasing returns to scale to physical capital accumulation. The justification for this assumption was that the accumulation of knowledge could be considered a by-product of the economic activities of firms. Later work by Romer, which will be studied in the next chapter, took a very different approach to modeling the process of economic growth, but the same key idea is present in both his early and later work: the nonrivalry of ideas matters.

By *nonrivalry,* Romer means that the use of an idea by one producer to increase efficiency does not preclude its use by others. While the same unit of labor or capital cannot be used by multiple producers, the same idea can be used by many, potentially increasing everybody's productivity. Let us consider a production function of the form $F(K, L, A)$, with A denoting technology. Romer argues that an important part of this technology is the ideas or blueprints concerning how to produce new goods, how to increase quality, or how to reduce costs.

Economists are generally comfortable assuming that the production function $F(K, L, A)$ exhibits constant returns to scale in capital and labor (K and L), and I adopted this assumption throughout the first three parts of the book. For example, replication arguments can be used to justify this type of constant returns to scale (unless land is an important factor of production): when capital and labor double, the society can always open a replica of the same production facility, and in the absence of externalities, this new facility will (at least) double output.

Romer argues that endogenizing A naturally leads to increasing returns to scale to all three inputs, K, L, and A. To understand why nonrivalry is important here, imagine that A is like any other input. Then the replication argument would require the new production facility to replicate A as well, and thus we should expect constant returns to scale when we vary all three inputs, K, L, and A. Instead, when ideas are nonrival, the new production facility does not need to re-create or replicate A, because it is already available for all firms to use. Then $F(K, L, A)$ will exhibit constant returns in K and L, and *increasing returns to scale* in K, L, and A.

Therefore the nonrivalry of ideas and increasing returns are intimately linked. This has motivated Romer and others to develop endogenous growth models with various conceptions of technology during the 1980s and 1990s. But the nonrivalry of ideas and the resulting increasing returns to scale have been a central element in most of these models.

Another important implication of the nonrivalry of ideas is the *market size effect*. If, once discovered, an idea can be used as many times as one wishes, then the size of its potential market will be a crucial determinant of whether it is profitable to implement it and whether to research it in the first place. This idea is well captured by a famous quote from Matthew Boulton, James Watt's business partner, who wrote to Watt: "It is not worth my while to manufacture your engine for three countries only, but I find it very well worth my while to make it for all the world" (quoted in Scherer, 1984, p. 13).

To see why nonrivalry is related to the market size effect, imagine another standard (rival) input that is also essential for production. A greater market size does not necessarily induce firms to use this alternate input more intensively, since a greater market size and thus greater sales means that more of this input has to be used. It is the fact that nonrival ideas can be embedded in as many units as desired, without incurring further costs, that makes the market size effect particularly important. In the next section, I discuss some empirical evidence on the importance of the market size effect.

Nevertheless the nonrivalry of ideas does not make ideas or innovations *pure public goods*. Recall that pure public goods are both nonrival and nonexcludable. While some discoveries may be, by their nature, nonexcludable (e.g., the "discovery" that providing excessively high-powered incentives to CEOs in the form of stock options leads to counterproductive incentives and cheating), most discoveries can be made partly excludable by patenting. An important aspect of the process of technological change is the protection of intellectual discoveries from rivals. For this reason, intellectual property rights protection and patent policy often play an important role in models of technological progress.

12.2 Science and Profits

Another major question for the economic analysis of technological change is whether innovation is mainly determined by scientific constraints and stimulated by scientific breakthroughs in particular fields, or whether it is, at least in part, driven by profit motives. Historians and economists typically give different answers to this question. Many historical accounts of technological change come down on the side of the science-driven view, emphasizing the autonomous progress of science and how important breakthroughs—perhaps macro innovations, as discussed above—have taken place as scientists build on one another's work with little emphasis on profit opportunities. For example, in his *History of Modern Computing,* Ceruzzi emphasizes the importance of a number of notable scientific discoveries and the role played by certain talented individuals rather than profit motives and the potential market for computers. He points out, for example, how important developments took place despite the belief of many important figures in the development of the computer, such as Howard Aiken, that there would not be a demand for more than a handful of personal computers in the United States (Ceruzzi, 2003, p. 13). Many economic historians (e.g., Rosenberg, 1976) similarly argue that a key determinant of innovation in a particular field is the largely exogenous growth of scientific and engineering knowledge in that field.

In contrast, most economists believe that profit opportunities play a much more important role, and that the demand for innovation is the key to understanding the process of technological change. John Stuart Mill provides an early and clear statement of this view in his *Principles of Political Economy* when he writes:

> The labor of Watt in contriving the steam-engine was as essential a part of production as that of the mechanics who build or the engineers who work the instrument; and was undergone, no less than theirs, in the prospect of a renumeration from the producers (quoted in Schmookler, 1966, p. 210).

In fact, profits were very much in the minds of James Watt and his business partner, Matthew Boulton, as the previous quote illustrates. James Watt also praised the patent system for the same reasons, arguing that "an engineer's life without patent was not worthwhile" (quoted in Mokyr, 1990, p. 248). The view that profit opportunities are the primary determinant of innovation and invention is articulated by Griliches and Schmookler (1963) and then most forcefully and eloquently by Schmookler's seminal study, *Invention and Economic Growth.* Schmookler (1966, p. 206) writes that "invention is largely an economic activity which, like other economic activities, is pursued for gain."

Schmookler concludes from his analysis of innovations in petroleum refining, papermaking, railroad construction, and farming that there is no evidence that past breakthroughs have been the major factor in new innovations. He (Schmookler, 1966, p. 199) argues: "Instead, in hundreds of cases the stimulus was the recognition of a costly problem to be solved or a potentially profitable opportunity to be seized."

If potential profits are a main driver of technological change, then the market size that will be commanded by new technologies or products will be a key determinant of innovations. A greater market size increases profits and makes innovation and invention more desirable. To emphasize this point, Schmookler called two of his chapters "The amount of invention is governed by the extent of the market." Schmookler's argument is most clearly illustrated by the example of the horseshoe. He documented that there was a very high rate of innovation throughout the late nineteenth and early twentieth centuries in the ancient technology of horseshoe making, and no tendency for inventors to run out of additional improvements. On the contrary, inventions and patents increased, because demand for horseshoes was high. Innovations came to an end only when "the steam traction engine and, later, internal combustion engine began to displace the horse" (Schmookler, 1966, p. 93). The classic study by Griliches (1957) on the spread of hybrid seed corn in U.S. agriculture also provides support for the view that technological change and technology adoption are closely linked to profitability and market size.

A variety of more recent papers also reach similar conclusions. Newell, Jaffee, and Stavins (1999) show that between 1960 and 1980, the typical air conditioner sold at Sears became significantly cheaper but not much more energy-efficient. On the other hand, between 1980 and 1990, there was little change in costs, but air conditioners became much more energy-efficient, which, they argue, was a response to higher energy prices. This example provides a clear case of the pace and type of innovation responding to profit incentives. In a related study, Popp (2002) documents evidence consistent with this pattern and finds a strong positive correlation between patents for energy-saving technologies and energy prices.

Evidence from the pharmaceutical industry also illustrates the importance of profit incentives and especially of the market size on the rate of innovation. Finkelstein (2004) exploits three different policy changes affecting the profitability of developing new vaccines against six infectious diseases. She finds that increases in vaccine profitability resulting from these policy changes are associated with a significant increase in the number of clinical trials to develop new vaccines against the relevant diseases. Acemoglu and Linn (2004) look at demographically driven exogenous changes in the market size for drugs and find a significant response in the rate of innovation to these changes in market sizes.

Overall, existing evidence suggests that market size is a major determinant of innovation incentives and the amount and type of technological change. This evidence motivates the types of models presented below, in which technological change is an economic activity and responds to profit incentives.

12.3 The Value of Innovation in Partial Equilibrium

Let us now turn to the analysis of the value of innovation and R&D to a firm. The equilibrium value of innovation and the difference between this private value and the social value (defined as the value to a social planner internalizing externalities) plays a central role in our analysis. As emphasized at the beginning of the book, economic growth is a process we can only understand in the context of dynamic general equilibrium analysis. Nevertheless it is useful to start our investigation of the value of innovation in partial equilibrium, where much of the industrial organization literature starts.

Throughout this section I consider a single industry. Firms in this industry have access to an existing technology to produce one unit of the product at the marginal cost $\psi > 0$ (in terms of some numeraire). The demand side of the industry is modeled with a demand curve

$$Q = D(p),$$

where p is the price of the product and Q is the demand at this price. Throughout I assume that $D(p)$ is strictly decreasing, differentiable, and satisfies the following conditions:

$$D(\psi) > 0, \quad \text{and} \quad \varepsilon_D(p) \equiv -\frac{p D'(p)}{D(p)} \in (1, \infty).$$

The first condition ensures that there is positive demand when price is equal to marginal cost, and the second ensures that the elasticity of demand, $\varepsilon_D(p)$, is greater than 1, so that there always exists a well-defined (profit-maximizing) monopoly price. Moreover this elasticity is less than infinity, so that the monopoly price is above marginal cost.

In this chapter, as in the rest of the book, when there are economies with monopolistic or oligopolistic competition, equilibrium refers to Nash Equilibrium or Subgame Perfect (Nash) Equilibrium (when the game in question is dynamic). A brief review of these concepts is contained in Appendix C.

12.3.1 No Innovation with Pure Competition

Suppose first that there is a large number N of firms with access to the existing technology. Now imagine that one of these firms, say firm 1, also has access to a research technology for generating a process innovation. In particular, let us simplify the discussion and suppose that there is no uncertainty in research, and if the firm incurs a cost $\mu > 0$, it can innovate and reduce the marginal cost of production to ψ/λ, where $\lambda > 1$. Let us suppose that this innovation is nonrival and is also nonexcludable, either because it is not patentable or because the patent system does not exist.

Let us now analyze the incentives of this firm to undertake this innovation. First, in the equilibrium without the innovation, the presence of a large number of N firms, all with the same technology, ensures that the equilibrium price is equal to marginal cost, $p^N = \psi$, where the superscript N denotes no innovation. The total quantity demanded is $D(\psi) > 0$ and can be distributed among the N firms in any arbitrary fashion. Since price is equal to marginal cost, the profits of firm 1 in this equilibrium is

$$\pi_1^N = (p^N - \psi)q_1^N = 0,$$

where q_1^N denotes the amount supplied by this firm.

Now imagine that firm 1 innovates, but because of nonexcludability, the innovation can and will be used by all firms in the industry. The same reasoning implies that the equilibrium price becomes $p^I = \lambda^{-1}\psi$, and total quantity supplied by all the firms will equal $D(\lambda^{-1}\psi) > D(\psi)$. Then the net profits of firm 1 after innovation will be

$$\pi_1^I = (p^I - \lambda^{-1}\psi)q_1^I - \mu = -\mu < 0.$$

Therefore if it undertakes the innovation, firm 1 will lose money. The reason is simple: the firm incurs the cost of innovation, μ, but because the knowledge generated by the innovation is nonexcludable, it is unable to *appropriate* any of the gains by the innovation. This simple example underlies a claim dating back to Schumpeter that pure competition will not generate innovation.

Clearly, this outcome is potentially very inefficient. To illustrate this point, let us calculate the social value of innovation, which is the additional gain resulting from innovation. A natural measure of social value is the sum of the consumer and producer surpluses generated from the innovation. Suppose that after innovation the good continues to be priced at marginal cost. Then this social value is

$$\mathcal{S}^I = \int_{\lambda^{-1}\psi}^{\psi} D(p)dp - \mu$$

$$= \int_{\lambda^{-1}\psi}^{\psi} [D(p) - D(\psi)]dp + D(\psi)\lambda^{-1}(\lambda - 1)\psi - \mu.$$

(12.1)

The first term in the second line is the increase in consumer surplus because of the expansion of output as the price falls from ψ to $\lambda^{-1}\psi$ (recall that price is equal to marginal cost). The second term is the savings in costs for already-produced units; in particular, there is a saving of $\lambda^{-1}(\lambda - 1)\psi$ on $D(\psi)$ units. Finally, the last term is the cost of innovation. It is straightforward to verify that, even though the equilibrium involves no innovation, $\mathcal{S}^I$ could be arbitrarily large.

For example, the cost of innovation, μ, could be arbitrarily small (but still positive) and the productivity gain from innovation, λ, could be arbitrarily large.

12.3.2 Some Caveats

The above example illustrates the problem of innovation under pure competition. The main problem is the inability of the innovator to exclude others from using this innovation. One way of ensuring such excludability is via the protection of intellectual property rights or a patent system, which will create *ex post monopoly power* for the innovator. This type of intellectual property right protection is present in most countries and plays an important role in many of the models we study below.

Before embarking on an analysis of the implications of ex post monopoly power of innovators, some caveats are worth noting. First, even without patents, trade secrecy may be sufficient to provide some incentives for innovation. Second, firms may engage in innovations that are only appropriate for their own firm, making their innovations de facto excludable. For example, imagine that at the same cost, the firm can develop a new technology that reduces the marginal cost of production by only $\lambda' < \lambda$. But this technology is specific to the needs and competencies of the current firm and cannot be used by any other (or alternatively, λ/λ' is the proportional cost of making the innovation excludable). The adoption of this technology may be profitable for the firm, since the specificity of the innovation acts exactly like patent protection (see Exercise 12.5). Therefore some types of innovations, in particular those protected by trade secrecy, can be undertaken under pure competition.

Finally, a number of authors have recently argued that innovations in competitive markets are possible. One strand of the literature shows that competitive growth may originate because firms are able to replicate new technologies (e.g., copy software or compact discs) and sell them to competitors during a certain interval of time before being imitated by others (see, e.g., Boldrin and Levine, 2003). Another strand incorporates diminishing returns at the firm level, which creates profits and potential innovation incentives even for price-taking firms (see, e.g., Hellwig and Irmen, 2001). This recent work on competitive growth constitutes a promising direction for future research, though existing models generate innovations and sustained growth in competitive equilibria only under somewhat special assumptions.

12.3.3 Innovation and Ex Post Monopoly

Let us now return to the simple environment introduced above and suppose that if firm 1 undertakes a successful innovation, it can obtain a fully enforced patent. Firm 1 then has a better technology than the rest of the firms and possesses ex post monopoly power. This monopoly power enables the firm to earn profits from the innovation, potentially encouraging its research activity in the first place. This is the basis of the claim by Schumpeter, Arrow, Romer, and others that there is an intimate link between ex post monopoly power and innovation.

Let us now analyze this situation in a little more detail. It is useful to separate two cases.

1. *Drastic innovation:* a drastic innovation corresponds to a sufficiently high value of λ such that firm 1 becomes an effective monopolist after the innovation. To determine which values of λ lead to a situation of this sort, let us first suppose that firm 1 does indeed act like a monopolist. Then chooses its price to maximize

$$\pi_1^I = D(p)(p - \lambda^{-1}\psi) - \mu.$$

Clearly this maximization gives the following standard monopoly pricing formula (see Exercise 12.1):

$$p^M \equiv \frac{\lambda^{-1}\psi}{1 - \varepsilon_D(p^M)^{-1}}. \tag{12.2}$$

We say that the innovation is *drastic* if $p^M \le \psi$. It is clear that this is the case when

$$\lambda \ge \lambda^* \equiv \frac{1}{1 - \varepsilon_D(p^M)^{-1}}.$$

When the innovation is drastic, firm 1 can set its unconstrained monopoly price, p^M, and capture the entire market.

2. *Limit pricing*: when the innovation is not drastic, so that $p^M > \psi$, or alternatively, when $\lambda < \lambda^*$, the unique equilibrium involves limit pricing, where firm 1 sets the price

$$p_1 = \psi,$$

so as to make sure that it still captures the entire market (if, in this case, it were to set $p_1 = p^M$, other firms can profitably undercut firm 1). This type of limit pricing arises in many situations. In this case, limit pricing results from process innovations by some firms that now have access to a better technology than their rivals. Alternatively, it can also arise when *a fringe* of potential entrants can imitate the technology of a firm (either at some cost or with lower efficiency) and the firm may be forced to set a limit price to prevent the fringe from stealing its customers.

Proposition 12.1 *Consider the above-described industry. Suppose that firm 1 undertakes an innovation reducing the marginal cost of production from ψ to $\lambda^{-1}\psi$. If $p^M \le \psi$ (or if $\lambda \ge \lambda^*$), then it sets the unconstrained monopoly price $p_1 = p^M$ and makes profits*

$$\hat{\pi}_1^I = D(p^M)(p^M - \lambda^{-1}\psi) - \mu. \tag{12.3}$$

If $p^M > \psi$ (if $\lambda < \lambda^*$), then firm 1 sets the limit price $p_1 = \psi$ and makes profits

$$\pi_1^I = D(\psi)\lambda^{-1}(\lambda - 1)\psi - \mu < \hat{\pi}_1^I. \tag{12.4}$$

Proof. The proof of this proposition involves solving for the equilibrium of an asymmetric cost Bertrand competition game. While this is standard, it is useful to repeat the argument to emphasize that, as claimed before the proposition, all demand must be met by the low-cost firm. Exercise 12.2 asks you to work through the steps of the proof. ■

The fact that $\hat{\pi}_1^I > \pi_1^I$ is intuitive, since the former refers to the case where λ is greater than λ^*, whereas in the latter firm 1 has a sufficiently low λ that it is forced to charge a price lower than the profit-maximizing monopoly price. Note further that $\hat{\pi}_1^I$ and π_1^I also correspond to the value of innovation to firm 1, since without innovation, it would make zero profits. Both of these expressions can be strictly positive, so that with ex post monopoly innovation is potentially profitable. This situation corresponds to one in which we start with pure competition, but one of the firms undertakes an innovation to escape competition and gains ex post monopoly power. The fact that the ex post monopoly power is important for innovation incentives is consistent with Schumpeter's emphasis on the role of monopoly in generating innovations.

Let us next contrast the value of innovation for firm 1 in these two regimes to the social value of innovation, which is still given by (12.1). Moreover, we can also compare social values in the equilibrium in which innovation is undertaken by firm 1 (which charges the profit-maximizing price) to the full social value of innovation in (12.1), which applies when the product is priced at marginal cost. The equilibrium social surplus in the regimes with monopoly and limit pricing (again corresponding to the cases in which λ is greater than or less than λ^*) can be computed as

$$\widehat{S}_1^I = D(p^M)(p^M - \lambda^{-1}\psi) + \int_{p^M}^{\psi} D(p)dp - \mu,$$

and
$$\tag{12.5}$$

$$S_1^I = D(\psi)\lambda^{-1}(\lambda - 1)\psi - \mu.$$

Proposition 12.2 *We have that*

$$\pi_1^I < \hat{\pi}_1^I < S^I$$

and

$$S_1^I < \widehat{S}_1^I < S^I.$$

Proof. See Exercise 12.3. ∎

This proposition states that the social value of innovation is always greater than the private value in two senses. The first line states that a social planner interested in maximizing consumer and producer surplus is always more willing to adopt an innovation, because of *an appropriability effect;* the firm, even if it has ex post monopoly rights, will be able to appropriate only a portion of the gain in consumer surplus created by the better technology. In addition, the second line implies that even conditional on innovation, the gain in social surplus is always less in the equilibrium supported by ex post monopoly than the gain that the social planner could have achieved (also by controlling prices). Therefore, even though ex post monopoly power (e.g., generated by patents) can induce innovation, the incentives for innovation and the equilibrium allocations following an innovation are still inefficient. Note also that $\widehat{S}_1^I$ might be negative, so that a potentially productivity-enhancing process innovation can reduce social surplus because of the cost of innovation, μ. This situation then corresponds to excessive innovation. However it can be shown that if $\hat{\pi}_1^I > 0$, then $\widehat{S}_1^I > 0$, which implies that excessive innovation is not possible in this competitive environment (see Exercise 12.4). This result is in contrast with the results in the next subsection.

12.3.4 The Value of Innovation to a Monopolist: The Replacement Effect

Let us now analyze the same environment as in the previous Section 12.3.3 but assume that firm 1 is already an unconstrained monopolist with the existing technology. Then with the existing technology, this firm sets the monopoly price of

$$\hat{p}^M \equiv \frac{\psi}{1 - \varepsilon_D(p^M)^{-1}}$$

and make profits equal to

$$\hat{\pi}_1^N = D(\hat{p}^M)(\hat{p}^M - \psi). \tag{12.6}$$

If it undertakes the innovation, it will reduce its marginal cost to $\lambda^{-1}\psi$ and still remain an unconstrained monopolist. Therefore its profits will be given by $\hat{\pi}_1^I$ as in (12.3), with the monopoly price p^M given by (12.2). Now the value of innovation to the monopolist is

$$\Delta\hat{\pi}_1^I = \hat{\pi}_1^I - \hat{\pi}_1^N = D(p^M)(p^M - \lambda^{-1}\psi) - D(\hat{p}^M)(\hat{p}^M - \psi) - \mu,$$

where $\hat{\pi}_1^I$ is given by (12.3) and $\hat{\pi}_1^N$ by (12.6).

Proposition 12.3 *We have $\Delta\hat{\pi}_1^I < \pi_1^I < \hat{\pi}_1^I$, so that a monopolist always has lower innovation incentives than does a competitive firm.*

Proof. See Exercise 12.6. ∎

This result, which was first pointed out in Arrow's (1962) seminal paper, is referred to as "Arrow's replacement effect." The terminology reflects the intuition for the result: the monopolist has lower incentives to undertake innovation than does the firm in a competitive industry because the innovation will replace its own already existing profits. In contrast, a competitive firm makes zero profits and has no profits to replace. An immediate corollary is as follows.

Corollary 12.1 *A potential entrant has stronger incentives to undertake an innovation than does an incumbent monopolist.*

The potential entrant would make zero profits without the innovation. If it undertakes the innovation, it becomes the ex post monopolist and makes profits equal to π_1^I or $\hat{\pi}_1^I$ (depending on whether there will be limit pricing). Both of these profits are greater than the additional profits that the incumbent would make by innovating, $\Delta\hat{\pi}_1^I$. This result is a direct consequence of the replacement effect: while the incumbent would be replacing its own profit-making technology, the entrant would be replacing the incumbent. The replacement effect and this corollary imply that in many models entrants have stronger incentives to invest in R&D than do incumbents.

The observation that entrants are often the engines of process innovations takes us to the realm of Schumpeterian models. Joseph Schumpeter characterized the process of economic growth as one of *creative destruction*, meaning a process in which economic progress is driven by the prospect of monopoly profits and is accompanied by the destruction of existing productive units. Because of the replacement effect, it is often entrants, not incumbents, that undertake greater R&D for inventing and implementing process innovations. Consequently innovations displace incumbents and destroy their rents. According to Schumpeter, this process of creative destruction is the essence of the capitalist economic system. Chapter 14 shows that the process of creative destruction can be the engine of economic growth as well.

In addition to providing an interesting description of the process of economic growth and highlighting the importance of the market structure, creative destruction is important because it also brings political economy interactions to the fore of the question of economic growth. If economic growth takes place through creative destruction, it will create losers—in particular, the incumbents who are currently enjoying profits and rents. Since incumbents may be politically powerful, many economic systems may create powerful barriers against the process of economic growth. The political economy of growth is partly about understanding the opposition of certain firms, individuals, and groups to technological progress and whether this opposition will be successful.

There is another, perhaps more surprising, implication of the analysis in this section. This relates to *the business stealing effect,* which is closely related to the replacement effect. The entrant, by replacing the incumbent, is also stealing the business—profits—of the incumbent. The above discussion suggests that this business stealing effect helps to close the gap between the private and social values of innovation. It is also possible, however, for the business stealing effect to lead to excessive innovation by the entrant. To see the possibility of excessive innovation, let us first look at the total surplus gain from an innovation starting with the monopolist. To simplify the discussion, suppose that the innovation is drastic, so that if the entrant undertakes this innovation, it can set the unconstrained monopoly price p^M in (12.2). Therefore the social value of innovation is $\widehat{S}_1^I$, as given by (12.5).

Proposition 12.4   *It is possible that $\widehat{S}_1^I < \hat{\pi}_1^I$. Thus the entrant may have excessive incentives to innovate.*

Proof.   See Exercise 12.8.   ∎

Intuitively, the social planner values the profits made by the monopolist, since these are part of the producer surplus. In contrast, the entrant only values the profits that it will make if it undertakes the innovation. This is the essence of the business stealing effect and creates the possibility of excessive innovations. This result is important because it points out that, in general, it is not clear whether the equilibrium involves too little or too much innovation. Whether or not it does so depends on how strong the business stealing effect is relative to the appropriability effect discussed in Section 12.3.3.

12.4   The Dixit-Stiglitz Model and Aggregate Demand Externalities

The analysis in Section 12.3 focused on the private and the social values of innovations in a partial equilibrium setting. Growth theory is largely about general equilibrium models of innovation. Such models require a tractable framework of industry equilibrium, which can then be embedded in a general equilibrium framework. The most widely used model of industry equilibrium is the one developed by Dixit and Stiglitz (1977) and Spence (1976), which captures many of the key features of Chamberlin's (1933) discussion of monopolistic competition. Chamberlin (1933) suggested that a good approximation to the market structure of many industries is one in which each firm faces a downward-sloping demand curve (and thus has some degree of monopoly power), but there is also free entry into the industry, so that each firm (or at the very least, the marginal firm) makes zero profits.

The Dixit-Stiglitz model not only formalizes Chamberlin's account but also allows us to specify a structure of preferences that leads to constant monopoly markups. This feature turns out to be very convenient in many growth models, though it also implies that this model may not be particularly well suited to situations in which market structure and competition affect markups.

12.4.1   The Dixit-Stiglitz Model with a Finite Number of Products

Consider a static economy that admits a representative household with preferences given by

$$U(c_1, \ldots, c_N, y) = u(C, y), \tag{12.7}$$

where

$$C \equiv \left(\sum_{i=1}^{N} c_i^{\frac{\varepsilon-1}{\varepsilon}} \right)^{\frac{\varepsilon}{\varepsilon-1}} \tag{12.8}$$

is a consumption index of N differentiated varieties $c_1, \ldots, c_N$, of a particular good, and y stands for a generic good, representing all other consumption. The function $u(\cdot, \cdot)$ is strictly increasing, differentiable in both of its arguments, and jointly strictly concave. The parameter ε in (12.8) represents the elasticity of substitution between the differentiated varieties, and we assume that $\varepsilon > 1$. The key feature of (12.8) is that it features *love-for-variety*, meaning that the greater is the number of differentiated varieties that the individual consumes, the higher is his utility. The aggregator over the different consumption varieties in (12.8) appears in many different models of technological change and economic growth in the remainder of the book. I refer to it as a "Dixit-Stiglitz aggregator" or "CES aggregator" (where "CES" stands for constant elasticity of substitution).

To see the love-for-variety feature, consider the case in which

$$c_1 = \cdots = c_N = \frac{\bar{C}}{N},$$

so that the household purchases a total of $\bar{C}$ units of differentiated varieties, distributed equally across all N varieties. Substituting this equation into (12.7) and (12.8), we obtain

$$U\left(\frac{\bar{C}}{N}, \ldots, \frac{\bar{C}}{N}, y\right) = u\left(N^{\frac{1}{\varepsilon-1}}\bar{C}, y\right),$$

which is strictly increasing in N (since $\varepsilon > 1$) and implies that for a fixed total $\bar{C}$ units of differentiated commodities, the larger is the number of varieties over which this total number of units are distributed, the higher is utility. This property is the essence of the love-for-variety utility function. What makes this utility function convenient is not only this feature, but also the fact that it yields isoelastic demands. To derive the demand for individual varieties, let us normalize the price of the y good to 1 and denote the price of variety i by p_i and the total income of the household by m (in terms of good y). Then the budget constraint of the individual takes the form

$$\sum_{i=1}^{N} p_i c_i + y \leq m. \tag{12.9}$$

The maximization of (12.7) subject to (12.9) implies the following first-order condition between varieties:

$$\left(\frac{c_i}{c_{i'}}\right)^{-\frac{1}{\varepsilon}} = \frac{p_i}{p_{i'}} \quad \text{for any } i, i'.$$

Next let P denote the *ideal price index,* that is, the price index corresponding to the consumption index C. This price index is defined such that the following first-order condition for the consumption index holds:

$$\left(\frac{c_i}{C}\right)^{-\frac{1}{\varepsilon}} = \frac{p_i}{P} \quad \text{for } i = 1, \ldots, N \tag{12.10}$$

(see Exercise 12.10). Equation (12.10) then gives the ideal price index as

$$P \equiv \left(\sum_{i=1}^{N} p_i^{1-\varepsilon}\right)^{\frac{1}{1-\varepsilon}}. \tag{12.11}$$

In many circumstances, it is convenient to choose this ideal price index as the numeraire. Note, however, that we cannot use (12.11) as the numeraire index in this particular instance, since the budget constraint is already written with good y as the numeraire. The choice between C and y is straightforward in this case and boils down to the maximization of the utility function $u(C, y)$ subject to the budget constraint

$$PC + y \leq m, \tag{12.12}$$

which combines (12.10) and (12.11) with (12.9), to obtain a budget constraint expressed in terms of C and y. This maximization yields the intuitive first-order condition

$$\frac{\partial u(C, y)/\partial y}{\partial u(C, y)/\partial C} = \frac{1}{P},$$

which assumes that the solution is interior, an assumption I maintain throughout this section to simplify the discussion. The strict joint concavity of u, combined with the budget constraint, implies that this first-order condition can be expressed as

$$y = g(P, m) \text{ and } C = \frac{m - g(P, m)}{P}, \tag{12.13}$$

for some function $g(\cdot, \cdot)$.

Next let us consider the production of the varieties. Suppose that each variety can only be produced by a single firm, which is thus an effective monopolist for this particular commodity. Also assume that all monopolists maximize profits (and are owned by the representative household).

Recall that the marginal cost of producing each of these varieties is constant and equal to ψ. Let us first write down the profit maximization problem of one of these monopolists:

$$\max_{p_i \geq 0} \left(\left(\frac{p_i}{P} \right)^{-\varepsilon} C \right) (p_i - \psi), \tag{12.14}$$

where the term in the first parentheses is c_i (recall (12.10)) and the second is the difference between price and marginal cost. The complication in this problem comes from the fact that P and C are potentially functions of p_i. However for N sufficiently large, the effect of p_i on these quantities can be ignored and the solution to this maximization problem becomes very simple (see Exercise 12.11). This simplification enables us to derive the profit-maximizing price in the form of a constant markup over marginal cost:

$$p_i = p = \frac{\varepsilon}{\varepsilon - 1} \psi \quad \text{for each } i = 1, \ldots, N. \tag{12.15}$$

This result follows because when the effect of firm i's price choice on P and C is ignored, the demand function facing the firm, (12.10), is isoelastic with an elasticity $\varepsilon > 1$. Since each firm charges the same price, the ideal price index P can be computed as

$$P = N^{-\frac{1}{\varepsilon-1}} \frac{\varepsilon}{\varepsilon - 1} \psi. \tag{12.16}$$

Using (12.16), the profits for each firm are obtained as

$$\pi_i = \pi = N^{-\frac{\varepsilon}{\varepsilon-1}} C \frac{1}{\varepsilon - 1} \psi \quad \text{for each } i = 1, \ldots, N.$$

Profits are decreasing in the price elasticity for the usual reasons. In addition, profits are increasing in C, which is a measure of total demand for these differentiated goods, and they are decreasing in N, since, for given C, a larger number of varieties means less spending on each variety.

Despite this last effect, the total impact of N on profits can be positive. To see this, let us substitute for P from (12.16) into (12.13) to obtain

$$C = N^{\frac{1}{\varepsilon-1}} \frac{\varepsilon-1}{\varepsilon\psi} \left(m - g\left(N^{-\frac{1}{\varepsilon-1}} \frac{\varepsilon}{\varepsilon-1} \psi, m \right) \right),$$

and

$$\pi = \frac{1}{\varepsilon N} \left(m - g\left(N^{-\frac{1}{\varepsilon-1}} \frac{\varepsilon}{\varepsilon-1} \psi, m \right) \right).$$

It can be verified that depending on the form of the $g(\cdot)$ function in (12.13), which in turn depends on the shape of the utility function u in (12.7), profits can be increasing in the number of varieties (see Exercise 12.12). This result may at first appear somewhat surprising: typically we expect a greater number of competitors to reduce profits. But the love-for-variety effect embedded in the Dixit-Stiglitz preferences creates a countervailing effect, potentially increasing demand. This is often referred to as an "aggregate demand externality" in the macroeconomics literature. The basic idea is that a higher N raises the utility from consuming each of the varieties because of the love-for-variety effect. It constitutes an "externality" because the impact of a new variety (or the impact of the increase in the production of a particular variety) on the demand for other varieties corresponds to a pecuniary externality. This pecuniary externality can have first-order welfare effects because markets are no longer competitive and complete (and the First Welfare Theorem no longer applies). This idea plays an important role in many of the models of endogenous technological change, and we will encounter it again in models of poverty traps in Chapter 21.

12.4.2 The Dixit-Stiglitz Model with a Continuum of Products

As discussed in the Section 12.4.1 and analyzed further in Exercise 12.12, when N is finite, the equilibrium in which each firm charges the price given by (12.15) may be viewed as an approximation (where each firm has only a small effect on the ideal price index and thus ignores this effect). An alternative modeling assumption would be to assume that there is a continuum of varieties. When there is a continuum of varieties, (12.15) is no longer an approximation. Moreover such a model will be more tractable, because the number of firms N need not be a natural number. For this reason, the version of the Dixit-Stiglitz model with a continuum of products is often used in the literature and is also used in the rest of this book.

This version of the model is very similar to the one discussed in Section 12.4.1, except that the utility function of the representative household now takes the form

$$U\left([c_i]_{i\in[0,N]}, y \right) = u(C, y),$$

where

$$C \equiv \left(\int_0^N c_i^{\frac{\varepsilon-1}{\varepsilon}} di \right)^{\frac{\varepsilon}{\varepsilon-1}},$$

and N denotes the measure of varieties. The budget constraint facing the representative household is

$$\int_0^N p_i c_i di + y \leq m.$$

An identical analysis to that in Section 12.4.1 leads to the utility-maximizing decisions given by (12.10) and to the ideal price index

$$P = \left(\int_0^N p_i^{1-\varepsilon} di \right)^{\frac{1}{1-\varepsilon}}.$$

The budget constraint is again given by (12.12). Equation (12.13) then determines y and C. Since the supplier of each variety is infinitesimal, their price has no effect on P and C. Consequently, the profit-maximizing pricing decision in (12.15) applies exactly, and each firm has profits given by

$$\pi = \frac{1}{\varepsilon N} \left(m - g \left(N^{-\frac{1}{\varepsilon-1}} \frac{\varepsilon}{\varepsilon - 1} \psi, m \right) \right),$$

where $g(\cdot)$ is defined in (12.13).

Using this expression, the entry margin can also be endogenized. Imagine, for example, that there is an infinite number of potential different varieties, and a particular firm can adopt one of these varieties at some fixed cost $\mu > 0$ and enter the market. Consequently, as in Chamberlin's (1933) model of monopolistic competition, the following free-entry condition has to hold for all entrants:

$$\frac{1}{\varepsilon N} \left(m - g \left(N^{-\frac{1}{\varepsilon-1}} \frac{\varepsilon}{\varepsilon - 1} \psi, m \right) \right) = \mu, \tag{12.17}$$

and because all firms are ex ante identical, they all make zero profits.

As discussed in the next chapter, there is an intimate link between entry by new products (firms) and technological change. Leaving a detailed discussion of this connection to the next chapter, here we can ask a simpler question: do the aggregate demand externalities imply that there is too little entry? The answer is not necessarily. While the aggregate demand externalities imply that firms do not take into account the positive benefits their entry creates on other firms, the business stealing effect identified in Section 12.3.4 is still present and implies that entry may also reduce the demand for existing products. Thus, in general, whether there is too little or too much entry in models of product differentiation depends on the details of the model and the values of the parameters (see Exercise 12.13).

12.4.3 Objectives of Monopolistic Firms

It is useful to briefly discuss the objectives of monopolistically competitive firms. Throughout this section, I follow the industrial organization and the growth literatures and assume that all firms maximize profits, even when they are owned by a representative household. One may object to this assumption, noting that, since this economy is monopolistically competitive and the First Welfare Theorem does not hold, the representative household might be made better off if firms pursued a non-profit-maximizing strategy. However, profit maximization is still the right objective function for firms, because an allocation in which firms do not maximize profits (and instead act in the way that a social planner would like them to act) cannot be an equilibrium. To see this, note that the representative household itself takes prices as given—for example, it represents a large number of identical price-taking households. If some firms did not maximize profits, then the households would refuse to hold the stocks of these firms in their portfolios, and there would be entry by other profit-maximizing firms instead. Thus as long as the representative household or the set of households on the consumer side act as price takers (as has been assumed to be the case throughout), profit maximization is the only consistent strategy for the monopolistically competitive firms.

The only caveat to this arises from a different type of deviation on the production side. In particular, a single firm may buy all monopolistically competitive firms and act as the single producer in the economy. This firm might then ensure an allocation that makes the representative household better off relative to the equilibrium allocation considered here (while also increasing its profits). Nevertheless, I ignore this type of deviation for two reasons. First, as usual we are taking the market structure as given, and the market structure here is monopolistic competition, not pure monopoly (by a single firm). A single firm owning all production units would correspond to an entirely different market structure, with much less realism and relevance to the issues studied here. Second, different firms typically specialize in different sectors of the economy, and it is generally impossible for a single monopolist to operate all of the economic activities at once. Finally, in a related model, Acemoglu and Zilibotti (1997) show that a single firm owning all production units cannot be an equilibrium in the presence of free entry. This issue is discussed further at the end of Chapter 17. Given these considerations, throughout the book I assume that firms are profit maximizing.

12.4.4 Limit Prices in the Dixit-Stiglitz Model

We have already encountered how limit prices can arise in Section 12.3, when process innovations are nondrastic relative to the existing technology. Another reason limit prices can arise is because of the presence of a competitive fringe of firms that can imitate the technology of monopolists. Such a competitive fringe is straightforward to incorporate into the Dixit-Stiglitz model and will be useful in later chapters as a way of parameterizing competitive pressures.

Let us assume that there is a large number of fringe firms that can imitate the technology of the incumbent monopolists. Suppose that this imitation is equivalent to the production of a similar good and is not precluded by patents. It may be reasonable to assume that the imitating firms will be less efficient than those who have invented the variety in question and produced it for a while. A simple way of capturing this would be to assume that while the monopolist creates a new variety by paying the fixed cost μ and then having access to a technology with the marginal cost of production of ψ, the fringe firms do not pay any fixed costs but can only produce with a marginal cost of $\gamma\psi$, where $\gamma > 1$.

Similar to the analysis in the Section 12.3, if $\gamma \geq \varepsilon/(\varepsilon - 1)$, then the fringe firms are sufficiently unproductive that they cannot profitably produce even when the monopolists charge the unconstrained monopoly price given in (12.15). Instead, when $\gamma < \varepsilon/(\varepsilon - 1)$, the monopolists are forced to charge a limit price. The same arguments as in the Section 12.3 establish that this limit price must take the form

$$p = \gamma\psi < \frac{\varepsilon}{\varepsilon - 1}\psi.$$

It is then straightforward to see that the entry condition that determines the number of varieties in the market changes to

$$\frac{(\gamma - 1)}{\gamma N} \left(m - g \left(N^{-\frac{1}{\varepsilon-1}} \gamma \psi, m \right) \right) = \mu.$$

12.4.5 Limitations

The most important limitation of the Dixit-Stiglitz model is the feature that makes it tractable: the constancy of markups as in (12.15). In particular, the model implies that the markup of each firm is independent of the number of varieties in the market. But this is a very special feature. Most industrial organization models imply that markups over marginal cost decline in the number of competing products (see, e.g., Exercise 12.14). While plausible, this property makes endogenous growth models less tractable, because in many classes of models, endogenous technological change corresponds to a steady increase in the number of products N. If markups decline toward zero as N increases, the process of innovation would ulitmately stop, and thus sustained economic growth would be impossible. The alternative would be to have a model in which some other variable, perhaps capital, simultaneously increases the potential markups that firms can charge. While such models can be developed, they are more difficult to analyze than the standard Dixit-Stiglitz setup. For this reason, the literature typically focuses on Dixit-Stiglitz specifications.

12.5 Individual R&D Uncertainty and the Stock Market

The final issue I discuss in this chapter involves uncertainty in the research process. As discussed at the beginning of the chapter, it is reasonable to presume that the output of research will be uncertain. Thus individual firms undertaking research face a stochastic revenue stream. When individuals are risk averse, there perhaps should be a risk premium associated with such stochastic streams of income. This is not necessarily the case, however, when the following three conditions are satisfied:

1. there are many firms involved in research;
2. the realization of the uncertainty across firms is independent; and
3. households and firms have access to a "stock market," where each consumer can hold a *balanced portfolio* of various research firms.

In many of the models presented in the next two chapters, firms face uncertainty (e.g., regarding whether their R&D will be successful or how long their monopoly position will last), but the three conditions outlined here are satisfied. In this case, even though each firm's revenue is risky, the balanced portfolio held by the representative household has deterministic returns. Here I illustrate this with a simple example.

Example 12.2 *Suppose that the representative household has a utility function over consumption given by $u(c)$, where $u(\cdot)$ is strictly increasing, differentiable, strictly concave (so that the household is risk averse), and satisfies $\lim_{c \to 0} u'(c) = \infty$. The household starts with an endowment equal to $y > 0$. This endowment can be consumed, or it can be invested in a risky R&D project. Imagine that the R&D project is successful with probability p and will have a return equal to $1 + R > 1/p$ per unit of investment. It is unsuccessful with probability $1 - p$, in which case it will have zero return. When this project is the only one available, the* *household would be facing consumption risk if it invested in this project. In particular, the maximization problem that determines how much it should invest is a solution to the following expected utility maximization:*

$$\max_{x\in[0,y]} (1-p)u(y-x) + pu(y+Rx).$$

The first-order condition of this problem implies that the optimal amount of investment in the risky research activity is given by

$$\frac{u'(y-x)}{u'(y+Rx)} = \frac{pR}{1-p}.$$

The assumption $\lim_{c\to 0} u'(c) = \infty$ implies that $x < y$; thus less than the full endowment of the individual will be invested in the research activity, even though this project has positive expected returns. Intuitively, the household requires a risk premium to bear the consumption risk associated with the risky investment.

Next imagine a situation in which many different firms can invest in similar risky research ventures. Suppose that the success or failure of each project is independent of the others. Imagine that the household invests an amount x/N in each of N projects. The Strong Law of Large Numbers implies that as $N \to \infty$, a fraction p of these projects will be successful, and the remaining fraction $1 - p$ will be unsuccessful. Therefore the household receives (almost surely) a utility of

$$u(y + (p(1+R) - 1)x).$$

Since $1 + R > 1/p$, this is strictly increasing in x and implies that the household prefers to invest all of its endowment in the risky projects, that is, $x = y$. Therefore the ability to hold a balanced portfolio of projects with independently distributed returns allows the household to diversify the risks and act in a risk-neutral manner.

A similar logic applies in many of the models presented in the remainder of the book; even though individual firms have stochastic returns, the representative household holds a balanced portfolio of all the firms in the economy and diversifies idiosyncratic risks. This observation also implies that the objective of each firm is to maximize expected profits (without a risk premium).

12.6 Taking Stock

This chapter has reviewed several conceptual and modeling issues related to the economics of R&D. I discussed why ex post monopoly power is important in creating incentives for innovation, how innovation incentives differ between competitive firms and monopolies, and how these compare to the social value of innovation. In this context, I emphasized the importance of the appropriability effect, which implies that the private value of innovation often falls short of its social value, because even with ex post monopoly power, an innovating firm is not able to appropriate the entire consumer surplus created by a better product or a cheaper process. I also discussed Arrow's replacement effect, which implies that incumbent monopolists typically have weaker incentives for innovation than do entrants. Despite the appropriability effect, the amount of innovation in equilibrium can be excessive, because of another, countervailing, force: the business stealing effect, which encourages firms to undertake innovations to become the new monopolist and take over ("steal") the monopoly rents. Therefore, whether there is too little or too much innovation in equilibrium depends on the market structure and the parameters of the model.

This chapter has also introduced the Dixit-Stiglitz model, which plays an important role in the analysis of the next few chapters. This model offers a simple formalization of Chamberlin's approach to monopolistic competition, in which each firm has some monopoly power, but free entry ensures that all firms (or the marginal entrants) make zero profits. The Dixit-Stiglitz model is particularly tractable, because the markup charged by monopolists is independent of the number of competing firms. This property makes it an ideal model to study endogenous growth, because it enables innovation to remain profitable even when the number of products (or the number of machines) increases continuously.

12.7 References and Literature

The literature on R&D in industrial organization is vast. My purpose in this chapter has not been to review this literature but to highlight the salient features that are used in the remainder of the book. The reader who is interested in this area can start with Tirole (1988, Chapter 10), which contains an excellent discussion of the contrast between the private and the social values of innovation. A more up-to-date reference that surveys the recent developments in the economics of innovation is Scotchmer (2005).

The classic reference on the private and social values of innovation is Arrow (1962). Schumpeter (1934) was the first to emphasize the role of monopoly in R&D and innovation. The importance of monopoly power for innovation and the implications of the nonrival nature of ideas are discussed in Romer (1990, 1993). Most of the industrial organization literature also emphasizes the importance of ex post monopoly power and patent systems in providing incentives for innovation. See, for example, Scotchmer (2005). This perspective has recently been criticized by Boldrin and Levine (2003).

The idea of creative destruction was also originally developed by Schumpeter (1942). Models of creative destruction in the industrial organization literature include Reinganum (1981, 1985). Similar models in the growth literature are developed in Aghion and Howitt (1992, 1998).

Chamberlin (1933) is the classic reference on monopolistic competition. The so-called Dixit-Stiglitz model is developed in Dixit and Stiglitz (1977) and in Spence (1976). This model was first used for an analysis of R&D in Dasgupta and Stiglitz (1980). An excellent exposition of the Dixit-Stiglitz model is provided in Matsuyama (1995). Tirole (1988) also discusses the Dixit-Stiglitz model as well as other models of product innovation, including Salop's (1979) model, which is presented in Exercise 12.14.

A stimulating general discussion of issues of innovation and the importance of market size and profit incentives is provided in Schmookler (1966). Recent evidence on the effect of market size and profit incentives on innovation is discussed in Newell, Jaffee, and Stavins (1999); Popp (2002); Finkelstein (2004); and Acemoglu and Linn (2004).

Mokyr (1990) contains an excellent history of innovation. Freeman (1982) also provides a survey of the qualitative literature on innovation and discusses the different types of innovation.

The rest of this part of the book, like this chapter, focuses on monopolistic environments, in which the appropriate equilibrium concept is not the competitive equilibrium but one that incorporates game-theoretic interactions. Since all games in this book have complete information, the appropriate notion of equilibrium is the standard Nash Equilibrium concept, or when the game is multistage or dynamic, it is the Subgame Perfect Equilibrium or the Markov Perfect Equilibrium. In these situations, equilibrium always refers to Nash, Subgame Perfect, or Markov Perfect Equilibrium. The treatment here presumes that the reader is familiar with these concepts. A quick introduction to the necessary game theory is provided in the Appendix of Tirole (1988), and a more detailed treatment can be found in Myerson (1991), Fudenberg and Tirole (1994), and Osborne and Rubinstein (1994). A brief overview of dynamic (infinite-horizon) games is provided in Appendix C.

12.8   Exercises

12.1   Derive (12.2).

12.2   Prove Proposition 12.1. In particular, do the following.

(a) Show that even if $p^M = \psi$, the unique (Nash) equilibrium involves $q_1 = D(p^M)$ and $q_j = 0$ for all $j > 1$. Why?

(b) Show that when $p^M > \psi$, any price $p_1 > \psi$ or $p_1 < \psi$ cannot be profit-maximizing. Show that there cannot be an equilibrium in which $p_1 = \psi$ and $q_j > 0$ for some $j > 1$ [Hint: find a profitable deviation for firm 1.]

(c) Prove that $\hat{\pi}_1^I > \pi_1^I$.

12.3   Derive (12.5). Using these relationships, prove Proposition 12.2.

12.4   Prove that if $\hat{\pi}_1^I > 0$, then $\widehat{\mathcal{S}}_1^I > 0$ (where these terms are defined in Proposition 12.2).

12.5   Consider the model in Section 12.3, and suppose that there is no patent protection for the innovating firm. The firm can undertake two different types of innovations at the same cost μ. The first is a general technological improvement, which can be copied by all firms. It reduces the marginal cost of production to $\lambda^{-1}\psi$. The second is specific to the needs of the current firm and cannot be copied by others. It reduces the marginal cost of production by $\lambda' < \lambda$. Show that the firm would never adopt the λ technology but may adopt λ' technology. Calculate the difference in the social values generated by these two technologies.

12.6   Prove Proposition 12.3. In particular, verify that the conclusion is also true with limit pricing, that is, $\Delta\hat{\pi}_1^I < \pi_1^I$.

12.7   Consider the model in Section 12.3 with an incumbent monopolist and an entrant. Suppose that the cost of innovation for the incumbent is μ, while for the entrant it is $\chi\mu$, where $\chi \geq 1$. Show that there exists $\bar{\chi} > 1$ such that if $\chi < \bar{\chi}$, the entrant has greater innovation incentives, and if $\chi > \bar{\chi}$, the incumbent has greater innovation incentives. What is the effect of the elasticity of demand on the relative innovation incentives of the incumbent and the entrant? Provide an intuition for this effect.

12.8   (a) Prove Proposition 12.4 by providing an example in which there are excessive innovation incentives.

(b) What factors make excessive innovation more likely?

12.9   The discussion in the text presumed a particular form of patent policy, which provided ex post monopoly power to the innovator. An alternative intellectual property rights policy is licensing: firms that have made an innovation can license the rights to use this innovation to others. This exercise asks you to work through the implications of this type of licensing. Throughout, think of the licensing stage as follows: the innovator can make a take-it-or-leave-it-offer to one or many firms so that they can buy the rights to use the innovation (and produce as many units of the output as they like) in return for some licensing fee ν. Consider a competitive environment, and show that if firm 1 is allowed to license its innovation to others, this can never raise its profits and can never increase its incentives to undertake the innovation. Provide an intuition for this result.

Now modify the model, so that each firm has a strictly convex and increasing cost of producing, $\psi_1(q)$, and also has to pay a fixed cost of $\psi_0 > 0$ to be active (so that the average costs take the familiar inverted U shape). Show that licensing can be beneficial for firm 1 in this case and therefore increase innovation incentives. Explain why the results differ between the two cases.

12.10 Derive the expression for the ideal price index, (12.11), from (12.10) and the definition of the consumption index C.

12.11 Consider the maximization problem in (12.14) and write down the first-order conditions, taking into account the impact of p_i on P and C. Show that as $N \to \infty$, the solution to this problem converges to (12.15).

12.12 In the Dixit-Stiglitz model in Section 12.4.1, determine the conditions on the function $u(\cdot, \cdot)$ in (12.7) such that an increase in N raises the profits of a monopolist.

12.13 Suppose that $U(C, y) = C + v(y)$, where $v(y) = y^{1-\alpha}/(1 - \alpha)$ with $\alpha \in (0, 1)$. Suppose also that new varieties can be introduced at the fixed cost μ.

(a) Consider the allocation determined by a social planner who also controls prices. Characterize the number of varieties that a social planner would choose to maximize the utility of the representative household in this case.

(b) Suppose that prices are given by (12.15). Characterize the number of varieties that the social planner would choose to maximize the utility of the representative household in this case.

(c) Characterize the equilibrium number of varieties (at which all monopolistically competitive variety producers make zero profits) and compare this number with the answers to the previous two parts. Explain the sources of differences between the equilibrium and the social planner's solution in each case.

12.14 This exercise asks you to work through the Salop (1979) model of product differentiation, which differs from the Dixit-Stiglitz model in that equilibrium markups are declining in the number of firms. Imagine that consumers are located uniformly around a circle with perimeter equal to 1. The circle indexes both the preferences of heterogeneous consumers and the types of goods. The point where the consumer is located along the circle corresponds to the type of product that he most prefers. When a consumer at point x around the circle consumes a good of type z, his utility is $R - t \, |z - x| - p$, while if he chooses not to consume, his utility is 0. Here R can be thought of as the reservation utility of the individual, while t parameterizes the "transport" costs that the individual has to pay in order to consume a good that is away from his ideal point along the circle. Suppose that each firm has a marginal cost of ψ per unit of production.

(a) Imagine a consumer at point x, with the two neighboring firms at points $z_1 > x > z_2$. As long as the prices of these firms are not much higher than those farther away, the consumer will buy from one of these two firms. Denote the prices of these two firms by p_1 and p_2. Show that the price difference that would make the consumer indifferent between purchasing from the two firms satisfies $p_1 - p_2 = (2x - z_1 - z_2)t$, with $t(z_1 - x) + p_1 \leq R$.

(b) Suppose that p_1 and p_2 satisfy the above relationships. Then show that all $x' \in [z_2, x)$ strictly prefer to buy from firm 2, and all $x' \in (x, z_1]$ strictly prefer to buy from firm 1.

(c) Now assume that there are three firms along the circle at locations $z_1 > z_2 > z_3$. Show that firm 2's profits are given by

$$\pi_2(p_1, p_2, p_3 \mid z_1, z_2, z_3) = (p_2 - \psi) \left(\frac{p_1 - p_2}{2t} + \frac{z_1 - z_2}{2} + \frac{p_3 - p_2}{2t} + \frac{z_2 - z_3}{2} \right),$$

and calculate its profit-maximizing price.

(d) Suppose that $p_1 = p_3$. Show that firm 2 would like to locate half way between z_1 and z_3. Prove that an equilibrium with N firms charging the same price must have the distance between any two firms equal to $1/N$.

(e) Show that when there are N equidistant firms, it is an equilibrium for all firms to charge $p = \psi + t/N$. Explain why the markup here is a decreasing function of the number of firms, whereas it was independent of the number of firms in the Dixit-Stiglitz model.

13

Expanding Variety Models

The simplest models of endogenous technological change are those in which R&D expands the variety of inputs or machines used in production. This chapter focuses on models with expanding input varieties; research leads to the creation of new varieties of inputs (machines), and a greater variety of inputs increases the "division of labor," raising the productivity of final good firms (Romer, 1987, 1990). This dynamic can therefore be viewed as a form of process innovation. An alternative, formulated and studied by Grossman and Helpman (1991a,b), focuses on product innovation. In this model, research leads to the invention of new goods, and because households have love-for-variety preferences, they derive greater utility when they consume a greater variety of products. Consequently "real" income increases as a result of these product innovations. Models of product innovation have a mathematical structure very similar to the models of process innovation with expanding input variety and will be discussed at the end of the chapter.

In all of these models, and also in the models of quality competition in the next chapter, I use the Dixit-Stiglitz constant elasticity structure introduced in the Chapter 12.

13.1 The Lab-Equipment Model of Growth with Input Varieties

An important element of all endogenous technology models is the innovation possibilities frontier (R&D technology). Let us start with a particular version of the endogenous growth model with expanding varieties of inputs and an R&D technology that only uses output for creating new inputs. This model is sometimes referred to as the "lab-equipment" model, since all that is required for research is investment in equipment or laboratories—rather than the employment of skilled or unskilled workers or scientists.

13.1.1 Demographics, Preferences, and Technology

Imagine an infinite-horizon economy in continuous time admitting a representative household with preferences

$$\int_0^\infty \exp(-\rho t) \frac{C(t)^{1-\theta} - 1}{1-\theta} dt. \tag{13.1}$$

There is no population growth, and the total population of workers, L, supplies labor inelastically. As discussed in the previous chapter, the representative household owns a balanced portfolio of all firms in the economy.

The unique final good is produced competitively with the production function

$$Y(t) = \frac{1}{1-\beta} \left(\int_0^{N(t)} x(v, t)^{1-\beta} dv \right) L^\beta, \tag{13.2}$$

where L is the aggregate labor input, $N(t)$ denotes the different number of varieties of inputs (machines) available to be used in the production process at time t, and $x(v, t)$ is the total amount of input of variety v used at time t. Let us assume that x depreciate fully after use; thus they can be interpreted as generic inputs, intermediate goods, machines, or even capital, as long as we are comfortable with the assumption that there is immediate depreciation. Throughout the chapter I refer to these inputs as "machines." The assumption that machines (or inputs) are "used up" in production or depreciate fully after being used ensures that the amounts (numbers) of these machines used in the past are not additional state variables. This assumption simplifies the exposition considerably (though the results are identical without this assumption; see Exercise 13.23).

The term $(1 - \beta)$ in the denominator is included for notational simplicity. Notice that for a given $N(t)$, which final good producers take as given, (13.2) exhibits constant returns to scale. Since some firms have monopoly power in this economy, Theorem 5.4 no longer applies, and we will not work with the aggregate production function of the entire economy. Nevertheless, since final good producers are competitive, there is no loss of generality in modeling the final good sector simply using the production function (13.2).

One can also write (13.2) in the following form:

$$Y(t) = \frac{1}{1-\beta} \tilde{\mathbf{X}}(t)^{1-\beta} L^\beta,$$

where

$$\tilde{\mathbf{X}}(t) \equiv \left(\int_0^{N(t)} x(v, t)^{\frac{\varepsilon_\beta - 1}{\varepsilon_\beta}} dv \right)^{\frac{\varepsilon_\beta}{\varepsilon_\beta - 1}},$$

with $\varepsilon_\beta \equiv 1/\beta$ as the elasticity of substitution between machines. This form emphasizes both the constant returns to scale properties of the production function and the continuity between the model here and the Dixit-Stiglitz model of the previous chapter. Throughout I normalize the price of the final good at each date to 1.

The resource constraint of the economy at time t is

$$C(t) + X(t) + Z(t) \le Y(t), \tag{13.3}$$

where $X(t)$ is spending on machines (the equivalent of "investment"), and $Z(t)$ is expenditure on R&D at time t.

Let us next turn to how machines are produced and how new machines are invented. Suppose that once the blueprint for a particular machine variety is invented, one unit of that machine can be produced at marginal cost equal to $\psi > 0$ units of the final good. The innovation possibilities frontier takes the form

$$\dot{N}(t) = \eta Z(t), \tag{13.4}$$

where $\eta > 0$, and the economy starts with some initial technology stock $N(0) > 0$. Equation (13.4) implies that greater spending on R&D leads to the invention of new machines. Throughout I assume that there is free entry into research, which means that any individual or firm can spend one unit of the final good at time t to generate a flow rate η of new blueprints. The firm that discovers a blueprint for a new machine receives a fully enforced perpetual patent on this machine variety. I also assume that the $N(0)$ initial varieties are supplied by monopolists with perpetual patents.

There is no aggregate uncertainty in the innovation process. Naturally there is idiosyncratic uncertainty, but with many different research labs undertaking such expenditures, at the aggregate level, (13.4) holds deterministically.

Given the patent structure specified above, a firm that invents a new machine variety v is the sole (monopolist) supplier of that machine variety and sets a price of $p^x(v, t)$ at time t to maximize profits. Since machines depreciate after use, $p^x(v, t)$ can also be interpreted as a rental price or the user cost of this machine.

The demand for machine variety v is obtained by maximizing net aggregate profits of the final good sector. Since machines depreciate after use and labor is hired on the spot market, the maximization problem of the final good sector can be considered for each point in time separately and simply requires the maximization of the instantaneous profits of a representative final good producer. These instantaneous profits can be obtained by subtracting total costs—the user costs of renting machines and the labor costs—from the value of production. Therefore the maximization problem at time t is

$$\max_{[x(v,t)]_{v \in [0, N(t)], L}} \frac{1}{1-\beta} \left(\int_0^{N(t)} x(v, t)^{1-\beta} dv \right) L^\beta - \int_0^{N(t)} p^x(v, t) x(v, t) dv - w(t) L.$$

$$(13.5)$$

The first-order condition of this maximization problem with respect to $x(v, t)$ for any $v \in [0, N(t)]$ yields the demand for machines from the final good sector. These demands take the following convenient isoelastic form:

$$x(v, t) = p^x(v, t)^{-1/\beta} L,$$

$$(13.6)$$

which is intuitive, since the elasticity of demand for different machine varieties is $\varepsilon_\beta \equiv 1/\beta$ (so that $x(v, t) = p^x(v, t)^{-\varepsilon_\beta} L$). Equation (13.6) implies that the demand for machines only depends on the user cost of the machine and on equilibrium labor supply, but not directly on the interest rate $r(t)$, the wage rate $w(t)$, or the total measure of available machines $N(t)$. This feature makes the model very tractable.

Next consider the (net present discounted) value of owning the blueprint of a machine of variety v. This value is

$$V(v, t) = \int_t^\infty \exp\left(-\int_t^s r(s') ds' \right) \pi(v, s) ds,$$

$$(13.7)$$

where

$$\pi(v, t) \equiv p^x(v, t) x(v, t) - \psi x(v, t)$$

denotes the profits of the monopolist producing machine ν at time t, $x(\nu, t)$ and $p^x(\nu, t)$ are the profit-maximizing choices for the monopolist, and $r(t)$ is the market interest rate at time t.[1] Alternatively, assuming that the value function is differentiable in time, this equation could be written in the form of a HJB equation as in Theorem 7.10 in Chapter 7:

$$r(t)V(\nu, t) - \dot{V}(\nu, t) = \pi(\nu, t). \tag{13.8}$$

Exercise 13.1 provides a different derivation of this equation than in Theorem 7.10.

13.1.2 Characterization of Equilibrium

An *allocation* in this economy is defined by the following objects: time paths of consumption levels, aggregate spending on machines, and aggregate R&D expenditure, $[C(t), X(t), Z(t)]_{t=0}^\infty$; time paths of available machine varieties, $[N(t)]_{t=0}^\infty$; time paths of prices and quantities of each machine, $[p^x(\nu, t), x(\nu, t)]_{\nu \in [0, N(t)], t=0}^\infty$; and time paths of interest rates and wage rates, $[r(t), w(t)]_{t=0}^\infty$.

An *equilibrium* is an allocation in which all monopolists (research firms) choose $[p^x(\nu, t), x(\nu, t)]_{\nu \in [0, N(t)], t=0}^\infty$ to maximize the discounted value of profits, the evolution of $[N(t)]_{t=0}^\infty$ is determined by free entry, the evolution of $[r(t), w(t)]_{t=0}^\infty$, is consistent with market clearing, and the evolution of $[C(t), X(t), Z(t)]_{t=0}^\infty$ is consistent with household maximization. Note that this equilibrium is not "competitive," since machine producers have market power.

Let us start with the firm side. Since (13.6) defines isoelastic demands, the solution to the maximization problem of any monopolist $\nu \in [0, N(t)]$ involves setting the same price in every period (see Exercise 13.2):

$$p^x(\nu, t) = \frac{\psi}{1 - \beta} \quad \text{for all } \nu \text{ and } t.$$

All monopolists thus charge a constant rental rate equal to a markup over their marginal cost of production, ψ. Let us normalize the marginal cost of machine production to $\psi \equiv (1 - \beta)$, so that

$$p^x(\nu, t) = p^x = 1 \quad \text{for all } \nu \text{ and } t. \tag{13.9}$$

Profit-maximization also implies that each monopolist rents out the same quantity of machines in every period, equal to

$$x(\nu, t) = L \quad \text{for all } \nu \text{ and } t. \tag{13.10}$$

This gives monopoly profits as

$$\pi(\nu, t) = \beta L \quad \text{for all } \nu \text{ and } t. \tag{13.11}$$

Equation (13.11) implies that each monopolist sells the same amount of machines, charges the same price, and makes the same amount of profits at all points in time.

---

1. As usual, the interest rate $r(t)$ is determined from the prices of (zero net supply) Arrow securities that households can trade to transfer consumption across dates. The aggregate economy can only transfer resources across dates by changing the stock of machine varieties, $N(t)$.

Substituting (13.6) and the machine prices into (13.2) yields a (derived) production function for the final good:

$$Y(t) = \frac{1}{1 - \beta} N(t)L. \qquad (13.12)$$

Equation (13.12) is one of the main equations of the expanding variety models. It shows that even though the aggregate production function exhibits constant returns to scale from the viewpoint of final good firms (which take $N(t)$ as given), there are increasing returns to scale for the entire economy. Moreover, (13.12) makes it clear that an increase in the variety of machines, $N(t)$, raises the productivity of labor and that when $N(t)$ increases at a constant rate so does output per capita.

The demand for labor from the final good sector follows from the first-order condition of maximizing (13.5) with respect to L and gives the equilibrium wage rate at time t as

$$w(t) = \frac{\beta}{1 - \beta} N(t). \qquad (13.13)$$

Finally, free entry into research implies

$$\eta V(v, t) \le 1, \quad Z(v, t) \ge 0, \quad \text{and} \quad (\eta V(v, t) - 1)Z(v, t) = 0 \quad \text{for all } v \text{ and } t, \qquad (13.14)$$

where $V(v, t)$ is given by (13.7). To understand (13.14), recall that one unit of final good spent on R&D leads to the invention of η units of new machines, each with a net present discounted value of profits given by (13.7). This free-entry condition is written in the complementary slackness form, since research may not be sufficiently profitable for there to be positive R&D. In this case, $\eta V(v, t)$ could be strictly less than 1. Nevertheless for the relevant parameter values there is positive R&D and economic growth (and technological *progress*), so I often simplify the exposition by writing the free-entry condition as

$$\eta V(v, t) = 1.$$

Note also that since each monopolist $v \in [0, N(t)]$ produces a total amount of machines given by (13.10) and there are $N(t)$ monopolists, the total expenditure on machines is

$$X(t) = (1 - \beta)N(t)L. \qquad (13.15)$$

Finally, the representative household's problem implies the usual Euler equation for consumption,

$$\frac{\dot{C}(t)}{C(t)} = \frac{1}{\theta}(r(t) - \rho), \qquad (13.16)$$

and the transversality condition,

$$\lim_{t \to \infty} \left[\exp\left(-\int_0^t r(s)\, ds\right) \int_0^{N(t)} V(v, t) dv \right] = 0, \qquad (13.17)$$

which is written in the market value form and requires the value of the total wealth of the representative household, which is equal to the value of corporate assets $\int_0^{N(t)} V(v, t)dv$, not to grow faster than the discount rate (see Exercise 13.3).

In light of the previous equations, an equilibrium can be defined more formally as time paths of consumption, expenditures, R&D decisions, and total number of machine varieties,

$[C(t), X(t), Z(t), N(t)]_{t=0}^{\infty}$, such that (13.3), (13.7), (13.14), (13.15), (13.16), and (13.17) are satisfied; time paths of prices and quantities of each machine, $[p^x(v, t), x(v, t)]_{v \in N(t), t=0}^{\infty}$, that satisfy (13.9) and (13.10); and time paths of interest rate and wages, $[r(t), w(t)]_{t=0}^{\infty}$, such that (13.13) and (13.16) hold.

A *balanced growth path (BGP)* is an equilibrium path where consumption $C(t)$ and output $Y(t)$ grow at a constant rate. Equation (13.12) then implies that $N(t)$ must also grow at a constant rate in a BGP. A BGP can alternatively be referred to as a "steady state," since it is a steady state in transformed variables (even though the original variables grow at a constant rate).

13.1.3 Balanced Growth Path

A BGP requires that consumption grows at a constant rate, say g_C^*. This is possible from (13.16) only if the interest rate is constant. Let us therefore look for an equilibrium allocation in which

$$r(t) = r^* \quad \text{for all } t,$$

where the asterisk ($*$) refers to BGP values. Since profits at each date are given by (13.11) and the interest rate is constant, (13.8) implies that $\dot{V}(t) = 0$. Substituting this in either (13.7) or in (13.8), we obtain

$$V^* = \frac{\beta L}{r^*}. \tag{13.18}$$

This equation is intuitive: a monopolist makes a flow profit of βL, and along the BGP this profit is discounted at the constant interest rate r^*.

Let us next suppose that the (free-entry) condition (13.14) holds as an equality, in which case we also have

$$\frac{\eta \beta L}{r^*} = 1.$$

This equation pins down the BGP interest rate r^* as

$$r^* = \eta \beta L.$$

The consumption Euler equation (13.16) then implies that the rate of growth of consumption in BGP must be given by

$$g_C^* = \frac{\dot{C}(t)}{C(t)} = \frac{1}{\theta}(r^* - \rho). \tag{13.19}$$

Moreover it can be verified that the current-value Hamiltonian for the representative household's maximization problem is concave. Thus this condition, together with the transversality condition, is sufficient to characterize the unique optimal consumption plan of the representative household (recall Theorem 7.14 in Chapter 7 and Exercise 8.11 in Chapter 8).

In a BGP, consumption cannot grow at a different rate than total output (see Exercise 13.6); thus the growth rate of output in the economy must be

$$g^* = g_C^*.$$

Given the BGP interest rate, the long-run growth rate of the economy is then obtained as

$$g^* = \frac{1}{\theta}(\eta\beta L - \rho). \tag{13.20}$$

Let us next assume that

$$\eta\beta L > \rho, \quad \text{and} \quad (1-\theta)\eta\beta L < \rho. \tag{13.21}$$

The first inequality ensures that $g^* > 0$, while the second one ensures that the representative household's utility is finite and the transversality condition is satisfied.

Proposition 13.1 *Suppose that condition (13.21) holds. Then in the above-described lab-equipment expanding input variety model, there exists a unique BGP in which technology, output, and consumption all grow at the same rate g^* given by (13.20).*

Proof. The preceding discussion establishes all the claims in the proposition except that the transversality condition holds. Exercise 13.4 verifies this and also shows that the resource constraint (13.3) is satisfied with positive consumption at all points. ∎

An important feature of this class of endogenous technological progress models is the presence of the scale effect, which was already discussed in Section 11.4 in the context of Romer's (1986a) model: the larger is L, the greater is the growth rate. The scale effect comes from a very strong form of the market size effect discussed in the previous chapter. The increasing returns to scale nature of the technology (e.g., as highlighted in (13.12)) is responsible for this strong form of the market size effect and thus for the scale effect. We will see in Section 15.5 that it is possible to have variants of the current model that feature the market size effect but not the scale effect.

13.1.4 Transitional Dynamics

It is straightforward to see that there are no transitional dynamics in this model. To derive this result, let us go back to the value function for each monopolist in (13.8). Substituting for profits from (13.11), noting that $V(\nu, t)$ is independent of ν, and denoting it by $V(t)$, this equation implies that

$$r(t)V(t) - \dot{V}(t) = \beta L.$$

The key observation is that positive growth of output at any point implies that $\eta V(t) = 1$ for all t. In other words, if $\eta V(t) = 1$ for $t \in (t' - \varepsilon, t' + \varepsilon)$ for some t' and $\varepsilon > 0$, then $\eta V(t) = 1$ for all t. Moreover, given (13.21), zero growth at all points is not possible and thus we must have $\eta V(t) = 1$ at least for some interval of time (see Exercise 13.5). Then differentiating $\eta V(t) = 1$ with respect to time yields $\dot{V}(t) = 0$ for all t, which is only consistent with $r(t) = r^*$ for all t, thus yielding

$$r(t) = \eta\beta L \quad \text{for all } t.$$

Proposition 13.2 *Suppose that condition (13.21) holds and that the initial technology stock is $N(0) > 0$. Then there exists a unique equilibrium path. In this equilibrium, technology, output, and consumption always grow at the rate g^*, as in (13.20).*

Proof. See Exercise 13.5. ∎

At some level, this result is not too surprising. The mathematical structure of the expanding variety model is similar to the AK model of Chapter 11 (as most clearly illustrated by the derived equation for aggregate output (13.12)). Consequently, as in the AK model, the economy always grows at a constant rate. Even though the mathematical structures of the two models are similar, the economics of the model presented here are very different. The equilibrium in Proposition 13.2 exhibits endogenous technological progress. In particular, research firms spend resources to invent new machines. They do so because, given their patents, they can profitably sell these machines to final good producers. It is thus profit incentives that drive R&D, and R&D drives economic growth. We have therefore arrived at our first model in which market-driven incentives determine the rate at which the technology possibilities of the economy evolve over time.

13.1.5   Pareto Optimal Allocations

The presence of monopolistic competition implies that the equilibrium is not necessarily Pareto optimal (and the First Welfare Theorem no longer applies). First, there is a markup over the marginal cost of production of machines. Second, the number of machines produced at any point in time may not be optimal. The first source of inefficiency is familiar from models of static monopoly, while the second emerges from the endogenous determination of the set of traded (Arrow-Debreu) commodities in this economy.[2]

To contrast the equilibrium and the Pareto optimal allocations, let us set up the optimal growth problem. The optimal growth path is a solution to the social planner's problem of maximizing the utility of the (normative) representative household, (13.1), subject to the resource constraint (13.3) and the innovation possibilities frontier (13.4), with an initial condition $N(0) > 0$. The social planner chooses $[x(v, t)]_{v \in [0, N(t)]}$ at each t and the time paths of $C(t)$, $Z(t)$, and $N(t)$. The resource constraint can be alternatively written as

$$C(t) + Z(t) \leq \frac{1}{1-\beta} \left(\int_0^{N(t)} x(v, t)^{1-\beta} dv \right) L^\beta - \int_0^{N(t)} \psi x(v, t) dv, \quad (13.22)$$

where the right-hand side is simply equal to net output, defined as $\tilde{Y}(t) \equiv Y(t) - X(t)$.

It is convenient to characterize the solution to the optimal growth problem in two steps. The first involves the characterization of the static allocation (for given $N(t)$). The second step then characterizes the optimal path of consumption $C(t)$ and the number of varieties, $N(t)$. The first step is equivalent to maximizing net output $\tilde{Y}(t)$ (i.e., the right-hand side of (13.22)). Maximization gives

$$x^S(v, t) = (1 - \beta)^{-1/\beta} L.$$

Substituting this equation into (13.2), we find the output level in the Pareto optimal allocation as

$$Y^S(t) = \frac{(1 - \beta)^{-(1-\beta)/\beta}}{1 - \beta} N^S(t) L$$

$$= (1 - \beta)^{-1/\beta} N^S(t) L,$$

---

2. The latter source of potential inefficiency relates to the issue of endogenously incomplete markets (there is no way to purchase a machine that is not supplied in equilibrium). Its role is clarified in Section 13.1.6. It is also discussed in greater detail in Section 17.6.

where superscript "S" is used to emphasize that the level of technology and thus the level of output differ between the social planner's and the equilibrium allocations. Net output $\tilde{Y}^S(t)$ can then be written as

$$\tilde{Y}^S(t) = (1-\beta)^{-1/\beta} N^S(t) L - \int_0^{N^S(t)} \psi x^S(v, t) dv$$

$$= (1-\beta)^{-1/\beta} N^S(t) L - (1-\beta)^{-(1-\beta)/\beta} N^S(t) L$$

$$= (1-\beta)^{-1/\beta} \beta N^S(t) L.$$

Given this expression and (13.4), the second step of the characterization of the optimal growth path takes the form (dropping the superscript S to simplify notation)

$$\max \int_0^\infty \exp(-\rho t) \frac{C(t)^{1-\theta} - 1}{1 - \theta} dt,$$

subject to

$$\dot{N}(t) = \eta[(1-\beta)^{-1/\beta} \beta N(t) L - C(t)].$$

In this problem, $N(t)$ is the state variable, and $C(t)$ is the control variable. Let us set up the current-value Hamiltonian as

$$\hat{H}(N, C, \mu) = \frac{C(t)^{1-\theta} - 1}{1 - \theta} + \mu(t)[\eta(1-\beta)^{-1/\beta} \beta N(t) L - \eta C(t)].$$

Once again using Theorem 7.13, a candidate solution to this problem is given by

$$\hat{H}_C(N, C, \mu) = C(t)^{-\theta} - \eta \mu(t) = 0,$$

$$\hat{H}_N(N, C, \mu) = \mu(t) \eta (1-\beta)^{-1/\beta} \beta L = \rho \mu(t) - \dot{\mu}(t),$$

$$\lim_{t \to \infty} [\exp(-\rho t) \mu(t) N(t)] = 0.$$

It can be easily verified that this current-value Hamiltonian is strictly concave and satisfies the conditions of Theorem 7.14. Therefore the above conditions uniquely characterize the optimal growth path (see Exercise 13.8).

Combining these conditions, we obtain the following growth rate for consumption in the optimal growth path (see again Exercise 13.8):

$$\frac{\dot{C}^S(t)}{C^S(t)} = \frac{1}{\theta}(\eta(1-\beta)^{-1/\beta} \beta L - \rho). \tag{13.23}$$

Like the equilibrium, the optimal growth allocation involves a constant rate of consumption growth (thus there are no transitional dynamics). This optimal growth rate of consumption, (13.23), can be directly compared to the growth rate in the decentralized equilibrium, (13.20). The comparison boils down to that of

$$(1-\beta)^{-1/\beta} \beta \quad \text{compared to } \beta.$$

The former is always greater, since $(1-\beta)^{-1/\beta} > 1$, so that the (Pareto) optimal growth rate is always greater than the equilibrium growth rate.

Proposition 13.3 *In the above-described expanding input variety model, the decentralized equilibrium is always Pareto suboptimal. Moreover, provided that $(1 - \theta)\eta(1 - \beta)^{-1/\beta}\beta L < \rho$, starting with any $N(0) > 0$, the Pareto optimal allocation involves a constant growth rate of*

$$g^S = \frac{1}{\theta}(\eta(1 - \beta)^{-1/\beta}\beta L - \rho),$$

which is strictly greater than the equilibrium growth rate g^* given in (13.20).

Proof.   See Exercises 13.9 and 13.10.   ∎

Intuitively, the Pareto optimal growth rate is greater than the equilibrium growth rate because of the greater social value of innovations. This greater social value stems from the fact that the Pareto optimal allocation involves no markups and thus uses the available set of machines more intensively. So the source of inefficiency in equilibrium is related to the pecuniary externality resulting from monopoly markups, which affect the set of traded commodities (and thus the rate of growth of machines and technology). Other models of endogenous technological progress incorporate technological spillovers and thus generate inefficiencies both because of the pecuniary externality isolated here and because of the technological spillovers.

13.1.6   Policy in Models of Endogenous Technological Progress

The divergence between the decentralized equilibrium and the Pareto optimal allocation introduces the possibility of Pareto improving policy interventions. There are two natural alternatives to consider:

1. *Subsidies to research:* by subsidizing research, the government can increase the growth rate of the economy, and this can be turned into a Pareto improvement if taxation is not distortionary (and in the presence of heterogeneity, if there is appropriate redistribution of resources so that all parties benefit).

2. *Subsidies to machines and/or inputs:* inefficiencies also arise because the decentralized economy is not using as many units of the machines and/or inputs (because of the monopoly markup), so subsidies to the use of machines by the final good sector would also increase the growth rate.

Moreover, as in the first-generation endogenous growth models, a variety of different policy interventions, including taxes on investment income and subsidies of various forms, have growth effects (rather than merely level effects; see, e.g., Exercise 13.12).

Naturally, once we start thinking of policy as potentially closing the gap between the decentralized equilibrium and the Pareto optimal allocation, we also have to consider the objectives of policy makers, and this brings us to issues of political economy, which are the subject matter of Part VIII. For that reason I do not present a detailed discussion of optimal policy (leaving some discussion to Exercises 13.11–13.13). Nevertheless it is useful to briefly discuss the role of competition policy in models of endogenous technological progress.

Recall that the profit-maximizing price that the monopolist charges for machines is $p^x = \psi/(1 - \beta)$. Imagine instead that a fringe of competitive firms can copy the innovation of any monopolist, but they are not able to produce at the same level of costs (because the inventor has more know-how). In particular, as in the previous chapter, suppose that instead of a marginal cost ψ, the fringe companies have marginal cost of $\gamma\psi$ with $\gamma > 1$. If $\gamma > 1/(1 - \beta)$, then this fringe is not a threat to the monopolist, since the monopolist could set its ideal, profit-maximizing, markup and the fringe would not be able to enter without making losses. However, if $\gamma < 1/(1 - \beta)$, then the fringe would prevent the monopolist from setting its ideal monopoly price. In particular, in this case the monopolist would be forced to set a limit price of

$$p^x = \gamma \psi, \tag{13.24}$$

which has an explanation identical to the limit price in the previous chapter.[3]

When the monopolist charges this limit price, its profits per unit would be

$$(\gamma - 1)\psi = (\gamma - 1)(1 - \beta),$$

which is less than monopoly profits per unit in the absence of a competitive fringe. What does this imply for economic growth? It is straightforward to see that in this case the economy would grow at a slower rate. For example, in the baseline model with the lab-equipment technology, this growth rate would be (see Exercise 13.14)

$$\hat{g} = \frac{1}{\theta}(\eta \gamma^{-1/\beta}(\gamma - 1)(1 - \beta)^{-(1-\beta)/\beta}L - \rho),$$

which is less than g^* given in (13.20). Therefore in this model greater competition, which reduces markups (and thus static distortions), also reduces long-run growth. This result might at first appear to be counterintuitive, since the monopoly markup may be thought to be the key source of inefficiency, and greater competition (lower γ) reduces this markup. Nevertheless as mentioned above, inefficiency results both because of monopoly markups and because the set of available machines may not be chosen appropriately. As γ declines, monopoly markups decline, but the problem of underprovision of machines becomes more severe. This is because when monopoly profits are reduced, incentives for research are also reduced. Since γ can also be interpreted as a parameter of antitrust (competition) policy, this result implies that in the baseline endogenous technological change models, stricter antitrust policy reduces economic growth.

Welfare is not the same as growth, and some degree of competition to reduce prices below the unconstrained monopolistic level might be useful for welfare, depending on the discount rate of the representative household. Essentially, with a lower markup, households will enjoy a higher level of consumption for a given level of N, but they will also suffer slower consumption growth (slower growth of N). The trade-off between these two opposing effects depends on the discount rate of the representative household (see Exercise 13.14).

Similar results apply when we consider patent policy. In practice, patents are for limited durations. In the baseline model, we assumed that patents are perpetual: once a firm invents a new good, it has a fully enforced patent forever. If patents are strictly enforced, then this might prevent the competitive fringe from competing, restoring the growth rate of the economy to (13.20). And even in the absence of a competitive fringe, we can imagine that once the patent runs out, the firm ceases to make profits on its innovation. In this case, it can easily be shown that growth is maximized by having patents last as long as possible, but there is again a welfare trade-off.

The results of this baseline endogenous technology model on the effects of competition and patent duration on growth are extreme, partly because this model does not incorporate

---

3. More specifically, if the price of the monopolist were higher than $\gamma \psi$, the fringe could undercut the price of the monopolist, take over the market, and make positive profits. If it were below this amount, then the monopolist could increase its price toward the unconstrained monopoly price and make more profits. Thus there is a unique equilibrium price given by (13.24).

rich competitive interactions among firms. The quality competition (Schumpeterian) models introduced in the next chapter allow a more nuanced analysis of the effects of competition and patents on innovation and economic growth.

13.2 Growth with Knowledge Spillovers

In the previous section, growth resulted from the use of final output for R&D. At some level, this is similar to that of Rebelo's (1991) model of sustained growth discussed in Chapter 11, since the innovation possibilities frontier (R&D technology) is linear in accumulable factors.

An alternative is to have "scarce factors" used in R&D. In other words, instead of the lab-equipment specification, researchers and scientists are now the key creators of R&D. The lab-equipment model generated sustained economic growth by investing more and more resources in the R&D sector. This is impossible with scarce factors, since, by definition, a sustained increase in the use of these factors in the R&D sector is not possible. Consequently, with this alternative specification, there cannot be endogenous growth unless there are knowledge spillovers from past R&D, making the scarce factors used in R&D increasingly productive over time. In other words, we now need current researchers to "stand on the shoulder of past giants." The original formulation of the endogenous technological change model by Romer (1990) relied on this type of knowledge spillovers. While such knowledge spillovers might be important in practice, the lab-equipment model studied in the previous section was a better starting point, because it clearly delineated the role of technology accumulation and showed that growth need not be generated by technological externalities or spillovers.

Since knowledge spillovers play an important role in many models of economic growth, it is useful to see how the baseline model of endogenous technological progress works in the presence of such spillovers. I now present the simplest version of the endogenous technological change model with knowledge spillovers. The environment is identical to that of the previous section, with the exception of the innovation possibilities frontier, which now takes the form

$$\dot{N}(t) = \eta N(t) L_R(t), \tag{13.25}$$

where $L_R(t)$ is labor allocated to R&D at time t. The term $N(t)$ on the right-hand side captures spillovers from the stock of existing ideas. The greater is $N(t)$, the more productive is an R&D worker. Notice that (13.25) requires that these spillovers are proportional, or linear. This linearity is the source of endogenous growth in the current model.

In (13.25), $L_R(t)$ is research employment, which comes out of the regular labor force. An alternative, which was originally used by Romer (1990), would be to suppose that only skilled workers or scientists can work in the knowledge-production (R&D) sector. Here I use the assumption that a homogeneous workforce is employed both in the R&D sector and in the final good sector. Competition between the production and the R&D sectors for workers then ensures that the cost of workers to the research sector is given by the wage rate in the final good sector. The only other change is that now the total labor input employed in the final good sector, represented by the production function (13.2), is $L_E(t)$ rather than L, since some of the workers are employed in the R&D sector. Labor market clearing requires that

$$L_R(t) + L_E(t) \leq L.$$

Aggregate output is then given by

$$Y(t) = \frac{1}{1-\beta} N(t) L_E(t), \tag{13.26}$$

and profits of monopolists from selling their machines are

$$\pi(t) = \beta L_E(t). \tag{13.27}$$

The net present discounted value of a monopolist (for a blueprint v) is still $V(v, t)$ as in (13.7) or (13.8), with the flow profits given by (13.27). However the free-entry condition is no longer the same as that which followed from (13.4). Instead (13.25) implies the following free-entry condition (when there is positive research):

$$\eta N(t)V(v, t) = w(t). \tag{13.28}$$

The left-hand side of (13.28) is the return from hiring one more worker for R&D. The term $N(t)$ is on the left-hand side, because higher $N(t)$ translates into higher productivity of R&D workers. The right-hand side is the flow cost of hiring one more worker for R&D, $w(t)$.

The equilibrium wage rate must be the same as in the lab-equipment model of the previous section; in particular, $w(t) = \beta N(t)/(1 - \beta)$, as in (13.13). Moreover, balanced growth again requires that the interest rate be constant at some level r^*. Using these observations together with the free-entry condition (13.28), BGP requires that

$$\eta N(t)\frac{\beta L_E(t)}{r^*} = \frac{\beta}{1 - \beta}N(t). \tag{13.29}$$

Hence the BGP equilibrium interest rate must be

$$r^* = (1 - \beta)\eta L_E^*,$$

where L_E^* is the number of workers employed in production in BGP (given by $L_E^* = L - L_R^*$). The fact that the number of workers in production must be constant in BGP follows from (13.29). Now using the Euler equation of the representative household, (13.16), we obtain

$$\frac{\dot{C}(t)}{C(t)} = \frac{1}{\theta}((1 - \beta)\eta L_E^* - \rho) \equiv g^* \quad \text{for all } t. \tag{13.30}$$

To complete the characterization of the BGP equilibrium, the BGP level of employment, L_E^*, needs to be determined. The innovation possibilities frontier, (13.25), implies $\dot{N}(t)/N(t) = \eta L_R^* = \eta(L - L_E^*)$. Moreover, by definition, the BGP growth rate of consumption must be equal to the rate of technological progress; thus $g^* = \dot{N}(t)/N(t)$. This implies that the BGP level of employment is uniquely pinned down as

$$L_E^* = \frac{\theta\eta L + \rho}{(1 - \beta)\eta + \theta\eta}. \tag{13.31}$$

The rest of the analysis is unchanged. It can also be verified that there are again no transitional dynamics in the decentralized equilibrium (see Exercise 13.17).

Proposition 13.4 *Consider the above-described expanding input variety model with knowledge spillovers, and suppose that*

$$(1 - \theta)(1 - \beta)\eta L_E^* < \rho < (1 - \beta)\eta L_E^*, \tag{13.32}$$

where L_E^* is the number of workers employed in production in BGP, given by (13.31). Then starting from any initial level of technology stock $N(0) > 0$, there exists a unique equilibrium *path. In this equilibrium, technology, output, and consumption grow at the same rate $g^* > 0$, given by (13.30).*

Proof.   See Exercise 13.16.   ∎

As in the lab-equipment model, the equilibrium allocation is Pareto suboptimal, and the Pareto optimal allocation involves a higher rate of output and consumption growth. Intuitively, while firms disregard future increases in the productivity of research resulting from their own R&D spending, the optimal growth allocation internalizes this effect (see Exercise 13.17). Finally, it is also useful to note that there is again a scale effect here—greater L increases the interest rate and the growth rate in the economy.

13.3   Growth without Scale Effects

The models used so far feature a scale effect in the sense that a larger population, L, translates into a higher interest rate and a higher growth rate. This connection is problematic for three reasons as argued in a series of papers by Chad Jones and others:

1. Larger countries do not necessarily grow faster (though the larger market of the U.S. or European economies may have been an advantage during the early phases of the industrialization process; see also Chapter 21).

2. The population of most nations has not been constant. With population growth as in the standard neoclassical growth model (e.g., $L(t) = \exp(nt)L(0)$), these models would not feature balanced growth. Instead the growth rate of the economy would steadily increase over time, and output per capita would reach infinity in finite time ("explode").

3. In the data, the fraction of resources (e.g., of employment and output) devoted to R&D appears to increase steadily, but there is no associated increase in the growth rate.

Each of these arguments against scale effects can be debated (e.g., by arguing that countries do not provide the right level of analysis because of international trade linkages, or that the growth rate of the world economy has indeed increased when we look at the past 2,000 years rather than the past 100 years). Nevertheless together these observations do suggest that the strong form of scale effects embedded in the baseline endogenous technological change models may not provide a good approximation to reality. These observations have motivated Jones (1995) to suggest a modified version of the baseline endogenous technological progress model. While this modification to remove scale effect can be formulated in the lab-equipment model (see Exercise 13.22), it is conceptually simpler to do so in the context of the model with knowledge spillovers discussed in the previous section. In particular, in that model the scale effect can be removed by reducing the impact of knowledge spillovers.

More specifically, consider the model of the previous section with only two differences. First, there is population growth at the constant exponential rate n, so that $\dot{L}(t) = nL(t)$. The economy admits a representative household, with CRRA preferences.

$$\int_0^\infty \exp(-(\rho - n)t)\frac{c(t)^{1-\theta} - 1}{1 - \theta}dt, \tag{13.33}$$

where $c(t)$ is per capita consumption of the final good of the economy at time t. The production function for the final good is again given by (13.2).

Second, in contrast to the knowledge spillover model studied in the previous section, the R&D sector only admits limited knowledge spillovers, and (13.25) is replaced by

$$\dot{N}(t) = \eta N(t)^\phi L_R(t), \tag{13.34}$$

where $\phi < 1$ and $L_R(t)$ is labor allocated to R&D activities at time t. Labor market clearing requires that

$$L_E(t) + L_R(t) \le L(t), \tag{13.35}$$

where $L_E(t)$ is the level of employment in the final good sector, and $L(t)$ is population at time t. The key assumption for the model is that $\phi < 1$. The case where $\phi = 1$ is the one analyzed in the previous section, and as mentioned above, with population growth it would lead to an exploding path and to infinite utility for the representative household.

Aggregate output and profits are given by (13.26) and (13.27), as in the previous section. An equilibrium is also defined similarly. Let us focus on the BGP, where a constant fraction of workers are allocated to R&D, and the interest rate and the growth rate are constant. Suppose that this BGP involves positive growth, so that the free-entry condition holds as equality. Then provided that $r^* > n$, the BGP free-entry condition can be written as (see Exercise 13.18)

$$\eta N(t)^\phi \frac{\beta L_E(t)}{r^* - n} = w(t). \tag{13.36}$$

As before, the equilibrium wage is determined by the production side and is given by (13.13). Combining (13.13) with (13.36) gives the following free-entry condition:

$$\eta N(t)^{\phi-1} \frac{(1-\beta)L_E(t)}{r^* - n} = 1.$$

Now differentiating this condition with respect to time, we have

$$(\phi - 1)\frac{\dot{N}(t)}{N(t)} + \frac{\dot{L}_E(t)}{L_E(t)} = 0.$$

Since in BGP, the fraction of workers allocated to research is constant, $\dot{L}_E(t)/L_E(t) = n$. Thus the BGP growth rate of technology is given by

$$g_N^* \equiv \frac{\dot{N}(t)}{N(t)} = \frac{n}{1-\phi}. \tag{13.37}$$

Using (13.12), (13.37) implies that total output grows at the rate $g_N^* + n$. But now there is population growth, so consumption per capita grows only at the rate

$$g_C^* = g_N^* = \frac{n}{1-\phi}. \tag{13.38}$$

The consumption Euler equation then determines the BGP interest rate as

$$r^* = \theta g_N^* + \rho = \frac{\theta n}{1-\phi} + \rho.$$

Proposition 13.5 *Suppose that $\rho > (1 - \phi - \theta)n/(1-\phi)$. Then in the expanding input variety model with limited knowledge spillovers, there exists a unique BGP in which technology* *and consumption per capita grow at the rate g_N^*, as given by (13.37), and output grows at the rate $g_N^* + n$.*

This analysis therefore shows that sustained (and stable) equilibrium growth of per capita income is possible in an economy with a growing population. Intuitively, instead of the linear (proportional) spillovers in the baseline Romer model, the current model allows only a limited amount of spillovers. Without population growth, these spillovers would not be sufficient to sustain long-run growth. Continuous population growth steadily increases the market size for new technologies and generates growth from these limited spillovers. While this pattern is referred to as "growth without scale effects," it is useful to note that there are two senses in which there are limited scale effects in these models. First, a faster rate of population growth translates into a higher equilibrium growth rate. Second, a larger population size leads to higher output per capita (see Exercise 13.20). It is not clear whether the data support these types of scale effects either. Put differently, some of the evidence suggested against the scale effects in the baseline endogenous technological change models may be inconsistent with this class of models as well. For example, there does not seem to be any evidence in the postwar data or from the historical data of the past 200 years that faster population growth leads to a higher equilibrium growth rate.

It is also worth noting that these models are sometimes referred to as "semi-endogenous growth" models, because while they exhibit sustained growth, the per capita growth rate of the economy, (13.38), is determined only by population growth and technology and does not respond to taxes or other policies. The literature has also developed models of endogenous growth without scale effects, with equilibrium growth responding to policies, though this normally requires a combination of restrictive assumptions.

13.4 Growth with Expanding Product Varieties

Finally, I now briefly present the equivalent model in which growth is driven by product innovations instead of process innovations—that is, by expanding product varieties rather than expanding varieties of inputs. The economy is in continuous time and has a constant population equal to L. It admits a representative household with preferences given by

$$\int_0^\infty \exp(-\rho t) \log C(t) dt, \tag{13.39}$$

where

$$C(t) \equiv \left(\int_0^{N(t)} c(v, t)^{\frac{\varepsilon-1}{\varepsilon}} dv \right)^{\frac{\varepsilon}{\varepsilon-1}} \tag{13.40}$$

is the consumption index, which is a Dixit-Stiglitz (CES) aggregate of the consumption of different varieties. Here $c(v, t)$ denotes the consumption of product v at time t, while $N(t)$ is the total measure of products. I assume throughout that $\varepsilon > 1$. Therefore expanding input varieties have been replaced with expanding product varieties. The log specification in this utility function is for simplicity and can be replaced by a CRRA utility function.

The patent to produce each product $v \in [0, N(t)]$ belongs to a monopolist, and the monopolist who invents the blueprints for a new product receives a fully enforced perpetual patent on this product. Each product can be produced with the technology

$$y(v, t) = l(v, t), \tag{13.41}$$

where $l(v, t)$ is labor allocated to the production of this variety. Since the economy is closed, we have

$$c(v, t) = y(v, t).$$

As in the model with knowledge spillovers of Section 13.2, I assume that new products can be invented with the production function given by

$$\dot{N}(t) = \eta N(t) L_R(t). \tag{13.42}$$

The reader will notice that there is a very close connection between the model here and the models of expanding input variety studied so far, especially the model with knowledge spillovers in Section 13.2. For instance, if the $y(v, t)$ were interpreted as intermediate goods or inputs instead of products and if $C(t)$ in (13.40) were interpreted as the production function for the final good rather than as part of the utility function of the representative household, the two models would be nearly identical. The only difference would be that, with this interpretation, labor would be used in the production of the inputs, while in Section 13.2 it is used only in the final good sector.

Equilibrium and BGP are defined similarly to before. The representative household now determines both the allocation of its expenditure on different varieties and the time path of consumption expenditures. Since the economy is closed and there is no capital, all output must be consumed. The consumption Euler equation then determines the equilibrium interest rate. Labor market clearing requires that

$$\int_0^{N(t)} l(v, t)dv + L_R(t) \le L. \tag{13.43}$$

Let us start with expenditure decisions. Given the Dixit-Stiglitz preferences, the represented household's demands are (see Exercise 13.25)

$$c(v, t) = \frac{p^c(v, t)^{-\varepsilon}}{\left(\int_0^{N(t)} p^c(v, t)^{1-\varepsilon}dv\right)^{-\frac{\varepsilon}{1-\varepsilon}}} C(t), \tag{13.44}$$

where $p^c(v, t)$ is the price of product variety v at time t, and $C(t)$ is defined in (13.40). The term in the denominator is the ideal price index raised to the power $-\varepsilon$. Let us set this ideal price index as the numeraire, so that the price of output at every instant is normalized to 1; that is,

$$\left(\int_0^{N(t)} p^c(v, t)^{1-\varepsilon}dv\right)^{\frac{1}{1-\varepsilon}} = 1 \quad \text{for all } t. \tag{13.45}$$

With this choice of numeraire, the Euler equation again becomes (see Exercise 13.26):

$$\frac{\dot{C}(t)}{C(t)} = r(t) - \rho. \tag{13.46}$$

With an argument similar to those used before, the net present discounted value of the monopolist owning the patent for product v can be written as

$$V(v, t) = \int_t^\infty \exp\left(-\int_t^s r(s')\, ds'\right) \left[p^c(v, s)c(v, s) - w(s)c(v, s)\right] ds,$$

where $w(t)c(v, t)$ is the total expenditure of the firm to produce a total quantity of $c(v, t)$ (given the production function (13.41) and the wage rate at time t, $w(t)$), while $p^c(v, t)c(v, t)$ is its revenue, consistent with the demand function (13.44). The maximization of the net present discounted value again requires profit maximization at every instant. Since each monopolist faces the isoelastic demand curve given in (13.44), the profit-maximizing monopoly price is

$$p^c(v, t) = \frac{\varepsilon}{\varepsilon - 1} w(t) \quad \text{for all } v \text{ and } t.$$

All firms thus charge the same price, produce the same amount, and employ the same amount of labor. At time t, there are $N(t)$ products, so the labor market clearing condition (13.43) implies that

$$c(v, t) = l(v, t) = \frac{L_E(t)}{N(t)} \quad \text{for all } v \text{ and } t, \tag{13.47}$$

where $L_E(t) = L - L_R(t)$. The instantaneous profits of each monopolist are

$$\pi(v, t) = p^c(v, t)c(v, t) - w(t)c(v, t) = \frac{1}{\varepsilon - 1}\frac{L_E(t)}{N(t)} w(t) \quad \text{for all } v \text{ and } t. \tag{13.48}$$

Since prices, sales, and profits are equal for all monopolists, we can simplify notation by letting

$$V(t) = V(v, t) \quad \text{for all } v \text{ and } t.$$

In addition, since $c(v, t) = c(t)$ for all v, we have

$$C(t) = N(t)^{\frac{\varepsilon}{\varepsilon - 1}} c(t) = L_E(t)N(t)^{\frac{1}{\varepsilon - 1}}, \tag{13.49}$$

where the second equality uses (13.47).

Labor demand comes from the research sector as well as from the final good producers. Labor demand from research can again be determined using the free-entry condition. Assuming that there is positive research, so that the free-entry condition holds as equality, this demand takes the form

$$\eta N(t)V(t) = w(t). \tag{13.50}$$

Combining (13.50) with (13.48) yields

$$\pi(t) = \frac{1}{\varepsilon - 1} L_E(t)\eta V(t), \tag{13.51}$$

where $\pi(t)$ denotes the profits of all monopolists at time t. In BGP, where the fraction of the workforce working in research is constant, (13.51) implies that profits and the net present discounted value of monopolists must grow at the same rate. Let us denote the BGP growth rate of the number of products, $N(t)$, by g_N, the growth rate of profit and values by g_V, and the growth rate of wages by g_w. Moreover, given the choice of numeraire, the consumption growth rate in this economy, g^*, must equal the wage growth rate g_w. The free-entry condition (13.50) then implies that $g^* = g_N + g_V$. Given these constant growth rates and the constant BGP interest rate r^*, (13.48) implies that in BGP:

$$V(t) = \frac{\pi(t)}{r^* - g^* + g_N}. \tag{13.52}$$

Intuitively, at time t, profits are equal to $\pi(t)$. Subsequently, because of product expansion, the number of employees per product decreases at the rate g_N, reducing profits, and wages increase at the rate g^*, increasing profits. Taking into account discounting at the rate r^* yields (13.52). Now combining (13.51) with (13.52) gives

$$r^* = \frac{\eta}{\varepsilon - 1}(L - L_R^*) + g^* - g_N,$$

with L_R^* denoting the BGP level of employment in the research sector. Combined with the R&D sector production function (13.42), this equation gives the growth rate of products as

$$\frac{\dot{N}(t)}{N(t)} = g_N = \eta L_R^*.$$

Then from (13.46), the BGP growth rate is $g^* = r^* - \rho$. Combining this expression with the previous two equations, we obtain the BGP level of research employment as

$$L_R^* = \frac{\eta L - (\varepsilon - 1)\rho}{\eta \varepsilon}. \tag{13.53}$$

Let us assume that $L_R^* > 0$ (i.e., $\eta L > (\varepsilon - 1)\rho$), so that there is positive growth (otherwise, the free-entry condition would hold as inequality and there would be zero growth). Moreover, from (13.49), $g^* = g_N/(\varepsilon - 1)$, and therefore we have

$$g^* = \frac{\eta L - (\varepsilon - 1)\rho}{\varepsilon(\varepsilon - 1)}. \tag{13.54}$$

Finally, since $r^* > g^*$ (because of logarithmic preferences), household utility is always finite, and the relevant transversality condition is satisfied.

Proposition 13.6 *Suppose that $\eta L > (\varepsilon - 1)\rho$. Then there exists a unique BGP in which aggregate consumption expenditure $C(t)$ and the wage rate $w(t)$ grow at the rate g^* given by (13.54).*

In this equilibrium, there is growth of real income, even though the production function of each good remains unchanged. This is because, while there is no process innovation reducing costs or improving quality, the number of products available to households expands because of product innovations. Since the utility function of the representative household, (13.39), exhibits love for variety, the expanding variety of products increases utility. What happens to income depends on the choice of numeraire. The natural numeraire is the one setting the ideal price index (13.45) equal to 1, which amounts to measuring incomes in similar units at different dates. With this choice of numeraire, real incomes grow at the same rate as $C(t)$, i.e., at the rate g^*. Exercise 13.24 further highlights the similarity between the expanding product and machine variety models. Exercise 13.27 shows that, as in other expanding variety models, there are no transitional dynamics in the current model and the equilibrium is again Pareto suboptimal. Finally, it can be verified that there is again a scale effect here. This discussion then reveals that whether one wishes to use the expanding input variety or the expanding product model is mostly a matter of taste, and perhaps one of context. Both models lead to similar structures of equilibria, similar effects of policy on equilibrium growth, and similar welfare properties.

13.5   Taking Stock

In this chapter, we had our first look at models of endogenous technological progress. The distinguishing feature of these models is the fact that profit incentives shape R&D spending and investments, which in turn determines the rate at which the technology of the economy evolves over time. At some level, there are many parallels between the models studied here and the Romer (1986a) model of growth with externalities discussed in Section 11.4: both have a mathematical structure similar to the neoclassical AK models (constant long-run growth rate, no transitional dynamics), both generate endogenous growth (as a function of preferences and policies), and in both (technological or pecuniary) externalities make the equilibrium growth rate less than the Pareto optimal growth rate. Nevertheless the fundamental difference between the Romer (1986a) model and the endogenous technological change model should not be understated. While one may interpret the Romer (1986a) model as involving "knowledge accumulation," this accumulation is not the outcome of purposeful economic activity—it is a by-product of other decisions (in this particular instance, those involving individual physical capital accumulation). While such a model may "endogenize" technology, it does so without explicitly specifying the costs and benefits of investing in new technologies. Since, as discussed in Chapter 3, technology differences across countries are likely to be important in accounting for their income differences, understanding the sources of technology differences is an essential part of our effort to understand the mechanics of economic growth. In this respect, the models presented in this chapter constitute a major improvement over those in Chapter 11.

The models studied in this chapter, like those of the previous chapter, emphasize the importance of profits in shaping technology choices. We have also seen the role of monopoly power and patent length on the equilibrium growth rate. In addition, the same factors that influence the equilibrium growth rate in the neoclassical AK model also affect equilibrium economic growth. These include the discount rate ρ as well as taxes on capital income or corporate profits. Nevertheless the effect of the market structure on equilibrium growth and innovation rates is somewhat limited in the current models, because the Dixit-Stiglitz structure and expanding product or input varieties limit the extent to which firms can compete with one another. The models of quality competition in the next chapter feature a richer interaction between market structure and equilibrium growth.

An important shortcoming of the models in this chapter (and those in the next two chapters) should also be noted at this point. In these models, the technology stock of a society is determined only by its own R&D. Thus technological differences result simply from R&D differences. In our current world of relatively free knowledge flows, many countries not only generate technological know-how from their own R&D but also benefit from the advances in the world technology frontier. Consequently, in practice technology adoption decisions and the patterns of technology diffusion may be equally important as, or more important than, R&D toward the invention of new technologies (see Chapter 18). Therefore the major contribution of the approaches studied in this chapter to our understanding is not necessarily in pinpointing the exact source of technology differences across countries but in their emphasis on the endogenous nature of technology and in the perspective they provide for modeling technological investments. In addition, even if technology adoption and imitation may be more important than innovation for the growth of some countries, models of endogenous technological change are essential for understanding world economic growth, since the world technology frontier advances (in large part) because of R&D.

13.6   References and Literature

Models of endogenous technological progress were introduced in Romer (1987, 1990) and then subsequently analyzed and advanced by, among others, Aghion and Howitt (1992); Grossman and Helpman (1991a,b); and Segerstrom, Anant, and Dinopoulos (1990). The lab-equipment model presented in Section 13.1 appears in Rivera-Batiz and Romer (1991). The model in Romer (1990) is similar to that presented in Section 13.2 but with skilled workers working in R&D. Gancia and Zilibotti (2005) provide an excellent survey of many of the models discussed in this chapter. Matsuyama (1995) gives a lucid discussion of the sources of inefficiency in Dixit-Stiglitz type models, which is related to the sources of inefficiency in the lab-equipment model presented in Section 13.1.

The critique of endogenous growth models because of scale effect is contained in Backus, Kehoe, and Kehoe (1992) and in Jones (1995). Backus, Kehoe, and Kehoe pointed out that more populous countries did not grow faster in the postwar era. Jones focused on time series patterns and pointed out the substantial increase in R&D inputs, for example, the total number of workers involved in research, with no corresponding increase in the equilibrium growth rate. Others have argued that looking at twentieth-century data may not be sufficient to reach a conclusion on whether there is a scale effect. Kremer (1993) argues, on the basis of estimates of world population, that there must have been an increase in economic growth over the past one million years.

The model in Section 13.3 is similar to that presented in Jones (1995, 1999). Dinopoulos and Thompson (1998), Segerstrom (1998), Young (1998), and Howitt (1999) develop generalizations of this model where policy affects the equilibrium growth rate.

The model of expanding product varieties was first suggested by Judd (1985). Endogenous growth models with expanding product varieties were first developed by Grossman and Helpman (1991a,b). The exposition here is different because I used the ideal price index rather than Grossman and Helpman's choice of total expenditure as the numeraire.

13.7   Exercises

13.1   Derive (13.8) from (13.7).

(a) Rewrite (13.7) at time t as

$$V(v, t) = \int_t^{t+\Delta t} \exp\left(-\int_t^s r(\tau)\,d\tau\right) [p^x(v, s) - \psi]x(v, s)\,ds$$
$$+ \int_{t+\Delta t}^{\infty} \exp\left(-\int_t^s r(\tau)\,d\tau\right) [p^x(v, s)x(v, s) - \psi x(v, s)]\,ds,$$

which is just an identity for any Δt. Interpret this equation and relate this to the Principle of Optimality in discrete-time problems (Theorem 6.2).

(b) Show that for small Δt, this equation can be written as

$$V(v, t) = [p^x(v, t) - \psi]x(v, t)\Delta t + \exp(r(t)\Delta t)V(v, t + \Delta t) + o(\Delta t),$$

and thus derive the following equation:

$$(p^x(v, t) - \psi)x(v, t)\Delta t + \exp(r(t)\Delta t)V(v, t + \Delta t) - \exp(r(t) \times 0)V(v, t) + o(\Delta t) = 0.$$

Interpret this equation and the significance of the term $o(\Delta t)$.

(c) Divide both sides of the equation in part b by Δt, take the limit $\Delta t \to 0$, and show that when the value function is differentiable, you obtain (13.8).

13.2 Derive (13.9) and (13.10) from the profit maximization problem of a monopolist.

13.3 Formulate the household optimization problem in terms of the current-value Hamiltonian and derive the necessary conditions for an interior continuous solution. Show that these are equivalent to (13.16) and (13.17).

13.4 Complete the proof of Proposition 13.1. In particular, show that when (13.21) holds, the utility of the representative household is finite, and the transversality condition is satisfied. Show also that in equilibrium the resource constraint (13.3) is always satisfied with positive consumption at all points.

13.5 Prove that in the model of Section 13.1 $V(v, t) = V(t)$ for all v and t. Moreover, show that if $\eta V(t) = 1$ for $t \in (t' - \varepsilon, t' + \varepsilon)$ for some t' and $\varepsilon > 0$, then $\eta V(t) = 1$ for all t, and conversely that if this condition does not hold for any t' and any $\varepsilon > 0$, then $\eta V(t) < 1$ for all t, and there is no entry at any t. Then show that, given (13.21), no entry at any t cannot be an equilibrium. Using these observations, provide a proof of Proposition 13.2.

13.6 Consider the expanding variety model of Section 13.1 and denote the BGP growth rates of consumption and total output by g_C^* and g^*, respectively.

(a) Show that $g_C^* > g^*$ is not feasible.

(b) Show that $g_C^* < g^*$ violates the transversality condition.

13.7 Consider a world economy consisting of $j = 1, \ldots, J$, economies. Suppose that each of these is closed and has access to the same production and R&D technology as described in Section 13.1. Countries differ in terms of labor force L_j, productivity of R&D η_j, and discount rate ρ_j. Also assume that one unit of R&D expenditure costs ζ_j units of final good in country j. There are no technological exchanges across countries.

(a) Define the "world equilibrium" in which each country is in equilibrium in analogy with the equilibrium path of the one-country economy in Section 13.1.

(b) Characterize the world equilibrium. Show that in the world equilibrium, each country grows at a constant rate starting at $t = 0$. Provide explicit solutions for these growth rates.

(c) Show that except in "knife-edge" cases, output in each country grows at a different long-run rate.

(d) Now return to the discussion in Chapters 3 and 8 regarding the effect of policy and taxes on long-run income per capita differences. Show that, in the model discussed in this exercise, arbitrarily small differences in policy or discount factors across countries lead to infinitely large differences in long-run income per capita. Does this property resolve the empirical challenges discussed in those chapters?

13.8 (a) Verify that Theorem 7.14 from Chapter 7 can be applied to the social planner's problem in Section 13.1.

(b) Derive the consumption growth rate in the optimal growth path (13.23).

13.9 Consider the expanding input variety model of Section 13.1. Show that it is possible for the equilibrium allocation to satisfy the transversality condition, while the optimal growth path may violate it. Interpret this result. Does it imply that the solution to the optimal growth problem is less compelling? Show that when the condition in Proposition 13.3 is satisfied, the optimal growth path satisfies the transversality condition and yields a finite level of utility for the representative household.

13.10 Complete the proof of Proposition 13.3, in particular showing that the Pareto optimal allocation always involves a constant growth rate and no transitional dynamics.

13.11 Consider the expanding input variety model of Section 13.1.

(a) Suppose that a benevolent government has access only to research subsidies, which can be financed by lump-sum taxes. Can these subsidies be chosen to ensure that the equilibrium growth rate is the same as the Pareto optimal growth rate? Can they be used to replicate the Pareto optimal equilibrium path? Would it be desirable for the government to use subsidies to achieve the Pareto optimal growth rate (from the viewpoint of maximizing social welfare at time $t = 0$)?

(b) Suppose that the government now has access only to subsidies to machines, which can again be financed by lump-sum taxes. Can these be chosen to induce the Pareto optimal growth rate? Can they be used to replicate the Pareto optimal equilibrium path?

(c) Will the combination of subsidies to machines and subsidies to research be better than either of these two policies by themselves?

13.12 Consider the expanding input variety model of Section 13.1, and assume that corporate profits are taxed at the rate τ.

(a) Characterize the equilibrium allocation.

(b) Consider two economies with identical technologies and identical initial conditions but with different corporate tax rates, τ and τ'. Determine the relative income of these two economies (as a function of time).

* 13.13 Consider the expanding input variety model of Section 13.1 with one difference. A firm that invents a new machine receives a patent, which expires at the Poisson rate ι. Once the patent expires, that machine is produced competitively and is supplied to final good producers at marginal cost.

(a) Characterize the BGP equilibrium in this case and show how the growth rate depends on ι. [Hint: notice that there will be two different machine varieties supplied at different prices.]

(b) Characterize the transitional dynamics. [Hint: show that the growth rate of consumption is constant but output growth is not.]

(c) What is the value of ι that maximizes the equilibrium rate of economic growth?

(d) Show that a policy of $\iota = 0$ does not necessarily maximize social welfare at time $t = 0$.

13.14 Consider the formulation of competition policy in Section 13.1.6.

(a) Characterize the equilibrium fully.

(b) Write down the welfare of the representative household at time $t = 0$ in this equilibrium.

(c) Maximize the welfare function derived in part b by choosing a value of γ.

(d) Why is the optimal value of γ not equal to some $\gamma^* \geq 1/(1 - \beta)$? Provide an interpretation in terms of the trade-off between level and growth effects.

(e) What is the relationship between the optimal value of γ and ρ?

13.15 This exercise asks you to construct and analyze the equivalent of the lab-equipment expanding variety model of Section 13.1 in discrete time. Suppose that the economy admits a representative household with preferences at time 0 given by

$$\sum_{t=0}^{\infty} \beta^t \frac{C(t)^{1-\theta} - 1}{1 - \theta},$$

with $\beta \in (0, 1)$ and $\theta \geq 0$. Production technology is the same as in the text, and the innovation possibilities frontier of the economy is given by $N(t + 1) - N(t) = \eta Z(t)$.

(a) Define the equilibrium in BGP allocations.

(b) Characterize the BGP and compare the structure of the equilibrium to that in Section 13.1.

(c) Show that there are no transitional dynamics, so that starting with any $N(0) > 0$, the economy grows at a constant rate.

13.16 Complete the proof of Proposition 13.4. In particular, show that the equilibrium path involves no transitional dynamics and that under (13.32), utility is finite and the transversality condition is satisfied.

13.17 Characterize the Pareto optimal allocation in the economy of Section 13.2. Show that it involves a constant growth rate greater than the equilibrium growth rate in Proposition 13.4 and has no transitional dynamics.

13.18 Derive (13.36) and explain why the denominator is equal to $r^* - n$.

13.19 Consider the model of endogenous technological progress with limited knowledge spillover as discussed in Section 13.3.

(a) Characterize the transitional dynamics of the economy starting from an arbitrary $N(0) > 0$.

(b) Characterize the Pareto optimal allocation, and compare it to the equilibrium allocation in Proposition 13.5.

(c) Analyze the effect of the following two policies: first, a subsidy to research; second, a patent policy, in which each patent expires at the rate $\iota > 0$. Explain why the effects of these policies on economic growth are different than their effects in the baseline endogenous growth model.

13.20 Consider the model in Section 13.3. Suppose that there are two economies with identical preferences, technology, and initial conditions, except country 1 starts with population $L_1(0)$ and country 2 starts with $L_2(0) > L_1(0)$. Show that income per capita is always higher in country 2 than in country 1.

13.21 Characterize the equilibrium dynamics in the model of Section 13.3 starting with an initial level of technology $N(0) > 0$.

13.22 Consider the lab-equipment model of Section 13.1, but modify the innovation possibilities frontier to be

$$\dot{N}(t) = \eta N(t)^{-\phi} Z(t),$$

where $\phi > 0$.

(a) Define an equilibrium and characterize the market clearing factor prices and determine the free-entry condition.

(b) Show that without population growth, there will be no sustained growth in this economy.

(c) Now consider population growth at the exponential rate n, and show that this model generates sustained equilibrium growth, as in the model analyzed in Section 13.3.

13.23 Consider the baseline endogenous technological change model with expanding machine varieties in Section 13.1. Suppose that x now denotes machines that do not immediately depreciate. In contrast, once produced, these machines depreciate at an exponential rate δ. Preferences and the rest of the production structure remain unchanged.

(a) Define the equilibrium in BGP allocations.

(b) Formulate the maximization problem of producers of machines. [Hint: it is easier to formulate the problem in terms of machine rentals rather than machine sales.]

(c) Characterize the equilibrium in this economy, and show that all the results are identical to those in Section 13.1.

13.24 Consider the following model. Population at time t is $L(t)$ and grows at the constant rate n (i.e., $\dot{L}(t) = nL(t)$). All agents have preferences given by

$$\int_0^\infty \exp(-\rho t) \frac{C(t)^{1-\theta} - 1}{1 - \theta} dt,$$

where C is consumption of the final good produced as

$$Y(t) = \left(\int_0^{N(t)} y(v, t)^\beta dv \right)^{1/\beta},$$

where $y(v, t)$ is the amount of intermediate good v used in production at time t, and $N(t)$ is the number of intermediate goods at time t. The production function of each intermediate is $y(v, t) = l(v, t)$, where $l(v, t)$ is labor allocated to this good at time t. New goods are produced by allocating workers to R&D, with the production function $\dot{N}(t) = \eta N^\phi(t) L_R(t)$, where $\phi \leq 1$ and $L_R(t)$ is labor allocated to R&D at time t. Labor market clearing requires that

$$\int_0^{N(t)} l(v, t)dv + L_R(t) = L(t).$$

Risk-neutral firms hire workers for R&D. A firm that discovers a new good becomes the monopoly supplier, with a perfectly enforced patent.

(a) Characterize the BGP in the case where $\phi = 1$ and $n = 0$, and show that there are no transitional dynamics. Why is this? Why does the long-run growth rate depend on θ? Why does the growth rate depend on L? Do you find this dependence plausible?

(b) Suppose that $\phi = 1$ and $n > 0$. What happens? Interpret.

(c) Characterize the BGP when $\phi < 1$ and $n > 0$. Does the growth rate depend on L? Does it depend on n? Why? Do you think that the configuration $\phi < 1$ and $n > 0$ is more plausible than the one with $\phi = 1$ and $n = 0$?

13.25 Derive (13.44). [Hint: use the first-order condition between two products v and v', and then substitute into the budget constraint of the representative household with total expenditure, denoted by $C(t)$.]

13.26 Using (13.44) and the choice of numeraire in (13.45), set up the household maximization problem in the form of the current-value Hamiltonian (derive the budget constraint explicitly). Derive the consumption Euler equation (13.46).

13.27 Consider the model analyzed in Section 13.4.

(a) Show that the allocation described in Proposition 13.6 always involves finite utility and satisfies the transversality condition.

(b) Show that in this model there are no transitional dynamics.

(c) Characterize the Pareto optimal allocation, and show that the equilibrium growth rate in Proposition 13.6 is less than the growth rate in the Pareto optimal allocation.

14

Models of Schumpeterian Growth

The previous chapter presented the basic endogenous technological change models based on expanding input, machine, or product varieties. The advantage of these models is their tractability. While the expansion of the variety of machines used in production captures certain aspects of the economics of innovation, most process innovations in practice either increase the quality of an existing product or reduce the costs of production. Therefore typical process innovations have a number of distinct features compared to the "horizontal innovations" of the previous chapter. For example, in the expanding machine variety model a newly invented computer is used alongside all previous vintages of computers; in reality, a newly invented computer often replaces existing vintages. Thus models of expanding machine variety may not provide a good description of innovation dynamics in practice because they do not capture the competitive aspect of innovations. These competitive aspects bring us to the realm of Schumpeterian creative destruction in which economic growth is driven, at least in part, by new firms replacing incumbents and new machines and products replacing old ones. For this reason, the models discussed in this chapter are referred to as "Schumpeterian growth models." My purpose in this chapter is to develop tractable models of Schumpeterian growth.

Schumpeterian growth raises a number of novel and important issues. First, in contrast to the models of expanding varieties, there may be direct price competition among various producers with different vintages of quality or different costs of producing the same product. This competition affects both the description of the growth process and several of its central implications. For example, market structure and antitrust policy can play potentially richer roles in models exhibiting this type of price competition. Second, competition between incumbents and entrants brings the replacement and business stealing effects discussed in Chapter 12 to the forefront and raises the possibility of excessive innovation.

This description suggests that a number of new and richer issues arise in the context of Schumpeterian growth models. One may then expect models of Schumpeterian models to be significantly more complicated than expanding varieties models. This is not necessarily the case, however. This chapter presents the basic models of competitive innovations, first proposed by Aghion and Howitt (1992) and then further developed by Grossman and Helpman

(1991a,b) and Aghion and Howitt (1998). The literature on models of Schumpeterian economic growth is now large, and an excellent survey is presented in Aghion and Howitt (1998). My treatment here highlights the most important implications of these models and maximizes the similarity to the mathematical structure of the expanding varieties models. Several applications of these models are discussed later in the chapter and in the exercises.

14.1 A Baseline Model of Schumpeterian Growth

14.1.1 Preferences and Technology

The economy is in continuous time and admits a representative household with the standard CRRA preferences (e.g., (13.1) in the previous chapter). Population is constant at L, and labor is supplied inelastically. The resource constraint at time t again takes the form

$$C(t) + X(t) + Z(t) \leq Y(t), \tag{14.1}$$

where $C(t)$ is consumption, $X(t)$ is aggregate spending on machines, and $Z(t)$ is total expenditure on R&D at time t.

There is a continuum of machines used in the production of a unique final good. Since there is no expansion of machine varieties, the measure of machines can be normalized to 1 without loss of generality. Each machine line is denoted by $v \in [0, 1]$. The engine of economic growth here is process innovations that lead to *quality improvements*. Let us first specify how the qualities of different machine lines change over time. Let $q(v, t)$ be the quality of machine line v at time t. The following "quality ladder" determines the quality of each machine variety:

$$q(v, t) = \lambda^{n(v,t)} q(v, 0) \quad \text{for all } v \text{ and } t, \tag{14.2}$$

where $\lambda > 1$, $q(v, 0) \in \mathbb{R}_+$, and $n(v, t)$ denotes the number of innovations on this machine line between time 0 and time t. This specification implies that there is a quality ladder for each machine variety, and each innovation takes the machine quality up by one rung on this ladder. These rungs are proportionally equidistant, so that each improvement leads to a proportional increase in quality by an amount $\lambda > 1$. Growth is the result of these quality improvements. Note that the number of innovations in machine line v by time t, $n(v, t)$, is a random variable, and thus $q(v, t)$ is also a random variable. Therefore there are stochastic changes in machine qualities.

The production function of the final good is similar to that in the previous chapter, except that now the quality of the machines matters for productivity. The aggregate production function takes the form

$$Y(t) = \frac{1}{1 - \beta} \left(\int_0^1 q(v, t) x(v, t \mid q)^{1-\beta} dv \right) L^\beta, \tag{14.3}$$

where $x(v, t \mid q)$ is the quantity of machine variety v of quality q used in the production process. In writing this expression, I conditioned on the qualities of machines, the $q(v, t)$s, at time t. In addition, as we will see below, because the realizations of different qualities are independent, aggregate output in (14.3) will be nonstochastic.

Note also that as in the previous chapter, this production function can be written as

$$Y(t) = \frac{1}{1 - \beta} \tilde{\mathbf{X}}(t)^{1-\beta} L^\beta,$$

where

$$\tilde{\mathbf{X}}(t) \equiv \left(\int_0^1 q(v, t) x(v, t \mid q)^{\frac{\varepsilon_\beta - 1}{\varepsilon_\beta}} \, dv \right)^{\frac{\varepsilon_\beta}{\varepsilon_\beta - 1}},$$

with $\varepsilon_\beta \equiv 1/\beta$. This form emphasizes the continuity with the expanding variety models of Chapter 12.

An implicit assumption in (14.3) is that at any point in time only one quality of any machine is used. This assumption is without loss of generality, because different qualities of the same machine are perfect substitutes and in equilibrium only the *leading-edge* (highest quality) machine of each machine line is employed. This feature is the source of creative destruction: when a higher quality machine is invented it will replace ("destroy") the previous vintage of the same machine.

I next specify the technology for producing machines of different qualities and the innovation possibilities frontier of this economy. New machine vintages are invented by R&D. The R&D process is cumulative, in the sense that new R&D builds on the know-how of existing machines. For example, consider the machine line v that has quality $q(v, t)$ at time t. R&D on this machine line attempts to improve over this quality. If a firm spends $Z(v, t)$ units of the final good for research on this machine line, then it generates a flow rate

$$\frac{\eta Z(v, t)}{q(v, t)}$$

of innovation. The innovation advances the know-how of the production of this machine to the new rung of the quality ladder, creating a machine variety v with quality $\lambda q(v, t)$. Note that one unit of R&D spending is proportionately less effective when applied to a more advanced machine. This result is intuitive, since we expect research on more advanced machines to be more difficult. It is also convenient from a mathematical point of view, because the benefit of research is also increasing with the quality of the machine (in particular, the quality improvements are proportional: an innovation increases quality from $q(v, t)$ to $\lambda q(v, t)$). Note also that the costs of R&D are identical for the current incumbent and new firms.

There is again free entry into research; thus any firm or individual can undertake this type of research on any of the machine lines. As in the expanding varieties models of the previous chapter, the firm that makes an innovation has a perpetual patent on the new machine that it has invented. But the patent system does not preclude other firms undertaking research based on the machine invented by this firm.

Once a particular machine of quality $q(v, t)$ has been invented, any quantity of this machine can be produced at marginal cost $\psi q(v, t)$. Once again, the fact that the marginal cost is proportional to the quality of the machine is natural, because producing higher-quality machines should be more expensive.

One noteworthy issue here concerns the identity of the firm that undertakes R&D and innovation. In the expanding varieties model, this was irrelevant, since machines could not be improved upon, so there was only R&D for new machines, and who undertook the R&D was not important. Here, in contrast, existing machines can be (and are) improved, and this is the source of economic growth. We have already seen in Chapter 12 that if the costs of R&D are identical for incumbents and new firms, Arrow's replacement effect implies that it will be entrants that undertake the R&D. The same applies in this model. The incumbent has weaker incentives to innovate, since it would replace its own machine (thus destroying the profits that it is already making). In contrast, a new entrant does not have this replacement calculation in mind. As a result, with the same technology of innovation, it is always the entrants that undertake the R&D investments (see Exercise 14.2). In practice, established firms contribute significantly to innovations and productivity growth, and this issue is discussed in Sections 14.3 and 14.4.

14.1.2 Equilibrium

An *allocation* in this economy consists of time paths of consumption levels, aggregate spending on machines, and aggregate R&D expenditure, $[C(t), X(t), Z(t)]_{t=0}^{\infty}$; time paths of qualities of leading-edge machines denoted by $[q(v, t)]_{v \in [0,1], t=0}^{\infty}$; time paths of prices and quantities of each machine and the net present discounted value of profits from that machine, $[p^x(v, t \mid q), x(v, t \mid q), V(v, t \mid q)]_{v \in [0,1], t=0}^{\infty}$; and time paths of interest rates and wage rates, $[r(t), w(t)]_{t=0}^{\infty}$. Recall that $q(v, t)$ and thus the corresponding prices, quantities, and values are stochastic (and thus the paths referred to above are stochastic processes). Nevertheless the aggregates are nonstochastic, simplifying the analysis. An equilibrium is defined below.

Let us start with the final good producers. A similar analysis to that in the previous chapter implies that the demand for machines from final good producers is

$$x(v, t \mid q) = \left(\frac{q(v, t)}{p^x(v, t \mid q)} \right)^{1/\beta} L \quad \text{for all } v \in [0, 1] \text{ and all } t, \tag{14.4}$$

where $p^x(v, t \mid q)$ refers to the price of machine of variety v of quality $q(v, t)$ at time t. This expression stands for $p^x(v, t \mid q(v, t))$, where $q(v, t)$ is the highest quality of this machine available at time t, but there should be no confusion in this notation, since it is clear that q here refers to $q(v, t)$. I use this notation for other variables as well. The price $p^x(v, t \mid q)$ is determined by the profit-maximization of the monopolist holding the patent for machine variety v of quality $q(v, t)$. Note that the demand from the final good sector for machines in (14.4) is isoelastic as in the previous chapter, so the unconstrained monopoly price is again a constant markup over marginal cost. However, in contrast to the previous chapter, there is now competition between firms that have access to different vintages of a particular machine variety. Thus, as in Chapter 12, we need to consider two regimes, one in which the innovation is drastic, so that each firm can charge the unconstrained monopoly price, and the other one in which limit prices have to be used. Which regime we are in does not affect the mathematical structure or the substantive implications of the model. Nevertheless we have to choose one of these two alternatives for consistency. Here let us assume that the quality gap between a new machine and the machine that it replaces, λ, is sufficiently large. In particular, it satisfies

$$\lambda \geq \left(\frac{1}{1 - \beta} \right)^{\frac{1-\beta}{\beta}}, \tag{14.5}$$

so that we are in the drastic innovations regime (see Exercise 14.9 for the derivation of this condition and Exercise 14.10 for the structure of the equilibrium under the alternative assumption). Let us also normalize $\psi \equiv 1 - \beta$ as in the previous chapter, which implies that the profit-maximizing monopoly price (for the highest quality machine at time t) is

$$p^x(v, t \mid q) = q(v, t). \tag{14.6}$$

Combining (14.6) with (14.4) implies

$$x(v, t \mid q) = L. \tag{14.7}$$

Consequently, the flow profits of a firm with the monopoly rights on the leading-edge machine of quality $q(v, t)$ can be computed as

$$\pi(v, t \mid q) = \beta q(v, t) L. \tag{14.8}$$

This only differs from the flow profits in the previous chapter because of the presence of the quality term, $q(v, t)$. Next, substituting (14.7) into (14.3), total output is given by

$$Y(t) = \frac{1}{1 - \beta} Q(t) L, \tag{14.9}$$

where

$$Q(t) \equiv \int_0^1 q(v, t) dv \tag{14.10}$$

is the average total quality of machines. While the $q(v, t)$s are stochastic, their average $Q(t)$ is deterministic with a law of large numbers type of reasoning (since the realizations of the quality of different machine lines are independent).[1] This expression closely parallels the derived production function (13.12) in the previous chapter, except that labor productivity is now determined by the average quality of the machines, $Q(t)$ (instead of the number of machine varieties, $N(t)$, in the previous chapter). This expression also clarifies the reasoning for the choice of functional forms above. In particular, the reader can verify that it is the linearity of the aggregate production function of the final good in the quality of machines that makes labor productivity depend on average quality. With alternative assumptions, an expression similar to (14.9) would still apply but would typically involve a different aggregator of machine qualities rather than the simple average (see, e.g., Section 14.4).[2] Next, aggregate spending on machines is obtained as

$$X(t) = (1 - \beta) Q(t) L. \tag{14.11}$$

As in the previous chapter, labor, which is only used in the final good sector, receives an equilibrium wage rate of

$$w(t) = \frac{\beta}{1 - \beta} Q(t). \tag{14.12}$$

I next specify the value function for the monopolist of variety v of quality $q(v, t)$ at time t. As before, even though each firm generates a stochastic stream of revenues, the presence of many firms with independent "draws" implies that each should maximize expected profits. The net present value of expected profits can be written in the HJB form as

$$r(t) V(v, t \mid q) - \dot{V}(v, t \mid q) = \pi(v, t \mid q) - z(v, t \mid q) V(v, t \mid q), \tag{14.13}$$

where $z(v, t \mid q)$ is the rate at which new innovations occur in sector v at time t, while $\pi(v, t \mid q)$ is the flow of profits. This value function is somewhat different from the ones in the previous

---

1. Some care is necessary here, since the typical laws of large numbers apply to the average of a countable sequence of random variables, whereas $Q(t)$ is the "average" of a continuum of random variables. This may sometimes create technical problems, though in the present context $Q(t)$ is well defined. See, for example, Uhlig (1996) for more details.

2. Another functional form that makes the relevant aggregate the average of the qualities is used in (14.33) below.

chapter (e.g., (13.8)) because of the last term on the right-hand side, which captures the essence of Schumpeterian growth. When a new innovation occurs, the existing monopolist loses its monopoly position and is replaced by the producer of the higher quality machine. From then on, it receives zero profits and thus has zero value. Moreover, in writing this equation, I made use of the fact that because of Arrow's replacement effect, it is an entrant that is undertaking the innovation; thus $z(v, t \mid q)$ corresponds to the flow rate at which the incumbent will be replaced by a new entrant.

Free entry again implies

$$\eta V(v, t \mid q) \leq \lambda^{-1} q(v, t) \ \text{ and } \ \eta V(v, t \mid q) = \lambda^{-1} q(v, t) \quad \text{if } Z(v, t \mid q) > 0. \quad (14.14)$$

In other words, the value of spending one unit of the final good should not be strictly positive. Recall that one unit of the final good spent on R&D for a machine of quality $\lambda^{-1} q$ has a flow rate of success equal to $\eta/(\lambda^{-1} q)$, and in this case, it generates a new machine of quality q, which has a net present value gain of $V(v, t \mid q)$. If there is positive R&D, that is, if $Z(v, t \mid q) > 0$, then the free-entry condition must hold as equality.

Note also that even though the qualities of individual machines, the $q(v, t)$s, are stochastic (and depend on success in R&D), as long as R&D expenditures, the $Z(v, t \mid q)$s, are non-stochastic, average quality $Q(t)$ and thus total output $Y(t)$ and total spending on machines $X(t)$ are nonstochastic. This feature significantly simplifies the analysis.

Household maximization again implies the familiar Euler equation

$$\frac{\dot{C}(t)}{C(t)} = \frac{1}{\theta}(r(t) - \rho), \quad (14.15)$$

and the transversality condition

$$\lim_{t \to \infty} \left[\exp\left(-\int_0^t r(s)ds \right) \int_0^1 V(v, t \mid q)dv \right] = 0. \quad (14.16)$$

This transversality condition is intuitive, since the total value of corporate assets is now $\int_0^1 V(v, t \mid q)dv$. Even though the evolution of the quality of each machine line is stochastic, the value of machine v of quality q at time t, $V(v, t \mid q)$, is nonstochastic. Either q is not the highest quality in this machine line, in which case $V(v, t \mid q)$ is equal to 0, or alternatively, it is given by (14.13).

These equations complete the description of the environment. An *equilibrium* can then be represented as time paths of consumption, aggregate spending on machines, and aggregate R&D, $[C(t), X(t), Z(t)]_{t=0}^{\infty}$, that satisfy (14.1), (14.11), (14.13), and (14.14); stochastic paths of prices and quantities for machines that have highest quality in their lines at that point, $[p^x(v, t \mid q), x(v, t \mid q)]_{v \in [0,1], t=0}^{\infty}$, given by (14.6) and (14.7); and time paths of aggregate machine quality, $[Q(t)]_{t=0}^{\infty}$, interest rates and wage rates, $[r(t), w(t)]_{t=0}^{\infty}$, and value functions, $[V(v, t \mid q)]_{v \in [0,1], t=0}^{\infty}$, that satisfy (14.12)–(14.16). I again start the analysis with the BGP, where output and consumption grow at constant rates.

14.1.3 Balanced Growth Path

In the BGP, consumption grows at the constant rate g_C^*. With familiar arguments, this must be the same rate as output growth g^*. Moreover from (14.15), the interest rate must be constant, that is, $r(t) = r^*$ for all t.

If there is positive growth in this BGP equilibrium, then there must be research at least in some sectors. Since both profits and R&D costs are proportional to quality, when the free-entry condition (14.14) holds as equality for one machine line, it holds as equality for all of them. Thus

$$V(v, t \mid q) = \frac{q(v, t)}{\lambda \eta}. \tag{14.17}$$

Note that if this condition holds between t and $t + \Delta t$, then $\dot{V}(v, t \mid q) = 0$. This is because $q(v, t)$ on the right-hand side of (14.17) refers to the quality of the machine supplied by the incumbent, which is constant over time (until there is innovation in this machine line). In BGP, R&D expenditures, $z(v, t)$, must be constant and the same for all machine lines, and I denote this common value by z^* (see Exercise 14.1). Then (14.13) implies

$$V(v, t \mid q) = \frac{\beta q(v, t)L}{r^* + z^*}. \tag{14.18}$$

Notice the difference between this value function and those in the previous chapter: instead of the discount rate r^*, the denominator has the "effective discount rate" $r^* + z^*$, because incumbent monopolists understand that new innovations will replace them.

Combining this equation with (14.17), we obtain

$$r^* + z^* = \lambda \eta \beta L. \tag{14.19}$$

Moreover, from the fact that $g_C^* = g^*$ and from (14.15), we have

$$r^* = \theta g^* + \rho. \tag{14.20}$$

To solve for the BGP equilibrium, we need a final equation relating the BGP growth rate of the economy, g^*, to z^*. From (14.9), this is given by

$$\frac{\dot{Y}(t)}{Y(t)} = \frac{\dot{Q}(t)}{Q(t)}.$$

Note that, by definition, in an interval of time Δt, there are $z(t)\Delta t$ sectors that experience one innovation, and this increases their productivity by λ. The measure of sectors experiencing more than one innovation within this time interval is $o(\Delta t)$—that is, it is second-order in Δt, so that as $\Delta t \to 0$, $o(\Delta t)/\Delta t \to 0$. Therefore

$$Q(t + \Delta t) = \lambda Q(t)z(t)\Delta t + (1 - z(t)\Delta t)Q(t) + o(\Delta t).$$

Now subtracting $Q(t)$ from both sides, dividing by Δt, and taking the limit as $\Delta t \to 0$ yields

$$\dot{Q}(t) = (\lambda - 1)z(t)Q(t). \tag{14.21}$$

Therefore

$$g^* = (\lambda - 1)z^*. \tag{14.22}$$

Now combining (14.19)–(14.22), the BGP growth rate of output and consumption is

$$g^* = \frac{\lambda \eta \beta L - \rho}{\theta + (\lambda - 1)^{-1}}. \tag{14.23}$$

This analysis establishes the following proposition.

Proposition 14.1 *Consider the model of Schumpeterian growth described above. Suppose that*

$$\lambda \eta \beta L > \rho > (1 - \theta)(\lambda - 1)\eta \beta L.$$

Then there exists a unique BGP in which average quality of machines, output, and consumption grow at rate g^* given by (14.23). The rate of innovation is $g^*/(\lambda - 1)$.

Proof. Most of the proof is given in the preceding analysis. Exercise 14.4 asks you to check that the BGP equilibrium is unique and satisfies the transversality condition. ∎

The above analysis illustrates that the mathematical structure of the model is similar to those analyzed in the previous chapter. Nevertheless creative destruction—the process of incumbent monopolists being replaced by new entrants—is an important new element and provides a different interpretation of the growth process. I return to some of the applications of creative destruction below.

Before doing this, let us briefly look at transitional dynamics in this economy. Similar arguments to those used in the previous chapter establish the following result.

Proposition 14.2 *In the model of Schumpeterian growth described above, starting with any average quality of machines $Q(0) > 0$, there are no transitional dynamics, and the equilibrium path always involves constant growth at the rate g^* given by (14.23).*

Proof. See Exercise 14.5. ∎

As noted above, only the average quality of machines, $Q(t)$, matters for the allocation of resources. Moreover, the incentives to undertake research are identical for two machine varieties v and v', with different quality levels $q(v, t)$ and $q(v', t)$. Thus there are no differential incentives for R&D in more and less advanced machines. Both features are a result of the functional form in (14.3). Exercise 14.14 investigates the conditions under which these results may not apply. Nevertheless the specification chosen in this section is appealing, since it implies that research is directed toward a broad range of machines rather than a specific subset of machines.

14.1.4 Pareto Optimality

This equilibrium, like that of the endogenous technology model with expanding varieties, is Pareto suboptimal. The first reason for this is the appropriability effect, which results because monopolists are not able to capture the entire social gain created by an innovation. However Schumpeterian growth also introduces the business stealing effect discussed in Chapter 12. Consequently the equilibrium rate of innovation and growth can now be too high or too low relative to the social optimum.

Let us proceed as in the previous chapter, first deriving the quantities of machines that are used in the final good sector in the optimal growth allocation (for given $Q(t)$). In this allocation, there are no markups, and thus

$$x^S(v, t \mid q) = \psi^{-1/\beta} L = (1 - \beta)^{-1/\beta} L. \tag{14.24}$$

Substituting (14.24) into (14.3), we obtain

$$Y^S(t) = (1 - \beta)^{-1/\beta} Q^S(t) L,$$

where again the superscript S refers to the optimal (social planner's) allocation. The net output that can be distributed between consumption and research expenditure is then

$$\tilde{Y}^S(t) \equiv Y^S(t) - X^S(t)$$

$$= (1 - \beta)^{-1/\beta} Q^S(t)L - \int_0^1 \psi q(v, t) x^S(v, t \mid q) dv$$

$$= (1 - \beta)^{-1/\beta} \beta Q^S(t)L. \tag{14.25}$$

Moreover, given the specification of the innovation possibilities frontier above (in particular, recall (14.21)), the social planner can improve the aggregate technology as follows:

$$\dot{Q}^S(t) = \eta(\lambda - 1)Z^S(t),$$

because R&D spending of $Z^S(t)$ leads to the discovery of better vintages at the flow rate η, and each new vintage increases average quality by a proportional amount $\lambda - 1$.

Given this equation, the optimal growth problem becomes

$$\max \int_0^\infty \exp(-\rho t) \frac{C^S(t)^{1-\theta} - 1}{1 - \theta} dt$$

subject to

$$\dot{Q}^S(t) = \eta(\lambda - 1)[(1 - \beta)^{-1/\beta} \beta Q^S(t)L - C^S(t)], \tag{14.26}$$

where (14.26) is obtained by using the expression for net output (14.25) and the resource constraint (14.1). In this problem, $Q^S(t)$ is the state variable, and $C^S(t)$ is the control variable. To characterize this solution, let us set up the current-value Hamiltonian as

$$\hat{H}(Q^S, C^S, \mu^S) = \frac{C^S(t)^{1-\theta} - 1}{1 - \theta} + \mu^S(t)[\eta(\lambda - 1)(1 - \beta)^{-1/\beta} \beta Q^S(t)L - \eta(\lambda - 1)C^S(t)].$$

Again using Theorem 7.13, a candidate interior solution satisfies

$$\hat{H}_C(Q^S, C^S, \mu^S) = C^S(t)^{-\theta} - \mu^S(t)\eta(\lambda - 1) = 0,$$

$$\hat{H}_Q(Q^S, C^S, \mu^S) = \mu^S(t)\eta(\lambda - 1)(1 - \beta)^{-1/\beta} \beta L = \rho\mu^S(t) - \dot{\mu}^S(t),$$

$$\lim_{t \to \infty} [\exp(-\rho t)\mu^S(t)Q^S(t)] = 0.$$

Because the current-value Hamiltonian is concave in C and Q, the sufficiency conditions in Theorem 7.14 are satisfied. Moreover an argument similar to that in Exercise 8.11 in Chapter 8 establishes that the solution to these conditions gives the unique optimal plan (see Exercise 14.8). Combining these conditions, we obtain the following growth rate for consumption in the Pareto optimal allocation (see again Exercise 14.8):

$$\frac{\dot{C}^S(t)}{C^S(t)} = g^S \equiv \frac{1}{\theta}(\eta(\lambda - 1)(1 - \beta)^{-1/\beta} \beta L - \rho). \tag{14.27}$$

Clearly, total output and average quality also grow at the rate g^S in this allocation.

It is straightforward to see that the Pareto optimal allocation is always different than the equilibrium allocation (because of the monopoly markups in the latter). However, in contrast to the expanding varieties models, the Pareto optimal growth rate is not always greater than the equilibrium growth rate. This can be seen by comparing g^S to g^* in (14.23). In particular, when λ is very large, $g^S > g^*$, and there is insufficient growth in the decentralized equilibrium. For example, as $\lambda \to \infty$, we have $g^S/g^* \to (1 - \beta)^{-1/\beta} > 1$. In contrast, to obtain an example in which there is excessive growth in equilibrium, suppose that $\theta = 1$, $\beta = 0.9$, $\lambda = 1.3$, $\eta = 1$, $L = 1$, and $\rho = 0.38$. In this case, it can be verified that $g^S \approx 0$, while $g^* \approx 0.18 > g^S$.[3] This example illustrates the counteracting influences of the appropriability and business stealing effects discussed above. The following proposition summarizes this result.

Proposition 14.3 *In the model of Schumpeterian growth described above, the decentralized equilibrium is Pareto suboptimal. The equilibrium may have a higher or lower rate of growth than the Pareto optimal allocation.*

It is also straightforward to verify that as in the models of the previous chapter, there is a scale effect, and thus population growth would lead to an exploding growth path. Exercise 14.11 asks you to construct a Schumpeterian growth model without scale effects.

14.1.5 Policy in Models of Schumpeterian Growth

As in the previous chapter, antitrust policy, patent policy, and taxation affect equilibrium growth. For example, two economies that tax corporate incomes at different rates grow at different rates.

Nevertheless the current model may be more appropriate for conducting policy analysis than the expanding varieties models. In these previous models, there was no reason for any agent in the economy to support distortionary taxes.[4] In contrast, the fact that growth here takes place through creative destruction implies that there is an inherent conflict of interest and certain types of distortionary policies may have a natural constituency. To illustrate this point, which is to be discussed in greater detail in Part VIII of the book, suppose that there is a tax τ imposed on R&D spending. This has no effect on the profits of existing monopolists and only influences their net present discounted value via replacement. Since taxes on R&D discourage R&D, there will be replacement at a slower rate; that is, BGP R&D effort z^* falls. A slower replacement rate directly increases the steady-state value of all monopolists given by (14.18). In particular, the value of a monopolist with a machine of quality q is

$$V(q) = \frac{\beta q L}{r^*(\tau) + z^*(\tau)},$$

where the equilibrium interest rate and the replacement rate have been written as functions of τ. With the tax rate on R&D, the free-entry condition (14.14) becomes

$$V(q) = \frac{(1 + \tau)}{\lambda \eta} q.$$

This equation shows that $V(q)$ is increasing in the tax rate on R&D, τ. Combining the previous two equations, it can be seen that in response to a positive rate of taxation, $r^*(\tau) + z^*(\tau)$ must adjust downward, so that the value of current monopolists increases (consistent with

---

3. Notice that the combination of $\beta = 0.9$ and $\lambda = 1.3$ is consistent with (14.5), which was used in deriving the equilibrium growth rate g^*.

4. Naturally, one can enrich these models so that tax revenues are distributed unequally across agents, for example, with taxes on capital distributed to workers. In this case, even in the basic neoclassical growth model, some groups could prefer distortionary taxes. Such models is discussed in Part VIII of the book.

the previous equation). Intuitively, when the costs of R&D are raised because of tax policy, the value of a successful innovation, $V(q)$, must increase to satisfy the free-entry condition. This can only happen through a decline in the effective discount rate $r^*(\tau) + z^*(\tau)$. A lower effective discount rate, in turn, is achieved by a decline in the equilibrium growth rate of the economy, which now takes the form

$$g^*(\tau) = \frac{(1+\tau)^{-1}\lambda\eta\beta L - \rho}{\theta + (\lambda - 1)^{-1}}.$$

This growth rate is strictly decreasing in τ. But as the previous expression shows, incumbent monopolists benefit from an increase in τ and would be in favor of such a "growth-retarding" policy.

Therefore an important advantage of models of Schumpeterian growth is that they provide us with clues about why some societies may adopt policies that reduce the equilibrium growth rate. Since taxing R&D by new entrants benefits incumbent monopolists, when incumbents are politically powerful such distortionary taxes can emerge in the political economy equilibrium, even though they are not in the interest of the society at large.

14.2 A One-Sector Schumpeterian Growth Model

The model of Schumpeterian growth presented in the previous section was designed to maximize the parallels between this class of models and those based on expanding varieties. I now discuss a model more closely related to the original Aghion and Howitt (1992) paper. There are two major differences from the previous section. First, there is only one sector experiencing quality improvements rather than a continuum of machine varieties. Second, the innovation possibilities frontier uses a scarce factor, labor, as in the model of knowledge spillovers in Section 13.2 of the previous chapter. Since there are many parallels between this model and the one in the previous section, I only provide a brief exposition.

14.2.1 The Basic Aghion-Howitt Model

The household side is the same as before, with the only difference being that we now assume households are risk neutral, so that the interest rate is determined as $r^* = \rho$ at all points in time. Population is again equal to L, and labor is supplied inelastically. The aggregate production function of the unique final good is

$$Y(t) = \frac{1}{1-\beta}x(t \mid q)^{1-\beta}(q(t)L_E(t))^{\beta}, \tag{14.28}$$

where $q(t)$ is the quality of the unique machine used in production and is written in the labor-augmenting form for simplicity; $x(t \mid q)$ is the quantity of this machine used at time t; and $L_E(t)$ denotes the amount of labor used in production at time t, which is less than L, since $L_R(t)$ workers are employed in the R&D sector. Market clearing requires that

$$L_E(t) + L_R(t) \leq L.$$

Once invented, a machine of quality $q(t)$ can be produced at the constant marginal cost ψ in terms of the final good. Let us again normalize $\psi \equiv 1 - \beta$. The innovation possibilities frontier now involves labor being used for R&D. In particular, each worker employed in the R&D sector generates a flow rate η of a new machine. When the current machine used in production has quality $q(t)$, the new machine has quality $\lambda q(t)$.

Let us once again assume that (14.5) is satisfied, so that the monopolist can charge the unconstrained monopoly price. Then an analysis similar to that in the previous section implies that the demand for the leading-edge (highest quality) machine is given by

$$x(t \mid q) = p^x(t)^{-1/\beta} q(t) L_E(t),$$

where again q is the quality of this machine, and $p^x(v, t)$ denotes its price. Let the monopoly price for the highest quality machine be $p^x(t \mid q) = \psi/(1 - \beta) = 1$ for all q and t.[5] Consequently the demand for the machine of quality q at time t is $x(t \mid q) = q(t) L_E(t)$, and monopoly profits are $\pi(t \mid q) = \beta q(t) L_E(t)$. Aggregate output can then be written as

$$Y(t \mid q) = \frac{1}{1 - \beta} q(t) L_E(t),$$

which again conditions on the quality of the machine available at the time, q. This equation also implies that the equilibrium wage, determined from (14.28), is given by

$$w(t \mid q) = \frac{\beta}{1 - \beta} q(t).$$

When there is no need to emphasize time dependence, I write this wage rate as a function of machine quality, that is, as $w(q)$.

Let us now focus on a "steady-state equilibrium" in which the flow rate of innovation is constant and equal to z^*. Steady state here is in quotation marks since, even though the flow rate of innovation is constant, consumption and output growth are not constant because of the stochastic nature of innovation (and this is the reason I do not use the term "BGP" in this context). In any case, steady state implies that a constant number of workers, L_R^*, work in research. Since the interest rate is equal to $r^* = \rho$, this implies that the steady-state value of a monopolist with a machine of quality q is given by

$$V(q) = \frac{\beta q \left(L - L_R^*\right)}{\rho + z^*},$$

where I used the fact that in steady state total employment in the final good sector is equal to $L_E^* = L - L_R^*$. Free entry requires that when the current machine quality is q, wages in the R&D sector should be equal to the flow benefits. These flow benefits from R&D are equal to $\eta V(\lambda q)$, since, when current machine quality is q, one more worker in R&D leads to the discovery of a new machine of quality λq at the flow rate η. In addition, given the R&D technology, we must have $z^* = \eta L_R^*$. Combining these relations, we obtain

$$\frac{\lambda(1 - \beta)\eta \left(L - L_R^*\right)}{\rho + \eta L_R^*} = 1,$$

5. This expression follows the original Aghion and Howitt (1992) paper and assumes that innovators ignore their effect on equilibrium wages. In the baseline model presented in Section 14.1, since there was a continuum of monopolistically competitive firms, each had no effect on equilibrium wages. Here, instead, the single monopolist could recognize that its price also affects equilibrium wages and thus the cost of R&D for its competitors. In this case, it may want to set a lower price than $\psi/(1 - \beta)$. Following Aghion and Howitt (1992), I ignore this issue.

which uniquely determines the steady-state number of workers in research as

$$L_R^* = \frac{\lambda(1-\beta)\eta L - \rho}{\eta + \lambda(1-\beta)\eta}, \tag{14.29}$$

as long as this expression is positive (otherwise the free-entry condition would be slack and there would be zero growth).

In contrast to the model in the previous section, output does not grow at a constant rate. Since there is only one sector undergoing technological change and this sector experiences growth only at finite intervals, the growth rate of the economy has an *uneven* nature. In particular, it can be verified that the economy has constant output for an interval of time (of average length $1/(\eta L_R^*)$; see Exercise 14.16) and then experiences a burst of growth when a new machine is invented. This pattern of uneven growth is a consequence of having only one sector rather than a continuum (or a large number of them). Whether it provides a better approximation to reality than the model of the previous section is open to debate. While modern capitalist economies do not grow at constant rates, they also do not have as jagged a growth performance as that implied by this model.

The results of this analysis are summarized in the next proposition.

Proposition 14.4 *Consider the one-sector Schumpeterian growth model presented in this section and suppose that*

$$\rho < \lambda(1-\beta)\eta L < \frac{\log \lambda + 1 + \lambda(1-\beta)}{\log \lambda} \rho. \tag{14.30}$$

Then there exists a unique steady-state equilibrium in which L_R^* workers work in the research sector, where L_R^* is given in (14.29). The economy has an average growth rate of $g^* = \eta L_R^* \log \lambda$. Equilibrium growth is "uneven," in the sense that the economy has constant output for a while and then grows by a discrete amount when an innovation takes place.

Proof. Much of the proof is provided by the preceding analysis. Exercise 14.17 asks you to verify that the average growth is given by $g^* = \eta L_R^* \log \lambda$ and that (14.30) is necessary for the above-described equilibrium to exist and to satisfy the transversality condition. ■

Therefore this analysis shows that the basic insights of the one-sector Schumpeterian model, as originally developed by Aghion and Howitt (1992), are very similar to the baseline model of Schumpeterian growth presented the Section 14.1. The main difference is that growth has an uneven flavor in the one-sector model, because it is driven by infrequent bursts of innovation, preceded and followed by periods of no growth.

14.2.2 Uneven Growth and Endogenous Cycles

Section 14.2.1 showed how the basic one-sector Schumpeterian growth model involves an uneven pattern of economic growth. There is another source of uneven growth in this basic model, which is more closely related to the process of creative destruction. Schumpeterian growth implies that future growth reduces the value of current innovations, because it causes more rapid replacement of existing technologies. This effect has not played a role in our analysis so far, because in the model with a continuum of sectors, growth takes a smooth form and as Proposition 14.2 shows, there is a unique equilibrium path with no transitional dynamics. The one-sector growth model analyzed in this section allows these effects to manifest themselves.

To show the potential for these creative destruction effects, I now construct a variant of the model which exhibits endogenous growth cycles.

The only difference from the setup Section 14.2.1 is that the R&D technology now implies that L_R workers in research leads to innovation at the rate

$$\eta(L_R)L_R,$$

where $\eta(\cdot)$ is a strictly decreasing function, representing an externality in the research process. When more firms try to discover the next generation of technology, there is more crowding-out in the research process, making it less likely for each of them to innovate. Each firm ignores its effect on the aggregate rate of innovation and thus takes $\eta(L_R)$ as given (this assumption is not important, as shown by Exercise 14.22). Consequently when the current machine quality is q, the free-entry condition takes the form

$$\eta(L_R(q))V(\lambda q) = w(q),$$

where $L_R(q)$ is employment in research when the current machine quality is q.

Let us now look for an equilibrium with the following cyclical property: the rate of innovation differs when the innovation in question is an odd-numbered innovation versus an even-numbered innovation (say with the number of innovations counted starting from some arbitrary date $t = 0$). This type of equilibrium is possible when all agents in the economy expect there to be such an equilibrium (i.e., it is a "self-fulfilling" equilibrium). Denote the number of workers in R&D for odd- and even-numbered innovations by L_R^1 and L_R^2. Then, following the analysis in the previous subsection, in any equilibrium with a cyclical pattern the values of odd- and even-numbered innovations (with a machine of quality q) can be written as (see Exercise 14.20):

$$V^2(\lambda q) = \frac{\beta q(L - L_R^2)}{\rho + \eta(L_R^2)L_R^2}, \quad \text{and} \quad V^1(\lambda q) = \frac{\beta q(L - L_R^1)}{\rho + \eta(L_R^1)L_R^1}, \tag{14.31}$$

and the free-entry conditions take the form

$$\eta(L_R^1)V^2(\lambda q) = w(q), \quad \text{and} \quad \eta(L_R^2)V^1(\lambda q) = w(q),$$

where $w(q)$ is the equilibrium wage with technology of quality q. The reason $\eta(L_R^1)$ multiplies the value for an even-numbered innovation is because L_R^1 researchers are employed for innovation today, when the current technology is odd-numbered, but the innovation that this research will produce is even-numbered and thus has value $V^2(\lambda q)$. Therefore the following two conditions must hold in equilibrium:

$$\eta(L_R^1)\frac{\lambda(1 - \beta)q(L - L_R^2)}{\rho + \eta(L_R^2)L_R^2} = 1, \quad \text{and} \quad \eta(L_R^2)\frac{\lambda(1 - \beta)q(L - L_R^1)}{\rho + \eta(L_R^1)L_R^1} = 1. \tag{14.32}$$

It can then be verified that these two equations can have solutions L_R^1 and $L_R^2 \neq L_R^1$, which would correspond to the possibility of a two-period endogenous cycle (see Exercise 14.21).

14.2.3 Labor Market Implications of Creative Destruction

Another important implication of creative destruction is related to the fact that growth destroys existing productive units. So far this only led to the destruction of the monopoly rents of incumbent producers without any loss of employment. In more realistic economies, creative destruction may dislocate previously employed workers, and these workers may experience some unemployment before finding a new job. How creative destruction may lead to unemployment is discussed in Exercise 14.19.

A final implication of creative destruction that is worth noting relates to the destruction of firm-specific skills. It may be efficient for workers to accumulate human capital that is specific to their employers. Creative destruction implies that productive units will have shorter horizons in an economy with rapid economic growth. An important consequence might be that in rapidly-growing economies, workers (and sometimes firms) may be less willing to make a range of relationship-specific investments.

14.3 Innovation by Incumbents and Entrants

A key aspect of the growth process is the interplay between innovations and productivity improvements by existing firms on the one hand and entry by more productive new firms on the other. The evidence from industry studies, which is discussed in greater detail in Section 18.1, suggests that a large part of productivity growth at the industry level (and thus in the aggregate) comes from productivity improvements by continuing plants, though entry by new plants also makes a nontrivial contribution to industry productivity growth. The Schumpeterian models presented in this chapter have emphasized entry by new firms as the engine of growth. Interpreted literally, these models predict that all growth should be driven by entry, which is at odds with the facts. The expanding variety models presented in the previous chapter also do not provide a framework for the analysis of the interplay between existing firms and new entrants.[6] In this and the next sections, I discuss models that feature productivity growth by continuing plants (firms). The model in this section features productivity growth by both incumbents and entrants. The model in the next section is richer in many respects, but does not allow entry. The two models together provide a first glimpse at the types of models that might be useful for studying the industrial organization of innovation and productivity growth.

14.3.1 Model

The economy is largely identical to that in Section 14.1, with a representative household with the standard CRRA preferences. Population is constant at L, and labor is supplied inelastically. The resource constraint is given by (14.1). The production function of the unique final good is

$$Y(t) = \frac{1}{1 - \beta} \left(\int_0^1 q(v, t)^\beta x(v, t \mid q)^{1-\beta} dv \right) L^\beta, \tag{14.33}$$

where $x(v, t \mid q)$ is the quantity of machine variety v of quality q used in the production process, and the measure of machines is again normalized to 1. This aggregate production function is similar to (14.3), except that the quality of machines has an exponent β. This modification has no effects on the results concerning growth, but implies that firms with different productivity levels will have different levels of sales (see Exercise 14.28). The engine of economic growth

---

6. In the expanding variety models, the identity of the firms that are undertaking the innovation does not matter, so one could assume that it is the existing producers that are inventing new varieties, though this is tantamount to determining the distribution of productivity improvements across firms by assumption.

is again quality improvements, but these are driven by two types of innovations: (1) innovation by incumbents and (2) creative destruction by entrants.

Let $q(v, t)$ be the quality of machine line v at time t. In particular, the quality ladder for each machine variety again takes the form

$$q(v, t) = \lambda^{n(v,t)} q(v, s) \quad \text{for all } v \text{ and } t,$$

where $\lambda > 1$, and $n(v, t)$ now denotes the number of *incremental* innovations on this machine line between times $s \leq t$ and t, where time s is the date at which this particular type of technology was first invented, and $q(v, s)$ refers to its quality at that point. The incumbent has a fully enforced patent on the machines that it has developed (though this patent does not prevent entrants leapfrogging the incumbent's machine quality). I assume that at time $t = 0$ each machine line starts with some quality $q(v, 0) > 0$ and is owned by an incumbent. Incremental innovations can only be performed by the incumbent producer. So we can think of those as "tinkering" innovations that improve the quality of the machine. More specifically, if the current incumbent spends an amount $z(v, t)q(v, t)$ of the final good for incremental innovation on a machine of quality $q(v, t)$, it has a flow rate of innovation equal to $\phi z(v, t)$ for $\phi > 0$. The resulting new machine is of quality $\lambda q(v, t)$.

Alternatively, a new firm (entrant) can undertake R&D to innovate over the existing machines in machine line v at time t. If the current quality of machine is $q(v, t)$, then by spending one unit of the final good this new firm innovates at the flow rate $\eta(\hat{z}(v, t))/q(v, t)$, where $\eta(\cdot)$ is a strictly decreasing, continuous, and differentiable function, and $\hat{z}(v, t)$ is R&D expenditure by new entrants for machine line v at time t. Incumbents also have access to the same technology for radical innovation as the entrants. However Arrow's replacement effect implies that incumbents would never use this technology (since entrants make zero profits from this technology, the profits of incumbents would be negative; see Exercise 14.24). Incumbents still find it profitable to use the technology for incremental innovations, which is not available to entrants.

The presence of the strictly decreasing function η, which was also used in Section 14.2.2, captures the fact that when many firms are undertaking R&D to replace the same machine line, they are likely to try similar ideas; thus there will be some amount of external diminishing returns (new entrants are "fishing out of the same pond"). Since each entrant attempting R&D on this line is potentially small, they all take $\eta(\hat{z}(v, t))$ as given. Throughout I assume that $z\eta(z)$ is strictly increasing in z, so that greater aggregate R&D toward a particular machine line increases the overall probability of discovering a superior machine. I also suppose that $\eta(z)$ satisfies the following Inada-type assumptions:

$$\lim_{z \to \infty} \eta(z) = 0, \quad \text{and} \quad \lim_{z \to 0} \eta(z) = \infty. \tag{14.34}$$

An innovation by an entrant leads to a new machine of quality $\kappa q(v, t)$, where $\kappa > \lambda$. Therefore innovations by entrants are more radical than those of incumbents. Existing empirical evidence from studies of innovation support the notion that innovations by new entrants are more significant or radical than those of incumbents.[7] Whether the entrant was a previous incumbent on this specific machine line or whether it is currently an incumbent in some other machine line does not matter for its technology of innovation.

---

7. Nevertheless, it may take a while for the successful entrants to realize the full productivity gains from these innovations, and the treatment here abstracts from this aspect.

Once a particular machine of quality $q(v, t)$ has been invented, any quantity of this machine can be produced at the marginal cost ψ. I again normalize $\psi \equiv 1 - \beta$. Total expenditure on R&D is

$$Z(t) = \int_0^1 [z(v, t) + \hat{z}(v, t)] q(v, t) dv, \tag{14.35}$$

where $q(v, t)$ refers to the highest quality of machine variety v at time t. Notice also that total R&D is the sum of R&D by incumbents and entrants ($z(v, t)$ and $\hat{z}(v, t)$, respectively).

An *allocation* in this economy consists of time paths of consumption, aggregate spending on machines, and aggregate R&D expenditure, $[C(t), X(t), Z(t)]_{t=0}^{\infty}$; (stochastic) time paths for R&D efforts by incumbent and entrants, $[z(v, t), \hat{z}(v, t)]_{v \in [0,1], t=0}^{\infty}$; (stochastic) time paths of prices and quantities of leading-edge machines and the net present discounted value of profits from those machines, $[p^x(v, t \mid q), x(v, t \mid q), V(v, t \mid q)]_{v \in [0,1], t=0}^{\infty}$; and time paths of interest rates and wage rates, $[r(t), w(t)]_{t=0}^{\infty}$. An *equilibrium* is given by an allocation in which R&D decisions by entrants maximize their discounted value; pricing, quantity, and R&D decisions by incumbents maximize their discounted value; the representative household chooses the path of consumption optimally; and the labor and capital markets clear. As usual, a BGP is an equilibrium path in which output and consumption grow at a constant rate.

Profit maximization by the final good sector implies that the demand for machines of highest quality is given by a slight variant of (14.4) in Section 14.1:

$$x(v, t \mid q) = p^x(v, t \mid q)^{-1/\beta} q(v, t) L \quad \text{for all } v \in [0, 1] \text{ and all } t, \tag{14.36}$$

where $p^x(v, t \mid q)$ refers to the price of machine variety v of quality $q(v, t)$ at time t. Since the demand from the final good sector for machines in (14.36) is isoelastic, the unconstrained monopoly price is given by the usual formula, as a constant markup over marginal cost. In this context, I introduce the analogue of condition (14.5),

$$\kappa \geq \left(\frac{1}{1 - \beta} \right)^{\frac{1-\beta}{\beta}}, \tag{14.37}$$

which ensures that new innovations can charge the unconstrained monopoly price. By implication, incumbents that make further innovations can also charge the unconstrained monopoly price.

14.3.2 Equilibrium

Since the demand for machines in (14.36) is isoelastic and $\psi \equiv 1 - \beta$, the profit-maximizing monopoly price (for the highest quality machine) is

$$p^x(v, t \mid q) = 1. \tag{14.38}$$

Combining (14.38) this with (14.36) implies that

$$x(v, t \mid q) = qL. \tag{14.39}$$

Consequently, the flow profits of a firm with the monopoly rights on the machine of quality q is again given by (14.8). Substituting (14.39) into (14.33), total output is given by (14.9), that is, $Y(t) = Q(t)L/(1 - \beta)$, with the average quality of machines $Q(t)$ given as in (14.10).

Moreover, since the labor market is competitive, the wage rate at any point in time is given by (14.12) as before.

Let us next determine R&D effort levels by incumbents and entrants. To do this, let us write the net present value of a monopolist with the highest quality of machine q at time t in machine line v. This value satisfies the standard HJB equation

$$r(t)V(v, t \mid q) - \dot{V}(v, t \mid q) = \max_{z(v,t\mid q) \geq o} \{\pi(v, t \mid q) - z(v, t \mid q)q(v, t) \tag{14.40}$$

$$+ \phi z(v, t \mid q)(V(v, t \mid \lambda q) - V(v, t \mid q)) - \hat{z}(v, t \mid q)\eta(\hat{z}(v, t \mid q))V(v, t \mid q)\},$$

where $\hat{z}(v, t \mid q)\eta(\hat{z}(v, t \mid q))$ is the rate at which radical innovations by entrants occur in sector v at time t, and $\phi z(v, q \mid q)$ is the rate at which the incumbent improves its technology. The first term in (14.40), $\pi(v, t \mid q)$, is the flow of profits given by (14.8), while the second term is the expenditure of the incumbent for improving the quality of its product. The second line includes changes in the value of the incumbent due to innovation either by itself (at the rate $\phi z(v, t \mid q)$, the quality of its product increases from q to λq) or by an entrant (at the rate $\hat{z}(v, t \mid q)\eta(\hat{z}(v, t \mid q))$, the incumbent is replaced and receives zero value from then on).[8] The value function is written with a maximum on the right-hand side, since $z(v, t \mid q)$ is a choice variable for the incumbent.

Free entry by entrants implies a free-entry condition similar to (14.14) in Section 14.1,

$$\eta(\hat{z}(v, t \mid q))V(v, t \mid \kappa q) \leq q(v, t), \hat{z}(v, t \mid q) \geq 0 \text{ and}$$

$$\eta(\hat{z}(v, t \mid q))V(v, t \mid \kappa q) = q(v, t) \text{ if } \hat{z}(v, t \mid q) > 0, \tag{14.41}$$

which takes into account that by spending an amount $q(v, t)$, the entrant generates a flow rate of innovation equal to $\eta(\hat{z})$, leading a product of quality κq, thus earning the value $\eta(\hat{z}(v, t \mid q))V(v, t \mid \kappa q)$.

In addition, the incumbent's choice of R&D effort implies a similar complementary slackness condition:

$$\phi(V(v, t \mid \lambda q) - V(v, t \mid q)) \leq q(v, t), \ z(v, t \mid q) \geq 0 \text{ and}$$

$$\phi(V(v, t \mid \lambda q) - V(v, t \mid q)) = q(v, t) \text{ if } z(v, t \mid q) > 0. \tag{14.42}$$

Finally, household maximization implies the familiar Euler equation and the transversality condition given by (14.15) and (14.16) as before.

As usual, in the BGP we have $r(t) = r^*$ (from (14.15)). Moreover $z(v, t \mid q) = z(q)$, and $\hat{z}(v, t \mid q) = \hat{z}(q)$. These together imply that in the BGP, $\dot{V}(v, t \mid q) = 0$ and $V(v, t \mid q) = V(q)$. Furthermore, since profits and costs are both proportional to quality q, we can also see that $\hat{z}(q) = \hat{z}$ and $V(q) = vq$ (Exercise 14.23, in fact, shows that $\hat{z}(v, t \mid q) = \hat{z}(t)$ and $V(v, t \mid q) = v(t)q$ in any equilibrium, even outside the BGP). These results enable a straightforward characterization of the BGP and the dynamic equilibrium.[9]

Let us first look for an interior BGP equilibrium. This solution implies that incumbents undertake research, and thus

$$\phi(V(v, t \mid \lambda q) - V(v, t \mid q)) = q(v, t). \tag{14.43}$$

---

8. The fact that the incumbent receives a zero value from then on follows from the assumption that a previous incumbent has no advantage relative to other entrants in competing for another round of innovations.

9. While $\hat{z}(q) = \hat{z}$ for all q, it is not necessarily true that $z(q) = z$ for all q. In fact, as we will see, the equilibrium only pins down the average R&D intensity of incumbents.

Given the linearity of V in q, (14.43) implies the following convenient equation for the value of a firm with a machine of quality q:

$$V(q) = \frac{q}{\phi(\lambda - 1)}. \tag{14.44}$$

Moreover, from the free-entry condition (again holding as equality), we have

$$\eta(\hat{z}) V(\kappa q) = q, \ \text{ or } \ V(q) = \frac{q}{\kappa \eta(\hat{z})}.$$

Combining this expression with (14.44), we obtain

$$\frac{\phi(\lambda - 1)}{\kappa \eta(\hat{z})} = 1.$$

Thus the BGP R&D level by entrants, $\hat{z}^*$, is implicitly defined by

$$\hat{z}(q) = \hat{z}^* \equiv \eta^{-1}\left(\frac{\phi(\lambda - 1)}{\kappa}\right) \quad \text{for all } q > 0. \tag{14.45}$$

In addition, in BGP (14.40) implies that

$$V(q) = \frac{\beta L q}{r^* + \hat{z}^* \eta(\hat{z}^*)}. \tag{14.46}$$

Next, combining (14.46) with (14.44) and (14.45), the BGP interest rate is obtained as

$$r^* = \phi(\lambda - 1)\beta L - \hat{z}^* \eta(\hat{z}^*). \tag{14.47}$$

From (14.15), the growth rate of consumption and output is therefore given by

$$g^* = \frac{1}{\theta}(\phi(\lambda - 1)\beta L - \hat{z}^* \eta(\hat{z}^*) - \rho). \tag{14.48}$$

Equation (14.48) already has some interesting implications. In particular, it determines the relationship between the rate of innovation by entrants $\hat{z}^*$ and the BGP growth rate g^*. In standard Schumpeterian models, this relationship is positive. In contrast, here it is straightforward to see that there is a negative relationship between $\hat{z}^*$ and g^*.

Equations (14.45) and (14.48) determine the BGP growth rate of the economy but do not specify how much of productivity growth is driven by creative destruction (innovation by entrants) and how much of it by productivity improvements by incumbents. To determine this breakdown, it is useful to repeat the analysis in Section 14.1. Recall, at this point, that $z(v, t \mid q)$ is not a function of v but could still depend on q. Consequently the law of motion of $Q(t)$ is

$$Q(t + \Delta t) = (\lambda \phi z(t) \Delta t) Q(t) + (\kappa \hat{z}(t) \eta(\hat{z}(t)) \Delta t) Q(t)$$
$$+ (1 - \phi z(t) \Delta t - \hat{z}(t) \eta(\hat{z}(t)) \Delta t) Q(t) + o(\Delta t), \tag{14.49}$$

where

$$z(t) \equiv \frac{\int_0^1 z(v, t \mid q) q(v, t) dv}{Q(t)} \tag{14.50}$$

is the average R&D effort of incumbents at time t. Now subtracting $Q(t)$ from both sides of (14.49), dividing by Δt, and taking the limit as $\Delta t \to 0$, we obtain

$$\frac{\dot{Q}(t)}{Q(t)} = (\lambda - 1)\phi z(t) + (\kappa - 1)\hat{z}(t)\eta(\hat{z}(t)). \tag{14.51}$$

Therefore an alternative expression for the growth rate of the economy, which decomposes growth into the component coming from incumbent firms (the first term) and that coming from new entrants (the second term), is given by

$$g^* = (\lambda - 1)\phi z^* + (\kappa - 1)\hat{z}^*\eta(\hat{z}^*), \tag{14.52}$$

where z^* is the average BGP R&D effort of incumbents. The constancy of this average R&D effort in BGP follows from (14.51) together with the facts that in BGP the growth rate of average quality is g^* and the R&D effort by entrants on each machine line is $\hat{z}^*$. While (14.48) pins down the BGP growth rate of output and consumption, (14.52) determines z^* and thus how much of growth is driven by innovation by incumbents and how much of it by innovation by entrants. Moreover it can also be verified that this economy does not have any transitional dynamics (see Exercise 14.23). Therefore if an equilibrium with growth exists, it involves growth at the rate g^*. To ensure that such an equilibrium exists, we need to verify that R&D is profitable both for entrants and for incumbents. The condition that the BGP interest rate r^*, given by (14.47), should be greater than the discount rate ρ is sufficient for there to be positive aggregate growth. In addition, this interest rate should not be so high that household utility reaches an infinite value (or that the transversality condition is violated). Finally, we need to ensure that there is also innovation by incumbents. The following condition ensures all three of these requirements (see again Exercise 14.23):

$$\phi(\lambda - 1)\beta L - (\theta(\kappa - 1) + 1)\hat{z}^*\eta(\hat{z}^*) > \rho > (1 - \theta)(\phi(\lambda - 1)\beta L - \hat{z}^*\eta(\hat{z}^*)), \tag{14.53}$$

with $\hat{z}^*$ given by (14.45).

Another set of interesting implications of this model concern firm-size dynamics. The size of a firm can be measured by its sales and is equal to

$$x(v, t \mid q) = qL \quad \text{for all } v \text{ and } t.$$

To determine the law of motion of firm sales, let us focus on the equilibrium where $z(v, t \mid q) = z^*$ for all q. Then the quality of each incumbent firm increases at the flow rate ϕz^*, with z^* given by (14.48) and (14.52). At the same time, each incumbent is also replaced at the flow rate $\hat{z}^*\eta(\hat{z}^*)$. Therefore for Δt sufficiently small, the stochastic process for the size of a particular firm is given by

$$x(v, t + \Delta t \mid q) = \begin{cases} \lambda x(v, t \mid q) & \text{with probability } \phi z^*\Delta t + o(\Delta t), \\ 0 & \text{with probability } \hat{z}^*\eta(\hat{z}^*)\Delta t + o(\Delta t), \\ x(v, t \mid q) & \text{with probability } (1 - \phi z^*\Delta t - \hat{z}^*\eta(\hat{z}^*)\Delta t) + o(\Delta t), \end{cases} \tag{14.54}$$

for all v and t, where $\hat{z}^*$ is given by (14.45) and z^* by (14.48) and (14.52). Therefore firms have random growth, and surviving firms expand on average. However firms also face a probability of replacement (extinction), and in fact, eventually each firm will necessarily be replaced.

Proposition 14.5 *Consider the above-described economy starting with an initial condition $Q(0) > 0$. Suppose that (14.34) and (14.53) are satisfied, and focus on an equilibrium in which* *all incumbents exert the same level of R&D effort. Then there exists a unique equilibrium. In this equilibrium growth is always balanced, and technology $Q(t)$, aggregate output $Y(t)$, and aggregate consumption $C(t)$, grow at the rate g^* as in (14.48), with $\hat{z}^*$ given by (14.45). Equilibrium growth is driven by both innovation by incumbents and creative destruction by entrants. Any given firm expands on average as long as it survives, but it is eventually replaced by a new entrant with probability one.*

Proof. See Exercise 14.23. ∎

Proposition 14.5 focuses on equilibria in which all incumbents exert the same R&D effort. Exercise 14.27 shows that the same conclusions hold when we do not focus on such equilibria. It is also straightforward to verify that for plausible parameter values, the BGP characterized here involves a significant fraction of productivity improvements generated by incumbents. Therefore this class of models can lead to richer equilibrium patterns with both incumbents and entrants contributing to innovation and productivity growth.

14.3.3 The Effects of Policy on Growth

Let us now use this model to analyze the effects of policies on equilibrium productivity growth and its decomposition between incumbents and entrants. Since the model has a Schumpeterian structure (with quality improvements as the engine of growth and creative destruction playing a major role), it may be conjectured that entry barriers (or taxes on potential entrants) will have a negative effect on economic growth as in the baseline model earlier in this chapter. To investigate whether this is the case, let us suppose that there is a tax τ_e on R&D expenditure applied to entrants and a tax τ_i on R&D expenditure paid by incumbents (naturally, these quantities can be taken to be negative and interpreted as subsidies as well). Note also that the tax on entrants, τ_e, can be interpreted as a more strict patent policy than the one in the baseline model, where the entrant did not have to pay the incumbent for partially benefiting from its accumulated knowledge. Nevertheless, to keep the analysis brief, I only focus on the case in which tax revenues are collected by the government rather than rebated back to incumbents as patent fees.

Repeating the above analysis yields the following equilibrium conditions:

$$\eta(\hat{z}^*)V(\kappa q) = (1 + \tau_e)q, \quad \text{or} \quad V(q) = \frac{q(1 + \tau_e)}{\kappa \eta(\hat{z}^*)}. \tag{14.55}$$

The equation that determines the optimal R&D decisions of incumbents, (14.43), is also modified because of the tax rate τ_i and becomes $\phi(V(\lambda q) - V(q)) = (1 + \tau_i)q$. Combining this with (14.55), we obtain

$$\phi\left(\frac{(\lambda - 1)(1 + \tau_e)}{\kappa \eta(\hat{z}^*)(1 + \tau_i)}\right) = 1.$$

Consequently the BGP R&D level by entrants $\hat{z}^*$, when their R&D is taxed at the rate τ_e, is given by

$$\hat{z}^* \equiv \eta^{-1}\left(\frac{\phi(\lambda - 1)(1 + \tau_e)}{\kappa(1 + \tau_i)}\right). \tag{14.56}$$

Equation (14.46) still applies, so that the BGP interest rate is $r^* = (1 + \tau_e)^{-1} \kappa \eta(\hat{z}^*)\beta L - \hat{z}^* \eta(\hat{z}^*)$, which, by substituting for (14.56), can be written as

$$r^* = \frac{\phi(\lambda - 1)\beta L}{1 + \tau_i} - \hat{z}^* \eta(\hat{z}^*),$$

and the BGP growth rate is

$$g^* = \frac{1}{\theta}\left(\frac{\phi(\lambda - 1)\beta L}{1 + \tau_i} - \eta(\hat{z}^*)\hat{z}^* - \rho\right),$$

with $\hat{z}^*$ given by (14.56). The following result is now immediate.

Proposition 14.6 *The growth rate of the economy is decreasing in the tax rate on incumbents, that is, $dg^*/d\tau_i < 0$, and is increasing in the tax rate on entrants, that is, $dg^*/d\tau_e > 0$.*

The result in this proposition is rather surprising and extreme. As shown above, in the baseline Schumpeterian model, making entry more difficult, either by using entry barriers or by taxing R&D by entrants, has negative effects on economic growth. Despite the Schumpeterian nature of the current model, blocking entry increases equilibrium growth. Moreover, as Exercise 14.25 shows, in the decentralized equilibrium of this economy there tends to be too much entry, so a tax on entry also tends to improve welfare. The intuition for this result is related to the main departure of this model from the standard Schumpeterian models. In contrast to the baseline Schumpeterian models, the engine of growth is still quality improvements, but these are undertaken by both incumbents and entrants. Entry barriers, by protecting incumbents, increase their value, and greater value of incumbents encourages more R&D investments and faster productivity growth. Taxing entrants makes incumbents more profitable, and this encourages further innovation by the incumbents. Taxes on entrants or entry barriers also further increase the contribution of incumbents to productivity growth.

Nevertheless this result should be interpreted with considerable caution. The model in this section is special in that the R&D technology of incumbents is linear. This linearity is important for Proposition 14.6. Exercise 14.26 characterizes the equilibrium when $\phi(z)$ is a concave function of z and shows that the effect of taxes on entrants in this case is ambiguous. Therefore Proposition 14.6 should be read as emphasizing a particular new channel in the starkest possible way, not as a realistic description of how innovation responds to tax policies.

14.4 Step-by-Step Innovations *

In the baseline Schumpeterian model and also in the extended Schumpeterian model of the previous section, new entrants could undertake innovation on any machine and did not need to have developed any know-how on a particular line of business. This assumption led to a simple structure, in many ways parallel to the models of expanding varieties studied in the previous chapter. However, quality improvements in practice may have a major cumulative aspect. Often, only firms that have already reached a certain level of knowledge in a particular product or machine line can engage in further innovations. Abernathy (1978, p. 70), for instance, concludes his study of a number of diverse industries by stating that "each of the major companies seems to have made more frequent contributions in a particular area," and he argues that this is because previous innovations in a field facilitate future innovations. This aspect is entirely absent from the baseline model of Schumpeterian growth, where any firm can engage in research to develop the next higher quality machine (and in addition, Arrow's replacement effect implies that incumbents do not undertake R&D, though this aspect was relaxed and generalized in the Section 14.3). A more realistic description of the research process may involve only a few firms engaging in continuous and cumulative innovation. These firms are then in continuous competition in a particular product or machine line.

This section presents a model of cumulative innovation of this type. Following Aghion et al. (2001), I refer to this model as one of *step-by-step innovation*. Such models are not only useful in providing a different conceptualization of the process of Schumpeterian growth, but they also enable us to endogenize the equilibrium market structure and allow a richer analysis of the effects of competition and intellectual property rights (IPR) policy. Together with the model of innovation by incumbents and entrants presented in the previous section, this model is a first step toward a framework in which existing firms (continuing establishments) contribute to productivity growth and build on their own past innovations (consistent with the empirical evidence as discussed in Section 18.1). In fact, the model in this section has a number of distinctive features relative to those presented so far. For instance, previous models predict that weaker patent protection and greater competition should reduce economic growth. Nevertheless existing empirical evidence suggests that industries with greater competition typically exhibit faster growth. Schumpeterian models with an endogenous market structure show that, under certain circumstances, greater competition (and weaker IPR protection) may increase growth.

14.4.1 Preferences and Technology

The economy admits a representative household with labor endowment normalized to 1 and supplied inelastically. To simplify the analysis, I assume that the instantaneous utility function takes a logarithmic form. Thus the representative household has preferences given by

$$\int_0^\infty \exp(-\rho t) \log C(t) dt, \tag{14.57}$$

where $\rho > 0$ is the discount rate, and $C(t)$ is consumption at date t.

Let $Y(t)$ be the total production of the final good at time t. The economy is closed, and the final good is used only for consumption (there is no investment or spending on machines), so that $C(t) = Y(t)$. The standard Euler equation from (14.57) then implies that

$$g(t) \equiv \frac{\dot{C}(t)}{C(t)} = \frac{\dot{Y}(t)}{Y(t)} = r(t) - \rho, \tag{14.58}$$

where this equation defines $g(t)$ as the growth rate of consumption and output, and $r(t)$ is the interest rate at date t.

The final good Y is produced using a continuum 1 of intermediate goods according to the Cobb-Douglas production function

$$Y(t) = \exp\left(\int_0^1 \log y(v, t) dv\right), \tag{14.59}$$

where $y(v, t)$ is the output of vth intermediate at time t. Throughout, I take the price of the final good (or the ideal price index of the intermediates) as the numeraire and denote the price of intermediate v at time t by $p^y(v, t)$. I also assume that there is free entry into the final good sector. These assumptions, together with the Cobb-Douglas production function (14.59), imply that each final good producer has the following demand for intermediates:

$$y(v, t) = \frac{Y(t)}{p^y(v, t)} \quad \text{for all } v \in [0, 1]. \tag{14.60}$$

Intermediate $v \in [0, 1]$ comes in two different varieties, each produced by one of two firms. These two varieties are perfect substitutes and compete à la Bertrand. No other firm is able to produce in this industry. Firm $i = 1$ or 2 in industry v has the following technology:

$$y_i(v, t) = q_i(v, t)l_i(v, t), \tag{14.61}$$

where $l_i(v, t)$ is the employment level of the firm, and $q_i(v, t)$ is its level of technology at time t. The only difference between the two firms is their technology, which is determined endogenously. Equation (14.61) implies that the marginal cost of producing intermediate v for firm i at time t is

$$MC_i(v, t) = \frac{w(t)}{q_i(v, t)}, \tag{14.62}$$

where $w(t)$ is the wage rate in the economy at time t.

Let us denote the *technological leader* in each industry by i and the *follower* by $-i$, so that

$$q_i(v, t) \geq q_{-i}(v, t).$$

Bertrand competition between the two firms implies that all intermediates are supplied by the leader at the limit price (see Exercise 14.29):

$$p_i^y(v, t) = \frac{w(t)}{q_{-i}(v, t)}. \tag{14.63}$$

Equation (14.60) then implies the following demand for intermediates:

$$y_i(v, t) = \frac{q_{-i}(v, t)}{w(t)} Y(t). \tag{14.64}$$

R&D leads to stochastic innovations. When the leader innovates, its technology improves by a factor $\lambda > 1$. The follower, on the other hand, can undertake R&D to catch up with the frontier technology. Let us assume that because this innovation is for the follower's variant of the product and results from its own R&D efforts, it does not constitute infringement of the patent of the leader, and the follower does not have to make any payments to the technological leader in the industry.

I simplify the analysis by assuming that R&D investments by the leader and the follower have the same costs and probability of success. In particular, in all cases, each firm (in every industry) has access to the following R&D technology (innovation possibilities frontier):

$$z_i(v, t) = \Phi(h_i(v, t)), \tag{14.65}$$

where $z_i(v, t)$ is the flow rate of innovation at time t, and $h_i(v, t)$ is the number of workers hired by firm i in industry v to work in the R&D process at time t. Let us assume that Φ is twice continuously differentiable and satisfies $\Phi'(\cdot) > 0$, $\Phi''(\cdot) < 0$, and $\Phi'(0) < \infty$, and that there exists $\bar{h} \in (0, \infty)$ such that $\Phi'(h) = 0$ for all $h \geq \bar{h}$. The assumption that $\Phi'(0) < \infty$ implies that there is no Inada condition when $h_i(v, t) = 0$. The last assumption, on the other hand, ensures that there is an upper bound on the flow rate of innovation. Recalling that the wage rate for labor is $w(t)$, the cost for R&D is therefore $w(t)G(z_i(v, t))$, where $G(z_i(v, t)) \equiv \Phi^{-1}(z_i(v, t))$, and the assumptions on Φ immediately imply that G is twice differentiable and satisfies $G'(\cdot) > 0$, $G''(\cdot) > 0$, $G'(0) > 0$, and $\lim_{z \to \bar{z}} G'(z) = \infty$, where $\bar{z} \equiv \Phi(\bar{h})$ is the maximal flow rate of innovation (with $\bar{h}$ defined above).

Let us next turn to the evolution of technologies within each industry. Suppose that leader i in industry v at time t has a technology level of

$$q_i(v, t) = \lambda^{n_i(v,t)}, \tag{14.66}$$

and that the follower $-i$'s technology at time t is

$$q_{-i}(v, t) = \lambda^{n_{-i}(v,t)}, \tag{14.67}$$

where, naturally, $n_i(v, t) \geq n_{-i}(v, t)$. Let us denote the technology gap in industry v at time t by $n(v, t) \equiv n_i(v, t) - n_{-i}(v, t)$. If the leader undertakes an innovation within a time interval of Δt, then the technology gap rises to $n(v, t + \Delta t) = n(v, t) + 1$ (the probability of two or more innovations within the interval Δt is again $o(\Delta t)$). If, on the other hand, the follower undertakes an innovation during the interval Δt, then $n(v, t + \Delta t) = 0$. In addition, let us assume that there is an IPR policy of the following form: the patent held by the technological leader expires at the exponential rate $\kappa < \infty$, in which case, the follower can close the technology gap. Given this specification, the law of motion of the technology gap in industry v can be expressed as

$$n(v, t + \Delta t) = \begin{cases} n(v, t) + 1 & \text{with probability } z_i(v, t)\Delta t + o(\Delta t), \\ 0 & \text{with probability } (z_{-i}(v, t) + \kappa)\Delta t + o(\Delta t), \\ n(v, t) & \text{with probability } 1 - (z_i(v, t) + z_{-i}(v, t) + \kappa)\Delta t - o(\Delta t)), \end{cases} \tag{14.68}$$

In the first line, when $n(v, t) = 0$ so that the two firms are *neck-and-neck*, by convention $z_i(v, t) = 2z_0(v, t)$. Here $o(\Delta t)$ again represents second-order terms, in particular, the probabilities of more than one innovation within an interval of length Δt. The terms $z_i(v, t)$ and $z_{-i}(v, t)$ are the flow rates of innovation by the leader and the follower, respectively, while κ is the flow rate at which the follower is allowed to copy the technology of the leader.

We next write the instantaneous *operating* profits for the leader (the profits exclusive of R&D expenditures and license fees). Profits of leader i in industry v at time t are

$$\Pi_i(v, t) = \left(p_i^y(v, t) - MC_i(v, t)\right) y_i(v, t)$$

$$= \left(\frac{w(t)}{q_{-i}(v, t)} - \frac{w(t)}{q_i(v, t)}\right) \frac{Y(t)}{p_i^y(v, t)}$$

$$= \left(1 - \lambda^{-n(v,t)}\right) Y(t), \tag{14.69}$$

where recall that $n(v, t)$ is the technology gap in industry v at time t. The first line simply uses the definition of operating profits as price minus marginal cost times quantity sold. The second line uses the fact that the equilibrium limit price of firm i is $p_i^y(v, t) = w(t)/q_{-i}(v, t)$ as given by (14.63), and the final equality uses the definitions of $q_i(v, t)$ and $q_{-i}(v, t)$ from (14.66) and (14.67). The expression in (14.69) also implies that there will be zero profits in an industry that is neck-and-neck (i.e., with $n(v, t) = 0$). Followers also make zero profits, since they have no sales. Since the profits $\Pi_i(v, t)$ in (14.69) only depend on $Y(t)$ and the gap between the leader and the follower, $n(v, t)$, let us denote them by $\Pi_n(t)$.

The Cobb-Douglas aggregate production function in (14.59) is responsible for the simple form of the profits (14.69), since it implies that profits only depend on the technology gap of the industry and aggregate output. This simplifies the analysis below by making the technology gap in each industry the only industry-specific state variable relevant to payoff.

The objective function of each firm is to maximize the net present discounted value of net profits. In doing this, each firm takes the paths of interest rates $[r(t)]_{t=0}^{\infty}$, aggregate output levels $[Y(t)]_{t=0}^{\infty}$, wages $[w(t)]_{t=0}^{\infty}$, the R&D decisions of all other firms, and policies as given. Note that as in the baseline model of Schumpeterian growth in Section 14.1, even though technology and output in each sector are stochastic, total output $Y(t)$, given by (14.59), is nonstochastic.

14.4.2 Equilibrium

Let $\mu(t) \equiv \{\mu_n(t)\}_{n=0}^{\infty}$ denote the distribution of industries over different technology gaps, with $\sum_{n=0}^{\infty} \mu_n(t) = 1$. For example, $\mu_0(t)$ denotes the fraction of industries in which the firms are neck-and-neck at time t. Throughout, I focus on Markov Perfect Equilibria (MPE), where strategies are only functions of the payoff-relevant state variables. MPE is a natural equilibrium concept in this context, since it does not allow for implicit collusive agreements between the follower and the leader (see Appendix C for references and a further discussion of MPE). While such collusive agreements may be likely when there are only two firms in the industry, in most industries there are many more firms and also many potential entrants, making collusion more difficult. To simplify notation, I drop the dependence on industry v and refer to R&D decisions by z_n for the technological leader that is n steps ahead and by z_{-n} for a follower that is n steps behind. I also denote the list of decisions by the leader and follower with technology gap n at time t by $\xi_n(t) \equiv \left(z_n(t), p_i^y(v, t), y_i(v, t) \right)$ and $\xi_{-n}(t) \equiv z_{-n}(t)$, respectively. Throughout, ξ indicates the whole sequence of decisions at every state: $\xi(t) \equiv \{\xi_n(t)\}_{n=-\infty}^{\infty}$.[10]

An MPE is represented by time paths $[\xi^*(t), w^*(t), r^*(t), Y^*(t)]_{t=0}^{\infty}$ such that

1. $[p_i^{y*}(v, t)]_{t=0}^{\infty}$ and $[y_i^*(v, t)]_{t=0}^{\infty}$ implied by $[\xi^*(t)]_{t=0}^{\infty}$ satisfy (14.63) and (14.64);
2. R&D policies $[\mathbf{z}^*(t)]_{t=0}^{\infty}$ are best responses to themselves; that is, $[\mathbf{z}^*(t)]_{t=0}^{\infty}$ maximizes the expected profits of firms taking aggregate output $[Y^*(t)]_{t=0}^{\infty}$, factor prices $[w^*(t), r^*(t)]_{t=0}^{\infty}$, and the R&D policies of other firms $[\mathbf{z}^*(t)]_{t=0}^{\infty}$ as given;
3. aggregate output $[Y^*(t)]_{t=0}^{\infty}$ is given by (14.59); and
4. the labor and capital markets clear at all times given the factor prices $[w^*(t), r^*(t)]_{t=0}^{\infty}$.

Let us now characterize this equilibrium. Since only the technological leader produces, labor demand in an industry with technology gap $n(v, t) = n$ can be expressed as

$$l_n(t) = \frac{\lambda^{-n} Y(t)}{w(t)} \quad \text{for } n \geq 0. \tag{14.70}$$

---

10. There are two sources of abuse of notation here. First, pricing and output decisions, given by (14.63) and (14.64), depend on the aggregate level of output $Y(t)$ as well. However, profits, as given by (14.69), and other choices do not depend on $Y(t)$, and I suppress this dependence without any effect on the analysis. Second, the sequences $[p_i^{y*}(v, t)]_{t=0}^{\infty}$ and $[y_i^*(v, t)]_{t=0}^{\infty}$ are stochastic, while the rest of the objects specified above are not. Since the stochastic nature of these sequences has no effect on the analysis, I suppress this feature as well.

In addition, there is demand for labor coming from R&D of both followers and leaders in all industries. Using (14.65) and the definition of the G function, we can express demand for R&D labor in an industry with technology gap n as

$$h_n(t) = G(z_n(t)) + G(z_{-n}(t)). \tag{14.71}$$

The labor market clearing condition can then be expressed as

$$1 \geq \sum_{n=0}^{\infty} \mu_n(t) \left(\frac{1}{\omega(t)\lambda^n} + G(z_n(t)) + G(z_{-n}(t)) \right), \tag{14.72}$$

and $\omega(t) \geq 0$, with complementary slackness, where

$$\omega(t) \equiv \frac{w(t)}{Y(t)} \tag{14.73}$$

is the labor share at time t. The labor market clearing condition (14.72) uses the fact that total supply is equal to 1, and the demand cannot exceed this amount. If demand falls short of 1, then the wage rate $w(t)$ and thus the labor share $\omega(t)$ have to be equal to zero (though this will never be the case in equilibrium).

The relevant index of aggregate quality in this economy is no longer the average but instead reflects the Cobb-Douglas aggregator in the production function (14.59). It is

$$\log Q(t) \equiv \int_0^1 \log q(\nu, t)d\nu. \tag{14.74}$$

Given (14.74), the equilibrium wage can be written as (see Exercise 14.30)

$$w(t) = Q(t)\lambda^{-\sum_{n=0}^{\infty} n\mu_n(t)}. \tag{14.75}$$

14.4.3   Steady-State Equilibrium

Let us now focus on steady-state MPEs, where the distribution of industries $\mu(t) \equiv \{\mu_n(t)\}_{n=0}^{\infty}$ is stationary, and $\omega(t)$ defined in (14.73) and the growth rate g^* are constant over time. If the economy is in steady state at time $t = 0$, then by definition, $Y(t) = Y_0 e^{g^* t}$, and $w(t) = w_0 \exp(g^* t)$. The two equations also imply that $\omega(t) = \omega^*$ for all $t \geq 0$.

Standard arguments imply that the value function for a firm that is n steps ahead (when the follower chooses $z_{-n}^*(t)$) is given by

$$r(t)V_n(t) - \dot{V}_n(t) = \max_{z_n(t)}\{[\Pi_n(t) - w^*(t)G(z_n(t))] \tag{14.76}$$

$$+ z_n(t)[V_{n+1}(t) - V_n(t)] + [z_{-n}^*(t) + \kappa][V_0(t) - V_n(t)]\}.$$

In steady state, the net present value of a firm that is n steps ahead, $V_n(t)$, also grows at a constant rate g^* for all $n \geq 0$. Let us then define normalized values as

$$v_n(t) \equiv \frac{V_n(t)}{Y(t)} \tag{14.77}$$

for all n, which will be independent of time in steady state—that is, $v_n(t) = v_n$.

Using (14.77) and the fact that, from (14.58), $r(t) = g(t) + \rho$, the steady-state value function (14.76) can be written as

$$\rho v_n = \max_{z_n} \{(1 - \lambda^{-n}) - \omega^* G(z_n) + z_n[v_{n+1} - v_n] \tag{14.78}$$

$$+ [z_{-n}^* + \kappa][v_0 - v_n]\} \quad \text{for all } n \geq 1,$$

where z_{-n}^* is the equilibrium value of R&D for a follower that is n steps behind, and ω^* is the steady-state labor share (while z_n is now explicitly chosen to maximize v_n).

Similarly the value for neck-and-neck firms is

$$\rho v_0 = \max_{z_0} \left\{ -\omega^* G(z_0) + z_0[v_1 - v_0] + z_0^*[v_{-1} - v_0] \right\}, \tag{14.79}$$

while the values for followers do not depend on how many steps behind the leader they are (because a single innovation is sufficient to catch up with the leader) and are given by

$$\rho v_{-1} = \max_{z_{-1}} \left\{ -\omega^* G(z_{-1}) + [z_{-1} + \kappa][v_0 - v_{-1}] \right\}. \tag{14.80}$$

The maximization problems involved in the value functions are straightforward and immediately yield the following profit-maximizing R&D decisions:

$$z_n^* = \max \left\{ G'^{-1} \left(\frac{[v_{n+1} - v_n]}{\omega^*} \right), 0 \right\}, \tag{14.81}$$

$$z_{-1}^* = \max \left\{ G'^{-1} \left(\frac{[v_0 - v_{-1}]}{\omega^*} \right), 0 \right\}, \tag{14.82}$$

$$z_0^* = \max \left\{ G'^{-1} \left(\frac{[v_1 - v_0]}{\omega^*} \right), 0 \right\}, \tag{14.83}$$

where z_{-1}^* is the R&D decision by all followers, and $G'^{-1}(\cdot)$ is the inverse of the derivative of the G function. Since G is twice differentiable and strictly convex, G'^{-1} is differentiable and strictly increasing. These equations therefore imply that innovation rates, the z_n^*s, are increasing in the incremental value of moving to the next step and decreasing in the cost of R&D, as measured by the normalized wage rate ω^*. Note also that since $G'(0) > 0$, these R&D levels can be equal to zero, which is taken care of by the max operator.

The response of innovation rates, z_n^*, to the increments in values, $v_{n+1} - v_n$, is the key economic force in this model. For example, a policy that reduces the patent protection of leaders that are $n + 1$ steps ahead (by increasing κ) will make being $n + 1$ steps ahead less profitable, thus reducing $v_{n+1} - v_n$ and z_n^*. This corresponds to the standard *disincentive effect* of relaxing IPR protection. However, relaxing IPR protection may also create a beneficial *composition effect:* because $\{v_{n+1} - v_n\}_{n=0}^{\infty}$ is a decreasing sequence, it implies that z_{-1}^* is higher than z_n^* for $n \geq 1$ (see Proposition 14.9 below). Weaker patent protection (in the form of shorter patent lengths) shifts more industries into the neck-and-neck state and potentially increases the equilibrium level of R&D in the economy.

Given the equilibrium R&D decisions, the steady-state distribution of industries across states μ^* has to satisfy the following accounting identities:

$$(z_{n+1}^* + z_{-1}^* + \kappa)\mu_{n+1}^* = z_n^*\mu_n^* \text{ for } n \geq 1, \tag{14.84}$$

$$(z_1^* + z_{-1}^* + \kappa)\mu_1^* = 2z_0^*\mu_0^*, \tag{14.85}$$

$$2z_0^*\mu_0^* = z_{-1}^* + \kappa. \tag{14.86}$$

The first expression equates exit from state $n + 1$ (which takes the form of the leader going one more step ahead or the follower catching up to the leader) to entry into this state (which takes the form of a leader from the state n making one more innovation). Equation (14.85) performs the same accounting for state 1, taking into account that entry into this state comes from innovation by either of the two firms that are competing neck-and-neck. Finally, (14.86) equates exit from state 0 with entry into this state, which comes from innovation by a follower in any industry with $n \geq 1$.

The labor market clearing condition in steady state can then be written as

$$1 \geq \sum_{n=0}^{\infty} \mu_n^* \left(\frac{1}{\omega^*\lambda^n} + G(z_n^*) + G(z_{-n}^*) \right), \text{ and } \omega^* \geq 0, \tag{14.87}$$

with complementary slackness.

The next proposition characterizes the steady-state growth rate in this economy.

Proposition 14.7 *The steady-state growth rate in the above economy is given by*

$$g^* = \log \lambda \left(2\mu_0^*z_0^* + \sum_{n=1}^{\infty} \mu_n^*z_n^* \right). \tag{14.88}$$

Proof. Equations (14.73) and (14.75) imply

$$Y(t) = \frac{w(t)}{\omega(t)} = \frac{Q(t)\lambda^{-\sum_{n=0}^{\infty} n\mu_n^*(t)}}{\omega(t)}.$$

Since $\omega(t) = \omega^*$ and $\{\mu_n^*\}_{n=0}^{\infty}$ are constant in steady state, $Y(t)$ grows at the same rate as $Q(t)$. Therefore

$$g^* = \lim_{\Delta t \to 0} \frac{\log Q(t + \Delta t) - \log Q(t)}{\Delta t}.$$

During an interval of length Δt, in a fraction μ_n^* of the industries with technology gap $n \geq 1$ the leaders innovate at a rate $z_n^*\Delta t + o(\Delta t)$, and in the fraction μ_0^* of the industries with technology gap of $n = 0$ both firms innovate, so that the total innovation rate is $2z_0^*\Delta t + o(\Delta t)$). Since each innovation increases productivity by a factor λ, we obtain the preceding equation. Combining these observations yields

$$\log Q(t + \Delta t) = \log Q(t) + \log \lambda \left(2\mu_0^*z_0^*\Delta t + \sum_{n=1}^{\infty} \mu_n^*z_n^*\Delta t + o(\Delta t) \right).$$

Subtracting $\log Q(t)$, dividing by Δt, and taking the limit as $\Delta t \to 0$ gives (14.88). ∎

This proposition clarifies that the steady-state growth comes from two sources: (1) R&D decisions of leaders or of firms in neck-and-neck industries and (2) the distribution of industries across different technology gaps, $\mu^* \equiv \{\mu_n^*\}_{n=0}^{\infty}$. The latter channel reflects the composition effect discussed above. This type of composition effect implies that the relationship between competition and growth (or IPR protection and growth) is more complex than in the models discussed so far, because such policies change the equilibrium market structure (the composition of industries).

A steady-state equilibrium can be summarized by $\langle \mu^*, \mathbf{v}, \mathbf{z}^*, \omega^*, g^* \rangle$ such that the distribution of industries μ^* satisfies (14.84), (14.85), and (14.86); the values $\mathbf{v} \equiv \{v_n\}_{n=-\infty}^{\infty}$ satisfy (14.78), (14.79), and (14.80); the R&D decisions $\mathbf{z}^*$ are given by (14.81), (14.82), and (14.83); the steady-state labor share ω^* satisfies (14.87); and the steady-state growth rate g^* is given by (14.88). I next provide a characterization of the steady-state equilibrium. The first result is a technical one that is necessary for this characterization.

Proposition 14.8 *In a steady-state equilibrium, $v_{-1} \leq v_0$, and $\{v_n\}_{n=0}^{\infty}$ forms a bounded and strictly increasing sequence converging to some positive value v_∞. Moreover there exists $n^* \geq 1$ such that $z_n^* = 0$ for all $n \geq n^*$.*

Proof. Let $\{z_n\}_{n=-1}^{\infty}$ be the R&D decisions of a firm and $\{v_n\}_{n=-1}^{\infty}$ be the sequence of values, taking the decisions of other firms and the industry distributions, $\{z_n^*\}_{n=-1}^{\infty}$, $\{\mu_n^*\}_{n=-1}^{\infty}$, ω^*, and g^*, as given. By choosing $z_n = 0$ for all $n \geq -1$, the firm guarantees $v_n \geq 0$ for all $n \geq -1$. Let π_n denote normalized flow profits when the technology gap is n. Then, since $\pi_n \leq 1$ for all $n \geq -1$, $v_n \leq 1/\rho$ for all $n \geq -1$, establishing that $\{v_n\}_{n=-1}^{\infty}$ is a bounded sequence, with $v_n \in [0, 1/\rho]$ for all $n \geq -1$.

Proof of $v_1 > v_0$: Suppose, first, that $v_1 \leq v_0$. Then (14.83) implies $z_0^* = 0$, and by the symmetry of the problem in equilibrium, (14.79) would imply $v_0 = v_1 = 0$. As a result, from (14.82) we obtain $z_{-1}^* = 0$. Equation (14.78) then implies that when $z_{-1}^* = 0$, $v_1 \geq (1 - \lambda^{-1})/(\rho + \kappa) > 0$, yielding a contradiction and proving that $v_1 > v_0$.

Proof of $v_{-1} \leq v_0$: Suppose, to obtain a contradiction, that $v_{-1} > v_0$. Then (14.82) implies $z_{-1}^* = 0$, which leads to $v_{-1} = \kappa v_0/(\rho + \kappa)$. The last equation contradicts $v_{-1} > v_0$, since $\kappa/(\rho + \kappa) < 1$ (given that $\kappa < \infty$).

Proof of $v_n < v_{n+1}$: Suppose, to obtain a contradiction, that $v_n \geq v_{n+1}$. Now (14.81) implies $z_n^* = 0$, and (14.78) becomes

$$\rho v_n = (1 - \lambda^{-n}) + z_{-1}^*[v_0 - v_n] + \kappa[v_0 - v_n]$$

Also from (14.78), the value for state $n + 1$ satisfies

$$\rho v_{n+1} \geq (1 - \lambda^{-n-1}) + z_{-1}^*[v_0 - v_{n+1}] + \kappa[v_0 - v_{n+1}].$$

Combining the two previous expressions yields

$$(1 - \lambda^{-n}) + z_{-1}^*[v_0 - v_n] + \kappa[v_0 - v_n] \geq 1 - \lambda^{-n-1} + z_{-1}^*[v_0 - v_{n+1}] + \kappa[v_0 - v_{n+1}].$$

Since $\lambda^{-n-1} < \lambda^{-n}$, this implies $v_n < v_{n+1}$, contradicting the hypothesis that $v_n \geq v_{n+1}$ and establishing the desired result: $v_n < v_{n+1}$.

Consequently $\{v_n\}_{n=-1}^{\infty}$ is nondecreasing and $\{v_n\}_{n=0}^{\infty}$ is (strictly) increasing. Since a nondecreasing sequence in a compact set must converge, $\{v_n\}_{n=-1}^{\infty}$ converges to its limit point v_∞, which must be strictly positive, since $\{v_n\}_{n=0}^{\infty}$ is strictly increasing and has a nonnegative initial value. Exercise 14.31 completes the proof by showing that there exists $n^* \geq 1$ such that $z_n^* = 0$ for all $n \geq n^*$. ∎

The next proposition provides the most important economic insights of this model and shows that $\mathbf{z}^* \equiv \{z_n^*\}_{n=0}^{\infty}$ is a decreasing sequence. Thus technological leaders that are further ahead undertake less R&D. Intuitively, the benefits of further R&D investments are decreasing in the technology gap, since greater values of the technology gap translate into smaller increases markups and profits (recall (14.69)). The fact that leaders who are sufficiently ahead of their competitors undertake little R&D is the main reason composition effects play an important role in this model. For example, all else equal, closing the technology gaps between leaders and followers increases R&D spending and equilibrium growth.

Proposition 14.9 *In any steady-state equilibrium, $z_{n+1}^* \leq z_n^*$ for all $n \geq 1$, and moreover $z_{n+1}^* < z_n^*$ if $z_n^* > 0$. Furthermore, $z_0^* > z_1^*$, and $z_0^* \geq z_{-1}^*$.*

Proof. From (14.81),

$$\delta_{n+1} \equiv v_{n+1} - v_n < v_n - v_{n-1} \equiv \delta_n \tag{14.89}$$

is sufficient to establish that $z_{n+1}^* \leq z_n^*$. Let us write

$$\bar{\rho} v_n = \max_{z_n}\{(1 - \lambda^{-n}) - \omega^* G(z_n) + z_n[v_{n+1} - v_n] + (z_{-1}^* + \kappa)v_0\}, \tag{14.90}$$

where $\bar{\rho} \equiv \rho + z_{-1}^* + \kappa$. Since z_{n+1}^*, z_n^*, and z_{n-1}^* are maximizers of the value functions v_{n+1}, v_n, and v_{n-1}, respectively, (14.90) implies

$$\bar{\rho} v_{n+1} = 1 - \lambda^{-n-1} - \omega^* G(z_{n+1}^*) + z_{n+1}^*[v_{n+2} - v_{n+1}] + (z_{-1}^* + \kappa)v_0,$$

$$\bar{\rho} v_n \geq 1 - \lambda^{-n} - \omega^* G(z_{n+1}^*) + z_{n+1}^*[v_{n+1} - v_n] + (z_{-1}^* + \kappa)v_0,$$

$$\bar{\rho} v_n \geq 1 - \lambda^{-n} - \omega^* G(z_{n-1}^*) + z_{n-1}^*[v_{n+1} - v_n] + (z_{-1}^* + \kappa)v_0, \tag{14.91}$$

$$\bar{\rho} v_{n-1} = 1 - \lambda^{-n+1} - \omega^* G(z_{n-1}^*) + z_{n-1}^*[v_n - v_{n-1}] + (z_{-1}^* + \kappa)v_0.$$

Now taking differences with $\bar{\rho} v_n$ and using the definition of δ_n yields

$$\bar{\rho}\delta_{n+1} \leq \lambda^{-n}(1 - \lambda^{-1}) + z_{n+1}^*(\delta_{n+2} - \delta_{n+1})$$

$$\bar{\rho}\delta_n \geq \lambda^{-n+1}(1 - \lambda^{-1}) + z_{n-1}^*(\delta_{n+1} - \delta_n).$$

Therefore

$$(\bar{\rho} + z_{n-1}^*)(\delta_{n+1} - \delta_n) \leq -k_n + z_{n+1}^*(\delta_{n+2} - \delta_{n+1}),$$

where $k_n \equiv (\lambda - 1)^2 \lambda^{-n-1} > 0$. Now to obtain a contradiction, suppose that $\delta_{n+1} - \delta_n \geq 0$. From the previous equation, this implies that $\delta_{n+2} - \delta_{n+1} > 0$ since k_n is strictly positive. Repeating this argument successively, we have that if $\delta_{n'+1} - \delta_{n'} \geq 0$, then $\delta_{n+1} - \delta_n > 0$ for all $n \geq n'$. However we know from Proposition 14.8 that $\{v_n\}_{n=0}^{\infty}$ is strictly increasing and converges to a constant v_∞. Thus $\delta_{n+1} - \delta_n < 0$ for sufficiently large n (with $\delta_n \uparrow 0$), which contradicts the hypothesis that $\delta_{n+1} - \delta_n \geq 0$ for all $n \geq n' \geq 0$ and establishes that $z_{n+1}^* \leq z_n^*$. To see that the inequality is strict when $z_n^* > 0$, it suffices to note that (14.89) has already been established, that is, $\delta_{n+1} - \delta_n < 0$. Thus if (14.81) has a positive solution, then we necessarily have $z_{n+1}^* < z_n^*$.

Proof of $z_0^* \geq z_{-1}^*$: (14.79) can be written as

$$\rho v_0 = -\omega^* G(z_0^*) + z_0^*[v_{-1} + v_1 - 2v_0]. \tag{14.92}$$

We have $v_0 \geq 0$ from Proposition 14.8. Suppose $v_0 > 0$. Then (14.92) implies $z_0^* > 0$ and

$$v_{-1} + v_1 - 2v_0 > 0, \text{ or} \qquad (14.93)$$

$$v_1 - v_0 > v_0 - v_{-1}.$$

This inequality combined with (14.83) and (14.82) yields $z_0^* > z_{-1}^*$. Suppose next that $v_0 = 0$. The Inequality (14.93) now holds as a weak inequality and implies that $z_0^* \geq z_{-1}^*$. Moreover, since $G(\cdot)$ is strictly convex and z_0^* is given by (14.83), (14.92) implies $z_0^* = 0$, and thus $z_{-1}^* = 0$.

Proof of $z_0^* > z_1^*$: See Exercise 14.32. ■

This proposition therefore shows that the greatest amount of R&D is undertaken in neck-and-neck industries. This explains why composition effects can increase aggregate innovation. Exercise 14.33 shows how a relaxation of IPR protection can increase growth.

So far, I have not provided a closed-form solution for the growth rate in this economy. It turns out that this is generally not possible because of the endogenous market structure in these types of models. Nevertheless it can be proved that a steady-state equilibrium exists in this economy, though the proof is somewhat more involved and does not generate additional insights for our purposes (see Acemoglu and Akcigit, 2006).

An important feature is that equilibrium markups are endogenous and evolve over time as a function of competition between the firms producing in the same product line. More importantly, Proposition 14.9 implies that when a particular firm is sufficiently ahead of its rival, it undertakes less R&D. Therefore this model, in contrast to the baseline Schumpeterian model and also contrary to all expanding varieties models, implies that greater competition (e.g., that generated by closing the gap between the followers and leaders) may increase growth because it induces the leaders to undertake more R&D to escape the competition from the followers. Similarly the model can be extended to incorporate different market structures and entry barriers, and in this case, the effect of competition on growth can be positive or negative.

14.5 Taking Stock

This chapter presented the basic Schumpeterian model of economic growth. Schumpeterian growth incorporates the process of creative destruction, where new products or machines replace older models and new firms replace incumbent producers.

The baseline model features process innovations leading to quality improvements. The description of economic growth that emerges from this model is, in many ways, more realistic than the expanding variety models. In particular, technological progress does not always correspond to new products or machines complementing existing ones but instead involves the creation of higher quality producers replacing incumbents. Arrow's replacement effect, discussed in Chapter 12, implies that there is a strong incentive for new entrants to undertake research because the new, higher-quality products will replace the products of incumbents, leading to Schumpeterian creative destruction as the engine of economic growth. Even though the description of economic growth in this model is richer, the mathematical structure turns out to be quite similar to the models with expanding varieties. In reduced form, the model again resembles an AK economy. An important difference is that now the growth rate of the economy, through the rate of replacement of old products, affects the value of innovation.

A major insight of Schumpeterian models is that growth comes with potential conflicts of interest. The process of creative destruction destroys the monopoly rents of previous incumbents. This raises the possibility that distortionary policies may arise endogenously as a way of protecting the rents of politically powerful incumbents. Models of creative destruction thus naturally raise the political economy issues that are central for understanding the fundamental causes of economic growth and provide us with insights about both the endogenous nature of technology and the potential resistance to technological change.

Schumpeterian models also enable us to make greater contact with the industrial organization of innovation. The process of creative destruction implies that market structures may be evolving endogenously over time. Nevertheless the baseline Schumpeterian models have a number of shortcomings, and addressing these is an interesting and important area for future research. An important discrepancy between the baseline models and the data is that, while the models predict all productivity growth should come from creative destruction and entry, in the data much of it comes from the incumbent firms and plants. Section 14.3 provided a first look at how the baseline models can be extended to account for these patterns and to provide a richer framework for the analysis of the industrial organization of innovation. A second important shortcoming of the baseline models is that they predict that markups are constant, and there is always a single firm supplying the entire market. These implications can also be relaxed by considering a richer framework, for example, by allowing cumulative or step-by-step innovation and competition between multiple firms that engage in innovation. Section 14.4 showed how the baseline model can be extended in this direction. Perhaps more interestingly, in models that incorporate different aspects of the industrial organization of innovation, the effects of competition and patent protection on economic growth are potentially richer. This observation suggests that (extensions of) Schumpeterian models might provide a useful framework for the analysis of a range of policies, including antitrust, licensing, and IPR policies, on growth.

14.6 References and Literature

The baseline model of Schumpeterian growth presented in Section 14.1 is based on the work by Aghion and Howitt (1992). Similar models have also been developed by Segerstrom, Anant, and Dinopoulos (1990) and Grossman and Helpman (1991a,b). Aghion and Howitt (1998) provide an excellent survey of many Schumpeterian models of economic growth and numerous extensions. The specific modeling assumptions made in the presentation here draw on Acemoglu (1998). The original Aghion and Howitt (1992) approach is very similar to that used in Section 14.2. Aghion and Howitt (1992) also discuss uneven growth and potential growth cycles, which were presented in Section 14.2. Uneven growth and cycles are also possible in other models of endogenous technology, as shown by Matsuyama (1999). I only discussed the possibility of such cycles in the context of Schumpeterian growth, since the forces leading to such cycles are more pronounced in these models.

The effect of creative destruction on unemployment was first studied in Aghion and Howitt (1994). The implications of creative destruction for firm-specific investments are discussed in François and Roberts (2003) and in Martimort and Verdier (2004).

The model in Section 14.3 draws on Acemoglu (2008b) and is a first attempt to introducing productivity growth driven both by incumbents and by entrants. Klette and Kortum (2004) construct a related model of firm and aggregate innovation dynamics based on expanding product varieties. Klepper (1996) documents various facts about the firm size, entry and exit, and innovation.

Step-by-step or cumulative innovations have been analyzed in Aghion, Harris, and Vickers (1999) and Aghion et al. (2001). The model presented here is a simplified version of Acemoglu and Akcigit (2006). The notion of MPE used in Section 14.4 is further discussed in Appendix C and in Fudenberg and Tirole (1994).

Nickell (1996); Blundell, Griffith, and Van Reenen (1999); and Aghion et al. (2005) provide evidence that greater competition may encourage economic growth and technological progress. The last paper shows that industries in which the technology gap between firms is smaller are typically more innovative. Aghion et al. (2001, 2005) show that in step-by-step models of innovation greater competition may increase growth.

14.7 Exercises

14.1   Prove that in the baseline model of Schumpeterian growth in Section 14.1, BGP R&D toward different machine varieties must be equal to some z^*. [Hint: use (14.14) together with (14.13).]

14.2   (a) Prove that in the baseline model of Schumpeterian growth in Section 14.1, all R&D is undertaken by entrants, and R&D is never done by incumbents. [Hint: rewrite (14.13) by allowing for a choice of R&D investments.]

(b) Now suppose that the flow rate of success of R&D is $\phi\eta/q$ for an incumbent as opposed to η/q for an entrant. Show that for any value of $\phi \leq \lambda/(\lambda - 1)$, the incumbent still chooses zero R&D. Explain this result.

14.3   The baseline endogenous technological change models, including the model of Schumpeterian growth in this chapter, assume that new products are protected by perpetual patents. This assumption is not strictly necessary for the logic of these models. Suppose that there is no patent protection for any innovation, but copying an innovator requires a fixed cost $\varepsilon > 0$. Any firm, after paying this cost, has access to the same technology as the innovator. Prove that in this environment there is no copying and all the results of the model with fully enforced perpetual patents apply.

14.4   Complete the proof of Proposition 14.1. In particular, verify that the equilibrium growth rate is unique, strictly positive, and such that the transversality condition (14.16) is satisfied.

14.5   Prove Proposition 14.2.

14.6   Modify the baseline model of Section 14.1 so that the aggregate production function for the final good is

$$Y(t) = \frac{1}{1-\beta} \left(\int_0^1 (q(v,t)x(v,t\mid q))^{1-\beta} dv \right) L^\beta.$$

All the other features of the model remain unchanged. Show that a BGP does not exist. What would you change in the model to ensure the existence of a BGP?

* 14.7   In the baseline Schumpeterian growth model, instead of (14.3), suppose that the production function of the final good sector is given by

$$Y(t) = \frac{1}{1-\beta} \left(\int_0^1 q(v,t)^{\zeta_1} x(v,t\mid q)^{1-\beta} dv \right) L^\beta.$$

Suppose also that producing one unit of an intermediate good of quality q costs ψq^{ζ_2} and that one unit of final good devoted to research on the machine line with quality q generates a flow rate of innovation equal to η/q^{ζ_3}. Characterize the equilibrium of this economy and determine what combinations of the parameters ζ_1, ζ_2, and ζ_3 ensure balanced growth.

14.8   (a) Verify that Theorem 7.14 from Chapter 7 can be applied to the optimal growth problem in the baseline Schumpeterian model of Section 14.1.

(b) Show that the solution to this problem is unique. [Hint: recall Exercise 8.11 in Chapter 8.]

(c) Derive (14.27).

14.9 Show that condition (14.5) is sufficient to ensure that a firm that innovates will set the unconstrained monopoly price. [Hint: First suppose that the innovator sets the monopoly price $\psi q/(1-\beta)$ for a product of quality q. Then consider the firm with the next highest quality, $\lambda^{-1}q$. Suppose that this firm sells at marginal cost, $\psi\lambda^{-1}q$. Find the value of λ such that final good producers are indifferent between buying a machine of quality q at the price $\psi q/(1-\beta)$ versus a machine of quality $\lambda^{-1}q$ at the price $\psi\lambda^{-1}q$.]

14.10 Analyze the baseline model of Schumpeterian growth in Section 14.1 assuming that (14.5) is not satisfied.

    (a) Show that monopolists set a limit price.

    (b) Characterize the BGP equilibrium growth rate.

    (c) Characterize the Pareto optimal allocation, and compare it to the equilibrium.

    (d) Now consider a hypothetical economy in which the previous highest quality producer disappears, so that the monopolist can charge a markup of $1/(1-\beta)$ instead of the limit price. Show that the BGP growth rate in this hypothetical economy is strictly greater than the growth rate characterized in part b. Explain this result.

14.11 Suppose that there is constant exponential population growth at the rate n. Modify the baseline model of Section 14.1 so that there is no scale effect and the economy grows at the constant rate (with positive growth of income per capita). [Hint: suppose that one unit of final good spent on R&D for improving the machine of quality q leads to flow rate of innovation equal to η/q^{ϕ}, where $\phi > 1$.]

* 14.12 Consider a model of Schumpeterian growth where the xs do not depreciate fully after use (similar to Exercise 13.23 in the previous chapter). Preferences and the rest of technology are the same as in Section 14.1.

    (a) Formulate the maximization problem of a monopolist with the highest quality machine, and define the equilibrium and BGP allocations.

    (b) Show that, contrary to Exercise 13.23 in the previous chapter, the results are different than those in Section 14.1. Explain why depreciation of machines was not important in the expanding varieties model but is important in Schumpeterian models.

14.13 Consider a version of the model of Schumpeterian growth in which innovations reduce costs instead of increasing quality. In particular, suppose that the aggregate production function is given by

$$Y(t) = \frac{1}{1-\beta}\left(\int_0^1 x(v, t)^{1-\beta}dv\right)L^{\beta},$$

and the marginal cost of producing machine variety v at time t is given by $MC(v, t)$. Every innovation reduces this cost by a factor λ.

    (a) Define the equilibrium and BGP allocations.

    (b) Specify a form of the innovation possibilities frontier that is consistent with balanced growth.

    (c) Derive the BGP growth rate of the economy, and show that there are no transitional dynamics.

    (d) Compare the BGP growth rate to the Pareto optimal growth rate of the economy. Can there be excessive innovation?

14.14 Consider the model in Section 14.2, with R&D performed by workers. Suppose instead that the aggregate production function for the final good is given by

$$Y(t) = \frac{1}{1-\beta}\left(\int_0^1 q(v, t)x(v, t \mid q)^{1-\beta}dv\right)L_E(t)^{\beta},$$

where $L_E(t)$ denotes the number of workers employed in final good production at time t.

(a) Show that in this case, there will only be R&D for the machine with the highest $q(v, t)$.

(b) How would you modify the model so that the equilibrium has balanced R&D across sectors?

14.15 Consider the model of Schumpeterian growth in Section 14.1, with one difference: conditional on success, an innovation generates a random improvement of λ over the previous technology, where the distribution function of λ is $H(\lambda)$ and has support $[(1 - \beta)^{-(1-\beta)/\beta}, \bar{\lambda}]$.

(a) Define and characterize the BGP.

(b) Why is the lower support of λ taken to be $(1 - \beta)^{-1}$? How would the analysis change if this condition were relaxed?

(c) Show that there are no transitional dynamics in this economy.

(d) Compare the BGP growth rate to the Pareto optimal growth rate of the economy. Can there be excessive innovation?

14.16 In the model of Section 14.2 show that the economy experiences no growth of output for intervals of average length $1/(\eta L_R^*)$.

14.17 (a) Prove Proposition 14.4, in particular verifying that the allocation described there is unique, the average growth rate is given by $g^* = \log \lambda \eta L_R^*$, and condition (14.30) is necessary and sufficient for the existence of the equilibrium described in the proposition.

(b) Explain why the growth rate features $\log \lambda$ rather than $\lambda - 1$ as in the model of Section 14.1.

14.18 Consider the one-sector Schumpeterian model in discrete time. Suppose as in the model in Section 14.2 that households are risk neutral, there is no population growth, and the final good sector has the production function given by (14.28). There is a linear production technology for intermediate goods whereby any intermediate good (that has been invented) can be produced at the marginal cost of ψ units of the final good. Assume also that the R&D technology is such that $L_R > 0$ workers employed in research at time t necessarily leads to an innovation at time $t + 1$, and the number of workers used in research simply determines the quality (size) of the innovation via the function $\Lambda(L_R)$; that is, if date t quality is q, the new, date $t + 1$, machine has quality $q' = \Lambda(L_R)q$. Assume that there will be innovation only if $L_R > 0$ and $\Lambda(\cdot)$ is strictly increasing, differentiable, strictly concave, and satisfies the appropriate Inada conditions.

(a) Characterize the BGP and specify restrictions on parameters so that the transversality condition is satisfied. [Hint: to simplify the algebra, you may wish to assume that once the new machine is invented, the old one cannot be used any longer, so that there is no limit pricing.]

(b) Compare the BGP growth rate to the Pareto optimal growth rate of the economy. Show that the size of innovations is always too small relative to the size of innovations in the Pareto optimal allocation.

* 14.19 Consider the one-sector Schumpeterian model in discrete time analyzed in the previous exercise, except that now $\Lambda(\cdot)$ denotes the probability of innovation, and each innovation improves the quality of a machine q to λq, where $\lambda > 1$. Suppose that when a new innovation arrives a fraction φ of workers employed in the final good production are unable to adapt to this new technology and need to remain unemployed for one time period to "retool."

(a) Define the equilibrium and steady-state (BGP) allocations. [Hint: also specify the number of unemployed workers in equilibrium.]

(b) Define the appropriate generalization of the steady state for this economy, and determine the number of unemployed workers in this equilibrium.

(c) Show that the economy experiences bursts of unemployment followed by periods of full employment.

(d) Show that a decline in ρ increases the average growth rate and the average unemployment rate in the economy.

* 14.20 Derive (14.31)–(14.32).

* 14.21 Consider the model discussed in Section 14.2.2.

(a) Choose a functional form for $\eta(\cdot)$ such that equations (14.32) have solutions L_R^1 and $L_R^2 \neq L_R^1$. Explain why, when such solutions exist, there is an equilibrium with two-period endogenous cycles.

(b) Show that even when such solutions exist, there also exists a steady-state equilibrium with constant research.

(c) Show that when such solutions do not exist, there exists an equilibrium that exhibits oscillatory transitional dynamics converging to the steady state in part b.

* 14.22 Show that the qualitative results in Section 14.2.2 generalize when there is a single firm undertaking research, thus internalizing the effect of L_R on $\eta(L_R)$.

* 14.23 This exercise sketches the proof of Proposition 14.5.

(a) Note that in an interior BGP where $\phi(V(\nu, t \mid \lambda q) - V(\nu, t \mid q)) = q$, V must be linear in q, and thus $V(\nu, t \mid q) = vq$ as used in the text. Given this observation, show that $\hat{z}^*$ is uniquely determined by (14.45) and is strictly positive, and (14.48) gives the unique BGP growth rate, which is also strictly positive. Next use (14.48) and (14.52) to show that z^* is also strictly positive. Finally, show that the transversality condition (14.16) is satisfied when (14.53) holds.

(b) Now show that the interior BGP from part a also gives the unique dynamic equilibrium path. First, show that when (14.43) holds, $V(\nu, t \mid q)$ is everywhere linear in q and thus can be written as $V(\nu, t \mid q) = v(t)q$ for some function $v(t)$. Therefore, from (14.43), $\phi(\lambda - 1)v(t) = 1$ for all t. Differentiating this equation with respect to time, establish that (14.41) must hold as equality, so that $\eta(\hat{z}(\nu, t \mid \kappa^{-1}q))v(t) = 1$ for all t. From this conclude that $r(t)v = \beta L - \hat{z}\eta(\hat{z})v$ for all t, and thus all variables must immediately take their BGP values, $r(t) = r^*$ and $\hat{z}(t) = \hat{z}^*$ for all t.

Second, sketch the argument for the case in which (14.43) does not hold for some $\nu \in \mathcal{N} \subset [0, 1]$, q, and t. [Hint: use (14.40) to derive a differential equation for $\hat{z}(\nu, t \mid q)$, and show that the unique steady state of this differential equation is the BGP allocation above and this steady state is unstable.]

14.24 Suppose that in the model of Section 14.3 incumbents also have access to the radical innovation technology used by entrants. Show that there cannot exist an equilibrium where incumbents undertake positive R&D with this technology.

14.25 Set up the social planner's problem (of maximizing the utility of the representative household) in Section 14.3.

(a) Show that this maximization problem corresponds to a concave current-value Hamiltonian, and derive the unique solution to this problem. Show that this solution involves the consumption of the representative household growing at a constant rate at all points.

(b) Show that the social planner may choose higher growth, because she avoids the monopoly markup over machines. Alternatively, she may choose lower entry because of the negative externality in the research process. Give numerical examples in which the growth rate in the Pareto optimal allocation is greater than or less than the decentralized growth rate.

14.26 Consider the model of Section 14.3, and suppose that the R&D technology of the incumbents for innovation is such that if an incumbent with a machine of quality q spends an amount zq for incremental innovations, then the flow rate of innovation is $\phi(z)$ (and this innovation again increases the quality of the incumbent's machine to λq). Assume that $\phi(z)$ is strictly increasing, strictly concave, differentiable, and satisfies $\lim_{z \to 0} \phi'(z) = \infty$ and $\lim_{z \to \infty} \phi'(z) = 0$.

(a) Focus on steady-state (BGP) equilibria and conjecture that $V(q) = vq$. Using this conjecture, show that incumbents choose R&D intensity z^* such that $(\lambda - 1)v = \phi'(z^*)$. Combining this equation with the free-entry condition for entrants and the equation for growth rate given by (14.52), show that there exists a unique BGP equilibrium (under the conjecture that $V(q)$ is linear).

(b) Is it possible for an equilibrium to involve different levels of z for incumbents with different-quality machines?

(c) In light of your answer to part b, what happens if we consider the "limiting case" of this model where $\phi(z)=$ constant?

(d) Show that this equilibrium involves positive R&D both by incumbents and entrants.

(e) Now introduce taxes on R&D by incumbents and entrants at the rates τ_i and τ_e, respectively. Show that, in contrast to the results in Proposition 14.6, the effects of both taxes on growth are ambiguous. What happens if $\eta(z) =$ constant?

* 14.27 Prove Proposition 14.5 for the case in which $z(v, t \mid q)$ could differ across incumbents with different levels of q. Show that the same BGP as in Proposition 14.5 applies and is essentially unique, in the sense that average incumbent R&D effort is always equal to z^*.

  14.28 Consider the model of Section 14.3, but modify the production function to $Y(t) = [\int_0^1 q(v, t)x(v, t \mid q)^{1-\beta}dv]L^\beta/(1 - \beta)$ and assume that production of an input of quality q requires ψq units of the final good as in the baseline model of Section 14.1. Show that the equilibrium growth rate and the decomposition of productivity growth between incumbents and entrants are identical in this case to the results in Section 14.3, but there are no firm-size dynamics. Explain why. Are there dynamics in profits? How does the distribution of profits across firm evolve over time?

* 14.29 Derive (14.63).

* 14.30 Derive (14.75). [Hint: write

$$\log Y(t) = \int_0^1 \log q(v, t)l(v, t)dv = \int_0^1 \left[\log q(v, t) + \log \frac{Y(t)}{w(t)} \lambda^{-n(v)} \right] dv,$$

and rearrange this equation.]

* 14.31 Complete the proof of Proposition 14.8 by showing that there exists $n^* \geq 1$ such that $z_n^* = 0$ for all $n \geq n^*$.

* 14.32 Complete the proof of Proposition 14.9; in particular, prove that $z_0^* > z_1^*$ [Hint: use similar arguments to the first part of the proof.]

* 14.33 Consider a steady-state equilibrium in the model of Section 14.4. Suppose that $\kappa = 0$ and $G'(0) < (1 - \lambda)/\rho$. Let $z^* \equiv G'^{-1}((1 - \lambda)/\rho)$, and suppose also that

$$G'(0) < \frac{z^*(1 - \lambda)/\rho + G(z^*)}{\rho + z^*}.$$

(a) Show that in this case the steady-state equilibrium has zero growth.

(b) Show that $\kappa > 0$ leads to a positive growth rate. Interpret this result, and contrast it to the negative effects of relaxing the protection of IPR in the baseline model of Schumpeterian growth.

* 14.34 Modify the model presented in Section 14.4 such that followers can now use the innovation of the technological leader and immediately leapfrog the leader, but in this case they have to pay a license fee of ζ to the leader.

(a) Characterize the BGP in this case.

(b) Write the value functions.

(c) Explain why licensing can increase the growth rate of the economy in this case, and contrast this result to the one in Exercise 12.9, where licensing was never used in equilibrium. What is the source of the difference between the two sets of results?

  14.35 Consider the following one-period model. There are two Bertrand duopolists producing a homogeneous good. At the beginning of each period, duopolist 1's marginal cost of production is determined as a draw from the uniform distribution $[0, \bar{c}_1]$, and the marginal cost of the second duopolist is determined as an independent draw from $[0, \bar{c}_2]$. Both cost realizations are observed, and then prices are set. Demand is given by $Q = A - P$, with $A > 2 \max\{\bar{c}_1, \bar{c}_2\}$.

(a) Characterize the equilibrium pricing strategies and calculate expected ex ante profits of the two duopolists.

(b) Now imagine that both duopolists start with a cost distribution $[0, \bar{c}]$ and can undertake R&D at cost μ. If they do, with probability η, their cost distribution shifts to $[0, \bar{c} - \alpha]$, where $\alpha < \bar{c}$. Find the conditions under which one of the duopolists invests in R&D and the conditions under which both do.

(c) What happens when $\bar{c}$ declines? Interpreting the decline in $\bar{c}$ as increased competition, discuss the effect of increased competition on innovation incentives. Why is the answer different from that implied by the baseline endogenous technological change models of expanding varieties or Schumpeterian growth?

Directed Technological Change

The previous two chapters introduced the basic models of endogenous technological change. These models provide us with a tractable framework for the analysis of aggregate technological change but focus on a single type of technology. Even when there are multiple types of machines, they all play the same role in increasing aggregate productivity. There are two important respects in which these models are incomplete. First, technological change in practice is often not "neutral": it benefits some factors of production and some agents in the economy more than others. Only in special cases, such as in economies with Cobb-Douglas aggregate production functions, can these types of biases be ignored. The study of why technological change is sometimes biased toward certain factors or sectors is both important for understanding the nature of endogenous technology and also for clarifying the distributional effects of technological change, which determine which groups embrace new technologies and which oppose them. Second, limiting the analysis to only one type of technological change potentially obscures the different competing effects that determine the nature of technological change.

The purpose of this chapter is to extend the models of the last two chapters to consider *directed technological change,* which endogenizes the direction and bias of new technologies that are developed and adopted. Models of directed technological change not only generate new insights about the nature of endogenous technological progress, but also enable us to ask and answer new questions about recent and historical technological developments.

I start with a brief discussion of a range of economic problems in which considering the endogenous bias of technology is important and also present some of the general economic insights that are important in models of directed technological change. The main results are presented in Section 15.3. The rest of the chapter generalizes these results and presents a few of their applications. Section 15.6 uses these models to return to the question raised in Chapter 2 concerning why technological change might take a purely labor-augmenting (Harrod-neutral) form. Section 15.8 presents an alternative approach to this question suggested by Jones (2005).

15.1   Importance of Biased Technological Change

To see the potential importance of the biased technological change, let us first review a number of examples.

1. Perhaps the most important example of biased technological change is the so-called *skill-biased technological change,* which plays an important role in the analysis of recent changes in the wage structure. Figure 15.1 plots a measure of the relative supply of skills (defined as the number of college equivalent workers divided by noncollege equivalents) and a measure of the return to skills, the college premium. It shows that over the past 60 years, the U.S. relative supply of skills has increased rapidly, but there has been no tendency for the returns to college to fall—on the contrary, there has been an increase in the college premium over this time period. The standard explanation for this pattern is that new technologies over the postwar period have been *skill biased*. In fact, at some level this statement is tautological; if skilled and unskilled workers are imperfect substitutes, an increase in the relative supply of skills, without some countervailing skill-biased changes in demand, will necessarily reduce the skill premium.

   The figure also shows that beginning in the late 1960s, the relative supply of skills increased more rapidly than before (compare the slope of the relative supply curve before and after 1969). Starting in the late 1970s, the skill premium also increases more rapidly than before. The standard explanation for this increase is an acceleration in the skill bias of technological change that happens to be coincidental with (or following shortly after) the significant changes in the relative supply of skills.

   An obvious question concerns why technological changes have been skill-biased over the past 60 or even 100 years. Relatedly, why does it appear that skill-biased technological change accelerated starting in the 1970s, precisely when the supply

FIGURE 15.1   Relative supply of college graduates and the college premium in the U.S. labor market.

of skills increased rapidly? While some economists are happy to treat the bias of technological change as exogenous, this is not entirely satisfactory. We have seen that understanding the endogenous nature of technology is important for our study of cross-country income differences and the process of modern economic growth. It is unlikely that while the amount of aggregate technological change is endogenous, the bias of technological change is entirely exogenous. It is therefore important to study the determinants of endogenous bias of technological change and ask why technological change has become more skill-biased in recent decades.

2. This conclusion is strengthened when we look at the historical process of technological change. In contrast to the developments during recent decades, technological changes during the eighteenth and nineteenth centuries appear to have been *unskill-biased*. The artisan shop was replaced by the factory and later by interchangeable parts and the assembly line. Products previously manufactured by skilled artisans started to be produced in factories by workers with relatively few skills, and many previously complex tasks were simplified, reducing the demand for skilled workers. Mokyr (1990, p. 137) summarizes this process as follows:

> First in firearms, then in clocks, pumps, locks, mechanical reapers, typewriters, sewing machines, and eventually in engines and bicycles, interchangeable parts technology proved superior and replaced the skilled artisans working with chisel and file.

Even though the types of skills valued in the labor market during the nineteenth century were different from those supplied by college graduates in today's labor markets, the juxtaposition of technological change biased toward college graduates in the recent past and biased against the most skilled workers of the time in the nineteenth century is both puzzling and intriguing. It raises the question: why was technological change, which has been generally skill-biased over the twentieth century, biased toward unskilled workers in the nineteenth century?

3. As another example, consider the potential effect of labor market conditions on technological change. Beginning in the late 1960s and the early 1970s, both unemployment and the share of labor in national income increased rapidly in a number of continental European countries. During the 1980s, unemployment continued to increase, but the labor share started a steep decline, and in many countries it fell below its initial level. Blanchard (1997) interprets the first phase as the response of these economies to a wage push by workers, and the second phase as a possible consequence of *capital-biased* technological changes. Is there a connection between capital-biased technological changes in European economies and the wage push preceding it?

4. The other obvious example of the importance of directed technological change is the common restriction to Harrod-neutral (purely labor-augmenting) technological progress in growth models. Recall from Chapters 2 and 8 that if technological change is not labor-augmenting, equilibrium growth will not be balanced. But a range of evidence suggests that modern economic growth has been relatively balanced. Is there any reason to expect technological change to be endogenously labor-augmenting?

This chapter shows that a framework of directed technological change can provide potential answers to these questions. The main insight is to think of profit incentives as affecting not only the amount but also the direction of technological change. Before presenting detailed models, let us review the basic arguments, which are quite intuitive.

Imagine an economy with two different factors of production, say L and H (corresponding, e.g., to unskilled and skilled workers), and two different types of technologies that can complement (augment) either one or the other factor. We would expect that when the profitability of H-augmenting technologies is greater than the L-augmenting technologies, more of the former type will be developed by profit-maximizing (research) firms. What determines the relative profitability of developing different technologies? The answer to this question summarizes most of the economics in the models of directed technological change. Two potentially counteracting effects shape the relative profitabilities of different types of technologies:

1. *The price effect:* there are stronger incentives to develop technologies when the goods produced by these technologies command higher prices.

2. *The market size effect:* it is more profitable to develop technologies that have a larger market (e.g., for the reasons discussed in Chapter 12).

An important result of the analysis in this chapter is that this market size effect is powerful enough to outweigh the price effect. In fact, under fairly general conditions the following two results hold.

Weak Equilibrium (Relative) Bias   An increase in the relative supply of a factor always induces technological change that is biased in favor of this factor.

Strong Equilibrium (Relative) Bias   If the elasticity of substitution between factors is sufficiently large, an increase in the relative supply of a factor induces sufficiently strong technological change bias toward this factor that the endogenous-technology relative demand curve becomes upward sloping.

To explain these concepts in a little more detail, suppose that the (inverse) relative demand curve takes the form $w_H/w_L = D(H/L, A)$, where w_H/w_L is the relative price of the H factor, relative to the L factor, H/L is the relative supply of the H factor, and $A \in \mathbb{R}_+$ is a technology term, for now taken to be one-dimensional for simplicity. Technology A is H-biased if D is increasing in A, so that a higher A increases the relative demand for the H factor. Standard microeconomic theory implies that D is always decreasing in H/L. Equilibrium bias concerns the behavior of A as H/L changes, so let us write this as $A(H/L)$. As a normalization, suppose that A is H-biased, so that $D(H/L, A)$ is increasing in A. Weak equilibrium bias then corresponds to $A(H/L)$ being increasing (nondecreasing) in H/L. Strong equilibrium bias, on the other hand, implies that $A(H/L)$ is sufficiently responsive to an increase in H/L that the total effect of the change in relative supply H/L is to increase w_H/w_L. In other words, let the endogenous-technology relative demand curve be $w_H/w_L = D(H/L, A(H/L)) \equiv \tilde{D}(H/L)$. Then strong equilibrium bias corresponds to this endogenous-technology relative demand curve, $\tilde{D}$, being increasing.

At first, both the weak and the strong equilibrium bias results appear surprising. However they become quite intuitive once the logic of directed technological change is understood. Moreover they have a range of important implications. In particular, Section 15.3.3 shows how the weak and the strong relative bias results provide us with potential answers to the questions posed at the beginning of this section.

15.2 Basics and Definitions

Before studying directed technological change, it is useful to clarify the difference between factor-augmenting and factor-biased technological changes, which are sometimes confused in the literature. Suppose that the production side of the economy can be represented by an aggregate production function

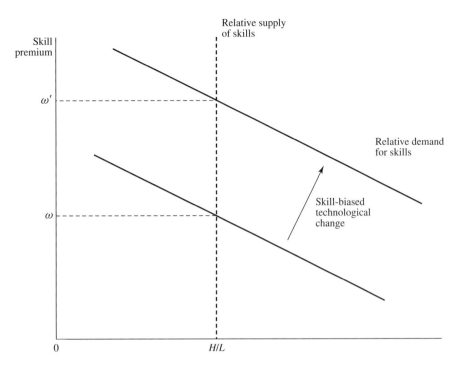

FIGURE 15.2 The effect of H-biased technological change on relative demand and relative factor prices.

$$Y(t) = F(L(t), H(t), A(t)),$$

where $L(t)$ is labor, and $H(t)$ denotes another factor of production (which could be skilled labor, capital, land, or some intermediate goods), and $A(t) \in \mathbb{R}_+$ represents technology. For concreteness, let us refer to H as skilled labor. Without loss of generality imagine that $\partial F/\partial A > 0$, so a greater level of A corresponds to better technology. Recall that technological change is (everywhere) L-augmenting if the production function can be written as $F(AL, H)$. Conversely, H-augmenting technological change corresponds to the production function taking the special form $F(L, AH)$.

Though often equated with factor-augmenting changes, the concept of factor-biased technological change is very different. We say that technological change is L-*biased* if it increases the relative marginal product of factor L compared to factor H. Mathematically, this corresponds to

$$\frac{\partial \frac{\partial F(L,H,A)/\partial L}{\partial F(L,H,A)/\partial H}}{\partial A} \geq 0.$$

Put differently, biased technological change shifts out the relative demand curve for a factor, so that its relative price increases at given factor proportions (given relative quantity of factors). Conversely, technological change is H-biased if this inequality holds in reverse. Figure 15.2 plots the effect of an H-biased (skill-biased) technological change on the relative demand for factor H and on its relative price (the skill premium).

These concepts can be further clarified using the CES production function (recall Example 2.3 in Chapter 2), which can be written as

$$Y(t) = \left[\gamma_L (A_L(t)L(t))^{\frac{\sigma-1}{\sigma}} + \gamma_H (A_H(t)H(t))^{\frac{\sigma-1}{\sigma}} \right]^{\frac{\sigma}{\sigma-1}},$$

where $A_L(t)$ and $A_H(t)$ are two separate technology terms, the γ_is determine the importance of the two factors in the production function, and $\gamma_L + \gamma_H = 1$. Finally, $\sigma \in (0, \infty)$ is the elasticity of substitution between the two factors. Recall that when $\sigma = \infty$, the two factors are perfect substitutes, and the production function is linear; when $\sigma = 1$, the production function is Cobb-Douglas; and when $\sigma = 0$, there is no substitution between the two factors, and the production function is Leontief. Let us refer to the case where $\sigma > 1$ as "gross substitutes," and to $\sigma < 1$ as "gross complements." While there are multiple definitions of complementarity in the microeconomics literature, this terminology is useful to distinguish between $\sigma < 1$ and $\sigma > 1$, which have very different implications in the current context.

Clearly, by construction, $A_L(t)$ is L-augmenting, while $A_H(t)$ is H-augmenting. Interestingly, whether technological change that is L-augmenting (or H-augmenting) is L-biased or H-biased depends on the elasticity of substitution σ. Let us first calculate the relative marginal product of the two factors (see Exercise 15.1):

$$\frac{MP_H}{MP_L} = \gamma \left(\frac{A_H(t)}{A_L(t)}\right)^{\frac{\sigma-1}{\sigma}} \left(\frac{H(t)}{L(t)}\right)^{-\frac{1}{\sigma}}, \tag{15.1}$$

where $\gamma \equiv \gamma_H/\gamma_L$. The relative marginal product of H is decreasing in its relative abundance, $H(t)/L(t)$. This is simply the consequence of the usual substitution effect, leading to a negative relationship between relative supplies and relative marginal products (or prices) and thus to a downward-sloping relative demand curve as drawn in Figure 15.2. The effect of $A_H(t)$ on this relative marginal product depends on σ, however. If $\sigma > 1$, an increase in $A_H(t)$ (relative to $A_L(t)$) increases the relative marginal product of H. In contrast, when $\sigma < 1$, an increase in $A_H(t)$ reduces the relative marginal product of H. Therefore when the two factors are gross substitutes, H-augmenting technological change is also H-biased. In contrast, when the two factors are gross complements, the relationship is reversed, and H-augmenting technological change is now L-biased. Naturally, when $\sigma = 1$, the production function is Cobb-Douglas, and neither a change in $A_H(t)$ nor in $A_L(t)$ is biased toward either of the factors.[1]

The intuition for why, when $\sigma < 1$, H-augmenting technological change is L-biased is simple but important: with gross complementarity ($\sigma < 1$), an increase in the productivity of H increases the demand for labor L by more than the demand for H. As a result, the marginal product of labor increases by more than the marginal product of H. This can be seen most clearly in the extreme case where $\sigma \to 0$, so that the production function becomes Leontief. In this case, starting from a situation in which $\gamma_L A_L(t)L(t) = \gamma_H A_H(t)H(t)$, a small increase in $A_H(t)$ creates an "excess supply of the services" of the H factor (and thus "excess demand" for L), and the price of factor H falls to 0.

I have so far defined the meaning of H-biased and L-biased technological changes. It is also useful to define two concepts that play a major role in the remainder of this chapter. There is *weak equilibrium bias* of technology if an increase in the relative supply of H, H/L, induces technological change biased toward H. Mathematically, this is equivalent to

$$\frac{\partial MP_H/MP_L}{\partial A_H/A_L} \frac{dA_H/A_L}{dH/L} \geq 0.$$

---

1. Also note for future reference that it can be easily verified from (15.1) that σ indeed satisfies the definition of the elasticity of substitution: $\sigma = -[d \log(MP_H/MP_L)/d \log(H/L)]^{-1}$.

From (15.1), it is clear that this condition will hold if

$$\frac{d(A_H(t)/A_L(t))^{\frac{\sigma-1}{\sigma}}}{dH/L} \geq 0,$$

so that in response to the change in relative supplies, $A_H(t)/A_L(t)$ changes in a direction that is biased toward the factor that has become more abundant.

On the other hand, there is *strong equilibrium bias* if an increase in H/L induces a sufficiently large change in the bias of technology so that, following the change in factor supplies, the marginal product of H *relative* to that of L increases. Mathematically, this is equivalent to

$$\frac{dMP_H/MP_L}{dH/L} > 0,$$

where I now use a strict inequality to distinguish strong equilibrium bias from the case in which relative marginal products are independent of relative supplies (e.g., because factors are perfect substitutes). These equations make it clear that the major difference between weak and strong equilibrium bias is whether the relative marginal product of the two factors are evaluated at the initial relative supplies (in the case of weak bias) or at the new relative supplies (in the case of strong bias). Consequently strong equilibrium bias is a much more demanding concept than weak equilibrium bias.

15.3 Baseline Model of Directed Technological Change

In this section, I present the baseline model of directed technological change, which uses the expanding varieties model of endogenous technological change and the lab-equipment specification of the innovation possibilities frontier introduced in Chapter 13. The former choice is motivated by the fact that the expanding varieties model is somewhat simpler to work with than the model of Schumpeterian growth introduced in the previous chapter. The lab-equipment specification, on the other hand, highlights that none of the results here depend on technological externalities. Section 15.4 considers a model of directed technological change with knowledge spillovers, and Exercise 15.18 shows that the main results generalize to a model of Schumpeterian growth.

The baseline economy has a constant supply of two factors, L and H, and admits a representative household with the standard CRRA preferences given by

$$\int_0^\infty \exp(-\rho t)\frac{C(t)^{1-\theta} - 1}{1-\theta}dt, \tag{15.2}$$

where, as usual, $\rho > 0$. The supply side is represented by an aggregate production function combining the outputs of two intermediate sectors with a constant elasticity of substitution:

$$Y(t) = \left[\gamma_L Y_L(t)^{\frac{\varepsilon-1}{\varepsilon}} + \gamma_H Y_H(t)^{\frac{\varepsilon-1}{\varepsilon}}\right]^{\frac{\varepsilon}{\varepsilon-1}}, \tag{15.3}$$

where $Y_L(t)$ and $Y_H(t)$ denote the outputs of two intermediate goods. As the indices indicate, the first is L-intensive, while the second is H-intensive. The parameter $\varepsilon \in [0, \infty)$ is the elasticity of substitution between these two intermediate goods. The assumption that (15.3) features a CES simplifies the analysis but is not crucial for the results. How relaxing this assumption affects the results is discussed at the end of this chapter.

The resource constraint of the economy at time t takes the form

$$C(t) + X(t) + Z(t) \leq Y(t), \tag{15.4}$$

where, as before, $X(t)$ denotes total spending on machines, and $Z(t)$ is aggregate R&D spending. The two intermediate goods are produced competitively with the following production functions:

$$Y_L(t) = \frac{1}{1-\beta} \left(\int_0^{N_L(t)} x_L(v, t)^{1-\beta} dv \right) L^\beta, \tag{15.5}$$

$$Y_H(t) = \frac{1}{1-\beta} \left(\int_0^{N_H(t)} x_H(v, t)^{1-\beta} dv \right) H^\beta, \tag{15.6}$$

where $x_L(v, t)$ and $x_H(v, t)$ denote the quantities of the different machine varieties (used in the production of one or the other intermediate good) and $\beta \in (0, 1)$.[2] These machines are again assumed to depreciate after use. The parallel between these production functions and the aggregate production function of the economy in the baseline expanding product varieties model of Chapter 13 is obvious. There are two important differences, however. First, these are now production functions for intermediate goods rather than the final good. Second, the two production functions (15.5) and (15.6) use different types of machines. The range of machines complementing labor, L, is $[0, N_L(t)]$, while the range of machines complementing factor H is $[0, N_H(t)]$.

Again as in Chapter 13, all machines in both sectors are supplied by monopolists that have a fully enforced perpetual patent on the machines. I denote the prices charged by these monopolists at time t by $p_L^x(v, t)$ for $v \in [0, N_L(t)]$ and $p_H^x(v, t)$ for $v \in [0, N_H(t)]$. Once invented, each machine can be produced at the fixed marginal cost $\psi > 0$ in terms of the final good, which I again normalize to $\psi \equiv 1 - \beta$. Thus total resources devoted to machine production at time t are

$$X(t) = (1 - \beta) \left(\int_0^{N_L(t)} x_L(v, t) dv + \int_0^{N_H(t)} x_H(v, t) dv \right).$$

The innovation possibilities frontier, which determines how new machine varieties are created, is assumed to take a form similar to the lab-equipment specification in Chapter 13:

$$\dot{N}_L(t) = \eta_L Z_L(t), \quad \text{and} \quad \dot{N}_H(t) = \eta_H Z_H(t), \tag{15.7}$$

where $Z_L(t)$ is R&D expenditure directed at discovering new labor-augmenting machines at time t, while $Z_H(t)$ is R&D expenditure directed at discovering H-augmenting machines. Total R&D spending is the sum of these two, that is,

$$Z(t) = Z_L(t) + Z_H(t).$$

---

2. Note that the range of machines used in the two sectors are different (there are two disjoint sets of machines); I use the index v to denote either set of machines for notational simplicity.

The value of a monopolist that discovers one of these machines is again given by the standard formula for the present discounted value of profits:

$$V_f(v, t) = \int_t^\infty \exp\left(-\int_t^s r(s')ds'\right) \pi_f(v, s)ds, \tag{15.8}$$

where $\pi_f(v, t) \equiv p_f^x(v, t)x_f(v, t) - \psi x_f(v, t)$ denotes instantaneous profits for $f = L$ or H, and $r(t)$ is the market interest rate at time t. The HJB version of this value function is

$$r(t)V_f(v, t) - \dot{V}_f(v, t) = \pi_f(v, t). \tag{15.9}$$

Throughout, the price of the final good is normalized to one at each t, which is equivalent to setting the ideal price index of the two intermediates equal to one, that is,

$$\left[\gamma_L^\varepsilon p_L(t)^{1-\varepsilon} + \gamma_H^\varepsilon p_H(t)^{1-\varepsilon}\right]^{\frac{1}{1-\varepsilon}} = 1 \quad \text{for all } t, \tag{15.10}$$

where $p_L(t)$ is the price index of Y_L at time t, and $p_H(t)$ is the price of Y_H. Intertemporal prices are therefore given by the interest rates $[r(t)]_{t=0}^\infty$. Finally, factor prices for L and H are denoted by $w_L(t)$ and $w_H(t)$, respectively.

15.3.1 Characterization of Equilibrium

An *allocation* in this economy is defined by the following objects: time paths of consumption levels, aggregate spending on machines, and aggregate R&D expenditure, $[C(t), X(t), Z(t)]_{t=0}^\infty$; time paths of available machine varieties, $[N_L(t), N_H(t)]_{t=0}^\infty$; time paths of prices and quantities of each machine, $[p_L^x(v, t), x_L(v, t)]_{v\in[0,N_L(t)],t}^\infty$ and $[p_H^x(v, t), x_H(v, t)]_{v\in[0,N_H(t)],t}^\infty$; and time paths of factor prices, $[r(t), w_L(t), w_H(t)]_{t=0}^\infty$.

An *equilibrium* is an allocation in which all existing monopolists (research firms) choose $[p_f^x(v, t), x_f(v, t)]_{v\in[0,N_f(t)],t=0}^\infty$ for $f = L$, H to maximize profits; the evolution of $[N_L(t), N_H(t)]_{t=0}^\infty$ is determined by free entry; the time paths of factor prices, $[r(t), w_L(t), w_H(t)]_{t=0}^\infty$, are consistent with market clearing; and the time paths of $[C(t), X(t), Z(t)]_{t=0}^\infty$ are consistent with household maximization.

To characterize the (unique) equilibrium, let us first consider the maximization problem of producers in the two sectors. Since machines depreciate fully after use, these maximization problems are static and can be written as

$$\max_{L, [x_L(v,t)]_{v\in[0,N_L(t)]}} p_L(t)Y_L(t) - w_L(t)L - \int_0^{N_L(t)} p_L^x(v, t)x_L(v, t)dv, \tag{15.11}$$

$$\max_{H, [x_H(v,t)]_{v\in[0,N_H(t)]}} p_H(t)Y_H(t) - w_H(t)H - \int_0^{N_H(t)} p_H^x(v, t)x_H(v, t)dv. \tag{15.12}$$

The main difference between these problems and the maximization problem facing final good producers in Chapter 13 is the presence of prices $p_L(t)$ and $p_H(t)$, which reflect the fact that these sectors produce intermediate goods, whereas factor and machine prices are expressed in terms of the numeraire, the final good.

These two maximization problems (15.11) and (15.12) immediately imply the following demand for machines in the two sectors:

$$x_L(v, t) = \left(\frac{p_L(t)}{p_L^x(v, t)} \right)^{1/\beta} L \quad \text{for all } v \in [0, N_L(t)] \text{ and all } t, \tag{15.13}$$

$$x_H(v, t) = \left(\frac{p_H(t)}{p_H^x(v, t)} \right)^{1/\beta} H \quad \text{for all } v \in [0, N_H(t)] \text{ and all } t. \tag{15.14}$$

Similar to the demands for machines in Chapter 13, these are isoelastic, so profit maximization implies that each monopolist sets a constant markup over marginal cost and thus

$$p_L^x(v, t) = p_H^x(v, t) = 1 \quad \text{for all } v \text{ and } t.$$

Substituting these prices into (15.13) and (15.14), we have

$$x_L(v, t) = p_L(t)^{1/\beta} L \text{ and } x_H(v, t) = p_H(t)^{1/\beta} H \quad \text{for all } v \text{ and all } t.$$

Since these quantities do not depend on the identity of the machine, only on the sector that is being served, profits are also independent of machine variety. In particular,

$$\pi_L(t) = \beta p_L(t)^{1/\beta} L, \text{ and } \pi_H(t) = \beta p_H(t)^{1/\beta} H. \tag{15.15}$$

Equation (15.15) implies that the net present discounted values of monopolists only depend on which sector they are supplying and can be denoted by $V_L(t)$ and $V_H(t)$.

Next, combining the demand for machines with (15.5) and (15.6) yields the *derived* production functions for the two intermediate goods:

$$Y_L(t) = \frac{1}{1 - \beta} p_L(t)^{\frac{1-\beta}{\beta}} N_L(t) L, \tag{15.16}$$

$$Y_H(t) = \frac{1}{1 - \beta} p_H(t)^{\frac{1-\beta}{\beta}} N_H(t) H. \tag{15.17}$$

These derived production functions are similar to (13.12) in Chapter 13, except for the presence of the price terms.

Finally, the prices of the two intermediate goods are derived from the marginal product conditions of the final good technology, (15.3), which imply

$$p(t) \equiv \frac{p_H(t)}{p_L(t)} = \gamma \left(\frac{Y_H(t)}{Y_L(t)} \right)^{-\frac{1}{\varepsilon}}$$

$$= \gamma \left(p(t)^{\frac{1-\beta}{\beta}} \frac{N_H(t) H}{N_L(t) L} \right)^{-\frac{1}{\varepsilon}}$$

$$= \gamma^{\frac{\varepsilon\beta}{\sigma}} \left(\frac{N_H(t) H}{N_L(t) L} \right)^{-\frac{\beta}{\sigma}}, \tag{15.18}$$

where again $\gamma \equiv \gamma_H / \gamma_L$, and

$$\sigma \equiv \varepsilon - (\varepsilon - 1)(1 - \beta) = 1 + (\varepsilon - 1)\beta.$$

is the (derived) elasticity of substitution between the two factors. The first line of this expression simply defines $p(t)$ as the relative price between the two intermediate goods and uses the fact that the ratio of the marginal productivities of the two intermediate goods must be equal to this relative price. The second line substitutes from (15.16) and (15.17). Using (15.18), the relative factor prices in this economy are obtained as

$$
\omega(t) \equiv \frac{w_H(t)}{w_L(t)}
$$

$$
= p(t)^{1/\beta} \frac{N_H(t)}{N_L(t)}
$$

$$
= \gamma^{\frac{\varepsilon}{\sigma}} \left(\frac{N_H(t)}{N_L(t)} \right)^{\frac{\sigma-1}{\sigma}} \left(\frac{H}{L} \right)^{-\frac{1}{\sigma}}. \tag{15.19}
$$

The first line defines $\omega(t)$ as the relative wage of factor H compared to factor L. The second line uses the definition of marginal product combined with (15.16) and (15.17), and the third line, (15.19), uses (15.18). I refer to σ as the (derived) elasticity of substitution between the two factors, since it is equal to

$$
\sigma = - \left(\frac{d \log \omega(t)}{d \log(H/L)} \right)^{-1}.
$$

To complete the description of equilibrium in the technology side, we need to impose the following free-entry conditions:

$$
\eta_L V_L(t) \leq 1, \ Z_L(t) \geq 0, \ \text{and} \ \eta_L V_L(t) = 1 \ \text{if} \ Z_L(t) > 0, \tag{15.20}
$$

$$
\eta_H V_H(t) \leq 1, \ Z_H(t) \geq 0, \ \text{and} \ \eta_H V_H(t) = 1 \ \text{if} \ Z_H(t) > 0. \tag{15.21}
$$

Finally, household optimization implies

$$
\frac{\dot{C}(t)}{C(t)} = \frac{1}{\theta}(r(t) - \rho), \tag{15.22}
$$

and

$$
\lim_{t \to \infty} \left[\exp \left(- \int_0^t r(s)ds \right) (N_L(t)V_L(t) + N_H(t)V_H(t)) \right] = 0, \tag{15.23}
$$

which uses the fact that $N_L(t)V_L(t) + N_H(t)V_H(t)$ is the total value of corporate assets in this economy.

Let us next define the BGP equilibrium as an equilibrium path where consumption grows at the constant rate g^* and the relative price $p(t)$ is constant. From (15.10) this definition implies that $p_L(t)$ and $p_H(t)$ are also constant.

Let V_L and V_H be the BGP net present discounted values of new innovations in the two sectors. Then (15.9) implies that

$$
V_L = \frac{\beta p_L^{1/\beta} L}{r^*}, \ \text{and} \ V_H = \frac{\beta p_H^{1/\beta} H}{r^*}, \tag{15.24}
$$

where r^* is the BGP interest rate, while p_L and p_H are the BGP prices of the two intermediate goods. The comparison of these two values is of crucial importance. As discussed intuitively above, the greater is V_H relative to V_L, the greater are the incentives to develop H-augmenting machines, N_H, rather than N_L. Taking the ratio of these two expressions yields

$$\frac{V_H}{V_L} = \left(\frac{p_H}{p_L}\right)^{\frac{1}{\beta}} \frac{H}{L}.$$

This expression highlights the two effects on the direction of technological change discussed in Section 15.1.

1. The price effect manifests itself because V_H/V_L is increasing in p_H/p_L. The greater is this relative price, the greater is V_H/V_L and thus the greater are the incentives to invent technologies complementing the H factor. Since goods produced by relatively scarce factors are relatively more expensive, the price effect favors technologies complementing scarce factors.

2. The market size effect is a consequence of the fact that V_H/V_L is increasing in H/L. The market for a technology is the workers (or other factors) that use and work with this technology. Consequently an increase in the supply of a factor translates into a greater market for the technology complementing that factor. The market size effect encourages innovation for the more abundant factor.

The above discussion is incomplete, however, since prices are endogenous. Combining (15.24) with (15.18), relative prices can be eliminated, and the relative profitability of the technologies becomes

$$\frac{V_H}{V_L} = \gamma^{\frac{\varepsilon}{\sigma}} \left(\frac{N_H}{N_L}\right)^{-\frac{1}{\sigma}} \left(\frac{H}{L}\right)^{\frac{\sigma-1}{\sigma}}. \tag{15.25}$$

Note for future reference that an increase in the relative factor supply, H/L, will increase V_H/V_L as long as $\sigma > 1$, and it will reduce it if $\sigma < 1$. Thus the elasticity of substitution between the factors, σ, regulates whether the price effect dominates the market size effect. Since σ is not a primitive but a derived parameter, we would like to know when it is greater than 1. It is straightforward to check that

$$\sigma \gtreqqless 1 \iff \varepsilon \gtreqqless 1.$$

So the two factors will be gross substitutes when the two intermediate goods are gross substitutes in the production of the final good.

Next, using the two free-entry conditions (15.20) and (15.21) and assuming that both of them hold as equalities, we obtain the following BGP *technology market clearing* condition:

$$\eta_L V_L = \eta_H V_H. \tag{15.26}$$

Combining (15.26) with (15.25), we obtain the following BGP ratio of relative technologies:

$$\left(\frac{N_H}{N_L}\right)^* = \eta^\sigma \gamma^\varepsilon \left(\frac{H}{L}\right)^{\sigma-1}, \tag{15.27}$$

where $\eta \equiv \eta_H/\eta_L$, and the asterisk ($*$) denotes that this expression refers to the BGP value. The notable feature here is that relative productivities are determined by the innovation possibilities frontier and the relative supply of the two factors. Equation (15.27) contains most of the economics of directed technology. However, before discussing (15.27), it is useful to characterize the BGP growth rate of the economy. This is done in the next proposition.

Proposition 15.1 *Consider the directed technological change model described above. Suppose that*

$$\beta \left[\gamma_H^\varepsilon (\eta_H H)^{\sigma-1} + \gamma_L^\varepsilon (\eta_L L)^{\sigma-1} \right]^{\frac{1}{\sigma-1}} > \rho, \ \text{and}$$

$$(1-\theta)\beta \left[\gamma_H^\varepsilon (\eta_H H)^{\sigma-1} + \gamma_L^\varepsilon (\eta_L L)^{\sigma-1} \right]^{\frac{1}{\sigma-1}} < \rho.$$

(15.28)

Then there exists a unique BGP equilibrium in which the relative technologies are given by (15.27), and consumption and output grow at the rate

$$g^* = \frac{1}{\theta} \left(\beta \left[\gamma_H^\varepsilon (\eta_H H)^{\sigma-1} + \gamma_L^\varepsilon (\eta_L L)^{\sigma-1} \right]^{\frac{1}{\sigma-1}} - \rho \right).$$

(15.29)

Proof. The derivation of (15.29) is provided by the argument preceding the proposition. Exercise 15.2 asks you to check that (15.28) ensures that free-entry conditions (15.20) and (15.21) must hold, to verify that this is the unique relative equilibrium technology, to calculate the BGP equilibrium growth rate, and to verify that household utility is finite and the transversality condition is satisfied. ∎

It can also be verified that there are simple transitional dynamics in this economy whereby starting with technology levels $N_H(0)$ and $N_L(0)$, there always exists a unique equilibrium path, and it involves the economy monotonically converging to the BGP equilibrium of Proposition 15.1. This result is stated in the next proposition.

Proposition 15.2 *Consider the directed technological change model described above. Starting with any $N_H(0) > 0$ and $N_L(0) > 0$, there exists a unique equilibrium path. If $N_H(0)/N_L(0) < (N_H/N_L)^*$ as given by (15.27), then $Z_H(t) > 0$ and $Z_L(t) = 0$ until $N_H(t)/N_L(t) = (N_H/N_L)^*$. If $N_H(0)/N_L(0) > (N_H/N_L)^*$, then $Z_H(t) = 0$ and $Z_L(t) > 0$ until $N_H(t)/N_L(t) = (N_H/N_L)^*$.*

Proof. See Exercise 15.3. ∎

More interesting than the aggregate growth rate and the transitional dynamics behavior of the economy are the results concerning the direction of technological change and its effects on relative factor prices. These are studied next.

15.3.2 Directed Technological Change and Factor Prices

Let us start by studying (15.27). This equation implies that when $\sigma > 1$, there is a positive relationship between the relative supply of the H factor, H/L, and the relative factor-augmenting technologies, N_H^*/N_L^*. In contrast, if the derived elasticity of substitution σ is less than 1, the relationship is reversed. This might suggest that, depending on the elasticity of substitution between factors (or between the intermediate goods), changes in factor supplies may induce technological changes that are biased in favor of or against the factor that is becoming more abundant. However, this conclusion is not correct. Recall from Section 15.2 that N_H^*/N_L^* refers to the ratio of factor-augmenting technologies (or to the ratio of *physical* productivities). What matters for the bias of technology is *the value of marginal product* of factors, which is affected by changes in relative prices. We have already seen that the relationship between factor-augmenting technologies and factor-biased technologies is reversed precisely when σ is less than 1. Thus when $\sigma > 1$, an increase in N_H^*/N_L^* is relatively biased toward H, while when $\sigma < 1$, it is a decrease in N_H^*/N_L^* that is relatively biased toward H.

This argument immediately establishes the following *weak equilibrium bias result*.

Proposition 15.3 *Consider the directed technological change model described above. There is always weak equilibrium (relative) bias in the sense that an increase in H/L always induces relatively H-biased technological change.*

Recall that weak bias was defined in Section 15.2 with a weak inequality, so that the proposition is also correct when $\sigma = 1$, even though in this case it can be verified easily from (15.27) that N_H^*/N_L^* does not depend on H/L.

Proposition 15.3 is the basis of the discussion about induced biased technological change in Section 15.1 and already gives us a range of insights about how changes in the relative supplies of skilled workers may be at the root of the skill-biased technological change. These implications are further discussed in Section 15.3.3.

The results of this proposition reflect the strength of the market size effect discussed above. Recall that the price effect creates a force favoring factors that become relatively scarce. In contrast, the market size effect, which is related to the nonrivalry of ideas discussed in Chapter 12, suggests that technology should change in a way that favors factors that are becoming relatively abundant. Proposition 15.3 shows that the market size effect always dominates the price effect.

Proposition 15.3 characterizes the direction of the induced technological change but does not specify whether this induced effect is strong enough to make the endogenous-technology relative demand curve for factors upward sloping. As mentioned in Section 15.1, directed technological change can lead to the seemingly paradoxical result that relative demand curves can be upward sloping once the endogeneity of technology is taken into account. To obtain this result, let us substitute for $(N_H/N_L)^*$ from (15.27) into the expression for the relative wage given technologies, (15.19), and obtain the following BGP relative factor price ratio (see Exercise 15.4):

$$\omega^* \equiv \left(\frac{w_H}{w_L}\right)^* = \eta^{\sigma-1}\gamma^\varepsilon \left(\frac{H}{L}\right)^{\sigma-2}. \tag{15.30}$$

Inspection of this equation establishes conditions for *strong equilibrium (relative) bias*.

Proposition 15.4 *Consider the directed technological change model described above. If $\sigma > 2$, there is strong equilibrium (relative) bias in the sense that an increase in H/L raises ω^*.*

Figure 15.3 illustrates the results of Propositions 15.3 and 15.4, referring to H as skilled labor and L as unskilled labor as in the first application discussed in Section 15.1. The curve marked with CT corresponds to the constant-technology relative demand from (15.19). It is always downward sloping because it holds the relative technologies, N_H/N_L, constant, and thus only features the usual substitution effect. The fact that this curve is downward sloping follows from basic producer theory. The curve marked as ET_1 applies when technology is endogenous, but the condition in Proposition 15.4, that $\sigma > 2$, is not satisfied. Proposition 15.3 states that even in this case an increase in H/L induces skill-biased (H-biased) technological change. Thus when H/L is higher than its initial level, the induced-technology effect will shift the constant-technology demand curve CT to the right (i.e., as technology changes, another CT curve, above the original one, applies). The skill premium following the increase in H/L is therefore ω_{ET1} rather than ω_{CT}. When H/L is below its initial level, the same effect shifts CT to the left. Consequently, the locus of points corresponding to the endogenous-technology demand, ET_1, is shallower than the constant-technology demand curve CT. (This can be also verified comparing the relative demand functions with constant and endogenous technology, (15.19) and (15.30), and noting that $\sigma - 2$ is never less than $-1/\sigma$).

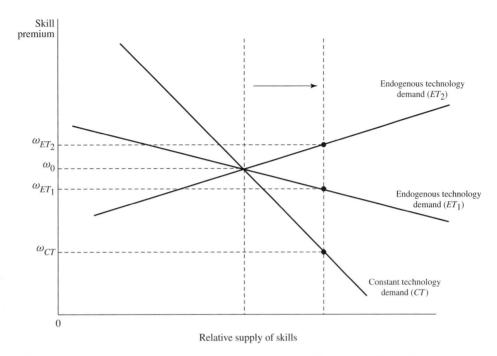

FIGURE 15.3 The relationship between the relative supply of skills and the skill premium in the model of directed technical change.

There is an obvious analogy between this result and Samuelson's *LeChatelier Principle,* which states that long-run demand curves, which apply when all factors can adjust, must be more elastic than the short-run demand curves, which hold some factors constant. We can think of the endogenous-technology demand curve as adjusting the "factors of production" corresponding to technology. However, the analogy is imperfect, because the effects here are caused by general equilibrium changes, while the LeChatelier Principle focuses on partial equilibrium effects. In fact, in basic producer theory, with or without the LeChatelier effects, all demand curves must be downward sloping, whereas here ET_2, which applies when the conditions of Proposition 15.4 hold, is upward sloping: higher levels of relative supply of skills correspond to higher skill premiums (ω_{ET2} is greater than ω_0 in Figure 15.3).

A complementary intuition for this result can be obtained by going back to the importance of the nonrivalry of ideas discussed in Chapter 12. Here, as in the basic endogenous technology models of the last two chapters, the nonrivalry of ideas leads to an aggregate production function that exhibits increasing returns to scale (in all factors, including technologies). It is this increasing returns to scale that leads to potentially upward-sloping relative demand curves. Put differently, the market size effect, which results from the nonrivalry of ideas and is at the root of aggregate increasing returns, can create sufficiently strong induced technological change to increase the relative marginal product and the relative price of the factor that has become more abundant.

15.3.3 Implications

One of the most interesting applications of Propositions 15.3 and 15.4 is to changes in the wage structure and the skill premium. For this application, suppose that H stands for college-educated workers. In the U.S. labor market, the skill premium has shown no tendency to decline despite a large increase in the supply of college-educated workers. On the contrary, following a brief period of decline during the 1970s in the face of the large increase in the supply of college-educated workers, the skill (college) premium has increased sharply throughout the 1980s and 1990s, to reach a level not experienced in the postwar era. Figure 15.1 above showed these general patterns.

The most popular explanation for these patterns is skill-biased technological change. For example, computers or new information technologies (IT) are argued to favor skilled workers relative to unskilled workers. But why should the economy adopt and develop more skill-biased technologies throughout the past 30 years, or more generally throughout the entire twentieth century? This question becomes more relevant once we remember that during the nineteenth century many of the technologies that were fueling economic growth, such as the factory system and the spinning and weaving innovations, were unskill-biased rather than skill-biased. Thus, in summary, the following stylized facts are relevant:

1. secular skill-biased technological change increasing the demand for skills throughout the twentieth century;

2. possible acceleration in skill-biased technological change over the past 25 years; and

3. a range of important technologies biased against skilled workers during the nineteenth century.

Propositions 15.3 and 15.4 provide us with a framework for thinking about these issues.

1. According to Propositions 15.3 and 15.4, the increase in the number of skilled workers that has taken place throughout the twentieth century should cause steady skill-biased technological change. Therefore models of directed technological change offer a natural explanation for the secular skill-biased technological developments of the past century.

2. The more rapid increase in the number of skilled workers over the past 25 years, shown in Figure 15.1, should also induce an acceleration in skill-biased technological change. If $\sigma > 2$ and Proposition 15.4 applies, then this acceleration can also lead to a rapid increase in the skill premium. How this class of models might account for the dynamics of factor prices in the face of endogenously changing technologies is discussed later in this section.

3. Can the framework also explain the prevalence of skill-replacing/labor-biased technological change in the late eighteenth and nineteenth centuries? While we know less about both changes in relative supplies and technological developments during these historical periods, available evidence suggests that there were large increases in the number of unskilled workers available to be employed in the factories. Bairoch (1988, p. 245), for example, describes this rapid expansion of unskilled labor in the cities as follows: "between 1740 and 1840 the population of England . . . went up from 6 million to 15.7 million. . . . while the agricultural labor force represented 60–70% of the total work force in 1740, by 1840 it represented only 22%." Habakkuk's well-known account of nineteenth-century technological development (1962, pp. 136–137) also emphasizes the increase in the supply of unskilled labor in English cities, and attributes it to a variety of factors. First, "technical changes in agriculture increased the supply of labor available to industry" (p. 137). Second, "population was increasing very rapidly" (p. 136). Third, labor reserves of rural industry came to the cities. Fourth, "there was a large influx of labor from Ireland" (p. 137).

In addition to accounting for the recent skill-biased technological developments and for the historical technologies that appear to have been biased toward unskilled workers, this framework also gives a potential interpretation for the dynamics of the college premium during

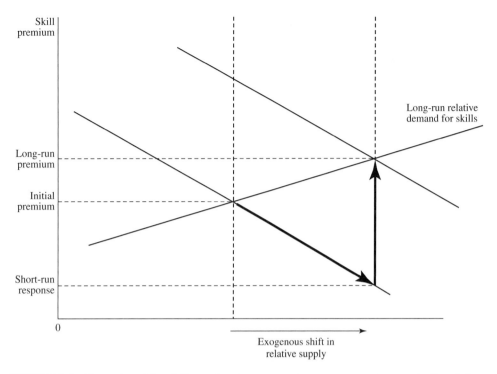

FIGURE 15.4 Dynamics of the skill premium in response to an exogenous increase in the relative supply of skills, with an upward-sloping endogenous-technology relative demand curve.

the 1970s and 1980s. It is reasonable to presume that N_H/N_L changes slowly as a result of the gradual buildup and development of new technologies (as the analysis of transitional dynamics in Proposition 15.2 shows). In this case, a rapid increase in the supply of skills first reduces the skill premium as the economy moves along a constant technology (constant N_H/N_L) curve as shown in Figure 15.4. After a while technology starts adjusting and the economy moves back to the upward-sloping relative demand curve, with a relatively sharp increase in the college premium. This approach can therefore explain both the decline in the college premium during the 1970s and its subsequent large surge, and relates both of these phenomena to the large increase in the supply of skilled workers.

If, on the other hand, $\sigma < 2$, then the long-run relative demand curve is downward sloping, though again it is shallower than the short-run relative demand curve. Following the increase in the relative supply of skills, there is again an initial decline in the college premium, and as technology starts adjusting, the skill premium increases. But it ends up below its initial level (Figure 15.5).

Consequently, a model of directed technological change can shed light both on the secular skill bias of technology and on the relatively short-run changes in technology-induced factor prices. Before discussing other implications of these results, a couple of further issues are worth noting. First, Proposition 15.4 shows that upward-sloping relative demand curves arise only when $\sigma > 2$. In the context of substitution between skilled and unskilled workers, an elasticity of substitution much higher than 2 is unlikely. Most estimates put the elasticity of substitution between 1.4 and 2. Section 15.4 shows that whether or not $\sigma > 2$ is not critical for this result; what is necessary for upward-sloping relative demand curves is that σ should be greater than a certain threshold (see, in particular, Proposition 15.8). Second, we would like to understand the relationship between the market size and the scale effects, in particular whether the results on

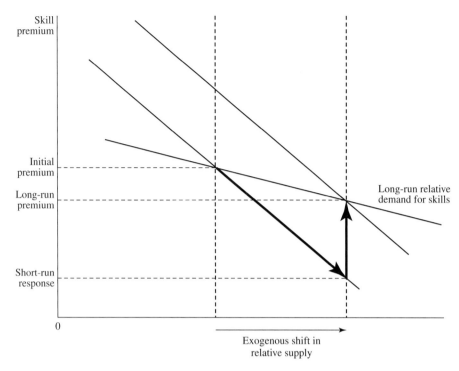

FIGURE 15.5 Dynamics of the skill premium in response to an increase in the relative supply of skills, with a downward-sloping endogenous-technology relative demand curve.

induced technological change are an artifact of the scale effect (which many economists do not view as an attractive feature of endogenous technological change models). Section 15.5 shows that this is not the case and exactly the same results apply when scale effects are removed. Third, we would like to apply these ideas to investigate whether there are reasons for technological change to be endogenously labor-augmenting in the neoclassical growth model. This issue is investigated in Section 15.6. Finally, it is also useful to contrast the equilibrium allocation to the Pareto optimal allocation, which is done in Exercise 15.6. This exercise shows that the qualitative results here, including the weak and the strong equilibrium bias results, also hold in the Pareto optimal allocation.

15.4 Directed Technological Change with Knowledge Spillovers

I now consider the directed technological change model of the previous section with knowledge spillovers. This exercise has three purposes. First, it shows how the main results on the direction of technological change can be generalized to a model using the other common specification of the innovation possibilities frontier. Second, this analysis shows that the strong bias result in Proposition 15.4 can hold under somewhat weaker conditions. Third, this formulation is essential for the study of labor-augmenting technological change in Section 15.6.

The lab-equipment specification of the innovation possibilities frontier is special in one respect: it does not feature *state dependence*. State dependence refers to the phenomenon in which the path of past innovations affects the relative costs of different types of innovations. The lab-equipment specification implied that R&D spending always leads to the same increase in the number of L-augmenting and H-augmenting machines. I now introduce a specification with knowledge spillovers, which allows for state dependence. Recall that, as discussed in Section 13.2 in Chapter 13, when there are scarce factors used for R&D, then growth cannot be sustained by continuously increasing the amount of these factors allocated to R&D. Therefore, to achieve sustained growth, these factors need to become more and more productive over time, because of spillovers from past research. Here for simplicity, let us assume that R&D is carried out by scientists and that there is a constant supply of scientists equal to S (Exercise 15.17 shows that the results are similar when workers can be employed in the R&D sector). With only one sector, the analysis in Section 13.2 indicates that sustained endogenous growth requires $\dot{N}/N$ to be proportional to S. With two sectors, there is instead a variety of specifications with different degrees of state dependence, because productivity in each sector can depend on the state of knowledge in both sectors. A flexible formulation is the following:

$$\dot{N}_L(t) = \eta_L N_L(t)^{(1+\delta)/2} N_H(t)^{(1-\delta)/2} S_L(t), \text{ and } \dot{N}_H(t) = \eta_H N_L(t)^{(1-\delta)/2} N_H(t)^{(1+\delta)/2} S_H(t),$$

(15.31)

where $\delta \leq 1$, and $S_L(t)$ is the number of scientists working to produce L-augmenting machines, while $S_H(t)$ denotes the number of scientists working on H-augmenting machines. Clearly, market clearing for scientists requires that

$$S_L(t) + S_H(t) \leq S.$$

(15.32)

In this specification, δ measures the degree of state dependence: when $\delta = 0$, there is no state dependence—$(\partial \dot{N}_H/\partial S_H)/(\partial \dot{N}_L/\partial S_L) = \eta_H/\eta_L$ regardless of the levels of N_L and N_H—because both N_L and N_H create spillovers for current research in both sectors. In this case, the results are identical to those in the previous section. In contrast, when $\delta = 1$, there is an extreme amount of state dependence. In this case, $(\partial \dot{N}_H/\partial S_H)/(\partial \dot{N}_L/\partial S_L) = \eta_H N_H/\eta_L N_L$, so an increase in the stock of L-augmenting machines today makes future labor-complementary innovations cheaper but has no effect on the cost of H-augmenting innovations. This discussion clarifies the role of the parameter δ and the meaning of state dependence. In some sense, state dependence adds another layer of "increasing returns," this time not for the entire economy, but for specific technology lines. In particular, a significant amount of state dependence implies that when N_H is high relative to N_L, it becomes more profitable to undertake more N_H-type innovations.

With this formulation of the innovation possibilities frontier, the free-entry conditions become (see Exercise 15.7)

$$\eta_L N_L(t)^{(1+\delta)/2} N_H(t)^{(1-\delta)/2} V_L(t) \leq w_S(t),$$
$$\eta_L N_L(t)^{(1+\delta)/2} N_H(t)^{(1-\delta)/2} V_L(t) = w_S(t) \quad \text{if } S_L(t) > 0.$$

(15.33)

and

$$\eta_H N_L(t)^{(1-\delta)/2} N_H(t)^{(1+\delta)/2} V_H(t) \leq w_S(t),$$
$$\eta_H N_L(t)^{(1-\delta)/2} N_H(t)^{(1+\delta)/2} V_H(t) = w_S(t) \quad \text{if } S_H(t) > 0,$$

(15.34)

where $w_S(t)$ denotes the wage of a scientist at time t. When both of these free-entry conditions hold, BGP technology market clearing implies

$$\eta_L N_L(t)^\delta \pi_L = \eta_H N_H(t)^\delta \pi_H,$$

(15.35)

where δ captures the importance of state dependence in the technology market clearing condition, and profits are not conditioned on time, since they refer to the BGP values, which are constant as in the previous section (recall (15.15)). When $\delta = 0$, this condition is identical to (15.26). Therefore, as claimed above, all results concerning the direction of technological change are the same as those in the lab-equipment specification.

This is no longer true when $\delta > 0$. To characterize the results in this case, let us combine condition (15.35) with (15.15) and (15.18). This yields the equilibrium relative technology as (see Exercise 15.8)

$$\left(\frac{N_H}{N_L}\right)^* = \eta^{\frac{\sigma}{1-\delta\sigma}} \gamma^{\frac{\varepsilon}{1-\delta\sigma}} \left(\frac{H}{L}\right)^{\frac{\sigma-1}{1-\delta\sigma}}, \tag{15.36}$$

where recall that $\gamma \equiv \gamma_H/\gamma_L$ and $\eta \equiv \eta_H/\eta_L$. This expression shows that the relationship between the relative factor supplies and relative physical productivities now depends on δ. This result is intuitive: as long as $\delta > 0$, an increase in N_H reduces the relative costs of H-augmenting innovations, so for technology market equilibrium to be restored, π_L needs to increase relative to π_H. Substituting (15.36) into the expression for relative factor prices for given technologies, which is still given by (15.19), yields the following long-run (endogenous-technology) relationship between relative factor prices and relative factor supplies:

$$\omega^* \equiv \left(\frac{w_H}{w_L}\right)^* = \eta^{\frac{\sigma-1}{1-\delta\sigma}} \gamma^{\frac{(1-\delta)\varepsilon}{1-\delta\sigma}} \left(\frac{H}{L}\right)^{\frac{\sigma-2+\delta}{1-\delta\sigma}}. \tag{15.37}$$

As claimed above, when $\delta = 0$, both (15.36) and (15.37) are identical to their counterparts in the previous section, (15.27) and (15.30).

The growth rate of this economy is determined by the number of scientists. In BGP, both sectors grow at the same rate, so we need $\dot{N}_L(t)/N_L(t) = \dot{N}_H(t)/N_H(t)$, or

$$\eta_H N_H(t)^{\delta-1} S_H(t) = \eta_L N_L(t)^{\delta-1} S_L(t).$$

Combining this equation with (15.32) and (15.36), we obtain the following BGP condition for the allocation of researchers between the two different types of technologies:

$$\eta^{\frac{1-\sigma}{1-\delta\sigma}} \left(\frac{1-\gamma}{\gamma}\right)^{-\frac{\varepsilon(1-\delta)}{1-\delta\sigma}} \left(\frac{H}{L}\right)^{-\frac{(\sigma-1)(1-\delta)}{1-\delta\sigma}} = \frac{S_L^*}{S - S_L^*}. \tag{15.38}$$

Notice that given H/L, the BGP researcher allocations, S_L^* and S_H^*, are uniquely determined, and this determines the BGP growth rate as in the next proposition.

Proposition 15.5 *Consider the directed technological change model with knowledge spillovers and state dependence in the innovation possibilities frontier. Suppose that*

$$(1-\theta)\frac{\eta_L \eta_H (N_H/N_L)^{(\delta-1)/2}}{\eta_H (N_H/N_L)^{(\delta-1)} + \eta_L} S < \rho,$$

where N_H/N_L is given by (15.36). Then there exists a unique BGP equilibrium in which the relative technologies are given by (15.36), and consumption and output grow at the rate

$$g^* = \frac{\eta_L \eta_H (N_H/N_L)^{(\delta-1)/2}}{\eta_H (N_H/N_L)^{(\delta-1)} + \eta_L} S. \tag{15.39}$$

Proof. See Exercise 15.9. ∎

In contrast to the model with the lab-equipment technology, transitional dynamics do not always take the economy to the BGP equilibrium, however. This is because of the additional increasing returns to scale mentioned above. With a high degree of state dependence, when $N_H(0)$ is very high relative to $N_L(0)$, it may no longer be profitable for firms to undertake further R&D directed at labor-augmenting (L-augmenting) technologies. Whether this is so depends on a comparison of the degree of state dependence δ and the elasticity of substitution σ. The elasticity of substitution matters because it regulates how prices change as a function of the composition of technology, and thus determines the strength of the price effect on the direction of technological change. The next proposition analyzes the transitional dynamics in this case.

Proposition 15.6 *Consider the directed technological change model with knowledge spillovers and state dependence in the innovation possibilities frontier. Suppose that $\sigma < 1/\delta$. Then starting with any $N_H(0) > 0$ and $N_L(0) > 0$, there exists a unique equilibrium path. If $N_H(0)/N_L(0) < (N_H/N_L)^*$ as given by (15.36), then $Z_H(t) > 0$ and $Z_L(t) = 0$ until $N_H(t)/N_L(t) = (N_H/N_L)^*$. If $N_H(0)/N_L(0) > (N_H/N_L)^*$, then $Z_H(t) = 0$ and $Z_L(t) > 0$ until $N_H(t)/N_L(t) = (N_H/N_L)^*$.*

If $\sigma > 1/\delta$, then starting with $N_H(0)/N_L(0) > (N_H/N_L)^*$, the economy tends to $N_H(t)/N_L(t) \to \infty$ as $t \to \infty$, and starting with $N_H(0)/N_L(0) < (N_H/N_L)^*$, it tends to $N_H(t)/N_L(t) \to 0$ as $t \to \infty$.

Proof. See Exercise 15.11. ∎

Of greater interest for the focus here are the results on the direction of technological change. The first result on weak equilibrium bias immediately generalizes from the previous section.

Proposition 15.7 *Consider the directed technological change model with knowledge spillovers and state dependence in the innovation possibilities frontier. Then there is always weak equilibrium (relative) bias in the sense that an increase in H/L always induces relatively H-biased technological change.*

Proof. See Exercise 15.12. ∎

While the results regarding weak bias have not changed, inspection of (15.37) shows that it is now easier to obtain *strong equilibrium (relative) bias*.

Proposition 15.8 *Consider the directed technological change model with knowledge spillovers and state dependence in the innovation possibilities frontier. Then if*

$$\sigma > 2 - \delta,$$

there is strong equilibrium (relative) bias in the sense that an increase in H/L raises the relative marginal product and the relative wage of the H factor compared to the L factor.

Intuitively, the additional increasing returns to scale coming from state dependence makes strong bias easier to obtain, because the induced technology effect is stronger. When a particular factor, say H, becomes more abundant, this encourages an increase in N_H relative to N_L (in the case where $\sigma > 1$). State dependence makes further increases in N_H more profitable, culminating in a larger effect on N_H/N_L. Since with $\sigma > 1$ greater values of N_H/N_L increase the relative price of factor H compared to L, this tends to make the strong bias result more likely.

Returning to the discussion of the implications of the strong bias results for the behavior of the skill premium in the U.S. labor market, Proposition 15.8 implies that values of the elasticity of substitution between skilled and unskilled labor significantly less than 2 may be sufficient to generate strong equilibrium bias. How much lower than 2 the elasticity of substitution can be depends on the parameter δ. Unfortunately, this parameter is not easy to measure in practice, even though existing evidence suggests that there is some amount of state dependence in the R&D technologies. For example, state dependence is confirmed by the empirical finding that most patents developed in a particular industry build upon and cite previous patents in the same industry.

15.5 Directed Technological Change without Scale Effects

This section shows that the market size effect and its implications for the direction of technological change are independent of whether there are scale effects. The market size effect here refers to the relative market sizes of the users of two different types of technologies, whereas the scale effect concerns the impact of the size of the population on the equilibrium growth rate. The results in this section show that it is possible to entirely separate the market size effect responsible for the weak and strong endogenous bias results from the scale effect.

Consider the knowledge-based R&D model of the previous section, but only with limited spillovers from past research. In particular, suppose that (15.31) is modified to

$$\dot{N}_L = \eta_L N_L^{\lambda} S_L, \text{ and } \dot{N}_H = \eta_H N_H^{\lambda} S_H, \tag{15.40}$$

where $\lambda \in (0, 1]$. In the case where $\lambda = 1$, the knowledge-based R&D formulation of the previous section applies but now with extreme state dependence. When $\lambda < 1$, the extent of spillovers from past research are limited, and this economy does not have steady growth in the absence of population growth.

Let us also modify the baseline environment by assuming that total population, including the population of scientists, grows at the exponential rate n. With a similar argument to that in Section 13.3 in Chapter 13, it can be verified that when $\lambda < 1$, output per capita in this economy grows at the rate (see Exercise 15.14)

$$g^* = \frac{n}{1 - \lambda}. \tag{15.41}$$

The important point for the focus here concerns the market size effect on the direction of technological change. To investigate this issue, note that the technology market clearing condition implied by (15.40) is (see Exercise 15.16)

$$\eta_L N_L^{\lambda} \pi_L = \eta_H N_H^{\lambda} \pi_H, \tag{15.42}$$

which is analogous to (15.35). The same analysis as above implies that equilibrium relative technology can be derived as

$$\left(\frac{N_H}{N_L}\right)^* = \eta^{\frac{\sigma}{1-\lambda\sigma}} \gamma^{\frac{\varepsilon}{1-\lambda\sigma}} \left(\frac{H}{L}\right)^{\frac{\sigma-1}{1-\lambda\sigma}}. \tag{15.43}$$

Now combining (15.43) with (15.19)—which still determines the relative factor prices given technology—we obtain

$$\omega^* \equiv \left(\frac{w_H}{w_L}\right)^* = \eta^{\frac{\sigma-1}{1-\lambda\sigma}} \gamma^{\frac{(1-\lambda)\varepsilon}{1-\lambda\sigma}} \left(\frac{H}{L}\right)^{\frac{\sigma-2+\lambda}{1-\lambda\sigma}}. \tag{15.44}$$

This equation shows that even without scale effects, the same results as before apply.

Proposition 15.9 *Consider the directed technological change model with no scale effects described above. Then there is always weak equilibrium (relative) bias, meaning that an increase in H/L always induces relatively H-biased technological change. Moreover, if*

$$\sigma > 2 - \lambda,$$

then there is strong equilibrium (relative) bias in the sense that an increase in H/L raises the relative marginal product and the relative wage of the H factor compared to the L factor.

15.6 Endogenous Labor-Augmenting Technological Change

One of the advantages of the models of directed technological change is that they allow us to investigate why technological change might be purely labor-augmenting as required for balanced growth (recall Theorem 2.6 in Chapter 2). This section shows that models of directed technological change create a natural reason for technology to be more labor-augmenting than capital-augmenting. However, under most circumstances, the resulting equilibrium is not purely labor-augmenting and as a result, a BGP fails to exist. Nevertheless, in one important special case, the model delivers long-run purely labor-augmenting technological changes exactly as in the neoclassical growth model, thus providing a rationale for one of the strong assumptions of the standard growth models.

In thinking about labor-augmenting technological change, it is useful to consider a two-factor model with H corresponding to capital, that is, $H(t) = K(t)$, in the aggregate production function (15.3). Correspondingly, let us use N_L and N_K to denote the varieties of machines in the two sectors. Let us also simplify the discussion by assuming that there is no depreciation of capital, so that the price of capital $K(t)$ is equal to the interest rate $r(t)$.

Let us first note that in the context of capital-labor substitution, the empirical evidence suggests that an elasticity of substitution of $\sigma < 1$ is much more plausible (whereas in the case of substitution between skilled and unskilled labor, the evidence suggests that $\sigma > 1$). An elasticity less than 1 is not only consistent with the available empirical evidence, but it is also economically plausible. For example, with the CES production function an elasticity of substitution between capital and labor greater than 1 would imply that production is possible without labor or without capital, which appears counterintuitive.

Now recall that when $\sigma < 1$, factor-augmenting and factor-biased technologies are reversed. Therefore labor-augmenting technological change corresponds to capital-biased technological change. Then the question becomes: Under what circumstances would the economy generate relatively capital-biased technological change? And when will the equilibrium technology be sufficiently capital biased that it corresponds to Harrod-neutral technological change? What distinguishes capital from labor is the fact that it accumulates. In other words, most growth models feature some type of capital deepening, with $K(t)/L$ increasing as the economy grows. Then in contrast to the analysis so far, which looked at the effect of one-time changes in relative supplies, the focus must now be on the implications of continuous changes in the relative supply of capital on technological change. In light of this observation, the answer to the first question above is straightforward: capital deepening, combined with Proposition 15.3, implies that technological change should be more labor- than capital-augmenting.

The next proposition summarizes the main idea of the previous paragraph. For simplicity, this proposition treats the increase in $K(t)/L$ as a sequence of one-time increases (full equilibrium dynamics are investigated in the next two propositions).

Proposition 15.10 *In the baseline model of directed technological change with $H(t) = K(t)$ as capital, if $K(t)/L$ is increasing over time and $\sigma < 1$, then $N_L(t)/N_K(t)$ will also increase over time, that is, technological change will be relatively labor-augmenting.*

Proof. Equation (15.27) or (15.36) together with $\sigma < 1$ implies that an increase in $K(t)/L$ raises $N_L(t)/N_K(t)$. ∎

This result already gives us important economic insights. The logic of directed technological change indicates that there are natural reasons for technology to be more labor- than capital-augmenting. While this is encouraging, the next proposition shows that the results are not easy to reconcile with the fact that technological change should be *purely* labor-augmenting (Harrod neutral). To state this result in the simplest possible way and to facilitate the analysis in the rest of this section, let us simplify the analysis and suppose that capital accumulates at an exogenous rate, that is,

$$\frac{\dot{K}(t)}{K(t)} = s_K > 0. \tag{15.45}$$

Proposition 15.11 *Consider the baseline model of directed technological change with the knowledge spillovers specification and state dependence. Suppose that $\delta < 1$ and capital accumulates according to (15.45). Then there exists no BGP.*

Proof. See Exercise 15.21. ∎

Intuitively, even though technological change is more labor- than capital-augmenting, there is still capital-augmenting technological change in equilibrium. This, combined with capital accumulation, is inconsistent with balanced growth. In fact, an even more negative result can be proved (see again Exercise 15.21): in any asymptotic equilibrium, the interest rate cannot be constant, and thus consumption and output growth cannot be constant.

In contrast to these negative results, there is a special case that justifies the basic structure of the neoclassical growth model. This takes place when there is extreme state dependence, that is, $\delta = 1$. Though somewhat extreme, this case is also a natural benchmark. In particular, it posits that knowledge spillovers are limited to the same class of technologies, so that the innovation possibilities frontier (written in terms of labor- and capital-augmenting technologies) takes the form

$$\frac{\dot{N}_L(t)}{N_L(t)} = \eta_L S_L(t), \quad \text{and} \quad \frac{\dot{N}_K(t)}{N_K(t)} = \eta_K S_K(t).$$

In this case, it can be verified that technology market equilibrium implies the following relationship in BGP between the shares of capital and labor in national income (see Exercise 15.22):

$$\frac{r(t)K(t)}{w(t)L} = \eta^{-1}. \tag{15.46}$$

Thus directed technological change implies that in the long run, the share of capital is constant in national income. Long-run constant factor shares (combined with capital deepening) means that asymptotically all technological change must be purely labor-augmenting. More specifically, recall from (15.19) that

$$\frac{r(t)}{w(t)} = \gamma^{\frac{\varepsilon}{\sigma}} \left(\frac{N_K(t)}{N_L(t)} \right)^{\frac{\sigma-1}{\sigma}} \left(\frac{K(t)}{L} \right)^{-\frac{1}{\sigma}},$$

where $\gamma \equiv \gamma_K / \gamma_L$ and γ_K replaces γ_H in the production function (15.3). Consequently

$$\frac{r(t)K(t)}{w(t)L(t)} = \gamma^{\frac{\varepsilon}{\sigma}} \left(\frac{N_K(t)}{N_L(t)} \right)^{\frac{\sigma-1}{\sigma}} \left(\frac{K(t)}{L} \right)^{\frac{\sigma-1}{\sigma}}.$$

In this case, (15.46) combined with (15.45) implies that

$$\frac{\dot{N}_L(t)}{N_L(t)} - \frac{\dot{N}_K(t)}{N_K(t)} = s_K. \tag{15.47}$$

Moreover it can be verified that the equilibrium interest rate is given by (see Exercise 15.23)

$$r(t) = \beta \gamma_K N_K(t) \left[\gamma_L \left(\frac{N_L(t)L}{N_K(t)K(t)} \right)^{\frac{\sigma-1}{\sigma}} + \gamma_K \right]^{\frac{1}{\sigma-1}}. \tag{15.48}$$

Let us now define a BGP as an equilibrium path in which consumption grows at a constant rate (though the two sectors and the two technology stocks need not grow at the same rate). From (15.22), this is possible only if $r(t)$ is constant and equal to some r^*. Equation (15.47) then implies that $(N_L(t)L)/(N_K(t)K(t))$ is constant, and (15.48) implies that $N_K(t)$ must also be constant. Therefore (15.47) implies that for the economy to ultimately converge to a BGP, long-run technological change must be purely labor-augmenting. This argument is summarized in the following proposition.

Proposition 15.12 *Consider the baseline model of directed technological change with the two factors corresponding to labor and capital. Suppose that the innovation possibilities frontier is given by the knowledge spillovers specification with extreme state dependence, that is, $\delta = 1$, and that capital accumulates according to (15.45). Then there exists a unique BGP allocation in which there is only labor-augmenting technological change, the interest rate is constant and consumption and output grow at constant rates.*

Proof. Part of the proof is provided by the argument preceding the proposition. Exercise 15.24 asks you to complete the proof and show that no other constant BGP allocation can exist. ∎

Notice that Proposition 15.12 does not imply that all technological change must be Harrod neutral (purely labor-augmenting). Along the transition path, there can be (and in fact there will be) capital-augmenting technological change. However, in the long run (i.e., asymptotically or as $t \to \infty$), all technological change is labor-augmenting.

It can also be verified that the BGP allocation with purely labor-augmenting technological change is globally stable if $\sigma < 1$ (see Exercise 15.25). This result is reasonable, especially in view of the results in Proposition 15.6, which indicated that the stability of equilibrium dynamics in the model with the knowledge spillovers requires $\sigma < 1/\delta$. Since here there is extreme state dependence ($\delta = 1$), stability requires $\sigma < 1$. Intuitively, if capital and labor were gross substitutes ($\sigma > 1$), the equilibrium would involve rapid accumulation of capital and capital-augmenting technological change, leading to an asymptotically increasing growth rate of consumption. However when capital and labor are gross complements ($\sigma < 1$), capital accumulation increases the price of labor more than proportionately, and the profits from labor-augmenting technologies increase more than the profits from capital-augmenting ones. This encourages further labor-augmenting technological change. These strong price effects are responsible for the stability of the BGP allocation in Proposition 15.12. Intuitively, an elasticity of substitution between capital and labor that is less than 1 induces the economy to strive toward a balanced allocation of effective capital and labor units (where "effective" here refers to capital and labor units augmented with their complementary technologies). Since capital accumulates at a constant rate, a balanced allocation implies that the productivity of labor should increase faster; in particular, the economy should converge to an equilibrium path with purely labor-augmenting technological progress.

15.7   Generalizations and Other Applications

The results presented so far rely on a range of specific assumptions that are inherent in endogenous technological change models (e.g., Dixit-Stiglitz preferences and linear structure to ensure sustained growth). One may naturally wonder whether the results on weak and strong equilibrium biases generalize to situations in which these assumptions are relaxed. The answer is broadly yes. In Acemoglu (2007a), I show that, as long as only factor-augmenting technological changes are possible, the main results presented here also apply in an environment in which production and cost functions take more general forms. In particular, in this general environment, there is always weak (relative) equilibrium bias in response to increases in relative supplies, and there will be strong equilibrium bias when the elasticity of substitution is sufficiently high. However, once we allow for a richer menu of technological changes, these results do not necessarily hold. Nevertheless the essence of the results is much more general. In Acemoglu (2007a), I define the complementary notions of weak and strong *absolute* equilibrium biases, which refer to whether the equilibrium price of a factor changes as the supply of that factor changes (rather than the price of a factor relative to the price of another factor, which is what I have focused on in this chapter). Under very weak regularity assumptions, there is always weak absolute equilibrium bias, in the sense that an increase in the supply of a factor always induces technological change biased in favor of that factor. Moreover, even though standard producer theory implies that an increase in the supply of a factor should reduce its price, under plausible assumptions the induced technology effect can be strong enough that the price of the factor that has become more abundant can increase. In this case, there is strong absolute equilibrium bias, and the (general equilibrium) demand curves for factors are upward sloping. Since these results require additional notation and somewhat different mathematical arguments, I do not present them here.

It is also useful to briefly discuss a number of other important applications of the models of directed technological change. To save space, these are left as exercises. In particular, Exercise 15.19 shows how this model can be used to shed light on the famous Habakkuk hypothesis in economic history, which relates the rapid technological progress in nineteenth-century United States to relative labor scarcity. Despite the importance of this hypothesis in economic history, there have been no compelling models of this process. This exercise shows why neoclassical models may have difficulties in explaining these patterns and how a model of directed technological change can account for this phenomenon as long as the elasticity of substitution between capital and labor is less than 1.

Exercise 15.20 shows the effects of international trade on the direction of technological change. It highlights that international trade often affects the direction in which new technologies are developed and this often works through the price effect emphasized above.

Exercise 15.26 returns to the discussion of the technological change and unemployment experiences of continental European countries discussed above. It shows how a "wage push shock" can first increase equilibrium unemployment and then induce endogenous capital-biased technological change, which reduces the demand for employment, further increasing unemployment.

Finally, Exercise 15.27 shows how the relative supply of factors can be endogenized and studies the two-way causality between relative supplies and relative technology.

15.8 An Alternative Approach to Labor-Augmenting Technological Change*

The models presented so far in this chapter are all based on the basic directed technological change framework developed in Acemoglu (1998, 2002a). Section 15.6 showed how this approach can be used to provide conditions under which technological change is endogenously labor-augmenting. An alternative approach to this problem is suggested in a recent paper by Jones (2005). I now briefly discuss this alternative approach.

The models developed so far treat the different types of technologies (e.g., N_L and N_H in the previous sections) as state variables. Thus short-run production functions correspond to the production possibilities sets for given state variables, while long-run production functions apply when technology state variables also adjust. Jones proposes a different approach, building on a classic paper by Houthakker (1955). Houthakker suggested that the aggregate production function should be derived as the upper envelope of different ideas (or "activities"). Each technique or activity corresponds to a particular way of combining capital and labor (thus to a Leontief production function of these two factors of production). However, when a producer has access to multiple ways of combining capital and labor, the resulting envelope is different than Leontief. In a remarkable result, Houthakker showed that if the distribution of techniques is given by the Pareto distribution (defined formally below), this upper envelope of a large number of activities corresponds to a Cobb-Douglas production function. Houthakker thus suggested a justification for Cobb-Douglas production functions based on "activity analysis."

Jones builds on and extends these insights. He argues that the long-run production function should be viewed as the upper envelope of a large number of ideas generated over time. At a given point in time, the set of ideas that the society has access to is fixed, and these ideas determine the short-run production function of the economy. In the long run, however, the society generates more ideas (either exogenously or via R&D), and the long-run production function is obtained as the upper envelope of this expanding set of ideas. Using a combination of Pareto distribution and Leontief production possibilities for a given idea, Jones shows that there is a major difference between short-run and long-run production functions. In particular, as in Houthakker's analysis, the long-run production function takes a Cobb-Douglas form and implies a constant share of capital in national income. However, this is not necessarily the case for short-run production functions. Then, with an argument similar to that in Section 15.6, the economy adjusts from the short-run to long-run production functions by undergoing a form of labor-augmenting technological change.

I now provide a brief sketch of Jones's model, focusing on the main economic insights. As pointed out above, the key building block of Jones's model are "ideas." An idea is a technique for combining capital and labor to produce output. At any given point in time, the economy has access to a set of ideas. Let us denote the set of possible ideas by $\mathcal{I}$ and the set of ideas available at time t by $\mathcal{I}(t) \subset \mathcal{I}$. Each idea $i \in \mathcal{I}$ is represented by a vector (a_i, b_i). The essence of the model is to construct the production possibilities set of the economy from the set of available ideas. To do this, we first need to specify how a given idea is used for production. Let us suppose that there is a single final good Y that can be produced using any idea $i \in \mathcal{I}$ with a Leontief production function given by

$$Y(t) = \min\{b_i K(t), a_i L(t)\}, \tag{15.49}$$

where $K(t)$ and $L(t)$ are the amounts of capital and labor, respectively, in the economy. In general, the economy may use multiple ideas; thus $K(t)$ and $L(t)$ should be indexed by i to denote the amount of capital and labor allocated to idea i. However, I follow Jones and assume that at any point in time the economy uses a single idea. This assumption is restrictive but simplifies the model and its exposition significantly (see Exercise 15.29). The production function (15.49) makes it clear that a_i corresponds to the labor-augmenting productivity of idea i and b_i is its capital-augmenting productivity.

Recall from Section 15.6 that the standard model delivers purely labor-augmenting technological change only under the (special) assumption of extreme state dependence, that is, $\delta = 1$ (see Proposition 15.12). In this model, we also have to make a special assumption, which, following Houthakker, is that ideas are independently and identically drawn from a Pareto distribution. A random variable y has a Pareto distribution if its distribution function is given by $G(y) = 1 - \Gamma y^{-\alpha}$ for $\Gamma > 0$ and $\alpha > 0$. Now assuming that each component of the idea, a_i and b_i, is independently drawn from two Pareto distributions, we have

$$\Pr[a_i \leq a] = 1 - \left(\frac{a}{\gamma_a}\right)^{-\alpha}, \quad \text{and} \quad \Pr[b_i \leq b] = 1 - \left(\frac{b}{\gamma_b}\right)^{-\beta},$$

for $a \geq \gamma_a > 0, b \geq \gamma_b > 0, \alpha > 0, \beta > 0$, and $\alpha + \beta > 1$ (see Exercise 15.31 for the importance of this last inequality).

This Pareto assumption plays a crucial role in the result of this model. It is therefore appropriate to understand what the special features of the Pareto distribution are and why this distribution plays an important role in many different areas of economics. The Pareto distribution has two related special features. One is that its tails are "thick" (and for this reason, the variance of a variable that has a Pareto distribution may be infinite; see Exercise 15.30). The second special feature is that if y has a Pareto distribution, then its expected value conditional on being greater than some y', $\mathbb{E}[y \mid y \geq y']$, is proportional to y'. Thus loosely speaking, the Pareto distribution has a certain degree of proportionality built into it. The expectation of something better in the future is proportional to what has been achieved today. This property makes it quite convenient in the modeling of growth-related processes.

Now, given this structure, let us define the function

$$\mathbb{G}(b, a) \equiv \Pr\left[a_i \geq a \text{ and } b_i \geq b\right] = \left(\frac{b}{\gamma_b}\right)^{-\beta} \left(\frac{a}{\gamma_a}\right)^{-\alpha} \tag{15.50}$$

as the joint probability $a_i \geq a$ and $b_i \geq b$. Denote the level of aggregate output that can be produced using technique i with capital K and labor L by $\tilde{Y}_i(K, L)$. Before the realization of a_i and b_i for idea i, this level of output is a random variable. Since the production function is Leontief, the distribution of $\tilde{Y}_i$ can be represented by the distribution function of this variable,

$$H(y) \equiv \Pr[\tilde{Y}_i \leq y] = 1 - \Pr[a_i L \geq y \text{ and } b_i K \geq y] \tag{15.51}$$

$$= 1 - \mathbb{G}\left(\frac{y}{K}, \frac{y}{L}\right)$$

$$= 1 - \gamma K^\beta L^\alpha y^{-(\alpha+\beta)},$$

where the second line follows from the definition of the function $\mathbb{G}$ and the third line from (15.50) with $\gamma \equiv \gamma_a^\alpha \gamma_b^\beta$. Thus the distribution of $\tilde{Y}_i$ is also Pareto (provided that $y \geq \min\{\gamma_b K, \gamma_a L\}$).

Let us next turn to the "global" production function, which describes the maximum amount of output that can be produced using any of the available techniques. In other words, let $\tilde{Y}(K, L) = \max_{i \in \mathcal{I}(t)} \tilde{Y}_i(K, L)$. Let $N(t)$ denote the total number of production techniques (ideas) that are available in the set $\mathcal{I}(t)$ (at time t). Then by time t $N(t)$ distinct ideas have been discovered. Since, by assumption, these $N(t)$ ideas are drawn independently, the global production function can be alternatively written as

$$\tilde{Y}(t; N(t)) = F(K(t), L(t); N(t)) \equiv \max_{i=1,\ldots,N(t)} \min\{b_i K(t), a_i L(t)\} \tag{15.52}$$

Since the realization of the $N(t)$ ideas are random, output at time t, $\tilde{Y}(t; N(t))$, conditional on capital $K(t)$ and $L(t)$, is also a random variable. We are interested in determining its distribution. Here the fact that the $N(t)$ draws of ideas are independent simplifies the analysis. The probability that the realization of $\tilde{Y}(t; N(t))$ is less than y is equal to the probability that each of the $N(t)$ ideas produces less than y. Therefore

$$\Pr[\tilde{Y}(t; N(t)) \leq y] = H(y)^{N(t)}. \tag{15.53}$$

$$= (1 - \gamma K(t)^\beta L(t)^\alpha y^{-(\alpha+\beta)})^{N(t)}.$$

Equation (15.53) makes it clear that as the number of ideas $N(t)$ becomes large, the probability that $\tilde{Y}(t; N(t))$ is less than any level of y will go to zero. This is simply a restatement of the fact that output grows without bound, which here follows from the fact that the Pareto distribution has unbounded support. Therefore we cannot simply determine the distribution of output as $N(t) \to \infty$. Instead we have to look at aggregate output normalized by an appropriate variable, such as its expected value (and apply a type of reasoning similar to the Central Limit Theorem). Given the Pareto distribution, the normalizing factor turns out to be $n(t) \equiv (\gamma N(t) K(t)^\beta L(t)^\alpha)^{\frac{1}{\alpha+\beta}}$, so that

$$\Pr[\tilde{Y}(t; N(t)) \leq (\gamma N(t) K(t)^\beta L(t)^\alpha)^{\frac{1}{\alpha+\beta}} y] = (1 - \gamma K(t)^\beta L(t)^\alpha (n(t)y)^{-(\alpha+\beta)})^{N(t)}$$

$$= \left(1 - \frac{y^{-(\alpha+\beta)}}{N(t)}\right)^{N(t)}, \tag{15.54}$$

where the second line, (15.54), makes it clear that $n(t) \equiv (\gamma N(t) K(t)^\beta L(t)^\alpha)^{\frac{1}{\alpha+\beta}}$ was indeed the correct normalizing factor. Now recalling that $\lim_{N \to \infty}(1 - x/N)^N = \exp(-x)$, we have

$$\lim_{N(t) \to \infty} \Pr[\tilde{Y}(t; N(t)) \leq (\gamma N(t) K(t)^\beta L(t)^\alpha)^{\frac{1}{\alpha+\beta}} y] = \exp(-y^{-(\alpha+\beta)}) \tag{15.55}$$

for $y > 0$. Equation (15.55) gives the famous *Fréchet distribution*, which is one of the three limiting distributions for extreme values.[3] More specifically, (15.55) implies that

$$\frac{\tilde{Y}(t; N(t))}{(\gamma N(t) K(t)^\beta L(t)^\alpha)^{1/\alpha+\beta}} \sim \text{Fréchet}(\alpha + \beta),$$

---

3. In particular, a fascinating result in statistics shows that regardless of the distribution $F(y)$, if we take N independent draws from F and look at the probability distribution of the highest draw, then as $N \to \infty$, this distribution converges to one of the following three distributions: the Weibull, the Gumbel, or the Fréchet. See, for example, Billingsley (1995, Section 14).

so that the long-run distribution of output, appropriately normalized, converges asymptotically to a Fréchet distribution. Then as $N(t)$ becomes large (i.e., as $t \to \infty$ and more ideas are discovered), the long-run global production function behaves approximately as

$$\tilde{Y}(t; N(t)) \approx \varepsilon(t)(\gamma N(t) K(t)^{\beta} L(t)^{\alpha})^{\frac{1}{\alpha+\beta}}, \qquad (15.56)$$

where $\varepsilon(t)$ is a random variable drawn from a Fréchet distribution. The intuition for this result is similar to Houthakker's result that aggregation over different units producing with techniques drawn independently from a Pareto distribution leads to a Cobb-Douglas production function. The implications are different, however. In particular, since the long-run production function behaves approximately as Cobb-Douglas, it implies that factor shares must be constant in the long run. However the short-run production function (for a finite number of ideas) is not Cobb-Douglas. Therefore as $N(t)$ increases, the production function evolves endogenously toward the Cobb-Douglas limit with constant factor shares, and as in the analysis in Section 15.6, this means that technological change must ultimately become purely labor-augmenting. Therefore Jones's model shows that insights related to Houthakker's derivation of a static production function also imply that the short-run production function evolves endogenously on average, with labor-augmenting technological change dominating the limiting behavior and making sure that the economy, in the long run, acts as if it has a Cobb-Douglas production function.

Although this idea is interesting and the Pareto distribution appears in many important contexts and has various desirable properties, it is not clear whether it provides a compelling reason for technological change to be labor-augmenting in the long run. Labor-augmenting technological change should be an equilibrium outcome (resulting from the research and innovation incentives of firms and workers). The directed technological change models emphasized how these incentives play out under various equilibrium scenarios. In the current model, the Cobb-Douglas production function arises purely from aggregation. There are no equilibrium interactions, price, or market size effects. Related to this, the unit of analysis is unclear. The same argument can be applied to a single firm, to an industry, or to a region. Thus if we are happy with this argument for the economy as a whole, we may also wish to apply it to firms, industries, and regions, concluding that the long-run production function of every unit of production or every firm, industry, and region should be Cobb-Douglas. However, existing evidence indicates that there are considerable differences in the production functions across industries, and they cannot be well approximated by Cobb-Douglas production functions (see the overview of the evidence on industry and aggregate production functions in Acemoglu, 2003a). This suggests that it would be interesting to combine the aggregation of different activities or "ideas" as in Houthakker's and Jones's papers with equilibrium interactions, which might delineate at what level the aggregation should take place and why it may apply to (some) economies but not necessarily to single firms or industries.

15.9   Taking Stock

This chapter introduced the basic models of directed technological change. These approaches differ from the endogenous technological change models of the previous two chapters because they not only determine the evolution of aggregate technology but also the direction and bias of technological change. Models of directed technological change enable us to investigate a range of new questions. These include the sources of skill-biased technological change over the past 100 years, the causes of acceleration in skill-biased technological change during more recent decades, the causes of unskilled-biased technological developments during the nineteenth century, the impact of international trade on the direction of technological change, and the relationship between labor market institutions and the types of technologies that are developed and adopted. Last but not least, they also enable an investigation of why technological change in neoclassical-type models may be largely labor-augmenting.

A relatively simple class of directed technological change models can shed light on all these questions. These models are quite tractable and allow closed-form solutions for equilibrium relative technologies and long-run growth rates. Their implications for the empirical questions mentioned above stem from two important, and perhaps at first surprising, results, which we can refer to as "weak equilibrium bias" and "strong equilibrium bias" results. The first states that, under fairly weak assumptions, an increase in the relative supply of a factor always induces endogenous changes in technology that are relatively biased toward that factor. Consequently any increase in the ratio of skilled to unskilled workers or in the capital-labor ratio has major implications for the relative productivities of these factors. The more surprising result is that for the strong equilibrium bias, which states that contrary to basic producer theory, (relative) demand curves can slope up. In particular, if the elasticity of substitution between factors is sufficiently high, a greater relative supply of a factor causes sufficiently strong induced technological change to make the resulting relative price of the more abundant factor increase. In other words, the long-run (endogenous-technology) relative demand curve becomes upward sloping. The possibility that relative demand curves may be upward sloping not only has a range of important empirical implications, but also illustrates the strength of induced technology effects.

This chapter also presented a number of applications of these ideas to several empirically important areas. Models of directed technological change are in their infancy, and there are many theoretical dimensions in which further developments are possible. Perhaps more importantly, there are also numerous applications of these ideas.

Finally, the models in this chapter have further emphasized that technology should not be thought of as a black box; instead it should be modeled as the outcome of decisions by firms, individuals, and other agents in the economy. This implies that profit incentives play a major role both in the aggregate rate of technological progress and in the biases of the technologies that are being developed and adopted.

15.10 References and Literature

Models of directed technological change were developed in Acemoglu (1998, 2002a, 2003a,b, 2007a), Kiley (1999), and Acemoglu and Zilibotti (2001). These papers use the term "directed technical change," but here I used the related term "directed technological change," to emphasize continuity with the models of endogenous technological change studied in the previous chapters. The framework presented here builds on Acemoglu (2002a). A more general framework, without functional form restrictions, is presented in Acemoglu (2007a).

Other papers modeling the direction of technological change include Xu (2001), Gancia (2003), Thoenig and Verdier (2003), Ragot (2003), Duranton (2004), Benabou (2005), Caselli and Coleman (2005), and Jones (2005).

Models of directed technological change are closely related to the earlier literature on induced innovation. The induced innovation literature was started indirectly by Hicks, who in *The Theory of Wages* (1932, pp. 124–25), argued: "A change in the relative prices of the factors of production is itself a spur to invention, and to invention of a particular kind—directed to economizing the use of a factor which has become relatively expensive." An important paper by Kennedy (1964) introduced the concept of "innovation possibilities frontier" and argued that it is the form of this frontier—rather than the shape of a given neoclassical production function—that determines the factor distribution of income. Kennedy, furthermore, argued that induced innovations would push the economy to an equilibrium with a constant relative factor share (see also Drandakis and Phelps, 1965, and Samuelson, 1965). Around the same time, Habakkuk (1962) published his important treatise, *American and British Technology in the Nineteenth Century: The Search for Labor-Saving Inventions*, where he argued that labor scarcity and the search for labor-saving inventions were central determinants of technological progress. The flavor of Habakkuk's argument was one of induced innovations: labor scarcity increased wages, which in turn encouraged labor-saving technological change. Nevertheless neither Habakkuk nor the induced innovation literature provided micro-founded approaches to technological change or technology adoption. For example, in Kennedy's specification the production function at the firm level exhibited increasing returns to scale because, in addition to factor quantities, firms could choose "technology quantities," but this increasing returns to scale was not taken into account in the analysis. Similar problems are present in other earlier works as well. It was also not clear who undertook the R&D activities and how they were financed and priced. These shortcomings reduced the interest in this literature.

The analysis in Acemoglu (1998) and the subsequent work in this area, instead, starts from the explicit microfoundations of the endogenous technological change models discussed in the previous two chapters. The presence of monopolistic competition avoids the problems that the induced innovations literature had with increasing returns to scale.

Acemoglu (2002a, b) shows that the specific way in which endogenous technological change is modeled does not affect the major results on the direction of technological change. This is also illustrated in Exercises 15.18 and 15.28. In addition, even though the focus here has been on technological progress, in Acemoglu (2007a), I show that all results generalize to models of technology adoption. There I also introduce the alternative concepts of weak absolute bias and strong absolute bias, which focus on the marginal product of a factor rather than on the relative marginal product, and I prove that there are considerably more general theorems on weak and strong absolute biases. In the text here, I refer to weak relative bias and strong relative bias to distinguish the results here from the absolute bias results. The results in Acemoglu (2007a) also show that the CES aggregator used here is unnecessary for the results. Nevertheless I have kept the CES structure to simplify the exposition.

Changes in U.S. wage inequality over the past 60 years are surveyed in Autor, Katz, and Krueger (1998); Katz and Autor (2000); and Acemoglu (2002b). The last paper also discusses how models on directed technological change can provide a good explanation for changes in wage inequality over the past 100 years and also for changes in the direction of technological change in the U.S. and UK economies over the past 200 years. There are many studies estimating the elasticity of substitution between skilled and unskilled workers. The estimates are typically between 1.4 and 2. See, for example, Katz and Murphy (1992), Angrist (1995), Krusell et al. (1999). A number of these estimates are summarized and discussed in Hammermesh (1993) and Acemoglu (2002b).

Evidence that nineteenth-century technologies were generally labor complementary (unskilled biased) is provided in James and Skinner (1985) and Mokyr (1990), while Goldin and Katz (1998) argue the same for a range of important early twentieth-century technologies.

Blanchard (1997) discusses the persistence of European unemployment and argues that the phase during the 1990s can only be understood by changes in technology reducing demand for high-cost labor. This idea is the basis of Exercise 15.26. Caballero and Hammour (1999) provide an alternative and complementary explanation to that suggested here.

Acemoglu (2003b) suggested that increased international trade can cause endogenous skill-biased technological change. Exercise 15.20 is based on this idea. Variants of this story have been developed by Xu (2001), Gancia (2003), and Thoenig and Verdier (2003).

The model of long-run purely labor-augmenting technological change presented in Section 15.6 was first proposed in Acemoglu (2003a), and the model presented here is a simplified version of the one in that paper (see also Funk, 2002). The assumption that the elasticity of substitution between capital and labor is less than 1 receives support from a variety of different empirical strategies. The evidence is summarized in Acemoglu (2003a). Section 15.8 builds on Jones (2005). See also Houthakker (1955) and Lagos (2001).

15.11 Exercises

15.1 Derive (15.1).

15.2 Complete the proof of Proposition 15.1. In particular, verify that in any BGP, (15.27) must hold, and derive the equilibrium growth rate as given by (15.29). Also prove that (15.28) ensures that the two free-entry conditions, (15.20) and (15.21), must hold as equalities. Finally, check that this condition is also sufficient to guarantee that household utility is finite and the transversality condition is satisfied. [Hint: calculate the equilibrium interest rate and then use (15.22).]

15.3 Prove Proposition 15.2. [Hint: use (15.9) to show that when $N_H(0)/N_L(0)$ does not satisfy (15.27), then (15.20) and (15.21) cannot both hold as equalities.]

15.4 Derive (15.30).

15.5 Explain why in Proposition 15.1 the effect of γ on the BGP growth rate, (15.29), is ambiguous. When is this effect positive? Provide an intuition.

15.6 This exercise asks you to characterize the Pareto optimal allocation in the model of Section 15.3. Set up the optimal growth problem in this model. Show that in the optimal growth (Pareto optimal) allocation, there are no markups and thus

$$x_L^S(v, t) = (1 - \beta)^{-1/\beta} p_L(t)^{1/\beta} L, \text{ and } x_H^S(v, t) = (1 - \beta)^{-1/\beta} p_H(t)^{1/\beta} H.$$

Using these expressions, show that the optimal growth problem can be characterized using the current-value Hamiltonian

$$\mathcal{H}(N_L^S, N_H^S, Z_L^S, Z_H^S, C^S, \mu_L, \mu_H) = \frac{C^S(t)^{1-\theta} - 1}{1 - \theta} + \mu_L(t)\eta_L Z_L^S(t) + \mu_H(t)\eta_H Z_H^S(t),$$

where

$$C^S(t) = (1 - \beta)^{-1/\beta} \beta \left[\gamma_L^{\varepsilon/\sigma} \left(N_L^S(t)L \right)^{\frac{\sigma-1}{\sigma}} + \gamma_H^{\varepsilon/\sigma} \left(N_H^S(t)H \right)^{\frac{\sigma-1}{\sigma}} \right]^{\frac{\sigma}{\sigma-1}} - Z_L^S(t) - Z_H^S(t).$$

Show that this problem has a unique solution, where, as $t \to \infty$, $\left(N_H^S/N_L^S\right)$ converges to a unique $\left(N_H^S/N_L^S\right)^*$ that is identically given by (15.27) and that the growth rate of consumption converges to

$$g^S = \frac{1}{\theta} \left((1 - \beta)^{-1/\beta} \beta \left[\gamma_H^{\varepsilon}(\eta_H H)^{\sigma-1} + \gamma_L^{\varepsilon}(\eta_L L)^{\sigma-1} \right]^{\frac{1}{\sigma-1}} - \rho \right).$$

Show that this growth rate is strictly greater than the BGP equilibrium growth rate g^* given by (15.29). Finally, show that the equivalents of weak and strong equilibrium bias results hold in this optimal growth allocation.

15.7 Derive the free-entry conditions (15.33) and (15.34). Provide an intuition for these conditions.

15.8 Derive (15.36).

15.9 Prove Proposition 15.5. In particular, check that there is a unique BGP and that the BGP growth rate satisfies the transversality condition.

15.10 In the model of Section 15.4, show that an increase in η_H raises the number of scientists working in H-augmenting technologies in the BGP, S_H^*, when $\sigma > 1$ (and $\sigma < 1/\delta$) and reduces it when $\sigma < 1$. Interpret this result.

15.11 (a) Prove Proposition 15.6. In particular, use (15.9) and show that when (15.36) is not satisfied, both free-entry conditions cannot hold simultaneously. Then show that if $\sigma < 1/\delta$, there are greater incentives to undertake research for the technology that is relatively scarce, and the opposite holds when $\sigma > 1/\delta$.

 (b) Interpret the economic significance of the condition $\sigma < 1/\delta$. [Hint: relate this to the fact that when $\sigma < 1/\delta$, $\partial(N_H^\delta V_H / N_L^\delta V_L)/\partial(N_H/N_L) < 0$, but the inequality is reversed when $\sigma > 1/\delta$.]

15.12 Prove Proposition 15.7.

15.13 Characterize the Pareto optimal allocation in the model with knowledge spillovers and state dependence (Section 15.4). Show that the relative technology ratio in the stationary Pareto optimal allocation no longer coincides with the BGP equilibrium. Explain why this result differs from that in Section 15.3.

15.14 Derive (15.41).

15.15 Show that in the model of Section 15.5 if $\lambda = 1$, there exists no BGP.

15.16 Derive (15.42) and (15.43).

* 15.17 Generalize the model of Section 15.4 so that there are no scientists and the R&D sector also uses skilled and unskilled workers. Thus the labor market clearing conditions now become

$$H^E(t) + H_L^R(t) + H_H^R(t) \leq H, \text{ and}$$

$$L^E(t) + L_L^R(t) + L_H^R(t) \leq L,$$

where $H^E(t)$ and $L^E(t)$ denote employment in the final good sector, and $H_L^R(t)$, $H_H^R(t)$, $L_L^R(t)$, and $L_H^R(t)$ denote the employment in the two R&D sectors. Suppose that the R&D technologies for both sectors combine skilled and unskilled workers according to the same constant returns to scale production function.

 (a) Define the equilibrium and BGP allocations, and specify the free-entry conditions.

 (b) Characterize the BGP equilibrium.

 (c) Show that the equivalents of Propositions 15.3 and 15.4 hold in this environment.

 (d) Characterize the transitional dynamics, and show that they are similar to those in Proposition 15.2.

 (e) Characterize the Pareto optimal allocation in this economy and show that the Pareto optimal ratio of technologies in the stationary equilibrium are also given by (15.27).

* 15.18 Consider a version of the baseline directed technological change model introduced in Section 15.3 with the only difference being that technological change is driven by quality improvements rather than expanding machine varieties. In particular, let us suppose that the intermediate goods are produced with the production functions

$$Y_L(t) = \frac{1}{1-\beta} \left(\int_0^1 q_L(\nu, t) x_L(\nu, t \mid q)^{1-\beta} d\nu \right) L^\beta, \text{ and}$$

$$Y_H(t) = \frac{1}{1-\beta} \left(\int_0^1 q_H(\nu, t) x_H(\nu, t \mid q)^{1-\beta} d\nu \right) H^\beta.$$

Producing a machine of quality q costs ψq, where we again normalize $\psi \equiv 1 - \beta$. R&D of amount $Z_f(\nu, t)$ directed at a particular machine of quality $q_f(\nu, t)$ leads to an innovation at the flow rate

$\eta_f Z_f(v, t)/q_f(v, t)$ and leads to an improved machine of quality $\lambda q_f(v, t)$, where $f = L$ or H, and $\lambda \geq (1 - \beta)^{-(1-\beta)/\beta}$, so that firms that undertake an innovation can charge the unconstrained monopoly price.

(a) Define and characterize the equilibrium and BGP allocations.

(b) Show that the relative technologies in the BGP equilibrium are given by (15.27).

(c) Show that the equivalents of Propositions 15.3 and 15.4 hold in this environment.

(d) Characterize the transitional dynamics, and show that they are similar to those in Proposition 15.2.

(e) Characterize the Pareto optimal allocation in this economy, and show that the Pareto optimal ratio of technologies in the stationary equilibrium is also given by (15.27).

(f) What are the pros and cons of this model relative to the baseline model studied in Section 15.3?

15.19 As a potential application of the models of directed technological change, consider the famous Habakkuk hypothesis, which claims that technology adoption in the U.S. economy during the nineteenth century was faster than in Britain because of relative labor scarcity in the former (which increased wages and encouraged technology adoption).

(a) First, consider a neoclassical-type model with two factors, labor and technology, $F(A, L)$, where F exhibits constant returns to scale, and A is a technology term, chosen by each firm with costs $\Gamma(A)$ in terms of the final good. Assume that Γ is continuous, differentiable, strictly increasing, and convex. Show that an increase in wages (caused by a decline in labor supply or an exogenous increase in wages because of a minimum wage) cannot increase A.

(b) Next, consider the directed technological change model studied in this chapter with H interpreted as land, and assume that N_H is fixed (so that only R&D increases N_L). Show that if $\sigma > 1$, the opposite of the Habakkuk hypothesis obtains. If in contrast σ is sufficiently smaller than 1, the model delivers results consistent with the Habakkuk hypothesis. Interpret this result, and explain why the implications are different from the neoclassical model considered in part a.

15.20 Consider the baseline model of directed technological change in Section 15.3 and assume that it is in steady state.

(a) Show that in steady state the relative price p of the two intermediate goods is proportional to $(H/L)^{-\beta}$.

(b) Now assume that the economy opens up to world trade and faces a relative price of intermediate goods $p' < p$. Derive the implications of this for the endogenous changes in technology. Explain why the results are different from those in the text. [Hint: relate your results to the price effect.]

15.21 (a) Prove Proposition 15.11. Show that in any BGP equilibrium (15.36) holds, and that this equation is inconsistent with capital accumulation.

(b) Prove that there exists no equilibrium allocation in which consumption grows at a constant rate. [Hint: show that a relationship similar to (15.36) must hold, and this leads to an increase in $N_K(t)$, which then implies that the interest rate cannot be constant.]

15.22 Derive (15.46).

15.23 Derive (15.48).

* 15.24 Complete the proof of Proposition 15.12 and show that there cannot exist any other BGP equilibrium.

* 15.25 Show that if $\sigma < 1$ and $S_K < \eta_L S$, then the BGP equilibrium in Proposition 15.12 is globally stable. Show that if $\sigma > 1$, it is unstable. Relate your results to Proposition 15.6.

15.26 Now let us use the results of Proposition 15.12 to revisit the discussion of the unemployment experiences of continental European economies provided in Blanchard (1997). Consider the model of Section 15.6. Discuss how a wage push, in the form of a wage floor above the market clearing level, first causes unemployment and then, if $\sigma < 1$, it will cause capital-biased technological change. Can this model shed light on the persistent unemployment dynamics in continental Europe? [Hint: distinguish two cases: (1) the minimum wage floor is constant and (2) the minimum wage floor increases at the same rate as the growth of the economy.]

* 15.27 The analysis in the text has treated the supply of the two factors as exogenous and examined the impact of relative supplies on factor prices. This exercise investigates at the joint determination of relative supplies and technologies. Let us focus on a model with the two factors corresponding to skilled and unskilled labor. Suppose a continuum υ of unskilled agents are born every period, and each faces a flow rate of death equal to υ, so that population is constant at 1 (as in Section 9.8). Each agent chooses upon birth whether to acquire education and become a skilled worker. For agent x, schooling of length K_x is necessary to become skilled, and during this time, he earns no labor income. The distribution of K_x is given by $\Gamma(K)$. The rest of the setup is the same as in the text. Suppose that $\Gamma(K)$ has no mass points. Define a BGP as a situation in which H/L and the skill premium remain constant.

(a) Show that in BGP if an individual with cost of education K_x chooses schooling, another with $K_{x'} < K_x$ must also acquire skills and that there exists $\bar{K}$ such that individuals with $K_x > \bar{K}$ do not become skilled.

(b) Show that as $\upsilon \to 0$, BGP relative supplies can be approximated by

$$\frac{H}{L} \approx \frac{\Gamma(\bar{K})}{1 - \Gamma(\bar{K})}.$$

(c) Show that as in BGP, $\bar{K} = \log \omega/(r^* + \upsilon - g^*)$, where r^* and g^* refer to the BGP interest rate and growth rate, respectively.

(d) Determine the BGP skill premium by combining the expressions in parts b and c with (15.30). Can there be multiple equilibria? Explain the intuition.

* 15.28 Consider an economy with a constant population and risk-neutral households discounting the future at the rate r. The population consists of L unskilled workers, H skilled workers and S scientists. Utility of each agent is defined over the final good, which is produced as

$$Y(t) = \left(\int_0^n y(v, t)^{\frac{\varepsilon-1}{\varepsilon}} dv \right)^{\frac{\varepsilon}{\varepsilon-1}},$$

where $\varepsilon > 1$, and intermediate $y(v, t)$ can be produced using either skilled or unskilled labor. When a new intermediate is invented, it is first produced using skilled labor only, with the production function $y(v, t) = h(v, t)$, and eventually, another firm may find a way to produce this good using unskilled labor with the production function $y(v, t) = l(v, t)$. Assume that new goods are created using scientists according to the innovation possibilities frontier

$$\dot{n}(t) = b_n n(t)^\delta m(t)^{1-\delta} S_n(t), \text{ and } \dot{m}(t) = b_m m(t)^\delta n(t)^{1-\delta} S_m(t),$$

with $\delta < 1$, and $S_n(t)$ and $S_m(t)$ are the number of scientists allocated to the two types of goods with $S_n(t) + S_m(t) \leq S$. Denote the wage of scientists at time t by $\omega(t)$. A firm that invents a new good becomes the monopolist producer, but can be displaced by a new monopolist who finds a way of producing the good using unskilled labor.

(a) Denote the unskilled wage by $w(t)$ and the skilled wage by $v(t)$. Show that, as long as $v(t)$ is sufficiently larger than $w(t)$, the instantaneous profits of a monopolist producing skill-intensive and labor-intensive goods at time t are

$$\pi_h(t) = \frac{1}{\varepsilon - 1} \frac{v(t)H}{n(t) - m(t)}, \quad \text{and} \quad \pi_l(t) = \frac{1}{\varepsilon - 1} \frac{w(t)L}{m(t)}.$$

Interpret these equations. Why is the condition that $v(t)$ is sufficiently larger than $w(t)$ necessary?

(b) Assume moreover that a firm that undertakes R&D to replace the skill-intensive good has an equal probability of replacing any of the existing $n - m$ skill-intensive goods. Define a BGP as an allocation where n and m grow at the same rate g. Show that this condition implies that output and wages of skilled and unskilled workers must grow at the rate $g/(\varepsilon - 1)$. [Hint: use the equation for the numeraire setting the price of the final good equal to 1 at each date.]

(c) Show that in BGP the wages of scientists also grow at the same rate as the wages of skilled and unskilled workers.

(d) Show that the BGP must satisfy the following condition

$$b_n \mu^{1-2\delta} \frac{vH}{r - (2 - \varepsilon)g/(1 - \varepsilon) + \mu g/(1 - \mu)} = b_m \frac{wL}{r - (2 - \varepsilon)g/(1 - \varepsilon)},$$

where $\mu \equiv m/n$. [Hint: note that a monopolist producing a labor-intensive good will never be replaced, but a monopolist producing a skill-intensive good faces a constant flow rate of being replaced; also use the fact that $\dot{m}/(n - m) = g\mu/(1 - \mu)$.]

(e) Using demands over varieties (i.e., $y(v, t)/y(v', t) = (p(v, t)/p(v', t))^{-\varepsilon}$), characterize the BGP path level of μ. What is the effect of an increase in H/L on μ? Interpret.

(f) Why was it necessary to impose $\delta < 1$ in the innovation possibilities frontier? Briefly discuss how the analysis would change if $\delta = 1$.

* 15.29 Consider the model presented in Section 15.8.

(a) Show that if capital and labor are allocated in competitive markets, in general more than one technique is used in equilibrium. [Hint: construct an example in which there are three ideas $i = 1, 2,$ and 3, such that when only one can be used, it is $i = 1$, but output can be increased by allocating some of labor and capital to ideas 2 and 3.]

(b) Show that in this case the aggregation result used in Section 15.8 does not apply.

* 15.30 Suppose that y has a Pareto distribution given by $G(y) = 1 - By^{-\alpha}$. Determine the variance of y and show that it may be infinite.

* 15.31 Suppose that y has a Pareto distribution given by $G(y) = 1 - By^{-\alpha}$ with $\alpha > 1$. Show that

$$\mathbb{E}[y \mid y \geq y'] = \frac{\alpha}{\alpha - 1} y'.$$

What happens if $\alpha < 1$?

PART V

STOCHASTIC GROWTH

This part of the book focuses on stochastic growth models and provides a brief introduction to basic tools of stochastic dynamic optimization. Stochastic growth models are useful for two related reasons. First, a range of interesting growth problems involve either aggregate uncertainty or nontrivial individual-level uncertainty interacting with investment decisions and the growth process. Some of these models are discussed in Chapter 17. Second, the stochastic neoclassical growth model has a wide range of applications in macroeconomics and in other areas of dynamic economic analysis. Various aspects of the stochastic neoclassical growth model are discussed in the next two chapters. The study of stochastic models requires us to extend the dynamic optimization tools of Chapters 6 and 7 to an environment in which either returns or constraints are uncertain (governed by probability distributions).[1] Unfortunately, dynamic optimization under uncertainty is considerably harder than the nonstochastic optimization. The generalization of continuous-time methods to stochastic optimization requires fairly advanced tools from measure theory and stochastic differential equations. While continuous-time stochastic optimization methods are very powerful, they are not used widely in macroeconomics and economic growth, and here I focus on discrete-time stochastic models. Thus the next chapter includes the most straightforward generalization of the discrete-time dynamic programming techniques presented in Chapter 6 to stochastic environments. A fully rigorous development of stochastic dynamic programming also requires further mathematical investment than is typically necessary in most courses on macroeconomics and economic growth. To avoid a heavy dose of new mathematical tools (in particular, a lengthy detour into measure theory at this stage of the book), the next chapter develops the basics of stochastic dynamic programming without measure theory.

---

1. Throughout, I do not draw a distinction between risk and uncertainty. Some economists follow Frank Knight and identify risk with situations in which there is a known probability distribution of events and uncertainty with situations in which such a probability distribution cannot be specified. While "Knightian uncertainty" may be important in a range of situations, given the set of models being studied here, there is little cost of following the standard practice of using the word "uncertainty" interchangeably with "risk."

16

Stochastic Dynamic Programming

T his chapter provides an introduction to basic stochastic dynamic programming. To avoid the use of measure theory in the main body of the text, I first focus on economies in which stochastic variables take finitely many values. This restriction enables us to use Markov chains, instead of general Markov processes, to represent uncertainty. Since many commonly used stochastic processes, such as those based on normal or uniform distributions, fall outside this class, I then indicate how the results can be generalized to situations in which stochastic variables can be represented by continuous—or a mixture of continuous and discrete—random variables. Throughout, my purpose is to provide a basic understanding of the tools of stochastic dynamic programming and how they can be used in dynamic macroeconomic models. For this reason, I make a number of judicious choices rather than attempting to provide the most general results. Throughout, I focus on stationary problems, that is, the equivalents of Problems 6.2 and 6.3 in Chapter 6. Analogues of Theorems 6.11 and 6.12, which applied to nonstationary optimization problems under certainty, can be proved using the same arguments in the stochastic case, and I omit these results to save space.

16.1 Dynamic Programming with Expectations

I use a notation similar to that in Chapter 6. Let us first introduce the *stochastic* (random) variable $z(t) \in Z \equiv \{z_1, \ldots, z_N\}$, with $z_1 < z_2 < \cdots < z_N$. Note that the set Z is finite and thus compact, which simplifies the analysis considerably. Let the instantaneous payoff at time t be

$$U(x(t), x(t+1), z(t)), \tag{16.1}$$

where $x(t) \in X \subset \mathbb{R}^K$ for some $K \geq 1$ and $U : X \times X \times Z \to \mathbb{R}$. Equation (16.1) extends the payoff function in Chapter 6, which took the form $U(x(t), x(t+1))$, by making payoffs directly a function of the stochastic variable $z(t)$. As usual, returns are discounted by some discount factor $\beta \in (0, 1)$, $x(t)$ again denotes the *state variables* (state vector), and $x(t+1)$ the *control variables* (control vector) at time t. The initial values of the state vector, $x(0)$, and of stochastic variable, $z(0)$, are taken as given.

An additional difference from Problem 6.2 in Chapter 6 is that the constraint on $x(t + 1)$ is no longer of the form $x(t + 1) \in G(x(t))$. Instead the constraint also incorporates the stochastic variable $z(t)$ and is written as

$$x(t + 1) \in G(x(t), z(t)),$$

where again $G(x, z)$ is a set-valued mapping (correspondence):

$$G : X \times \mathcal{Z} \rightrightarrows X.$$

Suppose that the stochastic variable $z(t)$ follows a (first-order) *Markov chain*.[1] The important property implied by the Markov chain assumption is that the current value of $z(t)$ only depends on its value from the last period, $z(t - 1)$. Mathematically, this can be expressed as

$$\Pr\left[z(t) = z_j \mid z(0), \dots, z(t - 1)\right] \equiv \Pr\left[z(t) = z_j \mid z(t - 1)\right].$$

The simplest example of an economic model with uncertainty represented by a Markov chain would be one in which the stochastic variable takes finitely many values and is independently distributed over time. In this case, clearly $\Pr[z(t) = z_j \mid z(0), \dots, z(t - 1)] = \Pr[z(t) = z_j]$, and the Markov property is trivially satisfied. More generally, Markov chains enable us to model economic environments in which stochastic shocks are correlated over time. Markov chains are widely used in probability theory, the study of stochastic processes, and various areas of dynamic economic analysis. While the theory of Markov chains is relatively straightforward, not much of this theory is necessary for the basic treatment of stochastic dynamic programming here.

The Markov property not only simplifies the mathematical structure of economic models but also allows us to use relatively simple notation for the probability distribution of the random variable $z(t)$. We can also represent a Markov chain as

$$\Pr\left[z(t) = z_j \mid z(t - 1) = z_{j'}\right] \equiv q_{jj'},$$

for any $j, j' = 1, \dots, N$, where $q_{jj'} \geq 0$ for all j, j', and

$$\sum_{j=1}^{N} q_{jj'} = 1 \quad \text{for each } j' = 1, \dots, N.$$

Here $q_{jj'}$ is also referred to as a *transition probability*, meaning the probability of the stochastic state z transitioning from $z_{j'}$ to z_j. I make use of this notation in some of the proofs in the next section.

To see how this particular way of introducing stochastic elements into dynamic optimization is useful in economic problems, let us start with a simple example, which is also useful for introducing some additional notation.

Example 16.1 *Recall the optimal growth problem, where the objective is to maximize*

$$\mathbb{E}_0 \sum_{t=0}^{\infty} \beta^t u(c(t)).$$

---

[1]. I adopt the standard terminology that $z(t)$ follows a Markov chain when it takes finitely (or countably) many values and that it follows a general Markov process when it has a continuous distribution or a mixture of the continuous and discrete distributions.

As usual, $c(t)$ denotes per capita consumption at time t, and $u(\cdot)$ is the instantaneous utility function. The maximand in this problem differs from those studied so far only because of the presence of the expectations operator $\mathbb{E}_0$, which stands for expectations conditional on information available at (the beginning of) time $t = 0$. Expectations are necessary here because the future values of consumption per capita are stochastic (as they depend on the realizations of future z values). In particular, suppose that the production function (per capita) takes the form

$$y(t) = f(k(t), z(t)),$$

where $k(t)$ again denotes the capital-labor ratio, and $z(t) \in \mathcal{Z} \equiv \{z_1, \ldots, z_N\}$ represents a stochastic variable that affects how much output is produced with a given amount of inputs. The most natural interpretation of $z(t)$ in this context is as a stochastic TFP term. The resource constraint (written as an equality) takes the form

$$k(t + 1) = f(k(t), z(t)) + (1 - \delta)k(t) - c(t), \tag{16.2}$$

and $k(t) \geq 0$ for all t with $k(0) > 0$ given. Again δ represents the depreciation rate. This formulation implies that at the time consumption $c(t)$ is chosen, the random variable $z(t)$ has been realized. Thus $c(t)$ depends on the realization of $z(t)$, and in fact on the entire history of $z(t)$. In particular, let us define

$$z^t \equiv (z(1), \ldots, z(t))$$

as the history of $z(t)$ up to date t. As a convention, this history does not include $z(0)$, which is taken as given, and this ensures that z^t indeed has t elements. In particular, let $\mathcal{Z}^t \equiv \mathcal{Z} \times \cdots \times \mathcal{Z}$ (the t-times product), so that $z^t \in \mathcal{Z}^t$. For given $k(0)$, the level of consumption at time t can be most generally written as

$$c(t) = \tilde{c}[z^t],$$

which simply states that consumption at time t is a function of the entire sequence of random variables observed up to that point. Clearly consumption at time t cannot depend on future realizations of the random variable—those values have not yet been realized. A function of the form $c(t) = \tilde{c}[z^t]$ is thus natural. Nevertheless not all functions $\tilde{c}[z^t]$ could be admissible as feasible plans, because they may violate the resource constraints. (I return shortly to additional restrictions to ensure feasibility.) There is also no point in making consumption a function of the history of capital stocks at this stage, since those are endogenously determined by the choice of past consumption levels and by the realization of past stochastic variables. (When we turn to the recursive formulation of this problem, we will write consumption as a function of the current capital stock and the current value of the stochastic variable.) In terms of (16.1), here $x(t) = k(t)$, so that

$$x(t + 1) = k(t + 1)$$
$$= f(k(t), z(t)) + (1 - \delta)k(t) - \tilde{c}[z^t]$$
$$\equiv \tilde{k}[z^t],$$

where the second line simply uses the resource constraint with equality and the third line defines the function $\tilde{k}[z^t]$. With this notation, feasibility is easier to express, since

$$k(t + 1) \equiv \tilde{k}[z^t]$$

by definition depends only on the history of the stochastic shocks up to time t and not on $z(t + 1)$. In addition, from the resource constraint we have

$$\tilde{k}[z^t] = f(\tilde{k}[z^{t-1}], z(t)) + (1 - \delta)\tilde{k}[z^{t-1}] - \tilde{c}[z^t] \quad \text{for all } z^{t-1} \in \mathcal{Z}^{t-1} \text{ and } z(t) \in \mathcal{Z}.$$

(16.3)

The maximization problem can then be expressed as

$$\max_{\{\tilde{c}[z^t], \tilde{k}[z^t]\}_{t=0}^{\infty}} \mathbb{E}_0 \sum_{t=0}^{\infty} \beta^t u(\tilde{c}[z^t])$$

subject to (16.3), $\tilde{c}[z^t] \geq 0$ and $\tilde{k}[z^t] \geq 0$ for all $z^t \in \mathcal{Z}^t$ and all $t = 0, 1, \ldots$, and starting with the initial conditions $\tilde{k}[z^{-1}] = k(0)$ and $z(0)$. This maximization problem can also be written using the instantaneous payoff function $U(x(t), x(t + 1), z(t))$ introduced in (16.1). In this case, the maximization problem takes the form

$$\max_{\{\tilde{k}[z^t]\}_{t=0}^{\infty}} \mathbb{E}_t \sum_{t=0}^{\infty} \beta^t U(\tilde{k}[z^{t-1}], \tilde{k}[z^t], z(t)),$$

(16.4)

where now $U(\tilde{k}[z^{t-1}], \tilde{k}[z^t], z(t)) = u(f(k(t), z(t)) - k(t + 1) + (1 - \delta)k(t))$. Notice the timing convention here: $\tilde{k}[z^{t-1}]$ is the value of the capital stock at time t, which is inherited from the investments at time $t - 1$ and thus depends on the history of stochastic shocks up to time $t - 1$, z^{t-1}, whereas $\tilde{k}[z^t]$ is the choice of capital stock for the next period (made at time t) given the history of stochastic shocks up to time t, z^t.

This example can also be used to show how the same maximization problem can be represented recursively. Since $z(t)$ follows a Markov chain, the current value of $z(t)$ contains both information about the available resources for consumption and future capital stock and information regarding the stochastic distribution of $z(t + 1)$. Thus we might naturally expect the policy function determining the capital stock at the next date to take the form

$$k(t + 1) = \pi(k(t), z(t)).$$

(16.5)

With the same reasoning, the recursive characterization would naturally take the form

$$V(k, z) = \sup_{y \in [0, f(k,z) + (1-\delta)k]} \left\{ u(f(k, z) + (1 - \delta)k - y) + \beta \mathbb{E}[V(y, z') \mid z] \right\}, \quad (16.6)$$

where $\mathbb{E}[\cdot \mid z]$ denotes the expectation conditional on the current value of z and incorporates the fact that the random variable z follows a Markov chain. Notice that this expectation is different from that in (16.4). In (16.4), the expectation is over the entire set of future values of z, whereas in (16.6), it is over next period's value of z, z'. Thus one might wish to distinguish this expectation by writing it as $\mathbb{E}^{z'}[V(y, z') \mid z]$. But since this notation is cumbersome and the context makes it clear whether the expectation is over the entire future sequence or just next period's value, I do not use it.

Let us suppose that this program has a solution, meaning that there exists a feasible plan that achieves the value $V(k, z)$ starting with capital-labor ratio k and stochastic variable z. Then the set of the next date's capital stock that achieves this maximum value can be represented by a correspondence $\Pi(k, z)$ for $k \in \mathbb{R}_+$ and $z \in \mathcal{Z}$. For any $\pi(k, z) \in \Pi(k, z)$, we have

$$V(k, z) = u(f(k, z) + (1 - \delta)k - \pi(k, z)) + \beta \mathbb{E}[V(\pi(k, z), z') \mid z].$$

When the correspondence $\Pi(k, z)$ is single valued, then $\pi(k, z)$ is uniquely defined and the optimal choice of next period's capital stock can be represented as in (16.5).

Example 16.1 already indicates how a stochastic optimization problem can be written in sequence form and also gives us a hint about how to express such a problem recursively. I now do this more systematically. Let a *plan* be denoted by $\tilde{x}[z^t]$. This plan specifies the value of the vector $x \in \mathbb{R}^K$ for time $t + 1$ (i.e., $x(t + 1) = \tilde{x}[z^t]$) for any $z^t \in \mathcal{Z}^t$. Using the same notation as in Chapter 6, the sequence problem takes the form

Problem 16.1

$$V^*(x(0), z(0)) = \sup_{\{\tilde{x}[z^t]\}_{t=0}^{\infty}} \mathbb{E}_0 \sum_{t=0}^{\infty} \beta^t U(\tilde{x}[z^{t-1}], \tilde{x}[z^t], z(t))$$

subject to

$$\tilde{x}[z^t] \in G(\tilde{x}[z^{t-1}], z(t)) \quad \text{for all } t \geq 0,$$

$$\tilde{x}[z^{-1}] = x(0) \text{ given.}$$

Here expectations at time $t = 0$, denoted by $\mathbb{E}_0$, are conditioned on $z(0)$ and are over the possible infinite sequences of $(z(1), z(2), z(3), \ldots)$. Throughout the symbols $\mathbb{E}_0$ and $\mathbb{E}[\cdot \mid z(0)]$ are used interchangeably. In this problem, as in the rest of this and the next chapters, I also adopt the convention that $\tilde{x}[z^{-1}] = x(0)$ and $z^0 = z(0)$, and write the maximization problem with respect to the sequence $\{\tilde{x}[z^t]\}_{t=0}^{\infty}$ (with $\tilde{x}[z^{-1}] = x(0)$ implicitly taken as given). The function V^* is conditioned on $x(0) \in \mathbb{R}^K$, since this is the initial value of the vector x, taken as given, and also on $z(0)$, since the choice of $x(1)$ is made after $z(0)$ is observed (and the expectations are also conditioned on $z(0)$). Finally, the first constraint in Problem 16.1 ensures that the sequence $\{\tilde{x}[z^t]\}_{t=0}^{\infty}$ is feasible.

Similar to (16.6) in Example 16.1, the functional equation corresponding to the recursive formulation of this problem can be written as follows.

Problem 16.2

$$V(x, z) = \sup_{y \in G(x,z)} \{U(x, y, z) + \beta \mathbb{E}[V(y, z') \mid z]\}, \quad \text{for all } x \in X \text{ and } z \in \mathcal{Z}. \quad (16.7)$$

Here $V : X \times \mathcal{Z} \to \mathbb{R}$ is a real-valued function, and $y \in G(x, z)$ represents the constraint on next period's state vector as a function of the realization of the stochastic variable z. Problem 16.2 is a direct generalization of the Bellman equation in Problem 6.3 of Chapter 6 to a stochastic dynamic programming setup. One can also write Problem 16.2 as

$$V(x, z) = \sup_{y \in G(x,z)} \left\{ U(x, y, z) + \beta \int V(y, z') Q(z, dz') \right\} \quad \text{for all } x \in X \text{ and } z \in \mathcal{Z},$$

where $Q(z, \cdot)$ is the state transition function, which gives the distribution of z' (tomorrow's stochastic variable) given the current value z, and $\int f(z') Q(z, dz')$ denotes the Lebesgue (or more properly, the Lebesgue-Stieltjes) integral of the function f with respect to the Markov process for z given the current value z. This notation is useful in emphasizing that an expectation is nothing but a Lebesgue integral (and thus contains regular summation as a special case). Remembering the equivalence between expectations and integrals is important both for a proper appreciation of the theory and for recognizing where some of the difficulties in the use of stochastic methods may lie.[2] There is typically little gain in rigor or insight in using the explicit Lebesgue integral instead of the expectation, and I do not do so unless absolutely necessary.

As in Chapter 6, let us first introduce the set of feasible plans starting with an initial value $x(t)$ and a value of the stochastic variable $z(t)$ as

$$\Phi(x(t), z(t)) = \{\{\tilde{x}[z^s]\}_{s=t}^{\infty} : \tilde{x}[z^s] \in G(\tilde{x}[z^{s-1}], z(s)) \quad \text{for } s = t, t+1, \ldots\}.$$

We denote a generic element of $\Phi(x(0), z(0))$ by $\mathbf{x} \equiv \{\tilde{x}[z^t]\}_{t=0}^{\infty}$. In contrast to Chapter 6, the elements of $\Phi(x(0), z(0))$ are not infinite sequences of vectors in $\mathbb{R}^K$, but infinite sequences of feasible plans $\tilde{x}[z^t]$ that assign a value $x \in \mathbb{R}^K$ for any history $z^t \in \mathcal{Z}^t$ for any $t = 0, 1, \ldots$. We are interested in using the formulation in Problem 16.2 to characterize the solution to Problem 16.1; thus we will investigate (1) when the solution $V(x, z)$ to Problem 16.2 coincides with the solution $V^*(x, z)$ and (2) when the set of maximizing plans $\Pi(x, z) \subset \Phi(x, z)$ also generates an optimal feasible plan for Problem 16.1 (presuming that both problems have feasible plans attaining their supremums). Recall that the set of maximizing plans $\Pi(x, z)$ is defined such that for any $\pi(x, z) \in \Pi(x, z)$,

$$V(x, z) = U(x, \pi(x, z), z) + \beta \mathbb{E}[V(\pi(x, z), z') \mid z]. \tag{16.8}$$

Let us now introduce analogues of Assumptions 6.1–6.5 from Chapter 6 and the appropriate generalizations of Theorems 6.1–6.6.

Assumption 16.1 *The correspondence $G(x, z)$ is nonempty-valued for all $x \in X$ and $z \in \mathcal{Z}$. Moreover for all $x(0) \in X$, $z(0) \in \mathcal{Z}$, and $\mathbf{x} \in \Phi(x(0), z(0))$, the limit of expected discounted utility $\lim_{n \to \infty} \mathbb{E}[\sum_{t=0}^{n} \beta^t U(\tilde{x}[z^{t-1}], \tilde{x}[z^t], z(t)) \mid z(0)]$ exists and is finite.*

Assumption 16.2 *X is a compact subset of $\mathbb{R}^K$, and G is nonempty-valued, compact-valued, and continuous. Moreover let $\mathbf{X}_G = \{(x, y, z) \in X \times X \times \mathcal{Z} : y \in G(x, z)\}$, and suppose that $U : \mathbf{X}_G \to \mathbb{R}$ is continuous.*

Observe that Assumption 16.2 only imposes the compactness of X, since $\mathcal{Z}$ is already compact in view of the fact that it consists of a finite number of elements. Moreover the continuity of U in (x, y, z) is equivalent to its continuity in (x, y), since $\mathcal{Z}$ is a finite set, so we endow it with the discrete topology, and thus continuity is automatically guaranteed (see Fact A.12 in Appendix A). As in Chapter 6, these assumptions enable us to establish a number of useful results about the equivalence between Problems 16.1 and 16.2 and the solution to the dynamic optimization problems specified above. I state these results without proof here. Some of the proofs are provided in Section 16.2 and the rest are left as exercises.

Our first result is a generalization of Theorem 6.1 from Chapter 6.

Theorem 16.1 (Equivalence of Values) *Suppose Assumptions 16.1 holds. Then for any $x \in X$ and any $z \in \mathcal{Z}$, $V^*(x, z)$ that is a solution to Problem 16.1 is also a solution to Problem 16.2. Moreover any solution $V(x, z)$ to Problem 16.2 is also a solution to Problem 16.1, so that $V^*(x, z) = V(x, z)$ for any $x \in X$ and any $z \in \mathcal{Z}$.*

The next theorem establishes the Principle of Optimality for stochastic problems. As in Chapter 6, the Principle of Optimality enables us to break the returns from an optimal plan into two parts, the current return and the expected continuation return.

---

2. In particular, potential difficulties arise when one needs to exchange limits and expectations.

Theorem 16.2 (Principle of Optimality) *Suppose Assumptions 16.1 holds. For $x(0) \in X$ and $z(0) \in \mathcal{Z}$, let $\mathbf{x}^* \equiv \{\tilde{x}^*[z^t]\}_{t=0}^{\infty} \in \Phi(x(0), z(0))$ be a feasible plan that attains $V^*(x(0), z(0))$ in Problem 16.1. Then we have*

$$V^*(\tilde{x}^*[z^{t-1}], z(t)) = U(\tilde{x}^*[z^{t-1}], \tilde{x}^*[z^t], z(t)) + \beta \mathbb{E}[V^*(\tilde{x}^*(z^t), z(t+1)) \mid z(t)] \quad (16.9)$$

for $t = 0, 1, \ldots$.

Moreover if $\mathbf{x}^* \in \Phi(x(0), z(0))$ satisfies (16.9), then it attains the optimal value for Problem 16.1.

The next result establishes the uniqueness of the value function and existence of solutions.

Theorem 16.3 (Existence of Solutions) *Suppose that Assumptions 16.1 and 16.2 hold. Then there exists a unique function $V : X \times \mathcal{Z} \to \mathbb{R}$ that satisfies (16.7). This function V is continuous and bounded in x for each $z \in \mathcal{Z}$. Moreover an optimal plan $\mathbf{x}^* \in \Phi(x(0), z(0))$ exists for any $x(0) \in X$ and any $z(0) \in \mathcal{Z}$.*

The remaining results, as in their analogues in Chapter 6, use further assumptions to establish concavity, monotonicity, and the differentiability of the value function.

Assumption 16.3 *U is concave. That is, for any $\alpha \in (0, 1)$ and any (x, y, z), and (x', y', z) in $\mathbf{X}_G$, we have*

$$U(\alpha x + (1-\alpha)x', \alpha y + (1-\alpha)y', z) \geq \alpha U(x, y, z) + (1-\alpha)U(x', y', z).$$

Moreover if $x \neq x'$, then

$$U(\alpha x + (1-\alpha)x', \alpha y + (1-\alpha)y', z) > \alpha U(x, y, z) + (1-\alpha)U(x', y', z).$$

In addition, $G(x, z)$ is convex in x. That is, for any $z \in \mathcal{Z}$, any $\alpha \in [0, 1]$, and any $x, x', y, y' \in X$ such that $y \in G(x, z)$ and $y' \in G(x', z)$, we have

$$\alpha y + (1-\alpha)y' \in G(\alpha x + (1-\alpha)x', z).$$

Assumption 16.4 *For each $y \in X$ and $z \in \mathcal{Z}$, $U(\cdot, y, z)$ is strictly increasing in its first K arguments, and G is monotone in x in the sense that $x \leq x'$ implies $G(x, z) \subset G(x', z)$ for each $z \in \mathcal{Z}$.*

Assumption 16.5 *$U(x, y, z)$ is continuously differentiable in x in the interior of its domain $\mathbf{X}_G$.*

Theorem 16.4 (Concavity of the Value Function) *Suppose that Assumptions 16.1–16.3 hold. Then the unique function V that satisfies (16.7) is strictly concave in x for each $z \in \mathcal{Z}$. Moreover the optimal plan can be expressed as $\tilde{x}^*[z^t] = \pi(x^*(t), z(t))$, where the policy function $\pi : X \times \mathcal{Z} \to X$ is continuous.*

Theorem 16.5 (Monotonicity of the Value Function I) *Suppose that Assumptions 16.1, 16.2, and 16.4 hold, and let $V : X \times \mathcal{Z} \to \mathbb{R}$ be the unique solution to (16.7). Then for each $z \in \mathcal{Z}$, V is strictly increasing in x.*

Theorem 16.6 (Differentiability of the Value Function) *Suppose that Assumptions 16.1, 16.2, 16.3, and 16.5 hold. Let π be the policy function defined above and assume that $x' \in \text{Int } X$ and $\pi(x', z) \in \text{Int } G(x', z)$ at $z \in \mathcal{Z}$. Then $V(x, z)$ is continuously differentiable at (x', z) with the gradient with respect to x given by*

$$D_x V(x', z) = D_x U(x', \pi(x', z), z). \quad (16.10)$$

These theorems have exact analogues in Chapter 6. Since the value function now depends on the stochastic variable z, an additional monotonicity result can also be obtained. To do this, let us introduce the following assumption.

Assumption 16.6

1. *G is monotone in z in the sense that $z \leq z'$ implies $G(x, z) \subset G(x, z')$ for each any $x \in X$ and $z, z' \in \mathcal{Z}$ such that $z \leq z'$.*

2. *For each $(x, y, z) \in \mathbf{X}_G$, $U(x, y, z)$ is strictly increasing in z.*

3. *The Markov chain for z is monotone in the sense that for any nondecreasing function $f : \mathcal{Z} \to \mathbb{R}$, $\mathbb{E}[f(z') \mid z]$ is also nondecreasing in z (where z' is next period's value of z).*

To interpret the last part of this assumption, suppose that $z_j \leq z_{j'}$ when $j < j'$. Then this condition is satisfied if and only if for any $\bar{j} = 1, \dots, N$ and any $j'' > j'$, $\sum_{j=\bar{j}}^N q_{jj''} \geq \sum_{j=\bar{j}}^N q_{jj'}$ (see Exercise 16.1).

Theorem 16.7 (Monotonicity of the Value Function II)   *Suppose that Assumptions 16.1, 16.2, and 16.6 hold, and let $V : X \times \mathcal{Z} \to \mathbb{R}$ be the unique solution to (16.7). Then for each $x \in X$, V is strictly increasing in z.*

16.2   Proofs of the Stochastic Dynamic Programming Theorems *

This section provides proofs for Theorems 16.1–16.3. The proofs of Theorems 16.5–16.7 are similar to those of corresponding theorems in Chapter 6 and are left as exercises.

Before proving the theorems presented in the previous section, let us introduce some additional definitions. For any feasible $\mathbf{x} \equiv \{\tilde{x}[z^t]\}_{t=0}^\infty$ and any initial conditions $x(0) \in X$ and $z(0) \in \mathcal{Z}$, define

$$\bar{\mathbf{U}}(\mathbf{x} \mid x(0), z(0)) \equiv \mathbb{E}\left[\sum_{t=0}^\infty \beta^t U\left(\tilde{x}[z^{t-1}], \tilde{x}[z^t], z(t) \right) \Big| z(0) \right],$$

and note that for any $x(0) \in X$ and $z(0) \in \mathcal{Z}$,

$$V^*(x(0), z(0)) = \sup_{\mathbf{x} \in \Phi(x(0), z(0))} \bar{\mathbf{U}}(\mathbf{x} \mid x(0), z(0)).$$

In view of Assumption 16.1, which ensures that all values are bounded, it follows that V^* must satisfy

$$V^*(x(0), z(0)) \geq \bar{\mathbf{U}}(\mathbf{x} \mid x(0), z(0)) \quad \text{for all } \mathbf{x} \in \Phi(x(0), z(0)), \tag{16.11}$$

and

$$\begin{aligned} &\text{for any } \varepsilon > 0, \text{ there exists } \mathbf{x}' \in \Phi(x(0), z(0)) \\ &\text{such that } V^*(x(0), z(0)) \leq \bar{\mathbf{U}}(\mathbf{x}' \mid x(0), z(0)) + \varepsilon. \end{aligned} \tag{16.12}$$

The conditions for V to be a solution to Problem 16.2 are similar. For any $x(0) \in X$ and $z(0) \in \mathcal{Z}$,

$$V(x(0), z(0)) \geq U(x(0), y, z) + \beta \mathbb{E}[V(y, z(1)) \mid z(0)] \quad \text{for all } y \in G(x(0), z(0)), \tag{16.13}$$

and

for any $\varepsilon > 0$, there exists $y' \in G(x(0), z(0))$

such that $V(x(0), z(0)) \leq U(x(0), y', z(0)) + \beta\mathbb{E}[V(y', z(1)) \mid z(0)] + \varepsilon.$ (16.14)

The following lemma is a straightforward generalization of Lemma 6.1 in Chapter 6.

Lemma 16.1 *Suppose that Assumption 16.1 holds. Then for any $x(0) \in X$, $z(0) \in \mathcal{Z}$, and*
$\mathbf{x} \equiv \{\tilde{x}[z^t]\}_{t=0}^{\infty} \in \Phi(x(0), z(0))$, *we have*

$$\bar{\mathbf{U}}(\mathbf{x} \mid x(0), z(0)) = U(x(0), \tilde{x}[z^0], z(0)) + \beta\mathbb{E}\big[\bar{\mathbf{U}}\big(\{\tilde{x}[z^t]\}_{t=1}^{\infty} \mid \tilde{x}[z^0], z(1)\big) \mid z(0)\big].$$

Proof.   See Exercise 16.2. ■

Proof of Theorem 16.1..   Suppose that $V^*(x(0), z(0))$ is a solution to Problem 16.1 for $x(0) \in X$ and $z(0) \in \mathcal{Z}$ (and thus (16.11) and (16.12) hold). Then (16.12) implies that given $x(1) \in X$, for each $\varepsilon > 0$ and each $z(1) = z_j$ ($j = 1, 2, \ldots, N$) there exists $\mathbf{x}_{\varepsilon}^j \in \Phi(x(1), z_j)$ such that

$$V^*(x(1), z_j) \leq \bar{\mathbf{U}}(\mathbf{x}_{\varepsilon}^j \mid x(1), z_j) + \varepsilon.$$

Then, letting j' be such that $z(0) = z_{j'}$, we have

$$\mathbb{E}[V^*(x(1), z(1)) \mid z(0)] = \sum_{j=1}^{N} q_{jj'} V^*(x(1), z_j)$$

$$\leq \sum_{j=1}^{N} q_{jj'} \bar{\mathbf{U}}(\mathbf{x}_{\varepsilon}^j \mid x(1), z_j) + \varepsilon$$

$$= \mathbb{E}[\bar{\mathbf{U}}(\mathbf{x}_{\varepsilon}^j \mid x(1), z_j) \mid z(0)] + \varepsilon,$$

where the second line exploits the fact that $\sum_{j=1}^{N} q_{jj'} = 1$, and the third line uses the definition of the conditional expectation $\mathbb{E}[\cdot \mid z(0)]$. Next, let $\mathbf{x}_{\varepsilon} \equiv (\mathbf{x}_{\varepsilon}^1, \ldots, \mathbf{x}_{\varepsilon}^N)$. Then (16.11), Lemma 16.1, and the previous string of inequalities yield

$$V^*(x(0), z(0)) \geq U(x(0), \tilde{x}'[z^0], z(0)) + \beta\mathbb{E}[\bar{\mathbf{U}}(\mathbf{x}_{\varepsilon} \mid x(1), z_j) \mid z(0)]$$

$$\geq U(x(0), \tilde{x}'[z^0], z(0)) + \beta\mathbb{E}[V^*(x(1), z(1)) \mid z(0)] - \beta\varepsilon.$$

Since the last inequality is true for any $\varepsilon > 0$, it follows that the function V^* satisfies (16.13).

Next, take an arbitrary $\varepsilon > 0$. By (16.12), there exists an alternative plan $\mathbf{x}_{\varepsilon} = (\tilde{x}_{\varepsilon}[z^0], \tilde{x}_{\varepsilon}[z^1], \ldots) \in \Phi(x(0), z(0))$ such that

$$\bar{\mathbf{U}}(\mathbf{x}_{\varepsilon} \mid x(0), z(0)) \geq V^*(x(0), z(0)) - \varepsilon.$$

Condition (16.11) implies that for any $z(1) \in \mathcal{Z}$,

$$V^*(\tilde{x}_{\varepsilon}[z^0], z(1)) \geq \bar{\mathbf{U}}(\{\tilde{x}_{\varepsilon}[z^t]\}_{t=1}^{\infty} \mid \tilde{x}[z^0], z(1)).$$

Then from Lemma 16.1, for any $\varepsilon > 0$,

$$V^*(x(0), z(0)) - \varepsilon \leq U(x(0), \tilde{x}_\varepsilon[z^0], z(0)) + \beta \mathbb{E}\big[\bar{U}\big(\{\tilde{x}_\varepsilon[z^t]\}_{t=1}^\infty\big) \mid \tilde{x}[z^0], z(1)\big) \mid z(0)\big]$$

$$\leq U(x(0), \tilde{x}_\varepsilon[z^0], z(0)) + \beta \mathbb{E}\big[V^*\big(\tilde{x}_\varepsilon[z^0], z(1)\big) \mid z(0)\big],$$

so that V^* also satisfies (16.14). This argument establishes that any solution to Problem 16.1 satisfies (16.13) and (16.14), and is thus a solution to Problem 16.2.

To establish the converse, note that (16.13) implies that for any $\tilde{x}[z^0] \in G(x(0), z(0))$,

$$V(x(0), z(0)) \geq U(x(0), \tilde{x}[z^0], z(0)) + \beta \mathbb{E}\big[V\big(\tilde{x}[z^0], z(1)\big) \mid z(0)\big].$$

Now for $n \in \mathbb{N}$, recursively substituting for $V(\tilde{x}[z^0], z(1))$, $V(\tilde{x}[z^1], z(2))$, $\ldots$, $V(\tilde{x}[z^{n-1}], z(n))$ and taking expectations, we obtain

$$V(x(0), z(0)) \geq \mathbb{E}\Big[\sum_{t=0}^n \beta^t U\big(\tilde{x}[z^{t-1}], \tilde{x}[z^t], z(t)\big) \mid z(0)\Big]$$

$$+ \beta^{n+1} \mathbb{E}\big[V\big(\tilde{x}[z^n], z(n+1)\big) \mid z(0)\big].$$

By definition, we have

$$\lim_{n \to \infty} \mathbb{E}\Big[\sum_{t=0}^n \beta^t U\big(\tilde{x}[z^{t-1}], \tilde{x}[z^t], z(t)\big) \mid z(0)\Big] = \bar{U}(\mathbf{x} \mid x(0), z(0))$$

and by Assumption 16.1,

$$\lim_{n \to \infty} \beta^{n+1} \mathbb{E}[V(\tilde{x}[z^n], z(n+1)) \mid z(0)]$$

$$= \lim_{n \to \infty} \mathbb{E}\Big[\lim_{m \to \infty} \sum_{t=n+1}^m \beta^t U\big(\tilde{x}[z^{t-1}], \tilde{x}[z^t], z(t)\big) \mid z(0)\Big] = 0,$$

so that (16.11) is verified.

Next, let $\varepsilon > 0$. From (16.14), for any $\varepsilon' = \varepsilon(1 - \beta) > 0$ there exists $\tilde{x}_\varepsilon[z^0] \in G(x(0), z(0))$ such that

$$V(x(0), z(0)) \leq U\big(x(0), \tilde{x}_\varepsilon[z^0]\big) + \beta \mathbb{E}\big[V\big(\tilde{x}_\varepsilon[z^0], z(1)\big) \mid z(0)\big] + \varepsilon'.$$

Let $\tilde{x}_\varepsilon[z^t] \in G(\tilde{x}_\varepsilon[z^{t-1}], z(t))$, and define $\mathbf{x}_\varepsilon \equiv (\tilde{x}_\varepsilon[z^0], \tilde{x}_\varepsilon[z^1], \tilde{x}_\varepsilon[z^2], \ldots)$. Again substituting recursively for $V(\tilde{x}[z^0], z(1))$, $V(\tilde{x}[z^1], z(2))$, $\ldots$, $V(\tilde{x}[z^{n-1}], z(n))$ and taking expectations yields

$$V(x(0), z(0)) \leq \mathbb{E}\Big[\sum_{t=0}^n \beta^t U\big(\tilde{x}_\varepsilon[z^{t-1}], \tilde{x}_\varepsilon[z^t], z(t)\big) \mid z(0)\Big]$$

$$+ \beta^{n+1} \mathbb{E}[V(\tilde{x}_\varepsilon[z^n], z(n+1)) \mid z(0)] + \varepsilon' + \varepsilon'\beta + \cdots + \varepsilon'\beta^n$$

$$\leq \bar{U}(\mathbf{x}_\varepsilon \mid x(0), z(0)) + \varepsilon,$$

where the last step follows using $\varepsilon = \varepsilon' \sum_{t=0}^{\infty} \beta^t$ and

$$\lim_{n \to \infty} \mathbb{E}\Big[\sum_{t=0}^{n} \beta^t U\big(\tilde{x}_\varepsilon[z^{t-1}], \tilde{x}_\varepsilon[z^t], z(t)\big) \mid z(0)\Big] = \bar{U}(\mathbf{x}_\varepsilon \mid x(0), z(0)).$$

This establishes that V satisfies (16.12) and completes the proof. ∎

Proof of Theorem 16.2.   Suppose that

$$\mathbf{x}^* \equiv (\tilde{x}^*[z^0], \tilde{x}^*[z^1], \tilde{x}^*[z^2], \ldots) \in \Phi(x(0), z(0))$$

is a feasible plan attaining the solution to Problem 16.1. Let $\mathbf{x}_t^* \equiv (\tilde{x}^*[z^t], \tilde{x}^*[z^{t+1}], \ldots)$ be the continuation of this plan from time $t \geq 1$.

We first show that for any $t \geq 0$, $\mathbf{x}_t^*$ attains the supremum starting from $\tilde{x}^*[z^{t-1}]$ and any $z(t) \in \mathcal{Z}$, that is,

$$\bar{U}(\mathbf{x}_t^* \mid \tilde{x}^*[z^{t-1}], z(t)) = V^*(\tilde{x}^*[z^{t-1}], z(t)). \tag{16.15}$$

The proof is by induction. The hypothesis is trivially satisfied for $t = 0$, since by definition, $\mathbf{x}_0^* = \mathbf{x}^*$ attains $V^*(x(0), z(0))$.

Next suppose that the statement is true for t, so that $\mathbf{x}_t^*$ attains the supremum starting from $\tilde{x}^*[z^{t-1}]$ and any $z(t) \in \mathcal{Z}$. Then (16.15) holds for t and for $z(t) \in \mathcal{Z}$. Now using this relationship we will establish that (16.15) holds for $t + 1$ and $\mathbf{x}_{t+1}^*$ attains the supremum starting from $\tilde{x}^*[z^t]$ and any $z(t + 1) \in \mathcal{Z}$.

First, note that (16.15) implies

$$V^*(\tilde{x}^*[z^{t-1}], z(t)) = \bar{U}(\mathbf{x}_t^* \mid \tilde{x}^*[z^{t-1}], z(t)) \tag{16.16}$$

$$= U(\tilde{x}^*[z^{t-1}], \tilde{x}^*[z^t], z(t))$$

$$+ \beta \mathbb{E}[\bar{U}(\mathbf{x}_{t+1}^* \mid \tilde{x}^*[z^t], z(t + 1)) \mid z(t)].$$

Let $\mathbf{x}_{t+1} = (\tilde{x}^*[z^{t+1}], \tilde{x}[z^{t+2}] \ldots) \in \Phi(\tilde{x}^*[z^t], z(t + 1))$ be any feasible plan starting with state vector $\tilde{x}^*[z^t]$ and stochastic variable $z(t + 1)$. By definition, $\mathbf{x}_t = (\tilde{x}^*[z^t], \mathbf{x}_{t+1}) \in \Phi(\tilde{x}^*[z^{t-1}], z(t))$. Since by the induction hypothesis, $V^*(\tilde{x}^*[z^{t-1}], z(t))$ is the supremum starting with $\tilde{x}^*[z^{t-1}]$ and $z(t)$, we also have

$$V^*(\tilde{x}^*[z^{t-1}], z(t)) \geq \bar{U}(\mathbf{x}_t \mid \tilde{x}^*[z^{t-1}], z(t))$$

$$= U(\tilde{x}^*[z^{t-1}], \tilde{x}^*[z^t], z(t)) + \beta \mathbb{E}[\bar{U}(\mathbf{x}_{t+1} \mid \tilde{x}^*[z^t], z(t + 1)) \mid z(t)]$$

for any $\mathbf{x}_{t+1}$. Combining this inequality with (16.16) yields

$$\mathbb{E}[\bar{U}(\mathbf{x}_{t+1}^* \mid \tilde{x}^*[z^t] z(t + 1)) \mid z(t)] \geq \mathbb{E}[\bar{U}(\mathbf{x}_{t+1} \mid \tilde{x}^*[z^t], z(t + 1)) \mid z(t)] \tag{16.17}$$

for all $\mathbf{x}_{t+1} \in \Phi(\tilde{x}^*[z^t], z(t + 1))$.

The last step is by contradiction. Suppose that $\mathbf{x}_{t+1}^*$ does not attain the supremum starting from $\tilde{x}^*[z^t]$ and any $z(t+1) \in \mathcal{Z}$. Then there exists $\hat{\mathbf{x}}_{t+1} \in \Phi(\tilde{x}^*[z^t], z(t+1))$ for some $z(t+1) = \hat{z}$ (with positive probability) such that

$$\bar{\mathbf{U}}\big(\mathbf{x}_{t+1}^* \mid \tilde{x}^*[z^t], \hat{z}\big) < \bar{\mathbf{U}}\big(\hat{\mathbf{x}}_{t+1} \mid \tilde{x}^*[z^t], \hat{z}\big).$$

Construct the sequence $\hat{\mathbf{x}}_{t+1}^* = \mathbf{x}_{t+1}^*$ if $z(t) \neq \hat{z}$ and $\hat{\mathbf{x}}_{t+1}^* = \hat{\mathbf{x}}_{t+1}$ if $z(t+1) = \hat{z}$. Since $\mathbf{x}_{t+1}^* \in \Phi(\tilde{x}^*[z^t], \hat{z})$ and $\hat{\mathbf{x}}_{t+1} \in \Phi(\tilde{x}^*[z^t], \hat{z})$, we also have $\hat{\mathbf{x}}_{t+1}^* \in \Phi(\tilde{x}^*[z^t], \hat{z})$. Then without loss of generality take $z(t) = z_{j'}$ and $\hat{z} = z_1$ (with $q_{1j'} > 0$) to obtain

$$\mathbb{E}[\bar{\mathbf{U}}(\hat{\mathbf{x}}_{t+1}^* \mid \tilde{x}^*[z^t], z(t+1)) \mid z(t)] = \sum_{j=1}^{N} q_{jj'}\bar{\mathbf{U}}(\hat{\mathbf{x}}_{t+1}^* \mid \tilde{x}^*[z^t], z_j)$$

$$= q_{1j'}\bar{\mathbf{U}}(\hat{\mathbf{x}}_{t+1} \mid \tilde{x}^*[z^t], z_1) + \sum_{j=2}^{N} q_{jj'}\bar{\mathbf{U}}(\mathbf{x}_{t+1}^* \mid \tilde{x}^*[z^t], z_j)$$

$$> q_{1j'}\bar{\mathbf{U}}(\mathbf{x}_{t+1}^* \mid \tilde{x}^*[z^t], z_1) + \sum_{j=2}^{N} q_{jj'}\bar{\mathbf{U}}(\mathbf{x}_{t+1}^* \mid \tilde{x}^*[z^t], z_j)$$

$$= \mathbb{E}[\bar{\mathbf{U}}(\mathbf{x}_{t+1}^* \mid \tilde{x}^*[z^t], z(t+1)) \mid z(t)],$$

which contradicts (16.17). This completes the induction step and establishes that $\mathbf{x}_{t+1}^*$ attains the supremum starting from $\tilde{x}^*[z^t]$ and any $z(t+1) \in \mathcal{Z}$. Equation (16.15) then implies that

$$V^*(\tilde{x}^*[z^{t-1}], z(t)) = \bar{\mathbf{U}}(\mathbf{x}_t^* \mid \tilde{x}^*[z^{t-1}], z(t))$$

$$= U(\tilde{x}^*[z^{t-1}], \tilde{x}^*[z^t], z(t)) + \beta\mathbb{E}[\bar{\mathbf{U}}(\mathbf{x}_{t+1}^* \mid \tilde{x}^*[z^t], z(t+1)) \mid z(t)]$$

$$= U(\tilde{x}^*[z^{t-1}], \tilde{x}^*[z^t], z(t)) + \beta\mathbb{E}[V^*(\tilde{x}^*(z^t), z(t+1)) \mid z(t)],$$

establishing (16.9) and thus completing the proof of the first part of the theorem.

For the second part, suppose that (16.9) holds for $\mathbf{x}^* \in \Phi(x(0), z(0))$. Then substituting repeatedly for $\mathbf{x}^*$ yields

$$V^*(x(0), z(0)) = \sum_{t=0}^{n} \beta^t U\big(\tilde{x}^*[z^{t-1}], \tilde{x}^*[z^t], z(t)\big) + \beta^{n+1}\mathbb{E}[V^*(\tilde{x}^*(z^n), z(n+1)) \mid z(0)].$$

Since V^* is bounded, $\lim_{n \to \infty} \beta^{n+1}\mathbb{E}[V^*(\tilde{x}^*(z^n), z(n+1)) \mid z(0)] = 0$ and thus

$$\bar{\mathbf{U}}(\mathbf{x}^*, z(0)) = \lim_{n \to \infty} \sum_{t=0}^{n} \beta^t U\big(\tilde{x}^*[z^{t-1}], \tilde{x}^*[z^t], z(t)\big)$$

$$= V^*(x(0), z(0)),$$

Thus $\mathbf{x}^*$ attains the optimal value in Problem 16.1. This completes the proof of the theorem. ∎

I now provide a proof of Theorem 16.3, working with the value function V in Problem 16.2. An alternative proof working directly with Problem 16.1 is developed in Exercise 16.3.

Proof of Theorem 16.3. Consider Problem 16.2. In view of Assumptions 16.1 and 16.2, there exists some $M < \infty$ such that $|U(x, y, z)| < M$ for all $(x, y, z) \in \mathbf{X}_G$. Then $\left| V^*(x, z) \right| \leq M/(1 - \beta)$ for all $x \in X$ and all $z \in \mathcal{Z}$. Now, consider the function $V^*(\cdot, \cdot) \in \mathbf{C}(X \times \mathcal{Z})$, where $\mathbf{C}(X \times \mathcal{Z})$ denotes the set of continuous functions defined on $X \times \mathcal{Z}$, where X is endowed with the sup norm, $\| f \| = \sup_{x \in X} |f(x)|$, and $\mathcal{Z}$ is endowed with the discrete topology (recall Fact A.12 in Appendix A). All functions in $\mathbf{C}(X \times \mathcal{Z})$ are bounded, because they are continuous and X and $\mathcal{Z}$ are compact.

Now define the operator T as

$$T V(x, z) = \max_{y \in G(x,z)} \left\{ U(x, y, z) + \beta \mathbb{E}[V(y, z') \mid z] \right\}. \tag{16.18}$$

Suppose that $V(x, z)$ is continuous and bounded. Then $\mathbb{E}[V(y, z') \mid z]$ is also continuous and bounded, since it is simply given by

$$\mathbb{E}[V(y, z') \mid z] \equiv \sum_{j=1}^{N} q_{jj'} V(y, z_j),$$

with j' defined such that $z = z_{j'}$. Moreover $U(x, y, z)$ is also continuous and bounded over $\mathbf{X}_G$. Thus the maximization problem on the right-hand side of (16.18) is one of maximizing a continuous function over a compact set, and by Weierstrass's Theorem (Theorem A.9), it has a (bounded) solution. Consequently the operator T is well defined and maps the space of continuous bounded functions over the set $X \times \mathcal{Z}$, $\mathbf{C}(X \times \mathcal{Z})$, into itself. It can be verified that T also satisfies Blackwell's sufficient conditions for a contraction (Theorem 6.9). Therefore, applying Theorem 6.7, a unique fixed point $V \in \mathbf{C}(X \times \mathcal{Z})$ to (16.18) exists and is the unique solution to Problem 16.2.

Now consider the maximization in Problem 16.2. Since U and V are continuous and $G(x, z)$ is compact-valued, we can apply Weierstrass's Theorem once more to conclude that there exists $y \in G(x, z)$ that achieves the maximum. This defines the set of maximizers $\Pi(x, z) \subset \Phi(x, z)$ for Problem 16.2. Let $\mathbf{x}^* \equiv (\tilde{x}^*[z^0], \tilde{x}^*[z^1], \tilde{x}^*[z^2], \ldots) \in \Phi(x(0), z(0))$ with $\tilde{x}^*[z^t] \in \Pi(\tilde{x}^*[z^{t-1}], z(t))$ for all $t \geq 0$ and each $z(t) \in \mathcal{Z}$. Then from Theorems 16.1 and 16.2, $\mathbf{x}^*$ is also an optimal plan for Problem 16.1. ∎

The proofs of Theorems 16.4–16.6 are similar to those of Theorems 6.4–6.6 from Chapter 6 and are left as exercises (see Exercises 16.4–16.6). The proof of Theorem 16.7 is similar to 16.5 and is left to Exercise 16.7.

16.3 Stochastic Euler Equations

In Chapter 6 Euler equations and transversality conditions played a central role. In the present context, instead of the standard Euler equations, we have to work with stochastic Euler equations. While not conceptually any more involved than the standard Euler equations, stochastic Euler equations are not always easy to manipulate. Sometimes, as in the permanent income hypothesis model studied in Section 16.5 below, the stochastic Euler equation can be used directly. In other instances we may be able to combine the stochastic Euler equation and the appropriate transversality condition to characterize certain qualitative features of optimal plans.

Let us follow the treatment in Chapter 6 and also build on the results from Section 16.1. I use asterisks ($*$) to denote optimal values and D for gradients. Using Assumption 16.5 and Theorem 16.6, we can write the necessary conditions for an interior optimal plan as

$$D_y U(x, y^*, z) + \beta \mathbb{E}[D_x V(y^*, z') \mid z] = 0, \tag{16.19}$$

where $x \in \mathbb{R}^K$ is the current value of the state vector, $z \in \mathcal{Z}$ is the current value of the stochastic variable, and $D_x V(y^*, z')$ denotes the gradient of the value function evaluated at next period's state vector y^*. Now using the stochastic equivalent of the Envelope Theorem for dynamic programming and differentiating (16.8) with respect to the state vector x yields

$$D_x V(x, z) = D_x U(x, y^*, z). \tag{16.20}$$

There are no expectations, since this equation is conditioned on the realization of $z \in \mathcal{Z}$. Note that y^* here is a shorthand for $\pi(x, z)$. Using this notation and combining (16.19) and (16.20), we obtain the canonical form of the stochastic Euler equation

$$D_y U(x, \pi(x, z), z) + \beta \mathbb{E}\big[D_x U(\pi(x, z), \pi(\pi(x, z), z'), z') \mid z\big] = 0,$$

where, as in Chapter 6, $D_x U$ represents the gradient vector of U with respect to its first K arguments, and $D_y U$ represents its gradient with respect to the second set of K arguments. Writing this equation in the notation more congruent with the sequence version of the problem, the stochastic Euler equation takes the form

$$D_y U(\tilde{x}^*[z^{t-1}], \tilde{x}^*[z^t], z(t)) + \beta \mathbb{E}[D_x U(\tilde{x}^*[z^t], \tilde{x}^*[z^{t+1}], z(t+1)) \mid z(t)] = 0 \tag{16.21}$$

for $z^{t-1} \in \mathcal{Z}^{t-1}$.

How do we write the transversality condition in this case? The transversality condition again requires the discounted marginal return from the state variable to tend to zero as the planning horizon goes to infinity. In a stochastic environment we clearly have to look at expected returns. In the present context it is sufficient to condition on the information available at date $t = 0$, that is, on $z(0) \in \mathcal{Z}$. Consequently the transversality condition associated with this stochastic Euler equation takes the form

$$\lim_{t \to \infty} \beta^t \mathbb{E}[D_x U(\tilde{x}^*[z^{t-1}], \tilde{x}^*[z^t], z(t)) \cdot \tilde{x}^*[z^{t-1}] \mid z(0)] = 0. \tag{16.22}$$

The next theorem generalizes Theorem 6.10 from Chapter 6 to an environment with uncertainty. In particular, it shows that the transversality condition together with the transformed Euler equations in (16.21) are both necessary and sufficient to characterize a solution to Problem 16.1 and therefore to Problem 16.2.

Theorem 16.8 (Euler Equations and the Transversality Condition)   *Let $X \subset \mathbb{R}_+^K$, and suppose that Assumptions 16.1–16.5 hold. Then the sequence of feasible plans $\{\tilde{x}^*[z^t]\}_{t=0}^{\infty}$, with $\tilde{x}^*[z^t] \in \text{Int } G(\tilde{x}^*[z^{t-1}], z(t))$ for each $z(t) \in \mathcal{Z}$ and each $t = 0, 1, \ldots$, is optimal for Problem 16.1 given $x(0)$ and $z(0) \in \mathcal{Z}$ if and only if it satisfies (16.21) and (16.22).*

Proof.   The proof is similar to that of Theorem 6.10 in Chapter 6.

(Sufficiency) Consider an arbitrary $x(0) \in X$ and $z(0) \in \mathcal{Z}$, and let $\mathbf{x}^* \equiv \{\tilde{x}^*[z^t]\}_{t=0}^{\infty} \in \Phi(x(0), z(0))$ be a feasible plan satisfying (16.21) and (16.22). For any $\mathbf{x} \equiv \{\tilde{x}[z^t]\}_{t=0}^{\infty} \in \Phi(x(0), z(0))$ and any $z^{\infty} \in \mathcal{Z}^{\infty}$, define

$$\Delta_{\mathbf{x}}(z^{\infty}) \equiv \lim_{T \to \infty} \inf \sum_{t=0}^{T} \beta^t \big[U\big(\tilde{x}^*[z^{t-1}], \tilde{x}^*[z^t], z(t)\big) - U\big(\tilde{x}[z^{t-1}], \tilde{x}[z^t], z(t)\big)\big]$$

as the difference of the *realized* objective function between the feasible sequences $\mathbf{x}^*$ and $\mathbf{x}$.

From Assumptions 16.2 and 16.5, U is continuous, concave, and differentiable, so that for any $z^\infty \in \mathcal{Z}^\infty$ and any $\mathbf{x} \in \Phi(x(0), z(0))$,

$$\Delta_{\mathbf{x}}(z^\infty) \geq \lim_{T \to \infty} \inf \sum_{t=0}^{T} \beta^t \big[D_x U\big(\tilde{x}^*[z^{t-1}], \tilde{x}^*[z^t], z(t)\big) \cdot \big(\tilde{x}^*[z^{t-1}] - \tilde{x}[z^{t-1}]\big)$$
$$+ D_y U\big(\tilde{x}^*[z^{t-1}], \tilde{x}^*[z^t], z(t)\big) \cdot \big(\tilde{x}^*[z^t] - \tilde{x}[z^t]\big) \big].$$

Since this inequality is true for any $z^\infty \in \mathcal{Z}^\infty$, we can take expectations on both sides to obtain

$$\mathbb{E}[\Delta_{\mathbf{x}}(z^\infty) \mid z(0)]$$
$$\geq \lim_{T \to \infty} \inf \mathbb{E}\Big[\sum_{t=0}^{T} \beta^t D_x U\big(\tilde{x}^*[z^{t-1}], \tilde{x}^*[z^t], z(t)\big) \cdot \big(\tilde{x}^*[z^{t-1}] - \tilde{x}[z^{t-1}]\big)\Big|z(0)\Big]$$
$$+ \lim_{T \to \infty} \inf \mathbb{E}\Big[\sum_{t=0}^{T} \beta^t D_y U\big(\tilde{x}^*[z^{t-1}], \tilde{x}^*[z^t], z(t)\big) \cdot \big(\tilde{x}^*[z^t] - \tilde{x}[z^t]\big)\Big|z(0)\Big]$$

for $z(0) \in \mathcal{Z}$. Rearranging the previous expression yields

$$\mathbb{E}[\Delta_{\mathbf{x}}(z^\infty) \mid z(0)] \geq$$
$$\lim_{T \to \infty} \inf \mathbb{E}\Big[\sum_{t=0}^{T} \beta^t D_y U\big(\tilde{x}^*[z^{t-1}], \tilde{x}^*[z^t], z(t)\big) \cdot \big(\tilde{x}^*[z^t] - \tilde{x}[z^t]\big)\Big|z(0)\Big]$$
$$+ \lim_{T \to \infty} \inf \mathbb{E}\Big[\sum_{t=0}^{T} \beta^{t+1} D_x U\big(\tilde{x}^*[z^t], \tilde{x}^*[z^{t+1}], z(t+1)\big) \cdot \big(\tilde{x}^*[z^t] - \tilde{x}[z^t]\big)\Big|z(0)\Big]$$
$$- \lim_{T \to \infty} \sup \mathbb{E}\Big[\beta^{T+1} D_x U\big(\tilde{x}^*[z^T], \tilde{x}^*[z^{T+1}], z(T+1)\big) \cdot \tilde{x}^*[z^T]\Big|z(0)\Big]$$
$$+ \lim_{T \to \infty} \inf \mathbb{E}\Big[\beta^{T+1} D_x U\big(\tilde{x}[z^T], \tilde{x}[z^{T+1}], z(T+1)\big) \cdot \tilde{x}[z^T]\Big|z(0)\Big].$$

Since $\mathbf{x}^* \equiv \{\tilde{x}^*[z^t]\}_{t=0}^{\infty}$ satisfies (16.21), the terms in first and second lines are all equal to zero. Moreover, since $\mathbf{x}^* \equiv \{\tilde{x}^*[z^t]\}_{t=0}^{\infty}$ satisfies (16.22), the third line is also equal to zero. Finally, since U is increasing in x, $D_x U \geq 0$, and $x \geq 0$, the fourth line is nonnegative, establishing that $\mathbb{E}[\Delta_{\mathbf{x}}(z^\infty) \mid z(0)] \geq 0$ for any $\mathbf{x} \in \Phi(x(0), z(0))$. Consequently $\mathbf{x}^*$ yields (weakly) greater value than any feasible $\mathbf{x} \in \Phi(x(0), z(0))$ and is therefore optimal.

(Necessity) The proof of necessity mirrors that of the necessity part of Theorem 6.10. In particular, again define $\Delta'_{\mathbf{x}}$ as in the proof of that theorem. Consider a feasible plan $\mathbf{x} \in \Phi(x(0), z(0))$ such that $\tilde{x}[z^t] = \tilde{x}^*[z^t] + \varepsilon a[z^t]$ for some variation $a[z^t] \in \mathbb{R}^K$ for each $z^t \in \mathcal{Z}^t$ and $\varepsilon > 0$ sufficiently small ($\mathbf{x}$ is feasible, since $\mathbf{x}^* \equiv \{\tilde{x}^*[z^t]\}_{t=0}^{\infty}$ is interior). This establishes the necessity of the stochastic Euler equations (16.21). Choosing a feasible plan $\tilde{x}[z^t] = (1 - \varepsilon)\tilde{x}^*[z^t]$ and using (16.21) gives

$$\mathbb{E}[\Delta_{\mathbf{x}}'(z^\infty) \mid z(0)] =$$

$$- \varepsilon \lim_{T \to \infty} \inf \mathbb{E}\big[\beta^{T+1} D_x U\big(\tilde{x}^*[z^T], \tilde{x}^*[z^{T+1}], z(T+1)\big) \cdot \tilde{x}^*[z^T]\big|z(0)\big]$$

$$+ \lim_{T \to \infty} \sum_{t=0}^{T} \beta^t o(\varepsilon, t).$$

If (16.22) is violated, the first term can be made negative and if so, it remains negative as $\varepsilon \to 0$. This contradicts the fact that $\mathbf{x}^* \equiv \{\tilde{x}^*[z^t]\}_{t=0}^{\infty}$ is an optimal plan, establishing the necessity part of the theorem. ∎

16.4 Generalization to Markov Processes *

What happens if z does not take on finitely many values? For example, z may be represented by a general Markov process, taking values in a compact metric space. The simplest example would be a one-dimensional stochastic variable $z(t)$ given by the process $z(t) = \rho z(t - 1) + \sigma \varepsilon(t)$, where $\varepsilon(t)$ has a standard normal distribution. At some level, most of the results we care about generalize to such cases. At another level, however, greater care needs to be taken in formulating these problems both in the sequence form of Problem 16.1 and in the recursive form of Problem 16.2. The main difficulty in this case arises in ensuring that there exist appropriately defined feasible plans, which now need to be "measurable" with respect to the information set available at the time. To avoid a lengthy detour into measure theory, I assume that both $\mathcal{Z}$ and X are compact and impose sufficient continuity in payoffs and constraints (which ensures the existence of measurable optimal plans). Under these assumptions, I state the main theorems for stochastic dynamic programming with general Markov processes. Throughout I use expectations instead of explicit integrals.

Let us first define $\mathcal{Z}$ as a compact subset of $\mathbb{R}$, which includes $\mathcal{Z}$ consisting of a finite number of elements and $\mathcal{Z}$ corresponding to a closed interval as special cases. Suppose that $z(t) \in \mathcal{Z}$ represents the uncertainty in this environment and follows a Markov process, that is,

$$\Pr[z(t) \mid z(0), \dots, z(t - 1)] \equiv \Pr[z(t) \mid z(t - 1)].$$

This Markov process can also be represented by the state transition function $Q(z, \cdot)$ as defined above. Let us again use the notation $z^t \equiv (z(1), \dots, z(t))$ to represent the history of the realizations of the stochastic variable. The objective function and the constraint sets are represented as in Section 16.1, so that $\tilde{x}[z^t]$ again denotes a feasible plan, which now also needs to be measurable with respect to the information sets generated by each $z^t \in \mathcal{Z}^t$. Let the set of feasible plans after history z^t be denoted by $\Phi(\tilde{x}[z^{t-1}], z(t))$. The set of feasible plans starting with $z(0)$ is then $\Phi(x(0), z(0))$. Also when there exists a function V that is a solution to Problem 16.2, let us define $\Pi(x, z) \subset \Phi(x, z)$ as the set of all $\pi(x, z)$ satisfying

$$V(x, z) = U(x, \pi(x, z), z) + \beta \mathbb{E}[V(\pi(x, y), z') \mid z].$$

Finally, the same assumptions as in Section 16.1 are necessary. In addition we now require the relevant functions to be measurable with respect to the appropriate information sets, and the correspondence $\Phi(x(t), z(t))$ to admit a measurable selection for all $x(t) \in X$ and $z^t \in \mathcal{Z}^t$.

However the continuity of U and G imposed in Assumptions 16.1 and 16.2 are sufficient to ensure such measurability. The only additional assumption we need to impose is the following (sometimes referred to as the "Feller property").

Assumption 16.7 *The Markov process $Q(z, \cdot)$ is such that for any $f : \mathcal{Z} \to \mathbb{R}$ that is bounded and continuous, $\mathbb{E}[f(z') \mid z] \equiv \int f(z')Q(z, dz')$ is a bounded and continuous function of z on $\mathcal{Z}$.*

This assumption is automatically satisfied when Q is a Markov chain (just endow $\mathcal{Z}$ with the discrete topology).

Theorem 16.9 (Existence of Solutions) *Suppose that Assumptions 16.1, 16.2, and 16.7 hold. Then any solution $V(x, z)$ to Problem 16.2 coincides with the solution $V^*(x, z)$ to Problem 16.1. Moreover if $\Pi(x, z)$ is nonempty for all $(x, z) \in X \times \mathcal{Z}$, then any plan $\tilde{x}[z^t]$ generated by $\pi(x, z) \in \Pi(x, z)$ achieves $V^*(x, z)$.*

This theorem implicitly imposes a lot of structure on Problem 16.1 or 16.2. In particular, Assumption 16.1 ensures that $\Phi(x, z)$ is nonempty and that for any $\mathbf{x} \in \Phi(x(0), z(0))$, $\mathbb{E}[\sum_{t=0}^{\infty} \beta^t U(\tilde{x}[z^{t-1}], \tilde{x}[z^t], z(t)) \mid z(0)]$ is well defined and finite valued. Moreover, with the same arguments as in the proof of Theorem 16.3, Assumption 16.2 ensures that $\Pi(x, z)$ is an upper hemicontinuous correspondence and thus allows a measurable selection for any $z \in \mathcal{Z}$ and $x \in X$ (and thus $\Phi(x(0), z(0))$ also admits a measurable selection for any $z(0) \in \mathcal{Z}$ and $x(0) \in X$).

Theorem 16.10 (Continuity of Value Functions) *Suppose that Assumption 16.1, 16.2, and 16.7 hold. Then there exists a unique function $V : X \times \mathcal{Z} \to \mathbb{R}$ that satisfies (16.7). Moreover V is continuous and bounded. Finally, an optimal plan $\mathbf{x}^* \in \Phi(x(0), z(0))$ exists for any $x(0) \in X$ and any $z(0) \in \mathcal{Z}$.*

Theorem 16.11 (Concavity of Value Functions) *Suppose that Assumptions 16.1, 16.2, 16.3, and 16.7 hold. Then the unique function V that satisfies (16.7) is strictly concave in x for each $z \in \mathcal{Z}$. Moreover the optimal plan can be expressed as $\tilde{x}^*[z^t] = \pi(x(t), z(t))$, where the policy function $\pi : X \times \mathcal{Z} \to X$ is continuous in x for each $z \in \mathcal{Z}$.*

Theorem 16.12 (Monotonicity of Value Functions) *Suppose that Assumptions 16.1, 16.2, 16.4, and 16.7 hold. Then the unique value function $V : X \times \mathcal{Z} \to \mathbb{R}$ that satisfies (16.7) is strictly increasing in x for each $z \in \mathcal{Z}$.*

Theorem 16.13 (Differentiability of Value Functions) *Suppose that Assumptions 16.1, 16.2, 16.3, 16.5, and 16.7 hold. Let π be the policy function defined above and assume that $x' \in$ Int X and $\pi(x', z) \in$ Int $G(x', z)$ for each $z \in \mathcal{Z}$. Then $V(x, z)$ is continuously differentiable at x', with gradient with respect to x given by*

$$D_x V(x', z) = D_x U(x', \pi(x', z), z).$$

The proofs of these theorems are not difficult, though they are long and require a little care. Their proofs can be found in Stokey, Lucas, and Prescott (1989, Chapter 9), who also develop the necessary measure theory and some of the theory of general Markov processes to state slightly more general versions of these theorems.

Finally, note also that Theorem 16.8 continues to apply in this case, since the statement or the proof of this theorem did not make use of the fact that z followed a Markov chain.

16.5 Applications of Stochastic Dynamic Programming

I now present a number of applications of the methods of stochastic dynamic programming. Some of the most important applications, related to stochastic growth and growth with incomplete markets, are left for the next chapter. In each application, I point out how formulating the problem recursively and using stochastic dynamic programming methods simplify the analysis.

16.5.1 The Permanent Income Hypothesis

One of the most important applications of stochastic dynamic optimization is to the consumption smoothing problem of a household facing an uncertain income stream. This problem was first discussed by Irving Fisher (1930) and then received its first systematic analysis in Milton Friedman's (1957) classic book on consumption theory. With Robert Hall's (1978) seminal paper on dynamic consumption behavior, it became one of the most celebrated macroeconomic models.

Consider a household maximizing discounted lifetime utility

$$\mathbb{E}_0 \sum_{t=0}^{\infty} \beta^t u(c(t)),$$

with $c(t) \geq 0$ as usual denoting consumption. To start with, assume that $u(\cdot)$ is strictly increasing, continuously differentiable, and concave, and denote its derivative by $u'(\cdot)$.

The household can borrow and lend freely at a constant interest rate $r > 0$; thus its lifetime budget constraint takes the form

$$\sum_{t=0}^{\infty} \frac{1}{(1+r)^t} c(t) \leq \sum_{t=0}^{\infty} \frac{1}{(1+r)^t} w(t) + a(0), \tag{16.23}$$

where $a(0)$ denotes its initial assets, and $w(t)$ is its labor income. Suppose that $w(t)$ is random and takes values from the set $\mathcal{W} \equiv \{w_1, \ldots, w_N\}$. This corresponds to potential labor income fluctuations due to aggregate or idiosyncratic shocks facing the household. To simplify the analysis, let us suppose that $w(t)$ is distributed independently over time and the probability that $w(t) = w_j$ is q_j (naturally with $\sum_{j=1}^{N} q_j = 1$). Consequently the lifetime budget constraint (16.23) has to be interpreted as a stochastic constraint. We therefore require this constraint to hold *almost surely* (with probability 1), so that there are no positive probability sample paths where the constraint is violated.

The fact that the lifetime budget constraint is stochastic has important economic implications. In particular, although there are no explicit borrowing constraints, the fact that the lifetime budget constraint must hold with probability 1 imposes *endogenous borrowing constraints*. For example, suppose that $w_1 = 0$ and $q_1 > 0$ (so that this state corresponds to unemployment and zero labor income). Then there is a positive probability that the household receives zero income for any sequence of periods of length $T < \infty$. Then, if the household ever chooses a negative asset holding, $a(t) < 0$, there will be a positive probability of violating its lifetime budget constraint, even if it were to choose zero consumption in all future periods. Therefore there is an endogenous borrowing constraint, which takes the form

$$a(t) \geq - \sum_{s=0}^{\infty} \frac{1}{(1+r)^s} w_1 \equiv -b_1,$$

with w_1 denoting the minimum value of w within the set $\mathcal{W}$.

Let us first solve this problem by treating it as a sequence problem, that is, the problem of choosing a sequence of feasible plans $\{\tilde{c}[w^t]\}_{t=0}^{\infty}$. This can be done simply by forming the Lagrangian. Even though there is a single lifetime budget constraint (16.23), it would be incorrect to treat the problem as if there were a unique Lagrange multiplier λ. This is because consumption plans are made conditional on the realizations of events up to a certain date. In particular, consumption at time t is conditioned on the history of shocks up to that date, $w^t \equiv (w(0), w(1), \ldots, w(t))$, and in fact I used the notation $\tilde{c}[w^t]$ to emphasize that consumption at date t is a mapping from the history of income realizations, w^t. At that point, since there is also more information about how much the household has earned and how much it has spent, it is also natural to think that the Lagrange multiplier, which represents the marginal utility of money, also depends on the realizations of the shocks up to date t, w^t. I therefore write this multiplier as $\tilde{\lambda}[w^t]$.

The first-order conditions for this problem give

$$\beta^t u'(\tilde{c}[w^t]) = \frac{1}{(1+r)^t} \tilde{\lambda}[w^t], \tag{16.24}$$

which requires the (discounted) marginal utility of consumption after history w^t to be equated to the (discounted) marginal utility of income after history w^t, $\tilde{\lambda}[w^t]$. While economically interpretable, this first-order condition is not particularly useful unless we know the law of motion of the marginal utility of income, $\tilde{\lambda}[w^t]$. This law of motion is not straightforward to derive in this formulation. An alternative formulation of the sequence problem, where prices for all possible claims to consumption contingent on any realization of history are introduced, is more tractable and gives similar results to the recursive approach below. I introduce this contingent-claims formulation in the analysis of the competitive equilibrium of the neoclassical growth model under uncertainty in the next chapter.

Instead let us formulate the same problem recursively, which enables sharper results. The flow budget constraint of the household can be written as

$$a' = (1+r)a + w - c,$$

where a' refers to next period's asset holdings. Conversely, this implies $c = (1+r)a + w - a'$. Then the value function of the household, conditioned on current asset holding a and current realization of the income shock w, can be written as

$$V(a, w) = \max_{a' \in [-b_1, (1+r)a+w]} \left\{ u((1+r)a + w - a') + \beta \mathbb{E} V(a', w') \right\},$$

where I have made use of the fact that w is distributed independently across periods, so the expectation of the continuation value is not conditioned on the current realization of w. Analogous to Example 6.5 in Chapter 6, where we studied the nonstochastic version of this problem, we need to restrict the set of feasible asset levels to apply Theorems 16.1–16.6 from Section 16.1. In particular, let us take $\bar{a} \equiv a(0) + w_N/r$, where w_N is the highest level of labor income. We can then impose that $a(t) \in [0, \bar{a}]$ and then again verify the conditions under which this has no effect on the solution (in particular the condition for $a(t)$ to be always in the interior of the set; see Exercise 16.11).

The first-order condition for the maximization problem gives

$$u'(c(t)) = \beta \mathbb{E}_t \frac{\partial V(a(t+1), w(t+1))}{\partial a}, \tag{16.25}$$

where $\mathbb{E}_t$ denotes the expectations given the information at time t. Noting that $\partial V(a', w')/\partial a$ is also the marginal utility of income, this equation is similar to (16.24). The additional mileage now comes from the Envelope condition in Theorem 16.6, (16.10), which implies that

$$\frac{\partial V(a(t), w(t))}{\partial a} = (1 + r)u'(c(t)).$$

Combining this equation with (16.25), we obtain the famous stochastic Euler equation of the permanent income hypothesis:

$$u'(c(t)) = \beta(1 + r)\mathbb{E}_t u'(c(t + 1)). \tag{16.26}$$

The notable feature here is that on the right-hand side we have the expectation of the marginal utility of consumption at date $t + 1$.

This equation becomes even simpler and perhaps more insightful when the instantaneous utility function is quadratic, for example, taking the form

$$u(c) = \phi c - \tfrac{1}{2}c^2,$$

with ϕ sufficiently large that in the relevant range $u(\cdot)$ is increasing in c. Using this quadratic form with (16.26), we obtain Hall's famous stochastic equation

$$c(t) = (1 - \kappa)\phi + \kappa\mathbb{E}_t c(t + 1), \tag{16.27}$$

where $\kappa \equiv \beta(1 + r)$. A striking prediction of this equation is that variables, such as current or past income, should not predict (future) consumption growth. A large empirical literature investigates whether this is the case in aggregate or individual data, focusing on *excess sensitivity* tests. The dependence of future consumption growth on current income is interpreted as evidence for excess sensitivity, rejecting (16.27). This rejection is often considered as evidence in favor of credit constraints (in addition to the endogenous borrowing constraints highlighted above). Nevertheless excess sensitivity can also emerge without credit constraints when the utility function is not quadratic (see, e.g., Zeldes, 1989; Caballero, 1990).

Equation (16.27) takes an even simpler form when $\beta = (1 + r)^{-1}$, that is, when the discount factor is the inverse of the gross interest rate. In this case, $\kappa = 1$ and $c(t) = \mathbb{E}_t c(t + 1)$ or $\mathbb{E}_t \Delta c(t + 1) = 0$, so that the expected value of future consumption should be the same as today's consumption. This last property is sometimes referred to as the "martingale property." Recall that a random variable $z(t)$ is a *martingale* with respect to some information set Ω_t if $\mathbb{E}[z(t + 1) \mid \Omega_t] = z(t)$. It is a *submartingale* if $\mathbb{E}[z(t + 1) \mid \Omega_t] \geq z(t)$ and a *supermartingale* if $\mathbb{E}[z(t + 1) \mid \Omega_t] \leq z(t)$. Thus consumption is a martingale, submartingale, or supermartingale, depending on the value of the interest rate relative to the discount factor. Exercises 16.8 and 16.11 further discuss the implications of (16.27).

16.5.2   Search for Ideas

This section provides another example of an economic problem where dynamic programming techniques are useful. This example also provides us with an alternative and complementary way of thinking about the endogeneity of technology to those presented in Part IV.

Consider the problem of a single entrepreneur with a risk-neutral objective function

$$\sum_{t=0}^{\infty} \beta^t c(t).$$

This entrepreneur's consumption is given by the income he generates in that period (there is no saving or borrowing). If the entrepreneur uses an idea of quality $a(t)$, he can then produce income equal to

$$y(t) = a(t)$$

at time t.[3] At $t = 0$, the entrepreneur starts with $a(0) = 0$. From then on, at each date, he can either engage in production using one of the techniques he has already discovered or spend that period searching for a new technique. Let us assume that each period in which he engages in such a search, he gets an independent draw from a time-invariant distribution function $H(a)$ defined over a bounded interval $[0, \bar{a}]$.

Therefore the decision of the entrepreneur at each date is whether to search for a new technique or to produce with one of the techniques he has discovered so far. Since there is no saving or borrowing, the entrepreneur simply consumes his current income $c(t) = y(t)$.

This problem introduces a slightly different perspective on some of the ideas already discussed in the book. As in the endogenous technological change models studied so far, the entrepreneur has a nontrivial choice that affects the technology available to him: by searching more, which is a costly activity in terms of foregone production, he can potentially improve the set of techniques available to him. Moreover this economic decision is related to the trade-offs in the standard models of technological progress and technology adoption: whether to produce with what he has available today or make an "investment" in one more round of search with the hope of discovering something better. This trade-off is complementary to the incentives to invest in new technology in the models of endogenous technology.

Here my main objective is to show how dynamic programming techniques can be used to analyze this problem. Let us first write the maximization problem facing the entrepreneur as a sequence problem. Let us begin with the class of decision rules of the agent. In particular, let $\mathbf{a}^t \in \mathbf{A}^t \equiv [0, \bar{a}]^t$ be a sequence of techniques observed by the entrepreneur over the past t periods, with $a(s) = 0$, if at time s the entrepreneur engaged in production, and write $\mathbf{a}^t = (a(0), \ldots, a(t))$. Then a decision rule for this entrepreneur is

$$q(t) : \mathbf{A}^t \rightarrow \{a(t)\} \cup \{\text{search}\},$$

which denotes the action of the agent at time t, which is either to produce with the current technique he has discovered, $a(t)$, or to choose $q(t) =$"search" and spend that period searching for a new technique. Let $\mathcal{P}_t$ be the set of functions from $\mathbf{A}^t$ into $a(t) \cup \{\text{search}\}$, and $\mathcal{P}^\infty$ the set of infinite sequences of such functions. The most general way of expressing the problem of the entrepreneur is

$$\max_{\{q(t)\}_{t=0}^\infty \in \mathcal{P}^\infty} \mathbb{E} \sum_{t=0}^\infty \beta^t c(t)$$

subject to $c(t) = 0$ if $q(t) =$"search" and $c(t) = a$ if $q(t) = a$, for $a(s) = a$ and for some $s \leq t$. $\mathbb{E}$ denotes the expectations operator. Naturally, written in this way, the problem looks complicated, even daunting. The point of writing it in this way is to show that in certain classes of models, the dynamic programming formulation is quite tractable even when the sequence problem may look quite complicated.

To demonstrate this, I now write this optimization problem recursively using dynamic programming techniques. Let us simplify the formulation of the recursive form of this problem

---

3. The use of a here for the quality of ideas, rather than as asset holdings of individual before, should cause no confusion.

by making two observations (which are both proved in Exercise 16.12). First, because the problem is stationary, we can discard all techniques that the entrepreneur has sampled except the current one and thus write the value of the entrepreneur simply conditioning on the current technique a, as $V(a)$. Second, we suppose that once the entrepreneur starts producing at some technique a, he continues to do so forever instead of going back to searching again at some future date. This observation is also intuitive due to the stationarity of the problem: if the entrepreneur is willing to accept production at technique a rather than searching further at time t, he would also do so at time $t + 1$. This last observation implies that if the entrepreneur accepts production at some technique a at date t, he will consume $c(s) = a$ for all $s \geq t$. Consequently we obtain the value of accepting technique a as

$$V^{\text{accept}}(a) = \frac{a}{1 - \beta}.$$

Therefore we can write

$$V(a') = \max\left\{ V^{\text{accept}}(a'), \beta \mathbb{E}V \right\}$$

$$= \max\left\{ \frac{a'}{1 - \beta}, \beta \mathbb{E}V \right\}, \tag{16.28}$$

where

$$\mathbb{E}V = \int_0^{\bar{a}} V(a) dH(a) \tag{16.29}$$

is the expected continuation value of not producing at the available techniques. The expression in (16.28) follows from the fact that the entrepreneur chooses whichever option, starting production or continuing to search, gives him higher utility. That the value of continuing to search is given by (16.29) follows by definition. At the next date, the entrepreneur has value $V(a)$ as given by (16.28) when he draws a from the distribution $H(a)$, and thus integrating over this expression gives $\mathbb{E}V$. The integral is written as a Lebesgue integral, since $H(a)$ may not have a continuous density.

A SLIGHT DIGRESSION.* Even though the special structure of the search problem enables a direct solution, it is also useful to see that optimal policies can be derived by applying the techniques developed in Section 6.4 of Chapter 6. For this, combine the two previous equations and write

$$V(a') = \max\left\{ \frac{a'}{1 - \beta}, \beta \int_0^{\bar{a}} V(a) dH(a) \right\}, \tag{16.30}$$

$$= TV(a'),$$

where the second line defines the mapping T. Blackwell's Sufficiency Theorem (Theorem 6.9) applies directly to (16.30) and implies that T is a contraction, since it is monotone and satisfies discounting.

Next let $V \in \mathbf{C}([0, \bar{a}])$, that is, the set of real-valued continuous (hence bounded) functions defined over the set $[0, \bar{a}]$, which is a complete metric space with the sup norm. Then the Contraction Mapping Theorem (Theorem 6.7) implies that a unique value function $V(a)$ exists. Thus the dynamic programming formulation of the sequential search problem immediately leads to the existence of a solution (and thus of optimal strategies, which are characterized below).

Moreover, Theorem 6.8 also applies by taking S' to be the space of nondecreasing continuous functions over $[0, \bar{a}]$, which is a closed subspace of $\mathbf{C}([0, \bar{a}])$. Therefore $V(a)$ is nondecreasing. In fact, using Theorem 6.8 we could also prove that $V(a)$ is piecewise linear with a flat portion first, followed by an increasing portion. Let the space of such functions be S'', which is another (not necessarily closed) subspace of $\mathbf{C}([0, \bar{a}])$. Nevertheless now the second part of Theorem 6.8 applies, since starting with any nondecreasing function $V(a)$, $TV(a)$ will be such a piecewise linear function. Therefore the theorem implies that the unique fixed point, $V(a)$, must have this property too. ∎

The digression above used Theorem 6.8 to argue that $V(a)$ would take a piecewise linear form. In fact, in this case this property can also be deduced directly from (16.30), since $V(a)$ is a maximum of two functions, one of them constant and the other one linear. Therefore $V(a)$ must be piecewise linear, with a flat portion first.

Our next task is to determine the optimal policy using the recursive formulation of Problem 16.2. The fact that $V(a)$ is linear (and strictly increasing) after a flat portion immediately tells us that the optimal policy takes a *cutoff rule,* meaning that there exists a cutoff technology level R such that the entrepreneur accepts all techniques above R, while those $a < R$ are turned down and the entrepreneur continues to search. This cutoff rule property follows because $V(a)$ is strictly increasing after some level; thus if some technology a' is accepted, all technologies with $a > a'$ will also be accepted.

Moreover, this cutoff rule must satisfy the following equation:

$$\frac{R}{1-\beta} = \int_0^{\bar{a}} \beta V(a) dH(a), \tag{16.31}$$

so that the entrepreneur is just indifferent between accepting the technology $a = R$ and waiting for one more period. Next, since $a < R$ are turned down, we have that for all $a < R$,

$$V(a) = \beta \int_0^{\bar{a}} V(a) dH(a)$$

$$= \frac{R}{1-\beta},$$

and for all $a \geq R$,

$$V(a) = \frac{a}{1-\beta}.$$

Using these observations yields

$$\int_0^{\bar{a}} V(a) dH(a) = \frac{RH(R)}{1-\beta} + \int_{a \geq R} \frac{a}{1-\beta} dH(a).$$

Combining this equation with (16.31), we obtain

$$\frac{R}{1-\beta} = \beta \left[\frac{RH(R)}{1-\beta} + \int_{a \geq R} \frac{a}{1-\beta} dH(a) \right]. \tag{16.32}$$

Manipulating this equation gives

$$R = \frac{\beta}{1 - \beta H(R)} \int_R^{\bar{a}} a \, dH(a),$$

which is a convenient way of expressing the cutoff rule R. Equation (16.32) can also be expressed in an alternative and more intuitive way. Rewrite this equation as

$$\frac{R}{1-\beta} = \beta \left[\int_{a<R} \frac{R}{1-\beta} dH(a) + \int_{a\geq R} \frac{a}{1-\beta} dH(a) \right].$$

Now subtracting

$$\frac{\beta R}{1-\beta} = \frac{\beta R}{1-\beta} \int_{a<R} dH(a) + \frac{\beta R}{1-\beta} \int_{a\geq R} dH(a)$$

from both sides, we obtain

$$R = \frac{\beta}{1-\beta} \int_R^{\bar{a}} (a-R) dH(a). \tag{16.33}$$

The left-hand side is best understood as the cost of foregoing production with a technology of R, while the right-hand side is the expected benefit of one more round of search. At the cutoff threshold, these two terms have to be equal, since the entrepreneur must be indifferent between starting production and continuing search.

Let us now define the right-hand side of equation (16.33), the expected benefit of one more search, as

$$\gamma(R) = \frac{\beta}{1-\beta} \int_R^{\bar{a}} (a-R) dH(a).$$

Suppose also that H has a continuous density, denoted by h. Then γ is differentiable and

$$\gamma'(R) = -\frac{\beta}{1-\beta}(R-R)h(R) - \frac{\beta}{1-\beta} \int_R^{\bar{a}} dH(a) = -\frac{\beta}{1-\beta}[1-H(R)] < 0.$$

Thus (16.33) has a unique solution. It can be easily verified that a higher β, by making the entrepreneur more patient, increases the cutoff threshold R.

16.5.3 Other Applications

There are numerous other applications of stochastic dynamic programming. In addition to the four growth models studied in the next chapter, the following are noteworthy.

1. *Asset Pricing*: following Lucas (1978), we can consider an economy in which a set of identical agents trade claims on stochastic returns of a set of given assets ("trees"). Each agent solves a consumption smoothing problem similar to that in Section 16.5.1, with the major difference that he or she can now save in assets with stochastic returns rather than (or in addition to) at a constant interest rate. Market clearing is achieved when the total supply of assets is equal to total demand. Thus equilibrium prices have to be such that each agent is happy to hold the appropriate amount of claims on the returns from these assets. Given the marginal utility of consumption derived from the recursive formulation, these assets can be priced. Exercise 16.14 considers this case.

2. *Investment under Uncertainty*: the model of investment with adjustment costs discussed in Section 7.8 of Chapter 7 has much wider application in macroeconomics and indus-

trial organization once augmented by the possibility that firms are uncertain about future demand and/or productivity. Exercise 16.15 considers this case.

3. *Optimal Stopping Problems*: the search model discussed in Section 16.5.2 is an example of an optimal stopping problem. More general optimal stopping problems can also be set up and analyzed as stochastic dynamic programming problems. Exercise 16.16 considers an example of such an optimal stopping problem.

16.6 Taking Stock

The material in this chapter is technical in nature and is more useful for its applications than for its own sake. It has widespread applications in macroeconomics and economic growth. The stochastic neoclassical growth model, presented in the next chapter, utilizes the methods developed here.

In addition to presenting the basic tools of stochastic dynamic programming, this chapter has presented two important economic models. The first, the stochastic permanent income hypothesis model, is one of the most famous macroeconomic models and has led both to a large theoretical and empirical literature. The early empirical literature focused on excess sensitivity tests as discussed in Section 16.5.1 using aggregate data. The more recent literature focuses on micro and panel data to derive sharper results about the behavior of individual consumption.

The other substantial model introduced in this chapter is the search-for-ideas model in Section 16.5.2, which is adapted from McCall's (1970) labor market search model. McCall's model is the basis of much of the modern equilibrium theory of unemployment. While the model here has been cast in terms of searching for ideas, the reader can easily adapt it to unemployment and use it as an introduction to equilibrium unemployment theory (see Exercise 16.13). In addition, some of the other applications, mentioned above and treated in the exercises (including the asset pricing model based on Lucas (1978) and the model of investment under uncertainty) are widely used in other areas of macroeconomics.

16.7 References and Literature

Most of the references from Chapter 6 are relevant to stochastic dynamic programming as well. The reader may want to look at Howard (1960), Blackwell (1965), and Puterman (1994) for advanced treatments. The most complete treatment of discounted stochastic dynamic programming problems with economic applications is in Stokey, Lucas, and Prescott (1989). This chapter covers the same material as Stokey, Lucas, and Prescott, though at a slightly less technical level. In particular, I presented all the major results of stochastic dynamic programming without introducing measure theory. A thorough study of stochastic dynamic programming requires a nontrivial investment in these methods. The reader should consult Stokey, Lucas, and Prescott (1989, Chapters 8–13), who present a more measure-theoretic approach and develop the necessary material on Markov processes.

The reader may also wish to consult Rudin (1976) or the very lively and readable treatment in Williams (1991) for some of the basic definitions and results in measure theory used in the discussion of Markov processes. These references also provide a formal definition of the Lebesgue integral, which I used informally a number of times throughout the text. A slightly more advanced but excellent treatment of measure theory is contained in Royden (1994). Williams (1991) also contains an excellent introductory treatment of martingales, which were mentioned in Section 16.5.

Futia (1982) presents a compact and excellent treatment of Markov processes and their applications to stochastic dynamic models. More advanced and complete treatments of Markov processes can be found in Gikhman and Skorohod (1974) or Ethier and Kurtz (1986).

A more detailed treatment of the necessity and sufficiency of stochastic transversality conditions (Theorem 16.8) can be found in Zilcha (1978) and Kamihigashi (2003).

The best survey of work on consumption is Deaton (1992). A survey of recent work can be found in Browning and Crossley (2001). Exercise 16.11 is based on Chamberlain and Wilson (2000), and the reader is referred to this paper for some of the subtle mathematical issues that arise in determining the limiting behavior of the stochastic consumption distribution when the discount factor is equal to the inverse of the gross interest rate. The search-for-ideas example in Section 16.5.2 is adapted from McCall's (1970) labor market search model. Kortum (1997) provides the first search-theoretical model of technology choice that I am aware of. Kortum's model is richer and more insightful than the model presented in Section 16.5.2. Ljungqvist and Sargent (2005) contains an excellent exposition of the basic McCall model. Pissarides (2000) and Rogerson, Shimer, and Wright (2004) provide excellent surveys of recent work in search theory applied to labor market problems.

16.8 Exercises

16.1   Show that Assumption 16.6 part 3 is satisfied if and only if for any $j'' > j'$ and any $\bar{j} = 1, \ldots, N$, $\sum_{j=\bar{j}}^{N} q_{jj''} \geq \sum_{j=\bar{j}}^{N} q_{jj'}$. What does this condition imply about the relationship between the conditional distribution of z given $z_{j''}$ and given $z_{j'}$?

* 16.2   Prove Lemma 16.1.

* 16.3   This exercise develops an alternative proof of Theorem 16.3.

   (a) Choose the appropriate topology on $\mathcal{Z}$ so that U is continuous on $X \times X \times \mathcal{Z}$.

   (b) Use Theorem A.12 in Appendix A to show that the objective function in Problem 16.1 is continuous in the product topology; Theorem A.13 and Lemma A.2 to show that the constraint set is compact; and Theorems A.9 and A.16 to show that $V^*(x(0), z(0))$ is well defined, continuous, and bounded over $X \times \mathcal{Z}$.

   (c) Deduce the same results for $V(x(0), z(0))$ by applying Theorem 16.1.

* 16.4   Prove Theorem 16.4.

* 16.5   Prove Theorem 16.5.

* 16.6   Prove Theorem 16.6.

* 16.7   Prove Theorem 16.7.

16.8   Consider the stochastic permanent income hypothesis model studied in Section 16.5 with a general instantaneous utility function $u(c)$. Explain the conditions under which the excess sensitivity tests described in that section would fail even when the stochastic Euler equation (16.26) holds. [Hint: you may want to consider the CRRA preferences for concreteness.]

16.9   (a) Consider the stochastic permanent income hypothesis model studied in Section 16.5 and assume that the interest rate r is no longer constant but is equal to $r(t) > 0$ at time t. Derive the equivalent of (16.26) in this case. Show that excess sensitivity tests can be applied in this case as well.

   (b) Now suppose that $r(t)$ is a random variable taking one of finitely many values, $r_1, \ldots, r_N$, and to simplify the analysis, suppose that the realizations of the interest rate are independent over time. Derive the equivalent of (16.26) in this case. Show that excess sensitivity tests can be applied in this case as well.

16.10 Consider the stochastic permanent income hypothesis model studied in Section 16.5. Suppose that instead of being distributed independently, $w(t)$ follows a Markov chain. Show that (16.26) still holds. Now suppose that $u(c)$ takes a quadratic form, and assume that the econometrician incorrectly believes that $w(t)$ is independently distributed, so that the household has superior information relative to the econometrician. Show that a regression of consumption growth on past income realizations still leads to a zero coefficient (thus the excess sensitivity test will not reject). [Hint: make use of the law of iterated expectations, which states that if Ω is an information set that is finer than Ω' and z is a random variable, then $\mathbb{E}[\mathbb{E}[z \mid \Omega] \mid \Omega'] = \mathbb{E}[z \mid \Omega']$.]

* 16.11 In the stochastic permanent income hypothesis model studied in Section 16.5, suppose that $c(t) \geq 0$; $u(\cdot)$ is twice continuously differentiable, everywhere strictly concave, and strictly increasing; and $u''(\cdot)$ is increasing. Suppose also that $w(t)$ has a nondegenerate probability distribution with lower support equal to 0.

   (a) Show that consumption can never converge to a constant level.

   (b) Prove that if $u(\cdot)$ takes the CRRA form and $\beta < (1+r)^{-1}$, then there exists some $\bar{a} < \infty$ such that $a(t) \in (0, \bar{a})$ for all t.

   (c) Prove that when $\beta \leq (1+r)^{-1}$, there may not exist $\bar{a} < \infty$ such that $a(t) \in (0, \bar{a})$ for all t. [Hint: first suppose $u(\cdot)$ takes the CRRA form, consider the case where $\beta = (1+r)^{-1}$, and take the stochastic sequence with $w(t) = w_N$ for an arbitrarily large number of periods, which is a positive probability sequence. Then generalize this argument to the case where $\beta \leq (1+r)^{-1}$.]

   (d) Suppose that $u''(\cdot)$ is nondecreasing. Prove that when $\beta \leq (1+r)^{-1}$, marginal utility of consumption follows a (nondegenerate) supermartingale, and therefore consumption must converge to infinity. [Hint: note that in this case (16.26) implies $u'(c(t)) \geq \mathbb{E}u'(c(t+1))$, and use this equation to argue that consumption must be increasing "on average."]

   (e) How is the analysis in part d modified if $u''(\cdot)$ is decreasing?

16.12 Consider the model of searching for ideas introduced in Section 16.5.2. Suppose that the entrepreneur can use any of the techniques he has discovered in the past to produce at any point in time, and he can also stop production at any point and go back to searching.

   (a) Formulate the maximization problem of the entrepreneur recursively.

   (b) Prove that if the entrepreneur has turned down production with some technique a' at date t, he will never accept technique a' at date $t + s$, for $s > 0$ (i.e., he will not accept it for any possible realization of events between dates t and $t + s$).

   (c) Prove that if the entrepreneur accepts technique a' at date t, he will continue to produce with this technique for all dates $s \geq t$ rather than stopping production and going back to searching.

   (d) Using parts a and b, show that the maximization problem of the entrepreneur can be formulated as in the text without loss of any generality.

   (e) Now suppose that when not producing, the entrepreneur receives income b. Write the recursive formulation for this case and show that as b increases, the cutoff threshold R increases.

16.13 Formulate the problem in Section 16.5.2 as one of an unemployed worker sampling wages from an exogenously given stationary wage distribution $H(w)$. The objective of the worker is to maximize the net present discounted value of his income stream. Assume that once the worker accepts a job he can work at that wage forever.

   (a) Formulate the dynamic maximization problem of the worker recursively, assuming that once the worker finds a job he never quits.

   (b) Prove that the worker never quits a job that he has accepted.

   (c) Prove that the worker uses a reservation wage R.

   (d) Calculate the expected duration of unemployment for the worker.

(e) Show that if the wages in the distribution $H(w)$ are offered by firms and all workers are identical, the wage offers of all firms other than those offering $w = R$ are not profit maximizing. What does this observation imply about the McCall search model?

16.14 Consider an economy populated by identical households, each with preferences given by $\mathbb{E}[\sum_{t=0}^{\infty} \beta^t u(c(t))]$, where $u(\cdot)$ is strictly increasing, strictly concave, and twice differentiable. Normalize the measure of agents in the economy to 1. Each household has a claim to a single tree, which delivers $z(t)$ units of consumption good at time t. Assume that $z(t)$ is a random variable taking values from the set $\mathcal{Z} \equiv \{z_1, \ldots, z_N\}$ and is distributed according to a Markov chain (all trees have exactly the same output, so there is no gain in diversification). Each household can sell any fraction of its trees or buy fractions of new trees, though it cannot sell trees short (i.e., negative holdings are not allowed). Suppose that the price of a tree when the current realization of $z(t)$ is z is given by the function $p : \mathcal{Z} \to \mathbb{R}_+$. There are no other assets to transfer resources across periods.

(a) Show that for a given price function $p(z)$, the flow budget constraint of a representative household can be written as

$$c(t) + p(z(t))x(t + 1) \leq [z(t) + p(z(t))]x(t),$$

where $x(t)$ denotes the tree holdings of the household at time t. Interpret this constraint.

(b) Show that for a given price function $p(z)$, the maximization problem of the representative household subject to the flow budget constraint and the constraints that $c(t) \geq 0$, $x(t) \geq 0$ can be written in a recursive form as follows:

$$V(x, z) = \sup_{y \in [0, p(z)^{-1}(z + p(z))x]} \left\{ u((z + p(z))x - p(z)y) + \beta \mathbb{E}[V(y, z') \mid z] \right\}.$$

(c) Use the results from Section 16.1 to show that $V(x, z)$ is increasing, strictly concave, and differentiable in x (in the interior of its domain).

(d) Derive the stochastic Euler equations for this maximization problem.

(e) Now impose market clearing, which implies that $x(t) = 1$ for all t. Explain why this condition is necessary and sufficient for market clearing.

(f) Under market clearing, derive $p(z)$, the equilibrium prices of trees as a function of the current realization of z.

(g) Now assume that households can also trade a riskless bond (which, in equilibrium, will be in zero net supply). Determine the price of the riskless bond.

16.15 Consider a discrete stochastic version of the investment model from Section 7.8, where a firm maximizes the net present discounted value of its profits, with discount factor given by $(1 + r)^{-1}$ and instantaneous returns given by

$$f(K(t), z(t)) - I(t) - \phi(I(t)).$$

Here $f(K(t), z(t))$ is the revenue or profit of the firm as a function of its capital stock $K(t)$ and a stochastic variable $z(t)$, representing productivity or demand. As in Section 7.8, $I(t)$ is investment, and $\phi(I(t))$ represents adjustment costs.

(a) Assume that $z(t)$ has a distribution represented by a Markov chain. Formulate the sequence version of the maximization problem of the firm.

(b) Formulate the recursive version of the maximization problem of the firm.

(c) Provide conditions under which the two problems have the same solutions.

(d) Derive the stochastic Euler equation for the investment decision of the firm and compare the results to those in Section 7.8.

* 16.16 Consider a general stopping problem, where the objective of the individual is to maximize $\mathbb{E}[\sum_{t=0}^{\infty} \beta^t u(y(t))]$. A random variable $z(t)$ follows a Markov chain, and at any t, the individual can "stop" the process. Let $y(t) = 0$ while the individual has not stopped and $y(t) = z(s)$ if the individual has stopped the process at some $s \leq t$.

(a) Formulate the problem of the individual as a stochastic dynamic programming problem. Provide sufficient conditions for there to exist some R^* such that the individual stops the process at time t if $z(t) \geq R^*$.

(b) Now assume that $z(t)$ has a distribution at time t given by $H(z \mid \zeta(t))$ and $\zeta(t)$ follows a Markov chain with values in the finite set $\mathcal{Z}$. Formulate the problem of the individual as a stochastic dynamic programming problem. Prove that there exists a function $R^* : \mathcal{Z} \to \mathbb{R}_+$ such that the individual stops the process when $z(t) \geq R^*(\zeta(t))$ when the current state is $\zeta(t)$. Explain why the stopping rule is no longer constant. What does this result imply for the job acceptance decisions of unemployed workers studied in Exercise 16.13 when the distribution of wages is different during periods of booms and recessions?

17

Stochastic Growth Models

I n this chapter I present four models of stochastic growth emphasizing different aspects of the interaction between growth and uncertainty. The first is the baseline neoclassical growth model (with complete markets) augmented with stochastic productivity shocks, first studied by Brock and Mirman (1972). This model is not only an important generalization of the baseline neoclassical growth of Chapter 8, but also provides the starting point of the influential *Real Business Cycle* models, which are used extensively for the study of a range of short- and medium-run macroeconomic questions. I present this model and some of its implications in the next three sections. The baseline neoclassical growth model incorporates complete markets in the sense that households and firms can trade using any Arrow-Debreu commodity. In the presence of uncertainty, this implies that a full set of *contingent claims* is traded competitively. For example, a household can buy an asset that pays one unit of the final good after a prespecified history. The presence of complete markets—or the full set of contingent claims—implies that households can fully insure themselves against idiosyncratic risks. The source of interesting uncertainty in these models is aggregate shocks. For this reason, the standard neoclassical growth model under uncertainty does not even introduce idiosyncratic shocks (had they been present, they would have been diversified away).

This discussion shows the importance of contingent claims in the basic neoclassical model under uncertainty. Moreover, trading in contingent claims is not only sufficient, but it is essentially also necessary for the representative household assumption to hold in environments with uncertainty. This result is illustrated in Section 17.4, which considers a model in which households cannot use contingent claims and can only trade in riskless bonds. This model, which builds on Bewley's seminal work in the 1970s and the 1980s, explicitly prevents risk sharing across households and thus features "incomplete markets"—in particular, one of the most relevant types of market incompleteness for macroeconomic questions: preventing the sharing or diversification of idiosyncratic risk. Households face a stochastic stream of labor income and can only achieve consumption smoothing by "self-insurance," that is, by borrowing and lending at a market interest rate. Like the OLG model of Chapter 9, the Bewley model does not admit a representative household. The Bewley model is not only important in illustrating the role of contingent claims in models under uncertainty, but also because it is a tractable model for the study of a range of macroeconomic questions related to risk, income fluctuations, and policy. Consequently over the past decade or so it has become another workhorse model for macroeconomic analysis.

The last two sections, Sections 17.5 and 17.6, turn to stochastic OLG models. The first presents a simple extension of the canonical OLG model that includes stochastic elements.

Section 17.6 shows how stochastic growth models can be useful in understanding the process of takeoff from low growth to sustained growth, which was discussed in Chapter 1. A notable feature of the long-run experience of many societies is that the early stages of economic development were characterized by little growth in income per capita and by frequent economic crises. The process of takeoff not only led to faster growth but also to a more steady (less variable) growth process. An investigation of these issues requires a model of stochastic growth. Section 17.6 presents a model that provides a unified framework for the analysis of the variability of economic performance and takeoff. The key feature is the tradeoff between investment in risky activities and safer activities with lower returns. At the early stages of development, societies do not have enough resources to invest in sufficiently many activities to achieve diversification and are thus forced to bear considerable risk. As a way of reducing this risk, they also invest in low-return safe activities, such as a storage or safe technology and low-yield agricultural products. The result is an equilibrium process that features a lengthy period of slow or no growth associated with high levels of variability in economic performance. An economy can escape this stage of development and take off into sustained growth only when its risky investments are successful for a number of consecutive periods. When this happens, the economy achieves better diversification and also better risk management through more developed financial markets. Better diversification reduces risk and also enables the economy to channel its investments in higher return activities, increasing its productivity and growth rate. Thus this simple model of stochastic growth presents a stylistic account of the process of takeoff from low and variable growth to sustained and steady growth. The model I use to illustrate these ideas features both a simple form of stochastic growth and endogenously incomplete markets. I therefore use this model to show how some simple ideas from Markov processes can be used to characterize the stochastic equilibrium path of a dynamic economy and to highlight potential inefficiencies that can arise in models with endogenous incomplete markets. Finally, this model gives us a first glimpse of the relationship between financial development and economic growth, a topic that is discussed more extensively in Chapter 21.

17.1 The Brock-Mirman Model

The first systematic analysis of economic growth with stochastic shocks was undertaken by Brock and Mirman in their 1972 paper. Brock and Mirman focused on the optimal growth problem and solved for the social planner's maximization problem in a dynamic neoclassical environment with uncertainty. Since, with competitive and complete markets, the First and Second Welfare Theorems still hold, the equilibrium growth path is identical to the optimal growth path. Nevertheless the analysis of equilibrium growth is more involved and also introduces a number of new concepts. I start with the Brock-Mirman approach and then discuss competitive equilibrium growth under uncertainty in the next section.

The economy is similar to the baseline neoclassical growth model studied in Chapters 6 and 8. It is in discrete time, and the aggregate production function is now given by

$$Y(t) = F(K(t), L(t), z(t)), \tag{17.1}$$

where $z(t)$ denotes a stochastic aggregate productivity term affecting how productive a given combination of capital and labor is in producing the unique final good of the economy. Let us suppose that $z(t)$ follows a Markov chain with values in the set $\mathcal{Z} \equiv \{z_1, \ldots, z_N\}$. Many applications of the neoclassical growth model under uncertainty also assume that the stochastic shock is a labor-augmenting productivity term, so that the aggregate production function takes the form $Y(t) = F(K(t), z(t)L(t))$, though for the analysis here, we do not need to impose this additional restriction. Suppose that the production function F satisfies Assumptions 1 and 2 from Chapter 2, and define per capita output and the per capita production function as

$$y(t) \equiv \frac{Y(t)}{L(t)}$$

$$\equiv f(k(t), z(t)),$$

with $k(t) \equiv K(t)/L(t)$ once again corresponding to the capital-labor ratio. A fraction δ of the existing capital stock depreciates at each date. Finally, suppose also that the numbers $z_1, \ldots, z_N$ are arranged in ascending order and that $j > j'$ implies $f(k, z_j) > f(k, z_{j'})$ for all $k \in \mathbb{R}_+$. This assumption implies that higher values of the stochastic shock z correspond to greater productivity at all capital-labor ratios. In addition, let us assume that $z(t)$ follows a monotone Markov chain (as defined in Assumption 16.6), so that a higher value of z today makes higher values in the future more likely.

On the preference side, the economy admits a representative household with instantaneous utility function $u(c)$ that satisfies Assumption 3 in Chapter 8. The representative household supplies one unit of labor inelastically, so that $K(t)$ and $k(t)$ can be used interchangeably. Total consumption $C(t)$ and per capita consumption, here denoted by $c(t)$, are also used interchangeably. Finally, consumption and saving decisions at time t are made after observing the realization of the stochastic shock for time t, $z(t)$.

The sequence version of the social planner's problem of maximizing the expected utility of the representative household can be written as

$$\max \mathbb{E}_0 \sum_{t=0}^{\infty} \beta^t u(c(t)) \tag{17.2}$$

subject to

$$k(t+1) = f(k(t), z(t)) + (1-\delta)k(t) - c(t), \text{ and } k(t) \geq 0, \tag{17.3}$$

with given $k(0) > 0$. The resource constraint (17.3) must hold at each state and for each history of the stochastic shock, z_t (I have not yet introduced the conditioning on the history of these shocks to keep the formulation of the initial problem simple).

To characterize the optimal growth path using the sequence problem we would need to define feasible plans, in particular, the mappings $\tilde{k}[z^t]$ and $\tilde{c}[z^t]$ introduced in the previous chapter, with $z^t \equiv (z(0), \ldots, z(t))$ again standing for the history of (aggregate) shocks up to date t. Rather than going through these steps again, let us directly look at the recursive version of this program, which can be written as

$$V(k, z) = \max_{k' \in [0, f(k,z)+(1-\delta)k]} \left\{ u(f(k, z) + (1-\delta)k - k') + \beta \mathbb{E}[V(k', z') \mid z] \right\}, \tag{17.4}$$

where I used "max" rather than "sup," since this maximization problem does have a solution. In particular, the main theorems from the previous chapter immediately apply to this problem and yield the following result.

Proposition 17.1 *In the stochastic optimal growth problem described above, the value function $V(k, z)$ is uniquely defined, strictly increasing in both of its arguments, strictly concave in k, and differentiable in $k > 0$. Moreover there exists a uniquely defined policy function $\pi(k, z)$ such that the capital stock at date $t + 1$ is given by $k(t + 1) = \pi(k(t), z(t))$.*

Proof. The proof simply involves verifying that Assumptions 16.1–16.6 from the previous chapter are satisfied, so that Theorems 16.1–16.7 can be applied. To do this, first define $\bar{k}$ such that $\bar{k} = f(\bar{k}, z_N) + (1 - \delta)\bar{k}$, and show that starting with $k(0)$, the capital-labor ratio always remains within the compact set $[0, \max\{k(0), \bar{k}\}]$. ∎

In addition, the following proposition can also be established.

Proposition 17.2 *In the stochastic optimal growth problem described above, the policy function for next period's capital stock, $\pi(k, z)$, is strictly increasing in both of its arguments.*

Proof. From Assumption 3, u is differentiable, and from Proposition 17.1, V is differentiable in k. Then for $k > 0$ we have

$$u'(f(k, z) + (1 - \delta)k - k') - \beta\mathbb{E}[V'(k', z') \mid z] = 0,$$

where V' denotes the derivative of the $V(k, z)$ function with respect to its first argument. Since from Proposition 17.1 V is strictly concave in k, this equation can hold when the level of k or z increases only if k' also increases. For example, an increase in k reduces the first term (because u is strictly concave); hence an increase in k' is necessary to increase the first term and to reduce the second term (by the concavity of V). The argument for the implications of an increase in z is similar. ∎

It is also straightforward to derive the stochastic Euler equations corresponding to the neoclassical growth model with uncertainty. For this purpose, let us first define the policy function for consumption as

$$\pi^c(k, z) \equiv f(k, z) + (1 - \delta)k - \pi(k, z),$$

where $\pi(k, z)$ is the optimal policy function for next date's capital stock determined in Proposition 17.1. Using this notation, the stochastic Euler equation can be written as

$$u'(\pi^c(k, z)) = \beta\mathbb{E}\big[(f'(\pi(k, z), z') + (1 - \delta))u'(\pi^c(\pi(k, z), z')) \mid z\big], \qquad (17.5)$$

where f' denotes the derivative of the per capita production function with respect to the capital-labor ratio k. In this form, the Euler equation looks complicated. A slightly different way of expressing this equation makes it both simpler and more intuitive:

$$u'(c(t)) = \beta\mathbb{E}_t\big[p(t + 1)u'(c(t + 1))\big], \qquad (17.6)$$

where $\mathbb{E}_t$ denotes the expectation conditional on information available at time t, and $p(t + 1)$ is the stochastic marginal product of capital (including undepreciated capital) at date $t + 1$. This form of writing the stochastic Euler equation is also useful for comparison with the competitive equilibrium, because $p(t + 1)$ corresponds to the stochastic (date $t + 1$) dividends paid out by one unit of capital invested at time t. Finally, we can also write the transversality condition associated with the optimal plan as

$$\lim_{t \to \infty} \mathbb{E}\big[\beta^t(f'(k(t), z(t)) + (1 - \delta))u'(c(t))k(t) \mid z(0)\big] = 0 \qquad (17.7)$$

given $z(0) \in \mathcal{Z}$, where for notational simplicity I have again used $c(t) = \pi^c(k(t), z(t))$ and $k(t) = \pi(k(t - 1), z(t - 1))$. It is straightforward to verify that Theorem 16.8 applies to this environment and implies that (17.6) and (17.7) are sufficient to characterize the solution to the optimal growth problem specified here.

Although Proposition 17.1 characterizes the form of the value function and policy functions, it has two shortcomings. First, it does not provide us with an analogue of the "Turnpike

Theorem" (see Section 6.8) of the nonstochastic neoclassical growth model. In particular, it does not characterize the long-run behavior of the neoclassical growth model under uncertainty. Second, while the characterization provides a number of qualitative results about the value and the policy functions, it does not deliver comparative static results.

A full analysis of the long-run behavior of the stochastic growth model would take us too far afield into the analysis of Markov processes. Nevertheless a few simple observations are useful to appreciate the salient features of the stochastic law of motion of the capital-labor ratio in this model. The capital stock at date $t + 1$ is given by the policy function π, thus

$$k(t + 1) = \pi \left(k(t), z(t) \right),   \tag{17.8}$$

which defines a general Markov process, since before the realization of $z(t)$, $k(t + 1)$ is a random variable, with its law of motion governed by the last period's value of $k(t)$ and the realization of $z(t)$. If $z(t)$ has a nondegenerate distribution, $k(t)$ does not typically converge to a single value (see Exercise 17.4). Instead, we may hope that it converges to an *invariant limiting distribution*. It can indeed be verified that this is the case. The Markov process (17.8) defines a sufficiently well-behaved stochastic process that, starting with any $k(0)$, it converges to a unique invariant limiting distribution, meaning that when we look at sufficiently faraway horizons, the distribution of k should be independent of $k(0)$. Moreover the average value of $k(t)$ in this invariant limiting distribution is the same as the time average of $\{k(t)\}_{t=0}^{T}$ as $T \to \infty$ (so that the stochastic process for the capital stock is ergodic). Consequently a steady-state equilibrium now corresponds not to specific values of the capital-labor ratio and output per capita but to an invariant limiting distribution. If the stochastic variable $z(t)$ takes values within a sufficiently small set, this limiting invariant distribution would hover around some particular value, which we may wish to refer to as a "quasi-steady-state" value of the capital-labor ratio, because even though the equilibrium capital-labor ratio may not converge to this value, it has a tendency to return to a neighborhood thereof. But in general the range of the limiting distribution could be quite wide.

To obtain a better understanding of the behavior of the neoclassical growth model under uncertainty, I next provide a simple example, which allows us to obtain a closed-form solution for the policy function π.

Example 17.1   *Suppose that $u(c) = \log c$, $F(K, L, z) = zK^\alpha L^{1-\alpha}$, and $\delta = 1$. The stochastic shock z again follows a Markov chain over the set $\mathcal{Z} \equiv \{z_1, \ldots, z_N\}$, with transition probabilities denoted by $q_{jj'}$. Let $k \equiv K/L$. The stochastic Euler equation (17.5) implies that*

$$\frac{1}{zk^\alpha - \pi(k, z)} = \beta \mathbb{E} \left[\left. \frac{\alpha z' \pi(k, z)^{\alpha-1}}{z' \pi(k, z)^\alpha - \pi \left(\pi(k, z), z' \right)} \right| z \right],   \tag{17.9}$$

which is a relatively simple functional equation in a single function $\pi(\cdot, \cdot)$. Though simple, this functional equation would still be difficult to solve unless we had some idea about what the solution looked like. Here, fortunately, the method of "guessing and verifying" the solution of the functional equation becomes handy. Let us conjecture that

$$\pi(k, z) = B_0 + B_1 z k^\alpha.$$

Substituting this guess into (17.9), we obtain

$$\frac{1}{(1 - B_1)zk^\alpha - B_0} = \beta \mathbb{E} \left[\left. \frac{\alpha z'(B_0 + B_1 zk^\alpha)^{\alpha-1}}{z'(B_0 + B_1 zk^\alpha)^\alpha - B_0 - B_1 z'(B_0 + B_1 zk^\alpha)^\alpha} \right| z \right].   \tag{17.10}$$

It is straightforward to check that this equation cannot be satisfied for any $B_0 \neq 0$ (see Exercise 17.5). Thus imposing $B_0 = 0$ and writing out the expectation explicitly with $z = z_{j'}$, (17.10) becomes

$$\frac{1}{(1 - B_1)z_{j'}k^\alpha} = \beta \sum_{j=1}^{N} q_{jj'} \frac{\alpha z_j(B_1 z_{j'}k^\alpha)^{\alpha-1}}{z_j(B_1 z_{j'}k^\alpha)^\alpha - B_1 z_j(B_1 z_{j'}k^\alpha)^\alpha}.$$

Simplifying each term within the summation yields

$$\frac{1}{(1 - B_1)z_{j'}k^\alpha} = \beta \sum_{j=1}^{N} q_{jj'} \frac{\alpha}{B_1(1 - B_1)z_{j'}k^\alpha}.$$

Now taking $z_{j'}$ and k out of the summation and using the fact that, by definition, $\sum_{j=1}^{N} q_{jj'} = 1$, we can cancel the remaining terms and obtain $B_1 = \alpha\beta$, so that regardless of the exact Markov chain for z, the optimal policy rule is

$$\pi(k, z) = \alpha\beta z k^\alpha.$$

The reader can verify that this result is identical to that in Example 6.4 in Chapter 6, with z there corresponding to a nonstochastic productivity term. Thus in this case the stochastic elements have not changed the optimal policy function. Exercise 17.6 shows that the same result applies when z follows a general Markov process rather than a Markov chain.

Using this example, we can fully analyze the stochastic behavior of the capital-labor ratio and output per capita. In fact, the stochastic behavior of the capital-labor ratio in this economy is identical to that of the OLG model analyzed in Section 17.5, and Figure 17.1 in that section applies exactly to this example. A more detailed discussion of these issues is left to Exercise 17.7. Unfortunately, Example 17.1 is one of the few instances where the neoclassical growth model admits closed-form solutions. In particular, if the depreciation rate of the capital stock δ is not equal to 1, the neoclassical growth model under uncertainty does not admit an explicit form characterization (see Exercise 17.8).

17.2 Equilibrium Growth under Uncertainty

Let us now consider the competitive equilibria of the neoclassical growth model under uncertainty. The environment is identical to that in the previous section, and z corresponds to an aggregate productivity shock affecting all production units. We continue to assume that z follows a Markov chain. Defining the Arrow-Debreu commodities in the standard way, so that goods indexed by different realizations of the history z^t correspond to different commodities, this is an economy with a countable infinity of commodities. The Second Welfare Theorem (Theorem 5.7 from Chapter 5) applies and implies that the optimal growth path characterized in the previous section can be decentralized as a competitive equilibrium (see Exercise 17.9). This result justifies the frequent focus on the optimal growth problems in stochastic growth models.

Here I briefly discuss the explicit characterization of competitive equilibria of this economy both to show more explicitly the equivalence between the optimal growth problem and the equilibrium growth problem under complete markets, and also to introduce a number of important ideas related to the pricing of various contingent claims in competitive equilibrium under uncertainty. The complete markets assumption in this context implies that, in principle, any commodity—including any contingent claim—can be traded competitively. Nevertheless, as shown by our analysis in Section 5.8, in practice there is no need to specify or trade all of these commodities, and a subset of the available commodities is sufficient to provide the necessary trading opportunities to households and firms. The analysis in this section also shows which subsets of commodities or contingent claims are typically sufficient to ensure an equilibrium with complete markets. In particular, I first present the characterization of the competitive equilibrium under uncertainty when the full set of commodities are traded and all trades take place at time $t = 0$. I then show how an equivalent characterization of the competitive equilibrium can be obtained with sequential trading and with the help of a smaller set of contingent claims, *the Arrow securities* (recall Section 5.8). In both formulations, the key step in the characterization of the equilibrium is the formulation of the appropriate market clearing conditions and the resulting no-arbitrage conditions.

17.2.1 Competitive Equilibrium with the Full Set of Commodities

Preferences and technology are as in the previous section. Recall that the economy admits a representative household and that the production side of the economy can be represented by a representative firm (Theorem 5.4). Let us first consider the problem of the representative household. This household maximizes the objective function given by (17.2) subject to the lifetime budget constraint (written from the viewpoint of time $t = 0$).

To write the lifetime budget constraint of the household, let $\mathcal{Z}^t$ be the set of all possible histories of the stochastic variable z^t up to date t and $\mathcal{Z}^\infty$ be the set of infinite histories. With a slight abuse of notation, I write $z^t \in \mathcal{Z}^\infty$ to denote a possible history of length t. For any z^t, let $p_0[z^t]$ be the price of the unique final good at time t following history z^t in terms of the final good of date 0. Let $c[z^t]$ be the time t consumption of the household following history z^t. Let $w_0[z^t]$ be the wage rate and thus total labor earnings of the household, in terms of the final good dated 0 following history z^t. Finally, let $R_0[z^t]$ be the price of one unit of capital after the state has been revealed as z^t. Notice that $R_0[\cdot]$ here refers to the price of capital goods, not to the rental price (whereas in the deterministic growth models R was the rental price of capital). This convention is simply for notational convenience and without any substantive implications (see below). Using this notation, the household's lifetime budget constraint can be written as

$$\sum_{t=0}^{\infty} \sum_{z^t \in \mathcal{Z}^\infty} p_0[z^t] c[z^t] \leq \sum_{t=0}^{\infty} \sum_{z^t \in \mathcal{Z}^\infty} w_0[z^t] + R_0[z(0)] k(0). \tag{17.11}$$

Several features about this lifetime budget constraint are worth noting.[1] First and most importantly, there are no expectations. This is because the economy has complete markets, which implies that the household is making all of its (lifetime) trades in the initial period of the economy $t = 0$ at a well-defined price vector for all Arrow-Debreu commodities. Consequently the lifetime budget constraint applies in exactly the same way as a static budget constraint in the standard theory of general equilibrium. More explicitly, the household buys claims to

---

1. Here $c[z^t]$ can be interpreted as a policy mapping from possible histories of the stochastic variable to consumption levels, which was defined as $\tilde{c}[z^t]$ in the previous chapter. I use the simpler expression $c[z^t]$ in this chapter both to simplify notation and also to emphasize the slightly different interpretation of this object in the present context as "contingent claims" on consumption after history z^t placed at date $t = 0$.

different "contingent" consumption bundles. These bundles are contingent in the sense that they are conditioned on the history of the aggregate state variable (stochastic shock) z^t, and thus whether they are realized and delivered depends on the realization of the sequence of the stochastic shock. For example, $c[z^t]$ denotes units of final good allocated to consumption at time t if history z^t is realized. If a different history is realized, then this claim will not be exercised. This way of writing the lifetime budget constraint reiterates the importance of thinking in terms of Arrow-Debreu commodities.

Second, with this interpretation, the left-hand side is simply the total expenditure of the household taking the prices of all possible claims (i.e., the entire set of $p_0[z^t]$s) as given. The right-hand side has a similar interpretation, except that it denotes the labor earnings of the household rather than his expenditures. The last term on the right-hand side, $R_0[z(0)]k(0)$, is the value of the household's initial capital stock (taking the initial state $z(0)$ as given).

Finally, the right-hand side of (17.11) could also include profits accruing to the households (as in Definition 5.1 in Chapter 5). The fact that the aggregate production function exhibits constant returns to scale combined with the presence of competitive markets implies that equilibrium profits are equal to 0. This enables us to omit the additional term for profits in the representative household's budget constraint without loss of generality.

The objective function of the household at time $t = 0$ can also be written somewhat more explicitly as

$$\sum_{t=0}^{\infty} \beta^t \sum_{z^t \in \mathcal{Z}^\infty} q[z^t \mid z^0] u(c[z^t]), \tag{17.12}$$

where $q[z^t \mid z^0]$ is the probability at time 0 that the history z^t will be realized at time t. I have written this in the form of a conditional probability to create continuity between the models that assume all trades take place at date $t = 0$ and the models with sequential trading. Notice that the expectations operator is no longer in this objective function. Instead the explicit summation over all possible events weighted by their probabilities has been introduced.[2]

For the characterization of the competitive equilibrium from the viewpoint of trading at time $t = 0$, it is most convenient to consider the maximization of (17.12) subject to (17.11)—rather than specifying this problem recursively, which is the approach adopted in Section 17.2.2. Assuming an interior solution, the first-order conditions are

$$\beta^t q[z^t \mid z^0] u'(c[z^t]) = \lambda p_0[z^t] \tag{17.13}$$

for all t and all z^t, where λ is the Lagrange multiplier on (17.11) and corresponds to the marginal utility of income at date $t = 0$ (see Exercise 17.11 on why a single multiplier for the lifetime budget constraint is sufficient in this case). Combining this first-order condition for two different histories z^t and $\hat{z}^t$ (for date t) yields

$$\frac{u'(c[\hat{z}^t])}{u'(c[z^t])} = \frac{p_0[\hat{z}^t]/q[\hat{z}^t \mid z^0]}{p_0[z^t]/q[z^t \mid z^0]},$$

---

2. In fact, more generally we could think of the preferences of the representative household as defined over the entire set of commodities, that is, as a functional $U(c[z^t]_{z^t \in \mathcal{Z}^\infty})$. This representation emphasizes that the household is maximizing its utility defined over different commodities, which here correspond to consumption goods at different dates and different states. Equation (17.12) exploits—and emphasizes—the fact that the household has preferences that are additively separable over these different commodities.

which shows that the right-hand side is the relative price of consumption claims conditional on histories z^t and $\hat{z}^t$. Combining this first-order condition for histories z^t and z^{t+1} such that $z^{t+1} = (z^t, z(t+1))$, we obtain

$$\frac{\beta u'(c[z^{t+1}])}{u'(c[z^t])} = \frac{p_0[z^{t+1}]/q[z^{t+1} \mid z^0]}{p_0[z^t]/q[z^t \mid z^0]}, \tag{17.14}$$

so that the right-hand side now corresponds to the contingent interest rate between date t and $t+1$ conditional on z^t (and contingent on the realization of z^{t+1}). While these expressions are intuitive, they cannot be used to characterize equilibrium consumption or investment sequences until we know more about the prices $p_0[z^t]$. We will be able to derive these prices from the profit maximization problem of the representative firm.

Let us next write the value of the firm at date $t = 0$, which takes the form

$$\sum_{t=0}^{\infty} \beta^t \sum_{z^t \in Z^\infty} \big\{ p_0[z^t](F(K^e[z^t], L[z^t], z(t)) $$

$$+ (1-\delta)K^e[z^t]) - R_0[z^t]K^e[z^t] - w_0[z^t]L[z^t] \big\},$$

where recall that $R_0[z^t]$ is the price of capital and $w_0[z^t]$ is the wage rate conditional on history z^t, and $K^e[z^t]$ and $L[z^t]$ are the capital and labor employment levels, respectively, of the representative firm after history z^t. The superscript "e" is introduced specifically to emphasize that $K^e[z^t]$ refers to capital employed by the firm after history z^t (and not to capital that is saved by the households after history z^t). Profit maximization by the firm implies that

$$p_0[z^t] \left(\frac{\partial F(K^e[z^t], L[z^t], z(t))}{\partial K^e} + (1-\delta) \right) = R_0[z^t],$$

$$p_0[z^t] \frac{\partial F(K^e[z^t], L[z^t], z(t))}{\partial L} = w_0[z^t].$$

Using constant returns to scale and expressing everything in per capita terms, these first-order conditions can be written as

$$p_0[z^t](f'(k^e[z^t], z(t)) + (1-\delta)) = R_0[z^t], \tag{17.15}$$

$$p_0[z^t](f(k^e[z^t], z(t)) - k^e[z^t]f'(k^e[z^t], z(t))) = w_0[z^t],$$

where f' denotes the derivative of the per capita production function with respect to the capital-labor ratio, $k^e \equiv K^e/L$. The first equation relates the price of the final good to the price of capital goods and to the marginal productivity of capital, while the second equation determines the wage rate in terms of the price of the final good and the marginal (physical) product of labor. Equation (17.15) can also be interpreted as stating that the price of a unit of capital good after history z^t, $R_0[z^t]$, is equal to the value of the dividends paid out by this unit of capital inclusive of undepreciated capital (i.e., the price of the final good, $p_0[z^t]$) times the marginal product of capital $f'(k^e[z^t] z(t))$ plus the $(1-\delta)$ fraction of the capital that is not depreciated and paid back to the holder of the capital good in terms of date t final good. An alternative way of formulating the competitive equilibrium and writing (17.15) is to assume that capital goods are rented—not purchased—by firms, thus introducing a rental price sequence for capital goods. Exercise 17.12 shows that this alternative formulation leads to identical results. This is not surprising because, with complete markets, buying one unit of capital today and selling contingent claims on $1 - \delta$ units of capital tomorrow is equivalent to renting. Whether one uses the formulation in which capital goods are purchased or rented by firms is then just a matter of convenience and emphasis.

The key step in the characterization of a competitive equilibrium is the specification of the set of market clearing conditions. For labor, this is straightforward and requires

$$L[z^t] = 1 \quad \text{for all } z^t. \tag{17.16}$$

To write the market clearing condition for capital, recall that per capita production after history z^t is given by $f(k^e[z^t] z(t)) + (1 - \delta)k^e[z^t]$, and this is divided between consumption $c[z^t]$ and savings $k[z^t]$. The capital used at time $t + 1$ (after history z^{t+1}) must be equal to $k[z^t]$, since this is the amount of capital available at the beginning of date $t + 1$. Market clearing for capital therefore implies that for any $z^{t+1} = (z^t, z(t + 1))$,

$$k^e[z^{t+1}] = k[z^t], \tag{17.17}$$

because the amount of available capital at time t is fixed regardless of the realization of $z(t + 1)$. The capital market clearing condition can then be written as

$$c[z^t] + k[z^t] \leq f(k[z^{t-1}], z(t)) + (1 - \delta)k[z^{t-1}] \tag{17.18}$$

for any $z^{t+1} = (z^t, z(t + 1))$.

The *no-arbitrage* conditions that are essential in the characterization of the competitive equilibrium, which link the price of capital conditional on z^{t+1} ($R_0[z^{t+1}]$) to the price of the final good at time t ($p_0[z^t]$), are then directly implied by the capital market clearing conditions. In particular, consider the following *riskless arbitrage;* the household buys one unit of the final good after history z^t and saves it to be used as capital at time $t + 1$.[3] It simultaneously sells claims on capital goods for each $z^{t+1} = (z^t, z(t + 1))$. These combined transactions carry no risk, since the one unit of the final good bought after history z^t covers the obligation to pay one unit of capital good after any history $z^{t+1} = (z^t, z(t + 1))$. Consequently, this transaction should not make or lose money, which implies the no-arbitrage condition

$$p_0[z^t] = \sum_{z(t+1) \in \mathcal{Z}} R_0[(z^t, z(t + 1))]. \tag{17.19}$$

A *competitive equilibrium* is defined in a standard manner as feasible policies determining consumption, saving, and capital levels, $\{c[z^t], k[z^t], k^e[z^{t+1}]\}_{z^t \in \mathcal{Z}^t}$, and price sequences, $\{p_0[z^t], R_0[z^t], w_0[z^t]\}_{z^t \in \mathcal{Z}^t}$, such that households maximize utility (i.e., satisfy (17.13)), firms maximize profits (i.e., satisfy (17.15) and (17.19)), and labor and capital markets clear (i.e., (17.16), (17.17), and (17.18) are satisfied).

---

3. This assumes that households can themselves save current output to be used as capital at the next date. Since goods dated t and $t + 1$ are different Arrow-Debreu commodities, one might alternatively introduce firms that transform goods dated t into goods dated $t + 1$, and in this case, the no-arbitrage condition would correspond to the profit maximization condition of these firms. Whether or not these firms are introduced has no implications for the rest of the analysis.

To characterize the equilibrium path, let us substitute from (17.15) and (17.19) into the first-order condition for consumption given by (17.13) and rearrange to obtain

$$u'(c[z^t]) = \sum_{z(t+1)\in\mathcal{Z}} \frac{\lambda p_0[z^{t+1}]}{\beta^t q[z^t \mid z^0]}(f'(k[z^t], z(t+1)) + (1-\delta)). \tag{17.20}$$

Using (17.13) for $t+1$, we also have

$$\beta u'(c[z^{t+1}]) = \frac{\lambda p_0[z^{t+1}]}{\beta^t q[z^{t+1} \mid z^0]} \tag{17.21}$$

$$= \frac{\lambda p_0[z^{t+1}]}{\beta^t q[z^{t+1} \mid z^t] q[z^t \mid z^0]},$$

where the second line simply uses the fact that, by the law of iterated expectations, $q[z^{t+1} \mid z^0] = q[z^{t+1} \mid z^t]q[z^t \mid z^0]$. Substituting this into (17.20) gives

$$u'(c[z^t]) = \beta \sum_{z(t+1)\in\mathcal{Z}} q[z^{t+1} \mid z^t](f'(k[z^t], z(t+1)) + (1-\delta))u'(c[z^{t+1}])$$

$$= \beta\mathbb{E}[(f'(k[z^t], z(t+1)) + (1-\delta))u'(c[z^{t+1}]) \mid z^t] \tag{17.22}$$

which is identical to (17.6). Since from Theorem 16.8, the stochastic Euler equation (17.6) and the transversality condition (17.7) are sufficient for optimal growth, the equivalence between optimal and equilibrium growth under uncertainty follows by observing that the lifetime budget constraint (17.11) and the transversality condition of the representative household imply (17.7).

To establish this claim, first note that, with an argument similar to that in Section 8.6 of Chapter 8, the lifetime budget constraint of the representative household (17.11) is equivalent to

$$\lim_{t\to\infty}\left[\sum_{z^{t-1}\in\mathcal{Z}^{t-1}} p_0[z^{t-1}]k[z^{t-1}]\right] \geq 0. \tag{17.23}$$

Here $k[z^{t-1}]$ denotes the asset (capital) holdings of the representative household after history z^{t-1}, and $p_0[z^{t-1}]$ is the price of the final good after this history. If this expression were negative, the household would be accumulating debt and violating the stochastic equivalent of the no-Ponzi condition (and thus (17.11)). Moreover the transversality condition of the household (or local nonsatiation) implies that (17.23) must hold as equality. Now combining this with (17.21) for $t-1$ and noting that $\lambda > 0$, we obtain

$$\lim_{t\to\infty}\left[\beta^{t-1}\sum_{z^{t-1}\in\mathcal{Z}^{t-1}} q[z^{t-1} \mid z^0]u'(c[z^{t-1}])k[z^{t-1}]\right] = 0.$$

Next using (17.22) and the fact that $q[z^t \mid z^0] = q[z^t \mid z^{t-1}]q[z^{t-1} \mid z^0]$, this equation can be written as

$$\lim_{t \to \infty} \left[\beta^t \sum_{z^t \in \mathcal{Z}^t} q[z^t \mid z^0](f'(k[z^{t-1}], z(t)) + (1 - \delta)) \, u'(c[z^t])k[z^{t-1}] \right] = 0,$$

which is identical to (17.7). This establishes the following proposition.

Proposition 17.3 *In the above-described economy, optimal and competitive growth paths coincide.*

Proof. See Exercise 17.13. ∎

17.2.2 Competitive Equilibrium with Sequential Trading

Complementary insights can be obtained by considering the equilibrium problem in its equivalent form with sequential trading and using the appropriate Arrow securities rather than all trades taking place at the initial date $t = 0$. To do this, we write the budget constraint of the representative household somewhat differently. First, normalize the price of the final good at each date to 1 (recall the discussion in Section 5.8 in Chapter 5). The $a[z^t]$s now correspond to (basic) Arrow securities that pay out only in specific states on nature. More explicitly, $a[z^t]$ denotes the assets of the household in terms of the final good at date t conditional on history z^t. We interpret $\{a[z^t]\}_{z^t \in \mathcal{Z}^t}$ as a set of contingent claims that the household has purchased that pay $a[z^t]$ units of the final good at date t when history z^t is realized. We also denote the price of a claim to one unit of $a[z^t]$ at time $t - 1$ after history z^{t-1} by $\bar{p}[z(t) \mid z^{t-1}]$, where naturally $z^t = (z^{t-1}, z(t))$. The amount of these claims purchased by the household is denoted directly by the amount that these claims will pay out, $a[(z^{t-1}, z(t))]$. Consequently, the flow budget constraint of the household can be written as

$$c[z^t] + \sum_{z(t+1) \in \mathcal{Z}} \bar{p}[z(t + 1) \mid z^t] \, a[(z^t, z(t + 1))] \le w[z^t] + a[z^t],$$

where $w[z^t]$ is the equilibrium wage rate after history z^t in terms of final goods dated t, so the right-hand side is the total amount of resources available to the household after history z^t, which is spent on consumption, $c[z^t]$, and for purchasing contingent claims to the final good at the next date, $a[(z^t, z(t + 1))]$. The total expenditure on these claims is equal to $\sum_{z(t+1) \in \mathcal{Z}} \bar{p}[z(t + 1) \mid z^t] a[(z^t, z(t + 1))]$.

With this formulation, we can once again write the sequence version of the optimization problem of the household. To save space, let us directly go to the recursive formulation, leaving the sequence version of the problem with sequential trading to Exercise 17.14.

Preparing for the recursive formulation, let a denote the current asset holdings of the household (in terms of the notation above, you can think of this as the realization of the current assets after some history z^t). Then the flow budget constraint of the household can be written as

$$c + \sum_{z' \in \mathcal{Z}} \bar{p}[z' \mid z] \, a'[z' \mid z] \le w + a,$$

where $\bar{p}[z' \mid z]$ summarizes the prices of contingent claims (for next date's state z' given current state z), and $a'[z' \mid z]$ denotes the corresponding asset holdings. Let $V(a, z)$ be the value function of the household when it holds a units of the final good as assets, and the current realization of the stochastic variable is z. The choice variables of the household are contingent asset holdings for the next date, denoted by $a'[z' \mid z]$, and consumption today, denoted by $c[a, z]$. Let us also denote by $q[z' \mid z]$ the probability that next period's stochastic variable is equal to z' conditional on today's value being z. Then, taking the sequence of equilibrium prices $\bar{p}$ as given, the value function of the representative household is

$$V(a, z) = \max_{\{a'[z'|z]\}_{z' \in \mathcal{Z}}} \left\{ u\left(a + w - \sum_{z' \in \mathcal{Z}} \bar{p}[z' \mid z] a'[z' \mid z]\right) \right.$$

$$\left. + \beta \sum_{z' \in \mathcal{Z}} q[z' \mid z] V(a'[z' \mid z], z') \right\}. \tag{17.24}$$

Theorems 16.1–16.7 can again be applied to this value function (see Exercise 17.15). The first-order condition for current consumption can now be written as

$$\bar{p}[z' \mid z] u'(c[a, z]) = \beta q[z' \mid z] \frac{\partial V(a'[z' \mid z], z')}{\partial a} \tag{17.25}$$

for any $z' \in \mathcal{Z}$, with $c[a, z]$ denoting the optimal consumption conditional on asset holdings a and stochastic variable z.

The key to the characterization of the equilibrium is again the capital market clearing condition. Let us denote the amount of savings of the representative household given the current value of z by $k[z]$, which is decided before next period's stochastic shock z' is realized. Capital market clearing requires that

$$a'[z' \mid z] = R[z' \mid z] k[z] \tag{17.26}$$

for all $z' \in \mathcal{Z}$. In other words, in the aggregate, the same amount of savings will be present in all states at the next date, and thus the total claims to the final good in state z' given last period's state z must simply be given by this amount of savings multiplied by the price of capital $R[z' \mid z]$.

The capital market clearing condition (17.26) again provides the key no-arbitrage condition, which now takes the form

$$\sum_{z' \in \mathcal{Z}} \bar{p}[z' \mid z] R[z' \mid z] = 1, \tag{17.27}$$

where $R[z' \mid z]$ is the price of capital goods when the current state is z' and last period's state was z. Intuitively, the cost of one unit of the final good now, which is 1, has to be equal to the return that the household obtains by saving this good to be used as capital next period. When tomorrow's state is z', the gross rate of return in terms of tomorrow's goods is $R[z' \mid z]$, and the relative price of tomorrow's goods in terms of today's goods is $\bar{p}[z' \mid z]$. Summing over all possible states z' tomorrow must then have a total return of 1 to ensure no arbitrage (see Exercise 17.16). Let us now combine (17.25) with the Envelope condition,

$$\frac{\partial V(a, z)}{\partial a} = u'(c[a, z]),$$

and then multiply both sides of (17.25) by $R[z' \mid z]$ and sum over all $z' \in \mathcal{Z}$ to obtain the first-order condition of the household as

$$u'(c[a, z]) = \beta \sum_{z' \in \mathcal{Z}} q[z' \mid z] R[z' \mid z] u'(c[a', z']).$$

$$= \beta \mathbb{E}[R[z' \mid z] u'(c[a', z']) \mid z],$$

which is identical to (17.6). A similar argument to that in Section 17.2.1 establishes that the transversality condition of the optimal growth problem, (17.7), is again satisfied in the competitive equilibrium. Consequently the approach based on sequential trading also leads to a competitive equilibrium allocation identical to the solution to the optimal growth problem.

The analysis in Sections 17.2.1 and 17.2.2 illustrates the equivalence between the optimal growth problem (under uncertainty) and the competitive equilibrium allocation (with a complete set of markets). Given this equivalence, also implied directly by the Second Welfare Theorem (Theorem 5.7), and the fact that the former problem is considerably simpler, much of the literature focuses on the optimal growth problem rather than the explicit characterization of the competitive equilibrium under uncertainty. The (stochastic) equilibrium paths of the real variables are obtained from this optimal growth problem, and equilibrium prices are given by the Lagrange multipliers. For example, the prices of capital goods, the $R[z' \mid z]$s, which also give the key intertemporal prices, are given by (17.5) and (17.6) as the marginal product of capital in the optimal growth path.

17.3 Application: Real Business Cycle Models

One of the most important applications of the neoclassical growth model under uncertainty over the past 25 years has been to the analysis of short- and medium-run fluctuations. The approach, pioneered by Kydland and Prescott's seminal (1982) paper and referred to as the *Real Business Cycle* (RBC) theory, uses the neoclassical growth model with aggregate productivity shocks in order to provide a framework for the analysis of macroeconomic fluctuations. The Real Business Cycle (RBC) theory has been one of the most active research areas of macroeconomics in the 1990s and also one of the most controversial. On the one hand, its conceptual simplicity and relative success in matching certain moments of employment, consumption, and investment fluctuations for a given (appropriately chosen) sequence of aggregate productivity shocks have attracted a large following. On the other hand, the absence of monetary factors and demand shocks, the traditional pillars of Keynesian economics and previous research on macroeconomic fluctuations, has generated a ferocious opposition and much debate on the merits of this theory. The merits of the RBC theory are not relevant for our focus here and would take us too far afield from the key questions of economic growth. Nevertheless a brief exposition of the canonical RBC model is useful for two purposes. First, it constitutes one of the most important applications of the neoclassical growth model under uncertainty and has become one of the workhorse models for macroeconomic research over the past 25 years. Second, it illustrates how the introduction of labor supply choices into the neoclassical growth model under uncertainty generates new insights. So far I have assumed, except in Exercise 8.33 in Chapter 8, that labor is supplied inelastically. Because the issue of labor supply is central to a number of questions in macroeconomics, a brief analysis of the neoclassical growth model with labor supply is also useful.

The environment is identical to that in Sections 17.1 and 17.2, with the only difference being that the instantaneous utility function of the representative household now takes the form

$$u(C, L),$$

where C denotes consumption and L labor supply. I use uppercase letters for consistency with what comes below. I assume that u is jointly concave and differentiable in both of its arguments and is strictly increasing in C and strictly decreasing in L. I also assume that L lies in some convex compact set $[0, \bar{L}]$.

Given the equivalence between the optimal growth and competitive equilibrium allocations, I focus on the optimal growth formulation, which is the maximization of

$$\mathbb{E} \sum_{t=0}^{\infty} \beta^t u(C(t), L(t))$$

subject to the flow resource constraint

$$K(t+1) \leq F(K(t), L(t), z(t)) + (1 - \delta)K(t) - C(t),$$

where the aggregate productivity shock $z(t)$ again follows a monotone Markov chain.

The social planner's problem can be written recursively as

$$V(K, z) = \sup_{\substack{L \in [0, \bar{L}] \\ K' \in [0, F(K, L, z) + (1-\delta)K]}} \left\{ u(F(K, L, z) + (1 - \delta)K - K', L) + \beta \mathbb{E}[V(K', z') \mid z] \right\}.$$

$$(17.28)$$

The following proposition is once again a direct consequence of Theorems 16.1–16.7.

Proposition 17.4 *The value function $V(K, z)$ defined in (17.28) is continuous and strictly concave in K, strictly increasing in K and z, and differentiable in $K > 0$. There exist unique policy functions $\pi^k(K, z)$ and $\pi^l(K, z)$ that determine the capital stock for the next period and labor supply today as functions of the current capital stock K and the stochastic variable z.*

Proof. See Exercise 17.17. ∎

Under the assumption that an interior solution exists, the relevant prices can be obtained from the appropriate multipliers, and standard first-order conditions characterize the form of the equilibrium. In particular, the two key first-order conditions determine the evolution of consumption over time and the equilibrium level of labor supply. Denoting the derivatives of the u function with respect to its first and second arguments by u_c and u_l, respectively, the derivatives of the F function by F_k and F_l, and defining the policy function for consumption as

$$\pi^c(K, z) \equiv F(K, \pi^l(K, z), z) + (1 - \delta)K - \pi^k(K, z),$$

these first-order conditions take the form

$$u_c(\pi^c(K, z), \pi^l(K, z))$$

$$= \beta \mathbb{E}\left[R(\pi^k(K, z), z') u_c(\pi^c(\pi^k(K, z), z'), \pi^l(\pi^k(K, z), z')) \mid z\right],$$

$$w(K, z) u_c(\pi^c(K, z), \pi^l(K, z))$$

$$= -u_l(\pi^c(K, z), \pi^l(K, z)), \tag{17.29}$$

where

$$R(K, z) = F_k(K, \pi^l(K, z), z) + (1 - \delta), \text{ and } w(K, z) = F_l(K, \pi^l(K, z), z)$$

denote the gross rate of return to capital and the equilibrium wage rate respectively. Notice that the first condition in (17.29) is essentially identical to (17.5), whereas the second is a static condition determining the level of equilibrium (or optimal) labor supply. The second condition does not feature expectations, since it is conditional on the current value of the capital stock K and the current realization of the aggregate productivity variable z.

Why is this framework useful for the analysis of macroeconomic fluctuations? The answer lies in the fact that estimates of TFP, along the lines described in Chapter 3, indicate that it is procyclical—that is, it fluctuates considerably and is higher in periods during which output is above trend and unemployment is low. So let us think of a period in which z is low. Clearly, if there is no offsetting change in labor supply, output is low, so we can think of this period as a "recession." Moreover, under standard assumptions, the wage rate $w(K, z)$ and equilibrium labor supply declines.[4] Thus there is low employment as well as low output. Thus a negative productivity shock generates two of the important characteristics of a recessionary period. In addition, if the Markov chain (or more generally the Markov process) governing the behavior of z exhibits persistence, output will be low the following period as well, so output and employment exhibit *persistent fluctuations*. Finally, provided that the aggregate production function $F(K, L, z)$ takes a form such that low output is also associated with low marginal product of capital, the expectation of future low output will typically reduce savings and thus future levels of capital stock (though this depends on the form of the utility function, which regulates the desire for consumption smoothing and the balance between income and substitution effects).

This brief discussion suggests that the neoclassical growth model with aggregate productivity shocks and labor supply choices generates some of the major qualitative features of the business cycle. The RBC literature argues that this model, under suitable assumptions, also generates the major quantitative features, such as the correlations between output, investment, and employment. The bulk of the RBC debate focuses on: (1) whether the model indeed matches these moments in the data, (2) whether these are the right empirical objects to look at (e.g., as opposed to persistence in employment or output at different frequencies), and

---

4. There is no agreement as to whether wages are indeed procyclical. Average wages do not seem to be procyclical over the business cycle, but this may be because of selection bias, the fact that the composition of the labor force changes over the business cycle as those who lose their jobs during recessions are typically different from the average worker. Depending on how one corrects for this potential source of bias, wages appear to be either mildly procyclical or acyclical. See, for example, Bils (1985); Solon, Barsky, and Parker (1994); and Abraham and Haltiwanger (1995).

(3) whether a framework in which the driving force of fluctuations is exogenous changes in aggregate productivity is sidestepping the more interesting question of why there are shocks that cause recessions. It is fair to say that, while the RBC debate is not as active today as it was in the 1990s, there has not been a complete agreement on these questions. In the meantime, many extensions of the standard RBC model have improved over the bare-bones version presented here.

The model presented here considers the neoclassical growth model without exogenous technological progress. Exercise 17.18 introduces exogenous technological progress into this model and shows that the analysis is essentially unchanged. The next example considers a very simple case of the RBC model that can be solved in closed form (though the price of doing so is that some of the interesting features of the model are lost).

Example 17.2 *Consider an example economy similar to that studied in Example 17.1. In particular, suppose that $u(C, L) = \log C - \gamma L$, $F(K, L, z) = zK^\alpha L^{1-\alpha}$, and $\delta = 1$. Productivity z follows a monotone Markov chain over the set $\mathcal{Z} \equiv \{z_1, \ldots, z_N\}$, with transition probabilities denoted by $q_{jj'}$. As in the previous example, let us conjecture that*

$$\pi^k(K, z) = BzK^\alpha L^{1-\alpha}.$$

The stochastic Euler equation for consumption (17.29) then implies that

$$\frac{1}{(1-B)zK^\alpha L^{1-\alpha}} = \beta \mathbb{E}\left[\left. \frac{\alpha z'(BzK^\alpha L^{1-\alpha})^{-(1-\alpha)}(L')^{1-\alpha}}{(1-B)z'(BzK^\alpha L^{1-\alpha})^\alpha (L')^{1-\alpha}} \right| z \right],$$

where L' denotes next period's labor supply. Canceling constants within the expectations and taking terms that do not involve z' out of the expectations, this equation simplifies to

$$\frac{1}{zK^\alpha L^{1-\alpha}} = \beta \mathbb{E}\left[\left. \alpha (BzK^\alpha L^{1-\alpha})^{-1} \right| z \right],$$

which yields $B = \alpha\beta$. The resulting policy function for the capital stock is therefore

$$\pi^k(K, z) = \alpha\beta zK^\alpha L^{1-\alpha},$$

which is identical to that in Example 17.1. Next, the first-order condition for labor implies that

$$\frac{(1-\alpha)zK^\alpha L^{-\alpha}}{(1-B)zK^\alpha L^{1-\alpha}} = \gamma.$$

The resulting policy function for labor can be obtained as

$$\pi^l(K, z) = \frac{(1-\alpha)}{\gamma(1-\alpha\beta)},$$

which implies that labor supply is constant. This is because with the logarithmic preferences here, the income and substitution effects cancel out; thus the increase in wages induced by a change in aggregate productivity has no effect on labor supply. Exercise 17.19 shows that the same result obtains when the utility function takes the form of $u(C, L) = \log C + h(L)$ for some decreasing and concave function h. Overall, this simple version of the RBC model therefore generates positive covariation between output, consumption, and investment, but it does not lead to labor fluctuations.

17.4 Growth with Incomplete Markets: The Bewley Model

I now turn to a fundamentally different model of economic growth, where the economy does not admit a representative household, and idiosyncratic risks are not diversified. This model was first introduced and studied by Truman Bewley (1977, 1980). It has subsequently been revived, extended, and applied to a variety of new questions, including the structure of optimal fiscal policy, business cycle fluctuations, and asset pricing in Aiyagari (1994) and Krusell and Smith (1998, 2005). Many economists believe that, to a first approximation, such a structure provides a better approximation to reality than the complete markets neoclassical growth model. Unfortunately, this model, which is often referred to as the "Bewley economy," is considerably more complicated than the baseline neoclassical growth model. Moreover, as discussed below, the assumption that there is no insurance for individual income fluctuations—except through self-insurance, that is, the process of accumulating assets to be used on a rainy day—is extreme and may limit the applications of the current model in the growth context.

The economy is populated by a continuum 1 of households, and the set of households is denoted by $\mathcal{H}$. Each household has preferences given by (17.2) and supplies labor inelastically. Suppose also that the second derivative of this utility function, $u''(\cdot)$, is increasing. In contrast to the baseline neoclassical growth model, the efficiency units that each household supplies vary over time. In particular, each household $h \in \mathcal{H}$ has a labor endowment of $z^h(t)$ at time t, where $z^h(t)$ is an independent draw from the set $\mathcal{Z} \equiv [z_{min}, z_{max}]$ $(0 < z_{min} < z_{max} < \infty)$, so that the minimum labor endowment is z_{min}. Suppose that the labor endowment of each household is identically and independently distributed with distribution function $G(z)$ defined over $[z_{min}, z_{max}]$.

The production side of the economy is the same as in the canonical neoclassical growth model under certainty and is represented by an aggregate production function satisfying Assumptions 1 and 2 (see Chapter 2), as in (17.1). The only difference is that $L(t)$ is now the sum (integral) of the heterogeneous labor endowments of all agents and is written as

$$L(t) = \int_{h \in \mathcal{H}} z^h(t)dh.$$

Appealing to a law of large numbers–type argument, $L(t)$ is constant at each date and can be normalized to 1. Thus output per capita in the economy can be expressed as

$$y(t) = f(k(t)),$$

with $k(t) = K(t)$. Notice that there is no longer any aggregate productivity shock. The only source of uncertainty is idiosyncratic (at the individual household level). Consequently, while households experience fluctuations in their labor income and consumption, we can imagine a *stationary* equilibrium in which aggregates are constant over time. Throughout this section I focus on such a stationary equilibrium. In particular, in a stationary equilibrium the wage rate w and the gross rate of return on capital R are constant (though of course their levels are determined endogenously to ensure equilibrium). Let us first take these prices as given and look at the behavior of a typical household $h \in \mathcal{H}$ (I am using the language "typical" household, since, though not representative, this household faces an identical problem to all other households in the economy). This household solves the following maximization problem: maximize (17.2) subject to the flow budget constraint

$$a^h(t+1) \leq Ra^h(t) + wz^h(t) - c^h(t)$$

for all t, where $a^h(t)$ is the asset holding of household $h \in \mathcal{H}$ at time t. Consumption cannot be negative, so $c^h(t) \geq 0$. In addition, though we do not impose any exogenous borrowing constraints, with the same reasoning as in the model of the permanent income hypothesis (see Section 16.5.1 in the previous chapter), the requirement that the household should satisfy its lifetime budget constraint in all histories imposes the endogenous borrowing constraint

$$a^h(t) \geq -\frac{z_{\min}}{R-1} \equiv -b \qquad (17.30)$$

for all t (see Exercise 17.20). We can then write the maximization problem of household $h \in \mathcal{H}$ recursively as

$$V^h(a, z) = \max_{a' \in [-b, Ra+wz]} \left\{ u(Ra + wz - a') + \beta \mathbb{E}[V^h(a', z') \mid z] \right\}. \qquad (17.31)$$

Standard arguments then establish the following proposition.

Proposition 17.5 *The value function $V^h(a, z)$ defined in (17.31) is uniquely defined, continuous, and strictly concave in a; strictly increasing in a and z; and differentiable in $a \in (-b, Ra + wz)$. Moreover the policy function that determines next period's asset holding $\pi(a, z)$ is uniquely defined, continuous in a, and nondecreasing in a and z.*

Proof.   See Exercise 17.21.   ∎

The total amount of capital stock in the economy can be obtained by aggregating the asset holdings of all households in the economy; thus in a stationary equilibrium we have

$$k(t + 1) = \int_{h \in \mathcal{H}} a^h(t) dh$$

$$= \int_{h \in \mathcal{H}} \pi(a^h(t), z^h(t)) dh.$$

This equation integrates over all households, taking their asset holdings and the realization of their stochastic shock as given. It states that both the average of current asset holdings and also the average of tomorrow's asset holdings must be equal by the definition of a stationary equilibrium. To understand this condition, recall that, as in the neoclassical growth model, the policy function $a' = \pi(a, z)$ defines a Markov process. Under fairly weak assumptions this Markov process admits a unique invariant distribution. If this were not the case, the economy could have multiple stationary equilibria or there might even be problems of nonexistence. For our purposes here, we can ignore this complication and assume the existence of a unique invariant distribution, which is denoted by $\Gamma(a)$, so that the stationary equilibrium capital-labor ratio is given by

$$k^* = \int \int \pi(a, z) d\Gamma(a) dG(z),$$

which uses the fact that z is distributed identically and independently across households and over time.

Turning to the production side, factor prices are the same as in the neoclassical growth model under certainty, that is,

$$R = f'(k^*) + (1 - \delta), \text{ and } w = f(k^*) - k^* f'(k^*).$$

Recall from Chapters 6 and 8 that the neoclassical growth model with complete markets and no uncertainty implies that there exists a unique steady state in which $\beta R = 1$, that is,

$$f'(k^{**}) = \beta^{-1} - (1 - \delta), \tag{17.32}$$

where k^{**} refers to the capital-labor ratio of the neoclassical growth model under certainty.

In the Bewley economy, (17.32) is no longer true.

Proposition 17.6 *In any stationary equilibrium of the Bewley economy, the stationary equilibrium capital-labor ratio k^* is such that*

$$f'(k^*) < \beta^{-1} - (1 - \delta), \tag{17.33}$$

and

$$k^* > k^{**}, \tag{17.34}$$

where k^{**} is the capital-labor ratio of the neoclassical growth model under certainty.

Proof. Suppose $f'(k^*) \geq \beta^{-1} - (1 - \delta)$. Then the result in Exercise 16.11 from the previous chapter implies that each household's expected consumption is strictly increasing. Thus average consumption in the population, which is deterministic, is strictly increasing and would tend to infinity. This is not possible in view of Assumption 2, which implies that aggregate resources must always be finite. This argument establishes (17.33). Given this result, (17.34) immediately follows from (17.32) and from the strict concavity of $f(\cdot)$ (Assumption 1). ∎

Intuitively, the interest rate in the incomplete markets economy is depressed relative to the neoclassical growth model with certainty because each household has an additional self-insurance, or precautionary, incentive to save. These additional savings increase the capital-labor ratio and reduce the equilibrium interest rate. Interestingly, therefore, the Bewley economy, like the OLG model of Chapter 9, leads to a higher capital intensity of production than the standard neoclassical growth model. Observe that in both cases, the lack of a representative household plays an important role in this result.

While the Bewley model is an important workhorse for macroeconomic analysis, two of its features may be viewed as potential shortcomings. First, as already remarked in the context of the OLG model, the source of inefficiency coming from overaccumulation of capital is unlikely to be important for explaining income per capita differences across countries. Thus the Bewley model is not interesting because of the greater capital-labor ratio that it generates. Instead it is important as an illustration of how an economy might exhibit a stationary equilibrium in which aggregates are constant while households have uncertain and fluctuating consumption and income profiles. It also emphasizes the role of idiosyncratic risks in the context of the neoclassical growth model. Issues of individual risk bearing are important in the context of economic development as shown in Section 17.6 below and also in Chapter 21. Second, the incomplete markets assumption in this model may be extreme. In practice, when their incomes are low, households may receive transfers, either because they have entered into some form of private insurance or because of government-provided social insurance. Instead the current model exogenously assumes that there are no insurance possibilities. Models in which the lack of insurance opportunities are derived from microfoundations (e.g., from moral hazard or adverse selection) or models in which the set of active markets is determined endogenously would be more satisfactory. While models of limited insurance due to moral hazard or adverse selection are beyond the scope of this book, I present an economic growth model with endogenously incomplete markets in Section 17.6.

17.5 The Overlapping Generations Model with Uncertainty

Let us now briefly consider a stochastic version of the canonical OLG model from Section 9.3 in Chapter 9. Time is discrete and runs to infinity. Each household lives for two periods. Suppose as in Section 9.3 that the utility of a household in generation t is given by

$$U_t\left(c_1(t), c_2(t+1)\right) = \log c_1(t) + \beta \log c_2(t+1). \tag{17.35}$$

There is a constant rate of population growth equal to n, so that

$$L(t) = (1+n)^t L(0), \tag{17.36}$$

where $L(0)$ is the size of the first generation. As in Section 9.3, the aggregate production technology is Cobb-Douglas but now also includes an aggregate stochastic shock z, which is assumed to follow a Markov process. Consequently total output at time t is given by

$$Y(t) = z(t) K(t)^\alpha L(t)^{1-\alpha}.$$

Expressing this in per capita terms yields $y(t) = z(t)k(t)^\alpha$. To simplify the notation, suppose also that capital depreciates fully ($\delta = 1$). Factor prices clearly only depend on the current values of z and the capital-labor ratio k:

$$R(k, z) = \alpha z k^{\alpha-1}, \quad \text{and} \quad w(k, z) = (1-\alpha) z k^\alpha. \tag{17.37}$$

The consumption Euler equation for a household of generation t takes the form

$$\frac{c_2(t+1)}{c_1(t)} = \beta R(t+1) = \beta R(k, z),$$

with $R(k, z)$ given by (17.37). The total amount of savings at time t is then given by $s(t) = s(k(t), z(t))$ such that

$$s(k, z) = \frac{\beta}{1+\beta} w(k, z), \tag{17.38}$$

which, as in the canonical OLG and Solow growth models, corresponds to a constant savings rate, now equal to $\beta/(1+\beta)$.

Combining (17.38) with (17.36) and the fact that $\delta = 1$, the next date's capital stock $k(t+1)$ can be written as

$$k(t+1) = \pi(k, z)$$

$$= \frac{s(k, z)}{(1+n)}$$

$$= \frac{\beta(1-\alpha)z k^\alpha}{(1+n)(1+\beta)}. \tag{17.39}$$

Clearly, if $z = \bar{z}$, this equation would have a unique steady state with the capital-labor ratio given by

$$k^* = \left[\frac{\beta(1-\alpha)\bar{z}}{(1+n)(1+\beta)}\right]^{\frac{1}{1-\alpha}}. \tag{17.40}$$

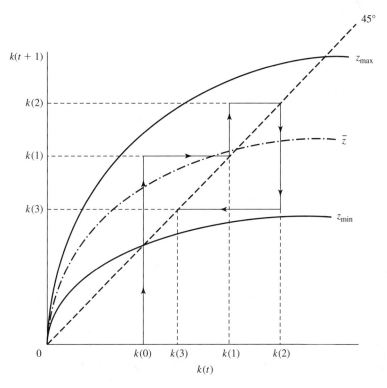

FIGURE 17.1 The stochastic correspondence of the overlapping generations model. Values for next period's capital-labor ratio within the two curves marked z_{min} and z_{max} are possible. The path $k(0) \to k(1) \to k(2) \to k(3)$ illustrates a particular sample path.

However, when z has a nondegenerate distribution, (17.39) defines a stochastic first-order difference equation. As in the neoclassical growth model under uncertainty, the long-run equilibrium of this model corresponds to an invariant distribution of the capital stock. In this particular case, (17.39) provides us with a tractable stochastic law of motion, and further insights about equilibrium behavior can be obtained from a diagrammatic analysis.

Suppose that z is distributed with support $[z_{min}, z_{max}]$, then the behavior of the economy can be analyzed by plotting *the stochastic correspondence* associated with (17.39), which is done in Figure 17.1. The stochastic correspondence plots the entire range of possible values of $k(t+1)$ for a given value of $k(t)$. The upper thick curve corresponds to the realization of z_{max}, while the lower thick curve corresponds to the realization of z_{min}. The dashed curve in the middle is for $z = \bar{z}$. Observe that the curves for both z_{min} and z_{max} start above the $45°$ line, which is a consequence of the Inada condition implied by the Cobb-Douglas technology—the marginal product of capital is arbitrarily large when the capital stock is close to zero. The stochastic correspondence enables a simple analysis of the dynamics of certain stochastic models. For example, Figure 17.1 plots a particular sample path of the capital-labor ratio in this economy, where starting with $k(0)$, the economy first receives a fairly favorable productivity shock moving to $k(1)$. Following this, there is another moderately favorable productivity realization, and the capital-labor ratio increases to $k(2)$. In the following period, however, the realization of the stochastic variable is quite bad, and the capital-labor ratio and thus output per capita decline sharply. This figure illustrates the type of dynamics that can emerge. Similar methods are used in the next section in a somewhat richer model.

Another noteworthy feature of this model is that, together with the stochastic Solow model discussed in Exercise 17.3 and the specific form of the neoclassical growth model in Example 17.1, it provides a much simpler model of stochastic growth than the neoclassical growth model under uncertainty. In the OLG model (with log preferences) and the Solow model, this is because saving decisions are myopic and remain unaffected by the distribution of stochastic shocks or even their realizations. Thus for a range of macroeconomic questions, these more myopic models or the simple neoclassical model of Example 17.1 might provide tractable alternatives to the full neoclassical growth model under uncertainty.

17.6   Risk, Diversification, and Growth

In this section, I present a stochastic model of long-run growth based on Acemoglu and Zilibotti (1997). This model is useful for two distinct purposes. First, because it is simpler than the baseline neoclassical growth model under uncertainty, it enables a complete characterization of the stochastic dynamics of growth and shows how simple ideas from the theory of Markov processes can be used in the context of the study of economic growth. Second and more important, this model introduces a number of issues in the theory of long-run growth. In particular, I have so far focused on models with balanced growth and relatively well-behaved transitional dynamics. The experience of economic growth over the past few thousand years has been much less orderly than implied by these models, however. Until about 200 years ago, growth in income per capita was relatively rare. Sustained growth in income per capita is a relatively recent phenomenon. Before this takeoff into sustained growth, societies experienced periods of growth followed by large slumps and crises. Acemoglu and Zilibotti (1997), Imbs and Wacziarg (2003), and Koren and Tenreyro (2007) document that even today richer countries have much more stable growth performances than less developed economies, which suffer from higher variability in their growth rates. In many ways, this pattern of relatively risky growth and low productivity followed by a process of capital-deepening, financial development, and better risk management is a major characteristic of the history of economic growth. The famous economic historian Fernand Braudel (1973, p. xi) describes the start of economic growth in Western Europe as follows:

> The advance occurred very slowly over a long period and was broken by sharp recessions. The right road was reached and thereafter never abandoned, only during the eighteenth century, and then only by a few privileged countries. Thus, before 1750 or even 1800 the march of progress could still be affected by unexpected events, even disasters.

In the model I present here, these patterns arise endogenously because the extent to which the economy can diversify risks by investing in imperfectly correlated activities is limited by the amount of capital it possesses. As the amount of capital increases, the economy achieves better diversification and faces fewer risks. The resulting equilibrium process thus generates greater variability and risk at the early stages of development, and these risks are significantly reduced after the economy manages to take off into sustained growth. Moreover, the desire of households to avoid risk makes them invest in lower return, less risky activities during the early stages of development; thus the growth rate of the economy is endogenously limited during this pre-takeoff stage. In addition, in this model, economic development goes hand-in-hand with financial development, as greater availability of capital enables better risk sharing through asset markets. Finally, because the model is one of endogenously incomplete markets, it also enables us to show that price-taking behavior by itself is not sufficient to guarantee

Pareto optimality; we will see that the form of inefficiency of the equilibrium in this economy is interesting both on substantive and methodological grounds.

17.6.1 Preferences, Technology, and Market Structure

Consider an OLG economy in which each generation lives for two periods. There is no population growth, and the size of each generation is normalized to 1. Production consists of two sectors. The first sector produces final goods with the Cobb-Douglas production function

$$Y(t) = K(t)^\alpha L(t)^{1-\alpha}, \tag{17.41}$$

where as usual $L(t)$ is total labor, and $K(t)$ is the total capital stock available at time t. Capital depreciates fully after use ($\delta = 1$ in terms of our previous notation).

The second sector transforms savings at time $t - 1$ into capital to be used for production at time t. This sector consists of a continuum $[0, 1]$ of intermediates, and stochastic elements only affect this sector. In particular, let us also represent possible states of nature with the unit interval and assume that intermediate sector $j \in [0, 1]$ pays a positive return only in state j and nothing in any other state. This formulation implies that investing in a sector is equivalent to buying a (basic) Arrow security that only pays in one state of nature. Since there is a continuum of sectors, the probability that a single sector has positive payoff is 0, but if a household invests in a subset $\bar{J}$ of $[0, 1]$, then there will be positive returns with probability equal to the (Lebesgue) measure of the set $\bar{J}$. This also implies that each intermediate sector is a risky activity, but a household (and in particular, the representative household in the economy) can diversify risks by investing in multiple sectors. In particular, if one were to invest in all of the sectors, then one would receive positive returns with probability 1. What makes the economic interactions in this model nontrivial is that investing in all sectors may not be possible at every date because of potential *nonconvexities*. More specifically, let us assume that each sector has a *minimum size requirement*, denoted by $M(j)$, and positive returns will be realized only if aggregate investment in that sector exceeds $M(j)$.

In light of this description, let $I(j, t)$ be the aggregate investment in intermediate sector j at time t. This investment generates date $t + 1$ capital equal to $QI(j, t)$ if state j is realized *and* $I(j, t) \geq M(j)$, and nothing otherwise. Thus aggregate investment in the intermediate sector exceeding the minimum size requirement is necessary for any positive returns.

In addition to the risky sectors, there is also a safe intermediate sector that transforms one unit of savings at date t into q units of date $t + 1$ capital. Suppose that

$$q < Q, \tag{17.42}$$

so that the safe option is also less productive.

The requirement that $I(j, t) \geq M(j)$ combined with the fact that the amount of capital obtained from savings $I(j, t)$ in state j is equal to $QI(j, t)$ implies that all intermediate sectors have linear technologies, but only after the minimum size requirement $M(j)$ is met. For any $I(j, t) < M(j)$, the output is equal to zero. To simplify the exposition and the computations, let us adopt a simple distribution of minimum size requirements by intermediate sector:

$$M(j) = \max\left\{0, \frac{D}{(1-\gamma)}(j - \gamma)\right\}. \tag{17.43}$$

This equation implies that intermediate sectors $j \leq \gamma$ have no minimum size requirement, so aggregate investments of any size can be made in these sectors. For the remaining sectors, the

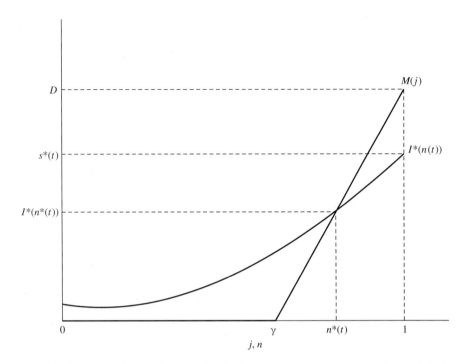

FIGURE 17.2 Minimum size requirements $M(j)$ of different sectors and demand for assets $I^*(n)$.

minimum size requirement increases linearly. Figure 17.2 shows the minimum size requirements (thick line). This figure is used to illustrate the determination of the set of open sectors once the equilibrium investments are specified.

It is worth noting that there are three important features introduced so far:

1. Risky investments have a higher expected return than the safe investment, which is captured by the assumption that $Q > q$.

2. The output of the risky investments (of the intermediate sectors) are imperfectly correlated so that there is safety in numbers.

3. The mathematical formulation here implies a simple relationship between investments and returns. As already hinted above, if a household holds a portfolio consisting of an equiproportional investment I in all sectors $j \in \bar{J} \subseteq [0, 1]$, and the (Lebesgue) measure of the set $\bar{J}$ is p, then the portfolio pays the return QI with probability p, and it pays nothing with probability $1 - p$.

The first two features imply that if the aggregate production set of this economy had been convex, for example because $D = 0$, all households would have invested an equal amount in all intermediate sectors and diversified all risks without sacrificing any of the high returns. However, in the presence of nonconvexities, as captured by the minimum size requirements, there is a trade-off between insurance and high productivity.

Let us next turn to the preferences of households. Recall that each generation has size normalized to 1. Consider a household from a generation born at time t. The preferences of this household are given by

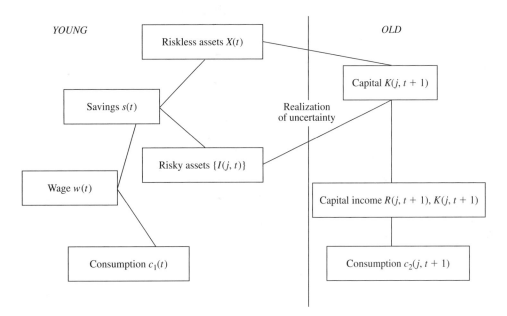

FIGURE 17.3 Life cycle of a typical household.

$$\mathbb{E}_t U_t(c_1(t), c_2(t+1)) = \log\big(c_1(t)\big) + \beta \int_0^1 \log c_2(j, t+1) dj, \qquad (17.44)$$

where $c_1(t)$ is the consumption of final goods in the first period of this household's life (which is at time t) and c_2 refers to consumption in the second period of this household. $\mathbb{E}_t$ is the expectations operator, which is necessary, because second-period consumption is risky. This is spelled out on the right-hand side of (17.44), with $c_2(j, t+1)$ denoting consumption in state j at time t. The integral replaces the expectation, using the fact that all states are equally likely. As in the canonical OLG model, each household has 1 unit of labor when young and no labor endowment when old. Thus the total supply of labor in the economy is equal to 1. Moreover, in the second period of their lives, households consume the return from their savings. For future reference, the set of young households at time t is denoted by $\mathcal{H}_t$, and Figure 17.3 depicts the life cycle and the various decisions of a typical household, emphasizing that uncertainty affects the return on their savings and thus the amount of capital they will have in the second period of their lives.

The aggregate capital stock depends on the realization of the state of nature, which determines how much of the investments in different intermediate sectors at time t is turned into capital. The capital stock at time $t+1$ therefore depends on the realization of the state of nature as well as the composition of investment of young households. In particular, in state j, the aggregate stock of capital is

$$K(j, t+1) = \int_{h \in \mathcal{H}_t} (q X^h(t) + Q I^h(j, t)) dh,$$

where $I^h(j, t)$ is the amount of savings invested by (young) household $h \in \mathcal{H}_t$ in sector j at time t, and $X^h(t)$ is the amount invested in the safe intermediate sector.

Since the capital stock is random, so are output and factor prices. In particular, both labor and capital are traded in competitive markets, so the equilibrium factor prices are given by their (realized) marginal products. Since the total capital stock in state j at time $t + 1$ is $K(j, t + 1)$ and the total supply of labor is equal to 1, these prices are given by

$$w(j, t + 1) = (1 - \alpha) K(j, t + 1)^{\alpha}$$

$$= (1 - \alpha) \left(\int_{h \in \mathcal{H}_t} (q X^h(t) + Q I^h(j, t)) dh \right)^{\alpha}, \tag{17.45}$$

and

$$R(j, t + 1) = \alpha K(j, t + 1)^{\alpha - 1}$$

$$= \alpha \left(\int_{h \in \mathcal{H}_t} (q X^h(t) + Q I^h(j, t)) dh \right)^{\alpha - 1}. \tag{17.46}$$

To complete the description of the environment, let us also specify the market structure of the intermediate sector. Suppose that households make investments in different intermediate sectors through financial intermediaries. There is free entry into financial intermediation (either by a large number of firms or by the households themselves). Any intermediary can form costlessly and mediate funds for a particular sector; that is, it can collect funds, invest them in a particular intermediate sector, and provide the corresponding Arrow securities to its investors. The important requirement is that, to be able to invest, any financial intermediary should raise enough funds to cover the minimum size requirement. For now, suppose that each financial intermediary can operate in only a single sector, which rules out the formation of a grand financial intermediary managing all investments.[5] I return to this issue in Section 17.6.5.

Let us denote the price charged for a security associated with intermediate sector j at time t by $P(j, t)$. Observe that $P(j, t) < 1$ cannot be part of an equilibrium, since one unit of the security requires one unit of the final good, so $P(j, t) < 1$ would lose money. What about $P(j, t) > 1$? This case is also ruled out by free entry. Imagine that a particular intermediary offers security j at some price $P(j, t) > 1$ and raises enough funds so that the total investment in this intermediate sector $I(j, t)$ is greater than the minimum size requirement $M(j)$. But in that case, some other intermediary can also enter, offer a lower price for the security, and attract all the funds that were otherwise received by the first intermediary. This argument shows that $P(j, t) > 1$ is not possible either, so that equilibrium behavior forces $P(j, t) = 1$ for all securities being supplied.

17.6.2 Equilibrium

I now characterize the equilibrium of the economy described in Section 17.6.1. Recall the two observations from the previous paragraph. First, not all intermediate sectors are *open* at each date, meaning that there are securities for only a subset of the intermediate sectors at any date.

---

5. To simplify the notation and the argument, I am sacrificing mathematical rigor here. Since there is a continuum of sectors, all (equilibrium) statements should be accompanied with the qualifier "almost everywhere." This implies that investment in a single sector (or in fact a countable subset of the [0, 1] sectors) may deviate from optimality. In addition, a fully rigorous analysis would require each financial intermediary to deal with a set of intermediate sectors of measure $\varepsilon > 0$ and then consider the limit $\varepsilon \to 0$. Throughout I ignore these qualifications and require that investment in each sector be consistent with equilibrium, and I assume that each intermediary controls a single sector.

Let the set of intermediate sectors that are open at date t be denoted by $J(t)$. Second, by the argument at the end of Section 17.6.1, for any $j \in J(t)$ free entry implies that $P(j, t) = 1$. These two observations enable us to write the problem of a representative household $h \in \mathcal{H}_t$ taking prices and the set of available securities at time t as given. This problem takes the following form:

$$\max_{s(t), X(t), [I(j,t)]_{0 \leq j \leq 1}} \log c(t) + \beta \int_0^1 \log c(j, t+1) dj \qquad (17.47)$$

subject to

$$X(t) + \int_0^1 I(j, t) dj = s(t), \qquad (17.48)$$

$$c(j, t+1) = R(j, t+1)(q X(t) + Q I(j, t)), \qquad (17.49)$$

$$I(j, t) = 0, \quad \forall j \notin J(t), \qquad (17.50)$$

$$c(t) + s(t) \leq w(t), \qquad (17.51)$$

where I have suppressed the superscript h to simplify the notation. Here (17.47) is the expected utility of the household. Equations (17.48)–(17.51) are the constraints on this maximization problem. The first one, (17.48), requires that the investment in the safe sector and the sum of the investments in all other securities equal the total savings of the household, $s(t)$. Equation (17.49) expresses consumption in state j at time $t + 1$. Two features are worth noting. First, recall that households supply labor only when young and consume capital income when old. Thus second-period consumption for the household is equal to its capital holdings times the rate of return to capital, $R(j, t+1)$ given by (17.46). This rate of return is conditioned on state j (at time $t + 1$) since the amount of capital and thus the marginal product of capital differs across states. Second, the amount of capital available to the household is equal to what it receives from the safe investment, $q X(t)$, plus the return from the Arrow security for state j, $Q I(j, t)$. Equation (17.50) encapsulates a major constraint on household behavior: it emphasizes that the household cannot invest in any security that is not being supplied in the market. In particular, recall that $I(j, t) \geq M(t)$ is necessary for an intermediate sector to be open, and thus there may be sectors that are not open in equilibrium and their securities will not be traded. Constraint (17.50) ensures that the household cannot invest in nontraded securities. Finally, (17.51) requires the sum of consumption and savings to be less than or equal to the income of the household, which only consists of its wage income, given by (17.45).

We are now in a position to define an equilibrium. A *static equilibrium* is an equilibrium for time t, taking the amount of capital available at time t, $K(t)$, and thus the wage $w(t)$ as given. The tuple

$$\left\langle s^*(t), X^*(t), [I^*(j, t)]_{0 \leq j \leq J^*(t)}, J^*(t), [P^*(j, t)]_{0 \leq j \leq J^*(t)}, w^*(j, t), R^*(j, t) \right\rangle$$

is a static equilibrium if $s^*(t)$, $X^*(t)$, $[I^*(j, t)]_{0 \leq j \leq 1}$ solve the maximization of (17.47) subject to (17.48)–(17.51) for given $[P^*(j, t)]_{0 \leq j \leq J^*(t)}$, $J^*(t)$, $w^*(j, t)$, and $R^*(j, t)$; $w^*(j, t)$ and $R^*(j, t)$ are given by (17.45) and (17.46), respectively. In addition, $J^*(t)$ and $[P^*(j, t)]_{0 \leq j \leq J^*(t)}$ are such that for all $j \in J^*(t)$, $P^*(j, t) = 1$ and the set $J^*(t)$ is determined by free entry in the sense that if some $j' \notin J^*(t)$ were offered for a price $P(j', t) \geq 1$, then the solution to the modified maximization problem (17.47) subject to (17.48)–(17.51) would involve $I(j', t) < M(j)$ (in other words, there is no more room for one more intermediate sector to open and attract sufficient funds to cover the minimum size requirement). A *dynamic equilibrium* is a sequence of static equilibria linked to one another through (17.45) given the realization of the state $j(t)$ at each $t = 1, 2, \ldots$

Because preferences in (17.47) are logarithmic, the saving rate of all households is constant, as in the canonical OLG model. Consequently the following saving rule applies regardless of the risk-return trade-off:

$$s^*(t) \equiv s^*(w(t)) = \frac{\beta}{1+\beta} w(t). \tag{17.52}$$

Given this result, a household's optimization problem can be broken into two parts: first, the amount of savings is determined, and then an optimal portfolio is chosen. This decomposition of the optimization problem is particularly useful because of two observations:

1. For any $j, j' \in J(t)$, $I^*(j, t) = I^*(j', t)$. Intuitively, since each household is facing the same price for all of the traded *symmetric* Arrow securities, it prefers to purchase an equal amount of each, thus achieving a *balanced portfolio* (see Exercise 17.23).

2. The set of open projects at time t takes the form $J^*(t) = [0, n^*(t)]$ for some $n(t) \in [0, 1]$. Intuitively, when only a subset of projects can be opened in equilibrium, intermediate sectors with small minimum size requirements will open before those with greater minimum size requirements. Consequently, if an intermediate sector j^* is open, all sectors $j \leq j^*$ must also be open (see Exercise 17.24).

These observations also imply that we can divide the states of nature at time t into two sets: states in $[0, n(t)]$ that are "good" in the sense that the society is lucky and its risky investments have delivered positive returns, and states in $(n(t), 1]$ that are "bad" in the sense that the society is unlucky and its risky investments have zero returns. Clearly the rate of return to capital (and the wage rate) take different values in these two sets of states. Let us denote the rate of return to capital when a good state is realized by $R^G(t + 1)$ and when a bad state is realized by $R^B(t + 1)$—these returns are dated $t + 1$, because they are paid out at time $t + 1$. In light of this structure, the maximization problem of a representative household can be written in much simpler form:

$$\max_{X(t), I(t)} n^*(t) \log\left[R^G(t + 1)(qX(t) + QI(t))\right] + \left(1 - n^*(t)\right) \log\left[R^B(t + 1)qX(t)\right] \tag{17.53}$$

subject to

$$X(t) + n^*(t)I(t) \leq s^*(t), \tag{17.54}$$

where $n^*(t)$, $R^G(t + 1)$, and $R^B(t + 1)$ are taken as given by the representative household, and $s^*(t)$ is given by (17.52). Clearly, from (17.46)

$$R^B(t + 1) = \alpha(qX(t))^{\alpha-1}$$

is the marginal product of capital in the bad state, when the realized state is $j > n^*(t)$ and no risky investment pays off, and

$$R^G(t) = \alpha(qX(t) + QI(t))^{\alpha-1}$$

applies in the good state (i.e., when the realized state is $j \in [0, n^*(t)]$).

Maximizing (17.53) subject to (17.54) yields the unique solution

$$X^*(t) = \frac{(1 - n^*(t))Q}{Q - qn^*(t)} s^*(t), \tag{17.55}$$

and

$$I^*(j, t) = \begin{cases} I^*(n^*(t)) \equiv \frac{Q-q}{Q-qn(t)} s^*(t), & \text{for } j \leq n^*(t), \\ 0 & \text{for } j > n^*(t). \end{cases} \tag{17.56}$$

Notably, (17.56) implies that the demand for each asset (or investment in each intermediate sector) grows as the measure of open sectors increases—that is, $I^*(n)$ is strictly increasing in n. This is because when more securities are available, the risk-diversification opportunities improve, and households become willing to reduce their investments in the safe asset and increase their investments in risky projects. This represents an important economic force. Investments in the high-productivity sectors are curtailed because these are riskier than the safe sector. But since there is "safety in numbers" (i.e., a first-order benefit from diversification), when there are more financial assets (more open sectors), each household is willing to invest more in risky assets in total. This complementarity between the set of traded assets and investments plays an important role in the dynamics of economic development described below.

Equations (17.52), (17.55), and (17.56) characterize the utility-maximizing behavior of the representative household given the set of intermediate sectors that are open. To completely characterize the equilibrium, we need to find the set of sectors that are open. This is equivalent to finding a threshold sector $n^*(t)$ such that all $j \leq n^*(t)$ can meet their minimum size requirements while no additional sector can enter and raise enough funds to meet its minimum size requirements. We can find this threshold diagrammatically by plotting the level of investment for each sector in a balanced portfolio, $I^*(n^*(t))$ given by (17.56), together with the minimum size requirement, $M(j)$ given by (17.43). The first curve can be loosely interpreted as the demand for assets in the financial market, and the curve for (17.43) can be thought of as corresponding to the supply of assets. The two curves and their intersection are plotted in Figure 17.2. The figure shows a unique intersection between the two curves. However, because both curves are upward sloping, more than one intersection is possible in general. It can be verified that the condition $Q \geq (2 - \gamma)q$ is sufficient to ensure a unique intersection (see Exercise 17.25). If this condition is violated, there might be multiple solutions, corresponding to multiple equilibria. These equilibria would involve different numbers of open sectors. When there are few open sectors, households invest a large fraction of their resources in the safe asset, and in equilibrium only a few risky sectors can be operated. In contrast, when there is a significant number of open risky sectors, each household invests a large fraction of its resources in risky assets. This enables more sectors to be open and creates better risk diversification for all households. When such multiple equilibria exist, the equilibrium with more open sectors gives higher ex ante utility to all households. While interesting for illustrating the forces at work, one would expect that financial intermediaries might be successful in avoiding this type of coordination failure. Motivated by this reasoning, let us focus on the part of the parameter space where $Q \geq (2 - \gamma)q$. In that case, the static equilibrium is uniquely defined, and the following proposition summarizes this equilibrium.

Proposition 17.7 *Suppose that $Q \geq (2 - \gamma)q$. Then given $K(t)$, there exists a unique time t equilibrium where all sectors $j \leq n^*(t) = n^*[K(t)]$ are open and those $j > n^*[K(t)]$ are shut, where*

$$n^*[K(t)] = \frac{(Q + q\gamma) - \left\{ (Q + q)^2 - 4q[D^{-1}(Q - q)(1 - \gamma)\Gamma K(t)^\alpha + \gamma Q] \right\}^{1/2}}{2q} \tag{17.57}$$

if $K(t) \leq D^{1/\alpha}\Gamma^{-1/\alpha}$, *and* $n^*[K(t)] = 1$ *if* $K(t) > D^{1/\alpha}\Gamma^{-1/\alpha}$, *with* Γ *defined as* $\Gamma \equiv (1-\alpha)\beta/(1+\beta)$. *In this equilibrium,*

$$s^*(t) = \frac{\beta}{1+\beta}(1-\alpha)K(t),$$

and $X^*(t)$ *and* $I^*(j, t)$ *are given by (17.55) and (17.56), respectively, with* $n^*(t) = n^*[K(t)]$.

Proof.   See Exercise 17.26.   ■

The equilibrium threshold sector $n^*[K]$ is increasing in K: when there is more capital, the economy is able to open more intermediate sectors and diversify risks better, encouraging greater investments in risky activities (see (17.56)).

17.6.3   Equilibrium Dynamics

Let us next turn to the characterization of equilibrium dynamics. Given the static equilibrium in Proposition 17.7, it is straightforward to characterize the full stochastic equilibrium process. The law of motion of the capital stock, $K(t)$, will be given by a simple Markov process. Recall that investments in risky sectors are successful with probability $n^*[K(t)]$ when the capital stock is $K(t)$, and they are unsuccessful with the complementary probability, $1 - n^*[K(t)]$. This implies the following stochastic law of motion for the capital stock:

$$K(t+1) = \begin{cases} \frac{q(1-n^*[K(t)])}{Q-qn^*[K(t)]} Q\Gamma K(t)^\alpha & \text{with probability } 1 - n^*[K(t)], \\ Q\Gamma K(t)^\alpha & \text{with probability } n^*[K(t)], \end{cases} \tag{17.58}$$

where $n^*[K(t)]$ is given by (17.57), and recall that $\Gamma \equiv (1-\alpha)\beta/(1+\beta)$. Notice that the first line of (17.58) is always less than the second line, because the second line refers to the case in which the investments in the intermediate sectors have been successful.

Equation (17.58) is a particularly simple Markov process, since given $K(t)$, $K(t+1)$ can only take two values.[6] A diagrammatic analysis of this Markov process is particularly illuminating. Consider Figure 17.4, which plots the stochastic correspondence of the Markov process in (17.58) and is thus similar to Figure 17.1. The main difference is that in Figure 17.1, any value between the two curves for z_{min} and z_{max} was possible. In contrast, here, only values exactly on the two curves plotted in the figure are possible. The upper curve corresponds to $Q\Gamma K(t)^\alpha$. This curve is the value of the capital stock that would result if households followed their equilibrium investment strategies given in (17.55) and (17.56), and at each date the economy turned out to be lucky, so that their investments always had positive returns. The lower, inverse U-shaped, curve corresponds to $q(1 - n^*[K(t)])Q\Gamma K(t)^\alpha/(Q - qn^*[K(t)])$ and thus applies if the economy is unlucky at each date. Both curves start above the $45°$ line near zero for the same reason as that given for the similar pattern in Figure 17.1 (because the aggregate production function (17.41) satisfies the Inada conditions). The economy is on the upper curve with probability $n^*[K(t)]$ and on the lower curve with probability $1 - n^*[K(t)]$. Thus not only do the probabilities of success and failure change with the aggregate capital stock but so does average productivity. To quantify this variation in average productivity, let us define *expected* TFP conditional on the proportion of intermediate sectors that are open:

---

6. It is a Markov process and not a Markov chain, since for different values of $K(t)$, the possible values of $K(t+1)$ belong to the entire $\mathbb{R}_+$.

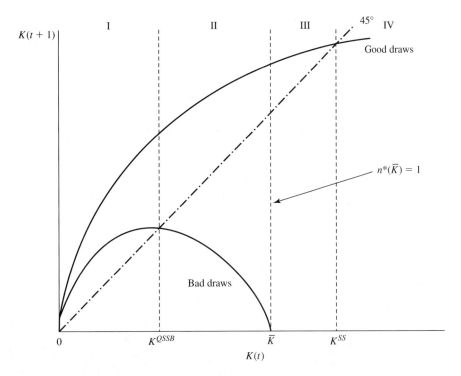

FIGURE 17.4 The stochastic correspondence of the capital stock.

$$\sigma^e(n^*[K(t)]) = (1 - n^*[K(t)]) \frac{q(1 - n^*[K(t)])}{Q - qn^*[K(t)]} Q + n^*[K(t)]Q. \qquad (17.59)$$

Straightforward differentiation establishes that $\sigma^e(n^*[K(t)])$ is strictly increasing in $n^*[K(t)]$. Thus as the economy develops and manages to open more intermediate sectors, its productivity increases endogenously. Since $n^*[K]$ is increasing in K, this implies that average productivity is increasing in the capital stock of the economy.

Proposition 17.8 *The expected TFP of the economy $\sigma^e(n^*[K])$ is increasing in n^* and thus increasing in K.*

Inspection of Figure 17.4 also suggests that the following two levels of capital stock are special and useful in the analysis:

1. K^{QSSB} refers to the "quasi–steady state" of an economy which always has unlucky draws. An economy would converge toward this quasi–steady state if it invests according to (17.55) and (17.56), but these sectors never have positive payoff due to bad luck.

2. K^{QSSG} refers to the "quasi–steady state" of an economy which always receives good news, meaning that it is always on the upper curve in Figure 17.4.

These two capital stock levels are plotted in the figure and are also easy to compute as

$$K^{QSSB} = \left[\frac{q(1 - n^*[K^{QSSB}])}{Q - qn^*[K^{QSSB}]} Q\Gamma \right]^{\frac{1}{1-\alpha}}, \text{ and } K^{QSSG} = (Q\Gamma)^{\frac{1}{1-\alpha}}. \qquad (17.60)$$

The form of K^{QSSG} is particularly noteworthy, since it refers to the case in which the economy never faces any risk and thus acts very much like a standard neoclassical growth model. In particular, if in equilibrium, $n^*[K^{QSSG}] = 1$, then K^{QSSG} becomes a proper steady state and the economy would stay at this level of capital stock once it reaches it. This is because once the economy accumulates sufficient capital to open all intermediate sectors, it eliminates all risk and would always be on the upper curve in Figure 17.4.

Equations (17.57) and (17.60) show that the condition for this good steady state to exist (i.e., $n^*[K^{QSSG}] = 1$) is that the saving level corresponding to K^{QSSG} be sufficient to ensure a balanced portfolio of investments, of at least D, in all the intermediate sectors. It is straightforward to show that the following condition is sufficient to ensure this:

$$D < \Gamma^{\frac{1}{1-\alpha}} Q^{\frac{\alpha}{1-\alpha}}. \tag{17.61}$$

Thus when (17.61) is satisfied, the good quasi–steady state indeed generates sufficient capital to open all sectors and eliminate all risk, becoming a proper steady state. In this case, we denote K^{QSSG} by K^{SS}. Under the assumption that (17.61) is satisfied, Figure 17.4 shows $n^*[K^{SS}]$. Now returning to this figure, we can get a better sense of the stochastic equilibrium dynamics. The figure divides the range of capital stocks into four regions. In region I, the capital stock is low enough so that both the curves conditional on good draws and on bad draws are above the 45° line, so that in this range the economy grows regardless of whether it experiences good or bad productivity realizations. Next comes region II, which in many ways is the most interesting one. Here the economy grows if it receives positive shocks but suffers a crisis if its investments are unsuccessful. Between these two regions lies the bad quasi–steady state K^{QSSB}. The figure justifies the terminology of calling this level of capital stock a "quasi–steady state," since when $K < K^{QSSB}$, the economy grows toward K^{QSSB}. When $K > K^{QSSB}$, the economy may grow or contract. Nevertheless, as noted above, because $n^*[K]$ is increasing in K, in the right-hand side neighborhood of K^{QSSB}, the economy has the highest probability of contracting (recall that to the left of K^{QSSB}, negative shocks do not lead to a contraction).

For plausible parameter values, the economy may spend a long time in region II. Acemoglu and Zilibotti (1997) provide examples where the number of periods the economy spends in regions I and II could be arbitrarily large. However, when the economy receives a sequence of good news, it ultimately exits region II and enters region III. The level of capital stock that divides these two regions, $\bar{K}$, is defined such that $n^*[\bar{K}] = 1$. This means that once the economy reaches the capital stock of $\bar{K}$, it has enough capital to open all sectors. Consequently, in region III all risk is diversified, and the dynamics are exactly the same as those of the canonical OLG model without uncertainty. Finally, starting anywhere in region III, the economy travels toward the steady state K^{SS}, which stands between regions III and IV. Region IV, on the other hand, has so much capital that even with the positive shocks, it contracts. Naturally, unless it starts there, the economy never enters region IV.

This discussion, combined with Figure 17.4, gives a complete characterization of the stochastic equilibrium growth path. In particular, an economy that starts with a low enough capital stock first experiences growth but then spends a long time fluctuating between successful periods and those of severe crises. Eventually, a string of good periods takes the economy to a level of capital stock such that much (here, all) of the risks can be diversified. At this level, we can think of the economy as achieving takeoff as in Rostow's account discussed in Chapter 1. After takeoff, the economy successfully diversifies all risk, so that growth from this point onward progresses steadily rather than being subject to significant fluctuations as in region II. In addition, Proposition 17.8 implies that the aggregate (labor and total factor) productivity increases after this level of capital. Thus takeoff comes with a decline in the fluctuations in economic activity and an increase in productivity.

It is also worth noting that as the economy develops by accumulating more capital, it achieves both higher productivity and also better diversification and management of risks. This latter takes the form of more sectors being open, which equivalently corresponds to greater financial intermediation. Thus in this model financial and economic development go hand-in-hand and are jointly determined in equilibrium (rather than one "causing" the other).

A natural question is whether the economy will reach region III and then region IV. The next proposition answers this question.

Proposition 17.9 *Suppose that condition (17.61) holds. Then the stochastic process $\{K(t)\}_{t=1}^{\infty}$ converges to the point K^{SS} with probability 1.*

Proof. See Exercise 17.27. ∎

This proposition establishes that the variability of growth in the economy will eventually decline (and in fact disappear). But one might wish to know whether the amplitudes of economic fluctuations are systematically related to the level of the capital stock or output in the economy. This is particularly relevant, since, as already discussed, both cross-sectional and time-series comparisons suggest that poorer nations suffer from greater economic variability. To answer this question, the natural variable to look at is the conditional variance of TFP (whose expected value was defined in (17.59)). Define $\sigma(n^*[K(t)])$ as a random variable that takes the values $q(1 - n^*[K(t)])Q/(Q - qn^*[K(t)])$ and Q with respective probabilities $(1 - n^*[K(t)])$ and $n^*[K(t)]$. The expectation of this random variable is $\sigma^e(n^*[K(t)])$ as defined in (17.59). Then taking logs, we can rewrite (17.58) as

$$\triangle \log(K(t + 1)) = \log \Gamma - (1 - \alpha) \log(K(t)) + \log(\sigma(n^*[K(t)])). \quad (17.62)$$

It is clear from (17.62) that capital (and output) growth volatility, after removing the deterministic convergence effects due to the standard neoclassical effects, are determined by the stochastic component σ. Denoting the (conditional) variance of $\sigma(n^*[K(t)]$ given $K(t)$ by $\mathcal{V}_n$, we can state the following proposition.

Proposition 17.10 *Let*

$$\mathcal{V}_n \equiv Var(\sigma(n^*) \mid n^*) = n^*(1 - n^*)[Q(Q - q)/(Q - qn^*)]^2.$$

If $\gamma \geq Q/(2Q - q)$, then $\partial \mathcal{V}_n/\partial K \leq 0$ for all $K \geq 0$. If $\gamma < Q/(2Q - q)$, then there exists $\tilde{K}$ defined such that $n^*(\tilde{K}) = Q/(2Q - q) < 1$, and

$$\frac{\partial \mathcal{V}_n}{\partial K} \leq 0 \quad \text{for all } K \geq \tilde{K}, \quad \text{and} \quad \frac{\partial \mathcal{V}_n}{\partial K_t} > 0 \quad \text{for all } K < \tilde{K}.$$

Proof. See Exercise 17.28. ∎

The behavior of the variability of growth in this proposition results from the counteracting effects of two forces: first, as the economy develops, more savings are invested in risky assets; and second, as more sectors are opened, idiosyncratic risks are better diversified. The proposition shows that if $\gamma \geq Q/(2Q - q)$, the second effect always dominates and thus richer economies are less risky. If $\gamma < Q/(2Q - q)$, then the first effect dominates for sufficiently low levels of capital stock, but once the capital stock reaches a critical threshold, $\tilde{K}$, the second effect dominates. Thus except for sufficiently low levels of capital, the variability of the growth rate is everywhere decreasing in the income level of the economy.

17.6.4 Efficiency

The Section 17.6.3 characterized the stochastic equilibrium of the economy. Is this equilibrium Pareto efficient? Since all households are price takers, it may be conjectured that the answer to this question must be yes. Here I show that this is not the case. Though at first surprising, this result is in fact intuitive and interesting. First, it results from an economically meaningful pecuniary externality. Second, it makes sense from the viewpoint of the theory of general equilibrium: though all households are price takers, this is not an Arrow-Debreu economy, because the set of traded commodities is determined endogenously by a zero profit condition. To illustrate these issues in the most transparent way I ignore any potential source of intertemporal inefficiency (which, we know from Chapter 9, may arise in OLG economies). I therefore condition on the level of savings $s(t)$ (or the capital stock $K(t)$) and investigate whether the way in which savings are allocated across different sectors of the economy is (constrained) efficient. Consider the social planner's problem of maximizing the expected utility of the representative household for given $s(t)$:

$$\max_{n(t), X(t), [I(j,t)]_{0 \le j \le n(t)}} \int_0^{n(t)} \log(qX(t) + QI(j,t))dj + (1 - n(t))\log(qX(t)) \quad (17.63)$$

subject to

$$X(t) + \int_0^{n(t)} I(j,t)dj \le s(t).$$

The social planner is choosing the set of open sectors, denoted by $[0, n(t)]$; the amount that will be invested in the safe sector, $X(t)$; and the allocation of funds among the open sectors, denoted by $[I(j, t)]_{0 \le j \le n(t)}$. In principle, the social planner could have chosen the set of open sectors not to be an interval of the form $[0, n(t)]$, but the same argument as in Exercise 17.24 ensures that there is no loss of generality in imposing this form. The constraint ensures that the sum of investments in the safe and the risky sectors is less than the amount of savings available to the planner. The main difference between this program and the maximization problem of the representative household, (17.47), is that the social planner also chooses $n(t)$, while the representative household takes the set of available assets as given. The social planner's allocation (and thus the Pareto optimal allocation) is given by the solution to this maximization problem. The next proposition characterizes the solution.

Proposition 17.11   *Let $n^*[K(t)]$ be given by (17.57), and $s(t)$ and $K(t)$ denote the current level of savings and capital stock available to the social planner. Then the unique solution to the maximization problem in (17.63) is as follows. For all $s(t) < D$, the set of open sectors is given by $[0, n^S[K(t)]]$, where $n^S[K(t)] > n^*[K(t)]$. The amount of investment in the safe sector is given by $X^S(t)$, where $X^S(t) < X^*(K(t))$. Finally, there exists $j^*(t) \in (0, n^S[K(t)])$ such that the portfolio of risky sectors for each household takes the form*

$$I^S(j, t) = M\left(j^*\right) > M(j) \quad \text{for } j < j^*(t)$$

$$I^S(j, t) = M(j) \qquad\qquad \text{for } j \in [j^*(t), n^S[K(t)]], \qquad (17.64)$$

$$I^S(j, t) = 0 \qquad\qquad\quad \text{for } j > n^S(K(t)).$$

For all $s(t) \ge D$, $n^S[K(t)] = n^*[K(t)] = 1$, and $I^S(j, t) = s(t)$ for all $j \in [0, 1]$.

Proof.   See Exercise 17.29. ∎

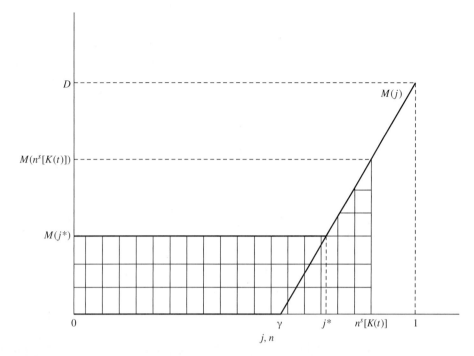

FIGURE 17.5 The Pareto optimal portfolio allocation.

This proposition implies that, when the economy has not achieved full diversification, the social planner will open more sectors than the decentralized equilibrium. She will finance these additional sectors by deviating from the *balanced portfolio,* which is always a feature of the equilibrium allocation. In other words, she will invest less in the sectors without the minimum size requirement. The Pareto optimal allocation of funds is shown in Figure 17.5.

The deviation from the balanced portfolio implies that the social planner is implicitly cross-subsidizing the sectors with high minimum size requirements at the expense of sectors with low or no minimum size requirements. This is because, starting with a balanced portfolio, opening a few more sectors always benefits all households, who will be able to achieve better risk diversification. The only way the social planner can achieve this is by implicitly taxing sectors that have low or no minimum size requirements (so that they have lower investments) and subsidizing the marginal sectors with high minimum size requirements.

Why does the decentralized equilibrium not achieve the same allocation? There are two complementary ways of providing the intuition for this. The first is that a marginal dollar of investment by a household in a sector with a high minimum size requirement creates a pecuniary externality, because this investment makes it possible for the sector to be active and to provide better risk diversification possibilities to all other households. However, each household, taking equilibrium prices as given, ignores this pecuniary externality and tends to underinvest in marginal sectors with high minimum size requirements. Thus the source of inefficiency is that each household ignores its impact on others' diversification opportunities. The second intuition for this result is related. Because households take the set of prices as given and in equilibrium $P(j, t) = 1$ for all open sectors, they will always hold a balanced portfolio. However, the Pareto optimal allocation involves cross-subsidization across sectors in a nonbalanced portfolio. Market prices do not induce the households to hold the right portfolio.

At this point, the reader may wonder why the First Welfare Theorem does not apply in this environment (especially since all households are price takers). This because the equilibrium here does not correspond to an Arrow-Debreu equilibrium. In particular, this is an equilibrium for an economy with endogenously incomplete markets, where the set of open markets is determined by a zero profit (free-entry) condition. All commodities that are traded in equilibrium are priced competitively, but there is no competitive pricing for commodities that are not traded. Instead, in an Arrow-Debreu equilibrium, all commodities, even those that are not traded in equilibrium, are priced, and in fact a potential commodity would not be traded in equilibrium only if its price were equal to zero and at zero prices, there were excess supply. In this sense, the equilibrium characterized here is not an Arrow-Debreu equilibrium. In fact, it can be verified that such an Arrow-Debreu equilibrium does not exist in this economy because of the nonconvexity of the production possibilities set. Instead the equilibrium concept used here is a more natural competitive equilibrium notion: it requires that all commodities that are traded in equilibrium are priced competitively and then determines the set of traded commodities by a free-entry condition. Some additional discussion of this equilibrium concept is provided in the References and Literature section below.

17.6.5　Inefficiency with Alternative Market Structures

Would the market failure in portfolio choices be overcome if some financial institution could coordinate households' investment decisions? Imagine that rather than all households acting in isolation and ignoring their impact on one anothers' decisions, funds are intermediated through a financial coalition-intermediary. This intermediary can collect all the savings and offer to each saver a *complex* security (as different from an Arrow security) that pays $QI^S(j, t) + qX^S(t)$ in each state j, where $I^S(j, t)$ and $X^S(t)$ are as in the optimal portfolio. Holding this security would make each household better off compared to the equilibrium.

Although from this discussion it may appear that the inefficiency identified here may not be robust to the formation of more complex financial institutions, this is not the case. The remarkable result is that unless some rather strong assumptions are made about the set of contracts that a financial intermediary can offer, equilibrium allocations resulting from competition among intermediaries are identical to the equilibrium allocation in Proposition 17.7. A full analysis of this issue is beyond our current scope, but a brief discussion gives the flavor. Let us model more complex financial intermediaries as "intermediary-coalitions," that is, as sets of households who join their savings together and invest in a particular portfolio of intermediate sectors. Such coalitions may be organized by a specific household, and if it is profitable for other households to join the coalition, the organizer of the coalition can charge a premium (or a joining fee), thus making profits. Let us assume that there is free entry into financial intermediation or coalition-building, so that any household can attempt to exploit profit opportunities if there are any. Let us also impose some structure on how the timing of financial intermediation works and also how households can participate in different coalitions. Let us adopt the following assumptions:

1. Coalitions maximize a weighted utility of their members at all points in time. In particular, a coalition cannot commit to a path of action that will be against the interests of its members in the continuation game.

2. Coalitions cannot exclude other households from investing in a particular project.

The following result is established in Acemoglu and Zilibotti (1997).

Proposition 17.12 *The set of equilibria of the financial intermediation game described above is always nonempty, and all equilibria have the same structure as those characterized in Section 17.6.2 and Proposition 17.7.*

I do not provide a proof of this proposition, since a formal statement and the proof require additional notation. But the intuition is straightforward: as shown in Proposition 17.11, the Pareto optimal allocation involves a nonbalanced portfolio and cross-subsidization across different sectors. Thus the shadow price of investing in some sectors should be higher than in others, even though the cost of investing in each sector is equal to 1 (in terms of date t final goods). These differences in shadow prices then support a nonbalanced portfolio. Recall also that it is the sectors with no or low minimum size requirements that are being implicitly taxed in this allocation. This kind of cross-subsidization is difficult to sustain, because each household can deviate by slightly reducing its investments in coalitions/intermediaries that engage in cross-subsidization and undertake investments on the side to move its portfolio toward a balanced one (by investing in sectors with no or low minimum size requirements). At the end, only allocations without cross-subsidization, that is, those as in Proposition 17.7, can survive as equilibria.

The most important implication of this result is that even with unrestricted financial intermediaries or coalitions, the inefficiency resulting from endogenously incomplete markets cannot be prevented. The key economic force is that each household creates a positive pecuniary externality by holding a nonbalanced portfolio, but in a decentralized equilibrium each household wishes to and can easily move toward a balanced portfolio, undermining efforts to sustain the efficient allocation.

17.7 Taking Stock

This chapter presented a number of different models of stochastic growth. My selection of topics was geared toward achieving two objectives. First, I introduced a number of workhorse models of macroeconomics, such as the neoclassical growth model under uncertainty and the basic Bewley model. These models are not only useful for the analysis of economic growth but also have a wide range of applications in the macroeconomics literature.

Second, the model in Section 17.6 demonstrated how stochastic models can significantly enrich the analysis of economic growth and economic development. In particular, this model showed how a simple extension of our standard models can generate an equilibrium path in which economies spend a long time with low productivity and suffer frequent crises. They take off into sustained and steady growth once they receive a sequence of favorable realizations. The takeoff process not only reduces volatility and increases growth, but is also associated with better management of risk and greater financial development. Though stylistic, this model provides a good approximation to the economic development process that much of Western Europe underwent over the past 700 years or so. It also emphasizes the possibility that luck may have played an important role in the timing of takeoff and perhaps even in determining which countries were early industrializers. Therefore this model provides an attractive formalization of the luck hypothesis discussed in Chapter 4. Nevertheless underlying the equilibrium in this model is a set of market institutions that enable trade and investment in competitive markets. Thus my interpretation is that the current model shows how random elements and luck can matter for the timing of takeoff among countries that satisfy the major prerequisites for modern growth. This could account for some of the current-day cross-country income differences and may also provide important insights about the beginning of the process of sustained growth. However institutional factors—which determine whether those prerequisites are satisfied— are more important for understanding why some parts of the world did not take off during the nineteenth century and have not yet embarked on a path of sustained and steady growth. These are topics that are discussed in the rest of the book.

Section 17.6 also introduced a number of important ideas related to incomplete markets. The Bewley model presented in Section 17.4 is a prototypical incomplete markets model, and as with most incomplete markets models in the literature, it takes the set of markets that are open as given. In contrast, the model in Section 17.6 incorporates endogenously incomplete markets. The fact that the set of open markets (the set of traded commodities) is determined in equilibrium with a free-entry condition can lead to a novel Pareto inefficiency due to pecuniary externalities (even though all households take prices as given). Although this type of Pareto inefficiency is different from those highlighted so far, there are some important parallels between the phenomena of an insufficient number of markets being open in this model and too few machine varieties being introduced in the baseline endogenous technological change model of Chapter 13.

17.8 References and Literature

The neoclassical growth model under uncertainty, presented in Section 17.1, was first analyzed by Brock and Mirman (1972). Because the optimal growth problem is considerably easier than the study of equilibrium growth under uncertainty, most analyses in the literature focus on the optimal growth problem and then appeal to the Second Welfare Theorem. Stokey, Lucas, and Prescott (1989) provide an example of this approach. An analysis of the full stochastic dynamics of this model requires a more detailed discussion of the general theory of Markov processes. Space restrictions preclude me from presenting these tools. The necessary material can be found in Stokey, Lucas, and Prescott (1989, Chapters 8, 11, 12, and 13), or the reader can look at Futia (1982) for a more compact treatment. More advanced and complete treatments are presented in Gikhman and Skorohod (1974) or Ethier and Kurtz (1986). The tools in Stokey, Lucas, and Prescott (1989) are sufficient to prove that the optimal path of capital-labor ratio in the neoclassical growth model under uncertainty converges to a unique invariant distribution, and they can also be used to prove the existence of a stationary equilibrium in the Bewley economy.

The first systematic analysis of competitive equilibrium under uncertainty is provided in Lucas and Prescott (1971). Ljungqvist and Sargent (2005, Chapter 12) provides an excellent textbook treatment. The material in Section 17.2 is similar to Ljungqvist and Sargent's treatment but is somewhat more detailed.

The RBC literature is enormous, and Section 17.3 only scratches the surface. The classic papers in this literature are Kydland and Prescott (1982) and Long and Plosser (1983). Ljungqvist and Sargent (2005) again provides a good introduction. The collection of papers in Cooley (1995) is an excellent starting point and provides a range of tools for theoretical and quantitative analysis. Blanchard and Fischer (1989) summarizes various critiques of the RBC approach. The interested reader is also referred to the exchange between Edward Prescott and Lawrence Summers (Prescott, 1986; Summers, 1986) and to the review of the more recent literature in King and Rebelo (1999).

Section 17.4 presents the incomplete markets model first introduced by Truman Bewley (1977, 1980). This model has become one of the workhorse models of macroeconomics and has been used for analysis of business cycle dynamics, income distribution, optimal fiscal policy, monetary policy, and asset pricing. A more modern treatment is provided in Aiyagari (1994), though the published version of the paper does not contain the proofs of the main results. The reader is referred to Bewley (1977, 1980) and to the working paper version of Aiyagari's paper, Aiyagari (1993), for more details on some of the propositions stated in Section 17.4 as well as a proof of existence of a stationary equilibrium. Krusell and Smith (1998, 2005), among others, have used this model for business cycle analysis and have also provided new quantitative tools for the study of incomplete market economies.

Section 17.6 builds on Acemoglu and Zilibotti (1997), and more details on some of the results stated in this section are provided there. Evidence on the relationship between economic development and volatility is provided in Acemoglu and Zilibotti (1997), Imbs and Wacziarg (2003) and Koren and Tenreyro (2007). Ramey and Ramey (1995) also provide related evidence. The concept of decentralized equilibrium used in this model is not Arrow-Debreu. Instead it imposes price-taking behavior in all open markets and determines the set of open markets via a free-entry condition. This equilibrium concept is natural and is used in various different contexts in general equilibrium theory; see, for example, Hart (1979), Makowski (1980), and Allen and Gale (1991).

17.9 Exercises

17.1 Proposition 17.2 shows that $k(t+1)$ is increasing in $k(t)$ and $z(t)$. Provide sufficient conditions such that $c(t)$ is also increasing in these variables.

17.2 Consider the neoclassical growth model under uncertainty analyzed in Section 17.1, and assume that $z(t)$ is realized after $c(t)$ and $k(t+1)$ are chosen.

(a) Show that if $z(t)$ is distributed independently across periods, the choice of capital stock and consumption in this economy is identical to that in a neoclassical growth model under certainty with a modified production function. Explain the intuition for this result.

(b) Now suppose that $z(t)$ is not distributed independently across periods. Establish the equivalent of Proposition 17.1. How does the behavior in this economy differ from the neoclassical growth model under uncertainty in Section 17.1?

17.3 Consider the same production structure as in Sections 17.1 and 17.2, but assume that regardless of the level of the capital stock and the realization of the stochastic variable, each household saves a constant fraction s of its income. Characterize the stochastic law of motion of this economy. How does equilibrium behavior in this economy differ from that in the canonical neoclassical growth model under uncertainty?

17.4 Consider the neoclassical growth model under uncertainty in Section 17.1.

(a) Provide conditions under which $\pi(k, z)$ is strictly increasing in both of its arguments.

(b) Show that when the conditions in part a hold, the capital-labor ratio can never converge to a constant unless z has a degenerate distribution (always taking the same value).

17.5 Consider Example 17.1.

(a) Prove that (17.10) cannot be satisfied for any $B_0 \neq 0$.

(b) Conjecture that the value function for this example takes the form $V(k, z) = B_2 + B_3 \log k + B_4 \log z$. Verify this guess and compute the parameters B_2, B_3, and B_3.

17.6 Show that the policy function in Example 17.1, $\pi(k, z) = \beta \alpha z k^\alpha$, applies when z follows a general Markov process rather than a Markov chain. [Hint: instead of the summation, replace the expectations sign with an appropriately defined integral, and cancel terms under the integral sign.]

17.7 (a) Consider the economy analyzed in Example 17.1 with $0 < z_1 < z_N < \infty$. Characterize the limiting invariant distribution of the capital-labor ratio, and show that the stochastic correspondence of the capital stock can be represented by Figure 17.1 in Section 17.5. Use this figure to show that the capital-labor ratio k always grows when it is sufficiently small and always declines when it is large.

(b) Consider the special case where z takes two values, z_h and z_l, with each value persisting with probability $q > 1/2$ and switching to the other value with probability $1 - q$. Show that as $q \to 1$, the behavior of the capital-labor ratio converges to its equilibrium in the neoclassical growth model under certainty.

17.8 Consider the economy studied in Example 17.1, but suppose that $\delta < 1$. Show that in this case there does not exist a closed-form expression for the policy function $\pi(k, z)$.

17.9 Write the maximization problem of the social planner explicitly as a sequence problem, with output, capital, and labor following different histories interpreted as different Arrow-Debreu commodities. Using this formulation, carefully show that all of the conditions of Theorem 5.7 are satisfied, so that the optimal growth path can be decentralized as a competitive equilibrium.

17.10 Consider an extended version of the neoclassical growth model under uncertainty such that the instantaneous utility function of the representative household is $u(c, b)$, where b is a random variable following a Markov chain.

   (a) Set up and analyze the optimal growth problem in this economy. Show that the optimal consumption sequence satisfies a modified stochastic Euler equation.

   (b) Prove that Theorem 5.7 can be applied to this economy and the optimum growth path can be decentralized as a competitive growth path.

17.11 Explain why in Section 16.5.1 in the previous chapter, the Lagrange multiplier $\tilde{\lambda}[y^t]$ was conditioned on the entire history of labor income realizations, while in the formulation of the competitive equilibrium with a full set of Arrow-Debreu commodities (contingent claims) in Section 17.2, there is a single multiplier λ associated with the lifetime budget constraint.

17.12 Consider the model of competitive equilibrium in Section 17.2. Repeat the analysis of the competitive equilibrium of the neoclassical growth model under uncertainty by assuming that instead of a price for buying and selling capital goods in each state ($R_0[z^t]$), there is a market for renting capital goods. Let the rental price of capital goods in terms of date 0 final good be $\tilde{R}_0[z^t]$ when the sequence of stochastic variables is z^t. Characterize the competitive equilibrium, and show that it is equivalent to that obtained in Section 17.2. Explain why the two formulations give identical results.

17.13 Prove Proposition 17.3. [Hint: use Theorem 16.8 together with (17.6) and (17.22) and then show that the lifetime budget constraint (17.11) implies (17.7).]

17.14 Characterize the competitive equilibrium path of the neoclassical growth model under uncertainty analyzed in Section 17.2 with sequential trading using the sequence (rather than the recursive) formulation of the household's maximization problem.

17.15 Show that Theorems 16.1–16.7 can be applied to $V(a, z)$ defined in (17.24), and establish that $V(a, z)$ is continuous, strictly increasing in both of its arguments, concave, and differentiable in a.

17.16 Derive (17.27).

17.17 Prove Proposition 17.4.

17.18 Consider the RBC model presented in Section 17.3, and suppose that the production function takes the form $F(K, zAL)$, with both z and A corresponding to labor-augmenting technological productivity terms. Suppose that z follows a Markov chain and $A(t + 1) = (1 + g)A(t)$ is an exogenous and deterministic productivity growth process. Set up the social planner's problem in this case. What restrictions do we need to impose on $u(C, L)$ to ensure that the optimal growth path corresponds to a "BGP," where labor supply does not (with probability 1) go to zero or infinity?

17.19 In Example 17.2, suppose that the utility function of the representative household is $u(C, L) = \log C + h(L)$, where $h(\cdot)$ is a continuous, decreasing, and concave function. Show that the equilibrium level of labor supply is constant and independent of the level of capital stock and the realization of the productivity shock.

17.20 Explain why in the Bewley model of Section 17.4, the budget constraint of the household must hold along all sample paths. Compare the resulting constraint, (17.30), to (17.11) in Section 17.2.

17.21 Prove Proposition 17.5.

17.22 What would happen if, instead of the logarithmic preferences (17.44), the utility function of the representative household in Section 17.6 took the more general form $u\left(c_1(t)\right) + \mathbb{E}_t u\left(c_2(t+1)\right)$? Could the growth rate of the economy be higher when $u(\cdot)$ becomes more concave? [Hint: distinguish between the effect of $u(\cdot)$ on asset allocation given the level of savings and its effect on the total amount of savings.]

17.23 In the model of Section 17.6, prove that the maximization problem of the representative household implies that for any $j, j' \in J(t)$, $I^*(j, t) = I^*(j', t)$.

17.24 In the model of Section 17.6, prove that if an intermediate sector $j^* \in J(t)$, then all sectors $j \leq j^*$ are also in $J(t)$.

17.25 In the model of Section 17.6, prove that the condition $Q \geq (2 - \gamma)q$ is sufficient to ensure that there is a unique intersection between the curves for (17.43) and (17.56) in Figure 17.2.

17.26 Prove Proposition 17.7. In particular, show that if $n < n^*[K]$, then there exists a profitable deviation for a financial intermediary to offer securities for a previously unavailable sector and make positive profits, and that if $n > n^*[K]$, feasibility is violated.

17.27 (a) Prove Proposition 17.9.

(b) Suppose that condition (17.61) is not satisfied. Does the stochastic process $\{K(t)\}_{t=0}^{\infty}$ converge? Does it converge to a point?

17.28 Prove Proposition 17.10.

17.29 Prove Proposition 17.11. [Hint: set up the Lagrangian, and show that when all sectors cannot be opened, the social planner will not choose a balanced portfolio.]

* 17.30 Consider the following two-period economy similar to Section 17.6. There are I financial intermediaries who compete à la Bertrand without using any resources. They invest funds on behalf of households in any of the projects of this economy. There are N projects in this economy, indexed by $j = 1, 2, \ldots, N$. Project j requires a minimum size investment $M(j)$, and without loss of generality rank the projects in ascending order of minimum size. There is continuum of households with measure normalized to 1, each with the utility function $u(c) + \mathbb{E}v(c')$, where c is consumption today, and c' is consumption tomorrow, so that $\mathbb{E}v(c')$ denotes expected utility from tomorrow's consumption. Each household has total resources equal to w and decides how much to consume, how much to save, and then how to allocate its savings. Assume that $u(\cdot)$ and $v(\cdot)$ are strictly concave and increasing. Funds today are turned into consumption tomorrow by financial intermediaries. Alternatively, funds can also be invested in a safe linear technology with rate of return q. Let the investment in asset j be $K(j)$, then if $K(j) \geq M(j)$, asset j has probability π of paying out $Qk(j)$ such that $\pi Q > q$. On the other hand if $K(j) < M(j)$, the pay-out is equal to zero.

(a) Denote the "share price" of \$1 invested in project j, which pays out \$Q with probability π and zero otherwise, by $p(j)$. Show that financial competition ensures that if $K(j), K(j') > 0$, then $p(j) = p(j') = 1$.

(b) Now assume that the returns of each project is independently drawn; that is, the probability that asset j pays out Q is equal to π independent of the realization of the returns of other projects. Show that $K(j) = K(j')$ for all j and j'.

(c) Characterize the decentralized equilibrium of this economy.

(d) Show that when some projects are inactive, the decentralized equilibrium may be constrained Pareto inefficient. Explain why the decentralized equilibrium may be constrained efficient in some cases even though some projects are inactive.

(e) Characterize the efficient allocation.

(f) Informally discuss what happens if $M(j)$ is not a minimum size requirement but a fixed cost (such that average costs are falling). [Hint: there are two cases to distinguish; (1) linear prices; (2) price discrimination.]

PART VI

TECHNOLOGY DIFFUSION, TRADE, AND INTERDEPENDENCES

One of the most important shortcomings of the models presented so far is that each country is treated as an isolated island that does not interact with the rest of the world. This is problematic for at least two reasons. The first is related to the technological interdependences across countries and the second to international trade (in commodities and in assets). In this part of the book, I investigate the implications of technological and trade interdependences on the process of economic growth.

The models presented so far treat technology either as exogenous or as endogenously generated within the boundaries of the economy in question. We have already seen how allowing for endogeneity of technology provides new and important insights about the process of growth. But should we think of the potential technology differences between Portugal and Nigeria as resulting from lower R&D in Nigeria? The answer to this question is most probably no. Nigeria, like most less-developed or developing countries, imports many of its technologies from the rest of the world. The same is the case for Portugal despite its substantially more developed economy. This observation suggests that a framework in which *frontier* technologies in the world are produced in the United States or other advanced economies and then copied or adopted by other "follower" countries provides a better approximation to reality. Therefore to understand technology differences between advanced and developing economies, we should focus not only, or not even primarily, on differential rates of endogenous technology generation in these economies, but also on their decisions concerning technology adoption and efficient technology use.

While the exogenous growth models of Chapters 2 and 8 have this feature, they too have important shortcomings. First, technology is entirely exogenous, so interesting economic decisions only concern investment in physical capital. There is a conceptually and empirically compelling sense in which technology is different from physical capital (and also from human capital), so we would like to understand sources of differences in technology arising endogenously across countries. Thus the recognition that technology adoption from the world frontier matters is not the same as accepting that the Solow or the neoclassical growth models are the best vehicles for studying cross-country income differences. Second, while the emphasis on technology adoption makes the process of growth resemble the exogenous growth models of Chapters 2 and 8, technological advances at the world level are unlikely to be "manna from heaven." Instead, economic growth at the world level results either from the interaction of the adoption and R&D decisions of all countries or perhaps from the innovations by frontier economies. Thus models in which the growth rate at the world level is endogenous and interacts (and coexists) with technology adoption may provide a better approximation to reality and a better framework for the analysis of the mechanics of economic growth. We will also see that international trade may play the same role of linking growth across countries while allowing for endogenous world growth.

In Chapter 18, I start with models of technology adoption and investigate the factors affecting the speed and nature of technology adoption. In addition to factors slowing down technology diffusion and the importance of barriers against new technologies, I discuss the role of whether technologies from the world frontier are appropriate for the needs of less-developed countries. Recall also that "technology differences" not only reflect differences in techniques used in production but also differences in the organization of production affecting the efficiency with which existing factors of production are utilized. A satisfactory theory of technology differences among countries must therefore pay attention to barriers to technology adoption and to potential inefficiencies in the organization of production, leading to apparent technology differences across countries. Chapter 18 also provides a simple model of inefficient technology adoption resulting from contracting problems among firms.

The second major element missing from our analysis so far, international trade and international capital flows, is discussed in Chapter 19. International trade in commodities and assets links the economic fortunes of the countries in the world as well. For example, economies with low capital-labor ratios may be able to borrow internationally, which would change equilibrium dynamics. Similarly and perhaps more importantly, less productive countries that export certain goods to the world economy will be linked with other economies because of changes in relative prices—because of changes in their terms of trade. This type of terms-of-trade effects may also work toward creating a framework in which, while the world economy grows endogenously, the growth rates of each country is linked to those of others through trading relationships. Finally, I emphasize the connections between international trade and technology adoption, in particular, emphasizing how trade and the "international product cycle" facilitate technology diffusion.

Throughout the rest of the book, including this part, my treatment will be less comprehensive than in the previous chapters. In particular, to economize on space I will be more selective in the range of models covered, focusing on the models that I believe provide the main insights in an economical fashion. I leave many alternative models and approaches to the discussion of the literature at the end or to exercises. In addition, I make somewhat greater use of simplifying assumptions and leave to exercises the proofs of results that are similar to those provided so far and the relaxation of some of the simplifying assumptions.

18

Diffusion of Technology

In many ways, the problem of innovation ought to be harder to model than the problem of technology adoption. Nevertheless the literature on economic growth and development has made more progress on models of innovation, such as those we discussed in Chapters 13–15, than on models of technology diffusion. This is in part because the process of technology adoption involves many challenging features. First, even within a single country, we observe considerable differences in the technologies used by different firms in the same narrowly defined industry. Second and relatedly, it is difficult to explain how in the globalized world in which we live some countries fail to import and use technologies that would significantly increase their productivity. In this chapter, I begin the study of these questions. Since potential barriers to technology adoption are intimately linked to the analysis of the political economy of growth, I return to some of these themes in Part VIII of the book. For now the emphasis is on how technological interdependences change the mechanics of economic growth and can thus enrich our understanding of the potential sources of cross-country income differences and economic growth over time.

I first provide a brief overview of some of the empirical patterns pertaining to technology adoption and diffusion within countries and industries, and how this appears to be important for within-industry productivity differences. I then turn to a benchmark model of world equilibrium with technology diffusion, which provides a reduced-form model for analyzing the slow diffusion of technological know-how across countries. I then enrich this model by incorporating investments in R&D and technology adoption. Next, I discuss issues of appropriate technology, and finally, I turn to the impact of contractual imperfections on technology adoption decisions. Throughout this chapter, the only interaction among countries is through technological exchange, and there is no international trade in goods or assets.

18.1 Productivity Differences and Technology

Let us first start with a brief overview of productivity and technology differences within countries. This overview will help us place the cross-country differences in productivity and technology into perspective. The most important lesson from the within-country studies is that productivity and technology differences are ubiquitous even across firms within narrow sectors in the same country.

18.1.1 Productivity and Technology Differences within Narrow Sectors

A large literature uses longitudinal micro-data (often for the manufacturing sector) to study labor and TFP differences across plants within narrow sectors (e.g., three- or four-digit manufacturing sectors). For our focus, the most important pattern that emerges from these studies is that, even within a narrow sector of the U.S. economy, there are significant differences in productivity across plants, with an approximately two- or threefold difference between the top and the bottom of the distribution (see, e.g., the survey in Bartelsman and Doms, 2000, for a summary of various studies and estimates). In addition, these productivity differences appear to be highly persistent (e.g., Baily, Hulten, and Campbell, 1992).

There is little consensus on the causes of these differences. Many studies find a correlation between plant productivity and plant or firm size, various measures of technology (in particular, IT technology), capital intensity, the skill level of the workforce, and management practices (e.g., Davis and Haltiwanger, 1991; Doms, Dunne, and Troske, 1997; Black and Lynch, 2005). Nevertheless, since all of these features are choice variables for firms, these correlations cannot be taken to be causal. Thus to a large extent the determinants of productivity differences across plants are still unknown. In this light, it should not appear as a surprise that there is no consensus on the determinants of cross-country differences in productivity.

Nevertheless the existing evidence suggests that technology differences are an important factor, at least as a proximate cause, for productivity differences. For example, Doms, Dunne, and Troske (1997) and Haltiwanger, Lane, and Spletzer (1999) document significant technology differences across plants within narrow sectors. Interestingly, as emphasized by Doms, Dunne, and Troske (1997) and Caselli and Coleman (2001a), a key determinant of technology adoption decisions seems to be the skill level of the workforce of the plant (often proxied by the share of nonproduction workers), though adoption of new technology does not typically lead to a significant change in the skill level of the employees of the plant. These results suggest that, consistent with some of the models discussed in Chapters 10 and 15, differences in the availability of skills and skilled workers might be an important determinant of technology adoption (and development).

The distribution of productivity across firms appears to be related to the entry of new and more-productive plants (and the exit of less-productive plants). For example, consistent with the basic Schumpeterian models of economic growth discussed in Chapter 14, Bartelsman and Doms (2000) and Foster, Haltiwanger, and Krizan (2000) document that entry of new plants makes an important contribution to industry productivity growth. Nevertheless entry and exit appear to account for only about 25% of average TFP growth, with the remaining productivity improvements accounted for by continuing plants. This suggests that models in which firms continually invest in technology and productivity (as in the models in Sections 14.3 and 14.4 in Chapter 14) may be important for understanding the productivity differences across firms and plants and also for the study of cross-country productivity differences.

18.1.2 Diffusion of New Technologies

A key implication of the sectoral studies is that, despite our presumption that technology and know-how are freely available and can be adopted easily, there are considerable technology and productivity differences among firms operating under similar circumstances. In addition, new and more productive technologies, once they arrive on the scene, diffuse and are gradually adopted by more firms and plants. The literature on technology diffusion studies this process of adoption of new technologies. As one might expect, there are parallels between the issue of technology diffusion across countries and slow technology diffusion across firms. Let us then briefly overview the main findings of the technology diffusion literature.

The classic paper in this area is Griliches's (1957) study of the adoption of hybrid corn in the United States. Griliches showed that the more productive hybrid corn diffused only slowly in U.S. agriculture and that this diffusion was affected by the local economic conditions of different areas. Consistent with the theoretical models presented so far, the likelihood of adoption appears to be related to the productivity contribution of the hybrid corn in a particular area, the market size, and the skill level of the workforce in the area. The importance of these factors has been found in other studies as well. Another important result of Griliches's study was to uncover the famous S-shape of diffusion, whereby a particular technology first spreads slowly and then once it reaches a critical level of adoption, it starts spreading much more rapidly. Finally, once a large fraction of the target population adopts the technology, the rate of adoption again declines. The overall pattern thus approximates an S curve or a logistic function.

The important lesson for our focus here is that productivity and technology differences are not only present across countries but also within countries. Moreover, even within countries better technologies are not immediately adopted by all firms. Nevertheless, the causes of within-country and cross-country productivity and technology differences might be different, and despite the presence of within-country differences, the significant cross-country differences are a major puzzle. For example, within-country productivity differences might be due to differences in managerial (entrepreneurial) ability or related to the success of the match between the manager and the technology (or the product). These types of explanations are unlikely to account for why almost all firms in many less-developed countries are much less productive than the typical firms in the United States and other advanced economies, or why the distribution of firm-level productivity is very different across countries. Motivated by the evidence briefly surveyed here, I discuss both models in which technology diffuses slowly across countries and models in which productivity differences may remain even when instantaneous technology diffusion and adoption are possible.

18.2 A Benchmark Model of Technology Diffusion

18.2.1 A Model of Exogenous Growth

In the spirit of providing the main insights with the simplest possible models, let us return to the Solow growth model of Chapter 2. Suppose that the world economy consists of J countries, indexed by $j = 1, \ldots, J$, each with access to an aggregate production function for producing a unique final good,

$$Y_j(t) = F(K_j(t), A_j(t)L_j(t)),$$

where $Y_j(t)$ is the output of this unique final good in country j at time t, and $K_j(t)$ and $L_j(t)$ are the capital stock and labor supply, respectively. Finally, $A_j(t)$ is the technology of this economy, which is both country-specific and time-varying. In line with the result in Theorem 2.6 in Chapter 2, technological change has already been assumed to be purely labor-augmenting (Harrod-neutral) in form. In addition, F satisfies the standard neoclassical assumptions, that is, Assumptions 1 and 2 from Chapter 2. Throughout this chapter and the next, whenever the world economy consists of J countries, I assume that J is large enough so that each country is "small" relative to the rest of the world and thus it ignores its effect on world aggregates.[1]

---

1. We can think of J as a large finite number or consider the limit where $J \to \infty$. Alternatively, we could have assumed that there is a continuum rather than a countable number of countries. None of the results in this and the next chapter depend on whether the number of countries is a continuum or finite. Throughout I work with a finite number of countries to simplify the exposition.

Using our usual approach, income per capita in country j at time t is

$$y_j(t) \equiv \frac{Y_j(t)}{L_j(t)}$$

$$= A_j(t) F\left(\frac{K_j(t)}{A_j(t)L_j(t)}, 1\right)$$

$$\equiv A_j(t) f(k_j(t)),$$

where the second line uses the fact that F exhibits constant returns to scale (Assumption 1) and the third line defines the per capita production function $f(\cdot)$ and the effective capital-labor ratio in country j at time t,

$$k_j(t) \equiv \frac{K_j(t)}{A_j(t)L_j(t)}.$$

Suppose that time is continuous, there is population growth at the constant rate $n_j \geq 0$ in country j, and there is an exogenous saving rate equal to $s_j \in (0, 1)$ in country j and a depreciation rate of $\delta \geq 0$ for capital, so that the law of motion of capital for each country is given by

$$\dot{k}_j(t) = s_j f(k_j(t)) - (n_j + g_j(t) + \delta)k_j(t), \qquad (18.1)$$

where

$$g_j(t) \equiv \frac{\dot{A}_j(t)}{A_j(t)} \qquad (18.2)$$

is the growth rate of technology of country j at time t (see Exercise 18.1). The initial conditions are $k_j(0) > 0$ and $A_j(0) > 0$ for each $j = 1, \ldots, J$.

To start with, technology diffusion is modeled in a reduced-form way. Let us assume that the world's technology frontier, denoted by $A(t)$, grows exogenously at the constant rate

$$g \equiv \frac{\dot{A}(t)}{A(t)} > 0,$$

with an initial condition $A(0) > 0$. I refer to $A(t)$ as the "world technology" or sometimes as the "world technology frontier." It encapsulates the maximal knowledge that any country can have, so that $A_j(t) \leq A(t)$ for all j and t. Each country's technology progresses as a result of absorbing the world's technological knowledge. In particular, let us posit the following law of motion for each country's technology:

$$\dot{A}_j(t) = \sigma_j(A(t) - A_j(t)) + \lambda_j A_j(t), \qquad (18.3)$$

where $\sigma_j \in (0, \infty)$ and $\lambda_j \in [0, g)$ for each $j = 1, \ldots, J$. Equation (18.3) implies that each country absorbs world technology at some exogenous technology absorption rate σ_j. In practice, absorption corresponds both to straightforward adoption of existing technologies and to adaptation of existing blueprints to the conditions prevailing in a specific country, so that they can be used with the other technologies and practices in place. This parameter varies across countries because of differences in their human capital or other investments (see below) and also because of institutional or policy barriers affecting technology adoption. The parameter multiplies the difference $A(t) - A_j(t)$, since it is this difference that remains to be absorbed by the country in question—if $A(t) = A_j(t)$, there is nothing to absorb from the world technology frontier. Though natural, this formulation has important economic consequences. In particular, it implies that countries that are relatively "backward" (in the sense of having a low $A_j(t)$ compared to the frontier) tend to grow faster, because they have more technology to absorb or more room for catch-up. This potential advantage of relatively backward economies plays an important role in ensuring a stable world income distribution across countries. It also formalizes an idea that originates in Gerschenkron's (1962) essay, *Economic Backwardness in Historical Perspective*, that rapid catch-up by relatively backward countries is important for understanding cross-country growth patterns.

Equation (18.3) also implies that technological progress can happen locally as well, that is, building upon the knowledge stock of country j, $A_j(t)$. The parameter λ_j captures the speed at which this happens. This equation therefore contains the two major forms of technological progress that a particular country can experience: absorption from the world technology frontier and local technological advances. Its functional form is adopted for simplicity.

Notice that (18.3) sidesteps one of the major issues raised at the beginning of this chapter: it posits that despite the relatively free flow of information across the globe, the process of technology transfer between countries is a slow one. The assumption that $\sigma_j < \infty$ imposes this feature. In particular, since $\sigma_j < \infty$, $A_j(t) < A(t)$ implies that $A_j(t + \Delta t) < A(t + \Delta t)$, at least for $\Delta t > 0$ sufficiently small. Consequently, countries that have access to only a subset of the production techniques (blueprints) available in the world do not immediately acquire all of the knowledge that they do not currently have access to.

To proceed with the analysis of this model, let us define

$$a_j(t) \equiv \frac{A_j(t)}{A(t)}$$

as an inverse measure of the proportional technology gap between country j in the world or alternatively as an inverse measure of country j's *distance to the frontier* (distance to the world technology frontier). We can then write the above equation as (see Exercise 18.3)

$$\dot{a}_j(t) = \sigma_j - (\sigma_j + g - \lambda_j)a_j(t). \tag{18.4}$$

Clearly the initial conditions $A(0) > 0$ and $A_j(0) > 0$ give a unique initial condition for the differential equation for a_j: $a_j(0) \equiv A_j(0)/A(0) > 0$.

Given the description of the environment above, the dynamics of the world income per capita levels and technology are determined by $2J$ differential equations. For each j, one of (18.1) and one of (18.4) applies. These equations characterize the steady-state distribution of technology and income per capita in the world economy and its transitional dynamics. What makes the analysis of this world equilibrium relatively straightforward is the *block recursiveness* of the system of differential equations governing the behavior of income per capita and technology across countries. The law of motion of (18.4) for country j only depends on $a_j(t)$, so it can be solved without reference to the law of motion of $k_j(t)$ and to the law of motion of $\{k_{j'}(t), a_{j'}(t)\}_{j' \neq j}$. Once (18.4) is solved, then (18.1) becomes a first-order nonautonomous differential equation in a single variable. The fact that it is nonautonomous is a consequence of the fact that $g_j(t)$ on the right-hand side is given as

$$g_j(t) = \frac{\dot{a}_j(t)}{a_j(t)} + g.$$

Once we solve for the law of motion of $a_j(t)$, this is simply a function of time, making (18.1) a simple nonautonomous differential equation.

Let us start the analysis with the steady-state world equilibrium. A *world equilibrium* is defined as an allocation $\{[k_j(t), a_j(t)]_{t \geq 0}\}_{j=1}^{J}$ such that (18.1) and (18.4) are satisfied for each $j = 1, \ldots, J$ and for all t, starting with the initial conditions $\{k_j(0), a_j(0)\}_{j=1}^{J}$. A *steady-state world equilibrium* is then defined as a steady state of this equilibrium path, that is, an equilibrium with $\dot{k}_j(t) = \dot{a}_j(t) = 0$ for each $j = 1, \ldots, J$. The steady-state equilibria studied in this chapter exhibit constant growth, so I could have alternatively referred to them as "balanced growth path equilibria." Throughout I use the term "steady-state equilibrium" for consistency.[2]

Proposition 18.1 *In the above-described model, there exists a unique steady-state world equilibrium in which income per capita in all countries grows at the same rate $g > 0$. Moreover, for each $j = 1, \ldots, J$, we have*

$$a_j^* = \frac{\sigma_j}{\sigma_j + g - \lambda_j},$$ (18.5)

and k_j^* is uniquely determined by

$$s_j \frac{f(k_j^*)}{k_j^*} = n_j + g + \delta.$$

The steady-state world equilibrium $\{k_j^*, a_j^*\}_{j=1}^{J}$ is globally stable in the sense that starting with any strictly positive initial values $\{k_j(0), a_j(0)\}_{j=1}^{J}$, the equilibrium path $\{k_j(t), a_j(t)\}_{j=1}^{J}$ converges to $\{k_j^*, a_j^*\}_{j=1}^{J}$.

Proof.   First solve (18.1) and (18.4) for each $j = 1, \ldots, J$, imposing the steady-state condition that $\dot{k}_j(t) = \dot{a}_j(t) = 0$. This yields a unique solution, establishing the uniqueness of the steady-state equilibrium. Then standard arguments show that the steady state a_j^* of the differential equation for $a_j(t)$ is globally stable. Using this result, the global stability of the steady state of the differential equation for $k_j(t)$ follows straightforwardly. Exercise 18.4 asks you to complete the details of this proof.   ■

Several features of this world equilibrium are noteworthy. First, there is a unique steady-state world equilibrium and it is globally stable. This enables us to perform simple comparative static and comparative dynamic exercises (see Exercise 18.5). Second and most importantly, despite differences in saving rates and technology absorption rates across countries, income per capita in all economies grows at the same rate, which is equal to the growth rate of the world technology frontier, g. Equation (18.3) clarifies the reason for this: the rate of technology diffusion (absorption) is higher when the gap between the world technology frontier and the technology level of a particular country is greater. Thus there is a force pulling backward economies toward the technology frontier, and in steady state this force is powerful enough to ensure that all countries grow at the same rate.

Does this imply that all countries will converge to the same level of income per capita? The answer is clearly no. Differences in saving rates and absorption rates translate into *level differences* (instead of growth rate differences) across countries. For example, a society with a low level of σ_j initially grows less than others, until it is sufficiently behind the world technology frontier. At this point, it will also grow at the world rate, g. This discussion

---

2. In the remainder, I sometimes write $[k_j(t), a_j(t)]_{t \geq 0}$ instead of $[k_j(t), a_j(t)]_{t=0}^{\infty}$ to simplify the notation.

illustrates that it is precisely the endogenous technology gap between a country and the world frontier that ensures growth at the rate g for all countries. Thus societies that are unsuccessful in absorbing world technologies, those that impose barriers slowing technology diffusion (those with low σ_j), and those that are not sufficiently innovative in developing their own local technologies (those with low λ_j) will be poorer. Moreover, as in the baseline Solow model, those with low saving rates will also be poorer. These results are summarized in the following proposition.

Proposition 18.2 *Steady-state income per capita level of country j can be written as $y_j^*(t) = \exp(gt)y_j^*$, where y_j^* is increasing in σ_j, λ_j, and s_j and decreasing in n_j and δ. It does not depend on $\sigma_{j'}$, $\lambda_{j'}$, $s_{j'}$ and $n_{j'}$ for any $j' \neq j$.*

Proof. See Exercise 18.7. ∎

A particularly convenient—but also restrictive—feature of the equilibrium studied here is that even though there is technology diffusion and interdependences in this world equilibrium, there is no interaction among countries. Each country's steady-state income per capita (and in fact path of income per capita) depends only on the behavior of the world technology frontier and its own parameters. Later in this chapter, we will see models in which there is more interaction between the decisions of individual countries.

18.2.2 Household Optimization

It is straightforward to incorporate household optimization into this benchmark model of technology transfer. In particular, let us now suppose that each country admits a representative household with preferences at time $t = 0$ given by

$$U_j = \int_0^\infty \exp(-(\rho - n_j)t)\frac{c_j(t)^{1-\theta} - 1}{1 - \theta}dt, \tag{18.6}$$

where $c_j(t) \equiv C_j(t)/L_j(t)$ is per capita consumption in country j at time t, and I imposed the restriction that all countries have the same time discount rate ρ. This latter feature is to simplify the discussion in the text, and Exercise 18.9 generalizes the results here to a world economy with different discount rates. This is an important generalization, since it highlights that a stable world income distribution does not depend on equal discount rates or asymptotically equal saving rates across countries.

As in the neoclassical growth model, the resource constraint takes the form

$$\dot{k}_j(t) = f(k_j(t)) - \tilde{c}_j(t) - (n_j + g_j(t) + \delta)k_j(t),$$

where $\tilde{c}_j(t) \equiv c_j(t)/A_j(t) \equiv C_j(t)/(A_j(t)L_j(t))$ is consumption normalized by effective units of labor. This equation now replaces (18.1) as the law of motion of the effective capital-labor ratio of country j.

The world equilibrium and the steady-state world equilibrium are defined in a similar fashion, except that now consumption decisions maximize the utility of the representative household in each country. The same analysis as in Chapter 8 leads to the next proposition.

Proposition 18.3 *Consider the above-described model with household optimization, with preferences given by (18.6), and suppose that $\rho - n_j > (1 - \theta)g$ for $j = 1, \ldots, J$. Then there* *exists a unique steady-state world equilibrium where for each j, a_j^* is given by (18.5) and k_j^* is uniquely determined by*

$$f'(k_j^*) = \rho + \delta + \theta g,$$

and consumption per capita in each country grows at the rate $g > 0$.

Moreover the steady-state world equilibrium is globally saddle-path stable: starting with any strictly positive initial values $\{k_j(0), a_j(0)\}_{j=1}^J$, the equilibrium path $\{k_j(t), a_j(t), \tilde{c}_j(t)\}_{j=1}^J$ converges to $\{k_j^*, a_j^*, \tilde{c}_j^*\}_{j=1}^J$, where $\tilde{c}_j^*$ is the steady-state consumption to effective labor ratio in economy j.

Proof. We can first show that a_j^* can be determined from the differential equation (18.4) without reference to any other variables and satisfies (18.5). The consumption Euler equations and the dynamics of capital accumulation are the same as in the baseline neoclassical growth model, taking into account that in steady state $g_j(t) = g$. To complete the proof of the proposition, we need to show the stability of a_j^*, and then taking into account the behavior of $g_j(t)$, we must establish the saddle-path stability of k_j^* using the same type of analysis as in Chapter 8—which is slightly more complicated here because the differential equation for capital accumulation is not autonomous. You are asked to complete these details in Exercise 18.8. ∎

This proposition shows that all qualitative results of the benchmark model of technology diffusion apply regardless of whether we assume constant saving rates or dynamic household maximization (as long as we ensure that the growth rate is not so high as to lead to infinite utility and violate the transversality condition). Naturally, an equilibrium now corresponds not only to paths of $\{k_j(t), a_j(t)\}$ but also includes the time path of consumption to effective labor, $\tilde{c}_j(t)$. Consequently, the appropriate notion of stability is saddle-path stability, which the equilibrium in Proposition 18.3 satisfies.

18.2.3 The Role of Human Capital in Technology Diffusion

The model presented above is in part inspired by the classic paper by Richard Nelson and Edmund Phelps (1966), which was already discussed in Chapter 10. Recall that the Becker-Mincer view emphasizes how human capital increases the productivity of the labor hours supplied by an individual. While this approach allows the effect of human capital to be different in different tasks, in most applications it is presumed that greater human capital translates into higher productivity in all or most tasks, with the set of productive tasks typically taken as given. In contrast, Nelson and Phelps (and Ted Schultz) emphasize the role of human capital in facilitating the adoption of new technologies and adaptation to changing environments.

In terms of the model described above, the simplest way of capturing this argument is to posit that the parameter σ_j is a function of the human capital of the workforce. The greater is the human capital of the workforce, the higher is the absorption capacity of the economy. If so, high human capital societies will be richer because, as shown in Proposition 18.2, economies with higher σ_j have higher steady-state levels of income.

While this modification leaves the mathematical exposition of the model unchanged, the implications for how we view the growth experiences of societies with different levels of human capital are potentially quite distinct from the Becker-Mincer approach (or at the very least, from the simplest version of the Becker-Mincer approach). The latter approach suggests that we can approximate the role of human capital in economic development by carefully accounting for its role in the aggregate production function. This, in turn, can be done by estimating individual returns to schooling and returns to other dimensions of human capital in the labor market. The

Nelson-Phelps-Schultz view, on the other hand, suggests that even if the contribution of human capital to productivity in regular activities is limited, lack of human capital may slow down the process of technology diffusion.

18.2.4 Barriers to Technology Adoption

As discussed in Chapter 8, one of the main criticisms against the neoclassical growth model has been its inability to generate quantitatively large differences in cross-country income per capita. Many economists view this as related to the fact that the basic neoclassical growth model does not provide an explanation for technology differences. The model in this section presents a reduced-form model of technology differences across countries and thus enables us to enrich the Solow or the neoclassical growth models to incorporate technology differences. Nevertheless, such a theory will be useful only to the extent that the key parameters, such as σ_j and λ_j, can be mapped to data. Section 18.2.3 discussed ideas linking the parameter σ_j to human capital. An alternative, emphasized by Parente and Prescott (1994), is to link σ_j to barriers to technology adoption. Parente and Prescott construct a variant of the neoclassical growth model in which investments affect technology absorption and countries differ in terms of the barriers that they place in the paths of firms in this process. In terms of the reduced-form model here, the Parente-Prescott mechanism can be captured by interpreting σ_j as a function of property rights institutions or other institutional or policy features.

This perspective is useful as it gives us a concrete way of thinking of the reasons that σ_j may vary across countries. Nevertheless, it is still unsatisfactory in two important respects. First, exactly how these institutions affect technology adoption is left as a black box. Second and more importantly, why some societies choose to create barriers against technology adoption while others do not is left unexplained. The models that combine technology diffusion with endogenous technology decisions, which are presented in the next section, make some progress on the first point. The question of why some societies block technology adoption will be the topic of Part VIII.

18.3 Technology Diffusion and Endogenous Growth

In the previous section, technology diffusion took place exogenously, in the sense that firms did not engage in R&D or investment-type activities to improve their technologies. In this section, I introduce these types of purposeful activities directed at improving technology. The section is separated into two parts. In the first, the world growth rate is taken as exogenous. In the second, it is endogenous.

18.3.1 Exogenous World Growth Rate

To keep the exposition as brief as possible, I use the baseline endogenous technological change model with expanding machine variety and lab-equipment specification as in Section 13.1 of Chapter 13, and I frequently refer to the analysis there. Clearly, different versions of the endogenous technological change models could be used for the same purposes.

The aggregate production function of economy $j = 1, \ldots, J$ at time t is

$$Y_j(t) = \frac{1}{1-\beta} \left(\int_0^{N_j(t)} x_j(v, t)^{1-\beta} dv \right) L_j^{\beta}, \qquad (18.7)$$

where L_j is the aggregate labor input, which is assumed to be constant over time; $N_j(t)$ denotes the number (measure) of varieties of machines available to country j at time t; and $x_j(v, t)$ is the total amount of machine variety v used at time t. Suppose again that each x depreciates fully after use. As in Chapter 13, each variety in economy j is owned by a technology monopolist, which sells machines embodying this technology at the profit-maximizing (rental) price $p_j^x(v, t)$. This monopolist can produce each unit of the machine at a cost of $\psi \equiv 1 - \beta$ units on the final good, where the normalization is again introduced to simplify the expressions.

Since there is no international trade, firms in country j can only use technologies supplied by technology monopolists in their country. This assumption introduces the potential differences in the knowledge stock available to different countries.

Each country admits a representative household with the same preferences as in (18.6), except that there is no population growth, that is, $n_j = 0$ for all j. New varieties are again produced by investment, and thus the resource constraint for each country at each point in time is

$$C_j(t) + X_j(t) + \zeta_j Z_j(t) \leq Y_j(t), \tag{18.8}$$

where $X_j(t)$ is investment or spending on inputs at time t, and $Z_j(t)$ is expenditure on technology adoption at time t, which may take the form of R&D or other expenditures, such as the purchase or rental of machines embodying new technologies. The parameter ζ_j is introduced as a potential source of differences in the cost of technology adoption across countries, which may result from institutional barriers against innovation as emphasized by Parente and Prescott (1994), from subsidies to R&D and to technology, or from other tax policies. It may also be a function of the human capital of the workforce of country j because of the role of human capital in technology adoption emphasized by Nelson and Phelps (1966).

The main difference from the environment in Chapter 13 is in the innovation possibilities frontier, which now takes the form

$$\dot{N}_j(t) = \eta_j \left(\frac{N(t)}{N_j(t)} \right)^\phi Z_j(t), \tag{18.9}$$

where $\eta_j > 0$ for all j, and $\phi > 0$ and is common to all economies. This form of the innovation possibilities frontier captures the same basic idea as (18.3), but what matters is not the absolute gap in technology but the proportional gap. This functional form is adopted for simplicity. I assume that each economy starts with some initial technology stock $N_j(0) > 0$. Finally, as noted above, the world technology frontier of varieties expands at an exogenous rate $g > 0$, that is,

$$\dot{N}(t) = g N(t). \tag{18.10}$$

The analysis in Chapter 13 implies that the flow profits of a technology monopolist at time t in economy j is given by $\pi_j(t) = \beta L_j$. Suppose a steady-state (BGP) equilibrium exists in which the interest rate is constant at some level $r_j^* > 0$. Then the net present discounted value of a new machine is

$$V_j^* = \frac{\beta L_j}{r_j^*}.$$

If the steady state involves the same rate of growth in each country, then $N_j(t)$ will also grow at the rate g, so that $N_j(t)/N(t)$ remains constant, say at some level μ_j^*. In that case, an additional unit of technology spending creates profits equal to $\eta_j(\mu_j^*)^{-\phi}V_j^*$ counterbalanced against the cost of ζ_j. Free entry (with positive activity) then requires

$$\mu_j^* = \left(\frac{\eta_j\beta L_j}{\zeta_j r^*}\right)^{1/\phi}, \tag{18.11}$$

where I have also used the fact that given the preferences in (18.6), equal growth rates across countries imply that the interest rates are the same in all countries (equal to $r^* = \rho + \theta g$).

Since a higher μ_j implies that country j is technologically more advanced and thus richer than others, (18.11) shows that societies with better innovation possibilities (as captured by the parameter η_j) and those with lower cost of R&D (corresponding to lower ζ_j) will be technologically more advanced and richer. This equation also incorporates a scale effect as in the standard endogenous technological change models, so a country with a greater labor force will also be richer. This is for the same reason that a greater labor force leads to faster growth in the baseline endogenous technological change model: a greater labor force creates more demand for machines, making R&D more profitable.

Proposition 18.4 *Consider the model with endogenous technology adoption described in this section. Suppose that $\rho > (1 - \theta)g$. Then there exists a unique steady-state world equilibrium where relative technology levels are given by (18.11) and all countries grow at the same rate $g > 0$.*

Moreover this steady-state equilibrium is globally saddle-path stable in the sense that starting with any strictly positive vector of initial conditions $N(0)$ and $(N_1(0), \ldots, N_J(0))$, the equilibrium path of $(N_1(t), \ldots, N_J(t))$ converges to $(\mu_1^* N(t), \ldots, \mu_J^* N(t))$.

Proof. First show that the specified steady-state equilibrium is the only steady-state equilibrium in which all countries grow at the same rate. Then consider the value function of technology monopolists in each country as in Chapter 13 and show that the number of varieties in each country must asymptotically grow at the rate g. Exercise 18.11 asks you to complete this proof. ∎

This result and the preceding analysis show that endogenizing investments in technology adoption leads to an equilibrium pattern similar to that in the previous section. The main difference is that we can now pinpoint the factors that affect the rates of technology adoption and relate them to the profit incentives of firms. An explicit model of technology decisions also allows us to investigate how differences in the cost of investing in technology might impact cross-country differences in technology and income (see Exercise 18.12).

18.3.2 Endogenous Growth in the World

The model in Section 18.3.1 was simplified by the fact that the world growth rate was exogenous. A more satisfactory model would derive the world growth rate from the technology adoption and R&D activities of each country. Such models are typically more involved, because they feature richer interactions among countries. In addition, a certain amount of care needs to be taken so that the world economy grows at a constant endogenous rate, while there are still forces that ensure relatively similar growth rates across countries. Naturally, one may also wish to construct models in which countries grow at permanently different long-run rates (see, e.g., Exercise 13.7 in Chapter 13). The evidence in Chapter 1 suggests that such long-run growth differences are present when we look at the past 200 or 500 years, but there are more limited differences in sustained growth rates over the past 60 years or so (implying only small changes in the postwar world income distribution). Thus whether one wants to have long-run growth rate differences across countries is a modeling choice—it partly depends on whether one thinks of a model with a long transition leading to the large income differences or wishes to approximate the past 200 or 500 years as corresponding to steady-state behavior. Since such differences in growth rates emerge straightforwardly in many models (including all of the endogenous technology models so far; see again Exercise 13.7), here I focus on forces that keep countries growing at similar rates in the presence of endogenous technological change at the world level.

The main difference from the model in Section 18.3.1 is that the world growth equation (18.10), which specified exogenous world growth at the rate g, is now replaced with an equation that links the improvements in the world technology to technological improvements in each country. In particular, let us adopt the simplest way of aggregating the technologies of different countries, which is by taking their arithmetic average:

$$N(t) = \frac{1}{J} \sum_{j=1}^{J} N_j(t). \tag{18.12}$$

With this new equation, $N(t)$ no longer corresponds to the world technology frontier. Instead, it represents average technology in the world, and as long as there are some differences across countries, it will naturally be the case that $N_j(t) > N(t)$ for at least some j. Nevertheless, having the world technology correspond to an average of the technology of each country is a natural generalization of the ideas presented so far in this chapter. One disadvantage of this formulation is that it implies that the contribution of each country to the world technology is the same. Exercise 18.18 discusses alternative ways of aggregating individual country technologies into a world technology term and shows that the qualitative results here do not depend on the specification in (18.12). Besides (18.12), all other equations from Section 18.3.1 continue to hold.

The main result of this section is that the pattern of cross-country growth is similar to that in Section 18.3.1, but now the growth rate of the world economy, g, is endogenous, resulting from the investments in technologies made by firms in each country. Suppose that there exists a steady-state world equilibrium in which each country grows at the rate g. Then (18.12) implies that the world technology $N(t)$ also grows at the same rate g. The net present discounted value of a new machine in country j is still $\beta L_j / r^*$, and the no-arbitrage condition in R&D investments implies that, for given g, each country j's relative technology μ_j^* should satisfy (18.11). However, now dividing both sides of equation (18.12) by $N(t)$ implies that the steady-state world equilibrium must satisfy

$$\frac{1}{J} \sum_{j=1}^{J} \mu_j^* = 1$$

$$\frac{1}{J} \sum_{j=1}^{J} \left(\frac{\eta_j \beta L_j}{\zeta_j (\rho + \theta g)} \right)^{1/\phi} = 1, \tag{18.13}$$

where the second line uses the definition of μ_j^* from (18.11) and substitutes for the common interest rate r^* as a function of the world growth rate. The only unknown in (18.13) is g. Moreover the left-hand side is clearly strictly decreasing in g, so this equation can be satisfied for at most one value of g, say g^*. The following condition is necessary and sufficient for the world growth rate to be positive (see Exercise 18.14):

$$\frac{1}{J} \sum_{j=1}^{J} \left(\frac{\eta_j \beta L_j}{\zeta_j \rho} \right)^{1/\phi} > 1. \tag{18.14}$$

Proposition 18.5 *Suppose that (18.14) holds and that the unique solution g^* to (18.13) satisfies $\rho > (1-\theta)g^*$. Then there exists a unique steady-state world equilibrium in which growth at the world level is given by g^* and all countries grow at this common rate. This growth rate is endogenous and is determined by the technologies and policies of each country. In particular, a higher η_j or L_j or a lower ζ_j for any country $j = 1, \ldots, J$ increases the world growth rate.*

Proof.   See Exercise 18.15.   ■

Several features of this equilibrium are noteworthy. First, taking the world growth rate as given, the structure of the equilibrium is similar to that in Proposition 18.4. Thus the fact that all countries grow at the same rate and that differences in the innovation possibilities frontier η_j, the size of the labor force L_j, and the extent of potential distortions in technology investments ζ_j translate into level differences across countries has exactly the same intuition as in that proposition. What is more interesting is that essentially the same model as in Section 18.3.1 now gives us an endogenous growth rate for the world economy. In particular, while growth for each country appears exogenous in the sense that each country accumulates toward a world-determined growth rate, the growth rate of the world economy is endogenous and results from the investments of the firms in each country. The current model thus provides a more satisfactory framework for the analysis of the process of world growth than both the purely exogenous growth models and the purely endogenous growth models. In the current model, technological progress and economic growth are the outcome of investments by all countries in the world, but there are sufficiently powerful forces in the world economy—here working through technological spillovers—that pull relatively backward countries toward the world average, ensuring equal long-run growth rates for all countries. Naturally, equal growth rates are still consistent with quite large level differences across countries (see Exercise 18.12).

Proposition 18.5 uses a number of simplifying assumptions. First, each country has the same discount rate. This is only for simplicity, and Exercise 18.13 considers the case in which countries differ according to their discount rates. Second, the proposition only describes the steady-state equilibrium. Transitional dynamics are now more complicated, since the block recursiveness of the dynamical system is lost. The differential equations describing the equilibrium path for all countries need to be analyzed together. Nevertheless, local stability of the steady-state world equilibrium can be established, and this is shown in Exercise 18.16.

18.4 Appropriate and Inappropriate Technologies and Productivity Differences

The models presented so far in this chapter explicitly introduce a slow process of technology diffusion from the world stock of knowledge to the set of techniques used in production in each country. This was motivated either by some process of costly (and slow) technology absorption or by barriers to technology adoption. However, as noted at the beginning of the chapter, in the highly globalized world we live in, where IT and information flows make a wide range of blueprints easily accessible to most individuals and firms around the world, we might have expected much faster technology transfer across countries. Why does rapid diffusion of ideas not remove all, or at least most, cross-country technology differences? Leaving the discussion of institutional or policy barriers preventing technology diffusion to later, in this section and the next I focus on how technology differences and income gaps can remain substantial even with free flow of ideas.

A first possibility is that productivity differences may remain even if all differences in techniques disappear, because production is organized differently and the extent of inefficiencies in production may vary across countries. The next section discusses this possibility. Another important idea is that technologies of the world technology frontier may be inappropriate to the needs of specific countries, so that importing the most advanced frontier technologies may not guarantee the same level of productivity for all countries. At some level, this idea is both simple and attractive. Technologies and skills consist of bundles of complementary attributes, and these bundles vary across countries, so that there is no guarantee that a new technology that works well given the skills and competences in the United States or Switzerland will also do so in Nigeria or Turkey. Nevertheless, without specifying these attributes that make some technologies work well in certain nations and not in others, this story has little explanatory power. In this section, I present three versions of this story that may have some theoretical and empirical appeal. First, I discuss how differences in exogenous (e.g., geographic) conditions may make the same set of technologies differentially productive in different areas. Second, I show how differences in capital intensity across countries may change the appropriateness of different types of technologies. Finally, most of this section is devoted to the implications of differences in skill supplies across countries for the appropriateness of frontier technologies to developing economies. In this context, I show how the degree of appropriateness of technologies may arise endogenously in the world equilibrium and also present a model of economic growth in which labor has to be allocated across different sectors, which is of independent interest.

18.4.1 Inappropriate Technologies

The idea of inappropriate technologies can be best illustrated by an example on health innovations. Suppose that productivity in country j at time t, $A_j(t)$, is a function of whether there are effective cures against certain diseases affecting their populations. Suppose that there are two different diseases: heart attack and malaria. Countries $j = 1, \ldots, J'$ are affected by malaria and not by heart attacks, while $j = J' + 1, \ldots, J$ are affected by heart attacks and not by malaria. If the disease affecting country j has no cure, then productivity in that country is given by $A_j(t) = \underline{A}$, while when a cure against this disease is introduced, then $A_j(t) = \overline{A}$. Now imagine that a new cure against heart attacks is discovered and becomes freely available to all countries. Consequently the productivity in countries $j = J' + 1, \ldots, J$ increases from $\underline{A}$ to $\overline{A}$, but productivity in countries $j = 1, \ldots, J'$ remains at $\underline{A}$. This simple example illustrates how technologies of the world frontier may be inappropriate to the needs of some countries (in this case, the J' countries affected by malaria). In fact, in this extreme case, a technological advance that is freely available to all countries in the world increases productivity in a subset of the countries and creates cross-country income differences.

Is there any reason to expect that issues of this sort might be important? The answer is both yes and no. There are natural reasons to expect that new technologies should be optimized for the conditions and the needs of OECD countries because these countries are both the largest market for new technologies and the producers of much of new world know-how (see Section 18.4.3 below). Nevertheless, other than the issue of disease prevention, there are not many obvious fixed country characteristics that will create this type of inappropriateness. Instead the issue of appropriate technology is much more likely to be important in the context of whether new technologies increasing productivity via process and product innovations function well at different factor intensities. Sections 18.4.2 and 18.4.3 focus on whether technologies developed in advanced economies can be productively used at different capital-labor and skilled-unskilled labor ratios than those for which they have been designed.

18.4.2 Capital-Labor Ratios and Inappropriate Technologies

Atkinson and Stiglitz's classic (1969) paper argued that a useful way of modeling technological change is to view it as shifting isoquants (increasing productivity) at a given capital-labor ratio. For example, a firm that is using a specific machine, say a particular type of tractor, with a single worker may discover a way to increase the productivity of the worker. This innovation can be used by any other firm employing the same tractor with a single worker. But it would be much less valuable to firms using oxen or less advanced tractors, or even to firms using more advanced tractors. Thus technological changes are localized for specific capital-labor ratios, and when used with different ratios, they do not bring the same benefits. The implications of this observation for cross-country income differences can be major. If new technologies are developed for high capital-intensive production processes in OECD countries, they may be of little use to labor-abundant less-developed economies, where most production units function at lower capital-labor ratios than those in the OECD. This point is developed in the context of a Solow-type growth model by Basu and Weil (1998). I provide a simple version of their argument here.

Suppose that output per worker in a country is given by

$$y \equiv \frac{Y}{L} = A(k \mid k')k^{1-\alpha},$$

where time and country indices are suppressed to simplify notation, $k \equiv K/L$ is the capital-labor ratio of the country in question, and $A(k \mid k')$ is the (total factor) productivity of the technology designed to be used with capital-labor ratio k' when used instead with capital-labor ratio k. Suppose that when a technology designed for the capital labor ratio k' is used with a lower capital-labor ratio, there is a loss in efficiency. In particular, let us assume that

$$A(k \mid k') = A \min \left\{ 1, \left(\frac{k}{k'} \right)^{\gamma} \right\}$$

for some $\gamma \in (0, 1)$. Suppose also that new technologies are developed in richer economies, which have greater capital-labor ratios. Then productivity in a less-developed country with the capital-labor ratio $k < k'$ is

$$y = A(k \mid k')k^{1-\alpha} = Ak^{1-\alpha+\gamma}(k')^{-\gamma}. \tag{18.15}$$

An immediate implication of (18.15) is that less-developed countries are less productive than advanced countries even when they are producing with the same techniques. Moreover this productivity disadvantage is larger when the gap in the capital intensity of production between these countries and in the technologically advanced economies is greater. Depending on the value of the parameter γ, the implication of this type of inappropriateness might be important for understanding cross-country income differences. With the same arguments as in Chapters 2 and 3, we may want to think of $\alpha \approx 2/3$. In this case, an economy with an eight times higher capital-labor ratio than another would be only twice as rich when both countries have access to the same technology and there is no issue of inappropriate technologies. But if $\gamma = 2/3$ and the country with the higher capital-labor ratio is the frontier one setting the level of k'

in terms of the function $A(k \mid k')$, the implied difference would be eightfold rather than the twofold difference implied by the model that overlooked the issue of appropriate technology. Thus inappropriateness of technologies has the potential to increase the implied cross-country income differences, even when all countries have access to the same technologies. Exercise 18.20 provides more details on this model.

18.4.3 Endogenous Technological Change and Appropriate Technology

The Atkinson-Stiglitz and Basu-Weil approach discussed in Section 18.4.2 emphasizes differences in capital intensity between rich and poor economies. The evidence discussed in Section 18.1 suggests that differences in human capital may be particularly important in the adoption of technology. Moreover the past 30 years have witnessed the introduction of a range of skill-biased technologies both in developed economies and in many developing countries. Given this evidence, a mismatch between the skill requirements of frontier technologies and the available skills of the workers in less-developed countries may be more important than differences in capital intensity. In this subsection, I outline the model introduced in Acemoglu and Zilibotti (2001), which emphasizes the implications of the mismatch between technologies developed in advanced economies and the skills of the workforce of the less-developed countries. Furthermore, this enables us to use the ideas related to directed technological change developed in Chapter 15 in the context of cross-country productivity differences and also provides us with a tractable multisector growth model.

The world economy consists of two groups of countries, the North and the South, and as in Chapter 15, two types of workers, skilled and unskilled. There are two differences between the North and the South. First, all R&D and new innovations take place in the North (so that the North approximates the OECD or the United States and some other advanced economies). The South simply copies technologies developed in the North. Because of lack of IPR in the South, the main market of new technologies is Northern firms. Second, the North is more skill abundant than the South; in particular,

$$H^n / L^n > H^s / L^s,$$

where H^j denotes the number of skilled workers in country j, and L^j denotes the number of unskilled workers. I use $j = n$ or s to denote the North or the South, and assume that there are many Northern and many Southern countries. There is no population growth and no trade between the countries. Throughout, all countries have access to the same set of technologies, so there is also no slow diffusion of technologies. All differences in productivity arise from the potential mismatch between technology and skills.

On the preference side, all economies are assumed to admit a representative household with the standard preferences, for example, as given in (18.6) with $n_j = 0$ for all countries, since there is no population growth. The final good in each country is produced as a Cobb-Douglas aggregate of a continuum 1 of intermediate goods as in (14.59) in Section 14.4 of Chapter 14. In particular, we have

$$Y_j(t) = \exp\left(\int_0^1 \log y_j(i, t) di\right), \tag{18.16}$$

where $Y_j(t)$ is the amount of final good in country j at time t, and $y_j(i, t)$ is the output of intermediate i. As usual, total output is spent on consumption $C_j(t)$, intermediate expenditures $X_j(t)$, and also in the North, there are R&D expenditures equal to $Z_j(t)$. The South does not undertake R&D but can adopt technologies developed in the North.

Let us assume that the technology for producing intermediate i in country j at time t is

$$y_j(i, t) = \frac{1}{1 - \beta} \left(\int_0^{N_L(t)} x_{L,j}(i, v, t)^{1-\beta} dv \right) ((1 - i)l_j(i, t))^\beta \qquad (18.17)$$

$$+ \frac{1}{1 - \beta} \left(\int_0^{N_H(t)} x_{H,j}(i, v, t)^{1-\beta} dv \right) (i\omega h_j(i, t))^\beta.$$

Several features of this intermediate production function are worth noting. First, each intermediate can be produced using two alternative technologies, one using skilled workers, the other one using unskilled labor. Here $l_j(i, t)$ is the number of unskilled workers working in intermediate i in country j at time t. The function $h_j(i, t)$ is defined similarly. Second, skilled and unskilled workers have different productivities in different industries—incorporating a pattern of cross-industry comparative advantages. In particular, the presence of the terms $1 - i$ and i in the production function (18.17) implies that skilled workers are relatively more productive in higher indexed intermediates, while unskilled workers have a comparative advantage in lower indexed intermediates. Third, skilled workers also have an absolute advantage, captured by the parameter ω, which is assumed to be greater than 1. Fourth, as in the standard models with machine varieties, $x_{L,j}(i, v)$ denotes the quantity of machines of type v used with unskilled workers, and $x_{H,j}(i, v)$ is defined similarly. This part of the production function parallels those used in Chapter 15. The numbers of machine varieties available to be used with skilled and unskilled workers differ and are equal to $N_L(t)$ and $N_H(t)$, respectively. The important point here is that these quantities are not indexed by j, since all technologies are available to all countries. Thus we are ignoring the issue of slow diffusion and focusing on differences arising purely from inappropriateness of technology. Finally, as usual, the term $1/(1 - \beta)$ is introduced as a convenient normalization.

Let us assume that the final good sectors and the labor markets are competitive. Again as in Chapters 13 and 15, a technology monopolist can produce these machines at marginal cost ψ. Let the prices of these machines be denoted by $p^x_{L,j}(v, t)$ and $p^x_{H,j}(v, t)$ for the two sectors in country j for machine variety v at time t. Note that these prices do not depend on i, since the machines are not sector specific. Instead, they are skill specific. As in Chapters 13 and 15, profit maximization by the final good producers leads to the following demands for machines:

$$x_{L,j}(i, v, t) = \left[p_j(i, t)((1 - i)l_j(i, t))^\beta / p^x_{L,j}(v, t) \right]^{1/\beta},$$

$$x_{H,j}(i, v, t) = \left[p_j(i, t)(i\omega h_j(i, t))^\beta / p^x_{L,j}(v, t) \right]^{1/\beta},$$

where $p_j(i, t)$ is the relative price of intermediate i in country j at time t in terms of the final good (which is set as the numeraire for each country). The technology monopolists in the North invent machine varieties, so here the analysis is identical to that in Chapters 13 and 15. In addition, to keep the treatment of Northern and Southern economies symmetric, I assume that in each Southern economy a technology firm adopts (copies) the new machines invented in the North (at no cost) and acts as the monopolist supplier of that machine for the producers in its own country. Moreover the marginal cost of producing machines for this Southern firm is the same as the inventor in the North, equal to $\psi > 0$.

As usual, the isoelastic demand for machines implies that the profit-maximizing price for the technology monopolists is a constant markup over marginal cost, and I normalize the cost to $\psi \equiv 1 - \beta$. The symmetry between the North and the South implies that the price of machines and thus the demand for machines takes the same form in all countries. In particular, we obtain output in sector i in any country j as

$$y_j(i, t) = \frac{1}{1-\beta} p_j(i, t)^{(1-\beta)/\beta} \left[N_L(t)(1-i)l_j(i, t) + N_H(t)i\omega h_j(i, t) \right]. \quad (18.18)$$

For each economy, $N_L(t)$ and $N_H(t)$ are the state variables. Given these state variables the equilibrium is straightforward to characterize. In particular, the following proposition determines the structure of equilibrium in each country.

Proposition 18.6 *In any country j, given the world technologies $N_L(t)$ and $N_H(t)$, there exists a threshold $I_j(t) \in [0, 1]$ such that skilled workers are employed only in sectors $i > I_j(t)$, that is, for all $i < I_j(t)$, $h_j(i, t) = 0$, and for all $i > I_j(t)$, $l_j(i, t) = 0$.*
Moreover prices and labor allocations across sectors are such that

$$\text{for all } i < I_j(t), \; p_j(i, t) = P_{L,j}(t)(1-i)^{-\beta} \text{ and } l_j(i, t) = L_j/I_j(t),$$

while

$$\text{for all } i > I_j(t), \; p_j(i, t) = P_{H,j}(t)i^{-\beta} \text{ and } h_j(i, t) = H_j/(1 - I_j(t)),$$

where the positive numbers $P_{L,j}(t)$ and $P_{H,j}(t)$ can be interpreted as the price indices for labor-intensive and skill-intensive intermediates, respectively.

Proof. See Exercise 18.21. ∎

Using Proposition 18.6, the characterization of equilibrium, given the level of world technologies $N_L(t)$ and $N_H(t)$, is straightforward. In particular, the technology for the final good sector in (18.16) implies that the price indices in country j at time t must satisfy

$$\frac{P_{H,j}(t)}{P_{L,j}(t)} = \left(\frac{N_H(t)\omega H_j/(1 - I_j(t))}{N_L(t)L_j/I_j(t)} \right)^{-\beta}. \quad (18.19)$$

Moreover the threshold sector $I_j(t)$ in country j at time t is indifferent between using skilled and unskilled workers (and technologies) for production, and thus $P_{L,j}(t)(1 - I_j(t))^{-\beta} = P_{H,j}(t)I_j(t)^{-\beta}$. Combining this expression with (18.19) yields

$$\frac{P_{H,j}(t)}{P_{L,j}(t)} = \left(\frac{N_H(t)}{N_L(t)} \frac{\omega H_j}{L_j} \right)^{-\beta/2}, \quad (18.20)$$

and the equilibrium threshold $I_j(t)$ is uniquely pinned down by

$$\frac{I_j(t)}{1 - I_j(t)} = \left(\frac{N_H(t)}{N_L(t)} \frac{\omega H_j}{L_j} \right)^{-1/2}. \quad (18.21)$$

Combining these two equations, we can also derive the level of total output in economy j as

$$Y_j(t) = \exp(-\beta)\left[(N_L(t)L_j)^{1/2} + (N_H(t)\omega H_j)^{1/2} \right]^2, \quad (18.22)$$

and the skill premium is obtained as

$$\frac{w_{H,j}(t)}{w_{L,j}(t)} = \omega \left(\frac{N_H(t)}{N_L(t)}\right)^{1/2} \left(\frac{\omega H_j}{L_j}\right)^{-1/2} \tag{18.23}$$

(see Exercise 18.22). An interesting feature of this characterization, apparent from (18.22), is that the multisector model in this section leads to an equilibrium allocation in which the level of output is identical to that given by a CES production function with an elasticity of substitution equal to 2. In fact, this phenomenon is more general, and by changing the pattern of comparative advantage of skilled and unskilled workers in different sectors, one can obtain aggregate production functions with different elasticities of substitution.

The characterization of the equilibrium above already shows that the type of technologies, $N_L(t)$ and $N_H(t)$, differentially affects productivity in economies with different factor proportions. For example, consider the extreme case in which $H^s = 0$, so that there are no skilled workers in the South. Then an increase in $N_H(t)$ increases productivity in the North, but has no effect in the South. Naturally, when there are skilled and unskilled workers in both the North and the South, the implications of the changes in these two technologies is not as extreme, but the general principle still applies: an increase in $N_H(t)$ relative to $N_L(t)$ benefits the skill-abundant North more than the skill-scarce South. But conversely, an increase in $N_L(t)$ tends to benefit Southern economies relatively more. Thus the question becomes whether the world technology is more appropriate to the needs of the North or the South. Here the features that new technologies are developed in the North and that there are no IPR for Northern R&D in the South become important. These features imply that new technologies are developed—*designed*—for the needs of the North.

Let us adopt the simplest version of the directed technological change model from Chapter 15 (i.e., the lab-equipment specification from Section 15.3) and suppose that

$$\dot{N}_L(t) = \eta Z_L(t), \text{ and } \dot{N}_H(t) = \eta Z_H(t), \tag{18.24}$$

which is the same as the innovation possibilities frontier in Section 15.3, except that η_L and η_H have been set equal to each other for simplicity. Equilibrium and BGP are defined in the usual way. The analysis from Section 15.3, combined with the fact that the relevant market sizes are given by H^n and L^n (because research firms can only sell their technologies to Northern firms), establishes the next proposition.

Proposition 18.7 *With the lab-equipment specification of directed technological change as in (18.24) and no IPR in the South, the unique BGP involves Northern relative prices*

$$\frac{P_H^n}{P_L^n} = \left(\frac{\omega H^n}{L^n}\right)^{-\beta},$$

and the world relative technology ratio is

$$\left(\frac{N_H}{N_L}\right)^* = \frac{\omega H^n}{L^n}. \tag{18.25}$$

Moreover in the North the threshold sector satisfies

$$\frac{1 - I^{n*}}{I^{n*}} = \frac{\omega H^n}{L^n},$$

and the skill premium is

$$\left(\frac{w_H^n}{w_L^n}\right)^* = \omega.$$

This unique BGP is globally (saddle-path) stable.

Proof. See Exercise 18.23. ∎

To understand the implications of directed technological change for cross-country productivity differences, let us next introduce three simple concepts. *Net output, income per capita, and income per effective unit of labor,* which are respectively given by

$$Y_j^N \equiv Y_j - X_j, \; y_j \equiv \frac{Y_j}{L_j + H_j}, \; \text{and} \; y_j^{\text{eff}} \equiv \frac{Y_j}{L_j + \omega H_j}.$$

These quantities are functions of labor supplies and of relative technologies, in particular of N_H/N_L. These dependences are suppressed to simplify notation.

The next result shows that the steady-state technologies are indeed appropriate for the conditions (factor proportions) in the North, and that this creates endogenous income differences between the North and the South.

Proposition 18.8 *Consider the above-described model. Then*

1. *The BGP technology ratio $(N_H/N_L)^*$ is such that, given a constant level of $N_H + N_L$, it achieves the unique maximum of net output in the North, Y_n^N, as a function of relative technology N_H/N_L.*

2. *At the steady-state equilibrium technology ratio $(N_H/N_L)^*$, $y_n > y_s$, and $y_n^{\text{eff}} > y_s^{\text{eff}}$.*

Proof. See Exercise 18.24. ∎

This proposition establishes two important results. First, the steady-state equilibrium technology is indeed appropriate for the needs of the North. This is intuitive, since research firms are targeting the Northern markets (in particular the relative supply of skills in the North). Moreover the statement that there is a unique maximum of Y_n^N (given the total amount of technology $N_H + N_L$) also implies that net output in the South, Y_s^N, given by a similar expression, will not be maximized by $(N_H/N_L)^*$. This is the essence of the second result contained in this proposition: because technologies are developed in the North (in practice, corresponding loosely to the OECD countries) and are designed for the needs (factor proportions) of Northern economies, they are inappropriate for the needs of the South. As a result, income per capita and income per effective units of labor in the North are higher than in the South. Thus the process of directed technological change acts as a force toward greater cross-country inequality. Using a simple calibration, Acemoglu and Zilibotti (2001) show that the technology-skill mismatch created by this channel might contribute significantly to cross-country income and productivity differences.

18.5 Contracting Institutions and Technology Adoption

An important determinant of differences in technology and technology adoption are institutional differences across societies. I have already noted how the parameter σ_j in the model of Section 18.2 can be interpreted as varying across countries because of differences in policies and institutions erecting barriers against technology adoption. Naturally, an approach that links σ_j to such technology barriers is rather reduced form. To make further progress, we need more micro-founded models of why there are barriers to technology adoptions and how these barriers affect technology choices. The reasons certain groups may want to erect barriers against the introduction of new technologies are discussed in detail in Part VIII, where I also discuss other factors affecting the efficiency of the organization of production. However, before turning to these models, it is useful to show how differences in the ability to write contracts between firms and their suppliers (or firms and their workers) may have first-order effects on technology adoption decisions. I now briefly discuss a model of endogenous technology adoption, which again builds on the framework developed in Chapter 13. The purpose of this model is to illustrate how contractual difficulties can lead to differences in productivity and technology adoption patterns across countries. The model is a slight simplification of that by Acemoglu, Antras, and Helpman (2007). The main focus is on how contracting institutions affect the relationship between producers and suppliers and thus change the profitability of technology adoption.

18.5.1 Preferences, Technology, and Market Structure

For simplicity, consider a static world and focus on a single country. There exists a continuum of final goods $q(z)$, with $z \in [0, M]$, where M represents the number (measure) of final goods (I use M here, since here N denotes technology choice). All households have identical CES preferences

$$u = \left(\int_0^M q(v)^\beta dv \right)^{1/\beta} - \psi e, \, 0 < \beta < 1, \tag{18.26}$$

where e is the total effort exerted by this individual, with ψ representing the cost of effort in terms of real consumption. The parameter $\beta \in (0, 1)$ determines the elasticity of demand and implies that the elasticity of substitution between final goods, $1/(1 - \beta)$, is greater than 1. The CES preferences in (18.26) imply the demand function

$$q(v) = \left(\frac{p(v)}{p^I} \right)^{-1/(1-\beta)} \frac{A}{p^I}$$

for each producer $v \in [0, M]$, where $p(v)$ is the price of good v, A is aggregate spending, and

$$p^I \equiv \left(\int_0^M p(v)^{-\beta/(1-\beta)} dv \right)^{-(1-\beta)/\beta}$$

is the ideal price index, which is taken as the numeraire, so that $p^I = 1$. Thus each final good producer faces a demand function of the form $q = Ap^{-1/(1-\beta)}$, where q denotes quantity and p denotes price, and I have dropped the conditioning on z, since I focus on the decisions of a single firm. The resulting revenue function for the firm can therefore be written as

$$R = A^{1-\beta} q^\beta. \tag{18.27}$$

Production depends on the technology choice of the firm, which is denoted by $N \in \mathbb{R}_+$. More advanced technologies involve a greater range of inputs (intermediates), supplied by different suppliers. The transactions between the producer and the suppliers necessitate contracting relationships. For each $j \in [0, N]$, let $X(j)$ be the quantity of input j. The production function of the firm also takes the standard CES form

$$q = N^{\kappa+1-1/\alpha} \left(\int_0^N X(j)^\alpha dj \right)^{1/\alpha}, \tag{18.28}$$

where $\alpha \in (0, 1)$, so that the elasticity of substitution between inputs, $\varepsilon \equiv 1/(1 - \alpha)$, is always greater than 1. In addition, $\kappa > 0$. The standard specification of the CES aggregator would not involve the term $N^{\kappa+1-1/\alpha}$ (i.e., it would implicitly set $\kappa = 1/\alpha - 1$). In that case, as in Section 12.4 in Chapter 12, when $X(j) = X$, total output is $q = N^{1/\alpha} X$, and both the elasticity of substitution between inputs and the elasticity of output to changes in technology, N, would be governed by the same parameter α. Introducing the term $N^{\kappa+1-1/\alpha}$ in front of the integral separates these two elasticities.

There is a large number of profit-maximizing suppliers that can produce the necessary inputs. Suppose that each supplier has the same outside option $w_0 > 0$. For now, let us take w_0 as given and also assume that each input needs to be produced by a different supplier with whom the firm needs to contract (see Exercise 18.31 on endogenizing this outside option). A supplier assigned to the production of an input needs to undertake relationship-specific investments in a unit measure of (symmetric) activities. The marginal cost of investment for each activity is ψ as specified in (18.26). The production function of inputs is Cobb-Douglas and is symmetric in the activities, that is,

$$X(j) = \exp\left(\int_0^1 \log x(i, j) di \right), \tag{18.29}$$

where $x(i, j)$ is the level of investment in activity i performed by the supplier of input j. This formulation allows a tractable parameterization of contractual incompleteness, whereby a subset of the investments necessary for production is nonverifiable and thus noncontractible. Finally, let us assume that adopting a technology N involves costs $\Gamma(N)$, such that:

1. For all $N > 0$, $\Gamma(N)$ is twice differentiable, with $\Gamma'(N) > 0$ and $\Gamma''(N) > 0$.
2. For all $N > 0$, $N\Gamma''(N)/[\Gamma'(N) + w_0] > [\beta(\kappa + 1) - 1]/(1 - \beta)$.

The second assumption introduces enough convexity to ensure interior solutions.

The relationship between the producer and its suppliers requires contracts to ensure that the suppliers deliver the required inputs. Let the payment to supplier j consist of two parts: an ex ante payment $\tau(j) \in \mathbb{R}$ before the investments, the $x(i, j)$, take place, and a payment $s(j)$ after the investments. Then the payoff to supplier j, also taking account of her outside option, is

$$\pi_x(j) = \max\left\{ \tau(j) + s(j) - \int_0^1 \psi x(i, j) di, \, w_0 \right\}. \tag{18.30}$$

Similarly, the payoff to the firm is

$$\pi = R - \int_0^N [\tau(j) + s(j)] dj - \Gamma(N), \tag{18.31}$$

where R is revenue, and the other two terms on the right-hand side represent costs. Substituting (18.28) and (18.29) into (18.27), revenue can be expressed as

$$R = A^{1-\beta} N^{\beta(\kappa+1-1/\alpha)} \left[\int_0^N \left(\exp\left(\int_0^1 \log x(i, j) di \right) \right)^\alpha dj \right]^{\beta/\alpha}. \quad (18.32)$$

18.5.2 Equilibrium under Complete Contracts

As a benchmark, consider the idealized case of complete contracts, where the firm has full control over all investments and pays each supplier her outside option. Conceptually, complete contracts correspond to the case in which markets are complete, and all inputs (of different qualities) can be bought and sold in a quasi-competitive fashion. Most of the models presented so far in this book have assumed complete contracts. While this is a good approximation for many commodities, complete contracts (or the corresponding complete markets) may not always capture the essence of the interaction between firms and their suppliers, especially when contracting institutions are imperfect, so that using courts or other legal sanctions against firms that breach their contractual agreements might be costly.

To prepare for the analysis of technology adoption under incomplete contracts, first consider a game in which the firm chooses a technology level N and makes a contract offer $[\{x(i, j)\}_{i \in [0,1]}, \{s(j), \tau(j)\}]$ for every input $j \in [0, N]$. If a supplier accepts this contract for input j, she is obliged to supply $\{x(i, j)\}_{i \in [0,1]}$ as stipulated in the contract in exchange for the payments $\{s(j), \tau(j)\}$. A *Subgame Perfect Equilibrium* (SPE) of this game is a strategy combination for the firm and the suppliers such that suppliers maximize (18.30) and the firm maximizes (18.31). An SPE can be alternatively represented as a solution to

$$\max_{N, \{x(i,j)\}_{i,j}, \{s(j), \tau(j)\}_j} R - \int_0^N (\tau(j) + s(j)) dj - \Gamma(N) \quad (18.33)$$

subject to (18.32) and the suppliers' *participation constraint*,

$$s(j) + \tau(j) - \psi \int_0^1 x(i, j) di \geq w_0 \quad \text{for all } j \in [0, N]. \quad (18.34)$$

Since the firm has no reason to provide rents to the suppliers, it chooses payments $s(j)$ and $\tau(j)$ that satisfy (18.34) with equality. Moreover, with complete contracts, $\tau(j)$ and $s(j)$ are perfect substitutes, so only the sum $s(j) + \tau(j)$ matters.

Moreover, since the firm's objective function (18.33) is (jointly) concave in the investment levels $x(i, j)$ and these investments are all equally costly, the firm chooses the same investment x for all activities in all inputs. Now, substituting for (18.34) in (18.33), we obtain the following simpler unconstrained maximization problem for the firm:

$$\max_{N, x} A^{1-\beta} N^{\beta(\kappa+1)} x^\beta - \psi N x - \Gamma(N) - w_0 N. \quad (18.35)$$

The first-order conditions of this problem imply that

$$(N^*)^{\frac{\beta(\kappa+1)-1}{1-\beta}} A\kappa \beta^{1/(1-\beta)} \psi^{-\beta/(1-\beta)} = \Gamma'(N^*) + w_0, \quad (18.36)$$

$$x^* = \frac{\Gamma'(N^*) + w_0}{\kappa \psi}. \quad (18.37)$$

Equations (18.36) and (18.37) can be solved recursively. The restrictions on the function Γ above ensure that (18.36) has a unique solution for N^*, which, together with (18.37), yields a unique solution for x^*.

When all investment levels are identical and equal to x, output is $q = N^{\kappa+1}x$. Since a total of $NX = Nx$ inputs are used in the production process, a natural measure of productivity is output divided by total input use, $P = N^\kappa$. In the case of complete contracts this productivity level is $P^* = (N^*)^\kappa$, which is increasing in the level of technology. The next proposition summarizes this analysis.

Proposition 18.9 *Consider the above-described model, take A as given, and suppose that there are complete contracts. Then there exists a unique SPE with technology and investment levels $N^* > 0$ and $x^* > 0$ given by (18.36) and (18.37), respectively. Furthermore in this SPE,*

$$\frac{\partial N^*}{\partial A} > 0, \ \frac{\partial x^*}{\partial A} \geq 0, \ \text{and} \ \frac{\partial N^*}{\partial \alpha} = \frac{\partial x^*}{\partial \alpha} = 0.$$

Proof. See Exercise 18.27. ∎

In the case of complete contracts, the size of the market (which corresponds to A and from the viewpoint of the individual firm is exogenous) has a positive effect on investments by suppliers of inputs and productivity, because a greater market size makes both suppliers' and the producer's investments more productive. The other noteworthy implication of this proposition is that under complete contracts, the level of technology and thus productivity do not depend on the elasticity of substitution between inputs, $1/(1-\alpha)$.

18.5.3 Equilibrium under Incomplete Contracts

Let us next consider the same environment under incomplete contracts. We model the imperfection of the contracting institutions by assuming that there exists $\mu \in [0, 1]$ such that for every input j, investments in activities $0 \leq i \leq \mu$ are observable and verifiable and therefore contractible, while investments in activities $\mu < i \leq 1$ are not contractible. Consequently a contract stipulates investment levels $x(i, j)$ for the μ contractible activities but does not specify the investment levels in the remaining $1 - \mu$ noncontractible activities. Instead suppliers choose their investments in noncontractible activities in anticipation of the ex post distribution of revenue, and they may decide to withhold their services in these activities from the firm. Economies with weak contracting institutions have a low μ and thus feature only a small set of tasks that are contractible, whereas more developed contracting institutions correspond to high levels of μ.

The ex post distribution of revenues in activities that are not ex ante contractible is determined by multilateral bargaining between the firm and its suppliers. The exact bargaining protocol determines investment incentives of suppliers and the profitability of investment for the firm. First, consider the timing of events:

- The firm adopts a technology N and offers a contract $[\{x_c(i, j)\}_{i=0}^{\mu}, \tau(j)]$ for every input $j \in [0, N]$, where $x_c(i, j)$ is an investment level in a contractible activity, and $\tau(j)$ is an upfront payment to supplier j. The payment $\tau(j)$ can be positive or negative.

- Potential suppliers decide whether to apply for the contracts. Then the firm chooses N suppliers, one for each input j.

- All suppliers $j \in [0, N]$ simultaneously choose investment levels $x(i, j)$ for all $i \in [0, 1]$. In the contractible activities $i \in [0, \mu]$ the suppliers invest $x(i, j) = x_c(i, j)$.

- The suppliers and the firm bargain over the division of revenue, and at this stage, suppliers can withhold their services in noncontractible activities.

- Output is produced and sold, and the revenue R is distributed according to the bargaining agreement.

Let us assume that the bargaining protocol leads to the *Shapley value*, which is a natural solution concept for this multilateral bargaining game (discussed further in Section 18.5.4). Taking this bargaining outcome as given, we now characterize the *symmetric Subgame Perfect Equilibria* (SSPE) of this game.

Behavior along the SSPE can be described by a tuple $\{\tilde{N}, \tilde{x}_c, \tilde{x}_n, \tilde{\tau}\}$ in which $\tilde{N}$ represents the level of technology, $\tilde{x}_c$ the investment in contractible activities, $\tilde{x}_n$ the investment in noncontractible activities, and $\tilde{\tau}$ the upfront payment to every supplier. That is, for every $j \in [0, \tilde{N}]$, the upfront payment is $\tau(j) = \tilde{\tau}$, and the investment levels are $x(i, j) = \tilde{x}_c$ for $i \in [0, \mu]$ and $x(i, j) = \tilde{x}_n$ for $i \in (\mu, 1]$. With a slight abuse of terminology, I denote the SSPE by $\{\tilde{N}, \tilde{x}_c, \tilde{x}_n\}$.

As is typically the case in extensive-form complete information games, the SSPE can be characterized by backward induction. First, consider the penultimate stage of the game, with N as the level of technology and x_c as the level of investment in contractible activities. Suppose also that each supplier other than j has chosen a level of investment in noncontractible activities equal to $x_n(-j)$ (these are all the same, because we are constructing a symmetric equilibrium), while the investment level in every noncontractible activity by supplier j is $x_n(j)$. Given these investments, the suppliers and the firm engage in multilateral bargaining. Denote the return to supplier j resulting from this bargaining by $\bar{s}_x[N, x_c, x_n(-j), x_n(j)]$. The optimal investment by supplier j implies that $x_n(j)$ must be chosen to maximize $\bar{s}_x[N, x_c, x_n(-j), x_n(j)]$ minus the cost of investment in noncontractible activities, $(1 - \mu)\psi x_n(j)$. In a symmetric equilibrium, $x_n(j) = x_n(-j)$; in other words, x_n needs to be a fixed-point given by

$$x_n \in \arg \max_{x_n(j)} \bar{s}_x(N, x_c, x_n, x_n(j)) - (1 - \mu)\psi x_n(j). \tag{18.38}$$

Equation (18.38) can be thought of as an incentive compatibility constraint, with the additional symmetry requirement. While this equation is written with "$\in$" to allow for the fact that there may be more than one maximizer of the expression on the right-hand side, the structure of the current model ensures that there is a unique maximizer; thus "$\in$" can be replaced with "$=$".

In a symmetric equilibrium with technology N, with investment in contractible activities given by x_c and investment in noncontractible activities equal to x_n, the revenue of the firm is given by $R = A^{1-\beta}(N^{\kappa+1} x_c^{\mu} x_n^{1-\mu})^{\beta}$. Moreover, let $s_x(N, x_c, x_n) = \bar{s}_x(N, x_c, x_n, x_n)$. Then the Shapley value of the firm is obtained as a residual:

$$s_q(N, x_c, x_n) = A^{1-\beta}(N^{\kappa+1} x_c^{\mu} x_n^{1-\mu})^{\beta} - N s_x(N, x_c, x_n).$$

Now consider the stage in which the firm chooses N suppliers from a pool of applicants. If suppliers expect to receive less than their outside option, w_0, this pool is empty. Therefore for production to take place, the final good producer has to offer a contract that satisfies the participation constraint of suppliers under incomplete contracts, that is,

$$\bar{s}_x(N, x_c, x_n, x_n) + \tau \geq \mu \psi x_c + (1 - \mu)\psi x_n + w_0 \tag{18.39}$$

for x_n that satisfies (18.38). In other words, given N and (x_c, τ), each supplier $j \in [0, N]$ should expect her Shapley value plus the upfront payment to cover the cost of investment in contractible and noncontractible activities and the value of her outside option.

The maximization problem of the firm can then be written as

$$\max_{N, x_c, x_n, \tau} s_q(N, x_c, x_n) - N\tau - \Gamma(N)$$

subject to (18.38) and (18.39). With no restrictions on τ, the participation constraint (18.39) is satisfied with equality; otherwise the firm could reduce τ without violating (18.39) and increase its profits. Therefore the upfront payment τ can be determined using this constraint and substituted into the firm's objective function. This yields the simpler problem,

$$\max_{N, x_c, x_n} s_q(N, x_c, x_n) + N\left[\bar{s}_x(N, x_c, x_n, x_n) - \mu\psi x_c - (1-\mu)\psi x_n\right] - \Gamma(N) - w_0 N$$

(18.40)

subject to (18.38).

The SSPE $\{\tilde{N}, \tilde{x}_c, \tilde{x}_n\}$ solves this problem, and the corresponding upfront payment satisfies

$$\tilde{\tau} = \mu\psi\tilde{x}_c + (1-\mu)\psi\tilde{x}_n + w_0 - \bar{s}_x(\tilde{N}, \tilde{x}_c, \tilde{x}_n, \tilde{x}_n).$$

(18.41)

The key issue in the presence of incomplete contracts is that the payments from the firm to its suppliers will be determined ex post through bargaining rather than through contractual arrangements. As noted above, different bargaining protocols between suppliers and the producer lead to somewhat different results. In the current context, the most natural choice is the Shapley value, since it provides a plausible and tractable division rule for multilateral bargaining problems. The derivation of this formula is not essential for the results here; thus it is included for completeness at the end of this section. The next proposition provides the form of this bargaining solution.

Proposition 18.10 *Suppose that supplier j invests $x_n(j)$ in her noncontractible activities, all the other suppliers invest $x_n(-j)$ in their noncontractible activities, every supplier invests x_c in her contractible activities, and the level of technology is N. Then the Shapley value of supplier j is*

$$\bar{s}_x(N, x_c, x_n(-j), x_n(j)) = (1-\gamma)A^{1-\beta}\left(\frac{x_n(j)}{x_n(-j)}\right)^{(1-\mu)\alpha} x_c^{\beta\mu} x_n(-j)^{\beta(1-\mu)} N^{\beta(\kappa+1)-1},$$

(18.42)

where

$$\gamma \equiv \frac{\alpha}{\alpha + \beta}.$$

(18.43)

Proof. See Section 18.5.4. ∎

Several features of (18.42) are worth noting. First, the derived parameter $\gamma \equiv \alpha/(\alpha + \beta)$ represents the bargaining power of the firm; it is increasing in α and decreasing in β. A higher elasticity of substitution between inputs—a higher α—raises the firm's bargaining power, because it makes every supplier less essential in production and therefore raises the share of revenue appropriated by the firm. In contrast, a higher elasticity of demand for the final good—higher β—reduces the firm's bargaining power, because, for any coalition, it reduces the marginal contribution of the firm to the coalition's payoff as a fraction of revenue.

Second, in equilibrium all suppliers invest equally in all noncontractible activities, that is, $x_n(j) = x_n(-j) = x_n$, and so

$$s_x(N, x_c, x_n) = \bar{s}_x(N, x_c, x_n, x_n) = (1-\gamma)A^{1-\beta}x_c^{\beta\mu}x_n^{\beta(1-\mu)}N^{\beta(\kappa+1)-1} = (1-\gamma)\frac{R}{N},$$

(18.44)

where $R = A^{1-\beta}x_c^{\beta\mu}x_n^{\beta(1-\mu)}N^{\beta(\kappa+1)}$ is the total revenue of the firm. Thus the joint Shapley value of the suppliers, $Ns_x(N, x_c, x_n)$, equals the fraction $1 - \gamma$ of the revenue, and the firm receives the remaining fraction γ, so that

$$s_q(N, x_c, x_n) = \gamma A^{1-\beta}x_c^{\beta\mu}x_n^{\beta(1-\mu)}N^{\beta(\kappa+1)} = \gamma R. \qquad (18.45)$$

Equation (18.45) is a relatively simple rule for the division of revenue between the firm and its suppliers.

Finally, when α is smaller, $\bar{s}_x[N, x_c, x_n(-j), x_n(j)]$ is more concave with respect to $x_n(j)$, because greater complementarity between the inputs implies that a given change in the relative employment of two inputs has a larger impact on their relative marginal products. The parameter β, on the other hand, affects the concavity of revenue in output (see (18.27)) but has no effect on the concavity of $\bar{s}_x$, because with a continuum of suppliers, a single supplier has an infinitesimal effect on output.

To characterize an SSPE, let us first derive the incentive compatibility constraint using (18.38) and (18.42):

$$x_n = \arg\max_{x_n(j)} (1-\gamma)A^{1-\beta}\left(\frac{x_n(j)}{x_n}\right)^{(1-\mu)\alpha} x_c^{\beta\mu}x_n^{\beta(1-\mu)}N^{\beta(\kappa+1)-1} - \psi(1-\mu)x_n(j).$$

Relative to the producer's first-best (complete) contracts characterized in Section 18.5.2, there are two differences. First, the term $(1-\gamma)$ implies that the supplier is not the full residual claimant of the return from her investment in noncontractible activities and thus underinvests in these activities. Second, as discussed above, multilateral bargaining distorts the perceived concavity of the private return relative to the social return. Using the first-order condition of this problem and solving for the fixed point by substituting $x_n(j) = x_n$ yields a unique x_n:

$$x_n = \bar{x}_n(N, x_c) \equiv [\alpha(1-\gamma)\psi^{-1}x_c^{\beta\mu}A^{1-\beta}N^{\beta(\kappa+1)-1}]^{1/(1-\beta(1-\mu))}. \qquad (18.46)$$

Equation (18.46) implies that investments in noncontractible activities are increasing in α. This follows from the fact that $\alpha(1-\gamma) = \alpha\beta/(\alpha+\beta)$ is increasing in α. The economics of this relationship is the outcome of two opposing forces. The share of the suppliers in revenue, $(1-\gamma)$, is decreasing in α, because greater substitution between the inputs reduces the suppliers' ex post bargaining power. But a greater level of α also reduces the concavity of $\bar{s}_x(\cdot)$ in x_n, increasing the marginal reward from investing further in noncontractible activities. Because the latter effect dominates, x_n is increasing in α.

Another interesting feature is that contractible and noncontractible activities are complements, and in particular, $\bar{x}_n(N, x_c)$ is increasing in x_c. Finally, the effect of N on x_n is ambiguous, since investment in noncontractible activities declines with the level of technology when $\beta(\kappa+1) < 1$ and increases with N when $\beta(\kappa+1) > 1$. This is because an increase in N has two opposite effects on a supplier's incentives to invest: a greater number of inputs increases the marginal product of investment due to the "love for variety" embodied in the technology (18.28), but at the same time, the bargaining share of a supplier, $(1-\gamma)/N$, declines with N. For large values of κ, the former effect dominates, while for small values of κ, the latter dominates.

Now, using (18.44), (18.45), and (18.46), the firm's optimization problem (18.40) can be expressed as the maximization of

$$A^{1-\beta}(x_c^\mu \bar{x}_n(N, x_c)^{1-\mu})^\beta N^{\beta(\kappa+1)} - \psi N \mu x_c - \psi N(1-\mu)\bar{x}_n(N, x_c) - \Gamma(N) - w_0 N$$

$$(18.47)$$

with respect to N and x_c, where $\bar{x}_n(N, x_c)$ is defined in (18.46). Substituting (18.46) into (18.47) and differentiating with respect to N and x_c results in two first-order conditions, which yield a unique solution $(\tilde{N}, \tilde{x}_c)$ to (18.47):

$$\left(\tilde{N}^{\frac{\beta(\kappa+1)-1}{1-\beta}} A\kappa\beta^{\frac{1}{1-\beta}}\psi^{-\frac{\beta}{1-\beta}}\right)\left(\frac{1-\alpha(1-\gamma)(1-\mu)}{1-\beta(1-\mu)}\right)^{\frac{1-\beta(1-\mu)}{1-\beta}}\left(\beta^{-1}\alpha(1-\gamma)\right)^{\frac{\beta(1-\mu)}{1-\beta}}$$

$$= \Gamma'(\tilde{N}) + w_0, \qquad (18.48)$$

$$\tilde{x}_c = \frac{\Gamma'(\tilde{N}) + w_0}{\kappa\psi}. \qquad (18.49)$$

As in the complete contracts case, these two conditions determine the equilibrium recursively. First, (18.48) gives $\tilde{N}$, and then given $\tilde{N}$, (18.49) yields $\tilde{x}_c$. Moreover, using (18.46), (18.48) and (18.49) imply that the level of investment in noncontractible activities is

$$\tilde{x}_n = \frac{\alpha(1-\gamma)(1-\beta(1-\mu))}{\beta(1-\alpha(1-\gamma)(1-\mu))}\left(\frac{\Gamma'(\tilde{N}) + w_0}{\kappa\psi}\right). \qquad (18.50)$$

Comparing (18.37) to (18.49), we see that for a given N the implied level of investment in contractible activities under incomplete contracts, $\tilde{x}_c$, is identical to the investment level in contractible activities under complete contracts, x^*. This highlights the fact that differences in investments in contractible activities between these economic environments only result from differences in technology adoption. In fact, comparing (18.36) with (18.48), we see that $\tilde{N}$ and N^* differ only because of the second and third bracketed terms on the left-hand side of (18.48). These represent the distortions created by bargaining between the firm and its suppliers. Intuitively, technology adoption is distorted because incomplete contracts reduce investments in noncontractible activities below the level of investment in contractible activities, and this underinvestment reduces the profitability of technologies with high N. As $\mu \to 1$ (and as contractual imperfections disappear), both of these bracketed terms on the left-hand side of (18.48) go to 1, and $(\tilde{N}, \tilde{x}_c) \to (N^*, x^*)$.

I next provide a number of comparative static results on the SSPE under incomplete contracts and compare the incomplete contracts equilibrium to that under complete contracts. The comparative static results are facilitated by the block recursive structure of the equilibrium: any change in A, μ or α that increases the left-hand side of (18.48) also increases $\tilde{N}$, and the effect on $\tilde{x}_c$ and $\tilde{x}_n$ can then be obtained from (18.49) and (18.50). The main results are provided in the next proposition.

Proposition 18.11 *Consider the above-described model with incomplete contracts, and suppose that the restrictions on Γ hold. Then there exists a unique SSPE under incomplete contracts, $\{\tilde{N}, \tilde{x}_c, \tilde{x}_n\}$, characterized by (18.48), (18.49), and (18.50). Furthermore $\{\tilde{N}, \tilde{x}_c, \tilde{x}_n\}$ satisfies $\tilde{N}, \tilde{x}_c, \tilde{x}_n > 0$, and*

$$\tilde{x}_n < \tilde{x}_c,$$

$$\frac{\partial \tilde{N}}{\partial A} > 0, \quad \frac{\partial \tilde{x}_c}{\partial A} \geq 0, \quad \frac{\partial \tilde{x}_n}{\partial A} \geq 0,$$

$$\frac{\partial \tilde{N}}{\partial \mu} > 0, \quad \frac{\partial \tilde{x}_c}{\partial \mu} \geq 0, \quad \frac{\partial (\tilde{x}_n / \tilde{x}_c)}{\partial \mu} > 0,$$

$$\frac{\partial \tilde{N}}{\partial \alpha} > 0, \quad \frac{\partial \tilde{x}_c}{\partial \alpha} \geq 0, \quad \frac{\partial (\tilde{x}_n / \tilde{x}_c)}{\partial \alpha} > 0.$$

Proof. See Exercise 18.28. ■

This proposition states that suppliers invest less in noncontractible activities than in contractible activities. In particular, we have

$$\frac{\tilde{x}_n}{\tilde{x}_c} = \frac{\alpha(1-\gamma)[1-\beta(1-\mu)]}{\beta[1-\alpha(1-\gamma)(1-\mu)]} < 1, \tag{18.51}$$

which follows from (18.49) and (18.50) and from the fact that $\alpha(1-\gamma) = \alpha\beta/(\alpha+\beta) < \beta$ (recall (18.43)). This result is intuitive: the producer is the full residual claimant of the return to investments in contractible activities, and it dictates these investments in the contract. In contrast, investments in noncontractible activities are decided by the suppliers, who are not the full residual claimants of the returns generated by these investments (recall (18.44)) and thus underinvest in these activities.

In addition, the level of technology and investments in both contractible and noncontractible activities are increasing in the size of the market, in the fraction of contractible activities (quality of contracting institutions), and in the elasticity of substitution between inputs. The impact of the size of the market is intuitive: a greater A makes production more profitable and thus increases investments and equilibrium technology. Better contracting institutions, on the other hand, imply that a greater fraction of activities receives the higher investment level $\tilde{x}_c$ rather than $\tilde{x}_n < \tilde{x}_c$. This makes the choice of a more advanced technology more profitable. A higher N, in turn, increases the profitability of further investments in $\tilde{x}_c$ and $\tilde{x}_n$. Better contracting institutions also close the (proportional) gap between $\tilde{x}_c$ and $\tilde{x}_n$, because with a higher fraction of contractible activities, the marginal return to investment in noncontractible activities is also higher.

A higher α (lower complementarity between inputs) also increases technology choices and investments. The reason is related to the discussion in Section 18.5.2, where it was shown that a higher α reduces the share of each supplier but also makes $\bar{s}_x(\cdot)$ less concave. Because the latter effect dominates, a lower degree of complementarity increases supplier investments and makes the adoption of more advanced technologies more profitable.

One of the main implications of this analysis is that contractual frictions cause underinvestment in quality. They therefore discourage technology adoption and reduce productivity. This result is summarized in the next proposition. Note that productivity under incomplete contracts is $\tilde{P} = \tilde{N}^\kappa$, while productivity under complete contracts is $P^* = (N^*)^\kappa$.

Proposition 18.12 Let $\{\tilde{N}, \tilde{x}_c, \tilde{x}_n\}$ be the unique SSPE with incomplete contracts and let $\{N^*, x^*\}$ be the unique equilibrium with complete contracts. Then

$$\tilde{N} < N^*, \quad \text{and} \quad \tilde{x}_n < \tilde{x}_c < x^*.$$

Proof. See Exercise 18.29. ■

Since incomplete contracts lead to the choice of less-advanced (lower N) technologies, they also reduce productivity and investments in contractible and noncontractible activities. Acemoglu, Antras, and Helpman (2007) also show that the technology and income differences resulting from relatively modest differences in contracting institutions can be quite large. Therefore the link between contracting institutions and technology adoption provides us with a theoretical mechanism that might generate significant technology differences across countries.

18.5.4 The Shapley Value and the Proof of Proposition 18.10*

The concept of Shapley value, first proposed by Shapley (1953), has both intuitive and game-theoretic appeal. In a bargaining game with a finite number of players, each player's Shapley value is the average of her contributions to all coalitions that consist of players ordered below her in all feasible permutations. More explicitly, in a game with $K + 1$ players, let $g = \{g(0), g(1), \ldots, g(K)\}$ be a permutation of $0, 1, 2, \ldots, K$, where player 0 is the firm and players $1, 2, \ldots, K$ are the suppliers, and let $z_g^j = \{j' \mid g(j) > g(j')\}$ be the set of players ordered below j in the permutation g. Let us denote the set of all feasible permutations by G, the set of all subsets of $K + 1$ players by S, and the value of a coalition consisting of a subset of the $K + 1$ players by $v : S \to \mathbb{R}$. Then the Shapley value of player j is

$$s_j = \frac{1}{(K+1)!} \sum_{g \in G} [v(z_g^j \cup j) - v(z_g^j)].$$

Let us now derive the asymptotic Shapley value proposed by Aumann and Shapley (1974), which involves considering the limit of this expression as the number of players goes to infinity. Let there be K suppliers, each one controlling a range $\xi = N/K$ of the continuum of inputs. Due to symmetry, all suppliers provide an amount x_c of contractible activities. As for the noncontractible activities, consider a situation in which a supplier j supplies an amount $x_n(j)$ per noncontractible activity, while the $K - 1$ remaining suppliers supply the same amount $x_n(-j)$ (note that I am again appealing to symmetry).

To compute the Shapley value for this particular supplier j, we need to determine the marginal contribution of this supplier to a given coalition of agents. A coalition of n suppliers and the firm yields a sales revenue of

$$F_{\text{IN}}(n, N; \xi) = A^{1-\beta} N^{\beta(\kappa+1-1/\alpha)} x_c^{\beta\mu} [(n-1)\xi x_n(-j)^{(1-\mu)\alpha} + \xi x_n(j)^{(1-\mu)\alpha}]^{\beta/\alpha};$$

when supplier j is in the coalition, and a sales revenue of

$$F_{\text{OUT}}(n, N; \xi) = A^{1-\beta} N^{\beta(\kappa+1-1/\alpha)} x_c^{\beta\mu} [n\xi x_n(-j)^{(1-\mu)\alpha}]^{\beta/\alpha}$$

when supplier j is not in the coalition. Notice that even when $n < N$, the term $N^{\beta(\kappa+1-1/\alpha)}$ remains, because it represents a feature of the technology affecting output independent of the amount and quality of the inputs provided by the suppliers. On the other hand, productivity suffers because the term in square brackets is lower.

The Shapley value of player j is then

$$s_j = \frac{1}{(K+1)!} \sum_{g \in G} [v(z_g^j \cup j) - v(z_g^j)]. \tag{18.52}$$

The fraction of permutations in which $g(j) = i$ is $1/(K+1)$ for every i. If $g(j) = 0$, then $v(z_g^j \cup j) = v(z_g^j) = 0$, because in this event the firm is necessarily ordered *after* j. If $g(j) = 1$, then the firm is ordered before j with probability $1/K$ and after j with probability $1 - 1/K$. In the former case $v(z_g^j \cup j) = F_{IN}(1, N; \xi)$, while in the latter case $v(z_g^j \cup j) = 0$. Therefore the conditional expected value of $v(z_g^j \cup j)$, given $g(j) = 1$, is $F_{IN}(1, N; \xi)/K$. By similar reasoning, the conditional expected value of $v(z_g^j)$ is $F_{OUT}(0, N; \xi)/K$. Repeating the same argument for $g(j) = i > 1$, the conditional expected value of $v(z_g^j \cup j)$, given $g(j) = i$, is $i F_{IN}(i, N; \xi)/K$, and the conditional expected value of $v(z_g^j)$ is $i F_{OUT}(i - 1, N; \xi)/K$. It then follows from (18.52) that

$$s_j = \frac{1}{(K+1)K} \sum_{i=1}^{K} i[F_{IN}(i, N; \xi) - F_{OUT}(i-1, N; \xi)]$$

$$= \frac{1}{(N+\xi)N} \sum_{i=1}^{K} i\xi[F_{IN}(i, N; \xi) - F_{OUT}(i-1, N; \xi)]\xi.$$

Substituting for the expressions of F_{IN} and F_{OUT}, yields

$$s_j = \frac{A^{1-\beta} N^{\beta(\kappa+1-1/\alpha)} x_c^{\beta\mu}}{(N+\xi)N} \sum_{i=1}^{K} i\xi \left\{ i\xi x_n(-j)^{(1-\mu)\alpha} + \xi \left[x_n(j)^{(1-\mu)\alpha} - x_n(-j)^{(1-\mu)\alpha} \right] \right\}^{\beta/\alpha} \xi$$

$$- \frac{A^{1-\beta} N^{\beta(\kappa+1-1/\alpha)} x_c^{\beta\mu}}{(N+\xi)N} \sum_{i=1}^{K} i\xi \left[i\xi x_n(-j)^{(1-\mu)\alpha} - \xi x_n(-j)^{(1-\mu)\alpha} \right]^{\beta/\alpha} \xi.$$

Now using a first-order Taylor expansion (see Theorem A.22 in Appendix A), we obtain

$$s_j = \frac{A^{1-\beta} N^{\beta(\kappa+1-1/\alpha)} x_c^{\beta\mu} (\beta/\alpha)\xi x_n(j)^{(1-\mu)\alpha}}{(N+\xi)N} \sum_{i=1}^{K} (i\xi) \left[i\xi x_n(-j)^{(1-\mu)\alpha} \right]^{(\beta-\alpha)/\alpha} \xi + o(\xi),$$

where $o(\xi)$ represents terms such that $\lim_{\xi \to 0} o(\xi)/\xi = 0$. Rearranging this expression and dividing by $o(\xi)$, we obtain

$$\frac{s_j}{\xi} = \frac{A^{1-\beta} N^{\beta(\kappa+1-1/\alpha)} (\beta/\alpha) \left(\frac{x_n(j)}{x_n(-j)} \right)^{(1-\mu)\alpha} x_c^{\beta\mu} x_n(-j)^{\beta(1-\mu)}}{(N+\xi)N} \sum_{i=1}^{K} (i\xi)^{\beta/\alpha} \xi + \frac{o(\xi)}{\xi}.$$

Taking the limit as $K \to \infty$ (which is also equivalent to the limit $\xi = N/K \to 0$, with $\lim_{\xi \to 0} o(\xi)/\xi = 0$) gives the Riemann integral (recall Section B.2 in Appendix B):

$$\lim_{K \to \infty} \left(\frac{s_j}{\xi} \right) = \frac{A^{1-\beta} N^{\beta(\kappa+1-1/\alpha)} (\beta/\alpha) \left(\frac{x_n(j)}{x_n(-j)} \right)^{(1-\mu)\alpha} x_c^{\beta\mu} x_n(-j)^{\beta(1-\mu)}}{N^2} \int_0^N z^{\beta/\alpha} dz.$$

Solving this integral gives (18.42) and completes the proof.

18.6 Taking Stock

This chapter presented models of technology differences across societies. While the baseline endogenous growth models, such as those studied in Part IV, are useful in understanding the incentives of research firms to create new technologies and can generate different rates of technological change across different economies, two factors suggest that a different perspective is necessary for understanding technology differences across nations. First, technology and productivity differences do not only exist across nations but are ubiquitous within countries. Even within narrowly defined sectors, there are substantial productivity differences across firms, and only a small portion of these differences can be attributed to differences in capital intensity of production. This within-country pattern suggests that technology adoption and use decisions of firms are complex, and new technologies only diffuse slowly across firms. This pattern gives us some clues about potential sources of productivity and technology differences across nations and suggests that a slow process of technology diffusion across countries may not be unreasonable. Second, while the United States, Germany, or Japan can be thought of as creating their own technologies via the process of R&D, most countries in the world are technology importers rather than technology leaders. This is not to deny that some firms in these societies do engage in R&D nor to imply that a number of important technologies, most notably those related to the Green Revolution, have been invented in developing countries. These exceptions notwithstanding, adoption of existing frontier technologies appears more important for most firms in developing countries than the creation of entirely new technologies. This perspective also suggests that a detailed analysis of technology diffusion and technology adoption decisions is necessary for obtaining a good understanding of productivity and technology differences across countries.

Several important lessons have emerged from our study in this chapter. First, we can make considerable progress in understanding technology and productivity differences across nations by positing a slow process of technology transfer across countries. Such an approach enables us to have a tractable model of technology differences across countries. An important element of most models of technology diffusion is a built-in advantage for countries (or firms) that are relatively behind: since there is a larger gap for them to close, it is relatively easier for them to close it. This catch-up advantage for backward economies ensures that models of slow technology diffusion lead to differences in income levels, not necessarily in growth rates. In other words, the canonical model of technology diffusion implies that countries that create barriers against technology diffusion (or those that are slow in adopting new technologies for other reasons) will be poor, but they eventually converge to the growth rate of the frontier economies. Thus a study of technology diffusion enables us to develop a model of world income distribution in which the position of each country in the world income distribution is determined by their ability to absorb new technologies from the world frontier. This theoretical machinery is also useful for developing a framework in which, while each country may act as a neoclassical exogenous growth economy importing its technology from the world frontier, the entire world behaves as an endogenous growth economy, with its growth rate determined by the investment in R&D decisions of all firms in the world. This class of models becomes particularly useful when we wish to think of the joint process of world growth and world income distribution across countries. Such models also emphasize that much is lost in terms of insights when we focus on the baseline neoclassical growth model in which each country is treated as an isolated island that does not interact with others in the world. Technological interdependences across countries implies that we should often consider the world equilibrium, not simply the equilibrium of each country on its own.

While slow diffusion of existing technologies across countries is reasonable, in the globalized world we live in today it is becoming increasingly easier for firms to adopt technologies that have already been tried and implemented in other parts of the world. Once we allow a relatively rapid diffusion of technologies, does there remain any reason for technology or productivity differences across countries (beyond differences in physical and human capital)? The second part of the chapter has argued that the answer to this question is also yes and is related to the appropriateness of technologies and to differences in contracting institutions that affect technology adoption (and productivity).

Issues of appropriateness imply that a given technology does not have the same impact on the productivity in all economies, because it may be a better match to the conditions or to the factor proportions of some countries than of others. A particularly important channel of (in)appropriateness is the potential (mis)match between technologies developed at the world frontier and the skills of the adopting country's workforce. A technology-skill mismatch can lead to large endogenous productivity differences. If the types of technologies developed at the world frontier were random, the possibility of the technology-skill mismatch creating a significant gap between rich and poor nations would be a mere possibility, no more. However there are reasons to suspect that technology-skill mismatch may be more important because of the organization of the world technology market. Two features are important here. First, the majority of frontier technologies are developed in a few rich countries. Second, the lack of effective IPR enforcement implies that technology firms in advanced countries target the needs of their own markets. This creates a powerful force for new technologies that are appropriate to (designed for) the needs of the advanced nations and thus are typically inappropriate to the factor proportions of developing nations. In particular, new technologies will often be too skill biased to be effectively used in developing countries. This source of inappropriateness of technologies can create a large endogenous technology and income gap across nations.

Finally, this chapter has also emphasized that productivity differences do not simply stem from differences in the use of different techniques of production, but also from differences in production organization around the world. A key reason for such differences is the institutions and policies in place in different parts of the world. The last part of the chapter showed how contracting institutions, affecting what types of contracts firms can write with their suppliers, can have an important effect on their technology adoption decisions and thus on cross-country differences in productivity. Contracting institutions are only one of many potential organizational differences across countries that might impact equilibrium productivity. Other sources of differences in the organization of production and technology are discussed in Chapter 21.

18.7   References and Literature

The large literature documenting productivity and technology differences across firms and the patterns of technology diffusion was discussed in Section 18.1 and the relevant references can be found there. The simple model of technology diffusion presented in Section 18.2 is inspired by Gerschenkron's (1962) essay and by Nelson and Phelps's (1966) seminal paper (and by Schultz, 1975). The Nelson-Phelps approach, which was discussed in greater detail in Chapter 10, has been important in a number of recent papers. Benhabib and Spiegel (1994) reinterpret and modify Barro-style growth regressions in light of Nelson-Phelps's view of human capital. Aghion and Howitt (1998) also provide a similar reinterpretation of growth regressions. Greenwood and Yorukoglu (1997), Caselli (1999), Galor and Moav (2000), and Aghion, Howitt, and Violante (2004) provide models inspired by the Nelson-Phelps-Schultz view of human capital and applied to understanding the recent increase in the returns to skills in the United States and other OECD economies.

The model in Section 18.3 is inspired by Howitt (2000) but is different in a number of important respects. Howitt constructs a model of Schumpeterian growth rather than the baseline expanding input variety model used here and introduces a variety of technological externalities. The model in Section 18.3 is a simpler benchmark model for the analysis of endogenous growth at the world level.

The ideas of appropriate technology presented in Section 18.4 have been discussed in Salter (1960), David (1975), and Stewart (1977). Atkinson and Stiglitz's classic (1969) paper suggested a simple and powerful formalization of how technological change can be localized and thus difficult to transfer from one productive unit to another (or from one country to another). Atkinson and Stiglitz's idea is incorporated into a growth model by Basu and Weil (1998), which was the basis of one of the models in Section 18.4. The last part of this section draws on Acemoglu and Zilibotti (2001). That paper also provided evidence that these effects could be quantitatively large, and patterns of sectoral differences are consistent with the importance of this type of technology-skill mismatch.

The model presented in Section 18.5 draws upon Acemoglu, Antras, and Helpman (2007). Other models also generate endogenous productivity or technology differences across countries as a result of differences in the organization of production. Some of these are discussed in Chapter 21.

18.8 Exercises

18.1 Derive (18.1).

18.2 Show that if the restriction that $\lambda_j \in [0, g)$ in Section 18.2 is relaxed, the requirement that $A_j(t) \leq A(t)$ can be violated.

18.3 Derive (18.4).

18.4 Complete the proof of Proposition 18.1.

18.5 Derive the effect of an increase in λ_j on the laws of motion of $a_j(t)$ and $k_j(t)$ ((18.4) and (18.1), respectively). How does this differ from the effect of an increase in σ_j? Explain why these two parameters have different effects on technology and capital stock dynamics.

18.6 In the model of Section 18.2, show that if $g = 0$, then all countries converge to the same level of technology. Explain carefully why $g > 0$ leads to steady-state technology differences, while these differences disappear when $g = 0$.

18.7 Prove Proposition 18.2.

18.8 (a) Why is the condition $\rho - n_j > (1 - \theta)g$ necessary in Proposition 18.3?

(b) Complete the proof of Proposition 18.3.

(c) Set up the world equilibrium problem in Section 18.2.2 as one in which the Second Welfare Theorem holds within each country. Under this assumption, carefully define an equilibrium path. Explain the significance of this assumption.

(d) Now set up the world equilibrium problem without appealing to the Second Welfare Theorem. Explain why the mathematical problem is identical to that in part a.

18.9 In the model of Section 18.2.2 with household optimization, suppose that preferences in country j are given by

$$U_j = \int_0^\infty \exp(-(\rho_j - n_j)t)[(c_j(t)^{1-\theta} - 1)/(1 - \theta)]dt,$$

where ρ_j differs across countries.

(a) Show that a unique steady-state world equilibrium still exists and all countries grow at the rate g.

(b) Provide an intuition for why countries grow at the same rate despite different rates of discounting.

(c) Show that this steady-state equilibrium is globally saddle-path stable.

* 18.10 Consider the model of Section 18.2 with F corresponding to the production function of an individual firm j (with a slight abuse of notation). Let (18.3) correspond to the law of motion of the technology of the firm, with $\sigma_j = \sigma(h_j)$, where h_j is the average human capital of the workers of firm j, and σ is a strictly increasing and differentiable function. To simplify the discussion, suppose that each firm employs a single worker.

(a) Derive the wage of the worker of human capital h_j. [Hint: this consists of the worker's value of marginal product in production plus the increase in the productivity of the firm because of the improvement in the firm's technology.]

(b) Show that an increase in g (at any t) increases wages. Derive the implications of changes in g on the returns to human capital. Contrast an increase in the returns to human capital driven by an increase in g with those discussed in Chapter 15.

18.11 Complete the proof of Proposition 18.4.

18.12 Consider the model in Section 18.3.1, and suppose that all countries have the same labor force size $L_j = 1$, have the same $\eta_j = \eta$, and only differ in terms of ζ_j. Imagine that the cross-country range of ζ_j is the same as used in the quantitative evaluation of the neoclassical growth model in Chapter 8.

(a) Evaluate the impact of these differences in ζ_j on cross-country technology and income differences for different values of ϕ.

(b) What value of ϕ is necessary so that a 4-fold difference in ζ_j translates into a 30-fold difference in income per capita?

(c) How would you interpret the economic significance of such a value of ϕ? Is this a more satisfactory model of cross-country technology and income differences than the neoclassical growth model?

* 18.13 Consider the model in Sections 18.3.1 and 18.3.2. Suppose that preferences are given by

$$U_j = \int_0^\infty \exp(-\rho_j t)[(c_j(t)^{1-\theta} - 1)/(1 - \theta)]dt,$$

where ρ_j differs across countries. Show that the equivalents of Propositions 18.4 and 18.5 apply, with a unique globally saddle-path stable world equilibrium where all countries grow at the same rate.

18.14 Show that (18.14) is necessary and sufficient for a positive world growth rate in the model of Section 18.3.2. Write down the conditions that characterize the world equilibrium when this condition is not satisfied.

18.15 Prove Proposition 18.5.

* 18.16 Analyze the local dynamics of the steady-state world equilibrium in Proposition 18.5. [Hint: linearize the system of differential equations around the steady state.]

* 18.17 Consider Proposition 18.5 with ρ_j differing across countries. Prove that a unique steady-state world equilibrium, with all countries growing at the same rate, still exists.

18.18 In the model of Section 18.3.2, replace (18.12) with

$$N(t) = G(N_1(t), \ldots, N_J(t)),$$

where G is increasing in all of its arguments and is homogeneous of degree 1.

(a) Generalize the results in Proposition 18.5 to this case, and derive an equation that determines the world growth rate implicitly.

(b) Derive an explicit equation for the world growth rate for the specific case in which $N(t) = \max_j N_j(t)$.

18.19 (a) Show that in the model in Section 18.3.2, if population grows at some constant rate $n > 0$ in each country, there does not exist a steady-state equilibrium.

(b) Construct a variation of this model along the lines of the semi-endogenous growth models of Section 13.3 in Chapter 13, where the strong scale effect is removed and there is long-run growth at a constant rate (when population grows at the rate $n > 0$ in each country). [Hint: modify (18.9) so that $\dot{N}_j(t) = \eta_j N(t)^\phi N_j(t)^{-\tilde{\phi}} Z_j(t)$, where $\tilde{\phi} > \phi$.]

(c) Provide a full characterization of the steady-state world equilibrium in the case described in part b.

18.20 Consider the model in Section 18.4.2. Suppose that the world consists of two countries with constant and equal populations, and constant savings rates, $s_1 > s_2$. Suppose that the production function in each country is given by (18.15), with k' corresponding to the highest capital-labor ratio in any country experienced until then. There is no technological progress, and both countries start with the same capital-labor ratio.

(a) Characterize the steady-state world equilibrium (i.e., the steady-state capital-labor ratios in both countries).

(b) Characterize the output per capita dynamics in the two economies. How does an increase in γ affect these dynamics?

(c) Show that the implied income per capita differences (in steady state) between the two countries are increasing in γ. Interpret this result.

(d) Do you think this model provides a plausible mechanism for generating large income differences across countries? Substantiate your answer with theoretical or empirical arguments.

18.21 Complete the proof of Proposition 18.6. Explicitly derive the expression for the threshold $I_j(t)$ and the skill premium $w_{H,j}(t)/w_{L,j}(t)$ in country j at time t.

18.22 Derive (18.20)–(18.23).

18.23 Prove Proposition 18.7. [Hint: in steady state the profits from owning a skill-complementary and unskilled labor-complementary machine must be equal.]

18.24 Prove Proposition 18.8.

18.25 Consider the model of appropriate technology in Section 18.4.3.

(a) Suppose that now research firms can sell their machines to all producers in the world, including those in the South, and can charge the same markup. Derive the steady-state equilibrium under these conditions. [Hint: assume that final good prices are the same in the North and the South.]

(b) Comparing your answer in part a to the analysis in the text, derive the implications of IPR enforcement in the South on equilibrium technologies. What are the implications for income per capita differences between the North and the South?

(c) In view of your answer to parts a and b, could it be the case that Southern economies prefer lack of IPR enforcement to full enforcement? [Hint: distinguish between a world in which there is a single Southern country versus one in which there are many.]

(d) What are the implications of IPR enforcement in the South for output and welfare in the North?

* 18.26 Instead of the multisector model in Section 18.4.3, suppose that output is given by an aggregate production function of the form

$$Y(t) = \left[\gamma Y_L(t)^{\frac{\varepsilon-1}{\varepsilon}} + (1-\gamma) Y_H(t)^{\frac{\varepsilon-1}{\varepsilon}} \right]^{\frac{\varepsilon}{\varepsilon-1}}$$

as in Section 15.3 in Chapter 15, with Y_L and Y_H being produced exactly as in that chapter. Assume, as in Section 18.4.3, that new technologies are developed in the North for the Northern market only.

(a) Characterize the steady-state (BGP) equilibrium of this economy. [Hint: use the same analysis as in Section 18.4.3.]

(b) Show that if $\sigma \equiv \varepsilon - (\varepsilon - 1)(1 - \beta)$ is equal to 2, the results are identical to those in Section 18.4.3.

(c) Derive the equivalents of Propositions 18.7 and 18.8.

(d) Do the implications of inappropriate technologies become more or less important when σ increases?

18.27 Prove Proposition 18.9.

18.28 Prove Proposition 18.11.

18.29 Prove Proposition 18.12.

* 18.30 Consider the model of Section 18.5. Suppose that there is a total population of L. Assume that each individual can work as a supplier for one of the M products, or he can work in the process of technology adoption. The cost of technology adoption is now given by $\Gamma(N) \equiv w\Gamma_0(N)$, where w is the wage rate, corresponding to the outside option of each supplier.

(a) Characterize the general equilibrium of the economy by endogenizing A for a given number of products M. In particular, show that in equilibrium the market clearing condition $M(\Gamma_0(N^*) + N^*) = L$ must be satisfied (where N^* is the equilibrium technology choice and thus the number of suppliers).

(b) What is the effect of an increase in μ on N^*? Explain the result.

(c) Now suppose that the M products differ according to their elasticity of substitution; in particular, each product has a different α, with the distribution of α across products given by a function $G(\alpha)$ with support within the interval $[0, 1]$. Let $N^*(\alpha)$ be the equilibrium technology choice (number of suppliers) for a product with parameter α. Show that the market clearing condition now takes the form

$$M \int_0^1 [\Gamma_0(N^*(\alpha)) + N^*(\alpha)]dG(\alpha) = L.$$

(d) What is the effect of an increase in μ on the equilibrium in this case?

(e) How would you endogenize M? What types of insights would this generate?

18.31 Consider the model of Section 18.5. What types of organizational forms might emerge when contracting institutions are imperfect (i.e., when μ is very low)? In particular, discuss how vertical integration and repeated interactions between suppliers and producers might change the results discussed in that section. How would you model each of these?

19

Trade and Growth

The previous chapter discussed how technological linkages across countries and technology adoption decisions lead to a pattern of interdependent growth across countries. This chapter studies world equilibria with international trade in financial assets or commodities. I start with growth in economies that can borrow and lend internationally and discuss how this affects cross-country income differences and growth dynamics. I then turn to the growth implications of international trade in commodities.

Our first task is to construct models of world equilibria that feature both international trade in commodities (or intermediate goods) and economic growth. The exact interactions between trade and growth depend on the nature of trade that countries engage in. I try to provide an overview of these different interactions. I start with a model in which trade is of the Heckscher-Ohlin type; that is, it originates only because of differences in factor abundance across countries, and growth is driven by capital accumulation. I then turn to a model of Ricardian type, where trade is driven by technological comparative advantage. A key difference between these two approaches concerns whether the prices of the goods that a country supplies to the world are affected by its own production and accumulation decisions. These models shed new light on the patterns of interdependences across countries, for example, showing that growth in one country cannot be analyzed in isolation from the growth experiences of other nations in the world.

Our second task is to turn to a central question of the literature on trade and growth: whether international trade encourages economic growth. The answer to this question also depends on exactly how trade is modeled, as well as on what the source of economic growth is (in particular learning-by-doing versus innovation). Throughout, the emphasis is on the importance of considering the world equilibrium rather than that of a closed economy in isolation.

19.1 Growth and Financial Capital Flows

In a globalized economy, if the rates of return to capital differ across countries, we would expect capital to flow toward areas where its rate of return is higher. This simple observation has a number of important implications for growth theory. First, it implies a different pattern of economic growth in a financially integrated world. Our first task in this section is to illustrate the implications of international capital flows for economic growth and show how they significantly change transitional dynamics in the basic neoclassical growth model. Our second task is to highlight what new lessons can be derived from the analysis of economic growth in the presence of international capital flows. The presence of international capital flows raises several puzzles, most notably, the one emphasized by Lucas (1990): "Why Doesn't Capital Flow from Rich to Poor Countries?" This simple question helps us think about a range of important issues in economic growth and economic development. While a model of free flow of capital around the world is a good starting point, the existing evidence is not entirely consistent with such free flows. In particular, free flows of capital lead to a pattern of growth that appears counterfactual. Moreover, a large literature in international finance, starting with Feldstein and Horioka (1980), points out that there is much less net flow of capital from countries with high saving rates toward those with lower saving rates than a theory of frictionless international capital markets would suggest. In the next section, I briefly discuss why capital flows across countries may be hampered and what the implications of this are for cross-country growth dynamics.

Consider a world economy consisting of J countries, indexed $j = 1, \ldots, J$, each with access to an aggregate production function for producing a unique final good:

$$Y_j(t) = F(K_j(t), A_j(t)L_j(t)),$$

where $Y_j(t)$ is the output of this unique final good in country j at time t; $K_j(t)$ and $L_j(t)$ are the capital stock and labor supply, respectively; and $A_j(t)$ is again the country-specific Harrod-neutral technology term. The production function F satisfies Assumptions 1 and 2 from Chapter 2. As in the previous chapter, each country is "small" and ignores its effects on world aggregates. Technological change occurs at a constant rate across countries, though there may be level differences in technology, that is,

$$A_j(t) = A_j \exp(gt),$$

where g is the common growth rate of technology in the world.

Suppose that each country admits a representative household with the standard preferences at time $t = 0$ given by

$$U_j = \int_0^\infty \exp(-(\rho - n)t) \frac{c_j(t)^{1-\theta} - 1}{1 - \theta} dt, \tag{19.1}$$

where $c_j(t)$ is per capita consumption in country j at time t, and I have assumed that all countries have the same time discount rate ρ and the same population growth rate n. Suppose that all countries start with the same population at time $t = 0$, which, without loss of generality, is normalized to 1, so that $L_j(0) = 1$ for $j = 1, \ldots, J$, and $L_j(t) = L(t) = \exp(nt)$ for each j. In addition, Assumption 4 from Chapter 8 continues to be satisfied, so that $\rho - n > (1 - \theta)g$.

The key feature of this economy is the presence of international borrowing and lending. Consistent with the permanent income hypothesis for individual consumption decisions, borrowing and lending allow a smoother consumption profile for households (in particular for the representative household) in each country. But since the desire for a smoother consumption profile was one of the main reasons why the capital stock did not adjust immediately to its steady-state (or BGP) value, the opportunities for international financial transactions will influence the dynamics of capital accumulation and growth.

More specifically, let $B_j(t) \in \mathbb{R}$ denote the net borrowing of country j from the world at time t. Let $r(t)$ denote the world interest rate. Free capital flows imply that this interest rate is independent of which country is borrowing and whether a country is a borrower or lender. Moreover, consistent with our assumption that each country is small relative to the world, all countries are price takers in the international financial markets, so they can borrow or lend as much as they like at this interest rate. Consequently the resource constraint in each country takes the form

$$\dot{k}_j(t) = f(k_j(t)) - \tilde{c}_j(t) + b_j(t) - (n + g + \delta)k_j(t), \qquad (19.2)$$

where, as usual, $k_j(t) \equiv K_j(t)/(A_j(t)L_j(t))$ is the effective capital-labor ratio in country j at time t, $\tilde{c}_j(t) \equiv C_j(t)/(A_j(t)L_j(t))$ is the ratio of consumption to effective labor, and

$$y_j(t) \equiv \frac{Y_j(t)}{L_j(t)} \equiv A_j(t)f(k_j(t))$$

is income per capita, while

$$b_j(t) \equiv \frac{B_j(t)}{A_j(t)L_j(t)}$$

denotes the net borrowing (international transfers) normalized by effective labor. The most important feature of (19.2) is that, in contrast to all other resource constraints so far, it does not require domestic consumption and investment to be equal to domestic production. Instead there are potential transfers of resources from the rest of the world, $B_j(t)$ or $b_j(t)$, which can be used for consumption or investment. Conversely, the country may be transferring resources to the rest of the world, so that it consumes and invests less than it produces. Naturally, once we allow for international borrowing and lending, we must ensure that each country (and thus each representative household) satisfies an international budget constraint. For this purpose, let $\mathcal{A}_j(t)$ denote the international asset position of country j at time t. If $\mathcal{A}_j(t)$ is positive, the country is a net lender and has positive claims on output produced in other countries, while if it is negative, the country is a net borrower. The flow budget constraint for country j at time t can then be written as

$$\dot{\mathcal{A}}_j(t) = r(t)\mathcal{A}_j(t) - B_j(t), \qquad (19.3)$$

which simply states that the country earns the world interest rate $r(t)$ on its existing asset position $\mathcal{A}(t)$ (or accumulates further debt if the latter is negative) and in addition receives transfers $B(t)$ from the rest of the world (or makes transfers to the rest of the world when $B(t)$ is negative). If transfers from the rest of the world exceed the interest earned on current assets, the asset position of the country deteriorates, that is, $\dot{\mathcal{A}}_j(t) < 0$. The no-Ponzi game condition (e.g., from Chapter 8) now applies to the representative household in each country and thus indirectly applies to the international asset position of a country. It requires that

$$\lim_{t \to \infty} \left[\mathcal{A}_j(t) \exp\left(-\int_0^t r(s)ds \right) \right] = 0$$

for each $j = 1, \ldots, J$. The intuition for this expression is the same as the no-Ponzi game condition, (8.16) in Chapter 8.

As with the other variables, it is convenient to express the net asset position of the country in terms of effective labor units, so let us define

$$\mathsf{a}_j(t) \equiv \frac{\mathcal{A}_j(t)}{A_j(t)L_j(t)},$$

which implies that (19.3) can be rewritten as

$$\dot{\mathsf{a}}_j(t) = (r(t) - g - n)\mathsf{a}_j(t) - b_j(t), \tag{19.4}$$

and the no-Ponzi game condition becomes

$$\lim_{t \to \infty} \left[\mathsf{a}_j(t) \exp\left(-\int_0^t (r(s) - g - n)ds \right) \right] = 0. \tag{19.5}$$

Naturally, the amount of borrowing and lending in the world has to balance. Thus the world capital market clearing condition

$$\sum_{j=1}^J B_j(t) = 0$$

must hold at all times t. Now dividing and multiplying each term by $A_j(t)L_j(t)$, and recalling that $A_j(t) = A_j \exp(gt)$ and $L_j(t) = L(t)$ for all j, the world capital market clearing condition can be written as

$$\sum_{j=1}^J A_j b_j(t) = 0 \tag{19.6}$$

for all $t \geq 0$.

With access to international capital markets, the problem of the representative household in each country is to maximize (19.1) subject to (19.2), (19.4), and (19.5).

A *world equilibrium* is now defined as paths of normalized consumption levels, capital stocks, and asset positions for each country, $\{[k_j(t), \tilde{c}_j(t), \mathsf{a}_j(t)]_{t \geq 0}\}_{j=1}^J$, and a time path of world interest rates, $[r(t)]_{t \geq 0}$, such that each country's allocation maximizes the utility of the representative household in each country, and the world financial market clears (i.e., (19.6) is satisfied). A steady-state world equilibrium is defined as a world equilibrium in which $k_j(t)$ and $\tilde{c}_j(t)$ are constant and output in each country grows at a constant rate. As in previous chapters, we could alternatively refer to this allocation as a BGP rather than a steady-state equilibrium.

The equilibrium of this world economy with free financial flows is straightforward to characterize. It is useful to first present a number of simple intermediate results to emphasize several important economic ideas.

Proposition 19.1 *In the world equilibrium of the economy with free flows of capital,*

$$k_j(t) = k(t) = f'^{-1}(r(t) + \delta) \text{ for all } j = 1, \ldots, J,$$

where $f'^{-1}(\cdot)$ is the inverse function of $f'(\cdot)$, and $r(t)$ is the world interest rate.

Proof. See Exercise 19.1. ∎

With free flows of capital, each firm in each country stops renting capital only when its marginal product is equal to the opportunity cost, which is given by the world rental rate (the world interest rate plus the depreciation rate). Consequently effective capital-labor ratios are equalized across countries. Note, however, that this does not imply equalization of capital-labor ratios. To the extent that two countries j and j' have different levels of productivity, $A_j(t)$ and $A_{j'}(t) \neq A_j(t)$, their capital-labor ratios are not, and *should not*, be equalized. This is an important point to which I return below.

The next proposition focuses on the steady-state world equilibrium.

Proposition 19.2 *Suppose that Assumption 4 in Chapter 2 is satisfied. Then in the world economy with free flows of capital, there exists a unique steady-state world equilibrium in which output, capital, and consumption per capita in all countries grow at the rate g, and effective capital-labor ratios are given by*

$$k_j^* = k^* = f'^{-1}(\rho + \delta + \theta g) \text{ for all } j = 1, \ldots, J.$$

Moreover in the steady-state equilibrium,

$$\lim_{t \to \infty} \dot{a}_j(t) = 0 \text{ for all } j = 1, \ldots, J.$$

Proof. See Exercise 19.1. ∎

This result is intuitive: with free capital flows, the world economy is *integrated*. This integrated world economy has a unique steady-state equilibrium similar to that in the standard neoclassical growth model. The steady-state equilibrium not only determines the effective capital-labor ratio and its growth rate but also the distribution of the available capital across different countries in the world economy. Even though this proposition is intuitive, its proof requires some care to ensure that no country runs a Ponzi scheme; the absence of a Ponzi scheme requires that the change in normalized asset position of each country (and each household within each country), $\dot{a}_j(t)$ for each j, asymptote to zero. This last feature is no longer the case when the model is extended so that countries differ according to their discount rates (see Exercise 19.2).

Let us next consider the transitional dynamics of the world economy. The analysis of transitional dynamics is simplified by the fact that the world behaves as an integrated economy rather than an independent collection of economies (see Exercise 19.2).

Proposition 19.3 *In the world equilibrium of the economy with free flows of capital, there exists a unique equilibrium path $\{[k_j(t), \tilde{c}_j(t), a_j(t)]_{t \geq 0}\}_{j=1}^J$ that converges to the steady-state world equilibrium. Along this equilibrium path, $k_j(t)/k_{j'}(t) = 1$ and $\tilde{c}_j(t)/\tilde{c}_{j'}(t) = constant$ for any two countries j and j'.*

Proof. See Exercise 19.3. ∎

Intuitively, the integrated world economy acts as if it has a single neoclassical aggregate production function; thus the characterization of the dynamic equilibrium path and of transitional dynamics from Chapter 8 applies. In addition, Proposition 19.1 implies that $k_j(t)/k_{j'}(t)$ is constant, and the consumption Euler equations imply that $\tilde{c}_j(t)/\tilde{c}_{j'}(t)$ must also be constant. Therefore both production and consumption in each economy grow in tandem. Notice, however, that Proposition 19.3 does not state that $\tilde{c}_j(t) = \tilde{c}_{j'}(t)$ (even though $k_j(t) = k_{j'}(t)$). This is because, while GDP and production per capita across countries are equalized, Gross National Product (GNP) need not be equalized, because different countries could have unequal asset positions. This point is further emphasized in Exercise 19.2.

The following is an important corollary to Proposition 19.3.

Corollary 19.1 *Consider the world economy with free flows of capital. Suppose that at time t, a fraction λ of the capital stock of country j is destroyed. Then capital flows immediately to this country ($\dot{a}_j(t) \to -\infty$) to ensure that $k_j(t')/k_{j'}(t') = 1$ for all $t' \geq t$ and for all $j' \neq j$.*

Proof. This corollary is a direct implication of Propositions 19.1 and 19.3. The latter implies that there exists a unique globally stable equilibrium, while the former implies that for all t, $k_j(t)/k_{j'}(t) = 1$. This is only possible if there is an immediate inflow of capital into country j.

∎

This result implies that in the world economy with free flows of capital, there are only transitional dynamics for the aggregate world economy but no transitional dynamics separately for each country (in particular, $k_j(t)/k_{j'}(t) = 1$ for all t and any j and j'). This is intuitive, since international capital flows ensure that each country has the same effective capital-labor ratio; thus dynamics resulting from slow capital accumulation are removed. The corollary therefore implies that any theory emphasizing the role of transitional dynamics in explaining the evolution of cross-country income differences must implicitly limit the extent or the speed of international capital flows. The evidence on this point is mixed. While the amount of gross capital flow in the world economy is large, the "Feldstein-Horioka puzzle," which is discussed below, highlights that countries that save more also tend to invest more. One reason for this might be the potential risk of sovereign default by countries that borrow significant amounts from the world financial markets. Exercise 19.4 investigates this issue.

Although the implications of this corollary for cross-country patterns of divergence can be debated, its implications for cross-regional convergence are clear: cross-regional patterns of convergence cannot be related to slow capital accumulation as in the baseline neoclassical growth model (see Exercise 19.5).

19.2 Why Does Capital Not Flow from Rich to Poor Countries?

The model studied in the previous section provides us with a framework to answer the question posed above and in the title of this section. In the basic Solow and neoclassical growth models, a key source of cross-country income differences is capital-labor ratios. For example, if we consider a world economy in which all countries have access to the same technology and there are no human capital differences, the only reason one country would be richer than another is differences in capital-labor ratios. But if two countries with the same production possibilities set differ in terms of their capital-labor ratios, then the rate of return to capital will be lower in the richer economy, and there will be incentives for capital to flow from rich to poor countries. I now discuss the reasons that capital may not flow from societies with higher capital-labor ratios to those with greater capital scarcity.

19.2.1 Capital Flows under Perfect International Capital Markets

One potential answer to the question posed above is provided by the analysis in the previous section. With perfect international capital markets, capital flows equalize effective capital-labor ratios. But this does not imply equalization of capital-labor ratios. This result, which follows directly from the analysis in the previous section, is stated in the next proposition. Note that this result does not give a complete answer to our question, since it takes productivity differences across countries as given. Nevertheless it explains how, given these productivity differences, there is no compelling reason to expect capital to flow from rich to poor countries.

Proposition 19.4 *Consider a world economy with identical neoclassical preferences across countries and free flows of capital. Suppose that countries differ according to their productivities, the A_js. Then, there exists a unique steady-state equilibrium in which capital-labor ratios differ across countries (in particular, effective capital-labor ratios, the k_js, are equalized).*

Proof. See Exercise 19.7. ■

There is thus no reason to expect capital flows when countries differ according to their productivities. The more productive countries should have higher capital-labor ratios. To the extent that two countries j and j' have different levels of productivity, $A_j(t)$ and $A_{j'}(t) > A_j(t)$, their capital-labor ratios should not be equalized; instead country j' should have a higher capital-labor ratio than that of j. Consequently capital need not flow from rich to poor countries. This explanation is similar to that suggested in Lucas (1990), except that Lucas also linked differences in A_js to differences in human capital (and in particular to human capital externalities). Instead Proposition 19.4 emphasizes that any source of differences in A_js generates this pattern.

The reader would be right to object at this point that this is only a proximate answer to the question, since it provides no reason for why productivity differs across countries. This objection is largely correct. Nevertheless, Proposition 19.4 is still useful, since it suggests a range of explanations for the lack of capital flows from rich to poor countries that do not depend on the details of the world financial system but instead focus on productivity differences across countries. We have already made some progress in understanding the potential sources of productivity differences across countries, and as we make more progress, we will start having better answers to the question of why capital does not flow from rich to poor countries (in fact, why it might sometimes flow from poor to rich countries).

19.2.2 Capital Flows under Imperfect International Financial Markets

There are other reasons, besides Proposition 19.4, why capital may not flow from rich to poor countries. The rate of return to capital may be higher in poor countries, but financial market frictions or issues of sovereign risk may prevent such flows. For example, lenders might worry that a country that has a negative asset position might declare international bankruptcy and not repay its debts. Alternatively, domestic financial problems in developing countries (which are discussed in Chapter 21) may prevent or slow down the flows of capital from rich to poor countries. For whatever reason, if the international financial markets are not perfect and capital cannot flow freely from rich to poor countries, we may expect large differences in the return to capital across countries.[1]

Existing evidence on this topic is mixed. Three different types of evidence are relevant. First, several studies, including Trefler's (1993) important work discussed in Chapter 3 and recent work by Caselli and Feyrer (2007), suggest that differences in the return to capital across countries are relatively limited. These estimates are directly relevant to the question of whether there are significant differences in the returns to capital across countries, but they are computed under assumptions that may not always hold in practice (in Trefler's case, they rely on data on factor contents of trade and make a variety of assumptions on the impact of trade on factor prices as discussed in Chapter 3; Caselli and Feyrer, on the other hand, require comparable and accurate measures of quality-adjusted differences in capital stocks across countries and assume that there are no costs of adjustment).

Second and somewhat in contrast to the aggregate results, some papers exploiting micro-data—for example, summarized in Banerjee and Duflo (2005)—suggest that the rate of return for additional investment in some firms in less-developed countries could be as high as 100%. Nonetheless, this evidence, even if taken at face value, does not suggest that there are strong incentives for capital to flow from rich to poor countries, since these higher rates of return may be generated by within-country credit market imperfections. In particular, it may be that the rate of return is very high for a range of credit-rationed firms, but various incentive problems make it impossible for domestic or foreign financial institutions to lend to these firms on profitable

---

1. Limits on capital flows may also contribute to productivity differences (e.g., by reducing productivity-enhancing investments), thus indirectly reducing the need for further capital flows.

terms. If these developing economies were to receive an infusion of additional foreign capital, the rate of return would not be given by the rate of return of credit-rationed firms but by the rate of return of unconstrained firms, which might be much lower. Consequently the incentives for capital to flow from rich to poor countries may be quite weak as suggested by Proposition 19.4.

Finally, Feldstein and Horioka's (1980) puzzle points out that differences in saving and investment rates across countries are highly correlated. Feldstein and Horioka reported the results from regressions of the form

$$\Delta \left(\frac{I_j(t)}{Y_j(t)} \right) = \alpha_0 + \alpha_1 \Delta \left(\frac{S_j(t)}{Y_j(t)} \right),$$

where $\Delta(I_j(t)/Y_j(t))$ is the change in the investment-GDP ratio of country j between some prior date and date t, and $\Delta(S_j(t)/Y_j(t))$ is the change in the savings-GDP ratio. Imagine that the savings-GDP ratio varies across countries and over time because of shocks to the saving rate or other reasons. In a world with free capital flows, we would expect these changes in savings to have no effect on investment; thus we should estimate a coefficient of $\alpha_1 \approx 0$. In contrast, Feldstein and Horioka estimated a coefficient close to 1 (about 0.9) for OECD economies. Similar results have been found for other samples of countries, though other studies argue that including additional controls removes the puzzle. Feldstein and Horioka and much of the literature that has followed them have interpreted the positive correlation between investment and savings as evidence against free capital flows. Naturally, in practice there are econometric and economic issues one needs to worry about before reaching a precise conclusion. For example, Exercise 19.6 shows how correlation between investment and savings can arise without imperfections in international financial markets (because the major difference across countries is in investment opportunities). Nevertheless the Feldstein-Horioka puzzle suggests that issues of sovereign risk might be important in practice and may create barriers to the free flow of capital across countries.

19.3 Economic Growth in a Heckscher-Ohlin World

We have so far focused on the growth implications of trade in financial assets, which enables countries to change the time profile of their consumption. Perhaps more important is international trade in commodities, which allows countries to exploit their comparative advantages (resulting from technology or differences in factor proportions). I now turn to a simple model of growth in a world consisting of countries that trade in commodities. My treatment builds on Ventura (1997), who constructed a tractable model of world equilibrium with *Heckscher-Ohlin* trade.

The Heckscher-Ohlin model posits that countries have access to the same (or similar) technologies, and the main source of trade is differences in factor proportions—for example, some countries have more physical or human capital relative to labor than others. Clearly an analysis of these issues necessitates the specification of models in which there are multiple commodities used either in consumption or as intermediates in production. For the sake of concreteness (without loss of generality), I pursue the second alternative, which also creates continuity with the models in Chapters 13 and 15.

Suppose that each country has access to an aggregate production function

$$Y_j(t) = F(X_j^K(t), X_j^L(t)), \tag{19.7}$$

where $Y_j(t)$ is final output in country j at time t, and $X_j^L(t)$ and $X_j^K(t)$ are respectively labor- and capital-intensive intermediates (inputs). I use the letter "X" to denote these inputs, since they refer to the amounts of these inputs used in production rather than the amount of inputs produced in country j. In the presence of international trade these two quantities will typically differ. In (19.7) F denotes a constant returns to scale production function and again satisfies Assumptions 1 and 2 from Chapter 2 (except that it is defined over two intermediate inputs rather than labor and capital). Notice that Assumption 2 also incorporates the Inada conditions. The production of the final good is competitive.

The theory of international trade is a well-developed and rich area and provides useful results on the structure of production and trade. Here my purpose is not to review these results but to illustrate the implications of Heckscher-Ohlin type international trade for economic growth. Therefore I adopt the simplest possible setting, which involves each intermediate input being produced by one factor. In particular,

$$Y_j^L(t) = A_j L_j(t), \text{ and} \tag{19.8}$$

$$Y_j^K(t) = K_j(t), \tag{19.9}$$

where the use of Y instead of X here emphasizes that these quantities refer to the local production, not the use, of these intermediates. Also, as usual, $L_j(t)$ is total labor input in country j at time t, supplied inelastically, and $K_j(t)$ is the total capital stock of the country. One feature about these intermediate production functions is worth noting: there are potential productivity differences across countries in the production of the labor-intensive good but not in the production of the capital-intensive good. This is the same assumption as the one adopted in Ventura (1997). Exercise 19.11 shows the implications of allowing differences in the productivity of the capital-intensive sector. For now, it suffices to note that this assumption makes it possible to derive a well-behaved world equilibrium, and it is in the spirit of allowing only labor-augmenting technological progress in the basic neoclassical model. One may also presume that differences in A_js reflect differences in the human capital embodied in labor. Finally, notice also that there is no technological progress. This is again to simplify the exposition, and Exercise 19.13 extends the model in this section to incorporate labor-augmenting technological progress.

Throughout the rest of this chapter, I assume that there is free international trade in commodities—in intermediate goods. This assumption is extreme, since trading internationally involves costs and many analyses of international trade incorporate the physical costs of transportation and tariffs. Nevertheless this assumption is useful to simplify the analysis and to highlight how international trade affects cross-country growth patterns. The most important implication of this assumption is that the prices of traded commodities—here the intermediate goods—in all countries are equal to their world prices, determined by the world supply and demand for these commodities. Let us denote the world prices of the labor-intensive and the capital-intensive intermediates at time t by $p^L(t)$ and $p^K(t)$, respectively. Both of these prices are in terms of the final good in the world market, which is taken as numeraire, with price normalized to 1.[2]

Given the production technologies in (19.8) and (19.9), competitive factor markets imply that the wage rate and the rental rate of capital in country j at time t are given by

---

2. In this model, there is no loss of generality in assuming that the price of the final good is normalized to 1 in each country even if there is no trade in the final good. This is because all goods are traded and there are no differences in costs of living (purchasing power parity) across countries. This will no longer be the case in the models studied in the next section.

$$w_j(t) = A_j p^L(t), \text{ and } R_j(t) = p^K(t).$$

These two equations summarize the most important economic insights of the model studied here. In closed-economy models, factor prices, which shape the incentives to accumulate capital, are determined by the capital-labor ratio in the economy (recall Chapter 8). In contrast, factor prices here are determined by world prices. In particular, since capital is used only in the production of the capital-intensive intermediate and there is free trade in intermediates, the rental rate of capital in each country is given by the world price of the capital-intensive intermediate. A similar reasoning applies to the wage rate, with the only difference being that, because of cross-country differences in the productivity of labor, wage rates are not equalized; instead it is the effective wage rates, $w_j(t)/A_j$, that are equalized. Let us follow Trefler (1993) in referring to this pattern as "conditional factor price equalization" across countries, meaning that, once we take into account intrinsic productivity differences of factors, there is equalization of (effective) factor prices across countries. Conditional factor price equalization is weaker than the celebrated factor price equalization of international trade theory, which would require $w_j(t)$s to be equalized across countries. Instead, here $w_j(t)/A_j$s are equalized.

In this model, conditional factor price equalization is a consequence of free and costless trade in goods, since each factor is used only in the production of a single traded intermediate. Nevertheless (conditional) factor price equalization results are more general than the specific structure here might suggest. In the jargon of international trade theory, with free trade of commodities, there exists *a cone of diversification* such that when factor proportions of different countries are within this cone, there will be (conditional) factor price equalization. The assumptions here that labor is used in the production of the labor-intensive intermediate and capital is used in the production of the capital-intensive intermediate (and that international trade is costless) ensure that the cone of diversification is large enough to include any possible configuration of the distribution of capital and labor stocks across countries.

Conditional factor price equalization is important because it implies that factor prices in each country are entirely independent of its capital stock and labor (provided that the country in question is small relative to the rest of the world; recall footnote 1 in the previous chapter). The distinguishing feature of the model in this section is this independence of factor prices from accumulation decisions.[3]

Because capital again depreciates at the rate δ, the interest rate in country j at time t is

$$r_j(t) = R_j(t) - \delta = p^K(t) - \delta. \tag{19.10}$$

Let us next specify the resource constraint. While there is free international trade in commodities, there is no intertemporal trade. Thus we are abstracting from international lending and borrowing discussed in the previous two sections. This enables us to isolate the effects of international trade in the simplest possible way. Lack of international lending and borrowing implies that at every date, each country must run a balanced international trade. Thus the following trade balance equation

$$p^K(t)[X_j^K(t) - Y_j^K(t)] + p^L(t)[X_j^L(t) - Y_j^L(t)] = 0 \tag{19.11}$$

must hold for all j and all t. This equation is intuitive; it requires that for each country (at each date), the value of its net sales of the capital-intensive good should be made up by its net purchases of the labor-intensive good. For example, if $X_j^K(t) - Y_j^K(t) < 0$, so that the country

---

3. This feature is common to many, but not all, Heckscher-Ohlin models of trade, and conditional factor price equalization may also hold in other trade models.

is a net supplier of the capital-intensive good (i.e., it uses less of the capital-intensive good in its final good sector than it produces), then it must be a net purchaser of the labor-intensive good (i.e., $X_j^L(t) - Y_j^L(t) > 0$).

In addition to this trade balance equation, there is the usual resource constraint affecting each country, which takes the form

$$\dot{K}_j(t) = F(X_j^K(t), X_j^L(t)) - C_j(t) - \delta K_j(t) \tag{19.12}$$

for all j and t. In addition, world market clearing requires that

$$\sum_{j=1}^{J} X_j^L(t) = \sum_{j=1}^{J} Y_j^L(t) \text{ and } \sum_{j=1}^{J} X_j^K(t) = \sum_{j=1}^{J} Y_j^K(t) \quad \text{for all } t. \tag{19.13}$$

The important feature here is that both the consumption good and the capital good are produced with the same technology—one unit of the final good can be transformed into one unit of consumption good or one unit of capital or the investment good. In the next section, we will see how different factor intensities of consumption and capital goods can be allowed in models of international trade and growth. But for our purposes, the simpler setup with the consumption and investment goods having the same factor intensities is sufficient.

Finally, on the preference side, I again assume that each country admits a representative household with standard preferences:

$$U_j = \int_0^\infty \exp(-(\rho - n)t) \frac{c_j(t)^{1-\theta} - 1}{1 - \theta} dt, \tag{19.14}$$

where $c_j(t) \equiv C_j(t)/L_j(t)$ is per capita consumption in country j at time t, all countries have the same time discount rate ρ, and they have the same rate of population growth. Without loss of generality, let us assume that all the decisions within each country are made by the representative household of that country and that $\rho > n$ to ensure positive discounting and finite lifetime utilities (see Chapter 8, in particular, Assumption 4′). To simplify the analysis let us also suppose that $L_j(0) = L$ for each $j = 1, 2, \ldots, J$, which, combined with the common population growth assumption, implies that

$$L_j(t) = L(t) \quad \text{for each } j = 1, 2, \ldots, J. \tag{19.15}$$

Exercise 19.12 allows population levels to vary across countries.

As in Chapter 8, a key object is the ratio of capital-like intermediates relative to labor-like intermediates in production. For this reason, let us define

$$x_j(t) \equiv \frac{X_j^K(t)}{X_j^L(t)},$$

so that

$$Y_j(t) = F(X_j^K(t), X_j^L(t))$$

$$= X_j^L(t) F\left(\frac{X_j^K(t)}{X_j^L(t)}, 1\right)$$

$$\equiv X_j^L(t) f(x_j(t)), \tag{19.16}$$

where the third line defines the per capita production function $f(\cdot)$ (exploiting the fact that F exhibits constant returns to scale). I refer to $x_j(t)$ as the "capital intermediate intensity of country j," and $k_j(t) \equiv K_j(t)/L_j(t)$ is again the capital-labor ratio.

A *world equilibrium* can be expressed as paths of consumption, capital accumulation, and capital intermediate intensity decision for each country and paths of world prices, $[\{c_j(t), k_j(t), x_j(t)\}_{j=1}^{J}, p^K(t), p^L(t)]_{t \geq 0}$, such that $[c_j(t), k_j(t), x_j(t)]_{t \geq 0}$ maximize the utility of the representative household in country j subject to (19.11) and (19.12) given world prices, $[p^K(t), p^L(t)]_{t \geq 0}$, and world prices are such that world markets clear (i.e., the equations in (19.13) hold). A *steady-state world equilibrium* is defined similarly as an equilibrium in which all of these quantities are constant.

The next proposition characterizes the allocation of production around the world.

Proposition 19.5 *Consider the above-described model. In any world equilibrium,*

$$x_j(t) = x_{j'}(t) = \frac{\sum_{j=1}^{J} k_j(t)}{\sum_{j=1}^{J} A_j} \quad \text{for any } j \text{ and } j' \text{ and any } t.$$

Proof. Given world prices at time t, the representative household in each country maximizes $F(X_j^L(t), X_j^K(t))$ subject to (19.11). Denoting the derivatives of this function by F_L and F_K, this problem implies that

$$\frac{F_K(X_j^K(t), X_j^L(t))}{F_L(X_j^K(t), X_j^L(t))} = \frac{p^K(t)}{p^L(t)} \quad \text{for any } j \text{ and any } t.$$

Using the definition in (19.16) and the homogeneity of degree 1 of F, this equation can be written as

$$\frac{f'(x_j(t))}{f(x_j(t)) - x_j(t)f'(x_j(t))} = \frac{p^K(t)}{p^L(t)} \quad \text{for any } j \text{ and any } t,$$

where the left-hand side is strictly decreasing in $x_j(t)$ and thus defines a unique $x_j(t)$ given the world price ratio. Since $x_j(t)$s are equal across countries, they must all be equal to the ratio of capital-intensive intermediates to labor-intensive intermediates in the world, so that

$$x_j(t) = \frac{\sum_{j=1}^{J} K_j(t)}{\sum_{j=1}^{J} A_j L_j(t)}$$

for $j = 1, \ldots, J$. Using the fact that $k_j(t) = K_j(t)/L_j(t) = K_j(t)/L(t)$ (because of (19.15)) completes the proof of the proposition. ∎

This proposition implies that regardless of differences in capital-labor ratios across countries, the ratio of capital-intensive to labor-intensive intermediates in production is equalized across countries. The equalization of the ratio of capital-intensive to labor-intensive intermediates in the production of the final good enables us to aggregate the production and capital stocks of different countries to obtain the behavior of world aggregates. In particular, let $c(t)$ be the average consumption per capita in the world and $k(t)$ be the average capital-labor ratio in the world, respectively given by

$$c(t) \equiv \frac{1}{J} \sum_{j=1}^{J} c_j(t), \quad \text{and } k(t) \equiv \frac{1}{J} \sum_{j=1}^{J} k_j(t).$$

The next proposition shows that world aggregates follow laws of motion very similar to those in the standard neoclassical closed economy.

Proposition 19.6 *Consider the above-described model. Then in any world equilibrium, the world averages follow the laws of motion given by*

$$\frac{\dot{c}(t)}{c(t)} = \frac{1}{\theta}\left(f'\left(\frac{k(t)}{A}\right) - \delta - \rho\right),$$

$$\dot{k}(t) = Af\left(\frac{k(t)}{A}\right) - c(t) - (n+\delta)k(t),$$

where $r(t) = p^K(t)$ is the world interest rate at time t, and

$$A = \frac{1}{J}\sum_{j=1}^{J} A_j$$

is average labor productivity.

Proof. Using (19.11), (19.12), and Proposition 19.5, the law of motion of the capital stock of country j can be written as

$$\dot{K}_j(t) = p^K(t)K_j(t) + p^L(t)A_jL(t) - C_j(t) - \delta K_j(t).$$

Now define

$$K(t) \equiv \frac{1}{J}\sum_{j=1}^{J} K_j(t),$$

sum over $j = 1, \ldots, J$, and use the definitions of $p^K(t)$ and $p^L(t)$, Proposition 19.5, and the homogeneity of degree 1 of F (together with Theorem 2.1) to obtain

$$\sum_{j=1}^{J}\dot{K}_j(t) = F\left(\sum_{j=1}^{J}K_j(t), \sum_{j=1}^{J}A_jL(t)\right) - \sum_{j=1}^{J}C_j(t) - \delta\sum_{j=1}^{J}K_j(t).$$

Dividing both sides by $JL(t)$ and using Theorem 2.1 once more yields

$$\frac{\dot{K}(t)}{L(t)} = Af\left(\frac{K(t)}{AL(t)}\right) - c(t) - \delta\frac{K(t)}{L(t)}.$$

Now using the definition of $k(t)$ gives the second differential equation in the proposition.

To obtain the differential equation for $c(t)$, sum over the Euler equations in each country, $\dot{c}_j(t)/c_j(t) = (r(t) - \rho)/\theta$. ∎

The result in this proposition is not surprising. With (conditional) factor price equalization, the world behaves as an integrated economy and thus obeys the two key differential equations of the neoclassical model. Now using the previous two propositions, we can characterize the form of the steady-state world equilibrium.

Proposition 19.7 *Consider the above-described model. There exists a unique steady-state world equilibrium for which*

$$f'(x_j^*) = f'\left(\frac{k^*}{A}\right) = \rho + \delta \quad \text{for all } j, \tag{19.17}$$

where

$$x_j^* = x^* = \frac{\sum_{j=1}^{J} K_j(t)}{L(t) \sum_{j=1}^{J} A_j}, \quad \text{and} \quad k^* = \frac{\sum_{j=1}^{J} K_j(t)}{JL(t)}. \tag{19.18}$$

Moreover

$$p^{K*} = \rho + \delta. \tag{19.19}$$

Proof. The proof follows from Proposition 19.6. The Inada conditions in Assumption 2 rule out sustained growth. Therefore world average consumption must remain constant in steady state, and the interest rate must satisfy $r^* = p^{K*} - \delta = \rho$. Propositions 19.5 and 19.6 then yield (19.17) and (19.18). ■

Proposition 19.7 shows that the steady-state world equilibrium takes a very simple form, with the ratio of capital-intensive to labor-intensive intermediates pinned down purely by the aggregate production function F (or its transform, f) and by the ratio of total capital to total labor in the world. The reason that steady-state production structure is determined by world supplies of capital and labor is simple: in the presence of (conditional) factor price equalization, the world economy is effectively integrated. We have already seen in the previous two sections how capital flows can make the world economy integrated. The analysis in this section shows that Heckscher-Ohlin trade (together with conditional factor price equalization) also leads to the same result.

While the structure of the steady-state equilibrium is rather straightforward, transitional dynamics in this world economy are more involved. In fact, the behavior of individual economies can be quite rich and complicated. Nevertheless, the fact that world averages obey the equations of the neoclassical growth model ensures that the steady-state world equilibrium is globally stable.

Proposition 19.8 *Consider the above-described economy. The steady-state equilibrium characterized in Proposition 19.7 is globally saddle-path stable.*

Proof. Using the arguments in the proof of Proposition 19.6, for any path of world prices $[p^L(t), p^K(t)]_{t \geq 0}$, the problem of the representative household in each country j at any time t satisfies the following differential equations:

$$\frac{\dot{c}_j(t)}{c_j(t)} = \frac{1}{\theta}(p^K(t) - \delta - \rho),$$

$$\dot{k}_j(t) = [p^K(t) - (n + \delta)]k_j(t) + p^L(t)A_j - c_j(t).$$

Standard arguments from Chapter 8 applied to world averages in Proposition 19.6 imply that world averages converge to the unique world steady-state equilibrium and $[p^K(t)]_{t \geq 0}$ converges to $\rho + \delta$. Thus consumption per capita and the capital-labor ratio of each country also converge to their steady-state values. With $p^{K*} = \rho + \delta$, the convergence is necessarily to the unique steady-state world equilibrium. ■

The analysis so far has shown that a world economy consisting of a collection of economies engaged in Heckscher-Ohlin trade (with conditional factor price equalization) generates a pattern of growth similar to that found in Chapter 8, with each country converging to a unique steady state. There is one important difference, however. As in the model with international borrowing and lending in the previous section, the nature of the transitional dynamics is very different from the closed-economy neoclassical growth models. Here, despite the absence of international capital flows, the rate of return to capital is equalized across countries. Thus there are no transitional dynamics, because a country with a higher rate of return to capital is accumulating capital faster than the rest. This model therefore also emphasizes the potential pitfalls of using the closed-economy growth model for the analysis of output and capital dynamics across countries and regions. Exercise 19.10 compares the equilibrium here to the closed-economy equilibrium of the same model.

Nevertheless, the results on transitional dynamics are perhaps the less interesting implications of the current model. One of the main objectives of this chapter is to illustrate how the presence of international trade changes the conclusions of closed-economy growth models. The current framework already points out how this can happen. Notice that while the world economy has a standard neoclassical technology satisfying Assumptions 1 and 2, each country faces an AK technology, since it can accumulate as much capital as it wishes without running into diminishing returns (as long as the country remains "small"). In particular, for every additional unit of capital at time t, a country receives a return of $p^K(t)$, which is independent of its own capital stock. So how is it that the world does not generate endogenous growth? The answer is that while each country faces an AK technology and thus can accumulate when the price of capital-intensive intermediates is high, accumulation by all countries drives down the price of capital-intensive intermediate goods to a level that is consistent with steady state. In other words, the price of capital-intensive intermediates adjusts to ensure the steady-state equilibrium where capital, output, and consumption per capita are constant (see the proof of Proposition 19.8).

While this process describes the long-run dynamics, it also opens the door for a very different type of short-run (or medium-run) dynamics, especially for countries that have different saving rates than others. To illustrate this possibility in the simplest possible way, consider the following thought experiment. Let us start with the world economy in steady state and suppose that one of the countries experiences a decline in its discount rate from ρ to $\rho' < \rho$. What happens? The answer is provided in the next proposition.

Proposition 19.9 *Consider the above-described model. Suppose that J is large and the world starts in steady state at time $t = 0$, and then the discount rate of country 1 declines to $\rho' < \rho$. After this change, there exists some $T > 0$ such that for all $t \in [0, T)$, country 1 grows at the rate*

$$g_1 = \frac{\dot{c}_1(t)}{c_1(t)} = \frac{1}{\theta}(\rho - \rho').$$

Proof. In steady state, Proposition 19.8 and (19.19) imply that $p^{K*} = \rho + \delta$. As long as country 1 is small (which will be the case during some interval $[0, T)$), it faces this price as the return on capital. Thus the country's dynamics will be identical to those of the AK economy in Chapter 11 (Section 11.1) with $A = \rho > \rho'$. The result that the growth rate is constant follows from the analysis there. ∎

Given conditional factor-price equalization, each country faces an AK technology and thus can accumulate capital and grow without experiencing diminishing returns. The price of capital-intensive intermediates and thus the rate of return to capital is pinned down by the discount rate of other countries in the world, so that country 1, with its lower discount rate, has an incentive to save faster than the rest of the world and can achieve positive growth of income per capita (while the rest of the world has constant income per capita).

Therefore the model of economic growth with Heckscher-Ohlin trade (and with conditional factor price equalization) can easily rationalize bouts of rapid growth ("growth miracles") by the countries that change their policies or their saving rates (or discount rates). Ventura (1997) suggests this model as a potential explanation for why, starting in the 1970s, the East Asian tigers grew rapidly without experiencing diminishing returns. Since in the 1970s and 1980s East Asian economies were indeed more open to international trade than many other developing economies and accumulated capital rapidly (e.g., Young, 1992, 1995; Vogel, 2006), this explanation is quite plausible. It shows how international trade can temporarily prevent the diminishing returns to capital that would set in because of rapid accumulation and can enable sustained growth at higher rates.

Nevertheless such behavior cannot go on forever. This follows from Assumption 2, which implies that world output cannot grow in the long run. So how is Proposition 19.9 consistent with Assumption 2? The answer is that this proposition describes behavior in the medium run. This is why the statement of the proposition is for $t \in [0, T)$. At some point, country 1 becomes so large relative to the rest of the world that it will essentially own almost all capital in the world. At that point (or in fact before this point is reached), country 1 can no longer be considered a small country: its capital accumulation will have a major impact on the relative price of the capital-intensive intermediate. Consequently the rate of return on capital will eventually fall so that accumulation by this country comes to an end. Naturally, an alternative path of adjustment could take place if, at some future date, the discount rate of country 1 increases back up to ρ, so that the world economy again settles into a steady state.

The important lesson from this discussion is that while the current model can generate growth miracles, these can only apply in the medium run. This feature is related to the result, highlighted in Exercise 19.9, that the current model does not admit a steady-state equilibrium (or even a well-defined distribution of world income) when discount rates differ across countries. In other words, the well-behaved world equilibrium that emerges from this model relies on the knife-edge case in which all countries have the same discount rate (and also the same productivity of the capital-intensive intermediates; see Exercise 19.11). This result is a consequence of the fact that in this Heckscher-Ohlin model, each country is small and factor prices are independent of domestic factor proportions. In the next section, we will see how a simple *Ricardian* model without these features leads to different interactions between international trade and growth.

19.4 Trade, Specialization, and the World Income Distribution

In this section I present a model of the world economy in which countries trade intermediate goods, because of Ricardian features—productivity or technology differences. Each country will affect the prices of the goods that it supplies to the world. This is a plausible feature. While countries typically take the prices of the goods that they import as given, they often influence the world prices of at least some of the goods that they export (e.g., copper for Chile, Microsoft Windows™ for the United States, or Lamborghinis for Italy). The key implication of this feature is that each country's *terms of trade* (the prices of its exports relative to its imports) are endogenous and depend on the rate at which it accumulates capital. Consequently, domestic factor prices are also affected by capital accumulation. We will see that such a model is more flexible than the one discussed in the previous section, since it can allow for differences in discount rates (and saving rates) and also enables us to obtain a richer set of comparative static results. The model economy presented here builds on Acemoglu and Ventura (2002). I start with a simplified version of this model, which features physical capital as the only factor of production. I then present the full model in which both physical capital and labor are used to produce consumption and investment goods.

Another major difference between the model in this section and the previous one will be that now, as in Section 18.3 in the previous chapter, the world economy exhibits endogenous growth, with the growth rate determined by the investment decisions of all countries. Despite endogenous growth at the world level, international trade (without any technological spillovers) creates sufficient interactions to ensure a common long-run growth rate for all countries. Therefore the current model shows how international trade, like technological spillovers, creates a powerful force limiting the extent of cross-country divergence.

19.4.1 Preferences and Technology

Consider a world economy consisting of a large number J of countries, again indexed by $j = 1, \ldots, J$. There is a continuum of intermediate products indexed by $v \in [0, N]$, and two final products that are used for consumption and investment. There is free trade in intermediate goods and no trade in final products or assets. Lack of trade in consumption and investment goods enables us to focus on trade in intermediates. Lack of trade in assets again rules out international borrowing and lending.

Countries differ in their technology, savings and economic policies. For example, country j is defined by its characteristics (μ_j, ρ_j, ζ_j), where μ is an indicator of how advanced the technology of the country is, ρ is its rate of time preference, and ζ is a measure of the effect of policies and institutions on the incentives to invest. All of these characteristics potentially vary across countries with a given distribution but are constant over time. In addition, I assume that each country has a population normalized to 1 and there is no population growth.

All countries admit a representative household with utility function

$$\int_0^\infty \exp(-\rho_j t) \log C_j(t) dt, \tag{19.20}$$

where $C_j(t)$ is consumption of country j date t. Preferences are logarithmic and thus more specialized than the typical CRRA preferences used so far (e.g., in terms of the preferences in (19.1), they involve $\theta \to 1$). Logarithmic preferences enable us to simplify the exposition without any substantive loss of generality. Note, however, that the preferences in (19.20) are significantly more flexible than those in the previous section, because they allow the discount rate ρ_j to differ across countries. We also assume that country j starts with a capital stock of $K_j(0) > 0$ at time $t = 0$.

The budget constraint of the representative household in country j at time t is

$$p_j^I(t)\dot{K}_j(t) + p_j^C(t)C_j(t) = Y_j(t) \tag{19.21}$$

$$= r_j(t)K_j(t) + w_j(t),$$

where $p_j^I(t)$ and $p_j^C(t)$ are the prices of the investment and consumption goods in country j at date t (in terms of the numeraire, which is the ideal price index of traded intermediates; see below). Despite international trade in intermediates, because consumption and investment goods are not traded, their prices might differ across countries. As usual, $K_j(t)$ is the capital stock of country j at time t, $r_j(t)$ is the rental rate of capital (which may also differ across countries), and $w_j(t)$ is the wage rate. Equation (19.21) requires investment plus consumption expenditures to be equal to total income and also requires that there be no depreciation. This assumption is adopted to reduce notation. The more important feature is that investment, $\dot{K}_j(t)$, is multiplied by $p_j^I(t)$, while consumption is multiplied by $p_j^C(t)$. This reflects the fact that investment and consumption goods have different production technologies and thus their prices will differ. In this respect, the model in this section is closely related to that in Section 11.3 in Chapter 11. The second equality in (19.21) specifies that total output is equal to capital income plus labor income—$r_j(t)$ is the rental rate of capital, $K_j(t)$ is the total capital holdings in country j, and $w_j(t)$ denotes total labor earnings (since the population is normalized to 1).

I introduce Ricardian specialization due to technology differences in the simplest possible way: the N intermediates available in the world economy are partitioned across the J countries such that each intermediate can only be produced by one country. This assumption, which is often referred to as the "Armington preferences" or technology in the international trade literature, ensures that while each country is small in import markets, it affects its terms of trades by the amount of the goods it exports. Denoting the measure of goods produced by country j by μ_j, this assumption implies that

$$\sum_{j=1}^{J} \mu_j = N. \tag{19.22}$$

It follows from (19.22) that a higher level of μ_j implies that country j has the technology to produce a larger variety of intermediates, so we can interpret μ as an indicator of how advanced the technology of the country is. I assume that all firms within each country have access to the technology to produce these intermediates, which ensures that all intermediates are produced competitively.

Moreover let us assume that in each country the production technology of intermediates is such that one unit of capital produces one unit of any of the intermediates that the country is capable of producing and that there is free entry into the production of intermediates. This assumption implies that production is competitive and the prices of all intermediates produced in country j at time t are given by

$$p_j(t) = r_j(t), \tag{19.23}$$

where recall that $r_j(t)$ is the rental rate of return in country j at time t.

19.4.2 The *AK* Model

Before presenting the full model, it is convenient to start with a simplified version, in which capital is the only factor of production. Consequently, in (19.21), $w_j(t) = 0$, and

$$Y_j(t) = r_j(t) K_j(t).$$

Suppose that both consumption and investment goods are produced using domestic capital as well as a bundle of all the intermediate goods in the world (which are all traded freely). In particular, the production function for consumption goods in country j is

$$C_j(t) = \chi K_j^C(t)^{1-\tau} \left(\int_0^N x_j^C(t, v)^{\frac{\varepsilon-1}{\varepsilon}} dv \right)^{\frac{\tau\varepsilon}{\varepsilon-1}}. \tag{19.24}$$

Several features of (19.24) are worth noting. First, K_j^C denotes domestic capital used in the consumption goods sector and enters the production function with exponent $1 - \tau$. Intuitively, this term corresponds to the services of the domestic capital stock used in the production of consumption goods. It represents the nontraded component of the production process, which depends on the services provided by nontraded goods using the capital available in the country. Since there is no international trade in assets, the domestic capital stock must be used to provide these nontraded services, and if a country has a relatively low capital stock, the relative price of capital will be high and less of it will be used in producing consumption goods (and investment goods; see Section 19.4.3). Second, the term in parentheses represents the bundle of intermediates purchased from the world economy. In particular, $x_j^C(t, v)$ is the quantity of intermediate good v purchased and used in the production of consumption goods in country j at time t. The expression implies that it is the CES aggregate of all the intermediates, with an elasticity of substitution ε, that matters in the production of consumption goods. I assume that $\varepsilon > 1$, which avoids the counterfactual and counterintuitive pattern of "immiserizing growth" (see Exercise 19.25). The use of CES aggregates is familiar by now and enables us to have tractable structure. The expression also makes it clear that there is a continuum N of intermediates (given by (19.22)). Notice that this CES aggregator has an exponent τ, which ensures that the production function for consumption goods exhibits constant returns to scale. The parameter τ is the elasticity of the production function of consumption goods with respect to traded intermediates and determines the share of trade in GDP (see Exercise 19.16). Finally, χ is a constant introduced for normalization (see Exercise 19.14).

The production function for investment goods in country j is

$$I_j(t) = \zeta_j^{-1} \chi K_j^I(t)^{1-\tau} \left(\int_0^N x_j^I(t, v)^{\frac{\varepsilon-1}{\varepsilon}} dv \right)^{\frac{\tau\varepsilon}{\varepsilon-1}}, \tag{19.25}$$

which is identical to that for consumption goods except for the presence of the term ζ_j. This allows differential levels of productivity, due to technology or policy, in the production of investment goods across countries. The assumption that these differences are in the investment good sector rather than in the production of consumption goods is consistent with results on the relative prices of investment goods discussed previously, which suggested that in poorer economies investment goods are relatively more expensive. In terms of the production functions specified here, we may want to think of greater distortions as corresponding to higher levels of ζ_j, since, as we will see, a high level of ζ_j reduces output and increases the relative price of investment goods. In the full model with both capital and labor, the relative price of investment goods is endogenous and depends on technology and discount rates.

Market clearing for capital naturally requires that

$$K_j^C(t) + K_j^I(t) + K_j^\mu(t) \le K_j(t), \tag{19.26}$$

where $K_j^\mu(t)$ is the capital used in the production of intermediates, and $K_j(t)$ is the total capital stock of country j at time t.

The reader can also see why this model is referred to as the "AK version": the production of both consumption and investment goods uses capital and intermediates that are directly produced from capital. Thus a doubling of the world capital stock doubles the output of all intermediates and of consumption and investment goods.

While we can directly work with the production functions for consumption and investment goods, (19.24) and (19.25), as in many trade models, it is simpler to work with *unit cost functions*, which express the cost of producing one unit of consumption and investment goods in terms of the numeraire (which will be chosen as the ideal price index for intermediates; see (19.32)). Exercise 19.14 shows that the production functions (19.24) and (19.25) are equivalent to the unit cost functions for consumption and production given by

$$B_j^C(r_j(t), [p(t, v)]_{v \in [0,N]}) = r_j(t)^{1-\tau} \left(\int_0^N p(t, v)^{1-\varepsilon} dv \right)^{\frac{\tau}{1-\varepsilon}}, \qquad (19.27)$$

$$B_j^I(r_j(t), [p(t, v)]_{v \in [0,N]}) = \zeta_j r_j(t)^{1-\tau} \left(\int_0^N p(t, v)^{1-\varepsilon} dv \right)^{\frac{\tau}{1-\varepsilon}}, \qquad (19.28)$$

where $p(t, v)$ is the price of the intermediate v at time t, and the constant χ in (19.24) and (19.25) is chosen appropriately (see Exercise 19.14). Notice that these prices are not indexed by j, since there is free trade in intermediates and thus all countries face the same intermediate prices. The specification using the unit cost functions simplifies the analysis.

A *world equilibrium* is defined by paths of prices, capital stock levels, and consumption levels for each country such that all markets clear and the representative household in each country maximizes utility given the paths for prices. It can be represented by

$$\left[\left\{ p_j^C(t), p_j^I(t), r_j(t), K_j(t), C_j(t) \right\}_{j=1}^J, [p(t, v)]_{v \in [0,N]} \right]_{t \geq 0}.$$

Notice that while the prices of consumption and investment goods and the return to capital are country specific, the prices of intermediates are not. A steady-state world equilibrium is also defined in the usual fashion, in particular, requiring that all prices are constant (as before, this "steady-state" equilibrium involves balanced growth).

The characterization of the world equilibrium in this case is made relatively simple by the AK technology (and the logarithmic preferences). In particular, the maximization of the representative household—that is, the maximization of (19.20) subject to (19.21) for each j—yields the following first-order conditions:

$$\frac{r_j(t) + \dot{p}_j^I(t)}{p_j^I(t)} - \frac{\dot{p}_j^C(t)}{p_j^C(t)} = \rho_j + \frac{\dot{C}_j(t)}{C_j(t)} \qquad (19.29)$$

for each j and t, and the transversality condition

$$\lim_{t \to \infty} \left[\exp(-\rho_j t) \frac{p_j^I(t) K_j(t)}{p_j^C(t) C_j(t)} \right] = 0, \qquad (19.30)$$

for each j (see Exercise 19.15).

Equation (19.29) is the consumption Euler equation. This equation might first appear slightly different from the standard Euler equations, but it is identical to the Euler equations implied by the two-sector model in Section 11.3 in Chapter 11 (recall, in particular, (11.31)). The difference from the standard Euler equations stems from the fact that we now have potentially different technologies for producing consumption and investment goods. Thus households that delay consumption have to take into account the change in the relative price of consumption versus investment goods—which explains the presence of the term $\dot{p}_j^I(t)/p_j^I(t) - \dot{p}_j^C(t)/p_j^C(t)$ in (19.29). In this light, it is clear that this equation simply requires the (net) rate of return to capital to be equal to the rate of time preference plus the slope of the consumption path. Equation (19.30) is the transversality condition.

Integrating the budget constraint and using the Euler and transversality conditions, we obtain a particularly simple consumption function,

$$p_j^C(t) C_j(t) = \rho_j p_j^I(t) K_j(t), \qquad (19.31)$$

which can be interpreted as households spending a fraction ρ_j of their wealth on consumption at every instant (recall that in this simplified model there is no labor income and $p_j^I(t)K_j(t)$ is household wealth at current prices).

The analysis so far has characterized the prices of intermediates and the behavior of the consumption and capital stock for each country. Let us next determine the prices of consumption and investment goods and the relative prices of intermediates in the world economy. As a first step, I define the numeraire for this world economy as the ideal price index for the basket of all the (traded) intermediates. Since the intermediates always appear in CES form, the corresponding ideal price index is simply

$$1 = \left(\int_0^N p(t, v)^{1-\varepsilon} dv \right)^{\frac{1}{1-\varepsilon}} \tag{19.32}$$

$$= \sum_{j=1}^{J} \mu_j p_j(t)^{1-\varepsilon}.$$

Here the first line defines the ideal price index, while the second uses the fact that country j produces μ_j intermediates, and each of these intermediates has the same price $p_j(t) = r_j(t)$ as given by (19.23).

This choice of numeraire has another convenient implication. Our assumption that each country is small implies that each exports practically all of its production of intermediates and imports the ideal basket of intermediates from the world economy. Consequently $p_j(t) = r_j(t)$ is not only the price of intermediates produced by country j but also its *terms of trade*—defined as the price of the exports of a country divided by the price of its imports.

Next, using the price normalization in (19.32), the unit cost functions (19.27) and (19.28) imply that the equilibrium prices of consumption and investment goods in country j at time t are

$$p_j^C(t) = r_j(t)^{1-\tau} \text{ and } p_j^I(t) = \zeta_j r_j(t)^{1-\tau}. \tag{19.33}$$

Equation (19.33) completes the characterization of all prices in terms of the rate of return to capital. To compute the rate of return to capital, we need to impose market clearing for capital in each country. In addition we also have a trade balance equation for each country. However, by Walras's Law, one of these equations is redundant. It turns out to be more convenient to use the trade balance equation, which can be written as

$$Y_j(t) = \mu_j r_j(t)^{1-\varepsilon} Y(t), \tag{19.34}$$

where $Y(t) \equiv \sum_{j=1}^{J} Y_j(t)$ is total world income at time t. To see why this equation ensures balanced trade, note that each country spends a fraction τ of its income on intermediates, and since each country is small, this implies that a fraction τ of its income is being spent on imports. At the same time, the rest of the world spends a fraction $\tau \mu_j p_j(t)^{1-\varepsilon}$ of its total income on intermediates produced by country j (because of the CES aggregator over intermediates combined with the observations that $p_j(t)$ is the relative price of country j's intermediates and there are μ_j of them). Noting that total world income is $Y(t)$ and that $p_j(t) = r_j(t)$, we obtain (19.34). Exercise 19.16 asks you to derive this equation from the capital market clearing equation (19.26), thus verifying the use of Walras's Law.

The equations derived so far—(19.23), (19.31), (19.33), and (19.34)—together with the resource constraint (19.21) fully characterize the world equilibrium.

Let us start by describing the state of the world economy, which can be represented by the distribution of capital stocks across the J economies (these are the only endogenous state variables). Their law of motion is obtained by combining (19.21), (19.31), and (19.33) on the one hand and (19.21) and (19.34) on the other. In particular, for each j and t, the law of motion of the capital stock is described by the following pair of differential equations:

$$\frac{\dot{K}_j(t)}{K_j(t)} = \frac{r_j(t)^\tau}{\zeta_j} - \rho_j, \tag{19.35}$$

$$r_j(t)K_j(t) = \mu_j r_j(t)^{1-\varepsilon} \sum_{i=1}^{J} r_i(t)K_i(t). \tag{19.36}$$

These two equations completely characterize the world equilibrium. Starting with a cross section of capital stocks at time t, $\{K_j(t)\}_{j=1}^{J}$, (19.36) gives the cross section of terms of trade and interest rates, $\{r_j(t)\}_{j=1}^{J}$. Given this cross section of interest rates, (19.35) describes exactly how the cross section of capital stocks evolves.

The simplicity of these laws of motion are noteworthy. The first, (19.35), determines the evolution of the capital stock of each country as a function of their own parameters, ζ_j; the distortions on the investment good producing sector; ρ_j, the discount rate; and the equilibrium rental rate. The second, (19.36), expresses the rental rate for each country as a function of the rental rates and capital stocks of other countries.

These two equations immediately establish the following important result.

Proposition 19.10 *There exists a unique steady-state world equilibrium where*

$$\frac{\dot{K}_j(t)}{K_j(t)} = \frac{\dot{Y}_j(t)}{Y_j(t)} = g^* \tag{19.37}$$

for $j = 1, \ldots, J$, and the world steady-state growth rate g^* is the unique solution to

$$\sum_{j=1}^{J} \mu_j [\zeta_j(\rho_j + g^*)]^{(1-\varepsilon)/\tau} = 1. \tag{19.38}$$

The steady-state rental rate of capital and the terms of trade in country j are given by

$$r_j^* = p_j^* = [\zeta_j(\rho_j + g^*)]^{1/\tau}. \tag{19.39}$$

This unique steady-state world equilibrium is globally saddle-path stable.

Proof. By definition, a steady-state world equilibrium must have constant prices and thus constant r_j^*s. Therefore, in any steady state, for each $j = 1, \ldots, J$, $\dot{K}_j(t)/K_j(t)$ must grow at some constant rate g_j. Suppose these rates are not equal for two countries j and j'. Taking the ratio of (19.36) for these two countries yields a contradiction, establishing that $\dot{K}_j(t)/K_j(t)$ is constant for all countries. Equation (19.34) then implies that all countries also grow at this common rate, say g^*. Given this common growth rate, (19.35) immediately implies (19.39). Substituting this back into (19.36) gives (19.38). The steady-state world equilibrium is unique because these equations are all uniquely determined and (19.38) is strictly decreasing in g^*, and thus has a unique solution.

To establish global stability, it suffices to note that (19.36) implies that $r_j(t)$ is decreasing in $K_j(t)$. Thus when a country has a high capital stock relative to the world, it has a lower rate of return on capital, which from (19.35) slows down capital accumulation. This process ensures that the world economy, and all economies, move toward the unique steady-state world equilibrium. Exercise 19.17 asks you to provide a formal proof of stability. ∎

The results summarized in this proposition are remarkable. First, despite the high degree of interaction among the various economies, there exists a unique globally stable steady-state world equilibrium. Second, this equilibrium takes a relatively simple form. Third and most important, in this equilibrium all countries grow at the same rate g^*. This third feature is quite surprising, since each economy has access to a AK technology: thus without any international trade (e.g., when $\tau = 0$, or see Exercise 19.18), each country would grow at a different rate (e.g., those with lower ζ_js or ρ_js would have higher long-run growth rates). The process of international trade acts as a powerful force keeping countries together, ensuring that in the long run they all grow at the same rate. In other words, international trade, together with terms-of-trade effects, leads to a stable world income distribution.

Why? The answer is related to the terms-of-trade effects encapsulated in (19.36). To understand the implications of this equation, consider the special case where all countries have the same technology parameter, that is, $\mu_j = \mu$ for all j. Suppose also that a particular country, say country j, has lower ζ_j and ρ_j than the rest of the world. Then (19.35) implies that this country accumulates more capital than others. But (19.36) makes it clear that this cannot go on forever, and country j, by virtue of being richer than the world average, will also have a lower rate of return on capital. This lower rate of return ultimately compensates the greater incentive to accumulate in country j, so that capital accumulation in this country converges to the same rate as in the rest of the world.

Intuitively, each country has "market power" in the goods that it supplies to the world: when it exports more of a particular good, the price of that good declines to ensure that world consumers purchase a greater amount of this good. So when a country accumulates faster than the rest of the world and thus increases the supply of its exports relative to the supplies of other countries' exports, it will face worse terms of trades. This negative terms-of-trade effect reduces its income and its rate of return to capital (recall (19.23)), and slows down capital accumulation. This mechanism ensures that in the steady-state equilibrium all countries accumulate and grow at the same rate.

Therefore this model shows how pure trade linkages are sufficient to ensure that countries that would otherwise grow at different rates pull one another toward a common growth rate, and the result is a stable world income distribution. The role of trade can be seen most clearly by comparing the equilibrium here to closed-economy equilibrium, which is done in Exercise 19.18.

Naturally, growth at a common rate does not imply that countries with different characteristics have the same level of income. Exactly as in models of technological interdependences in the previous chapter, countries with better characteristics (higher μ_j and lower ζ_j and ρ_j) grow at the same rate as the rest of the world, but will be richer than other countries. This is most clearly shown by the following equation, which summarizes the world income distribution. Let $y_j^* \equiv Y_j(t)/Y(t)$ be the relative income of country j in steady state. Then (19.34) and (19.39) yield

$$y_j^* = \mu_j[\zeta_j(\rho_j + g^*)]^{(1-\varepsilon)/\tau}. \tag{19.40}$$

This equation shows that countries with better technology (high μ_j), lower distortions (low ζ_j) and lower discount rates (low ρ_j) will be relatively richer. Equation (19.40) also highlights that the elasticity of income with respect to ζ_j and ρ_j depends on the elasticity of substitution between the intermediates, ε, and the degree of openness (which is a function of τ; see Exercise 19.16). When ε is high and τ is relatively low, small differences in ζ_js and ρ_js can lead to very large differences in income across countries. This observation is interesting for another reason: recall from Chapters 2 and 3 that the Solow growth model generates a similar equation linking the world income distribution to differences in saving rates and technology. In particular, recall that in a world with a Cobb-Douglas aggregate production function and no human capital differences, the Solow model implies that

$$y_j^* = A_j \left(\frac{s_j}{g^*} \right)^{\alpha/(1-\alpha)}, \tag{19.41}$$

where A_j is the relative labor-augmenting productivity of country j, s_j is its saving rate, g^* is again the world growth rate, and α is the exponent of capital in the Cobb-Douglas production function (which is also equal to the share of capital in national income). Equation (19.40) shows that the implications of the world economy with trade are very similar, except that (1) the role of the labor-augmenting technologies is played by the technological capabilities of the country, which determine the range of goods in which it has a comparative advantage; (2) the role of the saving rate is played by the discount rate ρ_j and the policy parameter affecting the distortions on the production of investment goods, ζ_j; and (3) instead of the share of capital in national income, the elasticity of substitution between intermediates and the degree of trade openness affect how spread out the world income distribution is. Exercise 19.19 develops these points further.

19.4.3 The General Model

The model presented in Section 19.4.2 has a number of striking implications. The most important is that, despite the possibility of endogenous growth at the country level, world relative prices adjust in such a way as to keep the world income distribution stable. Consequently differences in preferences and technology across countries translate into differences in income levels along a stable income distribution, rather than into differences in permanent growth rates. However the reader may wonder how general this result is. The result was derived in the context of a collection of AK economies. Here I show that the results generalize to an economy in which both capital and labor are used. To maintain the tractability of the model (and in fact to obtain almost identical equations to those in Section 19.4.2), I make use of the structure of production in Rebelo's (1991) model analyzed in Section 11.3 of Chapter 11. The production of investment goods only uses capital, but the production of consumption goods uses both capital and labor. While the exact mathematical derivations here depend on these specific assumptions, the general insights do not.

More specifically, preferences, demographics, and the production functions for intermediates and for investment goods are the same as in Section 19.4.2. The main difference is that the production function for consumption goods has now changed to

$$C_j(t) = \chi K_j^C(t)^{(1-\tau)\gamma} L_j(t)^{(1-\tau)(1-\gamma)} \left(\int_0^N x_j^C(t, v)^{\frac{\varepsilon-1}{\varepsilon}} dv \right)^{\frac{\tau\varepsilon}{\varepsilon-1}}$$

for some $\gamma \in (0, 1)$, and $L_j(t)$ is labor used in the consumption sector in country j at time t. Since neither the production of intermediates nor the production of the investment good use labor and population is equal to 1, we have that $L_j(t) = 1$. Thus in (19.21), $w_j(t)$ stands both for the wage rate per unit of labor and for total labor income. The associated unit cost function for the consumption good is

$$B_j^C(w_j(t), r_j(t), [p(t, v)]_{v \in [0,N]}) = w_j(t)^{(1-\tau)(1-\gamma)} r_j(t)^{(1-\tau)\gamma} \left(\int_0^N p(t, v)^{1-\varepsilon} dv \right)^{\frac{\tau}{1-\varepsilon}}.$$

Using the same price normalization, that is, (19.32), intermediate prices are still given by (19.23), and the price of the investment good in country j at time t is still given by $p_j^I(t) = \zeta_j r_j(t)^{1-\tau}$. The price of the consumption good is obtained, with a similar reasoning, as

$$p_j^C(t) = w_j(t)^{(1-\tau)(1-\gamma)} r_j(t)^{(1-\tau)\gamma}. \tag{19.42}$$

The maximization problem of the representative household in each country is essentially unchanged except for the stream of labor income that the household receives. This maximization problem again leads to the necessary and sufficient conditions given by (19.29) and (19.30). Combining these two equations, we again obtain that consumption expenditure is given as the fraction of the lifetime wealth of the household, which now consists of the value of capital plus the discounted value of future labor earnings (see Exercise 19.20):

$$p_j^C(t)C_j(t) = \rho_j \left(p_j^I(t)K_j(t) + \int_t^\infty \exp\left(- \int_t^z \frac{r_j(s) + \dot{p}_j^I(s)}{p_j^I(s)} ds \right) w(z) dz \right). \tag{19.43}$$

It is also straightforward to show that (19.34) still gives the necessary trade balance equation for each country.

The final condition we need to impose is market clearing for labor. Recall that labor demand comes only from the consumption goods sector, and given the Cobb-Douglas assumption, this demand is $(1 - \gamma)(1 - \tau)$ times consumption expenditure, $p_j^C C_j$, divided by the wage rate w_j. So the market clearing condition for labor in country j at time t is

$$1 = (1 - \gamma)(1 - \tau) \frac{p_j^C(t)C_j(t)}{w_j(t)}. \tag{19.44}$$

Because (19.44) implies that labor income $w_j(t)$ is always proportional to consumption expenditure, the optimal consumption rule (19.43) can be simplified to

$$p_j^C(t)C_j(t) = \frac{\rho_j}{1 - (1 - \gamma)(1 - \tau)} p_j^I(t)K_j(t). \tag{19.45}$$

Households again consume a constant fraction of the value of the capital stock, but this fraction now depends not only on their discount rate ρ_j but also on the technology parameters, τ and γ. In light of this derivation, the following two propositions characterize the world equilibrium.

Proposition 19.11 *In the general model with labor, the world equilibrium is characterized by (19.35) for each j and t, as well as the following two additional equations:*

$$r_j(t)K_j(t) + w_j(t) = \mu_j r_j(t)^{1-\varepsilon} \sum_{i=1}^J [r_i(t)K_i(t) + w_i(t)], \tag{19.46}$$

$$\frac{w_j(t)}{r_j(t)K_j(t) + w_j(t)} = \frac{(1 - \gamma)(1 - \tau)\rho_j}{[\gamma + (1 - \gamma)\tau]\zeta_j^{-1} r_j(t) + (1 - \gamma)(1 - \tau)\rho_j}. \tag{19.47}$$

Proof. See Exercise 19.21. ∎

The derivation and the intuition for this result follow those Section 19.4.2. For a given cross section of capital stocks, (19.46) and (19.47) determine the cross section of rental rates and wage rates, and given the cross section of rental rates, (19.35) determines the evolution of the distribution of capital stocks in the world economy.

The next proposition shows that the structure of the world equilibrium is essentially identical to that in Section 19.4.2.

Proposition 19.12 *In the general model with labor, there exists a unique steady-state world equilibrium. In this equilibrium, capital stock and output in each country grow at the constant rate g* as in (19.37), and the world steady-state growth rate g* is the unique solution to (19.38). This unique steady-state equilibrium is globally stable.*

Proof. See Exercise 19.22. ∎

This proposition implies that the results regarding the stable income distribution continue to apply in this more general model. Moreover (19.40) still gives the world income distribution in the steady-state world equilibrium.

This more general model does not simply replicate the results of the simpler AK model, however. One important implication concerns the relative prices of investment and consumption goods. As discussed previously, the available empirical evidence suggests that the price of investment goods relative to consumption goods is greater in poorer countries. Many models adopt a reduced-form approach to this empirical regularity and argue that it must be due to frictions affecting the investment sector in poor economies. Nevertheless, we need models that allow for trade and different production functions for consumption and investment goods for a satisfactory understanding of the sources of differences in these relative prices. The current model, which incorporates these features, generates this pattern of relative prices. The equilibrium derivation above implies that

$$\frac{p_j^I(t)}{p_j^C(t)} = \zeta_j \left(\frac{r_j(t)}{w_j(t)} \right)^{(1-\gamma)(1-\tau)},$$

so that the relative price of investment goods is higher in countries that have high ζ_j and low wages. The first part of this result, that countries with high ζ_j (high distortions on investment good sectors) have higher relative prices of investment goods, is natural and consistent with the presumption in the literature. However (19.47) shows that countries with worse technology (low μ_j) and higher discount rates (high ρ_j) will also have lower wages and, via this channel, they have higher relative prices of investment goods. Therefore the current model also generates a cross section of the relative prices of investment and consumption goods that is consistent with the patterns we observe in the data. It highlights that the relative price of investment goods may vary across countries for reasons other than distortions in the investment sector, so that considerable care is necessary when using the observed variation in these relative prices in the context of one-sector and/or closed-economy models as the previous literature has done.

In concluding this section, let us return to a comparison of the economic forces emphasized here with those of Section 19.3. Recall that in Section 19.3, each country can accumulate without running into diminishing returns to scale. In contrast, the model in this section has emphasized how capital accumulation by a country increases the world supply of goods in which it specializes, thus creating powerful terms-of-trade effects. These terms-of-trade effects are the reason that the long-run world income distribution is stable and the fast-growing countries tend to increase the growth rate of the rest of the world. Can the approaches in these two sections be reconciled? I believe the answer is yes. One way to reconcile them is to view them as applying to different stages of development and to different kinds of goods.

Imagine, for example, a world in which some goods are standardized and can be produced in any country. When a country is producing these goods, it does not face terms-of-trade effects and can accumulate without running into diminishing returns to capital. As discussed in Section 19.3, this might be a good approximation to the situation experienced by the East Asian tigers in the 1970s and 1980s, when they specialized in medium-tech goods (e.g., Vogel, 2006). However, as countries become richer, they produce more differentiated goods and run into terms-of-trade effects. Consequently, if a country is at the stage of development where it produces more of the differentiated goods, further capital accumulation results in diminishing returns because of terms-of-trade effects. An interesting research area would be to construct models combining these two forces.

19.5   Trade, Technology Diffusion, and the Product Cycle

The previous chapter highlighted the importance of technology diffusion in understanding cross-country income differences. But this analysis was done in the context of a world consisting of a collection of closed economies. The presence of international trade enriches the process of technology diffusion, since it introduces the possibility of the international product cycle, whereby technology diffusion goes hand-in-hand with certain products previously produced by technologically advanced economies migrating to less-developed nations. The idea of the international product cycle was first suggested by Vernon (1966). Here I present a simple model originally developed by Krugman (1979). The main advantage of this model is that, thanks to its simplicity, it has many applications in the study of various different issues in macroeconomics, international trade, and economic development.

19.5.1   The International Division of Labor

Consider the world economy consisting of two sets of countries, the North and the South. For the analysis in this section, it does not matter whether there is one Northern and one Southern country or many countries within each group. There is free international trade, without any trading costs.

All households in all countries have the same CES preferences with love-for-variety defined over a consumption index. This consumption index for country $j \in \{n, s\}$ at time t is

$$C_j(t) = \left(\int_0^{N(t)} c_j(t, \nu)^{\frac{\varepsilon-1}{\varepsilon}} dz \right)^{\frac{\varepsilon}{\varepsilon-1}}, \tag{19.48}$$

where $c_j(t, \nu)$ is the consumption of the zth good in country $j \in \{n, s\}$ at time t, $N(t)$ is the total number of goods in the world economy at time t that will be determined endogenously and traded freely, and $\varepsilon > 1$ is the elasticity of substitution between these goods. Naturally, without the free-trade assumption, the range of goods consumed by households in country j would not be $N(t)$ but a subset of those goods to which they have access to.

Each country admits a representative household with dynamic preferences defined over streams of consumption $C_j(t)$. For our purposes here, there is no need to specify what these dynamic preferences are, but for concreteness, the reader may want to assume that these are given by the standard CRRA preferences as in (19.1).

The key assumption of the model is that goods fall into two categories: new goods are invented in the North and can be produced only there; old goods have been invented in the past, and their production technology has been imitated by the South, so they can be produced both in the South and in the North.

The technology of production is simple: one worker produces one unit of any good to which his country has access. Workers in the North have access to all goods, but those in the South have access only to old goods. It is important to emphasize that when producing old goods, Northern workers have no productive advantage. Their only advantage (and the only difference in technology) arises because they have access to a larger set of goods.

Suppose that the total labor supply in the North is L^n at all times, and the labor supply in the South is L^s. All labor is supplied inelastically. An equilibrium is defined in the usual way as paths of prices for all goods and allocation of labor across goods.

This description of the environment implies that there can be two types of equilibria:

1. *Equalization equilibrium:* in this type of equilibrium there are sufficiently few new goods that workers in both the South and the North produce some of the old goods. We will see below that in this type of equilibrium both new goods and old goods command the same price, and incomes in the North and South are the same. This justifies the term "equalization equilibrium."

2. *Specialization equilibrium:* in this type of equilibrium the South specializes in the production of old goods, while the North specializes in the production of new ones.

Let us start by studying the international division of labor for a given set of new and old goods, $N^n(t)$ and $N^o(t)$, where naturally the total number of goods is $N(t) = N^n(t) + N^o(t)$. Since the North has access to all goods, while the South only has access to old goods, the ratio $N^n(t)/N^o(t)$ (or $N(t)/N^o(t)$) can be interpreted as a measure of the technology gap between the North and the South.

To start with, let us suppose that the world is in a specialization equilibrium. Clearly the prices of all new goods are equal and the prices of all old goods are also equalized. Denote these two sets of prices by $p^n(t)$ and $p^o(t)$. Let the wage rate in the North be $w^n(t)$ and that in the South be $w^s(t)$. Since one unit of labor produces one unit of a product and markets are competitive, in the specialization equilibrium we have

$$p^n(t) = w^n(t)$$
$$p^o(t) = w^s(t). \tag{19.49}$$

It must be the case that $w^n(t) \geq w^s(t)$, since otherwise Northern workers would prefer to produce old goods. Thus a specialization equilibrium can exist only when all old goods are produced in the South, and the implied equilibrium wage rate in the South is lower than that in the North. To find out when this condition holds is straightforward. The CES preferences specified in (19.48) imply that utility maximization requires the ratio of the consumption of new and old goods to satisfy

$$\frac{c^n(t)}{c^o(t)} = \left(\frac{p^n(t)}{p^o(t)}\right)^{-\varepsilon}. \tag{19.50}$$

Specialization implies that all labor in the South is used to produce old goods, while all labor in the North is employed in the production of new goods. Thus we have

$$c^n(t) = \frac{L^n}{N^n(t)}, \quad \text{and} \quad c^o(t) = \frac{L^s}{N^o(t)}. \tag{19.51}$$

Combining (19.49), (19.50), and (19.51) yields the following simple relationship between relative wages and labor supplies and technology:

$$\frac{w^n(t)}{w^s(t)} \equiv \omega(t) = \left(\frac{N^n(t)}{N^o(t)} \frac{L^s}{L^n} \right)^{1/\varepsilon}. \tag{19.52}$$

Notice that the right-hand side of (19.52) consists of predetermined (or constant) quantities at time t. Thus they determine a unique relative wage between the North and the South. A specialization equilibrium exists only if this ratio $\omega(t)$ is greater than or equal to 1. If it happens to be less than 1, then a specialization equilibrium does not exist; instead the equilibrium takes the form of an equalization equilibrium. In this equalization equilibrium, wages in the North and the South are equalized, and some of the old goods are produced in the North. In particular, suppose that $\omega(t)$ as defined by (19.52) is strictly less than 1. Then there exists a unique equilibrium, which takes the form of an equalization equilibrium, where new goods and old goods all command the same price and are consumed in the same quantity. Therefore we have

$$c^n(t) = \frac{\phi L^n}{N^n(t)} \quad \text{and} \quad c^o(t) = \frac{L^s + (1-\phi)L^n}{N^o(t)},$$

where $\phi \in (0, 1)$ is chosen such that $c^n(t) = c^o(t)$. We know that such a $\phi \in (0, 1)$ exists, since $\omega(t) < 1$, which implies that $c^n(t) > c^o(t)$ at $\phi = 1$.

The characterization of the equilibrium is shown diagrammatically in Figure 19.1. This figure shows that there is a downward-sloping relationship between the relative supply of labor in the North, L^n/L^s, and the earnings premium in the North, $\omega \equiv w^n/w^s$. It also shows that when $L^n/L^s = N^n(t)/N^o(t)$, the relationship becomes flat at $w^n/w^s = 1$, because in this case the relative supply of labor in the North is sufficiently large that we enter the region of equalization equilibrium.

An interesting implication of this equilibrium is that even when there is a technology gap between the North and the South, Northern and Southern incomes may be equalized. There will only be an income gap between the North and the South when the technology gap is relatively large or the labor supply in the South, L^s, is sufficiently large. This last feature is particularly interesting in the context of the current wave of globalization, which has involved the incorporation of India and China into the world economy as potential low-cost producers of old goods.[4]

While we may think that the case with a sufficiently large technology gap and sufficiently large L^s (which leads to a positive income gap between the North and the South) is more realistic, the possibility that such a gap may not exist is of theoretical interest and helps us to understand the impact of the international division of labor on cross-country income differences. The possibility that incomes in the North and the South are equalized may appear surprising at first, but the intuition is straightforward. International trade ensures that the Southern consumers have access to goods that their country does not have the technology to produce. Consequently, even though the South is technologically behind the North, it may achieve the same consumption bundle and the same level of income. This discussion therefore suggests that international trade is a powerful force limiting the extent of cross-country income inequality (e.g., that resulting from technological differences). This is typically the case, but perhaps surprisingly, not always so. Exercise 19.30 goes through the implications of trade on

---

4. Though it should be noted that, in addition to old goods, India and China also export some relatively high-tech electronics as well as high-quality software and provide a range of outsourcing opportunities to European and U.S. companies.

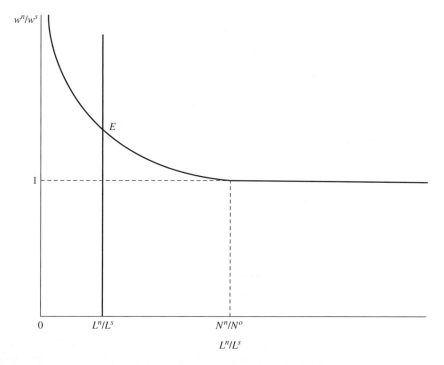

FIGURE 19.1 Determination of the relative wages in the North and the South in the international product cycle model.

cross-country income differences and shows that even in the context of the current model, it can sometimes lead to a larger gap between rich and poor countries.

19.5.2 Product Cycles and Technology Transfer

The characterization of the equilibrium in Section 19.5.1 was for a given number of new and old goods. Our interest in this model is because its relative simplicity enables us to endogenize the number of new and old goods and it generates a pattern of product cycles across countries. Here let us follow Krugman (1979) and endogenize the number of new and old goods using a model of exogenous technological change. Exercise 19.29 considers a version of this model with endogenous creation of new products.

In particular, let us suppose that new goods are created in the North according to the following simple differential equation:

$$\dot{N}(t) = \eta N(t),$$

with some initial condition $N(0) > 0$ and innovation parameter $\eta > 0$. Goods invented in the North can be imitated by the South. As in the models of technology diffusion in the previous chapter, this process is assumed to be slow and to follow the differential equation

$$\dot{N}^o(t) = \iota N^n(t),$$

where $\iota > 0$ is the imitation parameter. This differential equation has a motivation similar to that of the technology diffusion equations in the previous chapter and captures the idea that the South can only imitate from the set of goods that have not so far been imitated (of which there is a total of $N^n(t)$ at time t. Combining these equations with $N(t) = N^n(t) + N^o(t)$, we obtain a unique globally stable steady-state ratio of new to old goods given by

$$\frac{N^n(t)}{N^o(t)} = \frac{\eta}{\iota}. \tag{19.53}$$

This equation is intuitive: the ratio of new to old goods is high when the rate of innovation in the North, η, is high relative to the rate of imitation from the South, ι. Combining (19.53) with (19.52), the equilibrium wage ratio between the North and the South is

$$\frac{w^n(t)}{w^s(t)} = \max\left\{ \left(\frac{\eta}{\iota} \frac{L^s}{L^n} \right)^{1/\varepsilon}, 1 \right\}. \tag{19.54}$$

In this expression, when the max operator picks 1, the equalization equilibrium applies. Otherwise the specialization equilibrium is valid. Since the ratio $w^n(t)/w^s(t)$ also corresponds to the ratio of incomes between the North and the South, this equation also implies that a high rate of innovation by the North makes the South relatively poor (though not absolutely so), while a higher rate of imitation by the South makes the South relatively richer and the North relatively poorer (see Exercise 19.28). In view of the results from the previous chapter, these results are not surprising.

An important and interesting feature of this steady-state equilibrium is the product cycle. Let us focus on the specialization equilibrium. In this case, new goods are invented in the North and produced there by workers that receive relatively high wages (since in the specialization equilibrium, $w^n(t) > w^s(t)$). After a while, a given new good is imitated by the South, so its production shifts to the South, where labor costs are lower. Thus in this model we witness the international product cycle, starting with production at high labor costs in the North and then transitioning to a mode of cheap production in the South.

An important application of the product cycle model is to the implications of international protection of IPR. The rate of imitation ι can also be considered as an inverse measure of the international protection of IPR. Then, as shown in Exercise 19.28, in this baseline model, stronger international IPR protection always increases the income gap between the North and the South. Interestingly, however, the exercise also shows that it does not always lead to a welfare improvement in the North.

19.6 Trade and Endogenous Technological Change

The effect of trade on growth has attracted much academic and policy attention. Most economists believe that trade promotes growth, and there is both micro and macro evidence consistent with this belief. Some papers (e.g., Dollar (1992); Sachs and Warner (1995)) find a positive correlation between openness to international trade and economic growth. While these studies are not entirely convincing, owing to the typical difficulties of reaching causal conclusions from growth regressions (recall the discussion in Chapter 3), other papers have tried to overcome these difficulties by using instrumental-variables strategies. In this context, a well-known paper by Frankel and Romer (1999) exploits differences in the trade capacity of countries (as given by the gravity equations of trade) as a source of variation to estimate the effect of trade on long-run income differences. Gravity equations, which are widely used in the empirical trade literature, link the volume of trade between two countries to their geographic and economic characteristics and their interactions (e.g., size of country, GDP, distance). Frankel and Romer exploit the geographically determined component of these gravity equations to construct a measure of predicted trade for each country and use this as an instrument for actual trade openness. Using this strategy, they show that greater trade is associated with higher income per capita (thus with greater long-run growth). In addition, recent microeconomic evidence from Bernard et al. (2003), Bernard and Jensen (2004), and others show that firms that engage in exporting are typically more productive, which might be partly due to "learning-by-exporting," though at least some part of this correlation is likely due to selection (Melitz, 2003). Similarly, firms in developing countries that import machinery from more advanced economies appear to be more productive, and trade liberalization is associated with productivity increases both among continuing plants and due to reallocation (e.g., Pavcnik, 2002). Nevertheless some economists are skeptical of the growth effects of trade. Rodriguez and Rodrik (2000) criticize the empirical evidence that trade promotes growth. On the theoretical side, several authors (e.g., Matsuyama (1992); Young (1991)) have presented models in which international trade can slow down growth in some countries.

In this and the next sections, I investigate some of the simplest models that link trade to growth to investigate the potential impacts of international trade on economic growth. I start with a model illustrating how trade opening may change the pace of endogenous technological change. This model is inspired by Grossman and Helpman (1991b), who investigate many different interactions between international trade and endogenous technological change. Briefly, the model consists of two independent economies that can be approximated by the baseline endogenous technological change model with expanding input varieties as in Chapter 13. In fact, the model is identical to the lab-equipment specification in Section 13.1. The advantage of this model is that there are no knowledge spillovers; thus we do not have to make assumptions about how knowledge spillovers change with trade opening.[5] I compare innovation and growth in these two economies in the equilibria without any international trade and with costless international trade. Naturally, a smoother transition (in which trade costs decline slowly) is more realistic in practice, but the sharp thought experiment of moving from autarky to full trade integration is sufficient for us to obtain the main insights concerning the effect of international trade on technological progress.

Given the analysis in Section 13.1 of Chapter 13, there is no need to repeat the same steps here. It suffices to say that we consider two economies, say 1 and 2, with identical technologies, identical preferences, and identical labor forces normalized to 1 (and no population growth). Preferences and technologies are also the same as those specified in Section 13.1. Consequently a slight variation on Proposition 13.1 in that section immediately implies the following result.

Proposition 19.13 *Suppose that the conditions*

$$\eta\beta > \rho \text{ and } 2(1 - \theta)\eta\beta < \rho \tag{19.55}$$

hold. Then in autarky there exists a unique equilibrium where, starting from any level of technology, both countries innovate and grow at the same rate:

$$g^A = \frac{1}{\theta}(\eta\beta - \rho). \tag{19.56}$$

Proof. See Exercise 19.31. ∎

---

5. If instead of the lab-equipment specification, we were to use the specification with knowledge spillovers and the two countries produced different sets of inputs, we would need to decide whether and how much the inputs produced in the foreign country increase the productivity of R&D in the home country before and after trade opening. Exercise 19.33 shows that assumptions concerning how the extent of knowledge spillovers change with trade opening influence the conclusions regarding the effect of trade on growth.

Next, let us analyze what happens when these two economies start trading. The exact implications of trade depend on whether, before trade opening, the two countries were producing some of the same inputs (recall that there is a continuum of available inputs that can be produced). To the extent that they were producing some of the same inputs, the static gains from trade will be limited. If, on the other hand, the two countries were producing different inputs, there will be larger static gains. However our interest here is with the dynamic effects of trade opening, that is, with the effects of trade opening on economic growth. The analysis from Chapter 13 again leads to the following result.

Proposition 19.14 *Suppose that condition (19.55) holds. Then after trade opening, the world economy and both countries innovate and grow at the rate*

$$g^T = \frac{1}{\theta}(2\eta\beta - \rho) > g^A,$$

where g^A is the autarky growth rate given by (19.56).

Proof.   See Exercise 19.32.   ∎

This proposition shows that opening to international trade encourages technological change and increases the growth rate of the world economy. The reason is simple: international trade enables each input producer to access a larger market, and this makes inventing new inputs more profitable. This greater profitability translates into a higher rate of innovation and more rapid growth.

The main effect captured in this simple model is reasonably robust. Grossman and Helpman (1991b) provide a number of extensions and also richer models of international trade (e.g., with multiple factors). The economic force, a version of the market size effect that leads to the innovation gains from trade, is also reasonably robust. Nevertheless several caveats are necessary. First, as Exercise 19.33 shows, if the R&D sector competes with production, there are powerful offsetting effects, because trade also increases the demand for production workers. In this case, the qualitative result in this section—that trade opening increases the rate of technological progress—generally applies, but it is also possible to construct versions of this baseline model in which this effect is entirely offset. Exercise 19.33 also provides an example of this type of extreme offset, which should be borne in mind as a useful caveat. Second, Exercise 19.34 shows that if the full scale effect is removed and we focus on an economy with semi-endogenous growth (as the model studied in Section 13.3 in Chapter 13), trade opening increases innovation temporarily but not in the long run.

19.7   Learning-by-Doing, Trade, and Growth

The previous section showed how international trade can increase economic growth in all countries in the world by encouraging faster technological progress. In addition to this effect of trade on growth working via technological change, the static gains from trade are well recognized and understood. By improving the allocation of resources in the world economy, these static gains can also encourage economic growth. Nevertheless, as mentioned in Section 19.6, many commentators and some economists remain skeptical of the positive growth effects of international trade. A popular argument, often used to justify infant industry protection and industrial policy, is that the static gains from trade come at the cost of dynamic gains, because international trade induces some countries to specialize in industries with relatively low growth potential. In this section, I outline a simple model with this feature. Richer models that also lead to similar conclusions have been presented by, among others, Young (1991), Matsuyama

(1992), and Galor and Mountford (2008). There are also other arguments for why trade may have negative effects on growth based on institutional differences across countries, which are briefly discussed at the end of this chapter. My purpose here is to use the simplest model to illustrate the potential negative effects of trade. As in the models by Matsuyama and Young, the mechanism for potential dynamic losses from trade (for some countries) is the presence of learning-by-doing externalities in some sectors.

Consider a world economy consisting of two blocks of countries, the North and the South, and suppose that each block consists of many identical countries. The present thought experiment is a move from autarky to full international trade integration between these two blocks. To simplify the exposition and focus on the main ideas, let us assume that all countries are almost identical. In particular, each country has a total labor force of 1, and labor can be used to produce one of two intermediate goods with the production functions

$$Y_j^1(t) = A_j(t)L_j^1(t), \text{ and } Y_j^2(t) = L_j^2(t),$$

and with the labor market clearing condition

$$L_j^1(t) + L_j^2(t) \leq 1$$

for $j \in \{n, s\}$ denoting a Northern or Southern country. Moreover let us assume that the total number of Northern and Southern countries are equal, and denote the total number of countries in the world by $2J$.

The final good is produced as a CES aggregate of these two intermediates. Once again distinguishing between the production of intermediates and their use in the final good sector, we write this aggregate as

$$Y_j(t) = \left[\gamma X_j^1(t)^{\frac{\varepsilon-1}{\varepsilon}} + (1 - \gamma) X_j^2(t)^{\frac{\varepsilon-1}{\varepsilon}} \right]^{\frac{\varepsilon}{\varepsilon-1}},$$

where ε is the elasticity of substitution between the two intermediates and suppose that $\varepsilon > 1$. The case of $\varepsilon = 1$ (where the production function becomes Cobb-Douglas) is also of interest, and I treat this case separately. To simplify the algebra and the exposition below, I set $\gamma = 1/2$.

Learning-by-doing is modeled as follows:

$$\frac{\dot{A}_j(t)}{A_j(t)} = \eta L_j^1(t), \tag{19.57}$$

so that when more workers are employed in sector 1, the technology of sector 1 improves. There are no learning-by-doing opportunities in sector 2. Thus one might think of sector 1 as manufacturing or some high-tech sector, while sector 2 may correspond to agriculture or to relatively low-tech sectors (though whether there are greater opportunities for learning-by-doing in manufacturing than in agriculture is debatable). As in Romer's (1986a) growth model (recall Chapter 11), each producer ignores the positive externality that it creates on the future productivity of sector 1 by its production decisions today.

The only difference between the North and the South is a small comparative advantage for the North in the production of sector 1. In particular, I assume that

$$A_n(0) = 1, \text{ and } A_s(0) = 1 - \delta, \tag{19.58}$$

where $\delta > 0$, and it is taken to be a small number.

Given this structure, the equilibrium both without international trade and with it are relatively straightforward to characterize. The key in both cases is that the value of the marginal product of labor (the wage rates) in the two sectors has to be equalized or only one of the two sectors will be active. Let us start with the closed economy and suppose that both sectors have to be active at t. Then the marginal products have to be equalized in the two sectors, and thus

$$p_j^1(t)A_j(t) = p_j^2(t), \qquad (19.59)$$

where $p_j^1(t)$ and $p_j^2(t)$ denote the prices of the two intermediates in country j in terms of the final good, and $A_j(t)$ is the level of productivity in sector 1 in country j. Notice that prices are indexed by j, since we are in the closed-economy case. Profit maximization by the final good producers immediately implies that

$$\frac{p_j^1(t)}{p_j^2(t)} = \left(\frac{X_j^1(t)}{X_j^2(t)}\right)^{-\frac{1}{\varepsilon}} = \left(\frac{A_j(t)L_j^1(t)}{1 - L_j^1(t)}\right)^{-\frac{1}{\varepsilon}},$$

where $L_j^1(t)$ denotes the amount of labor allocated to sector 1 in country j at time t, and naturally, the amount of labor allocated to sector 2 is $L_j^2(t) = 1 - L_j^1(t)$. Combining this equation with (19.59) yields

$$L_j^1(t) = \frac{A_j(t)^{\varepsilon-1}}{1 + A_j(t)^{\varepsilon-1}}. \qquad (19.60)$$

The evolution of the productivity of sector 1 is then given by (19.57).

Proposition 19.15 *Consider the above-described model, and suppose that $\varepsilon > 1$ and $\delta \to 0$. Then in the absence of international trade the equilibrium involves the allocation of labor given by (19.60) for all j and t. In particular, $L_j^1(t=0) = 1/2$, and $L_j^1(t)$ monotonically converges to 1. The growth rate of each country $g_j(t)$ converges to $g^* = \eta$.*

If, on the other hand, $\varepsilon = 1$, then $L_j^1(t) = 1/2$ for all t, and the long-run growth rate of each country is $g^{**} = \eta/2$.

Proof. See Exercise 19.35. ∎

Next consider the same world economy with free international trade starting at time $t = 0$. For each intermediate good, there is now only a single world price, $p^1(t)$ for good 1 and $p^2(t)$ for good 2. With standard arguments, these prices satisfy

$$\frac{p^1(t)}{p^2(t)} = \left(\frac{X_n^1(t) + X_s^1(t)}{X_n^2(t) + X_s^2(t)}\right)^{-\frac{1}{\varepsilon}} = \left(\frac{A_n(t)L_n^1(t) + A_s(t)L_s^1(t)}{2 - L_n^1(t) - L_s^1(t)}\right)^{-\frac{1}{\varepsilon}},$$

where the subscripts n and s denote Northern and Southern countries.

It is straightforward to verify that as a result of the slight comparative advantage in (19.58), at $t = 0$ the marginal product of Northern workers in sector 1 is higher, and all of the labor force in the North is employed in sector 1, while all of the labor force in the South is employed in sector 2. Moreover all of sector 1 production is in Northern countries, and all of sector 2 production is in the South. In all subsequent periods, the productivity of Northern workers in sector 1 is even higher, while the productivity of Southern workers in sector 1 remains stagnant. The next proposition summarizes this result.

Proposition 19.16 *Consider the above-described model. Then with free international trade, the equilibrium is as follows: $L_n^1(t) = 1$ and $L_s^1(t) = 0$ for all t. In this equilibrium,*

$$\frac{\dot{A}_n(t)}{A_n(t)} = \eta, \text{ and } \frac{\dot{A}_s(t)}{A_s(t)} = 0.$$

The world economy converges to a growth rate of $g^* = \eta$ in the long run. The ratio of income in the North and the South is given by

$$\frac{Y_n(t)}{Y_s(t)} = A_n(t)^{\frac{\varepsilon-1}{\varepsilon}}$$

for all t. Consequently if $\varepsilon > 1$, then the North becomes progressively richer relative to the South, so that $\lim_{t\to\infty} Y_n(t)/Y_s(t) = \infty$. If, instead, $\varepsilon = 1$, then the relative incomes of the North and the South remain constant, so that $Y_n(t)/Y_s(t) = constant$ for all t.

Proof. See Exercise 19.36. ∎

This proposition contains the main result on how international trade can harm certain countries when there are learning-by-doing externalities in some sectors. The South has a slight comparative disadvantage in sector 1. Yet in the absence of trade, it devotes enough of its resources to that sector and achieves the same growth rate as the North. However, if there is free trade, the South specializes in sector 2 (because of its slight comparative disadvantage in sector 1) and fails to benefit from the learning-by-doing opportunities offered by sector 1. As a result, the South becomes progressively poorer relative to the North. This proposition therefore captures the main critique against international trade coming from models such as Young (1991) and proponents of the infant industry arguments.

However the proposition also shows some of the shortcomings of these arguments. For example, if $\varepsilon = 1$ (or sufficiently close to 1), specialization in sector 2 does not hurt the South. The reason is closely related to the effects highlighted in Section 19.4: the increase in the productivity of sector 1 in the North creates a negative terms-of-trade effect against the North. This effect is always present, but when $\varepsilon = 1$, it becomes sufficiently powerful to prevent the impoverishment of the South even though they have specialized in the sector with the low growth potential. Another caveat is highlighted in Exercise 19.36: in the world economy described here, infant industry protection will not help the South. Even if international trade is prevented in the South for a period of duration $T > 0$ for protecting some infant industry, the ultimate outcome is the same as in Proposition 19.16.

So what are we to make of the results in this section and the general issue of the impact of trade on growth? An immediate answer is that the juxtaposition of the models of this and the previous sections suggest that the effect of trade on growth must be an empirical one. Since there are models that highlight both the positive and the negative effects of trade on growth, the debate can be resolved only by empirical work.

Nevertheless, the theoretical perspectives are still useful. A couple of issues are particularly worth noting. First, the effect of trade integration on the rate of endogenous technological progress may be limited because of the factors already discussed at the end of Section 19.6. For example, significant effects are possible only when trade opening does not increase wages in the final good sector competing for workers against the R&D sector (which is the case when the R&D sector does not compete for workers with the final good sector). Moreover, if the extreme scale effects are removed, trade opening creates a temporary boost in innovation but does not necessarily change the long-run growth rate. Nonetheless the benefits of the greater market size for firms involved in innovation must be to some degree present in any model of endogenous technological change. Taking all these factors into account, we should expect some inducement to innovation from trade opening. Whether these effects are commensurate with, or even greater than, the static gains of international trade is much harder to ascertain. It may well be that the static gains from trade are more important than the subsequent innovation gains.

On the other side of the trade-off are the potential costs of trade in terms of inducing specialization in the wrong sectors. The model in this section illustrates this possibility. Nevertheless, I believe that the potential negative effects of trade on growth because of such "incorrect" specialization should not be exaggerated. First, there is no strong evidence that international trade leads to incorrect specialization in practice. Second, international flows of information, which often increase with trade opening, imply that improvements in productivity in some countries affect productivity in others that were not initially specializing in those sectors (e.g., South Korea was initially an importer of cars and is now a net exporter, its productivity in the automotive sector having increased with technology transfer). Finally, as the main result in this section showed, terms-of-trade effects ameliorate any negative impact of specialization.

19.8   Taking Stock

This chapter had three main objectives. The first was to emphasize the shortcoming of using the closed-economy models for the analysis of the economic growth patterns across countries or regions. We have seen that both intertemporal trade and trade in commodities change the dynamics and also possibly the long-run implications of the closed-economy neoclassical growth models. For example, international capital flows remove transitional dynamics, because economies that are short of capital do not need to accumulate it slowly but can borrow it in international markets. Naturally there are limits to how much international borrowing can take place. Countries are sovereign entities, and thus it is relatively easy for them to declare bankruptcy once they have borrowed a lot. Consequently the sovereign borrowing risk might place limits on the ability of countries to use international markets to smooth consumption and rapidly increase their investments. Even in this case, some amount of international lending takes place, and this has an important effect on the equilibrium dynamics of output and the capital stock. Nevertheless, the available evidence typically confirms the Feldstein-Horioka puzzle, which states that changes in investment are correlated with changes in savings. An investigation of why, despite significant gross capital flows, net international capital flows do not play a greater role in international consumption and investment smoothing and what the implications are for economic growth is an interesting area for future research.

We have further seen that international trade in commodities also changes the implications of the neoclassical growth model. For example, in the model of economic growth in Section 19.3, international trade in goods plays the same role as international lending and borrowing, and it significantly changes cross-country output dynamics. Thus even in the absence of international lending and borrowing, the implications of approaches that model the entire world equilibrium are significantly different from those focusing on closed-economy dynamics. The model of Ricardian trade and terms-of-trade effects in Section 19.4 also illustrated the potential sharp implications of international trade for economic growth. In that model, there would be no convergence across countries without trade, but international trade, via the terms-of-trade effects it induces, creates a powerful force that links incomes around the world. Consequently the long-run equilibrium involves a stable world income distribution, and the short-run dynamics are different from the closed-economy models.

The second objective was to highlight how the nature of international trade interacts with the process of economic growth. Sections 19.3 and 19.4 focused on this issue. The model of economic growth with Heckscher-Ohlin trade showed how economic growth increases the effective elasticity of output with respect to capital for each country because of conditional factor price equalization. This model is useful for understanding how certain economies, such as the East Asian tigers, can grow rapidly for extended periods, relying on capital accumulation without experiencing diminishing returns. However, our analysis also showed that conditional factor price equalization can lead to extreme results. In contrast, the model in Section 19.4 emphasized how a simple form of Ricardian trade, based on technological comparative advantage, creates a new source of diminishing returns to accumulation for each country based on terms-of-trade effects. As a country accumulates more capital, it starts exporting more of the goods in which it specializes. The result is a worsening of its terms of trade, reducing the rate of return to further capital accumulation. The analysis showed how this force leads to a stable world income distribution, whereby rapidly growing economies pull up the laggards to grow at the same rate as themselves. How are we to reconcile the different implications of the models in Sections 19.3 and 19.4? One possibility is to imagine a world that is a mixture of the models of these two sections. It may be that some goods are standardized and can be produced in any country. When producing these goods, there are no terms-of-trade effects. So if a country can grow only by producing these goods, it can escape the standard diminishing returns to capital thanks to international trade. This might be a good approximation to the situation experienced by the East Asian tigers in the 1970s and 1980s, when they specialized in medium-tech goods. However, as countries become richer they also produce more differentiated goods, and they may encounter terms-of-trade effects. Consequently, if a country is at the stage of development where it produces more of the differentiated goods, further capital accumulation result in diminishing returns through the mechanism highlighted in Section 19.4. Regardless of how the forces emphasized in these two approaches are combined, they both show the importance of modeling the world equilibrium and of viewing the changes in the rate of return to capital in the context of the international trading relations.

The third objective of this chapter was to investigate the effect of international trade on economic growth. Sections 19.6 and 19.7 illustrated two different approaches, one emphasizing the beneficial effects of trade on growth, the other one the potential negative effects. Both classes of models are useful to have in one's arsenal in the analysis of world equilibrium and economic growth. The usefulness of these models notwithstanding, the impact of international trade on economic growth is ultimately an empirical question, though our theoretical analysis has already highlighted some important mechanisms and also suggested that the negative effects of trade on growth are unlikely to be important. Whether the positive effects of trade on technological progress are quantitatively significant remains an open question. It may well be that the static gains of trade are more important than the dynamic ones. Nevertheless, any analysis of international trade must take into account its implications on economic growth and technological change.

19.9   References and Literature

This chapter covered a variety of models. Section 19.1 focused on the implications of international financial flows on economic growth. This topic is discussed in detail in Barro and Sala-i-Martin (2004, Chapter 3), both with and without limits to financial flows. Obstfeld and Rogoff (1996, Chapters 1 and 2) provide a more detailed analysis of international borrowing and lending. Chapter 6 of Obstfeld and Rogoff provides an introduction to the implications of imperfections in international capital markets. Work that models these imperfections and their implications includes Bulow and Rogoff (1989a,b), Atkeson (1991), Kehoe and Perri (2002), and Matsuyama (2004). The Feldstein-Horioka puzzle, which was also discussed in Section 19.1, is still an active area of research. Obstfeld and Taylor (2002) present a survey of much of the research on this topic. Taylor (1994), Baxter and Crucini (1993), and Kraay and Ventura (2007) propose potential resolutions for the Feldstein-Horioka puzzle.

Section 19.2 is motivated by Lucas's classic (1990) article. There is a large literature on why capital does not flow from rich to poor countries. Obstfeld and Taylor (1994) contain a survey of the work in this area. The work by Caselli and Feyrer (2007) discussed above provides a method for estimating cross-country differences in the marginal productive capital and argues that differences in the return to capital are limited. This work supports models that account for the lack of capital flows based on productivity differences, such as the model presented in Section 19.2. Recent work by Chirinko and Mallick (2007) argues that the Caselli and Feyrer (2007) procedure may lead to misleading results because they do not incorporate adjustment costs in investment in their calculations and that once these costs are incorporated, returns to capital differ significantly across countries. See also recent work by Gourinchas and Jeanne (2006) on the lack of major investment or growth gains following financial integration and Alfaro, Kalemli-Ozcan, and Volosovych (2005) on the links between institutional differences and capital flows.

The rest of the chapter relies on some basic knowledge of international trade theory. Space restrictions preclude a detailed review. The reader is referred to a standard text, for example, Dixit and Norman (1980). Section 19.3 provides a slight generalization of the model in Ventura (1997) (it considers a general constant returns to scale production function rather than CES production function used in Ventura). A similar but less-rich model was first analyzed by Stiglitz (1971). Stiglitz did not include labor-augmenting productivity differences across nations and assumed exogenous saving rates. Other papers that combine Heckscher-Ohlin trade with models of economic growth include Atkeson and Kehoe (2000) and Cunat and Maffezoli (2001). Section 19.4 builds on Acemoglu and Ventura (2002). This model uses the structure of preferences first introduced by Armington (1969) but in the production of the final good rather than in preferences (see also Ventura, 2005).

The model in Section 19.5 builds on Krugman's (1979) seminal article on the product cycle. Grossman and Helpman (1991b) provide richer models of the product cycle with endogenous technology, similar to the economy discussed in Exercise 19.29. Antras (2005) provides a new perspective on the international product cycle that relies on the importance of incomplete contracts. In his model, contractual problems between Northern producers and Southern subsidiaries constitute a barrier slowing down the transfer of goods to the South. Only after goods become sufficiently standardized do the contracting problems become less severe and can the transfer of production to the South take place.

There is a large empirical literature on the impact of trade on growth. Many of the best-known papers in this literature were discussed at the beginning of Section 19.6. The rest of Section 19.6 builds on Rivera-Batiz and Romer (1991) and Grossman and Helpman (1991b), but uses the formulation from Section 13.1 in Chapter 13. Grossman and Helpman (1991b) assume that R&D requires labor and introduce competition between the R&D sector and the final good sector. In this case, the nature of the knowledge spillovers becomes important for the implications of trade on the pace of endogenous technological progress. Rivera-Batiz and Romer (1991) also discuss the implications of the form of the innovation possibilities frontier for the effects of trade on technological change. This point, which is developed in Exercise 19.33, also features in recent work by Atkeson and Burstein (2007). Grossman and Helpman (1991b) also present models with multiple sectors and factor proportion differences across countries. Another potential effect of international trade on technology works by influencing the direction of technological change. This topic is analyzed in detail in Acemoglu (2003b), where I show that trade opening with imperfect IPR can make new technologies more skill-biased than before trade opening. Similar models are also analyzed in Thoenig and Verdier (2003) and Epifani and Gancia (2006).

Section 19.7 presents a model inspired by Young (1991) and Matsuyama (1992). Lucas (1988) and Galor and Mountford (2008) also present similar models, which feature interaction between specialization and learning-by-doing. Other models in which international trade may be costly for some countries rely on differences in the amount of rents generated by different sectors because of imperfections in the labor market or institutional problems. Nunn (2006) and Levchenko (2007) present models in which trade leads to the transfer of rent-creating jobs from countries with weak institutions to those with better institutions and may be harmful to countries with weak institutions.

19.10 Exercises

19.1   Prove Propositions 19.1 and 19.2. [Hint: for Proposition 19.2, use (19.5) together with the fact that consumption and output grow at the same rate in each country to show that in the steady state it is optimal for each country (or each household in each country) to choose $\dot{a}_j(t) \to 0$.]

19.2   Consider the world economy with free flows of capital, but assume that each country has a different discount factor ρ_j.

  (a) Prove that Proposition 19.1 still holds.

  (b) Show that there does not exist a steady-state equilibrium with $\dot{a}_j(t) = 0$ for all j. Explain the intuition for this result.

  (c) Characterize the asymptotic equilibrium (the equilibrium path as $t \to \infty$). Suppose that $\rho_{j'} < \rho_j$ for all $j \neq j'$. Show that the share of world net output that is consumed in country j' tends to 1. What does this imply for the relationship between GDP and GNP across countries?

  (d) How would you modify the model to make the asymptotic equilibrium in part c more realistic?

19.3   This exercise asks you to prove Proposition 19.3.

  (a) Show that $\tilde{c}_j(t)/\tilde{c}_{j'}(t)$ is constant for all j and j'.

  (b) Show that given the result in Proposition 19.1, the integrated world equilibrium can be represented by a single aggregate production function. [Hint: use an argument similar to that leading to Proposition 19.6.]

  (c) Relate this result and Proposition 19.6 to Theorem 5.4 in Chapter 5. Explain why these aggregation results would not hold without free capital flows.

  (d) Given the result in parts a and b, apply an analysis similar to that for the global stability of the equilibrium path in the basic neoclassical growth model to establish the global stability of the equilibrium path here. Given global stability, prove the uniqueness of the equilibrium path.

* 19.4 Consider a world economy with international capital flows, but suppose that because of sovereign default risk a country cannot borrow more than a fraction $\phi > 0$ of its capital stock. Consequently, in Section 19.1, we have the restriction that $\dot{a}_j(t) \leq \phi k_j(t)$.

  (a) Characterize the steady-state equilibrium of the world economy and show that the steady state is not affected by this constraint. Explain the intuition for this result carefully.

  (b) Characterize the transitional dynamics of the world economy under this constraint. Show that Corollary 19.1 no longer holds.

19.5   Barro and Sala-i-Martin (1991, 2004) use growth regressions to look at the patterns of convergence across U.S. regions and states. They find that there is a slow pattern of convergence across regions and states, and they interpret this through the lenses of the neoclassical growth model. Explain why Corollary 19.1 implies that this interpretation is not appropriate. Suggest instead an alternative explanation for why convergence across regions and states might be slow. [Hint: should we expect technology or capital to flow more rapidly across regions?]

19.6   Consider the baseline AK model studied in Chapter 11, and suppose that countries have the same production technology, but differ according to their discount rates ρ_j. Show that there are persistent differences in saving and investment rates across countries that are correlated, even in the presence of free financial flows across countries. Provide a precise intuition for this result. Explain why this model could not account for the Feldstein-Horioka puzzle (see Section 19.2.2), which does not refer to the correlation between saving and investment in levels but in differences. Can you extend this model to account for the Feldstein-Horioka puzzle?

19.7   Prove Proposition 19.4.

19.8   Show that in the model of Section 19.3 free capital flows across countries have no effect on the equilibrium allocation.

19.9   Consider the model in Section 19.3 with different discount rates across countries. Prove that there does not exist a steady-state equilibrium.

19.10 Characterize the closed-economy equilibrium in the model of Section 19.3 and compare it to the equilibrium with trade characterized in the text.

* 19.11 Consider the model in Section 19.3, but assume that (19.9) is now modified to be $Y_j^K(t) = B_j K_j(t)$, where B_js potentially differ across countries. Characterize the world equilibrium. What would happen if there were free capital flows in this case?

19.12 (a) Reformulate and prove the main results in Section 19.3 for the case in which population levels differ across countries. [Hint: instead of $k(t)/A$, relevant prices now depend on $\sum_{j=1}^{J} K_j(t) / \sum_{j=1}^{J} AL_j(t)$.]

        (b) What happens if each country has a different rate of population growth n_j?

* 19.13 (a) Show that the steady-state characterization in Section 19.3 continues to hold if the CRRA preferences in (19.14) is now modified to an arbitrary strictly increasing, strictly concave utility function $u(c)$. How would you analyze transitional dynamics in this case?

        (b) Now let us go back to the preferences as in (19.14), but suppose that productivity of labor in each country is given by $A_j(t) = A_j \exp(gt)$. Show that all results from the text continue to apply, and in particular, derive the equivalent of Proposition 19.6.

        (c) Finally, suppose that F in (19.7) does not satisfy Assumption 2. How does this affect the analysis and the results?

19.14 Derive the unit cost functions (19.27) and (19.28) from the production functions (19.24) and (19.25). Determine the value of the constant χ.

19.15 Derive (19.29) and (19.30).

19.16 Consider the model in Section 19.4.

        (a) Derive the trade balance equation (19.34) from the capital market clearing equation (19.26).

        (b) Determine the ratio of imports to GDP as a function of τ.

19.17 Provide a rigorous proof of the global (saddle-path) stability of the steady-state world equilibrium in Proposition 19.10.

19.18 Characterize the closed-economy equilibrium in the model of Section 19.4, where each country only uses the intermediates it produces. Compare this to the equilibrium with trade characterized in the text. Show that countries have different long-run growth rates in the closed-economy equilibrium. Can the households in the fastest-growing country be better off in this equilibrium than in the equilibrium with trade?

19.19 (a) Derive (19.40) and (19.41).

(b) Explain the roles of the different parameters in determining cross-country income dispersion. Using reasonable parameter values, discuss whether the model with international trade can generate larger differences in income per capita across countries than the neoclassical growth model.

19.20 Derive (19.43).

19.21 Prove Proposition 19.11.

19.22 Prove Proposition 19.12.

19.23 Consider the steady-state world equilibrium in the model of Section 19.4.

(a) Show that an increase in τ does not necessarily increase the steady-state world equilibrium growth rate g^* as given by (19.38). Provide an intuition for this result.

(b) Show that even when τ does not increase growth, it increases world welfare. [Hint: to simplify the answer to this part of the question, you can simply look at steady-state welfare.]

(c) Interpret the finding in part b in light of the debate about the effect of trade on growth.

(d) Provide a sufficient condition for an increase in τ to increase the world growth rate and interpret this condition.

19.24 Consider the model of Section 19.4, except that instead of utility maximization by a representative household, assume that each country saves a constant fraction s_j of its income. Characterize the equilibrium in this case, and show that terms-of-trade effects again lead to a stable world income distribution.

* 19.25 Consider the model of Section 19.4, but assume that $\varepsilon < 1$. Characterize the equilibrium. Show that in this case countries that have lower discount rates will be relatively poor. Provide a precise intuition for this result. Explain why the assumption that $\varepsilon < 1$ may not be plausible.

* 19.26 Consider the baseline AK model in Section 19.4. Suppose that production and allocation decisions within each country are made by a country-specific social planner (who maximizes the utility of the representative household within the country).

(a) Show that the allocation in the text is no longer an equilibrium. Explain.

(b) Characterize the equilibrium in this case and show that all of the qualitative results derived in the text apply. Provide generalizations of Propositions 19.11 and 19.12.

(c) Show that world welfare is lower in this case than in the equilibrium in the text.

(d) Do you find the equilibrium in this exercise or the one in the text more plausible? Justify your answer.

* 19.27 Consider the model with labor in Section 19.4. Suppose that countries can invest to create new varieties of products. Suppose that if a particular firm creates such a variety, it becomes the monopolist and can charge a markup equal to the monopoly price to all consumers in the world, until this variety is destroyed endogenously, which happens at the exponential rate $\delta > 0$.

(a) Show that the optimal monopoly price for a firm in country j at time t is given by $p_j(t) = \varepsilon r_j(t)/(\varepsilon - 1)$. Interpret this equation.

(b) Suppose that a new variety can be created by using $1/\eta$ units of labor. Show how this changes the labor market clearing condition, and specify the free-entry condition.

(c) Define a world BGP as an equilibrium in which all countries grow at the same rate. Show that such an equilibrium exists and is uniquely defined. Explain the economic forces that lead to the existence of such a "stable" equilibrium. [Hint: show that in this BGP, the number of varieties that each country produces is constant.]

(d) What is the effect of an increase in the discount rate ρ on the number of varieties that a country produces? Interpret this result.

(e) Discuss informally how the analysis and the results would be modified if new products were produced using a combination of labor and capital.

19.28 Show that in the model of Section 19.5 an increase in ι always (weakly) closes the relative income gap between the North and the South. Characterize the conditions under which an increase in ι makes the North worse off (in terms of reducing its real income).

19.29 This exercise asks you to endogenize innovation decisions in the model of Section 19.5. Assume that new goods are created by technology firms in the North as in the model in Section 13.4 in Chapter 13, and these firms are monopolist suppliers until the good they have invented is copied by the South. The technology of production is the same as before, and assume that new goods can be produced by using final goods with the technology $\dot{N}(t) = \eta Z(t)$, where $Z(t)$ is final good spending. Imitation is still exogenous and takes place at the rate ι. Once a good is imitated, it can be produced competitively in the South.

(a) Show that for a good that is not copied by the South, the equilibrium price is

$$p(t, v) = \frac{\varepsilon}{\varepsilon - 1} w^n(t).$$

(b) Characterize the static equilibrium for given levels of $N^n(t)$ and $N^o(t)$.

(c) Compute the net present value of a new product for a Northern firm. Why does it differ from (13.8) in Section 13.4?

(d) Impose the free-entry condition, and derive the equilibrium rate of technological change for the world economy. Compute the world growth rate.

(e) What is the effect of an increase in ι on the equilibrium? Can an increase in ι make the South worse off? Explain the intuition for this result.

19.30 Consider a variation of the product cycle model in Section 19.5. Suppose there is no trade, so that the number of goods consumed in each country differs.

(a) Show that wages and incomes in the North and the South at time t are

$$w^n(t) = N(t)^{\frac{1}{\varepsilon-1}}, \text{ and } w^s(t) = N^o(t)^{\frac{1}{\varepsilon-1}}.$$

(b) Derive a condition for relative income differences to be smaller in this case than in the model with international trade. Provide a precise intuition for why international trade may increase relative income differences.

(c) If trade increases the income differences between the North and the South, does it mean that it reduces welfare in the South? [Hint: if you wish, you can again use the steady-state welfare levels.]

19.31 Prove Proposition 19.13.

19.32 Prove Proposition 19.14.

19.33 Consider the model in Section 19.6, but assume that new products are created with the innovation possibilities frontier as in Section 13.2 in Chapter 13. Assume that before trade, knowledge spillovers are created by the entire set of available inputs in the world economy; that is, the innovation possibilities frontier is

$$\dot{N}^j(t) = \eta N(t) L_R^j(t)$$

for country j, where $N(t) = N^1(t) + N^2(t)$, and $L_R^j(t)$ is the number workers working in R&D in country j. Thus trade opening does not change knowledge spillovers.

(a) Show that in this model, trade opening has no effect on the equilibrium growth rate. Provide a precise intuition for this result.

(b) Assume that before trade opening the innovation possibilities frontier takes the form $\dot{N}^j(t) = \eta N^j(t) L_R^j(t)$. Show that in this case, trade opening leads to an increase in the equilibrium growth rate as in Proposition 19.14. Explain why the results are different.

(c) Which of the specifications in parts a and b is more plausible? In light of your answer to this question, how do you think trade opening should affect economic growth?

19.34 Consider the model in Section 19.6 with two differences. First, population grows at the rate n in both countries. Second, the innovation possibilities frontier is given by

$$\dot{N}^j(t) = \eta N(t)^{-\phi} Z^j(t)$$

for country j, where $N(t) = N^1(t) + N^2(t)$. Show that at first trade opening leads to more innovation, but the long-run growth rate of each country remains unchanged.

19.35 Prove Proposition 19.15.

19.36 (a) Prove Proposition 19.16.

(b) Explain why when $\varepsilon = 1$, specialization in the sector without learning-by-doing does not have an adverse effect on the relative income of the South.

(c) What are the implications of trade opening on relative incomes if $\varepsilon < 1$?

(d) Characterize the equilibrium if all economies are closed until time $t = T$ and then open to international trade at time T. What are the implications of this result for infant industry protection?

19.37 Consider the economy in Section 19.7, but suppose that the South is bigger than the North. In particular, assume that

$$(1 - \delta)^{-\varepsilon} < L^S / L^N < \varepsilon^{-1} + (1 - \delta)^{-\varepsilon}. \tag{19.61}$$

(a) Show that in this case not all Southern workers work in sector 2 and there is some learning-by-doing in the South. Why is (19.61) necessary for this result?

(b) How does this affect the long-run equilibrium? [Hint: show that the limiting value of L_s^1 is equal to 0.] Why is (19.61) necessary for this result?

PART VII

ECONOMIC DEVELOPMENT AND ECONOMIC GROWTH

In this part of the book I discuss the relationship between economic development and economic growth. The first question that the reader may rightly ask is why there is (or there should be) a distinction between economic development and economic growth. This question is particularly apt because I have argued in Chapter 1 that societies that are rich—developed—today are those that have grown steadily over the past 200 years and those that are poor (or less developed) are those that have not achieved this type of steady growth. This perspective suggests that economic development and economic growth are essentially the same thing and should be studied together. Nevertheless there are two reasons, one good and one bad, for drawing a distinction between development and growth. The good reason is that even though economic development and growth are part of the same process, models of growth emphasize different aspects of this process than models of economic development. In particular, the models studied so far focus on either balanced growth or transitional dynamics leading to balanced growth. Even though these transitional dynamics have been analyzed in a number of contexts, our main interest has been to ensure that they take us toward a BGP. Behavior along or near the BGP of a neoclassical or endogenous growth economy provides a good approximation to the behavior of relatively developed societies. But many salient features of economic growth at earlier stages of development are not easy to map to this orderly behavior of balanced growth. In fact, Kuznets and other economists have documented that even in more-developed economies, many aspects of the process of economic growth are far from the balanced benchmark implied by the standard neoclassical growth model.

Motivated by these patterns, in his classic book *Modern Economic Growth*, Kuznets (1966, p. 1) defines economic growth as follows:

> We identify the economic growth of nations as a sustained increase in per capita or per worker product, most often accompanied by an increase in population and usually by sweeping structural changes. In modern times these were changes in the industrial structure within which product was turned out and resources employed—away from agriculture toward nonagricultural activities, the process of industrialization; in the distribution of population between the countryside and the cities, the process of ur-banization; in the relative economic position of groups within the nation distinguished

by employment status, attachment to various industries, level of per capita income, and the like; in the distribution of product by use—among household consumption, capital formation, and the government consumption, and within each of these major categories by further subdivisions; in the allocation of product by its origin within the nation's boundaries and elsewhere; and so on.

Although one might debate whether this is the most functional definition of economic growth, it does capture a range of important changes that accompany economic growth in most societies. And yet the models of economic growth studied so far do not do justice to the complex process described by Kuznets. They provide a framework for explaining the sustained increase in income per capita or output per worker. But our models do not feature Kuznets's sweeping structural changes.

A complementary perspective to Kuznets's vision is provided by early development economists, such as Hirschman, Nurske, and Rosenstein-Rodan, who emphasized the importance of potential market failures and poverty traps in the process of development. If such market failures and poverty traps are an important determinant of economic performance, then we may expect them to be more widespread in less-developed, poorer economies.[1] Thus one might expect Kuznets's structural change to be accompanied by a process that involves the organization of production becoming more efficient and the economy moving from the interior of the aggregate production possibilities set toward its frontier. Throughout, I use the term "structural change" to describe changes in the composition of production and employment, while "structural transformations" refers to changes in the organization and efficiency of production accompanying the process of development.

A useful theoretical perspective might therefore be to consider the early stages of economic development taking place in the midst of—or even via—structural changes and transformations. We may then expect these changes to ultimately bring the economy to the neighborhood of balanced growth, where our focus has so far been. If this perspective is indeed useful, then we would like to develop models that can account for both the structural changes and transformations at the early stages of development and the behavior approximated by balanced growth at the later stages. We would also like to understand why some societies embark upon these transformations, while others do not.

Some of the models presented so far take steps in this direction. For example, the model of takeoff in Section 17.6 of Chapter 17 captures a specific type of transformation, from volatile, low-productivity growth into sustained, stable growth. In addition, many of the models in Chapter 18 emphasize the difference between frontier economies and technological followers. Nevertheless I have not offered a framework that can do justice to Kuznets's and other early development economists' vision. This is largely because the current growth literature is far from a satisfactory framework that can achieve this objective. In this light, the distinction between economic growth and economic development can be justified by arguing that, in the absence of a unified framework (or perhaps precisely as a prerequisite for developing a unified framework), we need to study the two aspects of the long-run growth process separately. Economic growth, according to this division of labor, focuses on balanced growth, the growth behavior of the world economy, and other aspects of the growth process approximating the behavior of relatively developed economies. Economic development, on the other hand, becomes the study of structural changes and transformations—and the efficiency implications of these transformations—at the early stages of development. Models of economic development would

---

1. In fact, these theoretical perspectives may be the justification for referring to relatively poor economies as "underdeveloped" rather than as "developing." In what follows, unless there is a special reason for using these terms, I stick with the less tainted adjectives "less-developed" or "relatively poor."

then focus on structural changes in production and consumption, on urbanization, on the size and the composition of the population, on the occupational structure, and on changes in living and social arrangements. The study of economic development would thus seek to understand when, why, and how these processes take place and whether they contribute to a less-developed economy moving toward the frontier of its production possibilities set. Since, as emphasized by Kuznets, economic growth in relatively developed economies also incorporates important elements of structural change, part of our analysis in the context of economic development also sheds light on the nature of economic growth in more advanced nations, for example, by helping us understand why and how relatively balanced growth can often go hand-in-hand with major changes in the sectoral composition of output and employment.

The second—not-so-satisfactory—reason for the distinction between economic growth and economic development is that there are separate literatures on these two topics, with very different emphases and often different questions. The economic growth literature focuses on the theoretical and empirical questions we have so far addressed in this book. The economic development literature, on the other hand, focuses on empirical analyses of education, poverty, discrimination, women's economic and social status, child outcomes, health, lending relations, and agriculture in less-developed economies. Much of this literature is nontheoretical. It documents how economic relationships work in less-developed economies or identifies specific market failures. This literature has provided us with numerous facts that are helpful in understanding the economic relations in less-developed economies and has sometimes acted as a conduit for micro reforms that have improved the lives of the citizens of these economies. But this literature does not ask questions about the aspects of the process of economic development I have emphasized here—that is, it does not pose the question of why some countries are less productive and poorer, and how these less-developed economies can undergo the process of structural transformation associated with, and necessary for, modern economic growth. Thus though the reason for drawing a distinction between economic growth and economic development might be literature-driven, it may still be useful. Moreover, based on this distinction one may attempt to bridge the gap between the development and growth literatures by combining the theoretical tools developed in this book with the wealth of evidence collected by the empirical development literature. Such a combination might ultimately lead to a more satisfactory framework for understanding the process of economic development (though unfortunately space restrictions preclude me from pursuing these issues in detail here).

These two reasons motivate my acceptance of the standard distinction between economic development and economic growth. Although I go along with this standard distinction, throughout I emphasize how it is exactly the same tools that are useful for understanding the process of economic development—the structural changes and transformations emphasized by Kuznets, Hirschman, Nurske, and Rosenstein-Rodan—as well as the more orderly process of economic growth. My hope is that this approach will engender both greater efforts to develop a unified theoretical framework useful for understanding the process of development and theoretical approaches that can make contact with and benefit from the wealth of evidence collected by the empirical development literature.

I organize this part of the book into two chapters. Chapter 20 focuses on models that make only a minimal departure from the balanced growth approaches studied so far while still shedding some light on the structural changes emphasized by Kuznets. The models in this chapter can thus be viewed as extensions of the neoclassical growth models in Chapters 8 and 11 designed to confront various important empirical patterns that are salient in the development process. However, these models neither do full justice to the process of sweeping structural changes emphasized by Kuznets nor do they capture the complex aspects of the process of economic development associated with the move from the interior of the production possibilities set toward the frontier. Chapter 21 presents several models that investigate various facets of this process, including financial development, the demographic transition, urbanization, and other social changes. Furthermore, they highlight the importance of potential market failures that may cause development traps. These models present a range of exciting questions and different modeling approaches, but at the expense of providing less unity. Each model makes a different set of assumptions, and the profession is far from having a unified framework for the analysis of the major structural transformations involved in the process of development. The purpose of Chapter 21 is not to provide such a unified framework but to introduce the reader to these interesting and important questions. It should also be noted that the division between the two chapters is not perfect. Some of the models of structural transformation studied in Chapter 21 can be seen as closely related to the structural change models in Chapter 20. Moreover some topics, such as the beginning of industrialization, can be treated both as a process of structural change and as an outcome of a society solving certain market failures. Thus the decision of whether a particular topic should be in Chapter 20 or Chapter 21 was somewhat arbitrary.

20

Structural Change and Economic Growth

Sections 20.1 and 20.2 focus on the shift of employment and production from agriculture to manufacturing, and then from manufacturing to services. This is a useful starting point both because changes in the composition of employment and production are an important part of the process of economic development and because, as emphasized by Kuznets and others, similar changes are present even beneath the façade of balanced modern growth. Consequently these two sections focus on preference-related ("demand-side") and technology-related ("supply-side") reasons for why we may expect structural change as an economy becomes richer, but they also emphasize how such structural changes can be reconciled with balanced growth. Section 20.3 turns to a related theme and shows how pre-industrial agricultural productivity may be a key determinant of the process of industrialization and takeoff.

20.1 Nonbalanced Growth: The Demand Side

Figure 20.1 provides a summary of some of the major changes in the structure of production that the U.S. economy has undergone over the past 150 years. It shows that the share of employment in agriculture stood at about 90% of the labor force at the beginning of the nineteenth century, while only a small fraction of the U.S. labor force worked in manufacturing and services. By the second half of the nineteenth century, both manufacturing and services had expanded to more than 20% of employment, accompanied by a steep decline in the share of agriculture. Over the past 150 years or so, the share of employment in agriculture has continued to decline and now stands at less than 5%, while more than 70% of U.S. workers are now employed in service industries. The share of manufacturing first increased when the share of agriculture started its decline but has been on a downward trend over the past 40 years or so and now stands at just over 20%. When we look at consumption shares, the general trends are similar, though the share of consumption expenditures on agricultural products is still substantial because of changes in relative prices and relative productivities (and also partly because of imports of agricultural goods). The changes in the composition of employment in the British economy toward the end of the eighteenth century are also consistent with the U.S. patterns shown in Figure 20.1 (see, e.g., Mokyr, 1993). Similar patterns are present in all OECD economies as

Employment shares

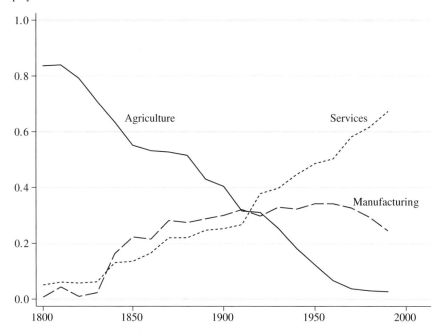

FIGURE 20.1 The share of U.S. employment in agriculture, manufacturing, and services, 1800–2000.

well. Some of the less-developed economies are still largely agricultural, but the time trend is inexorably toward a smaller share of agriculture.

Figure 20.1 paints a picture of changes in sectoral employment that includes a significant nonbalanced component. Kongsamut, Rebelo, and Xie (2001) refer to these changes in the composition of employment and production as the "Kuznets facts." They provide a tractable model to reconcile this type of structural change with the Kaldor facts emphasized so far in this book, that is, the relative constancy of factor shares and the interest rate. Even though it is designed to match the Kaldor facts regardless of the stage of development, the tractability of their model makes it a useful starting point for our analysis.

At the heart of Kongsamut, Rebelo, and Xie's approach is the so-called Engel's Law, which states that as a household's income increases, the fraction that it spends on food (agricultural products) declines. While calling this observation a law may exaggerate its status, this observation, first made by the nineteenth-century German statistician Ernst Engel, appears to be a remarkably robust pattern in the data. Kongsamut, Rebelo, and Xie extend Engel's Law by positing that as a household becomes richer, it not only desires to spend less on food but also more on services. In particular, consider the following infinite-horizon economy. Population grows at the exogenous rate n, so that total labor supply is $L(t) = \exp(nt)L(0)$. The economy admits a representative household that supplies labor inelastically and has standard preferences given by

$$\int_0^\infty \exp(-(\rho - n)t) \frac{c(t)^{1-\theta} - 1}{1 - \theta} dt, \qquad (20.1)$$

with $\theta \geq 0$, and $c(t)$ denoting the per capita consumption of a *Stone-Geary* aggregate consisting of agricultural, manufacturing, and services consumptions (recall Exercise 8.31 in Chapter 8):

$$c(t) = (c^A(t) - \gamma^A)^{\eta^A} c^M(t)^{\eta^M} (c^S(t) + \gamma^S)^{\eta^S}, \qquad (20.2)$$

where $c^A(t) \in [\gamma^A, \infty)$ denotes per capita agricultural consumption at time t, $c^M(t) \in \mathbb{R}_+$ is manufacturing consumption, and $c^S(t) \in \mathbb{R}_+$ is services consumption; γ^A, γ^S, η^A, η^M, and η^S are positive constants, and $\eta^A + \eta^M + \eta^S = 1$. This Stone-Geary form is a highly tractable way of introducing income elasticities that are different from one for different subcomponents of consumption and Engel's Law. In particular, this aggregator implies that there is a minimum, or *subsistence*, level of agricultural (food) consumption equal to γ^A. The household must consume at least this much food to survive and in fact, consumption and utility are not defined when the household does not consume the minimum amount of food. After this level of food consumption has been achieved, the household starts to demand other items, in particular, manufactured goods (e.g., textiles and durables) and services (e.g., health, entertainment, wholesale, and retail). However, as we will see shortly, the presence of the γ^S term in the aggregator implies that the household will spend a positive amount on services only after certain levels of agricultural and manufacturing consumption have been reached.

Suppose that the economy is closed; thus agricultural, manufacturing, and services consumption must be met by domestic production. I follow Kongsamut, Rebelo, and Xie and assume the following production functions:

$$Y^A(t) = B^A F(K^A(t), X(t)L^A(t)),$$

$$Y^M(t) = B^M F(K^M(t), X(t)L^M(t)), \tag{20.3}$$

$$Y^S(t) = B^S F(K^S(t), X(t)L^S(t)),$$

where $Y^j(t)$ for $j \in \{A, M, S\}$ denotes the output of agricultural, manufacturing, and services at time t; $K^j(t)$ and $L^j(t)$ for $j \in \{A, M, S\}$ are the levels of capital and labor, respectively, allocated to the agricultural, manufacturing, and services sectors at time t; B^j for $j \in \{A, M, S\}$ is a Hicks-neutral productivity term for the three sectors; and finally, $X(t)$ is a labor-augmenting (Harrod-neutral) productivity term affecting all sectors (I use the letter X instead of the standard A to distinguish this term from the agricultural good). The function F satisfies the usual neoclassical assumptions (Assumptions 1 and 2 from Chapter 2). Two other features in (20.3) are worth noting. First, the production functions for all three sectors are identical. Second, the same labor-augmenting technology term affects all three sectors. Both of these features are clearly unrealistic, but they are useful for isolating the demand-side sources of structural change and for contrasting them with the supply-side factors that will be discussed in the next section. Furthermore, Exercise 20.7 shows that they can be relaxed to some degree. Let us take the initial population, $L(0) > 0$, and the initial capital stock, $K(0) > 0$, as given, and also assume that there is a constant rate of growth of the labor-augmenting technology term, that is,

$$\frac{\dot{X}(t)}{X(t)} = g \tag{20.4}$$

for all t, with initial condition $X(0) > 0$. To ensure that the transversality condition of the representative household holds, I impose the same assumption as in the basic neoclassical growth model of Chapter 8—Assumption 4 (which implies that $\rho - n > (1 - \theta) g$).

Market clearing for labor and capital requires that

$$K^A(t) + K^M(t) + K^S(t) = K(t), \tag{20.5}$$

$$L^A(t) + L^M(t) + L^S(t) = L(t), \tag{20.6}$$

where $K(t)$ and $L(t)$ are the total supplies of capital and labor, respectively, at time t.

Another key assumption of the Kongsamut, Rebelo, and Xie model builds on Rebelo (1991) and requires that only the manufacturing good is used to produce the investment good. Consequently market clearing for the manufacturing good takes the form

$$\dot{K}(t) + c^M(t)L(t) = Y^M(t), \tag{20.7}$$

where, for simplicity, I ignore capital depreciation (otherwise there would be an additional term $\delta K(t)$ on the left-hand side). Equation (20.7) states that the total production of manufacturing goods is distributed between consumption of manufacturing goods and new capital stock, which will be used for the production of agricultural, manufacturing, and service goods in the future. Since the economy admits a representative household, (20.3)–(20.7) can also be taken to represent the representative household's budget constraint.

Market clearing for the agricultural and service goods take the standard forms

$$c^A(t)L(t) = Y^A(t) \text{ and } c^S(t)L(t) = Y^S(t), \tag{20.8}$$

where the left-hand sides of both equations are multiplied by $L(t)$ to turn per capita consumption levels into total consumptions.

All markets are competitive. Let us choose the price of the manufacturing good at each date as the numeraire, which leaves us with the prices of agricultural goods, $p^A(t)$, and of services, $p^S(t)$, and factor prices $w(t)$ and $r(t)$. The consumption aggregator (20.2) immediately implies that the prices of agricultural and service goods must satisfy

$$\frac{p^A(t)\left(c^A(t) - \gamma^A\right)}{\eta^A} = \frac{c^M(t)}{\eta^M}, \tag{20.9}$$

$$\frac{p^S(t)\left(c^S(t) + \gamma^S\right)}{\eta^S} = \frac{c^M(t)}{\eta^M}. \tag{20.10}$$

Competitive factor markets also imply that

$$w(t) = \frac{\partial B^M F\left(K^M(t), X(t)L^M(t)\right)}{\partial L^M}, \tag{20.11}$$

$$r(t) = \frac{\partial B^M F\left(K^M(t), X(t)L^M(t)\right)}{\partial K^M}, \tag{20.12}$$

where I could have equivalently used the marginal products from other sectors, with identical results.

A competitive equilibrium is defined in the usual manner as paths of sectoral factor demands, $[K^A(t), K^M(t), K^S(t), L^A(t), L^M(t), L^S(t)]_{t=0}^\infty$, that maximize profits given the paths of the total supplies of capital and labor, $[K(t), L(t)]_{t=0}^\infty$, and the paths of prices, $[p^A(t), p^M(t), w(t), r(t)]_{t=0}^\infty$; prices, $[p^A(t), p^M(t), w(t), r(t)]_{t=0}^\infty$, that satisfy (20.9)–(20.12) given $[K^A(t), K^M(t), K^S(t), L^A(t), L^M(t), L^S(t)]_{t=0}^\infty$; and paths of consumption and capital, $[c^A(t), c^M(t), c^S(t), K(t)]_{t=0}^\infty$, that maximize (20.1) subject to (20.3)–(20.7). In addition, suppose that

$$B^A F(K^A(0), X(0)L^A(0)) > \gamma^A L(0), \tag{20.13}$$

so that the economy starts with enough capital and technological know-how to produce more than the subsistence level of agricultural consumption.

An equilibrium is straightforward to characterize in this economy. Because the production functions of all three sectors are identical, the following result obtains immediately.

Proposition 20.1 *Suppose (20.13) holds. Then in any equilibrium, the following conditions are satisfied:*

$$\frac{K^A(t)}{X(t)L^A(t)} = \frac{K^M(t)}{X(t)L^M(t)} = \frac{K^S(t)}{X(t)L^S(t)} = \frac{K(t)}{X(t)L(t)} \equiv k(t) \qquad (20.14)$$

for all t, where the last equality defines k(t) as the aggregate effective capital-labor ratio of the economy, and also

$$p^A(t) = \frac{B^M}{B^A} \quad \text{and} \quad p^S(t) = \frac{B^M}{B^S} \quad \text{for all } t. \qquad (20.15)$$

Proof. See Exercise 20.2. ■

The results in this proposition are intuitive. First, the fact that the production functions are identical implies that the capital-labor ratios in the three sectors must be equalized. Second, given (20.14), the equilibrium price relationships (20.15) follow because the marginal products of capital and labor have to be equalized in all three sectors.

Proposition 20.1 does not make use of the preference side. Incorporating utility maximization on the side of the representative household (in particular, deriving the standard Euler equation for the representative household) and then using (20.9) and (20.10), we obtain the following additional equilibrium conditions.

Proposition 20.2 *Suppose (20.13) holds. Then in any equilibrium, we have*

$$\frac{\dot{c}^M(t)}{c^M(t)} = \frac{1}{\theta}(r(t) - \rho) \qquad (20.16)$$

for all t. Moreover, provided that Assumption 4 holds, household utility is finite, and the transversality condition is satisfied. In addition, we have

$$\frac{B^M(c^A(t) - \gamma^A)}{B^A \eta^A} = \frac{c^M(t)}{\eta^M} \quad \text{and} \quad \frac{B^M(c^S(t) + \gamma^S)}{B^S \eta^S} = \frac{c^M(t)}{\eta^M} \quad \text{for all } t. \qquad (20.17)$$

Proof. See Exercise 20.3. ■

Proposition 20.3 *Suppose that either $\gamma^A > 0$ and/or $\gamma^S > 0$. Then there does not exist an equilibrium in which all sectors grow at the same rate.*

Proof. See Exercise 20.4. ■

This result is not surprising. Since the preferences of the representative household incorporate Engel's Law, the household always wants to change the composition of its consumption, and this is reflected in a change in the composition of production. Nevertheless a "BGP," in which consumption (asymptotically) grows at a constant rate, still exists. I refer to this as a "constant growth path" (CGP) to emphasize that this notion allows for nonbalanced sectoral growth. In a CGP, the consumption aggregate grows at a constant rate, while output and employment in the three sectors grow at different rates. Given the preferences in (20.1), the constant growth rate of consumption also implies that the interest rate must be constant.

Proposition 20.4 *Suppose (20.13) holds. Then in the above-described economy a (unique) CGP exists if and only if*

$$\frac{\gamma^A}{B^A} = \frac{\gamma^S}{B^S}. \tag{20.18}$$

In a CGP $k(t) = k^*$ for all t, and

$$\frac{\dot{c}^A(t)}{c^A(t)} = g \frac{c^A(t) - \gamma^A}{c^A(t)}, \quad \frac{\dot{c}^M(t)}{c^M(t)} = g, \quad \frac{\dot{c}^S(t)}{c^S(t)} = g \frac{c^S(t) + \gamma^S}{c^S(t)}, \tag{20.19}$$

$$\frac{\dot{L}^A(t)}{L^A(t)} = n - g \frac{\gamma^A L(t)/L^A(t)}{B^A X(t) F(k^*, 1)}, \quad \frac{\dot{L}^M(t)}{L^M(t)} = n, \text{ and}$$

$$\frac{\dot{L}^S(t)}{L^S(t)} = n + g \frac{\gamma^S L(t)/L^S(t)}{B^S X(t) F(k^*, 1)} \quad \text{for all } t.$$

Moreover in a CGP the share of national income accruing to capital is constant.

Proof. See Exercise 20.5. ∎

This model therefore delivers a tractable framework for the analysis of structural change that has potential relevance both for the experience of economies at the early stages of development and for understanding the patterns of growth of relatively advanced countries. Engel's Law (augmented with the highly income-elastic demand for services) generates a demand-side force for nonbalanced growth. In particular, as their incomes grow, households wish to spend a greater fraction of their budgets on services and a smaller fraction on food (agricultural goods). This tendency makes an equilibrium with fully balanced growth impossible. Instead, different sectors grow at different rates, and there is reallocation of labor and capital across sectors. Nevertheless Proposition 20.4 shows that under condition (20.18) a CGP exists, and in this equilibrium structural change takes place even though the interest rate and the share of capital in national income are constant. This model therefore delivers many of the features that are useful for thinking about long-run economic development: the equilibrium path can be consistent with the Kaldor facts, and there is a continuous process of structural change whereby the share of agriculture in production and employment declines over the development process and the share of services increases.

On the downside, several potential shortcomings of the current model are worth noting. First, one may argue that the process of structural change in this model falls short of the sweeping changes discussed by Kuznets. Although I focused on the CGP, it is straightforward to incorporate transitional dynamics into the model. Exercise 20.6 shows that if the effective capital-labor ratio starts out below its CGP value of k^* in Proposition 20.4, then there will be additional transitional dynamics in this model complementing the structural changes. Nevertheless even these transitional dynamics fall short of the sweeping structural changes emphasized by Kuznets.

Second, the assumption that all three sectors have the same production function appears restrictive. This assumption can be relaxed to some degree. Exercise 20.7 discusses how this can be done. Perhaps more important is the assumption that investments for all three sectors use only the manufacturing good. This assumption is similar in nature to the assumption that only capital is used to produce capital (investment) goods in Rebelo's (1991) model (recall Chapter 11). Exercise 20.10 shows that if this assumption is relaxed, it is no longer possible to reconcile the Kuznets and the Kaldor facts in the context of this model.

Third, the model presented here is designed to generate a constant share of employment in manufacturing. Although this pattern is broadly consistent with the U.S. experience over the past 150 years, when we look at even earlier stages of development, almost all employment is in agriculture. Thus the early stages of structural change must also involve an increase in the share of employment in manufacturing. Several models in the literature generate this pattern by also introducing land as an additional factor of production. Exercise 20.8 provides an example, and Section 21.2 presents a model incorporating land as a major factor of production in the context of the study of population dynamics.

Finally and most importantly, the condition necessary for a CGP, (20.18), is a rather knife-edge condition. Why should this specific equality between technology and preference parameters hold? In the final analysis, there is no compelling argument that this condition should be satisfied (see Exercise 20.9).

20.2 Nonbalanced Growth: The Supply Side

The previous section showed how the process of structural change can be driven by a generalized form of Engel's Law, that is, by the desires of the households to change the composition of their consumption as they become richer. An alternative approach to why growth may be nonbalanced was first proposed by Baumol's (1967) seminal work. Baumol suggested that uneven growth (or what I am referring to here as "nonbalanced growth") will be a general feature of the growth process because different sectors grow at different rates owing to different rates of technological progress (e.g., technological progress might be faster in manufacturing than in agriculture or services). Although Baumol's original article derived this result only under a variety of special assumptions, the general insight that there might be technological "supply-side" forces pushing the economy toward nonbalanced growth is considerably more general. Here I review some ideas based on Acemoglu and Guerrieri (2008), who emphasize the technological causes of nonbalanced growth. Ultimately, both the rich patterns of structural change during the early stages of development and those we witness in more advanced economies today require models that combine technological and preference factors. Nevertheless, isolating these factors in separate models is both more tractable and conceptually more transparent. For this reason, in this section I focus on technological causes of nonbalanced growth, abstracting from Engel's Law throughout, and only return to the combination of technological and preference factors in Exercise 20.17.

20.2.1 General Insights

At some level, Baumol's theory of nonbalanced growth can be viewed as self-evident—if some sectors have higher rates of technological progress, there must be some nonbalanced elements in equilibrium. My first purpose in this section is to show that there are more subtle and compelling reasons for supply-side nonbalanced growth than those originally emphasized by Baumol. In particular, most growth models, like the Kongsamut, Rebelo, and Xie model presented in Section 20.1, assume that production functions in different sectors are identical. In practice, however, industries differ considerably in terms of their capital intensity and the intensity with which they use other factors (e.g., compare the retail sector to durables manufacturing or transport). In short, different industries have different factor proportions. The main economic point I emphasize in this section is that factor proportion differences across sectors combined with capital deepening lead to nonbalanced economic growth.

I illustrate this point first using a simple but fairly general environment. This environment consists of two sectors, each with a constant returns to scale production function and arbitrary preferences over the goods that are produced in these two sectors. Both sectors employ capital

K and labor L. To highlight that the exact nature of the accumulation process is not essential for the results, I take the path of capital and labor supplies, $[K(t), L(t)]_{t=0}^{\infty}$, as given and assume that $K(t)$ and $L(t)$ are differentiable functions of time. Labor is supplied inelastically.

Preferences are defined over the final output or a consumption aggregator as in (20.2) in the Section 20.1. Whether we use the specification with a consumption aggregator or a formulation with intermediates used competitively in the production of a final good makes no difference to any of the results. With this in mind, let final output be denoted by Y, and assume that it is produced as an aggregate of the output of two sectors, Y_1 and Y_2,

$$Y(t) = F(Y_1(t), Y_2(t)),$$

which again satisfies Assumptions 1 and 2 (see Chapter 2). Sectoral production functions are given by

$$Y_1(t) = A_1(t)G_1(K_1(t), L_1(t)), \text{ and} \tag{20.20}$$

$$Y_2(t) = A_2(t)G_2(K_2(t), L_2(t)), \tag{20.21}$$

where $L_1(t)$, $L_2(t)$, $K_1(t)$, and $K_2(t)$ denote the amount of labor and capital employed in the two sectors, and the functions G_1 and G_2 are also assumed to satisfy the equivalents of Assumptions 1 and 2. The terms $A_1(t)$ and $A_2(t)$ are Hicks-neutral technology terms.

Market clearing for capital and labor implies that

$$K_1(t) + K_2(t) = K(t), \text{ and } L_1(t) + L_2(t) = L(t) \tag{20.22}$$

at each t. Without loss of generality, I ignore capital depreciation.

Let us take the final good as the numeraire in every period and denote the prices of Y_1 and Y_2 by p_1 and p_2, and wage and rental rate of capital (interest rate) by w and r, respectively. Product and factor markets are competitive, so that product and factor prices satisfy

$$\frac{p_1(t)}{p_2(t)} = \frac{\partial F(Y_1(t), Y_2(t))/\partial Y_1}{\partial F(Y_1(t), Y_2(t))/\partial Y_2}, \tag{20.23}$$

and

$$w(t) = p_1(t)\frac{\partial A_1(t)G_1(K_1(t), L_1(t))}{\partial L_1} = p_2(t)\frac{\partial A_2(t)G_2(K_2(t), L_2(t))}{\partial L_2}$$

$$r(t) = p_1(t)\frac{\partial A_1(t)G_1(K_1(t), L_1(t))}{\partial K_1} = p_2(t)\frac{\partial A_2(t)G_2(K_2(t), L_2(t))}{\partial K_2}. \tag{20.24}$$

An equilibrium, given factor supply paths, $[K(t), L(t)]_{t=0}^{\infty}$, is a path of product and factor prices, $[p_1(t), p_2(t), w(t), r(t)]_{t=0}^{\infty}$ and factor allocations, $[K_1(t), K_2(t), L_1(t), L_2(t)]_{t=0}^{\infty}$, such that (20.22), (20.23) and (20.24) are satisfied.

Let the shares of capital in the two sectors be defined as

$$\sigma_1(t) \equiv \frac{r(t)K_1(t)}{p_1(t)Y_1(t)}, \text{ and } \sigma_2(t) \equiv \frac{r(t)K_2(t)}{p_2(t)Y_2(t)}. \tag{20.25}$$

There is *capital deepening* at time t if $\dot{K}(t)/K(t) > \dot{L}(t)/L(t)$. There are *factor proportion differences* at time t if $\sigma_1(t) \neq \sigma_2(t)$. And finally, technological progress is *balanced* at time t

if $\dot{A}_1(t)/A_1(t) = \dot{A}_2(t)/A_2(t)$. Notice that factor proportion differences, that is, $\sigma_1(t) \neq \sigma_2(t)$, refers to the equilibrium factor proportions in the two sectors at time t. It does not necessarily mean that these will not be equal at some future date. The following proposition shows the supply-side forces leading to structural change.

Proposition 20.5 *Suppose that at time t there are factor proportion differences between the two sectors in the above model, technological progress is balanced, and there is capital deepening. Then growth is not balanced, that is, $\dot{Y}_1(t)/Y_1(t) \neq \dot{Y}_2(t)/Y_2(t)$.*

Proof. First, define the capital-labor ratio in the two sectors as

$$k_1(t) \equiv \frac{K_1(t)}{L_1(t)}, \text{ and } k_2(t) \equiv \frac{K_2(t)}{L_2(t)},$$

and the per capita production functions (without the Hicks-neutral technology terms) as

$$g_1\left(k_1(t)\right) \equiv \frac{G_1(K_1(t), L_1(t))}{L_1(t)} \text{ and } g_2\left(k_2(t)\right) \equiv \frac{G_2(K_2(t), L_2(t))}{L_2(t)}. \tag{20.26}$$

Since G_1 and G_2 are twice differentiable by assumption, so are g_1 and g_2. Denote their first and second derivatives by g_1', g_2', g_1'', and g_2''.

Differentiating the production functions for the two sectors yields

$$\frac{\dot{Y}_1(t)}{Y_1(t)} = \frac{\dot{A}_1(t)}{A_1(t)} + \sigma_1(t)\frac{\dot{K}_1(t)}{K_1(t)} + \left(1 - \sigma_1(t)\right)\frac{\dot{L}_1(t)}{L_1(t)},$$

$$\frac{\dot{Y}_2(t)}{Y_2(t)} = \frac{\dot{A}_2(t)}{A_2(t)} + \sigma_2(t)\frac{\dot{K}_2(t)}{K_2(t)} + \left(1 - \sigma_2(t)\right)\frac{\dot{L}_2(t)}{L_2(t)}.$$

To simplify the notation, I drop the time arguments for the remainder of this proof.

Suppose, to obtain a contradiction, that $\dot{Y}_1/Y_1 = \dot{Y}_2/Y_2$. Since F exhibits constant returns to scale, $\dot{Y}_1/Y_1 = \dot{Y}_2/Y_2$ together with (20.23) implies that

$$\frac{\dot{p}_1}{p_1} = \frac{\dot{p}_2}{p_2} = 0. \tag{20.27}$$

Given the definitions in (20.26), equation (20.24) gives the following conditions characterizing the equilibrium interest rate and wage:

$$r = p_1 A_1 g_1'(k_1) = p_2 A_2 g_2'(k_2), \tag{20.28}$$

$$w = p_1 A_1 (g_1(k_1) - g_1'(k_1)k_1) = p_2 A_2 (g_2(k_2) - g_2'(k_2)k_2). \tag{20.29}$$

Differentiating the interest rate condition (20.28) with respect to time and using (20.27) yields

$$\frac{\dot{A}_1}{A_1} + \varepsilon_{g_1'}\frac{\dot{k}_1}{k_1} = \frac{\dot{A}_2}{A_2} + \varepsilon_{g_2'}\frac{\dot{k}_2}{k_2},$$

where

$$\varepsilon_{g_1'} \equiv \frac{g_1''(k_1)k_1}{g_1'(k_1)}, \text{ and } \varepsilon_{g_2'} \equiv \frac{g_2''(k_2)k_2}{g_2'(k_2)}.$$

Since $\dot{A}_1/A_1 = \dot{A}_2/A_2$,

$$\varepsilon_{g_1'}\frac{\dot{k}_1}{k_1} = \varepsilon_{g_2'}\frac{\dot{k}_2}{k_2}. \tag{20.30}$$

Differentiating the wage condition (20.29) with respect to time and using (20.27) and some algebra gives

$$\frac{\dot{A}_1}{A_1} - \frac{\sigma_1}{1-\sigma_1}\varepsilon_{g_1'}\frac{\dot{k}_1}{k_1} = \frac{\dot{A}_2}{A_2} - \frac{\sigma_2}{1-\sigma_2}\varepsilon_{g_2'}\frac{\dot{k}_2}{k_2}.$$

Since $\dot{A}_1/A_1 = \dot{A}_2/A_2$ and $\sigma_1 \neq \sigma_2$, this equation is inconsistent with (20.30), yielding a contradiction and proving the claim. ∎

The intuition for this result is straightforward. Suppose that there is capital deepening and that, for concreteness, sector 2 is more capital intensive ($\sigma_1 < \sigma_2$). If both capital and labor were allocated to the two sectors at constant proportions over time, the more capital-intensive sector, sector 2, would grow faster than sector 1. In equilibrium, the faster growth in sector 2 would change equilibrium prices, and the decline in the relative price of sector 2 would cause some of the labor and capital to be reallocated to sector 1. However this reallocation could not entirely offset the greater increase in the output of sector 2, since, if it did, the relative price change that stimulated the reallocation in the first place would not occur. Consequently equilibrium growth must be nonbalanced.

Proposition 20.5 is related to the well-known Rybczynski's Theorem in international trade. Rybczynski's Theorem states that in an open economy within the cone of diversification (where factor prices do not depend on factor endowments), changes in factor endowments are absorbed by changes in the sectoral output mix. Proposition 20.5 can be viewed both as a closed-economy analogue and as a generalization of Rybczynski's Theorem; it shows that changes in factor endowments (capital deepening) is absorbed by faster growth in one sector than the other, even though relative prices of goods and factors change in response to the change in factor endowments.

20.2.2 Balanced Growth and Kuznets Facts

The Section 20.2.1 provided general insights about how technological factors can lead to nonbalanced growth. To obtain a general result on the implications of capital deepening and factor proportion differences across sectors on nonbalanced growth, Proposition 20.5 was stated for a given (arbitrary) path of capital and labor supplies, $[K(t), L(t)]_{t=0}^{\infty}$. However, without endogenizing the path of capital accumulation (and specifying the pattern of population growth), we cannot address whether a model relying on technological factors can also provide a useful framework for thinking about the Kuznets facts without significantly deviating from the balanced growth patterns exhibited by many relatively developed economies.

For this purpose, I now specialize the environment of Section 20.2.1 by incorporating specific preferences and production functions and then provide a full characterization of a simpler economy. The economy is again in infinite horizon, and population grows at the exogenous rate $n > 0$. Let us also assume that the economy admits a representative household, with standard preferences given by (20.1), that also supplies labor inelastically. Proposition 20.5 emphasized the importance of capital deepening, which now results from exogenous technological progress.

Instead of a general production function for the final good as in Section 20.2.1, I now assume that the unique final good is produced with a CES aggregator,

$$Y(t) = \left[\gamma Y_1(t)^{\frac{\varepsilon-1}{\varepsilon}} + (1-\gamma) Y_2(t)^{\frac{\varepsilon-1}{\varepsilon}} \right]^{\frac{\varepsilon}{\varepsilon-1}}, \tag{20.31}$$

where $\varepsilon \in [0, \infty)$ is the elasticity of substitution between the two intermediates, and $\gamma \in (0, 1)$ determines the relative importance of the two goods in aggregate production. Let us ignore capital depreciation again and also assume that the final good is distributed between consumption and investment,

$$\dot{K}(t) + L(t)c(t) \leq Y(t), \tag{20.32}$$

where $c(t)$ is consumption per capita.

The two intermediates, Y_1 and Y_2, are produced competitively with aggregate production functions

$$Y_1(t) = A_1(t)K_1(t)^{\alpha_1}L_1(t)^{1-\alpha_1} \text{ and } Y_2(t) = A_2(t)K_2(t)^{\alpha_2}L_2(t)^{1-\alpha_2}. \tag{20.33}$$

Throughout I impose that

$$\alpha_1 < \alpha_2, \tag{20.34}$$

which implies that sector 1 is less capital intensive than sector 2. This assumption is without loss of generality, since in the case in which $\alpha_1 = \alpha_2$, there are no supply-side effects and thus the issues I am concerned with in this section do not arise.

In (20.33), A_1 and A_2 correspond to Hicks-neutral technology terms that grow at exogenous and potentially different rates given by

$$\frac{\dot{A}_1(t)}{A_1(t)} = a_1 > 0 \text{ and } \frac{\dot{A}_2(t)}{A_2(t)} = a_2 > 0. \tag{20.35}$$

Labor and capital market clearing again require that at each t,

$$L_1(t) + L_2(t) = L(t) \text{ and} \tag{20.36}$$

$$K_1(t) + K_2(t) = K(t). \tag{20.37}$$

Let us also denote the wage and the interest rate (the rental rate of capital) by $w(t)$ and $r(t)$, respectively, and the prices of the two intermediate goods by $p_1(t)$ and $p_2(t)$. We again normalize the price of the final good to 1 at each instant. An equilibrium is defined in the usual manner, as paths of labor and capital allocations and prices, such that $[K_1(t), K_2(t), L_1(t), L_2(t)]_{t=0}^{\infty}$ maximize intermediate sector profits given the prices, $[w(t), r(t), p_1(t), p_2(t)]_{t=0}^{\infty}$, and the aggregate capital and labor supplies, $[K(t), L(t)]_{t=0}^{\infty}$; intermediate and factor markets clear at the prices $[w(t), r(t), p_1(t), p_2(t)]_{t=0}^{\infty}$; and $[K(t), c(t)]_{t=0}^{\infty}$ maximize utility of the representative household given the prices $[w(t), r(t), p_1(t), p_2(t)]_{t=0}^{\infty}$.

It is useful to break the characterization of equilibrium in the two pieces: *static* and *dynamic*. The static part takes the state variables of the economy, which are the capital stock, the labor supply, and the technology (K, L, A_1, and A_2) as given and determines the allocation of capital and labor across sectors and the equilibrium factor and intermediate prices. The dynamic part of the equilibrium determines the evolution of the endogenous state variable K.

The choice of numeraire implies that

$$1 = \left[\gamma^{\varepsilon} p_1(t)^{1-\varepsilon} + (1-\gamma)^{\varepsilon} p_2(t)^{1-\varepsilon} \right]^{\frac{1}{1-\varepsilon}}$$

for all t, and profit maximization of the final good sector implies that

$$p_1(t) = \gamma \left(\frac{Y_1(t)}{Y(t)} \right)^{-\frac{1}{\varepsilon}} \quad \text{and} \quad p_2(t) = (1-\gamma) \left(\frac{Y_2(t)}{Y(t)} \right)^{-\frac{1}{\varepsilon}}. \qquad (20.38)$$

Given this specification (and the fact that capital does not depreciate), the equilibrium allocation of resources equates the marginal product of capital and labor into two sectors. The following equations give these equilibrium conditions and also provide expressions for the factor prices (see Exercise 20.12). The equilibrium conditions are

$$\gamma \left(1-\alpha_1\right) \left(\frac{Y(t)}{Y_1(t)} \right)^{\frac{1}{\varepsilon}} \frac{Y_1(t)}{L_1(t)} = (1-\gamma) \left(1-\alpha_2\right) \left(\frac{Y(t)}{Y_2(t)} \right)^{\frac{1}{\varepsilon}} \frac{Y_2(t)}{L_2(t)} \quad \text{and} \qquad (20.39)$$

$$\gamma \alpha_1 \left(\frac{Y(t)}{Y_1(t)} \right)^{\frac{1}{\varepsilon}} \frac{Y_1(t)}{K_1(t)} = (1-\gamma) \alpha_2 \left(\frac{Y(t)}{Y_2(t)} \right)^{\frac{1}{\varepsilon}} \frac{Y_2(t)}{K_2(t)}, \qquad (20.40)$$

while the factor prices can be expressed as

$$w(t) = \gamma \left(1-\alpha_1\right) \left(\frac{Y(t)}{Y_1(t)} \right)^{\frac{1}{\varepsilon}} \frac{Y_1(t)}{L_1(t)} \quad \text{and} \qquad (20.41)$$

$$r(t) = \gamma \alpha_1 \left(\frac{Y(t)}{Y_1(t)} \right)^{\frac{1}{\varepsilon}} \frac{Y_1(t)}{K_1(t)}. \qquad (20.42)$$

The key to the characterization of the static equilibrium is to determine the fraction of capital and labor employed in the two sectors. Let us define $\kappa(t) \equiv K_1(t)/K(t)$ and $\lambda(t) \equiv L_1(t)/L(t)$. Combining (20.36), (20.37), (20.39), and (20.40) yields

$$\kappa(t) = \left[1 + \frac{\alpha_2}{\alpha_1} \left(\frac{1-\gamma}{\gamma} \right) \left(\frac{Y_1(t)}{Y_2(t)} \right)^{\frac{1-\varepsilon}{\varepsilon}} \right]^{-1} \quad \text{and} \qquad (20.43)$$

$$\lambda(t) = \left[1 + \frac{\alpha_1}{\alpha_2} \left(\frac{1-\alpha_2}{1-\alpha_1} \right) \left(\frac{1-\kappa(t)}{\kappa(t)} \right) \right]^{-1}. \qquad (20.44)$$

Equation (20.44) makes it clear that the share of labor in sector 1, λ, is monotonically increasing in the share of capital in sector 1, κ. Thus in equilibrium capital and labor are reallocated to the same sector. The key feature of the structure of the equilibrium is how the allocation of capital and labor depends on the aggregate amount of capital and labor available in the economy. The following proposition answers this question.

Proposition 20.6 *In equilibrium the following conditions hold:*

$$\frac{d \log \kappa(t)}{d \log K(t)} = -\frac{d \log \kappa(t)}{d \log L(t)} = \frac{(1-\varepsilon)\left(\alpha_2 - \alpha_1\right)(1-\kappa(t))}{1 + (1-\varepsilon)\left(\alpha_2 - \alpha_1\right)(\kappa(t) - \lambda(t))} > 0 \qquad (20.45)$$

if and only if $(\alpha_2 - \alpha_1)(1 - \varepsilon) > 0$, *and*

$$\frac{d \log \kappa(t)}{d \log A_2(t)} = -\frac{d \log \kappa(t)}{d \log A_1(t)} = \frac{(1 - \varepsilon)(1 - \kappa(t))}{1 + (1 - \varepsilon)(\alpha_2 - \alpha_1)(\kappa(t) - \lambda(t))} > 0 \quad (20.46)$$

if and only if $\varepsilon < 1$.

Proof.   See Exercise 20.13.   ∎

Equation (20.45) states that when the elasticity of substitution between sectors, ε, is less than 1, the fraction of capital allocated to the capital-intensive sector declines in the stock of capital (and conversely, when $\varepsilon > 1$, this fraction is increasing in the stock of capital). Intuitively, if K increases and κ remains constant, then the capital-intensive sector, sector 2, will grow by more than sector 1. Equilibrium prices given in (20.38) then imply that when $\varepsilon < 1$, the relative price of the capital-intensive sector will fall more than proportionately, inducing a greater fraction of capital to be allocated to the less capital-intensive sector 1. The intuition for the converse result when $\varepsilon > 1$ is similar.

Moreover (20.46) implies that when the elasticity of substitution ε is less than 1, an improvement in the technology of a sector causes the share of capital going to that sector to fall. The intuition is again the same: when $\varepsilon < 1$, increased production in a sector causes a more than proportional decline in its relative price, inducing a reallocation of capital away from it to the other sector (again the converse results and intuition apply when $\varepsilon > 1$).

Combining (20.41) and (20.42), we also obtain relative factor prices as

$$\frac{w(t)}{r(t)} = \frac{1 - \alpha_1}{\alpha_1} \left(\frac{\kappa(t) K(t)}{\lambda(t) L(t)} \right), \quad (20.47)$$

and the capital share in the economy as

$$\sigma_K(t) \equiv \frac{r(t) K(t)}{Y(t)} = \gamma \alpha_1 \left(\frac{Y_1(t)}{Y(t)} \right)^{\frac{\varepsilon - 1}{\varepsilon}} \kappa(t)^{-1}. \quad (20.48)$$

Proposition 20.7   *In equilibrium the following conditions hold:*

$$\frac{d \log (w(t)/r(t))}{d \log K(t)} = -\frac{d \log (w(t)/r(t))}{d \log L(t)} = \frac{1}{1 + (1 - \varepsilon)(\alpha_2 - \alpha_1)(\kappa(t) - \lambda(t))} > 0,$$

$$(20.49)$$

$$\frac{d \log (w(t)/r(t))}{d \log A_2(t)} = -\frac{d \log (w(t)/r(t))}{d \log A_1(t)} = -\frac{(1 - \varepsilon)(\kappa(t) - \lambda(t))}{1 + (1 - \varepsilon)(\alpha_2 - \alpha_1)(\kappa(t) - \lambda(t))} < 0$$

$$(20.50)$$

if and only if $(\alpha_2 - \alpha_1)(1 - \varepsilon) > 0$,

$$\frac{d \log \sigma_K(t)}{d \log K(t)} < 0 \quad (20.51)$$

if and only if $\varepsilon < 1$, *and*

$$\frac{d \log \sigma_K(t)}{d \log A_2(t)} = -\frac{d \log \sigma_K(t)}{d \log A_1(t)} < 0 \quad (20.52)$$

if and only if $(\alpha_2 - \alpha_1)(1 - \varepsilon) > 0$.

Proof. The results in (20.49) and (20.51) follow from differentiating (20.47) and from Proposition 20.6. To prove the remaining claims, let me suppress time arguments and write

$$\left(\frac{Y_1}{Y}\right)^{\frac{\varepsilon-1}{\varepsilon}} = \left[\gamma + (1-\gamma)\left(\frac{Y_1}{Y_2}\right)^{\frac{1-\varepsilon}{\varepsilon}}\right]^{-1} = \gamma^{-1}\left(1 + \frac{\alpha_1}{\alpha_2}\left(\frac{1}{\kappa} - 1\right)\right)^{-1}.$$

Using the results of Proposition 20.6 and the definition of σ_K from (20.48), we have

$$\frac{d \log \sigma_K}{d \log K} = -\Omega \frac{1 - \sigma_K}{\sigma_K} \frac{\alpha_1}{\alpha_2} \frac{(1-\varepsilon)(\alpha_2 - \alpha_1)(1-\kappa)/\kappa}{1 + (1-\varepsilon)(\alpha_2 - \alpha_1)(\kappa - \lambda)}, \quad \text{and} \quad (20.53)$$

$$\frac{d \log \sigma_K}{d \log A_2} = -\frac{d \log \sigma_K}{d \log A_1} = \Omega \frac{1 - \sigma_K}{\sigma_K} \frac{\alpha_1}{\alpha_2} \frac{(1-\varepsilon)(1-\kappa)/\kappa}{1 + (1-\varepsilon)(\alpha_2 - \alpha_1)(\kappa - \lambda)}, \quad (20.54)$$

where

$$\Omega \equiv \left[\left(1 + \frac{\alpha_1}{\alpha_2}\left(\frac{1}{\kappa} - 1\right)\right)^{-1} - \left(\frac{1-\alpha_1}{1-\alpha_2} + \frac{\alpha_1}{\alpha_2}\left(\frac{1}{\kappa} - 1\right)\right)^{-1}\right].$$

Clearly, $\Omega > 0$ if and only if $\alpha_1 < \alpha_2$, which is satisfied in view of (20.34). Equations (20.53) and (20.54) then imply (20.51) and (20.52). ∎

The most important result in this proposition is (20.51), which links the equilibrium relationship between the capital share in national income and the capital stock to the elasticity of substitution. Since a negative relationship between the share of capital in national income and the capital stock is equivalent to capital and labor being gross complements in the aggregate, this result also implies that the elasticity of substitution between capital and labor is less than 1 if and only if ε is less than 1. Recall from the discussion in Section 15.6 in Chapter 15 that various empirical approaches suggest that the elasticity of substitution between capital and labor is less than 1, so in what follows, the case where $\varepsilon < 1$ is more relevant.

The intuition for Proposition 20.7 is informative about the workings of the model. Consistent with the discussion of Proposition 20.5 above, when $\varepsilon < 1$, an increase in the capital stock of the economy causes the output of the more capital-intensive sector, sector 2, to increase relative to the output in the less capital-intensive sector (even though the share of capital allocated to the less capital-intensive sector increases as shown in (20.45)). This then increases the production of the more capital-intensive sector and reduces the relative reward to capital (and the share of capital in national income). The converse result applies when $\varepsilon > 1$.

Recall also from Section 15.2 in Chapter 15 that when $\varepsilon < 1$, (20.52) in Proposition 20.7 implies that an increase in A_1 is capital biased and an increase in A_2 is labor biased. The intuition for why an increase in the productivity of the sector that is intensive in capital is biased toward labor (and vice versa) is again similar: when the elasticity of substitution between the two sectors, ε, is less than 1, an increase in the output of a sector (this time driven by a change in technology) decreases its price more than proportionately, thus reducing the relative compensation of the factor used more intensively in that sector. When $\varepsilon > 1$, the converse pattern applies, and an increase in A_2 is capital biased, while an increase in A_1 is labor biased.

I next turn to the characterization of the dynamic equilibrium path of this economy. The consumption Euler equation from the maximization of (20.1) takes the familiar form

$$\frac{\dot{c}(t)}{c(t)} = \frac{1}{\theta}(r(t) - \rho). \quad (20.55)$$

Since the only asset of the representative household in this economy is capital, the transversality condition takes the standard form

$$\lim_{t \to \infty} \left[K(t) \exp \left(- \int_0^t r(\tau) \, d\tau \right) = 0 \right],$$ (20.56)

which, together with the Euler equation (20.55) and the resource constraint (20.32), determines the dynamic behavior of consumption per capita c and capital stock K.

A dynamic equilibrium is given by paths of wages, interest rates, labor, and capital allocation decisions, $[w(t), r(t), \lambda(t), \kappa(t)]_{t=0}^{\infty}$, satisfying (20.41), (20.39), (20.42), (20.40), (20.43), and (20.44), and of consumption per capita and capital stock, $[c(t), K(t)]_{t=0}^{\infty}$, satisfying (20.55) and (20.56).

Let us also introduce the following notation for growth rates of the key objects in this economy:

$$\frac{\dot{L}_s(t)}{L_s(t)} \equiv n_s(t), \quad \frac{\dot{K}_s(t)}{K_s(t)} \equiv z_s(t), \quad \frac{\dot{Y}_s(t)}{Y_s(t)} \equiv g_s(t)$$

for $s = 1, 2$, and

$$\frac{\dot{K}(t)}{K(t)} \equiv z(t), \quad \frac{\dot{Y}(t)}{Y(t)} \equiv g(t).$$

When they exist, we can also define the corresponding (limiting) asymptotic growth rates as

$$n_s^* = \lim_{t \to \infty} n_s(t), \ z_s^* = \lim_{t \to \infty} z_s(t), \ \text{and} \ g_s^* = \lim_{t \to \infty} g_s(t),$$

for $s = 1, 2$. Similarly denote the asymptotic capital and labor allocation decisions by an asterisk ($*$),

$$\kappa^* = \lim_{t \to \infty} \kappa(t), \ \text{and} \ \lambda^* = \lim_{t \to \infty} \lambda(t).$$

With this terminology, the following useful proposition can be established.

Proposition 20.8

1. If $\varepsilon < 1$, then $n_1(t) \gtreqqless n_2(t) \Leftrightarrow z_1(t) \gtreqqless z_2(t) \Leftrightarrow g_1(t) \lesseqqgtr g_2(t)$.
2. If $\varepsilon > 1$, then $n_1(t) \gtreqqless n_2(t) \Leftrightarrow z_1(t) \gtreqqless z_2(t) \Leftrightarrow g_1(t) \gtreqqless g_2(t)$.

Proof. Omitting time arguments and differentiating (20.39) with respect to time,

$$\frac{1}{\varepsilon} g + \frac{\varepsilon - 1}{\varepsilon} g_1 - n_1 = \frac{1}{\varepsilon} g + \frac{\varepsilon - 1}{\varepsilon} g_2 - n_2,$$ (20.57)

which implies that $n_1 - n_2 = (\varepsilon - 1) (g_1 - g_2) / \varepsilon$ and establishes the first part of the proposition. Similarly differentiating (20.40) yields

$$\frac{1}{\varepsilon} g + \frac{\varepsilon - 1}{\varepsilon} g_1 - z_1 = \frac{1}{\varepsilon} g + \frac{\varepsilon - 1}{\varepsilon} g_2 - z_2$$ (20.58)

and establishes the second part of the result. ∎

This proposition establishes the straightforward, but at first counterintuitive, result that when the elasticity of substitution between the two sectors is less than 1, the equilibrium growth rate of the capital stock and labor force in the sector that is growing faster must be *less* than in the other sector. When the elasticity of substitution is greater than 1, the converse result obtains.

To see the intuition, note that terms of trade (relative prices) shift in favor of the more slowly growing sector. When the elasticity of substitution is less than 1, this change in relative prices is more than proportional with the change in quantities, and this encourages more of the factors to be allocated to the more slowly growing sector.

Proposition 20.9 *Suppose the asymptotic growth rates g_1^* and g_2^* exist. If $\varepsilon < 1$, then $g^* = \min\{g_1^*, g_2^*\}$. If $\varepsilon > 1$, then $g^* = \max\{g_1^*, g_2^*\}$.*

Proof. Differentiating the production function for the final good (20.31) yields

$$g(t) = \frac{\gamma Y_1(t)^{\frac{\varepsilon-1}{\varepsilon}} g_1(t) + (1-\gamma) Y_2(t)^{\frac{\varepsilon-1}{\varepsilon}} g_2(t)}{\gamma Y_1(t)^{\frac{\varepsilon-1}{\varepsilon}} + (1-\gamma) Y_2(t)^{\frac{\varepsilon-1}{\varepsilon}}}. \tag{20.59}$$

This equation, combined with $\varepsilon < 1$, implies that as $t \to \infty$, $g^* = \min\{g_1^*, g_2^*\}$. Similarly, combined with $\varepsilon > 1$, it implies that as $t \to \infty$, $g^* = \max\{g_1^*, g_2^*\}$. ■

Consequently, when the elasticity of substitution is less than 1, the asymptotic growth rate of aggregate output is determined by the sector that is growing more slowly, and the converse applies when $\varepsilon > 1$.

As in the previous section, let us focus on a CGP, again defined as an equilibrium path where the asymptotic growth rate of consumption per capita exists and is constant, so that $\lim_{t \to \infty} \dot{c}(t)/c(t) = g_c^*$. Let us also define the growth rate of total consumption as $\dot{C}(t)/C(t) \equiv g_C^* = g_c^* + n$, since it will be slightly more convenient to work with the growth rate of total consumption than the growth rate of consumption per capita. From the Euler equation (20.55), the fact that the growth rate of consumption or consumption per capita are asymptotically constant implies that the interest rate must also be asymptotically constant, that is, $\lim_{t \to \infty} \dot{r}(t) = 0$.

To establish the existence of a CGP, I impose the following parameter restriction:

$$\rho - n \geq (1-\theta) \max\left\{\frac{a_1}{1-\alpha_1}, \frac{a_2}{1-\alpha_2}\right\}, \tag{20.60}$$

which ensures that household utility is finite and that the transversality condition (20.56) holds. Terms of the form $a_1/(1-\alpha_1)$ or $a_2/(1-\alpha_2)$ appear naturally in equilibrium, since they capture the augmented rate of technological progress. In particular, recall that associated with the technological progress, there is also endogenous capital deepening in each sector. The overall effect on labor productivity (and output growth) depends on the rate of technological progress augmented with the rate of capital deepening. The terms $a_1/(1-\alpha_1)$ or $a_2/(1-\alpha_2)$ capture this augmented effect, since a higher α_s corresponds to a greater share of capital in sector $s = 1, 2$, and thus to a higher rate of augmented technological progress for a given rate of Hicks-neutral technological change. In this light, condition (20.60) can be understood as implying that the augmented rate of technological progress should be low enough to satisfy the transversality condition (20.56).

The next proposition characterizes the CGP. Rather than presenting the general case, it is useful to focus on parameter values such that

$$\text{either } a_1/(1-\alpha_1) < a_2/(1-\alpha_2) \text{ and } \varepsilon < 1,$$
$$\text{or } a_1/(1-\alpha_1) > a_2/(1-\alpha_2) \text{ and } \varepsilon > 1. \tag{20.61}$$

This condition will make it easier to describe the CGP. In particular, it ensures that sector 1 is the *asymptotically dominant* sector, either because it has a slower rate of technological progress and $\varepsilon < 1$, or it has more rapid technological progress and $\varepsilon > 1$. Notice also that, for the reasons noted above, the appropriate comparison is not between a_1 and a_2 but between $a_1/(1 - \alpha_1)$ and $a_2/(1 - \alpha_2)$. Exercise 20.14 generalizes the results in this proposition to the case in which the converse of condition (20.61) holds.

Proposition 20.10 *Suppose that (20.34), (20.60), and (20.61) hold. Then there exists a unique CGP such that*

$$g^* = g_C^* = g_1^* = z_1^* = n + g_c^* = n + \frac{1}{1 - \alpha_1} a_1, \tag{20.62}$$

$$z_2^* = n - (1 - \varepsilon)a_2 + (1 + (1 - \varepsilon)(1 - \alpha_2)) \frac{a_1}{1 - \alpha_1} < g^*, \tag{20.63}$$

$$g_2^* = n + \varepsilon a_2 + (1 - \varepsilon(1 - \alpha_2)) \frac{a_1}{1 - \alpha_1} > g^*, \tag{20.64}$$

$$n_1^* = n, \text{ and } n_2^* = n - (1 - \varepsilon)\left(1 - \alpha_2\right)\left(\frac{a_2}{1 - \alpha_2} - \frac{a_1}{1 - \alpha_1}\right) < n_1^*. \tag{20.65}$$

Proof. Suppose first that $g_2^* \geq g_1^* > 0$ and $\varepsilon > 1$. Then (20.43) and (20.44) imply that $\lambda^* = \kappa^* = 1$. In view of this, Proposition 20.9 implies $g^* = g_1^*$. This condition, together with (20.33), (20.57), and (20.58), solves uniquely for $n_1^*, n_2^*, z_1^*, z_2^*, g_1^*$, and g_2^* as given in (20.62), (20.63), (20.64), and (20.65). Note that this solution is consistent with $g_2^* > g_1^* > 0$, since conditions (20.34) and (20.60) imply that $g_2^* > g_1^*$ and $g_1^* > 0$. Finally, $C(t) \equiv c(t)L(t) \leq Y(t)$, (20.32), and (20.56) imply that the consumption growth rate g_C^* is equal to the growth rate of output g^*. To see why, suppose that this last claim is not correct; then since $C(t)/Y(t) \to 0$ as $t \to \infty$, the resource constraint (20.32) would imply that asymptotically $\dot{K}(t) = Y(t)$. Integrating this equation, we obtain $K(t) \to \int_0^t Y(s) \, ds$, and since Y is growing exponentially, this implies that the capital stock grows more than exponentially, violating the transversality condition (20.56).

Next, we can show that the solution with $z_1^*, z_2^*, m_1^*, m_2^*, g_1^*$, and g_2^* satisfies the transversality condition (20.56). In particular, (20.56) is satisfied if

$$\lim_{t \to \infty} \frac{\dot{K}(t)}{K(t)} < r^*, \tag{20.66}$$

where r^* is the constant asymptotic interest rate. Since from the Euler equation (20.55) $r^* = \theta g^* + \rho$, (20.66) is satisfied when $g^*(1 - \theta) < \rho$. Condition (20.60) ensures that this is the case with $g^* = n + a_1/(1 - \alpha_1)$. The argument for the case in which $g_1^* \geq g_2^* > 0$ and $\varepsilon > 1$ is similar and is left to Exercise 20.14.

To complete the proof, we need to establish that in all CGPs $g_2^* \geq g_1^* > 0$ when $\varepsilon < 1$ ($g_1^* \geq g_2^* > 0$ when $\varepsilon > 1$ is again left to Exercise 20.14). Let us separately derive a contradiction for two configurations: (1) $g_1^* \geq g_2^*$, or (2) $g_2^* \geq g_1^*$ but $g_1^* \leq 0$.

1. Suppose $g_1^* \geq g_2^*$ and $\varepsilon < 1$. Then, following the same reasoning as above, the unique solution to the equilibrium conditions (20.33), (20.57), and (20.58) when $\varepsilon < 1$ is

$$g^* = g_C^* = g_2^* = z_2^* = n + \frac{a_2}{1 - \alpha_2},$$

$$z_1^* = n - (1 - \varepsilon)a_1 + (1 + (1 - \varepsilon)(1 - \alpha_1)) \frac{a_1}{1 - \alpha_1},$$

$$g_1^* = n + \varepsilon a_1 + (1 - \varepsilon(1 - \alpha_1)) \frac{a_1}{1 - \alpha_1}, \tag{20.67}$$

and also similar expressions for n_1^* and n_2^*. Combining these equations implies that $g_1^* < g_2^*$, which contradicts the hypothesis $g_1^* \geq g_2^* > 0$. The argument for $\varepsilon > 1$ is analogous.

2. Suppose $g_2^* \geq g_1^*$ and $\varepsilon < 1$. Then the same steps as above imply that there is a unique solution to equilibrium conditions (20.33), (20.57), and (20.58), which is given by (20.62)–(20.65). But now (20.62) directly contradicts $g_1^* \leq 0$. Finally, suppose $g_2^* \geq g_1^*$ and $\varepsilon > 1$. Then the unique solution is given by the equations in part 1 above. But in this case, (20.67) contradicts the hypothesis that $g_1^* \leq 0$, completing the proof.   ∎

Several implications of this proposition are worth emphasizing. First, as long as $a_1/(1 - \alpha_1) \neq a_2/(1 - \alpha_2)$, growth is nonbalanced. The intuition for this result is the same as that for Proposition 20.5. Suppose, for concreteness, that $\varepsilon < 1$ and $a_1/(1 - \alpha_1) < a_2/(1 - \alpha_2)$ (which would be the case, e.g., if $a_1 \approx a_2$). Then differential capital intensities in the two sectors, combined with capital deepening in the economy (which itself results from technological progress), ensures faster growth in the more capital-intensive sector, sector 2. Intuitively, if capital were allocated proportionately to the two sectors, sector 2 would grow faster. Because of the changes in prices, capital and labor would be reallocated in favor of the less capital-intensive sector, and relative employment in sector 1 would increase. However, crucially, this reallocation would not be enough to fully offset the faster growth of real output in the more capital-intensive sector. This result also highlights that the assumption of balanced technological progress in Proposition 20.5 (which, in this context, corresponds to $a_1 = a_2$) was not necessary for the result there, but we simply needed to rule out the knife-edge case where the relative rates of technological progress between the two sectors were exactly in the right proportion to ensure balanced growth (in this context, $a_1/(1 - \alpha_1) = a_2/(1 - \alpha_2)$).

Second, the CGP growth rates are relatively simple, especially because I restricted attention to the set of parameters that ensure that sector 1 is the asymptotically dominant sector (see (20.61)). If in addition $\varepsilon < 1$, the model leads to the richest set of dynamics, where the more slowly growing sector determines the long-run growth rate of the economy, while the more rapidly growing sector continually sheds capital and labor but does so at exactly the rate to ensure that it still grows faster than the rest of the economy.

Third, in the CGP the share of capital and labor allocated to one of the sectors tends to 1 (e.g., when sector 1 is the asymptotically dominant sector, $\lambda^* = \kappa^* = 1$). Nevertheless, at all points in time both sectors produce positive amounts, so this limit point is never reached. In fact, at all times both sectors grow at rates greater than the rate of population growth in the economy. Moreover when $\varepsilon < 1$, the sector that is shrinking in terms of capital and labor share grows faster than the rest of the economy at all points in time, even asymptotically. Therefore the rate at which capital and labor are allocated away from this sector is determined in equilibrium to be exactly such that this sector still grows faster than the rest of the economy. This is the sense in which nonbalanced growth is not a trivial outcome in this economy (with one of the sectors shutting down) but results from the positive but differential growth of the two sectors.

Finally, it can be verified that the capital share in national income and the interest rate are constant in the CGP (see Exercise 20.15). For example, when (20.61) holds, $\sigma_K^* = \alpha_1$. In contrast, when this condition does not hold, then $\sigma_K^* = \alpha_2$. Thus the asymptotic capital share in national income always reflects the capital share of the (asymptotically) dominant sector. Therefore this model based on technological sources of nonbalanced growth is also broadly consistent with the Kaldor facts as well as the Kuznets facts (though this model also generates significant deviations from the orderly behavior implied by the Kaldor facts when the economy is away from the CGP). The analysis so far does not establish that the CGP is asymptotically stable. This is done in Exercise 20.16, which also provides an alternative proof of Proposition 20.10. Consequently, a model based on technological factors can also give useful insights about structural change. Naturally, to understand the sweeping long-run changes in the composition of output and employment, we need to combine the preference and the technological factors studied in the last two sections. Exercise 20.17 takes a first step in this direction.

20.3 Agricultural Productivity and Industrialization

Although the models presented in Sections 20.1 and 20.2 have highlighted how preference and technological factors can lead to structural change (and also how structural change can be consistent with a constant BGP and the Kaldor facts), they did not focus on the process of industrialization. Chapter 1 documented that the industrialization process, beginning at the end of the eighteenth century in Europe, lies at the root of modern economic growth and cross-country income differences. Thus a natural question is why industrialization started and then progressed rapidly in some countries, while it did not in others. In view of the general patterns presented in Chapter 1, this question might hold important clues about the cross-country differences in income per capita today.

It would therefore be useful to have several different approaches to this question and evaluate their pros and cons. While this is part of my objective, I do not present these models all in one place. The first approach, based on the model of Acemoglu and Zilibotti (1997), has already been presented as an application of stochastic growth models in Section 17.6. Although this theory focused on takeoff in general, the most relevant incident of takeoff in history is related to industrialization. Therefore the theory in Section 17.6 can be interpreted as offering a potential explanation for the origins of industrialization based on whether the investments in different sectors undertaken by different societies turned out to be successful. In particular, societies that happen to have put a substantial fraction of their resources in sectors that turned out to be unlucky, or were ex post discovered not to be as productive, have been less successful than those that have invested in sectors and projects that were ex post more successful. In the next chapter, we will see another approach to the origins of industrialization based on the idea of coordination failures and "the big push" as suggested by Rosenstein-Rodan.

Before turning to market failures in development, it is useful to consider another approach that can shed light on factors facilitating, or even spurring, industrialization. A common argument in the economic history literature is that eighteenth-century England was particularly well placed for industrialization because of its high agricultural productivity (e.g., Nurske, 1958; Rostow, 1960; Mokyr, 1993; Overton, 1996). The basic idea is that societies with a high agricultural productivity can afford to shift part of their labor force to industrial activities. Some type of increasing returns coming from technology or demand is then invoked to argue that the ability to shift a critical fraction of the labor force to industry is an important element of the early industrial experience.

In this section, I present a model based on Matsuyama (1992), which formalizes this intuition. Matsuyama's model naturally complements the models already studied in this chapter, because it is a model of structural change. It combines Engel's Law with learning-by-doing externalities in the industrial sector. The model is not only a tractable framework for the analysis of the relationship between agricultural productivity and industrialization, but it also enables an insightful analysis of the impact of international trade on industrialization (along the lines of the model in Section 19.7 in the previous chapter).

The economy is in continuous time. Population is normalized to 1. The preference side is modeled via a representative household with preferences given by

$$\int_0^\infty \exp\left(-\rho t\right) \left(c^A(t) - \gamma^A\right)^\eta c^M(t)^{1-\eta} dt. \tag{20.68}$$

These preferences are similar to those in (20.1): $c^A(t)$ again denotes the consumption of the agricultural good, $c^M(t)$ is the consumption of the manufacturing good at time t, and the parameter γ^A is the minimum (subsistence) food requirement. In addition ρ is the discount factor, and $\eta \in (0, 1)$ designates the importance of agricultural goods versus manufacturing goods in the utility function. The representative household supplies labor inelastically. Let us also focus on the closed economy in the text, leaving the extension to an open economy to Exercise 20.20.

Output in the two sectors is produced with the following production functions:

$$Y^M(t) = X(t)F(L^M(t)) \text{ and } Y^A(t) = B^A G(L^A(t)), \tag{20.69}$$

where, as before Y^M and Y^A denote the total production of the manufacturing and the agricultural goods, respectively, and L^M and L^A denote the total labor employed in the two sectors. Both production functions F and G exhibit diminishing returns to labor. More formally, F and G are differentiable and strictly concave. In particular, $F(0) = 0$, $F'(\cdot) > 0$, $F''(\cdot) < 0$, $G(0) = 0$, $G'(\cdot) > 0$, and $G''(\cdot) < 0$. Diminishing returns to labor might arise because they both use land or some other factor of production as well as labor. Nevertheless it is simpler to assume diminishing returns rather than introduce another factor of production. Diminishing returns implies that when labor is priced competitively, there are equilibrium profits, and these are redistributed to households.

The key feature for this model of industrialization is that there is no technological progress in agriculture, but the production function for the manufacturing good in (20.69) includes the term $X(t)$, which allows for technological progress in manufacturing. Although there is no technological progress in agriculture, the productivity parameter B^A potentially differs across countries, reflecting either previous technological progress in terms of new agricultural methods or differences in land quality (for simplicity, I am focusing on a single country). Existing evidence shows that there are very large differences in labor productivity and the TFP of agricultural activities among countries even today; thus allowing for potential productivity differences in agriculture is reasonable. Current research also shows that the image of agriculture as a quasi-stagnant sector without technological progress is not accurate, and in fact, this sector experiences both substantial capital-labor substitution and major technological change (including the introduction of new varieties of seeds, mechanization, and organizational changes affecting productivity). Nevertheless the current model provides a good starting point for our purposes.

Labor market clearing requires that

$$L^M(t) + L^A(t) \leq 1.$$

Let $n(t)$ denote the fraction of labor employed in manufacturing as of time t. Since there is full employment in this economy, $L^M(t) = n(t)$, and $L^A(t) = 1 - n(t)$.

The key assumption is that manufacturing productivity $X(t)$ evolves over time as a result of learning-by-doing externalities as in Romer's (1986a) model in Chapter 11. In particular, suppose that the growth of the manufacturing technology, $X(t)$, is proportional to the amount of current production in manufacturing:

$$\dot{X}(t) = \kappa Y^M(t), \tag{20.70}$$

where $\kappa > 0$ measures the extent of these learning-by-doing effects, and the initial productivity level is $X(0) > 0$ at time $t = 0$ taken as given. As in the Romer model, learning-by-doing is external to individual firms. This type of external learning-by-doing is too reduced-form to generate insights about how productivity improvements take place in the industrial sector. Nevertheless our analysis so far makes it clear that one can endogenize technology choices by introducing monopolistic competition, and under the standard assumptions made in Part IV, this richer model of endogenous technological change generates a market size effect and leads to an equation similar to (20.70). Exercise 20.19 asks you to consider such a model.

In equilibrium, each firm chooses its labor demand to equate the value of the marginal product to the wage rate $w(t)$. Let us choose the agricultural good as the numeraire (so that its price is normalized to 1) and also assume that the equilibrium is interior with both sectors being active. Then in equilibrium we have

$$w(t) = B^A G'(1 - n(t)) \text{ and } w(t) = p(t)X(t)F'(n(t)),$$

where $p(t)$ is the relative price of the manufactured good (in terms of the numeraire, the agricultural good). Market clearing then implies that

$$B^A G'(1 - n(t)) = p(t)X(t)F'(n(t)). \tag{20.71}$$

The term $\gamma^A > 0$ in (20.68) implies that as in Section 20.1, preferences in the economy are nonhomothetic and that the income elasticity of demand for agricultural goods is less than unity (while that for manufacturing goods is greater than unity). As we have already seen, this is the simplest way of introducing Engel's Law.

Suppose that productivity is high enough to meet the minimum agricultural consumption requirements of the entire population (which, here, is normalized to 1):

$$B^A G(1) > \gamma^A > 0. \tag{20.72}$$

If (20.72) were violated, the economy's agricultural sector would not be productive enough to provide the subsistence level of food to all households.

Finally, the budget constraint of the representative household at each date t can be written as

$$c^A(t) + p(t)c^M(t) \le w(t) + \pi(t),$$

where $\pi(t)$ is the profits per representative household, resulting from the diminishing returns in the production technologies.

An equilibrium in this economy is defined in the standard way as paths of consumption levels in the two sectors and allocations of labor between the two sectors at all dates such that households maximize utility and firms maximize profits given prices, and goods and factor prices are such that all markets clear.

Maximization of (20.68) implies that

$$c^A(t) = \gamma^A + \eta p(t)c^M(t)/(1 - \eta). \tag{20.73}$$

Since the economy is closed, production must equal consumption and thus

$$c^A(t) = Y^A(t) = B^A G(1 - n(t)) \text{ and } c^M(t) = Y^M(t) = X(t)F(n(t)).$$

Now combining these equations with (20.71) and (20.73) yields

$$\phi(n(t)) = \frac{\gamma^A}{B^A}, \tag{20.74}$$

where

$$\phi(n) \equiv G(1 - n) - \frac{\eta G'(1 - n)F(n)}{(1 - \eta) F'(n)}$$

is strictly decreasing. Moreover $\phi(0) = G(1)$, and $\phi(1) < 0$. Here ϕ can be interpreted as the aggregate relative demand function for manufacturing over agriculture. An equilibrium has to satisfy (20.74). From assumption (20.72) and the properties of the ϕ function, we can conclude that the equilibrium condition (20.74) has a unique interior solution in which

$$n(t) = n^* \in (0,\ 1)\ .$$

Notice an important implication. Even though the current model is one of structural change like those in Sections 20.1 and 20.2, it only generates changes in the composition of output—the fraction of the labor force working in agriculture remains constant at $1 - n^*$. Thus while the current model is useful for interpreting the onset of industrialization, it is not sufficient to generate insights about why the composition of employment in different sectors of the economy has been changing over the past 150 or 200 years.

Next, using (20.74), the unique equilibrium allocation of labor between the two sectors satisfies

$$n^* = \phi^{-1}\left(\frac{\gamma^A}{B^A}\right). \tag{20.75}$$

Since ϕ is strictly decreasing, so is its inverse function ϕ^{-1}, and thus the fraction of the labor force employed in manufacturing, n^*, is strictly increasing in B^A. This is the most important result of the current model and shows that a greater fraction of the labor force will be allocated to the manufacturing sector when agricultural productivity is higher. This result is intuitive: the Cobb-Douglas utility function combined with homothetic preferences would imply a constant allocation of employment between the two sectors independent of their productivity. But in the current model, preferences are nonhomothetic, and a certain amount of food production is necessary first. When agricultural productivity B^A is high, a relatively small fraction of the labor force is sufficient to generate this minimal level of food production, and thus a greater fraction of the labor force can be employed in manufacturing.

This result, combined with learning-by-doing in manufacturing (see (20.70)), is at the root of the relationship between agricultural productivity and industrialization. In particular, (20.70) implies that output in manufacturing grows at the constant rate $\kappa F(n^*)$, which is also positively related to B^A in view of (20.75). Therefore the current model generates a simple representation of the often-hypothesized relationship between agricultural productivity and the origins of industrialization.

It is also useful to note that in the equilibrium of this model, because the shares of employment in manufacturing and agriculture are constant and there is no technological progress in the agricultural sector, agricultural output remains constant. All growth is generated by growth of manufacturing production. However, since manufacturing and agricultural goods are imperfect substitutes, the relative prices change, so expenditure on agricultural goods increases (see Exercise 20.18). The next proposition summarizes this discussion.

Proposition 20.11 *In the above-described model, the combination of learning-by-doing and Engel's Law generates a unique equilibrium in which the share of employment of manufacturing is constant at $n^* \equiv \phi^{-1}(\gamma^A/B^A)$, and manufacturing output and consumption grow at the rate $\kappa F(n^*)$, which is increasing in agricultural productivity B^A.*

We have so far characterized the equilibrium in a closed economy. A major result is that higher agricultural productivity leads to faster industrial growth and thus to faster overall growth, because higher agricultural productivity enables the economy to allocate a larger fraction of its labor force to the knowledge-producing sector (here manufacturing).

An important advantage of the current model is its tractability. This enables us to adapt it easily to analyze related questions, such as the impact of trade opening on industrialization. This is done in Exercise 20.20, which shows that the role of agricultural productivity in closed and open economies can be very different. For example, in an open economy greater agricultural productivity may delay or prevent industrialization rather than encouraging it as in the closed economy. The reason for this is related to the forces highlighted in Section 19.7 of Chapter 19: specialization according to comparative advantage may have negative long-run consequences in the presence of sector-specific externalities. However, as already discussed in that section, the evidence for large externalities of this sort is not very strong. Consequently the role of international trade in the process of industrialization is likely to be more complex than that suggested by Exercise 20.20. Nevertheless, this exercise illustrates how open economy models enrich the study of structural change.

20.4 Taking Stock

This chapter took a first step toward the analysis of structural changes involved in the process of economic development. Our first step has been relatively modest. The focus has been on the structural changes associated with (1) the shifts in output and employment away from agriculture to manufacturing and to services and (2) the changes between sectors of different capital intensities. Section 20.1 focused on "demand-side" reasons, resulting from the structure of preferences, for why growth may be nonbalanced. It incorporated Engel's Law into the basic neoclassical growth model, so that households spend a smaller fraction of their budget on agricultural goods as they become richer. This framework is ideally suited to the analysis of the structural changes across broad sectors, such as agriculture, manufacturing, and services. Section 20.2, on the other hand, turned to "supply-side," technological, reasons for nonbalanced growth, which were first highlighted by Baumol's (1967) classic paper. However, instead of assuming exogenously given different rates of technological progress across sectors, this section emphasized how sectoral differences in capital intensity can lead to nonbalanced growth. Capital-intensive sectors tend to grow more rapidly as a result of an equiproportionate increase in the capital-labor ratio. This feature, combined with capital deepening at the economy level, naturally leads to a pattern of nonbalanced growth. Such nonbalanced growth may contribute to structural change across agricultural, manufacturing, and service sectors but becomes particularly relevant when we look at sectors differentiated according to their capital intensity. A particular focus of both Sections 20.1 and 20.2 was to reconcile nonbalanced growth at the sectoral level with the patterns of relatively balanced growth at the aggregate. As already noted in Chapter 2, balanced growth need not be taken literally. It is at best an approximation. Nevertheless it seems to be a good approximation to many features of the growth process in advanced economies, where interest rates and the share of capital income in GDP appear to have been relatively constant over the past 100 years or so. It is therefore important to understand how significant reallocation of resources at the sectoral level can coexist with the more balanced behavior at the aggregate. The models in Sections 20.1 and 20.2 suggested some clues about why this may be the case, but the answers provided here should be viewed as preliminary rather than definitive.

I also discussed a simple model of the origins of industrialization. This model showed how agricultural productivity might have a significant effect on the timing of industrialization. The study of the process of industrialization is important, in part because, as discussed in Chapter 1, existing evidence suggests that the timing and nature of industrialization may have important implications for the cross-country income differences we observe today. The study of economic development may therefore necessitate an analysis of why some countries industrialized early, while others were delayed or never started the process of industrialization.

Understanding the sources of structural changes and how they can be reconciled with the broad patterns of balanced growth in the aggregate sheds light on the process of economic growth and development. In this sense, the models in this section enrich our understanding of economic growth considerably. And yet, this is only a modest step toward the investigation of the sweeping structural changes emphasized by Kuznets, because we have not departed from the neoclassical approach to economic growth. In particular, Sections 20.1 and 20.2 used generalized versions of the basic neoclassical growth model of Chapter 8, and Section 20.3 used a variant of the Romer (1986a) model from Chapter 11.

It should be emphasized again that the topics discussed in this chapter, though closely related to the basic neoclassical growth model, are areas of frontier research. We are far from a satisfactory framework for understanding the process of reallocation of capital and labor across sectors, how this changes at different stages of development, and how it remains consistent with relatively balanced aggregate growth and the Kaldor facts. I have therefore not attempted to provide a unified framework that combines the transition from agriculture to industrialization, nonhomothetic preferences resulting from Engel's Law and technological factors leading to nonbalanced growth. The development of such unified models as well as richer models of nonbalanced growth are areas for future research.

20.5 References and Literature

The early development literature contains many important works documenting the major structural changes taking place in the process of development. Kuznets (1957, 1973) and Chenery (1960) provide some of the best overviews of the broad evidence and the literature, though similar issues were discussed by even earlier development economists, such as Rosenstein-Rodan (1943), Nurske (1958), and Rostow (1960). Figure 20.1, which uses data from *Historical Statistics of the United States* (Carter et al., 2006), gives a summary of these broad changes.

The model of nonbalanced growth based on Engel's Law presented in Section 20.1 is from Kongsamut, Rebelo, and Xie (2001). Previous works that have analyzed similar models include Murphy, Shleifer, and Vishny (1989); Echevarria (1997); and Laitner (2000). More recent work building on Kongsamut, Rebelo, and Xie (2001) includes Caselli and Coleman (2001b) and Gollin, Parente, and Rogerson (2002). Some of these models include land as an additional factor of production necessary for agriculture. Exercise 20.8 provides an example of such a model. The recent literature also places greater emphasis on sources of agricultural productivity and emphasizes that differences in agricultural productivity across countries are often as large as, or even larger than, productivity differences in other sectors. Gollin, Parente, and Rogerson (2002) is one of the first papers in this vein.

The works mentioned in the previous paragraph, like the model I presented in Section 20.1, appeal to Engel's Law and model the resulting nonhomothetic preferences by positing Stone-Geary preferences as in (20.2). A more flexible and richer approach is to allow for "hierarchies of needs" in consumption, whereby households consume different goods in a particular sequence (e.g., food needs to be consumed before textiles, and textiles need to be consumed before electronics, and so on). This and related approaches are used in Stokey (1988), Foellmi and Zweimuller (2002), Matsuyama (2002), and Buera and Kaboski (2006) to generate richer models of structural change. Space restrictions preclude me from presenting these hierarchy of needs models, even though they are both insightful and elegant alternatives to the standard approach of using Stone-Geary preferences.

Section 20.2 builds on Acemoglu and Guerrieri (2008). The precursor to this work is Baumol (1967), which emphasizes the importance of differential productivity growth on nonbalanced growth. However, Baumol did not derive a pattern of nonbalanced growth including reallocation of capital and labor across sectors, and assumed differential rates of productivity growth to be exogenous. Ngai and Pissarides (2006) and Zuleta and Young (2006) provide modern versions of Baumol's hypothesis. Instead, the approach in Section 20.2 emphasizes how the combination of different capital intensities and capital deepening in the aggregate can endogenously lead to this pattern.

The model in Section 20.3 is based on Matsuyama (1992) and is also closely related to the model presented in Section 19.7 in Chapter 19. The role of agriculture in industrialization is discussed in Mokyr (1993), Overton (1996), and Mundlak (2000).

20.6 Exercises

20.1 Show that the consumption aggregator in (20.2) leads to Engel's Law. Suggest alternative consumption aggregators that will generate similar patterns.

20.2 Prove Proposition 20.1.

20.3 (a) Set up the optimal control problem for a representative household in the model of Section 20.1.

(b) From the Euler equations and the transversality condition, verify (20.16) in Proposition 20.2.

(c) Use (20.9) and (20.10) to derive (20.17) of the proposition.

20.4 Prove Proposition 20.3. Show that an equilibrium path always exists (even though it never features equal rates of growth for all sectors).

20.5 (a) Prove Proposition 20.4. In particular, show that if (20.18) is not satisfied, a CGP cannot exist, and that this condition is sufficient for a unique CGP to exist.

(b) Characterize the CGP effective capital-labor ratio k^*.

20.6 In the model of Section 20.1 show that as long as condition (20.18) is satisfied, when the economy starts with an effective capital-labor ratio $K(0) / (X(0)L(0))$ different from k^*, the CGP is globally stable and the effective capital-labor ratio monotonically converges to k^* as $t \to \infty$.

* 20.7 Consider a generalization of the model of Section 20.1, in which the sectoral production functions are given by the following Cobb-Douglas forms:

$$Y^A(t) = K^A(t)^{\alpha^A} (B^A(t)L^A(t))^{1-\alpha^A},$$

$$Y^M(t) = K^M(t)^{\alpha^M} (B^M(t)L^M(t))^{1-\alpha^M},$$

$$Y^S(t) = K^S(t)^{\alpha^S} (B^S(t)L^S(t))^{1-\alpha^S},$$

and assume that $B^A(t)$, $B^M(t)$, and $B^S(t)$ grow at the rates g^A, g^M, and g^S, respectively.

(a) Derive the equivalents of Propositions 20.1 and 20.2.

(b) Show that there exists a generalization of condition (20.18) such that this model will have a CGP as defined in Section 20.1. [Hint: the generalization includes two separate conditions on technology growth rates and preferences.]

20.8 Consider a version of the model in Section 20.1 with only manufacturing and agricultural goods. The consumption aggregator is $c(t) = (c^A(t) - \gamma^A)^{\eta^A} c^M(t)^{\eta^M}$, with $\gamma^A > 0$. Assume that the production functions for agricultural and manufacturing goods take the form $Y^A(t) = X(t)(L^A(t))^\zeta (Z)^{1-\zeta}$ and $Y^M(t) = X(t)L^M(t)$, respectively, where Z is land. There are no savings or capital.

(a) Characterize the competitive equilibrium in this economy.

(b) Show that this economy also exhibits structural change; in particular, show that the share of manufacturing sector grows over time.

(c) What happens to land rents along the equilibrium path?

* 20.9 In the model of Section 20.1, suppose that condition (20.18) is not satisfied. Assume that the production function F is Cobb-Douglas. Characterize the asymptotic growth path of the economy (the growth path of the economy as $t \to \infty$).

20.10 Consider the model of Section 20.1, but assume that there exists a final good produced with the technology $Y(t) = (Y^A(t) - \gamma^A)^{\eta^A} Y^M(t)^{\eta^M} (Y^S(t) + \gamma^S)^{\eta^S}$.

(a) Show that all the results in Section 20.1 hold without any change as long as capital goods are produced out of intermediate Y^M as implied by (20.7).

(b) Next assume that capital goods are produced out of the final good, so that the resource constraint becomes $\dot{K}(t) + c(t)L(t) = Y(t)$, where $c(t)$ is the per capita consumption of the final good. Show that in this model a CGP does not exist.

20.11 In the model of Section 20.2.1, suppose that aggregate output is given by the constant returns to scale production function $Y = F(Y_1(t), Y_2(t), \dots, Y_N(t))$. Defining $\sigma_j(t)$ as the capital share in sector $j = 1, \dots, N$ as in (20.25), show that if at time t there are factor proportion differences among the N sectors in the sense that there exists i and $j \le N$ such that $\sigma_i(t) \ne \sigma_j(t)$, technological progress is balanced between i and j, that is, $\dot{A}_i(t)/A_i(t) = \dot{A}_j(t)/A_j(t)$, and there is capital deepening, that is, $\dot{K}(t)/K(t) > \dot{L}(t)/L(t)$, then growth is not balanced and $\dot{Y}_i(t)/Y_i(t) \ne \dot{Y}_j(t)/Y_j(t)$.

20.12 Derive (20.39), (20.40), (20.41), and (20.42).

20.13 Prove Proposition 20.6.

20.14 (a) Complete the proof of Proposition 20.10 by considering the case in which $\varepsilon > 1$ and $g_1^* \ge g_2^* > 0$.

(b) State and prove the equivalent of Proposition 20.10, when the converse of condition (20.61) holds.

20.15 Show that in the allocation in Proposition 20.10, the asymptotic interest rate is constant, and derive a closed-form expression for this interest rate.

* 20.16 In this exercise, you are first asked to provide an alternative proof of Proposition 20.10 and then characterize the local transitional dynamics in the neighborhood of the CGP. Throughout suppose that either $\varepsilon < 1$ and $a_1/(1 - \alpha_1) < a_2/(1 - \alpha_2)$ or that $\varepsilon > 1$ and $a_1/(1 - \alpha_1) > a_2/(1 - \alpha_2)$.

(a) Re-express the equilibrium equations in terms of the following three variables: $\varphi(t) \equiv c(t)/(L(t)A_1(t)^{1/(1-\alpha_1)})$, $\chi(t) \equiv K(t)/(L(t)A_1(t)^{1/(1-\alpha_1)})$, and $\kappa(t)$. In particular, show that the following three differential equations, together with the appropriate transversality condition and initial values $\chi(0)$ and $\kappa(0)$, characterize the dynamic equilibrium:

$$\frac{\dot{\varphi}(t)}{\varphi(t)} = \frac{1}{\theta}[\alpha_1 \gamma \eta(t)^{1/\varepsilon} \lambda(t)^{1-\alpha_1} \kappa(t)^{-(1-\alpha_1)} \chi(t)^{-(1-\alpha_1)} - \rho] - n - \frac{a_1}{1-\alpha_1},$$

$$\frac{\dot{\chi}(t)}{\chi(t)} = \lambda(t)^{1-\alpha_1} \kappa(t)^{\alpha_1} \chi(t)^{-(1-\alpha_1)} \eta(t) - \chi(t)^{-1} \varphi(t) - n - \frac{a_1}{1-\alpha_1}, \qquad (20.76)$$

$$\frac{\dot{\kappa}(t)}{\kappa(t)} = \frac{(1-\kappa(t))[(\alpha_2 - \alpha_1)\frac{\dot{\chi}(t)}{\chi(t)} + a_2 - \frac{1-\alpha_2}{1-\alpha_1}a_1]}{(1-\varepsilon)^{-1} + (\alpha_2 - \alpha_1)(\kappa(t) - \lambda(t))},$$

where $\kappa(t)$ and $\lambda(t)$ are given by (20.43) and (20.44), respectively, and

$$\eta(t) \equiv \gamma^{\frac{\varepsilon}{\varepsilon-1}} \left[1 + \frac{\alpha_1}{\alpha_2} \left(\frac{1-\kappa(t)}{\kappa(t)} \right) \right]^{\frac{\varepsilon}{\varepsilon-1}}. \tag{20.77}$$

[Hint: use the Euler equation of the representative household and the resource constraint of the economy; rearrange these to express the laws of motion of $\varphi(t)$ and $\chi(t)$ in terms of $\kappa(t)$, $\lambda(t)$, and $\eta(t)$ as defined in (20.77); and then differentiate (20.43).]

(b) State the appropriate transversality condition.

(c) Show that if an allocation satisfies the three differential equations in (20.76) and the appropriate transversality condition, then it corresponds to an equilibrium path.

(d) Show that in a CGP equilibrium $\varphi(t)$ must be constant. Using this result, show that the CGP requires that $\kappa(t) \to 1$ and that $\chi(t)$ must also be constant. From these observations, derive an alternative proof of Proposition 20.10.

(e) Now linearize the three equations in (20.76) around the CGP of Proposition 20.10, and show that the linearized system has two negative eigenvalues and one positive eigenvalue. Using this fact, conclude that the CGP is locally stable. [Hint: as part of this argument, explain why $\kappa(t)$ should be considered a state variable with $\kappa(0)$ taken as an initial value.]

20.17 Consider a model that combines the supply-side and the demand-side features of Sections 20.1 and 20.2. Suppose that the consumption aggregator is given by

$$c(t) = (c^S(t) + \gamma^S)^{\eta^S} c^M(t)^{\eta^M},$$

where c^S is the consumption of services, and c^M denotes the consumption of manufacturing goods. Assume that the economy is closed, and both services and manufacturing are produced by Cobb-Douglas technologies with the same Hicks-neutral rate of exogenous technological progress, but manufacturing is more capital-intensive. Assume also investment goods are produced from the manufacturing goods alone as in the model of Section 20.1. Characterize the equilibrium of this economy. Show that the relative price and the employment share of services will be increasing over time. Is it possible for the total consumption of manufacturing goods to increase faster than those of services?

20.18 Consider the model of Section 20.3.

1. Show that agricultural consumption and production stay constant at

$$B^A G(1 - \phi^{-1}(\gamma^A/B^A)) = \gamma^A + B^A \frac{\eta}{1-\eta} G'(1 - \phi^{-1}(\gamma^A/B^A)) \frac{F(\phi^{-1}(\gamma^A/B^A))}{F'(\phi^{-1}(\gamma^A/B^A))}.$$

2. Show that this is increasing in B^A and provide the intuition for this result.

3. Show that expenditure on agricultural goods increases at the same rate as aggregate output. [Hint: first characterize how $p(t)$ changes along the equilibrium path.]

* 20.19 Consider the model of Section 20.3 and suppose that the production function for the manufacturing sector is given by

$$Y^M(t) = \frac{1}{1-\beta} \left[\int_0^{N(t)} x(v, t)^{1-\beta} dv \right] L^M(t)^\beta,$$

which is similar to the production functions in Part IV of the book, with $N(t)$ denoting the range of machines and $x(v, t)$ corresponding to the amount of machine of type v used by the manufacturing sector. Assume as in Part IV that these machines are supplied by technology monopolists with perpetual patents and can be produced by using the manufacturing good at constant marginal cost of $(1 - \beta)$ units of the manufacturing good. Also assume the lab-equipment specification for creating new machines as in Section 15.7. Characterize the equilibrium of this economy and show that the qualitative features are the same as the model in the text.

20.20 Consider an open economy version of the model of Section 20.3. In particular, suppose that the economy trades with the rest of the world taking product prices as given. The rest of the world is characterized by the same technology, except that it has an initial level of productivity in the manufacturing sector equal to $X^F(0)$ and an agricultural productivity given by B^F. Suppose that there are no spillovers in learning-by-doing, so that (20.70) applies to the home economy and the law of motion of manufacturing productivity in the rest of the world is given by $\dot{X}^F(t) = \kappa Y^{M,F}(t)$, where $Y^{M,F}(t)$ is total foreign manufacturing production at time t.

(a) Show that comparative advantage in this economy is determined by the comparison of $X(0)/B^A$ to $X^F(0)/B^F$. Interpret this result.

(b) Suppose that $X(0)/B^A < X^F(0)/B^F$, so that the home economy has a comparative advantage in agricultural production. Show that the initial share of employment in manufacturing in the home economy, $n^*(0)$, must satisfy

$$\frac{X(0)F'(n^*(0))}{B^A G'(1-n^*(0))} = \frac{X^F(0)F'(n^{F*}(0))}{B^F G'(1-n^{F*}(0))}, \tag{20.78}$$

where $n^{F*}(0)$ is the share of manufacturing employment in the rest of the world. Show that $n^*(0)$ given by this equation is strictly less than n^* as given by (20.75).

(c) What happens to manufacturing employment in the home economy starting as in part b of this exercise? [Hint: derive an equivalent of (20.78) for any t, differentiate this with respect to time, and then use the laws of motion of X and X^F.]

(d) Explain why agricultural productivity, which was conducive to faster industrialization in the closed economy, may lead to delayed industrialization or to deindustrialization in the open economy.

(e) Consider an economy specializing in agriculture as in the earlier parts of this exercise. Is welfare at time $t = 0$ necessarily lower when this economy is open to trade than when it is closed to trade? Relate your answer to the analysis in Section 19.7 of Chapter 19.

Structural Transformations and Market Failures in Development

A more complex transformation of the economy than the changes in the structure of production studied in the previous chapter takes place with the process of economic development. Among other things this transformation involves major social changes and induces greater coordination of economic activities. Loosely speaking, we can think of a society that is relatively developed as functioning along (or at any rate, near) the frontier of its production possibilities set, while a less-developed economy may be in the interior of its "notional" production possibilities set. This may be because certain arrangements necessary for an economy to reach the frontier of its production possibility set require a large amount of capital or some specific technological advances (in which case, even though we may think of the society as functioning in the interior of its production possibility set, this may not be the outcome of market failure; thus the qualifier "notional" in the previous sentence). Alternatively, less-developed economies may be in the interior of their production possibility set because these societies are subject to severe market failures. In this chapter, I discuss these approaches to economic development.

I first focus on various dimensions of structural transformations and how these may be limited by the amount of capital or technology available in a society. I then discuss a number of approaches suggesting that less-developed economies might be suffering disproportionately from market failures or may even be "stuck" in development traps. In this context, I also discuss differences between models with multiple equilibria and with multiple steady states.

The topics covered in this chapter are part of a large and diverse literature. My purpose is not to do justice to this literature but to emphasize how certain major structural transformations take place as part of the process of economic development and also to highlight the potential importance of market failures in this process. Given this objective and the large number of potential models, my choice of models is selective, and my treatment is more informal than in the rest of the book. In addition, I often make reduced-form assumptions to keep the exposition brief and simple.

21.1 Financial Development

An important aspect of the structural transformation brought about by economic development is a change in financial relations and a deepening of financial markets. Section 17.6 in Chapter 17 presented a model in which economic growth goes hand-in-hand with financial deepening. However the model in that section only focused on a specific aspect of the role of financial institutions. In general, financial development brings about a number of complementary changes in the economy. First, there is greater depth in the financial market, allowing better diversification of aggregate risks—a feature also emphasized in the model of Section 17.6. Second, one of the key roles of financial markets is to allow risk sharing and consumption smoothing for individuals. In line with this role, financial development also allows better diversification of idiosyncratic risks. Section 17.6 showed that better diversification of aggregate risks leads to improved allocation of funds across sectors or projects. Similarly, better sharing of idiosyncratic risks leads to improved allocation of funds across individuals. Third, financial development might also reduce credit constraints on investors and thus may directly enable the transfer of funds to individuals with improvements in investment opportunities. The second and the third channels not only affect the allocation of resources in the society but also the distribution of income, because diversification of idiosyncratic risks and relaxation of credit market constraints might lead to improvements in income and risk sharing. On the other hand, as the possibility of such risk-sharing arrangements reduces consumption risk, individuals might take riskier actions, also potentially affecting the distribution of income.

To provide a brief introduction to these issues, I now present a simple model of financial development, focusing on the diversification of idiosyncratic risks and complementing the analysis in Section 17.6. The model is inspired by the work of Townsend (1979) and Greenwood and Jovanovic (1990). It illustrates how financial development takes place endogenously and interacts with economic growth; it also provides some simple insights into the implications of financial development for income distribution. Given the similarity of the model to that in Section 17.6, my treatment here is relatively informal.

I consider an OLG economy in which each individual lives for two periods and has preferences given by

$$\mathbb{E}_t U_t(c(t), c(t+1)) = \log c(t) + \beta \mathbb{E}_t \log c(t+1), \tag{21.1}$$

where $c(t)$ denotes the consumption of the unique final good of the economy, and $\mathbb{E}_t$ denotes the expectation operator given time t information.

There is no population growth, and the total population of each generation is normalized to 1. Let us assume that each individual is born with some labor endowment l. The distribution of endowments across agents is given by the distribution function $G(l)$ over some support $[\underline{l}, \bar{l}]$ This distribution of labor endowments is constant over time with mean $L = 1$, and labor is supplied inelastically by all individuals in the first period of their lives. In the second period of their lives, individuals simply consume their capital income.

The aggregate production function of the economy is given by

$$Y(t) = K(t)^\alpha L(t)^{1-\alpha} = K(t)^\alpha,$$

where $\alpha \in (0, 1)$, and the second equality uses the fact that total labor supply equals to 1 at each date. As in Section 17.6, the only risk is in transforming savings into capital; thus the life cycle of an individual looks identical to that shown in Figure 17.3. Moreover suppose that agents can either save all of their labor earnings from the first period of their lives using a safe technology with rate of return q (in terms of capital at the next date) or invest all of their labor income in the risky technology with return $Q + \varepsilon$, where ε is a mean zero independently and identically distributed stochastic shock, and as in Section 17.6, we assume that $Q > q$. Thus the risky technology is more productive. The assumption that individuals have to choose one of these two technologies rather than dividing their savings between the two is made for simplicity (see Exercise 21.1).

Although the model looks very similar to that in Section 17.6, there is a crucial difference. Because ε is identically and independently distributed across individuals, if individuals could pool their resources, they could perfectly diversify idiosyncratic risks. In particular, if a large number (a continuum) of individuals pooled their resources, they would guarantee an average return of Q. Let us assume that this is not possible because of a standard *informational problem*—the actual return of an individual's saving decision is not observed by others unless some financial monitoring is undertaken. Let us assume that this type of financial monitoring costs $\xi > 0$ for each individual. Then by paying the cost ξ, each individual can join the financial market (or in the language of Townsend, he can become part of a "financial coalition"). In this case, the actual returns of his savings become fully observable. Intuitively, this cost captures the fixed costs that individuals have to pay to be engaged in financial markets as well as the fixed costs associated with monitoring or being monitored. An immediate implication of this specification is that joining the financial markets is more attractive for richer individuals, since the fixed cost is less important for them. This feature is plausible and generates predictions consistent with microdata, where we observe richer individuals investing in more complex financial securities.

If an individual does not join the financial markets, then no other agent in the economy can observe the realization of the returns on his savings. In this case, no financial contract for sharing of idiosyncratic risks is possible, since such a contract would involve agents that have a high (realized) value of ε making transfers to those who are unlucky and have low realized values of ε. However, without monitoring, each agent will claim to have a low value of ε and thus receive ex post payments. The anticipation of this type of opportunistic behavior prevents any risk sharing in the absence of monitoring.

Let us also assume that ε has a distribution with positive probability of $\varepsilon = -Q$, so that if an individual undertakes the risky investments, there is a positive probability that all his savings will be lost. Thus without some type of risk sharing, individuals will choose the safe project. This observation simplifies the analysis of the model. Suppose that the economy starts with some initial capital stock of $K(0) > 0$, so an individual with labor endowment l_i has labor earnings of $W_i(0) = w(0)l_i$, where

$$w(t) = (1 - \alpha)K(t)^\alpha \tag{21.2}$$

is the competitive wage rate at time t. After labor incomes are realized, individuals first make their savings decisions and then choose which assets to invest in. The preferences in (21.1) imply that individuals save a constant fraction $\beta/(1 + \beta)$ of their income regardless of their income level or the rate of return (in particular, independent of whether they are investing in the risky or the safe asset). In view of this, the value of not participating in the financial markets for individual i at time t is

$$V_i^N(W_i(t), R(t+1)) = \log\left(\frac{1}{1+\beta}W_i(t)\right) + \beta \log\left(\frac{\beta R(t+1)q}{1+\beta}W_i(t)\right),$$

which takes into account that the rate of return on capital in the second period of the life of the individual is $R(t + 1)$ and the individual receives a gross return q on his savings of $\beta W_i(t)/(1 + \beta)$. Next, suppose that there are sufficiently many (i.e., a positive measure of) other individuals taking part in financial markets. When the individual decides to take part in financial markets, his value is

$$V_i^F(W_i(t), R(t+1)) = \log\left(\frac{1}{1+\beta}(W_i(t)-\xi)\right) + \beta \log\left(\frac{\beta R(t+1)Q}{1+\beta}(W_i(t)-\xi)\right),$$

which takes into account that the individual has to spend the amount ξ out of his labor income to join the financial market, leaving him a net income of $W_i(t) - \xi$. He then saves a fraction $\beta/(1+\beta)$ of this income, but in return, he is guaranteed to receive the higher return Q. The reason the individual receives Q, rather than a risky return, is that conditional on joining the financial market, each individual is able to fully diversify his idiosyncratic risks. The comparison of these two expressions gives the threshold level

$$W^* \equiv \frac{\xi}{1-(q/Q)^{\beta/(1+\beta)}} > 0 \tag{21.3}$$

such that individuals with first-period earnings greater than W^* join the financial market and those with less than W^* do not. A notable feature of this threshold W^* is that it is independent of the rate of return on capital in the second period of the lives of the individuals, R. This result is an implication of log preferences in (21.1).

Given the behavior of individuals concerning whether they join the financial market, let us next determine the evolution of the economy by studying the evolution of individual earnings. Individual earnings are determined by two factors: labor endowments and the capital stock at time t, which gives the wage per unit of labor, $w(t)$, as in (21.2). Given $w(t)$, the fraction of individuals who join the financial market at time t, $g^F(t)$, is given by the fraction of individuals who have $l_i \geq W^*/w(t)$. Alternatively, using the fact that labor endowments have a distribution given by $G(\cdot)$, the fraction of individuals investing in financial markets is obtained as

$$g^F(t) \equiv 1 - G\left(\frac{W^*}{w(t)}\right) = 1 - G\left(\frac{W^*}{(1-\alpha)K(t)^\alpha}\right). \tag{21.4}$$

Using (21.4) and defining $\chi(t) \equiv W^*/(1-\alpha)K(t)^\alpha$, the capital stock at time $t+1$ can be written as

$$K(t+1) = \frac{\beta}{1+\beta}\left[q\int_{\underline{l}}^{\chi(t)} l\,dG(l) + Q\int_{\chi(t)}^{\bar{l}} l\,dG(l)\right](1-\alpha)K(t)^\alpha$$

$$-\frac{\beta}{1+\beta}Q[1-G(\chi(t))]\xi, \tag{21.5}$$

which takes into account that all individuals with labor endowment less than $\chi(t)$ choose the safe project and receive the gross return q on their savings, while those above this threshold spend ξ on monitoring and receive the higher return Q (the last term in (21.5) subtracts the cost of monitoring from next period's capital stock). It can be verified that $K(t+1)$ is increasing in $K(t)$ and there is growth in the capital stock (and thus output) of the economy provided that $K(t)$ is less than the steady-state level of capital (see Exercise 21.2).

Inspection of the accumulation equation (21.5) together with the threshold rule for joining the financial market leads to a number of interesting conclusions.

1. As $K(t)$ increases, that is, as the economy develops, (21.4) implies that more individuals will join the financial market. Consequently, a greater level of capital leads to more risk taking, but these risks are also better shared. More importantly, economic development also induces a better composition of investment, as a greater fraction of the individuals

start using their savings more efficiently. Thus with a mechanism similar to that in Section 17.6, economic development improves the allocation of funds in the economy and increases productivity. Consequently this model, like the one in Section 17.6, implies that economic development and financial development go hand-in-hand.

2. However there is also a distinct sense in which the economy here allows for a potential causal effect of financial development on economic growth. Imagine that societies differ according to their values of ξ, which can be interpreted as a measure of the institutionally or technologically determined costs of monitoring (or some other costs associated with financial transactions that may depend on the degree of investor protection). Societies with lower ξ values have greater participation in financial markets, and this endogenously increases their productivity. Thus while the equilibrium behavior of financial and economic development are jointly determined, differences in financial development driven by exogenous institutional factors related to ξ have a potential causal effect on economic growth.

3. As noted above, at any given point in time it is the richer agents—those with greater labor endowment—that join the financial market. Therefore, initially, the financial market helps those who are already well off to increase the rate of return on their savings. This can be thought of as the unequalizing effect of the financial market.

4. The fact that participation in financial markets increases with $K(t)$ also implies that as the economy grows, at least at the early stages of economic development, the unequalizing effect of financial intermediation become stronger. Therefore, presuming that the economy starts with relatively few rich individuals, the first expansion of the financial market increases the level of overall inequality in the economy as a greater fraction of the agents in the economy now enjoy the greater returns.

5. As $K(t)$ increases even further, eventually the equalizing effect of the financial market starts operating. At this point, the fraction of the population joining the financial market and enjoying the greater returns is steadily increasing. If the steady-state level of capital stock K^* is such that $\underline{l} \geq W^*/((1-\alpha)(K^*)^{\alpha})$, then eventually all individuals join the financial market and receive the same rate of return on their savings.

The last two observations are interesting in part because the relationship between growth and inequality is a topic of great interest to development economics (one to which I return later in this chapter). One of the most important ideas in this context is that of the *Kuznets curve*, which claims that economic growth first increases and then reduces income inequality in the society. Whether the Kuznets curve is a good description of the relationship between growth and inequality is a topic of current debate. While many European societies seem to have gone through a phase of increasing and then decreasing inequality during the nineteenth century, the evidence for the twentieth century is more mixed. The last two observations show that a model with endogenous financial development based on risk sharing among individuals can generate a pattern consistent with the Kuznets curve. Whether there is indeed a Kuznets curve in general, and if so, whether the mechanism highlighted here plays an important role in generating this pattern are questions for future theoretical and empirical work.

21.2 Fertility, Mortality, and the Demographic Transition

Chapter 1 highlighted the major questions related to growth of income per capita over time and its dispersion across countries today. Our focus so far has been on these per capita income differences. Equally striking differences exist in the level of population across countries and

Population (millions)

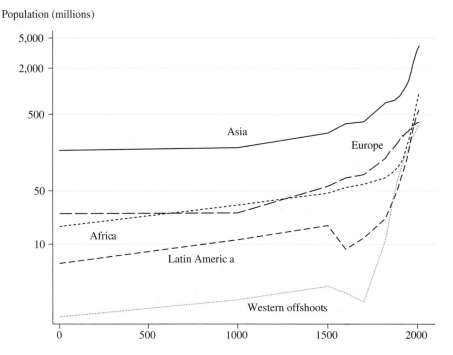

FIGURE 21.1 Total population in different parts of the world over the past 2,000 years.

over time. Figure 21.1 uses data from Maddison (2002) and shows the levels and the evolution of population in different parts of the world over the past 2,000 years. The figure is in log scale, so a linear curve indicates a constant rate of population growth. The figure shows that starting about 250 years ago there is a significant increase in the population growth rate in many areas of the world. This more rapid population growth continues in much of the world, but importantly, the rate of population growth slows down in Western Europe some time in the nineteenth century (though, thanks partly to immigration, not so in the Western offshoots). There is no similar slowdown of population growth in less-developed parts of the world. On the contrary, in many less-developed nations, the rate of population growth seems to have increased over the past 50 years or so. We have already discussed one of the reasons for this in Chapter 4—the spread of antibiotics, basic sanitation, and other health-care measures around the world that have reduced the high mortality rates in many countries. However, equally notable is the *demographic transition*, which, in the course of the nineteenth century, reduced fertility in Western Europe. Why population has grown slowly and then accelerated to reach a breakneck speed of growth over the past 150 years, and why population growth rates differ across countries, are major questions for economic development.

In this section, I present the most basic approaches to population dynamics and fertility. I first discuss a simple version of the famous Malthusian model and then use a variant of this model to investigate potential causes of the demographic transition. Thomas Malthus was one of the most brilliant and influential economists of the nineteenth century and is responsible for one of the first general equilibrium growth models. Section 21.2.1 presents a version of this model. The Malthusian model is responsible for earning the discipline of economics the name "the dismal science," because of its dire prediction that population will adjust up or down (by births or deaths) until all individuals are at the subsistence level of consumption. Nevertheless, this dire prediction is not the most important part of the Malthusian model. At the heart of this model is the negative relationship between income per capita and population, which is itself endogenously determined. In this sense, it is closely related to the Solow and the neoclassical growth models, augmented with a behavioral rule that determines the rate of population growth. It is this less-extreme version of the Malthusian model that is presented next. I then enrich this model by the important and influential idea due to Gary Becker that there is a trade-off between the quantity and quality of children and that this trade-off changes over the process of development. I show how a simple model can incorporate the notion that over the course of development, markets and parents may start valuing the quality (human capital) of their offspring more, and how this shift in valuation may lead to a pattern reminiscent of the demographic transition.

21.2.1 A Simple Malthusian Model

Consider the following non-OLG model that starts with a population of $L(0) > 0$ at time $t = 0$. A representative individual living at time t supplies one unit of labor inelastically and has utility

$$c(t)^{\beta}[y(t+1)n(t+1) - \tfrac{1}{2}\eta_0 n(t+1)^2] \tag{21.6}$$

where $c(t)$ denotes the consumption of the unique final good of the economy by the individual himself, $n(t + 1)$ denotes the number of offspring the individual begets, $y(t + 1)$ is the income of each offspring, and $\beta > 0$ and $\eta_0 > 0$. The last term in the square brackets represents the cost of child rearing and is assumed to be convex to reflect the fact that the costs of having more and more children will be higher (e.g., because of time constraints of parents, though one can also make arguments for why child rearing might exhibit increasing returns to scale over a certain range). Clearly these preferences introduce a number of simplifying assumptions. First, each individual is allowed to have as many offspring as he likes, which is unrealistic because it does not restrict the number of offspring to a natural number. The technology also does not incorporate possible specialization in child rearing and market work within the family. Second, these preferences introduce the warm glow type of altruism we encountered in Chapter 9, so that parents receive utility not from the future utility of their offspring but from some characteristic of their offspring. Here it is a transform of the total income of all the offspring that features in the utility function of the parent. Third, the costs of child rearing are in terms of "utils" rather than forgone income, and current consumption multiplies both the benefits and the costs of having additional children. This feature, which is motivated by a balanced growth type of reasoning, implies that the demand for children is independent of current income (otherwise, growth would automatically lead to greater demand for children). All three of these assumptions are adopted for simplicity. I have also written the number of offspring that an individual has at time t as $n(t + 1)$, since this determines population at time $t + 1$.

Each individual has one unit of labor, and there are no savings. The production function for the unique good takes the form

$$Y(t) = Z^{\alpha} L(t)^{1-\alpha}, \tag{21.7}$$

where Z is the total amount of land available for production, and $L(t)$ is total labor supply. There is no capital, and land is introduced to create diminishing returns to labor, which is an important element of the Malthusian model. Without loss of generality, I normalize the total amount of land to $Z = 1$. A key question in models of this sort is what happens to the returns to land. The most satisfactory way of dealing with this problem would be to allocate the property rights to land among the individuals and let them bequeath land to their offspring. This, however, introduces another layer of complication, and since my purpose here is to illustrate the basic ideas, I follow the unsatisfactory assumption often made in the literature that land is owned by another set of agents, whose behavior is not analyzed here.

By definition, population at time $t + 1$ is given by

$$L(t + 1) = n(t + 1)L(t), \tag{21.8}$$

which takes into account new births as well as the death of the parent.

Labor markets are competitive, so the wage at time $t + 1$ is given by

$$w(t + 1) = (1 - \alpha)L(t + 1)^{-\alpha}. \tag{21.9}$$

Since there is no other source of income, (21.9) is also equal to the income of each individual living at time $t + 1$, $y(t + 1)$. Thus an individual with income $w(t)$ at time t solves the problem of maximizing (21.6) subject to the constraint that $c(t) \leq w(t)$, together with the equation $y(t + 1) = (1 - \alpha)L(t + 1)^{-\alpha}$. Naturally, in equilibrium $n(t + 1)$ must be consistent with $L(t + 1)$ according to (21.8). Individual maximization implies that

$$n(t + 1) = (1 - \alpha)\eta_0^{-1}L(t + 1)^{-\alpha}.$$

Now substituting for (21.8) and rearranging, we obtain

$$L(t + 1) = (1 - \alpha)^{\frac{1}{1+\alpha}} \eta_0^{-\frac{1}{1+\alpha}} L(t)^{\frac{1}{1+\alpha}}. \tag{21.10}$$

This equation implies that $L(t + 1)$ is an increasing concave function of $L(t)$. In fact, the law of motion for population implied by (21.10) resembles the dynamics of capital-labor ratio in the Solow growth model (or the OLG model) and is plotted in Figure 21.2. The figure makes it clear that starting with any $L(0) > 0$, there exists a unique globally stable state L^* given by

$$L^* \equiv (1 - \alpha)^{1/\alpha} \eta_0^{-1/\alpha}. \tag{21.11}$$

If the economy starts with $L(0) < L^*$, then population slowly (and monotonically) adjusts toward this steady-state level. Moreover, (21.9) shows that as population increases, wages fall. If in contrast, $L(0) > L^*$, then the society experiences a decline in population and rising real wages. It is straightforward to introduce shocks to population and show that in this case, the economy fluctuates around the steady-state population level L^* (with an invariant distribution depending on the distribution of the shocks) and experience cycles reminiscent of the Malthusian cycles, with periods of increasing population and decreasing wages followed by periods of decreasing population and increasing wages (see Exercise 21.3).

The main difference between this model and the simplest (or crudest) version of the Malthusian model is that there is no biologically determined subsistence level of consumption. The steady-state level of consumption instead reflects technology and preferences and is given by

$$c^* = (1 - \alpha)(L^*)^{-\alpha} = \eta_0.$$

21.2.2 The Demographic Transition

To study the demographic transition, I now introduce a quality-quantity trade-off along the lines of the ideas suggested by Becker. Each parent can choose his offspring to be unskilled or skilled. To make them skilled, the parent has to exert the additional effort for child rearing denoted by $e(t) \in \{0, 1\}$. If he chooses not to do this, his offspring will be unskilled.

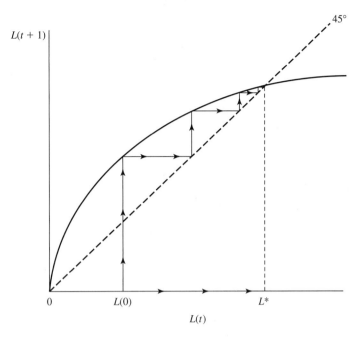

FIGURE 21.2 Population dynamics in a simple Malthusian model.

The total population of unskilled individuals at time t is denoted by $U(t)$, and the total population of the skilled is denoted by $S(t)$, clearly with

$$L(t) = U(t) + S(t).$$

The second modification is that there are now two production technologies that can be used for producing the final good. The traditional ("Malthusian") technology is still given by (21.7), and any worker can be employed with this technology. The modern technology is

$$Y^M(t) = X(t)S(t). \tag{21.12}$$

Equation (21.12) implies that productivity in the modern technology is potentially time varying and also states that only skilled workers can be employed with this technology. It also requires that all skilled workers be employed with this technology.[1]

To model the quality-quantity trade-off, individual preferences are now modified from (21.6) to

$$c(t)^\beta \left[y(t+1)n(t+1) - \tfrac{1}{2} \left(\eta_0(1 - e(t)) + \eta_1 X(t+1)e(t) \right) n(t+1)^2 \right]. \tag{21.13}$$

This formulation of the preferences states that if the individual decides to invest in his offspring's skills, instead of the fixed cost η_0, he must pay a cost that is proportional to the amount of knowledge $X(t+1)$ that the offspring has to absorb to use the modern technology. I assume

---

1. This need not be true in general, since wages in the traditional sector may be higher. However, in equilibrium this possibility is never the case, because parents would not choose to exert the additional effort to endow their offspring with skills if they would then work in the traditional sector. To keep the exposition simple (and with a slight abuse of notation), (21.12) already incorporates the fact that, in equilibrium, all skilled workers are employed in the modern sector.

that η_1 is sufficiently greater than η_0, and in particular, that $X(0)\eta_1 > \eta_0$, so that even at the initial level of the modern technology, rearing a skilled child is more costly than an unskilled child.

Finally, I assume learning-by-doing is external as in Romer (1986a), so that

$$X(t+1) - X(t) = \kappa S(t), \tag{21.14}$$

which implies that the improvement in the technology of the modern sector is a function of the number of skilled workers employed in this sector. This type of reduced-form assumption is clearly unsatisfactory, but as noted in Chapter 20 (in particular, recall Exercise 20.19), one could obtain similar results with an endogenous technology model featuring the market size effect. Another important feature of this production function is that it does not use land. This assumption is consistent with the fact that most modern production processes make little use of land, instead relying on technology, physical capital, and human capital.

The output of the traditional and the modern sectors are perfect substitutes—they both produce the same final good. In view of the observation that all unskilled workers work in the traditional sector and all skilled workers work in the modern sector, wages of skilled and unskilled workers at time t are

$$w^U(t) = (1-\alpha)U(t)^{-\alpha} \quad \text{and} \tag{21.15}$$

$$w^S(t) = X(t), \tag{21.16}$$

respectively, where (21.15) is identical to (21.9), except that it features only the unskilled workers instead of the entire labor force.

Let us next turn to the fertility and quality-quantity decisions of individuals. As before, current income has no effect on fertility and quality-quantity decisions. Thus we do not need to distinguish between high-skill and low-skill parents. Using this observation, let us simply look at the optimal number of offspring that an individual will have when he chooses $e(t) = 0$. This number is given by

$$n^U(t+1) = w^U(t+1)\eta_0^{-1} = (1-\alpha)\eta_0^{-1}U(t+1)^{-\alpha}, \tag{21.17}$$

where the second equality uses (21.15). If the parent instead decides to exert effort $e(t) = 1$ and invest in the skills of his offspring, then he will choose a number of offspring equal to

$$n^S(t+1) = \eta_1^{-1}w^S(t+1)X(t+1)^{-1} = \eta_1^{-1}. \tag{21.18}$$

The comparison of (21.17) and (21.18) suggests that unless unskilled wages are very low, an individual who decides to provide additional skills to his offspring will have fewer offspring. This is because bringing up skilled children is more expensive (i.e., because η_1 is sufficiently larger than η_0). Thus the comparison of these two equations captures the quality-quantity trade-off.

Substituting these equations back into the utility function (21.13), we obtain the utility from the two strategies (normalized by consumption, i.e., the utility divided by $c(t)^\beta$) as

$$V^U(t) = \tfrac{1}{2}(1-\alpha)^2\eta_0^{-1}U(t+1)^{-2\alpha} \quad \text{and} \quad V^S(t) = \tfrac{1}{2}\eta_1^{-1}X(t+1).$$

Inspection of these two expressions shows that in equilibrium, some workers must be unskilled, since otherwise V^U would become infinite. Therefore in equilibrium we have

$$V^U(t) \geq V^S(t) \quad \text{for all } t. \tag{21.19}$$

This equilibrium condition implies that there are two possible configurations. First, $X(0)$ can be so low that (21.19) holds as a strict inequality at all t and all individuals remain unskilled at all dates. The condition for inequality (21.19) to be strict at time $t = 0$ is

$$\eta_1^{-1} X(0) < (1 - \alpha)^2 \eta_0^{-1} L(1)^{-2\alpha},$$

which uses the fact that when there are no skilled workers, there is no production in the modern sector and thus $X(1) = X(0)$. If this inequality were satisfied, there would be no skilled children at date $t = 0$. However, as long as $L(1)$ is less than L^* as given in (21.11), the population grows. It is therefore possible that at some point (21.19) holds with equality. The condition ensuring that equality never happens is that

$$\eta_1^{-1} X(0) < (1 - \alpha)^2 \eta_0^{-1} (L^*)^{-2\alpha}. \tag{21.20}$$

In this case, (21.19) would hold as strict inequality at all dates, there would be no investment in skills, and the law of motion of population would be identical to that in Section 21.2.1. We can think of this case as a pure Malthusian economy.

If, on the other hand, (21.20) is not satisfied, then at least at some point individuals start investing in the skills of their offspring. From then on, (21.19) must hold as equality. Let the fraction of parents having unskilled children at time t be denoted by $u(t + 1)$. Then by definition it follows that

$$U(t + 1) = u(t + 1)n^U(t + 1)L(t)$$
$$= (1 - \alpha)^{2/(1+\alpha)} \eta_0^{-1/(1+\alpha)} u(t + 1)^{1/(1+\alpha)} L(t)^{1/(1+\alpha)}, \tag{21.21}$$

and

$$S(t + 1) = (1 - u(t + 1))n^S(t + 1)L(t)$$
$$= \eta_1^{-1}(1 - u(t + 1))L(t). \tag{21.22}$$

Moreover to satisfy (21.19) as equality, we need

$$(1 - \alpha)^2 \eta_0^{-1} U(t + 1)^{-2\alpha} = \eta_1^{-1} X(t + 1).$$

Rearranging this expression yields

$$X(t + 1) = (1 - \alpha)^{2/(1+\alpha)} \eta_0^{-(1-\alpha)/(1+\alpha)} \eta_1 u(t + 1)^{-2\alpha/(1+\alpha)} L(t)^{-2\alpha/(1+\alpha)}. \tag{21.23}$$

Equilibrium dynamics are then determined by (21.21)–(21.23) together with (21.16). While the details of the behavior of this dynamical system are somewhat involved, the general picture is clear. Most interestingly, if an economy has both a low level of $X(0)$ and a low level of $L(0)$ but does not satisfy condition (21.20), then it starts in the Malthusian regime, only making use of the traditional technology and not investing in skills. As population increases, wages fall, and at that point parents start finding it beneficial to invest in the skills of their children, and firms start using the modern technology. Parents who invest in the skills of their children will typically have fewer children than parents rearing unskilled offspring (because η_1 is sufficiently larger than η_0, (21.17) is greater than (21.18)). The aggregate rate of population growth and fertility are still high at first, but as the modern technology improves and the demand for skills increases, a larger fraction of parents start investing in the skills of their children, and the rate of population growth declines. Ultimately the rate of population growth approaches

η_1^{-1}. This model thus gives a stylized representation of the demographic transition based on the quality-quantity trade-off.

There exist substantially richer models of the demographic transition in the literature. For example, there are many ways of introducing quality-quantity trade-offs, and what spurs a change in this trade-off may be an increase in capital intensity of production, changes in the wages of workers, or changes in the wages of women differentially affecting the desirability of market and home activities. Nevertheless, the general qualitative features are similar to those in the model presented here, and in most of these approaches, the quality-quantity trade-off is the major reason for the demographic transition. Despite this emphasis on the quality-quantity trade-off, there is relatively little direct evidence that this trade-off is important in general or that it leads to the demographic transition. Other social scientists have suggested social norms, the large declines in mortality starting in the nineteenth century, and the reduced need for child labor as potential factors contributing to the demographic transition. As of yet, there is no general consensus on the causes of the demographic transition or on the role of the quality-quantity trade-off in determining population dynamics. The study of population growth and demographic transition is an exciting and important area, and theoretical and empirical analyses of the factors affecting fertility decisions and how they interact with the reallocation of workers across different tasks (sectors) remain important and interesting questions to be explored.

21.3 Migration, Urbanization, and the Dual Economy

Another major structural transformation that occurs during the process of development relates to changes in social and living arrangements. For example, as an economy develops, more individuals move from rural areas to cities and also undergo the social changes associated with separation from a small community and becoming part of a larger, more anonymous environment. Other social changes might also be important. For instance, certain social scientists regard the replacement of "collective responsibility systems" by "individual responsibility systems" as an important social transformation. This replacement is clearly related to changes in the living arrangements of individuals (e.g., villages versus cities, or extended versus nuclear families). It is also linked to whether different types of contracts are being enforced by social norms and community enforcement, and whether they are enforced by legal institutions. There may also be a similar shift in the importance of the market, as more activities are mediated by prices rather than taking place inside the home or using the resources of an extended family or broader community. This process of social change is both complex and interesting to study, though a detailed discussion of the literature and possible approaches to these issues is beyond the scope of this book.

Nevertheless, a brief discussion of some of these social changes is useful to illustrate other, more diverse, facets of structural transformations associated with economic development. I illustrate the main ideas by focusing on the process of migration from rural areas and on urbanization. Another reason to study migration and urbanization is that the reallocation of labor from rural to urban areas is closely related to the popular concept of *the dual economy,* which is an important theme of some of the older literature on development economics. According to this notion, less-developed economies consist of a modern sector and a traditional sector, but the connection between these two sectors is imperfect. The model of industrialization in the previous chapter (Section 20.3) featured a traditional and a modern sector, but these sectors traded their outputs and competed for labor in competitive markets. Dual economy approaches, instead, emphasize situations in which the traditional and the modern sectors function in parallel but with only limited interactions. Moreover the traditional sector is often viewed as less efficient than the modern sector; thus the lack of interaction may also be a way of shielding the traditional economy from its more efficient competitor. A natural implication of this approach is then to view the process of development as one in which the less-efficient traditional sector is replaced by the more-efficient modern sector. Lack of development may in turn correspond to the society's inability to generate such reallocation.

I first present a model of migration that builds on the work by Lewis (1954). A less-developed economy is modeled as a dual economy, with the traditional sector associated with villages and the modern sector with the cities. I then present a model that builds on Banerjee and Newman (1998) and Acemoglu and Zilibotti (1999), in which the traditional sector and the rural economy have a comparative advantage in community enforcement, even though—in line with the other dual economy approaches—the modern economy (the city) enables the use of more efficient technologies. This model also illustrates how certain aspects of the traditional sector can shield the less-productive firms from more-productive competitors and slow down the process of development. Finally, I show how the import of technologies from more-developed economies, along the lines of the models discussed in Section 18.4 of Chapter 18, may also lead to dual economy features as a by-product of the introduction of more skill-intensive, modern technologies into less-developed economies.

21.3.1 Surplus Labor and the Dual Economy

Lewis argued that less-developed economies typically have *surplus labor,* that is, unemployed or underemployed labor, often in the villages. The dual economy can then be viewed as the juxtaposition of the modern sector, where workers are productively employed, with the traditional sector, where they are underemployed. The general tendency of less-developed economies to have lower levels of employment-population ratios was one of the motivations for Lewis's model. A key feature of the model is the presence of some barriers preventing, or slowing down, the allocation of workers away from the traditional sector toward urban areas and the modern sector. I now present a reduced-form model that formalizes these notions.

Consider a continuous-time, infinite-horizon economy that consists of two sectors or regions, which I refer to as "urban" and "rural." Total population is normalized to 1. At time $t = 0$, $L^U(0)$ individuals are in the urban area and $L^R(0) = 1 - L^U(0)$ are in the rural area. In the rural area, the only economic activity is agriculture and, for simplicity, suppose that the production function for agriculture is linear. Thus total agricultural output is

$$Y^A(t) = B^A L^R(t),$$

where $B^A > 0$. In the urban area, the main economic activity is manufacturing. Manufacturing can only employ workers in the urban area and employs all available workers. The production function therefore takes the form

$$Y^M(t) = F(K(t), L^U(t)),$$

where $K(t)$ is the capital stock, with initial condition $K(0)$. The function F is a standard neoclassical production function satisfying Assumptions 1 and 2 (Chapter 2). Let us also assume, for simplicity, that the manufacturing and agricultural goods are perfect substitutes. Labor markets in both the rural and urban area are competitive. There is no technological change in either sector.

The key assumption is that because of barriers to mobility, there is only a slow migration of workers from rural to urban areas, even when manufacturing wages are greater than rural wages. In particular, let us capture the dynamics in this model in a reduced-form way, assuming that capital accumulates only out of the savings of individuals in the urban area and thus

$$\dot{K}(t) = sF(K(t), L^U(t)) - \delta K(t), \tag{21.24}$$

where s is the exogenous saving rate, and δ is the depreciation rate of capital. The important feature implied by (21.24) is that greater output in the modern sector leads to further accumulation of capital for the modern sector. An alternative, adopted in Section 20.3 of the previous chapter and also used in Section 21.3.2, is to allow the size of the modern sector to directly influence its productivity growth (e.g., because of learning-by-doing externalities as in Romer (1986a), or because of endogenous technological change depending on the market size commanded by this sector; see Exercise 20.19). For the purposes of the model here, which of these alternatives is adopted has no major consequences.

Given competitive labor markets, the wage rates in the urban and rural areas are

$$w^U(t) = \frac{\partial F(K(t), L^U(t))}{\partial L}, \text{ and } w^R(t) = B^A.$$

Let us assume that

$$\frac{\partial F(K(0), 1)}{\partial L} > B^A, \tag{21.25}$$

so that even if all workers are employed in the manufacturing sector at the initial capital stock, they will have a higher marginal product than working in agriculture.

Migration dynamics are assumed to take the following simple form:

$$\dot{L}^R(t) \begin{cases} = -\mu L^R(t) & \text{if } w^U(t) > w^R(t), \\ \in [-\mu L^R(t), 0] & \text{if } w^U(t) = w^R(t), \\ = 0 & \text{if } w^U(t) < w^R(t). \end{cases} \tag{21.26}$$

Equation (21.26) implies that as long as wages in the urban sector are greater than those in the rural sector, there is a constant rate of migration. The speed of migration does not depend on the wage gap, which is an assumption adopted only to simplify the exposition. We may want to think of μ as small, so that there are barriers to migration and so even when there are substantial gains to migrating to the cities, migration takes place slowly. When there is no wage gain to migrating, there will be no migration.

Now (21.25) implies that at date $t = 0$, there is migration from the rural areas to the cities. Moreover, assuming that $K(0)/L^U(0)$ is below the steady-state capital-labor ratio, the wage remains high and continues to attract further workers. To analyze this process in slightly greater detail, let us define

$$k(0) \equiv \frac{K(0)}{L^U(0)}$$

as the capital-labor ratio in manufacturing (the modern sector). As usual, let us also define the per capita production function in manufacturing as $f(k(t))$. Clearly, $w^U(t) = f(k(t)) - k(t)f'(k(t))$. Combining (21.24) and (21.26), we find that, as long as $f(k(t)) - k(t)f'(k(t)) > B^A$, the dynamics of this capital-labor ratio is given by

$$\dot{k}(t) = sf(k(t)) - (\delta + \mu v(t))k(t), \tag{21.27}$$

where $v(t) \equiv L^R(t)/L^U(t)$ is the ratio of the rural to urban population. Notice that when urban wages are greater than rural wages, the rate of migration μ times the ratio $v(t)$ plays the role of the rate of population growth in the basic Solow model. In contrast, when $f(k(t)) - k(t)f'(k(t)) \leq B^A$, there is no migration and we have

$$\dot{k}(t) = sf(k(t)) - \delta k(t). \tag{21.28}$$

Let us focus on the former case. Let $\bar{k}$ be the level of capital-labor ratio such that urban and rural wages are equalized, given by

$$f(\bar{k}) - \bar{k}f'(\bar{k}) = B^A. \tag{21.29}$$

Once this level is reached, migration stops and $v(t)$ remains constant. After this level, equilibrium dynamics are given by (21.28). Therefore the steady state must involve

$$\frac{sf(\hat{k})}{\hat{k}} = \delta. \tag{21.30}$$

For the analysis of transitional dynamics, which are our primary interest here, there are several cases to study. Let us focus on the one that appears most relevant for the experiences of many less-developed economies (leaving the rest to Exercise 21.4). In particular, suppose that the following conditions hold:

1. $k(0) < \hat{k}$, so that the economy starts with a lower capital-labor ratio (in the urban sector) than in the steady-state level. This assumption also implies that $sf(k(0)) - \delta k(0) > 0$.
2. $k(0) > \bar{k}$, which implies that $f(k(0)) - k(0)f'(k(0)) > B^A$; that is, wages are initially higher in the urban sector than in the rural sector.
3. $sf(k(0)) - (\delta + \mu v(0))k(0) < 0$, so that given the distribution of population between urban and rural areas, the initial migration leads to a decline in the capital-labor ratio.

In this case, the economy starts with rural to urban migration at date $t = 0$. Since initially $v(0)$ is high, this migration reduces the capital-labor ratio in the urban area (which evolves according to the differential equation (21.27)). There are then two possibilities. In the first, the capital-labor ratio never falls below $\bar{k}$; thus rural to urban migration takes place at the maximum possible rate of μ forever. Nevertheless the effect of this migration on the urban capital-labor ratio is reduced over time, as $v(t)$ declines with migration. Since we know that $sf(k(0)) - \delta k(0) > 0$, at some point the urban capital-labor ratio will start increasing, and it will eventually converge to the unique steady-state level $\hat{k}$. This convergence can take a long time, however, and notably, it is not necessarily monotone: the capital-labor ratio and urban wages first fall and then increase. The second possibility is that the initial surge in rural to urban migration reduces the capital-labor ratio to $\bar{k}$ at some point, say, at date t'. When this happens, wages remain constant at B^A in both sectors, and the rate of migration $\dot{L}^R(t)/L^R(t)$ adjusts exactly so that the capital-labor ratio remains at $\bar{k}$ for a while (recall that when urban and rural wages are equal, (21.26) admits any level of migration between zero and the maximum rate μ). In fact the urban capital-labor ratio can remain at this level for an extended period of time. During this time, wages in both sectors remain stagnant. Ultimately, however, $v(t)$ will again decline sufficiently that the capital-labor ratio in the urban sector must start increasing. Once this happens, urban wages also start increasing, migration takes place at the maximal rate μ, and the economy again slowly converges to the capital-labor ratio $\hat{k}$ in the urban sector.

Therefore, this discussion illustrates how a simple model of migration can generate rich population dynamics in rural and urban areas and also dynamics of wage difference between the modern and the traditional sectors.

The dynamics discussed above, especially in the first case, give the flavor of a dual economy. Wages and the marginal product of labor are higher in the urban area than in the rural one. If in addition, μ is low, the allocation of workers from the rural to the urban area is slow, despite the higher wages. Thus the pattern of dual economy may be pronounced and may persist for a long time. It is also notable that rural to urban migration increases total output in the economy, because it enables workers to be allocated to activities in which their marginal product is higher. This process of migration increasing the output level in the economy also happens slowly because of the relatively slow process of migration.

The above discussion implies that, for the parameter configurations on which we have focused, the dual economy structure not only affects the social outlook of the society, which remains rural and agricultural for an extended period of time (especially when μ is small), but also leads to lower output than the economy could have generated by allocating labor more rapidly to the manufacturing sector. One should be cautious in referring to this as a "market failure," however, since we did not specify the reason why migration is slow.

21.3.2 Community Enforcement, Migration, and Development

I now present a model that builds on Banerjee and Newman (1998) and Acemoglu and Zilibotti (1999). Banerjee and Newman consider an economy in which the traditional sector has low productivity but is less affected by informational asymmetries. Thus individuals can engage in borrowing and lending with limited monitoring and incentive costs. In contrast, the modern sector is more productive, but informational asymmetries create more severe credit market problems. Banerjee and Newman discuss how the process of development is associated with the reallocation of economic activity from the traditional to the modern sector and how this reallocation is slowed down by the informational advantage of the traditional sector. Acemoglu and Zilibotti (1999) view the development process as one of information accumulation and argue that greater information enables individuals to write more sophisticated contracts and enter into more complex production relations. This process is then associated with changes in technology, changes in financial relations, and social transformations, since greater availability of information and better contracts enable individuals to abandon less-efficient and less-information-dependent social and productive relationships.

The model in this subsection is simpler than those of both of these papers but features a similar economic mechanism. Individuals who live in rural areas are subject to community enforcement. Thus they can enter into economic and social relationships without being unduly affected by moral hazard problems. When individuals move to cities, they can take part in more productive activities, but other enforcement systems are necessary to ensure compliance to social rules, contracts, and norms. These systems are typically associated with certain costs. As in the model of industrialization in Section 20.3 in the previous chapter, I also assume that the modern sector is subject to learning-by-doing externalities. Thus the productivity advantage of the modern sector grows as more individuals migrate to cities and work there. However, the community enforcement advantage of villages slows down this process.

Both labor markets are competitive, and total population is normalized to 1. There are three differences between this model and the one in Section 21.3.1. First, migration between the rural and urban areas is costless. Thus at any point in time an individual can switch from one sector to another. Second, instead of capital accumulation, there is an externality, so that output in the modern sector is given by

$$Y^M(t) = X(t)F(L^U(t), Z),$$

where $X(t)$ denotes the productivity of the modern sector, which will be determined endogenously via learning-by-doing externalities. In addition, Z denotes another factor of production in fixed supply (so that there are diminishing returns to labor), and the production function F satisfies Assumptions 1 and 2. The returns to factor Z are distributed back to individuals (and how they are distributed has no effect on the results). Moreover let us assume that the technology in the modern sector evolves according to the differential equation

$$\dot{X}(t) = \eta L^U(t)X(t)^\zeta,$$

where $\zeta \in (0, 1)$. This equation builds in learning-by-doing externalities along the lines of Romer's (1986a) paper. The fact that $\zeta < 1$ implies that these externalities are less than those necessary for sustained growth.

Finally, let us also assume that rural areas have a comparative advantage in community enforcement. In particular, individuals engage in many social and economic activities, ranging from financial relations and employment to marriage and social relations. Many of these relationships in cities are anonymous, and enforcement is through some type of monitoring by the law and relies on complex institutions. Such institutions often work imperfectly in most societies and particularly in less-developed economies. In contrast, rural areas house a small number of individuals who are typically engaged in long-term relationships. These long-term relationships enable the use of community enforcement in many activities. Thus with long-term relationships, individuals can pledge their reputation to borrow money, to obtain information about which individual would be most appropriate for a particular job, or to ensure cooperation in other work or social relations. I represent these advantages in a reduced-form way by assuming that, when in the urban area, an individual pays a flow cost of $\xi > 0$ due to imperfect monitoring and lack of community enforcement.

All individuals maximize the net present discounted value of their lifetime incomes. Since moving between urban and rural areas is costless, each individual should work in the sector that has the higher net wage at that time. Thus in an interior equilibrium (where both the rural and the urban sectors are active), we must have

$$w^M(t) - \xi = w^A(t).$$

Competitive labor markets then imply that

$$w^M(t) = X(t)\frac{\partial F(L^U(t), Z)}{\partial L} \equiv X(t)\tilde{\phi}(L^U(t)),$$

where the second equation defines the function $\tilde{\phi}$, which is strictly decreasing (in view of Assumption 1 on the production function F). Substituting from the above relationships, labor market clearing implies that $X(t)\tilde{\phi}(L^U(t)) = B^A + \xi$, or

$$L^U(t) = \tilde{\phi}^{-1}\left(\frac{B^A + \xi}{X(t)}\right) \equiv \phi\left(\frac{X(t)}{B^A + \xi}\right),$$

where the second equality defines the function ϕ, which is strictly increasing in view of the fact that $\tilde{\phi}$ (and thus $\tilde{\phi}^{-1}$) is strictly decreasing. Therefore the evolution of this economy can be represented by the differential equation

$$\dot{X}(t) = \eta\phi\left(\frac{X(t)}{B^A + \xi}\right)X(t)^\zeta.$$

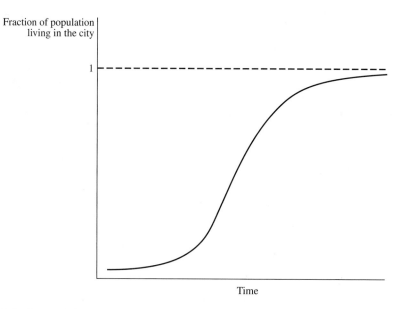

FIGURE 21.3 Dynamic behavior of the population in rural and urban areas.

Several features of this law of motion are worth noting. First, the typical evolution of $X(t)$ is given as in Figure 21.3, with an S-shaped pattern. This is because starting with a low initial value of $X(0)$, equilibrium urban employment, $\phi(X(t)/(B^A + \xi))$, is also low during the early stages of development. Thus there is limited learning-by-doing, and the modern sector technology progresses only slowly. However, as $X(t)$ increases, $\phi(X(t)/(B^A + \xi))$ also increases, raising the rate of technological change in the modern sector. Ultimately, however, $L^U(t)$ cannot exceed 1, so $\phi(X(t)/(B^A + \xi))$ tends to a constant, and thus the rate of growth of X declines. Therefore this reduced-form model generates an S-shaped pattern of technological change in the modern sector and an associated pattern of migration of workers from rural to urban areas.

Second and more importantly, the process of technological change in the modern sector and migration to the cities are slowed down by the comparative advantage of the rural areas in community enforcement. In particular, the greater is ξ, the slower is technological change and migration into urban areas. Since employment in the urban areas creates positive externalities, the community enforcement system in rural areas slows down the process of economic development in the economy as a whole. We may therefore conjecture that a higher ξ, corresponding to a greater community enforcement advantage of the traditional sector, generally reduces growth and welfare in the economy. Counteracting this effect, however, are the static gains created by the better community enforcement system in rural areas. A high level of ξ increases the initial level of consumption in the economy. Consequently there is a trade-off between the dynamic and static welfare implications of different levels of ξ. This trade-off is investigated formally in Exercise 21.5.

It is worth noting that unlike the model in Section 21.3.1, there are no barriers to migration here: workers in the villages and cities receive the same wage. However the functioning of the economy and the structure of social relations are different in these two areas. While villages and the rural economy rely on community enforcement, the city uses the modern technology and impersonal institutional checks to enforce various economic and social arrangements. Consequently the dual economy in this model manifests itself as much in the social as in the economic dimension.

21.3.3 Inappropriate Technologies and the Dual Economy

I now discuss how ideas related to appropriate and inappropriate technologies presented in Chapter 18 may provide promising clues about other important aspects of the dual economy. Recall from Section 18.4 that less-developed economies often import their technologies from more advanced economies and that these technologies are typically designed for different factor proportions than those of the less-developed economy. For example, in Section 18.4, I emphasized the implications of a potential mismatch between the skills of the workforce of a less-developed economy and the skill requirements of modern technologies. However in that model the equilibrium always involved all workers in the less-developed economy using the modern technology.

Here suppose that each technology is of the Leontief type, so that it requires a certain number of skilled and unskilled workers. For example, technology A_h produces a total of $A_h L$ units of the unique final good, where L is the number of unskilled workers, but this technology requires a ratio of skilled to unskilled workers exactly equal to h (e.g., the skilled workers are the managers of the unskilled workers). Suppose A_h is increasing in h, so that more advanced technologies are more productive.

Now consider a less-developed economy that has access to all technologies A_h for $h \in [0, \bar{h}]$ for some $\bar{h} < \infty$. Suppose that the population of this economy consists of H skilled and L unskilled workers, such that $H/L < \bar{h}$. This inequality implies that not all workers can be employed with the most skill-intensive technology. What is the form of equilibrium be in this economy?

To answer this question, imagine that all markets are competitive, so that the allocation of workers to tasks simply maximizes output (recall the Second Welfare Theorem, Theorem 5.7). Then the problem can be written as

$$\max_{[L(h)]_{h\in[0,\bar{h}]}} \int_0^{\bar{h}} A_h L(h)dh \tag{21.31}$$

subject to

$$\int_0^{\bar{h}} L(h)dh = L \text{ and } \int_0^{\bar{h}} hL(h)dh = H,$$

where $L(h)$ is the number of unskilled workers assigned to work with technology A_h. The first-order conditions for this maximization problem can be written as

$$A_h \leq \lambda_L + h\lambda_H \text{ for all } h \in [0, \bar{h}], \tag{21.32}$$

where λ_L is the multiplier associated with the first constraint, and λ_H is the multiplier associated with the second constraint. The first-order condition is written as an inequality, since not all technologies $h \in [0, \bar{h}]$ are used, and those that are not active might satisfy this condition with a strict inequality.

Inspection of the first-order conditions implies that if $A_{\bar{h}}$ is sufficiently high and if $A_0 > 0$, the solution to this problem has a simple feature. All skilled workers are employed at technology $\bar{h}$, and together with them are $L(\bar{h}) = H/\bar{h}$ unskilled workers employed with this technology. The remaining $L - L(\bar{h})$ workers are employed with the technology $h = 0$ (see Exercise 21.6). This equilibrium then has the features of a dual economy. Two very different technologies are used for production, one more advanced (modern), and the other corresponding to the least advanced technology that is feasible. This dual economy structure emerges because of a nonconvexity—to maximize output, it is necessary to operate the most advanced technology, but this exhausts all available skilled workers, implying that unskilled workers must be employed in technologies that do not require skilled inputs. This perspective therefore suggests that a dual economy structure may result from the import of technologies that are potentially mismatched with the supply of skills in an economy.

Models of dual economy based on this type of appropriate technology ideas have not been investigated in detail, though the literature on appropriate technology, which was discussed in Chapter 18, suggests that they may be important in practice. While this model focuses on the dual economy aspect in production, one can easily generalize the framework by assuming that the more advanced technology operates in urban areas with contractual arrangements enforced by modern institutions, while the less advanced technology operates in villages or rural areas. Thus models based on appropriate (or inappropriate) technology may be able to account for the broad patterns related to the dual economy, including rural to urban migration and changes in social arrangements.

21.4 Distance to the Frontier and Changes in the Organization of Production

In this section, I discuss how the structure of production changes over the process of development, and how this might be related both to changes in certain aspects of the internal organization of the firm and to a shift in the growth strategy of an economy—here, meaning whether the engine of growth is innovation or imitation. I illustrate these ideas using a simple model based on Acemoglu, Aghion, and Zilibotti (2006). Because of space restrictions, I only provide a sketch of the model, mainly focusing on the production side.

Consider an economy that is behind the world technology frontier. There is no need to use country indices, since I focus on a single country, taking the behavior of the world technology frontier as given. Time is discrete and the economy is populated by overlapping generations that live for two periods. Total population is normalized to 1. There is a unique final good, which is also taken as the numeraire. It is produced competitively using a continuum of machines with a technology similar to the Schumpeterian models in Chapter 14:

$$Y(t) = \int_0^1 A(v, t)^\beta x(v, t)^{1-\beta} \, dv, \tag{21.33}$$

where $A(v, t)$ is the productivity of machine variety v at time t, $x(v, t)$ is the amount of this machine variety used in the production of the final good at time t, and $\beta \in (0, 1)$.

Each machine variety is produced by a monopolist $v \in [0, 1]$ at a unit marginal cost in terms of the unique final good. The monopolist faces a competitive fringe of imitators that can copy its technology and also produce an identical machine with productivity $A(v, t)$, but can only do so at the cost of $\chi > 1$ units of final good. The existence of this competitive fringe forces the monopolist to charge a *limit price:*

$$p(v, t) = \chi > 1. \tag{21.34}$$

This limit price configuration is an equilibrium when χ is not so high that the monopolist can set the unconstrained monopoly price. The condition for this is

$$\chi \leq 1/(1 - \beta),$$

which I impose throughout. The parameter χ captures both technological factors and government regulations regarding competition policy. A higher χ corresponds to a less competitive market. Given the demand implied by the final goods technology in (21.33) and the equilibrium limit price in (21.34), equilibrium monopoly profits are simply given by

$$\pi(\nu, t) = \delta A(\nu, t), \tag{21.35}$$

where

$$\delta \equiv (\chi - 1)\chi^{-1/\beta}(1 - \beta)^{1/\beta}$$

is a measure of the extent of monopoly power. In particular it can be verified that δ is increasing in χ for all $\chi \leq 1/(1 - \beta)$.

In this model, the process of economic development is driven not by capital accumulation—which was the force emphasized in some of the earlier models—but by technological progress, that is, by increases in $A(\nu, t)$. Let us assume that each monopolist $\nu \in [0, 1]$ can increase its $A(\nu, t)$ by two complementary processes: (1) imitation (adoption of existing technologies) and (2) innovation (discovery of new technologies). The key economic trade-offs in the model arise from the fact that different economic arrangements (in terms of both the organization of firms and the growth strategy of the economy) lead to different amounts of imitation and innovation.

To illustrate this point, let us define the average productivity of the economy in question at date t as

$$A(t) \equiv \int_0^1 A(\nu, t)d\nu.$$

Let $\bar{A}(t)$ denote the productivity at the world technology frontier. The fact that this economy is behind the world technology frontier means that $A(t) \leq \bar{A}(t)$ for all t. The world technology frontier progresses according to the difference equation

$$\bar{A}(t) = (1 + g)\bar{A}(t - 1), \tag{21.36}$$

where the growth rate of the world technology frontier is taken to be

$$g \equiv \underline{\eta} + \bar{\gamma} - 1, \tag{21.37}$$

and $\underline{\eta}$ and $\bar{\gamma}$ are defined further below.

I assume that the process of imitation and innovation leads to the following law of motion of each monopolist's productivity:

$$A(\nu, t) = \eta \bar{A}(t - 1) + \gamma A(t - 1) + \varepsilon(\nu, t), \tag{21.38}$$

where $\eta > 0$, $\gamma > 0$, and $\varepsilon(\nu, t)$ is a random variable with zero mean that captures differences in innovation performance across firms and sectors.

In (21.38), $\eta \bar{A}(t - 1)$ stands for advances in productivity coming from the adoption of technologies from the frontier (and thus depends on the productivity level of the frontier, $\bar{A}(t - 1)$), while $\gamma A(t - 1)$ stands for the component of productivity growth coming from innovation (building on the existing knowledge stock of the economy in question at time $t - 1$, $A(t - 1)$). Let us also define

$$a(t) \equiv \frac{A(t)}{\bar{A}(t)}$$

as the (inverse) measure of the country's *distance to the technological frontier* at date t.

Integrate (21.38) over $v \in [0, 1]$, use the fact that $\varepsilon(v, t)$ has mean zero, divide both sides by $\bar{A}(t)$, and use (21.36) to obtain a simple linear relationship between a country's distance to frontier $a(t)$ at date t and its distance to the frontier $a(t-1)$ at date $t-1$:

$$a(t) = \frac{1}{1+g}(\eta + \gamma a(t-1)). \tag{21.39}$$

This equation is similar to the technological catch-up equation (18.4) in Section 18.2. It shows how the dual process of imitation and innovation may lead to a process of convergence. In particular, as long as $\gamma < 1 + g$, (21.39) implies that $a(t)$ eventually converges to 1. This equation also shows that the relative importance of imitation and innovation depends on the distance to the frontier of the economy in question. In particular when $a(t)$ is large (meaning the country is close to the frontier), innovation γ matters more for growth. In contrast when $a(t)$ is small (meaning the country is farther from the frontier), imitation η is relatively more important.

To obtain further insights, let us now endogenize η and γ using a reduced-form approach. Following the analysis in Acemoglu, Aghion, and Zilibotti (2006), I model the parameters η and γ as functions of the investments undertaken by the entrepreneurs and the contractual arrangement between firms and entrepreneurs. The key idea is that there are two types of entrepreneurs: high-skill and low-skill. When an entrepreneur starts a business, his skill level is unknown and is revealed over time through his subsequent performance. Thus two types of "growth strategies" are possible. The first one emphasizes selection of high-skill entrepreneurs and replaces any entrepreneur who is revealed to have low skill. This growth strategy involves a high degree of churning (creative destruction) and a large number of young entrepreneurs (as older unsuccessful entrepreneurs are replaced by new young entrepreneurs). The second strategy maintains experienced entrepreneurs in place even when they have low skills. This strategy therefore involves an organization of firms relying on longer-term relationships (here between entrepreneurs and the credit market), an emphasis on experience and cumulative earnings, and less creative destruction. While low-skill entrepreneurs are less productive than high-skill ones, there are potential reasons for preferring an experienced low-skill entrepreneur to a new young entrepreneur. For example, experience may increase productivity, at least in certain tasks. Alternatively, Acemoglu, Aghion, and Zilibotti (2006) show that in the presence of credit market imperfections, the retained earnings of an old entrepreneur may provide him with an advantage in the credit market (because he can leverage his existing earnings to raise more money and undertake greater productivity-enhancing investments). I denote the strategy based on selection by $R = 0$, while the strategy that maintains experienced entrepreneurs in place is denoted by $R = 1$.

The key reduced-form assumption here is that experienced entrepreneurs (either because of the value of experience or because of their retained earnings) are better at increasing the productivity of their company when this involves the imitation of technologies from the world frontier, which can be thought to correspond to relatively "routine" tasks. High-skill entrepreneurs, on the other hand, are more innovative and generate higher growth through innovation. Thus the trade-off between $R = 1$ and $R = 0$ and the associated trade-off between organizational forms boils down to the trade-off between imitation of technologies from the world technology frontier and innovation. For this reason, I refer to the first strategy as an "imitation-based growth strategy" and to the second as an "innovation-based growth strategy." Motivated by these considerations, let us assume that the equation for the law of motion of the distance to frontier, (21.39), takes the form

$$a(t) = \begin{cases} \frac{1}{1+g}(\bar{\eta} + \underline{\gamma} a(t-1)) & \text{if } R(t) = 1, \\ \frac{1}{1+g}(\underline{\eta} + \bar{\gamma} a(t-1)) & \text{if } R(t) = 0. \end{cases} \qquad (21.40)$$

Let us also impose the following conditions:

$$\bar{\eta} > \underline{\eta}, \text{ and } \underline{\gamma} < \bar{\gamma} < 1 + g. \qquad (21.41)$$

The first part of this assumption follows immediately from the notion that high-skill entrepreneurs are better at innovation, while the second part (in particular, that $\bar{\gamma} > \underline{\gamma}$) builds in the feature that experienced entrepreneurs are better at imitation. When the imitation-based growth strategy is pursued, experienced entrepreneurs are not replaced, and consequently, there is greater transfer of technology from the world technology frontier. The final part of this assumption, $\underline{\gamma} < 1 + g$, simply ensures that imitation-based growth does not lead to faster growth than the world technology frontier. We can thus interpret assumption (21.37) as stating that the world technology frontier advances due to innovation-based growth strategy, which is natural, since a country at the world technology frontier cannot imitate others.

Figure 21.4 plots (21.40) and shows that the economy with long-term contracts ($R = 1$) achieves greater growth (higher level of $a(t)$ for given $a(t-1)$) through the imitation channel but lower growth through the innovation channel. The figure also shows that which regime maximizes the growth rate of the economy depends on the level of $a(t-1)$, that is, on the distance of the economy to the world technology frontier. In particular, inspection of (21.40) is sufficient to establish that there exists a threshold

$$\hat{a} \equiv \frac{\bar{\eta} - \underline{\eta}}{\bar{\gamma} - \underline{\gamma}} \in (0, 1) \qquad (21.42)$$

such that when $a(t-1) < \hat{a}$, the imitation-based strategy ($R = 1$) leads to greater growth, and when $a(t-1) > \hat{a}$, the innovation-based strategy ($R = 0$) achieves higher growth. Thus for the economy to follow a growth-maximizing sequence of strategies, it should start with $R = 1$ and then switch to an innovation-based strategy, $R = 0$, once it is sufficiently close to the world technology frontier. In the imitation-based regime, incumbent entrepreneurs are sheltered from the competition of younger entrepreneurs, and this may enable the economy to make better use of the experience of older entrepreneurs or to finance greater investments out of their retained earnings. In contrast, the innovation-based regime is based on an organizational form relying on greater selection of entrepreneurs and places greater emphasis on maximizing innovation at the expense of experience, imitation, and investment.

Figure 21.4 describes the law of motion of technology in an economy as a function of the organization of firms (markets) as captured by R. It does not specify what the equilibrium sequence $\{R(t)\}_{t=0}^{\infty}$ is. To determine this sequence, we need to specify the equilibrium behavior, which involves the selection of entrepreneurs as well as the functioning of credit markets. Space restrictions preclude me from providing a full analysis of the equilibrium in such a model. Instead, I informally discuss some of the main insights of such an analysis.

Conceptually, one might want to distinguish among four configurations, which arise as equilibria under different institutional settings and parameter values.

1. *Growth-maximizing equilibrium:* the first and the most obvious possibility is an equilibrium that is growth maximizing. In particular, if markets and entrepreneurs have growth maximization as their objective and are able to solve the agency problems, have

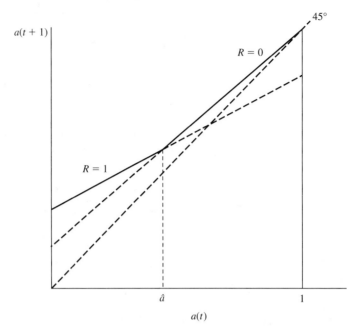

FIGURE 21.4 Dynamics of the distance to frontier in the growth-maximizing equilibrium.

the right decision-making horizon, and are able to internalize the pecuniary and non-pecuniary externalities, an efficient equilibrium would result. This equilibrium takes a simple form:

$$R(t) = \begin{cases} 1 & \text{if } a(t-1) < \hat{a}, \\ 0 & \text{if } a(t-1) \geq \hat{a}, \end{cases}$$

so that the economy achieves the upper envelope of the two solid lines in Figure 21.4. In this case, there is no possibility of outside intervention to increase the growth rate of the economy.[2] Moreover an economy starting with $a(0) < 1$ always achieves a growth rate greater than g and ultimately converges to the world technology frontier, that is, $a(t) \to 1$. In this growth-maximizing equilibrium, the economy first starts with a particular set of organizations or institutions, corresponding to $R = 1$. Then the economy undergoes a structural transformation—in this case, a change in its organizational form—switching from $R = 1$ to $R = 0$. In our simple economy, this structural transformation takes the form of long-term relationships disappearing and being replaced by shorter-term relationships, greater competition among entrepreneurs and firms, and better selection of entrepreneurs.

2. *Underinvestment equilibrium:* the second potential equilibrium configuration involves the following equilibrium organizational form:

$$R(t) = \begin{cases} 1 & \text{if } a(t-1) < a_r(\delta), \\ 0 & \text{if } a(t-1) \geq a_r(\delta), \end{cases}$$

2. However, recall that growth maximization is not necessarily the same as welfare maximization. Depending on how preferences and investments are specified, the growth-maximizing allocation may not maximize welfare.

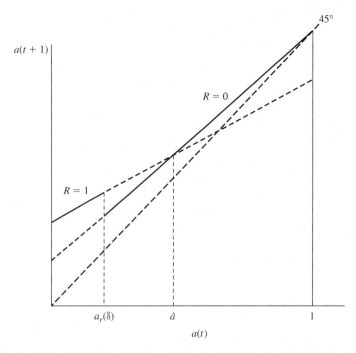

FIGURE 21.5 Dynamics of the distance to frontier in the underinvestment equilibrium.

where $a_r(\delta) < \hat{a}$. Figure 21.5 depicts this equilibrium visually, with the thick black lines corresponding to the equilibrium law of motion of the distance to the frontier, a. How is $a_r(\delta)$ determined? Acemoglu, Aghion, and Zilibotti (2006) show that when investment is important for innovation and credit markets are imperfect, then the retained earnings of old (experienced) entrepreneurs enable them to undertake greater investments. However, because of monopolistic competition, there is the standard *appropriability effect*, whereby an entrepreneur that undertakes a greater investment does not capture all the surplus generated by this investment, because some of it accrues to households in the form of greater consumer surplus. The appropriability effect discourages investments, and in this context, because greater investments are associated with more experienced entrepreneurs, it discourages the imitation-based strategy. This reasoning also explains why this equilibrium is referred to as the "underinvestment equilibrium": in the range $a \in (a_r(\delta), \hat{a})$, the economy could reach a higher growth rate (as shown in the figure) by choosing $R(t) = 1$, but because the appropriability effect discourages investments, a switch to the innovation-based equilibrium occurs before the growth-maximizing threshold is reached.

A notable feature is that although the underinvestment equilibrium is different from the previous case, it again starts with $R = 1$ and is followed by a structural transformation, that is, by a switch to the innovation-based regime ($R = 0$). Moreover the economy still ultimately converges to the world technology frontier; that is, $a(t) = 1$ is reached as $t \to \infty$. The only difference is that the structural transformation from $R = 1$ to $R = 0$ happens too soon, at $a(t - 1) = a_r(\delta)$, rather than at the growth-maximizing threshold $\hat{a}$.

Consequently, in this case, a temporary government intervention may increase the growth rate of the economy. The temporary aspect is important here, since the best that the government can do is to increase the growth rate while $a \in (a_r(\delta), \hat{a})$. How can the government achieve this? Subsidies to investment would be one possibility. Acemoglu, Aghion, and Zilibotti (2006) show that the degree of competition in the product market also has an indirect effect on the equilibrium, as emphasized by the notation $a_r(\delta)$. In particular, a higher level of δ, which corresponds to lower competition in the product market (higher χ), increases $a_r(\delta)$ and thus may close the gap between $a_r(\delta)$ and $\hat{a}$. Nevertheless it has to be noted that reducing competition creates other, static, distortions (because of higher markups). Moreover and more importantly, we will see in the next two configurations that reducing competition can have much more detrimental effects on economic growth, so any use of competition policy for this purpose must be subject to serious caveats.

3. *Sclerotic equilibrium:* the third possibility is a sclerotic equilibrium in which $a_r(\delta) > \hat{a}$, so that low-productivity incumbents survive even when they are potentially damaging to economic growth. Acemoglu, Aghion, and Zilibotti (2006) show that this configuration can also arise in equilibrium because the retained earnings of incumbent entrepreneurs act as a *shield* protecting them against the forces of creative destruction brought about by new entrepreneurs. Consequently, the retained earnings or other advantages of experienced entrepreneurs both have (social) benefits and costs, and which of these dominates depends on parameter values. When the benefits dominate, the equilibrium may feature too rapid a switch to the innovation-based strategy, and when the costs dominate, the economy may experience sclerosis in the imitation regime, with excessive protection of incumbents.

   The resulting pattern in this case is drawn in Figure 21.6. Now the economy fails to achieve the maximum growth rate for a range of values of a such that $a \in (\hat{a}, a_r(\delta))$. In this range, the innovation-based regime would be growth maximizing, but the economy is stuck with the imitation-based regime, because the retained earnings and the power of the incumbents prevent the transition to the more efficient organizational forms. An interesting feature is that, as Figure 21.6 shows, this economy also follows a pattern in line with Kuznets's vision: it starts with a distinct set of organizations, represented by $R = 1$, and then switches to a different set of arrangements, $R = 0$. Like the previous two types of equilibria, this case also features convergence to the world technology frontier, that is, to $a = 1$.

4. *Nonconvergence trap equilibrium:* the fourth possibility is related to the third one and also involves $a_r(\delta) > \hat{a}$. However, now the gap between $a_r(\delta)$ and $\hat{a}$ is larger (as depicted in Figure 21.7) and includes the level of a, a_{trap}, such that

$$a_{\text{trap}} \equiv \frac{\bar{\eta}}{1 + g - \underline{\gamma}}.$$

Inspection of (21.40) immediately reveals that if $a(t - 1) = a_{\text{trap}}$ and $R(t) = 1$, the economy remains at a_{trap}. Therefore in this case the retained earnings or the experience of incumbent firms afford them so much protection that the economy never transitions to the innovation-based equilibrium. This scenario not only retards growth for a temporary interval but also pushes the economy into a nonconvergence trap. In particular, this is the only equilibrium pattern in which the economy fails to converge to the frontier; in the imitation-based regime, $R = 1$, the economy does not grow beyond a_{trap}, and at this distance from the frontier, the equilibrium always involves $R = 1$.

   This equilibrium therefore illustrates the most dangerous scenario—that of nonconvergence. Encouraging imitation-based growth, for example by supporting incum-

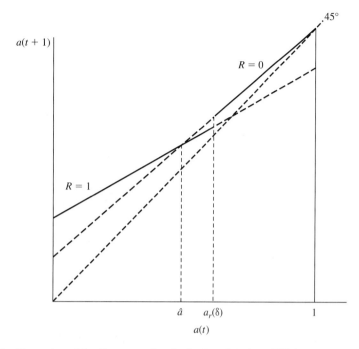

FIGURE 21.6   Dynamics of the distance to frontier in the sclerotic equilibrium.

bent firms, may at first appear to be a good policy. But in practice, it may condemn the economy to nonconvergence. This case is also the only one in which the switch to $R = 0$ and the associated structural transformation does not occur because the economy remains trapped. In many ways, this case might best illustrate Kuznets' vision: the resulting economy is an underdeveloped one, partly because it is unable to realize the structural transformation necessary for the process of economic development.

Taken together, the four scenarios suggest that depending on the details of the model, there should be no presumption that the efficient or the growth-maximizing sequence of growth strategies will be pursued. Thus some degree of government intervention might be useful. However the third and the fourth cases also emphasize that government intervention can have negative unintended consequences. It may improve growth during a limited period of time (in the second scenario, this is the case when $a \in (a_r(\delta), \hat{a})$), but it may subsequently create much more substantial costs by leading to a nonconvergence trap as shown in Figure 21.7.

Even though the implications of these four scenarios for government intervention are mixed, their implications for changes in the structure of organizations over the development process are clearer: regardless of which scenario applies, the economy starts with a distinct organization of production in which longer-term contracts, incumbent producers, experience, and imitation are more important, and then (except in the nonconvergence trap equilibrium) it ultimately switches to an equilibrium with greater creative destruction, shorter-term relationships, younger entrepreneurs, and more innovation. This is another facet of the structural transformations emphasized by Kuznets as part of the process of economic development. The framework presented here, though reduced-form, can also be used to study other aspects of changes in the organization of production over the process of development (see Exercise 21.7).

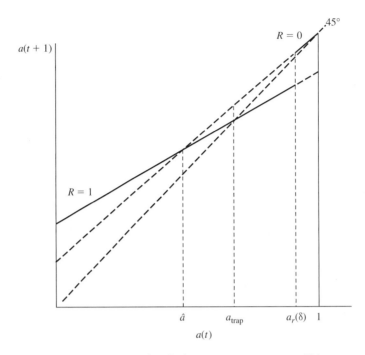

FIGURE 21.7 Dynamics of the distance to frontier in a nonconvergence trap. If the economy starts with $a(0) < a_{\text{trap}}$, it fails to converge to the world technology frontier and instead converges to a_{trap}.

21.5 Multiple Equilibria from Aggregate Demand Externalities and the Big Push

I now present a simple model of multiple equilibria arising from aggregate demand externalities, based on Murphy, Shleifer, and Vishny's (1989) "big push" model. This model formalizes ideas first proposed by Rosenstein-Rodan (1943), Hirschman (1958), and Nurske (1958) that economic development can (or should) be viewed as a move from one (Pareto inefficient) equilibrium to another, more efficient, equilibrium. Moreover these early development economists argued that this type of move requires coordination among different individuals and firms in the economy and thus a big push. As already discussed in Chapter 4, multiple equilibria, literally interpreted, are unlikely to be the root cause of persistently low levels of development, since if there is indeed a Pareto improvement—a change that will make all individuals better off—it is unlikely that the necessary coordination cannot be achieved for decades or even centuries. Nevertheless the forces leading to multiple equilibria highlight important economic mechanisms that can be associated with market failures slowing down, or even preventing, the process of development. Moreover dynamic versions of models of multiple equilibria can lead to multiple steady states such that once an economy ends up in a steady state with low economic activity, it may get stuck there (and there is no possibility of a coordination to jump to another steady state). Models with multiple steady states, which are more useful for thinking about the process of long-run development than models with multiple equilibria, are discussed in the next section.

Murphy, Shleifer, and Vishny formalize the ideas related to the big push using a model with multiple equilibria due to aggregate demand externalities. The economy has two periods, $t = 1$ and 2, and admits a representative household with preferences

$$U(C(1), C(2)) = \frac{C(1)^{1-\theta} - 1}{1-\theta} + \beta \frac{C(2)^{1-\theta} - 1}{1-\theta},$$

where $C(1)$ and $C(2)$ denote consumption at the two dates, β is the discount factor of the households, and θ plays a similar role to before ($1/\theta$ is the intertemporal elasticity of substitution and determines how willing individuals are to substitute consumption between date 1 and date 2). The representative household supplies labor inelastically, and the total labor supply is denoted by L.

The resource constraints are

$$C(1) + I(1) \le Y(1) \text{ and } C(2) \le Y(2), \tag{21.43}$$

where $I(1)$ denotes investment at date 1, $Y(t)$ is total output at date t, and investment is only possible at date 1.

Households can borrow and lend, so their budget constraint can be represented as

$$C(1) + \frac{C(2)}{1+r} \le w(1) + \pi(1) + \frac{w(2) + \pi(2)}{1+r},$$

where $\pi(t)$ denotes the profits accruing to the representative household, and $w(t)$ is the wage rate at time t. The parameter r is the interest rate between periods 1 and 2 and adjusts in equilibrium so that the aggregate resource constraints (21.43) hold.

The final good is produced from a CES aggregate of differentiated intermediate goods, with production function

$$Y(t) = \left(\int_0^1 y(v, t)^{\frac{\varepsilon-1}{\varepsilon}} dv \right)^{\frac{\varepsilon}{\varepsilon-1}},$$

where $y(v, t)$ is the output level of intermediate v at date t. As usual ε is the elasticity of substitution between intermediate goods, and we assume that $\varepsilon > 1$.

The production functions of intermediate goods in the two periods are as follows:

$$y(v, 1) = l(v, 1),$$

$$y(v, 2) = \begin{cases} l(v, 2) & \text{with old technology,} \\ \alpha l(v, 2) & \text{with new technology,} \end{cases} \tag{21.44}$$

where $\alpha > 1$, and $l(v, t)$ denotes labor devoted to the production of intermediate good v at time t. Labor market clearing requires that

$$\int_0^1 l(v, t) dv \le L. \tag{21.45}$$

At date 1, there is a designated producer for each intermediate, which I also refer to as a "monopolist." A competitive fringe of firms can also enter and produce each good as productively as the designated producer. At date 1, the designated producer can also invest in the new technology, which costs F in terms of the final good. If this investment is undertaken, this producer's productivity at date 2 will be higher by a factor $\alpha > 1$ as indicated by (21.44). In contrast, the fringe does not benefit from this technological improvement; thus the designated producer has some degree of monopoly power. The profits from intermediate producers are naturally allocated to the representative household.

We will look for the pure-strategy symmetric SPE (SSPE) of this two-period economy (see, e.g., Section 18.5 in Chapter 18). SSPE is defined in the usual fashion as a combination of production and investment decisions for firms and consumption decisions for households that are best responses to one another in both periods.

First, since all goods are symmetric, labor market clearing at date 1 is straightforward and requires that

$$l(v, 1) = L \quad \text{for all } v \in [0, 1]$$

(recall that the measure of sectors and firms is normalized to 1). Thus we have

$$Y(1) = L.$$

At date 2, the equilibrium depends on how many firms have adopted the new technology. Since the focus is on SSPE, it is sufficient to consider the two extreme allocations: all firms adopt the new technology and no firm adopts. In either case, the marginal productivity of all sectors is the same, so labor is allocated equally, resulting in

$$l(v, 2) = L \quad \text{for all } v \in [0, 1].$$

Consequently, when the technology is not adopted,

$$Y(2) = L,$$

and when the technology is adopted by all the firms,

$$Y(2) = \alpha L.$$

I now turn to the pricing decisions. In the first date, the designated producers have no monopoly power because of the competitive fringe; thus they charge a price equal to the marginal cost, which is $w(1)$, and they make zero profits (i.e., $p(v, 1) = w(1)$ and $\pi(v, 1) = 0$ for all $v \in [0, 1]$). Since total output is equal to $Y(1) = L$, this also implies that the equilibrium wage rate is $w(1) = 1$. In the second date, if the technology is not adopted, the equilibrium is identical to that at date 1, so $w(2) = 1$, and thus profits are again zero. In this case there is also no investment, so consumption at both dates is equal to L. Since the consumption Euler equation is $C(1)^{-\theta} = (1 + r)\beta C(2)^{-\theta}$, the equilibrium interest rate in this case is

$$\hat{r} = \beta^{-1} - 1. \tag{21.46}$$

Next consider the situation in which the designated producers have invested in the advanced technology. Now they can produce α units of output with one unit of labor, while the fringe of competitive firms still produces one unit of output with one unit of labor. Thus the designated producers have some monopoly power. The extent of this monopoly power depends on the comparison of ε and α.

Let us first determine the demand facing each producer, which is given as a solution to the following program of profit maximization for the final good sector:

$$\max_{[y(v,2)]_{v\in[0,1]}} \left[\int_0^1 y(v, 2)^{\frac{\varepsilon-1}{\varepsilon}} dv \right]^{\frac{\varepsilon}{\varepsilon-1}} - \int_0^1 p(v, 2) y(v, 2) dv,$$

where $p(\nu, 2)$ is the price of intermediate ν at date 2. The first-order condition to this program implies that

$$y(\nu, 2) = p(\nu, 2)^{-\varepsilon} Y(2) \quad \text{for each } \nu \in [0, 1]. \tag{21.47}$$

This expression is useful in laying the foundations for the aggregate demand externalities: the demand for intermediate ν depends on the total amount of production $Y(2)$. The familiar feature of the demand curve (21.47) is that it is isoelastic. To make further progress, first imagine the situation in which there is no fringe of competitive producers. In that case, each designated producer acts as an unconstrained monopolist and maximizes its profits given by price minus marginal cost times quantity, that is,

$$\pi(\nu, 2) = \left(p(\nu, 2) - \frac{w(2)}{\alpha} \right) y(\nu, 2) \quad \text{for each } \nu \in [0, 1].$$

Substituting from (21.47), the firm maximization problem is thus

$$\max_{p(\nu,2)} \left(p(\nu, 2) - \frac{w(2)}{\alpha} \right) p(\nu, 2)^{-\varepsilon} Y(2),$$

which gives the profit-maximizing price as

$$p(\nu, 2) = \frac{\varepsilon}{\varepsilon - 1} \frac{w(2)}{\alpha}.$$

This equation is the standard monopoly price formula with a markup related to demand elasticity over the marginal cost. The markup is constant, because the demand elasticity is constant.

However the monopolist can only charge this price if the competitive fringe cannot enter and make profits stealing the entire market at this price. Since the competitive fringe can produce one unit using one unit of labor, the monopolist can only charge this price if $\varepsilon/((\varepsilon - 1)\alpha) \leq 1$. Otherwise, the price would be too high, and the competitive fringe would enter. Let us assume that α is not so high as to make the monopolist unconstrained. In other words, assume that

$$\frac{\varepsilon}{\varepsilon - 1} \frac{1}{\alpha} > 1. \tag{21.48}$$

Under this assumption, the monopolist is forced to charge a *limit price*. It is straightforward to see that this equilibrium limit price is $p^* = w(2)$. Consequently, given (21.48), each monopolist would make per unit profits equal to

$$w(2) - \frac{w(2)}{\alpha} = \frac{\alpha - 1}{\alpha} w(2).$$

Total profits are then obtained from (21.47) as

$$\pi(\nu, 2) = \frac{\alpha - 1}{\alpha} w(2)^{1-\varepsilon} Y(2). \tag{21.49}$$

The wage rate can be determined from income accounting. Total production is equal to $Y(2) = \alpha L$, and this has to be distributed between profits and wages, thus yielding

$$\frac{\alpha - 1}{\alpha} w(2)^{1-\varepsilon} \alpha L + w(2)L = \alpha L,$$

which has a solution of $w(2) = 1$, exactly the same as in the case without the technological investments. Intuitively, wages in this economy are determined by the demand from the competitive fringe and thus the greater marginal product does not directly benefit workers. Instead it increases monopolists' profits. Nevertheless all of these profits are redistributed to households, who are the owners of the firms, and thus $C(2) = \alpha L$. However, because of investment in the new technology at date 1, $C(1) = L - F$. The consumption Euler equation now requires $(L - F)^{-\theta} = (1 + \tilde{r})\beta(\alpha L)^{-\theta}$, which gives the equilibrium interest rate in this case as

$$\tilde{r} = \beta^{-1}\left(\frac{\alpha L}{L - F}\right)^{\theta} - 1 > \hat{r},$$

where $\hat{r}$ is given by (21.46). The interest rate in this case, $\tilde{r}$, is higher than $\hat{r}$, because individuals are now being asked to forgo date 1 consumption for date 2 consumption. Note also that the greater is θ, the higher is $\tilde{r}$, since with a greater θ there is less intertemporal substitution. Also a higher F (meaning a greater consumption sacrifice at date 1) implies a higher interest rate.

The question is whether a monopolist finds it profitable to undertake the investment at date 1. The reason for the possibility of multiplicity of equilibria is that the answer to this question depends on whether other firms are undertaking the investment. Let us first consider a situation in which no other firm is undertaking the investment and consider the incentives of a single monopolist to undertake such an investment.

In this case total output at date 2 is equal to L (since the firm considering investment is infinitesimal), and the market interest rate is given by $\hat{r}$. Moreover, from (21.49) and the fact that $w(2) = 1$, profits at date 2 are

$$\pi^N(v, 2) = \frac{\alpha - 1}{\alpha}L \quad \text{for each } v\varepsilon[0, 1],$$

where the superscript N denotes that no other firm is undertaking the investment. Therefore the net discounted profits at date 1 for the firm in question are

$$\Delta\pi^N = -F + \frac{1}{1 + \hat{r}}\frac{\alpha - 1}{\alpha}L = -F + \beta\frac{\alpha - 1}{\alpha}L.$$

Next, consider the case in which all other firms are undertaking the investment. In this case, profits at date 2 are

$$\pi^I(v, 2) = (\alpha - 1)L \quad \text{for each } v \in [0, 1],$$

where the superscript I designates that all other firms are undertaking the investment. Consequently the profit gain from investing at date 1 is

$$\Delta\pi^I = -F + \frac{1}{1 + \tilde{r}}(\alpha - 1)L = -F + \beta\left(\frac{\alpha L}{L - F}\right)^{-\theta}(\alpha - 1)L.$$

As discussed above, the idea of the paper by Murphy, Shleifer, and Vishny (1989) (similar to the ideas of many economists writing on economic development before them) was to generate multiple equilibria, with one corresponding to backwardness and the other to industrialization. In the present context, this result means that for the same parameter values, both the allocations with no investment in the new technology and with all monopolists investing in the new technology should be equilibria. This is possible if

$$\Delta\pi^N < 0 \text{ and } \Delta\pi^I > 0, \tag{21.50}$$

that is, when nobody else invests, investment is not profitable; when all other firms invest, investment is profitable. This result is clearly possible because the *aggregate demand externalities* ensure that $\Delta\pi^I > \Delta\pi^N$: when other firms invest, they produce more, there is greater aggregate demand, and profits from the new technology are higher. Counteracting this effect is the fact that the interest rate is also higher when all firms invest. Therefore the existence of multiple equilibria requires that the interest rate effect not be too strong. For example, in the extreme case in which preferences are linear ($\theta = 0$), we have

$$\Delta\pi^I = -F + \beta(\alpha - 1)L > \Delta\pi^N = -F + \beta\frac{\alpha - 1}{\alpha}L,$$

so the configuration in (21.50) is certainly possible. More generally, the condition for the existence of multiple equilibria is that

$$\beta\left(\frac{\alpha L}{L - F}\right)^{-\theta}(\alpha - 1)L > F > \beta\frac{\alpha - 1}{\alpha}L. \tag{21.51}$$

It is also straightforward to see that when both equilibria exist, the equilibrium with investment Pareto dominates the one without investment, since (21.51) implies that all households are better off with the upward-sloping consumption profile, giving them higher consumption at date 2 (see Exercise 21.8). Therefore this analysis establishes that when (21.51) is satisfied, there exist two (pure-strategy) SSPE. In one of these, all firms undertake the investment at date 1 and households are better off, while in the other one there are no investments in new technology and greater market failures. Intuitively, investing in the new technology at date 1 is profitable only when there is sufficient aggregate demand at date 2; in turn, there is sufficient demand at date 2 when all firms invest in the new technology. Aggregate demand externalities are responsible for the multiple equilibria here. In particular, the investment decision of a firm creates a positive (pecuniary) externality on other firms by increasing the level of demand facing their products. These pecuniary externalities correspond to first-order effects because of monopoly markups: firms do not capture the full gains from increased production, which instead creates first-order gains for households and for other firms that can sell more.

The interpretation of this result suggested by Murphy, Shleifer, and Vishny is to consider the equilibrium with no investment in the new technology as representing a "development trap," where the economy remains in underdevelopment because no firm undertakes the investment in new technology. This behavior implies that the demand necessary to make such investments profitable is absent. In contrast, the equilibrium with investment in new technology is interpreted as corresponding to industrialization. According to this interpretation, societies that can somehow coordinate on the equilibrium with investment (either because private expectations are aligned or because of some type of government action) industrialize and realize both economic growth and Pareto improvement. Thus this model is argued to provide a formalization of the big push type of industrialization described by economists such as Nurske or Rosenstein-Rodan. Although the idea of the big push and the aggregate demand externalities are attractive, the model here suffers from a number of obvious shortcomings. First, even though the process of industrialization is a dynamic one, the model here is static. Therefore it does not allow a literal interpretation of a society being first in the no-investment equilibrium and then changing to the investment equilibrium and industrializing. Second, as already discussed in Chapter 4, models with multiple equilibria do not provide satisfactory theories of development, since it is difficult to imagine a society remaining unable to coordinate on a simple range of actions that would make all households (and firms) better off. Instead it is much more likely that the ideas related to aggregate demand externalities (or other potential forces leading to multiple equilibria) are more important as sources of persistence or as mechanisms generating multiple steady states (while still maintaining a unique equilibrium path).

21.6 Inequality, Credit Market Imperfections, and Human Capital

The previous section illustrated how aggregate demand externalities can generate development traps. Investment by different firms may require coordination, leading to multiple equilibria. Underdevelopment may be thought to correspond to a situation in which the coordination is on the bad equilibrium, and the development process starts with the big push, ensuring coordination to the high-investment equilibrium. Here I illustrate a related set of issues in the context of the impact of the distribution of income on human capital under imperfect credit markets. In contrast to the previous section, I emphasize the possibility of multiple steady states (rather than multiple equilibria). In addition, while I focus on human capital investments, inequality and credit market problems influence not only human capital investments but also business creation, occupational choices, and other aspects of the organization of production. Nevertheless models focusing on the link between inequality and human capital are more tractable and constitute a natural continuation of the theories of human capital investments presented in Chapter 10.

21.6.1 A Simple Case with No Borrowing

When credit markets are imperfect, a major determinant of human capital investments is the distribution of income (as well as the degree of imperfection in credit markets). I start with a discussion of the simplest case in which there is no borrowing or lending, which introduces an extreme form of credit market problems. I then enrich this model by introducing imperfect credit markets, where the cost of borrowing is greater than the interest rate received by households engaged in saving.

The economy consists of a continuum 1 of dynasties. Each individual lives for two periods, childhood and adulthood, and begets an offspring in his adulthood. There is consumption only at the end of adulthood. Preferences are given by

$$(1 - \delta) \log c_i(t) + \delta \log e_i(t),$$

where c is consumption at the end of the individual's life, and e is the educational spending on the offspring of this individual. The budget constraint is

$$c_i(t) + e_i(t) \leq w_i(t),$$

where w denotes the wage income of the individual. Notice that preferences here have the warm glow type of altruism encountered in Chapter 9 and in Section 21.2. In particular, parents do not care about the utility of their offspring but simply about what they bequeath to them (here, education). As usual, this assumption significantly simplifies the analysis.

The labor market is competitive, and the wage income of each individual is simply a linear function of his human capital, $h_i(t)$:

$$w_i(t) = A h_i(t).$$

The human capital of the offspring of individual i of generation t in turn is given by

$$h_i(t+1) = \begin{cases} e_i(t)^\gamma & \text{if } e_i(t) \geq 1, \\ \bar{h} & \text{if } e_i(t) < 1, \end{cases} \tag{21.52}$$

where $\gamma \in (0, 1)$, and $\bar{h} \in (0, 1)$ is some minimum level of human capital that the individual attains even without any educational spending. Once spending exceeds a certain level (here set equal to 1), the individual starts benefiting from the additional spending and accumulates further human capital (though with diminishing returns, since $\gamma < 1$).

Equation (21.52) introduces a crucial feature necessary for models of credit market imperfections to generate multiple equilibria or multiple steady states; a nonconvexity in the technology of human capital accumulation. Exercise 21.9 shows that this nonconvexity plays a pivotal role in the results here.

Given this description, the equilibrium is straightforward to characterize. Each individual chooses the spending on education that maximizes his own utility. This immediately implies the following "saving rate" in terms of education:

$$e_i(t) = \delta w_i(t) = \delta A h_i(t). \tag{21.53}$$

This rule has one unappealing feature (not crucial for any of the results): because parents derive utility from educational spending on their children, they invest in education even when $e_i(t) < 1$; but in this case, educational spending is wasted (it does not translate into higher human capital of the offspring).

To obtain stark results, let us also assume that

$$\delta A > 1 > \delta A \bar{h}. \tag{21.54}$$

Now, let us look at the dynamics of human capital for a particular dynasty i. If at time 0, $h_i(0) < (\delta A)^{-1}$, then (21.53) implies that $e_i(0) < 1$, so the offspring will have $h_i(1) = \bar{h}$. Given (21.54), $h_i(1) = \bar{h} < (\delta A)^{-1}$, and repeating this argument, $h_i(t) = \bar{h} < (\delta A)^{-1}$ for all t. Therefore a dynasty that starts with $h_i(0) < (\delta A)^{-1}$ never reaches a human capital level greater than $\bar{h}$.

Next consider a dynasty with $h_i(0) > (\delta A)^{-1}$. Then from (21.54), $h_i(1) = (\delta A h_i(0))^\gamma > 1$, so this dynasty gradually accumulates more and more human capital over generations and ultimately reaches the steady state given by $h^* = (\delta A h^*)^\gamma$, or

$$h^* = (\delta A)^{\frac{\gamma}{1-\gamma}} > 1.$$

Naturally, this description applies to any dynasty with $h_i(0) \in ((\delta A)^{-1}, h^*)$. If $h_i(0) > h^*$, then the dynasty would have too much human capital and would decumulate human capital.

Figure 21.8 illustrates the dynamics of individual human capital decisions. It shows that there are two steady-state levels of human capital for individuals, $\bar{h}$ and $h^* > \bar{h}$. An important question when there are multiple steady states is where, given initial conditions, the economy (or a particular individual) converges to. Assume for now that, even though there are multiple steady states, the equilibrium is unique (meaning that given initial conditions, there is a unique equilibrium path—this is the case in all the models discussed in this section). Then equilibrium dynamics are represented by a dynamical system with multiple steady states. Each (locally) asymptotically stable steady state will have a *basin of attraction*, meaning a set of initial conditions that ultimately lead to this particular steady state. Both steady states in the model studied here are asymptotically stable, and Figure 21.8 plots their basins of attractions. In

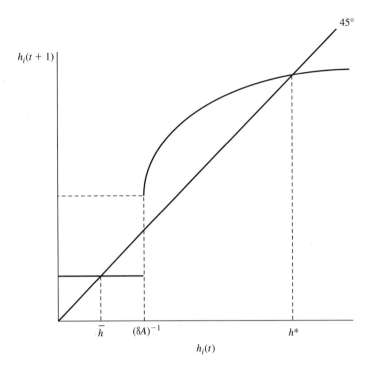

FIGURE 21.8 Dynamics of human capital with nonconvexities and no borrowing.

particular, inspection of this figure shows that the basin of attraction of steady state $\bar{h}$ is $(0, (\delta A^{-1}))$, that is, dynasties with $h_i(0) < (\delta A)^{-1}$ tend to the lower steady-state level of human capital, $\bar{h}$. Those with $h_i(0) > (\delta A)^{-1}$ are in the basin of attraction of h^* and tend to this higher level of human capital.

This figure also reveals why the dynamics in this model are so simple: the dynamics of the human capital of a single individual contain all the information relevant for the dynamics of human capital and income of the entire economy. This is because there are no prices (e.g., the rate of return to human capital, or the interest rate) that are determined in equilibrium here. For this reason, the dynamics in this type of model are sometimes described as *Markovian*—because they are summarized by the Markov process describing the behavior of the human capital of a single individual (without any general equilibrium interactions). Markovian models are much more tractable than those in which the dynamics of inequality depend on equilibrium prices. An example of this richer type of model is given in Exercise 21.13.

The most important implication of this analysis is again the presence of poverty traps. This is most clearly illustrated by an economy with two groups starting at income levels h_1 and $h_2 > h_1$ such that $(\delta A)^{-1} < h_2$. If inequality (poverty) is high, so that $h_1 < (\delta A)^{-1}$, a significant fraction of the population never accumulates much human capital. In contrast, if inequality is limited so that $h_1 > (\delta A)^{-1}$, all agents accumulate human capital, eventually reaching h^*. This example also illustrates that there are (many) multiple steady states in this economy. Depending on the fraction of dynasties that start with initial human capital below $(\delta A)^{-1}$, any fraction of the population may end up at the low level of human capital, $\bar{h}$. The greater is this fraction, the poorer is the economy.

There are certain parallels between the multiplicity of steady states here and the multiple equilibria highlighted in the model of the previous section. Nevertheless, the differences are more important. In the model in Section 21.5, there are multiple equilibria in a static model.

Thus nothing determines which equilibrium the economy will be in. At best, we can appeal to expectations, arguing that the better equilibrium will emerge when everybody expects the better equilibrium to emerge. One can informally appeal to the role of history, for example, suggesting that if an economy has been in the low investment equilibrium for a while, it is likely to stay there, but this argument is misleading. First of all, the model is a static one; thus a discussion of an economy "that has been in the low equilibrium for a while" is not quite meaningful. Second, even if the model were turned into a dynamic one by repeating it over time, the history of being in one equilibrium for a number of periods has no effect on the existence of multiple equilibria in the next period. In particular, each static equilibrium would still remain an equilibrium in the "dynamic" environment, and the economy could suddenly jump from one equilibrium to another. Thus models with multiple equilibria have a degree of indeterminacy that is both theoretically awkward and empirically difficult to map to reality. Models with multiple steady states avoid these thorny issues. The equilibrium is unique, but the initial conditions determine where the dynamical system will eventually end up. Because the equilibrium is unique, there is no issue of indeterminacy or expectations affecting the path of the economy. But because multiple steady states are possible, the model can be useful for thinking about potential development traps.

This model also shows the importance of the distribution of income in an economy with imperfect credit markets (here with no credit markets). In particular, the distribution of income affects which individuals are unable to invest in human capital accumulation and thus influences the long-run income level of the economy. For this reason, models of this sort are sometimes interpreted as implying that an unequal distribution of income leads to lower output (and growth). The above example with two classes seems to support this conclusion. However, it is not a general result, and it is important to emphasize that this class of models does not make specific predictions about the relationship between inequality and growth. To illustrate this, consider again the same economy with two classes, but now starting with $h_1 < h_2 < (\delta A)^{-1}$. In this case, neither group accumulates human capital, but redistributing resources away from group 1 to group 2 (thus increasing inequality), so that we push group 2 to $h_2 > (\delta A)^{-1}$, would increase human capital accumulation. This feature is general: in models with nonconvexities, there are no unambiguous results about whether greater inequality is good or bad for economic growth; it depends on whether greater inequality pushes more people below or above the critical thresholds. Somewhat sharper results can be obtained about the effect of inequality on human capital accumulation and development under additional assumptions. Exercise 21.10 presents a parameterization of inequality in the model here that shows that greater inequality leads to lower human capital and lower output per capita in relatively rich economies but to greater investments in human capital in poorer economies.

21.6.2 Human Capital Investments with Imperfect Credit Markets

I now enrich the environment in Section 21.6.1 by introducing credit markets, following Galor and Zeira's (1993) model. Each individual still lives for two periods. In his youth, he can either work or acquire education. The utility function of each individual is

$$(1 - \delta) \log c_i(t) + \delta \log b_i(t),$$

where again c denotes consumption at the end of the life of the individual. The budget constraint is

$$c_i(t) + b_i(t) \leq y_i(t),$$

where $y_i(t)$ is individual i's income at time t. Note that preferences still take the warm glow form, but the utility of the parent now depends on the monetary bequest to the offspring, $b_i(t)$, rather than on the level of education expenditures. It is now the individuals themselves who use the monetary bequests to invest in education. The logarithmic formulation once again ensures a constant saving rate equal to δ.

Education is a binary outcome, and educated (skilled) workers earn wage w_s, while uneducated workers earn w_u. The required education expenditure to become skilled is h, and workers acquiring education do not earn the unskilled wage w_u during the first period of their lives. The fact that education is a binary decision introduces the aforementioned nonconvexity in human capital investment decisions.[3]

Imperfect capital markets are modeled by assuming that there is some monitoring required for loans to be paid back. The cost of monitoring creates a wedge between the borrowing and lending rates. In particular, assume that there is a linear savings technology open to all agents, which fixes the lending rate at some constant r. However the borrowing rate is $i > r$, because of costs of monitoring necessary to induce agents to pay back the loans (see Exercise 21.12 for a more micro-founded version of these borrowing costs).

Also assume that

$$w_s - (1+r)h > w_u(2+r), \tag{21.55}$$

which implies that investment in human capital is profitable when financed at the lending rate r.

Consider an individual with wealth x. If $x \geq h$, (21.55) implies that the individual invests in education. If $x < h$, then whether it is profitable to invest in education depends on the wealth of the individual and on the borrowing interest rate i.

Let us now write the utility of this individual (with $x < h$) in the two scenarios, and also the bequest that he will leave to his offspring. These are

$$U_s(x) = \log(w_s + (1+i)(x-h)) + \log(1-\delta)^{1-\delta}\delta^\delta,$$

$$b_s(x) = \delta(w_s + (1+i)(x-h)),$$

when he invests in education. When he chooses not to invest, then the equations become

$$U_u(x) = \log((1+r)(w_u + x) + w_u) + \log(1-\delta)^{1-\delta}\delta^\delta,$$

$$b_u(x) = \delta((1+r)(w_u + x) + w_u).$$

Comparing these expressions, it is clear that an individual prefers to invest in education if and only if

$$x \geq f \equiv \frac{(2+r)w_u + (1+i)h - w_s}{i - r}.$$

The dynamics of individual wealth can then be obtained simply by using the bequests of unconstrained, constrained-investing, and constrained-noninvesting agents.

---

3. An alternative to nonconvexities in human capital investments is presented in Galor and Moav (2004), who show that multiple steady states are possible when there are no nonconvexities, credit markets are imperfect, and the marginal propensity to save is higher for richer dynasties. This assumption is motivated by Kaldor's (1957) paper and was discussed in Exercise 2.12 in Chapter 2.

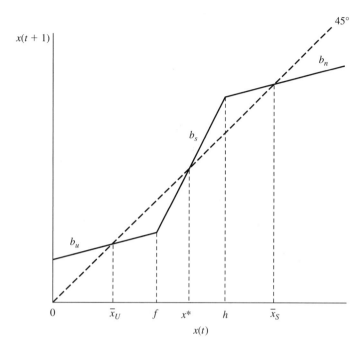

FIGURE 21.9 Multiple steady-state equilibria in the Galor and Zeira (1993) model.

More specifically, the equilibrium correspondence describing equilibrium dynamics is

$$x(t+1) = \begin{cases} b_u(x(t)) = \delta((1+r)(w_u + x(t)) + w_u) & \text{if } x(t) < f, \\ b_s(x(t)) = \delta(w_s + (1+i)(x(t) - h)) & \text{if } h > x(t) \geq f, \quad (21.56) \\ b_n(x(t)) = \delta(w_s + (1+r)(x(t) - h)) & \text{if } x(t) \geq h. \end{cases}$$

Equilibrium dynamics can now be analyzed diagrammatically by looking at the graph of (21.56), which is shown in Figure 21.9. As emphasized in the context of the model of Section 21.6.1, the curve corresponding to (21.56) describes both the evolution of the wealth of each individual and that of the aggregate wealth distribution in the aggregate economy. This is again a feature of the Markovian nature of the current model.

Now define x^* as the intersection of the equilibrium curve (21.56) with the $45°$ line when the equilibrium correspondence is steeper. Such an intersection exists when the borrowing interest rate i is large enough and the lending interest rate r is not too large (in particular, we need $i > (1 - \delta)/\delta > r$). Suppose this is the case. Then Figure 21.9 makes it clear that there will be three intersections between (21.56) and the $45°$ line: $\bar{x}_U, x^*,$ and $\bar{x}_S$. Moreover, the figure shows that x^* corresponds to an unstable steady state, while the other two are locally asymptotically stable.

The basin of attraction of the steady states for $\bar{x}_U$ and $\bar{x}_S$ are also easy to obtain from this figure. In particular, all individuals with $x(t) < x^*$ converge to the wealth level $\bar{x}_U$, while all those with $x(t) > x^*$ converge to the greater wealth level $\bar{x}_S$. Thus the basin of attraction of $\bar{x}_U$ is $(0, x^*)$, and this corresponds to a poverty trap, in the sense that individuals (dynasties) with initial wealth in this interval converge to $\bar{x}_U$. The initial distribution of income again has a first-order effect on the efficiency and income level of the economy. If the majority of individuals start with $x(t) < x^*$, the economy is characterized by low productivity, low human capital, and low wealth. Therefore this model extends the insights of the simple model with no borrowing from Section 21.6.1 to a richer environment in which individuals make forward-looking human capital investments. The key is again the interaction between credit market imperfections (which here make the interest rate for borrowing greater than the interest rate for saving) and inequality. As in the earlier model, it is straightforward to construct examples where an increase in inequality can lead to either worse or better outcomes, depending on whether the scenario pushes more individuals into the basin of attraction of the low steady state.

An important feature of the model here is that because it allows individuals to borrow and lend in financial markets, it enables an investigation of the implications of financial development for human capital investments. In an economy with better financial institutions, the wedge between the borrowing rate and the lending rate is smaller, that is, i is smaller for a given level of r. With a smaller i, more agents escape the poverty trap, and in fact, the poverty trap may not exist at all (there may not be an intersection between (21.56) and the $45°$ line where (21.56) is steeper). Thus financial development not only improves risk sharing (as demonstrated in Section 21.1), but by relaxing credit market constraints, it also contributes to human capital accumulation.

Although the model in this section is considerably richer than that in Section 21.6.1, it is still a partial equilibrium model. Multiple steady states are possible for different individuals as a function of their initial level of human capital (or wealth), but individual dynamics are not affected by general equilibrium prices. Galor and Zeira (1993), Banerjee and Newman (1993), Aghion and Bolton (1997), and Piketty (1997) consider richer environments in which income dynamics of each dynasty (individual) are affected by general equilibrium prices (e.g., interest rate or wage rate), which are themselves functions of the income inequality. Exercise 21.11 shows that the type of multiple steady states generated by the model presented here may not be robust to the addition of noise in income dynamics—instead of multiple steady states, the long-run equilibrium may generate a stationary distribution of human capital levels, though this stationary distribution would exhibit considerable persistence.[4] In contrast, models in which prices are determined in general equilibrium and affect wealth (income) dynamics can generate more robust multiplicity of steady states.

21.7   Toward a Unified Theory of Development and Growth?

A unifying theme recurs in to the models discussed in this chapter. They have either emphasized the transformation of the economy and the society during the process of development or potential reasons for the failure of such a transformation. This transformation takes the form of the structure of production changing, the process of industrialization getting underway, a greater fraction of the population migrating from rural areas to cities, financial markets becoming more developed, mortality and fertility rates changing through health improvements and the demographic transition, and the extent of inefficiencies and market failures becoming less pronounced over time. In many instances, the driving force for this process is reinforced by the structural transformation that it causes.

---

4. Note that this is related to the Markovian nature of the model. Markovian models can generate multiple steady states because the Markov chain or the Markov process implied by the model is not ergodic (e.g., poor individuals can never accumulate enough to become rich). A small amount of noise then ensures that different parts of the distribution "communicate," making the Markov process ergodic and thus removing the multiplicity of steady states.

My purpose in this section is not to offer a unified model of structural transformations and market failures in development. An attempt to pack many different aspects of development into a single model often leads to a framework that is complicated, whereas I believe that relatively abstract representations of reality are more insightful. Moreover the literature has not made sufficient progress for us to be able to develop a unified framework. Instead I provide a reduced-form model intended to bring out the salient common features of the models presented in this chapter.

In all of the models presented in this and the previous chapters, economic development is associated with capital deepening, that is, with greater use of capital instead of human labor. Thus we can also approximate the growth process with an increase in the capital-labor ratio of the economy, $k(t)$. This does not necessarily mean that capital accumulation is the engine of economic growth. In fact, previous chapters have emphasized how technological change is often at the root of the process of economic growth (and economic development), and thus capital deepening may be the result of technological change. Moreover Section 21.4 shows how the crucial variable capturing the stage of development might be the distance of an economy's technology from the world technology frontier. Nevertheless, even in these cases, an increase in the capital-labor ratio takes place along the equilibrium path and can thus be used as a proxy for the stage of development (though in this case one must be careful not to confuse increasing the capital-labor ratio with ensuring economic development). With this caveat in mind, in this section I take the capital-labor ratio as the proxy for the stage of development, and for analytical convenience, I use the Solow model to represent the dynamics of the capital-labor ratio.

In particular, consider a continuous-time economy, with output per capita given by

$$y(t) = f(k(t), x(t)), \tag{21.57}$$

where $k(t)$ is the capital-labor ratio, and $x(t)$ is some social variable, such as financial development, urbanization, the structure of production, or the structure of the family. As usual, f is assumed to be differentiable, increasing, and strictly concave in k. The social variable x potentially affects the efficiency of the production process and thus is part of the per capita production function in (21.57). As a convention, suppose that an increase in x corresponds to "structural change" (e.g., a move from the countryside to the cities). Therefore f is also increasing in x, and the partial derivative with respect to x is nonnegative, that is, $f_x \geq 0$. Naturally, not all structural change is beneficial. Nevertheless for simplicity, I focus on the case in which f is increasing in x.

Suppose that structural change can be represented by the differential equation

$$\dot{x}(t) = g(k(t), x(t)), \tag{21.58}$$

where g is assumed to be twice differentiable. Since x corresponds to structural change associated with development, g should be increasing in k, and in particular, its partial derivative with respect to k is strictly positive, that is, $g_k > 0$. The standard "mean-reversion" type of reasoning suggests that the case in which the derivative g_x is negative is the most reasonable benchmark. If x is above its natural level, it should decline, and if it is below its natural level, it should increase. Motivated by this reasoning, let us also assume that $g_x < 0$.

Capital accumulates according to the Solow growth model as in Chapter 2, so that

$$\dot{k}(t) = sf(k(t), x(t)) - \delta k(t), \tag{21.59}$$

where I have suppressed population growth, and there is no technological change for simplicity. For a fixed x, capital naturally accumulates in an identical fashion to that in the basic Solow model. The structure of this economy is slightly more involved, because $x(t)$ also changes.

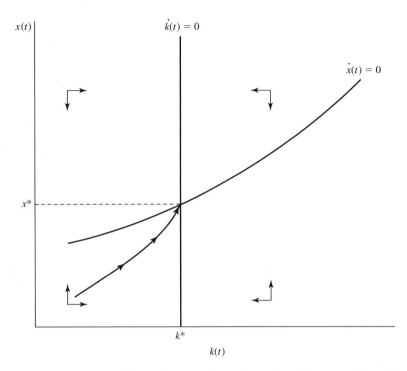

FIGURE 21.10 Capital accumulation and structural transformation without any effect of the social variable x on productivity.

First consider the case in which $f_x(k, x) \equiv 0$, so that the social variable x has no effect on productivity. The dynamics in this case are shown in Figure 21.10. The thick vertical line corresponds to the locus for $\dot{k}(t)/k(t) = 0$: it represents the steady state of the differential equation (21.59). This locus takes the form of a vertical line, since only a single value of $k(t)$, k^*, is consistent with steady state. The upward-sloping line, on the other hand, corresponds to (21.58) and shows the locus of the values of k and x such that $\dot{x}(t)/x(t) = 0$. It is upward sloping, since g is increasing in k and decreasing in x. The laws of motion, represented by the arrows in the figure, follow directly from (21.58) and (21.59). For example, when $k(t) < k^*$, (21.59) implies that $k(t)$ will increase. Similarly, when $x(t)$ is above the $\dot{x}(t)/x(t) = 0$ locus, (21.58) implies that $x(t)$ will decrease. Given these laws of motion, it is straightforward to see that the dynamical system representing the equilibrium of this model is globally stable, and starting with any $k(0) > 0$ and $x(0) > 0$, the economy travels toward the unique steady state (k^*, x^*). Now consider the dynamics of a less-developed economy, that is, an economy that starts with a low capital-labor ratio $k(0)$ and a low level of the social variable $x(0)$. Then development in this economy takes place with gradual capital deepening and a corresponding increase in $x(t)$ toward x^*, which can be viewed as a reduced-form representation of development-induced structural change.

Next, consider the more interesting case in which $f_x(k, x) > 0$. In this case, the locus for $\dot{k}(t)/k(t) = 0$ is also upward sloping, since $f_x > 0$ and the right-hand side of (21.59) is decreasing in k by the standard arguments (in particular, because by the strict concavity of $f(k, x)$ in k, $f(k, x)/k > f_k(k, x)$ for all k and x; see Exercise 21.14). A steady state is again given by the intersection of the loci for $\dot{k}(t)/k(t) = 0$ and $\dot{x}(t)/x(t) = 0$. Since both of these curves are now upward sloping, multiple steady states are possible (Figure 21.11). These multiple steady states may correspond to the multiple equilibria arising from aggregate demand

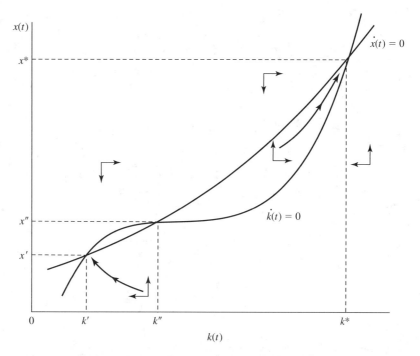

FIGURE 21.11 Capital accumulation and structural transformation with multiple steady states.

externalities or from the presence of imperfect credit markets. The low steady state (k', x') corresponds to a situation in which the social variable x is low, which depresses productivity and makes the economy settle into an equilibrium with a low capital-labor ratio. In contrast, in the high steady state (k^*, x^*) the high level of x supports greater productivity and thus a greater capital-labor ratio consistent with steady state. It can be verified that both the low and the high steady states are typically locally stable, so that starting from the neighborhood of one, the economy converges to that steady state and tends to stay there. This observation highlights the importance of historical factors in the development process. If historical factors or endowments placed the economy in the basin of attraction of the low steady state, the economy converges to this steady state, corresponding to a development trap. Interestingly, this development trap is, at least in part, caused by lack of structural change (i.e., by a low value of the social variable x).

Figure 21.11 makes it clear that such multiplicity requires the locus for $\dot{k}(t)/k(t) = 0$ to be relatively flat, at least over some range. Inspection of (21.59) shows that this is the case when $f_x(k, x)$ is large, at least over some range. Intuitively, multiple steady states can only arise when the social variable x (or structural change) has a large effect on productivity.

Perhaps more interesting than multiple steady states is the situation in which the same forces are present, but a unique steady state exists. The same reasoning suggests that this occurs when $f_x(k, x)$ is relatively small. In this case, the locus for $\dot{k}(t)/k(t) = 0$ is everywhere steeper than the locus for $\dot{x}(t)/x(t) = 0$. This case is plotted in Figure 21.12, and the unique steady state is given by (k^*, x^*). The laws of motion, represented by the arrows in the figure, again follow from the inspection of the differential equations (21.58) and (21.59). This figure shows that the unique steady state is globally stable (see Exercise 21.14 for a proof). Consider, once again, a less-developed economy starting with a low capital-labor ratio $k(0)$ and a low value of the social variable $x(0)$. The dynamics in this case are qualitatively similar to those in Figure 21.10. However the economics is slightly different. Capital accumulation (capital deepening) leads to an increase in $x(t)$ as before, but now this structural change also improves productivity (as

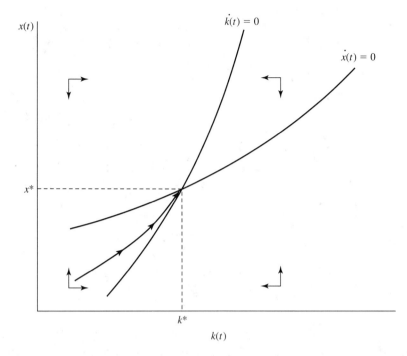

FIGURE 21.12   Capital accumulation and structural transformation when the social variable x affects productivity, but there exists a unique steady state.

in the models in Section 17.6 in Chapter 17 and in Sections 21.3 and 21.1). This increase in productivity leads to faster capital accumulation and there is a self-reinforcing (cumulative) process of development, with economic growth leading to structural changes that facilitate further growth. However, since the effect of x on productivity is limited, this process ultimately takes the economy toward a unique steady state.

This reduced-form representation of structural change therefore captures some of the salient features emphasized in this chapter. It is not meant to be a unified model; on the contrary, rather than combining multiple dimensions of structural change, it presents an abstract representation emphasizing how the process of development—corresponding to capital accumulation—can go hand-in-hand with structural change, which may in turn increase productivity and facilitate further capital accumulation. Developing a truly unified model of economic development and structural change is an area for future work.

21.8   Taking Stock

This chapter provided a large number of models focusing on various aspects of the structural transformation accompanying economic development. As emphasized in the previous section, there is no single framework unifying these distinct aspects, even though there are many common themes in these models. The previous section was an attempt to bring out these common themes. Instead of repeating these commonalities, here I conclude by pointing out that many of the topics covered in this chapter are at the frontier of current research, and much still remains to be done. Economic development is intimately linked to economic growth, but it may require different, even specialized, models that do not focus just on balanced growth and the orderly growth behavior captured by the neoclassical and endogenous technology models. These models may also need to take market failures and how these market failures change over time more seriously. This view stems from the recognition that the essence of economic development is the process of structural transformation, including financial development, the demographic transition, migration, urbanization, organizational change, and other social changes.

Another potentially important aspect of economic development is the possibility that the inefficiencies in the organization of production, credit markets, and product markets may culminate in development traps. These inefficiencies may stem from lack of coordination in the presence of aggregate demand externalities or from the interaction between imperfect credit markets and human capital investments. These topics not only highlight some of the questions that need to be addressed for understanding the process of economic development but also bring a range of issues that are often secondary in the standard growth literature to the forefront of analysis. These include, among other things, the organization of financial markets, the distribution of income and wealth, and issues of incentives (e.g., problems of moral hazard), adverse selection, and incomplete contracts in both credit markets and production relationships.

The recognition that the analysis of economic development necessitates a special focus on these topics also opens the way for a more constructive interaction between empirical development studies and the theories of economic development surveyed in this chapter. As already noted, there is now a large literature on empirical development economics, documenting the extent of credit market imperfections, the impact of inequality on human capital investments and occupation choices, the process of social change, and various other market failures in less-developed economies. By and large, this literature is about market failures in less-developed economies and sometimes also focuses on how these market failures can be rectified. The standard models of economic growth do not feature these market failures. A fruitful area for future research is then the combination of theoretical models of economic growth and development (that pay attention to market failures) with the rich empirical evidence on the incidence, characterization, and costs of these market failures. This combination has the advantage of being theoretically rigorous and empirically grounded, and perhaps most importantly, it can focus on what I believe to be the essence of development economics—the questions of why some countries are less developed, how they can grow more rapidly, and how they can jumpstart the process of structural transformation necessary for economic development.

21.9 References and Literature

By its nature, this chapter has covered a large amount of material. My selection of topics has reflected my own interests and was also motivated by a desire to keep this chapter from becoming even longer than it already is.

Section 21.1 scratches the surface of a rich literature on financial development and economic growth. On the theoretical side, Townsend (1979), Greenwood and Jovanovic (1990), and Bencivenga and Smith (1991) focus on the interaction between financial development on the one hand and risk sharing, the allocation of funds across different tasks, and individuals on the other. Obstfeld (1994) and Acemoglu and Zilibotti (1997) focus on the relationship between financial development and the diversification of risks. There is also a large empirical literature looking at the effect of financial development on economic growth. An excellent survey of this literature is provided in Levine (2005). Some of the best-known empirical papers include King and Levine (1993), which documents the cross-country correlation between measures of financial development and economic growth, Rajan and Zingales (1998), which shows that lack of financial development has particularly negative effects on sectors that have greater external borrowing needs, and Jayaratne and Strahan (1996), which documents how banking deregulation that increased competition in U.S. financial markets led to more rapid financial and economic growth in the United States. In discussing financial development, I also mentioned the literature on the Kuznets curve. There is no consensus on whether there is a Kuznets curve. Work that focuses on historical data, such as Lindert and Williamson (1976) or Bourguignon and Morrison (2002), reports aggregate patterns consistent with a Kuznets curve, while studies using panels of countries in the postwar era, such as Fields (1980), do not find a consistent pattern resembling this curve.

The literature on fertility, the demographic transition, and growth is also vast. The main trends in world population and cross-country differences in population growth are summarized in Livi-Bacci (1997) and Maddison (2003). The idea that parents face a trade-off between the numbers and the human capital of their children—the quality and quantity trade-off—was proposed by Becker (1981). The aggregate patterns in Livi-Bacci (1997) are consistent with this idea, though there is little micro evidence supporting this trade-off. Recent work on micro data (by Black, Devereux, and Salvanes (2005); Angrist, Lavy, and Schlosser (2006); and Qian (2007)) looks at evidence from Norway, Israel, and China but does not find strong support for the quality-quantity trade-off. Fertility choices were first introduced into growth models by Becker and Barro (1988) and Barro and Becker (1989). Becker, Murphy, and Tamura (1990) provide the first endogenous growth model with fertility choice. More recent work on the demographic transition and the transition from a Malthusian regime to one of sustained growth include Goodfriend and McDermott (1995), Galor and Weil (1996, 2000), Hansen and Prescott (2002), and Doepke (2004). Kalemli-Ozcan (2002) and Fernandez-Villaverde (2003) focus on the effect of declining mortality on fertility choices in a growth context. A recent series of papers by Galor and Moav (2002, 2004) combine fertility choice, quality-quantity trade-off, and natural selection. Galor (2005) provides an excellent overview of this literature. The first model presented in Section 21.2 is a simplified version of Malthus's classic model in his (1798) book, while the second model is a simplified version of Becker and Barro (1988) and Galor and Weil (2000).

Urbanization is another major aspect of the process of economic development. Bairoch (1988) provides an overview of the history of urbanization. The first model in Section 21.3 builds on Arthur Lewis's (1954) classic, which argued that early development can be viewed as a situation in which there is surplus labor available to the modern sector, and thus growth is constrained by capital and technology but not by labor. Harris and Todaro's well-known (1970) paper also emphasizes the importance of migration, though their model features free migration between rural and urban areas and suggests that unemployment in urban areas is the key equilibrating variable.

The second model, presented in Section 21.3.2, is based on Banerjee and Newman (1998) and Acemoglu and Zilibotti (1999). Banerjee and Newman emphasize the advantage of smaller rural communities in reducing moral hazard problems in credit relations and show how this interacts with the process of urbanization, which involves individuals migrating to areas where their marginal product is higher. Acemoglu and Zilibotti argue that development leads to information accumulation. In particular, as more individuals perform similar tasks, more socially useful information is revealed, which enables more complex contractual and production relations. Section 21.3.2 also touched on another important aspect of social and economic relations in less-developed economies: the importance of community enforcement. Clifford Geertz (1963) emphasizes the importance of community enforcement mechanisms and how they may sometimes conflict with markets. Section 21.4 builds on Acemoglu, Aghion, and Zilibotti (2006).

Section 21.5 is based on Murphy, Shleifer, and Vishny's famous (1989) paper, which formalized ideas first proposed by Rosenstein-Rodan (1943). Other models that demonstrate the possibility of multiple equilibria in monopolistic competition models featuring nonconvexities include Kiyotaki (1988), who derives a similar result in a model with endogenous labor supply choices as well as investment decisions. Matsuyama (1995) provides an excellent overview of these models and a clear discussion of why pecuniary externalities can lead to multiple equilibria in the presence of monopolistic competition.

The distinction between multiple equilibria and multiple steady states is discussed in Krugman (1991) and Matsuyama (1991). Both of these papers highlight the idea that in models with multiple equilibria, expectations determine which equilibria emerge, while with multiple steady states, there can be (or often is) a unique equilibrium, and initial conditions (history) determine where the economy will end up.

The model in Section 21.6.2 is based on the first model in Galor and Zeira (1993). Similar ideas are investigated in Banerjee and Newman (1993) in the context of the effect of inequality on occupational choice, and in Aghion and Bolton (1997) and Piketty (1997) in the context of the interaction between inequality and entrepreneurial investments. Other work on the dynamics of inequality and its interactions with efficiency include Loury (1981), Tamura (1991), Benabou (1996), Durlauf (1996), Fernandez and Rogerson (1996), Glomm and Ravikumar (1992), and Acemoglu (1997b).

21.10 Exercises

21.1 Analyze the equilibrium of the economy in Section 21.1, relaxing the assumption that each individual has to invest either all or none of his wealth in the risky saving technology. Does this generalization affect the qualitative results derived in the text?

21.2 Consider the economy in Section 21.1.

(a) Show that in (21.5), $K(t+1)$ is everywhere increasing in $K(t)$ and that there exists some $\bar{K}$ such that the capital stock grows over time when $K(t) > \bar{K}$.

(b) Can there be more than one steady-state level of capital stock in this economy? If so, provide an intuition for this type of multiplicity.

(c) Provide sufficient conditions for the steady-state level of capital stock K^* to be unique. Show that in this case $K(t+1) > K(t)$ when $K(t) < K^*$.

21.3 In the model of Section 21.2.1, suppose that the population growth equation takes the form $L(t+1) = \varepsilon(t)(n(t+1)-1)L(t)$ instead of (21.8), where $\varepsilon(t)$ is a random variable that takes one of two values, $1 - \bar{\varepsilon}$ or $1 + \bar{\varepsilon}$, reflecting random factors affecting population growth. Characterize the stochastic equilibrium. In particular, plot the stochastic correspondence representing the dynamic equilibrium behavior, and analyze how shocks affect population growth and income dynamics.

21.4 Characterize the full dynamics of migration, urban capital-labor ratio, and wages in the model of Section 21.3.1 (i.e., consider the cases in which conditions 1, 2, and 3 in that section do not all hold simultaneously).

21.5 Consider the model of Section 21.3.2, and suppose that all individuals have time $t = 0$ utility given by the standard CRRA preferences. Taking the equilibrium path in that section as given, find a level of community enforcement advantage ξ that would maximize time $t = 0$ utility. What happens if the actual comparative advantage of community enforcement of villages is greater than this level?

21.6 Consider the maximization problem (21.31).

(a) Explain why this maximization problem characterizes the equilibrium allocation of workers to tasks. What kind of price system would support this allocation?

(b) Derive the first-order conditions (21.32).

(c) Provide sufficient conditions such that the solution to this problem involves all skilled workers being employed at technology $\bar{h}$.

(d) Provide an example in which no worker is employed at technology $\bar{h}$, even though $A_{\bar{h}} > A_h$ for all $h \in [0, \bar{h}]$.

(e) Can there be a solution where more than two technologies are being used in equilibrium? If so, explain the conditions for such an equilibrium to arise.

21.7 Consider a variant of the model in Section 21.4, in which firms have to make a decision on organizational form; in particular, they decide whether to vertically integrate. For this purpose, consider a slight modification of (21.38):

$$A(v, t) = \eta \bar{A}(t - 1) + \gamma(v, t)A(t - 1),$$

with $\gamma(v, t) = \underline{\gamma} + \theta(v, t)$. Suppose that entrepreneurial effort increases $\theta(v, t)$, and the internal organization of the firm affects how much effort the entrepreneur devotes to innovation activities. In particular, suppose that $\theta(v, t) = 0$ if there is vertical integration, because the entrepreneur is overloaded and has limited time for innovation activities. In contrast, with outsourcing, $\theta(v, t) = \theta > 0$. However, when there is outsourcing, the entrepreneur has to share a fraction $\beta > 0$ of the profits with the manager (owner) of the firm to which certain tasks have been outsourced (whereas in a vertically integrated structure, he can keep the entire revenue).

(a) Determine the profit-maximizing outsourcing decision for an entrepreneur as a function of $a(t)$. In particular, show that there exists a threshold $\bar{a}$ such that there is vertical integration for all $a(t) \le \bar{a}$ and outsourcing for all $a(t) > \bar{a}$.

(b) Contrast this equilibrium behavior with the growth-maximizing internal organization of the firm.

21.8 Show that when multiple equilibria exist in the model of Section 21.5, the equilibrium with investment Pareto dominates the one without.

21.9 Consider the model of Section 21.6.1, and remove the nonconvexity in the accumulation equation (21.52), so that the human capital of the offspring of individual i is given by $h_i(t + 1) = e_i(t)^\gamma$ for any level of $e_i(t)$ and $\gamma \in (0, 1)$. Show that there exists a unique level of human capital to which each dynasty converges. Based on this result, explain the role of nonconvexities in generating multiple steady states.

21.10 Consider the model of Section 21.6.1, and suppose that the initial inequality is given by a uniform distribution with mean human capital of $h(0)$ and support over $[h(0) - \lambda, h(0) + \lambda]$. An increase in λ corresponds to greater inequality.

(a) Show that when $h(0)$ is sufficiently small, an increase in λ increases long-run average human capital and income, whereas when $h(0)$ is sufficiently large, an increase in λ reduces them. [Hint: use Figures 21.8 and 21.9.]

(b) What other types of distributions (besides uniform) would lead to the same result?

(c) Show that the same result generalizes to the model of Section 21.6.2.

(d) On the basis of this result, discuss whether we should expect greater inequality to lead to higher income in poor societies and lower income in rich societies. (If your answer is no, then sketch an environment in which this is not the case.)

21.11 Consider the model presented in Section 21.6.2. Make the following two modifications. First, the utility function is now

$$(1 - \delta)^{-(1-\delta)}\delta^{-\delta}c^{1-\delta}b^\delta, \tag{21.60}$$

and second, unskilled agents receive a wage of $w_u + \varepsilon$, where ε is a random shock with mean zero.

(a) Suppose that ε is distributed with support $[-\lambda, \lambda]$. Show that if λ is sufficiently close to zero, then the multiple steady states characterized in Section 21.6.2 survive, in the sense that depending on their initial conditions, some dynasties become highly skilled and others become low skilled.

(b) Why was it convenient to change the utility function from the log form used in the text to (21.60)?

(c) Now suppose that ε is distributed with support $[-\lambda, \infty)$, where $\lambda \leq w_u$. Show that in this case there is a unique ergodic distribution of wealth and no poverty trap. Explain why the results here are different from those in part a.

(d) How would the results be different if, in addition, the skilled wage is equal to $w_s + \upsilon$, where υ is another random shock of mean zero? [Hint: simply sketch the analysis and the structure of the equilibrium without repeating the full analysis of part c.]

21.12 (a) In the model of Section 21.6.2, suppose that each individual can run away without paying his debts, and if he does so, he is never caught. However a bank can prevent this by paying a monitoring cost per unit of borrowing equal to m. Suppose that there are many banks competing à la Bertrand for lending opportunities. Under these assumptions, show that all bank lending is accompanied with monitoring, and the lending rate satisfies $i = r + m$. Show that in this case all results in the text apply.

(b) Next suppose that the bank can prevent the individual from running away by paying a fixed monitoring cost of M. Under the same assumptions as in part a, show that in this case the interest rate charged to an individual who borrows an amount $x - h$ is $i = r + M/(x - h)$. Given this assumption, characterize the equilibrium of the model in Section 21.6.2. How do the conclusions change in this case?

(c) Next suppose that there is no way of preventing individuals from running away, but if an individual runs, he is caught with probability p, and if caught, a fraction $\lambda \in (0, 1)$ of his income is confiscated. Given this assumption, characterize the equilibrium dynamics of the model in Section 21.6.2. How do the conclusions change?

(d) Now consider an increase in w_s (for a given level of w_u), so that the skill premium in the economy increases. In which of the three scenarios outlined in parts a–c does this have the largest effect on human capital investments?

21.13 In this exercise, you are asked to study Banerjee and Newman's (1994) model of occupational choice. The utility of each individual is again

$$(1 - \delta)^{-(1-\delta)} \delta^{-\delta} c^{1-\delta} b^{\delta} - z,$$

where z denotes whether the individual is exerting effort, with cost of effort normalized to 1. Each agent chooses one of four possible occupations. These are (1) subsistence and no work, which leads to no labor income and has a rate of return on assets equal to $\hat{r} < 1/\delta$; (2) work for a wage v; (3) self-employment, which requires investment I plus the labor of the individual; and (4) entrepreneurship, which requires investment μI plus the employment of μ workers, and the individual becomes the boss, monitoring the workers (and does not take part in production). All occupations other than subsistence involve effort. Let us assume that both entrepreneurship and self-employment generate a rate of return greater than subsistence (i.e., the mean return for both activities is $\bar{r} > \hat{r}$).

(a) Derive the indirect utility function associated with the preferences above. Show that no individual will work as a worker for a wage less than 1.

(b) Assume that $\mu[I(\bar{r} - \hat{r}) - 1] - 1 > I(\bar{r} - \hat{r}) - 1 > 0$. Interpret this assumption. [Hint: it relates the profitabilities of entrepreneurship and self-employment at the minimum possible wage of 1.]

(c) Suppose that only agents who have wealth $w \geq w^*$ can borrow enough to become self-employed, and only agents who have wealth $w \geq w^{**} > w^*$ can borrow μI to become an entrepreneur. Provide an intuition for these borrowing constraints.

(d) Now compute the expected indirect utility from the four occupations. Show that if $v > \bar{v} \equiv (\mu - 1)(\bar{r} - \hat{r})I/\mu$, then self-employment is preferred to entrepreneurship.

(e) Suppose the wealth distribution at time t is given by $G_t(w)$. On the basis of the results in part d, show that the demand for labor in this economy is given by

$$
\begin{aligned}
x = 0 && \text{if } v > \bar{v}, \\
x \in [0, \mu(1 - G_t(w^{**}))] && \text{if } v = \bar{v}, \\
x = \mu(1 - G_t(w^{**})) && \text{if } v < \bar{v}.
\end{aligned}
$$

(f) Let $\tilde{v} \equiv (\bar{r} - \hat{r})I > \bar{v}$. Then show that the supply of labor is given by

$$
\begin{aligned}
s = 0 && \text{if } v < 1, \\
s \in [0, G_t(w^*)] && \text{if } v = 1, \\
s = G_t(w^*) && \text{if } 1 < v < \tilde{v}, \\
s \in [G_t(w^*), 1] && \text{if } v = \tilde{v}, \\
s = 1 && \text{if } v > \tilde{v}.
\end{aligned}
$$

(g) Show that if $G_t(w^*) > \mu[1 - G_t(w^{**})]$, there is an excess supply of labor and the equilibrium wage rate is $v = 1$. Show that if $G_t(w^*) < \mu[1 - G_t(w^{**})]$, there is an excess demand for labor and the equilibrium wage rate is $v = \bar{v}$.

(h) Now derive the wealth (bequest) dynamics (for a worker with wealth w) as follows: (1) subsistence and no work: $b(t) = \delta \hat{r} w$; (2) worker: $b(t) = \delta(\hat{r}w + v)$; (3) self-employment: $b(t) = \delta(\bar{r}I + \hat{r}(w - I))$; and (4) entrepreneurship: $b(t) = \delta(\bar{r}\mu I + \hat{r}(w - \mu I) - \mu v)$. Explain the intuition for each of these expressions.

(i) Now using the wealth dynamics in part b, show that multiple steady states with different wealth distributions and occupational choices are possible. In particular, show that the steady-state wealth level of a worker when the wage rate is v is $w_w(v) = \delta v/(1 - \delta \hat{r})$, while the steady-state wealth level of a self-employed individual is $w_{se} = \delta(\bar{r} - \hat{r})I/(1 - \delta \hat{r})$, and the wealth level of an entrepreneur is $w_e(v) = \delta(\bar{r}\mu I - \hat{r}\mu I - \mu v)/(1 - \delta \hat{r})$. Now show that when $w_w(v = 1) < w^*$ and $w_e(v = \bar{v}) > w^{**}$, a steady state in which the equilibrium wage rate is equal to $v = 1$ would involve workers not accumulating sufficient wealth to become self-employed, while entrepreneurs accumulate enough wealth to remain entrepreneurs. Explain why. [Hint: it depends on the equilibrium wage rate.]

(j) Given the result in part i, show that if we start with a wealth distribution such that $\mu(1 - G(w^{**})) < G(w^*)$, the steady state involves an equilibrium wage $v = 1$ and no self-employment, whereas for $\mu(1 - G(w^{**})) > G(w^*)$, the equilibrium wage is $v = \bar{v}$ and there is self-employment. Contrast the level of output in these two steady states.

(k) Is the comparison of the steady states in terms of output in this model plausible? Is it consistent with historical evidence? What are the pros and cons of this model relative to the Galor-Zeira model discussed in Section 21.6.2?

21.14 This exercise asks you to analyze the dynamics of the reduced-form model in Section 21.7 more formally than done in the text.

1. Show that when $f_x > 0$, the locus for $\dot{k}/k = 0$ implied by (21.58) is an upward-sloping curve.

2. Consider the differential equations (21.58) and (21.59) and a steady state (k^*, x^*). By linearizing the two differential equations around (k^*, x^*), show that if $f_x(k^*, x^*)$ is sufficiently small, the steady state is locally stable.

3. Provide a uniform bound on $f_x(k, x)$, so that there exists a unique steady state. Show that when this bound applies, the unique steady state is globally stable.

4. Construct a parameterized example where there are multiple steady states. Interpret the conditions necessary for this example. Do you find them economically likely?

PART VIII

THE POLITICAL ECONOMY OF GROWTH

In this part of the book, I turn from the mechanics of economic growth to an investigation of potential causes of economic growth. Almost all models studied so far take economic institutions (e.g., property rights and types of written contracts) policies (e.g., tax rates, distortions, and subsidies), and often the market structure as given. They then derive implications for economic growth and cross-country income differences. While these models constitute the core of growth theory, they leave unanswered some of the central questions raised in Chapters 1 and 4: why do some societies choose institutions and policies that discourage growth, while others choose growth-enhancing social arrangements? In this part of the book, I make a first attempt to provide some answers to these questions based on political economy—that is, on differences in institutions and policies arising from different ways of aggregating individual preferences across societies and on differences in the type and nature of social conflict. In particular, I emphasize a number of key themes and attempt to provide a tractable and informative formalization of these issues. The main themes are as follows.

1. Different institutions (policies) generate different economic allocations. In the context of growth models, this may correspond to distinct growth rates or steady-state levels of output. These institutions also generate different winners and losers, however. Consequently there will be social conflict concerning the types of policies and institutions that a society should adopt.

2. Two interrelated factors are central in shaping collective (equilibrium) choices in the presence of social conflict: the form of political institutions and the political power of different groups. Individuals and groups with significant political power are more likely to be influential and sway policies toward their preferences. Exactly how political power is distributed within the society and how individuals can exercise their political power (resulting from their votes, connections, or brute force) depends on political institutions. For example, a dictatorship that concentrates political power in the hands of a small group implies a different distribution of political power

in the society than a democracy, which corresponds to a society with a greater degree of political equality. We expect that these various political regimes induce different sets of economic institutions and policies and thus lead to different economic outcomes. The purpose of the next two chapters is to investigate this process of collective decision making and the implications of different choices of institutions and policies on economic growth.

3. The technology, the nature of the endowments, and the distribution of income and endowments in the economy influence both preferences and the distribution of political power. For example, the nature of political conflict and the resulting political economy equilibrium is likely to be different in a society where much of the land and the capital stock is concentrated in the hands of a few individuals and families than one in which there is a more equitable distribution of resources. We would also expect politics to function differently in a society where the major assets are in the form of human capital vested in individuals than in one where natural resources, such as diamonds or oil, are the major assets.

The issues raised and addressed in this part of the book are central to the field of political economy. Since this is a book on economic growth, not on political economy, I do not try to do justice to the large and growing literature in this area. Instead I focus on topics and models that I deem to be most important for the questions posed above. I also save space by focusing, when possible, on the neoclassical growth model (in discrete time) rather than some of the richer models that have been presented in this book. This might at first appear an odd choice. Why focus on the neoclassical growth model, which does not generate growth (other than by exogenous technological change), to study the political economy of growth? Yet the neoclassical growth model offers two significant advantages. First, it provides the most tractable framework to analyze the main political economy conflicts. Second, because competitive equilibria in this model are Pareto optimal, the role of political economy distortions become more transparent. Naturally, once the basic forces are understood, it is relatively straightforward to incorporate them into endogenous growth models or other richer structures. Some of the exercises consider these extensions. Finally, throughout I focus on discrete-time models because this makes game-theoretic interactions easier to study.

I have organized the material on the political economy of growth into two chapters. Chapter 22 takes political institutions as given and focuses on the implications of distributional conflict under different scenarios. In this chapter, I highlight why and when distributional conflict can lead to distortionary policies that retard growth. I also offer various complementary frameworks for the analysis of these questions. Chapter 23 then turns to the implications of different political regimes for economic growth and includes a brief discussion of how political institutions themselves are determined endogenously.

Before presenting this material, it is useful to start with an abstract discussion of the relationship between economic institutions, political institutions, and economic outcomes and of how individual preferences over economic and political institutions are formed. Much of the political science literature posits that individuals have (direct) preferences over political institutions (and perhaps also over economic institutions). For example, individuals might derive utility from living under a democratic system. While this assertion is plausible, the approach developed so far emphasizes another, potentially equally important, reason for individuals to have preferences over political institutions.

Economic institutions and policies have a direct effect on economic outcomes (e.g., the effects of tax policies, regulation, and contracting institutions described in previous chapters). Thus a major determinant of individual preferences over economic institutions (and policies) ought to be the allocations that result from these arrangements. Based on this viewpoint, throughout I focus on these induced preferences over economic institutions. The same reasoning applies to political institutions. These determine the political rules under which individuals interact. In direct democracy, for example, key decisions are made by majoritarian voting. In representative democracy, majorities choose representatives, who then make the policy choices and face the risk of being removed from office if they pursue policies that are not in line with the preferences of the electorate. In contrast, in nondemocratic regimes, such as dictatorships or autocracies, a small clique, such as an oligarchy of rich individuals or a junta of generals, make the key decisions. As a result, different policies and economic institutions are likely to emerge in different political systems, and individuals should have induced preferences over political institutions.

To emphasize this point, let us represent the chain of causation described above by a set of mappings. Let $\mathcal{P}$ denote the set of political regimes or institutions, $\mathcal{R}$ be the set of feasible policies (or economic institutions), and $\mathcal{X}$ denote the set of feasible allocations (which include different levels of consumption of all goods and services by all individuals in the society). Ignoring any stochasticity in outcomes for simplicity, we can think of each political institution in the set $\mathcal{P}$ leading to some specific set of economic institutions in the set $\mathcal{R}$. Let this be represented by the mapping $\pi\left(\cdot\right)$. Similarly, different policies lead to different allocations (ignoring again stochastic elements and multiple equilibria); let this be represented by the mapping $\rho\left(\cdot\right)$. Schematically, we can write

$$\mathcal{P} \xrightarrow{\pi(\cdot)} \mathcal{R} \xrightarrow{\rho(\cdot)} \mathcal{X}.$$

Now suppose that each individual i has a utility function $u_i : \mathcal{X} \to \mathbb{R}$, representing his preferences over possible allocations in $\mathcal{X}$. Suppose also that individuals are *consequentialist,* in the sense that they do not care about economic or political institutions beyond these institutions' influences on allocations. Then their preferences over some economic institution $R \in \mathcal{R}$ are simply given by $u_i\left(\rho\left(R\right)\right) \equiv u_i \circ \rho : \mathcal{R} \to \mathbb{R}$. This mapping therefore captures their induced preferences over economic institutions (as a function of the economic allocations that these institutions induce). Preferences over political institutions are also induced in the same manner. The utility that individual i derives from some political institution $P \in \mathcal{P}$ is $u_i\left(\rho\left(\pi\left(P\right)\right)\right) \equiv u_i \circ \rho \circ \pi : \mathcal{P} \to \mathbb{R}$. Induced preferences over institutions are important, since an equilibrium framework ought to explain the emergence and change of political institutions as a function of these preferences.

This brief introduction has therefore laid two types of foundations for the next two chapters. First, as taken up in Chapter 22, we must understand how different types of economic institutions (and policies) affect economic outcomes, including economic performance and the distribution of resources—the mapping $\rho\left(\cdot\right)$. Based on this understanding, we will analyze the preferences of different groups over these economic institutions (policies) and determine the conditions under which different groups will have a preference for distortionary, nongrowth-enhancing economic arrangements. Second, to understand political change and how it interacts with economic decisions and economic growth, we need to study induced preferences over political institutions—the mapping $\pi\left(\cdot\right)$. This is the topic of Chapter 23.

22

Institutions, Political Economy, and Growth

This chapter makes a first attempt at answering the following question that has been in the background of much of what we have done so far: why do similar societies choose different institutions and policies, leading to very different economic growth outcomes? The analysis so far has highlighted the role of capital accumulation, human capital, and technology in economic growth. Throughout I have stressed that the level of physical capital, the extent of human capital, and even the technology of societies should be thought of as endogenous, that is, as responding to incentives. This brings us to the fundamental question: why do different societies provide different incentives to firms and workers? Chapter 4 suggested that differences in institutions are important determinants of these incentives and of cross-country variations in investments in physical capital, human capital, and technology. The purpose of this and the next chapter is to provide models that can help us understand why institutions might have such an effect and why institutions themselves differ across societies.

22.1 The Impact of Institutions on Long-Run Development

As already emphasized in Chapter 4, institutions matter—at least when we look at clusters of economic and political institutions over long horizons. Most of the models in the book incorporate this feature, since they highlight various effects of economic institutions and policies on economic allocations. For example, tax and subsidy policies and market structures may affect physical capital accumulation, human capital investments, and technological progress; and contracting institutions and the structure of the credit markets influence technology choices and the efficiency of production. Perhaps even more important, all models studied so far assume a relatively orderly working of the market economy. Add to these models some degree of insecurity of property rights or entry barriers preventing activities by the more productive firms, and they imply major inefficiencies. Both theory and casual empiricism suggest that these factors are important. We must thus recognize that doing business is very different in the United States than in sub-Saharan Africa. Entrepreneurs and businessmen in the United States (or pretty much in any OECD country) face relatively secure property rights and a stable, orderly environment. Individuals or corporations that wish to create new businesses face relatively few barriers. The situation is starkly different in much of the rest of the world, for example, in sub-Saharan Africa, the Caribbean, and large parts of Central America and Asia. Similarly, the lives of the majority of the population are radically different across these societies: most citizens have access to a wide variety of public goods and the ability to invest in their human capital in most OECD countries but not in many less-developed economies.

Economists often summarize these variations across societies as "institutional differences" (or differences in institutions and policies). The term is slightly unfortunate, but is one that is widely used and accepted in the literature. "Institutions" mean different things in different contexts, and none of these exactly corresponds to the meaning intended here. As already emphasized in Chapter 4, by "institutional differences," we are referring to differences in a broad cluster of social arrangements, including security of property rights for businesses as well as for regular citizens, and the ability of firms and individuals to write contracts to facilitate their economic transactions (contracting institutions), the entry barriers faced by new firms, the socially imposed costs and barriers facing individual investments in human capital, and incentives of politicians to provide public goods. This definition of institutions is quite encompassing. To make theoretical and empirical progress, one typically needs a narrower definition. Toward this goal, I have already distinguished between *economic institutions* (and policies), which correspond to taxes, the security of property rights, contracting institutions, entry barriers, and other economic arrangements, and *political institutions,* which correspond to the rules and regulations affecting political decision making, including checks and balances against presidents, prime ministers, or dictators, as well as methods of aggregating the different opinions of individuals in the society (e.g., electoral laws). In terms of the notation introduced in the introduction to this part, the effect of economic institutions on economic outcomes is summarized by the mapping $\rho(\cdot)$, while the implications of political institutions for the types of economic institutions and policies is captured by the mapping $\pi(\cdot)$.

It is also useful to note that the difference between economic institutions and policies is not always clear, so it is often their combination, not one or the other, that is important. For example, we can refer to the security of property rights as economic institutions, but we would not typically refer to tax rates as institutions. Yet, entirely insecure property rights and 100% taxation of income have much in common. One difference might be that institutions are more durable than policies.[1] Thus in what follows I make a distinction between economic institutions and policies: economic institutions provide a framework in which policies are set. However, when the distinction between economic institutions and policies is unimportant, I typically use "economic institutions" as a stand-in for both.

The evidence presented in Chapter 4 suggests that institutional differences do matter for economic growth. The focus of this section is not to review this evidence, but to build on it and ask the next question: if economic institutions are so important for economic growth, why do some societies choose institutions that do not encourage growth? In fact, based on available historical evidence, we can go further: why do some societies choose institutions and policies that specifically block technological and economic progress? The rest of this chapter and much of the next one provide a framework for answering these questions. I start with an informal discussion of the main building blocks for constructing an answer.

The first important element of the political economy approach is social conflict. There are few (if any) economic changes that would benefit all agents in the society. Thus every change in institutions and policies creates winners and losers relative to the status quo. Take the

---

1. In Section 22.9, I discuss another potential reason that taxation and security of property rights might be different, which relates to how the proceeds are used.

simplest example: removing entry barriers so that a previously monopolized market becomes competitive. While consumers benefit from this policy because of lower prices, the monopolist, who was previously enjoying a privileged position and high profits, will be a loser. The effect on workers depends on the exact market structure. If the labor market is competitive, workers also benefit, since the demand for labor increases with the entry of new firms. But if there are labor market imperfections, so that the employees of the monopolist were previously sharing some of the rents accruing to this firm, they will also be potential losers from the reform. Consequently there will not be unanimous support for removing entry barriers even when removal increases growth and output in the economy.

This example highlights a general principle: because of the different allocations that they induce, individuals have different, conflicting preferences over economic institutions. So if there are conflicting preferences over collective choices in general (and over institutions and policies in particular), how do societies make decisions? Political economy is the formal analysis of this process of collective decision making. If there is social conflict between a monopolist who wishes to retain entry barriers and consumers who wish to dismantle them, the equilibrium of a political process decides the outcome. This process may be orderly in democracies, or disorderly or even chaotic in other political regimes as illustrated by the all-too-frequent civil wars throughout human history. Whether it is a democratic or a nondemocratic process that leads to the equilibrium policy, the political power of the parties with conflicting interests plays a central role. Put simply, if two individuals disagree over a particular choice (e.g., about how to divide a dollar), their relative powers determine the ultimate choice. In the political arena, this corresponds to the political power of different individuals and groups. For example, in the monopoly example, we may expect the monopolist to have political power because it has already amassed income and wealth and may be able to lobby politicians. In a nondemocratic society where the rule of law is tenuous, we can even imagine the monopolist utilizing thugs and paramilitaries to quash the opposition. On the other hand, in a democracy, consumers may have sufficient political power to overcome the interests and wishes of the monopolist through the ballot box or by forming their own lobbying groups.

The second key element of the political economy approach is commitment problems, which act as a source of inefficiency and augment the distortions created by social conflict. Political decisions at each date are made by the political process at that date (e.g., by those holding political power at that time); commitment to future sequences of political and economic decisions are not possible unless they happen to be equilibrium commitments (we will see that whether we use the concept of Subgame Perfect Equilibrium [SPE] or Markov Perfect Equilibrium [MPE] plays an important role).

At this point, it is important to distinguish between nongrowth-enhancing policies (or distortionary policies) and Pareto inefficiency. Many political economy models do not lead to Pareto inefficiency. This is because their equilibria can be represented as solutions to weighted social welfare functions (see Section 22.7). The resulting allocation is then a point along the constrained Pareto frontier of the economy (given the set of available instruments). Nevertheless many such allocations involve distortionary and nongrowth-enhancing policies.[2] In addition, when commitment problems are present, the political equilibrium can involve (constrained) Pareto inefficiencies as well, because there may exist future policy sequences that can make all parties better off, but they may not be implemented in equilibrium.

Consider a situation in which political power is in the hands of a specific group or an individual—the political elite. To simplify the thought experiment, let us ignore any constraints

---

2. Consider, for example, an allocation in which a dictator such as Mobutu Sese Seko in Zaire expropriates all the investors in the country; it is possible to change policies to increase investment and growth, but this will typically imply taking resources and power away from Mobutu and making him worse off.

on the exercise of this political power. Then the elite can set policies to induce allocations that are most beneficial for themselves, and thus the political equilibrium can be thought of as the solution to the maximization of a social welfare function giving all the weight to the elite. Even though the resulting equilibrium may not be Pareto inefficient, it typically involves non-growth-enhancing policies. The key question is: under what circumstances does the exercise of political power by the elite lead to such distortionary policies?

I argue that there are two broad reasons for why those with political power choose distortionary policies. The first is revenue extraction, that is, the attempt by the elite to extract resources from other members of the society. Central to this source of distortionary policies are two aspects of the society: (1) a decoupling between political power (which is in the hands of the elite) and economic opportunities (which lie with the entrepreneurs and the workers) and (2) a limited set of fiscal instruments. These two aspects combined imply that the elite will use the available (distortionary) fiscal instruments to transfer resources from the rest of the society to themselves. We will also see that the same type of distortionary policies emerge even when there is no political elite but decisions are made democratically (see Section 22.8). The restriction to a limited set of fiscal instruments, such as distortionary linear taxes, is important here. Had there been nondistortionary taxes, such as lump-sum taxes, the elite could extract resources from the rest of the society without discouraging economic growth. But lump-sum taxes are often not feasible, and more generally, most forms of redistribution create distortions by reducing incentives for work or effort or by discouraging investment.

Second, the elite may choose distortionary policies because they are in competition with other social groups. This competition may be economic. For example, the elite may be engaged in production and recognize that taxes on other producers will reduce the demand for factors, thus increasing the elite's profits indirectly. I refer to this as the "factor price manipulation" motive for distortionary policies. The competition between the elite and other social groups may also be political. Enrichment by other groups might pose a threat to the elite's ability to use and benefit from their political power in the future; distortionary taxes are then beneficial for the elite as a way of impoverishing their political competitors. I refer to this as the "political replacement" motive for distortionary policies. The rest of the chapter illustrates these various mechanisms. An important implication of the models I present is that factor price manipulation and political replacement motives often lead to greater distortions and are more damaging to the growth potential of a society than the revenue extraction motive.

This basic framework also clarifies the additional inefficiencies created by commitment problems. Because the elite cannot commit to future policies, there may be a *holdup problem*, whereby investments, once undertaken, are expropriated or taxed at prohibitively high rates. Holdup problems are likely to be important in a wide variety of circumstances; for example, when the relevant investments are in long-term projects, so that a range of policies is decided after these investments are undertaken. I also use this framework to illustrate how and under what conditions economic institutions can constrain equilibrium policies.

In Sections 22.7 and 22.8, I show how political economy equilibria can be studied in models with greater heterogeneity and how distributional conflicts in such societies also lead to distortionary policies. Finally I end this chapter by emphasizing the role of public goods provision by the government and how political economy considerations affect equilibrium investment by the state (and the politically powerful groups controlling it) in public goods.

22.2 Distributional Conflict and Economic Growth in a Simple Society

In this and the next four sections, I discuss the implications of distributional conflict for economic growth in *a simple society*. In a simple society individuals are permanently allocated to social groups (e.g., producers, landowners, or workers), and the main distributional conflict is among groups. The latter feature is ensured by assuming that individuals within each group are ex ante identical and restricting the set of fiscal instruments so that it is not possible to redistribute resources from one member of the group to another. The former feature, on the other hand, rules out issues of occupational choice and social mobility, which are discussed in the next chapter. The main advantage of a simple society for our purposes here is that it enables a tractable aggregation of political preferences of individuals. Models in which there is a nondegenerate distribution of endowments (e.g., wealth or productivity) across individuals are studied in Section 22.8. While these models are significantly richer than the simple society studied here, the economic forces that shape the political economy equilibrium are similar, which motivates my choice of presenting a detailed analysis of political economy equilibrium in a simple society in the next several sections.

The society we study comprises three groups of individuals. The first group consists of workers who supply their labor inelastically. The second consists of entrepreneurs who have access to a production technology and make the investment decisions. The third is the elite who make the political decisions (and may also engage in entrepreneurial activities). I first assume that the political system is an oligarchy dominated by the elite. The model is then enriched in various ways in this and the next chapter by introducing additional heterogeneity, incorporating occupational choice, and endogenizing the distribution of political power among the various members of the society.

22.2.1 The Basic Environment

The economy is populated by a continuum $1 + \theta^e + \theta^m$ of risk-neutral agents, each with a discount factor equal to $\beta \in (0, 1)$. There is a unique nonstorable final good denoted by Y. The expected utility of agent i at time 0 is given by

$$\mathbb{E}_0 \sum_{t=0}^{\infty} \beta^t C_i(t), \tag{22.1}$$

where $C_i(t) \in \mathbb{R}$ denotes the consumption of agent i at time t, and $\mathbb{E}_t$ is the expectations operator conditional on information available at time t. The most important feature about these preferences is their linearity (risk-neutrality). The gain in simplicity from linear preferences here more than makes up for the loss of generality—linear preferences remove transitional dynamics but in return enable a complete characterization of political economy equilibria.

There is a continuum of workers, with measure normalized to 1, who supply their labor inelastically. The elite, denoted by "e," initially hold political power in this society. There is a total of θ^e elites. Let us first suppose that the elite do not take part in productive activities (this is discussed in Section 22.4). Finally, there are θ^m "middle class" agents, denoted by "m," who are the entrepreneurs in the economy, with access to the production technology. The label of "middle class" for the entrepreneurs is motivated by some historical examples that are discussed in the next chapter and plays no role in the formal analysis. The sets of elite and middle-class producers are denoted by S^e and S^m, respectively. With a slight abuse of notation, I use i to denote either individual or group (though when referring to groups, I use i as a superscript, and when referring to individuals, as a subscript). The identity of the agents (their social group membership) does not change over time.

Each entrepreneur (middle-class agent) $i \in S^m$ has access to the following production technology for producing the final good:

$$Y_i(t) = F(K_i(t), L_i(t)), \tag{22.2}$$

where $Y_i(t)$ is final output produced by entrepreneur i, and $K_i(t)$ and $L_i(t)$ are the total amount of capital and labor, respectively, that he uses in production. I assume that F satisfies Assumptions 1 and 2 from Chapter 2. Since F exhibits constant returns to scale, without further restrictions a single entrepreneur can employ the entire labor force and the capital stock of the economy. To ensure a dispersed distribution of entrepreneurial activity, I assume that there is a maximum scale for each entrepreneur (e.g., because each entrepreneur has a limited span of control in managing his employees). In particular, suppose that $L_i(t) \in [0, \bar{L}]$ for some $\bar{L} > 0$. Thus at least after a certain level of employment, there are diminishing returns to additional capital investments by each entrepreneur. Since the total workforce in the economy is equal to 1, labor market clearing at time t requires that

$$\int_{S^m} L_i(t)di \leq 1, \tag{22.3}$$

with $L_i(t) \leq \bar{L}$. As in the standard neoclassical model, a fraction δ of capital depreciates.

The (competitive) equilibrium of this economy without taxes—and without considering the effects of political economy—is straightforward. Let $k \equiv K/L$ denote the capital-labor ratio, as usual, and $f(k) \equiv F(K/L, 1)$ the per capita production function. Standard arguments imply that, without taxes, each entrepreneur chooses the capital-labor ratio

$$k_i(t) = k^* \equiv (f')^{-1}(\beta^{-1} + \delta - 1) \tag{22.4}$$

for each t, where $(f')^{-1}(\cdot)$ is the inverse of the marginal product of capital (the derivative of the f function). Equation (22.4) is identical to the standard steady-state equilibrium condition from Chapters 6 and 8 and equates the gross marginal product of capital, $f'(k^*) + 1 - \delta$, with the inverse of the discount factor, β^{-1} (e.g., recall (6.52) in Chapter 6). The difference here is that because of linear preferences, (22.4) applies at all points in time, not only in steady state. Thus there are no transitional dynamics.

Another special feature of this economy is that it may fail to achieve full employment. Recall that the total labor force is equal to 1. However, (22.5) shows that the level of employment of each employer may be strictly less than $1/\theta^m$ because of the maximum size constraint on firms. When this is the case, $1 - \theta^m \bar{L}$ workers are unemployed, and wages are equal to 0. When there is an excess supply of labor, each entrepreneur $i \in S^m$ employs $\bar{L}$ workers, and total employment falls short of total supply. When there is no excess supply, the entire labor force is employed, and the allocation of these workers across the entrepreneurs is arbitrary (since all entrepreneurs would be making zero profits). To simplify the exposition, I assume, without loss of any generality, that even in this case, all entrepreneurs employ the same number workers, so that

$$L_i(t) = L^* \equiv \min \left\{ \bar{L}, \frac{1}{\theta^m} \right\} \tag{22.5}$$

for each $i \in S^m$ at each t.

In addition, in this section I assume that

$$\theta^m \bar{L} > 1, \tag{22.6}$$

which ensures that there is full employment and thus $L^* = 1/\theta^m$. Under this assumption, the equilibrium wage rate in the competitive equilibrium without taxes is

$$w(t) = w^* \equiv f(k^*) - k^* f'(k^*) \quad \text{for all } t, \tag{22.7}$$

where k^* is given in (22.4). I refer to this equilibrium without political economy (with capital-labor ratio k^* and wage rate w^*) as the "first-best equilibrium."

22.2.2 Policies and Economic Equilibrium

Before we can characterize political economy equilibria, we need to specify the set of available fiscal instruments (policies) and then define an economic equilibrium for a given sequence of policies. Throughout, economic equilibria given policies are identical to the competitive equilibria described in Chapters 6 and 8. Economic equilibria resulting from different policies involve different levels of welfare for different agents, thus implicitly defining induced preferences over the policies and economic institutions leading to these economic equilibria. The political equilibrium then aggregates these preferences over different sequences of policies. In the current model, this last step is simplified, given our focus on elite-dominated politics.

Suppose that the society has access to four different policy instruments: a linear tax rate on output $\tau(t) \in [0, 1]$ and lump-sum transfers to each of the three groups (workers, middle-class entrepreneurs, and the elite), $T^w(t) \geq 0$, $T^m(t) \geq 0$, and $T^e(t) \geq 0$. Since lump-sum transfers are nonnegative, they cannot be used for nondistortionary lump-sum taxation. Instead revenues can only be raised using the linear tax on output. While lump-sum taxes might sometimes be possible, the ability of individuals to move into the informal sector or stop working puts limits on the use of lump-sum taxes. Nevertheless the restriction to a simple linear tax rate is quite restrictive, and there might often exist more efficient ways of raising revenues. In political economy models, such restrictions are sometimes made to ensure the existence of equilibrium (e.g., when using the Median Voter Theorem; see Section 22.7). Here they are imposed to emphasize how the interaction between the decoupling of political and economic power and a limited menu of fiscal instruments can lead to distortionary policies.

Let us next specify the timing of events at each date. The most important aspect here is the timing of taxes relative to investments (and this is the main reason that discrete-time models are slightly more convenient in this context). To start with, let us assume that taxes are set before the relevant investment decisions. In particular, the timing of events is such that at each t, we start with a predetermined tax rate on output $\tau(t)$, as well as the capital stocks of the entrepreneurs, $[K_i(t)]_{i \in S^m}$. Entrepreneurs decide how much labor to hire $[L_i(t)]_{i \in S^m}$ (and in the process the labor market clears). Output is produced, and a fraction $\tau(t)$ of the output is collected as tax revenue. The political process (e.g., the politically powerful social group) then decides the transfers, $T^w(t) \geq 0$, $T^m(t) \geq 0$, and $T^e(t) \geq 0$, subject to the government budget constraint

$$T^w(t) + \theta^m T^m(t) + \theta^e T^e(t) \leq \tau(t) \int_{S^m} F(K_i(t), L_i(t))di, \qquad (22.8)$$

where the left-hand side denotes total government expenditure in transfers, and the right-hand side is the predetermined tax rate times output. Next, the political process announces the tax rate $\tau(t+1)$ that will apply at the next date. Entrepreneurs choose their capital stocks for the next date, $[K_i(t+1)]_{i \in S^m}$, after observing this tax rate, so that they know exactly what tax rate they will face at the next date. The alternative, where the capital stock is chosen before the tax rate, is discussed in Section 22.5. For now it suffices to say that this alternative leads to greater distortions because of holdup problems.

More formally, let $p^t = \{\tau(s), T^w(s), T^m(s), T^e(s)\}_{s=t}^{\infty}$ denote a feasible (infinite) sequence of policies starting at time t. An economic equilibrium (from time t on) is a *competitive equilibrium* given p^t and the distribution of capital stocks among the entrepreneurs at time t,

$[K_i(t)]_{i \in S^m}$. This economic equilibrium specifies a sequence of capital stock and labor decisions for each entrepreneur, $\{[K_i(s+1), L_i(s)]_{i \in S^m}\}_{s=t}^{\infty}$, and wage rates, $\{w(s)\}_{s=t}^{\infty}$, such that given $[K_i(t)]_{i \in S^m}$, p^t and $w^t \equiv \{w(s)\}_{s=t}^{\infty}$, $\{K_i(s+1), L_i(s)\}_{s=t}^{\infty}$ maximizes the utility of entrepreneur i for each $i \in S^m$, and given $\{[L_i(s)]_{i \in S^m}\}_{s=t}^{\infty}$, the labor market clears.[3]

Since workers supply labor inelastically, the only nontrivial decisions are by the entrepreneurs. Given any feasible policy sequence p^t and equilibrium wages w^t, the utility of an entrepreneur with capital stock $K_i(t)$ at time t as a function of these policies is

$$\mathbf{U}_i(\{K_i(s), L_i(s)\}_{s=t}^{\infty} \mid p^t, w^t) = \sum_{s=t}^{\infty} \beta^{s-t}[(1 - \tau(s)) F(K_i(s), L_i(s)) \tag{22.9}$$
$$- (K_i(s+1) - (1-\delta)K_i(s)) - w(s)L_i(s) + T^m(s)].$$

This expression makes use of the fact that preferences are linear, and thus the value of the entrepreneur can be written in terms of the discounted sum of his consumption levels. Consumption is simply given by the term in square brackets, since output is taxed at the rate $\tau(t)$ at time t and moreover a fraction $(1-\delta)$ of last period's capital stock is left, so an additional investment of $K_i(t+1) - (1-\delta)K_i(t)$ is made for the next period. Finally, the labor costs at the current wage are subtracted, and the lump-sum transfer to middle-class entrepreneurs is added. Note that (22.9) is formulated for a given sequence of policies p^t. Although we are interested in political economy equilibria where there is no commitment to future policies, from the viewpoint of an individual entrepreneur (or of the competitive equilibrium) the sequence of policies p^t is taken as given.[4]

Maximizing (22.9) with respect to the sequences of capital stock and labor choices, we obtain the following simple first-order condition:

$$\beta[(1 - \tau(t+1)) f'(k_i(t+1)) + (1-\delta)] = 1, \tag{22.10}$$

where $k_i(t+1)$ denotes the capital-labor ratio chosen by entrepreneur i for time $t+1$ given the tax rate $\tau(t+1)$, which has already been announced (and committed to) at the time of the investment decision. Thanks to the Inada conditions in Assumption 2, this first-order condition holds as equality for any $\tau(t+1) \in [0, 1)$, and Exercise 22.1 shows that there will never be 100% taxation. Thus we do not need the complementary slackness conditions.

Equation (22.10) determines the equilibrium capital-labor ratio. Since $\theta^m \bar{L} > 1$, there is full employment, so the total capital stock is also given by (22.10).

It can be easily verified that if all taxes were equal to zero ($\tau(t) = 0$ for all t), the unique solution to (22.10) would be identical to the first-best capital-labor ratio k^* in (22.4). Naturally, when there are positive taxes, the level of capital-labor ratio is less than k^* (this follows immediately, since $f(\cdot)$ is strictly concave; see (22.12)).

---

3. One has to be a little careful about feasibility of policies here, because whether a policy sequence is feasible cannot be determined without reference to the actions of the entrepreneurs (e.g., any policy sequence with positive transfers cannot be feasible if all entrepreneurs choose zero capital stock). In the present context, linear preferences again simplify the analysis considerably, since only the tax rate sequence matters for capital, and production decisions and transfers can be determined as residuals to satisfy the government budget constraint (22.8).

4. This way of writing the maximization problem of the entrepreneur does not give information about how he would react if the political process (here the elite) deviated from p^t, since this might also be associated with a change in the remainder of the policy sequence. Nevertheless linear preferences again ensure that we do not need to worry about this issue, since, as we will see momentarily, entrepreneurial decisions only depend on current taxes.

The most noteworthy feature of the equilibrium capital-labor ratio given in (22.10) is that, thanks to linear preferences, the choice of the capital-labor ratio by each entrepreneur at time $t + 1$ only depends on the tax rate $\tau(t + 1)$ and not on future taxes. We can therefore write the equilibrium capital-labor ratio at time t for all entrepreneurs as $\hat{k}(\tau(t))$:

$$\hat{k}(\tau(t)) \equiv (f')^{-1} \left(\frac{\beta^{-1} + \delta - 1}{1 - \tau(t)} \right). \tag{22.11}$$

For future reference, note also that since $F(\cdot, \cdot)$, and thus $f(\cdot)$, is twice differentiable, $\hat{k}(\tau)$ is also differentiable, with derivative

$$\hat{k}'(\tau) = \frac{f'(\hat{k}(\tau))}{(1 - \tau)f''(\hat{k}(\tau))} < 0, \tag{22.12}$$

which follows by directly differentiating (22.11). The derivative is negative, since $f'(k) > 0$ and $f''(k) < 0$ for all k (from Assumption 1).

Given the expression for the equilibrium capital-labor ratio in (22.11) and full employment as implied by (22.6), the equilibrium wage at time t is given by the usual expression:

$$\hat{w}(\tau(t)) = (1 - \tau(t))\left[f(\hat{k}(\tau)) - \hat{k}(\tau(t))f'(\hat{k}(\tau)) \right], \tag{22.13}$$

which is similar to (22.7) except for the presence of the tax rate in front of the square brackets.

The analysis so far establishes the following proposition.

Proposition 22.1 *Suppose that (22.6) holds. Then for any initial distribution of capital stocks among entrepreneurs, $[K_i(0)]_{i \in S^m}$, and for any feasible sequence of policies, $p^t = \{\tau(s), T^w(s), T^m(s), T^e(s)\}_{s=0}^{\infty}$, there exists a unique (competitive) equilibrium in which the sequence of capital-labor ratios for each entrepreneur is $\{\hat{k}(\tau(s))\}_{s=0}^{\infty}$ and the equilibrium wage sequence is $\{\hat{w}(\tau(s))\}_{s=0}^{\infty}$, with $\hat{k}(\tau(t))$ and $\hat{w}(\tau(t))$ given by (22.11) and (22.13), respectively.*

This proposition is convenient not only because the form of the equilibrium is particularly simple, but also because for any given sequence of policies, the aggregate equilibrium allocation is unique.[5]

22.2.3 Political Economy under Elite Control

Our task of characterizing the political economy equilibrium here is considerably simplified by two features. First, political power is vested in the elite and there is no issue of political power changing hands or the elite choosing policies to appease voters or other social groups.

---

5. Notice the slight abuse of notation here, which I commit throughout this and the next chapter: the equilibrium is not "unique" in general, since the allocation of capital and labor across middle-class entrepreneurs is not pinned down. As with competitive equilibria with constant returns in general, only the aggregate allocation and capital-labor ratios are uniquely determined. In the present context, "uniqueness" is achieved by the assumption that, when indifferent, all firms employ the same amount of labor. Throughout this chapter when the issue arises again, rather than explicitly state that the aggregate allocation implied by the equilibrium is unique, I refer to the equilibrium as "unique."

Second, there are no fiscal instruments that would redistribute income among the elite. Thus the political economy choices here involve only the choice of fiscal policies that maximize the net present discounted utility of a representative elite agent.[6]

Throughout this section, I focus on the MPE of the dynamic political game described here. Recall that this equilibrium notion requires the policy sequence p^t to be such that policies at time t only depend on the date t *payoff-relevant* variables (see Appendix C for a formal definition of MPE). Here the only payoff-relevant variables are the capital stocks of the entrepreneurs. Thus current policies should depend on the current distribution of capital stocks. Linear preferences again simplify the analysis and imply that we do not need to keep track of the entire distribution of capital stocks as the relevant state variable. Moreover it is straightforward to see that the elite would never choose to redistribute to workers or to the middle class; thus in what follows we can restrict attention to sequences of policies that involve $T^w(t) = T^m(t) = 0$ for all t. Next, let us combine this fact with the government budget constraint (22.8), which must hold as equality (since otherwise the elite could increase their consumption and utility by increasing transfers to themselves), to obtain

$$
\begin{aligned}
T^e(t) &= \frac{1}{\theta^e} \tau(t) \int_{S^m} F(K_i(t), L_i(t)) di \\
&= \frac{1}{\theta^e} \tau(t) f(\hat{k}(\tau)),
\end{aligned}
\tag{22.14}
$$

where the first line simply uses the government budget constraint (22.8), while the second uses the equilibrium characterization in Proposition 22.1 together with the fact that with full employment, the total number of workers is equal to 1.

The maximization problem of the elite can then be written recursively as

$$
V^e(\tau(t), [K_i(t)]_{i \in S^m}) = \max_{\tau(t+1) \in [0,1]} \{ T^e(t) + \beta V^e(\tau(t+1), [K_i(t+1)]_{i \in S^m}) \}, \tag{22.15}
$$

where $V^e(\tau(t), [K_i(t)]_{i \in S^m})$ is the value of an elite agent given the tax rate announced last period for today, $\tau(t)$, and the distribution of capital stocks by the entrepreneurs, $[K_i(t)]_{i \in S^m}$. The per capita transfer today, $T^e(t)$, is given by the first line of (22.14) as a function of $\tau(t)$ and $[K_i(t)]_{i \in S^m}$. The elite choose the tax rate for tomorrow, $\tau(t+1)$, to maximize their current value, recognizing the effect of the tax rate on the investments of the entrepreneurs as given by the second line of (22.14). This recursive formulation is conditioned only on payoff-relevant state variables and thus imposes the MPE requirement.[7]

To characterize the equilibrium tax sequence, note that $T^e(t)$ depends only on the tax rate at time t. The utility-maximizing tax rate for the elite is then the same at all dates and is given by the solution $\hat{\tau}$ to the following first-order condition:

$$
f(\hat{k}(\hat{\tau})) + \hat{\tau} f'(\hat{k}(\hat{\tau})) \hat{k}'(\tau) = 0.
$$

---

6. Given this limited menu of policies, we can equivalently think of the political economy choices as being made by voting among the elite or by one of the elite agents chosen at random.

7. Again, without linear preferences this maximization problem would be more complicated. The value function V^e would also need to be conditioned on a *policy rule*, mapping from the distribution of capital stocks into future policies. Consequently, optimal policies would be a function of this policy rule. An MPE would then require the solution to this maximization problem to coincide with this policy rule.

This tax rate $\hat{\tau}$ maximizes tax revenues from middle-class entrepreneurs and puts the elite at the peak of the Laffer curve. Substituting for $\hat{k}'(\tau)$ from (22.12), we obtain the following expression for $\hat{\tau}$:

$$f(\hat{k}(\hat{\tau})) + \frac{\hat{\tau}}{1 - \hat{\tau}} \frac{(f'(\hat{k}(\hat{\tau})))^2}{f''(\hat{k}(\hat{\tau}))} = 0. \tag{22.16}$$

Intuitively, the utility-maximizing tax rate for the elite trades off the increase in revenues resulting from a small increase in the tax rate, $f(\hat{k}(\hat{\tau}))$, against the loss in revenues that results because the increase in the tax rate reduces the equilibrium capital-labor ratio, $\hat{\tau} f'(\hat{k}(\hat{\tau}))\hat{k}'(\tau)$. This tax rate $\hat{\tau}$ is always between 0 and 1 (see Exercise 22.1), though the maximization problem of the elite is not necessarily concave, and (22.16) may have more than one solution. If this is the case, $\hat{\tau}$ always corresponds to the global maximum for the elite.[8]

This analysis so far establishes the following result.

Proposition 22.2 *Suppose that (22.6) holds. Then for any initial distribution of capital stocks among entrepreneurs, $[K_i(0)]_{i \in S^m}$, there exists a unique MPE, where at each $t = 0, 1, \ldots$, the elite set the tax $\hat{\tau} \in (0, 1)$ as given in (22.16), all entrepreneurs choose the capital-labor ratio $\hat{k}(\hat{\tau})$ as given by (22.11), and the equilibrium wage rate is $\hat{w}(\hat{\tau})$ as given by (22.13). We have that $\hat{k}(\hat{\tau}) < k^*$, where k^* is given by (22.4), and $\hat{w}(\hat{\tau}) < w^*$, where w^* is given by (22.7).*

This proposition shows that the unique political equilibrium involves positive taxation of entrepreneurs by the elite. Consequently the capital-labor ratio, the output level, and the wage rate are strictly lower than they would be in an economy without taxation. Exercise 22.2 shows how this framework can be extended so that policies also affect the equilibrium growth rate.

Let us now return to the fundamental question raised at the beginning of this chapter: why would a society impose distortionary taxes on businesses/entrepreneurs? The model in this section gives a simple answer: political power is in the hands of the elite, who would like to extract revenues from the entrepreneurs. Given the available tax instruments, the only way they can achieve this is by imposing distortionary taxes. Thus the source of "inefficiencies" in this economy is the combination of revenue extraction motive by the politically powerful combined with a limited menu of fiscal instruments.

While the analysis so far shows how distortionary policies can emerge and reduce the level of investment and output below the first-best level, it is important to emphasize that the equilibrium here is not Pareto inefficient. In fact, given the set of fiscal instruments, the equilibrium allocation is the solution to the maximization of a social welfare function that puts all the weight on the elite. Pareto inefficiency requires that, given the set of instruments and informational constraints, there should exist an alternative feasible allocation that would make each agent either better off or at least as well off as they were in the initial allocation. Given the restriction to linear taxes, there is no way of improving the utility of the middle-class entrepreneurs and the workers without making the elite worse off.[9] This observation implies that when we explicitly incorporate political economy aspects into the analysis, there

---

8. Here I ignore the cases in which there might be multiple global maxima.

9. In a slightly modified environment there exist mechanisms that would lead to Pareto improvements, though these mechanisms could not be supported as MPE (but could be supported as SPE). For example, with a finite number of entrepreneurs, there exist SPEs in which each entrepreneur makes voluntary donations to the elite and chooses the first-best capital-labor ratio, and the elite refrain from distortionary taxation (see Exercise 22.4). This example shows that the MPE could easily lead to Pareto inefficient equilibria, even though this is not the case in our baseline economy. It also highlights why models with a continuum of agents, where such mechanisms are not possible, are often more intuitive.

are typically no "free lunches"—that is, there is often no easy way of making all agents better off. Thus political economy considerations typically involve trade-offs between winners and losers. Since the allocation in Proposition 22.2 involves distortionary policies and reduces output relative to the first-best allocation, we might want to refer to this outcome as "inefficient" (even though it is not Pareto inefficient). In fact, this label is often used for such allocations in the literature, and I follow this practice. But it is important to remember that inefficiencies here do not mean Pareto inefficiencies.

As a preliminary answer to our motivating question, Proposition 22.2 is a useful starting point. However it leaves a number of important questions unanswered. First, it does not provide useful comparative statics regarding when we should expect more distortionary policies. Second, it takes the distribution of political power as given. If political power were in the hands of the middle-class entrepreneurs rather than the nonproductive elite, the choice of fiscal instruments would be very different. Third, this analysis takes the menu of available fiscal instruments as given. If the elite had access to lump-sum taxes, they could extract revenues from the entrepreneurs without creating distortions. I extend the current framework to provide answers to these questions in this and the next chapters. Before doing this, let us first consider a more specific version of the economy analyzed so far where the production function is Cobb-Douglas. This Cobb-Douglas economy, by virtue of its tractability, is a workhorse model for Sections 22.4–22.6. Exercise 22.17 briefly discusses how the approach here can be generalized when individuals have concave preferences.

22.3 The Canonical Cobb-Douglas Model of Distributional Conflict

Consider a specialized version of the economy analyzed in the previous section, with two differences. First, the production function of each entrepreneur takes the form

$$Y_i(t) = \frac{1}{\alpha}(K_i(t))^\alpha (A_i(t)L_i(t))^{1-\alpha}, \tag{22.17}$$

where $A_i(t)$ is a labor-augmenting group-specific or individual-specific productivity term. For now, we can set $A_i(t) = A^m$ for all $i \in S^m$. The term $1/\alpha$ in the front is included as a convenient normalization. This Cobb-Douglas form enables an explicit-form characterization of the political equilibrium and also links equilibrium taxes to the elasticity of output with respect to capital. Second, the analysis so far has shown that with linear preferences, incomplete depreciation of capital plays no qualitative role, so I also simplify the notation by assuming full depreciation of capital, that is, $\delta = 1$.

Given (22.17), the per capita production function is

$$f(k_i) = \frac{1}{\alpha}(A^m)^{1-\alpha}k_i^\alpha.$$

Combining this production function with the assumption that $\delta = 1$, (22.10) implies that at date $t + 1$ each entrepreneur chooses a capital-labor ratio $k(t + 1)$ such that

$$k(t + 1) = [\beta(1 - \tau(t + 1))]^{1/(1-\alpha)} A^m. \tag{22.18}$$

The utility-maximizing tax policy of the elite is still given by (22.16), which combined with (22.17) implies that the utility-maximizing tax for the elite at each date is

$$\hat{\tau} = 1 - \alpha.$$

This formula is both simple and economically intuitive. When α is high, the production function is nearly linear in capital. Thus the demand for capital as a function of its effective price is highly elastic. With such an elastic demand for capital, high taxes would lead to a large decline in the capital stock and tax revenues. Consequently, the peak of the Laffer curve for the elite is at a relatively low tax rate. On the other hand, if α is low, the production function is highly concave in capital; thus even a significant tax rate does not lead to a large decline in the equilibrium capital-labor ratio choice of the entrepreneurs. In this case, the elite would find it profitable to charge relatively high taxes.

22.4 Distributional Conflict and Competition

In this and the next section, I use the model introduced in the previous section to illustrate two important issues. I first investigate how competition (in the marketplace or the political arena) between those with political power and the rest can lead to significantly more distortionary policies than the revenue extraction motive discussed so far. I then use this framework to derive some preliminary insights on how distributional conflict can provide perspectives on equilibrium economic institutions regulating the formation of policies.

Consider the canonical Cobb-Douglas model, with two differences. First, the elite as well as the middle class can become entrepreneurs. The productivity of each middle-class agent in terms of this production function is A^m ($A_i = A^m$ for all $i \in S^m$), and the productivity of each elite agent is A^e ($A_i = A^e$ for all $i \in S^e$). Productivity of the two groups may differ, for example, because they are engaged in different economic activities (e.g., agriculture versus manufacturing, old versus new industries) or they have different human capital or talent. Workers do not have access to these production functions and supply their labor inelastically. As in Section 22.2, each entrepreneur can hire at most $\bar{L}$ workers, but assumption (22.6) is no longer imposed. Second, I now allow group-specific taxes, so that the elite choose two tax rates: $\tau^e(t)$, applying to their own output, and $\tau^m(t)$, applying to middle-class entrepreneurs. The government budget constraint then takes the form

$$T^w(t) + \theta^m T^m(t) + \theta^e T^e(t) \leq \phi \int_{S^m \cup S^e} \tau^i(t) F(K_i(t), L_i(t)) di + R^N \quad (22.19)$$

where $\phi \in [0, 1]$ is a parameter that captures how much of the tax revenue can be redistributed (with the remaining $1 - \phi$ being wasted). This parameter can be thought of as a measure of state capacity—with high ϕ, the state has the capacity to raise and redistribute significant revenues. R^N denotes rents from natural resources. In Section 22.2, we set $\phi = 1$ and $R^N = 0$ (recall (22.8)). These parameters will be useful for the comparative static exercises below.

Since there are entrepreneurs both from the elite and the middle class, the condition for full employment is different from (22.6). In particular, I assume throughout that $\theta^e \bar{L} < 1$ and $\theta^m \bar{L} < 1$, so that neither of the two groups generates enough labor demand by itself to employ the entire labor force. The following condition then determines whether the elite and the middle class together generate enough labor demand for the entire labor force:

Condition 22.1 $(\theta^e + \theta^m)\bar{L} > 1$.

When this condition holds, there is full employment. When it does not (by which I mean $(\theta^e + \theta^m)\bar{L} < 1$, excluding the knife-edge case $(\theta^e + \theta^m)\bar{L} = 1$), there is a shortage of labor demand, and equilibrium wages are equal to 0. Whether this condition holds or not affects the nature of the political equilibrium.

The analysis in Section 22.2, in particular, (22.11), implies that the capital-labor ratio choice of each entrepreneur $i \in S^m \cup S^e$ for time $t + 1$ is given by

$$k_i(t + 1) = \hat{k}_i(\tau(t + 1)) \equiv (\beta(1 - \tau(t + 1)))^{1/(1-\alpha)} A_i. \tag{22.20}$$

This expression is the same as (22.11) but is adapted to the Cobb-Douglas production function, with labor-augmenting productivity of entrepreneur i given by A_i. Substituting $\hat{k}_i(\tau)$ into the production function for each entrepreneur and subtracting the cost of investment, we obtain the net marginal product (profitability) per worker as

$$(1 - \alpha)\beta^{\alpha/(1-\alpha)}(1 - \tau(t))^{1/(1-\alpha)} A_i/\alpha.$$

Thus the labor demand for each entrepreneur takes the form

$$L_i(t) \begin{cases} = 0 & \text{if } w(t) > (1-\alpha)\beta^{\alpha/(1-\alpha)}(1-\tau(t))^{1/(1-\alpha)} A_i/\alpha, \\ \in [0, \bar{L}] & \text{if } w(t) = (1-\alpha)\beta^{\alpha/(1-\alpha)}(1-\tau(t))^{1/(1-\alpha)} A_i/\alpha, \\ = \bar{L} & \text{if } w(t) < (1-\alpha)\beta^{\alpha/(1-\alpha)}(1-\tau(t))^{1/(1-\alpha)} A_i/\alpha. \end{cases} \tag{22.21}$$

This expression states that if the wage exceeds the net marginal product, then the entrepreneur hires zero labor. If the wage is strictly less than this net marginal product, then he would like to hire up to the maximum possible amount of labor, $\bar{L}$. The next proposition characterizes the economic equilibrium in this case.

Proposition 22.3 *Suppose that the taxes on output of the elite and middle-class entrepreneurs at time t are equal to $\tau^e(t)$ and $\tau^m(t)$, respectively. Then the equilibrium capital-labor ratio of each entrepreneur is uniquely given by (22.20). In addition, if Condition 22.1 holds, then the equilibrium wage at time t is*

$$w(t) = \min\left\{ \frac{1-\alpha}{\alpha}\beta^{\alpha/(1-\alpha)}(1 - \tau^e(t))^{1/(1-\alpha)} A^e, \frac{1-\alpha}{\alpha}\beta^{\alpha/(1-\alpha)}(1 - \tau^m(t))^{1/(1-\alpha)} A^m \right\}. \tag{22.22}$$

If Condition 22.1 does not hold, then $w(t) = 0$ for all t.

The only part of this proposition that requires comment is the form of equilibrium wages, (22.22). When Condition 22.1 holds, this equation states that each worker receives the lower of the net marginal product of the elite and the middle class. Labor market clearing also implies that whichever group has lower net marginal product will not be able to employ to its full capacity.

22.4.1 Competition in the Marketplace: The Factor Price Manipulation Effect

The next proposition is the equivalent of Proposition 22.2, except that it requires that Condition 22.1 not hold. Proposition 22.5 applies when this condition holds.

Proposition 22.4 *Suppose that Condition 22.1 does not hold and $\phi > 0$. Then the unique MPE features*

$$\tau^m(t) = \tau^{RE} \equiv 1 - \alpha \text{ and } \tau^e(t) = T^m(t) = T^w(t) = 0 \qquad (22.23)$$

for all t, and $T^e(t)$ is then determined from (22.19) holding as equality.

Proof. See Exercise 22.5. ■

The equilibrium is therefore similar to that in Section 22.2. Notice however that this proposition is stated under the assumption that Condition 22.1 fails to hold—so that the equilibrium wage rate is $w(t) = 0$ for all t. If this were not the case, the elite would also recognize the effect of their taxation policy on equilibrium wages. This would introduce the competition motive in the choice of policies, which is our next focus. An extreme form of this factor price manipulation effect is shown in the next proposition.

Proposition 22.5 *Suppose that Condition 22.1 holds and $\phi = 0$. Then the unique MPE features $\tau^m(t) = \tau^{FPM} \equiv 1$ and $\tau^e(t) = T^m(t) = T^w(t) = 0$ for all t.*

Proof. See Exercise 22.6. ■

In this proposition, ϕ is set equal to 0, so that there is no revenue extraction motive. Instead, the only motive for taxation is to affect the equilibrium wage rate in (22.22). Clearly, for this we need Condition 22.1 to hold; otherwise the wage rate would be equal to zero and the elite would not have the ability or the desire to manipulate factor prices. Proposition 22.5 implies that the equilibrium tax rate in this case, τ^{FPM}, is greater than the tax rate when the only motive for taxation was revenue extraction, τ^{RE}. This might at first appear paradoxical, but is in fact quite intuitive. With the factor price manipulation mechanism, the objective of the elite is to reduce the profitability of the middle class, whereas for revenue extraction, the elite would like the middle class to invest and generate revenues. Consequently, τ^{RE} puts the elite at the top of the Laffer curve, while τ^{FPM} tries to harm middle-class entrepreneurs as much as possible so as to reduce their labor demand (and thus equilibrium wages). It is also worth noting that, unlike the pure revenue extraction case, the tax policy of the elite is indirectly extracting resources from the workers, whose wages are being reduced.

The role of the assumption that $\phi = 0$ in this context also needs to be emphasized. Taxing the middle class at the highest rate is clearly inefficient. Why is there not a more efficient way of transferring resources to the elite? The answer again relates to the limited fiscal instruments available to the elite. In particular, $\phi = 0$ implies that they cannot use taxes to extract revenues from the middle class, so they are forced to use inefficient means of increasing their consumption—by directly impoverishing the middle class. The absence of any means of transferring resources from the middle class to the elite is not essential for the factor price manipulation mechanism, however. This is illustrated next by combining the factor price manipulation motive with revenue extraction (though the absence of nondistortionary lump-sum taxes is naturally important).

The next proposition derives the equilibrium when Condition 22.1 holds and $\phi > 0$, so that both the factor price manipulation and the revenue extraction motives are present. In Proposition 22.5, the factor price manipulation motive by itself leads to the extreme result that the tax on the middle class should be as high as possible. Revenue extraction, though typically another motive for imposing taxes on the middle class, serves to reduce the power of the factor price manipulation effect. The reason is that high taxes also reduce the revenues extracted by the elite (moving the economy beyond the peak of the Laffer curve). To derive the political equilibrium in this case, first note that the elite will again neither tax themselves nor redistribute to other groups, that is, $\tau^e(t) = T^m(t) = T^w(t) = 0$ for all t. The maximization problem of the elite at time $t-1$ can then be written as

$$\max_{\tau^m(t)} \left[\frac{1-\alpha}{\alpha} \beta^{\alpha/(1-\alpha)} A^e - w(t) \right] L^e(t)$$

$$+ \frac{1}{\theta^e} \left[\frac{\phi}{\alpha} \tau^m(t) (\beta(1-\tau^m(t)))^{\alpha/(1-\alpha)} A^m \theta^m L^m(t) + R^N \right] \tag{22.24}$$

subject to (22.22),

$$\theta^e L^e(t) + \theta^m L^m(t) = 1, \quad \text{and} \tag{22.25}$$

$$L^m(t) = \bar{L} \quad \text{if } (1-\tau^m(t))^{1/(1-\alpha)} A^m \geq A^e, \tag{22.26}$$

where $L^m(t)$ denotes equilibrium employment by a middle-class entrepreneur, and $L^e(t)$ is equilibrium employment by an elite entrepreneur. The first term in (22.24) is the elite's net revenues, and the second term is the transfer they receive. Equation (22.25) is the labor market clearing constraint, while (22.26) ensures that middle-class producers employ as much labor as they wish, provided that their net productivity is greater than that of elite producers.

The solution to this problem can take two different forms, depending on whether (22.26) holds at the solution. If it does, then $w = (1-\alpha)\beta^{\alpha/(1-\alpha)} A^e/\alpha$. In this case, the elite make zero profits, and their only income is derived from transfers. The elite then prefer to let the middle class undertake all profitable activities and maximize tax revenues (which involves policy identical to that in Proposition 22.4). If, on the other hand, (22.26) does not hold at the solution, then the elite generate revenues both from their own production and from taxing the middle class. The next proposition focuses on this case.

Proposition 22.6 *Consider the canonical elite-dominated politics model with Cobb-Douglas technology. Suppose that Condition 22.1 holds, $\phi > 0$, and*

$$A^e \geq \phi \alpha^{\alpha/(1-\alpha)} A^m \frac{\theta^m}{\theta^e}. \tag{22.27}$$

Then the unique MPE features

$$\tau^m(t) = \tau^{COM} \equiv \frac{\kappa(\bar{L}, \theta^e, \alpha, \phi)}{1 + \kappa(\bar{L}, \theta^e, \alpha, \phi)} \tag{22.28}$$

for all t, where

$$\kappa(\bar{L}, \theta^e, \alpha, \phi) \equiv \frac{1-\alpha}{\alpha} \left(1 + \frac{\theta^e \bar{L}}{(1-\theta^e \bar{L})\phi} \right). \tag{22.29}$$

Proof.   See Exercise 22.7. ∎

Several features of this proposition are worth noting. First, $\kappa(\bar{L}, \theta^e, \alpha, \phi)$ is less than infinity, so that the equilibrium tax rate is always less than 1. Proposition 22.6 therefore shows that the prospect of raising revenues from the middle class reduces the desired tax rate of the elite below the 100% level that applied in the case of pure factor price manipulation. On the other hand, $\kappa(\bar{L}, \theta^e, \alpha, \phi)$ is strictly greater than $(1-\alpha)/\alpha$, so that τ^{COM} is always greater than $\tau^{RE} \equiv 1-\alpha$, and thus the factor price manipulation motive always increases taxes above the pure revenue maximizing level—beyond the peak of the Laffer curve.

Second, since Proposition 22.6 incorporates both the revenue extraction and the factor price manipulation motives, it contains the main comparative static results of interest. One result is that the equilibrium tax rate is decreasing in ϕ, because as ϕ increases, revenue extraction becomes more efficient, which has a moderating effect on the tax preferences of the elite. Intuitively, this shows the positive side of state capacity: with greater state capacity, the elite can raise revenues through taxation, and thus their motives to impoverish competing groups become weaker (we will see a potentially negative side of state capacity below). Another comparative static result is that the equilibrium tax rate is increasing in θ^e. The reason for this is again the interplay between the revenue extraction and factor price manipulation mechanisms. When there are more elite producers, reducing factor prices becomes more important relative to raising tax revenues. This comparative static thus reiterates that when the factor price manipulation effect is more important, there are typically greater distortions. A third result is that a decline in α raises equilibrium taxes for the same reason as in the pure revenue extraction case: taxes create fewer distortions, and this increases the revenue-maximizing tax rate. Finally, for future reference, note that rents from natural resources, R^N, have no effect on equilibrium policies.

22.4.2 Political Competition: The Political Replacement Effect

Section 22.4.1 illustrated how competition in the factor market induces the elite to choose distortionary policies to reduce the labor demand from the middle class. In this subsection, I discuss the implications of competition in the political arena. The main difference is that I now allow for switches of political power. In particular, let us denote the probability that in period t political power permanently shifts from the elite to the middle class by $\eta(t)$. Once they come to power, the middle class will pursue the policies that maximize their own utility. We can easily derive what these policies are using the same analysis as in Section 22.4.1 (see Exercise 22.8). Denote the utility of the elite when they are in control of politics and when the middle class are in control of politics by $V^e(E)$ and $V^e(M)$, respectively.

When the probability of the elite losing power to the middle class, η, is exogenous, the analysis in Section 22.4.1 applies without any significant change. New political economy effects arise when the probability that the elite will lose power is endogenous. To save space while communicating the main ideas, I use a reduced-form model and assume that the probability that the elite will lose power to the middle class is a function of the net income level of the middle class:

$$\eta(t) = \eta(\theta^m C^m(t)) \in [0, 1], \tag{22.30}$$

where $C^m(t)$ is the net income of a representative middle-class entrepreneur, which is also equal to his consumption. I assume that η is differentiable and strictly increasing, with derivative $\eta'(\cdot) > 0$. This assumption implies that when the middle class are richer, they are more likely to gain power (e.g., with greater resources, they may be more successful in solving their collective action problems or they may increase their military power).

To simplify the discussion, let us focus on the case in which Condition 22.1 does not hold, so that equilibrium wage is equal to 0 and there is no factor price manipulation motive. Thus in the absence of the political replacement motive, the only reason for taxation is revenue extraction (resulting in an equilibrium tax rate of τ^{RE}). Given these assumptions and the definitions of $V^e(E)$ and $V^e(M)$, we can write the maximization problem of the elite when choosing the tax rate $\tau^m(t)$ at $t-1$ as

$$V^e(E) = \max_{\tau^m}\{\beta^{\alpha/(1-\alpha)}A^e\bar{L}/\alpha + [\phi\beta^{\alpha/(1-\alpha)}\tau^m(1-\tau^m)^{\alpha/(1-\alpha)}A^m\theta^m\bar{L}/\alpha + R^N]/\theta^e$$

$$+ \beta[(1-\eta[\tau^m])V^e(E) + \eta[\tau^m]V^e(M)]\},$$

where I write $\eta[\tau^m]$ to emphasize the dependence of the replacement probability on the tax rate on the middle class (while economizing on notation by not explicitly spelling out the argument of $\eta(\cdot)$). Since $C^m(t)$ is decreasing in τ^m, $\eta[\tau^m]$ is also decreasing in τ^m.

The first-order condition for an interior solution for the tax rate τ^m is

$$\frac{\phi(\beta(1 - \tau^m(t)))^{\alpha/(1-\alpha)} A^m \theta^m \bar{L}}{\alpha \theta^e} \left(1 - \frac{\alpha}{1 - \alpha} \frac{\tau^m(t)}{1 - \tau^m(t)}\right)$$

$$- \beta \frac{d\eta[\tau^m]}{d\tau^m}(V^e(E) - V^e(M)) = 0.$$

The first term corresponds to the revenue extraction motive, while the second relates to the political replacement effect. Inspection of this condition shows that when $\eta'(\cdot) = 0$, we obtain $\tau^m = \tau^{RE} \equiv 1 - \alpha$ as above. However, when $\eta'(\cdot) > 0$ and $V^e(E) - V^e(M) > 0$, we have $\tau^m(t) = \tau^{PC} > \tau^{RE}$. The result that $V^e(E) - V^e(M) > 0$ follows from Exercise 22.8.

The important point here is that, as with the factor price manipulation mechanism, the elite tax beyond the peak of the Laffer curve. Now their objective is not to increase their current revenues, but to consolidate their political power (in fact, taxes beyond the peak of the Laffer curve reduce the current income of the elite). Instead, higher (more distortionary) taxes are still useful for the elite, because they reduce the income and political power of the middle class. Consequently there is a higher probability that the elite remain in power in the future, enjoying the benefits of controlling policy.

Several new comparative static results follow from the possibility that the elite might lose political power. First, as R^N increases, it is straightforward to verify that the gap between $V^e(E)$ and $V^e(M)$ increases (see Exercise 22.8). This translates into a higher equilibrium tax rate on the middle class. Intuitively, the party in power receives the revenues from natural resources, R^N, and when these revenues are higher, *political stakes*—defined as the value of controlling political power—are greater. Consequently the elite are more willing to sacrifice tax revenue (by overtaxing the middle class) to increase the probability that they remain in power (because remaining in power has now become more valuable). This scenario contrasts with the results before, where R^N has no effect on taxes. Moreover in this case a higher state capacity ϕ also increases the gap between $V^e(E)$ and $V^e(M)$ (because this enables the group in power to raise more tax revenues; see Exercise 22.8) and thus creates a force for higher equilibrium taxes. This effect therefore shows the potential dark side of greater state capacity: when there is no political competition, greater state capacity, by allowing more efficient forms of transfers, improves the allocation of resources. In contrast, in the presence of political competition, a greater state capacity increases the political stakes and may induce more distortionary policies.

Finally, when the replacement of the elite by the middle class is very likely (corresponding to $\eta(\cdot) \approx 1$), or when such political replacement is very unlikely ($\eta(\cdot) \approx 0$), we have that $\eta'(\cdot)$ is uniformly low. In these cases, there is only a limited increase in the tax rate above the revenue-maximizing level. It is only when η takes intermediate values and depends on the wealth level of the middle class that $\eta'(\cdot)$ will be high and the political replacement effect will induce further distortionary taxes. Therefore we expect the elite to choose more distortionary policies when they have an intermediate level of security (rather than when they are entirely secure in their political power [i.e., $\eta(\cdot) \approx 0$] or when they definitely expect to be replaced [i.e., $\eta(\cdot) \approx 1$]). This is the sense in which the political replacement effect here is similar to Arrow's replacement effect in the context of innovation (recall Chapter 12).

22.5 Subgame Perfect versus Markov Perfect Equilibria

The concept of equilibrium so far has been MPE. A natural question is whether the results are different when we turn to the concept of SPE. In general, the set of SPEs in dynamic games is larger than the set of MPEs, and some SPEs can lead to more efficient allocation of resources (see Appendix C). I first show that in the setup analyzed so far the SPEs and MPEs coincide. I then turn to two modified versions of the environment studied so far, where there are holdup problems resulting from the timing of taxation or from ex ante technology adoption decisions. In these environments, commitment problems lead to greater inefficiencies, and SPE may be more efficient than MPE, because it allows for greater equilibrium commitment on the part of the elite.

22.5.1 SPE versus MPE without Holdup

The MPEs are a subset of the SPEs, because the latter include equilibria supported by history-dependent punishment strategies. If there is no room for such history dependence, SPEs coincide with the MPEs. In the models analyzed so far, such punishment strategies are not possible. Intuitively, in the economic sphere, each individual is infinitesimal and acts competitively (taking prices as given). Therefore (22.20) and (22.21) determine factor demands uniquely in any equilibrium. Given the factor demands, the payoffs from various policy sequences are also uniquely pinned down. Thus payoffs to the elite from different strategies are independent of history and there cannot be any SPEs other than the MPE characterized above.

Proposition 22.7 *The MPEs characterized in Propositions 22.4–22.6 are the unique SPEs.*

Proof. See Exercise 22.10. ∎

Exercise 22.11 shows that the MPE in the model of Section 22.4.2 is also the unique SPE. This last result, however, depends on the assumption that there is only one possible power switch (from the elite to the middle class). If there were multiple power switches, potential punishment strategies could be constructed, and the set of SPEs could include non-Markovian equilibria.

22.5.2 Lack of Commitment—Holdup

The models discussed so far feature full commitment to one-period-ahead taxes by the elite. In particular, at the end of period t, the elite can commit to the tax rate on output that applies at time $t + 1$. Using a term from organizational economics, this corresponds to a situation without any "holdup." *Holdup,* on the other hand, corresponds to a situation without commitment to taxes or policies, so that after entrepreneurs have undertaken their investments, they can be "held up" by higher rates of taxation or by expropriation. These types of holdup problems are endemic in political economy, since (binding) commitments to future policies are difficult or impossible. Those who have political power at a certain point in time make the relevant decisions at that point. Moreover, when the key investments are long term (so that once an investment is made, it is irreversible), there is a holdup problem even if there is a one-period commitment (since there will be taxes on the revenue stream of this investment after the investment decisions are sunk).

The problem with holdup is that the elite are unable to commit to a particular tax rate before middle-class producers undertake their investments (because taxes are set after investments). This lack of commitment generally increases the amount of taxation and distortion. Moreover, in contrast to the allocations so far (which featured distortions but were Pareto efficient), the presence of commitment problems leads to Pareto inefficiency. To illustrate the main issues that arise in the presence of commitment problems, I consider the same model as above but change the timing of events such that taxes on output at time t are decided in period t, that is, after the capital investments for this period have already been made. The economic equilibrium is essentially unchanged, and in particular, (22.20) and (22.21) still determine factor demands, with the only difference being that τ^m and τ^e now refer to expected taxes. Naturally, in equilibrium expected and actual taxes coincide.

What is different is the calculus of the elite in setting taxes. Previously, they took into account that higher taxes on output at date t would discourage investment for production at date t. Since taxes are now set after investment decisions are sunk, this effect is absent. As a result, in the MPE, the elite always tax at the maximum rate, so in all cases, there is a unique MPE where $\tau^m(t) = 1$ for all t.

Proposition 22.8 *With holdup, there is a unique MPE with $\tau^m(t) = \tau^{HP} \equiv 1$ for all t.*

Clearly, this holdup equilibrium is more inefficient than the equilibria characterized above. For example, consider a situation in which Condition 22.1 does not hold, so that with the original timing of events (without holdup), the equilibrium tax rate is $\tau^m(t) = 1 - \alpha$. But with holdup, the equilibrium tax is $\tau^m(t) = 1$, and the middle class stop producing. This policy is not only costly for the middle-class entrepreneurs but also for the elite, since they lose all their tax revenues.

In this model, the unique MPE is no longer the only SPE, since there is room for an implicit agreement between different groups whereby the elite (credibly) promise a different tax rate than $\tau^{HP} \equiv 1$. The MPE is now Pareto inefficient, and a social planner with access to the same fiscal instruments can improve the utility of all agents in the economy.

To illustrate the difference between the MPE and the SPE (and the associated Pareto inefficiency of the MPE), consider the example where Condition 22.1 fails to hold. In the MPE, the elite raise no tax revenue (because the middle class produce zero output). Recall that the history of the game is the complete set of actions taken up to that point. Then consider the following *trigger-strategy* profile: the elite set $\tau^m(t) = 1 - \alpha$ for all t, and the middle-class producers invest according to (22.20) with $\tau^m(t) = 1 - \alpha$ as long as the history consists of $\tau^m(s) = 1 - \alpha$ and investments have been consistent with (22.20) for all $s < t$. If there is any other action in the history, then the elite set $\tau^m = 1$ and the middle-class producers invest zero. Does this strategy constitute an SPE? First, it is clear that the middle class have no profitable deviation, since at each t, they are choosing their best response to taxes along the equilibrium path implied by (22.20). To check whether the elite have a profitable deviation, note that with this strategy profile, they are raising a tax revenue of $\phi(1 - \alpha)\alpha^{\alpha/(1-\alpha)}\beta^{\alpha/(1-\alpha)}A^m\theta^m\bar{L}/\alpha$ in every period, thus receiving transfers worth

$$\frac{\phi}{(1 - \beta)}(1 - \alpha)\alpha^{-(1-2\alpha)/(1-\alpha)}\beta^{\alpha/(1-\alpha)}A^m\theta^m\bar{L}. \tag{22.31}$$

If, in contrast, they deviate at any point, the most profitable deviation for them is to set $\tau^m = 1$, and they will raise a tax revenue of

$$\phi\alpha^{-(1-2\alpha)/(1-\alpha)}\beta^{\alpha/(1-\alpha)}A^m\theta^m\bar{L} \tag{22.32}$$

in that period. Following such a deviation, consider a continuation equilibrium that switches to the unique MPE, which is the worst possible continuation SPE in this model and yields zero continuation utility to the elite (see Appendix C). Therefore the above-described trigger-strategy profile is an equilibrium as long as (22.31) is greater than or equal to (22.32), which requires $\beta \geq \alpha$. This argument establishes the following proposition.

Proposition 22.9 *Consider the holdup game, and suppose that Condition 22.1 does not hold. Then for $\beta \geq \alpha$, there exists an SPE where $\tau^m(t) = 1 - \alpha$ for all t.*

Proof. See Exercise 22.12. ∎

An important implication of this result is that in societies where there are major holdup problems (e.g., because typical investments involve relatively long horizons), the MPE is likely to lead to Pareto inefficient equilibrium allocations, and there is room for coordinating on an SPE supported by an implicit agreement (trigger-strategy profile) between the elite and the rest of the society. The SPE described above can make all agents in the society better off relative to the MPE. This analysis thus shows that whether we use the MPE or the SPE equilibrium concept has important implications for the structure of the equilibrium and its efficiency properties. While the use of the equilibrium concept is a choice for the modeler, different equilibrium concepts approximate different real-world situations. For example, MPE may be much more appropriate when the institutional structure, frequency of interactions, or past history makes coordination and mutual trust unlikely, while SPE may be useful in modeling equilibria in societies where some degree of mutual trust can be developed among the different parties with conflicting interests.

22.5.3 Technology Adoption

Another source of holdup comes from the technology adoption decisions of entrepreneurs, which may, in practice, be more important than the timing of taxes. Many important technology adoption decisions are made with the long horizon in mind; thus future tax rates matter for these decisions. The analysis earlier in the book highlighted the importance of technology adoption decisions for economic growth; therefore the new types of political economy interactions that arise in the presence of such decisions are of practical as well as of theoretical interest. This analysis also shows that in dynamic political economy environments SPE can be Pareto inefficient as well.

Let us go back to the original timing, where taxes for time $t + 1$ are set and committed to at time t (so that the source of holdup in Section 22.5.2 is now removed). Instead, at time $t = 0$, before any economic decisions or policy choices are made, the middle class can invest to increase their productivity. In particular, suppose that there is a cost $\Gamma(A^m)$ of investing in productivity A^m. The function Γ is nonnegative, differentiable, and strictly convex. This investment is made once, and the resulting productivity A^m applies forever after.

Once investments in technology are made, the game proceeds as before. Let us focus on the case where Condition 22.1 does not hold. Since investments in technology are sunk after date $t = 0$, the MPE and SPE are unique (see Proposition 22.7) and involve a tax rate equal to $\tau^{RE} \equiv 1 - \alpha$ at all dates. As a result the first-order condition for an interior solution to the middle-class producers' technology choice is

$$\Gamma'(A^m) = \frac{1 - \alpha}{\alpha(1 - \beta)} \beta^{\alpha/(1-\alpha)} (1 - \tau^{RE})^{1/(1-\alpha)} \bar{L}. \tag{22.33}$$

It is then clear that the MPE and SPE allocations are now Pareto inefficient; in fact if the elite could commit to a tax rate sequence at time $t = 0$, they would choose lower taxes. To illustrate this point, suppose that the elite can indeed commit to a constant tax rate at $t = 0$. The optimization problem of the elite is then to maximize tax revenues, taking the relationship between taxes and technology (22.33) as given. In other words, they maximize $\phi \tau^m (\beta(1 - \tau^m))^{\alpha/(1-\alpha)} A^m \theta^m \bar{L}/\alpha$ subject to (22.33). The constraint (22.33) incorporates the fact that (expected) taxes affect technology choice.

The first-order condition for an interior solution can be expressed as

$$A^m - \frac{\alpha}{1 - \alpha} \frac{\tau^m}{1 - \tau^m} A^m + \tau^m \frac{dA^m}{d\tau^m} = 0, \qquad (22.34)$$

where $dA^m/d\tau^m$ takes into account the effect of future taxes on technology choice at $t = 0$. The expression for this derivative can be obtained by differentiating (22.33) (with τ^m instead of τ^{RE}):

$$\frac{dA^m}{d\tau^m} = -\frac{(\beta(1 - \tau^m))^{\alpha/(1-\alpha)} \bar{L}}{\alpha(1 - \beta)\Gamma''(A^m)} < 0.$$

Thus the solution to (22.34) is some $\tau^{TA} < \tau^{RE} \equiv 1 - \alpha$. Hence, if they could, the elite would commit to a lower tax rate in the future to encourage the middle-class producers to undertake technological improvements. Their inability to commit to such a tax policy leads to more distortionary policies (and to Pareto inefficiency). The next proposition states this result.

Proposition 22.10 *Consider the game with technology adoption, and suppose that Condition 22.1 does not hold and $\phi > 0$. Then the unique MPE and the unique SPE involve $\tau^m(t) = \tau^{RE} \equiv 1 - \alpha$ for all t. If the elite could commit to a tax policy at time $t = 0$, they would prefer to commit to a tax level $\tau^{TA} < \tau^{RE}$ at $t = 0$.*

In contrast to the pure holdup problem, where SPE could prevent the additional inefficiency (when $\beta \geq \alpha$; recall Proposition 22.9), with the technology adoption game the inefficiency survives with the SPE. The reason is that, since middle-class producers invest in technology only once at the beginning and from then on have unique optimal strategies in the competitive equilibrium, there is no possibility of using history-dependent punishment strategies (whereby following the deviation, middle-class producers have a best response that involves switching to zero or lower investment). This proposition illustrates the limits of implicit agreements to keep tax rates low. Such agreements not only require a high discount factor ($\beta \geq \alpha$) but also frequent investments by the middle class, so that there is a credible threat against the elite if they deviate from the promised policies. When such implicit agreements are not possible, the role of economic institutions in restricting future policies becomes more important.

22.6 Inefficient Economic Institutions: A First Pass

Economic institutions provide the framework in which policies are set. I now use the model from the previous section to make a first attempt to understand (1) the conditions under which equilibrium economic institutions might put limits on distortionary policies and (2) the conditions under which economic institutions might evolve the other extreme, involving the elite using inefficient instruments to reduce output and block economic development. To communicate the ideas in the simplest possible way, I consider two prototypical economic institutions that affect the policy choices by the elite:

1. *Security of property rights:* there may be constitutional or other limits on the extent of redistributive taxation and expropriation. In particular, suppose that it is now feasible to establish a constitutionally binding maximum tax rate $\bar{\tau}$. Moreover, suppose that the level of $\bar{\tau}$ is decided at the beginning of the game and cannot be changed thereafter.

2. *Regulation of technology:* these institutions concern direct or indirect factors affecting the productivity of firms and individuals.

The analysis of factor price manipulation in Section 22.5.3 provides a partial answer to one of the questions raised above: why would the political system use inefficient instruments? A full analysis of this question requires a setup with a richer menu of fiscal instruments, such as lump-sum taxes. A glimpse of such an analysis is provided in Exercise 22.16. Propositions 22.5 and 22.6 provide the beginning of an answer, since they show that the equilibrium tax rate would be strictly above the revenue-maximizing level. Our first task is to derive some implications from these observations about constitutional limits on taxation by the elite.

22.6.1 Emergence of Secure Property Rights

The environment is the same as in the previous section, with the only difference being that at time $t = 0$, before any decisions are taken, the elite can choose some $\bar{\tau}$ in the interval $[0, 1]$ as the constitutionally mandated maximum tax rate. Thus future taxes must be less than $\bar{\tau}$. A lower $\bar{\tau}$ provides greater security of property rights to the middle class. Naturally, a key question is how a constitution that imposes $\bar{\tau} < 1$ would be made credible. I do not address this question here and take it as given that such a constitutional limit on future taxes can be imposed (though this assumption, to some degree, goes against the presumption that commitment to future policies is not possible). My objective is to investigate whether, when such constitutional guarantees are feasible, the elite would like to institute them—that is, whether they prefer $\bar{\tau} = 1$ or $\bar{\tau} < 1$.

Proposition 22.11 *Without holdup and technology adoption, the elite (weakly) prefer* $\bar{\tau} = 1$.

The proof is immediate: without holdup or technology adoption, putting further restrictions on the taxes can only reduce the elite's utility. This proposition implies that when economic institutions are decided by the elite (who will also hold political power in the future) and there are no holdup issues, then the elite derive no benefits from introducing constitutional limits on their future taxes and will not introduce further security of property rights.

The results are different when there are holdup problems. To illustrate this, let us first go back to the environment with holdup (where taxes for time t are decided after the capital stock for time t is determined). Let us focus on the MPE and on the general case where both the revenue extraction and factor price manipulation motives are present.

Proposition 22.12 *Consider the game with holdup and suppose that Condition 22.1 holds and $\phi > 0$. Then the unique MPE involves $\tau^m(t) = \bar{\tau}$ for all t. The elite prefer to set $\bar{\tau} = \tau^{COM} < 1$ at $t = 0$.*

Proof. See Exercise 22.13. ∎

The intuition for this proposition is simple: in the presence of holdup problems, Proposition 22.8 shows that the unique MPE involves $\tau^m = 1$. However, this is (Pareto) inefficient; in fact, if the elite could commit to a tax rate of $\bar{\tau} = \tau^{COM}$, they would increase their consumption (and also the consumption levels of the middle class and the workers). If the elite could use economic institutions to regulate future taxes, for example by setting constitutional limits, then they may wish to use these to encourage investment. By manipulating economic institutions, the elite may approach their desired policy (indeed, in this simple economy, they can commit to the tax rate that maximizes their utility).

This result shows that, under certain circumstances, the elite may wish to change economic institutions to provide additional property rights protection to producers. Note however that the restriction to MPE is important in this proposition. If we allow history-dependent punishment strategies and look at the SPE, then the elite would be able to improve over the MPE allocation in Proposition 22.9, and depending on parameters, they may even be able to implicitly (and credibly) commit to an equilibrium in which the tax rate at each date is equal to τ^{RE}. If this were the case, there would be less need for changing economic institutions to place limits on future taxes. Whether the MPE or the SPE is more relevant in such a situation depends on what the expectations of the different parties are and on the degree of coordination among the players (which is typically determined by historical or other institutional factors).

When the source of additional inefficiency is technology adoption rather than the holdup problem (resulting from the timing of taxes), there is a greater need for a change in economic institutions—even if we focus on the SPE. This result is stated in the next proposition.

Proposition 22.13 *Consider the game with technology adoption, and suppose that Condition 22.1 does not hold and $\phi > 0$. Then the unique MPE and the unique SPE involve $\tau^m(t) = \tau^{RE} \equiv 1 - \alpha$ given by (22.28). At $t = 0$, the elite prefer to set $\bar{\tau} = \tau^{TA} < 1 - \alpha$ as defined in Proposition 22.10.*

Proof. See Exercise 22.14. ∎

This proposition highlights that in environments where long-term investments or technology adoption decisions are important, implicit promises as in Proposition 22.9 are of limited use. Instead, explicit (credible) guarantees through economic institutions are necessary to provide incentives and security to middle-class entrepreneurs, so that they undertake the appropriate technology investments. Thus while implicit promises and other informal arrangements could play the same role as economic institutions under some circumstances, there are often limits to how well they can perform this role. Consequently constitutional limits on distortionary policies and expropriation (if feasible) may emerge endogenously in the political equilibrium as a substitute for and/or an improvement over such implicit promises.

22.6.2 Blocking Economic Development

The focus in Section 22.6.1 was on choosing economic institutions at $t = 0$ to provide more secure property rights and better investment incentives to middle-class entrepreneurs. These types of economic institutions play an important role in practice, and variation in the security of property rights for businesses across societies likely explains part of the variation in economic performance we observe. Nevertheless security of property rights and limits on taxes are only one aspect of economic institutions. In many societies, rather than encouraging economic activity, the elite actively try to block economic development. Why would the elite choose specifically inefficient policies to reduce the productivity of entrepreneurs and block economic development?

To provide the basic ideas in the simplest possible way, I extend the basic framework in this section in one direction: at time $t = 0$, the government (thus the elite controlling political power) chooses a policy affecting the technology choices of producers, denoted by $g \in \{0, 1\}$. This choice can be thought of as investment in infrastructure or the provision of law and order (with $g = 1$ corresponding to creating a better business environment). Alternatively, $g = 0$ may directly correspond to actions taken by the elite to block technology adoption by middle-class entrepreneurs. Let us assume that $g \in \{0, 1\}$ affects the productivity of middle-class producers in all future periods, and in particular $A^m = A^m(g)$, with $A^m(1) > A^m(0)$. To simplify the discussion, suppose further that $g = 1$ is costless and has no effect on the productivity of the elite. The key question is whether the elite will choose $g = 1$, increasing the middle-class entrepreneurs' productivity, or choose to block technology adoption.

When the only mechanism at work is revenue extraction, the answer is that the elite would like the middle class to have the best technology.

Proposition 22.14 *Suppose that Condition 22.1 fails to hold and $\phi > 0$. Then the economic equilibrium always involves $w(t) = 0$, and in the unique MPE the elite choose $g = 1$.*

This proposition delineates a range of situations in which the elite would not block the technology adoption decisions of middle-class entrepreneurs. This result follows immediately, since $g = 1$ increases the tax revenues and has no other effect on the elite's consumption. Consequently in this case the elite benefit from the increase in the output of the middle-class entrepreneurs and thus would like them to be as productive as possible. Intuitively, there is no competition between the elite and the middle class (either in factor markets or in the political arena), and when the middle-class entrepreneurs are more productive, they generate greater tax revenues for the elite.

The situation is different when the elite wish to manipulate factor prices. To illustrate this possibility, suppose that there exists an upper bound on taxes equal to $\bar{\tau} < 1$.

Proposition 22.15 *Suppose Condition 22.1 holds, $\phi = 0$, $\bar{\tau} < 1$, and $(1 - \bar{\tau})^{1/(1-\alpha)} < A^e/A^m$. Then in any MPE or SPE, the elite choose $g = 0$.*

Proof. See Exercise 22.15. ∎

Intuitively, with $\bar{\tau} < 1$, labor demand from the middle class is high enough to generate positive equilibrium wages even at the maximum tax rate. Since $\phi = 0$, taxes raise no revenues for the elite, and their only objective is to reduce the labor demand from the middle class (and thus wages) as much as possible. This makes $g = 0$ their preferred policy. Consequently the factor price manipulation mechanism suggests that, when it is within their power to do so, the elite will choose economic institutions to reduce the productivity of competing (middle-class) producers. Proposition 22.15 shows how the elite may take actions to directly reduce the productivity of other competing entrepreneurs, thus retarding or blocking economic development. A similar effect applies when the political power of the elite is contested (see Exercise 22.16).

This section has demonstrated how the elite's preferences over policies translate into preferences over economic institutions. When the elite prefer to commit to lower taxes, this can lead to the emergence of economic institutions that provide greater security of property rights. On the other hand, the factor price manipulation or the political replacement effects may also induce the elite to choose arrangements that block technology adoption or more generally reduce the productivity of competing groups.

22.7 Heterogeneous Preferences, Social Choice, and the Median Voter *

My next objective is to relax the focus on simple societies and investigate how a richer and more realistic form of heterogeneity among the members of the society influences policy choices. I do this in two steps. In this section, I provide a brief overview of how political economy decisions are made in a society with heterogeneous agents. The main tool in this context is the *Median Voter Theorem*, and its cousin, the *Downsian Policy Convergence Theorem*. I show that these two theorems together provide a useful characterization of democratic politics under (limited) heterogeneity among agents. In Section 22.8 I then use these results to show that the qualitative results derived in Section 22.2 generalize to a model with heterogeneity among entrepreneurs. The bottom line of the analysis in Section 22.8 is that the source of distortionary (inefficient) policies that arise from the desire of the political system to extract revenues from a subset of the population holds more generally than in the simple society investigated in Section 22.2.

The Median Voter Theorem (MVT) has a long pedigree in economics and has been applied in many different contexts. Given its wide use in political economy models, I start with a section stating and outlining this theorem. Despite its simplicity and elegance, the MVT is not applicable to situations in which the menu of policies cannot be reduced to a one-dimensional policy choice. I end this section by outlining some alternative ways of aggregating heterogeneous preferences when there are multiple-dimensional decisions. This analysis also illustrates why in many circumstances the determination of political equilibria can be represented as the maximization of a weighted social welfare function.

22.7.1 Basics

Let us consider an abstract economy consisting of a set of individuals $\mathcal{H}$. Throughout this section, I take $\mathcal{H}$ to be a finite set and denote the number of individuals by H, though the results here can be extended to the case in which $\mathcal{H}$ consists of a continuum of individuals. Individual $i \in \mathcal{H}$ has a utility function

$$u(x_i, Y(p), p \mid \alpha_i).$$

Here x_i is his action, with a set of feasible actions denoted by X_i; p denotes the vector of political choices (e.g., institutions, policies, or other collective choices), with the menu of policies denoted by $\mathcal{R}$ (since $\mathcal{P}$ was used for the set of political institutions at the beginning of this part); and $Y(p)$ is a vector of general equilibrium variables, such as prices or externalities that result from all agents' actions as well as policies. Instead of writing a different utility function u_i for each agent, I have parameterized the differences in preferences by the variable α_i. This is without loss of generality (simply define $u_i(\cdot) \equiv u_i(\cdot \mid \alpha_i)$) and is convenient for some of the analysis that follows. Clearly, the equilibrium variables, such as prices, represented by $Y(p)$ here, need not be uniquely defined for a given set of policies p. Nevertheless, since multiple equilibria are not the focus here, I ignore these complications and assume that $Y(p)$ is uniquely defined.

I also assume that individual objective functions are strictly quasi-concave, so that each individual has a unique optimal action

$$x_i(p, Y(p), \alpha_i) = \arg \max_{x_i \in X_i} u(x_i, Y(p), p \mid \alpha_i).$$

Substituting this maximizing choice of individual i into his utility function, we obtain individual i's *indirect utility function* $U(p; \alpha_i)$, which summarizes his ranking of the policies $p \in \mathcal{R}$. It is also sometimes convenient to write $p \succeq_i p'$ when individual i weakly prefers p to p' (according to $U(p; \alpha_i)$) and $p \succ_i p'$ when he has a strict preference.

22.7.2 Voting and the Condorcet Paradox

Aggregating the preferences of heterogeneous agents, through voting or other mechanisms, is not always easy or feasible. Arrow's Impossibility Theorem in social choice theory highlights this issue from a normative perspective. The same problem arises in the context of voting and is most clearly illustrated by the well-known *Condorcet paradox* example, which I present next.

Imagine a society consisting of three individuals, 1, 2, and 3, and three choices. The individuals' preferences are as follows:

$$1 \quad a \succ c \succ b,$$
$$2 \quad b \succ a \succ c,$$
$$3 \quad c \succ b \succ a.$$

Moreover, let us make the political mechanism somewhat more specific and assume that it satisfies the following three requirements, which together make up the "open agenda direct democracy" system.

A1. *Direct democracy.* The citizens make the policy choices by majoritarian voting.

A2. *Sincere voting.* In every vote, each citizen votes for the alternative that gives her the highest utility according to her policy preferences, $U(p; \alpha_i)$. *Strategic voting,* where each individual chooses a utility-maximizing vote, is discussed below.

A3. *Open agenda.* Citizens vote over pairs of policy alternatives, such that the winning policy in one round is posed against a new alternative in the next round, and the set of alternatives includes all feasible policies. Later, I replace the open agenda assumption with parties offering policy alternatives, thus moving from direct democracy some way toward indirect or representative democracy.

Consider a contest between policies a and b. Agents 2 and 3 vote for b over a, so b is the majority winner. Next, by the open agenda assumption, policy alternative c is run against b. Now agents 1 and 3 prefer c to b, which is the new majority winner. Then c runs against a, but now agents 1 and 2 prefer a, so a is the majority winner. Therefore in this case we have cycling over the various alternatives, or put differently, there is no equilibrium of the voting process that selects a unique policy outcome.

For future reference, let us now define a *Condorcet winner* as a policy choice that does not lead to such cycling.

Definition 22.1 *A Condorcet winner is a policy p^* that beats any other feasible policy in a pairwise vote.*

Clearly, in the example of the Condorcet paradox there is no Condorcet winner.

22.7.3 Single-Peaked Preferences

Suppose that the policy space is unidimensional, so that p is a real number, that is, $\mathcal{R} \subset \mathbb{R}$. In this case, a simple way to rule out the Condorcet paradox is to assume that preferences are *single peaked* for all voters. We will see below that the restriction that $\mathcal{R}$ is unidimensional is essential and single-peaked preferences are generally not well defined when there are multiple policy dimensions. Let us first define the *preferred policy,* or the (political) bliss point, of voter i. To simplify notation, suppose that this preference is uniquely defined and denote it by

$$p(\alpha_i) \equiv \arg \max_{p \in \mathcal{R}} U(p; \alpha_i).$$

We say that voter i has single-peaked preferences if his preference ordering for alternative policies is dictated by their relative distance from his bliss point, $p(\alpha_i)$. More generally we have the following definition.

Definition 22.2 *Let $p(\alpha_i) \in \mathcal{R}$ be individual i's unique bliss point over $\mathcal{R}$. Then the policy preferences of citizen i are* single peaked *if and only if for all p'', $p' \in \mathcal{R}$, such that $p'' < p' \leq p(\alpha_i)$ or $p'' > p' \geq p(\alpha_i)$, we have*

$$U(p''; \alpha_i) < U(p'; \alpha_i).$$

When $\mathcal{R} \subset \mathbb{R}$, single-peaked preferences are equivalent to the strict quasi-concavity of $U(p'; \alpha_i)$. We can easily verify that in the Condorcet paradox, not all agents possess single-peaked preferences. For example, taking the ordering to be a, b, c, agent 1, who has preferences $a \succ c \succ b$, does not have single-peaked preferences (if we took a different ordering of the alternatives, then the preferences of one of the other two agents would violate the single-peakedness assumption; see Exercise 22.18).

The next theorem shows that with single-peaked preferences, there always exists a Condorcet winner. Before stating this theorem, let us define the *median voter* of the society. Given the assumption that each individual has a unique bliss point over $\mathcal{R}$, we can rank individuals according to their bliss points, the $p(\alpha_i)$s. Also, to remove uninteresting ambiguities, let us imagine that H is an odd number. Then the median voter is the individual who has exactly $(H-1)/2$ bliss points to his left and $(H-1)/2$ bliss points to his right. Put differently, his bliss point is exactly in the middle of the distribution of bliss points. We denote this individual by α_M and his bliss point (ideal policy) by p_M.

Theorem 22.1 (Median Voter Theorem) *Suppose that H is an odd number, that A1 and A2 (from Section 22.7.2) hold, and that all voters have single-peaked policy preferences over a given ordering of policy alternatives, $\mathcal{R}$. Then a Condorcet winner always exists and coincides with the median-ranked bliss point, p_M. Moreover p_M is the unique equilibrium policy (stable point) under the open agenda majoritarian rule, that is, under A1–A3.*

Proof. The proof is by a separation argument. Order the individuals according to their bliss points $p(\alpha_i)$, and label the median-ranked bliss point by p_M. By the assumption that H is an odd number, p_M is uniquely defined (though α_M may not be). Suppose that there is a vote between p_M and some other policy $p' < p_M$. By definition of single-peaked preferences, for every individual with $p_M < p(\alpha_i)$, we have $U(p_M; \alpha_i) > U(p'; \alpha_i)$. By A2, these individuals vote sincerely and thus in favor of p_M. The coalition voting for supporting p_M thus constitutes a majority. The argument for the case where $p' > p_M$ is identical. ∎

The assumption that the society consists of an odd number of individuals was made only to shorten the statement of the theorem and the proof. Exercise 22.19 asks you to generalize the theorem and its proof to the case in which H is an even number.

More important than whether there is an odd or even number of individuals in the society is the assumption of sincere voting. Clearly, rational agents could deviate from truthful reporting of their preferences (and thus from sincere voting) when this is beneficial for them. So an obvious question is whether the MVT generalizes to the case in which individuals do not vote sincerely. The answer is yes. To see this, let us modify the sincere voting assumption to strategic voting.

A2′. *Strategic voting.* Define a *vote function* of individual i in a pairwise contest between p' and p'' by $v_i(p', p'') \in \{p', p''\}$. Let a voting (counting) rule in a society with H citizens be $V:\{p', p''\}^H \to \{p', p''\}$ for any $p', p'' \in \mathcal{R}$ (e.g., the majoritarian voting rule V^{maj} picks p' over p'' when this policy receives more votes than p''). Let $V(v_i(p', p''), v_{-i}(p', p''))$ be the policy outcome from voting rule V applied to the pairwise contest $\{p', p''\}$, when the remaining individuals cast their votes according to the vector $v_{-i}(p', p'')$ and individual i votes $v_i(p', p'')$. Strategic voting requires that the voting behavior of each individual is a best response to those of others, that is,

$$v_i(p', p'') \in \arg \max_{\tilde{v}_i(p', p'')} U(V(\tilde{v}_i(p', p''), v_{-i}(p', p'')); \alpha_i).$$

In other words, strategic voting implies that each individual chooses the voting strategy that maximizes his utility given the voting strategies of other agents.

Finally, recall that a *weakly-dominant* strategy for individual i is a strategy that gives weakly higher payoff to individual i than any of his other strategies regardless of the strategy profile of other players

Theorem 22.2 (Median Voter Theorem with Strategic Voting) *Suppose that H is an odd number, A1 and A2' hold, and all voters have single-peaked policy preferences over a given ordering of policy alternatives $\mathcal{R}$. Then sincere voting is a weakly-dominant strategy for each player, and there exists a unique weakly-dominant equilibrium. This equilibrium features the median-ranked bliss point p_M as the Condorcet winner.*

Proof. The voting rule (the political system) in this case is majoritarian, denoted by V^{maj}. Consider two policies p', $p'' \in \mathcal{R}$, and fix an individual $i \in \mathcal{H}$. Assume without loss of generality that $U(p'; \alpha_i) \geq U(p''; \alpha_i)$. Suppose first that for any $v_i \in \{p', p''\}$, $V^{\text{maj}}(v_i, v_{-i}(p', p''))$ $= p'$ or $V^{\text{maj}}(v_i, v_{-i}(p', p'')) = p''$, that is, i is *not* pivotal. Thus $v_i(p', p'') = p'$ is a best response for individual i. Suppose next that i is pivotal, that is,

$$V^{\text{maj}}(v_i(p', p''), v_{-i}(p', p'')) = p' \quad \text{if } v_i(p', p'') = p', \text{ and}$$

$$V^{\text{maj}}(v_i(p', p''), v_{-i}(p', p'')) = p'' \quad \text{otherwise.}$$

In this case, the action $v_i(p', p'') = p'$ is clearly a best response for i. Since this argument applies for each $i \in \mathcal{H}$, it establishes that voting sincerely is a weakly-dominant strategy, and the conclusion of the theorem follows from Theorem 22.1. ∎

Notice that the second part of the Theorem 22.1, which applied to open agenda elections, is absent in Theorem 22.2. This is because the open agenda assumption does not lead to a well-defined game, so a game-theoretic analysis of strategic voting is not possible. In fact, there is no guarantee that sincere voting is optimal in dynamic situations even with single-peaked preferences (see Exercise 22.20).

22.7.4 Party Competition and the Downsian Policy Convergence Theorem

The focus so far has been on voting between two alternative policies or on open agenda voting, which can be viewed as an extreme form of direct democracy. The MVT becomes potentially more relevant, and more powerful, when applied in the context of indirect democracy, that is, when combined with a simple model of party competition. I now give a brief overview of this situation and derive the Downsian Policy Convergence Theorem, which is the basis of much applied work in political economy.

Suppose that there is a Condorcet winner and there are two parties, A and B, competing for political office. Assume that the parties do not have an ideological bias and would like to come to power. In particular, they both maximize the probability of coming to power, for example, because they receive a rent or utility of $Q > 0$ when they are in power.

Assume also that parties simultaneously announce their respective policies and are committed to these policies. Then the behavior of the two parties can be represented by the Nash Equilibrium corresponding to the following pair of maximization problems:

$$\text{Party } A: \max_{p_A} \ \mathbb{P}(p_A, p_B)Q, \quad \text{and } \text{Party } B: \max_{p_B}(1 - \mathbb{P}(p_A, p_B))Q,$$

where $Q > 0$ denotes the rents of being in power, and $\mathbb{P}(p_A,\, p_B)$ is the probability that party A comes to power when the two parties' platforms are p_A and p_B, respectively. Let the bliss point of the median voter be p_M. When the MVT applies, we have

$$\mathbb{P}(p_A,\, p_B = p_M) = 0, \ \ \mathbb{P}(p_A = p_M,\, p_B) = 1, \ \text{ and } \ \mathbb{P}(p_A = p_M,\, p_B = p_M) \in [0,\, 1]\,. \ (22.35)$$

The last equation in (22.35) follows, since when both parties offer exactly the same policy, it is a best response for all citizens to vote for either party. However the literature typically assumes randomization.

> A4. *Randomization:* $\mathbb{P}(p_A = p_M,\, p_B = p_M) = 1/2$. This assumption can be rationalized by arguing that when they are indifferent, individuals randomize between the two parties with equal probabilities.

Theorem 22.3 (Downsian Policy Convergence Theorem)   *Suppose that there are two parties competing for office, A4 holds, and all voters have single-peaked policy preferences over a given ordering of policy alternatives. Then both parties choose the median-ranked bliss point p_M as their policy platform.*

Proof.   Suppose this is not the case. Then there is a profitable deviation for one of the parties. For example, if $p^A > p^B > p_M$, one of the parties can announce p_M and is sure to win the election. When $p^A \neq p_M$ and $p^B = p_M$, party A can also announce p_M and so increase its chance of winning to 1/2. ∎

Exercise 22.21 provides a generalization of this theorem without assumption A4.

This theorem demonstrates that policy converges between the two parties and that party competition implements the Condorcet winner. Therefore, in situations in which the MVT applies, the democratic process of decision making with competition between two parties leads to a situation in which both parties choose their policy platform to coincide with the bliss point of the median voter. Thus the MVT and the Downsian Policy Convergence Theorem together enable us to simplify the process of aggregating the heterogeneous preferences of individuals over policies and assert that, under the appropriate assumptions, democratic decision making leads to the preferred policy of the median voter. The Downsian Policy Convergence Theorem is useful in this context, since it gives a better approximation to democratic policy making than do open agenda elections.

There is a sense in which Theorem 22.3 is slightly misleading, however. While the theorem is correct for a society with two parties, it gives the impression of a general tendency toward policy convergence in all democratic societies. Many democratic societies have more than two parties. A natural generalization of this theorem would be to consider three or more parties. Unfortunately, as Exercise 22.22 shows, these results do not generalize to three parties. Thus some care is necessary in applying the Downsian Policy Convergence Theorem in the context of different political institutions. Theorem 22.3 also does not apply when there is no Condorcet winner. In particular, if we take a situation in which there is cycling, as in the Condorcet paradox example of Section 22.7.2, there is typically no pure-strategy equilibrium in the political competition game. This is further discussed in Exercise 22.22.

22.7.5   Beyond Single-Peaked Preferences

Single-peaked preferences play a very important role in the results of Theorem 22.1 by ensuring the existence of a Condorcet winner. However, single peakedness is a very strong assumption and does not have a natural analogue in situations in which voting concerns more than one policy choice (see Exercise 22.25). When there are multiple policy choices (or when voting is over functions, e.g., in the problem of nonlinear taxation), much more structure needs to be imposed on voting procedures to determine equilibrium policies. It is possible to relax the assumption of single-peaked preferences to some degree and also introduce a set of preferences that are close to single-peaked in multidimensional spaces. The latter task would take us too far afield from our focus, and so is left to Exercise 22.24. Instead, here I introduce the useful concept of *single-crossing property*, which enables us to prove a version of Theorem 22.1 under somewhat weaker assumptions.

Definition 22.3 *Consider an ordered policy space $\mathcal{R}$, and order voters according to their α_i values. Then the preferences of voters satisfy the* single-crossing property *over the policy space $\mathcal{R}$ when the following statement is true:*

$$\text{if } p > p' \text{ and } \alpha_{i'} > \alpha_i, \text{ or } \text{ if } p < p' \text{ and } \alpha_{i'} < \alpha_i, \text{ then}$$

$$U(p; \alpha_i) > U(p'; \alpha_i) \text{ implies that } U(p; \alpha_{i'}) > U(p'; \alpha_{i'}).$$

Example 22.1 *Consider the following example:*

$$1 \quad a \succ b \succ c,$$
$$2 \quad a \succ c \succ b,$$
$$3 \quad c \succ b \succ a.$$

It can be verified that these preferences are not single peaked. For example, with the ordering $a > b > c$, the preferences of player 2 have two peaks, at a and c. To see why these preferences satisfy single crossing, take the same ordering, and order players as 1, 2, 3. Then we have

$$\alpha = 2: \ c \succ b \Longrightarrow \alpha = 3: \ c \succ b,$$

$$\alpha = 2: \ \begin{matrix} a \succ c \\ a \succ c \end{matrix} \Longrightarrow \alpha = 1: \ \begin{matrix} a \succ c, \\ a \succ b. \end{matrix}$$

Notice that while single peakedness is a property of preferences only, the single-crossing property refers to a set of preferences over a given policy space $\mathcal{R}$ and is thus a joint property of preferences and policy alternatives. The following theorem generalizes Theorem 22.1.

Theorem 22.4 (Extended Median Voter Theorem) *Suppose that A1 and A2 hold and that the preferences of voters satisfy the single-crossing property. Then a Condorcet winner always exists and coincides with the bliss point of the median voter (voter α_M).*

Proof. The proof works with exactly the same separation argument as in the proof of Theorem 22.1. Consider the median voter with α_M and bliss policy p_M. Consider an alternative policy $p' > p_M$. Naturally, $U(p_M; \alpha_M) > U(p'; \alpha_M)$. Then by the single-crossing property, for all $\alpha_i > \alpha_M$, $U(p_M; \alpha_i) > U(p'; \alpha_i)$. Since α_M is the median, there is a majority in favor of p_M. The same argument for $p' < p_M$ completes the proof. ■

Given this theorem, the following result is immediate.

Theorem 22.5 (Extended Downsian Policy Convergence Theorem) *Suppose that two parties are competing for office, A4 holds, and all voters have preferences that satisfy the single-crossing property. Then both parties choose the median-ranked bliss point p_M as their policy platform.*

Proof. See Exercise 22.23. ■

22.7.6 Equilibrium Social Welfare Functions

The MVT and the Downsian Policy Convergence Theorem (Theorems 22.1–22.5) are useful for the analysis of many models of political economy. However, as Exercise 22.25 illustrates, the assumptions necessary for these theorems do not apply in many interesting (even simple) models. The political economy literature has thus developed a variety of other plausible approaches for the aggregation of heterogeneous preferences in democratic societies. A full analysis of these approaches is beyond the scope of this book. Nevertheless, one feature of many of these formulations is worth noting in light of the discussion of the issue of Pareto efficiency above. Many simple versions of these models, just like the MVT, lead to equilibria that are equivalent to maximizing a reduced-form weighted social welfare function and thus yield (constrained) Pareto efficient equilibria.

To illustrate this point, I now discuss one such approach, the *probabilistic voting model*. This model adds noise to the voting behavior of individuals (e.g., because individuals care about some nonpolicy or ideological characteristic of the parties that are competing for office). My purpose is to highlight how this model, under a variety of plausible assumptions, leads to a tractable equilibrium that can be represented by the maximization of a (weighted) social welfare function.

Let the society consist of G distinct groups, with a continuum of voters within each group having the same economic characteristics and preferences. As in the Downsian model, there is electoral competition between two parties, A and B. Let π_J^g be the fraction of voters in group g voting for party J, where $J = A, B$, and let λ^g be the share of voters in group g. Naturally $\sum_{g=1}^G \lambda^g = 1$. The expected vote share of party J is

$$\pi_J = \sum_{g=1}^G \lambda^g \pi_J^g.$$

In our analysis so far, all voters in group g would have cast their votes identically (unless they were indifferent between the two parties). The idea of probabilistic voting is to smooth out this behavior by introducing other considerations in the voting behavior of individuals. In particular, suppose that individual i in group g has the following preferences:

$$\tilde{U}_i^g(p, J) = U^g(p) + \tilde{\sigma}_i^g(J) \tag{22.36}$$

when party J comes to power, where p is the vector of economic policies chosen by the party in power. The term $\tilde{\sigma}_i^g(J)$ captures the nonpolicy benefits that the individual receives if party $J = A, B$ comes to power. Suppose that $p \in \mathcal{R} \subset \mathbb{R}^K$, where K is a natural number, possibly greater than 1. Thus $p \equiv (p^1, \ldots, p^K)$ is a potentially multidimensional vector of policies. The function $U^g(p)$ is the indirect utility of agents in group g (previously denoted by $U(p; \alpha_i)$ for individual i) and captures their economic interests.

Let us normalize $\tilde{\sigma}_i^g(A) = 0$, so that

$$\tilde{U}_i^g(p, A) = U^g(p), \text{ and } \tilde{U}_i^g(p, B) = U^g(p) + \tilde{\sigma}_i^g. \tag{22.37}$$

In that case, the voting behavior of individual i can be represented as

$$v_i^g(p_A, p_B) = \begin{cases} 1 & \text{if } U^g(p_A) - U^g(p_B) > \tilde{\sigma}_i^g, \\ \frac{1}{2} & \text{if } U^g(p_A) - U^g(p_B) = \tilde{\sigma}_i^g, \\ 0 & \text{if } U^g(p_A) - U^g(p_B) < \tilde{\sigma}_i^g, \end{cases} \tag{22.38}$$

where $v_i^g(p_A, p_B)$ denotes the probability that the individual votes for party A, p_A is the platform of party A, and p_B is the platform of party B. If an individual is indifferent between the two parties (inclusive of the ideological benefits), she randomizes her vote.

Let us now assume that the distribution of nonpolicy-related benefits $\tilde{\sigma}_i^g$ for individual i in group g is given by a smooth cumulative distribution function H^g defined over $(-\infty, +\infty)$, with the associated probability density function h^g. The draws of $\tilde{\sigma}_i^g$ across individuals are independent. Consequently the vote share of party A among members of group g is

$$\pi_A^g = H^g(U^g(p_A) - U^g(p_B)).$$

Furthermore, to simplify the exposition here, suppose that parties maximize their expected vote share. In this case, party A sets policy platform p_A to maximize

$$\pi_A = \sum_{g=1}^{G} \lambda^g H^g(U^g(p_A) - U^g(p_B)). \tag{22.39}$$

Party B faces a symmetric problem and maximizes π_B, which is defined similarly. In particular, since $\pi_B = 1 - \pi_A$, party B's problem is to minimize π_A. Equilibrium policies are then determined as the Nash Equilibrium of a (zero-sum) game, where both parties make simultaneous policy announcements to maximize their vote share. Let us first look at the first-order condition of party A with respect to its own policy choice, p_A, taking the policy choices of the other party, p_B, as given. This first-order condition is

$$\sum_{g=1}^{G} \lambda^g h^g(U^g(p_A) - U^g(p_B)) DU^g(p_A) = 0,$$

where $DU^g(p_A)$ is the gradient of $U^g(\cdot)$ given by

$$DU^g(p_A) = \left(\frac{\partial U^g(p_A)}{\partial p_A^1}, \ldots, \frac{\partial U^g(p_A)}{\partial p_A^K} \right)^T,$$

with p_A^k corresponding to the kth component of the policy vector p_A. Since the problem of party B is symmetric, it is natural to focus on pure-strategy symmetric equilibria. In fact, if the maximization problems of both parties are strictly concave, such a symmetric equilibrium exists (see Exercise 22.26). Clearly in this case, we have policy convergence with $p_A = p_B = p^*$, and thus $U^g(p_A) = U^g(p_B)$. Consequently symmetric equilibrium policies satisfy

$$\sum_{g=1}^{G} \lambda^g h^g(0) DU^g(p^*) = 0. \tag{22.40}$$

It is now straightforward to see that (22.40) also corresponds to the solution to the maximization of the following weighted utilitarian (and concave) social welfare function

$$\sum_{g=1}^{G} \chi^g \lambda^g U^g(p), \tag{22.41}$$

where $\chi^g \equiv h^g(0)$ are the weights that different groups receive in the social welfare function. This analysis therefore establishes the following result.

Theorem 22.6 (Probabilistic Voting Theorem) *Consider a set of policy choices $\mathcal{R} \subset \mathbb{R}^K$, let $p \in \mathcal{R}$ be a policy vector and let preferences be given by the (22.37), with the distribution function of $\tilde{\sigma}_i^g$ as H^g. If a pure-strategy symmetric equilibrium exists, then equilibrium policy is given by the p^* that maximizes (22.41).*

The important point to note about this result is its seeming generality: as long as a pure-strategy symmetric equilibrium in the party competition game exists, it corresponds to a maximum of some weighted social welfare function. This generality is somewhat exaggerated, however, because such a symmetric equilibrium does not always exist. The sufficient conditions to guarantee the existence of such an equilibrium are rather restrictive and are discussed in Exercise 22.26.

22.8 Distributional Conflict and Economic Growth: Heterogeneity and the Median Voter

I now return to the model of Section 22.2 and relax the assumption that political power is in the hands of the elite. Instead, I now introduce heterogeneity among the agents and then apply the tools from Section 22.7, in particular, the MVT and Downsian Policy Convergence Theorem (Theorems 22.1–22.5) to analyze the political economy equilibrium of this model. Recall that these theorems show that if there is a one-dimensional policy choice and individuals have single-peaked preferences (or preferences over the menu of policies that satisfy the single-crossing property), then the political equilibrium coincides with the most preferred policy of the median voter.

To simplify the analysis, I modify the environment in Section 22.2 slightly. First, there are no longer any elites. Instead, economic decisions are made by majoritarian voting among all agents. Second, to abstract from political conflict between entrepreneurs and workers, I also assume that there are no workers. Instead the economy consists of a continuum 1 of yeoman-entrepreneurs, each denoted by $i \in [0, 1]$ and with access to a neoclassical production function

$$Y_i(t) = F(K_i(t), A_i L_i(t)),$$

where A_i is a time-invariant labor-augmenting productivity measure and is the only source of heterogeneity among the (yeoman-)entrepreneurs. In particular, F satisfies Assumptions 1 and 2 from Chapter 2. I assume that A_i has a distribution given by $\mu(A)$ among the entrepreneurs. The yeoman-entrepreneur assumption means that each entrepreneur can only employ himself as the worker, so $L_i(t) = 1$ for all $i \in [0, 1]$ and for all t. I also set the depreciation rate of capital δ equal to 1 to simplify notation.

All individuals have linear preferences given by (22.1). As in Section 22.2, the investment decisions at time $t + 1$ depend only on the tax rate announced for time $t + 1$. This latter feature is particularly important here, since we know from Section 22.7 that the MVT does not generally apply with multidimensional policy choices. The fact that at each point in time all actions depend on a single policy variable enables us to use the MVT.

The timing of events is similar to that in Section 22.2. At each date t, there is voting over a linear tax rate on output $\tau(t + 1) \in [0, 1]$ that will apply to all entrepreneurs in the next period (at $t + 1$). Voting is between two parties, so that Theorems 22.1–22.5 apply. The proceeds of taxation are redistributed as a lump-sum transfer $T(t + 1) \geq 0$ to all agents. Let us focus on MPE and first check that the conditions of the MVT are satisfied.

Let us define $k_i(t) \equiv K_i(t)/A_i$ as the effective capital-labor ratio (the ratio of capital to effective labor) of entrepreneur i, and recall that p^t includes the sequence of taxes starting from time t. With this definition, we can write the value of each entrepreneur recursively as

$$V_i(k_i(t) \mid p^t) = \max_{k_i(t+1) \geq 0} \{(1 - \tau(t))A_i f(k_i(t)) - A_i k_i(t+1) + T(t) + \beta V_i(k_i(t+1) \mid p^{t+1})\},$$

(22.42)

where the fact that total output is equal to $A_i f(k_i(t))$ at time t follows from the constant returns to scale property of F (Assumption 1), and the total amount of capital invested is, by definition, $K_i(t+1) = A_i k_i(t+1)$.

The maximization problem in (22.42) yields the first-order condition

$$\beta(1 - \tau(t+1))f'(k_i(t+1)) = 1 \quad \text{for all } i \text{ and } t.$$

(22.43)

The noteworthy feature of (22.43) is that the choice of the effective capital-labor ratio $k_i(t+1)$ is independent of A_i. This intuitive result implies that all entrepreneurs choose the same effective capital-labor ratio regardless of their productivity.

Proposition 22.16 *Let the tax rate announced for date $t+1$ be τ. Then in any MPE, each entrepreneur i chooses the effective capital-labor ratio $\hat{k}(\tau)$ for date $t+1$ given by*

$$\hat{k}(\tau) = (f')^{-1}((\beta(1 - \tau))^{-1}),$$

(22.44)

where $(f')^{-1}(\cdot)$ denotes the inverse of the marginal product of capital.

Given the result in Proposition 22.16, we can calculate total tax revenues at time $t+1$, and thus the lump-sum transfer from the government budget constraint, as

$$T(t+1) = \int_0^1 \tau(t+1)A_i f(\hat{k}(\tau(t+1)))di$$

$$= \tau(t+1)\bar{A} f(\hat{k}(\tau(t+1))),$$

(22.45)

where $\bar{A} \equiv \int_0^1 A_i di$ is the mean productivity among the entrepreneurs, and $\hat{k}(\cdot)$ is given by (22.44). The first line simply uses the definition of total tax revenue (and per capita lump-sum transfer) as the sum (integral) of output over all entrepreneurs; it also uses the fact that all entrepreneurs choose the effective capital-labor ratio $\hat{k}(\tau(t+1))$. The second line takes the terms that do not depend on the identity of the entrepreneur out of the integral and uses the definition of mean productivity $\bar{A}$.

Let us next determine the political bliss point of each entrepreneur, that is, their preferred tax rate. To do this, let us write their continuation utility from the end of period t. Substituting for best responses (i.e., for the effective capital-labor ratio from (22.44)), the expected discounted utility of entrepreneur i from (22.42) can be written as

$$\tilde{V}_i(\tau' \mid p^{t+1}) = -A_i \hat{k}(\tau') + \beta[(1 - \tau')A_i f(\hat{k}(\tau')) + \tau'\bar{A} f(\hat{k}(\tau')) + \tilde{V}_i(p^{t+2})], \quad (22.46)$$

where τ' denotes the tax rate announced for date $t+1$, and I use the notation $\tilde{V}_i$ to distinguish this value function defined over the current tax rate from the value function V_i defined in (22.42). In addition, $\tilde{V}_i(p^{t+1})$ is defined as the continuation value from the end of date $t+1$, and I have substituted for $T(t+1)$ from (22.45).

The most preferred tax rate for entrepreneur i can be obtained from the expression for $\tilde{V}_i(\tau' \mid p^{t+1})$. It can be verified easily that $\tilde{V}_i(\tau' \mid p^{t+1})$ is not necessarily quasi-concave in τ'; thus preferences are not single peaked. Nevertheless, they satisfy the single-crossing condition.

Proposition 22.17 *Preferences given by $\tilde{V}_i(\tau' \mid p^{t+1})$ in (22.46) over the policy menu $\tau' \in [0, 1]$ satisfy the single-crossing property in Definition 22.3.*

Proof.   See Exercise 22.29. ∎

In view of Proposition 22.17, we can apply Theorems 22.4 and 22.5 and conclude that at each date, the tax rate most preferred by the entrepreneur with the median productivity is implemented. Let this median productivity be denoted by A_M. From (22.46), this most preferred tax rate satisfies the following first-order condition:

$$(\bar{A} - A_M) f(\hat{k}(\tau_M)) + \tau' \bar{A} \frac{\left(f'(\hat{k}(\tau_M))\right)^2}{(1 - \tau^M) f''(\hat{k}(\tau_M))} \leq 0, \text{ and } \tau_M \geq 0, \qquad (22.47)$$

with complementary slackness. In writing this expression, I made use of condition (22.44) to simplify the expression and also differentiated (22.44) to obtain an expression for the derivative $\hat{k}'(\tau_M)$ (which is identical to (22.12)). It is easy to verify that $\hat{k}'(\tau_M) < 0$, so that, as in Section 22.2, higher taxes lead to lower capital-labor ratios and lower output. The emphasis on complementary slackness in (22.47) is important here, since the most preferred tax rate of the median voter (entrepreneur) may not satisfy the first-order condition as equality, instead corresponding to a corner solution of $\tau = 0$.

Proposition 22.18 *Consider the above-described model. Then there exists $\tau_M \in [0, 1)$ such that the unique MPE involves $\tau(t) = \tau_M$ for all t. If the distribution of productivity among the entrepreneurs, $\mu(A)$, is such that $A_M \geq \bar{A}$, then $\tau_M = 0$. If $A_M < \bar{A}$, then $\tau_M > 0$, and for given $\bar{A}$, τ_M is strictly decreasing in A_M.*

Proof.   The argument preceding the proposition combined with Theorems 22.4 and 22.5 shows that the tax rate most preferred by the entrepreneur with the median productivity is chosen at each period. Moreover $\tau' = 1$ cannot be preferred by any entrepreneur, since it would lead to zero output and zero tax revenues (Exercise 22.1); thus the result that there exists $\tau_M \in [0, 1)$ such that $\tau(t) = \tau_M$ for all t follows (where τ_M is the solution to (22.47)). Note that this equation might have more than one solution, and if so, τ_M corresponds to the global maximizer of (22.46) with productivity evaluated at A_M.

Next suppose that $A_M = \bar{A}$. Then the first expression in (22.47) is equal to zero, and the left-hand side of the equation is unambiguously negative for any $\tau' > 0$ and exactly equal to zero for $\tau' = 0$. This argument establishes that in this case $\tau_M = 0$. If, on the other hand, $A_M > \bar{A}$, then the first expression is strictly negative and the left-hand side of (22.47) is unambiguously negative and the conclusion that $\tau_M = 0$ follows from the complementary slackness condition.

Finally, suppose that $A_M < \bar{A}$. In this case, the first expression is strictly positive. Suppose, to obtain a contradiction, that $\tau_M = 0$. Then the second term must be 0. Consequently the left-hand side of (22.47) is strictly positive, and $\tau_M = 0$ cannot be a solution. Hence the unique equilibrium tax rate must be $\tau_M > 0$. To obtain the comparative static result, simply apply the Implicit Function Theorem (Theorem A.25) to (22.47) and use the fact that since τ_M is a global maximum, the derivative of (22.47) with respect to τ_M is negative. ∎

There are several important results in this proposition. First, it shows that linear preferences guarantee the existence of a well-defined MPE even when there is heterogeneity among the individuals in terms of their productivity.

Second, this proposition shows that if the productivity of the median voter is above average, there is no redistributive taxation. This result is intuitive. As the first term in (22.47) makes clear, the benefits of taxation are proportional to the average productivity in the economy, while the cost (to the median voter) is related to his productivity. If the median entrepreneur is more productive than the average, there are two forces making him oppose redistributive taxation; he is effectively redistributing away from himself, and there is also the distortionary effect of taxation captured by the second term in (22.47).

Third and most important, in the case in which the productivity of the median voter is below average, the political equilibrium involves positive (distortionary) taxation on all entrepreneurs. To obtain the intuition for this result, recall that tax revenues are equal to zero at $\tau = 0$. A small increase in taxes starting at $\tau = 0$ induces a second-order loss for each entrepreneur and, when $A_M < \bar{A}$, a first-order redistributive gain for the median voter. This result is important in part because most real-world wealth and income distributions appear to be skewed to the left (with the median lower than the mean); thus this configuration is more likely in practice. Furthermore, this result is most interesting in comparison with those in previous sections, which also led to positive distortionary taxation but in environments where the nonproductive elite were in power. Proposition 22.18 shows that the same qualitative result generalizes to the case in which there is democratic politics and the median voter is an entrepreneur himself but is less productive than the average.

Finally, Proposition 22.18 gives a new comparative static result. It shows that, holding average productivity constant, a decline in the productivity of the median entrepreneur (voter) leads to greater distortionary taxation. Since higher taxes correspond to lower output and the larger gap between the mean and the median of the productivity distribution can be viewed as a measure of inequality, this result suggests a political mechanism by which greater inequality may translate into higher distortions and lower output. Nevertheless some care is necessary in interpreting this last result, since the gap between the mean and the median is not an unambiguous measure of inequality. Exercise 22.30 gives an example in which a mean preserving spread of the distribution leads to a smaller gap between the mean and the median. This caveat notwithstanding, the literature often interprets this last result as providing a link between inequality and distortionary taxation. Exercise 22.31 presents a version of this model in which taxes affect the equilibrium growth rate.

22.9 The Provision of Public Goods: Weak versus Strong States

The analysis so far has emphasized the distortionary effects of taxation and expropriation. This paints a picture in which the major (political economy) determinant of poor economic performance is the extent of taxation and expropriation. While the disincentive effects of taxation are undoubtedly important, whether taxes are high is only one of the dimensions of policy that might affect economic growth. For example, in many endogenous growth models subsidies to R&D also encourage faster growth (even if this policy involves some taxation of capital and labor). More generally, public goods provision, investment in infrastructure, and provision of law and order are important functions of a government, and the failure to perform these functions may have significantly negative consequences for economic performance. In fact, existing evidence does not support the view that growth (or high levels of output) are strongly associated with (official) taxation. On the contrary, poor economies typically have lower levels of tax revenues and government spending. This is most stark if we compare OECD countries to sub-Saharan Africa. Consequently the political economy of growth must also pay attention to whether governments perform the roles that they are supposed to. The standard nonpolitical economy approach to this question starts by positing the existence of a benevolent government and looks for policy combinations that would maximize social welfare. Once we incorporate political economy considerations, we must also recognize that the government may not have an interest in investing in public goods. It thus becomes essential to investigate under what circumstances government undertakes investments in public goods, infrastructure, and law and order—as well as refraining from prohibitively high taxes and expropriation.

In this section, I present the simplest model that can shed light on this topic, which is based on Acemoglu (2005). The economy consists of a political elite controlling the government and a set of citizens with access to production opportunities. Productivity depends on public goods investments by the government. The government only undertakes these investments if they are beneficial to the political elite. In this environment, the extent of public goods provision depends on future returns that the political elite can secure by undertaking such investments. Thus the equilibrium provision of public goods is connected to the issue of weak versus strong states. If the state is very weak, the elite are unable to raise taxes in the future and reap the benefits of their investments. Anticipating this, they are unwilling to invest in public goods. On the other hand, if there are no checks on the ability of the elite to impose taxes on the population, then the state is too strong and private investment will be stifled. Thus in this context, states that have intermediate levels of strength may be most conducive to economic growth.

22.9.1 The Model

Preferences are again given by (22.1). The population consists of a set of yeoman-entrepreneurs (citizens), with size normalized to 1, and the political elite. The elite do not engage in production but control the government. In particular, they decide the levels of taxation and public goods provision. Without loss of generality, I also normalize the size of the political elite to 1.

Each citizen i has access to the following Cobb-Douglas production technology to produce the unique final good in this economy:

$$Y_i(t) = \frac{1}{\alpha} K_i(t)^\alpha (A(t) L_i(t))^{1-\alpha}, \qquad (22.48)$$

which differs from (22.17) only because here $A(t)$ is time varying. $A(t)$ is determined by the public goods investments of the government. Given the assumption that citizens correspond to yeoman-entrepreneurs, $L_i(t) = 1$ for all $i \in [0, 1]$ and for all t.

The timing of events is similar to the baseline model with holdup, in that taxes on output are set at time t, whereas capital investments for time t are decided at $t - 1$. Suppose that as in Section 22.5 there is a maximum tax rate $\bar{\tau}$. However, instead of the constitutional limits on taxation, here I suppose that this maximum tax rate arises from the possibility that producers might hide their output (or move to the informal sector) if they face very high taxes. For example, if they do so, they lose a fraction $\bar{\tau}$ of their output, so that with a tax rate above $\bar{\tau}$, all producers would prefer to move to the informal sector, and tax revenues would be equal to zero. Thus the tax rate must always satisfy $\tau(t) \in [0, \bar{\tau}]$. With this interpretation, $\bar{\tau}$ corresponds to the (economic) *strength of the state*. When $\bar{\tau}$ is high, we have a strong state, which can raise high taxes. When it is low, the state is weak and unable to raise high taxes.

Given a tax rate $\tau(t) \in [0, \bar{\tau}]$, tax revenues are

$$\text{Tax}(t) = \tau(t) \int_0^1 Y_i(t) di = \tau(t) Y(t), \qquad (22.49)$$

where $Y(t)$ is total output. Naturally, if the tax rate is above $\bar{\tau}$, tax revenues are equal to zero, because all production shifts to the informal economy.

The government (the political elite) at time t decides how much to spend on public goods for the next date, $A(t + 1)$. Assume that

$$A(t) = \left(\frac{\alpha \zeta}{1-\alpha} G(t) \right)^{1/\zeta}, \tag{22.50}$$

where $G(t)$ denotes government spending on public goods, and $\zeta > 1$, so that the technology for public goods exhibits diminishing returns (a greater ζ corresponds to greater decreasing returns). The term $(\alpha \zeta / (1-\alpha))^{1/\zeta}$ is included as a convenient normalization. In addition, (22.50) implies full depreciation of $A(t)$, which simplifies the analysis. The consumption of the elite is given by whatever is left over from tax revenues after expenditure and transfers and thus is equal to $C^E(t) = \text{Tax}(t) - G(t)$.

Let us again focus on the MPE, which, in this model, can be represented by the tuple $(\tau(A(t)), [k_i(A(t))]_{i \in [0,1]}, G(A(t)))$. Since each entrepreneur employs only himself, the capital-labor ratio k_i and the total capital stock K_i of each entrepreneur are identical. With an argument identical to that in Section 22.5, the unique MPE tax rate is

$$\tau(t) = \bar{\tau} \quad \text{for all } t, \tag{22.51}$$

since investment decisions are already sunk at the time the elite set the taxes.

Next, the capital-labor ratio of entrepreneurs is again given by the equivalent of (22.18):

$$k_i(t) = (\beta(1-\bar{\tau}))^{1/(1-\alpha)} A(t) \quad \text{for all } i \in [0, 1] \text{ and for all } t. \tag{22.52}$$

Combining (22.52) with (22.48) and (22.49), we obtain equilibrium tax revenue as a function of the level of public goods:

$$T(A(t)) = \frac{(\beta(1-\bar{\tau}))^{\alpha/(1-\alpha)} \bar{\tau} A(t)}{\alpha}. \tag{22.53}$$

Finally, the elite choose public investment $G(t)$ to maximize their consumption. To characterize this choice, let us write the discounted net present value of the elite as

$$V^e(A(t)) = \max_{A(t+1)} \left\{ T(A(t)) - \frac{1-\alpha}{\alpha \zeta} A(t+1)^{\zeta} + \beta V^e(A(t+1)) \right\}, \tag{22.54}$$

which simply follows from writing the discounted payoff to the elite recursively, after substituting for their consumption $C^E(t)$ as equal to taxes given by (22.53) minus their spending on public goods from (22.50).

Theorems 6.3, 6.4, and 6.6 in Chapter 6 imply that the value function $V^e(\cdot)$ is concave and differentiable. Hence the first-order condition of the ruler in choosing $A(t+1)$ is

$$\frac{1-\alpha}{\alpha} A(t+1)^{\zeta-1} = \beta(V^e)'(A(t+1)), \tag{22.55}$$

where $(V^e)'$ denotes the derivative of the value function of the elite. Equation (22.55) links the marginal cost of greater investment in public goods to the greater value that follows from this investment. To make further progress, I use the standard Envelope condition, which is obtained by differentiating (22.54) with respect to $A(t)$:

$$(V^e)'(A(t+1)) = T'(A(t)) = \frac{(\beta(1-\bar{\tau}))^{\alpha/(1-\alpha)} \bar{\tau}}{\alpha}. \tag{22.56}$$

The value of greater public goods for the elite is the additional tax revenue that these greater public goods generate, which is given by the expression in (22.56).

Combining these conditions, we obtain the unique MPE choice of the elite as

$$A(t+1) = A[\bar{\tau}] \equiv \left(\beta^{1/(1-\alpha)}(1-\alpha)^{-1}(1-\bar{\tau})^{\alpha/(1-\alpha)}\bar{\tau}\right)^{\frac{1}{\zeta-1}}. \tag{22.57}$$

Substituting (22.57) into (22.54) yields a simple form of the elite's value function:

$$V^e(A(t)) = \frac{(\beta(1-\bar{\tau}))^{\alpha/(1-\alpha)}\bar{\tau} A(t)}{\alpha} + \frac{\beta^{1/(1-\alpha)}(\zeta-1)(1-\bar{\tau})^{\alpha/(1-\alpha)}\bar{\tau}}{(1-\beta)\zeta\alpha} A[\bar{\tau}]. \tag{22.58}$$

The second term in (22.58) follows, since the level of public goods spending implied by (22.57) is equal to a fraction $1/\zeta$ of tax revenue. The value to the elite naturally depends on the current state of public goods, $A(t)$, inherited from the previous period, and from this point on, the equilibrium involves investment levels given by (22.52) and (22.57).

Proposition 22.19 *In the above-described economy, there exists a unique MPE. In this equilibrium, $\tau(A) = \bar{\tau}$ for all A, $A(t)$ is given by $A[\bar{\tau}]$ as in (22.57) for all $t > 0$, and the capital-labor ratio of each entrepreneur i at each t is given by (22.52). For all $t > 0$, the equilibrium level of aggregate output is*

$$Y(t) = Y[\bar{\tau}] \equiv \frac{1}{\alpha}(\beta(1-\bar{\tau}))^{\alpha/(1-\alpha)} A[\bar{\tau}]. \tag{22.59}$$

Proof.   See Exercise 22.32.   ■

22.9.2   Weak versus Strong States

The most noteworthy feature of Proposition 22.19 is the role played by the strength of the state, $\bar{\tau}$. When $\bar{\tau}$ is high, the state is economically powerful—citizens have little recourse against high rates of taxes. In contrast, when $\bar{\tau}$ is low, the state is economically weak (and there is limited government), since it is unable to raise taxes. With this interpretation, we can now ask whether greater economic strength of the state leads to worse economic outcomes. The answer is ambiguous: when $\bar{\tau} = 0$, the elite choose $G(t) = 0$; while when $\bar{\tau} = 1$, the citizens choose zero investments. In both cases, output is equal to zero.

It is straightforward to determine the level of $\bar{\tau}$ that maximizes output at all dates after the initial one (given by (22.59)). Exercise 22.32 shows that this tax rate is

$$\bar{\tau}^* \frac{1-\alpha}{1-\alpha+\alpha\zeta}. \tag{22.60}$$

If the economic power of the state is greater than $\bar{\tau}^*$, then the state is too powerful, and taxes are too high relative to the output-maximizing benchmark. This corresponds to the standard case on which most political economy models focus. In contrast, if the economic power of the state is less than $\bar{\tau}^*$, then the state is not powerful enough for there to be sufficient rents in the future to entice the elite to invest in public goods. This corresponds to the case of weak states, where the major problem is the underprovision of public goods.

There is an interesting parallel to the theory of the firm here. In the theory of the firm, the optimal structure of ownership and control gives ex post bargaining power to the parties that have more important investments. The same principle applies to the allocation of economic strength as captured by the parameter $\bar{\tau}$: greater power for citizens is beneficial when their investments matter more (here corresponding to a high value of α). When it is the state's investment that is more important for economic development (i.e., α is low), a higher $\bar{\tau}$ is required (justified).[10]

The main conclusion from this analysis is that when both the state and the citizens make productive investments, it is no longer true that limiting the rents that accrue to the state is always good for economic performance. Instead, there needs to be a certain degree of *balance of powers* between the state and its citizens. When the political elite controlling the power of the state expect too few rents in the future, they have no incentive to invest in public goods. Consequently, excessively weak states may be as damaging for economic development as the unchecked power and expropriation of excessively strong states.

A number of shortcomings of the analysis in this section should be noted. The first is that it relies on economic exit options of the citizens in the informal sector as the source of their control over the state, whereas in practice, political controls may be more important. The second is that it focuses on the MPE, without any possibility of an implicit agreement between the state and the citizens. In Acemoglu (2005), I generalize the results presented here in these directions. I show that similar results can be obtained when the constraints on the power of the state are not economic but political. In particular, we can envisage a situation in which citizens can (stochastically) replace the government if taxes are too high. In this case, when citizens are politically powerful, the extent of taxation and the amount of public goods provision are again limited. In addition, using a model with variable political checks on the state, one can analyze the SPE, where there might be an implicit agreement between the state and the citizens to allow for some amount of taxation and correspondingly high levels of public goods provision. This equilibrium configuration can be viewed as an example of a *consensually strong state,* since the citizens allow the economic power of the state to be high (partly because they believe they can control the state and the political elites by using elections or other means). The configuration with the consensually strong state might provide a potential explanation for the higher tax rates and higher levels of public goods provision in OECD countries than in many less-developed economies.

This perspective also suggests a useful distinction between taxation and expropriation. High taxes appear to have similar effects on investment and economic performance as does expropriation. One difference between expropriation and taxes might be uncertainty. It can be argued that producers know exactly at what rate they will be taxed, while expropriation is inherently risky. In the presence of risk aversion, expropriation could be more costly than taxation. The analysis here suggests another useful distinction, which comes not from the revenue side but from the expenditure side. Expropriation might correspond to the government taking a share of the output of the producers for its own consumption, while in an equilibrium with a consensually strong state, some of the revenues from taxation are spent on public goods, which are useful for the producers. If this distinction is important, one of the reasons why taxation is viewed as fundamentally different from expropriation may be because taxation is often associated with some of the proceeds being given back to the citizens in the form of public goods.

Perhaps the most important aspect of the analysis in this section is the emphasis on different facets of growth-enhancing institutions. Economic growth not only requires secure property rights and low taxes but also complementary investments, often most efficiently undertaken by the government. Provision of law and order, investment in infrastructure, and public goods are obvious examples. Thus growth-promoting institutions should not only provide some degree of security of property rights to individuals but also incentivize the government to undertake the appropriate public goods investments. In this light, excessively weak governments might be as costly to economic performance as the unchecked power of excessively strong governments.

---

10. This discussion focuses on the output-maximizing value of the parameter $\bar{\tau}$. Exercise 22.32 discusses how different taxes affect welfare of the elite and the citizens.

22.10 Taking Stock

To understand why some countries are poor and others are rich, we need to understand why some countries choose growth-enhancing policies while others choose policies that block economic development. This chapter emphasized a number of key themes in developing answers to these questions. First, the sources of institutional differences and non-growth-enhancing institutions must be sought in social conflict among different individuals and groups. Social conflict implies that there is no guarantee that the society will adopt economic institutions and policies that encourage economic growth. Such social arrangements benefit many individuals in the society, but they also create losers—individuals and groups whose rents are destroyed or eroded by the introduction of new technologies. When individuals in the society have conflicting preferences over institutions and policies, the distribution of political power in the society plays an important role in determining which institutions and policies are chosen (and whether non-growth-enhancing institutions will be reformed).

In this chapter, I emphasized that nongrowth-enhancing policies can emerge without any significant Pareto inefficiencies. I illustrated this point first by focusing on a simple society, in which individuals belong to a social group, the conflict of interest is among social groups, and all political power rests in the hands of the political elite. I showed that this environment, combined with linear preferences, implies that even the restrictive MPE concept leads to constrained Pareto efficient allocations. Despite their Pareto efficiency, equilibrium allocations may involve significant distortions (suggesting as a by-product that Pareto efficiency may not be the right concept to focus on in the analysis of the political economy of growth).

In addition to providing a simple useful framework for the analysis of policy, the model with political power vested in the hands of the elite also leads to a range of comparative static results that shed light on what types of societies adopt policies that encourage growth and which societies are likely to block economic development. The following are some of the main comparative static results: (1) taxes are likely to be higher when the demand for capital by entrepreneurs is inelastic, because in this case the revenue-maximizing tax rate for the elite is higher; (2) taxes are higher when the factor price manipulation effect is more important relative to the revenue extraction effect; (3) taxes are higher when the political power of the elite is contested and reducing the income level of the competing groups will lead to political consolidation for the elite; (4) taxes are higher and more distortionary when there are significant holdup problems because investments are long-term or entrepreneurs have ex ante technology adoption decisions; (5) in the absence of the political replacement effect, greater state capacity leads to lower taxes; and (6) when the political replacement effect is important, both greater state capacity and greater rents from natural resources may lead to more distortionary policies because they increase the political stakes (the value of holding on to political power).

This chapter has further illustrated that the revenue extraction mechanism emphasized in the context of elite-dominated politics is also present in more complex societies. If political decisions with heterogeneous productivity (or preferences) are made democratically, then they often reflect the policy preferences of the median voter. When the median voter is poorer than the average individual (entrepreneur) in the society, she may want to use distortionary policies to transfer resources to herself. This type of distortionary revenue extraction by the median voter is qualitatively similar to revenue extraction from middle-class entrepreneurs by the elite, though it is in the context of a more general environment with heterogeneity among the entrepreneurs. The analysis also leads to a new comparative static result: when the gap between the mean and the median of the productivity distribution is greater, the incentives to extract revenues are stronger, and policies are more likely to be distortionary.

Finally, I emphasized that taxation is not the only relevant policy affecting economic growth. The provision of public goods, in the form of securing law and order, investments in infrastructure, or even appropriate regulation, might also be important for inducing a high rate of economic growth. Will the state provide the appropriate amounts and types of public goods? In the context of a political economy model, the answer depends on whether the politically powerful groups controlling the state have the incentives to provide such goods. The economic or the political elite only invest in public goods if they expect to reap the benefits of these investments in the future. This raises the issue of weak versus strong states. While an emphasis on taxes suggests that checks on the economic or political power of the state should be conducive to more growth-enhancing policies, weak states are unwilling to invest in public goods because those controlling the state realize that they will not be able to tax future revenues created by these public goods investments. Consequently an intermediate strength of the state might be most conducive to growth-enhancing policies. The more important point here is that an analysis of the effect of economic institutions and policies on growth should take into account both individual incentives for investment and the government incentives for public goods provision.

The material in this chapter is no more than an introduction to the exciting and important field of the political economy of growth. Many issues have not been addressed. Among those omitted, the following appear most important. First, in addition to taxes, expropriation, and public goods, whether the society provides a level playing field to a broad cross section of society is important. For example, broad-based human capital investments, which are important for modern economic growth, require the provision of incentives and the ability to invest not only for a few businesses but for the entire population. Similarly, security of property rights for existing businesses must be balanced against the ease of entry for new firms. Second, the entire analysis in this chapter takes as given the distribution of political power in the society. It is clear, however, that different distributions of power in the society lead to different policies and thus to distinct growth trajectories. Consequently, it seems important to understand how the distribution of political power and equilibrium political institutions might evolve endogenously and how this distribution interacts with the economic equilibrium. Some of these issues are discussed in the next chapter.

22.11 References and Literature

The material in this chapter draws on the large political economy literature and also on some of the recent work on the political economy of growth. My purpose has not been to provide a balanced survey of these literatures but to emphasize the most important features pertaining to the sources of differences in economic institutions and policies across societies with the hope of shedding some light on differential cross-country growth performances. I focused throughout on the neoclassical growth model and its variants to isolate the contribution of political economy mechanisms and to keep the exposition manageable.

Persson and Tabellini (2000) and Drazen (2001) provide introductions to political economy. Eggertsson (2005) provides an informal discussion of institutions.

The material in Sections 22.2–22.6 and the discussion of revenue extraction and factor price manipulation effects draw on Acemoglu (2007b), but the setup has been modified to be more consistent with the neoclassical growth model. The factor price manipulation effect features in Acemoglu (2007b, 2008a). The political replacement effect is introduced in Acemoglu and Robinson (2000b) and is further discussed in Acemoglu (2007b). A detailed analysis of why the political elite may block technological innovations to increase the likelihood of their survival is presented in Acemoglu and Robinson (2006b). That paper also shows how both relatively secure elites and those in competitive political environments do not have incentives to block technological change, but those with intermediate levels of security that might be challenged by new technologies may try to block economic development. Models with competitive economic behavior by price-taking agents and strategic political decisions were first developed by Chari and Kehoe (1990) for the analysis of the time-consistency of the behavior of a benevolent government.

The material in Section 22.7 is standard. See, for example, Arrow (1951) and Austen-Smith and Banks (1999) for Arrow's Impossibility Theorem. Single-peaked preferences are first introduced in Black (1948). The single-crossing property is introduced in Roberts (1977) and further developed by Gans and Smart (1996). The notion of intermediate preferences introduced in Exercise 22.24 is due to Grandmont (1978). The Downsian model of political competition is introduced in Downs (1957) and builds heavily on Hotelling's seminal (1929) paper. Austen-Smith and Banks (1999) discuss the Downsian party competition model in detail. The probabilistic voting model is due to Lindbeck and Weibull (1987) and Coughlin (1992). My exposition here was simplified by the assumption that parties care about their vote share, not the probability of coming to power.

The Median Voter Theorem, presented in Section 22.8, was first applied to an economy with linear redistributive taxes by Romer (1975) and Roberts (1977). Meltzer and Richard (1981) used the Roberts-Romer model to relate taxation to inequality and to the extent of the voting franchise. Several authors have since applied the Roberts-Romer model in growth settings. The most notable examples are Alesina and Rodrik (1994), Persson and Tabellini (1994), Saint-Paul and Verdier (1993), and Benabou (2000). The models in Alesina and Rodrik (1994) and Persson and Tabellini (1994) are similar to the one I developed in Section 22.8, except that they do not characterize a well-defined MPE. Instead they assume that either (1) voting takes place at the beginning of time (at $t = 0$) and over a single tax rate that will apply at all future dates or (2) agents are myopic and do not take into account future votes (though they do take into account their own future economic decisions). In addition these papers focus on an economy with endogenous growth, so that differences in taxes lead to differences in equilibrium growth rates (see Exercise 22.31). Both Alesina and Rodrik (1994) and Persson and Tabellini (1994) emphasize the negative effects of inequality on economic growth, interpreting the gap between the mean and the median as a measure of inequality. They also present cross-country evidence suggesting that inequality is negatively correlated with economic growth. This cross-country growth evidence is difficult to interpret, however, both because there are many omitted variables in such growth regressions and also because other researchers find very different associations between inequality and growth (see, e.g., Forbes, 2000; Banerjee and Duflo, 2003). Saint-Paul and Verdier (1993), on the other hand, show that higher inequality can lead to greater growth when tax revenues are invested in human capital accumulation. Benabou (2000) shows how a negative relationship between inequality and growth is consistent with higher inequality, leading to less redistribution in a world in which greater redistribution may be growth-enhancing, again because tax revenues are invested in education. None of these papers characterize the MPE of a dynamic economy, instead assuming that voting is either myopic or takes place only once at the beginning of time. Krusell and Ríos-Rull (1996) and Hassler et al. (2005) provide characterizations of MPEs in related political environments.

Section 22.9 builds on Acemoglu (2005). The idea that weak states may be an important impediment to economic growth is popular among political scientists and political sociologists, and is most famously articulated in Migdal (1988), Wade (1990), Evans (1995), and Herbst (2000). These approaches do not analyze the incentives of the politicians or the government. Acemoglu (2005) provides the first formal framework to analyze these issues. The material in Section 22.9 embeds the baseline model in that paper into a neoclassical growth model.

22.12 Exercises

22.1 Prove that $\hat{\tau}$ given by (22.16) satisfies $\hat{\tau} \in (0, 1)$.

22.2 Consider the model in Section 22.2, the only difference being that the production technology is as in the Romer (1986a) model studied in Chapter 11. Each entrepreneur now has access to the production function $Y_i(t) = F(K_i(t), A(t)L_i(t))$, and

$$A(t) = B \int_0^1 K_i(t)di = BK(t).$$

Characterize the MPE in this case, and show that distortionary taxes imposed by the elite reduce the equilibrium growth rate of the economy. [Hint: assume that the elite do not take into account the effect of taxes on capital accumulation. How are the results affected if they do take this into account?]

22.3 Consider the model in Section 22.2, and assume that policies are decided by the middle class. Show that the middle class might prefer positive taxation on themselves (with the proceeds redistributed to themselves as lump-sum transfers). Provide a precise intuition for why such taxation may make political-economic sense for middle-class entrepreneurs. Would the same result apply if the proceeds of taxation were redistributed as a lump-sum transfer to every individual in the society (including workers)? Would it apply if the middle class had access to other policy instruments?

22.4 Consider the model of Section 22.2, but assume that there are $N < \infty$ middle-class entrepreneurs, and suppose that each entrepreneur can make a voluntary contribution to a fund that is paid out to the elite. Rather than assuming that middle-class entrepreneurs behave competitively, consider the SPE of this game. Show that for β sufficiently large, there exists an SPE in which the behavior along the equilibrium path involves each middle-class entrepreneur making a positive contribution to the fund and the elite setting zero taxes. [Hint: look for an equilibrium with the following structure: if total contributions to the fund fall below some $\tilde{T} > 0$ or if the elite set positive taxes at any $t' < t$, then the continuation play involves a tax rate $\tau = 1 - \alpha$ and zero contributions to the fund for all $t'' \geq t$.]

22.5 Prove Proposition 22.4.

22.6 Prove Proposition 22.5.

22.7 Prove Proposition 22.6.

22.8 Consider the model in Section 22.4, and suppose that the middle class are in political power. Characterize the MPE in this case. Derive the discounted utility of the elite when the middle class are in control of politics, denoted by $V^e(M)$, and compare this to their utility when they are in control, $V^e(E)$.

22.9 In the model with political replacement in Section 22.4.2, suppose that $\eta'(\cdot) < 0$. Show that in this case the tax rate preferred by the elite is less than $1 - \alpha$ and that when the elite can block technology adoption, they will not choose to do so. Explain the intuition for this result. What types of institutional structures might lead to $\eta'(\cdot) < 0$ as opposed to $\eta'(\cdot) > 0$?

22.10 Prove Proposition 22.7.

22.11 In the model with political replacement in Section 22.4.2, show that the unique MPE is also the unique SPE.

22.12 (a) Prove Proposition 22.9.

(b) Explain how Proposition 22.9 needs to be modified if $\bar{\tau} < 1$, and provide an analysis of the best stationary SPE in this case (where only stationary strategies are used).

22.13 Prove Proposition 22.12.

22.14 Prove Proposition 22.13.

22.15 Prove Proposition 22.15. Explain why the conditions that $\bar{\tau} < 1$ and $(1 - \bar{\tau})^{1/(1-\alpha)} < A^e/A^m$ are necessary in this theorem.

22.16   (a) Consider the economy with political replacement in Section 22.4.2. Suppose Condition 22.1 fails to hold and $\phi = 0$. Show that in any MPE or SPE, the elite prefer to block technology, that is, $g = 0$.

(b) Suppose that in this proposition ϕ is not equal to 0. Provide an example in which in the MPE, the elite would still prefer $g = 0$.

(c) Now suppose that the elite can charge lump-sum taxes to middle-class entrepreneurs. Provide an example in which in the MPE, the elite would still prefer $g = 0$. Explain why the political equilibrium might involve the use of inefficient fiscal instruments, even when more efficient alternatives exist.

* 22.17   Suppose that the economy consists of two groups, the elite and the producers. Suppose that both groups have equal size. Both groups have instantaneous utility $u(c) = \log c$ and discount factor β. Producers have access to the production technology $f(k) = Ak^\alpha$, where k is capital. The elite impose a linear tax rate of $\tau(t)$ on production at time t and consume the proceeds. The capital stock for time $t + 1$ must be chosen at time t after the tax rate $\tau(t)$ has been announced. There is full depreciation of capital.

(a) Given a tax sequence, set up the dynamic optimization problem of entrepreneurs and show that the evolution of the capital stock is given by

$$k(t + 1) = \alpha\beta(1 - \tau(t))Ak(t)^\alpha. \tag{22.61}$$

Explain why the capital stock for time $t + 1$ does not depend on the current tax rate but only on the past tax rate. [Hint: to derive (22.61), set up the maximization problem of the entrepreneur as a dynamic program and conjecture a decision rule of the form $k_i(t + 1) = \kappa y_i(t)$ for entrepreneur i, where $y_i(t)$ is his output at time t.]

(b) To determine the MPE tax rates, write the value to a representative elite agent at time $t + 1$ as a function of the tax rate $\tau = \tau(t + 1)$, taking into account that the capital stock of entrepreneurs at date $t + 1$, $k = k(t + 1)$, is from (22.61). Show that this value function takes the form

$$V^e(k) = \max_{\tau \in [0,1]} \left\{ \log(\tau Ak^\alpha) + \beta V^e(\alpha\beta(1 - \tau)Ak^\alpha) \right\}. \tag{22.62}$$

Use the results from Chapter 6 to conclude that V^e is strictly concave and differentiable for $k > 0$ (and denote the derivative by $(V^e)'$). Show that the Euler equation for the elite is

$$\frac{1}{\tau} = \beta^2 \alpha Ak^\alpha (V^e)'(k') = \beta \frac{k'(V^e)'(k')}{1 - \tau}.$$

(c) Conjecturing that $V^e(k) = \eta + \gamma \log k$ and using the Envelope condition, show that $\gamma = \alpha/(1 - \alpha\beta)$ and that the utility-maximizing strategy for the elite is

$$\tau(t) = 1 - \alpha\beta \tag{22.63}$$

for all t (regardless of the level of the capital stock at that point). Explain the role of logarithmic preferences in (22.63).

(d) Characterize the dynamics of capital stock in this economy.

* 22.18   In the Condorcet paradox example provided in Section 22.7.2, show that other orderings of the choices a, b, and c also imply that the preferences of at least one of the three individuals is not single peaked.

* 22.19   State and prove an analogue of Theorem 22.1 when H is even.

* 22.20   Consider three individuals with the following preferences:

$$
\begin{array}{ll}
1 & a \succ b \succ c, \\
2 & b \succ c \succ a, \\
3 & c \succ b \succ a.
\end{array}
$$

Suppose the following dynamic voting protocol is in effect: first, there is a vote between a and b; then the winner goes against c; and the winner of this contest will be implemented. Focus on SPE where voters do not use "weakly dominated" strategies at any stage.

(a) Show that these preferences are single peaked, but sincere voting is not equilibrium behavior. [Hint: suppose that players 1 and 2 are voting sincerely, and show that player 3 prefers not to vote sincerely.]

(b) Characterize the SPE of this game under strategic voting by all players.

(c) Consider a generalization in which the society $\mathcal{H}$ consists of H individuals and there are finite number of policies, $\mathcal{R} = \{p_1, p_2, \ldots, p_M\}$. For simplicity, suppose that H is an odd number. Voting takes $M - 1$ stages. In the first stage, there is a vote between p_1 and p_2. In the second stage, there is a vote between the winner of the first stage and p_3, until we have a final vote against p_M. The winner of the final vote is the policy choice of the society. Prove that if preferences of all agents are single peaked, then the unique SPE implements the bliss point of the median voter.

* 22.21 Modify and prove Theorem 22.3 without using assumption A4.

* 22.22 This exercise reviews Downsian party competition and then shows that Theorem 22.3 does not apply if there are three parties competing. In particular, consider Downsian party competition in a society consisting of a continuum 1 of individuals with single-peaked preferences. The policy space $\mathcal{R}$ is the $[0, 1]$ interval, and assume that the bliss points of the individuals are uniformly distributed over this space.

(a) To start with, suppose that there are two parties, A and B. They both would like to maximize the probability of coming to power. The game involves both parties simultaneously announcing $p^A \in [0, 1]$ and $p^B \in [0, 1]$, and then voters voting for one of the two parties. The platform of the party with most votes gets implemented. Determine the equilibrium of this game. How would the result be different if the parties maximized their vote share rather than the probability of coming to power?

(b) Now assume that there are three parties, simultaneously announcing their policies $p^A \in [0, 1]$, $p^B \in [0, 1]$, and $p^C \in [0, 1]$, and the platform of the party with most votes is implemented. Assume that parties maximize the probability of coming to power. Characterize all pure-strategy equilibria.

(c) Now assume that the three parties maximize their vote shares. Prove that there exists no pure-strategy equilibrium.

(d) In part c, characterize the mixed-strategy equilibrium. [Hint: assume the same symmetric probability distribution for two parties, and make sure that given these distributions, the third party is indifferent over all policies in the support of the distribution.]

* 22.23 Prove Theorem 22.5.

* 22.24 This exercise involves generalizing the idea of single-crossing property used in Theorem 22.4 to multidimensional policy spaces. The appropriate notion of preferences of individuals turns out to be intermediate preferences. Let $\mathcal{R} \subset \mathbb{R}^K$ (where $K \in \mathbb{N}$) and policies p belong to $\mathcal{R}$. We say that voters have "intermediate preferences" if their indirect utility function $U(p; \alpha_i)$ can be written as $U(p; \alpha_i) = G_1(p) + B(\alpha_i)G_2(p)$, where $B(\alpha_i)$ is monotone (monotonically increasing or monotonically decreasing) in α_i, and the functions $G_1(p)$ and $G_2(p)$ are common to all voters. Suppose that A2 holds and voters have intermediate preferences. The bliss point (vector) of individual i is $p(\alpha_i) \in \mathcal{R}$ that maximizes individual i's utility. Prove that when preferences are intermediate, a Condorcet winner always exists and coincides with bliss point of the voter with the median value of α_i, that is, $p_M = p(\alpha_M)$.

* 22.25 Consider a society consisting of three individuals, 1, 2, and 3, and a resource of size 1. The three individuals vote on how to distribute the resource among themselves and each individual prefers more of the resource for himself and does not care about consumption by the other two. Since all of the resource will be distributed among the three individuals, we can represent the menu of policies as $\{(x_1, x_2) : x_1 \geq 0, x_2 \geq 0, \text{ and } x_1 + x_2 \leq 1\}$, where x_i denotes the share of the resource consumed by individual i. A policy vector (x_1, x_2) is accepted if it receives two votes. Show that individual preferences over policy vectors do not satisfy single crossing or the conditions in Exercise 22.24. Show that there does not exist a policy vector that is a Condorcet winner. Show that if two parties compete to come to office by committing to policy platforms, then this game has no pure-strategy equilibria.

* 22.26 (a) Show that in Theorem 22.6, a necessary condition for a pure-strategy symmetric equilibrium, with $p_A = p_B = p^*$, to exist is that the matrix

$$\sum_{g=1}^{G} \lambda^g h^g(0) D^2 U^g(p^*) + \sum_{g=1}^{G} \lambda^g \left| \frac{\partial h^g(0)}{\partial \sigma} \right| (DU^g(p^*)) \cdot (DU^g(p^*))^T$$

is negative semidefinite, where $D^2 U^g$ denotes the Jacobian matrix of U^g. Explain why the condition takes the absolute values of $\partial h^g(0)/\partial \sigma$.

(b) Derive a sufficient condition for such a symmetric equilibrium to exist. [Hint: distinguish between local and global maxima.]

(c) Show that without any assumptions on $U^g(\cdot)$s (beyond concavity), the sufficient condition for a symmetric equilibrium can only be satisfied if all H^gs are uniform.

22.27 Consider the following one-period economy populated by a continuum 1 of agents. A fraction λ of these agents are capitalists, each owning capital k. The remainder have only human capital, with human capital distribution $\mu(h)$. Output is produced in competitive markets, with the aggregate production function

$$Y = K^{1-\alpha} H^{\alpha},$$

where uppercased letters denote total supplies. Assume that factor markets are competitive and denote the market clearing rental price of capital by r and that of human capital by w.

Suppose that agents vote over a linear income tax, τ. Because of tax distortions, total tax revenue is

$$\text{Tax} = (\tau - v(\tau)) \left(\lambda r k + (1 - \lambda) w \int h \, d\mu(h) \right),$$

where $v(\tau)$ is strictly increasing and convex, with $v(0) = v'(0) = 0$ and $v'(1) = \infty$. Tax revenues are redistributed lumpsum.

(a) Find the ideal tax rate for each agent. Find conditions under which preferences are single peaked, and determine the equilibrium tax rate. How does the equilibrium tax rate change when k increases? How does it change when λ increases? Explain the intuition for these results.

(b) Suppose now that agents vote over capital and labor income taxes, τ_k and τ_h, with corresponding costs $v(\tau_k)$ and $v(\tau_h)$, so that tax revenues are

$$\text{Tax} = (\tau_k - v(\tau_k)) \lambda r k + (\tau_h - v(\tau_h))(1 - \lambda) w \int h \, d\mu(h).$$

Determine the most preferred tax rates for each agent. Suppose that $\lambda < 1/2$. Does a voting equilibrium exist? How does it change when λ increases? Explain why the results are different from the case with only one tax instrument.

(c) In this model with two taxes, now suppose that agents first vote over the capital income tax, and then taking the capital income tax as given, they vote on the labor income tax. Does a voting equilibrium exist? If an equilibrium exists, how does the equilibrium tax rate change when k increases? How does it change when λ increases?

22.28 Derive (22.43).

22.29 Show that $\tilde{V}_i(\tau' \mid p^{t+1})$ defined in (22.46) is not necessarily quasi-concave, but it always satisfies the single-crossing property in Definition 22.3.

22.30 Consider an economy consisting of three groups, a fraction θ_p of poor agents each with income y_p, a fraction θ_m of middle-class agents with income $y_m > y_p$, and the remaining fraction $\theta_r = 1 - \theta_p - \theta_m$ of rich agents with income $y_r > y_m$. Suppose that both θ_p and θ_r are less than 1/2, so that the individual with the median income (the "median voter") is a middle-class individual.

(a) Construct a change in incomes that leaves mean income in the society unchanged and increases the gap between the mean and the median, but does not constitute a mean-preserving spread of the distribution.

(b) Construct a mean-preserving spread of the distribution such that the gap between the mean and the median narrows. [Hint: increase y_m and reduce y_p, holding y_r constant.]

22.31 Consider an economy with a continuum 1 of individuals. Each individual i has logarithmic instantaneous utility, so that

$$U_i = \sum_{t=0}^{\infty} \beta^t \log C_i(t),$$

and has one unit of labor, which he supplies inelastically. Final output is produced by competitive firms, indexed by j, that rent capital and labor from individuals. The production function of each firm is

$$Y_j(t) = A K_j(t)^{1-\alpha} G(t)^\alpha L_j(t)^\alpha,$$

where K_j and L_j denote capital and labor employed by firm j, respectively, and G is government investment in infrastructure. The only tax instrument is a linear tax on the capital holdings of all individuals at the rate $\tau(t)$ at time t. All the proceeds of this taxation are spent on government investment in infrastructure, so that

$$G(t) = \tau(t)\bar{K}(t), \tag{22.64}$$

where $\bar{K}(t)$ is the average (total) capital stock in the economy. This specification implies that government's provision of infrastructure creates a Romer-type externality. Denote the initial capital stock of the economy by $\bar{K}(0)$.

(a) Characterize the equilibrium with a constant tax rate $\tau > 0$ at each date, and show that with A sufficiently large, the economy achieves a constant and positive growth rate. Show that the growth rate of the economy is independent of the distribution of the initial capital stock among the individuals. [Hint: note that the net interest rate faced by households is equal to the marginal product of capital minus the tax rate τ.]

(b) Let the initial capital stock $\bar{K}(0)$ be distributed among the agents with shares ω_i, so that individual i's initial capital holding is $K_i(0) = \omega_i \bar{K}(0)$. Show that in equilibrium, we have $K_i(t) = \omega_i \bar{K}(t)$ for any $t = 1, 2, \ldots$.

(c) Suppose that the economy legislates a constant tax rate τ for all future periods. This tax rate is determined by the policy proposal of the party that receives the majority of the votes (from two competing parties). Determine the most preferred tax rate of individual i as a function of his share of initial capital ω_i at time $t = 0$. Show that individuals have single-peaked preferences. On the basis of this result, show that the tax rate most preferred by the individual with the median capital holdings, ω_M, will be implemented. Show that as this median capital holdings falls, the rate of capital taxation increases. What is the effect of this on economic growth?

(d) Show that the equilibrium characterized in part c is *not* an MPE. Explain why not. How would you set up the problem to characterize such an equilibrium? [Hint: just describe how you would set up the problem; no need to solve for the equilibrium.]

22.32 (a) Prove Proposition 22.19.

(b) Derive the output-maximizing tax rate as in (22.60).

(c) Let $\bar{\tau}^*$, $\bar{\tau}^{wm}$, $\bar{\tau}^e$ and $\bar{\tau}^c$ be the values of $\bar{\tau}$ that respectively maximize output, social welfare, the elite's utility, and citizens' utility for all $t > 0$. Show that $0 < \bar{\tau}^c < \bar{\tau}^* < \bar{\tau}^e < 1$ and $0 < \bar{\tau}^c < \bar{\tau}^{wm} < \bar{\tau}^e < 1$.

Political Institutions and Economic Growth

The previous chapter investigated why some societies choose "inefficient" economic institutions and policies. It emphasized the importance of social conflict among different groups and the lack of commitment to future policies as major sources of nongrowth-enhancing policies. Much of the discussion was in the context of a given set of political institutions, which shaped both the extent and kind of social conflict among different individuals and groups, and what types of policies were possible or could be committed to. A natural conjecture in this context is that political institutions influence a society's choices of economic institutions and policies and thus its growth trajectory. This conjecture leads to the following two questions: Do certain political institutions mediate social conflict more successfully, thus potentially avoiding nongrowth-enhancing policies? Why do different societies choose or end up with different political institutions?

This chapter provides some preliminary answers to these two questions. I start with a brief summary of the empirical evidence on the effect of different political regimes on economic growth. Section 23.2 then uses the baseline model in Section 22.2 from the previous chapter to illustrate that, once we take the existence of conflicting preferences into account, no political regime is perfect and each creates different types of costs and benefits associated with different losers and winners in the society. Whether a particular set of political institutions leads to growth-enhancing policies then depends on the details of how it functions, on the technology and the factor endowments of the society, and on which groups benefit from these institutions. Section 23.3 then turns to the dynamic trade-offs between different regimes, emphasizing how democratic regimes might compensate for the short-run distortions that they create by generating long-run benefits, both by avoiding sclerotic outcomes and by creating greater flexibility. This section also emphasizes how different political regimes deal with the process of creative destruction, which, as we saw in Chapter 14, is one of the engines of modern economic growth. The arguments in Section 23.3 suggest that democracies may be better at taking advantage of the forces of creative destruction. How political institutions themselves emerge and change is discussed briefly in Section 23.4.

23.1 Political Regimes and Economic Growth

In thinking about the impact of political institutions on economic outcomes and growth, most scholars would probably start with the contrast between democratic and nondemocratic regimes. But there are many different types and shades of democracy. Democracy is typically defined by a set of procedural rules; for instance, by whether there are free and fair elections in which most adults can participate and whether there is free entry of parties into politics. But this definition of democracy leaves many distinctive institutional features of democracies unspecified. Democracies can be parliamentary or presidential. They can use different electoral rules, giving varying degrees of voice to minorities. Perhaps more importantly, there are different degrees of "free and fair" and "most adults." Most elections, even those in Europe or the United States, involve some degree of fraud and some restrictions on the entry of parties or candidates. Moreover many individuals are effectively or sometimes explicitly disenfranchised. Similarly, political scientists consider Britain and the United States in the late nineteenth century to have been democratic, though only men had the right to vote. Few people would consider the United States in the 1960s to have been a nondemocracy, but many blacks were disenfranchised. These specifics create various shades of democracy that may affect the economic outcome.

The differences between nondemocratic societies are probably even more pronounced. China under the rule of the Communist Party since 1948 is an undisputed case of a nondemocratic regime, but it is very different in nature from the oligarchic regime in place in Britain before the process of democratization started with the First Reform Act of 1832. In Britain before 1832, there were prime ministers and parliaments, though they were elected by a small minority of the population—those with wealth, education, and privilege, who made up less than 10% of the adult population. Furthermore the powers of the state never rivaled those of the Communist Party in China. The Chinese example is also different from Augusto Pinochet's military dictatorship in Chile or that of Park Chung Hee in South Korea. Once we consider regimes based on personal rule, such as that of Mobutu Sese Seko in Zaire, and monarchies, such as the rule of the Saud family in Saudi Arabia, the contrast is even more marked.

Nevertheless there is an important commonality among these nondemocracies and an important contrast between nondemocratic and democratic regimes, making these categories still useful for conceptual and empirical analysis. Despite all their imperfections and different shades, democratic regimes, at least when they have a certain minimal degree of functionality, provide greater political equality than nondemocratic ones. The free entry of parties and the practice of one-person, one-vote in a democracy are the foundations of this and ensure some voice for each individual. When democracies function well, majorities have some (often a significant) influence on policies—though they themselves may be constrained by certain constitutional restrictions. In contrast, nondemocracies, rather than representing the wishes of the population at large, represent the preferences of a subgroup of the population, which I have so far referred to as the "elite." The identity of the elite differs across nondemocratic societies. In China, it is mainly the wishes of the leaders of Communist Party that matter. In Chile under Pinochet, most decisions were taken by a military junta, and it was their preferences (and perhaps those of certain affluent segments of the society supporting the dictatorship) that counted. In Britain before the First Reform Act of 1832, it was the small wealthy minority that was politically influential.

With this cautionary introduction on the distinctions between democracies and nondemocracies, what are the major differences between these political regimes? First, one might imagine that democracies and nondemocracies have different growth performances. The first place to look for such differences is the postwar era, for which there are better data on economic growth. Using cross-country regression evidence, Przeworski and Limongi (1993) and Barro (1999) conclude that democracies do not perform better than nondemocracies. However, there is no universal consensus on this matter. For example, Minier (1998) reports results showing both positive effects of democratizations and negative effects of transitions to nondemocracy on growth. Nevertheless the bulk of the available evidence suggests that, on average, democracies do not grow much faster than nondemocracies (at least, once one controls for other potential determinants of economic growth). This result is surprising and even perhaps disturbing. One might have expected significantly worse growth performances among nondemocracies, since this group includes highly unsuccessful countries, such as Iraq under Saddam Hussein, Zaire under Mobutu, and Haiti under the Duvaliers. Counteracting this group, however, are plenty of unsuccessful democracies, including India until the 1990s and many newly independent former colonies that started their independence as electoral democracies (though often quickly falling prey to coups or the personal rule of some strongman). There are also many successful non-democracies, including Singapore under Lee Kwan Yew, South Korea under General Park, or (more recently) China. Thus to understand how different political institutions affect economic decisions and economic growth, we need to go beyond the distinction between democracy and nondemocracy.

If there are no marked growth differences between democracies and nondemocracies, are there instead other significant policy or distributional differences? Rodrik (1999) documents that democracies have higher labor shares and interprets this as the outcome of greater redistribution in democracies. Acemoglu and Robinson (2006a) summarize a range of case studies showing how democracies pursue more redistributive policies. In contrast, Gil, Mulligan, and Sala-i-Martin (2004) use cross-sectional regressions to show that many policies, in particular overall government spending and spending on social security, do not differ between democracies and dictatorships. Therefore there is no consensus in the literature on whether democracies pursue different fiscal policies and whether this has a major impact on the distribution of resources in the society. But the evidence in Rodrik (1999) and some of the evidence summarized in Acemoglu and Robinson (2006a) indicate that, at least in some cases, democracies pursue significantly more redistributive policies than do nondemocracies, and we can take these differences as our starting point (or at least as a working hypothesis). But it is useful to bear in mind that the differences in policy between democracies and nondemocracies, even if present, appear to be much less pronounced than one might have expected on the basis of theory alone.

It should also be noted at this point that the comparison of democracies to nondemocracies over the postwar era might be overly restrictive. When we look at a longer time horizon, it appears that democracies experience better economic performance. Most of the countries that industrialized rapidly during the nineteenth century were more democratic than those that failed to do so. The comparisons of the United States to South American countries, or of Britain and France to Russia and Austria-Hungary, are particularly informative in this context. For example, the United States, which was one of the most democratic societies at the time, was not any richer, and may have been significantly poorer, than the highly nondemocratic and repressive Caribbean colonies at the end of the eighteenth century. However, the nineteenth century and early twentieth century witnessed rapid growth and industrialization in the United States and stagnation in the entire Caribbean area and in much of the rest of South America. This historical episode therefore suggests that the more democratic societies may have been better at taking advantage of the new investment and growth opportunities that came with the age of industrialization in the nineteenth century. The contrast of Britain and France to Russia and Austria-Hungary is similar. Even though the former two countries were already richer at the beginning of the nineteenth century than the latter two, the income differences were small. Differences in political institutions were much more marked, however. Britain was already on its way to becoming a parliamentary democracy, and France had already undergone the Revolution of 1789. Britain and France adopted pro-growth policies throughout much of the nineteenth century, even when this was costly to their existing landowning elites, whereas Russia and Austria-Hungary explicitly blocked industrialization to protect the economic and political interests of their landowning aristocracies.

Long-run regressions, such as those discussed in Chapter 4, are also consistent with this pattern and show a significant effect of a broad cluster of institutions on economic growth. While we cannot confidently say that this effect represents the impact of political institutions on growth, this cluster of institutions comprises both political and economic elements, and it is likely that the growth-enhancing cluster of institutions could not exist without the political institutions supporting the economic policies that encouraged investment and free entry.

I next turn to a theoretical investigation of how we might expect different political institutions to affect economic policies and economic outcomes.

23.2 Political Institutions and Growth-Enhancing Policies

Consider the canonical Cobb-Douglas model analyzed in Section 22.3 in the previous chapter. The model was analyzed under the assumption that a subset of the producers, the elite, was in power. I now briefly discuss the equilibrium in the same environment when the middle class or the workers are in power and then contrast the resulting allocations.

23.2.1 The Dictatorship of the Middle Class versus the Dictatorship of the Elite

First, let us suppose that the middle class hold political power, so that we have the *dictatorship of the middle class* instead of the dictatorship of the elite in the previous chapter. The situation is symmetric to that in the previous chapter with the middle class and the elite having exchanged places. In particular, the analysis leading to Proposition 22.6 immediately yields the following result.

Proposition 23.1   *Consider the environment of Section 22.3, but the middle class instead of the elite holding political power. Suppose that Condition 22.1 holds, $\phi > 0$, and*

$$A^m \geq \phi \alpha^{\alpha/(1-\alpha)} A^e \frac{\theta^e}{\theta^m}. \tag{23.1}$$

Then the unique MPE features $\tau^m(t) = 0$ and

$$\tau^e(t) = \bar{\tau}^{COM} \equiv \frac{\kappa(\bar{L}, \theta^m, \alpha, \phi)}{1 + \kappa(\bar{L}, \theta^m, \alpha, \phi)},$$

for all t, where $\kappa(\bar{L}, \theta^e, \alpha, \phi)$ is defined in (22.29).

Proof.   See Exercise 23.1.   ∎

This proposition shows that political equilibria under elite control and middle-class control are identical, except that the two groups have switched places. Political institutions therefore influence policies and the resulting equilibrium allocation of resources. In particular, in the elite-controlled society, the middle class are taxed both to create revenues for the elite and to reduce their labor demand. In the middle-class-dominated society, the competing group of producers that are out of political power are the elite (even though the name "elite" has the connotation of political power). So now the elite are taxed to generate tax revenues and create more favorable labor market conditions for the middle class. The contrast between the elite-dominated and the middle-class-dominated politics approximates certain well-known historical episodes. For example, in the context of the historical development of European societies, political power was first in the hands of landowners, who exercised it to keep labor tied to the land and reduce the power and profitability of merchants and early industrialists. With the economic and constitutional changes of the late medieval period, power shifted away from landowning aristocracies toward the merchants and industrialists (i.e., the middle class in terms of the model here), and it was their turn to adopt policies favorable to their own economic interests and costly for landowners.

So which one of these two sets of political institutions—the dictatorship of the middle class or that of the elite—is better? The answer is that they cannot be compared easily. First, as already emphasized in the previous chapter, the equilibrium in Section 22.4 is Pareto optimal: given the set of fiscal instruments, it is not possible to make any other member of the society better off without making the elite worse off. In the same way, the current allocation of resources is Pareto optimal, but it picks a different point along the Pareto frontier—a point that favors the middle class instead of the elite. What about the level of output? Even here, there is no straightforward ranking. Either of these two societies may achieve a higher level of income per capita depending on which group has more productive investment opportunities. When the middle class are more productive, a society in which the elite are in power creates significant distortions. In contrast, if the elite have more profitable and socially beneficial production opportunities, then having political power vested with the elite is more beneficial for economic performance than the dictatorship of the middle class.

The following proposition illustrates a particularly simple version of this result.

Proposition 23.2 *Consider the environment of Section 22.3 with Cobb-Douglas technology. Suppose that Condition 22.1 and the inequalities in (22.27) and (23.1) hold, $\theta^e = \theta^m$, and $\phi > 0$. Then the dictatorship of the middle class generates higher income per capita when $A^m > A^e$ and the dictatorship of the elite generates higher income per capita when $A^e > A^m$.*

Proof.   See Exercise 23.2.   ■

This proposition gives a simple example of a situation in which the political institutions that lead to better economic performance (in terms of income per capita) depend on whether more productive group also holds political power. When political and economic power are decoupled, there is greater inefficiency. An immediate implication of this result is that it is difficult to think about "efficient political institutions" without considering the self-interested objectives of those who hold and wield political power and without fully analyzing how their productivity and economic activities compare to those of others. Naturally, one can think of political institutions that will outperform both the elite-dominated politics of the previous chapter and the middle class–dominated politics of this section. In this case, the key question is whether such political institutions are feasible once more realistic political economy and economic interactions are introduced. The analysis of the design of feasible political institutions in the presence of political economy constraints is an interesting area but very much in its infancy. For now, we can simply note that under most circumstances, the choice of political institutions in practice is among arrangements that create different types of distortions and different winners and losers.

23.2.2   Democracy or Dictatorship of the Workers?

The Section 23.2.1 contrasted the dictatorship of the middle class to that of the elite. A third possibility is to have a more democratic political system in which the majority decides policies. Since in realistic scenarios, the workers outnumber both the elite and the middle-class entrepreneurs, policies that favor the economic interests of the workers (who have so far been passive in this model, simply supplying labor at the equilibrium wage rate) will then be implemented. While such a system resembles democracy in some ways (especially since it implies greater political equality than the dictatorship of the elite or the middle class), it can also be viewed as the "dictatorship of the workers": it is now the workers who dictate policies, in the same way that the elite or the middle class did under their own dictatorships.[1] This again emphasizes that different political institutions create different winners and losers, depending on which group has more political power.

As before, the analysis is straightforward, though the nature of the political equilibrium depends even more strongly on whether Condition 22.1 holds.

Proposition 23.3 *Consider the environment of Section 22.3, and suppose that workers hold political power.*

1. *Suppose that Condition 22.1 fails to hold (so that there is excess labor supply). Then the unique MPE features $\tau^m(t) = \tau^e(t) = \tau^{RE} \equiv 1 - \alpha$.*

2. *Suppose that Condition 22.1 holds (so that there is no excess labor supply) and that $\theta^e = \theta^m = \theta$. If, in addition, $A^m > A^e$, then in the unique MPE, $\tau^e(t) = 0$, and also $\tau^m(t) = \tau^{Dm}$, where*

$$(1 - \tau^{Dm})^{1/(1-\alpha)} A^m = A^e,$$

or $\tau^{Dm} = 1 - \alpha$, and $\alpha^{1/(1-\alpha)} A^m \geq A^e$. If $A^m < A^e$, then in the unique MPE, $\tau^m(t) = 0$, and also $\tau^e(t) = \tau^{De}$, where

$$(1 - \tau^{De})^{1/(1-\alpha)} A^e = A^m,$$

or $\tau^{De} = 1 - \alpha$, and $\alpha^{1/(1-\alpha)} A^e \geq A^m$.

Proof. See Exercise 23.3. ∎

The most interesting implication of this proposition comes from the comparison of the cases with and without excess supply. When Condition 22.1 fails to hold, there is excess labor supply and taxes have no effect on wages. Anticipating this, workers favor taxes on both groups of producers to raise revenues to be redistributed to themselves. Democracy then generates this outcome as the political equilibrium. Clearly, this result is more distortionary than either the dictatorship of the elite or that of the middle class, because in the latter two political scenarios, one of the producer groups was not taxed. The situation is very different when Condition 22.1 holds. In that case, recall that both the dictatorships of the elite and of the middle class generated significant distortions owing to the factor price manipulation effect—in particular, they imposed taxes on competing producers to keep wages low. In contrast, workers dislike taxes precisely because of their effect on wages. Consequently in this case, workers have more moderate preferences regarding taxation, and democracy generates lower taxes than both the dictatorships of the elite and of the middle class. This proposition therefore again highlights that which set of political institutions generates a greater level of income per capita (or higher economic growth) depends on investment opportunities and market structure. When workers (or a subgroup that is influential in democracy) can tax entrepreneurs without suffering the consequences, democracy generates high levels of redistributive taxation and can lead to a lower income per capita than elite- or middle class–dominated politics. However, when workers recognize the impact of taxes on their own wages, democracy generates more moderate political outcomes.

---

1. Distinguishing the dictatorship of workers or poor segments of the society from a true "democracy" is an important issue but falls beyond the scope of my focus here.

The simple analysis in this section therefore already gives us some clues about why there are no clear-cut relationships between political regimes and economic growth. When the equivalent of Condition 22.1 holds so that distortionary policies reduce wages, democracy is likely to generate higher aggregate output and growth than nondemocratic regimes. In contrast, democracy leads to worse economic performance by pursuing populist policies and imposing high taxes when the equivalent of Condition 22.1 fails to hold. Naturally, the model presented here is very simple in many ways, and Condition 22.1 or its close cousins may not be appropriate for evaluating whether democracy or other regimes are more growth-enhancing. Nevertheless, this analysis emphasizes that democracies, like other regimes, look after the interests of the groups that have political power, and the resulting allocations often involve different types of distortions. Whether these distortions are more or less severe than those generated by alternative political regimes depends on technology, factor endowments, and the types of policies available to the political system. In light of the analysis so far, this result is not surprising, but its implications are nonetheless important. In particular, it highlights that there are no a priori theoretical reasons to expect that there should be a simple empirical relationship between democracy and growth.

23.3 Dynamic Trade-offs

The previous section contrasted economic allocations under different political regimes. Although the underlying economic environment was a simplified version of the infinite-horizon neoclassical growth model, the trade-offs among the regimes were static. In this section, I examine an environment that also incorporates entry into entrepreneurship, social mobility, and a simple form of creative destruction. Using this environment, I contrast democracy to oligarchy. The emphasis is on the dynamic trade-offs between the two regimes.

23.3.1 The Baseline Model

The model economy is populated by a continuum of measure 1 of infinitely-lived agents, each with preferences given by (22.1) as in the previous chapter. In addition, for reasons that will soon become clear, I assume that each individual dies with a small probability $\varepsilon > 0$ in every period, and a measure ε of new individuals are born (with the convention that after death there is zero utility, and $\beta \in (0, 1)$ is the discount factor inclusive of the probability of death). I consider the limit of this economy with $\varepsilon \to 0$.

There are two occupations: production workers and entrepreneurs. This introduces the possibility of social mobility. In particular, each agent can either be employed as a worker or can become an entrepreneur. I assume that all agents have the same productivity as workers, but their productivity in entrepreneurship differs. In particular, agent i at time t has entrepreneurial talent/skills $a_i(t) \in \{A^L, A^H\}$, with $A^L < A^H$. To become an entrepreneur, an agent needs to set up a firm, if he does not have an active firm already. Setting up a new firm may be costly because of entry barriers created by existing entrepreneurs.

Each agent therefore starts period t with skill level $a_i(t) \in \{A^H, A^L\}$, some amount of capital $k_i(t)$ invested from the previous date (recall that capital investments are again made one period in advance), and another state variable denoting whether he already possesses a firm. I denote this variable by $e_i(t) \in \{0, 1\}$, with $e_i(t) = 1$ corresponding to the individual having chosen entrepreneurship at date $t - 1$ (for date t). The individual who is already an incumbent entrepreneur at t (i.e., $e_i(t) = 1$) may find it cheaper to become an entrepreneur at $t + 1$, because potential entry barriers into entrepreneurship do not apply to incumbents. I refer to an agent with $e_i(t) = 1$ as a member of the "elite" at t, both because he avoids the entry costs and because in an oligarchy, he will be a member of the political elite making the policy choices.

In summary, at date t, each agent chooses $e_i(t+1) \in \{0, 1\}$, and if $e_i(t+1) = 1$, he becomes an entrepreneur and also makes an investment decision for next period $k_i(t+1) \in \mathbb{R}_+$; at date $t+1$, he decides how much labor $l_i(t+1) \in \mathbb{R}_+$ to hire.

Agents also make the policy choices in this society. How the preferences of various agents map into policies differs depending on the political regime and is discussed below. There are three policy choices. Two of those are similar to the policies we have seen so far: a tax rate $\tau(t) \in [0, \bar{\tau}]$ on output and a lump-sum transfer distributed to all agents, denoted by $T(t) \in [0, \infty)$. Notice that I have already imposed an upper bound on taxes $\bar{\tau} < 1$. This bound may result from the ability of individuals to hide their output in the informal sector or from the distortionary effects of taxation; it is taken as given here. The new policy instrument is a cost $B(t) \in [0, \infty)$ imposed on new entrepreneurs when they set up a firm. I assume that the entry barrier $B(t)$ is pure waste, for example, corresponding to the bureaucratic procedures that individuals have to go through to open a new business. Thus lump-sum transfers are financed only from taxes.

An entrepreneur with skill level $a_i(t)$, capital level $k_i(t)$, and labor $l_i(t)$ produces

$$y_i(t) = \frac{1}{\alpha} k_i(t)^\alpha (a_i(t) l_i(t))^{1-\alpha} \tag{23.2}$$

units of the final good. As in Section 22.3, I assume that there is full depreciation of capital, so $k_i(t)$ is also the level of investment of entrepreneur i at time $t-1$ in terms of the unique final good.

I further simplify the analysis by assuming that all firms have to operate at the same size, $\bar{L}$, so $l_i(t) = \bar{L}$ (see Exercise 23.5 for the implications of relaxing this assumption). Finally, I adopt the convention that the entrepreneur himself can work in his firm as one of the workers, which implies that the opportunity cost of becoming an entrepreneur is 0.

The most important assumption here is that each entrepreneur has to run the firm himself, so it is his productivity, $a_i(t)$, that matters for output. An alternative would be to allow costly delegation of managerial positions to other, more productive agents. In this case, low-productivity entrepreneurs may prefer to hire more productive managers. Throughout I assume that delegation is prohibitively costly.

To simplify expressions, I also define $b(t) \equiv B(t)/\beta\bar{L}$, which corresponds to discounted per worker entry cost (and is the relevant object when we look at the profitability of different occupational choices). Profits (the returns to entrepreneur i gross of the cost of entry barriers) at time t are then equal to

$$\pi_i(t) = (1 - \tau(t)) y_i(t) - w(t) l_i(t) - \frac{1}{\beta} k_i(t),$$

which takes into account that the investment cost $k_i(t)$ was incurred in the previous period, and thus the opportunity cost of investment (which is forgone consumption) is multiplied by the inverse of the discount factor. This expression for profits takes into account that the entrepreneur produces output $y_i(t)$, pays a fraction $\tau(t)$ of this output in taxes, and also pays a total wage bill of $w(t) l_i(t)$. Given a tax rate $\tau(t)$ and a wage rate $w(t) \geq 0$ and using the fact that $l_i(t) = \bar{L}$, the net profits of an entrepreneur with talent $a_i(t)$ at time t are

$$\pi(k_i(t) \mid a_i(t), w(t), \tau(t)) = \frac{1}{\alpha}(1 - \tau(t)) k_i(t)^\alpha (a_i(t)\bar{L})^{1-\alpha} - w(t)\bar{L} - \frac{1}{\beta} k_i(t). \tag{23.3}$$

Given this expression, the (instantaneous) gain from entrepreneurship for an agent of talent $z \in \{L, H\}$ at time t as a function of the tax rate $\tau(t)$ and the wage rate $w(t)$ is

$$\Pi^z(\tau(t), w(t)) = \max_{k_i(t)} \pi(k_i(t) \mid a_i(t) = A^z, w(t), \tau(t)). \tag{23.4}$$

Note that this is the *net gain* to entrepreneurship, since the agent receives the wage rate $w(t)$ in all cases (either working for another entrepreneur when he is a worker or working for himself—thus having to hire one less worker—when he is an entrepreneur). More importantly, the gain to becoming an entrepreneur for an agent with $e_i(t-1) = 0$ and ability $a_i(t) = A^z$ is

$$\Pi^z(\tau(t), w(t)) - \frac{1}{\beta} B(t) = \Pi^z(\tau(t), w(t)) - b(t)\bar{L},$$

since this agent has to pay the additional cost imposed by the entry barriers, which, like the costs of investment, is incurred in the previous period and is thus divided by β.

Labor market clearing requires that the total demand for labor not exceed the supply. Since entrepreneurs also work as production workers, the supply is equal to 1, so that

$$\int_0^1 e_i(t) l_i(t) di = \int_{i \in S_t^E} \bar{L} di \leq 1, \tag{23.5}$$

where S_t^E is the set of entrepreneurs at time t.

Finally, I assume that there is imperfect correlation between the entrepreneurial skill over time. In particular, $a_i(t)$ follows the Markov chain

$$a_i(t+1) = \begin{cases} A^H & \text{with probability} & \sigma^H & \text{if } a_i(t) = A^H, \\ A^H & \text{with probability} & \sigma^L & \text{if } a_i(t) = A^L, \\ A^L & \text{with probability } 1 - \sigma^H & \text{if } a_i(t) = A^H, \\ A^L & \text{with probability } 1 - \sigma^L & \text{if } a_i(t) = A^L, \end{cases} \tag{23.6}$$

where $\sigma^H, \sigma^L \in (0, 1)$. Here σ^H is the probability that an agent has high skill in entrepreneurship conditional on having high skill in the previous period, and σ^L is the probability of transitioning from low to high skill. It is natural to suppose that $\sigma^H \geq \sigma^L > 0$, so that skills are persistent and low skill is not an absorbing state. The fact that $\sigma^H < 1$ implies that there is imperfect correlation of entrepreneurial talent over time. Therefore the identities of the entrepreneurs necessary to achieve productive efficiency change over time and thus necessitate a type of creative destruction, with new entrepreneurs replacing old ones.

The imperfect correlation over time in $a_i(t)$ can be interpreted in three alternative and complementary ways. First, we can suppose that the productivity of an individual is not constant over time, and changes in comparative advantage necessitate changes in the identity of entrepreneurs. Second, we can think of the infinitely-lived agents as representing dynasties, and the imperfect correlation over time in $a_i(t)$ may represent imperfect correlation between the skills of parents and children. Third and perhaps most interestingly, it may be that each individual has a fixed competence across different activities, and comparative advantage in entrepreneurship changes as the importance of different activities evolves over time. For example, some individuals may be better in industrial entrepreneurship, while others are better in agriculture, and as industrial activities become more profitable than agriculture, individuals who have a comparative advantage in industry should enter into entrepreneurship and those who have a comparative advantage in agriculture should exit. All three channels are parsimoniously captured by the Markov chain for talent given in (23.6).

This Markov chain also implies that the fraction of agents with high skill in the stationary distribution is (see Exercise 23.6)

$$M \equiv \frac{\sigma^L}{1 - \sigma^H + \sigma^L} \in (0, 1). \tag{23.7}$$

Since there is a large number (continuum) of agents, the fraction of agents with high skill at any point is M. I also assume that

$$M \bar{L} > 1,$$

so that, without entry barriers, high-skill entrepreneurs generate more than sufficient demand to employ the entire labor supply. Moreover suppose that M is small and $\bar{L}$ is large; in particular, $\bar{L} > 2$. Then the workers are always in the majority, which simplifies the political economy discussion below.

The timing of events is as follows. At the beginning of time t, $a_i(t)$, $e_i(t)$, and $k_i(t)$ are given for all individuals as a result of their decision at date $t - 1$ and the realization of uncertainty regarding ability. Then the following sequence of moves takes place.

1. Entrepreneurs demand labor, the labor market clearing wage rate $w(t)$ is determined, and production takes place.

2. The tax rate on entrepreneurs, $\tau(t) \in [0, \bar{\tau}]$, is set.

3. The skill level of each agent for the next period, $a_i(t + 1)$, is realized.

4. The entry barrier for new entrepreneurs, $b(t + 1)$, is set.

5. All agents make occupational choices $e_i(t + 1)$, and entrepreneurs make investment decisions $k_i(t + 1)$, for the next period.

Entry barriers and taxes are set by different agents in the various political regimes as specified below. Notice that taxes are set after the investment decisions. This raises the holdup problems discussed in the previous chapter and acts as an additional source of inefficiency. The fact that $\tau(t) \leq \bar{\tau} < 1$ puts a limit on these holdup problems. Individuals make their occupational choices and investment decisions knowing their ability level; that is, $a_i(t + 1)$ is realized before the decisions about $e_i(t + 1)$ and $k_i(t + 1)$. Notice also that if an individual does not operate his firm, he loses "the license," so next time he wants to set up a firm, he needs to incur the entry cost (and the assumption that $l_i(t) = \bar{L}$ rules out the possibility of operating the firm at a much smaller scale). Finally, we need to specify the initial conditions: I assume that the distribution of talent in the society is given by the stationary distribution and nobody starts out as an entrepreneur, so that $e_i(-1) = 0$ for all i. Given linear preferences, the initial level of capital holdings is not important.

Let us again focus on MPE, where strategies are a function only of the payoff-relevant states. For individual i the payoff-relevant state at time t includes his own state $(e_i(t), a_i(t), k_i(t), a_i(t + 1))$, and potentially the fraction of entrepreneurs that are high skill,[2] denoted by $\mu(t)$, and defined as

$$\mu(t) = \Pr(a_i(t) = A^H \mid e_i(t) = 1) = \Pr(a_i(t) = A^H \mid i \in S_t^E).$$

---

2. Here $e_i(t)$, $k_i(t)$, and $a_i(t)$ are part of the individual's state at time t, because they influence an entrepreneur's labor demand. In addition, $a_i(t + 1)$ is revealed at time t and influences his occupational choice and investment decisions $e_i(t + 1)$ and $k_i(t + 1)$ for $t + 1$ and so is also part of his state.

The *economic equilibrium* again corresponds to the competitive equilibrium for a given policy sequence $\{b(t), \tau(t)\}_{t=0,1,\ldots}$. Let $x_i(t) = (e_i(t+1), k_i(t+1))$ be the vector of choices of agent i at time t, $x(t) = [x_i(t)]_{i \in [0,1]}$ denote the choice profile for all agents, and $p(t) = (\tau(t), b(t+1))$ denote the vector of policies at time t. Let $p^t = \{p(s)\}_{s=t}^{\infty}$ denote the infinite sequence of policies from time t on, and similarly $w^t = \{w(s)\}_{s=t}^{\infty}$ and $x^t = \{x(s)\}_{s=t}^{\infty}$ denote the sequences of wages and choices, respectively, from t on. Then $\hat{x}^t$ and a sequence of wage rates $\hat{w}^t$ constitute an economic equilibrium given a policy sequence p^t if, given $\hat{w}^t$, p^t, and state $(e_i(t-1), a_i(t))$, $x_i(t)$ maximizes the utility of agent i, and $\hat{w}(t)$ clears the labor market at time t (i.e., (23.5) holds). Each agent's type in the next period, $(e_i(t), a_i(t+1))$, is then given by his decision at time t regarding whether to become an entrepreneur and by the law of motion in (23.6).

I now characterize this equilibrium. Since $l_i(t) = \bar{L}$ for all $i \in S_t^E$ (recall that S_t^E is the set of entrepreneurs at time t), profit-maximizing investments are given by

$$k_i(t) = (\beta(1 - \tau(t)))^{1/(1-\alpha)} a_i(t) \bar{L}, \tag{23.8}$$

where $\tau(t)$ is the equilibrium tax rate that entrepreneurs anticipate along the equilibrium path. Equation (23.8) implies that the level of investment is increasing in the skill level of the entrepreneur $a_i(t)$ and the level of employment $\bar{L}$, and decreasing in the tax rate $\tau(t)$.

Now using (23.8), the net current gain to entrepreneurship for an agent of type $z \in \{L, H\}$ (of skill level A^L or A^H) can be obtained as

$$\Pi^z(\tau(t), w(t)) = \frac{1-\alpha}{\alpha} \beta^{\alpha/(1-\alpha)} (1 - \tau(t))^{1/(1-\alpha)} A^z \bar{L} - w(t) \bar{L}. \tag{23.9}$$

Moreover the labor market clearing condition (23.5) implies that the total measure of entrepreneurs at any time is $\int_{i \in S_t^E} di = 1/\bar{L}$. Tax revenues at time t and the per capita lump-sum transfers are then given as

$$T(t) = \int_{i \in S_t^E} \tau(t) y_i(t) di = \frac{1}{\alpha} \tau(t) (\beta(1 - \tau(t)))^{\alpha/(1-\alpha)} \bar{L} \int_{i \in S_t^E} a_i(t) di. \tag{23.10}$$

To economize on notation, let us now denote the sequence of future policies and equilibrium wages by $q^t \equiv (p^t, w^t)$. Then the time t value of an agent with skill level $z \in \{L, H\}$ if he chooses production work (for time t) is

$$W^z(q^t) = w(t) + T(t) + \beta C W^z(q^{t+1}), \tag{23.11}$$

where $C W^z(q^{t+1})$ is the continuation value for a worker of type z from time $t + 1$ on, given by

$$C W^z(q^{t+1}) = \sigma^z \max\{W^H(q^{t+1}); V^H(q^{t+1}) - b(t+1)\bar{L}\} \tag{23.12}$$

$$+ (1 - \sigma^z) \max\{W^L(q^{t+1}); V^L(q^{t+1}) - b(t+1)\bar{L}\},$$

where $V^z(q^t)$ is defined similarly to $W^z(q^t)$ and is the time t value of an agent of skill z when he is an entrepreneur. Both (23.11) and (23.12) are intuitive. A worker of type $z \in \{L, H\}$ receives a wage income of $w(t)$ (independent of his skill), a transfer of $T(t)$, and the continuation value $C W^z(q^{t+1})$. This continuation value encodes the major dynamic trade-offs facing individuals in this model. A worker of type $z \in \{L, H\}$ today (with $e_i(t) = 0$) will be high skill in the next period with probability σ^z, and in this case, he can either choose to remain a worker, receiving value W^H, or incur the entry cost $b(t+1)\bar{L}$ and become an entrepreneur ($e_i(t+1) = 1$), receiving the value of a high-skill entrepreneur, V^H. The reason this individual has to pay $b(t+1)\bar{L}$ when he chooses $e_i(t+1) = 1$ is that he is not currently an entrepreneur; thus he has to pay the costs associated with the entry barriers. The max operator in (23.12) ensures that the individual chooses the option with the higher value. With probability $1 - \sigma^z$, the agent will be low skill and receive the corresponding low-skill values.

Similarly, the value functions for entrepreneurs are given by

$$V^z(q^t) = w(t) + T(t) + \Pi^z(\tau(t), w(t)) + \beta CV^z(q^{t+1}), \qquad (23.13)$$

where Π^z is given by (23.9) and depends on the skill level of the agent, and $CV^z(q^{t+1})$ is the continuation value for an entrepreneur of type z:

$$CV^z(q^{t+1}) = \sigma^z \max\{W^H(q^{t+1}); V^H(q^{t+1})\} + (1 - \sigma^z) \max\{W^L(q^{t+1}); V^L(q^{t+1})\}. \qquad (23.14)$$

An entrepreneur of ability A^z also receives wage $w(t)$ (working for his own firm) and transfer $T(t)$, and in addition makes profits equal to $\Pi^z(\tau(t), w(t))$. The following period, this entrepreneur has high skill with probability σ^z and low skill with probability $1 - \sigma^z$, and conditional on the realization of this event, he decides whether to remain an entrepreneur or to become a worker. Two points are noteworthy here. First, in (23.14), in contrast to (23.12), there is no additional cost of becoming an entrepreneur, since this individual already owns a firm. Second, if an entrepreneur decides to become a worker, he obtains the value (23.12), and the next time he wishes to operate a firm, he has to incur the entry cost.

Inspection of (23.12) and (23.14) reveals that the occupational choices of individuals for time t depend on the *net value* of entrepreneurship conditional on their current occupational status, $e_i(t-1) = \mathbf{e}$. Let us write this value as

$$NV(q^t \mid a_i(t) = A^z, e_i(t-1) = \mathbf{e}) = V^z(q^t) - W^z(q^t) - (1 - \mathbf{e})b(t)\bar{L}.$$

The last term is the entry cost incurred by agents with $\mathbf{e} = 0$. The max operators in (23.12) and (23.14) imply that if $NV > 0$ for an agent, then he prefers to become an entrepreneur.

Who becomes an entrepreneur in this economy? The answer depends on the values of NV. Standard dynamic programming arguments from Chapter 16, combined with the fact that instantaneous payoffs are strictly monotone, imply that $V^z(q^t)$ is strictly monotone in $w(t)$, $T(t)$, and $\Pi^z(\tau(t), w(t))$, so that $V^H(q^t) > V^L(q^t)$ (see Exercise 23.4). By the same arguments, $NV(q^t \mid a_i(t) = A^z, e_i(t-1) = \mathbf{e})$ is also increasing in $\Pi^z(\tau(t), w(t))$. Thus for all a and $\mathbf{e}$, we have

$$NV(q^t \mid a_i(t) = A^H, e_i(t-1) = 1) \geq NV(q^t \mid a_i(t) = a, e_i(t-1) = \mathbf{e})$$

$$\geq NV(q^t \mid a_i(t) = A^L, e_i(t-1) = 0).$$

In other words, the net value of entrepreneurship is highest for high-skill existing entrepreneurs and lowest for low-skill workers. However, it is unclear ex ante whether we have $NV(q^t \mid a_i(t) = A^H, e_i(t-1) = 0)$ or $NV(q^t \mid a_i(t) = A^L, e_i(t-1) = 1)$ greater; that is, whether entrepreneurship is more profitable for incumbents with low skill or for outsiders with high skill, who will have to pay the entry cost.

We can then define two types of equilibria:

1. *Entry equilibria*, where all entrepreneurs have $a_i(t) = A^H$; and

2. *Sclerotic equilibria,* where agents with $e_i(t-1) = 1$ remain entrepreneurs regardless of their productivity.

An entry equilibrium requires the net value of entrepreneurship to be greater for a nonelite high-skill agent than for a low-skill elite. Let us define $w^H(t)$ as the threshold wage rate such that high-skill nonelite agents are indifferent between entering and not entering entrepreneurship. That is, $w^H(t)$ has to be such that $NV(q^t \mid a_i(t) = A^H, e_i(t-1) = 0) = 0$. Using (23.11) and (23.13), this threshold is obtained as

$$w^H(t) \equiv \max \left\{ \frac{1-\alpha}{\alpha} \beta^{\alpha/(1-\alpha)} (1 - \tau(t))^{1/(1-\alpha)} A^H - b(t) \right.$$
$$\left. + \frac{\beta(CV^H(q^{t+1}) - CW^H(q^{t+1}))}{\bar{L}} ; 0 \right\}. \tag{23.15}$$

Similarly, define $w^L(t)$ as the wage such that low-skill incumbent producers are indifferent between retaining entrepreneurship or not. Then this wage $w^L(t)$ is such that $NV(q^t \mid a_i(t) = A^L, e_i(t-1) = 1) = 0$, or

$$w^L(t) \equiv \max \left\{ \frac{1-\alpha}{\alpha} \beta^{\alpha/(1-\alpha)} (1 - \tau(t))^{1/(1-\alpha)} A^L + \frac{\beta(CV^L(q^{t+1}) - CW^L(q^{t+1}))}{\bar{L}} ; 0 \right\}. \tag{23.16}$$

Both expressions are intuitive. For example, in equation (23.15), the first term $(1-\alpha)\beta^{\alpha/(1-\alpha)}(1 - \tau(t))^{1/(1-\alpha)} A^H / \alpha$ is the per worker profits that a high-skill entrepreneur makes before labor costs. Here $b(t)$ is the per worker entry cost (discounted total costs, $\beta^{-1}B(t)$, divided by $\bar{L}$). Finally, the term $\beta(CV^H(q^{t+1}) - CW^H(q^{t+1}))$ is the indirect (dynamic) benefit, the additional gain from changing status from a worker to a member of the elite for a high-skill agent. Naturally, this benefit depends on the sequence of policies; for example, it is larger when there are higher entry barriers in the future. If $w^L(t) < w^H(t)$, the total benefit of becoming an entrepreneur for a nonelite high-skill agent exceeds the cost. Equation (23.16) is explained similarly. Evidently a wage rate lower than both $w^L(t)$ and $w^H(t)$ would lead to excess demand for labor and could not be an equilibrium. Consequently the condition for an entry equilibrium to exist at time t can simply be written as a comparison of the two thresholds determined above:

$$w^H(t) \geq w^L(t). \tag{23.17}$$

A sclerotic equilibrium emerges, on the other hand, when the converse of (23.17) holds.

Moreover, in an entry equilibrium, that is, in any equilibrium where (23.17) holds, we have $NV(q^t \mid a_i(t) = A^H, e_i(t-1) = 0) = 0$. If it were strictly positive—in other words, if the wage were less than $w^H(t)$—then all agents with high skill would strictly prefer to become entrepreneurs, which is not possible, since by assumption, $M\bar{L} > 1$. This argument also shows that the total measure of entrepreneurs in the economy is $1/\bar{L}$. Then from (23.9), (23.11), and (23.13), the equilibrium wage $w^E(t)$ is

$$w^E(t) = w^H(t). \tag{23.18}$$

Note also that when (23.17) holds, $NV(q^t \mid a_i(t) = A^L, e_i(t-1) = 1) \leq 0$, so low-skill incumbents would be worse off if they remained as entrepreneurs at the wage $w^E(t)$.

Figure 23.1 illustrates the entry equilibrium diagrammatically by plotting labor demand and supply in this economy. Labor supply is constant at 1, while labor demand is decreasing

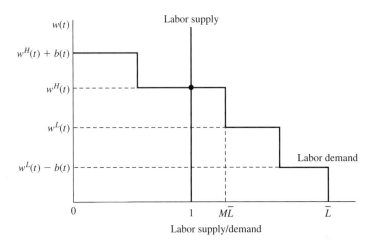

FIGURE 23.1 Labor market equilibrium when (23.17) holds.

as a function of the wage rate. This figure is drawn for the case where (23.17) holds, so that there exists an entry equilibrium. The first portion of the curve shows the willingness of high-skill incumbents (those with $e_i(t-1) = 1$ and $a_i(t) = A^H$) to pay, which is $w^H(t) + b(t)$. This result is intuitive, since entrepreneurship is as profitable for them as for high-skill potential entrants and they do not have pay the entry cost. The second portion is for high-skill potential entrants (those with $e_i(t-1) = 0$ and $a_i(t) = A^H$) and is equal to $w^H(t)$. These two groups together demand $M\bar{L} > 1$ workers, ensuring that labor demand intersects labor supply at the wage given in (23.18).

In a sclerotic equilibrium, on the other hand, $w^H(t) < w^L(t)$, and low-skill incumbents remain in entrepreneurship, that is, $e_i(t) = e_i(t-1)$. If there were no deaths, so that $\varepsilon = 0$, the total number of entrepreneurs would be $1/\bar{L}$ and for any $w \in [w^H(t), w^L(t)]$, labor demand would exactly equal labor supply (i.e., $1/\bar{L}$ agents would demand exactly $\bar{L}$ workers each, and the total supply would be 1). Hence there would be multiple equilibrium wages. In contrast, when $\varepsilon > 0$, the total number of entrepreneurs who could pay a wage of $w^L(t)$ will be less than $1/\bar{L}$ for all $t > 0$; thus there would be excess supply of labor at this wage, or at any wage above the lower support of this range. Thus the equilibrium wage must be equal to this lower support, $w^H(t)$, which is identical to (23.18). Since at this wage agents with $e_i(t-1) = 0$ and $a_i(t) = A^H$ are indifferent between entrepreneurship and production work, in equilibrium a sufficient number of them enter entrepreneurship, so that total labor demand is equal to 1. In the remainder, I focus on the limiting case of this economy, where $\varepsilon \to 0$, which picks $w^E(t) = w^H(t)$ as the equilibrium wage, even when labor supply coincides with labor demand for a range of wages.[3]

Figure 23.2 illustrates this case diagrammatically. Because (23.17) does not hold, the second flat portion of the labor demand curve is for low-skill incumbents ($e_i(t-1) = 1$ and $a_i(t) = A^L$), who, given the entry barriers, have a higher marginal product of labor than high-skill potential entrants.

The analysis also establishes that the equilibrium law of motion of the fraction of high-skill entrepreneurs, $\mu(t)$, is

---

3. The feature of multiple equilibrium wage levels in dynamic models with entry barriers applies much more generally than the setup here with two types of entrepreneurs (see Exercise 23.11).

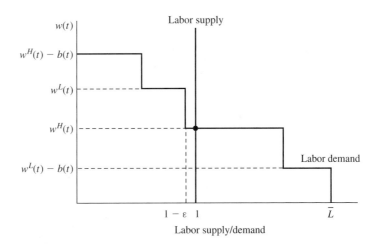

FIGURE 23.2 Labor market equilibrium when (23.17) does not hold.

$$\mu(t) = \begin{cases} \sigma^H \mu(t-1) + \sigma^L (1-\mu(t-1)) & \text{if (23.17) does not hold,} \\ 1 & \text{if (23.17) holds,} \end{cases} \qquad (23.19)$$

starting with $\mu(0)$. Recall that because $e_i(-1) = 0$ for all i, any $b(0)$ applies equally to all potential entrants, and thus in equilibrium we have $\mu(0) = 1$.

To obtain a full political equilibrium, we need to determine the policy sequence p^t. Here I consider two political regimes: (1) democracy—the policies $b(t)$ and $\tau(t)$ are determined by majoritarian voting, with each agent having one vote; and (2) oligarchy—the policies $b(t)$ and $\tau(t)$ are determined by voting among the elite (the current entrepreneurs) at time t.

23.3.2 Democracy

A democratic equilibrium is an MPE, where $b(t)$ and $\tau(t)$ are determined by majoritarian voting at time t. The timing of events implies that the tax rate at time t, $\tau(t)$, is decided after investment decisions, whereas the entry barriers are decided before. The assumption $\bar{L} > 2$ ensures that workers (nonelite agents) are always in the majority. At the time taxes are set, investments are sunk and agents have already made their occupation choices. Therefore taxes are chosen to maximize per capita transfers, given by

$$\frac{1}{\alpha} \tau(t) k(t)^\alpha \bar{L} \sum_{i \in S_t^E} a_i(t),$$

which takes into account that $k(t)$ is already given from the investment in the previous period. Since this expression is increasing in $\tau(t)$ and $\tau(t) \le \bar{\tau}$, the optimal tax for a worker is $\tau(t) = \bar{\tau}$ for all t. Thus total tax revenues are

$$T^E(t) = \frac{1}{\alpha} \bar{\tau} (\beta(1-\bar{\tau}))^{\alpha/(1-\alpha)} \bar{L} \sum_{i \in S_t^E} a_i(t). \qquad (23.20)$$

The entry barrier $b(t)$ is then set at the end of period $t-1$ (before occupational choices) to maximize (23.20). Low-productivity workers (with $e_i(t-1) = 0$ and $a_i(t) = A^L$) know that they will remain workers, and in MPE, the policy choice at time t has no influence on strategies in the future except through its impact on payoff-relevant state variables. Therefore, given $\tau(t) = \bar{\tau}$, the utility of agent i with $e_i(t-1) = 0$ and $a_i(t) = A^L$ depends on $b(t)$ only through the equilibrium wage $w^E(t)$ and the transfer $T^E(t)$. High-productivity workers (those with $e_i(t-1) = 0$ and $a_i(t) = A^H$) may become entrepreneurs, but as the above analysis shows, in this case, $NV(q^t \mid a_i(t) = A^H, e_i(t-1) = 0) = 0$, and $W^H = W^L$, so their utility is also identical to those of low-skill workers. Consequently all workers prefer a level of $b(t)$ that maximizes $w^E(t) + T^E(t)$. Since the preferences of all workers are the same and they are in the majority, the democratic equilibrium maximizes these preferences.

A democratic equilibrium (starting at time t) is therefore given by policy, wage, and economic decision sequences, $\hat{p}^t$, $\hat{w}^t$, and $\hat{x}^t$, respectively, such that $\hat{w}^t$ and $\hat{x}^t$ constitute an economic equilibrium given $\hat{p}^t$, and $\hat{p}^t = (\bar{\tau}, b(t+1))$ is such that

$$b(t+1) \in \arg\max_{b(t+1)\geq 0} \{w^E(t+1) + T^E(t+1)\}.$$

Inspection of (23.18) and (23.20) shows that wages and tax revenues are both maximized when $b(t+1) = 0$ for all t, so the democratic equilibrium will not impose any entry barriers. This result is intuitive: workers do not wish to protect incumbents, because such protection reduces labor demand and wages. Since there are no entry barriers, only high-skill agents become entrepreneurs—that is, $e_i(t) = 1$ only if $a_i(t) = A^H$ at all t. Given this stationary sequence of MPE policies, we can use the value functions (23.11) and (23.13) to obtain

$$V^H = W^H = W^L = W = \frac{w^D + T^D}{1 - \beta},$$

where w^D is the equilibrium wage in a democracy, and T^D is the level of transfers (when $\tau(t) = \bar{\tau}$ and $b(t) = 0$ for all t). Equation (23.15) implies that $w^D = (1-\alpha)(\beta(1-\bar{\tau}))^{\alpha/(1-\alpha)} A^H/\alpha$. The following proposition therefore follows immediately.

Proposition 23.4 *There exists a unique democratic equilibrium. In this equilibrium $\tau(t) = \bar{\tau}$ and $b(t) = 0$ for all t. Moreover $e_i(t) = 1$ if and only if $a_i(t) = A^H$, so $\mu(t) = 1$. The equilibrium wage rate is given by*

$$w(t) = w^D \equiv \frac{1-\alpha}{\alpha} \beta^{\alpha/(1-\alpha)} (1-\bar{\tau})^{1/(1-\alpha)} A^H,$$

and the aggregate output is

$$Y^D(t) = Y^D \equiv \frac{1}{\alpha} (\beta(1-\bar{\tau}))^{\alpha/(1-\alpha)} A^H.$$

Note that aggregate output is constant over time, and there is perfect equality in equilibrium (because the excess supply of high-skill entrepreneurs ensures that they receive no rents). These features will contrast with the oligarchic equilibrium.

23.3.3 Oligarchy

In oligarchy, policies are determined by voting among the elite.[4] At the time of voting over the entry barriers $b(t)$, the elite consist of those with $e_i(t-1) = 1$, and at the time of voting over

---

the taxes $\tau(t)$, the elite are those with $e_i(t) = 1$. Let us start with the taxation decision among those with $e_i(t) = 1$ and impose the following condition.

Condition 23.1

$$\bar{L} \geq \frac{1}{2} \frac{A^H}{A^L} + \frac{1}{2}.$$

When this condition is satisfied, both high- and low-skill entrepreneurs prefer zero taxes, $\tau(t) = 0$. I simplify the analysis here by assuming that this condition holds. Exercise 23.9 discusses the converse case. Intuitively, Condition 23.1 requires the productivity gap between low- and high-skill elites not to be so large that low-skill elites wish to tax profits to indirectly transfer resources from high-skill entrepreneurs to themselves.

When Condition 23.1 holds, the oligarchy always chooses $\tau(t) = 0$. At the stage of deciding the entry barriers, high-skill entrepreneurs would like to choose $b(t)$ to maximize V^H, and low-skill entrepreneurs would like to maximize V^L (both groups anticipating that $\tau(t) = 0$). Both of these expressions are maximized by setting a level of the entry barrier that ensures the minimum level of equilibrium wages. Recall from (23.18) that equilibrium wages in this case are still given by $w^E(t) = w^H(t)$, so they will be minimized at $w(t) = 0$ by choosing any

$$b(t) \geq b^E(t) \equiv \frac{1-\alpha}{\alpha} \beta^{\alpha/(1-\alpha)} A^H + \beta \left(\frac{CV^H(q^{t+1}) - CW^H(q^{t+1})}{\bar{L}} \right),$$

so that $w(t) = 0$. Without loss of any generality, let us assume that they set the entry barrier as $b(t) = b^E(t)$ in this case.

An oligarchic equilibrium (from time t on) then can be defined as a policy sequence $\hat{p}^t$, wage sequence $\hat{w}^t$, and economic decisions $\hat{x}^t$ such that $\hat{w}^t$ and $\hat{x}^t$ constitute an economic equilibrium given $\hat{p}^t$, and $\hat{p}^t$ involves $\tau(s) = 0$ and $b(s) = b^E(s)$ for all $s \geq t$. In the oligarchic equilibrium there is no redistributive taxation, and entry barriers are sufficiently high to ensure a sclerotic equilibrium with zero wages.

Imposing $w^E(s) = 0$ for all $s \geq t$, we can solve for the equilibrium values of high- and low-skill entrepreneurs from the value functions (23.13) as, respectively,

$$\tilde{V}^L = \frac{1}{1-\beta} \left[\frac{(1-\beta\sigma^H)A^L + \beta\sigma^L A^H}{(1-\beta(\sigma^H - \sigma^L))} \frac{1-\alpha}{\alpha} \beta^{\alpha/(1-\alpha)} \bar{L} \right], \quad \text{and}$$

$$\tilde{V}^H = \frac{1}{1-\beta} \left[\frac{(1-\beta(1-\sigma^L))A^H + \beta(1-\sigma^H)A^L}{(1-\beta(\sigma^H - \sigma^L))} \frac{1-\alpha}{\alpha} \beta^{\alpha/(1-\alpha)} \bar{L} \right].$$

These expressions are intuitive. First, consider $\tilde{V}^L$ and the case where $\beta \to 1$; then, starting in the state $e(t - 1) = L$, an entrepreneur will spend a fraction $\sigma^L/(1 - \sigma^H + \sigma^L)$ of his future with high skill A^H and a fraction $(1 - \sigma^H)/(1 - \sigma^H + \sigma^L)$ with low skill A^L. When $\beta < 1$, low-skill states occur sooner and are weighed more heavily, and thus they receive the weight $(1 - \beta\sigma^H)/(1 - \beta(\sigma^H - \sigma^L))$. The intuition for $\tilde{V}^H$ is identical.

---

are made by those who are politically powerful for historical or other reasons. The analysis in the previous chapter and in Section 23.2 in this chapter illustrated the distortionary policies that would arise from such decoupling. The model here goes to the other extreme: it places all political power in the hands of the current entrepreneurs and highlights a different set of resultant inefficiencies.

Since there are zero equilibrium wages and no transfers, it is clear that $W = 0$ for all workers. Therefore for a high-skill worker, $NV = \tilde{V}^H - b$, implying that

$$b(t) = b^E \equiv \frac{1}{1-\beta} \left[\frac{(1 - \beta(1 - \sigma^L))A^H + \beta(1 - \sigma^H)A^L}{(1 - \beta(\sigma^H - \sigma^L))} \frac{1 - \alpha}{\alpha} \beta^{\alpha/(1-\alpha)} \right] \quad (23.21)$$

is sufficient to ensure zero equilibrium wages.

In this oligarchic equilibrium, aggregate output is

$$Y^E(t) = \frac{1}{\alpha} \beta^{\alpha/(1-\alpha)} [\mu(t)A^H + (1 - \mu(t))A^L], \quad (23.22)$$

where $\mu(t) = \sigma^H \mu(t-1) + \sigma^L(1 - \mu(t-1))$ as given by (23.19), starting with $\mu(0) = 1$.

Recall that all individuals start with $e_i(-1) = 0$, and thus the equilibrium features $\mu(0) = 1$. In this case, (and in fact for any $\mu(0) > M$), $\mu(t)$ is a decreasing sequence converging to M, and aggregate output $Y^E(t)$ is also decreasing over time:

$$\lim_{t \to \infty} Y^E(t) = Y^E_\infty \equiv \frac{1}{\alpha} \beta^{\alpha/(1-\alpha)} [A^L + M(A^H - A^L)]. \quad (23.23)$$

Intuitively, the comparative advantage of the members of the elite in entrepreneurship gradually disappears because of the imperfect correlation over time between ability.[5]

Another important feature of the oligarchic equilibrium is that there is a high degree of (income) inequality. Wages are equal to 0, while entrepreneurs earn positive profits (in fact, total entrepreneurial earnings are equal to aggregate output). This contrasts with the relative equality in democracy. The next proposition summarizes this result.

Proposition 23.5 *Suppose that Condition 23.1 holds. Then there exists a unique oligarchic equilibrium. This equilibrium involves $\tau(t) = 0$, $b(t) = b^E$ as given by (23.21), $w^E(t) = 0$ for all t, and is sclerotic. The fraction of high-skill entrepreneurs in this equilibrium is given by $\mu(t) = \sigma^H \mu(t-1) + \sigma^L(1 - \mu(t-1))$, starting with $\mu(0) = 1$. Aggregate output is given by (23.22), is decreasing over time, and satisfies $\lim_{t \to \infty} Y^E(t) = Y^E_\infty$ as in (23.23).*

Proof. See Exercise 23.7. ∎

23.3.4 Comparison between Democracy and Oligarchy

Since $\mu(0) = 1$, aggregate output in the initial period of the oligarchic equilibrium, $Y^E(0)$, is greater than the constant level of output in the democratic equilibrium, Y^D. That is,

$$Y^D = \frac{1}{\alpha}(\beta(1 - \bar{\tau}))^{\alpha/(1-\alpha)}A^H < Y^E(0) = \frac{1}{\alpha}\beta^{\alpha/(1-\alpha)}A^H.$$

Therefore oligarchy initially generates greater output than does a democracy, because it is protecting the property rights of entrepreneurs (whereas democracy is imposing distortionary taxes on entrepreneurs). However the analysis also shows that $Y^E(t)$ declines over time, while Y^D is constant. Consequently the oligarchic economy may subsequently fall behind

---

5. Nevertheless, it is also possible to imagine societies in which $\mu(0) < M$, because there is some other process of selection into the oligarchy in the initial period that is negatively correlated with skills in entrepreneurship. In this case, somewhat paradoxically, $\mu(t)$ and thus $Y^E(t)$ would increase over time. While interesting in theory, this case appears less relevant in practice, where we would expect at least some positive selection in the initial period, so that high-skill agents are more likely to become entrepreneurs at time $t = 0$, and $\mu(0) > M$.

the democratic one. Whether it does so depends on whether Y^D is greater than Y^E_∞ as given by (23.23). This will be the case if $(1 - \bar{\tau})^{\alpha/(1-\alpha)} A^H > A^L + M(A^H - A^L)$, or if the following condition holds.

Condition 23.2

$$(1 - \bar{\tau})^{\alpha/(1-\alpha)} > \frac{A^L}{A^H} + M \left(1 - \frac{A^L}{A^H} \right).$$

If Condition 23.2 holds, then at some point the democratic society overtakes (leapfrogs) the oligarchic society. This result is stated in the next proposition.

Proposition 23.6 *Suppose that Condition 23.1 holds. Then at $t = 0$, aggregate output is higher in an oligarchic society than in a democratic society, that is, $Y^E(0) > Y^D$. If Condition 23.2 does not hold, then aggregate output in oligarchy is always higher than in democracy, that is, $Y^E(t) > Y^D$ for all t. If Condition 23.2 holds, then there exists t' such that for $t \leq t'$, $Y^E(t) \geq Y^D$, and for $t > t'$, $Y^E(t) < Y^D$, so that the democratic society leapfrogs the oligarchic society. Leapfrogging is more likely when $\bar{\tau}$, A^L/A^H, and M are low.*

Proof. See Exercise 23.8. ∎

This proposition implies that an oligarchic society starts out more productive than a democratic society but declines over time. It also shows that oligarchy is more likely to be relatively inefficient in the long run under the following conditions:

1. When $\bar{\tau}$ is low: in this case, democracy is unable to pursue highly populist policies with a high degree of redistribution away from entrepreneurs. The parameter $\bar{\tau}$ may correspond both to certain institutional impediments limiting redistribution, or more interestingly, to the specificity of assets in the economy: with greater specificity, taxes will be limited, and redistributive distortions may be less important.

2. When A^H is high relative to A^L: then the creative destruction process—the selection of high-skill agents for entrepreneurship—is important for the efficient allocation of resources.

3. When M is low: in this case a random selection contains a small fraction of high-skill agents, making oligarchic sclerosis highly distortionary. Alternatively, M is low when σ^H is low, so oligarchies are more likely to lead to low output in the long run when the efficient allocation of resources requires a high degree of churning in the ranks of entrepreneurs. This type of churning is another measure of the importance of creative destruction.

On the other hand, if the extent of taxation in democracy is high and the failure to allocate the right agents to entrepreneurship has only limited costs, then an oligarchic society generates greater output than a democracy in the long run.

These comparative static results may be useful in interpreting why, as discussed in Section 23.1, the northeastern United States so conclusively outperformed the Caribbean plantation economies during the nineteenth century. First, the American democracy was not highly redistributive, corresponding to low $\bar{\tau}$ in terms of the model here. Second, the nineteenth century was the age of industry and commerce, so that the allocation of high-skill agents to entrepreneurship is likely to have been important and potentially only a small fraction of the population were truly talented as inventors and entrepreneurs. This can be thought of as corresponding to low values of A^L/A^H and M.

This analysis therefore reiterates that there are no unambiguous theoretical results on whether democracy or nondemocracy generates greater growth. However it also highlights a different dimension of the trade-off between different regimes—that related to the dynamics they imply. While democracy may create short-run distortions, it can lead to better long-run performance because it avoids political sclerosis—that is, incumbents becoming politically powerful and erecting entry barriers against new and better entrepreneurs. This model also suggests the type of patterns we already discussed in Section 23.1: lack of a clear relationship between democracy and growth over the past 50 years combined with the examples of democracies that have been able to achieve industrialization during critical periods in the nineteenth century. In fact, a simple extension of the framework here provides additional insights that are useful for thinking about why democracies may be successful in preventing political sclerosis: the forces highlighted here also suggest that democracies are more flexible than oligarchies. For example, Exercise 23.10 shows that democracies are typically better able to adapt to the arrival of new technologies, because there are no incumbents with rents to protect, who can successfully block or slow down the introduction of new technology. This type of flexibility might be one of the more important advantages of democratic regimes.

Even though the model presented in this section provides ideas and results that are useful for understanding the comparative development experiences of democratic and nondemocratic regimes, like the model discussed in the previous section, it focuses on the costs of democracy resulting from its more redistributive nature. In particular, it emphasizes that democratic regimes redistribute income away from the rich and the entrepreneurs toward the poorer segments of the society, and this leads to distortions that reduce income per capita. An alternative source of distortions in democracy is that democratic regimes may become dysfunctional, because the elite still exercise power through corruption or other means despite the existence of democratic institutions. It is possible that when the society becomes democratic but the elite maintain significant political power, they may try to control the democratic agenda in potentially more inefficient ways than in nondemocracy—for example, by corruption rather than by direct decree. In this case, democracy can lead to worse economic outcomes not because it is pursuing populist redistributive policies as in the models presented here but because of political inefficiencies resulting from the continuing power of the elite.

23.4 Understanding Endogenous Political Change

23.4.1 General Insights

The analysis so far has focused on the implications of different political institutions on economic growth and how their economic consequences shape the preferences of different agents over these political institutions. How do equilibrium political institutions emerge? And why do institutions change? Returning to the model of Section 23.3, we can imagine that democracy emerges because oligarchs voluntarily give up power and institute a democracy. While this might be in their interest under some circumstances, it will generally be costly for them to give up their monopoly of political power and the economic rents that this monopoly brings. Not surprisingly, most institutional changes in practice do not happen voluntarily but result from social conflict.

Consider, for example, the democratization of most Western European nations during the nineteenth century and early twentieth century or the democratization experience in Latin America during the twentieth century. In these cases, democracy was not voluntarily granted by the existing elites but resulted from the process of social conflict, in which those previously disenfranchised demanded political rights and in some cases were able to secure them. But how does this happen? A nondemocratic regime, by its nature, vests political power with a narrow group. Those who are excluded from this group, the nonelites, do not have the right to vote, nor do they have any voice in collective decisions. So how can they influence the political equilibrium and induce equilibrium political change? The answer to this question lies in drawing a distinction between de jure (formal) and de facto political power. De jure political power refers to power that originates from the political institutions in society and has been the form of political power on which we have so far focused. Political institutions determine who gets to vote, how representatives make choices, and the general rules of collective decision making in society. However, there is another, equally important type of political power that features in equilibrium political changes. The political power of protesters that marched against the existing regime before the First Reform Act in Britain in 1832 was not of the de jure kind. The law of the land did not empower them to influence the political course of actions—in fact, they were quite explicitly disenfranchised. But they had a different kind of power, emanating from their majority in the population and their ability to solve the collective action problem and to organize protests. This type of political power, which lives outside the political institutions, is de facto political power.

De facto political power is important for political change, since de jure political power itself acts as a source of persistence—not of change. For example, consider the model of the previous section. The elite are typically content with the oligarchic regime. If de jure power is the only source of power, only the elite have decision-making powers in the society, and they are unlikely to change the political regime from oligarchy toward democracy. However, if the nonelites (citizens or workers) had some source of power—which, by its nature, has to be de facto power—then political change becomes a possibility. Perhaps in some periods, the nonelites will be able to solve their collective action problem and thus exercise enough pressure on the system to force some changes. In the extreme, they can induce the elite to disband the oligarchy and transition to democracy, or they can themselves topple the oligarchic regime.

The interaction between de jure and de facto political power is the most promising way to approach the analysis of equilibrium political change. Moreover this interaction becomes particularly interesting when studied in a dynamic framework. This is for at least two reasons. First, most of the issues we are discussing, such as commitment problems and institutional change, are dynamic in nature. Second, whether the distribution of de facto political power is permanent or changing stochastically over time has major consequences for the structure of political equilibrium. When a particular (disenfranchised) group has permanent de facto political power, it can use this power at each date to demand concessions from those holding de jure political power. Such a situation leads to a redistribution of resources in favor of this group, but not necessarily to institutional change, because the requisite redistribution can take place within the context of the existing political regime.

Next consider a situation in which the de facto political power of the disenfranchised group is highly transient—in the sense that they have been able to solve their collective action problem and can exercise de facto political power today, but it is unlikely that they will have the same type of power tomorrow. Then the disenfranchised group cannot rely on the use of their de facto political power in the future to receive concessions. To obtain redistribution of resources favorable to themselves in the future, they have to use their current power. This scenario generally involves a change in political institutions as a way of changing the future distribution of de jure power. More explicitly, consider a situation in which a particular group of (disenfranchised) individuals currently have the de facto political power to change the distribution of resources in their favor, but they also understand that this de facto power will be gone tomorrow. But any limited transfer of resources or other concessions made to this disenfranchised group today is likely to be reversed in the future. Therefore the transient nature of their de facto political power encourages this disenfranchised group to take actions to change political institutions to cement their power more firmly—so that they can change their transient de facto political power into more durable de jure political power. This informal discussion suggests a particular channel through which the interplay between de facto and de jure political power can lead to equilibrium changes in political institutions.

23.4.2 A Framework for the Study of the Dynamics of Political Institutions

The discussion so far illustrates how we can use the interaction between de facto and de jure political power to study equilibrium political changes. While the discussion has given some clues about what the incentives of different parties with and without de jure political power will be in a dynamic game, it is so far unclear how one would construct models to analyze these forces and generate useful comparative statics. I now suggest a general framework that is useful for thinking about the dynamic interactions between de facto and de jure political power.

Imagine a dynamic model in which there are two state variables, political institutions and the distribution of resources. For example, $P(t) \in \mathcal{P}$ denotes a specific set of political institutions at time t, such as democracy or nondemocracy, parliamentary versus presidential system, or different types of nondemocratic institutions. The set $\mathcal{P}$ denotes the set of feasible political institutions. Similarly, let $W(t) \in \mathcal{W}$ denote a variable encoding the distribution of resources at time t. For example, in a society consisting of two groups, the rich and the poor, $W(t)$, could be the relative incomes of the two groups. In a society with many individuals, it could be the distribution function of income or wealth. Again, $\mathcal{W}$ is the set of all possible distributions of resources. It is useful to think of both $P(t)$ and $W(t)$ as state variables for three reasons. First, they change relatively slowly, thus corresponding to the loose notion of a state variable. Second, they are typically the payoff-relevant Markovian states. Third, these two variables determine the two sources of political power essential for understanding equilibrium political change. $P(t)$ determines the distribution of de jure political power, $J(t) \in \mathcal{J}$, which, for example, determines who has the right to vote or the constraints on politicians. The distribution of resources, on the other hand, affects the distribution of de facto political power. De facto political power is typically the result of the ability of certain groups to solve their collective action problem, or it emerges when certain groups have the resources to hire their own armies, paramilitaries, and supporters, or simply use the money for lobbying and bribing. Let the distribution of de facto political power in the society at time t be $F(t) \in \mathcal{F}$. As in the beginning of Part VIII, let us also denote economic institutions by $R(t) \in \mathcal{R}$, and let $Y(t) \in \mathcal{Y}$ be a measure of economic performance, such as income per capita or growth.

A dynamic framework that is useful for thinking about political change and its implications for economic growth consists of a mapping $\varphi : \mathcal{P} \times \mathcal{Z} \to \mathcal{J}$, which determines the distribution of de jure power at time t as a function of political institutions at time t, $P(t) \in \mathcal{P}$, as well as some potential stochastic elements, captured by $z(t) \in \mathcal{Z}$. It also comprises a mapping that determines the equilibrium distribution of de facto power in a similar manner: $\phi : \mathcal{W} \times \mathcal{Z} \to \mathcal{F}$. Then given the realization of $J(t) \in \mathcal{J}$ and $F(t) \in \mathcal{F}$, another mapping $\iota : \mathcal{J} \times \mathcal{F} \to \mathcal{R} \times \mathcal{P}$ determines both economic institutions today, $R(t) \in \mathcal{R}$, and political institutions tomorrow, $P(t + 1) \in \mathcal{P}$. Put differently, the distributions of de facto and de jure political power regulate what types of economic institutions emerge in equilibrium (which thus corresponds to the mapping π introduced at the beginning of Part VIII), and they also determine whether there will be political reform leading to changes in future de jure power (e.g., example, a switch from nondemocracy to democracy to increase the future de jure power of the citizens who hold significant de facto power today). Finally, an economic equilibrium mapping $\rho : \mathcal{R} \to \mathcal{Y} \times \mathcal{W}$ determines both economic performance and the distribution of economic resources. For example, if economic institutions involve competitive markets and secure property rights, they lead to high aggregate output, whereas insecure property rights and entry barriers

$$
\begin{array}{ccc}
\begin{array}{c}\text{Political}\\ \text{institutions}(t)\end{array} & \Longrightarrow & \begin{array}{c}\text{De jure}\\ \text{political}\\ \text{power}(t)\end{array} \\
& & \text{and} \\
\begin{array}{c}\text{Distribution}\\ \text{of resources}(t)\end{array} & \Longrightarrow & \begin{array}{c}\text{De facto}\\ \text{political}\\ \text{power}(t)\end{array}
\end{array}
\left.\vphantom{\begin{array}{c}a\\a\\a\\a\\a\\a\\a\end{array}}\right\}
\begin{array}{ccc}
\Longrightarrow & \begin{array}{c}\text{Economic}\\ \text{institutions}(t)\end{array} & \Longrightarrow \left\{\begin{array}{c}\text{Economic}\\ \text{performance}(t)\\ \text{and}\\ \text{Distribution}\\ \text{of resources}(t+1)\end{array}\right. \\
\Longrightarrow & \begin{array}{c}\text{Political}\\ \text{institutions}(t+1)\end{array} &
\end{array}
$$

FIGURE 23.3 Components of a dynamic framework.

lead to lower output. These different economic institutions also result in different distributions of income and wealth in the society. Figure 23.3 summarizes this discussion diagrammatically.

This framework incorporates both the effects of economic institutions on economic outcomes—what we have tried to understand so far—and the dynamics of political power and political institutions. Of course, at this level of generality, such a dynamic framework is somewhat vacuous. It is only useful if we can put more content into the set of political institutions and the distribution of resources that need to be considered, derive the mappings φ, ϕ, ι, and ρ from economic interactions with sound microfoundations, and then conduct useful comparative statics. This is a tall order, and a full dynamic model of the sort does not currently exist. Nevertheless models focusing on political change and on the interaction between politics and economics exist, and these can be viewed through the lense of this framework. An abstract framework like the one presented here might be useful in clarifying what the important frontiers for research are and what types of models we may want to think about for advancing our understanding of political change and the relationship between political institutions and economic growth.

23.4.3 Example: The Emergence of Democracy

The framework sketched above builds on the approach to the emergence of democracy developed in Acemoglu and Robinson (2000a, 2006a). This approach emphasizes that institutional change, in particular democracy, emerges as a result of social conflict between the elite, who originally hold de jure political power, and the masses, who are initially without such political power. Even though the masses do not have de jure power, they can at times solve their collective action problems and gather significant de facto political power. Consider the emergence of democracy in nineteenth-century Europe. Many European nations during the nineteenth century were run by small groups of elites. Most had elected legislatures, often descendents of medieval parliaments, but the franchise was highly restricted to men with relatively large assets, high income, or established wealth. As the century and the Industrial Revolution progressed, this political monopoly was challenged by the disenfranchised, who were able to exercise their de facto power (resulting from their sheer numbers) and engaged in collective action to force political change.

In response to these developments, the elites responded in three ways. The first response was to use repression to prevent social unrest, as was the case in much of Europe during the revolutionary waves of 1848. The second response, used successfully by Bismarck in Germany, was to offer economic concessions to buy off or co-opt part of the opposition. Finally, if neither repression nor concessions were attractive or effective, as in Britain, the third response involved expanding the franchise and giving political power to the previously disenfranchised, which created the precedents for modern democracy.

In the context of European political history, the first important move toward democracy came in Britain with the First Reform Act of 1832. This act removed many of the worst inequities under the old electoral system and established the right to vote based strictly on property and income. The reform was passed in the context of rising popular unrest and discontent at the political status quo in Britain. By the 1820s the Industrial Revolution was well under way, and the decade prior to 1832 saw continual rioting and popular unrest. Notable were the Luddite Riots from 1811 to 1816, the Spa Fields Riots of 1816, the Peterloo Massacre in 1819, and the Swing Riots of 1830. Another catalyst for the reforms was the July revolution of 1830 in Paris. There is general agreement among historians that the motive for the 1832 Reform was to avoid social disturbances.

The 1832 Reform Act increased the total electorate from 492,700 to 806,000, which represented about 14.5% of the adult male population. Yet the majority of British population still could not vote. There is also evidence of continued corruption and intimidation of voters until the Ballot Act of 1872 and the Corrupt and Illegal Practices Act of 1883. The Reform Act therefore did not create mass democracy; it was instead designed as a strategic concession. As a result, parliamentary reform was still on the agenda in the middle of the century. Following the sharp business cycle downturn in the second half of the nineteenth century, the founding of the National Reform Union in 1864, the Reform League in 1865, and the Hyde Park Riots of July 1866, major electoral reforms were again instigated. The Second Reform Act in 1867 increased the total electorate from 1.36 million to 2.48 million and made working-class voters the majority in all urban constituencies. The electorate was doubled again by the Third Reform Act of 1884, which extended the same voting regulations that already existed in the boroughs (urban constituencies) to the counties (rural constituencies). The Redistribution Act of 1885 removed many remaining inequalities in the distribution of seats, and from this point on, Britain had only single-member electoral constituencies. After 1884, about 60% of adult males were enfranchised. Once again social disorder appears to have been an important factor behind the 1884 Act.

The Reform Acts of 1867–84 were a turning point in the history of the British state. Economic institutions also began to change. Liberal and Conservative governments introduced a considerable amount of labor market legislation, fundamentally changing the nature of industrial relations in favor of workers. During 1906–14, the Liberal Party, under the leadership of Henry Asquith and David Lloyd George, introduced the modern redistributive state into Britain, including health and unemployment insurance, government financed pensions, minimum wages, and a commitment to redistributive taxation. As a result of the fiscal changes, taxes as a proportion of GNP more than doubled in the 30 years following 1870, and then doubled again, and taxes became more progressive. Finally, the Education Act of 1870 committed the government to the systematic provision of universal education, and the educational attainment of the population increased dramatically at this time. As a result of these changes, inequality in Britain appears to have fallen sharply in the second half of the nineteenth century.

Overall the picture that emerges from British political history is clear. Beginning in 1832, when Britain was governed by the relatively rich, primarily rural aristocracy, a series of strategic concessions were made over an 86-year period. These concessions were aimed at incorporating the previously disenfranchised into politics, since the alternative was seen to be social unrest, chaos, and possibly revolution.

However, when faced with the threat of revolt and social chaos, the elite may also attempt to avoid giving away political power. They may instead make (economic) concessions, such as income redistribution or other policies that favor nonelites and the disenfranchised. Nevertheless because the promise of concessions is typically not credible when threats are transient, such promises are often insufficient to defuse social unrest. Democratization can then be viewed as a credible commitment to future redistribution. It is credible because it redistributes de jure political power away from the elite to the masses. In democracy, the poorer segments of the society become more powerful and can use their de jure political power to implement economic institutions and policies consistent with their interests. Thus democratization was a way of transforming the transient de facto power of the disenfranchised poor into more durable de jure political power.

The above account of events makes it clear that democracy in many Western societies, and particularly in Britain, did not emerge from the voluntary acts of an enlightened elite. Democracy was in many ways forced on the elite because of the threat of revolution. Nevertheless many other countries faced the same pressures, and political elites decided to repress the disenfranchised rather than make concessions to them. This happened with regularity in Europe in the nineteenth century, though by the turn of the twentieth century most West European nations had accepted that democracy was inevitable. Repression lasted much longer in much of South America and is still the preferred option for current political elites in China or Burma. And yet repression is costly not only for the repressed, but also for the elite, for example, because it destroys assets, disrupts production, and requires investments in repressive technologies. Therefore, faced with demands for democracy, political elites face a trade-off. In the urbanized environment of nineteenth century Europe (Britain was 70% urbanized at the time of the Second Reform Act), the disenfranchised masses were relatively well organized and therefore difficult to repress. Moreover industrialization had led to an economy based on physical, and increasingly human, capital. Such assets are easily destroyed by repression and conflict, making repression an increasingly costly option for the elite. In contrast, in predominantly agrarian societies, as in many parts of Latin America earlier in the century or current-day Burma, physical and human capital are relatively unimportant and repression is easier and cheaper. Moreover not only is repression cheaper in such environments, democracy is potentially much worse for the elite because of the prospect of radical land reform. Since physical capital is much harder to redistribute, the elites in Western Europe found the prospect of democracy much less threatening.

23.4.4 Modeling Democratization

So far I have offered a verbal account of how one might develop a model of the democratization process in line with the abstract framework of Section 23.4.2. Once the main ideas are understood, a formal framework is not difficult to construct. The following is a simplified version of framework in Acemoglu and Robinson (2006a). (See also Exercise 23.12.) The society consists of two groups, the elite and the "masses" (the poor or the citizens). Political power is initially in the hands of the elite, but the masses are more numerous. Thus if there is democratization, the masses become politically more powerful and dictate the policies. All individuals are infinitely lived, and the elite are richer than the masses. Because the society starts as a nondemocracy, de jure power is in the hands of the elite. Let us suppose that the only policy choice is a redistributive tax τ, the proceeds of which are distributed lumpsum. The elite prefer zero taxation, $\tau = 0$, since they are richer and any taxation redistributes income away from them to the poorer masses.

Let us imagine that while de jure power in the nondemocracy lies with the elite the poor sometimes have de facto political power. In particular, suppose that with probability q in each period, the masses are able to solve their collective action problem and can threaten to undertake a revolution. A revolution is very costly for the elite but generates only limited gains for the masses. These limited gains may nonetheless be better than living in a nondemocracy and the inequitable distribution of resources that it involves. So when they are able to solve their collective action problem, the *revolution constraint* of the masses becomes binding. In this case, the rich need to make concessions to avoid a revolution.

As in the historical account above, the elite have three options to defuse the revolutionary threat. The first is to make concessions through redistributive policies today, which will work if q is high. In the limit, where $q = 1$, a revolution is possible at each date; thus the elite can credibly commit to making redistribution toward the masses at each date, because if they fail to do so, the masses can immediately undertake a revolution. However the same strategy does not work when q is small. Consider the polar case where $q \to 0$. In this case, the masses expect never to have the same type of de facto political power in the future. Presuming that the amount to redistribution that the elite can give to the masses during a particular period is limited, they will not be satisfied by temporary concessions. In this case, the elite may prefer to use repression. Repression will be successful if the revolutionary threat is not well organized, and it will be profitable for the elite if they have a great deal to lose from democratization. Thus repression will be the action of choice for elites who fear major redistribution under democracy, such as the land-based elites in Central America and Burma. But in a highly urbanized and industrialized society like Britain, where the costs of repression are likely to be substantial and the elite have less to fear from democratization, the third option, enfranchisement, becomes an attractive choice. This option involves the elite changing the political system and initiating a transition to democracy to alter the distribution of de jure power in favor of the masses. With their newly gained decision-making power, the masses know that they can choose policies in the future that will create a more equitable distribution of resources for themselves and will typically be happy to accept democratic institutions instead of a revolution that is costly for themselves (as well as for the elite).

Compared to the abstract framework in Section 23.4.2, the model sketched here is stripped down (and to save space, I have not even provided the equations to establish the main claims). First, the distribution of resources is no longer a state variable (it is constant and does not affect transitions or the distribution of political power). Second, de jure political power is simply a nonstochastic outcome of political institutions: in a nondemocracy, the elite make the decisions; and in a democracy, there is a one-person one-vote policy, and the masses, thanks to their majority, become the decisive voters. Finally, there are limited economic decisions. Thus in its current form, this model is not satisfactory for analyzing the impact of political institutions on economic institutions or the relationship between political regimes and economic growth. Some of the extensions of this approach presented in Acemoglu and Robinson (2006a, 2008) go some way toward incorporating economic institutions and decisions. Nevertheless, much work still remains to be done on the dynamic interactions between political institutions and economic growth.

23.5 Taking Stock

This chapter provided a brief overview of some of the issues related to the effects of political institutions on economic growth. Based on the ideas presented in Chapter 22, we may expect differences in economic institutions to be related to political institutions. For example, if political power is in the hands of an elite that is opposed to growth, growth-enhancing policies are less likely to emerge. The empirical evidence in Chapter 4 also provides support for such a view, because the cluster of economic institutions that provide secure property rights to a broad cross section of society—together with political institutions that place constraints on the elite and on politicians—appear to be conducive to economic growth. Nevertheless the relationship between political regimes and growth is more complicated for a number of reasons. First, the empirical evidence is less clear-cut than we may have originally presumed—while there are historical examples of the positive effects of democratic institutions on economic growth, the postwar evidence does not provide strong support for the view that democracies and political institutions that constrain rulers and politicians always generate more economic growth. Second, political institutions themselves are endogenous and change dynamically. These two factors imply that we need to study how political institutions affect economic outcomes more carefully, and we should also consider the modeling of equilibrium political institutions. Both of these areas are at the forefront of research in political economy and are likely to play a more important role in the research on economic growth in the coming years.

I also presented a number of model approaches that can shed light on the relationship between political institutions and economic growth. I emphasized that ideal (or perfect) political institutions are unlikely to exist, because different political institutions create different sets of winners and losers and distinct distortions. Oligarchies, for example, favor the already rich and create distortions by protecting these established interests. Democracies, on the other hand, typically involve higher taxes on the rich and on businesses to generate income to redistribute to the less well off. In general, it is impossible to unambiguously conclude whether democracies or oligarchies (or yet other political systems favoring other groups) will be more growth enhancing. However certain ideas seem both plausible and consistent with the data. One aspect I tried to emphasize is that the dynamic trade-offs between democracies and other regimes may be different than the static trade-offs. While democracies may create static distortions because of their greater redistributive tendencies, they may outperform oligarchies in the long run, because they avoid political sclerosis that results when incumbents are able to dominate the political system and erect entry barriers to protect their businesses, even when efficiency dictates that new individuals and businesses should enter and replace theirs. Thus democracy may be more conducive than other political regimes to the process of creative destruction that is part of modern capitalist growth. Democracy may also be more flexible and adaptable to the arrival of new technologies.

Finally, I also gave a very brief overview of some of the issues that arise when we wish to model the dynamics of political institutions. Section 23.4 provided both a general discussion of the types of models that would be useful for such an analysis and examples of how these models can be developed. Once again, this is an area of active current research, and the material presented here is no more than the tip of the iceberg. It is meant to encourage the reader to think more about various aspects of the relationship between political institutions and economic growth.

23.6 References and Literature

This chapter relates to a large literature in political economy and political science. Because of space constraints, I do not provide a comprehensive literature review. The key references on the effect of political regimes on economic growth are provided in Section 23.1.

Section 23.2 built on the models presented in the previous chapter. Section 23.3 is directly based on Acemoglu (2008a). Other models that discuss the functioning of oligarchic societies include Leamer (1998), Bourguignon and Verdier (2000), Robinson and Nugent (2001), Sonin

(2003), and Galor, Moav, and Vollrath (2005). Coatsworth (1993), Eltis (1995), Engerman and Sokoloff (1997), and Acemoglu, Johnson, and Robinson (2002) provide information on the prosperity the United States in the seventeenth and eighteenth centuries relative to the Caribbean and South America. The contrast of industrialization in Britain and France against the experiences of Russia and Austria-Hungary draws on Acemoglu and Robinson (2006b), which includes references to the original literature.

Section 23.4 provided an abstract discussion of the issues related to the modeling of political change based on Acemoglu and Robinson (2006a). The distinction between de jure and de facto political power is introduced in Acemoglu and Robinson (2006a). The model sketched at the end of Section 23.4 builds on Acemoglu and Robinson (2000a, 2006a). The literature on democratization in Europe and Latin America is summarized in Acemoglu and Robinson (2006a). Modern historical references include Evans (1996), Lang (1999), and Collier (2000). The fiscal reforms following democratization are documented and discussed in Lindert (2000, 2004), and the educational reforms are discussed in Ringer (1979) and Mitch (1983).

23.7 Exercises

23.1 Prove Proposition 23.1.

23.2 (a) Prove Proposition 23.2.

(b) Generalize the result in Proposition 23.2 to the case where $\theta^e \neq \theta^m$. In particular, derive an inequality that determines when the dictatorship of the elite generates greater output per capita than does the dictatorship of the middle class.

23.3 Prove Proposition 23.3. [Hint: To prove the second part of this proposition, first note that equilibrium wages are determined by whichever group has lower net (after tax) productivity. Then write the utility of workers under two scenarios: (1) when the elite have lower net productivity and (2) when the middle class have lower net productivity. In writing these expressions, recall that the group with the lower productivity employs $1 - \theta \bar{L}$ workers, since Condition 22.1 holds. Derive the optimal tax policies for workers in these two scenarios, and then compare the utility at these optimal policies.]

23.4 In the model of Section 23.3, prove that $V^z(q^t)$ given in (23.13) is strictly monotone in $w(t)$, $T(t)$, and $\Pi^z(\tau(t), w(t))$ and therefore that $V^H(q^t) > V^L(q^t)$.

23.5 In the model of Section 23.3, suppose that $l_i(t)$ is unbounded above. What problems would this relaxation create? Next suppose that $l_i(t)$ could be arbitrarily small. What problems will this raise for the equilibrium in this section? Can you generalize the results in this section to an environment in which $l_i(t) \in [\underline{L}, \bar{L}]$, where $\underline{L} > 0$ and $\bar{L} < \infty$?

23.6 Derive (23.7).

23.7 Prove Proposition 23.5.

23.8 Prove Proposition 23.6.

23.9 Suppose that Condition 23.1 does not hold. Generalize the results in Propositions 23.5 and 23.6.

23.10 Consider the model in Section 23.3, starting with $\mu(0) = 1$ and an oligarchic regime. Suppose that at some time $t' < \infty$ a new technology arises, which is ψ-times as productive as the old technology, where $\psi > 1$. Entrepreneurial skills with this new technology are uncorrelated with skills relevant for the old technology and are given by

$$\hat{a}_i(t+1) = \begin{cases} A^H & \text{with probability} & \hat{\sigma}^H & \text{if } \hat{a}_i(t) = A^H, \\ A^H & \text{with probability} & \hat{\sigma}^L & \text{if } \hat{a}_i(t) = A^L, \\ A^L & \text{with probability } 1 - \hat{\sigma}^H & \text{if } \hat{a}_i(t) = A^H, \\ A^L & \text{with probability } 1 - \hat{\sigma}^L & \text{if } \hat{a}_i(t) = A^L. \end{cases}$$

(a) Show that there exists $\bar{\psi}$ such that if $\psi > \bar{\psi}$, all existing entrepreneurs raise the entry barriers and switch to the new technology.

(b) Show that if $\psi < \bar{\psi}$, then again the entry barriers will be raised, but now only entrepreneurs who have low skills with the old technology switch to the new technology.

(c) Analyze the response of a democracy to the arrival of the same technology.

(d) Compare output per capita in a democracy and an oligarchy after the arrival of new technology, and explain why democracy is more flexible in dealing with the arrival of new technologies.

23.11 This exercise shows that entry barriers typically lead to multiple equilibrium wages in dynamic models. Consider the following two-period model. The production function is given by (23.2), and the distribution of entrepreneurial talent is given by a continuous cumulative distribution function $G(a)$. There is an entry cost into entrepreneurship equal to b at each date, and each entrepreneur hires one worker (and does not work as a worker himself). Total population is equal to 1.

(a) Ignore the second period and characterize the equilibrium wage and determine which individuals become entrepreneurs. Show that the equilibrium is unique.

(b) Now introduce the second period, and suppose that all agents discount the future at the rate β. Show that there are multiple equilibrium wages in the second period and as a result, multiple equilibrium wages in the initial period.

(c) Suppose that a fraction ε of all agents die in the second period and are replaced by new agents. New agents have to pay the entry cost into entrepreneurship if they want to become entrepreneurs. Suppose that their talent distribution is also given by $G(a)$. Characterize the equilibrium in this case and show that it is unique.

(d) Consider the limiting equilibrium in part c with $\varepsilon \to 0$. Explain why this limit leads to a unique equilibrium while there are multiple equilibria at $\varepsilon = 0$.

23.12 Consider an economy populated by λ rich agents who initially hold power and $1 - \lambda$ poor agents who are excluded from power, with $\lambda < 1/2$. All agents are infinitely lived and discount the future at the rate $\beta \in (0, 1)$. Each rich agent has income θ/λ, while each poor agent has income $(1 - \theta)/(1 - \lambda)$, where $\theta > \lambda$. The political system determines a linear tax rate τ, the proceeds of which are redistributed lumpsum. Each agent can hide her money in an alternative nontaxable production technology, and in the process she loses a fraction ϕ of her income. There are no other costs of taxation. The poor can undertake a revolution, and if they do so, in all future periods, they obtain a fraction $\mu(t)$ of the total income of the society (i.e., an income of $\mu(t)/(1 - \lambda)$ per poor agent). The poor cannot revolt against democracy. The rich receive zero payoff after a revolution. At the beginning of every period, the rich also decide whether to extend the franchise. If the franchise is extended, the poor decide the tax rate in all future periods.

(a) Define the MPE in this game.

(b) First suppose that $\mu(t) = \mu^l$ at all times. Also assume that $0 < \mu^l < 1 - \theta$. Show that in the MPE, there is no taxation when the rich are in power, and the tax rate is $\tau = \phi$ when the poor are in power. Show that along the equilibrium path, there is no extension of the franchise and no taxation.

(c) Suppose that $\mu^l \in (1 - \theta, (1 - \phi)(1 - \theta) + \phi(1 - \lambda))$. Characterize the MPE in this case. Why is the restriction $\mu^l < (1 - \phi)(1 - \theta) + \phi(1 - \lambda)$ necessary?

(d) Now consider the SPE of this game when $\mu^l > 1 - \theta$. Construct an equilibrium where there is extension of the franchise along the equilibrium path. [Hint: To simplify, take $\beta \to 1$, and then consider a strategy profile where the rich are always expected to set $\tau = 0$ in the future. Then show that in this case the poor would undertake a revolution. Also explain why the continuation strategy of $\tau = 0$ by the rich in all future periods could be part of an SPE.] Why is there extension of the franchise now? Can you construct a similar non-Markovian equilibrium when $\mu^l < 1 - \theta$?

(e) Explain why the MPE led to different predictions than the non-Markovian equilibria. Which one is more satisfactory?

(f) Now suppose that $\mu(t) = \mu^l$ with probability $1 - q$, and $\mu(t) = \mu^h$ with probability q, where $\mu^h > 1 - \theta > \mu^l$. Construct an MPE where the rich extend the franchise, and from then on a poor agent sets that tax rate. Determine the parameter values that are necessary for such an equilibrium to exist. Explain why an extension of the franchise is useful for rich agents.

(g) Now consider non-Markovian equilibria again. Suppose that the unique MPE results in franchise extension. Can you construct an SPE equilibrium, as $\beta \to 1$, where there is no franchise extension?

Epilogue:
Mechanics and Causes
of Economic Growth

Instead of summarizing the models and ideas presented so far, I end with a brief discussion of what we have learned from the models in this book and how they offer a useful perspective on world growth and cross-country income differences. I then provide a quick overview of some of the many remaining questions, which are important to emphasize both as a measure of our ignorance and as potential topics for future research.

What Have We Learned?

Let us first summarize the most important aspects and takeaway lessons of our analysis.

Growth as the source of current income differences. At an empirical level, the investigation of economic growth is important not only for understanding the growth process, but also because the analysis of the sources of cross-country income differences today requires us to understand why some countries have grown rapidly over the past 200 years while others have not (Chapter 1).

The role of physical capital, human capital, and technology. Cross-country differences in economic performance and growth over time are related to physical capital, human capital, and technology. Part of our analysis has focused on the contributions of these factors to production and growth (Chapters 2 and 3). One conclusion that has emerged concerns the importance of technology in understanding both cross-country and over-time differences in economic performance. Here, technology refers to advances in techniques of production, advances in knowledge, and the general efficiency of the organization of production.

Endogenous investment decisions. While we can make empirical progress by taking cross-country differences in physical and human capital as given, we also need to endogenize these investment decisions to develop a more satisfactory understanding of the mechanics and the causes of income and growth differences across countries. A large part of the book has focused on understanding physical and human capital accumulation (Chapters 8–11). Investments in physical and human capital are forward-looking and depend on the rewards that individuals expect from their investments. Understanding differences in these investments is therefore intimately linked to understanding how reward structures—that is, the pecuniary and nonpecuniary rewards and incentives for different activities—differ across societies and how individuals respond to differences in reward structures.

Endogenous technology. I have also emphasized throughout that technology should be thought of as endogenous, not as manna from heaven. There are good empirical and theoretical reasons for thinking that new technologies are created by profit-seeking individuals and firms through research, development, and tinkering. In addition, decisions to adopt new technologies are likely to be highly responsive to profit incentives. Since technology appears to be a prime driver of economic growth over time and a major factor in cross-country differences in economic performance, we must understand how technology responds to factor endowments, market structures, and rewards. Developing a conceptual framework that emphasizes the endogeneity of technology has been one of the major objectives of this book. The modeling of endogenous technology necessitates ideas and tools that are somewhat different from those involved in the modeling of physical and human capital investments. Three factors are particularly important. First, the fixed costs of creating new technologies combined with the nonrival nature of technology necessitates the use of models in which innovators have ex post (after innovation) monopoly power. The same might apply, though perhaps to a lesser degree, to firms that adopt new technologies. The presence of monopoly power changes the welfare properties of decentralized equilibria and creates a range of new interactions and externalities (Chapters 12 and 13 and Section 21.5 in Chapter 21). Second, the process of innovation is implicitly one of competition and creative destruction. The modeling of endogenous technology necessitates more detailed models of the industrial organization of innovation. These models shed light on the impact of market structure, competition, regulation, and IPR protection on innovation and technology adoption (Chapters 12 and 14). Third, endogenous technology implies that not only the aggregate rate of technological change but also the types of technologies that are developed will be responsive to rewards. Key factors influencing the types of technologies that societies develop are again reward structures and factor endowments. For example, changes in relative supplies of different factors are likely to affect which types of technologies will be developed and adopted (Chapter 15).

Linkages across societies and balanced growth at the world level. While endogenous technology and endogenous growth are major ingredients in our thinking about the process of economic growth in general and the history of world economic growth in particular, it is also important to recognize that most economies do not invent their own technologies but adopt them from the world technology frontier or adapt them from existing technologies (Chapter 18). In fact, the process of technology transfer across nations might be one of the reasons why, after the initial phase of industrialization, countries that have been part of the global economy have grown at broadly similar rates (Chapter 1). Therefore the modeling of cross-country income differences and the process of economic growth for a large part of the world requires a detailed analysis of technology diffusion and international economic linkages. Two topics deserve special attention in this context. The first is the contracting institutions supporting contracts between upstream and downstream firms, between firms and workers, and between firms and financial institutions. These institutional arrangements affect the amount of investment, the selection of entrepreneurs and firms, and the efficiency with which different tasks are allocated across firms and workers. There are marked differences in contracting institutions across societies, and these differences appear to be a major factor influencing technology adoption and diffusion in the world economy. Contracting institutions not only have a direct effect on technology and prosperity, but they also shape the internal organization of firms, which contributes to the efficiency of production and influences how innovative firms will be (Section 18.5 in Chapter 18). The second is international trading relationships. International trade not only generates static gains familiar to economists but also influences the innovation and growth process. The international division of labor and the product cycle are examples of how international trading relationships help the process of technology diffusion and enhance the specialization of production (Chapter 19).

Takeoffs and failures. The past 200 years of world economic growth stand in stark contrast to the thousands of years before. Despite intermittent growth in some parts of the world during certain epochs, the world economy was largely stagnant until the end of the eighteenth century. This stagnation had multiple aspects. These included low productivity, high volatility in aggregate and individual outcomes, a largely rural and agricultural economy, and a Malthusian configuration in which increases in output were often accompanied by increases in population, thus having only a limited effect on per capita income. Another major aspect of stagnation has been the failed growth attempts: many societies grew for certain periods of time and then lapsed back into depressions and stagnation. This cycle changed at the end of the eighteenth century. We owe our prosperity today to the takeoff in economic activity, and especially in industrial activity, that started in Britain and Western Europe and spread to certain other parts of the world, most notably to Western European offshoots, such as the United States and Canada. The nations that are rich today are precisely those where this process of takeoff originated or those that were able to rapidly adopt and build on the technologies underlying this takeoff (Chapter 1). A study of current income differences across countries requires understanding why some countries failed to take advantage of the new technologies and production opportunities.

Structural changes and transformations. Modern economic growth and development are accompanied by a set of sweeping structural changes and transformations. These include changes in the composition of production and consumption (the shift from agriculture to industry and from industry to services), urbanization, financial development, changes in inequality of income and inequality of opportunity, the transformation of social and living arrangements, changes in the internal organization of firms, and the demographic transition. While the process of economic development is multifaceted, much of its essence lies in the structural transformation of the economy and the society at large (Section 17.6 in Chapter 17 and Chapters 20 and 21). Many of these transformations are interesting to study for their own sake. They are also important ingredients for sustained growth. Lack of structural transformation is not only a symptom of stagnation but is also often one of its causes. Societies may fail to take off and benefit from the available technology and investment opportunities, partly because they have not managed to undergo the requisite structural transformations and thus lack the type of financial relations, the appropriate skills, or the types of firms that are conducive to the adoption of new technologies.

Policy, institutions, and political economy. The reward structures faced by firms and individuals play a central role in shaping whether they undertake the investments in new technology and in human capital necessary for takeoff, industrialization, and economic growth. These reward structures are determined by policies and institutions. Policies and institutions also directly affect whether a society can embark on modern economic growth for a variety of interrelated reasons (Chapter 4). First, they directly determine the society's reward structure, thus shaping whether investments in physical and human capital and technological innovations are profitable. Second, they determine whether the infrastructure and contracting arrangements necessary for modern economic relations are present. For example, modern economic growth would be impossible in the absence of some degree of contract enforcement, the maintenance of law and order, and at least a minimum amount of investment in public infrastructure. Third, they influence and regulate the market structure, thus determining whether the forces of creative destruction are operational so that new and more efficient firms can replace less efficient incumbents. Finally, institutions and policies may sometimes (or perhaps often) block the adoption and use of new technologies to protect politically powerful incumbent producers or stabilize the established political regime. Thus to understand the process of modern economic growth, we need to study the institutional and policy choices that societies make. We then need to investigate the political economy of growth, paying special attention to which individuals and groups will be the winners from economic growth and which the losers. When losers cannot be compensated and have sufficient political power, we may expect the political economy equilibrium to lead to policies and institutions that are not growth enhancing. The basic analysis of the political economy of growth generates insights about what types of distortionary policies may block growth; when these distortionary policies will be adopted; and how technology, market structure, and factor endowments interact with the incentives of the social groups in power to encourage or discourage economic growth (Chapter 22).

Endogenous political institutions. Policies and institutions are central to understanding the growth process over time and cross-country differences in economic performance. These social choices are in turn determined in the context of a society's political institutions. Democracies and dictatorships are likely to make different policy choices and create distinct types of reward structures. But political institutions themselves are not exogenous. They can change along the equilibrium path as a result of their own dynamics and of stimuli coming from changes in technology, trading opportunities, and factor endowments (Chapter 23). For a more complete understanding of world economic growth and the income differences today, we therefore need to study (1) how political institutions affect policies and economic institutions, thus shaping incentives for firms and workers; (2) how political institutions themselves change, especially when interacting with economic outcomes and technology; and (3) why political institutions and the associated economic institutions did not lead to sustained economic growth throughout history, why they enabled economic takeoff 200 years ago, and why in some countries they blocked the adoption and use of superior technologies and derailed the process of economic growth.

In this summary, I have focused on the ideas most relevant for examining the process of world economic growth and cross-country income differences we observe today. The focus in the book has been not only on ideas but also on careful mathematical modeling of these ideas to develop coherent and rigorous theoretical approaches. I do not repeat here the theoretical foundations of these ideas, which range from basic consumer, producer, and general equilibrium theory to dynamic models of accumulation, models of monopolistic competition, models of world equilibria, and dynamic models of political economy. But I emphasize again that a thorough study of the theoretical foundations of these ideas is necessary both to develop a satisfactory understanding of the main issues and to find the best way of making them empirically operational.

A Possible Perspective on Growth and Stagnation over the Past 200 Years

The previous section summarized the most important ideas highlighted in this book. I now discuss how some of these ideas might be useful in shedding light on the process of world economic growth and cross-country divergence that have motivated our investigation from the start. The central questions are:

1. Why did the world economy not experience sustained growth before 1800?
2. Why did economic takeoff start around 1800 and in Western Europe?
3. Why did some societies manage to benefit from the new technologies and organizational forms that emerged starting in 1800, while others steadfastly refused or failed to do so?

I now offer a narrative that provides some tentative answers to these three questions. While certain parts of the mechanisms I propose here have been investigated econometrically and other parts are supported by historical evidence, the reader should view this narrative as a first attempt at providing coherent answers to these central questions. Two aspects of these answers are noteworthy. First, they build on the theoretical insights that the models presented so far generate. Second, in the spirit of the discussion in Chapter 4, they link the proximate causes of economic phenomena to fundamental causes, and in particular to institutions. And here I take a shortcut. Although I emphasized in Chapter 23 that there are no perfect political institutions and that each set of different political arrangements is likely to favor some groups at the expense of others, I simplify the discussion in this part by making a core distinction between two sets of institutional arrangements, one less conducive to growth than the other one. The first, which I refer to as *authoritarian political systems,* encompasses absolutist monarchies, dictatorships, autocracies, and various types of oligarchies that concentrate power in the hands of a small minority and pursue economic policies that are favorable to the interests of this minority. Authoritarian systems often rely on some amount of repression, because they seek to maintain an unequal distribution of political power and economic benefits. They also adopt economic institutions and policies that protect incumbents and create rents for those who hold political power. The second set of institutions are *participatory regimes.* These regimes place constraints on rulers and politicians, thus preventing the absolutist tendencies in political systems, and give voice to new economic interests, so that a strict decoupling between political and economic power is avoided. Such regimes include constitutional monarchies (where broader sections of the society take part in economic and political decision making) and democracies (where political participation is greater than in nondemocratic regimes). The distinguishing feature of participatory regimes is that they provide voice and (economic and political) security to a broader cross section of society than do authoritarian regimes. As a result, they are more open to entry by new businesses and provide a more level playing field and better security of property rights to a relatively broad section of the society. Thus in some ways, the contrast between authoritarian political systems and participatory regimes is related to the contrast between the growth-promoting cluster of institutions and the growth-blocking, extractive institutions emphasized and illustrated in Chapter 4. The reader should note that many different terms could have been used instead of "authoritarian" and "participatory," and some details of the distinction may be arbitrary. More importantly, it should be borne in mind that even the most participatory regime involves an unequal distribution of political power, and those who have more political power can use the fiscal and political instruments of the state for their own benefits and for the detriment of the society at large. Why this type of behavior is sometimes successfully curtailed or limited is a question at the forefront of current research, and I do not dwell on it here.

Why Did the World Not Experience Sustained Growth before 1800?

While sustained growth is a recent phenomenon, growth and improvements in living standards certainly have occurred many times in the past. Human history is also full of major technological breakthroughs. Even before the Neolithic Revolution, many technological innovations increased the productivity of hunter-gatherers. The transition to farming after about 9000 B.C. is perhaps the most significant technological revolution of all times: it led to increased agricultural productivity and the development of socially and politically more complex societies. Archaeologists have also documented various instances of economic growth in premodern periods. Historians estimate that consumption per capita doubled during the great flowering of ancient Greek society from 800 B.C. to 50 B.C. (Morris, 2004). Similar improvements in living standards were experienced by the Roman republic and empire after 400 B.C. (Hopkins, 1980) and also appear to have been experienced by pre-Columbian civilizations in South America, especially by the Olmec, the Maya, the Aztec, and even perhaps the Inca (Webster, 2002; Mann, 2004). Although data on these ancient growth experiences are limited, the available evidence suggests that the basic neoclassical model, in which growth relies mostly on physical capital accumulation, provides a good description of the developments in these ancient economies (see, e.g., Morris, 2004).

However, these growth experiences were qualitatively different from those that the world experienced after its economic takeoff starting in the late eighteenth and early nineteenth centuries. Four factors appear to have been particularly important and set these growth episodes apart from modern economic growth. First, earlier episodes were relatively short-lived or took place at a relatively slow pace.[1] In most cases, the initial spurt of growth soon crumbled for one reason or another, somehow reminiscent of the failed takeoffs in the model of Section 17.6 in Chapter 17. Secondly and relatedly, growth was never based on continuous technological innovations; thus it never resembled the technology-based growth described in Chapters 13–15. Third, in most cases economic institutions that would be necessary to support sustained growth did not develop. Financial relations were generally primitive, contracting institutions remained informal, markets were heavily regulated with various internal tariffs, and incomes and savings did not reach the levels necessary for the mass market and simultaneous investments in a range of activities to become profitable. Put differently, the structural transformations accompanying development discussed in Chapter 21 did not take place. Fourth (and arguably most important and the cause of the first three), all these episodes took place within the context of authoritarian political regimes. They were not broad-based growth experiences. Instead, this was elite-driven growth for the benefit of the elite that largely exploited existing comparative advantages. Thus it is not surprising that the improvements in living standards did not affect the entire society but only a minority.

Why did these growth episodes not turn into a process of takeoff, ultimately leading to sustained growth? My main answer is related to that offered in Section 23.3 in Chapter 23. Growth under authoritarian regimes is possible. Entrepreneurs and workers can become better at what they do, achieve a better division of labor, and improve the technologies they work with by tinkering and learning by doing. Moreover, those with political power and their allies do have the necessary security of property rights to undertake investments. And some technological breakthroughs can happen by chance. Nevertheless a distinguishing feature of growth under authoritarian institutions is that it protects the interests of the current elite. So in the final analysis, growth must always rely on existing techniques and production relationships. It will not unleash the process of creative destruction and the entry of new talent and new businesses necessary to carry a nation to the state of sustained growth. In addition, technological constraints may have also played a role. For example, the relatively rapid growth in the nineteenth century required skilled workers, and before the printing press was invented, it would have been prohibitively costly for a critical mass of workers to acquire the necessary skills. Although the progress of technological knowledge is not monotonic (and useful production techniques are sometimes forgotten), the technological know-how available to potential entrepreneurs at the end of the eighteenth century was undoubtedly greater than that available to potential entrepreneurs in Rome or ancient Greece.

---

1. For example, in ancient Greece, Morris (2004) estimates that income per capita doubled or at most tripled in the 500 years between 800 B.C. and 300 B.C., and this was largely caused by catch-up growth starting from unusually low levels in 800 B.C.

Let me next elaborate on the aspects of political economy that appear to be critical and provide a few examples to illustrate the limits to growth under authoritarian regimes. The available evidence shows that the Chinese empire was technologically innovative during many distinct phases of its history. Productivity in the Chinese economy, especially in the Yangtze Delta and other fertile lands, was high enough to support a high density of population. But the Chinese economy never came close to sustained growth. Authoritarian political institutions have regulated economic activity tightly for most of Chinese history. The society was hierarchical, with a clear distinction between the elite and the masses. This system did not allow free entry into business by new entrepreneurs who would adopt and exploit new technologies and unleash the powers of creative destruction. When prospects for economic growth conflicted with political stability, the elite opted for maintaining stability, even if this came at the expense of potential economic growth. Thus China tightly controlled overseas and internal trade, did not develop the broad-based property rights and contracting institutions necessary for modern economic growth, and did not allow an autonomous middle class to emerge as an economic and political force (Elvin, 1973; Mokyr, 1990; Wong, 1997).

The ancient Greek and Roman civilizations are often viewed as the first democratic societies. One might therefore be tempted to count them as participatory regimes that should have achieved sustained economic growth. But this is not necessarily the case. First, as noted above, participatory regimes do not guarantee sustained economic growth when other preconditions have not been met. But more importantly, these societies were democratic only in comparison to others at the time. Both societies were representative only for a small fraction of the population. Production relied on slavery and coercion. Moreover, despite certain democratic practices, there was a clear distinction between a small elite, which monopolized economic and political power, and the masses, which consisted of both free plebs and slaves. Economic growth in both ancient Greece and Rome did not rely on continuous innovation. Both societies managed to achieve high levels of productivity in agriculture but without changing the organization of production in a radical manner. Both societies benefited from their military superiority for a while, and challenges to their military power were also important factors in their decline.

The Ottoman Empire provides another example of a society that was successful for an extended period of time but without ever transitioning to sustained growth. The Ottoman Empire, especially during the fourteenth, fifteenth, and sixteenth centuries, achieved relative prosperity and military strength. Agricultural productivity was high in many parts of the empire, and military tribute contributed to state coffers and generated revenues to be distributed to parts of the population. But the state elite, who controlled decision making within the empire, never encouraged broad-based economic growth. There was no private property in land, trade was permitted as long as it was consistent with the state's objectives but was always tightly controlled, and any new technology that could destabilize the power of the state was blocked. Like China, Greece, and Rome, the Ottoman growth first tapered off and then turned into decline (Pamuk, 2004).

The final example I mention is the Spanish monarchy. By the beginning of the sixteenth century, the Spanish crown had achieved both political dominance over its own lands under Ferdinand and Isabella and control of a large overseas empire through its colonial enterprises. Many parts of greater Spain, including the lands of Aragon and the south that had been recently reconquered from the Moors, were already prosperous in the fifteenth century. The whole of Spain became much wealthier with the transfer of gold, silver, and other resources from the colonies in the sixteenth century. But this wealth did not translate into sustained growth. The colonial experiment was managed under a highly authoritarian regime set up by Ferdinand and Isabella, and the most lucrative businesses were allocated to the allies of the crown. The greater revenues generated from the colonies only helped to tighten the grip of the crown on the rest of the society and the economy. Instead of abating, absolutism increased. Trade and industry remained highly regulated, and groups not directly allied to the crown were viewed suspiciously and discriminated against. The most extreme example of this, the persecution of Jews that had started under the Inquisition, continued and spilled over to other independent merchants. Subsequent to the transfer of wealth from the colonies, Spain experienced a very lengthy period of stagnation, with economic and political decline (Elliott, 1963).

It is also remarkable that in none of these cases did complementary economic institutions develop. Financial institutions remained rudimentary. The Roman Republic developed a precursor to the modern corporation and allowed some contracts between free citizens, but by and large economic prosperity was built on traditional economic activities that did not necessitate complex relationships among producers and between firms and workers. Consequently the structural transformations that accompany economic growth never took place in these societies. Life was largely rural, and social relations were dominated by the state and community enforcement. Perhaps more important, there was little investment in human capital, except for the elite for whom education was seldom a means to higher productivity. Without broad-based human capital and political rights, creative destruction becomes even more difficult as a large fraction of the population is barred from entrepreneurial activities. All of the cases discussed here confirm this expectation.

Overall, these cases illustrate that societies that encourage increases in the productivity of the elite in traditional activities can secure growth for a while. But they are unlikely to engender creative destruction. Growth goes hand-in-hand with the political domination of the elite and thus with entry barriers protecting the status and the power of the elite. In this light, the answer to the question of "why not before 1800" is twofold. First, no society before 1800 invested in human capital, allowed new firms to bring new technology, and generally unleashed the powers of creative destruction. This failure might have been partly due to the difficulty of undertaking broad-based human capital investments in societies without the printing press and with only limited communication technologies. But it was also related to the reward structures for and constraints on workers and firms. An important consequence of this pattern of growth is that no society experienced the sweeping structural transformations that are an essential part of modern economic growth (Chapter 21). Second, no society took steps toward sustained growth, because all these societies lived under authoritarian political regimes.

Why Did Economic Takeoff Start around 1800 and in Western Europe?

The division of labor (emphasized by Adam Smith) and capital accumulation always present growth opportunities to societies. Furthermore human ingenuity is strong enough to create room for major technological breakthroughs in almost any environment. Thus there is always a growth impetus in human societies (Jones, 1988). Nevertheless this impetus may only be latent because it exists in the context of a set of political (and economic) institutions. When these institutions do not encourage growth—when they do not provide the right kind of reward structure and so punish rather than reward innovations—we do not expect the growth impetus to lead to sustained growth. Even in such environments, economic growth is possible, and this is why China, Greece, Rome, and other empires experienced growth for part of their history. But this prosperity did not exploit the full growth impetus; instead, it took place in the context of political regimes that, by their nature, had to control the growth impetus, because this impetus would ultimately bring these regimes down.

West European growth starting in the late eighteenth century was different, because Western Europe underwent three important structural transformations starting in the late Middle Ages. These structural transformations created an environment in which the latent growth impetus could turn into an engine of sustained growth.

The first was the collapse of one of the pillars of the ancient regime, the decline of feudal relations in Western Europe. Starting in the thirteenth century and especially after the Black Death during the mid-fourteenth century, feudal economic relations crumbled in many parts of Western Europe. Serfs were freed from their feudal dues either by default (because the relationship collapsed) or by fleeing to the expanding city centers (Postan, 1966). This emancipation heralded the beginning of an important social transformation: urbanization and changes in social relations. But perhaps more importantly, it created a labor force ready to work at cheap wages in industrial and commercial activities. It also removed one of the greatest sources of conflict between existing elites and new entrepreneurs—competition in the labor market (Chapter 22). The decline of the feudal order further weakened the power base of the European authoritarian regimes (Pirenne, 1937).

The second structural transformation was related. With the decline in population in the fourteenth century, real incomes increased in much of Europe, and many cities created sufficiently large markets for merchants to seek new imports and for industrialists to seek new products. During the Middle Ages, a range of important technologies in metallurgy, armaments, agriculture, and basic industry (e.g., textiles), were already perfected (White, 1964; Mokyr, 1990). Thus the European economy had reached the technological maturity to act as a platform for entrepreneurial activity in a range of areas, and income levels were sufficient to encourage investment in physical capital and technology to spearhead new production relations.

The third and most important change was political. The late Middle Ages also witnessed the start of a political process that inexorably led to the collapse of absolutist monarchies and to the rise of constitutional regimes. The constitutional regimes that emerged in the sixteenth and seventeenth centuries in Western Europe were the first examples of participatory regimes, because they shifted political power to a large group of individuals that were previously outsiders to political power. This group included the gentry, small merchants, proto-industrialists, as well as overseas traders and financiers. These regimes then provided secure property rights and growth-enhancing institutions for a broad cross section of society. These institutional changes created the requisite environment for new investments and technological changes and the beginning of sustained growth, which would culminate in the Commercial Revolution in the Netherlands and Britain during the seventeenth century and in the British Industrial Revolution at the end of the eighteenth century. By the nineteenth century, industry and commerce had spread to much of Western Europe (see Chapter 4; North and Thomas, 1973).

It is noteworthy that constitutional monarchies were not democracies as we understand them today. There was no one-person one-vote principle, and the distinction between the rich and the poor was quite palpable. Nevertheless these regimes emerged as responses to the demands by the merchants and industrialists. More importantly, these constitutional regimes not only reformed the political institutions of Western Europe but undertook a series of economic reforms facilitating modern capitalist growth. Internal tariffs and regulations were lifted. Entry into domestic businesses and foreign trade was greatly facilitated. For example, the process of financial development in Britain began with the founding of the Bank of England and other financial reforms.

These constitutional regimes, which emerged first in Britain and the Netherlands and then in France and other parts of Western Europe, paved the way for sustained economic growth based on property rights for a broad cross section of society, contract enforcement, the rule of law, and free entry into existing and new business lines. According to the theoretical perspective developed in earlier chapters, these improved conditions should have led to greater investments in physical capital, human capital, and technology. This is indeed what happened, and the process of modern economic growth was launched. Economic relations now relied on new businesses investing in industry, commerce, and the formation of complex organizational forms and production relations. Growth did not immediately accelerate. Economic growth was present but modest during the seventeenth and eighteenth centuries (Maddison, 2001). But these institutional changes laid the foundations for the more rapid growth that was soon to come. Financial institutions developed, the urban areas expanded further, new technologies were invented, and markets became the primary arena for transactions and competition (North and Thomas, 1973). By 1800, the process of technological change and investment had progressed so much as to be dubbed the "Industrial Revolution" (Ashton, 1969; Mokyr, 1993). The first phase of the Industrial Revolution was followed by the production of yet newer technologies, more complex organizations, greater reliance on skills and human capital in the production process, and increasing globalization of the world economy. By the second half of the nineteenth century, Western Europe had reached unprecedented growth levels.

Naturally, a complete answer to the question in the title of this subsection requires an explanation for why the constitutional regimes that were so important for modern economic growth emerged in Western Europe starting in the late sixteenth century and seventeenth century. These institutions had their roots in the late medieval aristocratic parliaments in Europe, but more importantly, they were the outcome of radical reform resulting from the change in the political balance of power in Europe starting in the sixteenth century (Ertman, 1997). The sixteenth century witnessed a major economic transformation of Europe, following the increase in international trade due to the discovery of the New World and the rounding of the Cape of Good Hope (Davis, 1973; Acemoglu, Johnson, and Robinson, 2005a). Together with increased overseas trade came greater commercial activity within Europe. These changes led to a modest increase in living standards, and more importantly, to greater economic and political power for a new group of merchants, traders, and industrialists. These new men were not the traditional allies of the European monarchies. They therefore demanded, and often were powerful enough to obtain, changes in political institutions that provided them with greater security of property rights and government action to help them in their economic endeavors. By this time, with the collapse of the feudal order, the foundations of the authoritarian regimes that were in place in the Middle Ages were already weak. Nevertheless the changes leading to the constitutional regimes did not come easy. The Dutch had to fight the Hapsburg monarchy to gain their independence as a republic. Britain had to endure its civil war and the Glorious Revolution. France had to go through the Revolution of 1789. But in all cases, the ancien regime gave way to more representative institutions, with greater checks on absolute power and greater participation by merchants, industrialists, and entrepreneurs. It was important that the social changes led to a new set of political institutions and not simply to concessions. This distinction is related to the theoretical ideas emphasized in Section 23.3 of Chapter 23: the nascent groups demanded long-term guarantees for the protection of their property rights and their participation in economic life. Such guarantees were most easily delivered by changes in political institutions, not by short-term concessions.

These changes created the set of political institutions that would then enable the emergence of the economic institutions mentioned above. The collapse of the authoritarian political regimes and the rise of the first participatory regimes then opened the way for modern economic growth.

Why Did Some Societies Manage to Benefit from New Technologies While Others Failed to Do So?

The economic takeoff started in Western Europe but quickly spread to certain other parts of the world. The chief importer of economic institutions and economic growth was the United States. The United States, founded by settler colonists who had just defeated the British crown to gain their independence and set up a smallholder society, already had participatory political institutions. This was a society built by the people who would live in it, and they were particularly willing to create checks and balances to prevent the subsequent emergence of a strong political or economic elite. This environment turned out to be a perfect conduit for modern economic growth. The lack of a strong political and economic elite meant that a broad cross section of society could take part in economic activity, import technologies from Western Europe, and then build their own technologies to quickly become the major industrial power in the world (Galenson, 1996; Engerman and Sokoloff, 1997; Keyssar, 2000; Acemoglu, Johnson, and Robinson, 2002). In the context of this example, the importance of technology adoption from the world technology frontier is in line with the emphasis in Chapter 18, while the growth-promoting effects of a lack of elite creating entry barriers is consistent with the approach in Section 23.3 in Chapter 23.

Similar processes took place in other West European offshoots, for example, in Canada. Yet in other parts of the world, adoption of new technologies and the process of economic growth came as part of a movement toward defensive modernization. Japan started its economic and political modernization with the Meiji restoration (or perhaps even before), and a central element of this modernization effort was the importation of new technologies.

However these attitudes to new technologies were by no means universal. New technologies were not adopted, but resisted, in many parts of the world. This included most of Eastern Europe—for example, Russia and Austria-Hungary—where the existing land-based elites saw new technologies as a threat both to their economic interests (because they would lead to the end of the feudal relations that still continued in this part of Europe) and to their political interests, which relied on limiting the power of new merchants and slowing down the process of peasants migrating to cities to become the new working class (see Freudenberger, 1967, and Mosse, 1992, for evidence, and Chapter 22 for a theoretical perspective). Similarly, the previously prosperous plantation economies in the Caribbean had no interest in introducing new technologies and allowing free entry by entrepreneurs. These societies continued to rely on their agricultural staples. Industrialization, competition in free labor markets, and workers investing in their human capital were seen as potential threats to the economic and political powers of the elite. The newly independent nations in Latin America were also dominated by a political elite, which continued the tradition of the colonial elite and showed little interest in industrialization. Much of Southeast Asia, the Indian subcontinent, and almost all of sub-Saharan Africa were still West European colonies and were governed under authoritarian and repressive regimes (often as producers of raw materials for the rapidly industrializing Western European nations or as sources of tribute). Free labor markets, factor mobility, creative destruction, and new technologies did not feature in the colonial political trajectories of these countries (Chapter 4).

Thus the nineteenth century was only to see the industrialization of a few select places. By the twentieth century, however, more and more nations started importing the technologies that had been developed and used in Western Europe. This process of technology transfer pulled the countries integrated into in the global economy toward higher income levels (Chapter 19). But this growth episode did not benefit all countries. Many had to wait for their independence from their colonial masters, and even then, the end of colonialism led to a period of instability and infighting among would-be elites. Once some degree of political stability was achieved and economic institutions that encourage growth were put in place, growth started. For example, growth in Australia and New Zealand was followed by that in Hong Kong, by that in South Korea, then by the rest of Southeast Asia, and finally by India. In each of these cases, as emphasized in Chapters 20 and 21, growth went hand-in-hand with structural transformations. Once the structural transformations were under way, they facilitated further growth. Consistent with the picture in Chapters 18 and 19, societies integrated into the global economy started importing technologies and achieved growth rates in line with the growth of the world technology frontier (and often exceeding those during their initial phase of catch-up). In most cases, this process meant growth for the new members of the global economy but not necessarily the disappearance of the income gap between these new members and the earlier industrializers.

Meanwhile many parts of the world continued to suffer political instability that discouraged investment in capital and new technology or even exhibited overt hostility to new technologies. These included parts of sub-Saharan Africa and, until recently, much of Central America. Returning to some of the examples discussed in Chapter 1, Nigeria and Guatemala failed to create incentives for their entrepreneurs or workers both during their colonial periods and after independence. Both these countries also experienced significant political instability and economically disastrous civil wars in the postwar era. Brazil managed to achieve some degree of growth, but it was mostly based on investment by large, heavily protected corporations and not on a sustained process of technological change and creative destruction (thus it was more similar to the oligarchic growth in terms of the model of Section 23.3 in Chapter 23). In these and other cases, policies that failed to provide secure property rights to new entrepreneurs and those that blocked the adoption of new technologies—as well as political instability and infighting among the elites—seem to have played an important role in the failure to join the world economy and its growth process. Overall, these areas fell behind the world average in the nineteenth century and continued to trail for most of the twentieth century. Many nations in sub-Saharan Africa, such as Congo, Sudan, and Zimbabwe, are still experiencing political turmoil and fail to offer even the most basic rights to their entrepreneurs and citizens. Consequently many are falling still further behind the world average.

Many Remaining Questions

The previous section provided a narrative emphasizing how technological changes transformed the world economy starting in the eighteenth century and how certain societies took advantage of these changes while others failed to do so. Parts of the story receive support from the data. The importance of industrialization to the initial takeoff is now well documented. There is a broad consensus that economic institutions protecting property rights and allowing for free entry and introduction of new technologies were important in the nineteenth century and continue to be important today in securing economic growth. There is also a general consensus that political instability, weak property rights, and lack of infrastructure are major impediments to growth in sub-Saharan Africa. Nevertheless the narrative here is speculative. These factors might be important, but they may not be the main explaination of the evolution of the world income distribution over the past 200 years. And as yet there is no consensus on the role of political institutions in this process.

Thus what I have presented here should be taken for what it is: a speculative answer that needs to be further investigated. My purpose in outlining it was not only that I suspect this answer has much truth to it but also to show how the various models developed in this book can help us better frame answers to fundamental questions of economic growth (and of economics and social sciences in general). I should add that further investigation of the causes of the world's takeoff into sustained growth and the failure of some nations to take advantage of this process is only one of the many remaining challenges. The political economy of growth is important because it enables us to ask and answer questions about the fundamental causes of economic growth. But many other aspects of the process of growth require further study. In some sense, the field of economic growth is one of the more mature areas in economics, and certainly within macroeconomics it is the area where there is broadest agreement on what types of models are useful for the study of economic dynamics and for empirical analysis. And yet there is so much that we still do not know.

I now end by mentioning a few areas with great potential for further theoretical and empirical advances. First, although here I have largely focused on factors facilitating or preventing the adoption of technologies in less-developed nations, there is still much to be done to understand the pace of technological progress in frontier economies. Our models of endogenous technological change give us the basic framework for thinking about how profit incentives shape investments in new technologies. But we still know relatively little about the industrial organization of innovation, for example, on how market structure affects economic growth. Chapters 12 and 14 highlighted how different market structures may create different incentives for technological change. But most of our understanding of these issues is qualitative. For example, in the context of the economics of innovation, we lack a framework—similar to that used for the analysis of the effects of capital and labor income taxes and indirect taxes in public finance—which could be used to analyze the effects of various regulations, IPR policies, and anticompetitive laws on innovation and economic growth. Since the pace at which the world technology frontier progresses has a direct effect on the growth of many nations, even small improvements in the environment for innovation in advanced economies could have important dividends for the rest of the world.

In addition to the industrial organization of innovation, the contractual structure of innovation needs further study. We live in a complex society in which most firms are linked to others as suppliers or downstream customers, and most firms are connected to the rest of the economy indirectly through their relationship with financial markets. These relationships are mediated by various explicit and implicit contracts. Similarly, the employment relationship that underlies the productivity of most firms relies on contractual relations between employers and employees. We know that moral hazard and holdup problems occur in these contractual relationships. But how important are they for the process of economic growth? Can improvements in contracting institutions improve innovation and technological upgrading in frontier economies? Can they also facilitate technology transfer? These are basic, but as yet, unanswered questions. The contractual foundations of economic growth are still in their infancy and require much work.

The previous section emphasized how several economies started the growth process by importing technologies and thus integrating into the global economy. Today we live in an increasingly globalized and globalizing economy. But there is still much to understand about how technology is transferred from some firms to others and from advanced economies to less-developed ones. The models I presented in Chapter 19 emphasized the importance of human capital, barriers to technology adoption, issues of appropriate technology, and contracting problems. Nevertheless most of the models are still at the qualitative level, and we lack a framework that can make quantitative predictions about the pace of technology diffusion. We have also not yet incorporated many important notions related to technology transfer into our basic frameworks. These include, among others, ideas related to tacit knowledge, appropriate technology, the workings of the international division of labor, the role of international IPR protection, and the interaction between trade and technology diffusion.

The reader will have also noticed that the material presented in Chapter 21 is much less unified and perhaps more speculative than that in the rest of the book. Although some of this reflects the fact that I had to simplify a variety of models to be able to present them in a limited space, much of it is because we are far from a satisfactory framework for understanding the process of economic development and the structural transformations that it involves. Some aspects of these structural transformations, such as the increased importance of manufacturing and then services relative to agriculture, can be viewed as a by-product of economic growth. But other aspects of this process, including financial development, changes in contract enforcement regimes, urbanization, and the amount and composition of human capital investments, may be facilitators or even preconditions for economic growth and development. Thus the lack of significant structural transformation might be an important factor in delaying or preventing economic growth. To understand these questions, we require models with stronger theoretical foundations, a systematic approach to these related issues, and a greater effort to link the models of economic development to the wealth of empirical evidence that the profession has now accumulated on economic behavior in less-developed economies.

Last but not least, given the narrative in the last section and the discussion in Chapters 4, 22, and 23, it comes as no surprise that I think many important insights about economic growth lie in political economy. But understanding politics is in many ways harder than understanding economics, because political relations are even more multifaceted. Although I believe that the political economy and growth literatures have made important advances in this area over the past decade or so, much remains to be done. The political economy of growth is in its infancy, and as we further investigate why societies make different collective choices, we will gain a better understanding of the process of economic growth.

PART IX

MATHEMATICAL APPENDIXES

A

Odds and Ends in Real Analysis and Applications to Optimization

This appendix reviews basic material from real analysis. Its main purpose is to make the book self-contained and to include explicit statements of some of the theorems that are used in the text. The material here is not meant to be a comprehensive treatment of real analysis. Accordingly, many results are stated without proof, and other important results are omitted as long as they are not referred to in the text and are not necessary for the results presented here. I state some useful results as "Facts" (often leaving their proofs as exercises). These results are typically used or referred to in the text. The more important results are stated as "Theorems."

The material here is not a substitute for a basic *Mathematics for Economists* review or textbook. An excellent book of this sort is Simon and Blume (1994), and I presume that the reader is familiar with most of the material in this or a similar book. In particular, I assume that the reader is comfortable with linear algebra, functions, relations, set theoretic language, multivariate calculus, and basic proof techniques.

To gain a deeper understanding and appreciation of the material here, the reader is encouraged to consult one of many excellent books on real analysis, functional analysis, and general topology. Some of the material here is simply a review of introductory real analysis more or less at the level of the classic books by Apostol (1975) or Rudin (1976). Some of the material, particularly that concerning topology and infinite-dimensional analysis, is more advanced and can be found in Kelley (1955), Kolmogorov and Fomin (1970), Conway (1990), Royden (1994), and Aliprantis and Border (1999). Excellent references for applications of these ideas to optimization problems include Berge (1963) and Luenberger (1969). A recent treatment of some of these topics with economic applications is presented in Ok (2007).

A.1   Distances and Metric Spaces

Throughout, X denotes a set, and $x \in X$ is a generic element of the set X. A set X can be viewed as a space or as a subset of a larger set (space) Z. I denote a subset Y of X as $Y \subset X$ (which includes the case where $Y = X$ as well as the empty set, $\emptyset$). For any $Y \subset X$, $X \backslash Y$ stands for the *complement* of Y in X, that is, $X \backslash Y = \{x : x \in X \text{ and } x \notin Y\}$.[1]

Of special importance for our purposes are two types of spaces: (1) finite-dimensional Euclidean spaces, which I denote by $X \subset \mathbb{R}^K$ ($K \in \mathbb{N}$) and (2) infinite-dimensional spaces, such as spaces of sequences or spaces of functions, which feature in discrete-time and continuous-time dynamic optimization problems. For us the most useful sets are those that are equipped with a *metric,* so that they can be treated as a *metric space.* Metric spaces play a major role in the analysis of dynamic programming problems in Chapters 6 and 16.

Definition A.1   *Let X be a nonempty set. A function $d : X \times X \rightarrow \mathbb{R}_+$ is a metric (distance function) if, for any x, y, and z in X, it satisfies the following three conditions:*

   1. *(**Properness**) $d(x, y) = 0$ if and only if $x = y$,*
   2. *(**Symmetry**) $d(x, y) = d(y, x)$, and*
   3. *(**Triangle Inequality**) $d(x, y) \leq d(x, z) + d(z, y)$.*

A nonempty set X equipped with a metric d constitutes a metric space (X, d).

In this definition, as in all mathematical definitions that follow, "if" is used instead of "if and only if," since the context makes it clearer that the notion (e.g., "metric") is being defined by the mathematical statements following it: thus "if and only if" is implicit.

The same set can be equipped with different metrics. In many cases, different metrics give equivalent results (in particular, they imply the same topological properties). When this is the case, we say that two metrics are *equivalent*, and the definition for this is given below in Definition A.4.

Example A.1   *The following are examples of metric spaces. In each case, properness and symmetry are easy to verify, but verifying that the triangle inequality holds requires some work (see Exercise A.2).*

   1. *For any $X \subset \mathbb{R}^K$, let x_i be the ith component of $x \in X$. Then the usual* Euclidean distance $d(x, y) = \left(\sum_{i=1}^{K} |x_i - y_i|^2\right)^{1/2}$ *is a metric, and thus the Euclidean space with its usual distance constitutes a metric space. It is typically referred to as the* K-dimensional Euclidean space. *Moreover, one can construct alternative metrics for Euclidean spaces that are equivalent. These metrics include the family $d_p(x, y) = \left(\sum_{i=1}^{K} |x_i - y_i|^p\right)^{1/p}$ for $1 \leq p < \infty$. An extreme element of this family, which also defines an equivalent metric on finite-dimensional Euclidean spaces, is $d_\infty(x, y) = \sup_i |x_i - y_i|$.*

   2. *For any nonempty set X, one can construct the* discrete metric, *defined as $d(x, y) = 1$ if $x \neq y$ and $d(x, y) = 0$ if $x = y$. In this case (X, d) is a* discrete space.

   3. *Let $X \subset \mathbb{R}^K$, and consider the set of continuous and bounded (real-valued) functions $f : X \rightarrow \mathbb{R}$, denoted by $\mathbf{C}(X)$. A natural metric for $\mathbf{C}(X)$ is the* sup metric $d_\infty(f, g) = \sup_{x \in X} |f(x) - g(x)|$. *Thus $(\mathbf{C}(X), d_\infty)$ is a metric space. The same metric can be used for the set of bounded (but not necessarily continuous) functions $\mathbf{B}(X)$, leading to the metric space $(\mathbf{B}(X), d_\infty)$.*

---

1. Throughout the appendixes I simplify the notation by using $=$ for definitions instead of $\equiv$.

4. Let $\ell \subset \mathbb{R}^\infty$ be a set consisting of infinite sequences of real numbers. For example, $x = (x_1, x_2, x_3, \ldots)$ would be a typical element of ℓ, provided that $x_i \in \mathbb{R}$ for each $i = 1, 2, \ldots$. A family of metrics for this set is given by $d_p(x, y) = \left(\sum_{i=1}^\infty |x_i - y_i|^p\right)^{1/p}$ for $1 \leq p < \infty$ (provided that $\left(\sum_{i=1}^\infty |x_i|^p\right)^{1/p} < \infty$ for all $x \in \ell$) or by $d_\infty(x, y) = \sup_i |x_i - y_i|$ (provided that $\sup_i |x_i| < \infty$ for all $x \in \ell$). For any $p \in [1, \infty]$, (ℓ, d_p) is a metric space, sometimes denoted by ℓ_p.

Metric spaces enable us to define neighborhoods and open sets, which are the building blocks of mathematical analysis and are essential in the study of optimization problems.

Definition A.2 *Let (X, d) be a metric space and $\varepsilon > 0$ be a real number. Then for any $x \in X$,*

$$\mathcal{N}_\varepsilon(x) = \{y \in X : d(x, y) < \varepsilon\}$$

is the ε-neighborhood of x.

Example A.2 *In the simplest case where $X \subset \mathbb{R}$ and $x \in X$, $d(x, y) = |x - y|$, $\mathcal{N}_\varepsilon(x) = (x - \varepsilon, x + \varepsilon) \cap X$.*

Definition A.3 *Let (X, d) be a metric space. Then $Y \subset X$ is* open *in X if for each $y \in Y$, there exists $\varepsilon > 0$ such that $\mathcal{N}_\varepsilon(y) \subset Y$; $Z \subset X$ is* closed *in X if $X \backslash Z$ is open in X.*

The *closure* of a set Y in X is $\overline{Y} = \{y \in X : \text{for each } \varepsilon > 0, \mathcal{N}_\varepsilon(y) \cap Y \neq \emptyset\}$, that is, every neighborhood of each point in $\overline{Y}$ contains at least one point of Y. Clearly, $Y \subset \overline{Y}$. Moreover if Y is closed, then $Y = \overline{Y}$. The *interior* of a set Y in X can then be defined as Int $Y = Y \backslash \overline{(X \backslash Y)}$. If Y is an open subset of X, then $\overline{(X \backslash Y)} = X \backslash Y$, and therefore Int $Y = Y$.

Example A.3 *Again in the simplest case where $X = [0, 1]$ and $d(x, y) = |x - y|$, for any $x \in (0, 1)$ and $\varepsilon > 0$ sufficiently small, $(x - \varepsilon, x + \varepsilon)$ is open in X, whereas the set $[0, 1] \backslash (x - \varepsilon, x + \varepsilon) = [0, x - \varepsilon] \cup [x + \varepsilon, 1]$ is closed in X. Also, Int$(x - \varepsilon, x + \varepsilon) = (x - \varepsilon, x + \varepsilon)$, Int$([0, 1] \backslash (x - \varepsilon, x + \varepsilon)) = (0, x - \varepsilon) \cup (x + \varepsilon, 1)$, $\overline{(x - \varepsilon, x + \varepsilon)} = [x - \varepsilon, x + \varepsilon]$, and $\overline{[0, 1] \backslash (x - \varepsilon, x + \varepsilon)} = [0, x - \varepsilon] \cup [x + \varepsilon, 1]$.*

Fact A.1 *Let (X, d) be a metric space. The sets X and $\emptyset$ are both open and closed sets.*

The importance of the following theorem will become clear once we turn to the somewhat more abstract topological characterization of closed and open sets. Let $\{X_\alpha\}_{\alpha \in A}$ denote a *collection of sets* in X (meaning that $X_\alpha \subset X$ for each $\alpha \in A$ and A is an arbitrary set). If A has a countable [finite] number of elements, then $\{X_\alpha\}_{\alpha \in A}$ is a countable [finite] collection of sets. Let us also use X_α^c to denote the complement of X_α in X (i.e., $X_\alpha^c = X \backslash X_\alpha$).

Theorem A.1 (Properties of Open and Closed Sets) *Let (X, d) be a metric space and $\{X_\alpha\}_{\alpha \in A}$ be a collection of sets with $X_\alpha \subset X$ for all $\alpha \in A$.*

1. *If each X_α is open in X, then $\bigcup_{\alpha \in A} X_\alpha$ is open.*
2. *If each X_α is open in X and $\{X_\alpha\}_{\alpha \in A}$ is a finite collection of sets (i.e., A is finite), then $\bigcap_{\alpha \in A} X_\alpha$ is open.*
3. *If each X_α is closed in X, then $\bigcap_{\alpha \in A} X_\alpha$ is closed.*
4. *If each X_α is closed in X and $\{X_\alpha\}_{\alpha \in A}$ is a finite collection of sets, then $\bigcup_{\alpha \in A} X_\alpha$ is closed.*

Proof. (**Part 1**) Let $\{X_\alpha\}_{\alpha \in A}$ be an arbitrary collection of open sets in X. If $\bigcup_{\alpha \in A} X_\alpha$ is empty, then it is open by Fact A.1. If it is nonempty, then for each $x \in \bigcup_{\alpha \in A} X_\alpha$, it must be the case that $x \in X_{\alpha'}$ for some $\alpha' \in A$. Since $X_{\alpha'}$ is open, there exists $\varepsilon > 0$ such that $\mathcal{N}_\varepsilon(x) \subset X_{\alpha'} \subset \bigcup_{\alpha \in A} X_\alpha$, establishing that for each $x \in \bigcup_{\alpha \in A} X_\alpha$ there exists an ε-neighborhood of x in $\bigcup_{\alpha \in A} X_\alpha$, so that $\bigcup_{\alpha \in A} X_\alpha$ is open.

(Part 2) Let $\{X_\alpha\}_{\alpha \in A}$ be a finite collection of open sets in X (enumerated by $\alpha = 1, 2, \ldots, N$). Once again, if $\bigcap_{\alpha \in A} X_\alpha$ is empty, then it is open by Fact A.1. If it is nonempty, then for each $x \in \bigcap_{\alpha \in A} X_\alpha$, $x \in X_\alpha$ for $\alpha = 1, 2, \ldots, N$. Since X_α is open, then by definition there exists $\varepsilon_\alpha > 0$ such that $\mathcal{N}_{\varepsilon_\alpha}(x) \subset X_\alpha$ for each $\alpha = 1, 2, \ldots, N$. Let $\varepsilon = \min\{\varepsilon_1, \varepsilon_2, \ldots, \varepsilon_N\}$. Clearly, $\varepsilon > 0$. Moreover by construction, $\mathcal{N}_\varepsilon(x) \subset \mathcal{N}_{\varepsilon_\alpha}(x) \subset X_\alpha$ for each $\alpha = 1, 2, \ldots, N$. Therefore $\mathcal{N}_\varepsilon(x) \subset \bigcap_{\alpha \in A} X_\alpha$, proving the claim.

(Parts 3 and 4) These follow immediately from De Morgan's Law, which states that

$$\left(\bigcup_{\alpha \in A} X_\alpha \right)^c = \bigcap_{\alpha \in A} X_\alpha^c. \quad \blacksquare$$

The restriction to finite collections is important in Part 2 of Theorem A.1. Consider the following example.

Example A.4 *Let $X = \mathbb{R}$, with the Euclidean metric $d(x, y) = |x - y|$. Take the subsets $X_\alpha = (0, 1 + \alpha^{-1})$ of X for $\alpha \in \mathbb{N}$, and consider the infinite intersection $\bigcap_{\alpha \in \mathbb{N}} X_\alpha$. It can be verified that $\bigcap_{\alpha \in \mathbb{N}} X_\alpha = (0, 1]$, which is not an open set. An even simpler example is the subsets $X_\alpha = (-1/\alpha, 1/\alpha)$, where $\bigcap_{\alpha \in \mathbb{N}} X_\alpha = \{0\}$, which is not open.*

Definition A.4 *Two metrics d and d' defined on X are* equivalent *if they both generate the same collection of open sets in X. Alternatively, let $\mathcal{N}_\varepsilon$ and $\mathcal{N}'_\varepsilon$ refer to neighborhoods defined by these metrics. Two metrics are equivalent if for each $x \in X$ and $\varepsilon > 0$, there exists $\delta > 0$ and $\delta' > 0$ such that $\mathcal{N}'_\varepsilon(x) \subset \mathcal{N}_\delta(x)$ and $\mathcal{N}_\varepsilon(x) \subset \mathcal{N}'_{\delta'}(x)$.*

Exercise A.4 verifies that the two parts of Definition A.4 imply each other.

Definition A.5 *Let (X, d) be a metric space. Then $Y \subset X$ is* bounded *if there exists $x \in X$ and $\delta \in (0, +\infty)$ such that $Y \subset \mathcal{N}_\delta(x)$. If $Y \subset X$ is not bounded, then it is* unbounded.

Example A.5 *Let $X = \mathbb{R}$ and $d(x, y) = |x - y|$. The subsets $(0, 1)$ and $[0, 1]$ of $\mathbb{R}$ are bounded, while the subset $\mathbb{R}_+ = [0, \infty)$ of $\mathbb{R}$ is unbounded.*

A.2 Mappings, Functions, Sequences, Nets, and Continuity

A *mapping* ϕ from X to Y is a subset of $X \times Y$ such that for each $x \in X$, there exists some $y \in Y$ with $(x, y) \in \phi$. As customary, I denote this mapping by $\phi : X \to Y$. Throughout the book $\phi : X \to Y$ implies that $\phi(x)$ is defined for each $x \in X$. I have also adopted the convention that ϕ assigns a single element of the set Y to $x \in X$, and thus I write $\phi(x)$ as an element of Y, that is, $\phi(x) \in Y$ (and in terms of the definition above, if $(x, y) \in \phi$ and $(x, z) \in \phi$, then $y = z$). This is without loss of generality, since the space Y is not restricted. For example, for a set Z, we could specify $Y = \mathcal{P}(Z)$ (recall that $\mathcal{P}(Z)$ denotes the set of all subsets of Z). In this case, an element of Y would be a subset of Z. Thus one can alternatively write that for $x \in X$, $\phi(x) \in Y$ or $\phi(x) \subset Z$. I also use the notation $\phi(X')$ for some $X' \subset X$ to designate the *image* of the set X', defined as

$$\phi(X') = \big\{ y \in Y : \exists x \in X' \text{ with } \phi(x) = y \big\}.$$

For a mapping $\phi : X \to Y$, X is also referred to as the *domain* of ϕ, while Y is its *range*. One might want to reserve the term "range" to $Y' \subset Y$ such that $Y' = \phi(X)$. For our purposes here, this distinction is not important.

The notation ϕ^{-1} is standard to denote the inverse of the mapping ϕ. Notice that ϕ^{-1} may not be single valued, even if ϕ is, since more than one x in X can have the same image in Y. For $Y' \subset Y$, let

$$\phi^{-1}(Y') = \left\{ x \in X : \exists y \in Y' \text{ with } \phi(x) = y \right\}.$$

By a *function* f I typically refer to a *real-valued* mapping (i.e., $f : X \to \mathbb{R}$ for some arbitrary set X). I use lowercased letters to refer to functions. I use the term "correspondence" to refer to a set-valued mapping (i.e., $F : X \to \mathcal{P}(Z)$ for some set Z). Thus the mapping F assigns a subset of Z to each element of x. I use uppercased letters to refer to correspondences. Since they play an important role below, the following common notation is used for correspondences: $F : X \rightrightarrows Z$. When the range of the correspondence is the real numbers, then we naturally have $F : X \rightrightarrows \mathbb{R}$.

Definition A.6 *Let (X, d) be a metric space. A sequence, denoted by $\{x_n\}_{n=1}^{\infty}$ (or simply by $\{x_n\}$), is a mapping ϕ with the domain given by the natural numbers $\mathbb{N}$ and the range given by X.*

The domain of the mapping ϕ that defines the sequence is $\mathbb{N}$, so that $\{x_n\}_{n=1}^{\infty}$ is a countable (infinite) sequence. One can easily generalize the notion of a sequence to that of *nets*, which are useful in continuous-time optimization. Let A be a *directed set* if there exists a reflexive and transitive relation $\succeq$ such that for any $a_1, a_2 \in A$, there exists $a \in A$ with $a \succeq a_1$ and $a \succeq a_2$. For example, the real numbers form a directed set with the "greater than or equal to" relation ($\geq$).

Definition A.7 *Let (X, d) be a metric space and A be a directed set. A net, denoted by $\{x_\alpha\}_{\alpha \in A}$, is a mapping with the domain given by A and the range given by X.*

When sequences and nets have real numbers as elements, the underlying metric space is $(\mathbb{R}, d)$, with d referring to the usual Euclidean metric $d(x, y) = |x - y| = \sqrt{|x - y|^2}$.

Example A.6 $\{x_n\}_{n=1}^{\infty}$ *such that* $x_n = 1/n$ *for each* $n \in \mathbb{N}$ *is a sequence, while* $\{x_\alpha\}_{\alpha \in A}$ $x_\alpha = 1/\alpha$ *for each* $\alpha \in (0, 1]$ *is a net.*

Definition A.8 *Consider the sequence $\{n_k\}_{k=1}^{\infty}$ of positive increasing natural numbers (such that $n_k > n_{k'}$ when $k > k'$). Then for a given sequence $\{x_n\}_{n=1}^{\infty}$, $\{x_{n_k}\}$ is a subsequence of $\{x_n\}_{n=1}^{\infty}$.*

A subnet can be defined in a similar manner.

Definition A.9 *Let (X, d) be a metric space. A sequence $\{x_n\}_{n=1}^{\infty}$ in X is* convergent *and has the* limit point *$x \in X$ if for every $\varepsilon > 0$, there exists $N(\varepsilon) \in \mathbb{N}$ such that $n \geq N(\varepsilon)$ implies $d(x_n, x) < \varepsilon$. We write this as $\lim_{n \to \infty} x_n = \lim x_n = x$ or simply as $\{x_n\}_{n=1}^{\infty} \to x$.*

Definition A.10 *Let $\{x_\alpha\}_{\alpha \in A}$ be a net in a metric space (X, d). Then, $\{x_\alpha\}_{\alpha \in A}$ is* convergent *and has* limit point *x if for each $\varepsilon > 0$, there exists $\bar{\alpha}$ such that for all $\alpha \geq \bar{\alpha}$, $x_\alpha \in \mathcal{N}_\varepsilon(x)$.*

Fact A.2 *If a sequence $\{x_n\}_{n=1}^{\infty}$ or a net $\{x_\alpha\}_{\alpha \in A}$ in a metric space X is convergent, then it has a unique limit point $x \in X$.*

Proof. See Exercise A.6. ∎

Fact A.3 $\{x_n\}_{n=1}^{\infty}$ *in X is convergent if and only if every subsequence of $\{x_n\}_{n=1}^{\infty}$ in X is convergent.*

Proof. See Exercise A.7. ∎

Example A.7   *Note, however, that convergence of a subsequence (or a subnet) does not guarantee convergence of the original sequence. Consider the sequence $\{x_n\}_{n=1}^{\infty}$ such that $x_n = (-1)^n$. Clearly, this sequence is not convergent. But picking $\{n_k\}_{n=1}^{\infty}$ as the even natural numbers, we construct a convergent subsequence $\{x_{n_k}\}$ with limit point 1.*

Let $\bar{\mathbb{R}}$ denote the *extended real numbers,* that is, $\bar{\mathbb{R}} = \mathbb{R} \cup \{-\infty\} \cup \{+\infty\}$. It is straightforward to verify that $(\bar{\mathbb{R}}, \bar{d})$ is a metric space, where $\bar{d}(x, y) = d(x, y)/(1 + d(x, y))$, with $d(x, y)$ denoting the standard Euclidean metric now allowed to take infinite values (with the convention that $\bar{d}(x, y) = 1$ if $d(x, y) = \infty$).

Fact A.4   *Let $\{x_n\}$ be a sequence or net in $\bar{\mathbb{R}}$ (equipped with the metric $\bar{d}$). If $\{x_n\}$ is monotone (nondecreasing or nonincreasing), then it is convergent.*

Proof.   See Exercise A.8.   ∎

Definition A.11   *Let $X \subset \mathbb{R}$. Then the supremum of X, denoted by $\sup X$, is the smallest $\bar{x} \in \bar{\mathbb{R}}$ such that $\bar{x} \geq x$ for all $x \in X$. If there does not exist $\bar{x} \in \mathbb{R}$ for which this is true, then clearly $\sup X = \infty$. Similarly, the infimum of X, denoted by $\inf X$, is the greatest $\underline{x}$ such that $\underline{x} \leq x$ for all $x \in X$, where again $\underline{x} = -\infty$ is allowed. If $\bar{x} = \sup X \in X$, then we refer to $\bar{x}$ as the maximum of X and denote it by $\bar{x} = \max X$. Similarly, if $\underline{x} = \inf X \in X$, then $\underline{x}$ is the minimum of X and is denoted by $\underline{x} = \min X$.*

Since X itself can be taken to be a sequence of numbers, supremum and infimum can be defined for sequences. In particular, for $\{x_n\}_{n=1}^{\infty}$ in $\mathbb{R}$, construct the sequences $\{x_n'\}_{n=1}^{\infty}$ and $\{x_n''\}_{n=1}^{\infty}$ such that $x_n' = \sup_{k \geq n}\{x_k\}$ and $x_n'' = \inf_{k \geq n}\{x_k\}$. Clearly $\{x_n'\}_{n=1}^{\infty}$ is monotone (nonincreasing) and $\{x_n''\}_{n=1}^{\infty}$ is monotone (nondecreasing). Therefore, by Fact A.4, $\lim_{n \to \infty} x_n'$ exists. Let us denote it by $\limsup x_n$, and also $\lim_{n \to \infty} x_n''$ exists and is denoted by $\liminf x_n$. The same construction works with nets.

Fact A.5   *Let $\{x_n\}$ be a sequence or net in $\bar{\mathbb{R}}$.*

1. $\inf_n x_n$, $\liminf x_n$, $\limsup x_n$, and $\sup_n x_n$ exist and satisfy

$$\inf_n x_n \leq \liminf x_n \leq \limsup x_n \leq \sup_n x_n.$$

2. $\{x_n\}$ is convergent if and only if

$$\liminf x_n = \limsup x_n,$$

and in this case, both of these are denoted as $\lim x_n = x$.

3. Let $\{y_n\}$ be such that $x_n \leq y_n$ for all n. Then

$$\liminf x_n \leq \liminf y_n, \quad \text{and} \quad \limsup x_n \leq \limsup y_n,$$

and moreover if the limits exist,

$$\lim x_n \leq \lim y_n.$$

4. If $\lim x_n y_n = 0$, then

$$\lim x_n |y_n| = \lim |x_n| y_n = \lim |x_n| |y_n| = 0.$$

Moreover either $\lim x_n = 0$ or $\lim y_n = 0$.

5. *Then*

$$\liminf(x_n + y_n) \geq \liminf x_n + \liminf y_n$$

$$\liminf(x_n - y_n) \geq \liminf x_n - \limsup y_n.$$

Proof. See Exercise A.12. ∎

The following two facts are also useful.

Fact A.6 *Let $\{x_n\}$ be a sequence or net in $\bar{\mathbb{R}}$. If all convergent subsequences or subnets $\{x_{n_k}\}$ have the same limit point $x^* \in \bar{\mathbb{R}}$, then $\{x_n\}$ also converges to x^*.*

Proof. If all convergent subsequences or subnets have the same limit point x^*, then $\liminf x_n = \limsup x_n = x^*$, so the result follows from Fact A.5(2). ∎

Fact A.7 *Let $\{x_n\}$ be a sequence in $\mathbb{R}$, and define the sequence $\{y_n\}$ by $y_n = \sum_{j=0}^{n} z_n$. We say that $\{y_n\}$ is absolutely convergent if $\{\bar{y}_n\} = \sum_{j=0}^{n} |z_n|$ converges to some $\bar{y}^* \in \mathbb{R}$. If $\{y_n\}$ is absolutely convergent, then it is also convergent; that is, there exists $y^* \in \mathbb{R}$ such that $\{y_n\} \to y^*$.*

Definition A.12 *Let (X, d) be a metric space. A sequence $\{x_n\}_{n=1}^{\infty}$ in X is a Cauchy sequence if for each $\varepsilon > 0$, there exists $M(\varepsilon) \in \mathbb{N}$ such that for any $n, m \geq M(\varepsilon)$, $d(x_n, x_m) < \varepsilon$.*

Lemma A.1 *Let (X, d) be a metric space and $\{x_n\}_{n=1}^{\infty}$ be a convergent sequence in X. Then it is a Cauchy sequence.*

Proof. Fix $\varepsilon > 0$. Since $\{x_n\}_{n=1}^{\infty}$ is convergent, $\lim_{n \to \infty} x_n = x$ exists. Then by the triangle inequality, for any x_n, x_m,

$$d(x_n, x_m) \leq d(x_n, x) + d(x_m, x). \tag{A.1}$$

Since $\lim_{n \to \infty} x_n = x$, by Definition A.9 there exists $M(\varepsilon)$ such that for any $n \geq M(\varepsilon)$, $d(x_n, x) < \varepsilon/2$. Combining this result with (A.1) implies that $d(x_n, x_m) < \varepsilon$, establishing the desired result. ∎

The converse of this lemma is not true, as illustrated by the following example.

Example A.8 *Let $X = (0, 1]$ and $d(x, y) = |x - y|$. Consider the sequence $x_n = 1/n$. This is clearly Cauchy, but does not converge to any point in X and thus is not convergent.*

Definition A.13 *A metric space (X, d) is complete if every Cauchy sequence in (X, d) is convergent.*

Examples of complete spaces include any closed subset of the Euclidean space and the metric space of continuous bounded (real-valued) functions with the sup metric, $(\mathbf{C}(X), d_\infty)$, introduced in Example A.1 (see Exercise A.9). The importance of complete metric spaces is illustrated by the Contraction Mapping Theorem (Theorem 6.7) which was presented in Section 6.4. The following fact is straightforward.

Fact A.8 *Let (X, d) be a complete metric space. A closed subset X' of X is also complete.*

I now briefly discuss continuity of mappings and functions in metric spaces.

Definition A.14 *Let (X, d_X) and (Y, d_Y) be metric spaces, and consider a mapping $\phi : X \to Y$. ϕ is continuous at $x \in X$ if for every $\varepsilon > 0$, there exists $\delta > 0$ such that when $d_X(x, x') < \delta$, then $d_Y(\phi(x), \phi(x')) < \varepsilon$. ϕ is continuous on X if it is continuous at each $x \in X$.*

Fact A.9 *Equivalently, ϕ is continuous at x if for all $\{x_n\}_{n=1}^{\infty} \to x$, $\{\phi(x_n)\}_{n=1}^{\infty} \to \phi(x)$.*

Fact A.10 *Let (X, d_X), (Y, d_Y), and (Z, d_Z) be metric spaces, and consider the mappings $\phi : X \to Y$ and $\gamma : Y \to Z$. If ϕ is continuous at x' and γ is continuous at $\phi(x')$, then $\gamma \circ \phi = \gamma(\phi(x))$ is continuous at x'.*

Proof. See Exercise A.13. ■

Similarly, sums and products of continuous functions are continuous, and ratios of real-valued continuous functions are continuous as long as the denominator is not equal to zero.

The following is an important theorem in its own right and also motivates the somewhat more general treatment of continuity in the next section.

Theorem A.2 (Open Sets and Continuity I) *Let (X, d_X) and (Y, d_Y) be metric spaces and consider the mapping $\phi : X \to Y$. ϕ is continuous if and only if for every $Y' \subset Y$ that is open in Y, $\phi^{-1}(Y')$ is open in X.*

Proof. ($\Longrightarrow$) Suppose that ϕ is continuous and Y' is open in Y. Then take any $x \in \phi^{-1}(Y')$. Since Y' is open, there exists $\varepsilon > 0$ such that $d_Y(\phi(x), y) < \varepsilon$ implies $y \in Y'$. Since ϕ is continuous at x, for the same $\varepsilon > 0$ there exists $\delta > 0$ such that for all x' with $d_X(x, x') < \delta$, $d_Y(\phi(x), \phi(x')) < \varepsilon$. Thus $\phi(x') \in Y'$ and so $\phi^{-1}(Y')$ is open in X.

($\Longleftarrow$) Suppose that $\phi^{-1}(Y')$ is open in X for every open Y' in Y. For given $\varepsilon > 0$ and $x \in X$, let $Y' = \mathcal{N}_\varepsilon(\phi(x))$ (i.e., $Y' = \{y \in Y : d_Y(\phi(x), y) < \varepsilon\}$), which is clearly an open set, and thus $\phi^{-1}(Y')$ is open in X. Therefore there exists $\delta > 0$ such that $x' \in \phi^{-1}(Y')$ when $d_X(x, x') < \delta$. Next $x' \in \phi^{-1}(Y')$ implies that $\phi(x') \in Y'$, so that $d_Y(\phi(x), \phi(x')) < \varepsilon$, completing the proof.

■

Theorem A.3 (Intermediate Value Theorem) *Let $f : [a, b] \to \mathbb{R}$ be a continuous function. Suppose that $f(a) \neq f(b)$. Then for c intermediate between $f(a)$ and $f(b)$ (e.g., $c \in (f(a), f(b))$ if $f(a) < f(b)$), there exists $x^* \in (a, b)$ such that $f(x^*) = c$.*

Proof. The image of the interval $[a, b]$ under the continuous function f, $f([a, b])$, is connected, in the sense that the set $f([a, b])$ cannot be the union of two disjoint open sets W, W' (i.e., $f([a, b]) \neq W \cup W'$ for any W, W' open and satisfying $W \cap W' = \emptyset$). Suppose not. Then there would exist two disjoint open sets V and V' such that $f([a, b]) \subset V \cup V'$. But from Theorem A.2, this implies that $f^{-1}(V)$ and $f^{-1}(V')$ are open in $[a, b]$, and by the fact that $f([a, b]) \subset V \cup V'$, we have $[a, b] \subset f^{-1}(V) \cup f^{-1}(V')$, which implies that $[a, b]$ is not connected. This yields a contradiction. Theorem A.3 then follows immediately, since $f([a, b])$ is connected and thus includes any value between $f(a)$ and $f(b)$. ■

The Intermediate Value Theorem is the simplest "fixed point theorem" that economists use (see Theorems A.18 and A.19 below for more general fixed point theorems). Fixed point theorems provide conditions such that given a mapping $\phi : X \to X$, there exists $x^* \in X$ with $x^* = \phi(x^*)$. The usefulness of this construction stems from the fact that many equilibrium problems can be formulated as fixed point problems. It is also clear that a fixed point is simply a "zero" of a slightly different mapping. In particular, define $\tilde{\phi}(x) = \phi(x) - x$. Then a fixed point of ϕ corresponds to a zero of $\tilde{\phi}$. Perhaps the most useful application of the Intermediate Value Theorem is for the case in which $\tilde{\phi}(a) < 0$ and $\tilde{\phi}(b) > 0$ (or $\tilde{\phi}(a) > 0$ and $\tilde{\phi}(b) < 0$). In this case, the theorem states that the continuous function $\tilde{\phi}$ has a "zero" over the interval $[a, b]$; that is, there exists some value $x^* \in (a, b)$ such that $\tilde{\phi}(x^*) = 0$. Thus ϕ has a fixed point.

A.3   A Minimal Amount of Topology: Continuity and Compactness *

Theorem A.2 implies that only the structure of open sets is relevant for thinking about the continuity of mappings. This motivates our brief introduction to topology. Topology is the study of open sets and their properties. Our main interest in introducing notions from topology is to be able to talk about *compactness*. While compactness can be discussed just using ideas from metric spaces, for some of the results on infinite-dimensional (dynamic) optimization, a slightly more general treatment of compactness is necessary.

Definition A.15   *A* topology *$\tau = \{V_\alpha\}_{\alpha \in A}$ on a nonempty set X is a collection of subsets $\{V_\alpha\}_{\alpha \in A}$ of X, such that*

1. *$\emptyset \in \tau$, and $X \in \tau$;*
2. *for any $A' \subset A$, $\bigcup_{\alpha \in A'} V_\alpha$ is in τ; and*
3. *for any finite $A' \subset A$, $\bigcap_{\alpha \in A'} V_\alpha$ is in τ.*

Given a topology τ on X, V is an open *set in X if $V \in \tau$ and it is a* closed *set in X if $X \backslash V \in \tau$. The pair (X, τ) is a* topological space.

The parallel between this definition and the properties of unions and intersections of open sets given in Theorem A.1 is obvious. Sometimes it is convenient to describe a topology not by all of the open sets but in a more economical fashion. Two convenient ways of doing this are as follows. First, a topological space can be derived from a metric space. In particular, since a topological space (X, τ) is defined by a collection of open sets and a metric space (X, d) defines the collection of open sets in the space X, it also defines a topological space with the topology *induced* by the metric d. Second, instead of the collection of all open sets, a topological space can be described by a smaller collection of sets, called a *base*.

Definition A.16   *Given a topological space (X, τ), $\{W_\alpha\}_{\alpha \in A'}$ is a* base *for (X, τ) if for every $V \in \tau$, there exist $A'' \subset A'$ such that $V = \bigcup_{\alpha \in A''} W_\alpha$.*

If $\{W_\alpha\}_{\alpha \in A'}$ is a base for (X, τ), we say that τ is *generated* by $\{W_\alpha\}_{\alpha \in A'}$.

Example A.9

1. *For any $X \subset \mathbb{R}^K$, define a collection of open sets (in the sense of Definition A.3) according to the family of metrics $d_p(x, y) = \left(\sum_{i=1}^K |x_i - y_i|^p \right)^{1/p}$ for $1 \leq p < \infty$ and $d_\infty(x, y) = \max_{i=1,\dots,K} |x_i - y_i|$ denoted by τ_p for $p \in [1, \infty]$. Then (X, τ_p) is a topological space. The pair (X, τ_2) is sometimes referred to as the* Euclidean topology, *though since the other metrics are also equivalent (Exercise A.11), it would not be wrong to refer to any (X, τ_p) as the "Euclidean topology."*

2. *For any nonempty set X, the* discrete topology *is defined equivalently either by the discrete metric in Example A.1 or by declaring all subsets of X as open sets.*

3. *The* indiscrete topology *τ' on X has only $\emptyset$ and X as open sets.*

4. *Consider the $(\mathbf{C}(X), d_\infty)$ metric space of all continuous, bounded, real-valued functions with the sup metric. Define the collection of open sets on $\mathbf{C}(X)$ according to d_∞ by τ_∞. Then $(\mathbf{C}(X), \tau_\infty)$ is a topological space.*

5. *Consider the set of infinite sequences of real numbers $\ell \subset \mathbb{R}^\infty$ and the family of metrics for this set given by $d_p(x, y) = \left(\sum_{i=1}^\infty |x_i - y_i|^p \right)^{1/p}$ for $1 \leq p < \infty$ and by $d_\infty(x, y) = \sup_i |x_i - y_i|$ (again provided that $\left(\sum_{i=1}^\infty |x_i|^p \right)^{1/p} < \infty$ for all $x \in \ell$ in the first case and $\sup_i |x_i| < \infty$ in the second case). For any $p \in [1, \infty]$, d_p defines*

a topology τ_p, and (ℓ, τ_p) is a topological space, which is sometimes denoted by the same symbol as the corresponding metric space ℓ_p.

As suggested by this example, many topological spaces of interest are derived from a metric space. In this case, we say that they are *metrizable* and for all practical purposes, we can treat metrizable topological spaces as metric spaces.

Definition A.17 *A topological space (X, τ) is* metrizable *if there exists a metric d on X such that when $V \in \tau$, then V is also open in the metric space (X, d) (according to Definition A.3).*

Fact A.11 *If a topological space (X, τ) is metrizable with some metric d, then it defines the same notions of convergence and continuity as the metric space (X, d).*

Proof. This follows immediately from the fact that (X, τ) and (X, d) have the same open sets. ∎

Not all general topological spaces have the nice properties of metric spaces. Fortunately, this is not an issue for the properties of topological spaces that are related to continuity and compactness, which we focus on here. Nevertheless it is useful to note that a particularly relevant property of general topological spaces is the *Hausdorff* property, which requires that any distinct points x and y of a topological space (X, τ) should be separated; that is, in a topological space with the Hausdorff property, there exist V_x, $V_y \in \tau$ such that $x \in V_x$, $y \in V_y$ and $V_x \cap V_y = \emptyset$. It is clear that every metric space has the Hausdorff property (see Exercise A.14). For our purposes, the Hausdorff property is not necessary.

Returning to general topological spaces, the notions of convergence of sequences, subsequences, nets, and subnets can be stated for general topological spaces. Here I only give the definitions for convergence of sequences and nets (those for subsequences and subnets are defined similarly).

Definition A.18 *Let (X, τ) be a topological space. A sequence $\{x_n\}_{n=1}^{\infty}$ [a net $\{x_\alpha\}_{\alpha \in A}$] in X is* convergent *and has* limit point $x \in X$ *if for each $V \in \tau$ with $x \in V$, there exists $N \in \mathbb{N}$ [there exists some $\bar{\alpha} \in A$] such that $x_n \in V$ for all $n \geq N$ [$x_\alpha \in V$ for all $\alpha \geq \bar{\alpha}$]. We write this as $\lim_{n \to \infty} x_n = \lim x_n = x$ or as $\{x_n\}_{n=1}^{\infty} \to x$.*

Continuity is defined in a similar manner.

Definition A.19 *Let (X, τ_X) and (Y, τ_Y) be topological spaces, and consider the mapping $\phi : X \to Y$. ϕ is* continuous at $x \in X$ *if for every $U \in \tau_Y$ with $\phi(x) \in U$, there exists $V \in \tau_X$ with $x \in V$ such that $\phi(V) \subset U$. ϕ is* continuous on X *if it is continuous at each $x \in X$.*

The parallel between this definition and the equivalent characterization of continuity in metric spaces in Definition A.14 is evident. This leads to the following theorem.

Theorem A.4 (Open Sets and Continuity II) *Let (X, τ_X) and (Y, τ_Y) be topological spaces, and consider the mapping $\phi : X \to Y$. ϕ is continuous if and only if for every $Y' \subset Y$ that is open in Y, $\phi^{-1}(Y')$ is open in X.*

The proof of this theorem is identical to that of Theorem A.2 and is thus omitted.

In general topological spaces, convergence in terms of sequences is not sufficient to characterize continuity, but convergence in terms of nets is.

Theorem A.5 (Continuity and Convergence of Nets) *Let (X, τ_X) and (Y, τ_Y) be topological spaces. The mapping $\phi : X \to Y$ is continuous at $x \in X$ if and only if $\{\phi(x_\alpha)\}_{\alpha \in A} \to \phi(x)$ for any net $\{x_\alpha\}_{\alpha \in A} \to x$.*

Proof. ($\Longrightarrow$) Suppose ϕ is continuous at x, and consider a net $\{x_\alpha\}_{\alpha \in A} \to x$. Take $U \in \tau_Y$, with $\phi(x) \in U$, $\phi^{-1}(U) \in \tau_X$, and $x \in \phi^{-1}(U)$. Therefore for some $\bar\alpha \in A$, we have that $\alpha \geq \bar\alpha$ implies that $x_\alpha \in \phi^{-1}(U)$, and thus $\phi(x_\alpha) \in U$ for all $\alpha \geq \bar\alpha$, establishing $\{\phi(x_\alpha)\}_{\alpha \in A} \to \phi(x)$.

($\Longleftarrow$) Suppose that ϕ is not continuous at x. Then there exists $U \in \tau_Y$, with $\phi(x) \in U$ such that $\phi^{-1}(U) \notin \tau_X$. Let $V = \mathcal{N}(x)$ denote a neighborhood x in X, that is, $V \in \tau_X$, with $x \in V$. Since there exists $U \in \tau_Y$ such that $\phi(x) \in U$ and $\phi^{-1}(U) \notin \tau_X$, for each $V \in \mathcal{N}(x)$ there exists $x_V \in V$ such that $\phi(x_V) \notin U$. Order the Vs in $\mathcal{N}(x)$ by inclusion (i.e., $V' \geq V$ if and only if $V' \subset V$). Then by construction, $\{x_V\}_{V \in \mathcal{N}(x)}$ is a net converging to x, but $\{\phi(x_V)\}_{V \in \mathcal{N}(x)} \not\to \phi(x)$, completing the proof. ∎

Fact A.12 *Consider a function $f : X \to \mathbb{R}$, and suppose that X is endowed with the discrete topology. Then f is continuous.*

Proof. This result immediately follows from the fact that any subset X' of X is open in X according to the discrete topology. ∎

Definition A.20 *Let (X, τ) be a topological space with $\tau = \{V_\alpha\}_{\alpha \in A}$ and $X' \subset X$. A collection of open sets $\{V_\alpha\}_{\alpha \in A'}$ for some $A' \subset A$ is an* open cover *of X' if $X' \subset \bigcup_{\alpha \in A'} V_\alpha$.*

Fact A.13 *Every $X' \subset X$ has an open cover.*

Proof. By Definition A.15 $X \in \tau$, so that $\{X\}$ is an open cover of X'. ∎

Definition A.21 *A subset X' of a topological space (X, τ) (where $X' = X$ is allowed) is* compact *if every open cover of X' contains a finite subcover; that is, for every open cover $\{V_\alpha\}_{\alpha \in A'}$ of X', there exists a finite set $A'' \subset A'$ such that $X' \subset \bigcup_{\alpha \in A''} V_\alpha$.*

Compactness is a major property, since compact sets have many nice features, and some of these are used below. Compactness has a particularly simple meaning in Euclidean spaces, which is given by the following famous theorem.

Theorem A.6 (Heine-Borel Theorem) *Let $X \subset \mathbb{R}^K$ be a Euclidean space (with a Euclidean metric or topology). Then $X' \subset X$ is compact if and only if X' is closed and bounded in $\mathbb{R}^K$.*

A proof of this proposition can be found in any real analysis textbook, and I do not repeat it here. Its main implication for us is that any K-dimensional segment $\prod_{i=1}^K [a_i, b_i]$, with $a_i, b_i \in \mathbb{R}$ and $a_i \leq b_i$, is compact.[2] The assumption that X is a Euclidean space is important for Theorem A.6, as illustrated by the following example.

Example A.10 *Consider the topological space (ℓ, τ), where ℓ is the space of infinite sequences, and τ is the topology induced by the discrete metric. Let us define $\ell' = \{x \in \{0, 1\}^\infty : \sum_{i=1}^\infty x_i^2 = 1\}$. Clearly ℓ' is a closed and bounded subset of ℓ, but not every open cover of ℓ' has a finite subcover. In particular, note that each point in ℓ' has the form $v_1 = (1, 0, 0, 0, \ldots)$, $v_2 = (0, 1, 0, 0, 0, \ldots)$, $v_3 = (0, 0, 1, 0, 0, \ldots)$, and so on. Since τ is the discrete topology, $v_n \in \tau$ for each n, and moreover the collection $\bigcup_{n \in \mathbb{N}} v_n$ is an open cover of ℓ'. But this open cover does not a have finite subcover. Equivalently, the sequence $\{v_n\}_{n=1}^\infty$ does not have a convergent subsequence. The same construction works as an example of a noncompact, closed, and bounded set if we take $\ell'_2 = \{x \in [0, 1]^\infty : \sum_{i=1}^\infty x_i^2 \leq 1\}$, which is a subset of ℓ_2, the space of infinite sequences with metric $d_2(x, y) = \left(\sum_{i=1}^\infty |x_i - y_i|^2\right)^{1/2}$. This subset is closed and bounded. But v_1, v_2, and v_3 above are elements of ℓ'_2, and the sequence $\{v_n\}_{n=1}^\infty$ does not have a convergent subsequence.*

---

2. The product of subsets can also be denoted by $\mathsf{X}_i\, [a_i, b_i]$ instead of $\prod_i [a_i, b_i]$.

Nevertheless, there are important connections between closed sets and compact sets.

Lemma A.2 *Let (X, τ) be a topological space, and suppose that $X' \subset X$ is compact. Then*

1. *any $X'' \subset X'$ that is closed is also compact (and hence X' itself is closed), and*
2. *for any $X'' \subset X$ that is closed, $X'' \cap X'$ is compact.*

Proof. See Exercise A.15. ■

One of the important implications of compactness is the following theorem.

Theorem A.7 (Bolzano-Weierstrass Theorem) *Let (X, d) be a metric space and $\{x_n\}_{n=1}^{\infty}$ be a sequence in X. If X is compact, then $\{x_n\}_{n=1}^{\infty}$ has a convergent subsequence.*

Proof. To obtain a contradiction suppose that no such convergent subsequence exists. Then each $x \in X$ must have neighborhood V_x that contains at most one element of the sequence $\{x_n\}_{n=1}^{\infty}$. Clearly $\{V_x\}_{x \in X}$ is an open cover of X with no finite subcover, contradicting compactness. ■

It is possible to state an equivalent of Theorem A.7 for nets and subnets, but this result is not necessary for our purposes here. The reader may also wonder whether an equivalent of Theorem A.7 applies in a general topological space. Unfortunately, this is not the case (but it is true for topological spaces that have the Hausdorff property and also have a countable base; see Kelley, 1955).

Theorem A.8 (Continuity and Compact Images) *Let (X, τ_X) and (Y, τ_Y) be topological spaces, and consider the mapping $\phi : X \to Y$. If ϕ is continuous and $X' \subset X$ is compact, then $\phi(X')$ is compact.*

Proof. Let $\{V_\alpha\}_{\alpha \in A'}$ be an open cover of $\phi(X')$. Since ϕ is continuous, Theorem A.4 implies that $\phi^{-1}(V_\alpha)$ is open for each $\alpha \in A'$. Since X' is compact, every open cover has a finite subcover, and therefore there exists a finite $A'' \subset A'$ such that $X' \subset \bigcup_{\alpha \in A''} \phi^{-1}(V_\alpha)$. Since by definition, $\phi(\phi^{-1}(Y'')) \subset Y''$ for any $Y'' \subset Y$, we have

$$\phi(X') \subset \bigcup_{\alpha \in A''} (V_\alpha),$$

and thus $\{V_\alpha\}_{\alpha \in A''}$ is a finite subcover of $\{V_\alpha\}_{\alpha \in A'}$, completing the proof. ■

Despite its simplicity Theorem A.8 has many fundamental implications. The most important is Weierstrass's Theorem.[3] Recall that for a real-valued function $f : X \to \mathbb{R}$, $\max_{x \in X} f(x)$ and $\min_{x \in X} f(x)$ are the maximum and the minimum of the function over the set X. These may not exist. When they do, we also define the following nonempty sets $\arg\max_{x \in X} f(x) = \{x' \in X : f(x') = \max_{x \in X} f(x)\}$ and $\arg\min_{x \in X} f(x) = \{x' \in X : f(x') = \min_{x \in X} f(x)\}$.

Theorem A.9 (Weierstrass's Theorem) *Consider the topological space (X, τ) and a function $f : X \to \mathbb{R}$. If X' is a compact subset of (X, τ), then $\max_{x \in X'} f(x)$ and $\min_{x \in X'} f(x)$ exist, and $\arg\max_{x \in X'} f(x)$ and $\arg\min_{x \in X'} f(x)$ are nonempty.*

---

3. In fact, there are many theorems that go under the name of "Weierstrass's Theorem," including one on uniform continuity of a family of functions and one on approximation of continuous functions by polynomials. However, since these theorems are not used commonly in economic applications, there should be little confusion in referring to Theorem A.9 as "Weierstrass's Theorem."

Proof. By Theorem A.8, $f(X')$ is compact. A compact subset of $\mathbb{R}$ contains a minimum and a maximum; thus $\max_{x \in X'} f(x)$ and $\min_{x \in X'} f(x)$ exist. The nonemptiness of arg $\max_{x \in X'} f(x)$ and arg $\min_{x \in X'} f(x)$ then follows immediately. ∎

This theorem implies that if we can formulate a maximization problem as one of maximizing a real-valued function subject to a constraint set that is a compact subset of a topological space, then the existence of solutions and nonemptiness of the set of maximizers are guaranteed. An immediate corollary is also useful in many applications. A real-valued function $f : X \to \mathbb{R}$ is *bounded on* X if there exists $M < \infty$ such that $|f(x)| < M$ for all $x \in X$.

Corollary A.1 *Consider a topological space* (X, τ). *If* $f : X \to \mathbb{R}$ *is continuous on* X *and* X *is compact, then* f *is bounded on* X.

Finally, a stronger version of continuity for real-valued functions is sometimes useful (e.g., in Theorem 7.15 in Chapter 7).

Definition A.22 *Let* (X, d) *be a metric space. Then* $f : X \to \mathbb{R}$ *is* uniformly continuous *on* X *if, given any* $\varepsilon > 0$, *there exists* $\delta > 0$ *such that for any* $x_1, x_2 \in X$ *with* $d(x_1, x_2) < \delta$, *we have* $|f(x_1) - f(x_2)| < \varepsilon$.

Notice the difference between continuity at some point $x \in X$ (e.g., Definition A.14) and uniform continuity. In the former, δ can vary with x, whereas with uniform continuity the same δ must be used for all $x \in X$.

Theorem A.10 (Uniform Continuity over Compact Sets) *Let* (X, d_X) *and* (Y, d_Y) *be metric spaces. If* (X, d_X) *is compact and* f *is continuous on* X, *then* F *is uniformly continuous on* X.

Proof. Suppose, to obtain a contradiction, that f is continuous on the compact metric space (X, d_X) but not uniformly so. Then for some $\varepsilon > 0$ and every $n = 1, 2, \ldots$, there exists $x_n, x'_n \in X$ such that

$$d_X(x_n, x'_n) < \frac{1}{n}, \tag{A.2}$$

$$d_Y(f(x_n), f(x'_n)) \geq \varepsilon. \tag{A.3}$$

Now consider the sequence $\{x_n\}_{n=1}^{\infty}$ in X. Since X is compact, Theorem A.7 implies that there exists a subsequence $\{x_{n_k}\}$ converging to $x \in X$. Then (A.2) implies that the corresponding subsequence of $\{x'_n\}_{n=1}^{\infty}$, $\{x'_{n_k}\}$, also converges to the same x. From (A.3), for each n_k,

$$\varepsilon \leq d_Y(f(x_{n_k}), f(x'_{n_k})) \leq d_Y(f(x), f(x'_{n_k})) + d_Y(f(x), f(x_{n_k})),$$

where the second inequality uses the triangle inequality. Thus either $d_Y(f(x), f(x_{n_k})) \geq \varepsilon/2$, or $d_Y(f(x), f(x'_{n_k})) \geq \varepsilon/2$, or both. But this contradicts the continuity of f on X. This contradiction establishes the uniform continuity of f on X. ∎

The converse of this theorem is obvious, since every uniform continuous function is continuous.

A.4 The Product Topology*

One of the main reasons for introducing topological spaces rather than simply working with metric spaces is to introduce the *product topology*. The product topology is particularly useful when dealing with infinite-dimensional optimization problems, since we can represent the space of sequences, ℓ, as the infinite product of $\mathbb{R}$, that is, as $\mathbb{R}^\infty$. What are the topological properties of such product spaces? The answer is provided by the famous Tychonoff Theorem. Before presenting this theorem, it is necessary to introduce a few more concepts. First, we need to rank topologies according to how "weak" or "strong" they are.

Definition A.23 *Let τ and τ' be topologies defined on some set X. Then τ is* weaker *than τ' (τ' is* stronger *than τ), if when V_α is open in τ, it is also open in τ'.*

Definition A.24 *Let $\{(X_\alpha, \tau_\alpha)\}_{\alpha \in A}$ be a collection of topological spaces. Then the* product topology *$\tau = \prod_{\alpha \in A} \tau_\alpha$ is the strongest topology such that all sets of the form $\bigcup_{j \in J} V^j$ are open, where $V^j = \prod_{\alpha \in A} V_\alpha^j$, with $V_\alpha^j \in \tau_\alpha$ and $V_\alpha^j = X_\alpha$ for all but finitely many αs.*

A different way of stating this definition is that sets of the form $V^j = \prod_{\alpha \in A} V_\alpha^j$, with $V_\alpha^j \in \tau_\alpha$ and $V_\alpha^j = X_\alpha$ for all but finitely many αs form a *base* for the product topology (recall Definition A.16).

The product topology is particularly useful, because it ensures continuity of the projection maps (which seems like a minimal requirement for any reasonable topology) without introducing too many open sets.

Definition A.25 *Let $X = \prod_{\alpha \in A} X_\alpha$. The* projection map *for $\alpha \in A$ is defined as $P_\alpha : X \to X_\alpha$ such that $P(x) = x_\alpha$.*

Theorem A.11 (Projection Maps and the Product Topology) *The product topology is the weakest topology that makes each projection map P_α continuous.*

Proof. Let τ be the product topology and τ' any other topology in which each projection map is continuous. Then for each $\alpha \in A$, when $V_\alpha \in X_\alpha$ is open in X_α, then $P_\alpha^{-1}(V_\alpha)$ is open according to τ' (i.e., $P_\alpha^{-1}(V_\alpha) \in \tau'$). But then finite intersections of all sets of the form $P_\alpha^{-1}(V_\alpha)$ are members of τ', and therefore all open sets in the product topology τ belong to τ'. Thus τ' must be stronger than τ, and the argument establishes that the product topology is the weakest topology in which each projection map is continuous. ∎

The product topology is also referred to as the *topology of pointwise convergence* because of the following fact.

Fact A.14 *A sequence $\{x_n\}_{n=1}^\infty$ or a net $\{x_j\}_{j \in J}$ in $X = \prod_{\alpha \in A} X_\alpha$ converges to some $\bar{x}$ if and only if the projections $P_\alpha(x_n)$ or $P_\alpha(x_j)$ converge to $P_\alpha(\bar{x})$ for any $\alpha \in A$.*

Thus in many situations, the product topology is the right tool for analyzing the convergence of infinite sequences. An alternative to the product topology would be the *box topology*, which is defined similarly, except that it does not have the last qualifier "$V_\alpha^j = X_\alpha$ for all but finitely many αs." Thus the box topology has an abundance of open sets and so is stronger than the product topology. Consequently, compactness is difficult to achieve in the box topology. Exercise A.16 investigates this issue further.

An implication of Theorem A.11 is that a mapping $\phi : Y \to \prod_{\alpha \in A} X_\alpha$ is continuous according to the product topology if $P_\alpha \circ \phi : Y \to X_\alpha$ is continuous for each $\alpha \in A$. The product topology is particularly useful in dynamic optimization problems (in discrete time) because of the following result.

Theorem A.12 (Continuity in the Product Topology) *Suppose that $f_n : X_n \to \mathbb{R}$ is continuous, X_n is a compact metric space for every $n \in \mathbb{N}$, the collection of functions $\{f_n\}_{n \in \mathbb{N}}$ is uniformly bounded (in the sense that there exists $M \in \mathbb{R}$ such that $\left| f_n(x_n) \right| \leq M$ for all*

$x_n \in X_n$ and $n \in \mathbb{N}$), and $\beta < 1$. Then $f = \sum_{n=1}^{\infty} \beta^n f_n : \prod_{n \in \mathbb{N}} X_n \to \mathbb{R}$ is continuous in the product topology.

Proof. First note that uniform boundedness of the functions $\{f_n\}_{n \in \mathbb{N}}$ ensures that f is well defined for all $x \in \prod_{n \in \mathbb{N}} X_n$. From Theorem A.5, f is continuous in the product topology if and only if for any $x^{\infty} \in \prod_{n \in \mathbb{N}} X_n$, $\{f(x_j)\}_{j \in J} \to f(x^{\infty})$ for any net $\{x_j\}_{j \in J} \in \prod_{n \in \mathbb{N}} X_n$ with $\{x_\alpha\}_{\alpha \in A} \to x^{\infty}$ in the product topology. Now take a net $\{x_j\}_{j \in J} \to x^{\infty}$. By Fact A.14, $\{x^j\}_{j \in J} \to x^{\infty}$ in the product topology if and only if $\{x_n^j\}_{j \in J} \to x_n^{\infty}$ for each $n \in \mathbb{N}$. Then by the continuity of each function f_n, $\{f_n(x_n^j)\}_{j \in J} \to f(x_n^{\infty})$. Fix $\varepsilon > 0$, and let $\bar{n}$ be such that $2M\beta^{\bar{n}}/(1 - \beta) < \varepsilon/2$. Since $\{f_n(x_n^j)\}_{j \in J} \to f(x_n^{\infty})$ for each $n < \bar{n}$, there exists $\bar{j} \in J$ such that

$$\left| f_n\left(x_n^j\right) - f\left(x_n^{\infty}\right) \right| \leq \varepsilon(1 - \beta)/2$$

for each $n < \bar{n}$ and $j \geq \bar{j}$. Therefore for all $j \in J$ such that $j \geq \bar{j}$, we have

$$\left| \sum_{n=1}^{\infty} \beta^n f_n(x_n^j) - \sum_{n=1}^{\infty} \beta^n f_n(x_n^{\infty}) \right| \leq \sum_{n=1}^{\bar{n}-1} \beta^n \left| f_n(x_n^j) - f\left(x_n^{\infty}\right) \right| + 2M \sum_{n=\bar{n}}^{\infty} \beta^n$$

$$\leq \sum_{n=1}^{\bar{n}-1} \beta^n \frac{\varepsilon(1 - \beta)}{2} + \frac{\varepsilon}{2} < \varepsilon,$$

where the first line uses the triangle inequality and the fact that $\{f_n\}_{n \in \mathbb{N}}$ is uniformly bounded, and the second line uses the definition of $\bar{j}$. This inequality shows that $\{f(x^j)\}_{j \in J} \to f(x^{\infty})$ and establishes the continuity of f. ∎

Discounting is important in the previous result. The following example shows why.

Example A.11 *Suppose that $f_n : X \to \mathbb{R}$ is continuous and X is a compact metric space, and let $f = \sum_{n=1}^{\infty} f_n : X^{\infty} \to \mathbb{R}$. It can be verified that f is not continuous and tends to infinity for any $\{x^j\}_{j=1}^{\infty} \to x^*$ such that $f_n(x^n) > \varepsilon$ for all n and for some $\varepsilon > 0$.*

Theorem A.13 (Tychonoff's Theorem) *Let $A \subset \mathbb{R}$, and consider the family of topological spaces $\{(X_\alpha, \tau_\alpha)\}_{\alpha \in A}$. If each X_α is compact, then $X = \prod_{\alpha \in A} X_\alpha$ is compact in the product topology, that is, (X, τ) is compact, where $\tau = \prod_{\alpha \in A} \tau_\alpha$.*

The proof of this theorem can be found in Kelley (1955) or Royden (1994).

Combined with Theorem A.12, this theorem implies that problems involving the maximization of discounted utility in standard dynamic economic environments have a continuous objective function in the product topology. We can then appeal to Tychonoff's Theorem to make sure that the relevant constraint set is compact (again in the product topology). This combination then enables us to apply Weierstrass's Theorem (Theorem A.9) to show the existence of solutions (see, e.g., Chapters 6 and 16).

A.5 Absolute Continuity and Equicontinuity *

In this section, I provide several more advanced results that are useful in establishing existence of solutions in optimal control problems in Section 7.6 of Chapter 7. Some of the results presented in this section are typically developed in the context of measure-theoretic analysis. Nevertheless, since I have avoided the use of concepts from measure theory throughout the book, I continue to do so here.

Definition A.26 *Let* $X \subset \mathbb{R}$. *Then* $f : X \to \mathbb{R}$ *is* absolutely continuous *if for any* $\varepsilon > 0$, *there exists* $\delta > 0$ *such that*

$$\sum_{k=1}^{n} \left| f(b_k) - f(a_k) \right| < \varepsilon$$

for any collection of pairwise disjoint intervals (a_k, b_k), *with* $\sum_{k=1}^{n}(b_k - a_k) < \delta$.

In this definition $X = \mathbb{R}$ is allowed; that is, a function can be absolutely continuous on the entire real line. Absolute continuity arises naturally in the context of (Lebesgue) integration. In particular, the following facts are straightforward and illustrate the context in which absolute continuity plays a useful role.

Fact A.15 *Let* $f(x) = \int_0^x g(s)ds$ *for all* $x \in X$. *If* $g(s)$ *is piecewise continuous on* X, *then* f *is absolutely continuous on* X.

Here the integral can be interpreted as the standard Riemann integral (see Appendix B). However the same result holds when the integral is the Lebesgue integral and $g(s)$ is (Lebesgue) integrable (rather than piecewise continuous).

Fact A.16 *If* $f : X \to \mathbb{R}$ *is absolutely continuous on* X, *then it is uniformly continuous (and thus continuous) on* X.

Fact A.17 *If* $f : X \to \mathbb{R}$ *is differentiable on* X, *then it is absolutely continuous on* X.

I next introduce several concepts that will be useful in establishing compactness of a subset of $\mathbf{C}(X)$. Recall that $\mathbf{C}(X)$ is the set of continuous and bounded real-valued functions defined on X, and in what follows, I take X to be a compact Euclidean space (a compact subset of the Euclidean space).

Definition A.27 *Let* (X, d) *be a metric space. For* $\varepsilon > 0$, $A \subset X$ *is an* ε-net *for* $X' \subset X$ *if for every* $x \in X'$, *there exists* $a \in A$ *such that* $d(a, x) \leq \varepsilon$.

Definition A.28 *Let* (X, d) *be a metric space. A subset* X' *of* X *is* totally bounded *if for every* $\varepsilon > 0$, *there exists a finite set* $A_\varepsilon \subset X$ *that is an* ε-net (*a finite* ε-net) *of* X'.

In this definition, we can, without loss of generality, set $A_\varepsilon \subset X'$. Also, as a subset of itself, X can be totally bounded with the same definition.

The following theorem, which I state without proof, is an alternative characterization of compactness (for a proof, see, e.g., Kolmogorov and Fomin, 1970, pp. 100–102).

Theorem A.14 (Totally Bounded and Compact Spaces) *A metric space* (X, d) *is compact if and only if it is totally bounded and complete.*

Definition A.29 *Let* X *be a compact Euclidean space. A subset* $\mathcal{F}$ *of* $\mathbf{C}(X)$ *is* uniformly bounded *if there exists* $K > 0$ *such that* $|f(x)| < K$ *for all* $x \in X$ *and all* $f \in \mathcal{F}$.

Definition A.30 *Let* X *be a compact Euclidean space. A subset* $\mathcal{F}$ *of* $\mathbf{C}(X)$ *functions is* equicontinuous *if for any* $\varepsilon > 0$, *there exists* $\delta > 0$ *such that*

$$\left| f(x_1) - f(x_2) \right| < \varepsilon$$

for any $x_1, x_2 \in X$ *with* $\left| x_1 - x_2 \right| < \delta$ *and any* $f \in \mathcal{F}$.

Theorem A.15 (Arzela-Ascoli Theorem) *Let* X *be a compact Euclidean space and* $\mathcal{F}$ *be a subset of* $\mathbf{C}(X)$. *The closure of* $\mathcal{F}$, $\overline{\mathcal{F}}$, *is compact in* $\mathbf{C}(X)$ *if and only if* $\mathcal{F}$ *is uniformly bounded* *and equicontinuous. That is, if $\mathcal{F}$ is uniformly bounded and equicontinuous, when $f^n \in \mathcal{F}$ for $n = 1, 2, \ldots$, there exists a subsequence $\{f^{n_k}\}$ of $\{f^n\}_{n=1}^{\infty}$ such that $\{f^{n_k}\} \to f \in \overline{\mathcal{F}}$.*

Proof. ($\Longleftarrow$) Suppose $\overline{\mathcal{F}}$ is compact in $\mathbf{C}(X)$. Then by Theorem A.14 and Definition A.28, for every $\varepsilon > 0$, there exists a finite $(\varepsilon/3)$-net $\{f_1, \ldots, f_n\}$ in $\mathcal{F}$. Thus for any $f \in \mathcal{F}$, there exists $i \in \{1, \ldots, n\}$ such that

$$\sup_{x \in X} \left| f(x) - f_i(x) \right| \leq \frac{\varepsilon}{3}. \tag{A.4}$$

Moreover each f_i is bounded, since it is continuous on compact X (Corollary A.1). Thus for each $i = 1, \ldots, n$, there exists $K_i < \infty$ such that

$$\left| f_i(x) \right| \leq K_i \quad \text{for all } x \in X.$$

Set $K = \max\{K_1, \ldots, K_n\} + \varepsilon/3$ and use the triangle inequality to rewrite (A.4) as

$$|f(x)| \leq \left| f_i(x) \right| + \frac{\varepsilon}{3} \leq K_i + \frac{\varepsilon}{3} \leq K$$

for all $x \in X$, which establishes that $\mathcal{F}$ is uniformly bounded. Moreover each one of $f_1, \ldots, f_n$ is uniformly continuous (this follows from Theorem A.10, since each f_i is continuous and X is compact). Therefore for each $i = 1, \ldots, n$ and for any $\varepsilon > 0$, there exists $\delta_i > 0$ such that

$$\left| f_i(x) - f_i(x') \right| < \frac{\varepsilon}{3}$$

when $\left| x - x' \right| < \delta_i$ for $x, x' \in X$. Set $\delta = \max\{\delta_1, \ldots, \delta_n\}$. Then for any $f \in \mathcal{F}$, choose $i \in \{1, \ldots, n\}$ such that (A.4) holds, and again use the triangle inequality to write

$$\left| f(x) - f(x') \right| \leq \left| f(x) - f_i(x) \right| + \left| f_i(x) - f_i(x') \right| + \left| f_i(x') - f(x') \right|$$

$$< \frac{\varepsilon}{3} + \frac{\varepsilon}{3} + \frac{\varepsilon}{3} = \varepsilon$$

for all $x, x' \in X$ with $\left| x - x' \right| < \delta$, implying that $\mathcal{F}$ is equicontinuous.

($\Longrightarrow$) Take $\varepsilon > 0$. Since $\mathcal{F}$ is equicontinuous, for each $x \in X$, there exists $\delta > 0$ such that

$$\left| f(x) - f(x') \right| < \frac{\varepsilon}{4}$$

for all $f \in \mathcal{F}$ when $x' \in N_\delta(x)$ (open δ-neighborhood of x). Since X is compact, it has a finite subcover (Definition A.21), and thus we can choose $X' = \{x_1, \ldots, x_n\}$ such that $X = \bigcup_{x_i \in X'} N_\delta(x_i)$. Moreover, since each $f \in \mathcal{F}$ is bounded on X (Corollary A.1), the set $\{f(x_i) : f \in \mathcal{F} \text{ and } i = 1, \ldots, n\}$ is a totally bounded subset of $\mathbf{C}(X)$. From Definition A.28, there exists a finite $(\varepsilon/4)$-net $A = \{g_1, \ldots, g_m\} \subset \mathcal{F}$ for $X'' = \{f(x_1), \ldots, f(x_n)\}$. Now consider the set of functions F_A such that $F_A = \{f : X' \to A\}$. Since both X' and A are finite, the set F_A is also finite. Let

$$\mathcal{F}_\phi = \left\{ f \in \mathcal{F} : \left| f(x_i) - \phi(x_i) \right| < \frac{\varepsilon}{4} \text{ for } i = 1, \ldots, n \right\}.$$

Since A is a $(\varepsilon/4)$-net for X'', $\bigcup_{\phi \in F_A} \mathcal{F}_\phi = \mathcal{F}$. Take $f, g \in \mathcal{F}_\phi$ for some $\phi \in F_A$ and observe that, from the triangle inequality, we have

$$\left| f(x_i) - g(x_i) \right| \le \left| f(x_i) - \phi(x_i) \right| + \left| \phi(x_i) - g(x_i) \right|$$

$$\le \frac{\varepsilon}{4} + \frac{\varepsilon}{4} = \frac{\varepsilon}{2}$$

for $x_i \in X'$. By the fact that $X = \bigcup_{x_i \in X'} \mathcal{N}_\delta(x_i)$, any $x \in X$ is in $\mathcal{N}_\delta(x_i)$ for some $i \in \{1, \dots, n\}$, and therefore for any $x \in X$ it follows that

$$\left| f(x) - g(x) \right| \le \left| f(x) - f(x_i) \right| + \left| f(x_i) - g(x_i) \right| + \left| g(x_i) - g(x) \right|$$

$$< \frac{\varepsilon}{4} + \frac{\varepsilon}{2} + \frac{\varepsilon}{4} = \varepsilon.$$

Thus $\mathcal{F}$ is totally bounded. Moreover, since $\mathbf{C}(X)$ is complete, $\overline{\mathcal{F}}$ is also complete (Fact A.8), and thus $\overline{\mathcal{F}}$ is compact in $\mathbf{C}(X)$, proving this sufficiency part of the theorem.

Finally, the sufficiency result also implies that if $f^n \in \mathcal{F}$ for $n = 1, 2, \dots$, then there exists a subsequence $\{f^{n_k}\}$ of $\{f^n\}$ with $\{f^{n_k}\} \to f \in \overline{\mathcal{F}}$, completing the proof of the theorem. ∎

The next corollary can be proved using an identical argument to that of Theorem A.15.

Corollary A.2   *Let X be a compact Euclidean space and $\mathcal{F}$ be the subset of $\mathbf{C}(X)$ consisting of the family of absolutely continuous functions defined on X. Suppose that $\mathcal{F}$ is uniformly bounded and equicontinuous. Then when $f^n \in \mathcal{F}$ for $n = 1, 2, \dots$, there exists a subsequence $\{f^{n_k}\}$ of $\{f^n\}_{n=1}^\infty$ such that $\{f^{n_k}\} \to f \in \mathcal{F}$.*

A.6   Correspondences and Berge's Maximum Theorem

In this section, I state one of the most important theorems in mathematical economic analysis, Berge's Maximum Theorem. This theorem is not only essential for dynamic optimization, but it also plays a major role in general equilibrium theory, game theory, political economy, public finance, and industrial organization. In fact, it is hard to imagine any area of economics where it does not play a major role. Despite its enormous importance, this theorem is left out of most basic "Mathematics for Economists" courses and textbooks. This motivates my somewhat detailed treatment of it here. The first step toward establishing this theorem is to briefly review correspondences, which have already been mentioned above.

In this and the next three sections, I focus on metric spaces. Recall that F is a correspondence from a metric space (X, d_X) into (Y, d_Y) if to each $x \in X$ it assigns a subset of Y. We write this as

$$F : X \rightrightarrows Y, \ \text{ or } \ F : X \to \mathcal{P}(Y) \backslash \emptyset,$$

where $\mathcal{P}(Y)$, is the power set of Y, and the empty set $\emptyset$ is explicitly subtracted so that the correspondence is not empty valued. We are interested in correspondences for three fundamental reasons. First, even when a mapping into real numbers is a well-behaved function, $f : X \to \mathbb{R}$, its inverse f^{-1} will typically be set-valued, and thus it is a correspondence. Second, our main interest in most economic problems is with the "arg max" sets defined above, which are the subsets of values in some set X that maximize a function. These correspond to utility-maximizing consumption, investment, or price levels in simple economic problems.

Finally, correspondences are also useful in expressing the properties of maximizers in Berge's Maximum Theorem (Theorem A.16).

As with functions, for a correspondence $F : X \rightrightarrows Y$, I use the notation $F(X')$ to denote the image of the set X' under the correspondence F, so that $F(X')$ is defined as $F(X') = \{y \in Y : \exists x \in X' \text{ with } y \in F(x)\}$.

Definition A.31 *Let (X, d_X) and (Y, d_Y) be metric spaces, and consider the correspondence $F : X \rightrightarrows Y$. Let $\mathcal{N}_\varepsilon(x)$ refer to neighborhoods in (X, d_X). Then*

1. *F is* upper hemicontinuous *at $x \in X$ if for every open subset Y' of Y with $F(x) \subset Y'$, there exists $\varepsilon > 0$ such that $F(\mathcal{N}_\varepsilon(x)) \subset Y'$ (F is* upper hemicontinuous *on X if it is upper hemicontinuous at each $x \in X$);*

2. *F is* lower hemicontinuous *at $x \in X$ if for every open subset Y' of Y for which $F(x) \cap Y' \neq \emptyset$, there exists $\varepsilon > 0$ such that $F(x') \cap Y' \neq \emptyset$ for all $x' \in \mathcal{N}_\varepsilon(x)$ (F is* lower hemicontinuous *on X if it is lower hemicontinuous at each $x \in X$); and*

3. *F is* continuous *at $x \in X$ if and only if it is both upper- and lower hemicontinuous at $x \in X$ (F is* continuous *on X if and only if it is continuous at each $x \in X$).*

These notions are slightly easier to understand if we specialize them to Euclidean spaces. First, we say that a correspondence $F : X \rightrightarrows Y$ is *closed-valued* [*compact-valued*] if $F(x)$ is closed [compact] in Y for each x. For Euclidean spaces, the following definition is equivalent to Definition A.31, and more generally, it implies Definition A.31 (see Exercise A.18 and Fact A.18).

Definition A.32 *Let $X \subset \mathbb{R}^{K_X}$ and $Y \subset \mathbb{R}^{K_Y}$ where $K_X, K_Y \in \mathbb{N}$, and consider a compact-valued correspondence $F : X \rightrightarrows Y$. Then*

1. *F is* upper hemicontinuous *at $x \in X$ if for every sequence $\{x_n\}_{n=1}^{\infty} \to x$ and every sequence $\{y_n\}_{n=1}^{\infty}$ with $y_n \in F(x_n)$ for each n, there exists a convergent subsequence $\{y_{n_k}\}$ of $\{y_n\}_{n=1}^{\infty}$ such that $\{y_{n_k}\} \to y \in F(x)$; and*

2. *F is* lower hemicontinuous *at $x \in X$ if $F(x)$ is nonempty-valued and for every $y \in F(x)$ and every sequence $\{x_n\}_{n=1}^{\infty} \to x$, there exists some $N \in \mathbb{N}$ and a sequence $\{y_n\}_{n=1}^{\infty}$ with $y_n \in F(x_n)$ for all $n \geq N$, and $\{y_n\}_{n=1}^{\infty} \to y$.*

Figure A.1 illustrates these notions diagrammatically. In this figure, the correspondence $F(x)$ is upper and lower hemicontinuous and thus continuous at x_1; it is upper hemicontinuous but not lower hemicontinuous at x_2; and it is lower hemicontinuous but not upper hemicontinuous at x_3.

Upper hemicontinuity and lower hemicontinuity according to Definition A.32 imply the corresponding concepts in Definition A.31 for general metric spaces.

Fact A.18 *Let (X, d_X) and (Y, d_Y) be metric spaces, and consider the correspondence $F : X \rightrightarrows Y$. If F is upper hemicontinuous [lower hemicontinuous] at $x \in X$ according to Definition A.32, then it is upper hemicontinuous [lower hemicontinuous] at $x \in X$ according to Definition A.31.*

Proof. Suppose, to obtain a contradiction, that part 1 of Definition A.32 holds at x, but F is not upper hemicontinuous at x. Then there exists an open set $Y' \subset Y$ such that $F(x) \subset Y'$, but for any $\varepsilon > 0$, $F(\mathcal{N}_\varepsilon(x))$ is not a subset of Y'. Then for any $\varepsilon > 0$, there exists $x_\varepsilon \in \mathcal{N}_\varepsilon(x)$ and $y_\varepsilon \in F(x_\varepsilon)$ such that $y_\varepsilon \notin Y'$. Construct the sequence $\{(x_n, y_n)\}_{n=1}^{\infty}$ such that each (x_n, y_n) satisfies this property for $\varepsilon = 1/n$. Clearly $\{x_n\}_{n=1}^{\infty} \to x$. Therefore by hypothesis, there exists a convergent subsequence $\{y_{n_k}\} \to y \in F(x)$. Since Y' is open, $Y \setminus Y'$ is closed, and since

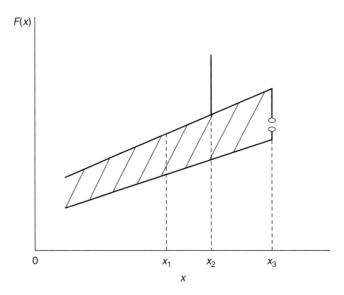

FIGURE A.1 Upper and lower hemicontinuity.

$y_{n_k} \in Y \setminus Y'$ for each n_k, the limit point y must also be in the closed set $Y \setminus Y'$. But $y \in Y \setminus Y'$ together with $y \in F(x)$ yields a contradiction, because $F(x) \subset Y'$, proving the first part of the Fact.

Suppose, to obtain a contradiction, that part 2 of Definition A.32 holds at x, but F is not lower hemicontinuous at x. Then there exists an open set $Y' \subset Y$ such that $F(x) \cap Y' \neq \emptyset$, but for any $\varepsilon > 0$, there exists $x_\varepsilon \in F(\mathcal{N}_\varepsilon(x))$ such that $F(x_\varepsilon) \cap Y' = \emptyset$. Consider the sequence $\{x_n\}_{n=1}^\infty$ with $x_n \to x$, let $\varepsilon = 1/n$, and suppose that this sequence satisfies the property just stated (i.e., for any $\varepsilon > 0$, there exists $x_\varepsilon \in F(\mathcal{N}_\varepsilon(x))$ such that $F(x_\varepsilon) \cap Y' = \emptyset$). Also let $y \in F(x) \cap Y'$. By part 2 of Definition A.32, there exists a sequence $\{y_n\}_{n=1}^\infty$ and some $N \geq 1$ such that $y_n \in F(x_n)$ for all $n \geq N$ and $\{y_n\}_{n=1}^\infty \to y$. However by the construction of the sequence $\{x_n\}_{n=1}^\infty$, $y_n \notin Y'$. Once again, since $Y \setminus Y'$ is closed, it must be the case that the limit point y also lies in the closed set $Y \setminus Y'$. This contradicts $y \in F(x) \cap Y'$ and establishes the second part of the Fact.

∎

Definition A.33 *Let (X, d_X) and (Y, d_Y) be metric spaces, and consider the correspondence $F : X \rightrightarrows Y$. Then F has a* closed graph *(is closed) at $x \in X$ if for every sequence $\{(x_n, y_n)\}_{n=1}^\infty \to (x, y)$ such that $y_n \in F(x_n)$ for each n, we also have $y \in F(x)$. In addition, F has a closed graph on the set X if it is closed at each $x \in X$.*

The following fact is a simple consequence of Definition A.32.

Fact A.19 *Let $X \subset \mathbb{R}^{K_X}$ and $Y \subset \mathbb{R}^{K_Y}$ where $K_X, K_Y \in \mathbb{N}$, and consider the correspondence $F : X \rightrightarrows Y$ that is upper hemicontinuous. If $F(x)$ is a closed set in Y (i.e., if F is* closed-valued*) for each $x \in X$, then F has a closed graph.*

Proof. See Exercise A.20. ∎

For finite-dimensional spaces, correspondences with closed graphs are also upper hemicontinuous, provided that they satisfy a simple boundedness hypothesis.

Fact A.20 *Let $X \subset \mathbb{R}^{K_X}$ and $Y \subset \mathbb{R}^{K_Y}$ where $K_X, K_Y \in \mathbb{N}$, and consider a correspondence $F : X \rightrightarrows Y$. Suppose that F has a closed graph at $x \in X$ and that there exists a neighborhood V_x of x such that $F(V_x)$ is bounded. Then F is upper hemicontinuous at x.*

Proof.   Consider sequences $\{x_n\}_{n=1}^{\infty}$ and $\{y_n\}_{n=1}^{\infty}$ such that $y_n \in F(x_n)$ for each n. Suppose that $\{x_n\}_{n=1}^{\infty} \to x$. Then by definition there exists $N \in \mathbb{N}$ such that $x_n \in V_x$ for all $n \geq N$, where V_x is the neighborhood specified in the statement of the claim, satisfying the property that $F(V_x)$ is bounded. Then since Y is a Euclidean space, the closure of V_x, $\overline{F(V_x)}$, is compact. Then by Theorem A.7, $\{y_n\}_{n=1}^{\infty}$ has a subsequence $\{y_{n_k}\}$ converging to some $y \in Y$. Thus the (sub)sequence $\{(x_{n_k}, y_{n_k})\} \to (x, y)$. Moreover since F has a closed graph at x, $y \in F(x)$, which establishes that F is upper hemicontinuous at $x \in X$ according to Definition A.32. Then from Fact A.18, it is upper hemicontinuous at $x \in X$ according to Definition A.31.   ∎

The hypothesis that there exists a neighborhood V_x with $F(V_x)$ bounded cannot be dispensed with in this result. This is shown by the following example.

Example A.12   *Consider the correspondence* $F : [0, 1] \to \mathbb{R}$ *given by* $F(x) = \{0\}$ *if* $x = 0$ *and* $F(x) = \{\log x, 0\}$ *if* $x \in (0, 1]$. *Then* F *has a closed graph but is not upper hemicontinuous at* $x = 0$. *It can be verified easily that* F *does not satisfy the hypothesis that there exists a neighborhood* V_x *with* $F(V_x)$ *bounded at* $x = 0$.

The following fact is useful for using continuous correspondences in optimization problems.

Fact A.21   *Let* (X, d_X) *be a metric space, and consider the continuous concave function* $g : Y \to \mathbb{R}$. *Then the set-valued mapping* $G(x) = \{y \in Y : y \leq g(x)\}$ *defines a continuous correspondence* $G : X \rightrightarrows Y$.

Proof.   See Exercise A.21.   ∎

Theorem A.16 (Berge's Maximum Theorem)   *Let* (X, d_X) *and* (Y, d_Y) *be metric spaces. Consider the maximization problem*

$$\sup_{y \in Y} f(x, y)$$

subject to

$$y \in G(x),$$

where $G : X \rightrightarrows Y$ *and* $f : X \times Y \to \mathbb{R}$. *Suppose that* f *is continuous and* G *is compact-valued and continuous at* x. *Then*

1. $M(x) = \max_{y \in Y}\{f(x, y) : y \in G(x)\}$ *exists and is continuous at* x, *and*
2. $\Pi(x) = \arg\max_{y \in Y}\{f(x, y) : y \in G(x)\}$ *is nonempty-valued, compact-valued, upper hemicontinuous, and has a closed graph at* x.

Proof.   In view of Fact A.18, let us work with Definition A.32. The fact that $M(x)$ exists and thus $\Pi(x)$ is nonempty-valued for all $x \in X$ follows from Theorem A.9. Consider a sequence $\{y_n\}_{n=1}^{\infty} \to y$ such that $y_n \in \Pi(x)$ for each n. Since $G(x)$ is closed, $y \in G(x)$. Moreover by definition $f(x, y_n) = M(x)$ for each n. Since f is continuous, $f(x, y) = M(x)$ follows. Therefore $y \in \Pi(x)$, and thus $\Pi(x)$ is closed. Since $\Pi(x)$ is a closed subset of the compact set $G(x)$, we can invoke Lemma A.2 to conclude that $\Pi(x)$ is compact-valued.

Now again take $\{x_n\}_{n=1}^{\infty} \to x$, $\{y_n\}_{n=1}^{\infty}$, with $y_n \in G(x_n)$ for all n, with a convergent subsequence $\{y_{n_k}\} \to y$. Since $G(x)$ is upper hemicontinuous, $y \in G(x)$. Take any $z \in G(x)$. Since $G(x)$ is continuous and thus lower hemicontinuous, there exists $\{z_{n_k}\} \to z$, with $z_{n_k} \in G(x_{n_k})$ for all n_k. Since $y_{n_k} \in \Pi(x_{n_k})$, $M(x_{n_k}) = f(x_{n_k}, y_{n_k}) \geq f(x_{n_k}, z_{n_k})$. Moreover, since f is continuous, by Fact A.5, $M(x) = f(x, y) \geq f(x, z)$. Since this holds for all $z \in G(x)$, $y \in \Pi(x)$, and therefore $\Pi(x)$ is upper hemicontinuous. Applying Fact A.19 once more, we conclude that $\Pi(x)$ also has a closed graph.

To complete the proof, we need to show that $M(x)$ is continuous at x. This follows from the fact that $\Pi(x)$ is upper hemicontinuous. Take $\{x_n\}_{n=1}^{\infty} \to x$, and consider $\{y_n\}_{n=1}^{\infty}$ such that $y_n \in \Pi(x_n)$ for each n. Since Π is upper hemicontinuous, Definition A.32 implies that there exists a subsequence $\{y_{n_k}\}$ converging to $y \in F(x)$. The continuity of f implies that $M(x_{n_k}) = f(x_{n_k}, y_{n_k}) \to f(x, y) = M(x)$ and establishes that $M(x)$ is continuous at x. ∎

Note that I wrote the maximization problem as $\sup_{y \in Y}$ instead of $\max_{y \in Y}$. There would have been no loss of generality in using the latter notation, since the theorem establishes that the maximum is attained. Nevertheless the former is slightly more appropriate, since when we first consider the problem we do not know whether the maximum is attained.

A.7 Convexity, Concavity, Quasi-Concavity, and Fixed Points

Theorem A.16 shows how we can ensure certain desirable properties of the set of maximizers in a variety of problems arising in economic analysis. However, it is not strong enough to assert the uniqueness of maximizers or the continuity of the set of maximizers (instead, we have upper hemicontinuity). In this section, I show how these results can be strengthened when we focus on problems with concave objective functions and convex constraint sets, and then I provide a brief illustration of how these stronger results can be used. Throughout the rest of this appendix, let V be a *vector space* (or a linear space) so that if $x, y \in V$ and λ is a real number, then $x + y \in V$ and $\lambda x \in V$. Let X and Y be subsets of V. Properties of vector spaces are discussed further in Section A.10.

Definition A.34 *A set X is* convex *if for any $\lambda \in [0, 1]$ and any $x, y \in X$, $\lambda x + (1 - \lambda)y \in X$.*

Definition A.35 *A correspondence $G : X \rightrightarrows Y$ is* convex-valued *at x if $G(x)$ is a convex set (in Y).*

Definition A.36 *Let X be convex, $f : X \to \mathbb{R}$ be a real-valued function and $\lambda \in (0, 1)$. Suppose that $f(x)$, $f(y)$, and $f(\lambda x + (1 - \lambda)y)$ are well defined. Then*

1. *f is* concave *if $f(\lambda x + (1 - \lambda)y) \geq \lambda f(x) + (1 - \lambda)f(y)$ for all $\lambda \in (0, 1)$ and all $x, y \in X$ (f is* strictly concave *if the inequality is strict for any $x \neq y$);*

2. *f is* convex *if $f(\lambda x + (1 - \lambda)y) \leq \lambda f(x) + (1 - \lambda)f(y)$ for all $\lambda \in (0, 1)$ and all $x, y \in X$ (f is* strictly convex *if the inequality is strict for any $x \neq y$);*

3. *f is* quasi-concave *if $f(\lambda x + (1 - \lambda)y) \geq \min\{f(x), f(y)\}$ for all $\lambda \in (0, 1)$ and all $x, y \in X$ (f is* strictly quasi-concave *if the inequality is strict for any $x \neq y$); and*

4. *f is* quasi-convex *if $f(\lambda x + (1 - \lambda)y) \leq \max\{f(x), f(y)\}$ for all $\lambda \in (0, 1)$ and all $x, y \in X$ (f is* strictly quasi-convex *if the inequality is a strict for any $x \neq y$).*

Naturally, one can define all these concepts for a subset X' of the domain X of the function f, since a function could be concave over a certain range but not everywhere.

The following result strengthens the conclusions of Theorem A.16 under additional assumptions.

Theorem A.17 (Properties of Maximizers) *Consider the maximization problem*

$$\sup_{y \in Y} f(x, y)$$

subject to

$$y \in G(x),$$

where $G : X \rightrightarrows Y$, *and* $f : X \times Y \to \mathbb{R}$. *Suppose that* f *is continuous and* G *is convex-valued, compact-valued, and continuous at* x:

1. *If* f *is quasi-concave, then* $\Pi(x) = \arg\max_{y \in Y} \{f(x, y) : y \in G(x)\}$ *is nonempty-valued, compact-valued, upper hemicontinuous; has a closed graph, and is convex-valued at* x.

2. *If* f *is strictly quasi-concave in a neighborhood of* x, *then* $\Pi(x)$ *is a singleton.*

3. *If* f *satisfies the conditions in part 2 everywhere in* X, *then* $\Pi(x)$ *is a continuous (single-valued) function in* X.

Proof. **(Part 1)** Most of the statements here follow from Theorem A.16. We only need to prove that $\Pi(x)$ is convex-valued. Suppose, to obtain a contradiction, that this is not the case. Then there exist y and $y' \neq y$ in $\Pi(x)$ such that for some $\lambda \in (0, 1)$, we have $y'' = \lambda y + (1 - \lambda) y' \notin \Pi(x)$. But since $G(x)$ is convex-valued, $y'' \in G(x)$. Then by quasi-concavity, $f(\lambda y + (1 - \lambda) y') \geq \min\{f(y), f(y')\}$. But since y, $y' \in \Pi(x)$, $f(y) = f(y')$, and thus $f(\lambda y + (1 - \lambda) y') \geq f(y) = f(y')$, implying that $y'' = \lambda y + (1 - \lambda) y' \in \Pi(x)$. This yields a contradiction and establishes that $\Pi(x)$ is convex-valued.

(Part 2) Suppose, to obtain a contradiction, that there exist y and $y' \neq y$ in $\Pi(x)$. Since $G(x)$ is convex-valued, $y'' = \lambda y + (1 - \lambda) y' \in G(x)$ for any $\lambda \in (0, 1)$. Moreover, by strict quasi-concavity of f, we have $f(\lambda y + (1 - \lambda) y') > \lambda f(y) + (1 - \lambda) f(y')$. Again since y, $y' \in \Pi(x)$, $f(y) = f(y')$, and thus $f(\lambda y + (1 - \lambda) y') > f(y) = f(y')$, contradicting the condition that y, $y' \in \Pi(x)$ and establishing the result.

(Part 3) Part 2 implies that $\Pi(x)$ is single-valued everywhere, and Part 1 implies that it is upper hemicontinuous. Then from Definition A.31, for every sequence $\{x_n\}_{n=1}^{\infty} \to x$ and every sequence $\{y_n\}_{n=1}^{\infty}$ with $y_n = \Pi(x_n)$ for each n, there exists a convergent subsequence $\{y_{n_k}\}$ of $\{y_n\}_{n=1}^{\infty}$ such that $\{y_{n_k}\} \to y = \Pi(x)$. When $\Pi(x)$ is single-valued, this implies continuity at x (recall Fact A.9). ∎

Clearly these results can be generalized to minimization problems (with quasi-convexity replacing quasi-concavity) by simply applying Theorems A.16 and A.17 to $-f$.

The following well-known and important theorem shows why convex-valuedness is important.

Theorem A.18 (Kakutani's Fixed Point Theorem) *Suppose* $X \subset \mathbb{R}^K$ *(where* $K \in \mathbb{N}$*) is a nonempty, compact, and convex set, and let* $F : X \rightrightarrows X$ *be a nonempty-valued, convex-valued, and upper hemicontinuous correspondence. Then* F *has a* fixed point *in* X *that is, there exists* $x^* \in X$ *such that* $x^* \in F(x^*)$.

The proof of this theorem can be found in Berge (1963), Aliprantis and Border (1999), or Ok (2007). Exercise A.22 shows why convex-valuedness is important, and Exercise A.23 presents an application of Theorem A.18 to the existence of pure-strategy Nash equilibria in normal-form games.

While some of the proofs of Kakutani's Fixed Point Theorem start from the slightly simpler Brouwer's Fixed Point Theorem, given Theorem A.18, Brouwer's Fixed Point Theorem can be obtained as a simple corollary.

Theorem A.19 (Brouwer's Fixed Point Theorem) *Suppose* $X \subset \mathbb{R}^K$ *(where* $K \in \mathbb{N}$*) is a nonempty, compact, and convex set, and let*

$$\phi : X \to X$$

be a continuous map. Then ϕ *has a* fixed point *in* X; *that is, there exists* $x^* \in X$ *such that* $x^* = \phi(x^*)$.

Proof.   The result follows immediately from Theorem A.18, using Part 3 of Theorem A.17, which shows that a continuous map is a nonempty-valued, convex-valued, and upper hemi-continuous correspondence.   ■

A.8   Differentiation, Taylor Series, and the Mean Value Theorem

In this and the next sections, I briefly discuss differentiation and some important results related to differentiation that are useful for the analysis in the text. The material in this section should be more familiar, thus I am somewhat more brief in my treatment than in other sections of this appendix. In this section the focus is on a real-valued function of one variable $f : \mathbb{R} \to \mathbb{R}$. Functions of several variables and vector-valued functions are discussed in the next section.

The reader will recall that the derivative (function) for $f : \mathbb{R} \to \mathbb{R}$ has a simple definition. Take a point x in an open set X' on which the function f is defined. Then when the limit exists (and is finite), the derivative of f at x is defined as

$$f'(x) = \lim_{h \to 0} \frac{f(x+h) - f(x)}{h}. \tag{A.5}$$

Clearly the term $f(x+h)$ is well defined for h sufficiently small, since x is in the open set X'. Moreover this limit exists at point x only if f is continuous at $x \in X$. This property is more general: differentiability implies continuity (see Fact A.22). Using the elementary properties of limits, (A.5) can be rearranged as

$$\lim_{h \to 0} \frac{f(x+h) - f(x) - L(x)h}{h} = 0, \tag{A.6}$$

where $L(x) = f'(x)$. This expression emphasizes that we can think of the derivative of the function $f(x)$, $f'(x)$, as a *linear operator*. In fact, one might want to define $f'(x)$ precisely as the *linear operator* $L(x)$ that satisfies equation (A.6). Note that $f'(x)$ is linear in h—not in x. It is generally a nonlinear function of x, but it defines a linear function from X' (the open subset of X where f is defined) to $\mathbb{R}$ that assigns the value $f'(x)h$ to each h such that $x + h \in X'$. This perspective is particularly useful in the next section.

Definition A.37   *When $f'(x)$ exists at x, f is* differentiable *at x. If $f'(x)$ exists at all x in some subset $X'' \subset X$, then f is* differentiable *on the entire X''. If in addition f' is a continuous function of x on X'', f is* continuously differentiable.

When X' is a closed set, then f being differentiable or continuously differentiable on X' is equivalent to f being differentiable or continuously differentiable in the interior of X' and then also having *an extension* (or a continuous extension) of its derivative to the boundary of X'. A slightly stronger requirement, which also guarantees (continuous) differentiability on X', is that there exists an open set $X'' \supset X'$ such that f is (continuously) differentiable on X''. When f is not differentiable at x (i.e., $f'(x)$ does not exist), it may still have *directional derivatives*—in particular, left and right derivatives. These derivatives are defined by

$$f^-(x) = \lim_{h \uparrow 0}[f(x+h) - f(x)]/h, \text{ and } f^+(x) = \lim_{h \downarrow 0}[f(x+h) - f(x)]/h$$

(which can be well defined even when (A.5) is not). Directional derivatives are used in the second version of the proof of Theorem 6.6 in Chapter 6. The next example illustrates how simple functions may have left and right derivatives but may fail to be differentiable.

Example A.13 *Let f be defined as $f(x) = x$ for $x \geq 0$ and $f(x) = -x$ for $x < 0$. f has left and right derivatives at 0 but is not differentiable according to (A.5), since a unique $f'(x)$ does not exist.*

Differentiability is a stronger requirement than continuity.

Fact A.22 *Let $X \subset \mathbb{R}$, and $f : X \to \mathbb{R}$ be a real-valued function. If f is differentiable at $x \in X$, then it is also continuous at x.*

Proof. See Exercise A.24. ■

It is also useful to note that differentiability over some set X' does not imply continuous differentiability. The following example illustrates this point.

Example A.14 *Consider the function f such that $f(x) = x^2 \sin(1/x)$ for all $x \neq 0$ and $f(0) = 0$. It can be verified that f is continuous and differentiable, with derivative $f'(x) = 2x \sin(1/x) - \cos(1/x)$ and $f'(0) = 0$. But clearly, $\lim_{x \downarrow 0} f'(x) \neq 0$.*

Higher-order derivatives are defined in a similar manner. Again starting with a real-valued function f, suppose that this function has a continuous derivative $f'(x)$. Taking x in some open set X', where $f'(X')$ is well defined, the second derivative of f, denoted $f''(x)$, is

$$f''(x) = \lim_{h \to 0} \frac{f'(x+h) - f'(x)}{h}.$$

Higher-order derivatives are defined similarly. If a real-valued function f has continuous derivatives up to order n on some set X', then it is said to be $\mathcal{C}^n$ on X'. If f is a $\mathcal{C}^1$ function, we also say that it is *continuously differentiable*. A $\mathcal{C}^\infty$ function has continuous derivatives of any order (which may be constant after some level, as is the case with polynomials).

The following simple fact shows how first- and second-order derivatives relate to concavity (equivalent results naturally hold for convexity).

Fact A.23 *Suppose that $X \subset \mathbb{R}$ and that $f : X \to \mathbb{R}$ is differentiable. Then:*

1. *f is concave on X if and only if, for all $x, y \in X$,*

$$f(y) - f(x) \leq f'(x)(y - x). \tag{A.7}$$

2. *f is concave on X if and only if $f'(x)$ is nonincreasing in x for all $x \in X$.*

3. *If, in addition, f is twice differentiable, then f is concave on X if and only if $f''(x) \leq 0$ for all $x \in X$.*

Proof. **(Part 1)** Suppose first that f is concave, and take, without loss of generality, $y > x$. Then $f(\lambda y + (1 - \lambda)x) \geq \lambda f(y) + (1 - \lambda) f(x)$ for all $\lambda \in (0, 1)$. Rearranging this expression yields

$$f(y) - f(x) \leq \frac{f(x + \lambda(y - x)) - f(x)}{\lambda(y - x)}(y - x).$$

Let $\varepsilon = \lambda(y - x)$, and note that this inequality is true for any $\lambda \in (0, 1)$ and thus for any $\varepsilon \geq 0$ in the neighborhood of 0. Therefore we have

$$f(y) - f(x) \leq \frac{f(x + \varepsilon) - f(x)}{\varepsilon}(y - x)$$

$$\leq f'(x)(y - x),$$

where the second line follows by taking the limit $\varepsilon \downarrow 0$ and using the fact that, by the differentiability of f, this limit uniquely defines $f'(x)$.

Conversely, suppose that (A.7) holds. Then for any $\lambda \in (0, 1)$ it follows that

$$f(y) - f(\lambda y + (1 - \lambda)x) \le (1 - \lambda)f'(\lambda y + (1 - \lambda)x)(y - x), \text{ and}$$

$$f(x) - f(\lambda y + (1 - \lambda)x) \le -\lambda f'(\lambda y + (1 - \lambda)x)(y - x).$$

Multiplying the first inequality by λ and the second by $(1 - \lambda)$ and summing the two, we obtain that, for all $\lambda \in (0, 1)$,

$$f(\lambda y + (1 - \lambda)x) \ge \lambda f(y) + (1 - \lambda)f(x).$$

(Part 2) Suppose f is concave (or equivalently (A.7) holds). Then for $y > x$, we have

$$f'(x) \ge \frac{f(y) - f(x)}{y - x}$$

$$= \frac{f(x) - f(y)}{x - y}$$

$$\ge f'(y),$$

where the last inequality uses the fact that $x - y < 0$.

Conversely, if $y > x$ and $f'(x) < f'(y)$, then the previous string of inequalities imply that either $f'(x)(y - x) < f(y) - f(x)$ or $f'(y)(x - y) > f(x) - f(y)$, thus violating (A.7).

(Part 3) This part follows immediately from Part 2 when f is twice differentiable. ∎

The next three results are often very useful in applications. The first one is a generalization of the Intermediate Value Theorem (Theorem A.3) to derivatives.

Theorem A.20 (Mean Value Theorem) *Suppose that $f : [a, b] \to \mathbb{R}$ is continuously differentiable on $[a, b]$ (with $b > a$). Then there exists $x^* \in [a, b]$ such that*

$$f'(x^*) = \frac{f(b) - f(a)}{b - a}.$$

Moreover if $f'(a) \ne f'(b)$, then for any c intermediate between $f'(a)$ and $f'(b)$, there exists $x^{**} \in (a, b)$ such that $f'(x^{**}) = c$.

Proof. See Exercise A.25. ∎

A particular difficulty often encountered in evaluating limits of the form $\lim_{x \to x^*} f(x)/g(x)$ (where f and g are continuous real-valued functions) is that we may have both $f(x^*) = 0$ and $g(x^*) = 0$. The following result, known as *l'Hôpital's Rule*, provides one way of evaluating these types of limits.

Theorem A.21 (l'Hôpital's Rule) *Suppose that $f : [a, b] \to \mathbb{R}$ and $g : [a, b] \to \mathbb{R}$ are differentiable functions on $[a, b]$, suppose that $g'(x) \ne 0$ for $x \in (a, b)$, and let $c \in [a, b]$. If*

$$\lim_{x \uparrow c} \frac{f'(x)}{g'(x)}$$

exists and

$$\text{either } \lim_{x \uparrow c} f(x) = \lim_{x \uparrow c} g(x) = 0, \text{ or } \lim_{x \uparrow c} f(x) = \lim_{x \uparrow c} g(x) = \infty,$$

then

$$\lim_{x \uparrow c} \frac{f(x)}{g(x)} = \lim_{x \uparrow c} \frac{f'(x)}{g'(x)}.$$

The same conclusions also hold for $\lim_{x \downarrow c}$.

Proof.   See Exercise A.26.   ∎

The final result in this section are the Taylor Theorem and the resulting Taylor Series approximation to differentiable real-valued functions. For this theorem, let the nth derivative of a real-valued function f be denoted by $f^{(n)}$ (e.g., $f' = f^{(1)}$, and so on).

Theorem A.22 (Taylor's Theorem I)   *Suppose that $f : [a, b] \to \mathbb{R}$ is a $\mathcal{C}^{n-1}$ function, and its nth derivative $f^{(n)}(x)$ exists for all $x \in (a, b)$. Then for any x and $y \neq x$ in $[a, b]$, there exists z between x and y such that*

$$f(y) = f(x) + \sum_{k=1}^{n-1} \frac{f^{(k)}(x)}{k!}(y - x)^k + \frac{f^{(n)}(z)}{n!}(y - x)^n.$$

Proof.   Suppose $y > x$. The proof requires that there exists $z \in (x, y)$ such that

$$f^{(n)}(z) = n!(y - x)^{-n} \left(f(y) - f(x) - \sum_{k=1}^{n-1} \frac{f^{(k)}(x)}{k!}(y - x)^k \right).$$

Let

$$g(t) = f(t) - f(x) - \sum_{k=1}^{n-1} \frac{f^{(k)}(x)}{k!}(t - x)^k$$

$$- \frac{(t - x)^n}{(y - x)^n} \left(f(y) - f(x) - \sum_{k=1}^{n-1} \frac{f^{(k)}(x)}{k!}(y - x)^k \right).$$

Clearly g is n-times differentiable. Thus the proof is equivalent to showing that there exists $z \in (x, y)$ such that $g^{(n)}(z) = 0$. It can be verified that $g^{(k)}(x) = 0$ for $k = 0, 1, \dots, n - 1$, and also $g(x) = g(y) = 0$. The Mean Value Theorem (Theorem A.20) then implies that $g^{(1)}(z_1) = 0$ for some $z_1 \in (x, y)$. Since $g^{(1)}(x) = g^{(1)}(z_1) = 0$, again from Theorem A.20, we have that there exists $z_2 \in (x, z_1)$ such that $g^{(2)}(z_2) = 0$. Continuing inductively for $n - 2$ more steps establishes the existence of $z \in (x, y)$ such that $g^{(n)}(z) = 0$.   ∎

Corollary A.3

1. *Suppose that $f : [a, b] \to \mathbb{R}$ is a $\mathcal{C}^n$ function. Then*

$$f(y) = f(x) + \sum_{k=0}^{n} \frac{f^{(k)}(x)}{k!}(y - x)^k + o(|y - x|^n),$$

   where recall that $o(k)/k \to 0$ as $k \to 0$.

2. *Suppose that $f : [a, b] \to \mathbb{R}$ is a $\mathcal{C}^{\infty}$ and that $\lim_{n \to \infty} \sum_{k=0}^{n} \frac{f^{(k)}(x)}{k!}(y - x)^k$ exists. Then*

$$f(y) = f(x) + \lim_{n \to \infty} \sum_{k=0}^{n} \frac{f^{(k)}(x)}{k!}(y - x)^k.$$

Proof.   See Exercise A.27.   ∎

Corollary A.4 *Suppose that $f : [a, b] \to \mathbb{R}$ is twice continuously differentiable and concave. Then for any $x, y \in [a, b]$, we have $f(y) \leq f(x) + f'(x)(y - x)$.*

Proof. By Theorem A.22, $f(y) = f(x) + f'(x)(y - x) + f''(z)(y - x)^2/2$ for some z between x and y. From Fact A.23, $f''(z) \leq 0$ for a concave function and thus the conclusion follows. ∎

A.9 Functions of Several Variables and the Inverse and Implicit Function Theorems

Throughout this section, I limit myself to differentiation in Euclidean spaces; that is, our interests are with mappings

$$\phi : X \to Y,$$

where $X \subset \mathbb{R}^{K_X}$ and $Y \subset \mathbb{R}^{K_Y}$, with $K_X, K_Y \in \mathbb{N}$. In the text, when mappings of this form arise and emphasis is needed, I refer to ϕ as a *vector* function or *vector-valued* function, since $\phi(x) \in \mathbb{R}^{K_Y}$ (for $x \in X$).

The theory of differentiation and the types of results that I present here can be developed in more general spaces than Euclidean spaces. For example, Luenberger's (1969) classic treatment of general optimization problems considers X and Y to be Banach spaces (complete normed vector spaces, which allow for a convenient definition of *linear operators;* see Section A.10). Nevertheless for the results presented here, restricting attention to Euclidean spaces is without loss of generality and enables me to reduce notation and avoid unnecessary complexities.

The case $K_x = K_Y = 1$ was treated in the previous section. Building on the results and the intuitions of that section, let us now move to more general mappings. For $\phi : X \to Y$ (where $X \subset \mathbb{R}^{K_X}$ and $Y \subset \mathbb{R}^{K_Y}$), the equivalent of the derivative is the linear operator $J(x) : X \to Y$. In particular, in analogy to (A.6), we have the following definition of differentiability.[4] Let $h \in X$ be a vector, and let $\|h\|$ denote its Euclidean norm. Then for $x \in X'$, where X' is an open set with $\phi(X') \subset Y$ well defined, ϕ is differentiable if the limit

$$\lim_{h \to 0} \frac{\|\phi(x + h) - \phi(x) - J(x)h\|}{\|h\|} = 0 \tag{A.8}$$

at x exists and defines a unique linear operator $J(x)$ (mapping from $\mathbb{R}^{K_X}$ onto $\mathbb{R}^{K_Y}$). In this case, the derivative of $\phi(x)$ is denoted by $J(x)$. The derivative is again a linear operator because it assigns the value $J(x)h$ to any vector h such that $x + h \in X'$.

We refer to $J(x)$ as the *Jacobian matrix* (or as simply the *Jacobian*) of ϕ at x and often denote it by $D\phi(x)$. The latter is a more convenient notation than $J(x)$, since it indicates which function we are referring to. We will see below that the Jacobian, when it exists, is also the matrix of partial derivatives of ϕ. We can also denote the matrix of partial derivatives by $D_{x_1}\phi(x_1, x_2)$ for $x_1 \in \mathbb{R}^{K_1}$, $x_2 \in \mathbb{R}^{K_2}$, and $K_1, K_2 \in \mathbb{N}$.

Fact A.24 *Let $X \subset \mathbb{R}^{K_X}$, $Y \subset \mathbb{R}^{K_Y}$ (where $K_X, K_Y \in \mathbb{N}$), and $\phi : X \to \mathbb{Y}$. If ϕ is differentiable at $x \in X$, then it is also continuous at x.*

---

4. More precisely, this is the definition of *Fréchet differentiability*. The alternative, weaker, notion of *Gateaux differentiability* is also useful in many instances (see, e.g., Luenberger, 1969). For our purposes, there is no need to distinguish between these two notions, since in finite-dimensional spaces they are equivalent.

Let us next take $X \subset \mathbb{R}^{K_X}$ and consider the mapping $\phi : X \to \mathbb{R}$, also referred to as a *function of several variables*. Its partial derivatives with respect to each component of X are defined identically to the derivative of a real-valued function of one variable (holding all the other variables constant). Let $x = (x_1, \ldots, x_{K_X})$, and assume that ϕ is differentiable with respect to its kth component. Then the kth partial derivative of ϕ is

$$\frac{\partial \phi(x_1, \ldots, x_{K_X})}{\partial x_k} = \phi_k(x),$$

where

$$\phi_k(x) = \lim_{h \to 0} \frac{\phi(x_1, \ldots, x_{k-1}, x_k + h, x_{k+1}, \ldots, x_{K_X}) - \phi(x_1, \ldots, x_{k-1}, x_k, x_{k+1}, \ldots, x_{K_X})}{h}.$$

Now assuming that ϕ has partial derivatives with respect to each x_k for $k = 1, \ldots, K_X$, the Jacobian in this case is simply a *row vector*,

$$J(x) = (\phi_1(x) \quad \cdot \quad \cdot \quad \cdot \quad \phi_{K_X}(x)).$$

A general mapping $\phi : X \to Y$, where Y is a subset of $\mathbb{R}^{K_Y}$ can then be thought of as consisting of K_Y real-valued functions of several variables, $\phi^1(x), \ldots, \phi^{K_Y}(x)$. We can define the partial derivatives of each of these functions in a similar fashion and denote them by $\phi_k^j(x)$. The Jacobian can then be written as

$$J(x) = \begin{pmatrix} \phi_1^1(x) & \cdot & \cdot & \cdot & \phi_{K_X}^1(x) \\ & \cdot & & \cdot & \\ & \cdot & & \cdot & \\ & \cdot & & \cdot & \\ \phi_1^{K_Y}(x) & \cdot & \cdot & \cdot & \phi_{K_X}^{K_Y}(x) \end{pmatrix}.$$

Higher-order derivatives can be defined in a similar fashion. When $\phi : X \to X$, $J(x)$ is a $K_X \times K_X$ matrix, and in this case, we can investigate whether it is invertible (i.e., whether the inverse $J^{-1}(x)$ at x exists). This property plays an important role in the Inverse Function and Implicit Function Theorems below.

When the matrix of partial derivatives exists, we refer to it as the "Jacobian," but this does not guarantee that the mapping in question is differentiable. The following example illustrates the problem.

Example A.15 *Consider the function of several variables $\phi(x_1, x_2)$ over the entire $\mathbb{R}^2$ such that $\phi(x_1, x_2) = 0$ if $x_1 = x_2 = 0$, and*

$$\phi(x_1, x_2) = \frac{x_1^2 x_2^2}{x_1 + x_2}$$

otherwise. The partial derivatives of this function are

$$\frac{\partial \phi(x_1, x_2)}{\partial x_1} = \frac{x_1^2 x_2^2 + 2x_1 x_2^3}{(x_1 + x_2)^2}, \text{ and}$$

$$\frac{\partial \phi(x_1, x_2)}{\partial x_2} = \frac{x_1^2 x_2^2 + 2x_1^3 x_2}{(x_1 + x_2)^2}.$$

It can be verified that these partial derivatives exist everywhere in $\mathbb{R}^2$, and in particular, $\partial\phi(0, 0)/\partial x_1 = \partial\phi(0, 0)/\partial x_2 = 0$. However, it is also clear that ϕ is not continuous at $x_1 = x_2 = 0$ (let $x = x_1 = x_2$ and evaluate the limit $x \to 0$ using L'Hospital's Rule as $\lim_{x\to 0}\phi(x, x) = 2$). Thus in view of Fact A.24, ϕ is not differentiable. The fact that ϕ is not differentiable can also be established using directly the definition of differentiability provided above.

The situation illustrated in Example A.15 is important to bear in mind, and it implies that a well-defined matrix of partial derivatives does not guarantee differentiability. Thus one may wish to distinguish between the linear operator $J(x)$ defined above and the Jacobian, consisting of the partial derivatives $D\phi(x)$. Nevertheless in this book there is no need to draw this distinction, and throughout $D\phi(x)$ refers to the Jacobian (i.e., to the matrix of partial derivatives).

Continuous differentiability is defined analogously to the one-dimensional case.

Definition A.38 *A mapping ϕ is of class $\mathcal{C}^n$ (n-times continuously differentiable) on some set X' if it has continuous derivatives up to the nth order.*

Fact A.25 *A mapping $\phi : X \to Y$, with $X \subset \mathbb{R}^{K_X}$, $Y \subset \mathbb{R}^{K_Y}$ (where K_X, $K_Y \in \mathbb{N}$), and X open, is of class $\mathcal{C}^1$ on X if its partial derivatives $\phi_k^j(x)$ for $k = 1, \ldots, K_X$ and $j = 1, \ldots, K_Y$ exist and are continuous functions of x for each $x \in X$.*

When there is no need for further generality, I require that the relevant utility or production functions are continuously differentiable (of class $\mathcal{C}^1$) or the stronger requirement that they are twice differentiable.

Taylor's Theorem and its corollaries can be generalized to mappings discussed here. I state this result for $\phi : X \to \mathbb{R}$, with $X \subset \mathbb{R}^{K_X}$. Let $D\phi$ and $D^2\phi$ denote the vector of first derivatives and the Jacobian of ϕ, respectively. Let $\|y - x\|$ be the Euclidean norm of the K_X-dimensional vector $y - x$ and z^T be the transpose of vector z. The following is a simpler version of the equivalent form of Taylor's Theorem in Corollary A.3. Its proof is similar to that of Theorem A.22 and is omitted.

Theorem A.23 (Taylor's Theorem II) *Suppose that $\phi : X \to \mathbb{R}$ is a $\mathcal{C}^1$ function and its second derivative $D^2\phi(x)$ exists for all $x \in X$. Then for any x and $y \neq x$ in X,*

$$\phi(y) = \phi(x) + D\phi(x)^T(y - x) + o(\|y - x\|).$$

If in addition $\phi : X \to \mathbb{R}$ is a $\mathcal{C}^2$ function with third derivative $D^3\phi(x)$ for all $x \in X$, then for any x and $y \neq x$ in X,

$$\phi(y) = \phi(x) + D\phi(x)^T(y - x) + (y - x)^T D^2\phi(x)(y - x) + o(\|y - x\|^2).$$

The following two theorems are the basis of much of the comparative static results in economics. They are therefore among the most important mathematical results for economic analysis. Consider a mapping $\phi : X \to X$ for $X \subset \mathbb{R}^{K_X}$. A key question is whether this mapping will have an inverse $\phi^{-1} : X \to X$. If for some subset X' of X, ϕ is single-valued and has an inverse ϕ^{-1} (which is also a single-valued) then we say that it is *one-to-one*.

Theorem A.24 (Inverse Function Theorem) *Consider a $\mathcal{C}^1$ mapping $\phi : X \to X$ for $X \subset \mathbb{R}^{K_X}$. Suppose that the Jacobian of ϕ, $J(x)$, evaluated at some interior point x^* of X is invertible. Then there exist open sets X' and X'' in X such that $x^* \in X'$, $\phi(x^*) \in X''$, and ϕ is one-to-one on X', with $\phi(X') = X''$. Moreover $\phi^{-1}(\phi(x)) = x$ for all x in X' and ϕ^{-1} is also a $\mathcal{C}^1$ mapping.*

The proof of this theorem can be found in any real analysis book and is omitted.

Theorem A.25 (Implicit Function Theorem) *Consider a $\mathcal{C}^1$ mapping $\phi : X \times Y \to Y$, with $X \subset \mathbb{R}^{K_X}$ and $Y \subset \mathbb{R}^{K_Y}$. Suppose that $(x^*, y^*) \in X \times Y$; $\phi(x^*, y^*) = 0$; all the entries of the Jacobian of ϕ with respect to (x, y), $D_{(x,y)}\phi(x^*, y^*)$, are finite; and $D_y\phi(x^*, y^*)$ is invertible. Then there exists an open set X' containing x^* and a unique $\mathcal{C}^1$ mapping $\gamma : X' \to Y$ such that $\gamma(x^*) = y^*$ and*

$$\phi(x, \gamma(x)) = 0 \tag{A.9}$$

for all $x \in X'$.

This theorem is called the Implicit Function Theorem because the mapping γ is defined implicitly. Exercise 6.5 in Chapter 6 provided the proof of a special case of this theorem. The more general case can also be proved with the same methods as in that exercise. An alternative proof uses the Inverse Function Theorem. Since the former proof has already been discussed and the latter one is contained in most real analysis books, I omit the proof.

The main utility of this theorem comes from the fact that since ϕ and γ are $\mathcal{C}^1$ and (A.9) holds for an open set around x^*, (A.9) can be differentiated with respect to x to obtain an expression for how the solution y to the set of equations $\phi(x, y) = 0$ behaves as a function of x. If we think of x as representing a set of parameters and y as the endogenous variables determined by some economic relationship summarized by (A.9), then this procedure can tell us how the endogenous variables change in response to the changes in the environment captured by the parameter x. I make repeated use of this approach throughout the book.

A.10 Separation Theorems *

In this section I briefly discuss the separation of convex disjoint sets using linear functionals (or hyperplanes). These results form the basis of the Second Welfare Theorem (Theorem 5.7). They also provide the basis of many important results in constrained optimization (see Section A.11).

For this section, I take X to be a *vector space* (linear space). Recall that linearity implies that if $x, y \in X$ and λ is a real number, then $x + y \in X$ and $\lambda x \in X$ (see Section A.7). The element of X with the property that $x = \lambda x$ for all $\lambda \in \mathbb{R}$ is denoted by θ.

Definition A.39 *The real-valued nonnegative function $\|\cdot\| : X \to \mathbb{R}_+$ is taken to be a* norm *on X, which implies that for any $x, y \in X$ and any $\lambda \in \mathbb{R}$,*

1. *(**Properness**) $\|x\| \geq 0$ and $\|x\| = 0$ if and only if $x = \theta$,*
2. *(**Linearity**) $\|\lambda x\| = |\lambda| \|x\|$, and*
3. *(**Triangle Inequality**) $\|x + y\| \leq \|x\| + \|y\|$.*

A vector space equipped with a norm is a normed *vector space. A complete normed vector space is a* Banach *space.*

If a function $p : X \to \mathbb{R}_+$ satisfies properness and the triangle inequality, but not necessarily the linearity condition, then it is a *semi-norm*.

Many of the metric spaces given in Example A.1 are also normed vector spaces with the appropriate norm. In fact, a simple way of obtaining the norm in many cases is to take the distance function d and try the norm $\|x\| = d(x, \theta)$. Notice, however, that this method will not always work, since metrics do not need to satisfy the linearity condition in Definition A.39.

Example A.16   *The first four spaces are normed vector spaces, while the fifth one is not.*

1. *For any $X \subset \mathbb{R}^K$, let x_i be the ith component of $x \in X$. Then the K-dimensional Euclidean space is a normed vector space, with norm given by $\|x\| = \left(\sum_{i=1}^{K} |x_i|^2\right)^{1/2}$.*

2. *Let $X \subset \mathbb{R}^K$, and consider the set of continuous, bounded, real-valued functions $f : X \to \mathbb{R}$ denoted by $\mathbf{C}(X)$. Then $\mathbf{C}(X)$ is a normed vector space, with norm $\|f\| = \sup_{x \in X} |f(x)|$.*

3. *The set $\ell \subset \mathbb{R}^\infty$, consisting of infinite sequences of real numbers, is a normed vector space, with norm $\|x\|_p = \left(\sum_{i=1}^{\infty} |x_i|^p\right)^{1/p}$ for $1 \le p < \infty$ and with $\|x\|_\infty = \sup_i |x_i|$. For any $p \in [1, \infty]$, the corresponding normed vector space is denoted by ℓ_p. The one of greatest interest for us is ℓ_∞.*

4. *Let $\mathbf{c} \subset \mathbb{R}^\infty$ be the set consisting of infinite sequences of real numbers that are equal to zero after some point (e.g., $(x_1, \ldots, x_M, 0, 0, \ldots)$, where $M \in \mathbb{N}$. Let the sup norm on $\mathbf{c}$ be defined as $\|x\|_\infty = \sup_i |x_i|$. Then $\mathbf{c}$ with the sup norm is a normed vector space.*

5. *For X nonempty, consider the discrete metric $d(x, y) = 1$ if $x \neq y$ and $d(x, y) = 0$ if $x = y$. The metric space (X, d) is not a normed vector space.*

When the norm is understood implicitly, we refer to X as a normed vector space.

Definition A.40   *Let X be a normed vector space. Then $\phi : X \to \mathbb{R}$ is a* linear functional *on X if for any $x, y \in X$ and any real numbers λ and μ,*

$$\phi(\lambda x + \mu y) = \lambda \phi(x) + \mu \phi(y).$$

Linear functionals on normed vector spaces have many nice properties. For example, if $X \subset \mathbb{R}^K$, then any linear functional on X can be expressed as an *inner product* of x with another K-dimensional vector η; that is,

$$\phi(x) = \eta \cdot x = \sum_{i=1}^{K} \eta_i x_i,$$

where $\eta = (\eta_1, \ldots, \eta_K) \in \mathbb{R}^K$. Therefore on Euclidean spaces, linear functionals correspond to inner products. Some useful properties of linear functionals are provided in the following result.

Theorem A.26 (Continuity of Linear Functionals)   *Let X be a normed vector space. Then*

1. *the linear functional $\phi : X \to \mathbb{R}$ is continuous on X if and only if it is continuous at θ and*

2. *the linear functional $\phi : X \to \mathbb{R}$ is continuous on X if and only if it is bounded in the sense that there exists $M \in \mathbb{R}$ such that $|\phi(x)| \le M \|x\|$ for all $x \in X$.*

Proof.   **(Part 1)** We need only prove that ϕ is continuous on X if it is continuous at θ. Suppose that it is continuous at θ. Fix an arbitrary $x \in X$, and consider a sequence in X, $\{x_n\}$, converging to x. By the linearity of ϕ,

$$\left|\phi(x_n) - \phi(x)\right| = \left|\phi(x_n - x + \theta) - \phi(\theta)\right|.$$

Since $x_n \to x$, we have $x_n - x + \theta \to \theta$, and since ϕ is continuous at θ, we also have that $\phi(x_n - x + \theta) \to \phi(\theta)$. Therefore $\left|\phi(x_n) - \phi(x)\right| \to 0$, proving that ϕ is continuous at x.

(**Part 2**) To prove the "if" part, suppose that ϕ is bounded. Consider a sequence $\{x_n\}$ converging to θ. Thus $|\phi(x_n)| \leq M \|x_n\|$, and since $x_n \to \theta$, we have $|\phi(x_n)| \to 0$, proving that ϕ is continuous at θ. Then by Part 1, ϕ is continuous on X.

To prove the "only if" part, suppose that ϕ is continuous at θ. Fix $\varepsilon > 0$. Then there exists $\delta > 0$ such that for $\|x\| \leq \delta$, $|\phi(x)| \leq \varepsilon$. Note that for $x \neq \theta$, the vector $\delta x / \|x\|$ has norm equal to δ. Therefore

$$
\begin{aligned}
|\phi(x)| &= \left| \phi \left(\frac{\delta x}{\|x\|} \right) \right| \cdot \frac{\|x\|}{\delta} \\
&\leq \varepsilon \cdot \frac{\|x\|}{\delta} \\
&= M \|x\|,
\end{aligned}
$$

with $M = \varepsilon / \delta$, completing the proof. ∎

The smallest M that satisfies $|\phi(x)| \leq M \|x\|$ for all $x \in X$ is defined as the norm of the linear functional ϕ and is denoted by $\|\phi\|$. Theorem A.26 therefore implies that a continuous linear functional has a finite norm.

Definition A.41 *Let X be a normed vector space. The space of all continuous linear functionals on X is the* normed dual *of X and is denoted by X^*.*

Dual spaces have many nice features.

Fact A.26 *If X is a normed vector space, then its dual X^* is a Banach space.*

The following example gives the duals of some common spaces (see Exercise A.29).

Example A.17

1. *For any $K \in \mathbb{N}$, the dual of $\mathbb{R}^K$ is $\mathbb{R}^K$.*
2. *For any $p \in (1, \infty)$, the dual of ℓ_p is ℓ_q, where $p^{-1} + q^{-1} = 1$.*

A nonobvious fact is the following. Let $\mathbf{c} = \{x = (x_1, x_2, \ldots) \in \ell_\infty : \lim_{n \to \infty} x_n = 0\}$.

Fact A.27

1. *The dual of ℓ_∞ is not ℓ_1 (it contains ℓ_1).*
2. *The dual of $\mathbf{c}$ is ℓ_1.*

Dual spaces are useful in economics, because when X is a commodity space, its dual X^* corresponds to the space of "price functionals" for X. For example, the dual of $X \subset \mathbb{R}^K$ is $X^* \subset \mathbb{R}^K$ and indeed consists of functionals of the form $\phi(x) = \sum_{i=1}^K \eta_i x_i$ as noted above. Loosely speaking, we can interpret the η_is as prices corresponding to the commodity vector x, so that $\phi(x)$ is the cost of x at the price vector η. The utility of this construction for economics stems from the following famous theorem. A linear functional ϕ defined on X is *nonzero* if it is not identically equal to zero for all $x \in X$.

Theorem A.27 (Geometric Hahn-Banach Theorem) *Let X be a normed vector space, and let $X^1, X^2 \subset X$. Suppose that X^1 and X^2 are convex, Int $X^1 \neq \emptyset$ and $X^2 \cap$ Int $X^1 = \emptyset$. Then there exists a nonzero continuous linear functional ϕ on X such that*

$$
\phi(x^1) \leq c \leq \phi(x^2)
$$

for all $x^1 \in X^1$, $x^2 \in X^2$, and some $c \in \mathbb{R}$.

This theorem is obtained from the Hahn-Banach Theorem. The latter states that if ϕ is a continuous linear functional on a subspace M of X and is dominated by a semi-norm $p(x)$ (i.e., $f(x) \leq p(x)$ for all $x \in M$), then there is an extension Φ of ϕ to the entire X such that Φ is a continuous linear functional on X, $\Phi(x) = \phi(x)$ for all $x \in M$, and $\Phi(x) \leq p(x)$ for all $x \in X$. This theorem therefore establishes that normed vector spaces are "abundant" in linear functionals. Since its proof is not particularly useful for our purposes here, it is omitted (see Luenberger, 1969; Kolmogorov and Fomin, 1970; or Conway, 1990).

Notice the nonintuitive requirement that Int $X^1 \neq \emptyset$, which implies that X^1 should contain an interior point. This is not a stringent requirement when X is a subset of the Euclidean space (and in fact, this condition is not even necessary in that case). However some common infinite-dimensional normed vector spaces, such as ℓ_p for $p < \infty$, do not contain interior points when we restrict attention to their economically relevant subspace, ℓ_p^+, which requires all sequences to consist of nonnegative numbers (this is not obvious, but Exercise A.30 illustrates why). This limitation might be a problem if we wish to model the allocations (e.g., the sequence of consumption levels or capital stocks) in an infinite-horizon economy as elements of ℓ_p^+. Nevertheless it is not an issue when we focus on the economically more natural space of sequences of allocations ℓ_∞, because ℓ_∞^+ does contain interior points (see Exercise A.31). The only complication that arises from the use of ℓ_∞ is that not all linear functionals on ℓ_∞ have an inner-product representation and thus may not correspond to economically meaningful price systems (recall Fact A.27). This problem can be handled, however, by making somewhat stronger assumptions on preferences and technology to ensure that the relevant linear functionals on ℓ_∞ have the desired inner-product representation. This is the reason why the Second Welfare Theorem (Theorem 5.7) imposes additional conditions on preferences and technology.

It is also useful to note the following immediate corollary of Theorem A.27.

Theorem A.28 (Separating Hyperplane Theorem) *Let $X \subset \mathbb{R}^K$ and $X^1, X^2 \subset X$. Suppose that X^1 and X^2 are convex and $X^2 \cap$ Int $X^1 = \emptyset$. Then there exists a hyperplane*

$$H = \left\{ x \in X : \sum_{i=1}^{K} \eta_i x_i = c \text{ for } \eta \in \mathbb{R} \text{ and } \eta \neq 0 \right\}$$

such the H separates X^1 and X^2; that is,

$$\eta \cdot x^1 \leq c \leq \eta \cdot x^2 \text{ for all } x^1 \in X^1, x^2 \in X^2,$$

where recall that $\eta \cdot x = \sum_{i=1}^{K} \eta_i x_i$.

Note that the statement of this theorem disposes of the hypothesis that Int $X^1 \neq \emptyset$, since the two sets are subsets of Euclidean spaces. Moreover the theorem does not add the qualification that the hyperplane H is nonzero (in the same way as Theorem A.27 did for linear functionals), since the definition of a hyperplane incorporates this requirement.

A.11 Constrained Optimization

Many of the problems we encountered in this book are formulated as constrained optimization problems. Chapters 6, 7, and 16 dealt with dynamic (infinite-dimensional) constrained optimization problems. Complementary insights about these problems can be gained by using the separation theorems of the previous section. Let me illustrate this by focusing on finite-dimensional optimization problems. Consider the maximization problem

$$\sup_{x \in X} f(x) \tag{A.10}$$

subject to

$$g(x) \leq 0,$$

where X is an open subset of $\mathbb{R}^K$; $f : X \to \mathbb{R}$; $g : X \to \mathbb{R}^N$; and $N, K \in \mathbb{N}$.

The constrained maximization problem (A.10) satisfies the *Slater* condition if there exists $x' \in X$ such that $g(x') < 0$ (meaning that each component of the mapping g takes a negative value). This condition is equivalent to the set $G = \{x : g(x) \leq 0\}$ having an interior point. We say that g is convex, if each component function of g is convex. Thus the set G is also convex (but the converse is not necessarily true; see Exercise A.32). As usual, we define the Lagrangian function as

$$\mathcal{L}(x, \lambda) = f(x) - \lambda \cdot g(x)$$

for $\lambda \in \mathbb{R}_+^N$. The vector λ is the *Lagrange multiplier*, and $\lambda \cdot g(x)$ denotes the inner product of the two vectors (here λ and the vector-valued function $g(\cdot)$ evaluated at x); thus it is equal to a real number. A central theorem in constrained maximization is the following.

Theorem A.29 (Saddle-Point Theorem) *Suppose that in (A.10) f is a concave function, g is convex, and the* Slater *condition is satisfied.*

1. *If x^* is a solution to (A.10), then there exists $\lambda^* \in \mathbb{R}_+^N$ such that*

$$\mathcal{L}(x, \lambda^*) \leq \mathcal{L}(x^*, \lambda^*) \leq \mathcal{L}(x^*, \lambda) \text{ for all } x \in X \text{ and } \lambda \in \mathbb{R}_+^N. \tag{A.11}$$

In this case, (x^*, λ^*) satisfies the complementary slackness condition

$$\lambda^* \cdot g(x^*) = 0. \tag{A.12}$$

2. *If $(x^*, \lambda^*) \in X \times \mathbb{R}_+^N$ satisfies $g(x^*) \leq 0$ and (A.11), then x^* is a solution to (A.10).*

Proof. (Part 1) Consider the space $Y = \mathbb{R}^{N+1}$, with subsets

$$Y^1 = \{(a, b) \in Y : a > f(x^*) \text{ and } b < 0\}, \text{ and}$$

$$Y^2 = \{(a, b) \in Y : \exists x \in X, \text{ with } a \leq f(x) \text{ and } b \geq g(x)\},$$

where $a \in \mathbb{R}$, $b \in \mathbb{R}^N$, and $b < 0$ means that each element of the N-dimensional vector b is negative. Y^1 is clearly convex. Moreover the concavity of f and the convexity of g ensure that Y^2 is also convex.

By the hypothesis that x^* is a solution to (A.10), the two sets are disjoint. Then Theorem A.28 implies that there exists a hyperplane separating these two sets. In other words, there exists a nonzero vector $\eta \in \mathbb{R}^{N+1}$ such that

$$\eta \cdot y^1 \leq c \leq \eta \cdot y^2$$

for all $y^1 \in Y^1$ and $y^2 \in Y^2$. Moreover the same conclusion holds for all $y^1 \in \overline{Y^1}$ and $y^2 \in \overline{Y^2}$. Then let $\eta = (\rho, \lambda)$, with $\rho \in \mathbb{R}$ and $\lambda \in \mathbb{R}^N$, so that

$$\rho a^1 + \lambda \cdot b^1 \leq \rho a^2 + \lambda \cdot b^2 \text{ for all } (a^1, b^1) \in Y^1, (a^2, b^2) \in \overline{Y^2}. \tag{A.13}$$

For $(f(x^*), 0) \in \overline{Y^2}$, we have

$$\rho a^1 + \lambda \cdot b^1 \leq \rho f(x^*) \tag{A.14}$$

for all $(a^1, b^1) \in \overline{Y^1}$. Now taking $a^1 = f(x^*)$ and $b^1 < 0$ implies $\lambda \geq 0$ (suppose instead that one component of the vector λ is negative; then take b^1 to have zeros everywhere except for that component, yielding a contradiction to (A.14)). Similarly, setting $b^1 = 0$ and $a^1 > f(x^*)$, we obtain $\rho \leq 0$. Moreover by the definition of a hyperplane, either ρ is negative or a component of λ must be strictly positive.

Next the optimality of x^* implies that for any $x \in X$, we have $(f(x), g(x)) \in \overline{Y^2}$. Since $(f(x^*), 0) \in \overline{Y^1}$, (A.13) implies that

$$\rho f(x^*) \leq \rho f(x) + \lambda \cdot g(x) \tag{A.15}$$

for all $x \in X$. Now to obtain a contradiction, suppose that $\rho = 0$. Then by the Slater condition, there exists $x' \in X'$ such that $g(x') < 0$, so that $\lambda \cdot g(x') < 0$ for any nonzero vector λ, violating (A.15). Therefore $\lambda = 0$. However this contradicts the fact that the separating hyperplane is nonzero (so that we cannot have both $\rho = 0$ and $\lambda = 0$). Therefore $\rho < 0$. Now define

$$\lambda^* = -\frac{\lambda}{\rho} \geq 0.$$

The complementary slackness condition then follows immediately from (A.15). In particular, evaluate the right-hand side at $x^* \in X$, which implies that $\lambda \cdot g(x^*) \geq 0$. Since $\lambda \geq 0$ and $g(x^*) \leq 0$, we must have

$$\lambda \cdot g(x^*) = -\rho(\lambda^* \cdot g(x^*)) = 0.$$

Now using the complementary slackness condition and (A.15) together with $\rho < 0$ yields

$$\mathcal{L}(x, \lambda^*) = f(x) - \lambda^* \cdot g(x) \leq f(x^*) = \mathcal{L}(x^*, \lambda^*)$$

for all $x \in X$, which establishes the first inequality in (A.11). To establish the second inequality, again use the complementary slackness condition and the fact that $g(x^*) \leq 0$ to obtain

$$\mathcal{L}(x^*, \lambda^*) = f(x^*) \leq f(x^*) - \lambda \cdot g(x^*) = \mathcal{L}(x^*, \lambda)$$

for all $\lambda \in \mathbb{R}^N_+$, which completes the proof of the first part.

(Part 2) Suppose, to obtain a contradiction, that (A.11) holds, but x^* is not a solution to (A.10). Thus there exists $x' \in X$ with $g(x') \leq 0$ and $f(x') > f(x^*)$. Then

$$f(x') - \lambda^* \cdot g(x') > f(x^*) - \lambda^* \cdot g(x^*),$$

which exploits the facts that $\lambda^* \cdot g(x^*) = 0$ and $\lambda^* \cdot g(x') \leq 0$ (since $\lambda^* \geq 0$ and $g(x') \leq 0$). But this expression contradicts (A.11) and so establishes the desired result. ∎

We often refer to maximization problems where, as in Theorem A.29, F is concave and g is convex, as *concave problems*.

Exercise A.33 shows that the Slater condition cannot be dispensed with in Theorem A.29. Despite their importance, constraint qualification conditions, such as the Slater condition or the linear independence condition in the next theorem, are often not stated explicitly in economic applications, because in most problems they are naturally satisfied. Nevertheless it is important to be aware that these conditions are necessary and that ignoring them can sometimes lead to misleading results.

An immediate corollary of the first inequality in (A.11) is that if $x^* \in$ Int X and if f and g are differentiable, then

$$D_x f(x^*) = \lambda^* \cdot D_x g(x^*), \tag{A.16}$$

where, as usual, $D_x f$ and $D_x g$ denote the Jacobians of f and g. Equation (A.16) is the usual first-order necessary condition for interior constrained maximum. In this case because the maximization problem is concave, (A.16), together with $g(x^*) \leq 0$, is also sufficient for a maximum.

The next result is the famous Kuhn-Tucker Theorem, which shows that (A.16) is necessary for an interior maximum (provided that f and g are differentiable) even when the concavity-convexity assumptions do not hold.

Theorem A.30 (Kuhn-Tucker Theorem) *Consider the constrained maximization problem*

$$\sup_{x \in \mathbb{R}^K} f(x)$$

subject to

$$g(x) \leq 0 \text{ and } h(x) = 0,$$

where $f : x \in X \to \mathbb{R}$, $g : x \in X \to \mathbb{R}^N$ and $h : x \in X \to \mathbb{R}^M$ (for some K, N, $M \in \mathbb{N}$). Let $x^* \in$ Int X be a solution to this maximization problem, and suppose that $N_1 \leq N$ of the inequality constraints are active, *in the sense that they hold as equality at x^*. Define $\bar{h} : X \to \mathbb{R}^{M+N_1}$ to be the mapping of these N_1 active constraints stacked with $h(x)$ (so that $\bar{h}(x^*) = 0$). Suppose that the following* constraint qualification condition *is satisfied: the Jacobian matrix $D_x(\bar{h}(x^*))$ has rank $N_1 + M$. Then the following Kuhn-Tucker condition is satisfied: there exist Lagrange multipliers $\lambda^* \in \mathbb{R}^N_+$ and $\mu^* \in \mathbb{R}^M$ such that*

$$D_x f(x^*) - \lambda^* \cdot D_x g(x^*) - \mu^* \cdot D_x h(x^*) = 0, \tag{A.17}$$

and the complementary slackness condition

$$\lambda^* \cdot g(x^*) = 0$$

holds.

Proof. (Sketch) The constraint qualification condition ensures that there exists an $(N_1 + M)$-dimensional manifold at x^*, defined by the equality and active inequality constraints. Since g and h are differentiable, this manifold is differentiable at x^*. Let $v_\varepsilon(x)$ denote a feasible direction along this manifold for small $\varepsilon \in \mathbb{R}^K$; in particular, such that $x^* \pm \varepsilon v_\varepsilon(x^* + \varepsilon)$ remains along this manifold and thus satisfies $D_x \bar{h}(x^*) \cdot \varepsilon v_\varepsilon(x^* + \varepsilon) = 0$. For ε sufficiently small, the $N - N_1$ nonactive constraints are still satisfied; thus $x^* \pm \varepsilon v_\varepsilon(x^* + \varepsilon)$ is feasible. If $D_x f(x^*) \cdot \varepsilon v_\varepsilon(x^* + \varepsilon) \neq 0$, then

$$f(x^* + \varepsilon v_\varepsilon(x^* + \varepsilon)) > f(x^*), \text{ or } f(x^* + \varepsilon v_\varepsilon(x^* + \varepsilon)) > f(x^*),$$

implying that x^* cannot be a local (and thus global) maximum. As a next step consider the $(M + N_1 + 1 \times K)$-dimensional matrix A, where the first row is $D_x f(x^*)^T$, and the rest is given by $D_x(\bar{h}(x^*))$. The preceding argument implies that for all nonzero $\varepsilon \in \mathbb{R}^K$ such that $D_x \bar{h}(x^*) \cdot \varepsilon v_\varepsilon(x^* + \varepsilon) = 0$, we also have $A \cdot (\varepsilon + v_\varepsilon(x^* + \varepsilon)) = 0$. Therefore both $D_x \bar{h}(x^*)$ and A have the same rank, which by the constraint qualification condition is equal to $M + N_1$.

Since A has $M + N_1 + 1$ rows, the first row of A must be a linear combination of its remaining $M + N_1$ rows, which equivalently implies that there exists an $(M + N_1)$-dimensional vector $\bar{\mu}$ such that $D_x f(x^*) = \bar{\mu} D_x \bar{h}(x^*)$. Assigning zero multipliers to all nonactive constraints, this result is equivalent to (A.17). The complementary slackness condition then follows immediately, since we have zero multipliers for the nonactive constraints and $g_j(x^*) = 0$ for the active constraints. ∎

The constraint qualification condition, which required that the active constraints should be linearly independent, plays a similar role to the Slater condition in Theorem A.29. Exercise A.34 shows that this constraint qualification condition cannot be dispensed with (though somewhat weaker conditions can be used instead of this full rank condition).

The complementary slackness condition in Theorem A.30 is a central result and has been used repeatedly in the text as a necessary condition for a maximum.

Let us end this Appendix with the famous and eminently useful Envelope Theorem.

Theorem A.31 (Envelope Theorem) *Consider the constrained maximization problem*

$$v(p) = \max_{x \in X} f(x, p)$$

subject to

$$g(x, p) \leq 0 \text{ and } h(x, p) = 0,$$

where $X \in \mathbb{R}^K$; $p \in \mathbb{R}$; and $f : X \times \mathbb{R} \to \mathbb{R}$, $g : X \times \mathbb{R} \to \mathbb{R}^N$, and $h : X \times \mathbb{R} \to \mathbb{R}^M$ are differentiable (K, N, $M \in \mathbb{N}$). Let $x^*(p) \in \text{Int } X$ be a solution to this maximization problem. Denote the Lagrange multipliers associated with the inequality and equality constraints by $\lambda^* \in \mathbb{R}_+^N$ and $\mu^* \in \mathbb{R}^M$. Suppose also that $v(\cdot)$ is differentiable at $\bar{p}$. Then we have

$$\frac{\partial v(\bar{p})}{\partial p} = \frac{\partial f(x^*(\bar{p}), \bar{p})}{\partial p} - \lambda^* \cdot D_p g(x^*(\bar{p}), \bar{p}) - \mu^* \cdot D_p(x^*(\bar{p}), \bar{p}). \quad \text{(A.18)}$$

Proof. Since $x^*(p)$ is the solution to the maximization problem, we have

$$v(\bar{p}) = f(x^*(\bar{p}), \bar{p}). \quad \text{(A.19)}$$

By hypothesis, $v(\cdot)$ is differentiable at $\bar{p}$, so $\partial v(\bar{p})/\partial p$ exists. Moreover, applying the Implicit Function Theorem to the necessary conditions for a maximum given in Theorem A.30, $x^*(\cdot)$ is also differentiable at $\bar{p}$. Therefore from (A.19) we can write

$$\frac{\partial v(\bar{p})}{\partial p} = \frac{\partial f(x^*(\bar{p}), \bar{p})}{\partial p} + D_x f(x^*(\bar{p}), \bar{p}) \cdot D_p x^*(\bar{p}), \quad \text{(A.20)}$$

where, once again, $D_x(x^*(\bar{p}), \bar{p}) \cdot D_p x^*(\bar{p})$ is the inner product and thus is a real number. Let $\tilde{g} : X \times \mathbb{R} \to \mathbb{R}^{N_1}$ denote the $N_1 \leq N$ active inequality constraints. Differentiating the active inequality constraints and the equality constraints with respect to p, we also have

$$-D_p \tilde{g}(x^*(\bar{p}), \bar{p}) = D_x \tilde{g}(x^*(\bar{p}), \bar{p}) \cdot D_p x^*(\bar{p}), \text{ and}$$

$$-D_p h(x^*(\bar{p}), \bar{p}) = D_x h(x^*(\bar{p}), \bar{p}) \cdot D_p x^*(\bar{p}).$$

The equivalent of (A.17) for this problem (recall Theorem A.30) implies that

$$D_x f(x^*(\bar{p}), \bar{p}) - \lambda^* \cdot D_x g(x^*(\bar{p}), \bar{p}) - \mu^* \cdot D_x(x^*(\bar{p}), \bar{p}) = 0.$$

Combining this expression with the previous two equations and noting that the Lagrange multipliers for the inactive constraints are equal to zero yields

$$D_x f(x^*(\bar{p}), \bar{p}) \cdot D_p x^*(\bar{p}) = -\lambda^* \cdot D_p g(x^*(\bar{p}), \bar{p}) - \mu^* \cdot D_x(x^*(\bar{p}), \bar{p}).$$

Substituting into (A.20) gives (A.18). ∎

A special case of this result applies when the problem is one of unconstrained maximization. In that case we simply have

$$\frac{\partial v(\bar{p})}{\partial p} = \frac{\partial f(x^*(\bar{p}), \bar{p})}{\partial p}.$$

A.12 Exercises

* A.1   (a) Prove the *Minkowski's inequality* that for any $x = (x_1, x_2, \ldots, x_K) \in \mathbb{R}^K$, $y = (y_1, y_2, \ldots, y_K)$ $\in \mathbb{R}^K$, with $K \in \mathbb{N}$, and any $p \in [1, \infty)$, we have

$$\left(\sum_{k=1}^{K} |x_k + y_k|^p \right)^{1/p} \leq \left(\sum_{k=1}^{K} |x_k|^p \right)^{1/p} + \left(\sum_{k=1}^{K} |y_k|^p \right)^{1/p}.$$

      (b) Formulate and prove the generalization of this inequality for $K = \infty$.

A.2   Using Minkowski's inequality (Exercise A.1), show that the metric spaces in Example A.1 part 1 satisfy the triangle inequality.

A.3   Show that the *sup metric* $d_\infty(f, g) = \sup_{x \in X} |f(x) - g(x)|$ on $\mathbf{C}(X)$ in Example A.1 satisfies the triangle inequality.

A.4   Using the definition of equivalent metrics in Definition A.4, show that if d and d' are equivalent metrics on X and a subset X' of X is open according to the collection of neighborhoods generated by the metric d, then it is open according to the collection of neighborhoods generated by the metric d'.

A.5   Prove that $X' \subset X$ is closed if and only if every convergent sequence $\{x_n\}_{n=1}^{\infty}$ in X' has a limit point $x \in X'$.

A.6   Prove Fact A.2.

A.7   Prove Fact A.3.

A.8   Prove Fact A.4. [Hint: use Theorem A.7.]

A.9   Prove that the metric space $(\mathbf{C}(X), d_\infty)$ introduced in Example A.1 is complete.

A.10   Using an argument similar to that in the proof of Theorem A.3, show that if (X, d) is a metric space and $\phi : X \to Y$ a continuous mapping, then $f(X')$ is a connected subset of Y for every connected subset X' of X.

A.11   Prove that all metrics of the family d_p defined on the Euclidean space in Example A.1 are equivalent according to Definition A.4.

A.12   Prove Fact A.5.

A.13   Prove Fact A.10.

A.14   Show that every metric space has the Hausdorff property.

A.15   Prove Lemma A.2.

A.16   (a) Show that if $X = \prod_{\alpha=1}^{K} X_\alpha$ (i.e., if X is a finite-dimensional product), then the box and the product topologies are equivalent in the sense that they define the same open sets (recall Definition A.4 for the equivalence of metrics, which applies to the equivalence of topologies as well).

(b) Show that if X is not finite-dimensional, then the box and the product topologies are not equivalent.

(c) Show that projection maps are always continuous in the box topology.

* A.17 Suppose that X_α is a metric space for each $\alpha \in A$. Show that the space $X = \prod_{\alpha \in A} X_\alpha$ endowed with the product topology satisfies the Hausdorff property.

A.18 Prove that the properties of upper and lower hemicontinuity in Definition A.31 imply the properties in Definition A.32 when X and Y are Euclidean.

A.19 (a) Show that $G(x, y) = \{(x, y) \in \mathbb{R}^2 : xy \leq 0\}$ is not a continuous correspondence.

(b) Show that if $G_1(x)$ and $G_2(x)$ are continuous, their nonempty intersection $G_1(x) \cap G_2(x)$ may fail to be continuous. [Hint: consider $G_1(x) = (-\infty, x]$ and $G_2(x) = \{a, b\}$ for some $a \neq b$.]

A.20 Prove Fact A.19.

A.21 Prove Fact A.21.

A.22 Give an example of an upper hemicontinuous correspondence from $[0, 1]$ into $[0, 1]$ that is not convex-valued and does not have a fixed point.

A.23 Consider an N-person normal-form game. Player i's strategy is denoted by $a_i \in A_i$, and her payoff function is given by the real-valued function $u_i(a_1, \ldots, a_N)$.

(a) Using Theorems A.16, A.17, and A.18, prove that if each A_i is nonempty, compact, and convex and each u_i is continuous in a_j for $j \neq i$ and is continuous and quasi-concave in a_i, there exists a strategy profile $(a_1^*, \ldots, a_N^*)$ that constitutes a pure-strategy Nash Equilibrium.

(b) Give counterexamples showing why each of the assumptions of (1) compactness of A_i, (2) convexity of A_i, (3) continuity of u_i, and (4) quasi-concavity of u_i in own strategy cannot be dispensed with.

A.24 Prove Fact A.22.

A.25 Prove Theorem A.20.

A.26 Prove Theorem A.21. [Hint: use Theorem A.20.]

A.27 Prove Corollary A.3.

A.28 Show that the first four spaces given in Example A.16 are normed vector spaces, while the fifth one is not. [Hint: in each case, verify the triangle inequality and the linearity conditions.]

A.29 Prove the claims in Example A.17.

A.30 Consider the subspace of ℓ_p, ℓ_p^+, where all elements of the sequence are nonnegative. Suppose $1 \leq p < \infty$. Now consider $x \in \ell_p^+$ and the ε-neighborhood of x, $N_\varepsilon(x)$. Show that for any $x \in \ell_p^+$ and any $\varepsilon > 0$, $N_\varepsilon(x) \not\subseteq \ell_p^+$. [Hint: fix $\varepsilon > 0$ and $x = (x_1, x_2, \ldots) \in \ell_p^+$. Since $x \in \ell_p$, for any $\varepsilon > 0$, there exists $N \in \mathbb{N}$ such that for all $n \geq N$, $|x_n| < \varepsilon/2$. Then define z such that $z_n = x_n$ for all $n \neq N$ and $z_N = x_N - \varepsilon/2$. Show that $z \in N_\varepsilon(x)$, but $z \notin \ell_p^+$.]

A.31 Show that $x = (1, 1, 1, \ldots)$ is an interior point of ℓ_∞^+. [Hint: consider $z_\varepsilon = (1 + \varepsilon, 1 + \varepsilon, \ldots)$, and show that $z \in N_\varepsilon(x) \subset \ell_\infty^+$.]

A.32 For the mapping $g : X \to \mathbb{R}^N$ for some $X \subset \mathbb{R}^K$, construct the set $G = \{x : g(x) \leq 0\}$. Show that even when each component of g is not a convex function, the set G can be convex.

A.33 Consider the problem of maximizing x subject to the constraint that $x^2 \leq 0$. Show that there exists a unique solution to this problem, but there exists no Lagrange multiplier. Show that this is because the Slater condition is not satisfied.

A.34 Consider the constrained maximization problem $\max_{x_1, x_2} -x_1$ subject to $x_1^2 \leq x_2$ and $x_2 = 0$. Show that there exists a unique solution, $(x_1, x_2) = (0, 0)$. Show that there does not exist a Lagrange multiplier vector (λ, μ) at which $(0, 0)$ satisfies (A.17). Explain how this is related to the failure of the constraint qualification condition.

Review of Ordinary Differential Equations

In this appendix, I give a brief overview of some basic results on differential equations and include a few results on difference equations. I limit myself to results that are useful for the material covered in the body of the text. In particular, I provide the background for the major theorems on stability, Theorems 2.2, 2.3, 2.4, 2.5, 7.18, and 7.19, which are presented and then extensively used in the text. I also provide some basic theorems on existence, uniqueness, and continuity of solutions to differential equations. Most of the material here can be found in basic differential equation textbooks, such as Boyce and DiPrima (1977). Luenberger (1979) is an excellent reference, since it gives a symmetric treatment of differential and difference equations. The results on existence, uniqueness, and continuity of solutions can be found in more advanced books, such as Walter (1991) or Perko (2001). Before presenting the results on differential equations, I also provide a brief overview of eigenvalues and eigenvectors, and some basic results on integrals. Throughout I continue to assume basic familiarity with matrix algebra and calculus.

B.1 Eigenvalues and Eigenvectors

Let $\mathbf{A}$ be an $n \times n$ (square) real matrix—meaning that all of its entries are real numbers. The $n \times n$ matrix $\mathbf{D}$ is *diagonal* if all of its nondiagonal elements are equal to zero, that is,

$$\mathbf{D} = \begin{pmatrix} d_1 & 0 & \cdot & 0 \\ 0 & d_2 & \cdot & \cdot \\ \cdot & \cdot & \cdot & 0 \\ 0 & \cdot & 0 & d_n \end{pmatrix}.$$

The $n \times n$ *identity matrix* $\mathbf{I}$ is the diagonal matrix with 1s on the diagonal:

$$\mathbf{I} = \begin{pmatrix} 1 & 0 & \cdot & 0 \\ 0 & 1 & \cdot & \cdot \\ \cdot & \cdot & 1 & 0 \\ 0 & \cdot & 0 & 1 \end{pmatrix}.$$

Throughout this appendix I denote matrices and vectors by boldface letters, so $\mathbf{0}$ is the vector or matrix of zeros, whereas 0 is simply the number zero.

Let the real number $\det \mathbf{A}$ denote the determinant of a square matrix $\mathbf{A}$. A matrix $\mathbf{A}$ is *nonsingular* or *invertible* if $\det \mathbf{A} \neq 0$, or alternatively if the only $n \times 1$ column vector $\mathbf{v}$ that is a solution to the equation

$$\mathbf{A}\mathbf{v} = \mathbf{0}$$

is the zero vector $\mathbf{v} = (0, \ldots, 0)^T$. If $\mathbf{A}$ is invertible, then there exists $\mathbf{A}^{-1}$ such that

$$\mathbf{A}^{-1}\mathbf{A} = \mathbf{I}.$$

Conversely, if there exists a nonzero solution $\mathbf{v}$ or if $\det \mathbf{A} = 0$, then $\mathbf{A}$ is singular and does not have an inverse.

Let $a, b \in \mathbb{R}$, and define the imaginary number i such that $i^2 = -1$, so that $i = \pm\sqrt{-1}$. Throughout this appendix, with no loss of generality, I take $i = \sqrt{-1}$. Then $\chi = a + bi$ is a *complex number*. A complex number ξ is an *eigenvalue* of $\mathbf{A}$ if

$$\det(\mathbf{A} - \xi\mathbf{I}) = 0.$$

If $\mathbf{A}$ is invertible, then none of its eigenvalues are equal to zero. Given an eigenvalue ξ of $\mathbf{A}$, the $n \times 1$ nonzero column vector $\mathbf{v}_\xi$ is an eigenvector of $\mathbf{A}$ if

$$(\mathbf{A} - \xi\mathbf{I})\,\mathbf{v}_\xi = \mathbf{0}.$$

Clearly, if $\mathbf{v}_\xi$ satisfies this equation, so does $\lambda\mathbf{v}_\xi$ for any $\lambda \in \mathbb{R}$. The linear space $\mathbf{V} = \{\mathbf{v} : (\mathbf{A} - \xi\mathbf{I})\mathbf{v} = \mathbf{0}\}$ is sometimes referred to as the *eigenspace* of $\mathbf{A}$. One of the major uses of eigenvalues and eigenvectors is in diagonalizing a nondiagonal square matrix $\mathbf{A}$. In particular, suppose that the $n \times n$ matrix $\mathbf{A}$ has n *distinct* real eigenvalues. Then a standard result in matrix algebra implies that

$$\mathbf{P}^{-1}\mathbf{A}\mathbf{P} = \mathbf{D},$$

where $\mathbf{D}$ is the diagonal matrix with the eigenvalues $\xi_1, \ldots, \xi_n$ on the diagonal, and $\mathbf{P} = (\mathbf{v}_{\xi_1}, \ldots, \mathbf{v}_{\xi_n})$ is a matrix of the eigenvectors corresponding to the eigenvalues. This result is used in the proof of Theorems B.5 and B.14 below.

Note that the eigenvalues of the matrix $\mathbf{A}$ with real entries can be complex numbers (corresponding to complex roots to the $\det(\mathbf{A} - \xi\mathbf{I}) = 0$). In addition, the polynomial $\det(\mathbf{A} - \xi\mathbf{I}) = 0$ may have repeated roots, so that the $n \times n$ matrix $\mathbf{A}$ might have repeated (rather than distinct) eigenvalues. Both of these possibilities create a range of difficulties in diagonalizing matrix $\mathbf{A}$. These difficulties are discussed in most linear algebra, matrix algebra, and differential equations textbooks, and are not discussed in detail here.

B.2 Some Basic Results on Integrals

Before proceeding to differential equations, it is useful to review some basic results on integrals. Throughout this section, I focus on Riemann integrals. In particular, for real numbers $b > a$, let $f : [a, b] \to \mathbb{R}$ be a continuous function. Then the Riemann integral of f between a and b, denoted by $\int_a^b f(x)dx$, is defined as follows. First create a partition of interval $[a, b]$; that is, divide $[a, b]$ into N subintervals of the form $[a, x_1), [x_1, x_2), \ldots, [x_{N-1}, b]$, with the convention that $a = x_0$ and $b = x_n$. Moreover, take N numbers, $\xi_1, \xi_2, \ldots, \xi_N$, respectively from one of each subinterval. Denote the vector of numbers $X_N = (x_1, x_2, \ldots, x_{N-1}, \xi_1, \xi_2, \ldots, \xi_N)$. Define the *Riemann sum* given X_N as

$$\mathbf{R}(X_N) = \sum_{j=0}^{N-1} f(\xi_j)(x_{j-1} - x_j).$$

Now consider the limit $\lim_{N \to \infty} \mathbf{R}(X_N)$ corresponding to the value of the preceding expression as we take finer and finer partitions of $[a, b]$; that is, as we increase N. If this limit exists and is independent of the partition X_N, it defines the *Riemann integral,* denoted by

$$\int_a^b f(x)dx. \tag{B.1}$$

For example, when it exists, the Riemann integral is equal to the Riemann sum resulting from the equal partition of the interval $[a, b]$:

$$\int_a^b f(x)dx = \lim_{N \to \infty} \frac{b-a}{N} \sum_{j=0}^{N-1} f\left(a + j\frac{b-a}{N}\right).$$

The assumption that f is continuous is not necessary for the Riemann integral to be well defined (e.g., the Riemann integral can be defined for monotone discontinuous functions). But for many functions the Riemann integral is not well defined. For this reason, it is often more convenient to work with more general integrals, such as the Lebesgue integral. Although I made references to Lebesgue integrals in the text, here I focus exclusively on Riemann integrals to simplify the discussion. When they both exist, the Riemann and Lebesgue integrals are equivalent. When a function f has a well-defined Riemann integral over the interval $[a, b]$, it is *Riemann integrable* over $[a, b]$.

The following four basic results are useful for our analysis. The proofs can be found in standard real analysis or calculus textbooks and are not repeated here.

Theorem B.1 (Fundamental Theorem of Calculus I) *Let $f : [a, b] \to \mathbb{R}$ be Riemann integrable on $[a, b]$. For any $x \in [a, b]$, define*

$$F(x) = \int_a^x f(t)dt.$$

Then $F : [a, b] \to \mathbb{R}$ is continuous on $[a, b]$. If f is continuous at some $x_0 \in [a, b]$, then $F(x)$ is differentiable at x_0 with derivative

$$F'(x_0) = f(x_0).$$

Theorem B.2 (Fundamental Theorem of Calculus II) *Let $f : [a, b] \to \mathbb{R}$ be continuous on $[a, b]$. Then there exists a differentiable function $F : [a, b] \to \mathbb{R}$ on $[a, b]$ (or only with the right derivative at a and the left derivative at b) such that $F'(x) = f(x)$ for all $x \in [a, b]$. Moreover for any such function*

$$\int_a^b f(x)dx = F(b) - F(a).$$

Theorem B.3 (Integration by Parts) *Let $f : [a, b] \to \mathbb{R}$ and $g : [a, b] \to \mathbb{R}$ be continuous functions, and let $F : [a, b] \to \mathbb{R}$ and $G : [a, b] \to \mathbb{R}$ be differentiable functions such that*

$F'(x) = f(x)$ and $G'(x) = g(x)$ for all $x \in [a, b]$. Then the (product) functions Fg and Gf are integrable, and

$$\int_a^b F(x)g(x)dx = F(b)G(b) - F(a)G(a) - \int_a^b G(x)f(x)dx.$$

Theorem B.4 (Leibniz's Rule) *Let $f(x, y)$ be continuous in x on $[a, b]$ and differentiable in y at y_0, and suppose that the functions $a(y)$ and $b(y)$ are differentiable at y_0 with derivatives denoted by a' and b'. Then*

$$\left. \frac{d}{dy} \int_{a(y)}^{b(y)} f(x, y)dx \right|_{y=y_0}$$

$$= \int_{a(y_0)}^{b(y_0)} \frac{\partial f(x, y_0)}{\partial y} dx + b'(y_0)f(b(y_0), y_0) - a'(y_0)f(a(y_0), y_0).$$

Riemann integrals as in (B.1), which specify lower and upper limits, are referred to as *definite integrals*. One can also define *indefinite integrals, $\int f(x)dx$*, which simply refer to the set of functions $F(x)$ with the property that $F'(x) = f(x)$ (this is a set, since if $F(x)$ satisfies this property, so does $F(x) + c$, where c is a constant). For this reason, the indefinite integral $\int f(x)dx$ is also sometimes referred to as an *antiderivative*. Definite integrals can also be defined for the cases in which $a = -\infty$ and/or $b = \infty$, provided that the limit is finite.

B.3   Linear Differential Equations

Recall the motivation for considering differential equations in dynamic economic models discussed in Chapter 2. In particular, consider a function $x : \mathcal{T} \to \mathbb{R}$, where $\mathcal{T}$ is an interval in $\mathbb{R}$. Suppose that given the real number Δt,

$$x(t + \Delta t) - x(t) = G(x(t), t, \Delta t),$$

where $G(x(t), t, \Delta t)$ is a real-valued function. Now divide both sides of this equation by Δt and consider the limit as $\Delta t \to 0$. Suppose that $\lim_{\Delta t \to 0} G(x(t), t, \Delta t)/\Delta t$ exists, and let

$$g(x(t), t) \equiv \lim_{\Delta t \to 0} \frac{G(x(t), t, \Delta t)}{\Delta t}.$$

Using this limit, we obtain the following *differential equation*

$$\frac{dx(t)}{dt} \equiv \dot{x}(t) = g(x(t), t). \tag{B.2}$$

This is an *explicit* first-order differential equation. The term "explicit" refers to the fact that $\dot{x}(t)$ is separated from the rest of the terms. This contrasts with *implicit* first-order differential equations of the form

$$H(\dot{x}(t), x(t), t) = 0.$$

For our purposes, it is sufficient to deal with explicit equations.

A differential equation is *autonomous* if it can be written in the form

$$\dot{x}(t) = g(x(t)),$$

or simply as

$$\dot{x} = g(x),$$

meaning that time is not a separate argument. Alternatively, if it cannot be written this way, it is a *nonautonomous* equation. In addition to first-order differential equations, we can consider second-order or nth-order equations, for example,

$$\frac{d^2 x(t)}{dt^2} = g\left(\frac{dx(t)}{dt}, x(t), t\right), \quad \text{or}$$

$$\frac{d^n x(t)}{dt^n} = g\left(\frac{d^{n-1} x(t)}{dt^{n-1}}, \ldots, \frac{dx(t)}{dt}, x(t), t\right). \tag{B.3}$$

I focus on first-order equations, since higher-order equations can always be transformed into a system of first-order equations (see Exercise B.3).

The most common form of differential equation is the *initial value* problem. In this case, a differential equation as in (B.2) is specified together with an initial condition $x(0) = x_0$. There are many examples of such initial value problems in the text. However many important problems in economics are not initial value problems, since some of the boundary conditions are specified by *transversality conditions,* that is, by what the terminal value of the solution $x(t)$ should be at some time $T < \infty$ or at $T = \infty$.

Suppose that a first-order differential equation (B.2) is defined for all $t \in \mathcal{D}$, where $\mathcal{D}$ is an interval in $\mathbb{R}$, and an initial value $x(0) = x_0$ has been specified. A *solution* to this initial value problem is given by a function $x : \mathcal{D} \to \mathbb{R}$ that satisfies (B.2) for all $t \in \mathcal{D}$ with $x(0) = x_0$. Sometimes a family of functions $\mathcal{X} = \{x : \mathcal{D} \to \mathbb{R} \text{ such that } x \text{ satisfies } (B.2) \text{ for all } t \in \mathcal{D}\}$ is referred to as the *general solution,* while an element of $\mathcal{X}$ that satisfies the boundary condition is called a *particular solution.*[1]

B.4 Solutions to Linear First-Order Differential Equations

Let us now first look at linear first-order differential equations. This is a good starting point both because such equations are commonly encountered in economics and because they have simple solutions. A linear first-order differential equation takes the general form

$$\dot{x}(t) = a(t)x(t) + b(t). \tag{B.4}$$

In addition, if $b(t) = 0$, (B.4) is referred to as a *homogeneous equation,* and if $a(t) = a$ and $b(t) = b$, then it is an equation with *constant coefficients.*

Let us start with the simplest case, which is a homogeneous linear equation with constant coefficients:

$$\dot{x}(t) = ax(t). \tag{B.5}$$

A solution to this equation is straightforward to obtain. One can simply guess the solution and then verify that the solution satisfies the differential equation (B.5). Or one can divide both

---

1. This terminology is somewhat confusing, since general and particular solutions are also used with different meanings in other contexts. In this book these other notions are not introduced, so there will be no cause for confusion.

sides by $x(t)$, integrate with respect to t, and recall that for $x(t) \neq 0$,

$$\int \frac{\dot{x}(t)}{x(t)} dt = \log |x(t)| + c_0,$$

and

$$\int a \, dt = at + c_1,$$

where c_0 and c_1 are constants of integration. Now taking exponents on both sides, the general solution to (B.5) is obtained as

$$x(t) = c \exp(at), \qquad (B.6)$$

where c is a constant of integration combining c_0 and c_1 (in fact, $c = \pm \exp(c_1 - c_0)$). Differentiating (B.6), one can easily obtain (B.5) and verify that (B.6) is indeed a general solution to (B.5). If (B.5) is specified as an initial value problem, then we also have a boundary condition, which, without loss of any generality, can be specified at $t = 0$ as $x(0) = x_0$. This boundary condition pins down the unique value of the constant of integration. In particular, since $\exp(a \times 0) = 1$, $c = x_0$. Therefore the particular solution with this initial value is

$$x(t) = x_0 \exp(at).$$

Next consider a slightly more general equation, one that is homogeneous but does not have constant coefficients:

$$\dot{x}(t) = a(t) x(t), \qquad (B.7)$$

defined over $t \geq 0$ with an initial condition $x(0) = x_0$. Once again, dividing both sides by $x(t)$, integrating and then finally taking exponents, we obtain

$$x(t) = c \exp\left(\int_0^t a(s) ds \right). \qquad (B.8)$$

Equation (B.8) follows since the integral of the right-hand side for a bounded function $a(t)$ is simply $\int_0^t a(s) ds + c_1$. Since

$$\lim_{t \to 0} \int_0^t a(s) ds = \int_0^0 a(s) ds = 0,$$

the constant of integration is again pinned down by the initial condition, that is, $c = x_0$. That (B.8) is a solution to (B.7) can be verified by differentiating (B.8) using Theorem B.1 or B.4.

Next consider an autonomous but nonhomogeneous first-order linear differential equation,

$$\dot{x}(t) = ax(t) + b. \qquad (B.9)$$

A similar analysis gives the general solution as

$$x(t) = -\frac{b}{a} + c \exp(at). \qquad (B.10)$$

Derivation of (B.10): To derive this solution, we use the following simple change of variables. Let

$$y(t) = x(t) + b/a.$$

It is clear that $\dot{y}(t) = \dot{x}(t)$ (simply differentiate both sides with respect to t). Then rewrite (B.9) in terms of $y(t)$, which gives

$$\dot{y}(t) = ay(t).$$

Now using the general solution to (B.5) derived above, $y(t) = c \exp(at)$, where c is the appropriate constant of integration. Transforming this equation back into $x(t)$, we obtain (B.10) as the general solution to (B.9). ∎

Finally, note that the constant of integration must be $c = x_0 + b/a$ to ensure that $x(0) = x_0$. Therefore the particular solution that satisfies the boundary condition is

$$x(t) = -\frac{b}{a} + \left(x_0 + \frac{b}{a} \right) \exp(at). \tag{B.11}$$

This equation also enables us to have a simple discussion of stability. Recall that, as in the text, a *steady state* of (B.9) refers to a situation which $\dot{x}(t) = 0$ for all t. Clearly in this case,

$$x(t) = x^* \equiv -\frac{b}{a},$$

is the unique steady state. Inspection of (B.11) immediately shows that $x(t)$ approaches the steady-state value x^* as t increases if $a < 0$, and it diverges from it if $a > 0$. This behavior is naturally what we would expect from Theorem 2.4, which states that the steady state is asymptotically stable if $a < 0$.

Finally, let us consider the most general case of the first-order linear differential equation, that given in (B.4). The general solution to (B.4) is

$$x(t) = \left[c + \int_0^t b\,(s) \left(\exp \int_0^s a(v)dv \right)^{-1} ds \right] \exp \left(\int_0^t a(s)ds \right). \tag{B.12}$$

Differentiation using Theorem B.4 verifies that (B.12) provides the solution to (B.4) (see Exercise B.4). The constant of integration is again obtained from the initial value $x(0) = x_0$ as $c = x_0$. Notice, however, that in this case there may not exist a steady-state value of x^* for which $\dot{x}(t) = 0$ in (B.4), since $\dot{x}(t) = 0$ implies that $x(t) = -b(t)/a(t)$, which is generally not constant.

Derivation of (B.12): The derivation of (B.12) as the solution to (B.4) requires a somewhat different argument than those used for the special cases above. Rewrite (B.4) as $\dot{x}(t) - a(t)x(t) = b(t)$, and multiply both sides by *the integrating factor* $\exp\left(-\int_0^t a(s)ds \right)$ to obtain

$$\dot{x}(t) \exp \left(-\int_0^t a(s)ds \right) - a(t)x(t) \exp \left(-\int_0^t a(s)ds \right) = b(t) \exp \left(-\int_0^t a(s)ds \right).$$

It can be verified that the left-hand side is the derivative of $x(t) \exp\left(-\int_0^t a(s)ds \right)$. Therefore, integrating both sides of this expression, we obtain

$$x(t) \exp \left(-\int_0^t a(s)ds \right) = \int_0^t b(s) \exp \left(-\int_0^s a(v)dv \right) ds + c,$$

where c is the constant of integration. Dividing both sides by $\exp\left(\int_0^t a(s)ds \right)$, we obtain (B.12). ∎

A by-product of this explicit derivation is that we have also established the existence of unique solutions to linear differential equations. This is a special case of Theorem B.8 below.

B.5   Systems of Linear Differential Equations

The results on the existence of solutions and explicit characterization of solutions for linear first-order differential equations can be extended to systems of differential equations. Before presenting the general characterization in Theorem B.6, it is useful to consider the following simpler system of first-order differential equations with constant coefficients:

$$\dot{\mathbf{x}}(t) = \mathbf{A}\mathbf{x}(t), \tag{B.13}$$

where $\mathbf{x}(t) \in \mathbb{R}^n$, $n \in \mathbb{N}$, and $\mathbf{A}$ is an $n \times n$ matrix. The boundary condition again takes the form of an initial value $\mathbf{x}(0) = \mathbf{x}_0 \in \mathbb{R}^n$. This system of equation does not include a constant, so that the steady state is $\mathbf{x}^* = \mathbf{0}$. This is simply a normalization, since as we just saw, a nonhomogeneous differential equation with constant coefficients can be transformed into a homogeneous one by a simple change of variables. This system of differential equations always has a unique solution (this result follows from Theorem B.6 or from Theorem B.10; see Exercise B.5). However when $\mathbf{A}$ has distinct real eigenvalues, the solution to (B.13) takes a particularly simple form. This case is presented in the next result.

Theorem B.5 (Solution to Systems of Linear Differential Equations with Constant Coefficients)   *Suppose that* $\mathbf{A}$ *has n distinct real eigenvalues* $\xi_1, \ldots, \xi_n$. *Then the unique solution to (B.13) with the initial value* $\mathbf{x}(0) = \mathbf{x}_0$ *takes the form*

$$\mathbf{x}(t) = \sum_{j=1}^{n} c_j \exp\left(\xi_j t\right) \mathbf{v}_{\xi_j},$$

where $\mathbf{v}_{\xi_1}, \ldots, \mathbf{v}_{\xi_n}$ *denote the eigenvectors corresponding to the eigenvalues* $\xi_1, \ldots, \xi_n$, *and* $c_1, \ldots, c_n$ *denote the constants of integration.*

Proof.   The proof follows by diagonalizing the matrix $\mathbf{A}$. In particular, since $\mathbf{A}$ has n distinct real eigenvalues, we have $\mathbf{P}^{-1}\mathbf{A}\mathbf{P} = \mathbf{D}$, where $\mathbf{D}$ is a diagonal matrix with the eigenvalues $\xi_1, \ldots, \xi_n$ on the diagonal, and $\mathbf{P} = (\mathbf{v}_{\xi_1}, \ldots, \mathbf{v}_{\xi_n})$ is the matrix of the eigenvectors corresponding to the eigenvalues. Let $\mathbf{z}(t) \equiv \mathbf{P}^{-1}\mathbf{x}(t)$, which also implies that

$$\dot{\mathbf{z}}(t) = \mathbf{P}^{-1}\dot{\mathbf{x}}(t)$$

$$= \mathbf{P}^{-1}\mathbf{A}\mathbf{x}(t)$$

$$= \mathbf{P}^{-1}\mathbf{A}\mathbf{P}\mathbf{z}(t)$$

$$= \mathbf{D}\mathbf{z}(t). \tag{B.14}$$

Since $\mathbf{D}$ is a diagonal matrix, writing $\mathbf{z}(t) = \left(z_1(t), \ldots, z_n(t)\right)$, (B.14) implies that $z_1(t) = c_1 \exp\left(\xi_1 t\right), \ldots, z_n(t) = c_n \exp(\xi_n t)$, where $c_1, \ldots, c_n$ are the constants of integration. Now since $\mathbf{x}(t) = \mathbf{P}\mathbf{z}(t)$, the result follows by multiplying the matrix $(\mathbf{v}_{\xi_1}, \ldots, \mathbf{v}_{\xi_n})$ with the vector of solutions $\mathbf{z}(t)$.   ■

When the matrix $\mathbf{A}$ has repeated or complex eigenvalues, explicit solutions can still be derived but are somewhat more complicated. Therefore I instead focus on the more general results in Theorem B.6 below. One important set of implications of Theorem B.5 are Theorems 2.4 and 7.18 in the text. In particular, Theorem B.5 implies that the steady-state value, here $\mathbf{x}^* = \mathbf{0}$, is stable only when all eigenvalues are negative. If instead, $m < n$ of the eigenvalues are negative, then there exists an m-dimensional subspace such that the solution tends to the steady state only starting with an initial value on this subspace.

Now consider the most general form of a system of linear differential equations:

$$\dot{\mathbf{x}}(t) = \mathbf{A}(t)\mathbf{x}(t) + \mathbf{B}(t), \tag{B.15}$$

where $\mathbf{x}(t) \in \mathbb{R}^n$, $n \in \mathbb{N}$, and $\mathbf{A}(t)$ and $\mathbf{B}(t)$ are $n \times n$ matrices for each t. Let us assume that each element of $\mathbf{A}(t)$ and $\mathbf{B}(t)$ is integrable.

I now characterize the solution to (B.15) in two steps. First, I introduce the *state-transition matrix* $\Phi(t, s)$ corresponding to $\mathbf{A}(t)$ as the $n \times n$ matrix function that is differentiable in its first argument and is uniquely defined by

$$\frac{d}{dt}\Phi(t, s) = \mathbf{A}(t)\Phi(t, s), \text{ and } \Phi(t, t) = \mathbf{I} \text{ for all } t \text{ and } s. \tag{B.16}$$

The state-transition matrix is useful because it enables us to express the solutions to homogeneous systems and then derive the solutions to (B.15) from the solutions to the corresponding homogeneous systems. In particular, if $\hat{\mathbf{x}}(t)$ is a solution to the homogeneous system

$$\dot{\mathbf{x}}(t) = \mathbf{A}(t)\mathbf{x}(t), \tag{B.17}$$

then it is straightforward to verify that (see Exercise B.6)

$$\hat{\mathbf{x}}(t) = \Phi(t, s)\hat{\mathbf{x}}(s) \quad \text{for any } t \text{ and } s. \tag{B.18}$$

Let us next define the *fundamental set of solutions* to (B.17). The $n \times n$ matrix $\mathbf{X}(t)$ is a fundamental set of solutions to (B.17) if its columns consist of vector-valued functions $\mathbf{x}^1(t), \mathbf{x}^2(t), \ldots, \mathbf{x}^n(t)$ that are linearly independent from one another and are solutions to (B.17). In this case clearly

$$\dot{\mathbf{X}}(t) = \mathbf{A}(t)\mathbf{X}(t).$$

Then it can be verified that (see Exercise B.7)

$$\Phi(t, s) = \mathbf{X}(t)\mathbf{X}(s)^{-1}. \tag{B.19}$$

We are now in a position to state the form of the unique solution to the general system of linear equations in (B.15).

Theorem B.6 (Solutions to General Systems of Linear Differential Equations) *The solution to (B.15) with initial condition* $\mathbf{x}(0) = \mathbf{x}_0$ *is given by*

$$\hat{\mathbf{x}}(t) = \Phi(t, 0)\mathbf{x}_0 + \int_0^t \Phi(t, s)\mathbf{B}(s)ds, \tag{B.20}$$

where $\Phi(t, s)$ *is the state transition matrix corresponding to* $\mathbf{A}(t)$.

Proof. We need only verify that $\hat{\mathbf{x}}(t)$ given in (B.20) is a solution to (B.15). Differentiating (B.20) with respect to time and using Theorem B.4, we obtain

$$\frac{d}{dt}\hat{\mathbf{x}}(t) = \frac{d}{dt}\Phi(t, 0)\mathbf{x}_0 + \int_0^t \frac{d}{dt}\Phi(t, s)\mathbf{B}(s)ds + \Phi(t, t)\mathbf{B}(t).$$

By the definition of the state transition matrix (B.16), $\Phi(t, t) = \mathbf{I}$, and

$$\frac{d}{dt}\Phi(t, s) = \mathbf{A}(t)\Phi(t, s).$$

Therefore

$$\frac{d}{dt}\hat{\mathbf{x}}(t) = \mathbf{A}(t)\Phi(t, 0)\mathbf{x}_0 + \mathbf{A}(t)\int_0^t \Phi(t, s)\mathbf{B}(s)ds + \mathbf{B}(t)$$

$$= \mathbf{A}(t)\hat{\mathbf{x}}(t) + \mathbf{B}(t),$$

completing the verification that (B.20) satisfies (B.15) with initial condition $\hat{\mathbf{x}}(0) = \mathbf{x}_0$. ∎

B.6 Local Analysis and Stability of Nonlinear Differential Equations

Systems of nonlinear differential equations can be analyzed in the neighborhood of the steady state by using Taylor's Theorem (Theorem A.23). In particular, consider the system of nonlinear autonomous differential equations

$$\dot{\mathbf{x}}(t) = \mathbf{G}(\mathbf{x}(t)), \tag{B.21}$$

where again $\mathbf{x}(t) \in \mathbb{R}^n, n \in \mathbb{N}$, and now $\mathbf{G} : \mathbb{R}^n \to \mathbb{R}^n$ is a continuously differentiable mapping. Suppose that this system of differential equations has a steady state $\mathbf{x}^* \in \mathbb{R}^n$, and consider $\mathbf{x}(t)$ in the neighborhood of $\mathbf{x}^*$. Then from Taylor's Theorem,

$$\dot{\mathbf{x}}(t) = D\mathbf{G}(\mathbf{x}^*)(\mathbf{x}(t) - \mathbf{x}^*) + o(\|\mathbf{x}(t) - \mathbf{x}^*\|^2),$$

where recall that

$$o(\|\mathbf{x}(t) - \mathbf{x}^*\|^2)/\|\mathbf{x}(t) - \mathbf{x}^*\|^2 \to \mathbf{0} \text{ as } \|\mathbf{x}(t) - \mathbf{x}^*\| \to 0$$

(and thus as $\mathbf{x}(t) \to \mathbf{x}^*$). We say that $\mathbf{x}^*$ is a *hyperbolic* steady state if the matrix $D\mathbf{G}(\mathbf{x}^*)$ does not have zero eigenvalues (or complex eigenvalues with zero real parts). Then as long as $\mathbf{x}^*$ is a hyperbolic steady state, the behavior of $\mathbf{x}(t)$ in the neighborhood of the steady state $\mathbf{x}^*$ can be approximated by the system of linear differential equations

$$\dot{\mathbf{x}}(t) = D\mathbf{G}(\mathbf{x}^*)\left(\mathbf{x}(t) - \mathbf{x}^*\right).$$

This result is the basis of Theorems 2.5 and 7.19. The following theorem formalizes this result and also implies Theorems 2.5 and 7.19. A rigorous proof can be found in Walter (1991, pp. 305–317).

Theorem B.7 (Grobman-Hartman Theorem) *Let $\mathbf{x}^*$ be a steady state of (B.21), and suppose that $\mathbf{G} : \mathbb{R}^n \to \mathbb{R}^n$ is a continuously differentiable mapping. If $\mathbf{x}^*$ is hyperbolic, then there exists an open set of trajectories U of (B.21) around $\mathbf{x}^*$ and an open set of trajectories V of the linear system $\dot{\mathbf{x}}(t) = D\mathbf{G}(\mathbf{x}^*)(\mathbf{x}(t) - \mathbf{x}^*)$ around $\mathbf{x}^*$ such that there exists a one-to-one continuous function $h : U \to V$ that preserves the direction of trajectories in U and V.*

Figure B.1 illustrates the implications of Theorem B.7. In this figure, N_c and N_d correspond to the convergent and the divergent manifolds, respectively, of a two-dimensional nonlinear system with a steady state at (x^*, y^*). E_c and E_d show the convergent and the divergent subspaces for the corresponding linearized system.

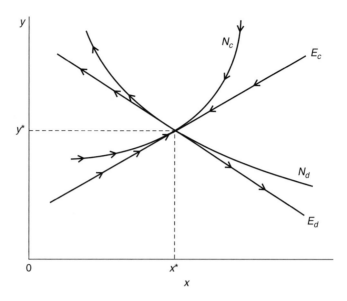

FIGURE B.1 Relationship between the convergent and the divergent manifolds of the nonlinear and the linearized systems.

B.7 Separable and Exact Differential Equations

Two important special classes of differential equations, separable and exact differential equations, often enable us to derive explicit solutions. A differential equation

$$\dot{x}(t) = g(x(t), t) \tag{B.22}$$

is *separable* if g can be written as

$$g(x, t) \equiv f(x)h(t).$$

In that case, (B.22) can be expressed as

$$\frac{dx(t)}{f(x(t))} = h(t)dt.$$

Integrating both sides, we obtain

$$\int \frac{dx}{f(x)} = \int h(t)dt.$$

This equation typically allows us to obtain an explicit solution. The following example illustrates a particular application.

Example B.1 *The differential equation*

$$\dot{x}(t) = \frac{4t^3 + 3t^2 + 2t + 1}{2x(t)}$$

with initial value $x(0) = 1$ at first looks difficult to solve. However, once we note that it is separable, we can write it as $2x \cdot dx = (4t^3 + 3t^2 + 2t + 1)dt$, and integrate it to obtain $x^2(t) = t^4 + t^3 + t^2 + t + c$, where c is a combination of the two constants of integration.

To satisfy the initial value, we need $c = 1$. Therefore the solution to this initial value problem is given by $x(t) = \sqrt{t^4 + t^3 + t^2 + t + 1}$, where the negative root to the quadratic is eliminated because it does not satisfy the initial value $x(0) = 1$. An example that is relevant for economic applications is provided in Exercise B.9.

Next, consider a differential equation of the form (B.22) again, and suppose that the function g can be written as

$$g(x(t), t) \equiv \frac{G_1(x(t), t)}{G_2(x(t), t)},$$

where

$$G_1(x(t), t) = \frac{\partial F(x(t), t)}{\partial t}, \quad \text{and} \quad G_2(x(t), t) = -\frac{\partial F(x(t), t)}{\partial x}.$$

Then (B.22) defines an *exact differential equation*. In particular, in this case, we can write

$$\dot{x}(t) = \frac{G_1(x(t), t)}{G_2(x(t), t)} = -\frac{\partial F(x(t), t)/\partial t}{\partial F(x(t), t)/\partial x},$$

or

$$\dot{x}(t)\frac{\partial F(x(t), t)}{\partial x} + \frac{\partial F(x(t), t)}{\partial t} = 0.$$

Let $\hat{x}(t)$ be a solution to this differential equation. Then we equivalently have that

$$\frac{d}{dt} F(\hat{x}(t), t) = 0, \tag{B.23}$$

where d/dt denotes the total derivative of the function F. Equation (B.23) then implies that

$$F\left(\hat{x}(t), t\right) = c, \tag{B.24}$$

where c is the constant of integration. Equation (B.24) implicitly defines the solution $\hat{x}(t)$.

Exact differential equations are straightforward to solve once they have been identified. The following provides a simple example.

Example B.2 *Consider the differential equation*

$$\dot{x}(t) = -\frac{2x(t) \log x(t)}{t},$$

with initial value $x(1) = \exp(1)$. While this differential equation looks difficult to solve at first, once we recognize that it can be written as

$$\dot{x}(t) = -\frac{2t \log x(t)}{t^2/x(t)} = -\frac{\partial(t^2 \log (x(t)))/\partial t}{\partial(t^2 \log(x(t)))/\partial x},$$

it can be seen to be an exact differential equation. Therefore its solution $\hat{x}(t)$ is given by $t^2 \log(\hat{x}(t)) = c$, which implies that $\hat{x}(t) = \exp(ct^{-2})$ is the general solution. The initial condition pins down the constant of integration as $c = 1$.

B.8 Existence and Uniqueness of Solutions

Initial value problems generally enable us to establish the existence and uniqueness of solutions under relatively weak conditions. In fact, there are many related existence theorems. I state the most basic existence theorem here, which extends the original theorem by Picard. Consider a first-order differential equation

$$\dot{x}(t) = g(x(t), t) \tag{B.25}$$

defined on some interval $\mathcal{D} \subset \mathbb{R}$ (i.e., defined for all $t \in \mathcal{D}$). Throughout this section I assume that 0 is in the interior of $\mathcal{D}$. Let us introduce the following Lipschitz condition.

Definition B.1 *The first-order differential equation (B.25) satisfies the* Lipschitz condition *on the strip $S = \mathcal{X} \times \mathcal{D}$ if there exists a real number $L < \infty$ such that*

$$\left| g(x, t) - g(x', t) \right| \leq L \left| x - x' \right|$$

for all $x, x' \in \mathcal{X}$ and for all $t \in \mathcal{D}$.

It can be verified that if $g : S \to \mathbb{R}$ satisfies the Lipschitz condition, then it must be continuous (see Exercise B.8).

Theorem B.8 (Picard's Theorem I) *Suppose that $g : \mathcal{X} \times \mathcal{D} \to \mathbb{R}$ is continuous in both of its arguments and satisfies the Lipschitz condition in Definition B.1. Then there exists $\delta > 0$ such that the initial value problem defined by (B.25) with $x(0) = x_0 \in \mathcal{X}$ has a unique solution $x(t)$ over the interval $[-\delta, \delta] \subset \mathcal{D}$.*

This theorem guarantees only the existence of a unique solution in the neighborhood of the initial value x_0. A stronger version of this theorem holds when $\mathcal{D}$ is compact.

Theorem B.9 (Existence and Uniqueness on Compact Sets I) *Suppose that g is continuous in both of its arguments and satisfies the Lipschitz condition in Definition B.1 and that $\mathcal{D}$ is compact. Then the initial value problem defined by (B.25) with $x(0) = x_0$ has a unique solution $x(t)$ over the entire interval $\mathcal{D}$.*

There are various proofs of these theorems. Example 6.3 and Exercise 6.4 in Chapter 6 provide proofs using the Contraction Mapping Theorem (Theorem 6.7).

This theorem can easily be extended to systems of first-order differential equations. Suppose that $\mathbf{x}(t) \in \mathcal{X} \subset \mathbb{R}^n$, where $n \in \mathbb{N}$. Let $\mathcal{D} \subset \mathbb{R}$ and $\mathbf{G} : \mathcal{X} \times \mathcal{D} \to \mathcal{X}$, and consider the system of first-order differential equations

$$\dot{\mathbf{x}}(t) = \mathbf{G}(\mathbf{x}(t), t). \tag{B.26}$$

Definition B.2 *The system of first-order differential equations (B.26) satisfies the* Lipschitz condition *over the strip $S = \mathcal{X} \times \mathcal{D}$ if there exists a real number $L < \infty$ such that*

$$\left\| \mathbf{G}(\mathbf{x}, t) - \mathbf{G}(\mathbf{x}', t) \right\| \leq L \left\| \mathbf{x} - \mathbf{x}' \right\|$$

for all $\mathbf{x}, \mathbf{x}' \in \mathcal{X}$ and for all $t \in \mathcal{D}$.

Theorem B.10 (Picard's Theorem II) *Suppose that $\mathbf{G}$ is continuous in all of its arguments and satisfies the Lipschitz condition in Definition B.2. Then there exists $\delta > 0$ such that the initial value problem defined by the system of differential equations in (B.26) with $\mathbf{x}(0) = \mathbf{x}_0$ has a unique solution $\mathbf{x}(t)$ over the interval $[-\delta, \delta] \subset \mathcal{D}$.*

Theorem B.11 (Existence and Uniqueness on Compact Sets II) *Suppose that* **G** *is continuous in all of its arguments and satisfies the Lipschitz condition in Definition B.2 and that* $\mathcal{D}$ *is compact. Then the initial value problem defined by the system of differential equations in (B.26) with* $\mathbf{x}(0) = \mathbf{x}_0$ *has a unique solution* $\mathbf{x}(t)$ *over the entire interval* $\mathcal{D}$.

The proofs of these theorems can be found in Walter (1991, pp. 108–110).

B.9 Continuity and Differentiability of Solutions

We would also like to know whether when some parameter or an initial condition of a differential equation is changed by a small amount, the solution also changes by a small amount. The following theorem provides conditions for this to be true (see Walter, 1991, pp. 145–146, for a proof).

Theorem B.12 (Continuity of Solutions to Differential Equations) *Suppose that* $g : \mathcal{X} \times \mathcal{D} \to \mathbb{R}$ *is continuous in both of its arguments and that* $\mathcal{D}$ *is compact. Let* $x(t)$ *be a solution to (B.26) with initial condition* $x(0) = x_0$. *For every* $\varepsilon > 0$, $x_0 \in \mathcal{X}$, *and continuous function* $\tilde{g} : \mathcal{X} \times \mathcal{D} \to \mathbb{R}$, *there exists* $\delta > 0$ *such that if*

$$\left| \tilde{g}(x, t) - g(x, t) \right| < \delta, \text{ and } \left| \tilde{x}_0 - x_0 \right| < \delta \text{ for all } (x, t) \in \mathcal{X} \times \mathcal{D},$$

then every solution $\tilde{x}(t)$ *to the perturbed initial value problem*

$$\dot{x}(t) = \tilde{g}(x(t), t), \quad \text{with } x(0) = \tilde{x}_0,$$

satisfies

$$\left| \tilde{x}(t) - x(t) \right| < \varepsilon \quad \text{for all } t \in \mathcal{D}.$$

This theorem can also be extended to systems of differential equations. Finally, under slightly stronger assumptions, the solution depends on initial values and parameters smoothly (see Walter, 1991, pp. 148–156).

Theorem B.13 (Differentiability of Solutions to Differential Equations) *Suppose that* $g : \mathcal{X} \times \mathcal{D} \to \mathbb{R}$ *is differentiable in both of its arguments and that* $\mathcal{D}$ *is compact. Let* $x(t)$ *be a solution to (B.26) with initial condition* $x(0) = x_0$. *For every* $\varepsilon > 0$ *and* $x_0 \in \mathcal{X}$, *there exists* $\delta > 0$ *such that if*

$$\left| x_0' - x_0 \right| < \delta \text{ for all } (x, t) \in \mathcal{X} \times \mathcal{D},$$

then every solution $x'(t)$ *to the perturbed initial value problem*

$$\dot{x}(t) = g(x(t), t), \quad \text{with } x(0) = x_0'$$

satisfies

$$\left| \dot{x}'(t) - \dot{x}(t) \right| < \varepsilon \quad \text{for all } t \in \mathcal{D}.$$

B.10 Difference Equations

Similar to first-order differential equations, a first-order difference equation is defined as

$$x(t + 1) = g(x(t), t),$$

where $g : \mathbb{R} \times \mathbb{R} \to \mathbb{R}$. Higher-order difference equations and systems of difference equations are defined similarly.

Solutions to difference equations have many features in common with the solutions to differential equations. For example, the simple first-order difference equation

$$x(t + 1) = ax(t) + b,$$

has a solution similar to the first-order linear differential equation with constant coefficients. In particular, if we specify the initial condition $x(0) = x_0$, then successive substitutions yield

$$x(1) = ax_0 + b,$$

$$x(2) = a^2 x_0 + ab + b,$$

and so on. By induction, the general solution to this equation is

$$x(t) = \begin{cases} x_0 + bt & \text{if } a = 1, \\ a^t \left(x_0 - \dfrac{b}{1-a} \right) + \dfrac{b}{1-a} & \text{otherwise.} \end{cases}$$

The reader will recognize $x^* \equiv b/(1 - a)$ as the steady-state value (when $a \neq 1$), and the solution makes it clear that if $|a| < 1$, then the first term tends to zero and $x(t) \to x^*$ (as $t \to \infty$), which is the essence of the stability results presented in the text. In contrast, when $|a| > 1$, the solution diverges from x^*.

Next consider the system of first-order linear difference equations

$$\mathbf{x}(t + 1) = \mathbf{A}\mathbf{x}(t), \tag{B.27}$$

where $\mathbf{x}(t) \in \mathbb{R}^n$, $n \in \mathbb{N}$, and $\mathbf{A}$ is an $n \times n$ real matrix. When $\mathbf{A}$ has n distinct real eigenvalues, the solution to the system of equations is very similar to that given in Theorem B.5.

Theorem B.14 (Solution to Systems of Linear Difference Equations with Constant Coefficients) *Suppose that $\mathbf{A}$ has n distinct real eigenvalues $\xi_1, \ldots, \xi_n$. Then the unique solution to (B.27) with the initial value $\mathbf{x}(0) = \mathbf{x}_0$ takes the form*

$$\mathbf{x}(t) = \sum_{j=1}^{n} c_j \xi_j^t \mathbf{v}_{\xi_j},$$

where $\mathbf{v}_{\xi_1}, \ldots, \mathbf{v}_{\xi_n}$ denote eigenvectors corresponding to the eigenvalues $\xi_1, \ldots, \xi_n$, and $c_1, \ldots, c_n$ denote constants determined by the initial conditions.

Proof. The proof again follows by diagonalizing the matrix $\mathbf{A}$. Recall that since $\mathbf{A}$ has n distinct real eigenvalues, we have $\mathbf{P}^{-1}\mathbf{A}\mathbf{P} = \mathbf{D}$, where $\mathbf{D}$ is a diagonal matrix with the eigenvalues $\xi_1, \ldots, \xi_n$ on the diagonal, and $\mathbf{P} = (\mathbf{v}_{\xi_1}, \ldots, \mathbf{v}_{\xi_n})$ is the matrix of the eigenvectors corresponding to the eigenvalues. Let $\mathbf{z}(t) \equiv \mathbf{P}^{-1}\mathbf{x}(t)$, and note that

$$\mathbf{z}(t + 1) = \mathbf{P}^{-1}\mathbf{x}(t + 1)$$

$$= \mathbf{P}^{-1}\mathbf{A}\mathbf{x}(t)$$

$$= \mathbf{P}^{-1}\mathbf{A}\mathbf{P}\mathbf{z}(t)$$

$$= \mathbf{D}\mathbf{z}(t). \tag{B.28}$$

Since $\mathbf{D}$ is a diagonal matrix, writing $\mathbf{z}(t) = \big(z_1(t), \ldots, z_n(t)\big)$, (B.28) implies that $z_1(t) = c_1\xi_1^t, \ldots, z_n(t) = c_n\xi_n^t$. Now since $\mathbf{x}(t) = \mathbf{Pz}(t)$, the result follows by multiplying the matrix $(\mathbf{v}_{\xi_1}, \ldots, \mathbf{v}_{\xi_n})$ with the vector of solutions $\mathbf{z}(t)$. ∎

The analogue of Theorem B.6 also applies to difference equations. The matrix of fundamental solutions $\mathbf{X}(t)$ is defined similarly to the matrix of fundamental solutions to differential equations. In addition, the state transition matrix again satisfies $\Phi(t, s) = \mathbf{X}(t)\mathbf{X}(s)^{-1}$ and $\Phi(t, t) = \mathbf{I}$. Now consider the system of first-order difference equations

$$\mathbf{x}(t + 1) = \mathbf{A}(t)\mathbf{x}(t) + \mathbf{B}(t). \tag{B.29}$$

The solution to this set of difference equations is characterized by the next theorem.

Theorem B.15 (General Solutions to Systems of Linear Difference Equations)

The solution to (B.29) with initial condition $\mathbf{x}(0) = \mathbf{x}_0$ *is given by*

$$\mathbf{x}(t) = \Phi(t, 0)\mathbf{x}_0 + \sum_{s=0}^{t-1} \Phi(t, s + 1)\mathbf{B}(s).$$

Proof. See Exercise B.10. ∎

Linearizing systems of nonlinear difference equations then leads to an analogue of Theorem B.7. Finally, the existence and uniqueness of solutions is somewhat more straightforward for difference equations.

Theorem B.16 (Existence and Uniqueness of Solutions to Difference Equations)

Consider the system of first-order nonlinear difference equations

$$\mathbf{x}(t + 1) = \mathbf{G}(\mathbf{x}(t)), \tag{B.30}$$

where $\mathbf{x}(t) \in \mathbb{R}^n$, $n \in \mathbb{N}$, *and* $\mathbf{G} : \mathbb{R}^n \to \mathbb{R}^n$ *is an arbitrary mapping. Suppose that the initial condition is specified as* $\mathbf{x}(0) = \mathbf{x}_0$. *Then (B.30) has a unique solution for all* $t \in \mathbb{N}$.

Proof. Given $\mathbf{x}_0$, $\mathbf{x}(1)$ is uniquely defined as $\mathbf{G}(\mathbf{x}_0)$. Proceeding iteratively, we determine a unique $\mathbf{x}(t)$ that satisfies (B.30) for any $t \in \mathbb{N}$. ∎

Using a similar method to that used for turning higher-order differential equations into a system of first-order differential equations (see Exercise B.3), this theorem also guarantees existence and uniqueness of solutions to higher-order difference equations when the appropriate initial values are specified (see Exercise B.11).

B.11 Exercises

B.1   Use integration by parts as in Theorem B.3 to evaluate $\int_a^b \log x\,dx$.

B.2   Consider a household with preferences given by

$$U(0) = \int_0^\infty \exp(-\rho t) \log C(t)dt.$$

Suppose that $C(0) = C_0$ and that $C(t)$ grows at a constant proportional rate g (i.e., $C(t) = \exp(gt)C(0)$). Derive the expression for $U(0)$.

B.3   Show that an nth order differential equation as in (B.3) can be written as a system of n first-order equations. [Hint: let $z_j(t) = d^j x(t)/dt^j$ for $j = 1, \ldots, n$.]

B.4 Show that (B.12) is the general solution to the first-order differential equation (B.4).

B.5 Verify that the system of linear differential equations (B.13) satisfies the conditions of Theorem B.10.

B.6 Verify (B.18).

B.7 Prove (B.19).

B.8 Show that if $g : \mathbb{R} \times \mathbb{R} \to \mathbb{R}$ satisfies the Lipschitz condition in Definition B.1, then $g(x, t)$ is continuous in x.

B.9 This exercise asks you to use the techniques for solving separable differential equations to characterize the family of utility functions with a constant coefficient of relative risk aversion. In particular, recall that the (Arrow-Pratt) measure of relative risk aversion of a twice differentiable utility function u is given by

$$\mathcal{R}_u(c) = -\frac{u''(c)c}{u'(c)}.$$

Suppose that $\mathcal{R}_u(c) = r > 0$, and let $v(c) = u'(c)$. Then we obtain

$$\frac{v'(c)}{v(c)} = -\frac{r}{c}.$$

Using this equation, characterize the family of utility functions that have a constant coefficient of relative risk aversion.

B.10 Prove Theorem B.15.

B.11 Consider the nth-order difference equation

$$x(t + n) = H(x(t + n - 1), \ldots, x(t), t),$$

where $H : \mathbb{R}^n \to \mathbb{R}$. Prove that if the initial values $x(0), x(1), \ldots, x(n - 1)$ are specified, this equation has a unique solution for any t.

C

Brief Review of Dynamic Games

This appendix provides a brief overview of basic definitions, results, and notation for infinite-horizon dynamic games. The reader is already assumed to be familiar with basic game theory and the notions of Nash Equilibrium and Subgame Perfect (Nash) Equilibrium. A review of these notions as well as much of the material covered here can be found in standard graduate game theory textbooks, such as Myerson (1991), Fudenberg and Tirole (1994), and Osborne and Rubinstein (1994). My focus here is on games of complete information (or the so-called games of *perfect monitoring*). These types of games are used in Section 14.4 in Chapter 14, as well as in Chapters 22 and 23.

C.1 Basic Definitions

I consider the following class of dynamic infinite-horizon games. There is a set of players denoted by $\mathcal{N}$. This set is either finite, or when it is infinite (especially uncountable), more structure is imposed to make the game tractable, and thus variants of the theorems presented below are still applicable. In particular, in many of the applications (especially in those considered in Chapters 22 and 23), there is a continuum of players, but these are in distinct finite groups, and the game can be viewed as one between the distinct groups. Thus I focus on the case in which $\mathcal{N}$ is finite and consists of N players. Each player $i \in \mathcal{N}$ has a strategy set $A_i(k) \subset \mathbb{R}^{n_i}$ (with $n_i \in \mathbb{N}$) at every date, and in addition, $k \in K \subset \mathbb{R}^n$ is the state vector (with $n \in \mathbb{N}$), with value at time t denoted by $k(t)$. A generic element of $A_i(k)$ at time t is denoted by $a_i(t)$, and $a(t) = (a_1(t), \ldots, a_N(t))$ denotes the *action profile* at time t:

$$a(t) \in A(k(t)) = \prod_{i=1}^{N} A_i(k(t)).$$

I use the standard notation $a_{-i}(t) = (a_1(t), a_{i-1}(t), a_{i+1}(t), \ldots, a_N(t))$ to denote the vector of actions without i's action; thus with a slight abuse of notation, we can write $a_i(t) = (a_i(t), a_{-i}(t))$. Consistent with the types of models analyzed in the text, the action set of each player $A_i(k)$ is a function only of the state variable k and not of calendar time.

934

Each player has an instantaneous utility function $u_i(k(t), a(t))$, where

$$u_i : K \times A \to \mathbb{R}$$

is assumed to be continuous and bounded. This notation emphasizes the dependence of each player's payoff on the entire action profile in that period (and not on past actions) and also on a common vector of state variables, denoted by $k(t)$. Past actions have an effect on current payoffs only through this vector of state variables.

As usual, each player's objective at time t is to maximize her discounted payoff

$$U_i[t] = \mathbb{E}_t \sum_{s=0}^{\infty} \beta^s u_i(k(t+s), a(t+s)), \tag{C.1}$$

where $\beta \in (0, 1)$ is the discount factor, and $\mathbb{E}_t$ is the expectations operator conditional on information available at time t. The games I focus on here contain potential uncertainty about the evolution of the state variable in the future and strategic uncertainty resulting from mixed strategies. However they do not feature *asymmetric information,* since I do not use incomplete information or asymmetric information dynamic games in this book. Consequently the expectations operator $\mathbb{E}_t$ is not indexed by i.

The law of motion of vector $k(t)$ is given by the following Markovian transition function

$$q(k(t+1) \mid k(t), a(t)), \tag{C.2}$$

which denotes the probability density that next period's state vector is equal to $k(t+1)$ when the time t action profile of all the agents is $a(t) \in A(k(t))$ and the state vector is $k(t) \in K$. I refer to transition function (C.2) as "Markovian," since it depends only on the current profile of actions and the current state. Naturally, we have

$$\int_{-\infty}^{\infty} q(k \mid k(t), a(t))dk = 1$$

for all $k(t) \in K$ and $a(t) \in A(k(t))$.

Next we need to specify the information structure of the players. We focus on games with perfect observability or perfect monitoring, so that individuals observe realizations of all past actions. Then the public history at time t, observed by all agents up to time t, is $h^t = (a(0), k(0), \ldots, a(t), k(t))$. With mixed strategies, the history naturally only includes the realizations of mixed strategies, not the actual strategy. Let the set of all potential histories at time t be denoted by H^t. It should be clear that any element $h^t \in H^t$ for any t corresponds to a subgame of this game.[1]

Let a (pure) strategy for player i at time t be

$$\sigma_i(t) : H^{t-1} \times K \to A_i,$$

that is, a mapping that determines what to play given the entire past history h^{t-1} and the current value of the state variable $k(t) \in K$. This is the natural specification of a strategy for time t given that h^{t-1} and $k(t)$ entirely determine the subgame.

---

1. Sometimes, it may be useful to distinguish calendar time from the nodes within a stage game. In this case, one might want to use the notation h^t to denote the history up to the beginning of time t and then some other variable, say, $j^t \in J^t$ to summarize actions within the stage game at time t. In that case, the proper history at time t would be given by an element of the set $H^t \times J^t$. For our purposes here, this distinction is not necessary.

A mixed strategy for player i at time t is

$$\sigma_i(t) : H^{t-1} \times K \to \Delta(A_i),$$

where $\Delta(A_i)$ is the set of all probability distributions over A_i, and I have used the same symbol, σ, for pure and mixed strategies to economize on notation. Let $\sigma = (\sigma_1, \ldots, \sigma_N)$ be the strategy profile in the infinite game, and let $\sigma_i(t) = (\sigma_1(t), \ldots, \sigma_N(t))$ be the *continuation strategy profile* after time t induced by the strategy profile of the infinite game, σ. Let S_i be the set of all feasible strategies for player i in the infinite game, and $S = \prod_{i=1}^{N} S_i$ be the set of all feasible strategy profiles. I also use the notation $S_i(t)$ for the set of continuation strategies for player i starting at time t. Naturally, $S(t) = \prod_{i=1}^{N} S_i(t)$ and $S_{-i}(t) = \prod_{j \neq i} S_j(t)$ are defined in the usual manner.

As is standard, define the best-response correspondence as

$$BR(\sigma_{-i}(t) \mid h^{t-1}, k(t)) = \left\{ \sigma_i(t) \in S_i(t) : \sigma_i(t) \text{ maximizes (C.1) given } \sigma_{-i}(t) \in S_{-i}(t) \right\}.$$

Definition C.1 *A Subgame Perfect Equilibrium (SPE) is a strategy profile* $\sigma^* = (\sigma_1^*, \ldots, \sigma_N^*) \in S$ *such that* $\sigma_i^*(t) \in BR(\sigma_{-i}^*(t) \mid h^{t-1}, k(t))$ *for all* $(h^{t-1}, k(t)) \in H^{t-1} \times K$, *for all* $i \in \mathcal{N}$, *and for* $t = 0, 1, \ldots$.

Therefore, an SPE requires strategies to be best responses to one another given all possible histories, which is a minimal requirement. What is "strong" (or "weak," depending on the perspective) about the SPE concept is that strategies are mappings from the entire history. Consequently in many infinitely repeated games, there will be numerous SPEs. This type of multiplicity sometimes makes it attractive to focus on subsets of equilibria. One possibility would be to look for stationary SPEs, motivated by the fact that the underlying game itself is stationary (i.e., payoffs do not depend on time). Another possibility would be to look at the best SPEs, (i.e., those that are on the Pareto frontier).

Perhaps the most popular alternative concept often used in dynamic games is that of Markov Perfect Equilibrium (MPE). The MPE differs from SPE in that it only conditions on the payoff-relevant state of the game. The motivation comes from dynamic programming where, as we have seen in Chapters 6 and 16, an optimal plan is a mapping from the state vector to the control vector. MPE can be thought of as an extension of this reasoning to game-theoretic situations. The advantage of the MPE relative to SPE is that many infinite games have far fewer MPEs than SPEs in general. The disadvantage, naturally, is that some economically interesting SPEs will be ignored when we focus on MPEs.

We could define payoff-relevant history at time t as the smallest (coarsest) partition $\mathcal{P}^t$ of H^t such that any two distinct elements of $\mathcal{P}^t$ necessarily lead to different payoffs or strategy sets for at least one of the players, holding the action profile of all other players constant.

In this case, it is clear that given the Markovian transition function (C.2), the payoff-relevant state is simply $k(t) \in K$. Then we define a pure Markovian strategy as

$$\hat{\sigma}_i : K \to A_i$$

and a mixed Markovian strategy as

$$\hat{\sigma}_i : K \to \Delta(A_i).$$

Define the set of Markovian strategies for player i by $\hat{S}_i$. Naturally, $\hat{S} = \prod_{i=1}^{N} \hat{S}_i$.

Notice that I have dropped the dependence on t, since time is not part of the payoff-relevant state. This is a feature of the infinite-horizon nature of the game. With finite horizons, time would necessarily be part of the payoff-relevant state. It is also possible to imagine more general infinite-horizon games in which the payoff function is $u_i(t, k(t), a_i(t))$, with time being part of the payoff-relevant state.

Note also that $\hat{\sigma}_i$ has a different dimension than σ_i above. In particular, $\hat{\sigma}_i$ assigns an action (or a probability distribution over actions) to each state $k \in K$, while σ_i does so for each subgame, that is, for all $(h^{t-1}, k(t)) \in H^{t-1} \times K$ and all t. To compare Markovian with non-Markovian strategies (in particular with non-Markovian deviations), it is useful to consider an *extension* of Markovian strategies to the same dimension as σ_i. In particular, let $\hat{\sigma}'_i$ be an extension of $\hat{\sigma}_i$ such that

$$\hat{\sigma}'_i : K \times H^{t-1} \to \Delta(A_i),$$

with $\hat{\sigma}'_i(k, h^{t-1}) = \hat{\sigma}_i(k)$ for all $h^{t-1} \in H^{t-1}$ and $k(t) \in K$. Define the set of extended Markovian strategies for player i by $\hat{S}'_i$ and $\hat{S}' = \prod_{i=1}^{N} \hat{S}'_i$. Moreover, as before, let $\hat{\sigma}'_i(t)$ be the continuation strategy of player i induced by $\hat{\sigma}'_i$ after time t, and let $\hat{\sigma}'_{-i}(t)$ be the continuation strategy profile of all players other than i induced by their Markovian strategies $\hat{\sigma}_{-i}$. I refer both to $\hat{\sigma}_i$ and to its extension $\hat{\sigma}'_i$ as "Markovian strategies."

Definition C.2 *A Markov Perfect Equilibrium (MPE) is a profile of Markovian strategies $\hat{\sigma}^* = (\hat{\sigma}_1^*, \ldots, \hat{\sigma}_N^*) \in \hat{S}$ such that the extension of these strategies satisfies $\hat{\sigma}_i'^*(t) \in BR(\hat{\sigma}_{-i}'^*(t) \mid h^{t-1}, k(t))$ for all $(h^{t-1}, k(t)) \in H^{t-1} \times K$, for all $i \in \mathcal{N}$, and for all $t = 0, 1, \ldots$.*

Therefore the only difference between MPEs and SPEs is that in the former attention is restricted to Markovian strategies. It is important to note that deviations are not restricted to be Markovian. This is implicitly emphasized by the extension of the Markovian strategies to $\hat{\sigma}_i'^* \in \hat{S}'_i$ and by the requirement that $\hat{\sigma}_i'^*(t) \in BR(\hat{\sigma}_{-i}'^*(t) \mid h^{t-1}, k(t))$ (which conditions on history h^t). In particular, for an MPE, a Markovian strategy $\hat{\sigma}_i^*$ must be a best response to $\hat{\sigma}_{-i}^*$ among all strategies $\sigma_i(t) : H^{t-1} \times K \to \Delta(A_i)$ available at time t.

It should also be clear that an MPE is an SPE, since the extended Markovian strategy satisfies $\hat{\sigma}_i'^*(t) \in BR(\hat{\sigma}_{-i}'^*(t) \mid h^{t-1}, k(t))$, ensuring that $\hat{\sigma}_i'^*$ is a best response to $\hat{\sigma}_{-i}'^*$ in all subgames, that is, for all $(h^{t-1}, k(t)) \in H^{t-1} \times K$ and for all t.

C.2 Some Basic Results

Recall that $\sigma(t) = (\sigma_1(t), \ldots, \sigma_N(t))$ denotes the continuation play for player i after date t, and therefore $\sigma_i(t) = (a_i(t), \sigma_i^*(t+1))$ designates the strategy involving action $a_i(t)$ at date t and the continuation play given by strategy $\sigma_i^*(t+1)$ subsequently.

Theorem C.1 (One-Stage Deviation Principle) *Suppose that the instantaneous payoff function of each player is uniformly bounded; that is, there exists $M < \infty$ such that*

$$\sup_{k \in K, a \in A(k)} u_i(a, k) < M$$

for all $i \in \mathcal{N}$. Then a strategy profile $\sigma^* = (\sigma_1^*, \ldots, \sigma_N^*) \in S$ is an SPE [$\hat{\sigma}^* = (\hat{\sigma}_1^*, \ldots, \hat{\sigma}_N^*) \in \hat{S}$ is an MPE] if and only if for all $i \in \mathcal{N}$, $(h^{t-1}, k(t)) \in H^{t-1} \times K$, and time t and for all $a_i(t) \in A(k(t))$,

$$\sigma_i^*(t) = (a_i(t), \sigma_i^*(t+1))$$

[$\hat{\sigma}'_i(t) = (a_{it}, \hat{\sigma}_i'^*(t+1))$] yields no higher payoff to player i than $\sigma_i^*(t)$ [$\hat{\sigma}_i'^*(t)$].

Proof.   **(Sketch)** Fix the strategy profile of other players. Then the problem of individual i is equivalent to a dynamic optimization problem. Since

$$\lim_{T \to \infty} \sum_{s=T}^{\infty} \beta^s u_i(k(t+s), a(t+s)) = 0$$

for all $\{k(t+s), a(t+s)\}_{s=0}^{T}$ and all t, given the uniform boundedness of instantaneous payoffs and $\beta < 1$, we can apply a slight variant of the Principle of Optimality (Theorem 16.2). In particular, given the uniform boundedness assumption, the same argument as in the proof of this theorem implies that an optimal plan for an individual, for a fixed profile of strategies of all other players, must be optimal for the next stage given her optimal continuation from then on. Moreover, any nonoptimal plan must violate the principle of optimality at some point.   ∎

This theorem implies that we can check whether a strategy is a best response to other players' strategy profiles by looking at one-stage deviations and keeping the rest of the strategy of the deviating player as given. The uniform boundedness assumption can be weakened to require continuity at infinity, which essentially means that discounted payoffs converge to zero along any history.

Lemma C.1   *Suppose that $\hat{\sigma}_{-i}^{\prime*}$ is Markovian (i.e., it is an extension of a Markovian strategy $\hat{\sigma}_{-i}^*$) and that for $h^{t-1} \in H^{t-1}$ and $k(t) \in K$, $BR(\hat{\sigma}_{-i}^{\prime*} \mid k(t), h^{t-1}) \neq \emptyset$. Then there exists $\hat{\sigma}_i^{\prime*} \in BR(\hat{\sigma}_{-i}^{\prime*} \mid k(t), h^{t-1})$ that is Markovian.*

Proof.   Suppose $\hat{\sigma}_{-i}^{\prime*}$ is Markovian. Suppose, to obtain a contradiction, that there exists a non-Markovian strategy σ_i^* that performs strictly better against $\hat{\sigma}_{-i}^{\prime*}$ than all Markovian strategies. Then by Theorem C.1, there exists $t, \tilde{t} > t, k \in K, h^{t-1} \in H^{t-1}$, and $\tilde{h}^{\tilde{t}-1} \in H^{\tilde{t}-1}$ such that the continuation play following these two histories given $k \in K$ are not the same; that is,

$$\sigma_i^*[t](k, h^{t-1}) \in BR(\hat{\sigma}_{-i}^{\prime*} \mid k, h^{t-1}), \; \sigma_i^*[\tilde{t}](k, \tilde{h}^{\tilde{t}-1}) \in BR(\hat{\sigma}_{-i}^{\prime*} \mid k, \tilde{h}^{\tilde{t}-1}), \quad \text{and}$$

$$\sigma_i^*[t](k, h^{t-1}) \neq \sigma_i^*[\tilde{t}](k, \tilde{h}^{\tilde{t}-1}),$$

where $\sigma_i^*[t](k, h^{t-1})$ denotes a continuation strategy for player i starting from time t with state vector k and history h^{t-1}. Now construct the continuation strategy $\hat{\sigma}_i^{\prime*}[\tilde{t}]$ such that $\hat{\sigma}_i^{\prime*}[\tilde{t}](k, \tilde{h}^{\tilde{t}-1}) = \sigma_i^*[t](k, h^{t-1})$. Since $\hat{\sigma}_{-i}^{\prime*}$ is Markovian, $\hat{\sigma}_{-i}^{\prime*}[t]$ is independent of h^{t-1} and $\tilde{h}^{\tilde{t}-1}$, and therefore

$$\hat{\sigma}_i^{\prime*}[t](k, h^{t-1}) = \hat{\sigma}_i^{\prime*}[t](k, \tilde{h}^{\tilde{t}-1}) \in BR(\hat{\sigma}_{-i}^{\prime*} \mid k, h^{t-1}) \cap BR(\hat{\sigma}_{-i}^{\prime*} \mid k, \tilde{h}^{\tilde{t}-1}).$$

Repeating this argument for all instances in which σ_i^* is not Markovian establishes that a Markovian strategy $\hat{\sigma}_i^{\prime*}$ is also best response to $\hat{\sigma}_{-i}^{\prime*}$.   ∎

This lemma states that when all other players are playing Markovian strategies, there exists a best response that is Markovian for each player. This does not mean that there are no other best responses, but since there is a Markovian best response, the lemma gives us hope that we can construct MPEs.

Theorem C.2 (Existence of Markov Perfect Equilibria)   *Let K and $A_i(k)$ for all $k \in K$ be finite sets. Then there exists an MPE $\hat{\sigma}^* = (\hat{\sigma}_1^*, \ldots, \hat{\sigma}_N^*)$.*

Proof. (Sketch) Consider an extended game in which the set of players is an element (i, k) of $\mathcal{N} \times K$, with payoff function given by the original payoff functions for player i starting in state k as in (C.1) and strategy set $A_i(k)$. The set $\mathcal{N} \times K$ is finite, and since $A_i(k)$ is also finite, the set of mixed strategies $\Delta(A_i(k))$ for player (i, k) is the simplex over $A_i(k)$. Therefore the standard proof of existence of Nash Equilibrium based on Kakutani's Fixed Point Theorem (Theorem A.18) applies and leads to the existence of an equilibrium $\left(\hat{\sigma}^*_{(i,k)}\right)_{(i,k) \in \mathcal{N} \times K}$ in this extended game.

Now going back to the original game, construct the strategy $\hat{\sigma}^*_i$ for each player $i \in \mathcal{N}$ such that $\hat{\sigma}^*_i(k) = \hat{\sigma}^*_{(i,k)}$, that is, $\hat{\sigma}^*_i : K \to \Delta(A_i)$. This strategy profile $\hat{\sigma}^*$ is Markovian. Consider the extension of $\hat{\sigma}^*$ to $\hat{\sigma}'^*$ as above, that is, $\hat{\sigma}'^*_i(k, h^{t-1}) = \hat{\sigma}^*_i(k)$ for all $h^{t-1} \in H^{t-1}$, $k(t) \in K$, $i \in \mathcal{N}$, and t. Then by construction, given $\hat{\sigma}'^*_{-i}$, it is impossible to improve over $\hat{\sigma}'^*_i$ with a deviation at any $k \in K$. Theorem C.1 implies that $\hat{\sigma}'^*_i$ is a best response to $\hat{\sigma}'^*_{-i}$ for all $i \in \mathcal{N}$ among all Markovian strategies. Lemma C.1 then implies that there exists no non-Markovian strategy that can perform strictly better than $\hat{\sigma}'^*_i$ against $\hat{\sigma}'^*_{-i}$ for all $i \in \mathcal{N}$. This argument establishes that $\hat{\sigma}'^*$ is an MPE strategy profile. ∎

Similar existence results can be proved for countably infinite sets K and $A_i(k)$ and for uncountable sets, but in the latter instance, some additional requirements are necessary, and these are rather technical in nature. Since they play no role in what follows, we do not need to elaborate on these requirements.

For the next result, let $\hat{\Sigma} = \left\{\hat{\sigma}^* \in \hat{S} : \hat{\sigma}^* \text{ is an MPE}\right\}$ be the set of MPE strategies and $\Sigma^* = \left\{\sigma \in S : \sigma^* \text{ is an SPE}\right\}$ be the set of SPE strategies. Let $\hat{\Sigma}'$ be the extension of $\hat{\Sigma}$ to include conditioning on histories. In particular, recall that $\hat{\sigma}'_i : K \times H^{t-1} \to \Delta(A_i)$ is such that $\hat{\sigma}'_i(k, h^{t-1}) = \hat{\sigma}_i(k)$ for all $h^{t-1} \in H^{t-1}$ and $k(t) \in K$, and let

$$\hat{\Sigma}' = \left\{ \begin{array}{c} \hat{\sigma}' \in S : \hat{\sigma}'_i(k, h^{t-1}) = \hat{\sigma}_i(k) \text{ for all } h^{t-1} \in H^{t-1}, k(t) \in K, \\ \text{and } i \in \mathcal{N}, \text{ and } \hat{\sigma} \text{ is an MPE} \end{array} \right\}.$$

Theorem C.3 (Markov versus Subgame Perfect Equilibria) $\hat{\Sigma}' \subset \Sigma^*$.

Proof. This theorem follows immediately by noting that since $\hat{\sigma}^*$ is an MPE strategy profile, the extended strategy profile, $\hat{\sigma}'^*$, is such that $\hat{\sigma}'^*_i$ is a best response to $\hat{\sigma}^*_{-i}$ for all $h^{t-1} \in H^{t-1}$, $k(t) \in K$, and for all $i \in \mathcal{N}$ and thus is subgame perfect. ∎

This theorem implies that every MPE strategy profile corresponds to an SPE strategy profile, and any equilibrium-path play supported by an MPE can be supported by an SPE.

Theorem C.4 (Existence of Subgame Perfect Equilibria) *Let K and $A_i(k)$ for all $k \in K$ be finite sets. Then there exists an SPE $\sigma^* = (\sigma^*_1, \ldots, \sigma^*_N)$.*

Proof. Theorem C.2 shows that an MPE exists, and since an MPE is an SPE (Theorem C.3), the existence of an SPE follows. ∎

When K and $A_i(k)$ are uncountable sets, existence of pure strategy SPEs can be guaranteed by imposing compactness and convexity of K and $A_i(k)$ and quasi-concavity of $U_i[t]$ in $\sigma_i[t]$ for all $i \in \mathcal{N}$ (in addition to the continuity assumptions above). In the absence of convexity of K and $A_i(k)$ or quasi-concavity of $U_i[t]$, mixed strategy equilibria can still be guaranteed to exist under some mild additional assumptions.

Finally, a well-known theorem for SPE from repeated games also generalizes to dynamic games. Let $p(a \mid \sigma)$ be the probability distribution over the equilibrium-path actions induced by the strategy profile σ, with the usual understanding that $\int_{a \in A} p(a \mid \sigma)\,da = 1$ for all $\sigma \in S$, where A is a set of admissible action profiles. With a slight abuse of terminology, I refer to $p(a \mid \sigma)$ as the "equilibrium-path action induced by strategy σ." Then let

$$U_i^M(k) = \min_{\sigma_{-i} \in \Sigma_{-i}} \max_{\sigma_i \in \Sigma_i} \mathbb{E} \sum_{s=0}^{\infty} \beta^s u_i(k(t+s), a(t+s)),$$

be the maximum payoff of player i when $k(t) = k$ and $k(t+s)$ is given by (C.2). Moreover let

$$U_i^N(k) = \min_{\sigma \in \Sigma} \mathbb{E} \sum_{s=0}^{\infty} \beta^s u_i(k(t+s), a(t+s)), \tag{C.3}$$

be the minimum SPE payoff of player i starting in state $k \in K$. In other words, (C.3) is player i's payoff in the equilibrium chosen to minimize this payoff (starting in state k).

Theorem C.5 (Punishment with the Worst Equilibrium)   *Suppose $\sigma^* \in S$ is a pure strategy SPE with the distribution of equilibrium-path actions given by $p(a \mid \sigma^*)$. Then there exists an SPE $\sigma^{**} \in S$ such that $p(a \mid \sigma^*) = p(a \mid \sigma^{**})$ and σ^{**} involves a continuation payoff of $U_i^N(k)$ to player i, if i is the first to deviate from σ^{**} at date t after some history $h^{t-1} \in H^{t-1}$ and when the resulting state in the next period is $k(t+1) = k$.*

Proof.   If σ^* is an SPE, then no player wishes to deviate from it. Suppose that i were to deviate from σ^* at date t after history $h^{t-1} \in H^{t-1}$ and when $k(t) = k$. Denote her continuation payoff starting at time t, with $k(t)$, and h^{t-1} by $U_i^d[t](k(t), h^{t-1} \mid \sigma^*)$. Denote her equilibrium payoff under σ^* by $U_i^c[t](k(t), h^{t-1} \mid \sigma^*)$. Then σ^* can be an SPE only if

$$U_i^c[t](k(t), h^{t-1} \mid \sigma^*) \geq$$

$$\max_{a_i(t) \in A_i(k)} \mathbb{E} \left\{ u_i(a_i(t), a_{-i}(\sigma_{-i}^*) \mid k(t), h^{t-1}) + \beta U_i^d[t+1](k(t+1), h^t \mid \sigma^*) \right\},$$

where $u_i(a_i(t), a_{-i}(\sigma_{-i}^*) \mid k(t), h^{t-1}, \sigma^*)$ is the instantaneous payoff of individual i when she chooses action $a_i(t)$ in state $k(t)$ following history h^{t-1} and other players are playing the (potentially mixed) action profiles induced by σ_{-i}^* (denoted by $a_{-i}(\sigma_{-i}^*)$). Recall that $U_i^d[t+1](k(t+1), h^t \mid \sigma^*)$ is the continuation payoff following this deviation, with $k(t+1)$ following from the transition function $q(k(t+1) \mid k(t), a_i(t), a_{-i}(\sigma_{-i}^*))$, and h^t incorporating the actions $a_i(t), a_{-i}(\sigma_{-i}^*)$. The continuation play, following the deviation, will correspond to an SPE, since σ_{-i}^* specifies an SPE action for all players other than i in all subgames, and in response, the best that player i can do is to play an equilibrium strategy.

By definition of an SPE and the minimum equilibrium payoff of player i defined in (C.3),

$$U_i^d[t+1](k(t+1), h^t \mid \sigma^*) \geq U_i^N(k(t+1)).$$

The preceding two inequalities imply that

$$U_i^c[t](k(t), h^{t-1} \mid \sigma^*) \geq \max_{a_i(t) \in A_i(k)} \mathbb{E} \left\{ u_i(a_i(t), a_{-i}(\sigma_{-i}^*) \mid k(t), h^{t-1}) + \beta U_i^N(k(t)) \right\}.$$

Therefore we can construct σ^{**}, which is identical to σ^* except that we replace $U_i^d[t+1](k(t+1), h^t \mid \sigma^*)$ with $U_i^N(k(t+1))$ following the deviation by player i from σ^* after history $h^{t-1} \in H^{t-1}$. Since $U_i^N(k(t+1))$ is an SPE payoff, σ^{**} is also an SPE.   ∎

This theorem states that in characterizing the set of sustainable payoffs in SPEs, we can limit attention to SPE strategy profiles involving the most severe equilibrium punishments. A stronger version of this theorem is the following.

Theorem C.6 (Punishment with Minmax Payoffs) *Suppose $\sigma^* \in S$ is a pure strategy SPE with the distribution of equilibrium-path actions given by $p(a \mid \sigma^*)$. Then for β sufficiently close to 1, there exists an SPE $\sigma^{**} \in S$ (possibly equal to σ^*) with $p(a \mid \sigma^*) = p(a \mid \sigma^{**})$, and σ^{**} involves a continuation payoff of $U_i^M(k)$ to player i, if i is the first to deviate from σ^{**} at date t after some history $h^{t-1} \in H^{t-1}$ and when $k(t) = k$.*

Proof. The proof is similar to that of Theorem C.5, except that it uses $U_i^M(k)$ instead of $U_i^N(k)$. When β is sufficiently high, the minmax payoff for player i, $U_i^M(k)$, can be supported as part of an SPE (see Abreu (1988) or Fudenberg and Tirole (1994)). ∎

C.3 Application: Repeated Games with Perfect Observability

For repeated games with perfect observability, both SPE and MPE are easy to characterize. Suppose that the same stage game is played an infinite number of times, so that

$$U_i[t] = \mathbb{E}_t \sum_{s=0}^{\infty} \beta^s u_i(a(t+s)),$$

which differs from (C.1) only in that there is no conditioning on the state variable $k(t)$. Let us refer to the game $\{u_i(a), a \in A\}$ as the *stage game*. Define $m_i = \min_{a_{-i}} \max_{a_i} u_i(a)$ as the minmax payoff in this stage game. Let $V \in \mathbb{R}^N$ be the set of feasible per period payoffs for the N players, with v_i corresponding to the payoff to player i (so that discounted payoffs correspond to $v_i/(1-\beta)$).

Theorem C.7 (The Folk Theorem for Repeated Games) *Suppose that $\{A_i\}_{i \in \mathcal{N}}$ are compact. Then for any $v \in V$ such that $v_i > m_i$ for all $i \in \mathcal{N}$, there exists $\bar{\beta} \in [0, 1)$ such that for all $\beta > \bar{\beta}$, v can be supported as the payoff profile of a SPE.*

Proof. (Sketch) Construct the following punishment strategies for any deviation: the first player to deviate, i, is held down to her minmax payoff m_i (which can be supported as a SPE). Then the payoff from any deviation $a \in A_i$ is $D_i(a \mid \beta) \leq d_i + \beta m_i/(1-\beta)$, where d_i is the highest payoff player i can obtain by deviating, which is finite, because u_i is continuous and bounded and A_i is compact. Then v_i can be supported if

$$\frac{v_i}{1-\beta} \geq d_i + \beta \frac{m_i}{1-\beta}.$$

Since d_i is finite and $v_i > m_i$, there exists $\bar{\beta}_i \in [0, 1)$ such that for all $\beta \geq \beta_i$ this inequality is true. Letting $\bar{\beta} = \max_{i \in \mathcal{N}} \bar{\beta}_i$ establishes the desired result. ∎

Theorem C.8 (Unique Markov Perfect Equilibrium in Repeated Games) *Suppose that the stage game has a unique equilibrium a^*. Then there exists a unique MPE in which a^* is played at each date.*

Proof. The result follows immediately, since K is a singleton and the stage payoff has a unique equilibrium. ∎

This last theorem is natural but is also very important. In repeated games, there is no state vector, so strategies cannot be conditioned on anything. Consequently in MPE we can only look at the strategies that are a best response in the stage game.

Example C.1 *(Prisoner's Dilemma) Consider the following standard prisoner's dilemma game, which, in fact, has many applications in political economy.*

	D	C
D	(0, 0)	(4,-1)
C	(-1, 4)	(2, 2)

The stage game has a unique equilibrium, which is (D,D). Now imagine this game being repeated an infinite number of times with both agents having discount factor β. The unique MPE is playing (D,D) at every date.

In contrast, when $\beta \geq 1/2$, then (C,C) at every date can be supported as an SPE. To see this, recall that we only need to consider the minmax punishment, which in this case is (0, 0). Playing (C,C) leads to a payoff of $2/(1 - \beta)$, whereas the best deviation leads to the payoff of 4 now and a continuation payoff of 0. Therefore $\beta \geq 1/2$ is sufficient to ensure that the following grim strategy profile implements (C,C) at every date: for both players, the strategy is to play C if h^t includes only (C,C) and to play D otherwise.

It is straightforward to see why the grim strategy profile is not an MPE. This profile conditions on whether one of the players defected at any point in the past. This history is not payoff relevant for the future of the game given the action profile of the other player.

C.4   Exercises

C.1   A simple application of the ideas in this appendix are *common pool games*. Consider a society consisting of $N + 1 < \infty$ players each with payoff function $\sum_{s=0}^{\infty} \beta^s \log(c_i(t + s))$ at time t, where $\beta \in (0, 1)$, and $c_i(t)$ denotes consumption of individual $i \in \mathcal{N}$ at time t. The society has a common resource, denoted by $K(t)$, which can be thought of as the capital stock at time t. This capital stock follows the nonstochastic law of motion

$$K(t + 1) = AK(t) - \sum_{i \in \mathcal{N}} c_i(t),$$

where $A > 0$, $K(0)$ is given, and $K(t) \geq 0$ must be satisfied in every period. The stage game is as follows: at every date all players simultaneously announce $\{c_i(t)\}_{i \in \mathcal{N}}$. If $\sum_{i \in \mathcal{N}} c_i(t) \leq AK(t)$, then each individual consumes $c_i(t)$. If $\sum_{i \in \mathcal{N}} c_i(t) > AK(t)$, then $AK(t)$ is equally allocated among the $N + 1$ players.

(a) First, suppose that $\{c_i(t)\}_{i \in \mathcal{N}}$ is chosen by a benevolent planner maximizing the total discounted payoff of all individuals:

$$\sum_{i \in \mathcal{N}} \sum_{s=0}^{\infty} \beta^s \log(c_i(t + s)).$$

Set up this problem as a dynamic programming problem and show that the value function of the planner given capital stock K, $V(K)$, is uniquely defined, continuous, concave, and differentiable when $S \in (0, AK)$. Also show that the saving level as a function of the capital stock is $\pi(K) = \beta AK$, and derive an explicit form equation for the value function $V(K)$.

(b) Now consider the MPEs of this game. First show that all individuals announcing $c_i(0) = AK(0)$ is an MPE. Next focus on continuous and symmetric MPEs, where each agent pursues a strategy of consuming $c^N(K)$ when the capital stock is K. Given symmetry, when all other agents are pursuing this strategy and agent i chooses consumption c, aggregate savings will be $S = AK - Nc^N(K) - c$. Using this observation, show that the value function of an individual is

$$V^N(K) = \max_{S \le AK - Nc^N(K)} \left\{ \log(AK - Nc^N(K) - S) + \beta V^N(S) \right\}. \qquad \text{(C.4)}$$

Assuming differentiability, derive the first-order condition of the maximization problem in (C.4) and show that there exists a symmetric equilibrium where the equilibrium aggregate saving level in the economy is given by

$$\pi(K) = \frac{\beta A}{1 + N - \beta N} K.$$

Verify that this is the unique solution to (C.4). What is the effect of an increase in N?

(c) Show that if $\beta A > 1 > \beta A/(1 + N - \beta N)$, then the single-person decision problem would involve growth over time, while the MPE would involve the resources shrinking over time.

(d) Next show that in this game there always exist SPEs that implement the single-person solution for any value of $\beta > 0$. Explain this result.

(e) Now suppose that $\beta A = 1$, and again focus on MPEs. Suppose that the game starts with capital stock $K(0)$, and consider the following discontinuous Markovian strategy profile:

$$c_i(K) = \begin{cases} \frac{\beta A K}{1+N} & \text{if } K \ge K(0), \\ K & \text{if } K < K(0). \end{cases}$$

Show that when all players other than i' pursue this strategy, it is a best response for player i' to play this strategy as well, and along the equilibrium path, the single-person solution is implemented. Show that the same result cannot be obtained when $\beta A \ne 1$. Why not?

D

List of Theorems

In this appendix, I list the theorems presented in various chapters for reference. Many of these theorems refer to mathematical results used in different parts of the book. Some of them are economic results that are more general and more widely applicable than the results I label as "propositions." To conserve space, I do not list additional mathematical results given in lemmas, corollaries, and facts.

Chapter 2

2.1: Euler's Theorem
2.2: Stability for Systems of Linear Difference Equations
2.3: Local Stability for Systems of Nonlinear Difference Equations
2.4: Stability of Linear Differential Equations
2.5: Local Stability of Nonlinear Differential Equations
2.6: Uzawa's Theorem I
2.7: Uzawa's Theorem II

Chapter 5

5.1: Debreu-Mantel-Sonnenschein Theorem
5.2: Gorman's Aggregation Theorem
5.3: Existence of a Normative Representative Household
5.4: Representative Firm Theorem
5.5: First Welfare Theorem I: Economies with Finite Number of Households
5.6: First Welfare Theorem II: Economies with Infinite Number of Households
5.7: Second Welfare Theorem
5.8: Equivalence of Sequential and Nonsequential Trading with Arrow Securities

Chapter 6

6.1: Equivalence of Sequential and Recursive Formulations
6.2: Principle of Optimality in Dynamic Programming

6.3: Existence of Solutions in Dynamic Programming
6.4: Concavity of the Value Function
6.5: Monotonicity of the Value Function
6.6: Differentiability of the Value Function
6.7: Contraction Mapping Theorem
6.8: Applications of Contraction Mappings
6.9: Blackwell's Sufficient Conditions for a Contraction
6.10: Euler Equations and the Transversality Condition
6.11: Existence of Solutions in Nonstationary Problems
6.12: Euler Equations and the Transversality Condition in Nonstationary Problems

Chapter 7

7.1: Necessary Conditions for an Interior Optimum with Free End Points
7.2: Necessary Conditions II for Interior Optimum with Fixed End Points
7.3: Necessary Conditions III for Interior Optimum with Inequality-Constrained End Points
7.4: Simplified Version of Pontryagin's Maximum Principle
7.5: Mangasarian's Sufficiency Conditions for an Optimum
7.6: Arrow's Sufficiency Conditions for an Optimum
7.7: Pontyagin's Maximum Principle for Multivariate Problems
7.8: Sufficiency Conditions for Multivariate Problems
7.9: Pontyagin's Infinite-Horizon Maximum Principle
7.10: Hamilton-Jacobi-Bellman Equation
7.11: Sufficiency Conditions for Infinite-Horizon Optimal Control
7.12: Transversality Condition for Infinite-Horizon Problems
7.13: Maximum Principle for Discounted Infinite-Horizon Problems
7.14: Sufficiency Conditions for Discounted Infinite-Horizon Problems
7.15: Existence of Solutions in Optimal Control
7.16: Concavity of the Value Function in Optimal Control
7.17: Differentiability of the Value Function in Optimal Control
7.18: Saddle-Path Stability in Systems of Linear Differential Equations
7.19: Saddle-Path Stability in Systems of Nonlinear Differential Equations

Chapter 10

10.1: Separation Theorem for Investment in Human Capital

Chapter 16

16.1: Equivalence of Sequential and Recursive Formulations
16.2: Principle of Optimality in Stochastic Dynamic Programming
16.3: Existence of Solutions in Stochastic Dynamic Programming
16.4: Concavity of the Value Function
16.5: Monotonicity of the Value Function in State Variables
16.6: Differentiability of the Value Function
16.7: Monotonicity of the Value Function in Stochastic Variables

16.8: Euler Equations and the Transversality Condition
16.9: Existence of Solutions with Markov Processes
16.10: Continuity of Value Functions with Markov Processes
16.11: Concavity of Value Functions with Markov Processes
16.12: Monotonicity of Value Functions with Markov Processes
16.13: Differentiability of Value Functions with Markov Processes

Chapter 22

22.1: Median Voter Theorem
22.2: Median Voter Theorem with Strategic Voting
22.3: Downsian Policy Convergence Theorem
22.4: Extended Median Voter Theorem
22.5: Extended Downsian Policy Convergence Theorem
22.6: Probabilistic Voting Theorem

Appendix A

A.1: Properties of Open and Closed Sets in Metric Spaces
A.2: Open Sets and Continuity in Metric Spaces
A.3: Intermediate Value Theorem
A.4: Open Sets and Continuity in Topological Spaces
A.5: Continuity and Convergence of Nets in Topological Spaces
A.6: Heine-Borel Theorem
A.7: Bolzano-Weierstrass Theorem
A.8: Continuity and Compact Images in Topological Spaces
A.9: Weierstrass's Theorem
A.10: Uniform Continuity over Compact Sets
A.11: Projection Maps and the Product Topology
A.12: Continuity of Discounted Utilities in the Product Topology
A.13: Tychonoff's Theorem
A.14: Totally Bounded and Compact Spaces
A.15: Arzela-Ascoli Theorem
A.16: Berge's Maximum Theorem
A.17: Properties of Maximizers under Quasi-Concavity
A.18: Kakutani's Fixed Point Theorem
A.19: Brouwer's Fixed Point Theorem
A.20: Mean Value Theorem
A.21: l'Hôpital's Rule
A.22: Taylor's Theorem I
A.23: Taylor's Theorem II: Functions of Several Variables
A.24: Inverse Function Theorem
A.25: Implicit Function Theorem
A.26: Continuity of Linear Functionals in Normed Vector Spaces
A.27: Geometric Hahn-Banach Theorem
A.28: Separating Hyperplane Theorem
A.29: Saddle-Point Theorem

A.30: Kuhn-Tucker Theorem
A.31: Envelope Theorem

Appendix B

B.1: Fundamental Theorem of Calculus I
B.2: Fundamental Theorem of Calculus II
B.3: Integration by Parts
B.4: Leibniz's Rule
B.5: Solutions to Systems of Linear Differential Equations with Constant Coefficients
B.6: Solutions to General Systems of Linear Differential Equations
B.7: Grobman-Hartman Theorem: Stability of Nonlinear Systems of Differential Equations
B.8: Picard's Theorem I: Existence and Uniqueness for Differential Equations
B.9: Existence and Uniqueness of Differential Equations on Compact Sets I
B.10: Picard's Theorem II: on Existence and Uniqueness for Systems of Differential Equations
B.11: Existence and Uniqueness for Systems of Differential Equations on Compact Sets II
B.12: Continuity of Solutions to Differential Equations
B.13: Differentiability of Solutions to Differential Equations
B.14: Solutions to Systems of Linear Difference Equations with Constant Coefficients
B.15: General Solutions to Systems of Linear Difference Equations with Constant Coefficients
B.16: Existence and Uniqueness of Solutions to Difference Equations

Appendix C

C.1: One-Stage Deviation Principle
C.2: Existence of Markov Perfect Equilibria in Finite Dynamic Games
C.3: Markov versus Subgame Perfect Equilibria
C.4: Existence of Subgame Perfect Equilibria in Finite Dynamic Games
C.5: Punishment with Worst Equilibrium
C.6: Punishment with Minmax Payoffs
C.7: Folk Theorem for Repeated Games
C.8: Unique Markov Perfect Equilibrium in Repeated Games

References

Abernathy, William J. (1978) *The Productivity Dilemma: Roadblock to Innovation in the Automotive Industry*. Baltimore: Johns Hopkins University Press.

Abraham, Kathrine G., and Jon Haltiwanger (1995) "Real Wages and the Business Cycle." *Journal of Economic Literature* 33: 1215–1264.

Abramowitz, Moses (1957) "Resources on Output Trends in the United States since 1870." *American Economic Review* 46: 5–23.

Abreu, Dilip (1988) "On the Theory of Infinitely Repeated Games with Discounting." *Econometrica* 56: 383–396.

Acemoglu, Daron (1995) "Reward Structures and the Allocation of Talent." *European Economic Review* 39: 17–33.

——— (1996) "A Microfoundation for Social Increasing Returns in Human Capital Accumulation." *Quarterly Journal of Economics* 111: 779–804.

——— (1997a) "Training and Innovation in an Imperfect Labor Market." *Review of Economic Studies* 64(2): 445–464.

——— (1997b) "Matching, Heterogeneity and the Evolution of Income Distribution."*Journal of Economic Growth* 2(1): 61–92.

——— (1998) "Why Do New Technologies Complement Skills? Directed Technical Change and Wage Inequality." *Quarterly Journal of Economics* 113: 1055–1090.

——— (2002a) "Directed Technical Change." *Review of Economic Studies* 69: 781–809.

——— (2002b) "Technical Change, Inequality and the Labor Market." *Journal of Economic Literature* 40(1): 7–72.

——— (2003a) "Patterns of Skill Premia." *Review of Economic Studies* 70: 199–230.

——— (2003b) "Labor- and Capital-Augmenting Technical Change." *Journal of European Economic Association* 1(1): 1–37.

——— (2003c) "Why Not a Political Coase Theorem?" *Journal of Comparative Economics* 31: 620–652.

——— (2005) "Politics and Economics in Weak and Strong States."*Journal of Monetary Economics* 52: 1199–1226.

——— (2007a) "Equilibrium Bias of Technology." *Econometrica* 75(5): 1371–1410.

——— (2007b) "Modeling Inefficient Institutions." In *Advances in Economic Theory, Proceedings of World Congress 2005*, Richard Blundell, Whitney Newey, and Torsten Persson (editors). Cambridge: Cambridge University Press, pp. 341–380.

——— (2008a) "Oligarchic versus Democratic Societies." *Journal of the European Economic Association* 6: 1–44.

——— (2008b) "Innovation by Incumbents and Entrants." MIT Economics Department Working Paper. Massachusetts Institute of Technology.

Acemoglu, Daron, and Ufuk Akcigit (2006) "State Dependent IPR Policy." NBER Working Paper 12775. National Bureau of Economic Research.

Acemoglu, Daron, and Joshua D. Angrist (2000) "How Large Are Human Capital Externalities? Evidence from Compulsory Schooling Laws." *NBER Macroeconomics Annual* 2000: 9–59.

Acemoglu, Daron, and Veronica Guerrieri (2008) "Capital Deepening and Non-Balanced Economic Growth." *Journal of Political Economy* 116: 467–498.

Acemoglu, Daron, and Simon Johnson (2005) "Unbundling Institutions." *Journal of Political Economy* 113: 949–995.

——— (2007) "Disease and Development." *Journal of Political Economy* 115: 925–985.

Acemoglu, Daron, and Joshua Linn (2004) "Market Size in Innovation: Theory and Evidence from the Pharmaceutical Industry." *Quarterly Journal of Economics* 119: 1049–1090.

Acemoglu, Daron, and James A. Robinson (2000a) "Why Did the West Extend the Franchise? Democracy, Inequality and Growth in Historical Perspective." *Quarterly Journal of Economics* 115: 1167–1199.

——— (2000b) "Political Losers as a Barrier to Economic Development."*American Economic Review* 90: 126–130.

——— (2006a) *Economic Origins of Dictatorship and Democracy.* New York: Cambridge University Press.

——— (2006b) "Economic Backwardness in Political Perspective." *American Political Science Review* 100: 115–131.

——— (2008) "Persistence of Power, Elites and Institutions." NBER Working Paper 12108. National Bureau of Economics Research. Forthcoming in *American Economic Review* 98: 267–293.

Acemoglu, Daron, and Jaume Ventura (2002) "The World Income Distribution." *Quarterly Journal of Economics* 117: 659–694.

Acemoglu, Daron, and Fabrizio Zilibotti (1997) "Was Prometheus Unbound by Chance? Risk, Diversification and Growth." *Journal of Political Economy* 105: 709–751.

——— (1999) "Information Accumulation in Development." *Journal of Economic Growth* 1999(4): 5–38.

——— (2001) "Productivity Differences." *Quarterly Journal of Economics* 116: 563–606.

Acemoglu, Daron, Philippe Aghion, and Fabrizio Zilibotti (2006) "Distance to Frontier, Selection, and Economic Growth." *Journal of the European Economic Association* 4(1): 37–74.

Acemoglu, Daron, Pol Antras, and Elhanan Helpman (2007) "Contracts and Technology Adoption." *American Economic Review* 97: 916–943.

Acemoglu, Daron, Simon Johnson, and James A. Robinson (2001) "The Colonial Origins of Comparative Development: An Empirical Investigation." *American Economic Review* 91: 1369–1401.

——— (2002) "Reversal of Fortune: Geography and Institutions in the Making of the Modern World Income Distribution." *Quarterly Journal of Economics* 117: 1231–1294.

——— (2005a) "Institutions as a Fundamental Cause of Long-Run Growth." In *Handbook of Economic Growth,* Philippe Aghion and Steven N. Durlauf (editors). Amsterdam: North-Holland, pp. 384–473.

——— (2005b) "The Rise of Europe: Atlantic Trade, Institutional Change and Growth." *American Economic Review* 95: 546–579.

Aczel, J. (1966) *Lectures on Functional Equations and Their Applications.* New York: Academic Press.

Aghion, Philippe, and Patrick Bolton (1997) "A Theory of Trickle-Down Growth and Development." *Review of Economic Studies* 64: 151–172.

Aghion, Philippe, and Peter Howitt (1992) "A Model of Growth through Creative Destruction." *Econometrica* 60: 323–351.

——— (1994) "Growth and Unemployment."*Review of Economic Studies* 61: 477–494.

——— (1998) *Endogenous Growth Theory.* Cambridge, Mass.: MIT Press.

——— (2008) *The Economics of Growth.* Cambridge, Mass: MIT Press, forthcoming.

Aghion, Philippe, Peter Howitt, and Gianluca Violante (2004) "General Purpose Technology and Wage Inequality." *Journal of Economic Growth* 7: 315–345.

Aghion, Philippe, Christopher Harris, Peter Howitt, and John Vickers (2001) "Competition, Imitation, and Growth with Step-by-Step Innovation." *Review of Economic Studies* 68: 467–492.

Aghion, Philippe, Nick Bloom, Richard Blundell, Rachel Griffith, and Peter Howitt (2005) "Competition and Innovation: An Inverted-U Relationship." *Quarterly Journal of Economics* 120: 701–728.

Aiyagari, S. Rao (1993) "Uninsured Indiosyncratic Risk and Aggregate Saving." Federal Reserve Bank of Minneapolis Working Paper 502.

———— (1994) "Uninsured Indiosyncratic Risk and Aggregate Saving." *Quarterly Journal of Economics* 109: 659–684.

Alesina, Alberto, and Dani Rodrik (1994) "Distributive Politics and Economic Growth." *Quarterly Journal of Economics* 109: 465–490.

Alfaro, Laura, Sebnem Kalemli-Ozcan, and Vadym Volosovych (2005) "Why Doesn't Capital Flow from Rich to Poor Countries? An Empirical Investigation." University of Houston, mimeo.

Aliprantis, Charalambos, and Kim Border (1999) *Infinite Dimensional Analysis: A Hitchhiker's Guide.* New York: Springer-Verlag.

Allen, Franklin, and Douglas Gale (1991) "Arbitrage, Short Sales and Financial Innovation." *Econometrica* 59: 1041–1068.

Allen, Robert C. (2004) "Agriculture during the Industrial Revolution: 1700–1850." In *Cambridge Economic History of Modern Britain,* Roderick Floud and Paul A. Johnson (editors). Cambridge: Cambridge University Press, pp. 96–116.

Andreoni, James (1989) "Giving with Impure Altruism: Applications to Charity and Ricardian Equivalence." *Journal of Political Economy* 97: 1447–1458.

Angrist, Joshua D. (1995) "The Economic Returns to Schooling in the West Bank and Gaza Strip." *American Economic Review* 85: 1065–1087.

Angrist, Joshua D., Victor Lavy, and Analia Schlosser (2006) "New Evidence on the Causal Link between the Quantity and Quality of Children." Massachusetts Institute of Technology, mimeo.

Antras, Pol (2005) "Incomplete Contracts and the Product Cycle." *American Economic Review* 95: 1054–1073.

Apostol, Tom M. (1975) *Mathematical Analysis,* 2nd edition. Reading, Mass: Addison-Wesley.

Araujo, A., and Jose A. Scheinkman (1983) "Maximum Principle and Transversality Condition for Concave Infinite Horizon Economic Models." *Journal of Economic Theory* 30: 1–16.

Armington, Paul S. (1969) "A Theory of Demand for Products Distinguished by Place and Production." *International Monetary Fund Staff Papers* 16: 159–178.

Arrow, Kenneth J. (1951) *Social Choice and Individual Values.* New York: Wiley.

———— (1962) "The Economic Implications of Learning by Doing." *Review of Economic Studies* 29: 155–173.

———— (1964) "The Role of Security in Optimal Allocation of Risk Bearing." *Review of Economic Studies* 31: 91–96.

———— (1968) "Applications of Control Theory to Economic Growth." In *Mathematics of Decision Sciences,* George B. Dantzig and Arthur F. Veinott (editors). Providence, R.I.: American Mathematical Society.

Arrow, Kenneth J., and Mordecai Kurz (1970) *Public Investment, the Rate of Return, and Optimal Fiscal Policy.* Baltimore: Johns Hopkins University Press.

Arrow, Kenneth J., Hollis B. Chenery, Bagicha S. Minhas, and Robert Solow (1961) "Capital-Labor Substitution and Economic Efficiency." *Review of Economics and Statistics* 43: 225–250.

Ashton, Thomas Southcliffe (1969) *The Industrial Revolution: 1760–1830.* Oxford: Oxford University Press.

Atkeson, Andrew (1991) "International Lending with Moral Hazard and Risk of Repudiation." *Econometrica* 59: 1069–1089.

Atkeson, Andrew, and Ariel Burstein (2007) "Innovation, Firm Dynamics and International Trade." University of California, Los Angeles, mimeo.

Atkeson, Andrew, and Patrick Kehoe (2002) "Paths of Development for Early and Late Boomers in a Dynamic Heckscher-Ohlin Model." Federal Reserve Bank of Minneapolis, mimeo.

Atkinson, Anthony, and Joseph Stiglitz (1969) "A New View of Technological Change." *Economic Journal* 79: 573–578.

Aumann, Robert J., and Lloyd S. Shapley (1974) *Values of Non-Atomic Games.* Princeton, N.J.: Princeton University Press.

Austen-Smith, David, and Jeffrey S. Banks (1999) *Positive Political Theory I: Collective Preference.* Ann Arbor: University of Michigan Press.

Autor, David, Lawrence Katz, and Alan Krueger (1998) "Computing Inequality: Have Computers Changed the Labor Market?" *Quarterly Journal of Economics* 113: 1169–1214.

Azariadis, Costas (1993) *Intertemporal Macroeconomics.* London: Blackwell.

Azariadis, Costas, and Allan Drazen (1990) "Threshold Externalities in Economic Development." *Quarterly Journal of Economics* 105: 501–526.

Backus, David, Patrick J. Kehoe, and Timothy J. Kehoe (1992) "In Search of Scale Effects in Trade and Growth." *Journal of Economic Theory* 58: 377–409.

Baily, Martin N., Charles Hulten, and David Campbell (1992) "The Distribution of Productivity in Manufacturing Plants." *Brookings Papers on Economic Activity: Microeconomics* 187–249.

Bairoch, Paul (1988) *Cities and Economic Development: From the Dawn of History to the Present,* translated by Christopher Braider. Chicago: University of Chicago Press.

Bairoch, Paul, Jean Batou, and Pierre Chèvre (1988) *La Population des villes Européennes de 800 a 1850: Banque de Données et Analyse Sommaire des Résultats.* Geneva: Centre d'histoire économique Internationale de l'Universite de Genève, Libraire Droz.

Banerjee, Abhijit V., and Esther Duflo (2003) "Inequality and Growth: What Can the Data Say?" *Journal of Economic Growth* 8: 267–299.

——— (2005) "Economic Growth through the Lenses of Development Economics." In *Handbook of Economic Growth,* Philippe Aghion and Steven N. Durlauf (editors). Amsterdam: North-Holland, pp. 384–473.

Banerjee, Abhijit V., and Andrew Newman (1991) "Risk Bearing and the Theory of Income Distribution." *Review of Economic Studies* 58: 211–235.

——— (1993) "Occupational Choice and the Process of Development." *Journal of Political Economy* 101: 274–298.

——— (1998) "Information, the Dual Economy and Development." *Review of Economic Studies* 65: 631–653.

Banfield, Edward C. (1958) *The Moral Basis of a Backward Society.* Chicago: University of Chicago Press.

Barro, Robert J. (1974) "Are Government Bonds Net Wealth?" *Journal of Political Economy* 81: 1095–1117.

——— (1991) "Economic Growth in a Cross Section of Countries." *Quarterly Journal of Economics* 106: 407–443.

——— (1997) *Determinants of Economic Growth: A Cross Country Empirical Study.* Cambridge, Mass.: MIT Press.

——— (1999) "Determinants of Democracy." *Journal of Political Economy* 107: S158–S183.

Barro, Robert J., and Gary S. Becker (1989) "Fertility Choice in a Model of Economic Growth." *Econometrica* 57: 481–501.

Barro, Robert J., and Jong-Wha Lee (2001) "International Data on Educational Attainment: Updates and Implications." *Oxford Economic Papers* 53: 541–563.

Barro, Robert J., and Rachel McCleary (2003) "Religion and Economic Growth." NBER Working Paper 9682. National Bureau of Economics Research.

Barro, Robert J. and Xavier Sala-i-Martin (1991) "Convergence across States and Regions." *Brookings Papers on Economic Activity* 1: 107–182.

——— (1992) "Convergence." *Journal of Political Economy* 100: 223–251.

——— (2004) *Economic Growth.* Cambridge, Mass.: MIT Press.

Bartelsman, Eric J., and Mark Doms (2000) "Understanding Productivity: Lessons from Longitudinal Microdata." *Journal of Economic Literature* 38: 569–594.

Basu, Susanto, and David Weil (1998) "Appropriate Technology and Growth." *Quarterly Journal of Economics* 113: 1025–1054.

Baum, R. F. (1976) "Existence Theorems for Lagrange Control Problems with Unbounded Time Domain." *Journal of Optimization Theory and Applications* 19: 89–116.

Baumol, William J. (1967) "Macroeconomics of Unbalanced Growth: The Anatomy of Urban Crisis." *American Economic Review* 57: 415–426.

——— (1986) "Productivity Growth, Convergence, and Welfare: What the Long-Run Data Show." *American Economic Review* 76: 1072–1085.

Baxter, Marianne, and Mario J. Crucini (1993) "Explaining Saving-Investment Correlations." *American Economic Review* 83: 416–436.

Becker, Gary S. (1965) "A Theory of the Allocation of Time." *Economic Journal* 75: 493–517.

——— (1981) *A Treatise on the Family.* Cambridge, Mass.: Harvard University Press.

Becker, Gary S., and Robert J. Barro (1988) "A Reformulation of the Economic Theory of Fertility." *Quarterly Journal of Economics* 103: 1–25.

Becker, Robert, and John Harvey Boyd (1997) *Capital Theory, Equilibrium Analysis and Recursive Utility.* Oxford: Blackwell.

Becker, Gary S., Kevin M. Murphy, and Robert Tamura (1990) "Human Capital, Fertility, and Economic Growth." *Journal of Political Economy* 98(part 2): S12–S37.

Bellman, Richard (1957) *Dynamic Programming.* Princeton, N.J.: Princeton University Press.

Benabou, Roland (1996) "Heterogeneity, Stratification, and Growth: Macroeconomic Implications of Community Structure and School Finance." *American Economic Review* 86: 584–609.

——— (2000) "Unequal Societies: Income Distribution and the Social Contract." *American Economic Review* 90: 96–129.

——— (2005) "Inequality, Technology and the Social Contract" In *Handbook of Economic Growth,* Philippe Aghion and Steven N. Durlauf (editors). Amsterdam: North-Holland, pp. 1595–1638.

Bencivenga, Valerie, and Bruce Smith (1991) "Financial Intermediation and Endogenous Growth." *Review of Economic Studies* 58: 195–209.

Benhabib, Jess, and Mark M. Spiegel (1994). "The Role of Human Capital in Economic Development: Evidence from Aggregate Cross-Country Data." *Journal of Monetary Economics* 34: 143–173.

Ben-Porath, Yoram (1967) "The Production of Human Capital and the Life Cycle of Earnings." *Journal of Political Economy* 75: 352–365.

Benveniste, Lawrence M., and Jose A. Scheinkman (1979) "On the Differentiability of the Value Function in Dynamic Models of Economics." *Econometrica* 47: 727–732.

——— (1982) "Duality Theory for Dynamic Organization Models of Economics: The Continuous Time Case." *Journal of Economic Theory* 27: 1–19.

Berge, Claude (1963) *Topological Spaces.* New York: MacMillan.

Bernard, Andrew, and Bradford Jensen (2004) "Why Some Firms Export." *Review of Economics and Statistics* 86: 561–569.

Bernard, Andrew, Jonathan Eaton, Bradford Jensen, and Samuel Kortum (2003) "Plants and Productivity in International Trade." *American Economic Review* 93: 1268–1290.

Bewley, Truman F. (1977) "The Permanent Income Hypothesis: A Theoretical Formulation." *Journal of Economic Theory* 16: 252–292.

——— (1980) "The Optimum Quantity of Money." In *Models of Monetary Economies,* John H. Kareken and Neil Wallace (editors). Minneapolis, Minn., Federal Reserve Bank of Minneapolis, pp. 169–210.

——— (2007) *General Equilibrium, Overlapping Generations Models, and Optimal Growth Theory.* Cambridge, Mass.: Harvard University Press.

Billingsley, Patrick (1995) *Probability and Measure,* 3rd edition. New York: Wiley.

Bils, Mark J. (1985) "Real Wages over the Business Cycle: Evidence from Panel Data." *Journal of Political Economy* 93: 666–689.

Black, Duncan (1948) *The Theory of Committees and Elections.* London: Cambridge University Press.

Black, Sandra E., and Lisa Lynch (2005) "Measuring Organizational Capital in the New Economy." University of California, Los Angeles, mimeo.

Black, Sandra E., Paul J. Devereux, and Kjell Salvanes (2005) "The More the Merrier? The Effect of Family Size and Birth Order on Education." *Quarterly Journal of Economics* 120: 669–700.

Blackwell, David (1965) "Discounted Dynamic Programming."*Annals of Mathematical Statistics* 36: 226–235.

Blanchard, Olivier J. (1979) "Speculative Bubbles, Crashes and Rational Expectations." *Economics Letters* 3: 387–389

——— (1985) "Debt, Deficits, and Finite Horizons." *Journal of Political Economy* 93: 223–247.

——— (1997) "The Medium Run" *Brookings Papers on Economic Activity* 2: 89–158.

Blanchard, Olivier J., and Stanley Fischer (1989) *Lectures on Macroeconomics.* Cambridge, Mass.: MIT Press.

Bloom, David E., and Jeffrey D. Sachs (1998) "Geography, Demography, and Economic Growth in Africa." *Brookings Papers on Economic Activity* 2: 207–295.

Blundell, Richard, Rachel Griffith, and Jon Van Reenen (1999) "Marketshare, Market Value, and Innovation in a Panel of British Manufacturing Firms." *Review of Economic Studies* 56: 529–554.

Boldrin, Michele, and David K. Levine (2003) "Innovation and the Size of the Market." University of Minnesota and University of California, Los Angeles, mimeo.

Boserup, Ester (1965) *The Conditions of Agricultural Progress*. Chicago: Aldine.

Bourguignon, François, and Christian Morrison (2002) "Inequality among World Citizens: 1820–1992." *American Economic Review* 92: 727–744.

Bourguignon, François, and Thierry Verdier (2000) "Oligarchy, Democracy, Inequality and Growth." *Journal of Development Economics* 62: 285–313.

Boyce, William E., and Richard C. DiPrima (1977) *Elementary Differential Equations and Boundary Value Problems*, 3rd edition. New York: Wiley.

Braudel, Fernand (1973). *Capitalism and Material Life: 1400–1800* translated by Miriam Kochan. New York: Harper and Row.

Broadberry, Stephen, and Bishnupriya Gupta (2006) "The Early Modern Great Divergence: Wages, Prices and Economic Development in Europe and Asia 1500–1800." CEPR Discussion Paper 4947. Centre for Economic Policy Research.

Brock, William A., and Leonard J. Mirman (1972) "Optimal Economic Growth under Uncertainty: Discounted Case." *Journal of Economic Theory* 4: 479–513.

Browning, Martin, and Thomas F. Crossley (2001) "The Lifecycle Model of Consumption and Saving." *Journal of Economic Perspectives* 15: 3–22.

Bryant, Victor (1985) *Metric Spaces, Iteration and Application.* Cambridge: Cambridge University Press.

Buera, Francisco, and Joseph Kaboski (2006) "The Rise of the Service Economy." Northwestern University, mimeo.

Bulow, Jeremy I., and Kenneth Rogoff (1989a) "A Constant Recontracting Model of Sovereign Debt." *Journal of Political Economy* 97: 155–178.

——— (1989b) "Sovereign Debt: Is to Forgive to Forget?" *American Economic Review* 79: 43–50.

Caballero, Ricardo J. (1990) "Consumption Puzzles and Precautionary Savings." *Journal of Monetary Economics* 25: 113–136.

——— (1999) "Aggregate Investment." In *Handbook of Macroeconomics,* volume 1, John B. Taylor and Michael Woodford (editors). Amsterdam: North-Holland, pp. 813–862.

Caballero, Ricardo J., and Mohammad Hammour (1999) "Jobless Growth: Appropriability, Factor Substitution and Unemployment." *Carnegie-Rochester Conference Proceedings* 48: 51–94.

Caputo, Michael (2005) *Foundations of Dynamic Economic Analysis: Optimal Control Theory and Applications*. Cambridge: Cambridge University Press.

Card, David (1999) "The Causal Effect of Education on Earnings." In *Handbook of Labor Economics,* volume 3A, Orley Ashenfelter and David Card (editors). Amsterdam: North-Holland, pp. 1801–1863.

Carter, Susan B., Scott Sigmund Gartner, Michael R. Haines, Alan L. Olmstead, Richard Sutch, and Gavin Wright, editors (2006) *Historical Statistics of the United States Earliest Times to the Present: Millennial Edition*. New York: Cambridge University Press.

Caselli, Francesco (1999) "Technological Revolutions." *American Economic Review* 87: 78–102.

——— (2005) "Accounting for Cross-Country Income Differences." In *Handbook of Economic Growth,* Philippe Aghion and Steven N. Durlauf (editors). Amsterdam: North-Holland, pp. 680–743.

Caselli, Francesco, and Wilbur John Coleman (2001a) "Cross-Country Technology Diffusion: The Case of Computers." *American Economic Review* 91: 328–335.

——— (2001b) "The U.S. Structural Transformation and Regional Convergence: A Reinterpretation." *Journal of Political Economy* 109: 584–616.

——— (2005) "The World Technology Frontier." *American Economic Review* 96: 499–522.

Caselli, Francesco, and James Feyrer (2007) "The Marginal Product of Capital." *Quarterly Journal of Economics* 123: 535–568.

Caselli, Francesco, and Jaume Ventura (2000) "A Representative Household Theory of Distribution." *American Economic Review* 90: 909–926.

Caselli, Francesco, Gerard Esquivel, and Fernando Lefort (1996) "Reopening the Convergence Debate: A New Look at Cross-Country Growth Empirics." *Journal of Economic Growth* 40: 363–389.

Cass, David (1965) "Optimum Growth in an Aggregate Model of Capital Accumulation." *Review of Economic Studies* 32: 233–240.

——— (1972) "On Capital Overaccumulation in the Aggregate Neoclassical Model of Economic Growth: A Complete Characterization." *Journal of Economic Theory* 4: 200–223.

Ceruzzi, Paul E. (2003) *A History of Modern Computing.* Cambridge, Mass.: MIT Press.

Cesari, Lamberto (1966) "Existence Theorems for Weak and Usual Optimal Solutions in Lagrange Problems with Unilateral Constraints. I." *Transactions of the American Mathematical Society* 124: 369–412.

Chamberlain, Gary, and Charles A. Wilson (2000) "Optimal Intertemporal Consumption under Uncertainty." *Review of Economic Dynamics* 3: 365–395.

Chamberlin, Edward (1933) *The Theory on Monopolistic Competition.* Cambridge, Mass.: Harvard University Press.

Chandler, Tertius (1987) *Four Thousand Years of Urban Growth: An Historical Census.* Lewiston, N.Y.: St. David's University Press.

Chari, V. V., and Patrick J. Kehoe (1990) "Sustainable Plans." *Journal of Political Economy* 98: 783–802.

Chari, V. V., Patrick J. Kehoe and Ellen McGrattan (1997) "The Poverty of Nations: A Quantitative Exploration." Federal Reserve Bank of Minneapolis, mimeo.

Chenery, Hollis (1960) "Patterns of Industrial Growth," *American Economic Review* 5: 624–654.

Chiang, Alpha C. (1992) *Elements of Dynamic Optimization.* New York: McGraw-Hill.

Chirinko, Robert S., and Debdulal Mallick (2007) "The Marginal Product of Capital: A Persistent International Puzzle." Camry University, mimeo.

Ciccone, Antonio, and Giovanni Peri (2006) "Identifying Human Capital Externalities: Theory with Applications." *Review of Economic Studies* 73: 381–412.

Coatsworth, John H. (1993) "Notes on the Comparative Economic History of Latin America and the United States." In *Development and Underdevelopment in America: Contrasts in Economic Growth in North and Latin America in Historical Perpsective,* Walter L. Bernecker and Hans Werner Tobler (editors). New York: Walter de Gruyter.

Collier, Ruth B. (2000) *Paths towards Democracy: The Working Class and Elites in Western Europe and South America.* New York: Cambridge University Press.

Conrad, Jon M. (1999) *Resource Economics.* Cambridge: Cambridge University Press.

Conway, John B. (1990) *A Course in Functional Analysis,* 2nd edition. New York: Springer-Verlag.

Cooley, Thomas F., editor (1995) *Frontiers of Business Cycle Research.* Princeton N.J.: Princeton University Press,

Coughlin, Peter J. (1992) *Probabilistic Voting Theory.* New York: Cambridge University Press.

Cunat, Alejandro, and Marco Maffezoli (2001) "Growth and Interdependence under Complete Specialization." Universita Bocconi, mimeo.

Curtin, Philip D. (1989) *Death by Migration: Europe's Encounter with the Tropical World in the Nineteenth Century.* New York: Cambridge University Press.

——— (1998) *Disease and Empire: The Health of European Troops in the Conquest of Africa.* New York: Cambridge University Press.

Dasgupta, Partha, and Geoffrey Heal (1979) *Economic Theory and Exhaustible Resources.* Cambridge: Cambridge University Press.

Dasgupta, Partha, and Joseph Stiglitz (1980) "Uncertainty, Industrial Structure, and the Speed of R&D." *Bell Journal of Economics* 11: 1–28.

David, Paul A. (1975) *Technical Choice, Innovation and Economic Growth: Essays on American and British Experience in the Nineteenth Century.* London: Cambridge University Press.

Davis, Ralph (1973) *The Rise of the Atlantic Economies.* Ithaca, N.Y.: Cornell University Press.

Davis, Steven, and John Haltiwanger (1991) "Wage Dispersion between and within U.S. Manufacturing Plants, 1963–86." *Brookings Papers on Economic Activity: Microeconomics* 115–200.

Davis, Y. Donald, and David E. Weinstein (2001) "An Account of Global Factor Trade." *American Economic Review* 91: 1423–1453.

Deaton, Angus S. (1992) *Understanding Consumption.* New York: Oxford University Press.

——— (2005) "Measuring Poverty in a Growing World (or Measuring Growth in a Poor World)." *Review of Economics and Statistics* 87: 1–19.

Deaton, Angus S., and John Muellbauer (1980) *Economics and Consumer Behavior.* Cambridge: Cambridge University Press.

Debreu, Gerard (1954) "Valuation Equilibrium and Pareto Optimum." *Proceedings of the National Academy of Sciences,* USA 40: 588–592.

——— (1959) *Theory of Value.* New York: Wiley.

——— (1974) "Excess Demand Functions." *Journal of Mathematical Economics* 1: 15–23.

De La Croix, David, and Philippe Michel (2002) *A Theory of Economic Growth: Dynamics and Policy in Overlapping Generations.* Cambridge, Mass.: Cambridge University Press.

Denardo, Eric V. (1967) "Contraction Mappings in the Theory Underlying Dynamic Programming." *SIAM Review* 9: 165–177.

Diamond, Jared M. (1997) *Guns, Germs and Steel: The Fate of Human Societies.* New York: W. W. Norton.

Diamond, Peter (1965) "National Debt in a Neoclassical Growth Model." *American Economic Review* 55: 1126–1150.

Dinopoulos, Elias, and Peter Thompson (1998) "Schumpterian Growth without Scale Effects." *Journal of Economic Growth* 3: 313–335.

Dixit, Avinash K., (2004) *Lawlessness and Economics: Alternative Modes of Economic Governance.* Gorman Lectures. Princeton, N.J.: Princeton University Press,

Dixit, Avinash K., and Victor Norman (1980) *Theory of International Trade: A Dual, General Equilibrium Approach.* Cambridge: Cambridge University Press.

Dixit, Avinash K., and Robert S. Pindyck (1994) *Investment under Uncertainty.* Princeton, N.J.: Princeton University Press.

Dixit, Avinash K., and Joseph E. Stiglitz (1977) "Monopolistic Competition and Optimum Product Diversity." *American Economic Review* 67: 297–308.

Doepke, Matthias (2004) "Accounting for the Fertility Decline during the Transition to Growth." *Journal of Economic Growth* 9: 347–383.

Dollar, David (1992) "Outward-Oriented Developing Economies Really Do Grow More Rapidly: Evidence from 95 LDCs, 1976–1985." *Economic Development and Cultural Change* 40: 523–544.

Domar, Evsey D. (1946) "Capital Expansion, Rate of Growth and Employment." *Econometrica* 14: 137–147.

Doms, Mark, and Timothy Dunne, and Kenneth Troske (1997) "Workers, Wages and Technology." *Quarterly Journal of Economics* 112: 253–290.

Dorfman, Robert (1969) "An Economic Interpretation of Optimal Control Theory." *American Economic Review* 64: 817–831.

Downs, Anthony (1957) *An Economic Theory of Democracy.* New York: Harper & Row.

Drandakis, E., and Edmund Phelps (1965) "A Model of Induced Invention, Growth and Distribution." *Economic Journal* 76: 823–840.

Drazen, Allan (2001) *Political Economy in Macroeconomics.* Princeton N.J.: Princeton University Press.

Duflo, Esther (2004) "Medium-Run Effects of Educational Expansion: Evidence from a Large School Construction Program in Indonesia." *Journal of Development Economics* 74: 163–197.

Duranton, Gilles (2004) "Economics of Productive Systems: Segmentations and Skill Biased Change." *European Economic Review* 48: 307–336.

Durlauf, Steven N. (1996) "A Theory of Persistent Income Inequality." *Journal of Economic Growth* 1: 75–94.

Durlauf, Steven N., and Marcel Fafchamps (2005) "Empirical Studies of Social Capital: A Critical Survey." In *Handbook of Economic Growth,* Philippe Aghion and Steven N. Durlauf (editors). Amsterdam: North-Holland, pp. 1639–1699.

Durlauf, Steven N., and Danny Quah (1999) "The New Empirics of Economic Growth." In *The Handbook of Macroeconomics,* John Taylor and Michael Woodruff (editors). Amsterdam: North-Holland and Elsevier, pp. 235–308.

Durlauf, Steven N., Paul A. Johnson, and Jonathan R. W. Temple (2005) "Growth Econometrics." In *Handbook of Economic Growth,* Philippe Aghion and Steven Durlauf (editors). Amsterdam: North-Holland, pp. 555–678.

Echevarria, Cristina (1997) "Changes in Sectoral Composition Associated with Economic Growth." *International Economic Review* 38: 431–452.

Eggertsson, Thrainn (2005) *Imperfect Institutions: Possibilities and Limits of Reform.* Ann Arbor: University of Michigan Press.

Eggimann, Gilbert (1999) *La Population des Villes des Tiers-Mondes, 1500–1950.* Geneva: Centre d'Histoire Economique Internationale de l'Université de Genève, Librairie Droz.

Ekeland, Ivar, and Jose A. Scheinkman (1986) "Transversality Condition for Some Infinite Horizon Discrete Time Optimization Problems." *Mathematics of Operations Research* 11: 216–229.

Elliott, John H. (1963) *Imperial Spain 1469–1716.* New York: St. Martin Press.

Eltis, David (1995) "The Total Product of Barbados, 1664–1701."*Journal of Economic History* 55: 321–336.

Elvin, Mark (1973) *The Pattern of the Chinese Past.* Stanford, Calif.: Stanford University Press.

Engerman, Stanley L., and Kenneth Sokoloff (1997) "Factor Endowments, Institutions, and Differential Paths of Growth among New World Economics: A View from Economic Historians of the United States." In *How Latin America Fell Behind,* Stephen Haber (editor). Stanford, Calif.: Stanford University Press.

Epifani, Paolo, and Gino Gancia (2006) "The Skill Bias of World Trade." Universitat Pompano Fabra, mimeo.

Epstein, Larry G., and Stanley E. Zin (1989) "Substitution, Risk Aversion, and the Temporal Behavior of Consumption and Asset Returns: A Theoretical Framework." *Econometrica* 57: 937–969.

Ertman, Thomas (1997) *Birth of the Leviathan: Building States and Regimes in Medieval and Early Modern Europe.* New York: Cambridge University Press.

Ethier, Stewart, and Thomas Kurtz (1986) *Markov Processes: Characterization and Convergence.* Hoboken, N.J.: Wiley.

Evans, Eric J. (1996) *The Forging of the Modern State: Early Industrial Britain: 1783–1870,* 2nd edition. New York: Longman.

Evans, Peter (1995) *Embedded Autonomy: States and Industrial Transformation.* Princeton N.J.: Princeton University Press.

Feinstein, Charles (2005) *An Economic History of South Africa.* Cambridge: Cambridge University Press.

Feldstein, Martin, and Charles Horioka (1980) "Domestic Savings and International Capital Flows." *Economic Journal* 90: 314–329.

Fernandez, Raquel, and Roger Rogerson (1996) "Income Distribution, Communities and the Quality of Public Education." *Quarterly Journal of Economics* 111: 135–164.

Fernandez-Villaverde, Jesus (2003) "Was Malthus Right? Economic Growth and Population Dynamics." University of Pennsylvania, mimeo.

Fields, Gary (1980) *Poverty, Inequality and Development.* Cambridge: Cambridge University Press.

Finkelstein, Amy (2004) "Static and Dynamic Effects of Health Policy: Evidence from the Vaccine Industry." *Quarterly Journal of Economics* 119: 527–564.

Fisher, Irving (1930) *The Theory of Interests.* New York: Macmillan.

Fleming, Wendell H., and Raymond W. Rishel (1975) *Deterministic and Stochastic Optimal Control.* New York: Springer-Verlag.

Foellmi, Reto, and Josef Zweimuller (2002) "Structural Change and the Kaldor Facts of Economic Growth." CEPR Discussion Paper 3300. Centre for Economic Policy Research.

Forbes, Kristen J. (2000) "A Reassessment of the Relationship between Inequality and Growth." *American Economic Review* 90: 869–887.

Foster, Andrew, and Mark Rosenzweig (1995) "Learning by Doing and Learning from Others: Human Capital and Technical Change in Agriculture." *Journal of Political Economy* 103: 1176–1209.

Foster, Lucia, John Haltiwanger, and Cornell J. Krizan (2000) "Aggregate Productivity Growth: Lessons from Microeconomic Evidence." NBER Working Paper 6803. National Bureau of Economic Research.

François, Patrick, and Joanne Roberts (2003) "Contracting Productivity Growth." *Review of Economic Studies* 70: 59–85.

Frankel, Jeffrey, and David Romer (1999) "Does Trade Cause Growth?" *American Economic Review* 89: 379–399.

Freeman, Christopher (1982) *The Economics of Industrial Innovation.* Cambridge, Mass.: MIT Press.

Freudenberger, Herman (1967) "State Intervention as an Obstacle to Economic Growth in the Hapsburg Monarchy." *Journal of Economic History* 27: 493–509.

Friedman, Milton (1957) *A Theory of the Consumption Function.* Princeton N.J.: Princeton University Press.

Fudenberg, Drew, and Jean Tirole (1994) *Game Theory.* Cambridge, Mass.: MIT Press.

Funk, Peter (2002) "Induced Innovation Revisited."*Economica* 69: 155–171.

Futia, Carl A. (1982) "Invariant Distributions and Limiting Behavioral Markovian Economic Models." *Econometrica* 50: 377–408.

Gabaix, Xavier (2000) "The Factor Content of Trade: A Rejection of the Heckscher-Ohlin-Leontief Hypothesis." Massachusetts Institute of Technology, mimeo.

Galenson, David W. (1996) "The Settlement and Growth of the Colonies: Population, Labor and Economic Development." In *The Cambridge Economic History of the United States,* Volume I, The Colonial Era, Stanley L. Engerman and Robert E. Gallman (editors). New York: Cambridge University Press.

Gallup, John Luke, and Jeffrey D. Sachs (2001) "The Economic Burden of Malaria." *American Journal of Tropical Medicine and Hygiene* 64: 85–96.

Galor, Oded (1996) "Convergence? Inference from Theoretical Models." *Economic Journal* 106: 1056–1069.

———— (2005) "From Stagnation to Growth: Unified Growth Theory." In *Handbook of Economic Growth,* Philippe Aghion and Steven N. Durlauf (editors). Amsterdam: North-Holland, pp. 171–293.

Galor, Oded, and Omer Moav (2000) "Ability Biased Technology Transition, Wage Inequality and Growth." *Quarterly Journal of Economics* 115: 469–498.

———— (2002) "Natural Selection and the Origin of Economic Growth." *Quarterly Journal of Economics* 117: 1133–1192.

———— (2004) "From Physical to Human Capital Accumulation: Inequality in the Process of Development."*Review of Economic Studies* 71: 1101–1026.

Galor, Oded, and Andrew Mountford (2008) "Trading Population for Productivity: Theory and Evidence." *Review of Economic Studies*, forthcoming.

Galor, Oded, and Harl E. Ryder (1989) "Existence, Uniqueness and Stability of Equilibrium in an Overlapping-Generations Model with Productive Capital." *Journal of Economic Theory* 49: 360–375.

Galor, Oded, and Daniel Tsiddon (1997) "Tecnological Progress, Mobility, and Growth." *American Economic Review* 87: 363–382.

Galor, Oded, and David N. Weil (1996) "The Gender Gap, Fertility, and Economic Growth." *American Economic Review* 86: 374–387.

———— (2000) "Population, Technology, and Growth: From Malthusian Stagnation to the Demographic Transition and Beyond." *American Economic Review* 90: 806–828.

Galor, Oded, and Joseph Zeira (1993) "Income Distribution and Macroeconomics." *Review of Economic Studies* 60: 35–52.

Galor, Oded, Omer Moav, and Dietrich Vollrath (2005) "Land Inequality and the Origin of Divergence in Overtaking in the Growth Process: Theory and Evidence." Brown University, mimeo.

Gancia, Gino (2003) "Globalization, Divergence and Stagnation." University of Pompeu Fabra, working paper.

Gancia, Gino, and Fabrizio Zilibotti (2005) "Horizontal Innovation in the Theory of Growth and Development." In *Handbook of Economic Growth,* Philippe Aghion and Steven N. Durlauf (editors). Amsterdam: North-Holland, pp. 111–170.

Gans, Joshua S., and Michael Smart (1996) "Majority Voting with Single-Crossing Preferences." *Journal of Public Economics* 59: 219–237.

Geary, Robert C. (1950) "A Note on a Constant Utility Index of the Cost of Living." *Review of Economic Studies* 18: 65–66.

Geertz, Clifford (1963) *Peddlers and Princes.* Chicago: University of Chicago Press.

Gelfand I. M., and Sergei V. Fomin (2000) *Calculus of Variation,* translated by Richard A. Silverman. New York: Dover Publications.

Gerschenkron, Alexander (1962) "Economic Backwardness in Political Perspective." In *The Progress of Underdeveloped Areas,* Bert Hoselitz (editor). Chicago: University of Chicago Press.

Gikhman, I. I., and A. V. Skorohod (1974) *The Theory of Stochastic Processes,* volume I, translated by Samuel Kotz. New York: Springer-Verlag.

Gil, Richard, Casey Mulligan, and Xavier Sala-i-Martin (2004) "Do Democracies Have Different Public Policies than Nondemocracies?" *Journal of Economic Perspectives* 18: 51–74.

Gilles, Christian, and Stephen F. LeRoy (1992) "Bubbles and Charges." *International Economic Review* 33: 323–339.

Glomm, Gerhard, and B. Ravikumar (1992) "Public vs. Private Investment in Human Capital: Endogenous Growth and Income Inequality." *Journal of Political Economy* 100: 818–834.

Goldin, Claudia, and Lawrence F. Katz (1998) "The Origins of Technology-Skill Complementarity." *Quarterly Journal of Economics* 113: 693–732.

Gollin, Douglas, Stephen Parente, and Richard Rogerson (2002) "Structural Transformation and Cross-Country Income Differences." University of Illinois, Urbana-Champaign, mimeo.

Gomez-Galvarriato, Aurora (1998) "The Evolution of Prices and Real Wages in Mexico from the Porfiriato to the Revolution." In *Latin America and the World Economy since 1800,* John H. Coatsworth and Alan M. Taylor (editors). Cambridge, Mass.: Harvard University Press.

Goodfriend, Marvin, and John McDermott (1995) "Early Development." *American Economic Review* 85: 116–133.

Gordon, Robert J. (1990) *The Measurement of Durable Goods Prices.* Chicago: University of Chicago Press.

Gorman, W. M. (1953) "Community Preference Fields." *Econometrica* 21: 63–80.

——— (1959) "Separable Utility and Aggregation." *Econometrica* 71: 469–481.

——— (1976) "Tricks with Utility Functions." In *Essays in Economic Analysis,* Michael Artis and A. R. Nobay (editors). Cambridge: Cambridge University Press, pp. 212–243.

——— (1980) "Some Engel Curves." In *Essays in Theory and Measurement of Consumer Behavior,* Angus S. Deaton (editor). Cambridge: Cambridge University Press, pp. 7–29.

Gourinchas, Pierre-Olivier, and Olivier Jeanne (2006) "The Elusive Gains from International Financial Integration." *Review of Economic Studies* 73: 715–741.

Grandmont, Jean-Michel (1978) "Intermediate Preferences and Majority Rule." *Econometrica* 46: 317–330.

Greenwood, Jeremy, and Boyan Jovanovic (1990) "Financial Development, Growth and the Distribution of Income." *Journal of Political Economy* 98: 1076–1107.

Greenwood, Jeremy, and Mehmet Yorukoglu (1997) "1974." *Carnegie-Rochester Conference Series on Public Policy* 46: 49–95.

Greenwood, Jeremy, Zvi Hercowitz, and Per Krusell (1997) "Long-Run Implications of Investment-Specific Technological Change." *American Economic Review* 87: 342–362.

Greif, Avner (1994) "Cultural Beliefs and the Organization of Society: A Historical and Theoretical Reflection on Collectivist and Individualist Societies." *Journal of Political Economy* 102: 912–950.

Griliches, Zvi (1957) "Hybrid Corn: An Exploration in the Economics of Technological Change." *Econometrica* 25: 501–522.

——— (1969) "Capital-Skill Complementarity." *Review of Economics and Statistics* 51: 465–468.

Griliches, Zvi, and Jacob Schmookler (1963) "Inventing and Maximizing." *American Economic Review* 53: 725–729.

Grossman, Gene M., and Elhanan Helpman (1991a) "Quality Ladders in the Theory of Growth." *Review of Economic Studies* 68: 43–61.

——— (1991b) *Innovation and Growth in the Global Economy.* Cambridge, Mass.: MIT Press.

Grossman, Herschel, and Minseong Kim (1995) "Swords or Ploughshares? A Theory of the Security of Claims to Property Rights." *Journal of Political Economy* 103: 1275–1288.

——— (1996) "Predation and Accumulation," *Journal of Economic Growth* 1: 333–350.

Guiso, Luigi, Paola Sapienza, and Luigi Zingales (2004) "Does Culture Affect Economic Outcomes?" CEPR working paper. Centre for Economic Policy Research.

Gutierrez, Hector (1986) "La Mortalite des Eveques Latino-Americains aux XVIIe et XVIII Siecles." *Annales de Demographie Historique* 53(2): 29–39.

Guvenen, Fatih, and Burhanettin Kuruscu (2006) "Understanding Wage Inequality: Ben-Porath Meets Skill Biased Technical Change." University of Texas, Austin, mimeo.

Habakkuk, H. J., (1962) *American and British Technology in the Nineteenth Century: Search for Labor-Saving Inventions*. Cambridge: Cambridge University Press.

Hakenes Hendrik, and Andreas Irmen (2006) "Something Out of Nothing: Neoclassical Growth and the Trivial Steady State." University of Heidelberg, mimeo.

Halkin, Hubert (1974) "Necessary Conditions for Optimal Control Problems with Infinite Horizons." *Econometrica* 42: 267–272.

Hall, Robert E. (1978) "Stochastic Implications of the Life-Cycle–Permanent Income Hypothesis: Theory and Evidence." *Journal of Political Economy* 86: 971–988. (Reprinted in Sargent, Thomas J., and Robert E. Lucas Jr., editors (1981) *Rational Expectations and Econometric Practice*. Minneapolis, Minn.: University of Minnesota Press.)

Hall, Robert E., and Charles I. Jones (1999) "Why Do Some Countries Produce So Much More Output per Worker than Others?" *Quarterly Journal of Economics* 114: 83–116.

Haltiwanger, John C., Julia I. Lane, and James R. Spletzer (1999) "Productivity Differences across Employers: The Roles of Employer Size, Age and Human Capital." *American Economic Review* 89: 94–98.

Hammermesh, Daniel (1993) *Labor Demand*. Princeton, N.J.: Princeton University Press.

Hansen, Gary D., and Edward C. Prescott (2002) "Malthus to Solow." *American Economic Review* 92: 1205–1217.

Harris, John, and Michael Todaro (1970) "Migration, Unemployment and Development: A Two-Sector Analysis." *American Economic Review* 60: 126–142.

Harrison, Lawrence E., and Samuel P. Huntington, editors (2000) *Culture Matters: How Values Shape Human Progress*. New York: Basic Books.

Harrod, Roy (1939) "An Essay in Dynamic Theory." *Economic Journal* 49: 14–33.

Hart, Oliver D. (1979) "On Shareholder Unanimity in Large Stockmarket Economies." *Econometrica* 47: 1057–1084.

Hassler, John, Sevi Mora, Kjetil Storesletten, and Fabrizio Zilibotti (2003) "Survival of the Welfare State." *American Economic Review* 93: 87–112.

Hassler, John, Per Krusell, Kjetil Storesletten, and Fabrizio Zilibotti (2005) "The Dynamics of Government: A Positive Analysis." *Journal of Monetary Economics* 52: 1331–1358.

Hayashi, Fumia (1982) "Tobin's Marginal q and Average q: A Neoclassical Interpretation." *Econometrica* 50: 213–234.

Heckman, James, Lance Lochner, and Christopher Taber (1998) "Tax Policy and Human Capital Formation." *American Economic Review Papers and Proceedings* 88: 293–297.

Hellwig, Martin, and Andreas Irmen (2001) "Endogenous Technical Change in a Competitive Economy." *Journal of Economic Theory* 101: 1–139.

Helpman, Elhanan (2005) *Mystery of Economic Growth*. Cambridge, Mass.: Harvard University Press.

Herbst, Jeffery I. (2000) *States and Power in Africa: Comparative Lessons in Authority and Control*. Princeton, N.J.: Princeton University Press.

Heston, Allen, Robert Summers, and Bettina Aten (2002) *Penn World Tables Version 6.1*. Downloadable Data Set. Philadelphia: Center for International Comparisons at the University of Pennsylvania.

Hicks, John (1932) *The Theory of Wages*. London: Macmillan.

Hildenbrand, Werner, and Alan Kirman (1988) *Equilibrium Analysis: Variations on Themes by Edgeworth and Walras*. Amsterdam: Elsevier.

Hirschman, Albert (1958) *The Strategy of Economic Development*. New Haven, Conn.: Yale University Press.

Hirshleifer, Jack (2001) *The Dark Side of the Force: Economic Foundations of Conflict Theory*. New York: Cambridge University Press.

Homer, Sydney, and Richard Sylla (1991) *A History of Interest Rates*. New Brunswick, N.J.: Rutgers University Press.

Hopkins, Keith (1980) "Taxes and Trade in the Roman Empire (200 B.C.–A.D. 400)." *Journal of Roman Studies* 70: 101–125.

Hotelling, Harold (1929) "Stability in Competition." *Economic Journal* 39: 41–57.

——— (1931) "The Economics of Exhaustible Resources." *Journal of Political Economy* 31: 137–175.

Houthakker, Hendrik S. (1955) "The Pareto Distribution and the Cobb-Douglas Production Function in Activity Analysis."*Review of Economic Studies* 23: 27–31.

Howard, Ronald A. (1960) *Dynamic Programming and Markov Processes.* Cambridge, Mass.: MIT Press.

Howitt, Peter (1999) "Steady Endogenous Growth with Population and R&D Inputs Growing." *Journal of Political Economy* 107: 715–730.

———— (2000) "Endogeous Growth and Cross–Country Income Differences." *American Economic Review* 90: 829–846.

Hsieh, Chang-Tai (2002) "What Explains the Industrial Revolution in East Asia? Evidence from the Factor Markets." *American Economic Review* 92: 502–526.

Hsieh, Chang-Tai, and Peter J. Klenow (2006) "Relative Prices and Relative Prosperity." *American Economic Review* 97: 562–585.

Imbs, Jean, and Romain Wacziarg (2003) "Stages of Diversification." *American Economic Review* 93: 63–86.

Inada, Ken-Ichi (1963) "On a Two-Sector Model of Economic Growth: Comments and a Generalization." *Review of Economic Studies* 30: 119–127.

Jacobs, Jane (1970) *The Economy of Cities.* New York: Vintage Books.

James, John A., and Jonathan S. Skinner (1985) "The Resolution of the Labor-Scarcity Paradox." *Journal of Economic History* 45: 513–540.

Jayaratne, Jay, and Philip Strahan (1996) "The Finance-Growth Nexus: Evidence from Bank Branch Deregulation." *Quarterly Journal of Economics* 111: 639–670.

Jones, Benjamin F., and Benjamin A. Olken (2005) "Do Leaders Matter? National Leadership and Growth since World War II." *Quarterly Journal of Economics* 120: 835–864.

Jones, Charles I. (1995) "R&D-Based Models of Economic Growth." *Journal of Political Economics* 103: 759–784.

———— (1997) "On the Evolution of the World Income Distribution." *Journal of Economic Perspectives* 11: 19–36.

———— (1998) *Introduction to Economic Growth.* New York: W. W. Norton.

———— (1999) "Growth: With or without Scale Effects." *American Economic Review* 89: 139–144.

———— (2005) "The Shape of Production Functions and the Direction of Technical Change." *Quarterly Journal of Economics* 2: 517–549.

Jones, Charles I., and Dean Scrimgeour (2006) "The Steady-State Growth Theorem: Understanding Uzawa (1961)." University of California, Berkeley, mimeo.

Jones, Eric (1988) *Growth Recurring.* Oxford: Oxford University Press.

Jones, Larry, and Rodolfo Manuelli (1990) "A Convex Model of Equilibrium Growth: Theory and Policy Indications." *Journal of Political Economy* 98: 1008–1038.

Jorgensen, Dale (2005) "Accounting for Growth in the Information Age." In *Handbook of Economic Growth,* Philippe Aghion and Steven N. Durlauf (editors). Amsterdam: North-Holland, pp. 744–815.

Jorgensen, Dale, F. M. Gollop, and Barbara Fraumeni (1987) *Productivity and U.S. Economic Growth.* Cambridge, Mass.: Harvard University Press.

Judd, Kenneth (1985) "On the Performance of Patents." *Econometrica* 53: 567–585.

———— (1998) *Numerical Methods in Economics.* Cambridge, Mass.: MIT Press.

Kaldor, Nicholas (1957) "Alternative Theories of Distribution." *Review of Economic Studies* 23: 83–100.

———— (1963) "Capital Accumulation and Economic Growth." In *Proceedings of a Conference Held by the International Economics Association,* Friedrich A. Lutz and Douglas C. Hague (editors). London: Macmillan.

Kalemli-Ozcan, Sebnem (2002) "Does Mortality Decline Promote Economic Growth?" *Journal of Economic Growth* 7: 411–439.

Kamien, Morton, and Nancy Schwartz (1981) *Dynamic Optimization: The Calculus of Variations and Optimal Control in Economics and Management.* Amsterdam: Elsevier.

Kamihigashi, Takashi (2001) "Necessity of Transversality Conditions for Infinite Horizon Problems." *Econometrica* 69: 995–1012.

———— (2003) "Necessity of Transversality Conditions for Stochastic Problems." *Journal of Economic Theory* 109: 140–149.

Karlin, Samuel (1955) "The Structure of Dynamic Programming Models." *Naval Research Logistics Quarterly* 2: 285–294.

Katz, Lawrence, and David Autor (2000) "Changes in the Wage Structure and Earnings Inequality." In *The Handbook of Labor Economics,* volume III, Orley Ashenfelter and David Card (editors). Amsterdam: North-Holland.

Katz, Lawrence F., and Kevin M. Murphy (1992), "Changes in Relative Wages, 1963–1987: Supply and Demand Factors." *Quarterly Journal of Economics* 107: 35–78.

Kehoe, Patrick J., and Fabrizio Perri (2002) "International Business Cycles with Endogenous Incomplete Markets." *Econometrica* 70: 907–928.

Kelley, John (1955) *General Topology.* New York: Van Nostrand.

Kennedy, Charles (1964) "Induced Bias in Innovation and the Theory of Distribution." *Economic Journal* 74: 541–547.

Keyssar, Alexander (2000) *The Right to Vote: The Contested History of Democracy in the United States.* New York: Basic Books.

Kiley, Michael (1999 "The Supply of Skilled Labor and Skill-Biased Technological Progress." *Economics Journal* 109: 708–724.

King, Robert G., and Ross Levine (1993) "Finance, Entrepreneurship, and Growth: Theory and Evidence." *Journal of Monetary Economics* 32: 513–542.

King, Robert G. and Sergio Rebelo (1999) "Resuscitating Real Business Cycles." In *Handbook of Macroeconomics,* volume 1, John B. Taylor and Michael Woodford (editors). Amsterdam: North-Holland, pp. 927–1007.

Kiyotaki, Nobuhiro (1988) "Multiple Expectational Equilibria under Monopolistic Competition." *Quarterly Journal of Economics* 103: 695–713.

Klenow, Peter J., and Andres Rodriguez (1997) "The Neoclassical Revival in Growth Economics: Has It Gone Too Far?" *NBER Macroeconomics Annual* 1997: 73–103.

Klepper, Steven (1996) "Entry, Exit, Growth and Innovation over the Product Life Cycle." *American Economic Review* 86: 562–583.

Klette, Tor Jacob, and Samuel Kortum (2004) "Innovating Firms and Aggregate Innovation." *Journal of Political Economy* 112: 986–1018.

Knack, Stephen, and Philip Keefer (1995) "Insititutions and Economic Performance: Cross-Country Tests Using Alternative Institutional Measures." *Economics and Politics* 7: 207–228.

——— (1997) "Does Social Capital Have an Economic Impact? A Cross-Country Investigation." *Quarterly Journal of Economics* 112: 1252–1288.

Kolmogorov, Andrei, and Sergei V. Fomin (1970) *Introductory Reak Analysis.* New York: Dover Press.

Kongsamut, Piyabha, Sergio Rebelo, and Danyang Xie (2001) "Beyond Balanced Growth." *Review of Economic Studies* 48: 869–882.

Koopmans, Tjalling C. (1965) "On the Concept of Optimal Economic Growth." In *The Econometric Approach to Development Planning,* Amsterdam: North-Holland, pp. 225–295.

Koren, Miklos, and Silvana Tenreyro (2007) "Volatility and Growth." *Quarterly Journal of Economics* 122: 243–287.

Kortum, Samuel (1997) "Research, Patenting and Technological Change." *Econometrica* 55: 1389–1431.

Kraay, Aart, and Jaume Ventura (2007) "Comparative Advantage and the Cross-Section of the Business Cycle." *Journal of the European Economic Association* 6: 1300–1333.

Kremer, Michael (1993) "Population Growth and Technological Change: One Million B.C. to 1990." *Quarterly Journal of Economics* 108: 681–716.

Kreps, David (1988) *Notes on the Theory of Choice.* Boulder, Colo.: Westview Press.

Kreyszig, Erwin (1978) *Introductory Functional Analysis with Applications.* New York: Wiley.

Krueger, Alan, and Mikael Lindahl (2001) "Education for Growth: Why and for Whom?" *Journal of Economic Literature* 39: 1101–1136.

Krugman, Paul (1979) "A Model of Innovation, Technology Transfer, and the World Distribution of Income." *Journal of Political Economy* 87: 253–266.

——— (1991) "History versus Expectations." *Quarterly Journal of Economics* 106: 651–667.

Krusell, Per, and José-Víctor Ríos-Rull (1996) "Vested Interests in a Theory of Stagnation and Growth." *Review of Economic Studies* 63: 301–330.

—— (1999) "On the Size of Government: Political Economy in the Neoclassical Growth Model." *American Economic Review* 89: 1156–1181.

Krusell, Per, and Anthony Smith (1998) "Income and Wealth Heterogeneity in the Macroeconomy." *Journal of Political Economy* 106: 867–896.

—— (2005) "Income and Wealth Heterogeneity, Portfolio Choice and Equilibrium Asset Returns." *Macroeconomic Dynamics* 1: 387–422.

Krusell, Per, Lee Ohanian, Victor Rios-Rull, and Giovanni Violante (1999) "Capital-Skill Complementarity and Inequality." *Econometrica* 58: 1029–1053.

Kupperman, Karen O. (1993) *Providence Island: 1630–1641: The Other Puritan Colony.* New York: Cambridge University Press.

Kuznets, Simon (1957) "Quantitative Aspects of the Economic Growth of Nations: II. Industrial Distribution of National Product and Labour Force." *Economic Development and Cultural Change* 5 (supplement): 1–111.

—— (1966) *Modern Economic Growth.* New Haven, Conn.: Yale University Press.

—— (1973) "Modern Economic Growth: Findings and Reflections." *American Economic Review* 53: 829–846.

Kydland, Finn E., and Edward C. Prescott (1982) "Time to Build and Aggregate Fluctuations." *Econometrica* 50: 1345–1370.

Lagos, Ricardo (2001) "A Model of TFP." New York University, working paper.

Laitner, John (2000) "Structural Change and Economic Growth." *Review of Economic Studies* 57: 545–561.

Landes, David S. (1998) *The Wealth and Poverty of Nations: Why Some Are So Rich and Some So Poor.* New York: W. W. Norton.

Lang, Sean (1999) *Parliamentary Reform: 1785–1928.* New York: Routledge.

Leamer, Edward (1998) "Does Natural Resource Abundance Increase Latin American Income Inequality?" *Journal of Development Economics* 59: 3–42.

Leonard, Daniel, and Ngo Van Long (1992) *Optimal Control Theory and Static Optimization in Economics.* Cambridge: Cambridge University Press.

Levchenko, Andrei (2007) "Institutional Quality and International Trade." *Review of Economic Studies* 74: 791–819.

Levine, Ross (2005) "Finance and Growth," In *The Handbook of Economic Growth,* Philippe Aghion and Steven N. Durlauf (editors). Amsterdam: North-Holland.

Lewis, William Arthur (1954) "Economic Development with Unlimited Supplies of Labor." *Manchester School of Economics and Social Studies* 22: 139–191.

Lindbeck, Assar, and Jörgen Weibull (1987) "Balanced-Budget Redistribution as the Outcome of Political Competition." *Public Choice* 12: 272–297.

Lindert, Peter H. (2000) "Three Centuries of Inequality in Britain and America." In *Handbook of Income Distribution,* Anthony B. Atkinson and François Bourguignon (editors). Amsterdam: North-Holland, pp. 167–216.

—— (2004) *Growing Public: Social Spending and Economics Growth since the Eighteenth Century.* Cambridge: Cambridge University Press.

Lindert, Peter H., and Jeffrey Williamson (1976) "Three Centuries of American Inequality." *Research in Economic History* 1: 69–123.

Livi-Bacci, Massimo (1997) *A Concise History of World Population.* Oxford: Blackwell.

Ljungqvist, Lars, and Thomas J. Sargent (2005) *Recursive Macroeconomic Theory.* Cambridge, Mass.: MIT Press.

Long, John B., and Charles I. Plosser (1983) "Real Business Cycles." *Journal of Political Economy* 91: 39–69.

López-Alonso, Moramay, and Rául Porras Condey (2004) "The Ups and Downs of Mexican Economic Growth: The Biological Standard of Living in Inequality: 1870–1950." *Economics and Human Biology* 1: 169–186.

Loury, Glenn (1981) "Intergenerational Transfers and the Distribution of Earnings." *Econometrica* 49: 834–867.

Lucas, Robert E. (1978) "Asset Prices in an Exchange Economy." *Econometrica* 46: 1426–1445.

Lucas, Robert E. (1988) "On the Mechanics of Economic Development." *Journal of Monetary Economics* 22: 3–42.

——— (1990) "Why Doesn't Capital Flow from Rich to Poor Countries?" *American Economic Review* 80: 92–96.

Lucas, Robert E., and Edward C. Prescott (1971) "Investment under Uncertainty." *Econometrica* 39: 659–681.

Luenberger, David (1969) *Optimization by Vector Space Methods*. New York: Wiley.

——— (1979) *Introduction to Dynamic Systems: Theory, Models and Applications*. New York: Wiley.

Maddison, Angus (1991) *Dynamic Forces in Capitalist Development: A Long-Run Comparative View*. New York: Oxford University Press.

——— (2001) *The World Economy: A Millennial Perspective*. Paris: Development Centre.

——— (2003) *The World Economy: Historical Statistics*. CD-ROM. Paris: Organisation for Economic Co-operation and Development.

Magill, Michael J. P. (1981) "Infinite Horizon Programs." *Econometrica* 49: 679–712.

Makowski, Louis (1980) "Perfect Competition, the Profit Criterion and the Organization of Economic Activity." *Journal of Economic Theory* 22: 222–242.

Malthus, Thomas R. (1798) *An Essay on the Principle of Population*. London: W. Pickering.

Mangasarian, O. O. (1966) "Sufficient Conditions for the Optimal Control of Nonlinear Systems." *SIAM Journal of Control* 4: 139–152.

Mankiw, N. Gregory, David Romer, and David N. Weil (1992) "A Contribution to the Empirics of Economic Growth." *Quarterly Journal of Economics* 107: 407–437.

Mann, Charles C. (2004) *1491: New Revelations of the Americas before Columbus*. New York: Vintage Books.

Mantel, Rolf R. (1976) "Homothetic Preferences and Community Excess Demand Function." *Journal of Economic Theory* 12: 197–201.

Manuelli, Rodolfo, and Anant Seshadri (2006) "Human Capital and the Wealth of Nations." University of Wisconsin, mimeo.

Marris, Robin (1982) "How Much of the Slowdown Was Catch-Up?" In *Slower Growth in the Western World*, Ruth C. O. Matthews (editor). London: Heinemann.

Marshall, Alfred [1890] (1949) *Principles of Economics*. London: Macmillan.

Martimort, David, and Thierry Verdier (2004) "Agency Costs of Internal Collusion and Schumpeterian Growth." *Review of Economic Studies* 71: 1119–1141.

Mas-Colell, Andreu, Michael D. Whinston, and Jerry R. Green (1995) *Microeconomic Theory*. New York: Oxford University Press.

Matsuyama, Kiminori (1991) "Increasing Returns, Industrialization, and the Indeterminacy of Equilibrium." *Quarterly Journal of Economics* 106: 617–650.

——— (1992) "Agricultural Productivity, Comparative Advantage and Economic Growth." *Journal of Economic Theory* 58: 317–334.

——— (1995) "Complementarities and Cumulative Processes in Models of Monopolistic Competition." *Journal of Economic Literature* 33: 701–729.

——— (1999) "Growing through Cycles." *Econometrica* 67: 335–348.

——— (2002) "The Rise of Mass Consumption Societies." *Journal of Political Economy* 110: 1035–1070.

——— (2004) "Financial Market Globalization, Symmetry-Breaking and Endogenous Inequality of Nations." *Econometrica* 72: 853–882.

Mauro, Paolo (1995) "Corruption and Growth." *Quarterly Journal of Economics* 110: 681–712.

McCall, John (1970) "Economics of Information and Job Search." *Quarterly Journal of Economics* 84: 113–126.

McCandless, George T., and Neil Wallace (1991) *Introduction to Dynamic Macroeconomic Theory: An Overlapping Generations Approach*. Cambridge, Mass.: Harvard University Press.

McEvedy, Colin, and Richard Jones (1978) *Atlas of World Population History*. New York: Facts on File.

Melitz, Mark (2003) "The Impact of Trade on Intra-Industry Reallocations and Aggregate Industry Productivity." *Econometrica* 71: 1695–1725.

Meltzer, Allan H., and Scott Richard (1981) "A Rational Theory of the Size of Government." *Journal of Political Economy* 89: 914–927.

Michel, Philippe (1982) "On the Transversality Condition in Infinite Horizon Optimal Problems." *Econometrica* 50: 975–985.

Migdal, Joel (1988) *Strong Societies and Weak States: State-Society Relations and State Capabilities in the Third World.* Princeton, N.J.: Princeton University Press.

Mincer, Jacob (1974) *Schooling, Experience, and Earnings.* New York: National Bureau of Economic Research.

Minier, Jenny A. (1998) "Democracy and Growth: Alternative Approaches." *Journal of Economic Growth* 3: 241–266.

Mirman, Leonard J., and Itzak Zilcha (1975) "On Optimal Growth under Uncertainty." *Journal of Economic Theory* 11: 329–339.

Mitch, David (1983) "The Role of Human Capital in the First Industrial Revolution." In *The British Industrial Revolution: An Economic Perspective,* Joel Mokyr (editor). San Francisco: Westview Press.

Mokyr, Joel (1990) *The Lever of Riches*: *Technological Creativity and Economic Progress.* New York: Oxford University Press.

——— (1993) "Introduction." In *The British Industrial Revolution,* Joel Mokyr (editor). Boulder, Colo.: Westview Press, pp. 1–129.

Montesquieu, Charles de Secondat [1748] (1989) *The Spirit of the Laws.* New York: Cambridge University Press.

Moretti, Enrico (2004) "Estimating the External Return to Education: Evidence from Repeated Cross-Sectional and Longitudinal Data." *Journal of Econometrics* 121: 175–212.

Morris, Ian (2004) "Economic Growth in Ancient Greece." *Journal of Institutional and Theoretical Economics* 160: 709–742.

Mosse, W. E. (1992) *An Economic History of Russia, 1856–1914.* London: I. B. Taurus Press.

Mundlak, Yair (2000) *Agriculture and Economic Growth: Theory and Measurement.* Cambridge, Mass.: Harvard University Press.

Murphy, Kevin M., Andrei Shleifer, and Robert W. Vishny (1989) "Industrialization and the Big Push." *Quarterly Journal of Economics* 106: 503–530.

Myerson, Rogerson (1991) *Game Theory.* Cambridge, Mass.: Harvard University Press.

Myrdal, Gunnar (1968) *Asian Drama: An Inquiry into the Poverty of Nations,* 3 volumes. New York: Twentieth Century Fund.

Nelson, Richard R., and Edmund S. Phelps (1966) "Investment in Humans, Technological Diffusion, and Economic Growth." *American Economic Review* 56: 69–75.

Newell, Richard, Adam Jaffee, and Robert Stavins (1999) "The Induced Innovation Hypothesis and Energy-Saving Technological Change." *Quarterly Journal of Economics* 114: 907–940.

Ngai, Rachel, and Christopher Pissarides (2006) "Structural Change in a Multi-Sector Model of Growth." London School of Economics, mimeo.

Nickell, Stephen (1996) "Competition and Corporate Performance." *Journal of Political Economy* 104: 724–746.

North, Douglass C. (1990) *Institutions, Institutional Change, and Economic Performance.* New York: Cambridge University Press.

North, Douglass C., and Robert Thomas (1973) *The Rise of the Western World: A New Economic History.* Cambridge: Cambridge University Press.

North, Douglass C., William Summerhill, and Barry R. Weingast (2000) "Order, Disorder, and Economic Change: Latin America versus North America." In *Governing for Prosperity,* Bruce Bueno de Mesquita and Hilton L. Root (editors). New Haven, Conn.: Yale University Press, pp. 17–58.

Nunn, Nathan (2006) "Relationship-Specificity, Incomplete Contracts and the Pattern of Trade." *Quarterly Journal of Economics* 123: 569–600.

Nurske, Ragnar (1958) *Problems of Capital Formation in Underdeveloped Countries.* New York: Oxford University Press.

Obstfeld, Maurice (1994) "Risk-Taking, Global Diversification, and Growth." *American Economic Review* 84: 1310–1329.

Obstfeld, Maurice, and Kenneth Rogoff (1996) *Foundations of International Macroeconomics.* Cambridge, Mass.: MIT Press.

Obstfeld, Maurice, and Alan M. Taylor (2002) "Globalization and Capital Markets." NBER Working Paper 8846. National Bureau of Economic Research.

Ok, Efe (2007) *Real Analysis with Economic Applications.* Princeton, N.J.: Princeton University Press.

Osborne, Martin, and Ariel Rubinstein (1994) *A Course in Game Theory.* Cambridge, Mass.: MIT Press.

Overton, Mark (1996) *Agricultural Revolution in England: The Transformation of the Agrarian Economy, 1500–1850.* New York: Cambridge University Press.

Pamuk, Sevket (2004) "Institutional Change and the Longevity of the Ottoman Empire: 1500–1800." *Journal of Interdisciplinary History* 35: 225–247.

Parente, Stephen L., and Edward C. Prescott (1994) "Barriers to Technology Adoption and Development." *Journal of Political Economy* 102: 298–321.

Pavcnik, Nina (2002) "Trade Liberalization, Exit, and Productivity Improvements: Evidence from Chilean Plants." *Review of Economic Studies* 69: 245–276.

Perko, Lawrence (2001) *Differential Equations and Dynamical System,* 3rd edition. New York: Springer Verlag.

Persson, Torsten, and Guido Tabellini (1994) "Is Inequality Harmful for Growth? Theory and Evidence." *American Economic Review* 84: 600–621.

——— (2000) *Political Economics: Explaining Economic Policy.* Cambridge, Mass.: MIT Press.

Phelps, Edmund S. (1966) *Golden Rules of Economic Growth.* New York: W. W. Norton.

Piketty, Thomas (1997) "The Dynamics of Wealth Distribution and the Interest Rate with Credit Rationing." *Review of Economic Studies* 64: 173–190.

Piketty, Thomas, and Emmanuel Saez (2003) "Income Inequality in the United States, 1913–1998." *Quarterly Journal of Economics* 118: 1–39.

Pirenne, Henri (1937) *Economic and Social History of Medieval Europe.* New York: Routledge.

Pissarides, Christopher (2000) *Equilibrium Unemployment Theory,* 2nd edition. Cambridge, Mass.: MIT Press.

Pollak, Richard (1971) "Additive Utility Functions and Linear Engel Curves." *Review of Economic Studies* 38: 401–413.

Pomeranz, Kenneth (2000) *The Great Divergence: China, Europe and the Making of the Modern World Economy.* Princeton, N.J.: Princeton University Press.

Pontryagin, Lev S., Vladimir Boltyanskii, Kevac Giamkelidze, and Eugene Mischenko (1962) *The Mathematical Theory of Optimal Processes.* New York: Interscience.

Popp, David (2002) "Induced Innovation and Energy Prices." *American Economic Review* 92: 160–180.

Postan, M. M. (1966) "Medieval Agrarian Society in its Prime: England." In *The Cambridge Economic History of Europe,* M. M. Postan (editor). London: Cambridge University Press, pp. 168–300.

Prescott, Edward C. (1986) "Theory Ahead of Business Cycle Measurement." *Federal Reserve Bank of Minneapolis Quarterly Review* 10: 1–22.

Pritchett, Lant (1997) "Divergence, Big Time." *Journal of Economic Perspectives* 11: 3–18.

Przeworski, Adam, and Fernando Limongi (1993) "Political Regimes and Economic Growth." *Journal of Economic Perspectives* 7: 51–69.

Puterman, Martin L. (1994) *Markov Decision Processes: Discrete Stochastic Dynamic Programming.* New York: Wiley.

Putnam, Robert, with Robert Leonardi, and Raffaella Y. Nanetti (1993) *Making Democracy Work: Civic Traditions in Modern Italy.* Princeton, N.J.: Princeton University Press.

Qian, Nancy (2007) "Quantity-Quality: The Positive Effect of Family Size on School Enrollment in China." Brown University, mimeo.

Quah, Danny (1993) "Galton's Fallacy and Tests of the Convergence Hypothesis." *Scandinavian Journal of Economics* 95: 427–443.

——— (1997) "Empirics for Growth and Distribution: Stratification, Polarization and Convergence Clubs." *Journal of Economic Growth* 2: 27–60.

Ragot, Xavier (2003) "Technical Change and the Dynamics of the Division of Labor." DELTA Working Papers 2003–09. DELTA.

Rajan, Raghuram, and Luigi Zingales (1998) "Financial Dependence and Growth." *American Economic Review* 88: 559–586.

Ramey, Garey, and Valerie Ramey (1995) "Cross-Country Evidence of the Link between Volatility and Growth." *American Economic Review* 88: 1138–1151.

Ramsey, Frank (1928) "A Mathematical Theory of Saving." *Economic Journal* 38: 543–559.

Rauch, James E. (1993), "Productivity Gains from Geographic Concentration of Human Capital: Evidence from the Cities." *Journal of Urban Economics* 34: 380–400.

Rebelo, Sergio (1991) "Long-Run Policy Analysis and Long-Run Growth." *Journal of Political Economy* 99: 500–521.

Reinganum, Jennifer (1981) "Dynamic Games of Innovation." *Journal of Economic Theory* 25: 21–24.

――― (1985) "Innovation and Industry Evolution." *Quarterly Journal of Economics* 100: 81–100.

Ringer, Fritz (1979) *Education and Society in Modern Europe.* Bloomington: University of Indiana Press.

Rivera-Batiz, Luis A., and Paul M. Romer (1991) "Economic Integration and Endogenous Growth." *Quarterly Journal of Economics* 106: 531–555.

Roberts, Kevin W. S. (1977) "Voting over Income Tax Schedules." *Journal of Public Economics* 8: 329–340.

Robinson, James, and Jeffrey Nugent (2001) "Are Endowments Fate?" University of California, Berkeley, mimeo.

Rockefeller, Tyrell R. (1971) "Existence in Duality Theorems for Convex Problems of Bolza." *Transactions of the American Mathematical Society* 159: 1–40.

Rodriguez, Francisco, and Dani Rodrik (2000) "Trade Policy and Economic Growth: A Skeptic's Guide to the Cross-National Evidence." *NBER Macroeconomics Annual* 2000: 261–325.

Rodrik, Dani (1999) "Democracies Pay Higher Wages." *Quarterly Journal of Economics* 114: 707–738.

Rogerson, Richard, Robert Shimer, and Randall Wright (2004) "Search-Theoretic Models of the Labor Market: A Survey." *Journal of Economic Literature* 43: 959–988.

Romer, David (2006) *Advanced Macroeconomics.* New York: McGraw-Hill.

Romer, Paul M. (1986a) "Increasing Returns and Long-Run Growth." *Journal of Political Economy* 94: 1002–1037.

――― (1986b) "Cake Eating, Chattering, and Jumps: Existence Results for Variational Problems." *Econometrica* 54: 897–908.

――― (1987) "Growth Based on Increasing Returns Due to Specialization." *American Economic Review* 77: 56–62.

――― (1990) "Endogenous Technological Change." *Journal of Political Economy* 98(part I): S71–S102.

――― (1993) "Idea Gaps and Object Gaps in Economic Development." *Journal of Monetary Economics* 32: 543–573.

Romer, Thomas (1975) "Individual Welfare, Majority Voting and the Properties of a Linear Income Tax." *Journal of Public Economics* 7: 163–168.

Rosenberg, Nathan (1976) *Perspectives on Technology.* Cambridge: Cambridge University Press.

Rosenstein-Rodan, Paul (1943) "Problems of Industrialization of Eastern and Southeastern Europe." *Economic Journal* 53: 202–211.

Rostow, Walt Whitman (1960) *The Stages of Economic Growth: A Non-Communist Manifetso.* Cambridge, Mass.: Cambridge University Press.

Royden, Halsey (1994) *Real Analysis.* New York: Macmillan.

Rudin, Walter (1976) *Introduction to Mathematical Analysis.* New York: McGraw-Hill.

Sachs, Jeffrey (2001) "Tropical Underdevelopment." NBER Working Paper 8119. National Bureau of Economic Research.

Sachs, Jeffrey, and Andrew Warner (1995) "Economic Reform in the Process of Global Integration." *Brookings Papers on Economic Activity* 1: 1–118.

Saint-Paul, Gilles, and Thierry Verdier (1993) "Education, Democracy, and Growth." *Journal of Development Economics* 42: 399–407.

Sala-i-Martin, Xavier (2005) "World Distribution of Income: Falling Poverty and . . . Convergence, Period." *Quarterly Journal of Economics* 121: 351–398.

Salop, Steven (1979) "Monopolistic Competition with Outside Goods." *Bell Journal of Economics* 10: 141–156.

Salter, W.E.G. (1960) *Productivity and Technical Change,* 2nd edition. Cambridge: Cambridge University Press.

Samuelson, Paul A. (1958) "An Exact Consumption-Loan Model of Interest with or without the Social Contrivance of Money." *Journal of Political Economy* 66: 467–482.

——— (1965) "A Theory of Induced Innovation along Kennedy-Weisäcker Lines." *Review of Economics and Statistics* 47: 343–356.

——— (1975) "Optimum Social Security in a Life–Cycle Growth Model." *International Economic Review* 16: 539–544.

Scherer, Frederick M. (1984) *Innovation and Growth: Schumpeterian Perspectives.* Cambridge, Mass.: MIT Press.

Schlicht, Ekkehart (2006) "A Variant of Uzawa's Theorem." *Economics Bulletin* 6: 1–5.

Schmookler, Jacob (1966) *Invention and Economic Growth.* Cambridge, Mass.: Harvard University Press.

Schultz, Theodore (1964) *Transforming Traditional Agriculture.* New Haven, Conn.: Yale University Press.

——— (1975) "The Value of the Ability to Deal with Disequilibria." *Journal of Economic Literature* 8: 827–846.

Schumpeter, Joseph A. (1934) *The Theory of Economic Development.* Cambridge, Mass.: Harvard University Press.

——— (1942) *Capitalism, Socialism and Democracy.* London: Harper & Brothers.

Scotchmer, Suzanne (2005) *Innovations and Incentives.* Cambridge, Mass.: MIT Press.

Segerstrom, Paul S. (1998) "Endogenous Growth without Scale Effects." *American Economic Review* 88: 1290–1310.

Segerstrom, Paul S., T. C. A. Anant, and Elias Dinopoulos (1990) "A Schumpterian Model of the Product Life Cycle." *American Economic Review* 80: 1077–1091.

Seierstad, Atle, and Knut Sydsaeter (1977) "Sufficient Conditions in Optimal Control Theory." *International Economic Review* 18: 367–391.

——— (1987) *Optimal Control Theory with Economic Applications.* Amsterdam: Elsevier.

Shapley, Lloyd (1953) "A Value for *n*-Person Games." In *Contributions to the Theory of Games,* Kuhn, H. and A. Tucker, (editors). Princeton, N.J.: Princeton University Press.

Shell, Karl (1971) "Notes on the Economics of Infinity." *Journal of Political Economy* 79: 1002–1011.

Simon, Carl, and Lawrence Blume (1994) *Mathematics for Economists.* New York: W. W. Norton.

Simon, Julian (1977) *The Economics of Population Growth.* Princeton, N.J.: Princeton University Press.

Skaperdas, Stergios (1992) "Cooperation, Conflict, and Power in the Absence of Property Rights," *American Economic Review* 82: 720–739.

Solon, Gary, Robert Barsky, and Jonathan A. Parker (1994) "Measuring the Cyclicality of Real Wages: How Important Is Composition Bias?" *Quarterly Journal of Economics* 109:1–25.

Solow, Robert M. (1956) "A Contribution to the Theory of Economic Growth." *Quarterly Journal of Economics* 70: 65–94.

——— (1957) "Technical Change and the Aggregate Production Function." *Review of Economics and Statistics* 39: 312–320.

——— (1970) *Growth Theory: An Exposition.* Oxford: Clarendon Press.

Sonin, Konstantin (2003) "Why the Rich May Favor Poor Protection of Property Rights." *Journal of Comparative Economics* 31: 715–731.

Sonnenschein, Hugo (1972) "Market Excess Demand Functions." *Econometrica* 40: 549–563.

Spence, Michael (1976) "Product Selection, Fixed Costs, and Monopolistic Competition." *Review of Economic Studies* 43: 217–235.

Stewart, Frances (1977). *Technology and Underdevelopment.* London: Macmillan Press.

Stiglitz, Joseph E. (1969) "Distribution of Income and Wealth among Individuals." *Econometrica* 37: 382–397.

——— (1971) "Factor Price Equalization in a Dynamic Economy." *Journal of Political Economy* 78: 456–488.

Stokey, Nancy (1988) "Learning by Doing and the Introduction of New Goods." *Journal of Political Economy* 96: 701–717.

Stokey, Nancy, and Robert E. Lucas, with Edward C. Prescott (1989) *Recursive Methods in Economic Dynamics*. Cambridge, Mass.: Harvard University Press.

Stone, Richard (1954) "Linear Expenditure Systems and Demand Analysis: An Application to the Pattern of British Demand." *Economic Journal* 64: 511–527.

Summers, Lawrence H. (1986) "Some Skeptical Observations on the Real Business Cycle Theory." *Federal Reserve Bank of Minneapolis Quarterly Review* 10: 23–27.

Summers, Robert, and Alan Heston (1991). "The Penn World Table (Mark 5): An Expanded Set of International Comparisons, 1950–1988." *Quarterly Journal of Economics* 106: 327–368.

Summers, Robert, Alan Heston, and Bettina Aten (2006) "Penn World Table Version 6.2." Center for International Comparisons of Production, Income and Prices, University of Pennsylvania.

Sundaram, Rangarajan (1996) *A First Course in Optimization Theory.* Cambridge: Cambridge University Press.

Swan, Trevor W. (1956) "Economic Growth and Capital Accumulation." *Economic Record* 32: 334–361.

Tabellini, Guido (2007) "Culture and Institutions: Economic Development in the Regions of Europe." University of Bocconi, mimeo.

Tamura, Robert (1991) "Income Convergence in an Endogeous Growth Model." *Journal of Political Economy* 99: 522–540.

Taylor, Alan M. (1994) "Domestic Savings and International Capital Flows." NBER Working Paper 4892. National Bureau of Economic Research.

Thoenig, Matthias, and Thierry Verdier (2003) "Trade-Induced Technical Bias and Wage Inequalities: A Theory of Defensive Innovations." *American Economic Review* 93: 709–728.

Tirole, Jean (1982) "On the Possibility of Speculation on the Rational Expectations." *Econometrica* 50: 1163–1181.

——— (1985) "Asset Bubbles and Overlapping Generations." *Econometrica* 53: 1499–1528.

——— (1988) *The Theory of Industrial Organization*. Cambridge, Mass.: MIT Press.

Tobin, James (1969) "A General Equilibrium Approach to Monetary Theory." *Journal of Money, Credit, and Banking* 1: 15–29.

Tornell, Aaron, and Andés Velasco (1992) "Why Does Capital Flow from Poor to Rich Countries? The Tragedy of the Commons and Economic Growth." *Journal of Political Economy* 100: 1208–1231.

Townsend, Robert (1979) "Optimal Contracts and Competitive Markets with Costly State Verification." *Journal of Economic Theory* 21: 265–293.

Trefler, Daniel (1993) "International Factor Price Differences: Leontief Was Right!"*Journal of Political Economy* 101: 961–987.

Uhlig, Harald (1996) "A Law of Large Numbers for Large Economies." *Economic Theory* 8: 41–50.

Uzawa, Hirofumi (1961) "Neutral Inventions and the Stability of Growth Equilibrium!" *Review of Economic Studies* 28: 117–124.

——— (1964) "Optimal Growth in a Two-Sector Model of Capital Accumulation." *Review of Economic Studies* 31: 1–24.

Véliz, Claudio (1994) *The New World of the Gothic Fox: Culture and Economy in English and Spanish America.* Berkeley: University of California Press.

Ventura, Jaume (1997) "Growth and Independence." *Quarterly Journal of Economics* 112: 57–84.

——— (2002) "Bubbles and Capital Flows." NBER Working Paper 9304. National Bureau of Economic Research.

——— (2005) "A Global View of Economic Growth." In *Handbook of Economic Growth,* Philippe Aghion and Steven N. Durlauf (editors). Amsterdam: North-Holland, pp. 1419–1498.

Vernon, Raymond (1966) "International Investment and International Trade in Product-Cycle." *Quarterly Journal of Economics* 80: 190–207.

Vogel, Ezra (2006) *Four Little Dragons: The Spread of Industrialization in East Asia.* Cambridge, Mass.: Harvard University Press.

Von Neumann, John (1945) "A Model of General Equilibrium." *Review of Economic Studies* 13: 1–9.

Wade, Robert (1990) *Governing the Market: Economic Theory and the Role of Government in East Asian Industrialization.* Princeton, N.J.: Princeton University Press.

Wallace, Neil (1980) "The Overlapping Generations Model of Fiat Money." In *Models of Monetary Economics,* John Karaken and Neil Wallace (editors). Minneapolis, Minn.: Federal Reserve Bank of Minneapolis.

Walter, Wolfgang (1991) *Ordinary Differential Equations.* New York: Springer-Verlag.

Wan, Henry, Jr. (1971) *Economic Growth.* New York: Harbrace.

Weber, Max (1930) *The Protestant Ethic and the Spirit of Capitalism.* London: Allen and Unwin.

———— (1958) *The Religion of India.* Glencoe: Free Press.

Webster, David L. (2002) *The Fall of the Ancient Maya: Solving the Mystery of the Maya Collapse.* New York: Thames & Hudson.

Weil, David N. (2005) *Economic Growth.* Boston: Addison-Wesley.

———— (2007) "Accounting for the Effect of Health on Growth." *Quarterly Journal of Economics* 122: 1265–1306.

Weil, Philippe (1987) "Confidence and the Real Value of Money in Overlapping Generation Models." *Quarterly Journal of Economics* 102: 1–22.

———— (1989) "Overlapping Families of Infinitely-Lived Agents." *Journal of Public Economics* 38: 183–198.

Weitzman, Martin L. (2003) *Income, Wealth, and the Maximum Principle.* Cambridge, Mass.: Harvard University Press.

White, Lynn T. (1964) *Medieval Technology and Social Change.* New York: Oxford University Press.

Wiarda, Howard J. (2001) *The Soul of Latin America: The Cultural and Political Tradition.* New Haven, Conn.: Yale University Press.

Williams, David (1991) *Probability with Martingales.* Cambridge: Cambridge University Press.

Wilson, Francis (1972) *Labour in the South African Gold Mines, 1911–1969.* Cambridge: Cambridge University Press.

Wong, R. Bin (1997) *China Transformed: Historical Change and the Limits of European Experience.* Ithaca, N.Y.: Cornell University Press.

Wooldridge, Jeffery M. (2002) *Econometric Analysis of Cross Section and Panel Data.* Cambridge, Mass.: MIT Press.

Xu, Bin (2001) "Endogenous Technology Bias, International Trade and Relative Wages." University of Florida, mimeo.

Yaari, Menahem E. (1965) "Uncertain Lifetime, Life Insurance, and the Theory of the Consumer." *Review of Economic Studies* 32: 137–150.

Young, Alwyn (1991) "Learning by Doing and the Dynamic Effects of International Trade." *Quarterly Journal of Economics* 106: 369–405.

———— (1992) "A Tale of Two Cities: Factor Accumulation and Technical Change in Hong Kong and Singapore." In *NBER Macroeconomics Annual* 1992: 13–54.

———— (1995) "The Tyranny of Numbers." *Quarterly Journal of Economics* 110: 641–680.

———— (1998) "Growth without Scale Effects." *Journal of Political Economy* 106: 41–63.

———— (2005) "The Gift of the Dying: The Tragedy of AIDS and the Welfare of Future African Generations." *Quarterly Journal of Economics* 120: 423–466.

Zeldes, Stephen P. (1989) "Consumption and Liquidity Constraints: An Empirical Investigation." *Journal of Political Economy* 97: 305–346.

Zilcha, Itzak (1978) "Transversality Condition in a Multisector Economy under Uncertainty." *Econometrica* 46: 515–525.

Zuleta, Hernando, and Andrew Young (2006) "Labor's Shares–Aggregate and Industry: Accounting for Both in a Model with Induced Innovation." University of Mississippi, mimeo.

Name Index

Page numbers for entries occurring in notes are followed by an *n*.

Abernathy, William J., 479
Abraham, Kathrine G., 581n
Abramowitz, Moses, 79
Abreu, Dilip, 941
Acemoglu, Daron, 24, 25, 129, 130, 133, 135, 136, 137, 138, 139, 141, 142, 143, 319, 380, 384, 416, 427, 430, 489, 490, 522, 523, 526, 527, 528, 529, 588, 598, 605, 626, 630, 631, 640, 644, 663, 686, 703, 715, 721, 737, 740, 744, 746, 749, 750, 769, 770, 771, 818, 821, 823, 824, 833, 853, 855, 857, 858, 870, 871
Aczel, J., 223
Aghion, Philippe, 23, 355, 384, 430, 453, 458, 459, 468, 469n, 470, 480, 490, 491, 643, 744, 746, 749, 750, 764, 770, 771
Aiken, Howard, 415
Aiyagari, S. Rao, 583, 604
Akcigit, Ufuk, 489, 490
Alesina, Alberto, 142, 824
Alfaro, Laura, 686
Aliprantis, Charalambos, 877
Allais, Maurice, 354
Allen, Franklin, 605
Allen, Robert C., 24
Anant, T. C. A., 453, 490
Andreoni, James, 355
Angrist, Joshua D., 380, 384, 528, 770
Antras, Pol, 631, 640, 644, 686
Apostol, Tom M., 877
Araujo, A., 277
Armington, Paul S., 686
Arrow, Kenneth J., 31, 54, 55, 70, 73, 171, 237, 277, 318, 418, 421, 430, 824

Ashton, Thomas Southcliffe, 24, 870
Aten, Bettina, 3n, 23
Atkeson, Andrew, 685, 686
Atkinson, Anthony, 625, 644
Aumann, Robert J., 640
Austen-Smith, David, 824
Autor, David, 384, 528
Azariadis, Costas, 354, 379, 384

Backus, David, 453
Baily, Martin N., 612
Bairoch, Paul, 143, 512, 770
Banerjee, Abhijit V., 355, 654, 737, 740, 764, 770, 771, 773, 824
Banfield, Edward C., 122, 142
Banks, Jeffrey S., 824
Barro, Robert J., 15, 17, 23, 24, 25, 69, 70, 80, 82, 83, 106, 142, 318, 319, 404, 685, 687, 770, 832–33
Barsky, Robert, 581n
Bartelsman, Eric J., 612
Basu, Susanto, 625, 644
Batou, Jean, 143
Baum, R. F., 276
Baumol, William J., 25, 82, 106, 703, 719, 721
Baxter, Marianne, 686
Becker, Gary S., 85, 359, 380, 384, 618, 732, 770
Becker, Robert, 178
Bellman, Richard, 185, 222
Benabou, Roland, 527, 771, 824
Bencivenga, Valerie, 769
Benhabib, Jess, 382, 384, 643
Ben-Porath, Yoram, 384
Beneviste, Lawrence M., 222, 277
Berge, Claude, 877

Bernard, Andrew, 679
Bewley, Truman F., 177, 355, 566, 583, 604
Billingsley, Patrick, 525
Bils, Mark J., 581n
Black, Duncan, 824
Black, Sandra E., 612, 770
Blackwell, David, 222, 561
Blanchard, Olivier J., 277, 318, 327, 346, 348, 352–53, 354, 355, 499, 528, 531, 604
Bloom, David E., 119, 141
Blume, Lawrence, 69, 70, 877
Blundell, Richard, 491
Boldrin, Michele, 418, 430
Bolton, Patrick, 355, 764, 771
Border, Kim, 877
Boserup, Ester, 141
Boulton, Matthew, 414, 415
Bourguignon, François, 142, 770, 857
Boyce, William E., 70, 917
Boyd, John Harvey, 178
Braudel, Fernand, 588
Broadberry, Stephen, 24
Brock, William A., 566, 604
Browning, Martin, 562
Bryant, Victor, 223
Buera, Francisco, 720
Bulow, Jeremy I., 685
Burstein, Ariel, 686

Caballero, Ricardo J., 277, 528, 556
Campbell, David, 612
Caputo, Michael, 277
Card, David, 384
Carter, Susan B., 720

Caselli, Francesco, 25, 107, 176, 384, 527, 612, 643, 654, 686, 720
Cass, David, 318, 355
Ceruzzi, Paul E., 415
Cesari, Lamberto, 276
Chamberlain, Gary, 562
Chamberlin, Edward, 422, 426, 430
Chandler, Tertius, 143
Chari, V. V., 319, 824
Chenery, Hollis, 720
Chèvre, Pierre, 143
Chiang, Alpha C., 276
Chirinko, Robert S., 686
Ciccone, Antonio, 380, 384
Coatsworth, John H., 858
Coleman, Wilbur John, 527, 612, 720
Collier, Ruth B., 858
Conrad, Jon M., 277
Conway, John B., 877, 910
Cooley, Thomas F., 604
Coughlin, Peter J., 824
Crossley, Thomas F., 562
Crucini, Mario J., 686
Cunat, Alejandro, 686
Curtin, Philip D., 143

Dasgupta, Partha, 277, 430
David, Paul A., 644
Davis, Ralph, 870
Davis, Steven, 612
Davis, Y. Donald, 107
Deaton, Angus S., 25, 153n, 176, 177, 562
Debreu, Gerard, 150, 177
De La Croix, David, 354
Denardo, Eric V., 222, 223
Devereux, Paul J., 770
Diamond, Jared M., 25, 118, 129, 141–42
Diamond, Peter, 327, 328, 353, 354, 355
Dinopoulos, Elias, 453, 490
DiPrima, Richard C., 70, 917
Dixit, Avinash K., 142, 277, 422, 430, 686
Doepke, Matthias, 770
Dollar, David, 678
Domar, Evsey D., 26, 75
Doms, Mark, 612
Dorfman, Robert, 277
Downs, Anthony, 824
Drandakis, E., 528
Drazen, Allan, 379, 384, 823
Duflo, Esther, 380, 384, 654, 824

Dunne, Timothy, 612
Duranton, Gilles, 527
Durlauf, Steven N., 25, 106, 142, 771

Echevarria, Cristina, 720
Eggertsson, Thrainn, 823
Eggimann, Gilbert, 143
Ekeland, Ivar, 223
Elliott, John H., 868
Eltis, David, 858
Elvin, Mark, 867
Engel, Ernst, 698
Engerman, Stanley L., 858, 871
Epifani, Paolo, 686
Epstein, Larry G., 178
Ertman, Thomas, 870
Esquivel, Gerard, 25
Ethier, Stewart, 562, 604
Evans, Eric J., 858
Evans, Peter, 824

Fafchamps, Marcel, 142
Feinstein, Charles, 25
Feldstein, Martin, 649, 655
Fernandez, Raquel, 771
Fernandez-Villaverde, Jesus, 770
Feyrer, James, 654, 686
Fields, Gary, 770
Finkelstein, Amy, 416, 430
Fischer, Stanley, 277, 318, 354, 604
Fisher, Irving, 554
Fleming, Wendell H., 276, 277
Foellmi, Reto, 720
Fomin, Sergei V., 177, 223, 275–76, 877, 910
Forbes, Kristen J., 824
Foster, Andrew, 382, 384
Foster, Lucia, 612
François, Patrick, 490
Frankel, Jeffrey, 678–79
Fraumeni, Barbara, 80, 106
Freeman, Christopher, 430
Freudenberger, Herman, 871
Friedman, Milton, 554
Fudenberg, Drew, 431, 490, 934, 941
Funk, Peter, 529
Futia, Carl A., 562, 604

Gabaix, Xavier, 107
Gale, Douglas, 605
Galenson, David W., 871
Gallup, John Luke, 119
Galor, Oded, 70, 141, 354, 355, 384,

643, 681, 687, 761, 762n, 763, 764, 770, 771, 858
Gancia, Gino, 453, 527, 528, 686
Gans, Joshua S., 824
Geary, Robert C., 319
Geertz, Clifford, 770
Gelfand, I. M., 275–76
Gerschenkron, Alexander, 615, 643
Gikhman, I. I., 562, 604
Gil, Richard, 833
Gilles, Christian, 355
Glomm, Gerhard, 771
Goldin, Claudia, 528
Gollin, Douglas, 720
Gollop, F. M., 80, 106
Gomez-Galvarriato, Aurora, 25
Goodfriend, Marvin, 770
Gordon, Robert J., 76
Gorman, W. M., 151, 176
Gourinchas, Pierre-Olivier, 686
Grandmont, Jean-Michel, 824
Green, Jerry R., 69, 150, 176, 177
Greenwood, Jeremy, 76, 384, 643, 726, 769
Greif, Avner, 142
Griffith, Rachel, 491
Griliches, Zvi, 384, 415, 613
Grossman, Gene M., 433, 453, 458, 490, 679, 680, 686
Grossman, Herschel, 142
Guerrieri, Veronica, 703, 721
Guiso, Luigi, 142
Gupta, Bishnupriya, 24
Gutierrez, Hector, 143
Guvenen, Fatih, 384

Habakkuk, H. J., 512, 528
Hakenes, Hendrik, 38n, 70–71
Halkin, Hubert, 277
Hall, Robert E., 96, 97, 106–7, 142, 554, 556
Haltiwanger, John C., 612
Haltiwanger, Jon, 581n
Hammermesh, Daniel, 528
Hammour, Mohammad, 528
Hansen, Gary D., 141, 770
Harris, Christopher, 490
Harris, John, 770
Harrison, Lawrence E., 142
Harrod, Roy, 26, 59, 75
Hart, Oliver D., 605
Hassler, John, 824
Hayashi, Fumia, 277

Heal, Geoffrey, 277
Heckman, James, 384
Hellwig, Martin, 418
Helpman, Elhanan, 23, 433, 453, 458, 490, 631, 640, 644, 679, 680, 686
Herbst, Jeffery I., 824
Hercowitz, Zvi, 76
Heston, Allen, 3n, 12, 23, 25, 91, 97
Hicks, John, 58, 527
Hildenbrand, Werner, 176, 177
Hirschman, Albert, 694, 695, 752
Hirshleifer, Jack, 142
Homer, Sydney, 57, 70
Hopkins, Keith, 866
Horioka, Charles, 649, 655
Hotelling, Harold, 277, 824
Houthakker, Hendrik S., 523, 524, 526, 529
Howard, Ronald A., 561
Howitt, Peter, 23, 384, 430, 453, 458, 459, 468, 469n, 470, 490, 643–44
Hsieh, Chang-Tai, 25, 319
Hulten, Charles, 612
Huntington, Samuel P., 142

Imbs, Jean, 588, 605
Inada, Ken-Ichi, 70
Irmen, Andreas, 38n, 70–71, 418

Jacobs, Jane, 379, 384
Jaffee, Adam, 415, 430
James, John A., 528
Jayaratne, Jay, 770
Jeanne, Olivier, 686
Jensen, Bradford, 679
Johnson, Paul A., 106
Johnson, Simon, 24, 25, 129, 130, 133, 135, 136, 137, 138, 139, 141, 142, 143, 858, 870, 871
Jones, Benjamin F., 117, 143
Jones, Charles I., 23, 25, 69, 70, 96, 97, 106–7, 142, 319, 446, 453, 497, 523, 526, 527, 529
Jones, Eric, 868
Jones, Larry, 404
Jones, Richard, 141, 142
Jorgensen, Dale, 80, 106
Jovanovic, Boyan, 726, 769
Judd, Kenneth, 221, 453

Kaboski, Joseph, 720
Kaldor, Nicholas, 57, 70, 72, 762n
Kalemli-Ozcan, Sebnem, 686, 770
Kamien, Morton, 277

Kamihigashi, Takashi, 223, 562
Karlin, Samuel, 222
Katz, Lawrence, 384, 528
Katz, Lawrence F., 528
Keefer, Philip, 142
Kehoe, Patrick J., 319, 453, 685, 686, 824
Kehoe, Timothy J., 453
Kelley, John, 877
Kennedy, Charles, 527–28
Keyssar, Alexander, 871
Kiley, Michael, 527
Kim, Minseong, 142
King, Robert G., 604, 769
Kirman, Alan, 176, 177
Kiyotaki, Nobuhiro, 771
Klenow, Peter J., 25, 96, 106–7, 319
Klepper, Steven, 490
Klette, Tor Jacob, 490
Knack, Stephen, 142
Knight, Frank, 535n
Kolmogorov, Andrei, 177, 223, 877, 910
Kongsamut, Piyabha, 698, 699, 720
Koopmans, Tjalling C., 318
Koren, Miklos, 588, 605
Kortum, Samuel, 490, 562
Kraay, Aart, 686
Kremer, Michael, 113, 141, 453
Kreps, David, 178
Kreyszig, Erwin, 177, 223
Krizan, Cornell J., 612
Krueger, Alan, 24, 528
Krugman, Paul, 674, 677, 686, 771
Krusell, Per, 76, 142, 528, 583, 604, 824
Kupperman, Karen O., 142
Kurtz, Thomas, 562, 604
Kuruscu, Burhanettin, 384
Kurz, Mordecai, 277, 318
Kuznets, Simon, 8, 693–94, 695, 697, 702, 720, 750, 751
Kydland, Finn E., 579, 604

Lagos, Ricardo, 529
Laitner, John, 720
Landes, David S., 142
Lane, Julia I., 612
Lang, Sean, 858
Lavy, Victor, 770
Leamer, Edward, 857
Lee, Jong-Wha, 23
Lefort, Fernando, 25

Leonard, Daniel, 277
LeRoy, Stephen F., 355
Levchenko, Andrei, 687
Levine, David K., 418, 430
Levine, Ross, 769
Lewis, William Arthur, 142, 737, 770
Limongi, Fernando, 832–33
Lindahl, Mikael, 24
Lindbeck, Assar, 824
Lindert, Peter H., 770, 858
Linn, Joshua, 416, 430
Livi-Bacci, Massimo, 770
Ljungqvist, Lars, 221, 318, 562, 604
Lochner, Lance, 384
Locke, John, 142
Long, John B., 604
López-Alonso, Moramay, 25
Loury, Glenn, 771
Lucas, Robert E., 177, 222–23, 379, 384, 399, 404, 407, 553, 560, 561, 604, 649, 654, 686, 687
Luenberger, David, 70, 177, 276, 877, 904, 904n, 910, 917
Lynch, Lisa, 612

Machiavelli, Niccolò, 141
Maddison, Angus, 12, 13, 24, 25, 126, 730, 770, 870
Maffezoli, Marco, 686
Magill, Michael J. P., 276
Makowski, Louis, 605
Mallick, Debdulal, 686
Malthus, Thomas R., 730, 770
Mangasarian, O. O., 236, 277
Mankiw, N. Gregory, 90, 91–93, 94, 95–96, 106
Mann, Charles C., 866
Mantel, Rolf R., 177
Manuelli, Rodolfo, 384, 404
Marris, Robin, 25
Marshall, Alfred, 118, 141, 384
Martimort, David, 490
Mas-Colell, Andreu, 69, 150, 176, 177
Matsuyama, Kiminori, 430, 453, 490, 679, 680–81, 685, 687, 715, 720, 721, 771
Mauro, Paolo, 142
McCall, John, 561, 562
McCandless, George T., 354
McCleary, Rachel, 142
McDermott, John, 770
McEvedy, Colin, 141, 142
McGrattan, Ellen, 319
Melitz, Mark, 679

Meltzer, Allan H., 824
Michel, Philippe, 277, 354
Migdal, Joel, 824
Mill, John Stuart, 142, 415
Mincer, Jacob, 85, 359, 361, 380, 384, 618
Minier, Jenny A., 833
Mirman, Leonard J., 222, 566, 604
Mitch, David, 858
Moav, Omer, 141, 384, 643, 762n, 763, 770, 858
Mokyr, Joel, 24, 25, 412, 415, 430, 499, 528, 697, 715, 721, 867, 869, 870
Montesquieu, Charles de Secondat, 117–18, 122, 124
Moretti, Enrico, 380n, 384
Morgenstern, Oskar, 156, 177
Morris, Ian, 866n
Morrison, Christian, 770
Mosse, W. E., 871
Mountford, Andrew, 681, 687
Muellbauer, John, 153n, 176, 177
Mulligan, Casey, 833
Mundlak, Yair, 721
Murphy, Kevin M., 528, 720, 752, 756, 757, 770, 771
Myerson, Rogerson, 431, 934
Myrdal, Gunnar, 141

Nelson, Richard R., 380, 382, 384, 618–19, 620, 643
Newell, Richard, 415, 430
Newman, Andrew, 355, 737, 740, 764, 770, 771, 773
Ngai, Rachel, 721
Nickell, Stephen, 491
Norman, Victor, 686
North, Douglass C., 25, 119, 141, 142, 870
Nugent, Jeffrey, 857
Nunn, Nathan, 687
Nurske, Ragnar, 694, 695, 715, 720, 752, 757

Obstfeld, Maurice, 685–86, 769
Ok, Efe, 877
Olken, Benjamin A., 117, 143
Osborne, Martin, 431, 934
Overton, Mark, 715, 721

Pamuk, Sevket, 867
Parente, Stephen, 720

Parente, Stephen L., 319, 619, 620
Park Chung Hee, 832
Parker, Jonathan A., 581n
Pavcnik, Nina, 679
Peri, Giovanni, 380, 384
Perko, Lawrence, 917
Perri, Fabrizio, 685
Persson, Torsten, 142, 823, 824
Phelps, Edmund, 528
Phelps, Edmund S., 70, 380, 382, 384, 618–19, 620, 643
Piketty, Thomas, 70, 355, 764, 771
Pindyck, Robert S., 277
Pinochet, Augusto, 832
Pirenne, Henri, 869
Pissarides, Christopher, 562, 721
Plosser, Charles I., 604
Pollak, Richard, 176
Pomeranz, Kenneth, 24
Pontryagin, Lev S., 227, 236, 248, 275, 276
Popp, David, 416, 430
Porras Condey, Raúl, 25
Postan, M. M., 869
Prescott, Edward C., 141, 177, 222–23, 319, 553, 561, 579, 604, 619, 620, 770
Pritchett, Lant, 25
Przeworski, Adam, 832–33
Puterman, Martin L., 222, 561
Putnam, Robert, 122, 142

Qian, Nancy, 770
Quah, Danny, 25, 106

Ragot, Xavier, 527
Rajan, Raghuram, 769–70
Ramey, Garey, 605
Ramey, Valerie, 605
Ramsey, Frank, 250, 318
Rauch, James E., 379, 380, 384
Ravikumar, B., 771
Rebelo, Sergio, 387, 395, 404, 444, 604, 671, 698, 699, 700, 702, 720
Reinganum, Jennifer, 430
Richard, Scott, 824
Ringer, Fritz, 858
Ríos-Rull, José-Víctor, 142, 824
Rishel, Raymond W., 276, 277
Rivera-Batiz, Luis A., 453, 686
Roberts, Joanne, 490
Roberts, Kevin W. S., 824
Robinson, James A., 24, 25, 129, 130,

133, 135, 141, 142, 143, 823, 824, 833, 853, 855, 857, 858, 870, 871
Rockefeller, Tyrell R., 276
Rodriguez, Andres, 25, 96, 106–7
Rodriguez, Francisco, 679
Rodrik, Dani, 142, 679, 824, 833
Rogerson, Richard, 562, 720
Rogerson, Roger, 771
Rogoff, Kenneth, 685
Romer, David, 90, 91–93, 94, 95–96, 106, 277, 318, 678–79
Romer, Paul M., 276, 387–88, 398, 399, 404, 413–14, 418, 430, 433, 439, 453, 681, 686, 720, 734, 738
Romer, Thomas, 824
Rosenberg, Nathan, 415
Rosenstein-Rodan, Paul, 694, 695, 715, 720, 752, 757, 771
Rosenzweig, Mark, 382, 384
Rostow, Walt Whitman, 13, 24, 598, 715, 720
Royden, Halsey, 561, 877
Rubinstein, Ariel, 431, 934
Rudin, Walter, 561, 877
Ryder, Harl E., 354

Sachs, Jeffrey, 118, 141, 678
Sachs, Jeffrey D., 119, 141
Saez, Emmanuel, 70
Saint-Paul, Gilles, 142, 824
Sala-i-Martin, Xavier, 15, 17, 23, 24, 25, 69, 70, 82, 83, 106, 142, 318, 404, 685, 687, 833
Salop, Steven, 430, 432
Salter W. E. G., 644
Salvanes, Kjell, 770
Samuelson, Paul A., 327, 328, 353, 354, 355, 511, 528
Sapienza, Paola, 142
Sargent, Thomas J., 221, 318, 562, 604
Scheinkman, Jose A., 222, 223, 277
Scherer, Frederick M., 414
Schlicht, Ekkehart, 60, 70
Schlosser, Analia, 770
Schmookler, Jacob, 415, 430
Schultz, Theodore, 85, 380, 384, 618–19, 643
Schumpeter, Joseph A., 8, 417, 418, 421, 430
Schwartz, Nancy, 277
Scotchmer, Suzanne, 430
Scrimgeour, Dean, 70
Segerstrom, Paul S., 453, 490
Seierstad, Atle, 277

Seshadri, Anant, 384
Shapley, Lloyd S., 222, 640
Shell, Karl, 328, 354–55
Shimer, Robert, 562
Shleifer, Andrei, 720, 752, 756, 757, 771
Simon, Carl, 69, 70, 877
Simon, Julian, 113, 141
Skaperdas, Stergios, 142
Skinner, Jonathan S., 528
Skorohod, A. V., 562, 604
Smart, Michael, 824
Smith, Adam, 142, 167, 868
Smith, Anthony, 583, 604
Smith, Bruce, 769
Sokoloff, Kenneth, 858, 871
Solon, Gary, 581n
Solow, Robert M., 26, 69, 77, 79, 106, 404
Sonin, Konstantin, 842, 857
Sonnenschein, Hugo, 177
Spence, Michael, 422, 430
Spiegel, Mark M., 382, 384, 643
Spletzer, James R., 612
Stavins, Robert, 415, 430
Stewart, Frances., 644
Stiglitz, Joseph E., 355, 422, 430, 625, 644, 686
Stokey, Nancy, 177, 222–23, 553, 561, 604, 720
Stone, Richard, 319
Strahan, Philip, 770
Summerhill, William, 142
Summers, Lawrence H., 604
Summers, Robert, 3n, 12, 23, 25, 91, 97
Sundaram, Rangarajan, 223
Swan, Trevor W., 26, 69
Sydsaeter, Knut, 277
Sylla, Richard, 57, 70

Tabellini, Guido, 142, 823, 824
Taber, Christopher, 384
Tamura, Robert, 770, 771

Taylor, Alan M., 685–86
Temple, Jonathan R. W., 106
Tenreyro, Silvana, 588, 605
Thoenig, Matthias, 527, 528, 686
Thomas, Robert, 25, 141, 142, 870
Thompson, Peter, 453
Tirole, Jean, 355, 430, 431, 490, 934, 941
Tobin, James, 274, 277
Todaro, Michael, 770
Tornell, Aaron, 142
Townsend, Robert, 726, 727, 769
Trefler, Daniel, 101–5, 107, 654, 657
Troske, Kenneth, 612
Tsiddon, Daniel, 384

Uhlig, Harald, 462n
Uzawa, Hirofumi, 60, 70, 404, 407

Van Long, Ngo, 277
Van Reenen, Jon, 491
Velasco, Andés, 142
Véliz, Claudio, 142
Ventura, Jaume, 176, 319, 355, 656, 663, 686
Verdier, Thierry, 142, 490, 527, 528, 686, 824, 857
Vernon, Raymond, 674
Vickers, John, 490
Violante, Gianluca, 384, 643
Vishny, Robert W., 720, 752, 756, 757, 771
Vogel, Ezra, 663, 674
Vollrath, Dietrich, 858
Volosovych, Vadym, 686
von Neumann, John, 156, 177, 318, 404

Wacziarg, Romain, 588, 605
Wade, Robert, 824
Wallace, Neil, 354, 355
Walter, Wolfgang, 917, 930
Wan, Henry, Jr., 70, 177

Warner, Andrew, 678
Watt, James, 414, 415
Weber, Max, 122, 142
Webster, David L., 866
Weibull, Jörgen, 824
Weil, David N., 23, 90, 91–93, 94, 95–96, 106, 137, 141, 143, 625, 644, 770
Weil, Philippe, 355
Weingast, Barry R., 142
Weinstein, David E., 107
Weitzman, Martin L., 277
Whinston, Michael D., 69, 150, 176, 177
White, Lynn T., 869
Wiarda, Howard J., 142
Williams, David, 561
Williamson, Jeffrey, 770
Wilson, Charles A., 562
Wilson, Francis, 25
Wong, R. Bin, 867
Wooldridge, Jeffery M., 106
Wright, Randall, 562

Xie, Danyang, 698, 699, 720
Xu, Bin, 527, 528

Yaari, Menahem E., 327, 346, 348, 354, 355
Yorukoglu, Mehmet, 384, 643
Young, Alwyn, 25, 143, 453, 663, 679, 680, 681, 687
Young, Andrew, 721

Zeira, Joseph, 355, 761, 764, 771
Zeldes, Stephen P., 556
Zilcha, Itzak, 222, 562
Zilibotti, Fabrizio, 427, 453, 527, 588, 598, 605, 626, 630, 644, 715, 737, 740, 744, 746, 749, 750, 769, 770
Zin, Stanley E., 178
Zingales, Luigi, 142, 769–70
Zuleta, Hernando, 721
Zweimuller, Josef, 720

Subject Index

Page numbers for entries occurring in figures are followed by an f; those for entries occurring in notes, by an n; and those for entries occurring in tables, by a t.

admissible pairs, 228, 228n, 238–39, 241

advanced countries: international division of labor, 674–77, 862–63; sectoral employment shares in, 697–98; tax rates in, 821; technologies optimized for conditions in, 624, 625, 643. *See also* cross-country income differences

Africa: disease burden in, 119, 133; European colonies in, 135, 871. *See also* less-developed countries

agents. *See* households

aggregate production function: with health capital, 137; with human capital, 85; in Solow model, 26, 28–29, 77

aggregate production possibilities set, 158–59

Aghion-Howitt model, 468–70

agricultural productivity: cross-country differences in, 716; employment shifts, 715; geographic factors in, 118–19; industrialization and, 715–19; in open economies, 719; technological change and, 865

agriculture: consumption expenditures on products of, 697, 698, 699; employment in, 697; history of, 865; technological change in, 716, 865

AK model: competitive equilibrium of, 389–92, 393–94; environment of, 388–89; with international trade, 665–71; neoclassical version of, 387, 388–92; with physical and human capital, 393–94; policy differences and, 392; sustained growth in, 55–56, 56f; two-sector, 395–98

altruism: impure, 342–45, 353; intergenerational, 157–58; pure, 342; warm glow, 342–45, 731

antitrust policies, 442–43

appropriability effect, 420, 429, 465, 749

appropriate technology, 626–30, 643

Arrow-Debreu equilibrium, 171, 173, 602

Arrow securities: definition of, 172n; sequential trading with, 171–72, 173, 577–79; symmetric, 594

Arrow's Impossibility Theorem, 806

Arrow's replacement effect, 421, 429

Arrow's sufficiency conditions, 237–38

Arzela-Ascoli Theorem, 892–94

Asia: economic growth miracles in, 20–21, 117, 123, 126, 663, 674, 685; European colonies in, 135–36, 871. *See also* less-developed countries

assets: bubbles on, 342; pricing, 560. *See also* investment; securities

asymptotic stability, 44

augmented Solow model, 85–89, 87f, 92–93

authoritarian political systems, 865, 866–68, 870. *See also* nondemocratic regimes

autocracies, 865

balanced growth: definition of, 57; Harrod-neutral technological change and, 64; models with, 58; in neoclassical growth model with technological change, 307; world, 862

balanced growth path (BGP), 65, 66, 67

balanced portfolios, 428–29, 594, 601

Barro growth regression, 15–16, 83

basin of attraction, 759–60

Bellman equation, 185

Ben-Porath model, 363–66, 365f, 366f, 383

bequests, 344–45. *See also* altruism

Berge's Maximum Theorem, 198, 199, 213, 894, 897–98

Bernoulli utility functions, 149

Bewley model, 583–85, 604

BGP. *See* balanced growth path

biased technological change: capital-biased, 499, 519–20; difference from factor-augmenting technological change, 500–502; importance of, 498–500; skill-biased, 498–99, 501, 501f, 512; strong equilibrium (relative) bias, 500, 503, 510, 517–18, 522, 527; unskill-biased, 499; weak equilibrium (relative) bias, 500, 502–3, 510, 517, 522, 527

big push model, 752

Blackwell's sufficient conditions for contraction, 193–94

block recursiveness, 615

Bolzano-Weierstrass Theorem, 888

borrowing, endogenous constraints on, 554. *See also* debt

Britain: agricultural productivity in, 715; democratization in, 832, 833–34, 853–54; economic growth in, 9; economic takeoff in, 863; financial development in, 869; First Reform Act of 1832, 832, 854; former colonies of, 134–35; Industrial Revolution in, 9, 715, 854, 869; sectoral employment shares in, 697

Brock-Mirman model, 566, 567–71

Brouwer's Fixed Point Theorem, 899–900

bubbles, 342

business stealing effect, 421–22, 429, 465

calculus, fundamental theorems of, 919–20

canonical overlapping generations model, 333–34, 335–36, 335f

capital: accumulation of, 598–99; depreciation of, 31–32, 97; diminishing returns to, 29, 47; expenditures on, 79; health, 137; measurement issues, 79; overaccumulation in, 585; rental rates of, 32; share in U.S. GDP, 57–58, 57f; in Solow model, 31; stock of, 596, 597–98. *See also* financial capital flows; human capital; physical capital

capital-augmenting technological change. *See* Solow-neutral technology

capital-biased technological change, 499, 519–20

capital deepening, 46, 398, 403, 519, 704, 706, 765

capital-labor ratios: capital flows and, 653–54; cross-country differences, 100; effective, 65; elasticity of substitution, 519, 710, 711; equalization across countries, 651, 653, 659; factor prices and, 101, 102, 657; inappropriate technologies and, 625–26; increases in, 765; in Solow model, 36, 38f, 40–41

capital markets: imperfect, 762; international, 653–54

capital-skill complementarity, 371–74

Cass-Koopmans model, 318. *See also* neoclassical growth model

CES. *See* constant elasticity of substitution

CES preferences (Dixit-Stiglitz preferences), 152–53, 425

CGP. *See* constant growth path

children, quality-quantity tradeoff of parents, 732–33, 734–36

cities: human capital externalities and, 379; lack of community enforcement in, 741. *See also* urbanization

climate, 118, 124. *See also* geography hypothesis

Cobb-Douglas production function, 36–37, 52–54, 81–82

colonies, European: contracting institutions in, 136–37; cultural influences of colonizing power, 134–36; disease environments in, 132–33; growth takeoff in former, 13–14, 14f, 863, 870–71; indigenous institutions in, 129n, 130; institutional differences among, 126–27, 129n, 130–34, 131f; institutions imposed by colonizers of, 128–29; latitudes of, 134; legal systems of, 136; property

rights institutions in, 130, 131f, 133, 134f, 135f, 136–37; reversals of fortune in, 127, 128–32, 129f; settler mortality in, 132–33, 134f, 135f; technological change in, 129–30

commitment problems, 783, 784, 799. *See also* holdup problems

commodities, sequential trading of, 171–74. *See also* markets

community enforcement, 740–42

comparative advantage, 655, 671, 685, 719. *See also* Ricardian model of international trade

comparative dynamics: with basic Solow model, 67–68; with standard neoclassical growth model, 313–15, 314f

competition, among political parties, 809–10, 812–13

competition policies, 442–43

competitive equilibria: definition of, 162–63; in optimal growth problem, 219–21; Pareto optimal, 161, 176; in stochastic growth models, 571–79; symmetric, 219–21; under uncertainty, 571–79; welfare theorems, 163–67

competitive markets, 30, 162

complete markets, 162, 566, 571–72

composition effect, 485, 487, 489

computational tools, 221

concave problems, 256, 258–59, 276–77, 912

concavity: of functions, 898, 901; of Hamiltonian, 239; of instantaneous payoff function, 188; of value function, 189, 199–200, 266–67, 543, 553

conditional convergence, 15–17, 83

conditional factor price equalization, 101, 102, 657, 660

Condorcet paradox, 806–7, 808

Condorcet winners, 807, 808

cone of diversification, 657

constant elasticity of substitution (CES) aggregator, 423

constant elasticity of substitution (CES) preferences, 152–53, 425

constant elasticity of substitution (CES) production function, 54–55

constant growth path (CGP), 701, 712

constant relative risk aversion (CRRA) utility function, 308–9

constant returns to scale, 29

constitutional monarchies, 865, 869, 870

constrained optimization, 910–15

consumption: constant growth path of, 701, 712; Engel curves, 151, 152, 698, 699, 701, 702, 715; hierarchies of needs, 720; intertemporal elasticity of substitution and, 297; love for variety, 423, 425; nonbalanced sectoral growth, 701, 702; of nonrenewable resources, 252–53; optimal plans, 209; permanent income hypothesis, 554–56, 561; relationship to income per capita, 7–8, 7f; in Solow model, 42

consumption Euler equation, 209

consumption set, 161

contingent claims: insuring against risk with, 566; pricing of, 571–72; sequential trading with, 577–79

continuous-time models: advantages of, 48; perpetual youth model, 347–53, 354; Solow model, 47–55, 64–67; stochastic growth, 535

continuous-time neoclassical growth model. *See* neoclassical growth model

continuous-time optimal growth problem, 268–69

continuous-time optimization problems, 227–28; applications of, 233–35, 269–74, 275; approach, 275; existence of solutions, 259–66; finite-horizon, 228–29; infinite-horizon control, 240–50; Maximum Principle, 235–39; transversality condition of, 232; variational approach, 229–35

contracting institutions, 782; as barrier to technology transfer, 686; effects of differences on technology adoption, 630–41, 862; emergence of, 869; in former European colonies, 136–37; future research on, 873; influence on economic outcomes, 136–37, 862; in less-developed countries, 136–37, 741

Contraction Mapping Theorem, 190–94

control variables, 183, 537

convergence: Cobb-Douglas production function and, 81–82; conditional, 15–17, 83; global, 82; in optimal growth model, 218, 219; of policies, 805, 809–10, 811; speed of, 81

convexity, 898

costate variables, 230–31, 236

creative destruction: in democracies, 857; economic growth and, 489; economic institutions and, 120–21; labor market implications of, 471–72; losers from, 421; productivity growth resulting from, 476–77; social and political tensions from, 8, 467, 489–90; source of, 460; uneven growth resulting from, 470–71. *See also* innovations; new entrants; Schumpeterian growth models

credit market imperfections, 746, 758, 761–64. *See also* debt

cross-country income differences: absolute gap between rich and poor countries, 4, 5f; conditional convergence, 15–17, 83; distribution of GDP per capita, 3–6, 4f, 5f; growth rate differences and, 9–11; growth regressions, 80–85; human and physical capital investment decisions and, 93, 861–62; human capital differences and, 370–71, 378, 380; inappropriate technologies and, 625–26, 630; increasing inequality, 4–6, 5f; with international trade, 670–71, 673–74; in nineteenth and twentieth centuries, 12–14, 13f, 14f, 15f; origins of, 11–14; per capita, 3–6, 9–10, 11f, 14, 15f; persistence of, 139–40, 139f; possible perspective on, 864–72; productivity differences and, 96–100, 98f, 99f; proximate causes of, 312–13; regression analysis using augmented Solow model, 90–96, 92t, 93t; stability of, 11, 685; technology differences and, 90–96, 105; timing of growth takeoffs and, 603; welfare impact of, 7–9

CRRA. *See* constant relative risk aversion

cultural differences hypothesis, 20, 21, 122–23; arguments against, 130, 136; channels affecting economic growth, 111, 122; distinction from institutional differences, 112; evidence in European colonies, 134–36

culture: definition of, 111, 112; influences on economic behavior, 111, 122; institutions and, 112; measurement issues, 122–23; religion and, 122, 135

current-value Hamiltonian, 254, 255

Debreu-Mantel-Sonnenschein Theorem, 150

debt: consumption-denominated loans, 396–97; international borrowing and lending, 317; international financial capital flows, 648–53; natural limit, 208, 290–91; no-Ponzi condition, 207; sovereign, 654, 684

demand-side sources of structural change, 697–703, 719

democracy: advantages of, 857; contrast with nondemocratic regimes, 832; definition of, 832; dictatorship of workers, 835–37; direct, 779, 807; dynamic trade-offs with oligarchy, 837–50, 857; dysfunctional, 850; economic growth in, 832–34, 850; electoral rules of, 832; elite political power in, 850; emergence of, 850–51, 853–56; equilibrium, 845–46, 848–50; flexibility of, 850, 857; indirect, 809; industrialization in, 833–34; Montesquieu on geography and, 124; open agenda, 807, 809; party competition in, 809–10, 812–13; political economy model of, 805–14; political equality in, 832, 836; political participation in, 865; redistributive policies in, 833, 836, 849, 850, 854–56, 857; representative, 779

demographics. *See* migration; population growth; urbanization

demographic transition, 730, 732–36, 764

developing countries. *See* less-developed countries

development. *See* economic development

development (poverty) traps, 757, 760, 764, 769

dictatorial allocations, 162

dictatorships, 832, 834–35, 865. *See also* authoritarian political systems; nondemocratic regimes

difference equations, 930–32; linear, 44, 51; nonlinear, 44–45, 51

differentiability, 900–907; Fréchet, 904n; Gateaux, 904n; of instantaneous payoff function, 188; of solutions, 930; of value function, 190, 200–201, 267, 543, 553

differential equations, 920–21; continuity of solutions, 930; differentiability of solutions, 930; linear first-order, 921–24; nonlinear, 926, 927f; separable and exact, 927–28; systems of linear, 924–26; systems of nonlinear, 926, 927f

directed technological change: factor prices and, 509–11; Harrod-neutral (purely labor-augmenting), 499; profit incentives and, 499–500; skill premium and, 498, 510, 511–13, 511f, 513f, 514f, 517; wage structure and, 498, 511–13. *See also* biased technological change directed technological change models: advantages of, 497, 526–27; applications of, 522–23; baseline, 503–14, 511f; with knowledge spillovers, 514–18, 520, 521; without scale effects, 518–19. *See also* endogenous technology models

discounted infinite-horizon optimization problems, 253–59, 275

discounting, 256. *See also* exponential discounting

discrete-time infinite-horizon optimization, 182–85

discrete-time models: neoclassical growth, 305–6; overlapping generations, 329–34; perpetual youth, 345–47; stochastic growth, 535. *See also* Solow model

disease burden: in European colonies, 132–33, 134f, 135f; influence on economic outcomes, 119, 137–40; influence on institutional development, 132–33, 134f, 135f; labor productivity effects of, 137

distance to world technology frontier, 615, 616, 745–46, 747, 748f, 749f, 751f

distortionary policies, 468, 783–84, 793, 802–5, 822, 864

distributional conflicts: Cobb-Douglas model of, 792–98; political power and, 822; in simple society, 784–92. *See also* social conflict

division of labor: economic growth and, 868; international, 674–77, 862–63

Dixit-Stiglitz aggregator, 423

Dixit-Stiglitz model: with continuum of products, 425–26; with finite number of products, 422–25; limitations of, 428; limit prices, 427–28; love-for-variety feature, 423, 425

Dixit-Stiglitz preferences. *See* CES preferences

Downsian Policy Convergence Theorem, 805, 809–10, 811, 814

dual economy: community enforcement in, 740–42; modern sector, 736–37; surplus labor in, 737; technologies in, 743–44; traditional sector, 736–37; urbanization rates in, 736, 739, 742, 742f; wages in, 737–38, 740

dynamic general equilibrium models, 161, 176

dynamic inefficiency: in overlapping generations model, 338–39, 353–54; in Solow model, 42–43

dynamic infinite-horizon games, 934–42

dynamic programming: computational tools, 221; contraction mapping theorem, 190–94; importance of, 221–22; Principle of Optimality, 186, 189, 197–98, 542–43, 547–48; sequence problem and, 210–11. *See also* stationary dynamic programming; stochastic dynamic programming

dynastic preferences, 158

Eastern Europe, 871

economic development: big push model, 752; capital deepening, 765, 766f, 767f, 768f; distinction from growth, 693–95; future research on, 873–74; institutional influences on long-term, 781–84; models of, 694–95, 768–69; policies blocking, 804–5, 822, 871; structural transformations in, 694, 764–68, 766f, 767f, 768f, 863, 873–74; traps, 757

economic growth: Asian miracles, 20–21, 117, 123, 126, 663, 685; balanced, 57, 58; correlates of, 18–19; definition of, 693–94; distinction from development, 693–95; future research on, 872–74; links to economic development, 764–68; in pre-modern periods, 865–66, 867, 868; pre-nineteenth century, 13, 588, 863, 865–68; proximate causes of, 19–20, 106, 109, 312–13; regression analysis of determinants of, 83–84; sustained, 55–56, 56f, 863; uneven, 470–71; winners and losers from, 8–9. *See also* fundamental causes; takeoff, growth

economic growth rates: cross-country differences in, 9–11; distribution of, 9, 10f; GDP per worker and, 16–17, 16f, 17f; geometric averages, 24; human capital investments and, 18–19; investment levels and, 18–19, 18f, 861–62; in nineteenth and twentieth centuries, 12–14, 13f, 14f, 15f, 112–14; regression analysis of, 80–85; technological diffusion and, 862; variability of, 588

economic institutions: distinction from policies, 782; distinction from political institutions, 782; distortionary policies and, 802–5; incentives provided by, 120–21; political institutions and, 779, 782, 852–53, 853f, 856–57; preferences over, 778, 779, 783; relationship to economic outcomes, 778, 782. *See also* contracting institutions; distortionary policies; entry barriers; institutions; property rights institutions; tax policies

economies of scale, 113–14

education. *See* human capital investments; schooling

eigenvalues, 917–18

eigenvectors, 917–18

elasticity of substitution, 519, 710, 711. *See also* constant elasticity of substitution

elections. *See* voters

electoral laws, 782, 832. *See also* political institutions; voting

elites: in democracies, 850; economic development blocked by, 804–5, 871; with political power, 783–84, 789–93, 795–97, 832, 866, 871; property rights protection provided by, 803–4; reactions to social conflict, 854–55. *See also* oligarchy

employment: sectoral shifts in, 715; in Solow model, 30; structural change in United States, 697, 698f. *See also* labor markets

endogenous borrowing constraints, 554

endogenous growth models, 387–88; *AK* model, 387, 388–92; application to data, 403; Romer model, 398–402; technological diffusion, 621–23

endogenous political change, 850–56

endogenous technology models: appropriate technology, 626–30; differences from Romer model, 452; with expanding input variety, 433–46, 451–52, 458; with expanding product variety, 448–52; generalizations of, 522; importance of, 452–53, 862; Jones's model, 523–

26; with knowledge spillovers, 444–48; lab-equipment model with input varieties, 433–44; labor-augmenting technological change, 523–26; limitations of, 452, 458, 497; linearity of, 402; policies in, 442–44; process innovation, 433; product innovation, 433, 448–52; Romer model, 398–402; scale effect in, 439, 446; technological diffusion, 619–21; technology adoption with contractual differences, 631–41; trade liberalization effects on, 679–80; uses of, 409. *See also* directed technological change; Romer model; Schumpeterian growth models

Engel curves, 151, 152

Engel's Law, 698, 699, 701, 702, 715

entrepreneurs: distortionary taxes on, 791; economic institutions and, 804; high-skill, 746, 747; innovations by, 747; low-skill, 746, 747; with political power, 814–17; retained earnings of, 750; search for ideas, 556–60, 561; social mobility and, 837–38; technology adoption by, 747, 801–2; in Western Europe, 869. *See also* new entrants

entry barriers, 479, 782, 838

Envelope Theorem, 190, 914–15

equilibrium: Arrow-Debreu, 171, 173, 602; democratic, 845–46, 848–50; dynamic, 707; entry, 842–44, 844f; equalization, 675, 678; meaning of, 43; multiple equilibria models, 114–15, 116, 752–58, 760–61; Nash, 416, 430, 939; nonconvergence trap, 750–51, 752f; oligarchic, 847–49; sclerotic, 750, 751f, 843, 844, 845f; specialization, 675, 678; static, 593–94, 707; stationary, 583, 584, 585; underinvestment, 748–50, 749f; world, 616, 651, 659, 667–68. *See also* competitive equilibria

Equivalence of Values Theorem, 542

Euler equations, 202–5, 212; consumption, 209; stochastic, 549–52

Euler's theorem, 29–30

Europe. *See* Eastern Europe; Western Europe

excess sensitivity tests, 556

existence theorems, 929–30

exogenous growth model, 613–17

expanding variety models, 433; input variety, 433–46, 451–52, 458; product variety, 448–52

expected utility functions, 149

expected utility theory, 156–57

exponential discounting, 148, 160–61, 253–59

expropriation: distinction from taxation, 821; holdup problems, 784, 799; protection against risk of, 123, 124f, 130, 131f, 133, 134f, 135f, 802, 804

Extended Downsian Policy Convergence Theorem, 811

Extended Median Voter Theorem, 811

externalities: aggregate demand, 425, 426, 752–58; human capital, 94, 378–80, 383; learning-by-doing, 681, 683, 715, 716, 738; pecuniary, 338–39, 378, 383, 442; physical capital, 399; technological, 398, 399–400, 444–48, 514–18, 520, 679n

factor-augmenting technological change, 500–502

factor price equalization, 101, 102, 657, 660

factor price manipulation effect, 784, 794–97, 803, 805, 822

factor proportion differences, 704, 705

factors of production. *See* capital; labor

feasible variations, 230

Feldstein-Horioka puzzle, 653, 655, 684, 685–86

felicity function, 148

fertility, 764. *See also* population growth

fiat money, 342

financial capital flows: growth and, 648–53; under imperfect international capital markets, 654–55; under perfect international capital markets, 653–54; to poor countries, 653–55

financial development: effects on economic growth, 729; model of, 726–29; risk sharing through, 588, 599; in Western Europe, 869, 870

financial intermediaries, 592, 599, 602–3

firms: optimization problem of, 32–34; production functions of, 158; profit maximization problem of, 32–33; representative, 27–28, 158–59; in Solow model, 27–28; value of investment to, 274

First Welfare Theorem, 163–66, 167; importance of, 176; with infinite number of households, 164–65; non-applicability to OLG models, 328–29, 339

fixed point theorems, 884

Fréchet distribution, 525–26

frontier technologies, 609, 642, 643; skill requirements of, 626–30. *See also* technological diffusion; world technology frontier

functional equations, 185–86

functions: absolute continuity of, 892; definition of, 881; of several variables, 905–6; vector, 904

fundamental causes of economic growth, 19–21; analysis with neoclassical growth model, 312–13; cultural differences, 20, 21, 111, 112, 122–23, 130, 134–36; distinction from proximate causes, 106, 109; geographic differences, 20–21, 111, 117–19, 123–24; importance of investigating, 110; luck, 20, 110–11, 114–17, 603. *See also* institutional differences hypothesis

game theory, dynamic infinite-horizon games, 934–42

general equilibrium models: Arrow-Debreu equilibrium of, 171; assumptions in, 176; competitive equilibria in, 163; dynamic, 161, 176; economic growth theory and, 161–67; infinite number of commodities in, 31

geography hypothesis, 20–21, 111, 117–19; arguments against, 129, 136; disease burden, 119, 137–40; empirical support for, 123–24, 125f; latitude and income relationship, 123–24, 125f, 134; sophisticated, 129–30

Geometric Hahn-Banach Theorem, 167, 909–10

globalization, 652, 871–72. *See also* international trade

"golden rule" saving rate, 42, 70

Gorman preferences, 151, 152, 154, 308

Gorman's Aggregation Theorem, 151

governments. *See* policies; political institutions; public goods; state

government spending, 34n, 317

Grobman-Hartman Theorem, 926

gross domestic product (GDP): distribution of per capita, 3–6, 4f, 5f; per capita increases in, 9–10, 11f, 57; per worker, 11, 12f, 16–17, 16f, 17f. *See also* cross-country income differences

growth. *See* economic growth; takeoff

growth accounting, 78

Habakkuk hypothesis, 522, 528

Hahn-Banach Theorem, 910; Geometric, 167, 909–10

Hamiltonian, 235; concavity of, 239; current-value, 254, 255; maximized, 237; notation of, 235n

Hamiltonian dynamical system, 236n

Hamilton-Jacobi-Bellman (HJB) equation, 243–44; economic intuitions from, 247–48; heuristic derivation of, 244–46; stationary version of, 244–46, 248

Harrod-Domar model, 26, 27, 29

Harrod-neutral (purely labor-augmenting) technology, 59, 59f, 60, 61, 62, 64, 499, 519

health: improvements in, 138–39, 730, 764; life expectancies at birth, 7–8, 8f, 138–39, 138f; productivity and, 119; relationship to economic growth, 139–40. *See also* disease burden

health capital, 137

Heckscher-Ohlin international trade theory, 101, 655–63, 684–85

Heine-Borel Theorem, 887

hemicontinuity, 895–97, 896f

Hicks-neutral technology, 40, 58, 59f

HJB. *See* Hamilton-Jacobi-Bellman equation

holdup problems, 784, 799–801, 803, 822

households: budget constraints of, 208, 290–92, 296, 554; infinite planning horizons of, 156–58; life cycles of typical, 591, 591f; lifetime budget constraint of, 554; local nonsatiation of, 163–64; maximization problem of, 290–92, 294–97, 309–11; normative representative, 150, 153–55; ownership of factors of production, 30–31; permanent income hypothesis, 554–56, 561; representative, 27, 149–52; in Solow model, 27; strong representative, 152, 153, 154. *See also* consumption; preferences

human capital: *AK* model with, 393–94; in augmented Solow model, 85–89, 87f, 92–93; cross-country income differences and, 370–71, 378, 380; definition of, 85, 359; depreciation of, 363; firm-specific skills, 472; imbalance between physical capital and, 367, 369–70, 371, 374, 377–78, 383; in imperfect labor markets, 374–79; in neoclassical growth model, 367–71; quality of, 383; role in technology diffusion, 612, 618–19, 626–30; stocks of, 96–97. *See also* capital; schooling

human capital externalities, 94, 378–80, 383

human capital investment models: Ben-Porath, 363–66, 365f, 366f, 383; Nelson-Phelps, 380–82, 383

human capital investments: barriers to, 370, 782; dynamics of individual decisions, 759–60, 760f; estimating, 94; in imperfect credit markets, 761–64, 763f; income distribution and, 758–61; on-the-job training, 366, 383; in pre-modern periods, 868; productivity increases from, 367, 383, 618; rates of, 91; relationship to economic growth, 18–19, 19f, 92–93, 382–83, 861–62; returns to education, 94–95, 96–97, 361–63, 382, 498, 498f, 512–13; schooling decisions, 359–63; separation theorem, 359–61; technological change and, 380–82, 383; training, 366, 383. *See also* schooling

human capital theory, 85, 359

ideas: nonrivalry of, 413–14; search for, 556–60, 561. *See also* innovations

Implicit Function Theorem, 41, 907

Inada conditions, 33, 34f

inappropriate technology, 624–26, 630, 643, 743–44

income differences. *See* cross-country income differences

income distribution: human capital investments and, 758–61; world, 4–6, 5f, 403, 615

income inequality: cross-country, 4–6, 5f; distortionary taxation and, 817; Kuznets curve, 729; relationship to economic growth, 729; wages, 528

income per capita: consumption per capita and, 7–8, 7f; cross-country differences in, 3–6, 9–10, 11f, 14, 15f; life expectancy and, 7–8, 8f; population density and, 127–28, 129f; population growth rates and, 730–32; urbanization rates and, 127–28, 127f, 128f

incomes: demand and, 151–52; Engel curves, 151, 152, 698, 699, 701, 702, 715. *See also* wages

incomplete markets, 338–39, 566, 583–85, 604

individuals. *See* households; voters

induced innovation, 527–28

industrialization, 13–14; big-push type of, 757; in Britain, 9, 715, 854, 869; in democracies, 833–34; distinction from takeoff, 24; in nineteenth century, 132, 715, 855, 870; political effects of, 855; Protestantism and, 122; relationship to agricultural productivity, 715–19; timing of, 719–20; trade liberalization effects on, 719. *See also* dual economy; takeoff, growth

industrial organization of innovation, 472, 490, 862, 873

inefficiency. *See* dynamic inefficiency; Pareto inefficiency

inequality. *See* income inequality

infant industry protection, 680, 683

Infinite-Horizon Maximum Principle, 243, 248–50

infinite-horizon optimization: continuous-time, 240–50; discounted, 253–59; discrete-time, 182–85; economic intuitions from, 246–48; necessary and sufficient conditions, 240–44, 246; nonstationary, 211–15; transversality condition, 246, 250–53

infinite planning horizons, 156–58

initial value problems, 921, 929–30

inner product, 158

innovation possibilities frontier, 413, 433, 434–35, 444, 527–28, 620

innovations: appropriability effect of, 420, 429, 749; cumulative, 479–80; drastic, 418–19; excessive, 422, 429; incremental, 473; induced, 527–28; industrial organization of, 472, 490, 862, 873; limit pricing and, 419; macro, 412–13, 414–15; micro, 412–13; by new entrants, 421–22, 747, 862; nonexcludability, 414, 417; policies affecting, 620; process, 411–12, 433, 458, 459; product, 411, 433, 448–52; profit incentives for, 440, 452; quality improvements, 459, 473, 479; replacement effect of, 420–21, 429; search for ideas, 556–60, 561; social value of, 419–20; step-by-step, 479–89; value in partial equilibrium, 416–22. *See also* creative destruction; Dixit-Stiglitz model; technological change

inputs, expanding variety models, 433–46, 451–52, 458

institutional differences hypothesis, 20, 21, 111–12; analysis with neoclassical growth model, 315–17; empirical support for, 123–25, 133–34; as factor in takeoff to modern economic growth, 863–64, 869–70; importance of investigating, 140–41; influence on investment decisions, 862; influence on technology adoption, 862; meaning of term, 782; natural experiments, 125–37; reversals of fortune in former colonies and, 130–32, 131f; role of incentives, 119–21, 863; sources of differences, 822; tax policy differences, 315–17

institutions: as constraints on individuals, 119–20; culture and, 112; definition of, 111, 119–20, 782; endogeneity of, 121; extractive, 132, 865; growth-promoting, 865, 869; incentives provided by, 119, 120, 313, 863; long-run development and, 781–84; political leaders and, 117; reforms, 112, 121; relationship to preferences, 778–79; resource allocation and, 30; societal choices of, 782. *See also* contracting institutions; economic institutions; policies; political institutions; property rights institutions

integrated world economy, 652, 871–72

intellectual property rights (IPR) protection: composition effect of changes, 485, 487, 489; disincentive effect of changes, 485; patents, 414, 435, 443, 485; relationship to growth, 489; relationship to North-South income gap, 678; weak enforcement as barrier to technology transfer, 643

interest rates: on consumption-denominated loans, 396–97; in Solow model, 31, 32

Intermediate Value Theorem, 39, 884

international division of labor, 674–77, 862–63

international financial capital flows. *See* financial capital flows

international product cycle model: division of labor, 674–77, 862–63; equilibrium in, 675–76, 677f; with incomplete contracts, 686; technology transfer in, 677–78

international trade: comparative advantage in, 655, 671, 685, 719; cone of diversification, 657; economic growth with, 655–63, 670, 678–85; Heckscher-Ohlin model of, 101, 655–63, 684–85; income differences with, 670–71; infant industry protection, 680, 683; liberalization of, 679–80, 683–84, 719; negative growth effects of, 679, 680–83; productivity differences and, 101–5, 103f; Ricardian model of, 663–74, 684, 685; Rybczynski's Theorem, 706; technological diffusion and, 674–78, 862–63; terms-of-trade effects, 670, 673–74, 684, 685; world income distribution and, 670–71, 673–74

intertemporal elasticity of substitution, 297

intertemporal utility maximization problem, 207–9

invariant limiting distribution, 570

Inverse Function Theorem, 906–7

investment: balanced portfolios, 601; endogenous decisions on, 861–62; financial intermediaries, 592, 599, 602–3; institutional differences and, 862; minimum size requirements, 589–90, 590f; Pareto efficient portfolio allocations, 600–602, 601f; in public goods, 817–21; q-theory of, 269–74; risk-return relationship, 590; saving rates and, 655; subsidies to, 750; taxes on returns, 313, 315–16, 392; under uncertainty, 560–61; value to firm, 274. *See also* assets; capital; human capital investments; securities

investment goods, prices of, 316

IPR. *See* intellectual property rights

Jacobian matrix, 904

Jones's model, 523–26

Kakutani's Fixed Point Theorem, 899

Kaldor facts, 57, 698, 702, 714

knowledge: accumulation of, 398; as nonrival and nonexcludable good, 398

knowledge spillovers: in directed technological change models, 514–18, 520, 521; in endogenous technology models, 444–48; international trade and, 679n; reduced effect of, 446–48

Kongsamut-Rebelo-Xie model, 698–703

Kuhn-Tucker Theorem, 913–14

Kuznets curve, 729

Kuznets facts, 698, 702, 714

lab-equipment model with input varieties: balanced growth path in, 438–39; environment of, 433–36; equilibrium characterization in, 436–38; innovation possibilities frontier, 434–35; Pareto optimal allocations in, 440–42; policy effects in, 442–44; sources of inefficiency in, 442, 443; transitional dynamics of, 439–40

labor: diminishing returns to, 29; elasticity of substitution between skilled and unskilled, 517–18; household ownership of, 30–31; inelastic supply of, 30–31; measurement issues, 79; share in U.S. GDP, 57–58, 57f. *See also* capital-labor ratios; wages

labor-augmenting technological change, 59, 62, 519–22, 523–26. *See also* Harrod-neutral technology labor markets: imperfect, 374–79; implications of creative destruction, 471–72; population growth and, 48–51; relationship to technological change, 499; search model, 561; supply choices, 579–82

Latin America: culture, 122; democratization in, 850; growth rates in, 10; political institutions in, 832, 871, 872; pre-Columbian civilizations in, 127, 129n, 130, 866; repression of social conflict in, 855. *See also* less-developed countries

leaders, political, 117

learning-by-doing externalities, 681, 683, 715, 716, 738

Lebesgue integral, 152n

LeChatelier principle, 511

Leibniz's Rule, 920

Leontief production function, 54–55

less-developed countries: appropriate technology for, 626–30, 643; contracting institutions in, 136–37, 741; debt, 654; development traps, 757, 760, 764, 769; former European colonies, 135, 871; inappropriate technologies for, 624–26, 630, 643, 743–44; integration into global economy, 871–72; international division of labor, 674–77, 862–63; lack of capital flows to, 653–55; market failures in, 725; population growth rates of, 730; skills available in, 626–30; variable growth rates of, 588. *See also* cross-country income differences; dual economy; technological diffusion

l'Hôpital's Rule, 39, 902–3

life expectancies at birth, 7–8, 8f, 138–39, 138f

limit prices, 419, 427, 744

linear difference equations, stability for systems of, 44, 51

linear differential equations: first-order, 921–24; systems of, 924–26

local nonsatiation, 163–64

love-for-variety feature, 423, 425

luck hypothesis, 20, 110–11, 114–17; drawbacks of, 116–17; formalization of, 603; multiple equilibria and, 114–15, 116

Malthusian model, 730–32, 733f

Mangasarian's sufficiency conditions, 236–37

manufacturing sector, 697, 699, 716. *See also* industrialization

market failures, 725, 752

markets: competitive, 30, 162; complete, 162, 566, 571–72; credit, 746, 758, 761–64; financial development, 588, 599, 726–29, 869, 870; incomplete, 338–39, 566, 583–85, 604; sequential trading, 171–74, 577–79. *See also* commodities; labor markets; stock market

market size effect: direction of technological change and, 500, 508, 510, 513–14, 518–19; distinction from scale effect, 518; innovation and, 414, 415, 416; on technology adoption, 634

Markov chains, 538

Markovian models, 760, 764n

Markov Perfect Equilibrium (MPE): comparison to Subgame Perfect Equilibria, 936, 937; definition of, 937; existence of, 938–39; in political economy model, 790; in repeated games, 941; in step-by-step innovation model, 482; versus Subgame Perfect Equilibria, 799–802, 939

Markov processes, 538n, 552–53

martingales, 556

maximized Hamiltonian, 237

Maximum Principle: for discounted infinite-horizon problems, 254–56; economic intuitions from, 246–48, 275; infinite-horizon, 243, 248–50; for multivariate problems, 239–40; simplified, 235–36; terminal value constraint on, 276

McCall labor market search model, 561

Mean Value Theorem, 902

Median Voter Theorem (MVT), 805, 806–9, 810, 814; extended, 811; with strategic voting, 809

metric spaces, 191, 878–80, 881–83

middle class: emergence of, 869, 870; with political power, 797–98, 834–35

migration: during economic development, 736; model of, 737–40. *See also* dual economy; urbanization

Mincer equation, 94, 96, 362–63

minimum size requirements, 589–90, 590f

monarchies: absolutist, 865; constitutional, 865, 869, 870; Spanish, 867–68

monopolistic firms: antitrust policies, 442–43; political power of, 468; profit maximization objective of, 426–27, 452

monopoly power of innovating firm, 418–22, 427

monotonicity: of instantaneous payoff function, 188; of value function, 190, 200, 544, 553

moral hazard, 585, 740, 770, 873

mortality rates, 133, 730, 764. *See also* disease burden

MPE. *See* Markov Perfect Equilibrium

multi-factor productivity. *See* total factor productivity

multiple equilibria models: aggregate demand externalities, 752–58; differences from multiple steady-state models, 760–61; luck hypothesis and, 114–15; Pareto-ranked equilibria, 116

multiple steady state models, 116, 117, 758–61, 764, 764n

multivariate problems: Maximum Principle for, 239–40; sufficiency conditions for, 240

MVT. *See* Median Voter Theorem

Nash equilibria, 416, 430, 939

natural debt limit, 208, 290–91, 298

natural resources, 21n, 111

Nelson-Phelps model of human capital, 380–82, 383

neoclassical growth model: advantages of, 311, 318; *AK* model, 387, 388–92; applications of, 317; canonical, 309–11; comparative dynamics with, 313–15, 314f; comparative static results of, 301; comparison to Solow model, 27, 318; competitive equilibrium of, 293, 299–

300; consumption behavior in, 297–98; in continuous time, 287; discounting assumption in, 288; discount rate and saving rate, 301; in discrete time, 305–6; environment of, 287–89; equilibrium characterization in, 293–98; explanations of cross-country income differences, 403; extensions of, 317; household maximization problem in, 290–92, 294–97, 309–11; infinite planning horizons of households in, 156–58; with labor supply, 579–82; linearity of, 402; normative representative household in, 153–55; optimal growth problem and, 298–304; with physical and human capital, 367–71; preference orderings of, 147–49; preferences in, 287; problem formulation in, 160–61; proximate and fundamental causes of growth, 312–13; quantitative evaluation of, 315–17; Ramsey model, 318; representative firm assumption in, 158–59; representative household assumption in, 149–52; sequential trading in, 171–74; steady-state equilibrium in, 300–301, 309–10; with technological change, 306–12; transitional dynamics of, 302–4, 303f; with uncertainty (Brock-Mirman model), 566, 567–71; uniqueness of equilibrium in, 302–4, 311; use of, 287; welfare theorems in, 161–71

nets, 255

new entrants: aggregate demand externalities and, 426; barriers to, 479, 782, 838; business stealing effect, 421–22, 429, 465; free entry by, 475, 823; fringe of potential competitors, 419, 427, 442–43; high-skill entrepreneurs, 746; innovation by, 421–22, 747, 862; productivity growth by, 472–79; research and development by, 460–61. *See also* creative destruction; entrepreneurs

no-arbitrage conditions, 575

nonbalanced sectoral growth. *See* structural change

nonconvergence trap, 750–51, 752f

nonconvexities, 589, 590

nondemocratic regimes: authoritarian, 865, 866–68, 870; contrast with democratic regimes, 832; economic growth in, 832–34; elite rule in, 832; Montesquieu on geography and, 124; variations, 832. *See also* dictatorships; oligarchy

nonexcludability, 28, 398, 414, 417

non-growth-enhancing policies. *See* distortionary policies

nonlinear difference equations, local stability for systems of, 44–45, 51

nonlinear differential equations, 926, 927f

nonrenewable resources, 252–53

nonrival goods, 28, 398

nonrivalry of ideas, 413–14

nonstationary infinite-horizon optimization, 211–15

no-Ponzi condition, 207, 291–92, 296, 318–19

normative representative households, 150, 153–55

normed vector spaces, 907–10

OLG models. *See* overlapping generations models

oligarchy, 865; British, 832; dynamic trade-offs with democracy, 837–50, 857; equilibrium, 847–49; long-run inefficiency of, 849; policy decisions in, 846–49. *See also* authoritarian political systems

omitted variable bias, 93

optimal control theory, 227, 238–39

optimal growth model, 218–19

optimal growth paths, Second Welfare Theorem and, 167

optimal growth problem, 174–75; application of stationary dynamic programming, 206–7; competitive equilibrium in, 219–21; in continuous time, 268–69; in discrete time, 215–19, 305–6; existence of solutions, 259–66; of neoclassical economy, 215–19

optimality, principle of, 186, 189, 197–98, 242–43, 542–43, 547–48

optimal plans, 183–84, 186, 189, 209

optimal stopping problems, 561

output per worker, 6, 6f. *See also* gross domestic product

overlapping generations (OLG) models: advantages of, 327; applications of, 354; baseline, 329–34, 353–54; canonical, 333–34, 335–36, 335f; capital-skill complementarity in, 371–74; competitive equilibrium of, 331, 336–39; consumption, 330–31; in continuous time, 347–53, 352f, 354; in discrete time, 329–34; dynamic inefficiency in, 338–39, 353–54; financial development model, 726–29; with impure altruism, 342–45, 353, 371–74; non-applicability of First Welfare Theorem to, 328–29, 339; overaccumulation in, 336–39, 353; Pareto optimality of competitive equilibrium in, 336–39; restrictions on utility and production functions of, 332–34; savings, 330–31; with social security, 339–42, 354; steady-state equilibria of, 331–34, 332f; stochastic, 566–67, 586–88, 587f; with warm glow preferences, 342–45. *See also* perpetual youth model

Pareto distribution, 524

Pareto inefficiency: distinction from non-growth-enhancing policies, 783; in political economy models, 800, 801

Pareto optimal allocations: decentralization as competitive equilibria, 166–71, 176; definition of, 153, 163; normative representative household and, 153–54; in Romer model, 401–2. *See also* optimal growth problem

Pareto optimal equilibria, 161, 176

participatory regimes, 865, 869, 870, 871. *See also* democracy

party competition, 809–10, 812–13

patents, 414, 435, 443, 485. *See also* intellectual property rights protection

pay-as-you-go social security system, 339, 340–42

pecuniary externalities, 338–39, 378, 383, 442

perfect monitoring games, 934

permanent income hypothesis, 554–56, 561

perpetual inventory method, 97

perpetual youth model, 156, 327; in continuous time, 347–53, 352f, 354; in discrete time, 345–47 physical capital: *AK* model with, 393–94; depreciation of, 97; imbalance between human capital and, 367, 369–70, 371, 374, 377–78, 383; investments and economic growth rates, 18–19, 18f, 92–93, 861–62; in neoclassical growth model, 367–71. *See also* capital

physical capital externalities, 399

Picard's Theorem, 929

plans, 187, 541; feasible, 542. *See also* optimal plans

Poisson death model. *See* perpetual youth model

policies: child labor laws, 380; competition, 442–43; convergence of, 805, 809–10, 811; distinction from economic institutions, 782; distortionary, 468, 783–84, 793, 802–5, 822, 864; economic development blocked by, 804–5, 822, 871; in endogenous technology models, 442–44; as factor in takeoff to modern economic growth, 863–64; growth-enhancing, 823, 863–64; holdup problems of, 784, 799–801; infant industry protection, 680, 683; investment subsidies, 750; mappings to allocations, 779; political conflicts over, 468, 489–90; preferred, 807; public goods provision, 817–21; research subsidies, 442, 478, 620, 817; in Schumpeterian growth models, 467–68, 478–79, 489–90; in stationary dynamic programming, 185; technology adoption barriers, 872. *See also* intellectual property rights protection; tax policies

policy correspondences, 186

policy functions, 186, 190

political economy: analysis with neoclassical growth model, 778; collective decision making, 783; commitment problems, 783, 784, 799; conflicts among societal interests, 121, 140, 777, 782–83, 822; future research on, 874; growth-enhancing policies, 823, 863–64; leaders' influence on economic growth, 117; models of, 140; tensions from economic growth, 8–9, 421; winners and losers, 792. *See also* institutions; policies

political economy models: Cobb-Douglas, 792–98, 834–37; dynamics of political institutions, 852–53, 853f, 855–56; dynamic trade-offs between regimes, 837–50, 857; with heterogeneous preferences, 805–14; probabilistic voting model, 812–14; public goods provision, 817–21; of simple society, 784–92; tax policy decisions with heterogeneous voters, 814–17

political institutions: distinction from economic institutions, 782; dynamic model of, 852–53, 853f, 855–56; dynamic trade-offs between, 837–50, 857; endogenous change in, 850–56, 864; geographic differences and, 124; impact on economic growth, 832–37, 857; influence of social conflict, 822, 850, 853, 855; mapping to economic institutions, 779, 782, 852–53, 853f, 856–57; participatory, 865, 869, 870, 871; power distribution and, 777–78, 870; preferences over, 778. *See also* democracy; institutions; nondemocratic regimes

political party competition, 809–10, 812–13

political power: de facto, 851–52; de jure, 851–52, 855;

distributional conflicts and, 784–92, 822; distribution of, 777–78, 822, 823, 870; of elites, 783–84, 789–93, 795–97, 832, 866, 871; of entrepreneurs, 814–17; factors influencing distribution of, 778; of middle class, 797–98, 834–35; of monopolistic firms, 468; support of non-growth-enhancing policies, 783–84, 822

political replacement effect, 784, 797–98, 822

political stakes, 798

Ponzi games, 207, 292, 341–42. *See also* no-Ponzi condition

poor countries. *See* less-developed countries

population density: economic institutions and, 130–32, 131f; relationship to income per capita, 127–28, 129f

population growth: demographic transition, 730, 732–36, 764; differences in rates of, 729–30, 730f; economic growth and, 113; health improvements as cause of, 139; Malthusian model of, 730–32, 733f; relationship to technological change, 113–14; in Solow model, 48–51. *See also* scale effects

poverty traps. *See* development traps

preferences: CES (Dixit-Stiglitz), 152–53, 425; dynastic, 158; Gorman, 151, 152, 154, 308; induced, 778–79, 787; orderings, 147–49; over economic institutions, 778, 779, 783; over political institutions, 778; relationship to institutions, 778–79; single-crossing property of, 811; of voters, 807–10, 822; warm glow, 342–45

price effect, direction of technological change and, 500, 508, 510

price index, ideal, 423–24

prices: asset, 560; limit, 419, 427, 744

Principle of Optimality, 186, 189, 197–98, 242–43, 542–43, 547–48

Prisoner's Dilemma, 942

private return to schooling, 379–80

probabilistic voting model, 812–14

Probabilistic Voting Theorem, 814

process innovations, 411–12, 433, 458, 459. *See also* innovations

product cycles, international, 674–78, 862–63

product innovations, 411, 433, 448–52. *See also* innovations

production functions: Cobb-Douglas, 36–37, 52–54, 81–82; constant elasticity of substitution, 54–55; with health capital, 137; with human capital, 85; Leontief, 54–55; meta, 413; in Solow model, 26, 28–29, 77; technology, 413

production structure, change in, 744–51, 764

productivity: cross-country differences in, 101–5, 103f, 624; differences within countries, 611–13, 642; effects of disease burden, 137; Hicks-neutral, 40; human capital investments and, 367, 383, 618; in manufacturing sector, 716; naïve estimation approach, 100–101, 102–4, 103f, 104f; relationship to earnings, 95; trade liberalization and, 679; Trefler estimation approach, 101–5, 103f, 104f. *See also* agricultural productivity; total factor productivity

productivity growth: creative destruction and, 476–77; models of, 472–79; role of innovation, 412–13, 433

products, expanding variety models, 448–52

product topology, 889–91

profit motives, technological change and, 414–16

property rights institutions, 782; emergence of, 803–4, 869; in former colonies, 130, 131f, 133, 134f, 135f, 136–37; importance of, 120; limits on policy choices, 802; protection against expropriation risk, 123, 124f, 130, 131f, 133, 134f, 135f; relationship to economic growth, 123, 124f, 136–37. *See also* intellectual property rights protection

proximate causes of economic growth, 19–20, 106, 109, 312–13

public goods: economic growth and, 817, 821, 823; nonrival and nonexcludable, 28, 398, 414; provision of, 817–21, 823; pure, 414

q-theory of investment, 269–74

R&D. *See* research and development

Real Business Cycle (RBC) models, 566, 579–82

Rebelo model, 395–98, 444, 671, 702

repeated games, 941–42

replacement effect, 420–21, 429

representative firm, 27–28, 158–59

representative household: assumption of, 27, 149–52, 159, 176; maximization problem of, 220; normative, 150, 153–55; strong, 152, 153, 154

research and development (R&D): cumulative, 460; employment, 444; investors in firms, 428–29; knowledge spillovers from past, 444–48, 514–18, 520, 679n; subsidies to, 442, 478, 620, 817; taxes on spending, 467–68, 478–79; uncertainty in, 428–29. *See also* innovations; technological change

resource allocations, 162; dictatorial, 162; institutional structures and, 30. *See also* optimal growth problem

revenue extraction effect, 784, 791, 795–97, 798, 803, 805, 822

reverse causality, 93

Ricardian model of international trade: economic growth implications of trade, 684, 685; environment of, 664–65; general, 671–74; simplified, 663–71

Riemann integral, 919

risk: aggregate, 726; diversification of, 566, 595, 598–99, 726, 727; idiosyncratic, 566, 599, 726, 727; relationship to returns, 590; sovereign, 654, 655, 684

riskless arbitrage, 575

Romer model, 398–402; competitive equilibrium of, 400–401; environment of, 399–400; knowledge accumulation in, 452; learning-by-doing externalities, 681, 716, 738; parallels to endogenous technology models, 452; Pareto optimal allocations in, 401–2; scale effect in, 401, 439

Roy's identity, 151

rural areas, community enforcement in, 740–42. *See also* agriculture; dual economy

Rybczynski's Theorem, 706

saddle-path stability, 269, 271–72, 302

Saddle-Point Theorem, 911–12

saving rates: correlation with investment rates, 655; "golden rule," 42, 70; relationship to discount rate, 301; in Solow model, 27, 35, 301

scale effects, 401, 439; direction of technological change and, 513–14, 518; distinction from market size effect, 518; growth without, 446–48; in technology adoption, 414

schooling: college premium, 498, 498f, 512–13; effects of child labor laws, 380; external return to, 380; measurement issues, 24; private return to, 379–80; relationship to earnings, 94–95, 96; relationship to economic growth, 18, 19f, 24–25; returns to, 94–95, 96–97, 361–63, 382; universal, 854. *See also* human capital investments

Schumpeterian growth models, 458–59; advantages of, 468; Aghion-Howitt model, 468–70; applications of, 490; balanced growth path in, 463–65; baseline, 459–68, 489, 490; equilibrium in, 461–63; extensions of, 490; limitations of, 472, 490; one-sector, 468–72; Pareto optimal allocations in, 465–67; policies in, 467–68, 478–79; productivity growth by incumbents and entrants, 472–79; step-by-step innovation, 479–89. *See also* creative destruction

sclerotic equilibrium, 750, 751f, 843, 844, 845f

search for ideas, 556–60, 561

Second Welfare Theorem, 163, 166–67, 907; application to optimal growth problem, 175; importance of, 176; proof of, 168–71

securities: balanced portfolios of, 428–29, 594; complex, 602; prices, 31. *See also* Arrow securities; assets; interest rates; investment

semi-endogenous growth models, 448

Separating Hyperplane Theorem, 910

separation theorems, 359–61, 907–10

sequence problem, 210–11

sequences, 881–83

sequential trading, 171–74, 577–79

services sector: consumption spending in, 698–99; employment in, 697

sets. *See* metric spaces

Shapley value, 635, 636, 640–41

Shell model, 328–29

Simon-Kremer model, 113–14

simple society: definition of, 784–85; model of, 784–92

Simplified Maximum Principle, 235–36

sincere voting, 807, 808

single-crossing property, 811

skill-biased technological change, 498–99, 501, 501f, 512

skill premium, 498, 510, 511–13, 511f, 513f, 514f, 517

skills, relative supply of, 498–99, 498f. *See also* human capital

Slater condition, 911

social capital, 122

social conflict, 121, 140, 777, 782–83; Cobb-Douglas model of, 792–98; elite reactions to, 854–55; influence on institutions, 822, 850, 853, 855; repression of, 855, 856; simple society model of, 784–92; urbanization rates and, 855

social mobility, 837–38

social planner. *See* optimal growth problem

social security: fully funded, 339–40; in overlapping generations model, 339–42, 354; unfunded, 339, 340–42

social welfare function, weighted, 812

societies: dysfunctional, 122; heterogeneity of, 805–14; mobility in, 837–38; simple society model, 784–92; structural transformations in, 736. *See also* culture; political economy

Solow model: aggregate production function in, 26, 28–29, 77; application to data, 79, 90–96, 105; augmented version, with human capital, 85–89, 87f, 92–93; capital-labor ratio in, 36, 38f, 40–41; comparative dynamics with, 67–68; comparison to neoclassical model, 27, 318; in continuous time, 47–55, 64–67; in discrete time, 27, 34–47, 56–64; economic development, 765–68; endowments in, 30–32; environment of, 27–34; equilibrium difference equation of, 37; equilibrium in, 32–34, 35–43; firm optimization problem in, 32–34; fundamental law of motion of, 34–35; growth accounting framework, 77–80; growth regressions with, 80–85; growth sources in, 81; saving rate in, 27, 35, 301; simplicity of, 26–27; steady-state equilibrium in, 37–43, 38f, 39f, 40f, 47; stochastic form of, 588; strengths and weaknesses of, 105; sustained growth in, 55–56; technological diffusion in, 613–19; with technological progress, 56–67, 78, 81; technology in, 28; transitional dynamics of, 43–47, 47f, 51–55; value of, 68–69

Solow-neutral technology, 58, 59f, 62

sovereign risk, 654, 655, 684

spaces: dual, 909; metric, 191, 878–80, 881–83; normed vector, 907–10; topological, 885–89; vector, 898

SPE. *See* Subgame Perfect Equilibrium

specialization in international trade, 665, 675, 678

stability: asymptotic, 44; global, 45, 46, 47; local, 44–45, 51; saddle-path, 269, 271–72, 302

stable arm, 271, 302–4, 303f

standards of living, cross-country differences in, 7–9

state: balance of powers with citizens, 821; capacity of, 797, 798; consensually strong, 821; strong, 818, 820–21, 823; weak, 818, 820–21. *See also* governments; political institutions

state dependence, 514–15, 517, 520

state variables, 183, 537

stationary dynamic programming: applications of, 201–11; assumptions in, 187–88; basic equations of, 202–9; Euler equations, 202–5; functional equations, 185–86; optimal growth problem, 216; policy functions, 186; recursive formulation, 185–86, 190, 221; theorems of, 187–90, 194–201; transversality condition, 203–5

stationary problems, 184–85

step-by-step innovations, 479–89

stochastic correspondence, 587, 587f, 596, 597f

stochastic dynamic programming: applications of, 554–61; with expectations, 537–44; general Markov processes, 552–53; proofs of theorems, 544–49; theorems of, 542–44; transversality condition, 550

stochastic Euler equations, 549–52

stochastic growth models: applications of, 535, 579–82; Bewley model, 583–85, 604; Brock-Mirman, 566, 567–71; in continuous time, 535; in discrete time, 535; equilibrium growth under uncertainty, 571–79; of long-run growth, 588–603; overlapping generations models, 566–67, 586–88, 587f; Solow model, 588

stochastic permanent income hypothesis model, 554–56, 561

stock market, 428–29, 594. *See also* capital markets; securities

Stone-Geary preferences, 319

strategic voting, 807

structural change: agricultural productivity and, 715–19; definition of, 694; demand-side sources of, 697–703, 719; in economic growth, 695, 863; Kongsamut-Rebelo-Xie model, 698–703; supply-side sources of, 703–15, 719; technological causes of, 703–15. *See also* industrialization

structural transformations, 725; definition of, 694; demographic transition, 730, 732–36; economic takeoff and, 868–70; factors slowing, 742; financial development, 588, 599, 726–29, 869, 870; future research on, 873–74; migration, 736; in organizations, 751; to production structure, 744–51, 764; social and living arrangements, 736; social tensions caused by, 8–9; sustained growth and, 863, 871–72. *See also* economic development; urbanization

Subgame Perfect Equilibrium (SPE), 416; comparison to Markov Perfect Equilibria, 936, 937; definition of, 936; existence of, 939; versus Markov Perfect Equilibria, 799–802, 939; payoffs in, 939–41; symmetric, 635, 636, 637; in technology adoption model, 633

subsidies: to investment, 750; to research, 442, 478, 620, 817

subsistence level of agricultural consumption, 699

supply-side sources of structural change, 703–15, 719

takeoff, growth: causes of, 112–14; explanation in stochastic growth models, 588, 598–99, 603; institutional and policy choices allowing, 863–64; population growth and, 113–14; structural change model and, 715–19; structural

transformations and, 868–70; timing of, 603; in Western Europe, 12, 13–14, 14f, 588, 603, 863, 868–70; in West European offshoots, 13–14, 14f, 863, 870–71. *See also* economic growth

tax policies: *AK* model and, 392; analysis with neoclassical growth model, 313–15, 314f; capital returns taxes, 313, 315–16, 392; chosen by elites, 790–91, 795–96; decision models, 814–17; distinction from expropriation, 821; distortionary, 787, 798, 817; effects on cross-country income differences, 315–17; as entry barriers, 838; human capital investment taxes, 370; limits on policy choices, 802; preferred rates, 815–16; redistributive, 313, 784, 793, 814, 816–17, 833, 836, 849, 854–56; taxes on R&D spending, 467–68, 478–79

Taylor's Theorem, 903, 906

technological change: in agriculture, 716, 865; balanced, 704–5; capital-augmenting, 58, 62; factor-augmenting, 500–502; future research on, 873; Harrod-neutral (purely labor-augmenting), 59, 59f, 60, 61, 62, 64, 499, 519; Hicks-neutral, 58, 59f; history of, 869; imitation and innovation levels, 745–47, 750–51; labor-augmenting, 59, 62, 519–22, 523–26; labor markets and, 499; learning-by-doing externalities, 681, 683; local innovations, 615; in manufacturing, 716; monopoly power of innovating firm, 418–22, 427; neutral, 58–59, 59f; in nineteenth century, 512; population growth and, 113–14; production costs reduced by, 411–12, 458; profit motives and, 414–16; quality improvements, 412, 458; scientific breakthroughs, 414–16; in Solow model, 56–67, 78, 81; Solow-neutral, 58, 59f, 62; in standard neoclassical growth model, 306–12; supply-side sources of structural change, 703–15; trade liberalization effects on, 679–80, 683–84; types of, 411–12; Uzawa's Theorem, 59–64; value of innovation to firm, 416–22. *See also* biased technological change; creative destruction; directed technological change; Dixit-Stiglitz model; endogenous technology models; industrialization; innovations

technological diffusion: advantages for backward economies, 642; balanced world growth and, 862; barriers to, 617, 619, 630–31, 639–40; benchmark model of, 613–19; distance to world technology frontier and, 615, 616, 745–46; empirical data on, 611–13; endogenous growth and, 619–23; to European colonies, 129–30; explanations of cross-country differences, 623–24; future research on, 873; human capital role in, 618–19, 626–30; international product cycle model, 674–78; international trade and, 674–78, 862–63; level differences, 616–17; models of, 609–10, 611; speed of transfer process, 615, 642–43; S-shape of, 613; in twentieth century, 871; from world technology frontier, 615, 862. *See also* technology adoption

technological spillovers, 398, 399–400, 444–48, 514–18, 520, 679n

technology: appropriate, 626–30, 643; cross-country income differences and, 90–96, 105; cross-country variations in, 19, 861, 862; differences within countries, 611–13, 642; inappropriate, 624–26, 630, 643, 743–44; increasing returns to scale, 414; meaning of, 19; nonrivalry of ideas, 413–14; orthogonal, 91, 93–94

technology adoption: contracting institutions and, 630–41, 862; costs of, 620; determinants of decisions, 612, 862; effects of economic institutions, 803, 804; entrepreneurs' decisions, 801–2; human capital and, 380–82, 383, 612; model of, 631–41; policies blocking, 872; relationship to economic growth, 861, 862. *See also* technological diffusion

technology transfer. *See* technological diffusion

terminal value constraint, 276, 291–92

terms-of-trade effects, 663, 670, 673–74, 684, 685

TFP. *See* total factor productivity

time consistency, 148–49

time-separable utility, 148

Tobin's q, 274

topological spaces, 885–89

topology: continuity and compactness, 885–89; product, 889–91

total factor productivity (TFP): calibrating differences across countries, 96–100, 98f, 99f; causes of differences in, 105–6; differences within countries, 612; expected, 596–97; growth of, 78; measurement issues, 403; procyclical nature of, 581

trade. *See* international trade

training, 366, 383. *See also* human capital investments

transitional dynamics: of equilibrium difference equation, 43–44; of lab-equipment model with input varieties, 439–40; in q-theory of investment, 272; of Solow model, 43–47, 47f, 51–55; of standard neoclassical growth model, 302–4, 303f; of world economy, 652–53

transversality condition: of continuous-time optimization problem, 232; for discounted infinite-horizon problems, 255, 256; Euler equations and, 212; in infinite-dimensional problems, 203–5; for infinite-horizon optimization problems, 246, 250–53; market value version of, 296; no-Ponzi condition and, 296; sequence problem and, 210–11; for stochastic dynamic programming, 550; stronger, 256; weaker, 255

Turnpike Theorems, 219

two-sector *AK* model, 395–98

Tychonoff's Theorem, 198, 213, 891

uncertainty: aggregate shocks as source of, 566, 571; investment under, 560–61; in research and development, 428–29. *See also* risk

unit cost functions, 666–67

United States: democracy in, 849, 871; economic growth in, 9; economic institutions in, 870–71; income per capita in, 3; relative labor scarcity in nineteenth century, 522; sectoral employment shares in, 697, 698f; settlers of, 870–71